THE HISTORY OF W

General Editor: GLANMOR W

WALES AND THE BRITONS 3

T. M. Charles-Edwards was Jesus Professor of Celtic and Fellow of Jesus College, Oxford from 1997 until 2011. He is a Fellow of the Royal Historical Society, an Honorary Member of the Royal Irish Academy, a Fellow of the Learned Society of Wales, and a Fellow of the British Academy.

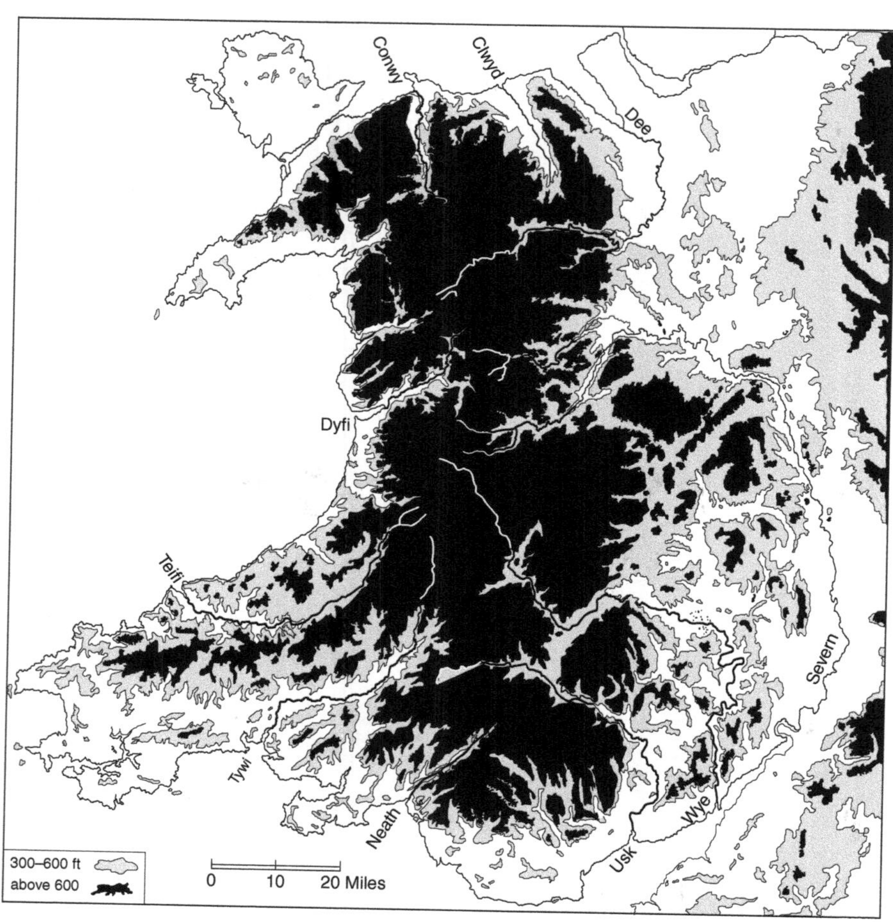

Map 1. Wales: rivers and mountains

Wales and the Britons 350–1064

T. M. CHARLES-EDWARDS

OXFORD
UNIVERSITY PRESS

Great Clarendon Street, Oxford, OX2 6DP,
United Kingdom

Oxford University Press is a department of the University of Oxford.
It furthers the University's objective of excellence in research, scholarship,
and education by publishing worldwide. Oxford is a registered trade mark of
Oxford University Press in the UK and in certain other countries

First Edition published 2013

First published in paperback 2014

Published in the United States of America by Oxford University Press
198 Madison Avenue, New York, NY 10016, United States of America

British Library Cataloguing in Publication Data
Data available

ISBN 978–0–19–821731–2 (Hbk)
ISBN 978–0–19–870491–1 (Pbk)

In memory of my parents, Tom and Imelda,
and of my wife, Gifford

Contents

List of Boxes

List of Figures

List of Illustrations

List of Maps

List of Tables

Abbreviations

ABT	'Achau Brenhinoedd a Thywysogion Cymru' in *EWGT*.
AC	*Annales Cambriae*
ASC	Anglo-Saxon Chronicle The versions cited here are denoted by letters A–E.
AT	Annals of Tigernach
AU	Annals of Ulster
BBCS	*Bulletin of the Board of Celtic Studies* (1923–1993)
Bede, *HE*	Bede, *Historia Ecclesiastica Gentis Anglorum* (references to book and chapter)
Brut	*Brut y Tywysogyon*, with references to the corrected dates as shown in *Brut y Tywysogyon or The Chronicle of the Princes, Peniarth MS. 20 Version*, trans. T. Jones, Cardiff, 1952. When the reference is to *Brut* without specifying the versions, there is no significant difference between the version in Peniarth MS 20 and the others.

Editions of the Welsh texts are:

Brut (Pen. 20)	*Brut y Tywysogyon, Peniarth MS. 20*, ed. T. Jones, Cardiff, 1941.
Brut (RBH)	*Brut y Tywysogyon or The Chronicle of the Princes, Red Book of Hergest Version*, ed. and trans. T. Jones, Cardiff, 1955.
BS	*Brenhinedd y Saeson or The Kings of the Saxons*, ed. and trans. T. Jones. Cardiff, 1971.
CA	*Canu Aneirin*, ed. I. Williams (Cardiff, 1938); references to lines.
Cart. Sax.	*Cartularium Saxonicum*, ed. W. de G. Birch, 3 vols. (London, 1885–93).
CBT	Cyfres Beirdd y Tywysogion, gen. ed. R. G. Gruffydd, 6 vols. (Cardiff, 1991–6). References are to vol., the number of the poem, and line.
CI	T. M. Charles-Edwards, *The Chronicle of Ireland*, Translated Texts for Historians, 44 (Liverpool, 2006).
CIB	P. Sims-Williams, *The Celtic Inscriptions of Britain: Phonology and Chronology, c. 400–1200*, Publications of the Philological Society 37 (Oxford, 2003).
CIH	*Corpus Iuris Hibernici*, ed. D. A. Binchy (Dublin, 1978).
CIIC	*Corpus Inscriptionum Insularum Celticarum*, ed. R. A. S. Macalister, 2 vols., Irish Manuscripts Commission (Dublin, 1945–49).

CLA E. A. Lowe, *Codices Latini Antiquiores*, 11 vols. and Supplement (Oxford, 1934–71).

CLlH *Canu Llywarch Hen*, ed. I. Williams (Cardiff, 1935); references to poem, stanza, and line.

CMCS *Cambridge Medieval Celtic Studies* (nos. 1–25), continued as *Cambrian Medieval Celtic Studies* (nos. 26–)

CS *Chronicum Scotorum*, ed. Hennessy

CSEL Corpus Scriptorum Ecclesiasticorum Latinorum (Vienna)

DB Domesday Book (references to folios)

ECI T. M. Charles-Edwards, *Early Christian Ireland* (Cambridge, 2000).

ECMW V. E. Nash-Williams, *The Early Christian Monuments of Wales* (Cardiff, 1950).

Edwards, *Corpus*, ii N. Edwards, *A Corpus of Early Medieval Inscribed Stones and Stone Sculpture*, ii, *South-West Wales* (Cardiff, 2007).

Edwards, *Corpus*, iii N. Edwards, *A Corpus of Early Medieval Inscribed Stones and Stone Sculpture*, iii, *North Wales* (Cardiff, forthcoming).

EIWK T. M. Charles-Edwards, *Early Irish and Welsh Kinship* (Oxford, 1993).

EWGT *Early Welsh Genealogical Tracts*, ed. P. C. Bartrum (Cardiff, 1966); references are to pages and to sections of individual texts, for which Bartrum's abbreviations are used: ABT, HG, JC.

Gregory of Tours *Hist.* Gregory of Tours, *Libri Historiarum Decem*, ed. B. Krusch and W. Levison, MGH SRM i. 1 (Hanover, 1951)

HB *Historia Brittonum* (Harleian recension; for editions see Bibliography: references are by chapters, which are the same in the editions by Faral, Mommsen, and Morris).

HG 'Welsh Genealogies from Harleian MS 3859' in *EWGT*.

Jackson, *Gododdin* K. H. Jackson, *The Gododdin* (Edinburgh, 1969).

Jarman, *Gododdin* A. O. H. Jarman, *Aneirin: Y Gododdin: Britain's Oldest Heroic Poem* (Llandysul, 1988); references are by line.

JC Genealogies from Jesus College, Oxford, MS 20 in *EWGT*.

JRSAI *Journal of the Royal Society of Antiquaries of Ireland*

Koch, *Gododdin* *The Gododdin of Aneirin: Text and Context from Dark-Age North Britain*, ed. J. T. Koch (Cardiff, 1997); references are by stanza; the line nos. of *CA* are included in this edn.

LHEB K. H. Jackson, *Language and History in Early Britain* (Edinburgh, 1953).

LL *Liber Landauensis*, ed. J. Gwenogvryn Evans with the cooperation of J. Rhys, *The Text of the Book of Llan Dâv* (Oxford, 1893); references are by charter; these are given by the page of the edition on which the charter starts, but with the

	addition of letters (e.g. 188a and 188b) whenever more than one charter begins on a given page.
Lloyd, *HW*	J. E. Lloyd, *A History of Wales*, 3rd edn., 2 vols. (London, 1939).
LTMW	D. Jenkins, *The Law of Hywel Dda: Law Texts from Medieval Wales* (Llandysul, 1986).
MGH	Monumenta Germaniae Historica
	AA Auctores Antiquissimi
	Epp. Epistolae
	Leges Leges in quarto
	SRG Scriptores Rerum Germanicarum
	SRM Scriptores Rerum Merovingicarum
	SS Scriptores
OP	*The Description of Pembrokeshire by George Owen of Henllys, Lord of Kemes*, ed. H. Owen, 4 vols. (London, 1892–1936)
PKM	*Pedeir Keinc y Mabinogi*, ed. I. Williams (Cardiff, 1930)
PL	J.-P. Migne (ed.), *Patrologia Latina*, 221 vols. (Paris, 1844–64)
PLRE	A. H. M. Jones, J. R. Martindale, and J. Morris, *The Prosopography of the Later Roman Empire*, 3 vols. in 4 (Cambridge, 1971–1992)
PLS	*Patrologiae Latinae Supplementum*, ed. A. Hamman (Paris, 1958–74)
PSAS	*Proceedings of the Society of Antiquaries of Scotland*
Redknap and Lewis, *Corpus*, i	M. Redknap and J. M. Lewis, *A Corpus of Early Medieval Inscribed Stones and Stone Sculpture*, i, *South-East Wales and the English Border* (Cardiff, 2007).
RIB	R. G. Collingwood and R. P. Wright, *The Roman Inscriptions of Britain*, i, *Inscriptions on Stone*, new edn. by R. S. O. Tomlin (Stroud, 1995); ii, *Instrumentum Domesticum*, Fascicules 1–7, ed. S. S. Frere, M. Roxan and R. S. O. Tomlin (Stroud, 1990–95); references are by the number of the inscription.
S	P. H. Sawyer, *Anglo-Saxon Charters: An Annotated List and Bibliography* (London, 1968); Anglo-Saxon charters are cited by their number in this list. For an updated online version see the bibliography.
VCH	Victoria County History
VSBG	*Vitae Sanctorum Britanniae et Genealogiae*, ed. A. W. Wade-Evans, History and Law Series 9 (Cardiff, 1944).
WATU	Melville Richards, *Welsh Administrative and Territorial Units* (Cardiff, 1969).
ZCP	*Zeitschrift für celtische Philologie*

Preface

This volume covers a shorter period than the first volume of J. E. Lloyd's *History of Wales*. The starting point of Lloyd's great work was long before there was any such people as the Welsh and long before the country called Wales by the English had become a separate part of Britain. I decided at the outset that I would begin at a date when one can see the processes beginning that would eventually create Wales and the Welsh. This was not because I wished to suggest that I gave the slightest assent to the notion that a history of Roman Britain should have been the first volume in an Oxford History of England rather than of the Britons. Nothing but the notion that one should begin with Imperial Rome and end with Imperial England could explain why such a plan seemed natural.

One excellent way to write a book such as this one is to begin with the land of Wales, as it came to be defined in the course of the period from 400 to 750. In that way one can ground history in the landscape, something which has huge benefits when writing about Wales. One reason why I have chosen a different route, beginning with the Britons and only coming later to Wales and the Welsh, is that Wendy Davies's *Early Medieval Wales* exists as a splendid example of what one can gain by beginning with the land and going on to its cultivators and, eventually, its rulers. It seemed that it would be helpful for the student of early Welsh history to have two quite distinct approaches to the subject. One of Lloyd's strengths, also, was his close appreciation of the land of Wales, in its physical aspect and in the ways in which Welsh culture was intertwined with the landscape. One of the remarkable things about this period—something true for the English as well as the Britons—is how quickly a people can give its special imprint to the land they inhabit; but in Lloyd's formative years what was more striking was the impact of the landscape on the people, an impact given special attention by such writers as O. M. Edwards. The first chapter of his *Wales*, described by himself as 'the first attempt at writing a continuous history of Wales', was entitled 'A Land of Mountains'.[1] For Lloyd's generation Wales formed the Welsh; and unsurprisingly those other Britons who did not inhabit Wales were not their concern.

The dedication marks the deepest debts I, and this book, have. My copy of Lloyd's *History of Wales*, the third edition of which was published in June 1939, was given by my mother to my father for his thirty-eighth birthday, 6 April 1940. It was only one of the many books about Wales, many of them in Welsh, which my father possessed and which he passed on to me. They have been a huge help in writing this book, all the more so because they were his. My mother's English patriotism was wholly natural, while my father's Welshness was something to be recovered across

[1] O. M. Edwards, *Wales* (London, 1901); Lloyd, however, saw the relationship as more complex than did Edwards: H. Pryce, *J. E. Lloyd and the Creation of Welsh History: Renewing a Nation's Past* (Cardiff, 2011), 132.

the chasm caused by the early death of his father. The interests and the loyalties which brought me to write this book were inherited from my father, but my mother was the rock on which the whole family happily perched. In the last years before her death my wife worked intensively on Welsh epigraphy: the third chapter of this book is, more or less, what I received from her work. My interest in Welsh epigraphy and my appreciation of how rewarding a source inscriptions might be was first stimulated by the teaching of Sir Idris Foster, but my wife's writings and conversation gave me what confidence in their interpretation I possess.

My work has been hugely facilitated by the riches of Oxford libraries, of the Celtic Library in Jesus College, of the Taylorian, the Sackler, the History Faculty Library, and, not least, the Bodleian itself. If I have missed any book or article which should have informed this book, the fault is most certainly not theirs but mine. I also owe a deep debt of gratitude to my two colleges, Corpus Christi and Jesus: it has been wonderful to have two extra homes and two extra families.

I am deeply indebted to my friends Fiona Edmonds and Paul Russell who unselfishly undertook the task of reading a draft. Their comments have markedly improved the book, and its shortcomings (much reduced by their hard work) are no responsibility of theirs but solely of the author. Oliver Padel gave guidance on Cornwall; Helen McKee helped with Chapter 19; and Nancy Edwards very kindly gave permission for me to use illustrations prepared for volume 3 of the *Corpus of Early Medieval Inscribed Stones and Stone Sculpture in Wales*. The two volumes of the *Corpus* so far published have been an invaluable aid in trying to understand early medieval Wales. The copy-editor, Angela Anstey-Holroyd, and the proof-reader, Kathleen Gill, saved me from numerous errors and inconsistencies; I am most grateful to them and to Emma Barber and Stephanie Ireland at OUP. My dear friend of Dublin days, Gearóid Mac Niocaill, wrote into the copy which he gave me of his *Ireland before the Vikings* the words of St Benedict and the author of the Book of Proverbs, *In multiloquio non effugies peccatum*, and I think, with some agitation, that in my case the sin must be made all the more grave by the great help which I have received.

Introduction: The Lands of the Britons

This is the first volume in a History of Wales; and, yet, it covers a period when, for contemporaries, Wales was merely part of a larger whole, the lands of the Britons. The modern terms for the Welsh, 'Cymry' and 'the Welsh' are at least as old as the early Middle Ages; but they then had wider meanings. 'Cymry' meant 'Britons' and 'Cymraeg' meant (Celtic) British; the Old English plural noun *Walas* or *Wealas*, the source of the modern 'Wales', and the adjective *Wielisc*, namely the Old English word that gave the modern 'Welsh', seem to have been used for all the people who had been part of the Roman Empire. True, there is no attestation of Cornish or Breton counterparts to 'Cymry', but *Cormac's Glossary* (*c.* 900) treats the language, normally called *Combrec* in Irish, as the language of the Britons; for him there seems to be no distinction between *Combrec* and *Bretnas* 'British' and both would thus cover the varieties spoken in Cornwall and Brittany as well as in Wales and the North.[1] These terms began to have much the same sense as they have today only when they ceased to mean all the Britons or all the people of the Roman Empire and were restricted to the land and people very roughly between Offa's Dyke, the Irish Sea, and the Bristol Channel. This did not happen until the twelfth century, after the period covered by this book.[2]

As a shorthand for the period up to the twelfth century, it is best to keep to the usage of Asser, at the end of the ninth century. Asser's *Britannia* had a double sense: on the one hand, it was the entire island, an island which the Britons had long conceived as their own, with other peoples as later intruders; on the other hand, it was Wales.[3] Similarly, *Britannia* is ambiguous in early Breton sources: it may be the island from which they had migrated; but it may also be Brittany.[4] (The term

[1] *Sanas Cormaic: An Old Irish Glossary*, ed. K. Meyer, in O. J. Bergin et al. (eds.), *Anecdota from Irish Manuscripts*, 5 (Halle a. S.), nos. 110, 124, 206, 883. For a full range of examples, see www.asnc.cam.ac.uk./irishglossaries.

[2] H. Pryce, 'British or Welsh? National Identity in Twelfth-Century Wales', *English Historical Review*, 116 (2001), 775–801.

[3] *Asser's Life of King Alfred*, ed. W. H. Stevenson (Oxford, 1904), trans. S. Keynes and M. Lapidge, *Alfred the Great: Asser's* Life of King Alfred *and Other Contemporary Sources*, Penguin Classics (Harmondsworth, 1983): *Britannia* is the island in the prefatory dedication to the king, p. 1, but in c. 80 (p. 66), *dexteralis Britannia* is South Wales. Cf. C. Plummer, *The Life and Times of Alfred the Great* (Oxford, 1902), 36–7.

[4] *Vita Prima S. Samsonis*, ed. and trans. P. Flobert, *La Vie ancienne de Saint Samson de Dol* (Paris, 1997); Eng. trans. T. Taylor, *The Life of St Samson of Dol* (London, 1925; reprinted Felinfach, 1991), i. 38, 41 (Britain), 59, 61 (Brittany). The same ambiguity is present in the sixth century in the work of an Italian settled in Gaul, Venantius Fortunatus, *Opera Poetica*, ed. F. Leo, MGH AA iv. 1 (Berlin, 1881), iii. 4; Appendix, 2. See below, 231–3.

Breton in English is a late import from French where it can mean either Britons or Bretons.) Brittany was, by the eleventh century, sometimes called *Brittania Minor*, 'Lesser Britain', to distinguish it from the homeland, the Greater Britain.[5] *Britannia* in the Scottish Chronicle (based on late-ninth and tenth-century sources) referred to Strathclyde.[6] Similarly, although *Cymry* is now the Welsh term for themselves, in this period it meant 'Britons'—not just 'Welsh', and, in the north, not just Cumbrians; Old English *Cumbras* was a rendering of an early form of *Cymry*, so that *Cumbra land*, 'Cumberland', was the northern land of the *Cymry*. The Welsh and Wales thus emerged slowly from the parent Britons and Britain; and until the twelfth century the emergence remained incomplete. Indeed, for some purposes it was never complete: the greatest dictionary of early modern Welsh proclaimed itself as a dictionary of 'the ancient British language'.[7] For the whole of the period up to 1064, the modern historian must maintain the distinction between modern terminology and the terms used at the time. It would be too draconian to prohibit 'Welsh' merely because the English could use *Walas* (later also *Wealas*) of the Cumbrians and the Cornishmen;[8] similarly, I shall use 'Cumbrians' as a convenient term for the Britons of the north and 'Bretons' for Britons resident in Armorica; but it would be fatal to import later senses into earlier periods as if they were as valid for, say, the seventh century as they were for the tenth or as they are for the twenty-first. 'Welsh', 'Bretons', and 'Cumbrians' are, in this book, convenient modern terms; contemporaries knew them all as Britons, *Cymry*, and *W(e)alas*. Admittedly the Anglo-Saxon Chronicle in the tenth century may have made a distinction by using *Cumbras* for the Cumbrians, alongside 'Strathclyde Welsh', whereas it did not use *Cumbras* for the Welsh of Wales; it thus used *Cumbra land* for Cumbria or Strathclyde rather than for Wales, but this has no relevance to how the Welsh and the Cumbrians saw themselves.[9] It may be that Old English *wealh* was used too regularly for someone inferior in status to an English freeman for it to be used so easily for the Cumbrians of the tenth century, who had taken over extensive territory that had formerly been English.[10]

[5] *Vita S. Cadoci*, § 35, *Vita Sancti Iltuti*, § 1, *Vita S. Bernachii*, § 3, ed. Wade-Evans, *VSBG* 4, 96, 194.

[6] Scottish Chronicle, ed. and trans. B. Hudson, 'The Scottish Chronicle', *Scottish Historical Review*, 77 (1998), 151/161; A. Woolf, *From Pictland to Alba, 789–1070* (Edinburgh, 2007), 209; corroboration comes from stanza 5 of the poem, *Carta dirige gressus*, ed. M. Lapidge, 'Some Latin Poems as Evidence for the Reign of Athelstan', *Anglo-Saxon England*, 9 (1981), 90, in which Constantine, king of Alba, is said to have rushed to *Bryttanium* (a variant of *Britanniam*) when he attended the meeting by the River Eamont in 927.

[7] J. Davies, *Antiquæ Linguæ Britannicæ, nunc vulgo dictæ Cambro-Britannicæ, a suis Cymraecae vel Cambricae, et Linguæ Latinæ, Dictionarium Duplex* (London, 1632).

[8] Stræcled Walas, ASC 875; Walas or Bretwalas referring to Britons of south-western England, ASC 753, 757, 825; North Walas for the Britons of Wales ASC 830; West Walas for the Cornishmen, ASC 838; but, in ASC D 927, West Walas refers to the subjects of Hywel Dda, probably because this annal sees the Britons from a Mercian rather than a West Saxon viewpoint.

[9] ASC 945; cf. Northumbrian annals attributed to Simeon of Durham *s.a.* 937 (*EHD* i, no. 3).

[10] K. Cameron, 'The Meaning and Significance of Old English *walh* in English Place-Names', *Journal of the English Place-Name Society*, 12 (1980), 1–53.

From its very conception, therefore, this book exploits the ambiguity of Asser. His narrower *Britannia*, our Wales, is in the centre of the picture; but that picture also embraces his wider *Britannia* in so far as it remained British territory. What was British territory will be defined by what may be called the 'small Britains' as opposed to the island of Britain: although *Britannia* in the sense of the whole island included the English and the Picts, the small Britains, those called *Britanniae* by contemporaries, such as Wales and Brittany, were doubly different: one *Britannia*, Brittany, lay outside the island of Britain; and, moreover, within the island the small Britains included only territory under British rule (or by dynasties of Irish origin, which had become assimilated to their British neighbours). My account of the lands of the northern Britons, of the Cornishmen, and of the Bretons will be far from complete; but they will be included whenever it helps us to understand the place of the Britons of Wales within the wider history of those who also called themselves Cymry or Britons. How completely Cumbrians, Cornishmen, and Bretons enter into the discussion will thus vary according to the circumstances. Relations between Britons and English are as central a theme for the history of the Cornishmen, and almost as central for the Cumbrians, as they are for the history of the Welsh; yet for the Bretons this is not so, even though their relations with the Franks and the Gallo-Romans will offer instructive comparisons and will sometimes play a direct role.

A Welsh poem of the second quarter of the tenth century has the phrase, 'from Manaw to Llydaw'—in modern terms 'from Clackmannanshire to Brittany'.[11] It was thinking of the lands which ought to be British, because it recalled a time when they had been British. Its idea was not the older one, found, for example, in Gildas, of the whole island as the inheritance of the Britons. For good reason, as we shall see, the contemporary Scotland (which only came south as far as the Firth of Forth) was excluded; but the phrase 'from Manaw to Llydaw' succeeds in conjuring up the lands of the Britons as they still were about 600, three years after the Gregorian missionaries led by St Augustine landed in Kent, and three years after St Columba died on Iona. These lands of the Britons were then a long strip from Stirling in the north almost to the Loire in the south. The strip had been squeezed by English conquest on the east and by Irish settlement in the west, but, at the same time, it had been expanding southwards. In the late sixth century Nantes on the Loire was a frontier city against the Bretons; but it would eventually be incorporated within Brittany.[12] The unity of these lands in the imaginations of contemporaries as late as the eleventh century is attested by the Breton Life of Gildas: it makes the saint a child of *Arecluta*, the land by the River Clyde—what would be called from *c.* 900 Strathclyde, Ystrad Glud—yet his destiny was to be the patron saint of

[11] *Armes Prydein*, ed. I. Williams (Cardiff, 1955; English version by R. Bromwich, Dublin, 1972), line 172: o Vynaw hyt Lydaw.

[12] Gregory of Tours, *Hist.*, ix. 24; x. 9; Erispoe was granted the counties of Nantes and Rennes and the pays de Retz by Charles the Bald in 851 in the aftermath of Erispoe's victory over Charles at Jengland on the River Vilaine: J. M. H. Smith, *Province and Empire: Brittany and the Carolingians* (Cambridge, 1992), 100–1.

Saint-Gildas-de-Rhuys on the southern coast of Brittany.[13] We may follow the hints of this Life and of *Armes Prydein* and pursue an even longer path than Gildas's, from the valley of the Forth to the valley of the Loire.

One 'Britain' is beyond the scope even of Gildas's journey, namely the *Britonia* established, probably in the fifth century, in the far north-west of Spain.[14] The evidence comes from the kingdom of the Suevi in Galicia, not long before it was forcibly incorporated into the kingdom of the Visigoths. The capital of the kingdom was at Braga, now in the northern part of Portugal, but the settlement of the Britons was further north around Mondoñedo, near the north coast of Spain and about halfway between La Coruña and Oviedo; their territory extended north to the sea and east across the River Eo into Asturia. After the Suevi had been converted from Arianism to Catholicism through the labours of St Martin of Braga, two councils were held at the capital; and in the second, in 572, one of the sees listed was *Britonensis ecclesia*, 'the (episcopal) church of the Britons', and its bishop was named as Mailoc. A list of local churches, of much the same date, arranged under their sees, includes, as the last see, the *sedes Britonorum*. What this Spanish *Britonia* reveals, even more than Brittany, is how much the Atlantic seaboard mattered for the history of the Britons in the post-Roman period.[15]

1. THE NORTH

Lothian, Lleuddinion (see Map 2), was the northern heart of the kingdom of the Gododdin, the Votadini of the Roman period, looking across the Firth of Forth to Pictish Fife. From Din Eidyn, Edinburgh, the army of the Gododdin set out to heroic defeat far to the south at Catterick in Yorkshire, and so came to be celebrated in the poem later named after the people, *Y Gododdin*.[16] Versions of the poem portray that expedition as including men from Gwynedd and from Ayrshire, Aeron, in addition to the Gododdin themselves.[17] A border province within the lands of the Gododdin was Manaw Gododdin, from which, according to the *Historia Brittonum*, came Cunedda,

[13] Ed. and trans. H. Williams, *Gildae De Excidio Britanniae, Fragmenta, Liber De Paenitentia, Lorica Gildae*, Cymmrodorion Record Series, 3 (London, 1899–1901), 322–89; ed. Th. Mommsen, *Chronica Minora Saec. IV. V. VI. VII*, iii, MGH AA 13 (Berlin, 1898), 91–106. For a discussion of why the hagiographer might have placed Gildas's birthplace in the land by the Clyde, see A. Woolf, *Where was Govan in the Early Middle Ages* (Govan, 2007); I am not persuaded by A. Breeze, 'Where was Gildas born', *Northern History*, 45 (2008), 347–50, who proposes that the Life had an early source for *Arecluta* and took the place-name to refer to the land by the Clyde, whereas, in Breeze's opinion, it is more likely to have been Arclid in Cheshire (SJ 78 61); there is also another Arclid in Cumbria (SD 29 88).

[14] E. A. Thompson, 'Britonia', in M. W. Barley and R. P. C. Hanson (eds.), *Christianity in Britain, 300–700* (Leicester, 1968), 201–5; P. David, *Études historiques sur la Galice et le Portugal* (Lisbon, 1947), 44, 57–64.

[15] E. G. Bowen, *Britain and the Western Seaways* (London, 1972); B. Cunliffe, *Facing the Ocean: The Atlantic and its Peoples, 8000 BC–AD 1500* (Oxford, 2001).

[16] See below, Chs. 11 § 3 and 12 § 1.

[17] Aeron and Gwynedd (or Gwyndyd, 'the people of Gwynedd') are in the A and B versions, *Canu Aneirin*, ed. I. Williams (Cardiff, 1938), lines 43, 809, 824, 1096 (for the importance of something being in both versions of the *Gododdin* see below, 365–78).

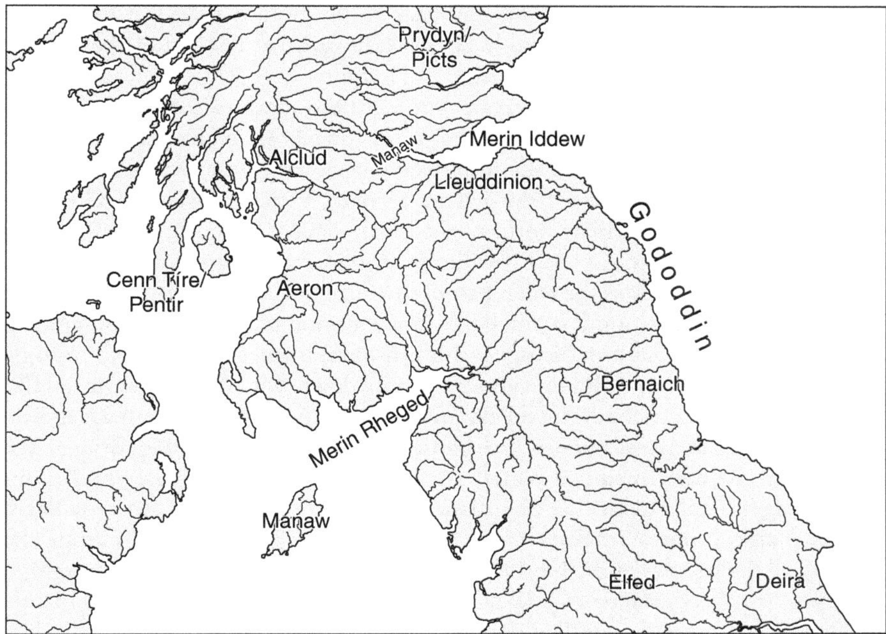

Map 2. The North, *c.* 550
The map shows northern Britain before the expansion of Bernicia north of the Tyne valley. Since Merin Rheged is likely to be the British name for the Solway Firth, it gives a clue as to the whereabouts of Rheged.

the ancestor of the early kings of north and west Wales as far south as the Teifi, 146 years before the reign of Maelgwn, king of Gwynedd.[18] The location of this Manaw, not to be confused with the island of Manaw, namely Man, can be fixed by two annalistic notices, one northern English, the other probably from Iona, on a battle between Picts and Northumbrians in 711. The annal derived from Iona places the battle in *Mag Manonn*, 'the plain of Manu', *Manu* (genitive *Manonn*) being the Irish name for what, in Welsh, was called Manaw. A northern annal in a version of the Anglo-Saxon Chronicle places the same battle 'between Avon and Carron'.[19] These are the two rivers which flow into the Forth on either side of Falkirk, formerly *Egles Breth*, 'the Speckled Church', for which 'Fawkirk', later Falkirk, was an English translation.[20] The plain along the Forth in the area of Falkirk was therefore within Manaw Gododdin. A hill south of Falkirk and just beyond the Avon bears the name Slamannan from Gaelic Sliabh Manann, 'the hill

[18] *HB*, c. 62; for discussion of the significance of this story see below 190, 328–9.

[19] AU 711. 3; ASC DE 710; Bede, *HE* v. 24, *s.a.* 711, confirms the date as 711.

[20] For the complexities of the evidence see W. F. H. Nicolaisen, *Scottish Place-Names* (London, 1976), 7–16; it suggests an interplay of Gaelic and 'Cumbric'.

of Manu'.[21] The name Manaw may go back to the Roman period, if the *Manavi* included in a list of northern British *loca*, special places, at the end of the Ravenna Cosmography refers to somewhere within this territory.[22]

Manaw, however, was not always confined to the south of the Forth: north of Falkirk and on the other side of the Forth is the town of Clackmannan, 'The Stone of Manu'.[23] This suggests that the strip of land enclosed by the Ochils to the north and the Forth to the south belonged to Manaw. Perhaps Picts and Gododdin shared Manaw, with Manaw north of the Forth usually being Pictish, or perhaps Britons held land north of the River Forth; in that case the river did not separate Manaw from the Picts, as the wider part of the Firth separated British Lothian from Pictish Fife.[24] Manaw south of the Forth, however, was to be the scene of several of the great battles of Scottish history: a short distance further up the Forth from the Carron is the tributary of Bannockburn, flowing down from the Gargunnock Hills, which the Britons called Mynydd Bannog, a name from which Bannock derives. Not long before Bannockburn the battles of Falkirk and Stirling Bridge were fought. In the early medieval period, also, this land was fought over by Britons, Picts, English, and the Irish of Dál Riata (roughly modern Argyll). An early Welsh poem praises a northern British king called Gwallog in terms of his reputation among all the peoples of the North: 'In *Prydyn* (Pictland), in *Eidyn* (Edinburgh), in *Gafran* (Kintyre, the land of Cenél nGabráin of Dál Riata) . . . it is admitted that the man who has not seen Gwallog does not see a man.'[25] We have noted a battle in Manaw between Picts and English in 711; earlier, in 642, the Irish of Dál Riata were defeated in the valley of the Carron by the Britons of Alclud and the Irish king was killed.[26] Although Manaw was remembered by the *Historia Brittonum* as a district within the lands of the Gododdin, possession of this strategically crucial plain was the prize of victory in the long struggle between the four peoples of northern Britain: Picts, English, Irish, and Britons. What is now the central belt of Scotland, where most Scots live, was by 650 a land disputed by three peoples, Picts, Britons, and English, with a fourth people, the Irish of Dál Riata, looking on covetously from across the Firth of Clyde; this made it unique within Britain.

The territory of the Votadini (later Gododdin) appears to have stretched from the Firth of Forth at least to the area of Hadrian's Wall. Ptolemy ascribed Bremenium, the

21 W. J. Watson, *The History of the Celtic Place-Names of Scotland* (Edinburgh, 1926), 103.

22 I. A. Richmond, 'Ancient Geographical Sources for Britain North of Cheviot', in I. A. Richmond (ed.), *Roman and Native in North Britain* (Edinburgh, 1958), 148.

23 Watson, *History of the Celtic Place-Names*, ibid.

24 J. Rhys, *Celtic Britain* (London, 1882), 110, suggested that the phrase *Manau Guotodin* 'Manaw of the Gododdin' (*HB*, c. 62, *EWGT*, HG 32) was used for the part of Manaw south of the Forth to distinguish it from the part north of the Forth.

25 *The Poems of Taliesin*, ed. I. Williams, Eng. version by J. E. Caerwyn Williams (Dublin, 1968), xi. 41–4. The later use of Pentir Gafran for the northern extremity of Britain, equivalent to John o' Groats, shows that the earlier meaning, 'Kintyre', had been forgotten in medieval Wales: CBT v. 1. 112. Hence this reference is likely to be early.

26 AU 642. 1.

Roman fort at High Rochester in Northumberland, to their territory. It thus appears to have embraced at least the coastlands from Manaw to the Tyne.[27]

Later Welsh texts sometimes conceive of Mynydd Bannog as the frontier between the Britons and their neighbours to the north;[28] yet this makes sense only if one looks north-east from the northern British stronghold at Dumbarton on the Clyde, and if Manaw was not then considered British territory. By 655, indeed, it was under English control, although much of it was lost to the Picts after 685. Earlier, in the sixth century, it may have been in, or on the edge of, the lands held by a Pictish people called the Maeatae or Miathi, whose name may be preserved in Dunmyat, on the edge of the Ochil Hills close to Stirling.[29]

The rock of Stirling, where Stirling Castle now stands and has stood since the Middle Ages, must have played a crucial role in the early medieval wars over what is now Scotland's central belt. It has been identified with a place named in Welsh as Iddew, earlier Iuddew; the identification is, however, disputed.[30] The same place, very probably, was named by Bede *urbs Giudi* (where *g* before *i* stands for a *y*-sound).[31] At this point in his *Historia Ecclesiastica* Bede was attempting to correct Gildas's description of the Picts as well as the Irish of Britain as 'transmarine peoples', namely peoples that invaded Britain from the sea. Bede's response is as follows:

> We call these peoples transmarine, not because they had been situated outside Britain, but because they were separated from the land of the Britons. Two bays of the sea lie between them, one coming from the eastern sea, the other from the western, and they penetrate far and wide into the lands of Britain, although they are not able to make contact between themselves. The eastern one has in its centre *urbs Giudi*, the western one above it, that is on its right-hand side, *urbs Alcluith*, a name which, in their language, means 'the Rock of the Clyde', for it lies by the river of that name.

It is important to remember that Bede was struggling in this passage to make sense of Gildas's 'transmarine peoples'; he wanted to make the sea separate the Britons from the Picts and the Irish. Yet, he is only imperfectly successful; and, as we shall see, the true explanation lies elsewhere. Bede rightly placed *Alcluith*, namely the British *Alclud*, Dumbarton Rock, on the right-hand, namely the north side of the

27 A. L. F. Rivet and C. Smith, *The Place-Names of Roman Britain* (London, 1979), 508–9. If the *civitas* capital were to have been Corbridge, as proposed by D. Breeze, 'Civil Government in the North: The Carvetii, Brigantes and Rome', *Transactions of the Cumberland and Westmorland Antiquarian and Archaeological Society*, 3rd Ser., 8 (2008), 63, 68–70, the southern boundary might have been the Wear; but I am not persuaded that they had a *civitas* capital in the same sense in which Carmarthen, Caerfyrddin, earlier *Moridunum*, was one for the Demetae.

28 e.g. *Vita S. Cadoci*, § 26, ed. Wade-Evans, *VSBG* 80–4.

29 Watson, *Celtic Place-Names*, 58–9.

30 *HB*, cc. 64–5; A. Graham, 'Giudi', *Antiquity*, 33 (1959), 63–5; K. H. Jackson, 'On the Northern British Section in Nennius', in N. K. Chadwick (ed.), *Celt and Saxon: Studies in the Early British Border* (Cambridge, 1963), 35–7; id., 'Varia: 1. Bede's *Urbs Giudi*: Stirling or Cramond', *CMCS* 2 (Winter 1981), 1–7; J. Fraser, 'Bede, the Firth of Forth and the Location of *Urbs Iudeu*', *Scottish Historical Review*, 87 (2008), 1–25, disputes the identification with Stirling and makes two new suggestions: Carlingnose Battery at North Queensferry in Fife (NGR NT 133 807) and Blackness, on the Forth west of Edinburgh, NGR NT 055 802. Both involve disregarding Bede's distinction between 'Orientalis (sinus) habet in medio sui' and 'occidentalis supra se, hoc est ad dexteram sui', *HE* i. 12.

31 *HE* i. 12.

Clyde; and, yet, his intention was to make the Firth of Clyde, rather than the River Clyde, separate the Britons from one of the 'transmarine peoples'. Moreover, when Bede uses the Latin word *sinus* for the firths, he chooses a term which suggests a curving indentation. This is probably the reason why his *Giudi* is placed *in medio* 'in the centre' or 'in the middle' of the eastern *sinus*, the Firth of Forth, which could only inaccurately be described as a curving bay. At all events, the contrast with the way Bede locates Alclud shows that, for him, *Giudi* was not on the south or the north bank of the Firth of Forth.

It used to be thought that the *urbs* or 'stronghold' of *Giudi* was an island in the middle of the Firth, and Inchkeith was proposed, a small island lying north of Edinburgh.[32] The principal objection to this identification is that *Giudi* or Iddew was an *urbs* in the sense of a fortified stronghold to be compared with Dumbarton Rock; yet Alclud was the capital of a kingdom and its capture in 870 by two Viking kings, Olaf and Ivar, after a siege lasting two months, would be a major turning point in the history of northern Britain. The solution, as argued by Kenneth Jackson, flows from Bede's use of *sinus*, whereby a stronghold at the end of the Firth of Forth could be imagined as being 'in the middle of' a bay. It has to be remembered, first, that Bede may well have had only a very general knowledge of the shape of the Firths of Forth and Clyde, and, secondly, that, as he undoubtedly combined the Firth of Clyde with the estuary of the River Clyde as the western *sinus*, so also he may have combined the Firth of Forth with the lower course of the River Forth as the eastern *sinus*. In Welsh, however, probably reflecting the names used by the northern Britons, the Firth of Forth was called Merin Iddew, but the River Forth itself was called Gweryd.[33]

While the main part of the Firth of Forth, Merin Iddew, was, therefore, a frontier with the Picts, first for the Gododdin and later for the Northumbrians, the River Forth and the upper part of the Firth was disputed land, now British, now Pictish, now Northumbrian.

Further west the kingdom of 'The Rock of the Clyde', Alclud (also Allt Glud), included what is now the district of Lennox and the rest of the lands around Loch Lomond.[34] The boundary between the Britons of Alclud and their northern neighbours may have been marked by Clach nam Breatann, 'The Rock of the Britons', on the west side of Glen Falloch, namely the pass leading from the top of Loch Lomond north-east to Crianlarich, over a watershed to the upper waters of the river system that flowed eastwards to make the Tay the great river of southern Pictland.[35] Loch Lomond was Llyn Llumonwy in Welsh: the *Historia Brittonum* of

[32] Cf. Plummer's note on Bede's *urbs Giudi*, *Baedae Opera Historica*, ii. 24.

[33] Jarman, *Gododdin*, line 944; *Canu Aneirin*, ed. I. Williams (Cardiff, 1938), line 1209. Cf. Irish *muir nGiudan*, 'The Sea of Giuda': Culross lay between it and Sliab nOchel, the Ochils, 'Culross in Strathearn among the Comgaill between the Ochils and the Firth of Forth', *Cuillennros hi Sraith Erenn i nComgellaibh eter Sliabh nOc[h]el ocus Mur nGiudan* : *Corpus Genealogiarum Sanctorum Hiberniae*, ed. P. Ó Riain (Dublin, 1985), § 722. 106.

[34] Both shorter and longer forms of the name are already attested in early copies of Bede, *HE* i. 1, where the Moore MS has *alcluith*, but the Namur MS *altclut*.

[35] Watson, *Celtic Place-Names*, 15; Clach nam Breatann is marked as Clach na Briton on OS maps at NN 3371 2161.

829 or 830 gives it as the first of the marvels of Britain.[36] The River Leven that flows south from Loch Lomond to meet the Clyde by Dumbarton was the Llyfn 'Smooth' in Welsh, Lemain in Gaelic; it later gave its name to the people of the district, the Lemnaig, anglicized as Lennox.[37] By the twelfth century, if not earlier, Lennox was a Gaelic-speaking district, but it had earlier been within the northern frontier of Alclud.

This may have been part of a shift of gravity southwards in the late ninth and tenth centuries, in the aftermath of the siege and capture of Alclud in 870 by the two Viking kings, Olaf and Ivar.[38] The capture of Alclud ranks alongside the capture of York in 867 and the defeat of the Northumbrians in the same year, when they attempted to retake the city as two pivotal events in the Viking onslaught on northern Britain. After 870 the kingdom was normally no longer named after Alclud (on the north side of the Clyde), but after the valley of the Clyde, Ystrad Glud, Strathclyde, that stretches south-east from Glasgow up into the Southern Uplands.[39] Its new capital may have been Govan, on the south side of the river. Strathclyde, *alias* Cumbria, profited by the decline of Northumbria. By 927, its frontier is likely to have shifted as far south as the River Eamont, close to Penrith.[40] This was how the lands around the head of the Solway Firth, including Carlisle, came to be part of Cumbria or Cumberland, once again the lands of the *Cymry* after they had been part of Northumbria for about 250 years; and the shift of the frontier southwards to the Eamont probably lies behind the later division between the counties of Cumberland and Westmorland. The *Westmoringas* first attested in 966 appear to have been those living west of Stainmore and north of Shap but on the English side of the boundary with Cumbria.[41]

This, however, was in the aftermath of the Viking conquest of York and the end of the old Northumbria. In its heyday Northumbria had conquered most of the lands between the Forth and Clyde in the north and Cheshire in the south. In 750, a year in which Alclud was preoccupied with a successful attempt to throw off the domination of the Pictish king, Óengus or Unust, the king of Northumbria, Eadberht, had 'added Kyle and other districts to his kingdom'.[42] To the north of Kyle is the district of Cunningham, on the south-west side of the Clyde valley; and

36 *HB*, c. 67; Watson, *Celtic Place-Names*, 212.

37 *HB*, c. 67 (Old Welsh *Lemn*); *Corpus Genealogiarum Hiberniae*, ed. M. A. O'Brien (Dublin, 1962), p. 358, LL 318 b 42.

38 AU 870.

39 The new name appears almost at once in AU 872. 5; ASC 875.

40 For this interpretation of ASC D 927 see below, 511–13. Cf. S. T. Driscoll, 'Church Archaeology in Glasgow and the Kingdom of Strathclyde', *Innes Review*, 49 (1998), 95–114.

41 ASC DEF 966; F. M. Stenton, 'Pre-Conquest Westmorland', *Royal Commission on Historical Monuments: Westmorland* (London, 1936), xlviii–lv; repr. in his *Preparatory to Anglo-Saxon England* (Oxford, 1970), 214–23.

42 Cont. Bede, *s.a.* 750. According to Watson, *Celtic Place-Names*, 127, the name Kyle was derived from the eponymous ancestor of a British dynasty called the Coeling. In the Irish version of the *Historia Brittonum*, *Lebor Bretnach*, ed. A. G. Van Hamel (Dublin, 1932), § 45, *Machlind*, namely Mauchlyne in Ayrshire, is *i Cuil*, 'in Kyle', which may have been understood as Gaelic *cúil*, a common place-name element bearing no relation to Coel. The usual British name of the district was taken from a river-name, Aeron.

it has been suggested that this was the area known as *In Cuneningum* 'Among the Cuneningas', in which Bede placed a Northumbrian of the days of King Aldfrith (685–705), Dryhthelm.[43] Cunningham and Kyle are respectively the northern and central divisions of Ayrshire, early medieval Aeron (Carrick being the third).[44] When King Aldfrith knew Dryhthelm, he was a monk of Melrose; and it is possible that English settlement had reached Cunningham in the previous reign, that of Ecgfrith, before Northumbrian power was dealt a heavy blow by the defeat and death of the king at Nechtanesmere on 20 May 685.

British political geography further south is largely obscure until we reach Wales. The best attested kingdoms are Elmet (Elfed) in West Yorkshire and Rheged, usually thought to be centred around Carlisle. Elmet was conquered by Edwin, king of Northumbria (616–633), but it survived as an English district name and its approximate situation is thus reasonably clear.[45] As for Rheged, its location around Carlisle is attested in a twelfth-century Welsh poem; and that makes it likely that the Merin Rheged mentioned in a prophetic poem in the Book of Taliesin was, for the Welsh, the Solway Firth just as Merin Iddew was the Firth of Forth.[46] The next major indentation of the sea, Morecambe Bay, retains its British name, but this was an antiquarian revival of the late eighteenth century; it is quite uncertain whether it still had the older British name in the early medieval period; if it did, that would make it less likely that it was Merin Rheged.[47] However, the medieval Welsh could make fundamental mistakes about early northern geography, as the example of Pentir Gafran cited earlier shows.[48] So, even if we accept that, for them, Rheged included Carlisle and the area around the Solway Firth, it is still possible that the original Rheged lay elsewhere.[49]

The main evidence for Rheged consists of poems in honour of Urien and his son Owain preserved in the Book of Taliesin.[50] The dating of these poems is controversial, but some, at least, are probably older and perhaps considerably older than the Gogynfeirdd of the twelfth and thirteenth centuries. Urien is described as 'lord

[43] *HE* v. 12.

[44] Cf. *The Charters of David I*, ed. G. W. S. Barrow (Woodbridge, 1999), no. 57, where Strathgriff corresponds to the deanery of Rutherglen on the south side of the Clyde, while Cunningham, Kyle, and Carrick are similarly all deaneries: P. G. B. McNeill and H. L. MacQueen (eds.), *Atlas of Scottish History to 1707* (Edinburgh, 1996), 350.

[45] The Elmedsætan were included in the Tribal Hidage, Dumville, 'The Tribal Hidage', in Bassett (ed.), *The Origins of Anglo-Saxon Kingdoms*, 227, 229. For Edwin's conquest, see below 345. R. G. Gruffydd, 'In Search of Elmet', *Studia Celtica*, 28 (1994), 63–79; M. L. Faull, 'Place-Names and the Kingdom of Elmet', *Nomina*, 4 (1980), 21–3, suggests that Elmet extended north-west into Craven, though the latter is also seen as an old British territory (cf. Domesday *Cravescire*: DB i. 380b), that its eastern boundary lay along the western edge of the magnesian limestone, the southern boundary on the River Sheaf, a tributary of the Don, and the northern perhaps on the River Wharfe.

[46] CBT ii. 6. 35–7 (Gorhoffedd Hywel ab Owain Gwynedd); The Book of Taliesin: Facsimile and Text, ed. J. G. Evans (Llanbedrog, 1910). 78. 15 (76. 15 – 78. 18, Yn wir dymbi Romani kar); *Poems of Taliesin*, Eng. version (Dublin, 1968), xli.

[47] Rivet and Smith, *Place-Names of Roman Britain*, 420–1.

[48] See above n. 25.

[49] M. McCarthy, 'Rheged: An Early Kingdom near the Solway', *PSAS* 132 (2002), 357–81, argues for the Rhinns of Galloway as the core of Rheged, but I am not persuaded.

[50] *Poems of Taliesin*, ed. Williams, nos. ii–x.

of Catraeth', as 'of *Yrechwyd*' (or *Erechwyd*) and 'lord of *Yrechwyd* , as 'of Rheged' and 'defender of Rheged', and his son Owain as 'lord of Rheged'.[51] Urien is also 'the rightful owner of Llwyfenydd', while his son, Owain, is 'lord of Llwyfenydd'.[52] As a result of Urien's generosity, the poet receives 'the riches of the lands of Llwyfenydd'.[53] We may take these names in turn, except that Rheged itself is postponed to the end. There is a strong chance that Catraeth is the Roman fort of Catterick or a site nearby, such as Richmond. (It has been argued that the 'falls' on the River Swale which gave their name to the Roman fort were close to Richmond.)[54] Admittedly, there was an English presence at Catterick from no later than *c.* 500, but in this part of Britain especially it would be very dangerous to suppose that the Britons never regained territory lost earlier.[55] *Yrechwyd* or *Erechwyd* cannot be located with any probability: the Lake District or Swaledale have been proposed, but there is nothing to add verisimilitude to a merely etymological speculation.[56] *Llwyfenyd* is more promising, since an identification with the River Lyvennet in Westmorland has found favour.[57] The Lyvennet flows north from the fells east of Shap and joins the Eden near Temple Sowerby. The best interpretation of the evidence, far from conclusive though it may be, is that the base of Urien's power lay in the Eden valley and that his ambitions extended south-east over Stainmore along the Roman road from Carlisle to Catterick.

If Rheged did indeed include Carlisle and the Eden valley, it may be, in part, a continuation of the Romano-British *civitas* of the Carvetii probably attested in an inscription, and indirectly by three milestones: Carlisle was the capital and it extended south at least as far as the Lune valley.[58] What may well have happened is that, after a rebellion about AD 153, and no later than 223, the date of the earliest attestation, the Brigantes lost much of their northern territory: in the west to a new *civitas* of the Carvetii, and in the east perhaps to a forerunner of the Bernicia or

[51] *Poems of Taliesin*, ed. Williams: *Catraeth*: viii. 9; *Yrechwyd*: iii. 1; vi. 13; Rheged: ii. 27; iii. 13, 14; x. 3.

[52] Ibid. viii. 27; x. 8.

[53] Ibid. ix. 10.

[54] J. T. Koch, *The Gododdin of Aneirin: Text and Context from Dark-Age Britain* (Cardiff, 1997), p. xiii.

[55] L. Alcock, *Economy, Society and Warfare among the Britons and Saxons* (Cardiff, 1987), 252–3; id., *Kings and Warriors, Craftsmen and Priests in Northern Britain 550–850* (Edinburgh, 2003), 140–4; P. R. Wilson, P. Cardwell, R. J. Cramp, J. Evans, R. H. Taylor-Wilson, A. Thompson, and J. Wacher, 'Early Anglian Catterick and *Catraeth*', *Medieval Archaeology*, 40 (1996), 1–61, with a general discussion at 50–4; they have shifted Alcock's dates a little later, but still well before any likely date for the *Gododdin* or Urien.

[56] *Poems of Taliesin*, ed. Williams, xlii–xliii.

[57] A. H. A. Hogg, 'Llwyfenydd', *Antiquity*, 20 (1946), 210–11; *Poems of Taliesin*, ed. Williams, xliv–xlv; A. H. Smith, *The Place-Names of Westmorland*, EPNS 42–3 (Cambridge 1967), i, p. xxv and n. 5, p. 10.

[58] *RIB* nos. 933, Old Penrith (see also Addenda and Corrigenda to the 2nd edn., p. 776, and R. P. Wright, 'Roman Britain in 1964: II. Inscriptions', *Journal of Roman Studies*, 55 (1965), 224, no. 11), 2283 (north of Kirby Lonsdale); C. E. Stevens, 'Gildas and the Civitates of Britain', *English Historical Review*, 52 (1937), 200 n. 3; R. S. O. Tomlin and M. W. Hassall, 'Roman Britain in 2004: II. The Inscriptions', *Britannia*, 36 (2005), 482; Breeze, 'Civil Government in the North', 67–8.

Berneich of the post-Roman period.[59] In 685 Carlisle was the seat of a Northumbrian reeve and contained the monastery of the queen's sister;[60] and thus it may have retained some political significance through the period from 400 to its incorporation into Northumbria in the seventh century.[61] The fort at the Mote of Mark, on the north side of the Solway Firth about halfway between Carlisle and Whithorn, has been excavated three times. The most recent excavators concluded that the rampart was built in the second half of the sixth century, namely at the period when the Britons were attempting to contain the newly expanding kingdom of Bernicia in the east. The fort was destroyed in the second half of the seventh century.[62] This is consistent with the hypothesis that the site was within Rheged; that at least part of the kingdom survived into the late seventh century; and that the Northumbrian occupation of Whithorn, which probably occurred *c.* 700, followed a further expansion along the southern coast of what is now Galloway after an earlier one in the area of Dumfries.

The description of Urien as 'lord of Catraeth' may, therefore, be taken as praise for his conquest of territory outside Rheged rather than evidence of where Rheged lay. How far Rheged extended into what is now southern Scotland is very uncertain. It has been suggested that a place-name, Dun Ragit, first attested as Dun Regate in 1535, preserves the name. The fort itself, the *dún*, is perhaps 'The Mote of Dunragit' at the head of Glenluce Bay.[63] If this were correct, Urien's kingdom might appear to have extended beyond the lands of the Carvetii to embrace the former territory of the Novantae in present-day Galloway. Apart from the lateness of the attestation of the name Dunragit, a reason for hesitation is that there may be echoes of the Novantae in medieval Welsh texts suggesting that their land was not subsumed into Rheged. One is the place-name, *Caer Neuenhyr*, 'the fortress of *Neuenhyr*'.[64] *Neuenhyr* has been understood as 'the king of the Nouantae'.[65] Secondly, a word *nouant* or *enouant* in *Y Gododdin* has been interpreted as an

[59] S. S. Frere, *Britannia: A History of Roman Britain*, 3rd edn. (London, 1987), 172 (London, 1999), 178–9; Salway, *Roman Britain*, 199–201; N. Higham and B. Jones, *The Carvetii* (Stroud, 1991), 9–14; for *Berneich* see below, 383–4.

[60] Anonymous Life of St. Cuthbert, iv. 8; Bede's Prose Life of St. Cuthbert, c. 27, ed. and trans. B. Colgrave, *Two Lives of Saint Cuthbert: A Life by an Anonymous Monk of Lindisfarne and Bede's Prose Life* (Cambridge, 1940), 122, 242.

[61] For a survey of the archaeology of the area, see D. O'Sullivan, 'Sub-Roman and Anglo-Saxon Finds from Cumbria', *Transactions of the Cumberland and Westmorland Antiquarian and Archaeological Society*, 2nd Ser. 93 (1993), 25–42, and M. McCarthy, *Roman Carlisle and the Lands of the Solway* (Stroud, 2002), 131–54.

[62] L. Laing and D. Longley, *The Mote of Mark: A Dark Age Hillfort in South-West Scotland* (Oxford, 2006), 24; the chronology is also summarized in D. Longley, 'The Mote of Mark: The Archaeological Context of the Decorated Metalwork', in M. Redknap et al. (eds.), *Pattern and Purpose in Insular Art* (Oxford, 2001), 85.

[63] Watson, *History of the Celtic Place-Names*, 156; National Grid Reference NX 148 579.

[64] The White Book Mabinogion, ed. J. G. Evans (Pwllheli, 1907), 458. 5 = *Culhwch and Olwen*, ed. R. Bromwich and D. Simon Evans (Cardiff, 1992), line 126; the name is spelt *Kaer Nefenhir* in *Legendary Poems*, ed. and trans. Marged Haycock, no. 5. 41, and *Newenhyr* CBT v. 23. 130.

[65] *Legendary Poems*, ed. Haycock, 170 (presumably assuming an alternation *w* / *f*, *GMW* § 10), developing J. Lloyd-Jones, 'Nefenhyr', *BBCS* 14 (1950–2), 35–7. The derivation would be easier if the form in *Culhwch* were correct and *-f-* an incorrect updating of *-u-*: see *LHEB* 384, P. Schrijver, *Studies in British Celtic Historical Phonology* (Amsterdam, 1995), VII. 2.

Old Welsh form of the name Novantae.[66] This is conceivable, but it involves the supposition that the scribe failed to modernize an old form, since he did not recognize what it signified. It is not the only explanation.[67] Yet a further difficulty arises if we accept that Dun Ragit does include the name Rheged: this is that such names may be more distinctive outside rather than inside the territory in question. If one does accept that 'The fort of Rheged' was within the normal territory of Rheged, it would naturally be taken as the pre-eminent royal seat of the country; yet, it seems unlikely that Urien's main fortress was so far to the west.

Another name, *Godeu*, occurs twice in the poems addressed to Urien.[68] In the poem celebrating the Battle of Llwyfain, 'Goddau and Rheged' are imagined as marshalling their forces together against the English general Fflamddwyn, 'Flame-bringer':[69]

> There was a great battle, Saturday morning,
> From the time the sun rose till it set.
> Fflamddwyn came on, in four war-bands.
> Goddau and Rheged were mustering,
> Summoned men, from Argoed to Arfynydd.

The same image of the two armies in alliance and drawing up their ranks recurs in the next poem. Goddau, therefore, has been taken as a territory on the same level as Rheged; and it has even been suggested that it was a name for what is now the western part of Galloway, though it has also been associated with 'the Forest' of Selkirk.[70]

The uncertainties are many; yet, there is acceptable evidence in favour of including within Rheged the area around Carlisle and the valley of the Eden, and no weighty evidence against it. Urien of Rheged appears as the leader of an alliance, a great warrior king whose power extended beyond Rheged—in the east to Catterick and in the west perhaps as far as Galloway. This is consistent with a sentence in the *Historia Brittonum*, according to which Urien was the outstanding war leader among the British kings of the north.[71] But the extent of the power enjoyed by Urien as the leader of an alliance is not the same thing as the extent of Rheged.

Rheged was the last known kingdom belonging to 'the north' on the west side of the Pennines. Further south, there was, as we have seen, Elmet, but its centre lay on the eastern side of the Pennines, close to what had been the *civitas* capital of the Brigantes and the likely core of their territory.[72] Whether Rheged and Elmet held

[66] Koch, *The Gododdin of Aneirin*, p. lxxxii *f.*

[67] Jarman, *Gododdin*, line 644, follows Williams, *Canu Aneirin*, p. 125, note on line 179, in taking the form as an adjective, *nofant*, meaning 'blood-stained'.

[68] *Poems of Taliesin*, ed. Williams, vi. 4; vii. 44.

[69] *Medieval Welsh Poems*, trans. J. P. Clancy (Dublin, 2003), 42.

[70] Haycock, *Legendary Poems*, 170; Watson, *History of the Celtic Place-Names*, 343–4.

[71] *Historia Brittonum*, c. 63.

[72] Breeze, 'Civil Government in the North', 63, is inclined to think that the Romano-British *civitas* only included this area, 'the Vale of York and south-west Yorkshire', and is sceptical of the usual view that the *civitas* of the Brigantes was a confederation of distinct peoples (including the Setantii and

land in what is now Lancashire is uncertain, although river names and other place-names indicate that, especially in the coastal area, British survived for a relatively long time.[73] One important link between north and south and east and west was, however, the Isle of Man. Its closest neighbour was to the north, what had been the land of the Novantae, the later Galloway; but, on a clear day, the inhabitant of Man might also look out eastwards and see the mountains of the Lake District, in 600 probably within Rheged, or southwards where, from the summit of Snaefell, he might glimpse Anglesey and the mountains of Snowdonia, or westwards, where he would see the Mountains of Mourne in Ulster. Post-Roman Man was a British land; but it also had an Irish component attested by inscriptions.[74] From Man would come Merfyn Frych, king of Gwynedd (*c.* 825–840), ancestor of the Merfynion, 'the Second Dynasty of Gwynedd'. Man was at the hub of the Irish Sea and thus crucial for the continuing links between the Britons of the north and those of Wales and between the Britons and Ireland.

2. WALES

If we return to the mainland of Britain and continue the long journey southwards from Manaw to Llydaw, we approach Chester and come to the borders of a kingdom that later formed part of the Wales of the twelfth and thirteenth centuries, Powys. About 850, Powys was one of the four main political units of that little Britain that would become Wales (see Map 3): the others were Gwent in the south-east (which often included Glywysing, the later Morgannwg or Glamorgan), Dyfed in the south-west, and Gwynedd in the north-west. The Powys of 600 was, however, a very different entity from the Powys of 850. First, there is the issue of the name: of the major kingdoms of Wales in 850, lying at the four corners of Wales, north-eastern Powys, south-eastern Gwent, south-western Dyfed and north-western Gwynedd, Powys was the last to be named in a surviving source. The name is not recorded until the ninth century, at which date it still referred primarily to the people rather than to the kingdom.[75] It has been explained as a borrowing from Latin *pagenses* 'country people', 'local people'.[76] Powys was

Gabrantovices of Ptolemy, and the Textoverdi of *RIB* 1695 from near Chesterholm, the ancient Vindolanda). In my opinion the view of I. A. Richmond, 'Queen Cartimandua', *Journal of Roman Studies*, 44 (1954), 44–6, remains preferable, especially in the light of Ptolemy's statement that the Brigantes stretched from sea to sea.

[73] *LHEB* 222–3, and the map on p. 220.

[74] See below, 148–52.

[75] *Pouis*, *AC* 808, 854, *Poyuis*, *AC* 822; *regio Pouisorum*, *HB*, c. 35.

[76] J. Lloyd-Jones, 'Rhai Geiriau Benthyg o'r Lladin', *BBCS* 2 (1925), 298; *LHEB* 443–4. Cf. *pagani uel decuriones*, *Cod. Theod.* 7. 21. 2; *pagensis* is well attested in Gregory of Tours and in an inscription from Numidia; it is also attested by derivatives in Romance languages: *Thesaurus Linguae Latinae*, s.v.; G. O. Pierce, *The Place-Names of Dinas Powys Hundred* (Cardiff, 1968), 219–21, notes that there is no direct evidence for the use in Britain of the word *pagus* for a subdivision of a *civitas*; but since there is such evidence for Gaul and it gave Welsh *pau*, this is not a major difficulty; part of his scepticism was based on the notion that the Latin *pagenses* is unattested, but this is incorrect.

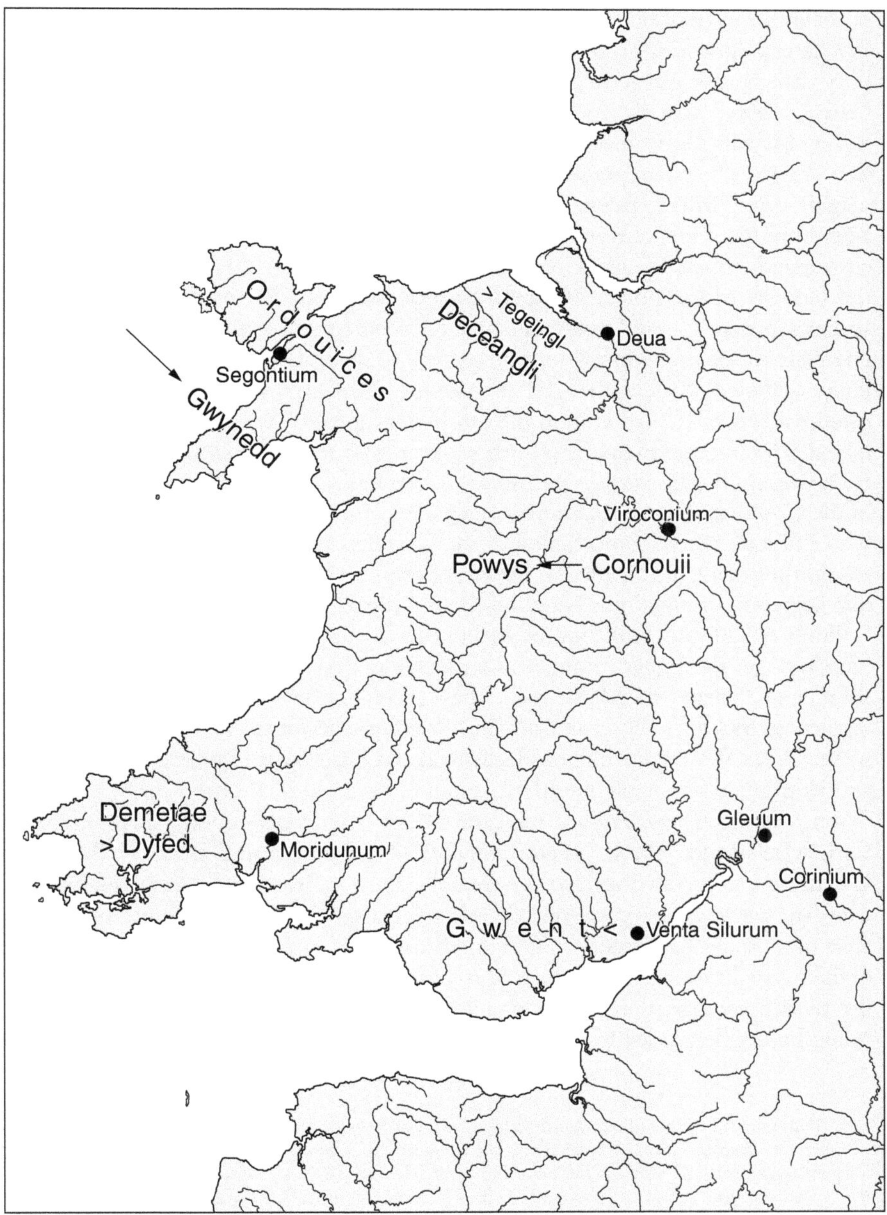

Map 3. From Roman *civitates* to British kingdoms.
This map covers the area that later became Wales and the neighbouring area, both *civitas* capitals (*Moridunum*, Carmarthen, and *Venta Silurum*, Caerwent) and major military settlements (*Segontium*, Caernarfon, *Deva*, Chester). An arrow, Ordovices → Gwynedd indicates that the kingdom of Gwynedd replaced the Ordovices; Demetae > Dyfed indicates that the later name is the lineal development from the earlier form.

probably a successor of the Romano-British *civitas* of the Cornovii, with its capital at Wroxeter (Viroconium), on the Severn five and a half miles south-east of Shrewsbury. But it may not have been the direct successor. A poem survives in praise of Cynan Garwyn son of Brochfael, an ancestor claimed by the later kings of Powys. A son of Cynan Garwyn, according to the genealogy, is likely to have died in battle in 615 or 616. The poem praises Cynan for his victories, not over the English, but over neighbouring British rulers and their peoples. One of these victims of Cynan's aggression is called Cernyw. In Welsh texts from the ninth century onwards Cernyw corresponds to the English Cornwall, and that is how Sir Ifor Williams understood the Cernyw of the poem. Marged Haycock, however, has made the unpublished suggestion that it would make much better geographical sense if the Cernyw of the poem stood for the Cornovii of Shropshire.[77] Cynan Garwyn, ancestor of the later kings of Powys, would then be threatening the Cernyw of the Shopshire plain, presumably still situated around the old *civitas* capital of Wroxeter. One might then take this interpretation one step further and suggest that the *pagenses* 'country people' from whom the name Powys derives were a break-away group from the former *civitas* of the Cornovii. They were, on this view, the 'country people' by contrast with those who still looked to the old capital of the Cornovii at Wroxeter. This interpretation would thus make the distinction between Powys and Cernyw a prime example of the disintegration of kingdoms based on the old *civitates*.

From *c.* 700, this limitation of territory to the upper valleys was typical of Welsh kingdoms on the English frontier as far south as Ergyng (now south-west Herefordshire) and Gwent. In Maelienydd, the valleys of the Teme and the Lugg were segmented by Offa's Dyke; similarly in Elfael the valley of the Arrow was also divided by the Dyke. West of the hills of Maelienydd and Elfael lay the upper valley of the Wye and its tributaries, notably the Ithon, draining southwards. Between the Wye and the Severn, *Rhwng Gwy a Hafren*, medieval Wales was divided among small territories, Ceri, Maelienydd, Elfael, Gwerthrynion (Gwrtheyrnion), and Buellt.[78] Buellt and Gwerthrynion or Gwrtheyrnion, were ruled in 830 by a single king, Ffernfael ap Tewdwr, whose ancestry was traced back to Vortigern; and the other territories in the areas may usually have attained the status of kingdoms in similar combinations.[79] Some of them may have constituted the region called *Cinlipiuc* in the *Historia Brittonum*.[80] In the twelfth century, these small kingdoms were claimed for Powys: several of their ruling houses descended from a common ancestor called Iorwerth Hirflawdd; and he

[77] I am grateful for her allowing me to include the suggestion here. The poem is *Trawsganu Kynan Garwyn mab Brochfael*, the first poem from the Book of Taliesin in *The Poems of Taliesin*, ed. Williams; the genealogy is HG 22 in *EWGT* 12. For the annal entry see T. M. Charles-Edwards, *The Chronicle of Ireland* (Liverpool, 2006), 128, *s.a.* 613. 3. The date of the poem is controversial: if G. Isaac, '*Trawganu Kynan Garwyn mab Brochuael*: A Tenth-Century Political poem', *ZCP* 51 (1999), 173–85, were correct in his dating, it would make it more difficult to regard the *Kernyw* of the poem as standing for the Cornovii. Conversely, if one were to accept the identification, as I am inclined to do, it constitutes evidence for a basis close to the time of Cynan Garwyn for the extant poem in the fourteenth-century manuscript.

[78] *OP* i. 202–3.

[79] *HB*, cc. 47–9. For the form Gwerthrynion, see CBT vi. 35. 59.

[80] *HB*, c. 70; *OP* iv. 606; Richards, Early Welsh Territorial Suffixes', *JRSAI* 95 (1965), 207.

may well be the person after whom was named the Iorweirthion, one of the *gwelygorddau*, 'kindreds', of Powys listed by Cynddelw, a poet of the second half of the twelfth century and himself from Powys.[81] Yet, although these kingdoms have also been attributed to the earlier Powys of the eighth and ninth centuries, whether they did indeed belong to that major kingdom is debatable.[82] For one thing, Powys is not mentioned again after the mid-ninth century until the eleventh and was probably subsumed into Gwynedd for much of that period.[83] There must, therefore, be some doubt as to whether, in the Powys reshaped in the late eleventh and twelfth centuries, anyone had any clear idea of what had been the bounds of the Powys of 850.[84] In an anonymous poem probably to be dated to 1101, Powys appears not to include Edeirnion, Iâl, Dyffryn Hafren, Dygen (probably the land by the Severn close to Breidden Hill, north-east of Welshpool), or Cyfeiliog, let alone the lands between Wye and Severn.[85] Perhaps, for this poet, Powys was restricted to the valleys of the Tanat, the Cain, and the Vyrnwy.

The land between the Wye and the Severn occupies one extreme in early Welsh politics. Roman Britain bequeathed *civitates* normally based on distinct peoples and kingdoms at the time of the Roman conquest.[86] In the area of Wales and the marches these were: the Cornovii, whom we have already met as the probable forerunners of Powys; the Silures of the south-east, whose territory lived on in the kingdom of Gwent, named after the *civitas* capital, *Venta Silurum*, medieval Caerwent; the Dobunni of the Cotswolds and lower Severn valley; the Demetae of the south-west, the later Dyfed; and, apparently without formal, self-governing *civitas* status, the Ordovices of the north-west, who survived past 400 as a distinct people but who were replaced by Gwynedd, and the Deceangli of the north-east, whose name survived as Tegeingl.[87] All but the last two of these received a *civitas* capital: Wroxeter, Caerwent, Cirencester, and Carmarthen. The Ordovices remained under a military administration, for which the most important centre was Caernarfon, Romano-British *Segontium*.[88] The principal units of government were, then, the *civitates*, illustrated by an inscription which, 'by a decree of their senate (*ordo*)', 'the commonwealth of the *civitas* of the Silures' erected in honour of a third-century commander of the Second Legion at Caerleon, Tiberius Claudius Paulinus.[89] There were, however, smaller units of population, such as the

[81] *EWGT*, JC 30, ABT §§ 2a, 11, 13, 14; CBT iii. 10. 29–32 (in the form Yorueirthyawn = Iorfeithiawn, a variant of Iorweirthiawn).

[82] Lloyd, *HW*, i. 242, 252; *OP* iv. 585–8, 605–7; D. Kirby, 'British Dynastic History in the Pre-Viking Period', *BBCS* 27 (1976–8), 102–10.

[83] See below, 552.

[84] See below, 487.

[85] CBT i. 1. 15–19. For the date, see N. A. Jones, 'Golwg Arall ar "Fawl Hywel ap Goronwy"', *Llên Cymru*, 21 (1988), 1–7, who favours 1096, and D. Stephenson, '*Mawl Hywel ap Goronwy*: Dating and Context', *CMCS* 57 (Summer 2009), 41–9, who favours dating the poem to Hywel's succession to Brycheiniog in 1101.

[86] M. G. Jarrett and J. C. Mann, 'The Tribes of Wales', *WHR* 4 (1968–9), 161–71.

[87] Rivet and Smith, *Place-Names of Roman Britain*, 331, 434. *Civitas* was also used more generally of the people of a pre-Roman kingdom or aristocracy, and in this sense the Ordovices were a *civitas*: Tacitus, *Agricola*, 18. 2. The last mention of them is in the Penbryn inscription, 354/126/Gso-41/CD28, for which see below, 137 (Illus. 3. 4), 176–9.

[88] P. J. Casey and J. L. Davies with J. Evans, *Excavations at Segontium (Caernarfon) Roman Fort, 1975–1979*, CBA Research Report 98 (London, 1993).

[89] *RIB*, no. 311 (Caerwent).

Deceangli of north-east Wales, named by Tacitus, or the Gangani, known only because they gave their name to the promontory at the end of the Llŷn peninsula.[90] In Latin, these subordinate units were usually termed *pagi*, a word which would be borrowed by Welsh and the other Brittonic languages, and the base of the *pagenses* that would give Powys.

Post-Roman Welsh politics could be seen as a tussle between the *civitas* (Welsh *ciwed* and *ciwdod*) and the *pagus* (Welsh *pau*). The issue was whether the *civitas* bequeathed by the Roman past would endure or would fragment into small units, an issue which is echoed, like so much of the earliest Welsh political vocabulary, in the verse of the twelfth-century poet Cynddelw, who describes the seven cantrefs, *seith cantref*, of Dyfed as 'seithbeu Dyued', the seven *pagi* of Dyfed.[91] There were four possible outcomes to this tussle: first, the *civitas* might survive relatively intact; secondly, it might survive as a smaller region around its old capital but lose outlying districts; thirdly, it might lose what had been the core region but nevertheless survive as the major kingdom of the area; finally, it might fragment entirely. The territory of the Dobunni was conquered by the English, probably leaving the small kingdom of Ergyng between the Wye and the Monnow as a relic. As for the others, the Ordovices of the north-west survived the end of Roman Britain, as demonstrated by an inscription, but were soon replaced by Gwynedd; the Cornovii lost the lowland core to the English, but the uplands survived as Powys; the Silures retained their south-eastern core, Gwent, but lost territory to the north and sometimes to the west; the Demetae (Dyfed) intermittently lost part of the old core to the east of the old capital at Carmarthen but survived further west. In the scheme of cantrefs and commotes, which may perhaps be ascribed to the eleventh century, Carmarthen is at the eastern edge of the easternmost cantref of 'the seven cantrefs of Dyfed';[92] and the name of that cantref was Cantref Gwarthaf, 'the uppermost cantref', namely the furthest from a centre to the west. In those terms, the lands further east lay outside Dyfed: Ystrad Tywi, the Vale of the Tywi, Gŵyr, and Cedweli (see Map 4).

Most of these changes are obscure for lack of evidence, but some sense of what happened is possible for the Silures and the Demetae.[93] By 1064, Gwent and Dyfed were no longer neighbours. They were divided from each other by Glamorgan (Gwlad Forgan, *alias* Morgannwg), by Gŵyr, by Ystrad Tywi (which included Carmarthen, the old *civitas* capital of Dyfed), and by Brycheiniog.[94] The *Historia Brittonum* (829–830) unhelpfully uses a single Latin word, *regio*, for all political units within Wales, from the small Gwerthrynion to the large Gwynedd; it separates the *regio* of Dyfed from its eastern neighbour, Gwent, by two other

[90] Tacitus, *Ann.* xii. 32; Rivet and Smith, *Place-Names of Roman Britain*, 331, 365–6, 430 (also the Octapitae whose name is attested in the name of St David's Head were not a people on the same level as the Demetae).

[91] CBT iv. 9. 187; cf. *PKM* 1, 27, 49.

[92] For cantrefs and commotes, see below, 568–9.

[93] For Dyfed, see *OP* i. 45–7 n., 199 n. 2, 224 n., 257 n., iv. 402–4.

[94] *Gliuising*, *AC* 864 (*Gwlad Vorgant, Brut*, 992), *Strat Tiui*, *AC* 894, 'Dyfed and Ystrad Tywi', The *Brut* 1047, *Broceniauc*, *AC* 848.

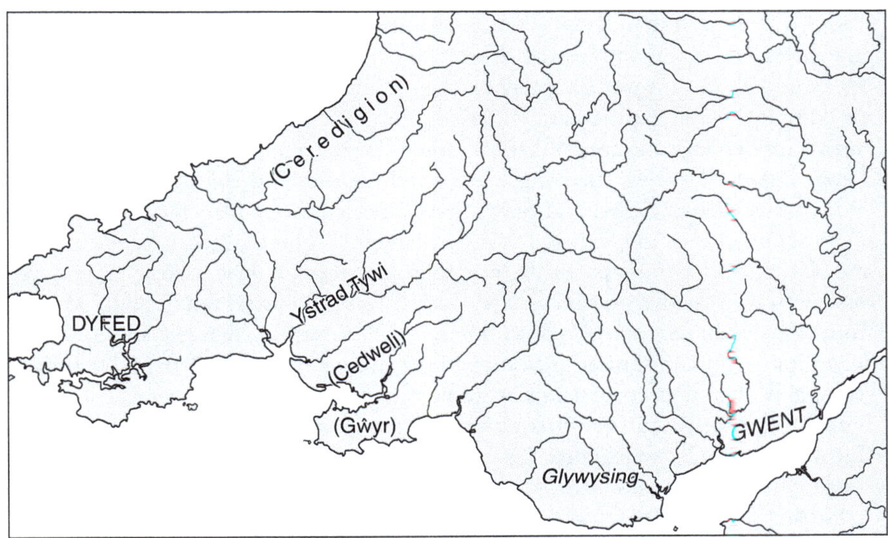

Map 4. Dyfed and Gwent: core and periphery
The major kingdoms of South Wales were the heirs of Roman *civitates*, but their territories varied in extent. The names in roman capitals refer to territories that always (capitals) or sometimes (lower case) belonged to Dyfed; those in italics always (italic capitals) or sometimes (lower case italic) belonged to Gwent. The names in capitals (roman or italic) thus refer to territory in the inner core; those in lower case (without brackets) refer to territories in the outer core; and those in brackets to peripheral territories.

intervening *regiones*, Gŵyr and Cedweli (Gower and Kidwelly).[95] Yet, in the post-Roman period, Dyfed and Gwent appear to have survived largely intact. The older Life of St Samson declares that the saint was of Dyfed, and that his father Amon belonged to the aristocracy of the kingdom, those who might foster the sons of kings; his mother, however, though she was of the same rank, belonged to *Ventia*, Gwent, a province said to have adjoined Dyfed.[96] What in Asser's time would be Glywysing and, later, Morgannwg or Gwlad Forgan, remained part of Gwent in the seventh century; and, indeed, even after the name Glywysing had come into use, the territory was tied to Gwent by dynastic links, and they often remained parts of the one kingdom.[97] Although Dyfed might have been separated from Ystrad Tywi, Ceredigion, Cedweli, and Gŵyr, it seems sometimes to have included at least Ystrad Tywi, as in 992, when 'the whole territory of Maredudd [ab Owain] in Deheubarth' was ravaged, 'that is, Ceredigion and Dyfed and Gŵyr and

[95] *HB*, c. 14.

[96] *Vita Prior S. Samsonis*, i. 1 (ed. and trans. Flobert, *La Vie ancienne de saint Samson de Dol*, 146; trans. Taylor, *The Life of St. Samson of Dol*, 8).

[97] W. Davies, *An Early Welsh Microcosm: Studies in the Llandaff Charters* (London, 1978), 88–98.

Cedweli';[98] here, Ystrad Tywi is not mentioned, although all the lands around are, and the easiest explanation is that it formed part of Dyfed. The whole kingdom of Maredudd ab Owain probably reflects the old, more extensive, Dyfed; but, within his kingdom, the contemporary Dyfed was still in 992 a preponderant part. A division between the core of Dyfed, called Rheinwg, and Ceredigion and Ystrad Tywi, called Seisyllwg, may have occurred in the mid-eighth century, if the eponymous Rhain (*Regin*) and Seisyll have been correctly identified; but it is not to be assumed that this division was permanent.[99] The boundary between Gŵyr and Gwent/Glywysing probably normally lay on the River Neath. The very difficult ford was guarded on the Gŵyr side by an early fort, Hen Gastell, occupied from the sixth century.[100] Both Dyfed and Gwent expanded or contracted according to circumstance, including or shedding outlying districts;[101] what is striking is that their core lands were at opposite extremes, a western extreme, roughly equivalent to Pembrokeshire and the part of Carmarthenshire west of Carmarthen itself, for Dyfed, and an eastern extreme, roughly equivalent to Monmouthshire, for Gwent.

Further north, away from the southern coastlands of Wales, Brycheiniog lay in the triangle of land between the mountain ranges of Mynydd Epynt to the north-west, the Brecon Beacons in the south, and the Black Mountain in the east; it occupied the upper valley of the Usk and touched upon the Wye as the latter swings north-east towards Hay. Brycheiniog is likely to have been part of Silurian territory in the Roman period, but it had broken away, perhaps as a result of Irish settlement in the immediately post-Roman period.[102] In the early tenth century, its capital was an artificial island on Llangors Lake—namely a crannog, a form of fortification characteristic of Ireland and Scotland.[103]

North Wales was very different. First, the old people of the north-west, the Ordovices, who, like the Silures, had been prominent in the resistance to Roman conquest, barely survived the end of Roman Britain. The people of the north-east, the Deceangli, are recalled in the name of a cantref, Tegeingl. The relationship between these two peoples and their territories is unclear in the Roman period. The

98 *Brut*, *s.a.* 992.

99 The *Regin* of HG 2, grandfather of Maredudd ap Tewdos, who died in 796, and the Seisyll of HG 26, whose son, Arthen, died in 809: D. P. Kirby, 'The Political Development of Ceredigion, *c.* 400–1081', in J. L. Davies and D. P. Kirby (eds.), *Ceredigion County History*, gen. ed. I. G. Jones, i, *From the Earliest Times to the Coming of the Normans* (Cardiff, 1994), 329. The name Ystrad Tywi is first attested in *AC s.a.* 893 (ed. Phillimore), *s.a.* 894 (ed. Dumville), and is there coupled with Ceredigion, but the name Seisyllwg is not used.

100 P. F. Wilkinson, 'Excavations at Hen Gastell, Briton Ferry, West Glamorgan', *Medieval Archaeology*, 39 (1995), 1–50. For the difficulty of the ford, see Gerald of Wales, *Itinerarium Kambriae*, i. 8.

101 A process of expansion is evoked at the end of *Pwyll Pendeuic Dyuet* and the beginning of *Math uab Mathonwy*, *PKM* 27, 67; trans. S. Davies, *The Mabinogion* (Oxford, 2007), 21, 47.

102 C. Thomas, *And shall these Mute Stones speak? Post-Roman Inscriptions in Western Britain* (Cardiff, 1994), 114, argues that the Irish element in Brycheiniog was due to movement from Dyfed in the late fifth century.

103 E. Campbell and A. Lane, 'Llangorse: A Tenth-Century Royal Crannog in Wales', *Antiquity*, 63 (1989), 675–81.

river behind which Caratacus's army, consisting of the Ordovices and their allies, faced Ostorius has been identified with the upper Severn, but with no good reason: Wales has several rivers behind which the Ordovices might have hoped to withstand the Roman army; and this river was overlooked by high mountains.[104] Tacitus's account of Agricola's first campaign, undertaken against the Ordovices immediately after his arrival as governor, makes it likely that Snowdonia lay within their territory. Although it was late in the summer, Agricola surprised his own troops, let alone the enemy, by attacking; he secured a decisive victory, and decided to complete his success by pushing on to Anglesey.[105] That special troops, accustomed to swimming, were used to cross the Menai Strait hardly implies that there were two quite distinct operations, one against the Ordovices and the other against an Anglesey understood to lie outside Ordovican territory.[106] A natural reading of the text would not allow that Snowdonia lay between the lands of the Ordovices and the Menai Straits, in the possession of another people, such as the Deceangli.[107] That would imply that imposing Roman power on Snowdonia was a matter of no consequence, not deserving even a mention. Moreover, if the Ordovices were based in the upper Severn valley (effectively what was later merely one part of Powys), while the Cornovii held the Shropshire plain, they would hardly have been so formidable a people as they appear in Tacitus's narrative. It is likely, therefore, that the Ordovices were the forerunners of the early medieval kingdom and people of Gwynedd. How the one replaced the other will be considered in Chapter 4.

North-west Wales was always likely to form part of an Irish-Sea zone. The richest lands lay in Anglesey—together with Man one of the two principal islands of the Irish Sea—in Arfon, the land opposite Môn, opposite Anglesey, and in the Llŷn peninsula. The heart of Gwynedd looked west, to Ireland and north to Man. Dyfed also looked west to Ireland, but particularly what remained the western part of Dyfed in Pembrokeshire, much less so the heart of the Romano-British Demetae, around Carmarthen.

3. SOUTH-WEST BRITAIN AND BRITTANY

In the Roman period south-west Britain was divided between the Dumnonii with their capital at Exeter, *Isca Dumnoniorum*, and the Durotriges of Dorset and Somerset with theirs at Dorchester, *Durnovaria*.[108] An outlier of the territory of the Belgae (with their capital at Winchester, *Venta Belgarum*) seems to have extended north-west to include Bath. All of these *civitates*, together with those of

[104] Tacitus, *Annals*, xii. 35.

[105] Tacitus, *Agricola*, c. 18.

[106] As argued by Salway, *Roman Britain*, 140.

[107] This is how the relationship between the two peoples, the Ordovices and the Deceangli, is represented by Salway, *Roman Britain*, Map II and p. 45.

[108] Attested by inscriptions commemorating work carried out on Hadrian's Wall in the fourth century, perhaps in AD 369 after the disaster of the 'Great Conspiracy' of 367: *RIB*, nos. 1672–3 (Great Chesters), 1843–4 (near Carvoran, NY 66 65).

Wales, belonged to the fourth-century province of *Britannia Prima* with its capital at Cirencester.

In 600 the territory of the Durotriges may have been largely untouched by English conquest: the very few early furnished burials of the type familiar from south-eastern England may be a relic of a wider conquest in the mid-fifth century that was partially reversed in the second half of the century.[109] One of the more credible early entries in the Anglo-Saxon Chronicle records a defeat of the Britons by Cenwealh in 658, after which he 'put them to flight as far as the Parret'. That might commemorate the first major English conquest of former Durotrigan territory. In the post-Roman period, what would become Somerset was a land of great hill forts: South Cadbury, Cadbury Congresbury, and Cannington.[110] Although the territory of the Durotriges was the most western to be much touched by Romanization of material culture, the hill forts of the subsequent period echoed the pre-Roman Iron Age, and, indeed, were typically refurbishments of Iron-Age sites.

In the sixth century, the old *civitas* of the far south-west, the Dumnonii, remained intact, but it lost territory in the mid-seventh. The clearest evidence is that Boniface, the later English missionary in Germany, is said by the late eighth-century author of his Life, Willibald, to have entered a monastery in Exeter at a date which must be about 680.[111] On the other hand, the group of British inscriptions at Wareham in Dorset, of approximately the same date, suggests caution about settlement if not conquest.[112] About 700, Aldhelm wrote a poem in which he described travelling through Dumnonia and on into Cornubia.[113] This seems to imply that Cornwall existed as an area within the kingdom of Dumnonia, perhaps with the Tamar as its boundary.[114] In the eighth century what would become the English county of Devon, *Defnascir*, 'the shire of the *Defnas*', was formed, leaving Cornwall, the *Cornwalas* 'Britons of the Horn of Britain', as a remnant.[115] Cornwall itself was conquered by the West Saxons in the ninth century; but whereas Devon was thoroughly anglicized, Cornwall was not, even though little more than a century separated the two conquests.

[109] E. O'Brien, *Post-Roman Britain to Anglo-Saxon England: Burial Practices Reviewed*, BAR, Brit. Ser., 289 (Oxford, 1999), 166–70.

[110] L. Alcock, *'By South Cadbury is that Camelot . . .' Excavations of Cadbury Castle 1966–70* (London, 1972); P. Rahtz, 'Celtic Society in Somerset AD 400–700', *BBCS* 30 (1982), 176–200; P. Rahtz et al., *Cadbury Congresbury 1968–73: A Late/Post Roman Hilltop settlement in Somerset*, BAR 223 (Oxford, 1992); P. Rahtz, 'Cannington Hillfort 1963', *Somerset Archaeology and Natural History*, 113 (1969), 56–68.

[111] Willibald, *Vita S. Bonifatii*, c. 1, ed. W. Levison, *Vitae Sancti Bonifatii*, MGH SRG (Hanover, 1905), pp.6–7; trans. C. H. Talbot, *The Anglo-Saxon Missionaries in Germany* (London, 1954), 28.

[112] Tedeschi, *Congeries*, DSD-15; Royal Commission on Historical Monuments in England, *An Inventory of Historical Monuments in the County of Dorset* (London, 1970), ii, *South-East*, Part 2, pp. 310–12 and Plates 165 and 166; and Yorke, *Wessex*, pp. 69–72.

[113] Aldhelm, *Carmen Rhythmicum*, ed. R. Ehwald, *Aldhelmi Opera Omnia*, MGH AA 15 (Berlin, 1919), 524, trans. in M. Lapidge and J. Rosier, *Aldhelm: The Poetic Works* (Cambridge, 1985), 177.

[114] This was suggested by O. J. Padel in an Oxford O'Donnell lecture, 29 April 2010.

[115] *Defnas* fight against *Walas* ASC 825; *bellum Hehil apud Cornuenses*, AC 722; *Hehil* was identified as the Camel river by W. G. Hoskins, *The Westward Expansion of Wessex* (Leicester, 1960), 19, but this seems to be unsustainable, since the earlier name of the main river was *Alan*: O. J. Padel, *A Popular Dictionary of Cornish Place-Names* (Penzance, 1988), 63.

The internal divisions of Cornwall are first attested, as a whole, in a Geld Inquest of *c.* 1084, preserved in the Exeter Domesday.[116] The country was laid out in hundreds along the north and south coasts (with the partial exception of the westernmost, Penwith, which has a coastline both to the north and to the south). In the Geld Inquest the hundreds were named after the hundred manor, the centre of administration, but the old names remained in popular use and resurfaced in the twelfth and thirteenth centuries.[117] The antiquity of some, at least, of these divisions is attested by the First Life of St Samson, which I would date to the seventh century.[118] When the saint left South Wales, he crossed 'the Severn Sea' and came to the monastery of St Docco at Lanow, now St Kew.[119] From there he set off in a cart drawn by two horses, transporting 'his holy vessels and his books'; he came to a '*pagus* which they call *Tricurius*'.[120] The name *Tricurius* is preserved in the Hundred of Trigg, which lies on the north-west side of Bodmin Moor and includes St Kew. The name belongs to a well-attested type of Celtic place-name, exemplified by Périgueux and its territory, Périgord, in France, from *Petrucorii*.[121] What it means is something like 'three battalions', whereas the *Petrucorii* were 'four battalions'; but it remains uncertain what was the size of group intended by a **corios* or **coria*. In Antiquity the custom was to estimate the size of a people by the number of full-armed soldiers it could muster, so that **corios* in these names may well have referred to a contingent of a specific size. In the Geld Inquest, the three later-attested hundreds of Trigg, Lesnewth, and Stratton were a single district, named after the administrative centre at Stratton in the far north-east, bordering Devon. What is likely is that the *Tricorii*—by the seventh century *Tricurius*—included the people of the whole area administered from Stratton in 1084 and otherwise divided between Trigg, Lesnewth, and Stratton; that the entire region was known as Trigg; and that the division into three continued, at least broadly, the threefold division suggested by the name *Tricorii*.[122]

One of the principal puzzles about the south-west in the early medieval period is its relationship with Brittany. The existence of close links is not in doubt; the Breton language, for example, is closer to Cornish than to Welsh; and both lay on the trade routes from the south to the Irish Sea; what is more mysterious is the way

[116] DB iii. ff. 63b and 72–3.

[117] C. Henderson, *Essays in Cornish History* (Oxford, 1935), 108–24; C. Thomas, 'Settlement-History in Early Cornwall, I. The Antiquity of the Hundreds', *Cornish Archaeology*, 3 (1964), 70–9; W. M. M. Picken, 'The Names of the Hundreds of Cornwall', *Devon and Cornwall Notes and Queries*, 30 (1965–7), 36–40, reprinted in his *A Medieval Cornish Miscellany*, ed. O. J. Padel (Chichester, 2000), 76–80.

[118] See below, 238–9.

[119] Cf. Lanow Farm (< Landochou), SX 025 777; Padel, *A Popular Dictionary of Cornish Place-Names*, 103 (under St Kew); W. M. M. Picken, 'The Landochou Charter', in Hoskins, *The Westward Expansion of Wessex*, 36–44, repr. in his *A Medieval Cornish Miscellany*, 1–11; L. Olson, *Early Monasteries in Cornwall* (Woodbridge, 1989), 82.

[120] *Vita I S. Samsonis*, i. 48.

[121] O. J. Padel, *Cornish Place-Name Elements*, English Place-Name Society, 56/57 (Nottingham, 1985), 64–5.

[122] Alfred left land to Edward the Elder at Stratton in Triggshire in Cornwall in his will, and to his younger son, Æthelweard land 'at Lifton and the lands which belong to it, namely all that I have in Cornwall except in Triggshire': Keynes and Lapidge, *Alfred the Great*, 175–6, *EHD* i, no. 96. Lifton is in Devon, just across the Tamar from Launceston.

Map 5. South-West Britain and Brittany
The names of territories in Dumnonia, of which Cornwall was a part, and in Brittany show the close connections between the two countries: Dumnonia/Domnonia, Cernew (Cornwall) / Kernev (Cornouaille), and Trigg and Treger (both from an earlier Trecorii).

in which names of territories north of the Channel find themselves repeated in Brittany (see Map 5). The *Tricorii* of Trigg in Cornwall correspond to Tregor (Tréguier) in Brittany; to Cornwall (Cornish Kernow, Welsh Cernyw) as a whole corresponds Kernev (Cornouaille); and to Dumnonia, the Domnonia of North Brittany.[123] Moreover, the coincidence of names pertains, in the main, to the sixth and seventh centuries, not to an earlier period.

Caesar records several peoples in the area of Gaul that would become Brittany. He includes them among a wider group, the *civitates Armoricae*, 'peoples by the sea', a description which he attributes to the Gauls themselves; the same peoples are attested for the late Roman period in the *Notitia Galliarum*.[124] By the late fourth century, at least, the capitals of two of these *civitates* had moved to coastal forts.

[123] Cf. Giot, Guigon and Merdrignac, *The British Settlement of Brittany*, 122.

[124] Caesar, *De Bello Gallico*, vii. 75; cf. the earlier list at ii. 34; for the late Roman period, see *Notitia Galliarum*, ed. Mommsen, *Chronica Minora*, i, MGH AA ix. 586–7.

Osismi — The westernmost *civitas* probably had Carhaix as its original capital, to judge by the layout of the roads. Coastal forts, such as Brest, came to be of major importance from the late third century, but it is doubtful whether Brest replaced Carhaix as Alet replaced Corseul among the Coriosolites.[125] The diocesan see came to be placed at Saint-Pol-de-Léon, perhaps no earlier than 845.[126] The territory of the Osismi was eventually divided between three bishoprics, Saint-Pol, Quimper, and Tréguier. References to a bishop of the Osismi do not show where, within their territory, he might have had his see.

Curiosolites — The native name is likely to have been Coriosolites, which Caesar adapted to suit readers familiar with Latin.[127] The capital was Corseul, about 11 km west-north-west of Dinan; the name of the town, Corseul, derives from the name of the people, a common feature of *civitas* capitals, but one that suggests that Corseul must have remained the capital until the Late-Roman period. It appears then to have been replaced by Alet or Aleth, probably 340 × 350, now part of St.-Servan-sur-Mer, in the southern part of St.-Malo. Alet, like Brest, was a coastal fort.[128] The rural population in the Roman period was denser towards the north coast; while the urban population recovered in the fourth century from the disasters of the third, the rural population did not.[129]

Veneti — Vannes was the capital in the Roman period; like Corseul it bears the name of the people, but, unlike Corseul, it survived as capital and, therefore, as the bishop's see into the Merovingian period and beyond.[130]

Redones — Rennes was the capital in the Roman period and again bears the name of the people. Like Vannes, it became the bishop's see and retained its status in the Merovingian period and beyond (Gregory of Tours, *Hist.*, viii. 32).

125 G. Le Duc, 'L'évêché mythique de Brest', *Britannia Monastica*, 3 (1994), 169–99; P. Guigon, *Les Églises du haut moyen âge en Bretagne*, 2 vols., Les Dossiers du Centre Régional d'Archéologie d'Alet, Suppléments T and U (Saint-Malo, 1997–8), i. 131–3; L. Pape, *La Civitas des Osismes à l'époque gallo-romaine* (Paris, 1978), 95–100; Fleuriot, *Origines de la Bretagne*, 30–2.

126 In the subscriptions to the first Council of Orléans, 511, 'Litardus episcopus de Vxuma', has been taken to be bishop of Saint-Pol-de-Léon: J. Gaudemet and B. Basdevant, *Les Canons des conciles mérovingiens (VIe – VIIe siècles)* (Paris, 1989), i. 90; cf. Fleuriot, *Origines*, 31, Giot, Guigon and Merdrignac, *The British Settlement of Brittany*, 135, who deny any link between Vxuma and the Osismi; but the supposition that Vxuma might be a Spanish see shows little sense of the history of Frankish–Visigothic relations at the time. L. Duchesne, *Fastes épiscopaux de l'ancienne Gaule* 3 vols. (Paris, 1894–1915), ii. 243 n., took it to be Exmes in the diocese of Séez. Similarly, in the Council of Paris, 614, 'Ex ciuitate Sammo Marcellus episcopus' has hesitantly been taken to refer to Saint-Pol-de-Léon: Gaudemet and Basdevant, *Les Canons des conciles mérovingiens*, ii. 524–5. Cf. Guigon, *Les Églises du haut moyen âge en Bretagne*, i. 125, 133.

127 *Ciuitas Coriosolitum* is the most likely reading of the *Notitia Galliarum* (395 × 455), ed. Mommsen, *Chron. Min.* i, MGH AA ix. 586; Fleuriot, *Les Origines de la Bretagne*, 251.

128 Marked as 'Cité d'Aleth' on the 1:100,000 IGN Map No. 16; L. Langouët, *Les Fouilles archéologiques de la zone des cathedrales d'Alet*, Les Dossiers du Centre Régional d'Archéologie d'Alet, Suppl. J (Saint-Malo, 1987); id., *La Cité d'Alet: de l'agglomeration gauloise à l'île de Saint-Malo*, Les Dossiers du Centre Régional d'Archéologie d'Alet, S (Saint-Malo, 1996), 73; L. Langouët, *Les Coriosolites: un peuple Armoricain de la période gauloise à l'époque gallo-romaine*, Les Dossiers du Centre Régional d'Archéologie d'Alet, suppl. K (Saint-Malo, 1988), 265–75; L. Pape, *La Bretagne romaine* (Rennes, 1995), 250–1, 261.

129 L. Langouët and M.Y. Daire, *La Civitas gallo-romaine des Coriosolites: le milieu rural* (Rennes, 1989), Figure 7, p. 17; pp. 28–9.

130 Council of Vannes, 461 × 491, ed. C. Munier, *Concilia Galliae A. 314–A. 506*, CCSL 148 (Turnhout, 1963), 150–7, *ecclesia Venetica*, 151; Gregory of Tours, *Hist.* x. 9.

Namnetes — Nantes was the capital and, again, bore the name of the people and retained its status to become an episcopal see.[131]

There is a clear distinction between those *civitates* that retained their capitals into the Merovingian period and those whose capitals were moved to coastal forts. The former also survived as *civitates*, but the latter did not. Whereas the Namnetes, Veneti, and Redones are all mentioned by Gregory of Tours, and their bishops appeared in Church councils or other great occasions, neither Gregory nor the councils attest the Osismi or the Coriosolites, with the single very doubtful exception of *Vxuma* in the first Council of Orléans (AD 511).[132] In Venantius Fortunatus's poem on the dedication of a new cathedral church for Nantes by its bishop, Felix, the assembled bishops are named: first Euphronius, metropolitan bishop of Tours, then the bishops of Angers, Rennes, Le Mans, and, from a neighbouring province, Coutances.[133] Even Vannes is not here represented, in spite of Felix's involvement with Brittany and Vannes in particular, well attested by Venantius Fortunatus and Gregory of Tours.[134] In the sixth century, Rennes and Nantes were outside Brittany, but subject to raids from the west.[135] Yet, even so, the division between surviving *civitates* and those subsumed into new political units did not coincide with the boundary between Brittany and the neighbouring *Romania*. Vannes was within Brittany and yet survived as a *civitas*.

The first evidence for the political geography of northern and north-western Brittany comes from the First Life of St Samson of Dol. The saint is shown as acting as emissary at the court of Childebert I (511–558) on behalf of a contender for the throne of Domnonia.[136] As far as one can tell, Domnonia then included the whole of northern Brittany from St Samson's church at Dol in the north-east to Léon in the north-west. At that period, Cornouaille (Kernev) and Tréguier (Tregor) are likely to have been districts within Domnonia, just as, across the Channel, Cornwall, including Trigg, was then part of Dumnonia.[137]

On the peninsula of Rhuys, south of the city of Vannes and enclosing the Morbihan, 'The Little Sea', lay the principal church of St Gildas, looking out to the south-west across the Bay of Quibéron to Belle-Ile and the Atlantic Ocean. Here, near to the southern limit of the lands of the Britons, the writer of his Life imagined Gildas to have ended his long journey from *Arecluta* in the north.[138]

[131] Venantius Fortunatus, *Opera Poetica*, ed. F. Leo, MGH AA iv.1 (Berlin, 1881), iii. 4–10, iv. 1.

[132] The most important council for the province of Tours is the Council of Tours, 567, *Les Canons des conciles mérovingiens*, ed. and trans. Gaudemet and Basdevant, ii. 346–99, which, although it encompassed bishops from outside the province, has an attached letter by four bishops of the province, those of Tours, Angers, Nantes, and Le Mans.

[133] Ibid. iii. 6.

[134] Venantius Fortunatus, *Opera Poetica*, iii. 5, line 7; Gregory of Tours, *Hist.*, iv. 4.

[135] Gregory of Tours, *Hist.*, v. 29, 31, ix. 24, x. 9.

[136] *Vita I S. Samsonis*, i. 59, ed. and trans. Flobert, *La Vie ancienne de Saint Samson de Dol*, 232; trans. Taylor, *The Life of St. Samson of Dol*, 58.

[137] The first attestation of the name Cornouaille/Kernev is in the Annals of Flodoard, *s.a.* 919, ed. Ph. Lauer, *Les Annales de Flodoard* (Paris, 1906), 1.

[138] *Vita S. Gildae, Auctore Monacho Ruiensi*, ed. and trans. H. Williams, *Gildae De Excidio Britanniae* (London, 1899), 348, 368, 370.

4. CHRONOLOGY

The history of Wales and the Britons between the Romans and the Normans falls naturally into three broad periods. First, there is the post-Roman phase: the period of war and loss of territory, and of a consequent steep decline in material culture, but the period also of the colonization of Brittany and the conversion of Ireland. At this stage it remained uncertain whether the Britons would continue to be regarded as one among the peoples of the former Empire or be relegated to the status of barbarians. A major change began when Gregory the Great formed his plan to convert the English by means of Frankish help, beginning in the south-east, closest to Francia and yet most distant from the British Christians in the west. It was completed when, in 664, the Synod of Whitby ended 'the episcopacy of the Irish' in Northumbria, and when in 669 Theodore of Tarsus arrived from Rome as archbishop of the whole Island of Britain and with the firm belief that the Britons and the northern Irish were schismatics and heretics.

Secondly, there is the period of isolation and the consolidation of the frontier. It is characteristic of this period that there survive fewer British place-names in Shropshire than in Staffordshire, in Devon than in Dorset. Although Staffordshire included the heartland of Mercia, whereas the Shropshire plain was a later acquisition, the anglicization of place-names was carried out more thoroughly in the latter, adjacent to the frontier. Instead of British populations living under English rule, as in the earlier period of English conquest, the frontier came to mark the limits of peoples as well as of kingdoms. Offa's Dyke, built to defend the heartland of Mercia from the Welsh, exemplified the much more impermeable frontier established by deliberate English policy in the eighth century. Trade no longer moved so much along the western seaways from the Bay of Biscay north into the Irish Sea, as in the first period, but instead flourished between the specialized trading towns of south-eastern and eastern England and those of north-eastern Francia and Frisia. As the centre of power in Francia moved eastwards in the second half of the seventh and the first half of the eighth century, so the power and the prosperity of the English in eastern Britain was enhanced at the expense of the Britons.

The third period is much less one of isolation; instead the growth of a united kingdom of the English on one side, and the Viking domination of the Irish Sea, on the other, ensured that the history of Wales and Cumbria would be shaped by outside powers. At the beginning of this period Cornwall was finally made a constituent part of Wessex. This was the period of the first rise and fall of an English Empire of Britain, an empire that could hardly match rhetoric with deeds without exerting effective authority over its British neighbours. Yet, its ability to exercise effective power over the Britons varied markedly from one period to another. This third period followed the conformity of the British churches to Rome, and thus the end of one source of isolation, and the drawing of Mercia into the shadow of Wessex, the first prerequisite of the tenth-century kingdom of the English.

The distribution and the problems of evidence change from period to period: for the first, post-Roman, phase the testimony of Gildas and the inscriptions of western Britain are crucial. They thus receive extended treatment. Also crucial, especially since this is the period in which Brittany was created, is the evidence of external observers such as Gregory of Tours, Venantius Fortunatus, and, even further afield, Procopius of Caesarea. In the period of isolation, Bede becomes a major source, and so too are the British, Irish, and English chronicles preserved in later copies: the *Annales Cambriae*, the various descendants of the Chronicle of Ireland, and those of the Anglo-Saxon Chronicle. In this period, also, the earlier charters preserved in the Book of Llandaff, in the margins of the Lichfield Gospels, and as an appendix to the Life of St Cadog, begin to throw light on the inner workings of Welsh society. In the third phase the annalistic sources become richer and it begins to be possible to include texts composed after 1064, our chronological limit, such as the Lives of St David and St Cadog or the Welsh laws. In the first phase, the historian inevitably looks forward in time from the Roman Empire of the fourth century; and in the last phase he would be unnecessarily austere not to make prudent use of the richer documentation that is to follow.

Some themes, however, continue in one shape or another from one period to the next. One, obviously, is the relationship between the Britons and the English; but another is the network of cultural connections linking Wales to Ireland and Wales to the northern Britons, Cornwall, and Brittany. Whether it is the welcome given to the writings of Gildas in Ireland or the intellectual one-upmanship at the court of Merfyn Frych, king of Gwynedd (825–840) between Irish and British scholars, or the tenth-century Cornish manuscript, probably from St Germans, preserved in the Bodleian Library, that contains Welsh alongside Cornish, the culture of the Britons of Wales was nourished from the seaways along the western side of Britain.[139]

[139] For these, see below, Chs. 5 § iii and 19.

PART I

AFTER ROME

1

Britain, 350–550

In 350 Britain was a prosperous 'diocese' within the Roman Empire, divided into four or even five provinces: Britannia Prima in the west, with its provincial capital close to its south-eastern edge, at Cirencester; Britannia Secunda in the north, with its capital at York; Flavia Caesariensis, roughly what eventually became England between the Humber and the Wash, with Lincoln as its capital; and Maxima Caesariensis in the south-east, with its capital at London. In the second half of the fourth century there appears to have been a fifth province, Valentia, named in honour of the Emperor Valentinian I after Count Theodosius's restoration of Roman power in 367–368, but its location is uncertain.[1] Since Britain was divided into a number of provinces, it was regularly known as 'the Britains' in the plural, *Britanniae*. In the elaborately hierarchical organization of the late Roman state, the diocese of 'the Britains' formed part of 'the Prefecture of the Gauls' that embraced most of what is now France and all of Spain, namely the dioceses that faced the Atlantic from Gibraltar to Scotland. Many levels of territorial government lay between the primary unit, the *civitas*, a city with its territory, and the emperor himself and the central government: above the Silures of what is now south-east Wales or the Demetae of south-west Wales came the province of Britannia Prima; above the province came the diocese of the Britains; and above the diocese came the Prefecture of the Gauls.

Rome was an empire but it was also a civilization—a civilization mainly of the elite but in which large segments of the population participated. Yet, the material impact of this Roman civilization was uneven in Britain as it was in many other dioceses. What would become Wales was only deeply affected in the south-east;[2] what would become Cornwall was largely untouched. The villae—namely country estates with their central buildings constructed according to Roman ideas of civilized life—reached no further northwards than the North Riding of Yorkshire.[3] The most Romanized areas in 350 were those that, by 550, would be most securely English; the least Romanized areas in 350 were those that two hundred years later

[1] Ammianus, *Res Gestae*, xxviii. 3. 7; P. Salway, *Roman Britain* (Oxford, 1981), 392–6; S. Frere, *Britannia*, 1999 edn. 205, suggests that York was the capital of Valentia, but in the 1987 edn. 200, Carlisle.

[2] Crops marks have been discovered indicating that there was a villa at Abermagwr near the Roman fort at Trawsgoed in the Ystwyth valley, south-east of Aberystwyth in Ceredigion: *Current Archaeology*, 240 (March 2010), 8–9; and this has been confirmed by excavation, *Current Archaeology*, 247 (October 2010), 10.

[3] Ordnance Survey, *Roman Britain*, 5th edn.: the most northerly is at Quarry Farm, close to Thornaby-on-Tees.

would still retain some continuity with the Roman past.[4] This paradox will be pursued further in succeeding chapters; first, however, we need some outline narrative of the events that changed a Roman diocese of the Britains into two Britains, the Britain of the Britons and the Britain of the English.

Since the second half of the third century there had been a series of forts along the eastern and southern coasts of Britain, forming part of a system of defence against Saxon raiders, a system known as 'the Saxon Shore'. On the western coasts there were more scattered forts designed to keep the Irish at bay. At least on the eastern side of the island, the forts were combined with fleets. In the north, Hadrian's Wall, closing off the narrow land between the mouth of the Tyne and the Solway, was the base for advance forts in the area between the Wall and the Forth–Clyde line. This defence was thus established in depth, whether by sea or by land, and it remained effective until 360. By then, however, the very prosperity of Britain and the power of the Empire had had a major impact on the political and military organization of its neighbours. Since the third century, major confederations had emerged east of the Rhine, the Franks opposite Lower Germany, the Alamans opposite Upper Germany, and the Saxons to the east and north-east of the Franks. For Britain, the Franks and the Saxons were of the greatest concern; both still remained confederations of small peoples, but both were capable, on occasion, of united attacks on the frontier. Similarly in the north, beyond the Forth and Clyde, a Pictish confederation had emerged, first attested in 297;[5] again it included distinct peoples, but relations with the Empire had encouraged some form of unity.[6] In Ireland, the *Scotti* may be of similar origin, since the name is only attested from the late Empire. The *Attacotti*, perhaps located in Northern Ireland, may have been another Irish confederation.[7]

An attempt has been made to question this account of the origin of the Picts using the evidence of finds of Roman objects on settlement sites.[8] The idea of a Pictish confederation emerging out of the relationship between the peoples beyond the Antonine Wall and the Roman Empire is held to imply a certain distribution of material resources: 'We might expect this [confederation] to be reflected in the emergence of regional-scale distributions of material culture and the development of larger scale power centres.'[9] Yet this depends on the nature of the confederation: only if the confederation was dominated by one or two centres of power would one expect any change in material culture or the development of a larger-scale centre of power.

[4] A. Sargent, 'The North–South Divide Revisited: Thoughts on the Character of Roman Britain', *Britannia*, 33 (2002), 219–26 (but rather than north–south, the division is, as Sargent sees it, north and west *versus* south and east).

[5] *XII Panegyrici Latini*, ed. R. A. B. Mynors, Oxford Classical Texts (Oxford, 1964), VI (VII). vii. 2, VIII. xi. 4, pp. 190, 222; F. T. Wainwright (ed.), *The Problem of the Picts* (Edinburgh, 1955), 2; N. K. Chadwick, 'The Name Pict', *Scottish Gaelic Studies*, 8 (1955–8), 146–76; J. Fraser, *From Caledonia to Pictland: Scotland to 795* (Edinburgh, 2009), 44–54.

[6] J. Mann, 'The Northern Frontier after AD 369', *Glasgow Archaeological Journal*, 3 (1974), 34–42.

[7] T. M. Charles-Edwards, *Early Christian Ireland* (Cambridge, 2000), 158–60.

[8] F. Hunter, *Beyond the Edge of Empire—Caledonians, Picts and Romans*, Groam House Lecture (Rosemarkie, 2007).

[9] Ibid. 45.

1. THE 'BARBARIAN CONSPIRACY' OF 367 AND ITS CONTEXT

In 360, the *Scotti* and *Picti* broke an existing treaty between themselves and the Roman authorities; they then mounted major attacks on Britain.[10] Irish participation indicates an ability to move men across the sea in large numbers; this is most easily explained if they had had the major share in the trade likely to have occurred under the terms of the treaty broken in 360. In 364, Britain continued to suffer from attacks by Picts, Saxons, *Attacotti*, and *Scotti*.[11] In 367, there occurred what was believed by the Romans to be a 'great conspiracy' between the *Scotti*, *Attacotti*, *Picti*, and *Saxones*, as well as Franks, leading to a major combined attack on Roman Britain and the northern coastlands of Gaul.[12] The primary target of the Saxons and Franks was apparently Gaul rather than Britain.[13] The *Scotti*, *Attacotti*, and *Picti* were able to defeat and demoralize the Roman army in Britain to such an extent that they could devote themselves to plundering the country. Some cities must have suffered, since they are said by Ammianus to have been restored by Count Theodosius.[14] When this Theodosius (father of the later emperor) was sent by the Emperor Valentinian to recover Britain, he established his base at Richborough, and was followed by four detachments of the field army, Batavians, Heruli, Iovii, and Victores.[15] He then made for London, encountering detachments of the enemy, burdened by plunder, on his way. The invaders, therefore, had been able to plunder even the far south-east. After he had entered London to the huge relief of the citizens, Count Theodosius was able to entice back many of those who had deserted from the Roman army in Britain in the face of barbarian invasion and victory. With these reinforcements and his four elite detachments from the field army, he was able to clear the British provinces of the barbarians and restore the Roman order.

A striking feature of Ammianus's contemporary account is that Theodosius was confronted almost as much by disloyalty within the former army of Britain as he was by barbarians. The invasion of 367 seems to have begun with the treachery of the frontier scouts, whose responsibility it was to monitor the peoples north of the Wall from advance forts at Bewcastle in the west and Risingham in the east.[16] Their treachery was then imitated by others in the army to the south.

The British peoples between Hadrian's Wall and the Forth are not mentioned as such in Ammianus's narrative, yet the implication of what he says about the frontier scouts, the *arcani* or *areani*, would appear to be that the Britons beyond Hadrian's

10 Ammianus, *Res Gestae*, xx. 1; Frere, *Britannia* (1999 edn.), 344.

11 Ammianus, *Res Gestae*, xxvi. 4. 5.

12 Ibid. xxvii. 8.

13 Assuming that the *Gallicani tractus* of Ammianus, xxvii. 8. 5, were the coastlands of Gaul, not the coastlands of Britain facing Gaul. I. N. Wood, 'The Channel from the Fourth to the Seventh Centuries AD', in S. McGrail (ed.), *Maritime Celts, Frisians and Saxons* (London, 1990), 94.

14 Ammianus, *Res Gestae*, xxviii. 3. 2.

15 Ibid. xxvii. 3.

16 Ammianus, xxviii. 3. 8. High Rochester may not have been occupied after 343: Salway, *Roman Britain*, 352.

Wall had joined, or been compelled to join, the great barbarian conspiracy. Although Ammianus portrays Theodosius's achievement as a general restoration of the Roman defences and administration, it is doubtful whether the forts north of the Wall were reoccupied after 367.[17] And it is certain that he abolished the frontier scouts, whose treachery had facilitated the barbarian invaders.[18] Yet, even though the northern Britons were probably part of the 'barbarian conspiracy', they were not, in the long run, assimilated into the Pictish confederation. Why this was so, is not easy to explain. After all, the Picts originated as a confederation of British peoples beyond the reach of Rome, so that one might imagine that any British people beyond Hadrian's Wall that shared in a major Pictish attack on Roman Britain would be likely to be brought into the Pictish federation itself. There may, therefore, have been a contrast between a short-term participation in the great attack of 367 and a quite different and more long-term policy in normal times. What was happening in northern Britain in the late fourth century cannot be understood without taking the long term into account.

So far as we can tell, the peoples north of the Forth were regarded in the first and second centuries as Britons; the leading people among them, according to Tacitus's Life of his father-in-law Agricola, was called the Caledonii (Welsh Celyddon); others mentioned elsewhere included the Verturiones and the Maeatae. Because of the predominance of the Caledonii, Tacitus used the term Caledonia for the land Agricola was attempting to conquer beyond the Forth and Clyde, and even speaks of 'the peoples inhabiting Caledonia'.[19] From the Renaissance, therefore, it was only natural to adopt Caledonia as a Latin name for Scotland. Yet any temptation to assume a distinction between Britons and Caledonians in Antiquity should be resisted: for Tacitus, the Caledonians were Britons. By the eighth century, however, the Picts were, for Bede, a distinct people with their own language—distinct both from the Britons to the south and from the Irish; and there is no reason to think that his perception was in any way idiosyncratic.[20] Yet, if the particular ways in which the Pictish language became distinct from British are examined, all of them can be dated later than the emergence of Picts in the written sources at the end of the third century.[21] The linguistic distinctiveness of the Picts, accepted without question by Bede, was, by the eighth century, real; but it appears to have been a consequence, not a precondition, of the Pictish confederation. Picts came first, Pictish only subsequently. The internal composition of the federations opposing Roman power in the north varied from one occasion to another. In the reign of Severus, the Maeatae, supported by Caledonii, opposed Roman power in the

[17] Salway, *Roman Britain*, 383, translates the *praetenturis* of Ammianus, xxviii. 3. 7, as 'frontier garrisons', but Rolfe has 'outposts' and W. Hamilton, *Ammianus Marcellinus: The Later Roman Empire (*AD *354–378)* (London, 1986), has 'defence-works'. The possible range of meanings for *praetentura* would encompass all of these, *Thesaurus Linguae Latinae, s.v.*

[18] Ammianus, xxviii. 3. 8.

[19] Tacitus, *Agricola*, c. 25.

[20] Bede, *HE* i. 1, where the phrase *quinque gentium linguis* 'five languages of peoples' is especially significant.

[21] They are listed by K. H. Jackson in Appendix I of F. T. Wainwright (ed.), *The Problem of the Picts* (Edinburgh, 1955), 161–6.

north.[22] According to Ammianus, the Picts were divided into two peoples, the *Dicalydones* and the *Verturiones*.[23] The latter gave the early medieval name for a territory, Fortriu, and strong arguments have been put forward for placing this north of the Mounth.[24] Throughout the late-Roman and post-Roman periods, therefore, the Picts remained a federation of peoples.

As we have seen, such federations of smaller peoples emerged in the late Empire on the Rhine frontier: the Franks on the lower Rhine and the Alamans on the upper Rhine. The Pictish federation is likely to be another such political effect of the Roman frontier: as the Franks emerged opposite Lower Germany and the Alamans opposite Upper Germany, so the Picts appear to have been the federation that emerged opposite the northern frontier of Britain. Yet, if this is the case, the effective frontier in this context was not Hadrian's Wall. In the end, it was not even precisely the Antonine Wall, but further north, especially in the west, where the main British centre of power in the post-Roman period was Alclud, Dumbarton Rock, on the north side of the Clyde and also to the north of the Antonine Wall. The boundary between Pict and Briton lay along the northern frontiers of peoples, the Votadini in the east and the Dumnonii in the west, not any Roman fortified *limes*.[25] It is difficult to see how this could have happened unless those northern peoples that remained British had been Roman clients on an enduring basis.[26] On the other hand, those peoples that were brought into the Pictish federation would either not have been Roman clients at all or clients only for a short period.

Whether this system of clientship was restored after the crisis of 367 has been debated. According to one view, the finds from the excavation of Traprain Law in Votadinian territory included plenty of ordinary Roman material from an earlier period, but after 367 only what was interpreted as 'a great treasure of stolen Roman plate'.[27] More recently, however, it has been argued that some of this bullion, at least, corresponds to Roman weights and might, therefore, have been a gift or gifts to clients or allies.[28] A parallel from the fifth century may be helpful here. During St Patrick's episcopate in Ireland, the soldiers of a British king called Coroticus allied themselves with Picts and Irish in order to carry out a raid within Ireland. The raid was successful in carrying off slaves, including some who had only recently been baptized. In response, Patrick wrote an open letter addressed to these soldiers. He did not say what territory Coroticus ruled, but a list of contents in the Book of Armagh identified him as king of Ail Cluaithe, namely Alclud. The alliance with Picts in a raid on Irish territory makes this very plausible, and the name Ceredig

[22] Dio Cassius, lxxvi. 8. 6; lxxvii. 12–13, 15. 2.

[23] Ammianus, xxvii. 8. 5.

[24] A. Woolf, 'Dún Nechtain, Fortriu and the Geography of the Picts', *Scottish Historical Review*, 85 (2006), 182–201.

[25] Admittedly the dividing line may have shifted northwards in the post-Roman period, but compare the way Brigantian territory extended north of Hadrian's Wall in the west: Salway, *Roman Britain*, 176.

[26] For example, D. J. Breeze, *The Northern Frontiers of Roman Britain* (London, 1982), 152, inferred from Traprain Law 'a special relationship between the Votadini and Rome'.

[27] Salway, *Roman Britain*, 386.

[28] A. S. Esmonde Cleary, *The Ending of Roman Britain* (London, 1989), 99.

appears in the pedigree of the kings of Alclud.[29] If this is correct, what is striking is the way Patrick denounced the king's soldiers: 'I do not describe them as my citizens nor as citizens of Roman Christians, but as citizens of the demons.'[30] These words would have no point unless the soldiers of Coroticus would have considered themselves to be Patrick's fellow-citizens and citizens of the Romans. The date at which this letter was written is probably in the second half of the fifth century, approximately a century after 'the barbarian conspiracy' of 367 and long after the Roman army had been withdrawn from Britain. What it shows, provided Coroticus is correctly identified, is that a British king could ally with Picts and *Scotti* to mount a raiding expedition on Ireland of much the same kind as those that devastated Roman Britain a century earlier, and that he could be denounced on these grounds for flouting the obligations of a 'citizen'. The geographical limit of 'the citizens' would appear now to be identical with the limit of British territory. This could hardly have happened unless the kind of alliance of northern Britons with Picts and *Scotti* that apparently took place in the 360s, and again with Coroticus, had been exceptional. Otherwise the major divide would have come to be on the Tyne–Solway line, not on the Forth and the watershed on the north side of the Clyde basin.

Any ethnic distinction, then, between Pict and Briton was only slowly emerging in the late Roman period. The division between those who were part of the Pictish federation and the Britons was not initially ethnic but a political and cultural division between a normal adhesion to Rome and normal independence. The northern Britons' adhesion to Rome was not just a matter of clientship, but extended into broader aspects of culture. The Britons adopted the habit of putting up inscriptions from Rome; they accepted Christianity earlier and more readily than did the Picts.[31] Part of the significance of 367, therefore, lay in an abnormality: the northern Britons, on this occasion, would appear to have combined their forces with those of the Picts, the *Scotti*, and the *Attacotti*, whereas, normally, they sided with Rome. The significance of Patrick's encounter with Coroticus is the same. The king's alliance with Picts and *Scotti* is treated as an aberration, showing that the normal allegiance endured long after the Roman army had been withdrawn.

2. MAGNUS MAXIMUS AND BRITAIN

After the crisis of 367, Britain slipped out of Ammianus's narrative. A brief reference in his summary of the virtues and vices of Valentinian I as an emperor indicates that all was not well. The emperor, we are told, was a severe disciplinarian when dealing with lower ranks, but allowed his senior commanders to get away with far too much: 'Hence, discontent in Britain, disasters in Africa and the devastation of Illyricum'.[32] Evidently, the government of the diocese between 367 and 375 was not always to the liking of the Britons, but Ammianus appears

[29] HG § 5 in *EWGT* 10.
[30] Patrick, *Epistola ad Milites Corotici*, § 2.
[31] See below, 139–48.
[32] Ammianus, *Res Gestae*, xxx. 9. 1.

to have thought that the troubles in Britain were less serious than those in Africa and Illyricum.

In 378 Ammianus's narrative comes to an end, and the quality of the surviving sources for the subsequent period is much poorer. The next point at which Britain emerges into the limelight is with the usurpation of Magnus Maximus in 381.[33] He was, like the Theodosii, father and son, a Spaniard and a career soldier. He had been linked with Count Theodosius both in Britain and, later, in Africa when the revolt of Firmus was suppressed. Theodosius, however, was executed at the outset of Gratian's reign, perhaps as part of a general move against successful generals who might endanger the new regime.[34] At the date of the usurpation, Maximus held high office in the army in Britain; and in 382 he showed himself to be a successful general in defeating another incursion of Picts and *Scotti*.[35]

In 383 he took an army across to Gaul; the western emperor, Gratian, was caught and killed by one of Maximus's generals, and Maximus took over his capital at Trier. From 383 until 387, Maximus ruled the three dioceses forming the Prefecture of the Gauls: Gaul, Spain, and Britain. Gratian's younger brother, Valentinian II, ruled in Italy and received the solid support of a large section of the Italian aristocracy, but Maximus's hope was that he would receive recognition as senior western emperor—senior, that is, to Valentinian II—from the eastern emperor, Theodosius, the son of Count Theodosius. In this, he was apparently briefly successful in 386; but, in 387, he invaded Italy and drove Valentinian II into flight. This led, however, to a countermove by Theodosius the next year, 388, in which Maximus was defeated and killed.

Maximus was remembered in two very different ways by later Britons: as the ancestor of many of their royal dynasties,[36] but also as a tyrant, who had killed a legitimate emperor. Gildas's verdict was the most hostile:[37]

> Applying cunning rather than virtue, Maximus turned the neighbouring lands and provinces against Rome, and attached them to his own kingdom of wickedness with the nets of his perjury and lying. One of his wings he stretched out to Spain, one to Italy; the throne of his wicked empire he placed at Trier, where he raged so madly against his masters that of the two legitimate emperors he drove one from Rome, the other from his life—which was a very holy one.

[33] For his career, see A. Birley, *The Roman Government of Britain* (Oxford, 2005), 443–50.

[34] J. F. Matthews, *Western Aristocracies and Imperial Court, A.D. 364–425* (Oxford, 1975), 64; A. Demandt, 'Der Tod des älteren Theodosius', *Historia*, 17 (1969), 598–626, emphasizes the role of personal rivals taking advantage of the sudden death of Valentinian and Theodosius's absence in Africa.

[35] The Gallic Chronicle of 452, ed. R. W. Burgess, 'The Gallic Chronicle of 452: A New Critical Edition with a Brief Introduction', in R. W. Mathisen and D. Shanzer (eds.), *Society and Culture in Late Antiquity: Revisiting the Sources* (Aldershot, 2001), 52–84, at 67; ed. Th. Mommsen, *Chronica Minora*, i. 646, § 7.

[36] For example, HG §§ 2, 4, JC §§ 4, 13, 19, in *EWGT* 10, 44, 46. For the mention of Maximus on the Pillar of Eliseg see below, 417, 450–1.

[37] Gildas, *De Excidio*, c. 13, trans. M. Winterbottom, *Gildas: The Ruin of Britain and Other Documents* (London, 1978), 20–1.

As a consequence of Maximus's tyrannical usurpation, so Gildas wrote, 'Britain was despoiled of her whole army, her military resources, her governors, brutal as they were, and her sturdy youth, who had followed in the tyrant's footsteps, never to return home.' This was the beginning of the misery of Britain, when the Picts and the *Scotti* laid waste a defenceless land.

Gildas placed the attacks of the Picts and *Scotti* in the period between Maximus and an appeal made by the Britons to Aëtius, when he had been consul three times, namely between 446 and his death in 454.[38] He placed the attacks of the Saxons after the failure of the appeal to Aëtius. In both cases, he was dating events too late. As we have seen, the usurpation by Maximus came more than twenty years after the treaty with Picts and *Scotti* had broken down and fourteen years after 367; and, as we shall see later, the attacks of the Saxons were also placed much too late. Similarly, there is no reason to suppose that Maximus deprived Britain of the shield of the Roman army. Roman coins seem to have been supplied to the garrison at Caernarfon until the last decade of the fourth century, but not in the reign of Honorius: it may be that the rebellion of Eugenius, 392–394, caused the withdrawal of the garrison.[39] What Gildas may well have done was to conflate two or even three usurpers: Maximus, perhaps Eugenius, and someone whose career was to be critical for the administrative and military detachment of Britain from Rome, Constantine III.

3. CONSTANTINE III

The end of Roman military and governmental power in Britain came about as a result of two things: the desperate military crisis in Italy and Gaul and the failure of a usurpation mounted from Britain itself, the usurpation of Constantine III. However, in judging the significance of these events, we also need to bear in mind a distinction between acknowledgement of the emperor's authority as the supreme ruler of the Christian world and a wish to be subject to the direct power of the emperor, his army, and his tax-gatherers. The distinction emerges from the way Gregory of Tours, in his *Histories*, described the Emperor Justinian's invasion of Visigothic Spain. Gregory regarded himself as a Roman of senatorial rank. As a Catholic bishop he deeply disapproved of Visigothic Arianism. Yet, when he recounts Justinian's invasion against the Visigothic king Agila, who was not only an Arian but a tyrant, he describes the conquest of Spanish cities by the emperor's army as wrongful.[40] To restrict the Empire to those regions over which its armies

[38] Gildas, *De Excidio*, c. 20. The Aëtius who was consul in 454 was a different man: E. A. Thompson, 'Gildas and the History of Britain', *Britannia*, 10 (1979), 215 n. 60; *PLRE* ii. 29; see also N. J. Higham, *The English Conquest: Gildas and Britain in the Fifth Century* (Manchester, 1994), 125–34, and, more briefly, id. *Rome, Britain and the Anglo-Saxons* (London, 1992), 156–7, who argues that Gildas may well have had no text of the appeal. This is conceivable, but hardly the most likely interpretation. For the spelling Agitius, see J. M. Wallace-Hadrill, *Bede's Ecclesiastical History of the English People: An Historical Commentary* (OMT; Oxford, 1988), 210–11.

[39] Casey et al., *Excavations at Segontium*, 16.

[40] Gregory of Tours, *Hist.*, iv. 8 (he may have been influenced in part by the fact that some of the cities were recaptured by Athanagild, Agila's successor, and father of Brunhild, who married Sigibert,

had control and from which its tax-gatherers exacted tribute would be to neglect its wider influence and authority. This distinction is necessary in order to assess fairly what happened to Britain in the early fifth century, when, traditionally, Roman rule over Britain came to an end, in large part through a failure at the centre. For example, Bede, in his chronological summary in Book V, chapter 24, of the *Historia Ecclesiastica* stated it succinctly: 'In the year 409 Rome was subdued by the Goths and from that time the Romans ceased to rule in Britain.'[41] He thus tied together events in the heart of the Empire and on its outer fringe.

In modern scholarship, the relationship is less direct, but it is still there. The essential background is, as Bede implied, that when Alaric was threatening Italy, and still more after the fall of Stilicho in 408, the western Emperor Honorius was entirely unable to come to the rescue of the Britons, themselves subject to renewed Saxon attacks and also endangered by barbarian incursions into Gaul.[42] Stilicho, who held the reins of power in the West between the death of Theodosius in 395 and his own fall, may already have been obliged to move some troops from Britain, while strengthening fortifications.[43] In 401 Alaric had made his first descent into Italy and in 405 Stilicho was obliged to confront and defeat another invader, King Radagaisus. By this time, the imperial government in Italy was in desperate straits, casting about for ways to rescue its finances, appealing for self-help from citizens and even slaves.[44]

Under Stilicho one can see three fateful changes. The first was a shift in the balance between taxation and expenditure in frontier provinces. In the late Roman period, taxes were raised across the Empire but a high proportion was spent on the army, both the frontier troops and the field army. The pattern is evident in the West from the role of Trier as an imperial capital, well placed so that the emperor, with the field army, could bring help to the Rhine frontier. After 401, however, as military operations against Alaric and Radagaisus shifted to Italy, expenditure moved away from the frontier to the centre. The second shift that now becomes evident is from military emperors, such as Magnus Maximus or Theodosius, to an emperor who relied on someone else to conduct military affairs, as Stilicho did for Honorius. The third shift followed the second: since the emperor no longer conducted military operations himself, there was no reason why he should reside at such places as Trier or Milan. Instead, from the winter of 402/3 he took refuge behind the marshes at Ravenna, secure even from an enemy within Italy. The

king of the eastern Franks; Sigibert and Brunhild ensured that Gregory secured the see of Tours against local opposition).

41 Bede's dating was out by one year. Cf. *Historia Brittonum*, c. 28, probably derived from Bede, since it uses 409 for the length of Roman rule in Britain (that it is quite wrong only makes the derivation more likely).

42 The Chronicle of 452, ed. Burgess, 73 (AD 407: Gaul), 74 (AD 410: Britain); ed. Th. Mommsen, *Chron. Min.*, i. 652, 654, §§ 55 (Gaul), 62 (Britain).

43 Salway, *Roman Britain*, 420–5 (but I would regard any attempt to tie together the evidence of Gildas with that of Claudian as excessively hazardous).

44 Matthews, *Western Aristocracies and Imperial Court*, 276, citing *Codex Theodosianus*, vii. 13. 16–17.

danger from all this was that an implicit bargain exchanging taxes for defence on the frontier was now threatened.

In Britain, the initial response to the crisis was that the army set up tyrants; military usurpers who hoped by force to gain recognition as legitimate emperors. Three followed in quick succession: Marcus in the summer of 406; Gratian in October of the same year, and, finally, Constantine III in February 407.[45] During Gratian's brief ascendancy there occurred the celebrated incursion across the frozen Rhine on the last day of 406 by the Vandals, Suevi, and Alans. Constantine and his advisers appear to have concluded, or perhaps taken it for granted, that the fate of Britain was bound up with that of Gaul and Spain, with which Britain was joined in 'the Prefecture of the Gauls'. Although Britain was also threatened by its own enemies, it was necessary to cross the Channel with an army capable of meeting this new barbarian invasion of Gaul.

The so-called end of Roman rule in Britain was a direct consequence of the failure of Constantine III. He attempted to take control of Spain as well as of the western Alpine passes into Italy. His forces were overextended and he managed to alienate his principal military lieutenant, Gerontius. By 409, his regime, although now recognized by Honorius, was crumbling. Also, in 409, Britain as well as Gaul suffered major incursions which Constantine was unable to repel. This is the point reached in a famous passage from Zosimus (an East-Roman historian writing a century later but with a good source for this period in the early fifth-century history of Olympiodorus).[46] It begins with Constantine sending his son, Constans, back to Spain and so causing a rebellion by Gerontius:[47]

> . . . Constans was sent back to Spain by his father with Justus as his Magister. Angered at this, Gerontius won over his soldiers and incited the barbarians in Gaul to revolt against Constantine. The latter was not able to oppose them because most of his army was in Spain, which allowed the barbarians over the Rhine to make unrestricted incursions. They reduced the inhabitants of Britain and some of the Gallic peoples to such straits that they revolted from the Roman empire, no longer submitted to Roman law, and reverted to their native customs. The Britons, therefore, armed themselves and ran many risks to ensure their own safety and free their cities from the attacking barbarians. The whole of Armorica and other Gallic provinces, in imitation of the Britons, freed themselves in the same way, by expelling the Roman magistrates and establishing the government they wanted.

[45] E. A. Thompson, 'Britain AD 406–410', *Britannia*, 8 (1977), 208–18, whose chronology I follow, but not his interpretation of events, which is criticized by P. Bartholomew, 'Fifth-Century Facts', *Britannia*, 13 (1982), 261–70; Birley, *The Roman Government of Britain*, 455–60.

[46] The source seems to have been Olympiodorus from V. 26 to VI. 13: J. F. Matthews, 'Olympiodorus of Thebes and the History of the West (A.D. 407–425)', *Journal of Roman Studies*, 60 (1970), 81; Olympiodorus's information is likely to have come from among the pagan supporters of Stilicho, ibid. 89–90.

[47] Zosimus, *Historia Nova*, vi. 5.2–3, ed. and trans. F. Paschoud, *Zosime: Histoire nouvelle*, iii. 2 (Paris, 1989), 9. Trans. R. T. Ridley, *Zosimus: New History* (Sydney, 1982), 128–9. Important confirmatory evidence is supplied by a passage of the lost history by Renatus Profuturus Fregeridus preserved by Gregory of Tours, *Hist.*, ii. 9.

At the beginning of the revolt Constantine's officials were still in place in Britain, but his policies had led to the current disastrous situation: the barbarians were in Britain but Constantine's British army was scattered across Spain and Gaul. The revolt of which Zosimus writes was thus against Constantine's regime, now, of course, recognized as legitimate by Honorius, even though everyone knew that it had begun as a tyranny. The actions of the British *civitates* were portrayed by Zosimus as a revolt against the Roman Empire, presumably because his source (thought to be Olympiodorus) took a legitimist stance: Constantine had been recognized by Honorius.

There may, however, have been more to it than that: native British law evidently survived the Roman period as local custom. To give it the same authority as the law of the emperor would be revolutionary in the eyes of a Roman official. The phrases of Ridley's translation, 'they revolted from the Roman empire, no longer submitted to Roman law, and reverted to their native customs', might however be more literally translated as: 'they rejected the rule of the Romans and lived according to their own decisions, no longer submitting to their laws' (namely the laws of the Romans). Zosimus asserts this not just of the inhabitants of Britain but also of the whole of Armorica and some other Gallic provinces, that is, a considerable proportion of Gaul. Yet, we know for a certainty that a sizeable proportion of Gaul did not reject Roman law at this period, for we meet it still in operation in the sixth century even in the north, and, what is more, reflecting the Theodosian Code, which, in 409, still lay in the future.[48]

The standpoint of Zosimus's text is of a 'top-down' view of law: it comes from the emperor down through his officials to be obeyed by the inhabitants of each province. It is also a standpoint which expects there to be a clear distinction between a professional army and a civilian population: the emperor should control the army through which, in the last analysis, he can enforce his laws and raise his taxes. By law civilians were unarmed. It was this political order and this standpoint against which the Britons, by sheer necessity, rebelled. As one can see from Zosimus's text, they armed themselves and by their own efforts freed their cities—that is, their *civitates*—from the barbarians. A wholesale rejection of Roman law was not, therefore, in question, although some change in Britain may have occurred. In the next century Gildas would write of the Britons submitting to Roman law only superficially;[49] his own grasp of Roman legal terms seems to be excellent;[50] and yet medieval Welsh law is remarkably unRoman.

This was the context in which, in the next year, 410, the emperor Honorius wrote the celebrated letter understood to have instructed the British *civitates* to defend themselves; it is possible, however, that Honorius was actually writing to the people of Bruttium in southern Italy.[51] If it was directed to Britain, the

[48] *The Testament of Remigius*, ed. B. Krusch, MGH SRM iii. 336–47, short version repr. CCSL cxvii. 1, 473–9.

[49] Gildas, *De Excidio*, 5. 2.

[50] See below, 214–15.

[51] Zosimus, *Historia Nova*, vi. 10. 2; Birley, *The Roman Government of Britain*, 461–2, favours Bruttium.

implications were profound but also straightforward: Honorius was not in a position, in the year in which Rome fell to Alaric, to establish a new Roman army and a new *vicarius* for the diocese of Britain; he thus instructed the Britons to do what they had already been doing since the previous year. Indeed, the emperor had earlier, in 406, issued a law to provincials in general encouraging civilians and even slaves to take up arms against the barbarians; this applied in Italy let alone Britain.[52] Honorius gave his authority to the existing situation and by so doing legitimated a political order that was, in traditional Roman eyes, revolutionary. As he had been forced to legitimate Constantine III, so now he legitimated the *civitates* that had rebelled against Constantine. Britain was no longer defended by Roman armies and governed by Roman officials; it had ceased to pay taxes to a central government. In that sense, as a taxing, bureaucratic, monarchical government, Rome now lost Britain; and the loss was indeed mourned, for, after all, the taxes of Britain would have been very welcome to the cash-starved Roman government of the fifth century.[53] What is not true is that the Britons ceased to give their allegiance to a Roman emperor, even though they may well have been happy to see their taxes, which they may well have continued to pay, but in kind not in coin, remaining within the island.[54] Even Roman taxes were preferable to Anglo-Saxon conquest: the appeal to Aëtius, thrice consul, for military help, an appeal made between 446 and 454, came to nothing; but if it had, the appearance of a Roman army would have entailed the appearance, also, of Roman tax-gatherers.[55] In any event, to appeal to Aëtius presupposed an allegiance to an empire of which he was then the principal military leader in the West.

The end of Roman taxation plays a major role in some accounts of the end of Roman civilization in Britain.[56] The essence of the argument turns on the effects of the cycle of taxation and expenditure on the relationship between peasants and towns. The imperial government minted gold and silver coins for its own purposes, not to serve as a medium of exchange among the general population. The coins used by the latter were the lower-value bronze coins. Taxation was either in coin or in kind. If it was not imposed in kind, as had been common in the third century, the government required it to be paid in the high-value gold and silver coins. In order for the taxpayers to obtain such coins, various methods were followed: peasants might band together so that they could offer enough bronze coins to *nummularii*, money changers, to get higher-value coins in exchange; alternatively, they might rely on their landlords to bring together enough bronze coins to exchange for gold and silver; and, in that case, their obligations to the state became

52 Matthews, *Western Aristocracies*, 276.

53 'Brittaniae Romano nomini in perpetuum sublatae', 'the British provinces removed for ever from the Roman dominion', *Narratio de Imperatoribus Domus Valentinianae et Theodosianae*, ed. Th. Mommsen, *Chron. Min.*, i. 630; dated to 423 × 450 by E. A. Thompson, 'Zosimus 6. 10. 2 and the Letters of Honorius, *Classical Quarterly*, 82 (1982), 445–62, at 461.

54 That they continued to be paid is suggested by the ability of the British authorities to offer *annonae* or *epimenia*: Gildas, *De Excidio*, 23. 5.

55 Gildas, *De Excidio*, c. 20.

56 A. S. Esmonde Cleary, *The Ending of Roman Britain*, 72–4; C. Wickham, *Framing the Early Middle Ages: Europe and the Mediterranean, 400–800* (Oxford, 2005), 309–10.

entangled with their obligations to their landlords. To obtain the bronze coins that were to be contributed to the sum required before they could be exchanged for gold or silver, peasants needed to sell produce; towns offered a market, but even in towns an important purchaser of peasant produce was the state itself, which required supplies for the army; and it may well be the case that the state operated through the same *nummularii* now functioning as grain merchants. The Empire both imposed taxes and bought the produce with which peasants could earn the wherewithal to pay the taxes. The consequence of imperial taxation, therefore, was to make towns essential to peasant agriculture. The existence of towns, however, was essential for the survival of a Roman way of life as well as a Roman economy. Just as the army was necessary for the peaceful order required for long-distance trade, so the taxation system that paid for the army also played a major role in promoting the towns through which such trade could be pursued. The implication of all this is that once the army was withdrawn from Britain and the *civitates* had to defend themselves, Roman tax-gatherers left with the army; without taxation peasants ceased to have a market, towns were likely to wither and, with them, the Roman way of life. This, so it is argued from the archaeological evidence, was what happened: no coins minted by the state reached Britain after the early years of the fifth century; and town life in the Roman manner did not survive in Britain beyond *c.* 430. So far as Wales was concerned, the most favourably placed town was the *civitas* capital at Caerwent. Yet, there too, there seems to have been a break between the Romano-British town, which did not endure beyond the early fifth century, and the later ecclesiastical Caerwent.[57]

There are some complications. First, what survived into subsequent centuries in the lands of the Britons and, through influence from Britain, in Ireland was not a coinage but the use of Roman weights of silver and gold as a medium of exchange.[58] In the long term, bronze rather than higher-value metals was what ceased to be used in conventional units when buying and selling. Secondly, the late Roman state sometimes taxed in kind rather than in coin, and the economic effects of this would have been different; the role of the *nummularii*, for example, would no longer be central. What happened to the relationship between defence and taxation after 410 is not clear. On the one hand, the implication of the urgings of Honorius's government as early as 405 that civilians take up arms against the barbarians was that the traditional divide between soldier and civilian would be eroded. Soldiering would no longer be a paid profession but rather a duty of all able-bodied men (normally only if they were free; an appeal to slaves was the ultimate mark of desperation). It would then be an aspect of gender and of status. To that extent, the Roman would come to live under the same conditions as his barbarian neighbour. On the other hand, Gildas wrote of the Saxon *foederati*, 'allied troops', receiving

[57] This is the conclusion of E. Campbell and P. Macdonald, 'Excavations at Caerwent Vicarage Orchard Garden, 1973: An Extramural Post-Roman Cemetery', *Archaeologia Cambrensis*, 142 (1993), 74–98.

[58] T. M. Charles-Edwards, *Early Irish and Welsh Kinship* (Oxford, 1993), 478–85; F. Kelly, *Early Irish Farming* (Dublin, 1997), 593–5.

from British authorities in the fifth century *annonae* and *epimenia*.[59] *Annona* was the normal word for the grain, and any other foodstuffs, taken in tax and supplied to the army; *epimenia* 'monthly rations' was more specific, indicating that such supplies were provided month by month. If this was what happened—and Gildas says that the *annona* or *epimenia* continued to be handed over to the Saxon *foederati* for a considerable period—it presupposed an ability on the part of the British authorities to tax in kind. Certainty, as usual, is impossible, but one may suggest that fifth-century Britain saw elements of both situations: both military force sustained by taxation in kind and military service as an aspect of gender and status. The first may perhaps have been more characteristic of the south and east, the second of the north and west. A military force sustained by taxation in kind could be British but could also be an army, or armies, of Saxon *foederati*.

Fifth-century Britain is best understood if it is put together with northern Gaul, north, that is, of the Loire. South of that line, Gaul was ruled either by the remnants of Roman imperial government—the Auvergne would even produce its own short-lived emperor, Avitus—or by relatively large and relatively Romanized Arian kingdoms, those of the Visigoths in the south-west and of the Burgundians in the Rhône valley. North of the Loire there emerged a mixture of small kingdoms—of the Britons in the west, of the Franks in the east, and even, for a time, a 'king of the Romans' in Soissons.[60] North of the Loire, therefore, such communities as survived from the Roman Empire, whether they derived ultimately from Britain or not, tended to be ruled by minor local kings, just like their pagan barbarian neighbours.[61] These minor kings imitated a distant Roman emperor and hoped to receive his alliance and his subsidies—or, failing that, those of an Ostrogothic king who, in his diplomacy, behaved as if he were a virtual emperor and whose letters could treat Germanic kingdoms further west and north as barbarian, unlike his own.[62] The world of Gildas was not very different from the world into which Clovis, the founder of the Frankish hegemony in north-western Europe, was born about 466.

4. THE ENGLISH SETTLEMENTS AND CONQUESTS

Speakers of Germanic languages had lived in Britain for centuries before 400; they had served in the Roman army and set up their altars to their own gods. Some Germans, after all, lived within the Roman Empire in the provinces of Germania Inferior and Germania Superior. These Germans in Britain, however, served Rome

[59] Gildas, *De Excidio*, c. 23. 5.

[60] Gregory of Tours, *Hist.*, ii. 27.

[61] At the end of the fifth century there were kings among the Bretons, Gregory of Tours, *Hist.* iv. 4, of Franks in Le Mans, Cambrai, Cologne, and elsewhere, ibid. ii. 40–2.

[62] Compare the coins of Zeno and the signet-ring in the grave of Childeric, J. J. Chifflet, *Anastasis Childerici I Francorum Regis, sive Thesaurus Sepulchralis Tornaci Nerviorum Effossus* (Antwerp, 1655), 96, 252, and Gregory of Tours, *Hist.*, ii. 38; Cassiodorus, *Variae*, ed. Th. Mommsen, MGH AA xii (Berlin, 1894), iii. 1–4, iv. 1–2, v. 1.

as individuals. Even if they settled in Britain and passed on their language to their children, their contribution to the huge change by which almost all lowland Britain became English-speaking was probably slight. We need to distinguish individual settlement from the settlement of whole communities, and we need to distinguish settlement from conquest and political control. In discussing the Germanic presence in Britain, it is essential to distinguish three phases: first, the presence of Germans within the structure of the Roman Empire; secondly, the presence of Germanic material alongside late Romano-British material within the same context; and, thirdly, Germanic material in new sites ancestral to later Anglo-Saxon phases. Only the third archaeological phase corresponds to the traditional concept of the *adventus Saxonum*.[63]

An intervening case is supplied by Ammianus, who records that, in 372, the emperor Valentinian I attacked one of the kings of the Alamanni, Macrianus.[64] Although he failed to catch his enemy, he replaced Macrianus as king of an Alamannic tribe, the Bucinobantes, by Fraomar. Shortly afterwards the territory of the Bucinobantes, which lay on the opposite side of the Rhine from Mainz, was devastated by attack, and Valentinian transferred Fraomar to Britain, with the title of tribune, where he was placed in command of a *numerus* of Alamanni, 'which at that time was distinguished for its numbers and strength'.[65] As king, Fraomar briefly ruled just one of the Alamannic peoples, the Bucinobantes; but the detachment of Alamanni that he came to command was apparently already in Britain before Valentinian transferred him from his territory opposite Mainz, and there is no reason to suppose that they had been recruited from the Bucinobantes in particular. The late Roman army made a habit of recruiting such detachments from across the frontier; they were composed of individual barbarians recruited from a particular area; and they did not normally bring their wives and children with them. This is to be distinguished from what later happened when entire peoples, men, women, and children, settled in the Empire.

The fact and distribution of settlement by communities emerges from the widespread appearance in eastern Britain of a burial rite uncharacteristic of the native Britons. During the Roman period the practice of supine extended inhumation had become general—that is, the body was buried rather than cremated and it was placed on its back with the legs extended rather than 'crouched'. Increasingly, also, people were buried with their heads to the west and their feet to the east. This, it should be noted, was the norm: local variations existed and sometimes survived through the processes of anglicization in Britain that created England.[66] The survival of such local variations is an important indication that a portion of the population continued in the same areas in spite of a shift of nationality from British

63 J. Hines, 'Philology, Archaeology, and the *Adventus Saxonum vel Anglorum*', in A. Bammesberger and A. Wollmann (eds.), *Britain 400–600: Language and History* (Heidelberg, 1990), 19–20.

64 Ammianus, *Res Gestae*, xxix. 4. 7.

65 This use of *numerus* 'number' for a detachment of an army is ubiquitous in the late Roman army, and is the source of Welsh *nifer*, in the sense of 'retinue' as well as 'number'.

66 This is one of the main conclusions of E. O'Brien, *Post-Roman Britain to Anglo-Saxon England: Burial Practices Reviewed*, BAR, Brit. Ser. 289 (Oxford, 1999), summarized on p. 185.

to English. Another important point is that the normal late Roman rite of burial was used by British pagans as well as Christians: it, as well as local varieties such as 'long-cist' burials, cannot be used without further corroboration as evidence for the spread of Christianity.

Two intrusive burial rites spread in the fifth century. One was cremation, by which the ashes were placed in a decorated pot, which also contained the burnt remnants of jewellery. The suggestion is, therefore, that a clothed and adorned body was burnt on a pyre, and the ashes were then placed in the pot and buried. The second was extended inhumation, very much as in the normal late Roman rite, but furnished with grave goods. It may be characterized as follows:

1. The corpse is buried clothed, not shrouded or naked. Such items as brooches and belt buckles thus appear in relation to the skeleton roughly where they were when the person was clothed.
2. The clothing is generally 'Sunday-best', so that wealth and status are marked by the presence of rich items.
3. The clothing and associated possessions are strongly gendered: males towards a warrior model;[67] females towards domesticity and the display of wealth through jewellery and metalwork.
4. Bodies are normally buried supine—on their backs with legs extended—not prone or crouched.
5. Bodies are generally buried with the head approximately towards the west, the feet towards the east.

In cemeteries of this type in Francia and occasionally in Britain, perhaps particularly in the south-east, graves may be in rows.[68] That is why the type as a whole has been termed 'the row-grave civilization' (*Reihengräberzivilisation*), but 'furnished inhumation' is a more helpful designation.[69] Furnished inhumation of this type has a marked distribution: the main concentrations occur in what was, in the fourth century, Roman territory: between the upper Danube and the Alps, from the valley of the Rhine to the Seine basin, extending south-east to the area of Lake Geneva and so linking up with the Danubian concentration; and south-eastern England. The effect is that the main distribution of such graves is in a strip, of varying breadth, between East Yorkshire and Linz on the Danube in Austria. Although such burials occur in Germany east of the Rhine, cremation was there the dominant

[67] H. Härke, 'The Anglo-Saxon Weapon Burial Rite', *Past & Present*, 126 (1990), 22–43.

[68] This may perhaps arise from burial guilds clubbing together to assist burial and each having one or more rows to themselves.

[69] J. Werner, 'Zur Enstehung der Reihengräberzivilisation', *Archaeologia Geographica*, 1 (1950), 23–32; G. Halsall, 'The Origins of the *Reihengräberzivilisation*: Forty Years on', in J. F. Drinkwater and H. Elton (eds.), *Fifth-Century Gaul: A Crisis of Identity* (Cambridge, 1992), 196–207, argued that these graves were the outcome of the need for local elites to emphasize their wealth and status in a zone lacking stable political authority; these elites he identified with the *Bacaudae* as portrayed by R. Van Dam, *Leadership and Community in Late Antique Gaul* (Berkeley, 1985), 25–56; but if this were the explanation, one might have expected to see such graves spread more or less evenly across the whole of Armorica as well as the lands between the Seine valley and the Rhine.

burial rite. The principal homes of the furnished inhumation rite were, therefore, in the lands of the Alamanni, the Burgundians, the Franks, and the English, all settled in former Roman territory. This makes it likely that the rite has something to do with relationships between barbarian and Roman.

An outstanding example of a furnished inhumation at the richest end of a spectrum of wealth is the grave of Childeric, Clovis's father, whom we know to have died *c.* 481. Use of the rite continued, however, into the seventh century. Its main period may have begun during or in the immediate aftermath of the Hunnic Empire, and it is possible that some of the characteristic forms of goldsmith work—in particular, gold cloisonnée and garnet decoration—may have gained their very wide distribution in the mixture of Germanic, Roman, and other influences facilitated by the power of the Huns. The chronology shows that it long survived conversion of the Franks to Christianity. A story told by Gregory of Tours proves that it was used by the military leaders of the East-Frankish kingdom in the second half of the sixth century. What moved the bishop to adverse comment in this case was not the practice of furnished burial but the way Duke Guntram Boso first organized a rich burial at Metz for a female relative of his wife; and then, shortly afterwards, when the citizens had processed out of the town on St Remigius's feast day, his slaves proceeded to rob the grave; he was brought to trial and convicted of having given the orders.[70] Grave-robbing, not furnishing a grave with treasures, was what Gregory denounced and East-Frankish royal officials prosecuted.[71] It may also be significant that Guntram Boso arranged for this lavish burial when his own position was already in danger and only a year before he was killed. The richness of the grave may have had more to do with Guntram Boso's own status and with the fragility of his political position at the time than with the status of his wife's female relative.

In general, it is likely that the majority of those given furnished burial were Franks, Burgundians, Alamans, or Anglo-Saxons, but it is far from inconceivable that some Gallo-Romans were buried in the same manner. There were degrees of *Romanitas*. Gregory of Tours had two great-uncles on his mother's mother's side, both of them from the Gallo-Roman senatorial aristocracy: one, Nicetius, became bishop of Lyons, dying in 573; the other, Gundulf, became a duke, namely a military leader, at the East-Frankish court. His name is Germanic: its first element was the same as the first element of Gundobad, the Burgundian king under whose rule he was born about 510; and the name may well have been given as a compliment to the king. To give a Germanic name to a Gallo-Roman aristocrat was unusual at that date, but it fitted his subsequent military career; and a military leader with a Germanic name might perhaps have been given a furnished burial that, for men of high rank, emphasized their status as warriors. It would have been startling in the extreme if Nicetius, bishop of Lyons, had been given a furnished burial, but much less surprising if this had happened to his brother Gundulf.

70 Gregory of Tours, *Hist.*, viii. 21.

71 Compare *Pactus Legis Salicae*, ed. K. A. Eckhardt, MGH, Legum Sectio I, iv. 1 (Hanover, 1962), lv. 4.

In Britain any such rapprochement between native and incomer was much less likely: there was the religious difference; and the Anglo-Saxon elite was less Romanized than was its Frankish counterpart. No Anglo-Saxon king in the sixth century is in the least likely to have composed Latin verses in praise of a saintly bishop, as did Chilperic I in praise of St Medard.[72] It is therefore probably safe to see furnished burial, especially in the earlier phases, as an indication of Anglo-Saxon settlement. On this basis we can conclude that the Anglo-Saxons first settled in what became East Anglia and spread their settlements across a swathe of country on the north side of the Chilterns to reach the Thames in the area around Dorchester, not far from Oxford, with another extension into Lindsey.[73] In terms of the Romano-British political landscape, this settlement included all or most of the territory of the Iceni and much of that of the Catuvellauni.

Unfortunately, this first major settlement cannot be closely dated. The pattern of reasoning has to be indirect, following types of metalwork back from Britain to the Continent and then relying on a more definite dating for the continental sequence. Reasoning along these lines leads to the conclusion that the first major settlement probably belonged to the first half of the fifth century.

The archaeological evidence can be related to three textual sources or groups of source. The first is provided by the references in Zosimus and the Gallic Chronicle to Saxons attacking Britain and the response of the Britons. In the passage of Zosimus quoted earlier is the statement: 'The Britons, therefore, armed themselves and ran many risks to ensure their own safety and free their cities from the attacking barbarians.' If this is accurate, it seems unlikely that a major invasion had already taken much territory by the first decade of the century. The second is a brief notice in the Chronicle of AD 452: 'The British provinces, having hitherto been subject to various disasters and events, are brought under the authority of the Saxons'.[74] It has been suggested that the chronicler either was, or was close to, Faustus of Riez, a Briton by origin and subsequently abbot of Lérins and then bishop of Riez.[75] This would explain the interest in Britain. Although the place where the Chronicle was written may have been distant from Britain, the chronicler would have comprehended the significance of the events. The chronology of the text is not entirely clear, so that, although this entry has been placed under the year 441 or 442, it is safer to think of this date as a reasonably close approximation. If, then, the entry is broadly accurate, it was referring to a much more extensive military conquest than the corridor from the coast of Norfolk to the

[72] MGH, *Poetae*, iv. 455–7.

[73] H. Böhme, 'Das Ende der Römerherrschaft in Britannien und die angelsächsische Besiedlung Englands im 5. Jahrhundert', *Jahrbuch des Römisch-Germanischen Zentralmuseums Mainz*, 33 (1986), 469–574 (with a summary of the archaeological conclusions, 558–9, and a discussion of the relationship of the archaeology to the written evidence, 559–61); and Hines, 'Philology, Archaeology and the *Adventus Saxonum vel Anglorum*', 25, with the circles marked in Fig. 1, p. 34.

[74] The Gallic Chronicle of 452, ed. Burgess, 79–80; ed. Mommsen, 660, § 126.

[75] I. N. Wood, 'Continuity or Calamity: The Constraints of Literary Models', in Drinkwater and Elton (eds.), *Fifth-Century Gaul*, 14. On Faustus, see below, 199–202.

Thames valley around Dorchester and Oxford; and that means that we must distinguish at this date, even more emphatically than usual, between settlement and conquest. The scale of the conquest would, however, suggest that it was based upon an existing Saxon settlement in Britain; and from this one may infer that the area of settlement defined by the earliest cemetery evidence was already Saxon by *c.* 440.

The third textual source, Constantius's Life of St Germanus of Auxerre, is more complex.[76] The hagiographer is usually identified as a priest of the church of Lyons in the episcopates of Eucherius (*c.* 434–450) and Patiens (450–*c.* 480).[77] He is known to us principally through his friendship with Sidonius Apollinaris, an aristocrat of the Auvergne, whose grandfather had briefly been Constantine III's praetorian prefect; Sidonius's career took him to Rome as Prefect of the City and back to Clermont as bishop; and he probably died *c.* 488.[78] Sidonius's first collection of letters was assembled in response to a request from Constantius; and, in the aftermath of Visigothic ravages in the Auvergne and the siege of Clermont itself, Constantius came to Clermont and helped Sidonius by raising the citizens' morale through his preaching.[79] He appears to have been considerably older than Sidonius, who was born *c.* 430, but of similar social status.[80] He wrote the Life on the instructions of Patiens, who himself also came to the aid of Sidonius and the Auvergne.[81] The date at which the Life was written cannot be defined precisely, but it would fit well into the 470s, that is, about forty years after the likely date for Germanus's death. On the other hand, if Constantius was considerably older than Sidonius, he would have been alive at the time of Germanus's first journey to Britain, let alone the second. There is no reason why he could not have met good informants about both journeys to Britain (429 and an uncertain date in the 430s or 440s).[82]

Germanus himself was one of the first Gallic bishops to be of aristocratic status; he had been a provincial governor before he entered the Church; and his personality, social status, and administrative experience all fitted him to be a leader of local

[76] Constantius, *Vita S. Germani*, ed. W. Levison, MGH SRM 7, 285–83; ed. R. Borius, *Constance de Lyon: Vie de S. Germain*, Sources chrétiennes, no. 112 (Paris, 1965).

[77] For the normal view, see *PLRE* ii, under Constantius 10; that he was a priest was doubted by E. A. Thompson, *Saint Germanus of Auxerre and the End of Roman Britain* (Woodbridge, 1984), 78, citing Levison, MGH SRM vii. 230 n. 8; a similarly sceptical view is taken by A. Gillett, *Envoys and Political Communication in the Late Antique West* (Cambridge, 2003), 117 n. 10; however, Loyen, *Sidoine Apollinaire*, ii, *Lettres (Livres I–V)* (Paris, 1970), p. xxxi, had already seen the problems, but pointed out that the phrase *sanctum pedem* in letter iii. 2, makes it very likely that Constantius was a cleric by 473, although he may still have been a layman in 469 or early 470, when Sidonius wrote letter i. 1 to Constantius revealing that the latter had encouraged Sidonius to revise and publish a collection of his letters.

[78] J. Harries, *The World of Sidonius Apollinaris* (Oxford, 1994), 7–9, 27, 227–9.

[79] Sidonius, *Epp.* iii. 2.

[80] He was described as *aetate grauis, infirmitate fragilis, nobilitate sublimis* in *Epp.* iii. 2.

[81] Sidonius, *Epp.* vi. 12. 5.

[82] R. Scharf, 'Germanus von Auxerre—Chronologie seiner Vita', *Francia*, 18/1 (1991), 1–19, who argues, 11–12, in favour of 440 × 441 for the second visit. A. Barrett, 'Saint Germanus and the British Missions', *Britannia*, 40 (2009), 197–217, argues that there was only one mission, but he takes a more pessimistic view of the quality of Constantius's information than I have taken here.

society in the face of political uncertainty and barbarian attack.[83] Patiens and Sidonius were in the same mould; and the Life of Germanus was thus a statement of what they were trying to achieve. It wastes little time on Germanus's career before his consecration as bishop. Most strikingly, however, its primary concern is with Germanus's role in shaping events in Gaul and Britain rather than his pastoral activity in the Auxerrois. The scale of Germanus's activities far exceeded anything that Patiens might have contemplated. In the eight sections into which it may be divided, the first two are centred on Auxerre and its territory; the others are shaped by a series of journeys: to Britain, to Arles, seat of the Prefect of the Gauls, a second journey to Britain; and a journey to Ravenna in the interests of the Bagaudae whom Goar, king of the Alans, had been sent by Aëtius to repress. At Ravenna Germanus died, so that his last journey was as a holy corpse being brought back to its resting place at Auxerre.[84]

The primary purpose of Germanus's journeys to Britain was to combat the Pelagian heresy. According to Constantius, an appeal for help came from Britain to the bishops of Gaul. A well-attended synod responded by sending Germanus and Lupus of Troyes to support the cause of orthodoxy. Up to a point, as we shall see in a later chapter, this is corroborated by a source contemporary with the events, the chronicle of Prosper of Aquitaine. Prosper also gives us something lacking in Constantius's Life, namely a date: the first journey to Britain was in 429 and thus a little more than midway between the collapse of Constantine III's regime in 409 and the Saxon victories of *c.* 441. The journey may have been facilitated by Aëtius's victory over the Franks in 428.[85] In the present context, two things about Constantius's narrative are of interest: that the Britons were fighting the Saxons, on this occasion with success, and that Germanus and Lupus were able to travel to the shrine of St Alban outside the Roman city of Verulamium.[86] The narrative of a British victory over the Saxons is heavily stylized and needed to be: it was not normally thought acceptable for bishops to lead armies.[87] Germanus was therefore cast in the mould of Joshua before Jericho, but in place of the insistent Old Testament motif of seven priests blowing seven trumpets circling the city for seven days, Constantius used a Trinitarian motif, with Germanus's army, led by the bishops, shouting three Allelujas; and whereas Joshua anathematized Jericho so that man, woman, child, and animal were all slain, Germanus's victory was achieved without bloodshed. The narrative reveals the skills of Constantius as a hagiographer; but it does not tell us that the Saxons were established in the island, even though this is likely. It does not present the battle as being close to the coast. The accessibility of St Albans should be reliable information, since Germanus took

83 Van Dam, *Leadership and Community*, 142–4.

84 Gillett, *Envoys and Political Communication*, 115–37, is interesting on these journeys as the keynote of the Life.

85 Prosper, *Chron. s.a.* 428; E. Zöllner, *Geschichte der Franken bis zur Mitte des sechsten Jahrhunderts* (Munich, 1970), 28; Scharf, 'Germanus von Auxerre', 12.

86 *Vita S. Germani*, §§ 17–18.

87 Compare, in the next century, Gregory of Tours, *Hist.*, iv. 42, on Bishops Salonius and Sagittarius.

back relics of the martyr, which he installed in a basilica built for the purpose in Auxerre.[88] This is helpful, since in the next phase of furnished burials after the first extension from East Anglia to the middle-Thames, they were distributed along the north of Kent from Thanet into the north of Surrey, on the other side of the Thames from London, so coming close to isolating any British area in the Chilterns.[89] Constantius's evidence would thus allow one to place 429 between the first and second phases of Anglo-Saxon settlement, although the first phase could have been later.

The Saxon victories at the beginning of the 440s were a major turning point. What they gave the settlers was a military dominance in lowland Britain that they would rarely ever lose thereafter. The victories do not represent a mass replacement of population, but an ability to extend the area open to settlement and to compel the Britons to pay tribute. The broad shape of the Saxon settlement, as represented by furnished burials, was already there in the second phase, the one that can be attributed to the middle of the fifth century, up to *c.* 475. Subsequent burials represent consolidation and infilling within an area already marked out, east of a line from York to Salisbury and Poole Bay. There may well have been areas still under local British rule east of this line, as for example, in the Chilterns, but these are likely to have been under continuous Saxon overlordship.[90]

The middle of the fifth century is also the date at which the evidence of Gildas's *De Excidio Britanniae* becomes usable. As we have seen already, the broad framework of Gildas's narrative—attacks of Picts and *Scotti* after Maximus's usurpation (383), Saxon settlement and conquest after an appeal by the Britons to Aëtius (446 × 454)—was entirely wrong. It is important for the sixth century that he could conceive of recent history in that manner, but there is nothing to be gained by attempting to rely on details of his narrative before the appeal to Aëtius, and major difficulties remain even after that date. Because of his erroneous framework, some of the events that he ascribed to the period after the appeal will belong to the period before the third consulship of Aëtius. Some of these are, if not reliable, at least suggestive. Once we understand what Gildas was attempting, his *De Excidio Britanniae* becomes a light in the darkness, as will be shown in the next chapter, but it is a light for the darkness of the sixth century and only casts the occasional uncertain gleam on the fifth.

One of these gleams of light is his account of an appeal made by 'the miserable remnants' of the Britons to Aëtius, then the outstanding general in the Western Empire:[91]

[88] Borius's introduction to his edition, 74.

[89] This is given by the squares in Hines, 'Philology, Archaeology and the Adventus', Fig. 1, p. 34. Survival in the Chilterns would allow for the late evidence at Verulamium, if it is to be dated as Frere proposed, *c.* 450–70: S. S. Frere, *Verulamium Excavations*, 3 vols. (Oxford and London, 1972–84), ii. 226.

[90] As argued by K. R. Davis, *Britons and Saxons: The Chiltern Region AD 400–700* (Chichester, 1982).

[91] Gildas, *De Excidio*, 20. 1, trans. Winterbottom, 23–4.

> So the miserable remnants sent off a letter again, this time to the Roman commander Aëtius, in the following terms: 'To Aëtius, thrice consul: the groans of the British.' Further on came this complaint: 'The barbarians push us back to the sea, the sea pushes us back to the barbarians; between these two kinds of death, we are either drowned or slaughtered.' But they got no help in return.

That the Britons got no help is hardly surprising: this was the heyday of the Hunnic Empire under their feared ruler Attila; by *c.* 450 the earlier friendship between Aëtius and Attila had been undermined; and Aëtius now had much more urgent threats to handle than the enemies of the Britons.[92] Three important features of this passage stand out: that Aëtius was consul for the third time, and had not yet been killed, gives us the date-range 446 × 454; what the Britons sent to Aëtius was a letter; and the scale of the disasters of which the Britons complained recalls the entry in the Chronicle of 452 for 441. Gildas did not claim to have read the letter (giving such detail on his sources was not his habit). Although the detail 'thrice consul' about the salutation at the beginning of the letter strongly argues that Gildas had information deriving from a text, one might argue that he himself may not have read it. Yet, his indications of its content have been seen as very different from his own style and are thus best understood as deriving from a text written by someone else.[93]

The temptation for us, therefore, is to combine this passage of Gildas with the Chronicle of 452 and to treat both of them as referring to the same Saxon victories. On the whole, this may well be the right interpretation, but it should be noted that Gildas thought that the onslaught that elicited the letter to Aëtius was unleashed by Picts and *Scotti*, not by Saxons. If we do combine the two pieces of evidence, we are doing so because we are already entitled to reject Gildas's overall framework, by which Picts and *Scotti* came first and Saxons only later. That we are thus entitled has been sufficiently established in the discussion of Constantine III. Another qualification is that, if the Chronicle's entry belongs to 441, at least five years separated the Saxon victories from the appeal to Aëtius. Yet a good reason for the timing of the appeal is that Aëtius and Majorian had restored relative stability in the Rhineland and Armorica at this date: only if Roman rule had been restored in northern Gaul would a British appeal to Aëtius have had any point.[94]

Another difficulty is whether we should attach any weight at all to the sequence of events that, in Gildas's narrative, followed the appeal to Aëtius, but which we would place between 410 and *c.* 441. The crucial issue here is whether there is any

[92] The connection with the Huns was perceived by Bede, *HE* i. 13, whose quotation from Gildas has the correct spelling, *Aetio*, in place of the unanimous testimony of the MSS of Gildas, which have a Vulgar Latin *Agitio*: D. N. Dumville, 'The Chronology of *De Excidio Britanniae*, Book I', in M. Lapidge and D. N. Dumville, *Gildas: New Approaches* (Woodbridge, 1984), 67; cf. Wallace-Hadrill, *Commentary*, 210–11.

[93] Winterbottom in the preface to his edition and translation, *Gildas: The Ruin of Britain*, 8; cf. the detailed discussion by P. Sims-Williams, 'The Settlement of England in Bede and the *Chronicle*', *Anglo-Saxon England*, 12 (1983), 6–15.

[94] I. N. Wood, 'The Fall of the Western Empire and the End of Roman Britain', *Britannia*, 18 (1987), 256–7.

truth in his picture of the British council, headed by 'the proud tyrant', inviting Saxons to settle as *foederati* in 'the eastern part of the island'.[95] The proud tyrant was named as Vortigern by Bede, and it is possible that the name was present in the copy of Gildas which he used; but Vortigern played a leading role in the Kentish origin legend, which has been attributed to the reign of Æthelberht, king of Kent (*ob.* 616), and was used by Bede and the *Historia Brittonum*.[96] The origin legend is not a good source for the fifth century; and, if Bede deduced from it that 'the proud tyrant' was Vortigern, no reliance can be placed on his use of the name.

Gildas's narrative immediately after the failure of their appeal to Aëtius has four main stages:

1. The Britons were gripped by famine while suffering from attacks by Picts and *Scotti*; some gave in, other fought back successfully, leading to a period of peace.
2. Peace led to *luxuria*, self-indulgence, especially sexual.
3. A renewed attack by Picts and *Scotti* was threatened, and this led the council and the proud tyrant to give the Saxons land in the east of the island on the basis of a *foedus*, a treaty, by which the Saxons would defend the Britons from the Picts and the *Scotti* in exchange for *annonae*, food-supplies.
4. The Saxons *foederati* first complained that their *epimenia*, monthly supplies, were inadequate. They threatened to break the treaty and attack the Britons; this they soon did. The Saxon onslaught 'spread from sea to sea'.

This sequence poses a temptation: the culmination of the fourth stage, the Saxon onslaught 'from sea to sea', appears similar in its scale to the Saxon subjection of the British provinces recorded by the Chronicle of 452, under the year *c.* 441. Yet, if we regard them as the same and also accept the historicity of the appeal to Aëtius, we have to do considerable violence to Gildas's narrative, since in that narrative all four stages were subsequent to the appeal to Aëtius, subsequent, that is, to some year in the range 446 × 454. Gildas puts the Saxon onslaught from sea to sea after the appeal to Aëtius; we are now contemplating putting it before the appeal, and yet accepting the rest of the sequence. It might be argued that a narrative sequence that has to be rescued in this high-handed fashion can have little evidential value.[97]

What makes the temptation to rearrange the sequence in this manner very strong is Gildas's use of the correct late Roman terms for the relationship between the British authorities and the first Saxon settlers. The relationship was, as we have seen, a *foedus*, a treaty by which a Saxon army was to fight against 'the northern peoples' in exchange for *annonae* and *epimenia*. The use of *foedus* is not significant on its own, since it was a normal term for 'treaty', but the use of *annonae* and

[95] Gildas, *De Excidio*, c. 23.

[96] N. Brooks, 'Canterbury, Rome and the Construction of English Identity', in J. M. H. Smith (ed.), *Early Medieval Rome and the Christian West: Essays in Honour of Donald A. Bullough* (Leiden, 2000), 221–47, esp. 245–6; id., *Bede and the English*, Jarrow Lecture 1999 (Jarrow, [2000]); id., 'The English Origin Myth', in his *Anglo-Saxon Myths: State and Church* (London, 2000), 79–89.

[97] For other discussions of this problem, see Sims-Williams, 'The Settlement of England', 6–15; Higham, *The English Conquest*, 120–38.

epimenia is much more striking. The inclusion of such supplies as part of the terms of a *foedus* was, for example, critical in allowing the movement of Alaric's Goths from Illyricum into Italy: the supply system of the Roman army enabled barbarian peoples, associated with the army by a *foedus*, to move within the Empire along the roads that had been constructed precisely to facilitate the movement of armies.[98] It is unlikely that the Britain of Gildas's day had any experience of such relationships; and that increases the likelihood that Gildas took the terminology from some source closer to the events.

On the basis of this argument, it is possible to associate the first, East-Anglian settlement of the Saxons with the treaty made by the Britons according to Gildas, provided we remember that the association is as fragile as the argument that sustains it. A weak point concerns the motivation for the treaty: in Gildas, the British council made the treaty with the Saxons in order to meet the threat from 'the northern peoples', that is, the Picts and the *Scotti*; but once Gildas's narrative has been rearranged as proposed, the serious threat to the Britons now appears to have been from the Saxons—as, indeed, one would expect given the written evidence from Zosimus and Constantius. Yet, how should we explain a treaty hiring Saxons to defend Britain against Saxons? A speculative answer to this conundrum would be to appeal to the diversity of origin of what the late Roman and post-Roman written sources tended to label 'Saxons'. Archaeology suggests that the settlers were recruited from a wide range of countries, from Scandinavia down to Frisia and even Francia. This would allow one to suppose that the British council hired, say, Angles to defend Britain against Saxons, and then to make a link between this hypothesis and the emergence of an Anglian identity in the material evidence from East Anglia, as well as their being called *East Engle*.[99]

There is an objection to this idea, not entirely fatal, but serious. The Anglian identity of the East Angles seems to have been less marked at the outset of the settlement than it was by the beginning of the seventh century. On the whole, the first settlements were the most mixed in terms of associations with parts of the Continent.[100] The reason, however, why this objection is not entirely fatal is that one may distinguish between the origins of the settlers in general and the origins of their leaders in particular. The reason why an Anglian identity emerged in East Anglia, looking more to Scandinavia than to Francia or Frisia, may be that the leadership was Anglian, even though this leadership recruited its manpower more widely.

Related to this issue is another. Some scholars have proposed a model of Anglo-Saxon settlement resting on small-scale groups as opposed to whole armies.[101] The later kingdoms would then be understood as having emerged through competition

[98] P. Heather, *Goths and Romans, 332–489* (Oxford, 1991), 205–6, 216–18.

[99] J. Hines, *The Scandinavian Character of Anglian England in the Pre-Viking Period*, BAR, Brit. Ser. 124 (Oxford, 1984); id., 'The Scandinavian Character of Anglian England', in M. Carver (ed.), *The Age of Sutton Hoo* (Woodbridge, 1992), 315–30.

[100] C. Hills, *The Origins of the English* (London, 2006), 105–7.

[101] This the first of the 'ideal types' proposed by S. Bassett, 'In Search of the Origins of Anglo-Saxon Kingdoms', in S. Bassett (ed.), *The Origins of Anglo-Saxon Kingdoms* (Leicester, 1989), 23.

between these small groups. Another view envisages larger-scale groups of settlers, at the level of something one might call an army, taking over an existing Romano-British *civitas* territory, such as Kent.[102] On this model, something like the later kingdoms might have been there from the start. The line of argument that has been followed so far, however, allows for an intermediate position. If the East-Anglian settlement was the starting point, it could be identified with the territory of the Iceni, with an extension west-south-west into that of the Catuvellauni. The lands of the Iceni would be the territory in the east of Britain granted to the *foederati*. The conquests of *c.* 441, however, vastly extended the area of Saxon control; and for a century there was infilling of settlement but relatively little extension of the conquered area. In the 440s, therefore, we can envisage the leaders of the victorious army—and it must have been an army rather than a mere war band to defeat the Britons on such a scale—seeking to recruit as many settlers as possible in order to hold their conquered territory. Many of those who responded to such a call will have been organized in quite small groups. One may propose, therefore, that wide settlement by small groups occurred under the protection of an army that had already won major victories against the Britons.

This picture of an extensive conquest of British territory in the 440s followed by a prolonged period in which little new conquest was made has a possible corollary. The proposition advanced in the previous paragraph is that the rapidity of the conquest created a problem of consolidation, and that this problem was met by recruiting more settlers from the Continent. It is possible that the ubiquity of the unit of land known as the 'hide' across several Anglo-Saxon kingdoms is a product of this need to recruit and of a competition between different nascent kingdoms for settlers.[103] The hide was described by Bede as the land of one family, a family that appears to have been a nuclear family rather than a whole kindred. It was also normally seen as approximately equivalent to a ploughland. With the plough agriculture characteristic of early historic and prehistoric Europe, the critical divide was between those who had a share in a plough team and those who did not. Among those who did have a share, a peasant aristocracy was composed of those who had an entire plough team. The hide, 'the land of one family', appears to have approximated to this level. If there was a competition for settlers and thus an impetus to offer holdings at the top end of the range between the man who had only one ox and the man who had an entire plough team, this might explain why the hide ended by being a common English unit, apart from Kent which had its equivalent, the sulung or ploughland.

According to Gildas, the Britons responded to the Saxon victories in three ways: some submitted to the power of the Saxons; some went into exile; others took refuge in the mountains.[104] Only later, some time after the Saxon army had gone

[102] This the second 'ideal type', ibid. 24–6.

[103] This is a summary of the theory proposed in T. M. Charles-Edwards, 'Social Structure', in P. Stafford (ed.), *A Companion to the Early Middle Ages: Britain and Ireland c. 500–c. 1100* (Chichester, 1009), 116–18, itself a development of id., 'Kinship, Status and the Origins of the Hide', *Past and Present*, 56 (1972), 3–33.

[104] Gildas, *De Excidio*, 25. 1.

back to its base, presumably the area of settlement after the great victory of the 440s, did those Britons who had not gone into exile or submitted to the Saxons, come together under the leadership of Ambrosius Aurelianus, 'who, perhaps alone of the Romans, had survived the shock of this notable storm', to challenge their enemies and to win an initial victory.[105] 'From then on victory went now to our countrymen, now to their enemies.'[106] This period of shifting fortunes ended with the battle of Mount Badon, in the same year as the birth of Gildas.[107] This battle Gildas described as 'pretty well the last defeat of the villains, and certainly not the least'. Since then, namely through Gildas's lifetime up to the date of the *De Excidio*, 'External wars may have stopped, but not civil ones.'

The impression given by Gildas's brief and allusive narrative is that the main acquisition of territory by the Saxons came in the initial victories—those that have been ascribed, though not by him, to *c.* 441. Initially, they seemed likely to effect a complete conquest of what had been Roman Britain, very much as the conquests of Clovis and his sons effected an almost complete conquest of Gaul. What prevented this was the resistance of 'the survivors' under the leadership of Ambrosius Aurelianus. He was apparently in the same generation as Gildas's grandparents: 'His descendants in our day have become greatly inferior to their grandfather's excellence.'[108]

5. THE ORIGINS OF BRITTANY

Among those who survived the Saxon victories, Gildas distinguished three groups: those who submitted to the victors, those who took refuge in the mountains and forests and then emerged under Ambrosius Aurelianus to challenge the Saxons to battle, and those who went into exile beyond the sea.[109] It is likely that this third group has something to do with the origins of Brittany, even though it is conceivable that some went to Ireland; and it is also likely that refugees from the Irish settlement in south-west Britain may have played their part. Later sources, such as the *Historia Brittonum*, ascribed the origins of Brittany to the Emperor Magnus Maximus (or Maximianus), who is said not to have allowed his British forces to return to Britain.[110] The story in the *Historia Brittonum* was elaborated in Geoffrey of Monmouth and in the Middle Welsh tale, *Breuddwyd Maxen*, for both of whom Maximus's supporter Conan Meriadoc (Cynan mab Eudaf Hen) was the founder of Brittany.[111] The ultimate source for this is probably Gildas's own statement that Maximus took British soldiers to the Continent, so that 'Britain was despoiled of her whole army'.[112] As we have seen already, this claim by Gildas cannot be correct.

By the late sixth century the territories of the Osismi and the Veneti, and, to a lesser extent, the territory of the Coriosolites, would be the heartland of a new

[105] Ibid. 25. 3.

[106] *Ex eo tempore nunc ciues, nunc hostes, uincebant*, ibid. 26. 1.

[107] Ibid.

[108] Ibid. 25. 3.

[109] Ibid. 22.

[110] *HB*, c. 27.

[111] *Trioedd Ynys Prydein: The Welsh Triads*, ed. and trans. R. Bromwich (3rd edn. Cardiff, 2006), 320–1, under Cynan, brawd Elen Luydawc.

[112] Gildas, *De Excidio*, 14.

Brittania south of the Channel. Gregory of Tours allows us to glimpse the process by which the Britons were, in his lifetime, gaining control over the Veneti and penetrating the territory of the Namnetes and Redones. In 590, King Guntram, the senior Frankish king, sent an army against Waroc, the leader of the Bretons in the territory of Vannes.[113] The Frankish army was, however, under the divided command of two Dukes, Ebrachar and Beppolen, who were at odds. Beppolen engaged Waroc in battle between the River Oust and the city of Vannes, but Waroc defeated and killed him while Ebrachar kept his troops out of the battle. With his rival safely dead, Ebrachar advanced to Vannes where they were welcomed by the bishop, Regalis, and his clergy. The speech that Gregory put into the mouth of Regalis shows that the latter was a Roman and so too were many, if not all, of his clergy: 'We have to do as the Bretons tell us and this irks us very much.'[114] However, when Gregory told how Ebrachar's army left Brittany, he makes it clear that the River Vilaine, to the east of Vannes, was the boundary. By 590, therefore, the Vannetais was effectively under Breton rule, even though significant elements of the population, perhaps centred on the city and its bishop, still regarded themselves as Romans. At least when a Frankish army was in the city, the bishop of Vannes could be portrayed by Gregory as making a direct link between Gallo-Roman identity and a preference for direct Frankish rule rather than subjection to the Bretons. Gregory does not mention any such Roman elements in the population further west, even though they are likely to have existed.[115] On the other hand, Breton incursions into the *civitates* of Rennes and Nantes were directed at the countryside rather than the cities. Only the Guérande district in the west of the territory of Nantes would subsequently form part of the solidly Breton-speaking area. This suggests three zones: in the old territory of the Osismi in the far west Romance-speaking islands survived, but, for Gregory, they were below the horizon; in the Vannetais, they were visible, but in the city rather than in the countryside; in the territories of Nantes and Rennes, Bretons raided the countryside, made limited settlements, but left the cities largely untouched.

All this goes to suggest that the lands of the Osismi saw the earliest mass British settlement, since control of the Vannetais was still imperfect. Settlement by individuals and small groups will, of course, have occurred before and during Roman rule, but such settlement was widely distributed throughout northern Gaul and has little to do with the origins of Brittany.[116] What we must distinguish is, first, such 'Bretons de la dispersion', to use the phrase of Léon Fleuriot;[117] second, the Britons who first established British control over the land of the Osismi; and, third, any subsequent migration after the territory of the Osismi had become an enclave dominated by Britons in the far north-west of Armorica (see Map 6).

[113] Gregory of Tours, *Hist.*, x. 9.

[114] Ibid., trans. L. Thorpe, *Gregory of Tours: The History of the Franks*, Penguin Classics (London, 1974).

[115] L. Fleuriot, 'Recherches sur les enclaves romanes anciennes en territoire bretonnant', *Études Celtiques*, 8 (1958), 164–78; id., *Les Origines de la Bretagne*, 87–9.

[116] Fleuriot, *Les Origines de la Bretagne*, 134–62.

[117] Ibid., 134–62.

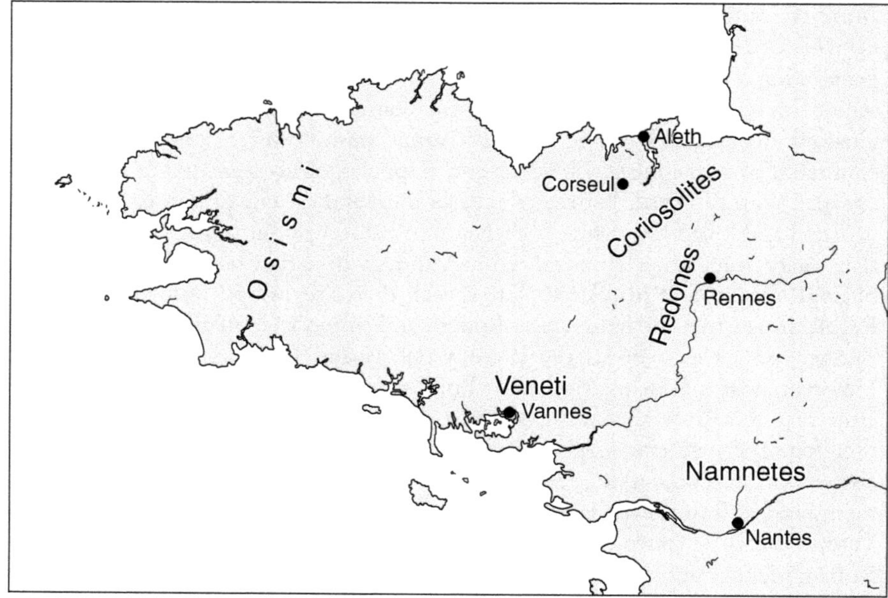

Map 6. North-West Armorica, *c.* 400
The map shows the *civitates* of that part of Armorica that later, in the ninth century, formed part of Brittany. The *civitas* capital of the Osismi is unknown but may have been at Carhaix. The capital of the Coriosolites moved from Corseul to Aleth.

Some Britons settling in Gaul are likely themselves to have been Latin-speakers from south-eastern Britain;[118] and they would soon become assimilated into the *Romani* of Gaul. By contrast, British-speaking Britons from further west in Britain may have been attracted more to the British-speaking part of Brittany.

The first strong evidence for the emergence of a distinct British settlement in the north-west of Armorica does not come until 461, when subscriptions to the Council of Tours (AD 461) included 'Mansuetus, bishop of the Britons'.[119] This indicates that there was already a British settlement within the province of Lugdunensis Tertia, the metropolitan see of which was Tours; it included the whole of the later Brittany as well as Maine, Anjou, and the Touraine. The synod was of the bishops of the province with three additions, so that Mansuetus's Britons are most

[118] P. Schrijver, 'The Rise and Fall of British Latin: Evidence from English and Brittonic', in M. Filppula et al. (eds.), *The Celtic Roots of English* (Joensuu, 2002), 102–8.

[119] *Concilia Galliae, A. 314–A. 506*, ed. C. Munier, CCSL 148 (Turnhout, 1963), subscriptions to the Council of Tours (AD 461), p. 148, include: *Mansuetus episcopus Britannorum*. The suggestion that the name of a bishop who attended the earlier Council of Angers (453), Chariatone, was the Celtic equivalent of Mansuetus and referred to the same person (Fleuriot, *Les Origines*, 145) is too speculative to carry much weight.

likely to have been in that part of Gaul.[120] This settlement could, therefore, have been in the *civitas* of the Osismi, where, in the late-sixth century, the Britons were most heavily concentrated.[121] The Council of Vannes, 461 × 491, included the bishops of Tours, Vannes, Rennes, Nantes, and Corseul, but not Mansuetus or his equivalent.[122]

Another guise in which Britons appeared in fifth-century Gaul, apart from the widely dispersed settlements of British individuals or small groups, the 'Bretons of the dispersal', emerged shortly after the Council of Tours: an organized British army under the leadership of a king, Riothamus. This army was part of the Emperor Anthemius's coalition intended to defend the province of Aquitania Prima (the northern part of Aquitania) from the Visigoths.[123] Anthemius was the western emperor promoted by his eastern colleague, Leo I, and proclaimed near Rome on 12 April 467 with the acceptance of Ricimer, the principal general (*Magister Militum*); but Anthemius was not universally welcome in the west, and his power was undermined by the failure of a combined eastern and western expedition in 468 organized by his patron, Leo I, against Gaiseric, king of the Vandals.

A witness to the divisions among the Romans and the diminished support for Anthemius was a letter written by Sidonius Apollinaris on behalf of the Prefect Arvandus from Lyons in 469 addressed to Euric, king of the Visigoths. It advised him against making an alliance with 'the Greek emperor', namely Anthemius, and urged him to attack the 'Britons situated on the far side of the Loire'.[124] The implication of this plea is that the Britons in question were already in alliance with the Emperor Anthemius when they were still north of the Loire and thus in Armorica. The British army under King Riothamus subsequently moved south into Aquitania Prima, the capital of which was Bourges, but was defeated by Euric's Visigoths at Bourg-de-Déols in Berry in 469.[125] It was then driven to take refuge with the Burgundians, who were also in alliance with the Emperor Anthemius. The letter of Arvandus to Euric indicates, therefore, that the British army came from Armorica, north of the Loire, at a date only a few years after the Council of Tours which Mansuetus, bishop of the Britons, attended. From a later letter of Sidonius Apollinaris, it is clear that it remained a coherent force after its defeat by the Visigoths, but it is not clear where it went after seeking refuge with the Burgundians.[126]

If we put the two letters of Sidonius together, it becomes very probable that Riothamus's army had been based north of the Loire, in Armorica. We are not told

120 Included from outside the province were the bishops of Bourges, Chalons-sur-Marne, and Rouen. The see of one bishop, Venerandus, is unidentified.

121 Fleuriot, *Les Origines*, 161.

122 *Concilia Galliae, A. 314–A. 506*, ed. Munier, 150, 157. Munier, in his index, attributes both Albinus and Liberalis to Corseul, which is hardly possible. The text was addressed to two absent bishops, Victorius of Le Mans and Thalassius of Angers.

123 E. Stein, *Histoire du Bas-Empire* (Paris, 1959), i. 389–93; Jordanes, *Getica*, XLV, §§ 236–8, ed. Th. Mommsen, *Iordanis Romana et Getica*, MGH AA v. 1 (Berlin, 1882), 118–19.

124 Sidonius Apollinaris, *Letters*, i. 7 (ed. Loyen, ii. 22).

125 Cf. Gregory of Tours, *Hist.*, ii. 18.

126 Apollinaris, *Letters*, iii. 9 (ed. Loyen, ii. 249).

whether it had previously come from Britain and was thus part of a migration to Armorica, and we are not told where it went after it took refuge in Burgundy. What is true is that there is no trace of a large-scale settlement among 'the Britons of the dispersal' to be compared, for example, to the Taifali of Poitou (a Sarmatian people), who gave their name to Tiffauges, about 20 kilometres south-east of Nantes. The latter were important enough to have, for a time, their own bishop.[127] The most economical explanation is that Riothamus's army returned to Armorica. It is important to remember that this army had been part of an imperial alliance, and that its settlement in Armorica may well have been with imperial authority.[128]

If we assume that, within Armorica, a British army, led by someone with royal status, was established from *c.* 465, it becomes easier to account for the implied background to Gregory of Tours's narrative in the next century. For Gregory, the Britons settled within Armorica in his own day were the direct continuation of the Britons in the same area who had their own kings until the reign of Clovis, and probably also those, further back, who fought the Visigoths at the battle of Bourg-de-Déols in 469.[129] To appreciate the fragments of narrative about Brittany in his *Histories*, however, it is best to begin at the end, at a time when Gregory was bishop of Tours. The Bretons only appear in Gregory's *Histories* at intervals, in *c.* 546, 560, 577–9, 587, and 590. On some, at least, of these occasions, particular difficulties between Frankish kings explain why relations with the Bretons should have deteriorated into violence. This calls into question any assumption that relations between Bretons and Franks were normally violent. Moreover, for the later episodes, not only was Gregory a contemporary with reason to be concerned about the situation on the Breton frontier, but his narrative supplies enough detail to enable us to see something of the context of events. After his *Histories* break off, we have the odd reference, but not enough to make much sense of what happened. Fredegar tells us, for example, of a battle between the Franks and the Bretons in 594 in which both sides suffered heavy losses.[130] Given the scope of Fredegar's interests, it is more likely than not that this army was sent by Childebert II, who had succeeded Guntram in 593. If so, it may have raised the same issues as had arisen, as we shall see, between Guntram and the regime of the boy-king Chlothar II. All we can make of this evidence with confidence is to note the contrast with the next year, 595, when the Franks, this time certainly Childebert II's Franks, bloodily suppressed a revolt of the Warni, 'so that few of them survived'.[131] Whatever the context of the battle of 594 may have been, it did not result in a close subjection of the Bretons either to Childebert II or to Chlothar II.

[127] Gregory of Tours, *Hist.*, iv. 18. E. Ewig, 'Volkstum und Volksbewusstsein im Frankenreich des 7. Jahrhunderts', *Settimane*, 5 (1958), 584, repr. in his *Spätantikes und fränkisches Gallien: Gesammelte Schriften (1952–1973)*, ed. H. Atsma, i. 236. Champtoceaux is some distance from Tiffauges.

[128] C. Brett, 'Soldiers, Saints, and States? The Breton Migrations Revisited', *CMCS* 61 (Summer 2011), 1–56, at 5–18, critically reviews the 'military settlement' hypothesis.

[129] Gregory of Tours, *Hist.*, ii. 18; iv. 4.

[130] Fredegar, *Chronica*, iv. 15.

[131] Ibid.

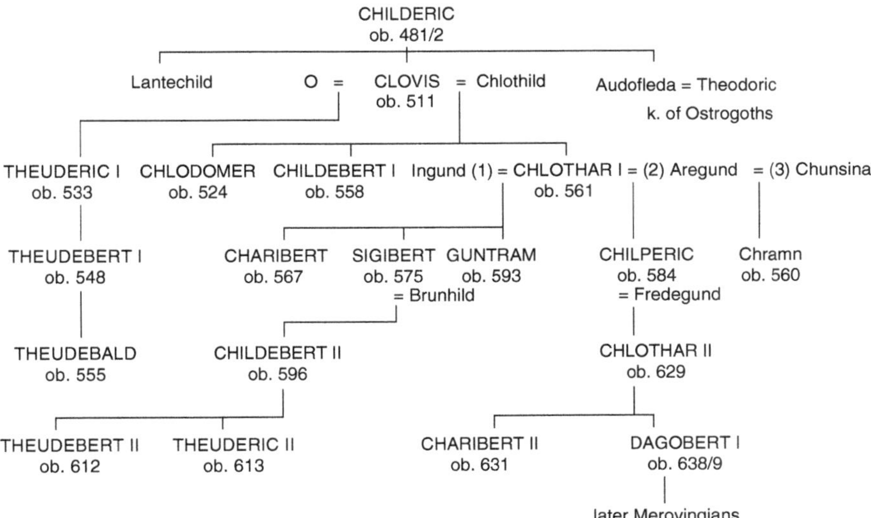

Figure 1.1. The earlier Merovingian kings

Note: The names of kings are in capitals

The violence of 587 and 590 belonged to a period when it was unclear who should, and who did, exercise royal authority in the *civitates* bordering Brittany. Chilperic I had exercised power over western Gaul in the years running up to his assassination not long after 1 September 584; but he left only a single surviving son, Chlothar II; and he was only a month or two old at his father's death. Moreover, relations had recently worsened between Chilperic and the other two Frankish kings, namely his brother Guntram and his nephew, Childebert II: they had made an alliance against Chilperic earlier in 584 reversing an alliance between Childebert II and Chilperic made in 581.[132] After Chilperic's death Guntram aimed to exercise power as the senior Frankish king, the uncle of two under-age nephews. This was easier to accomplish in the former kingdom of Chilperic: to take only one example, Chilperic had conquered two neighbouring *civitates*, the Touraine and Poitou, although they had been subject to his brother, Sigibert I, the king who, in 573, had commanded that Gregory be consecrated bishop of Tours. After Chilperic's death in 584, both *civitates* wanted to revert to the kingdom of Sigibert's son, Childebert II; yet they were forced to submit to Guntram.[133] As for the *civitates* along the Breton frontier, Nantes, Rennes, and Avranches, they had long been part of Chilperic's kingdom; and their loyalties lay with his son, Chlothar II. Yet,

132 Gregory of Tours, *Hist.*, vi. 3, 31, 33, 41.
133 Gregory of Tours, *Hist.*, vii. 12, 24.

Guntram also sought to control the whole of this region, not just Nantes to which he had a claim.[134]

After Chilperic's assassination in the autumn of 584, the faction within the eastern kingdom of Childebert II, that had promoted the earlier alliance of 581 with Chilperic against Guntram, was in danger from the latter's vengeance. They allied with magnates in other kingdoms hostile to Guntram to promote a bid for the kingship by the pretender Gundovald. Because of the threat from Gundovald, Guntram became much more sympathetic to the claims of Childebert II, in the hope that he could use the young king and other interests within his nephew's kingdom to weaken the faction behind Gundovald. Part of this drive to wean Childebert away from supporting Gundovald was a shift from claiming to promote the interests of both his nephews towards a preference for Childebert II over Chlothar II. This emerged most evidently in what Guntram said should happen to his kingdom after his death. To gain Childebert's backing, Guntram was prepared to promise that his kingdom would all go to Childebert. The shifts in Guntram's stance towards the Bretons were part of these manoeuvrings.

In the autumn of 584, in the aftermath of the assassination of Chilperic, the leading nobles of his kingdom, led by Ansovald, rallied to his son and his widow, Fredegund. They formally named the son Chlothar, recalling the name of the first Chlothar, the father of Chilperic, Sigibert, and Guntram.[135] The boy's regnal years began from this act of naming late in 584. Yet, he was not baptized until 591, more than six years later.[136] When it did occur, the baptism saw Guntram acting as Chlothar II's godfather, a role that placed heavy responsibilities of care. It was, therefore, the act that assured the boy's political survival. One might suppose that Ansovald and the boy's mother, Fredegund, would have been eager to bring the boy to meet Guntram as soon as possible, so that the king could sponsor him and so commit himself to respecting his claims as a Merovingian. That it did not happen until 591 betrays the depth of the suspicion that Fredegund, together with Ansovald and his fellow magnates, had of Guntram, their former enemy.

In 590, as we have seen, King Guntram, the senior Frankish king, sent two dukes, Beppolen and Ebrachar, with an army to attack the Breton ruler Waroc.[137] The expedition was ill-fated: the two dukes quarrelled and the widowed queen Fredegund, mother of Guntram's nephew, the future Chlothar II, was an enemy of Beppolen and sent the Saxons of the Bessin, disguised as Bretons, to aid Waroc against him. Duke Beppolen crossed the rivers Vilaine and the Oust, went into battle without Ebrachar's support, and was killed on the third day of fighting.

[134] Ibid. viii. 42. The division of Charibert's kingdom in 567 gave Nantes to Guntram and Avranches to Sigibert I: E. Ewig, 'Die fränkischen Teilungen und Teilreiche (511–613)', *Akademie der Wissenschaften und der Literatur, Mainz, Abhandlungen der Geistes- und sozialwissenschaftlichen Klasse*, 9 (1953), 679; repr. in his *Spätantikes und fränkisches Gallien*, i. 138–9; I. N. Wood, *The Merovingian Kingdoms: 450–751* (London, 1994), Map 3, p. 369. But this division did not survive the civil war of 573–5.

[135] Gregory of Tours, *Hist.*, vii. 7; E. Ewig, 'Studien zur merowingischen Dynastie', *Frühmittelalterliche Studien*, 8 (1974), 16–19.

[136] Gregory of Tours, *Hist.*, x. 28.

[137] Gregory of Tours, *Hist.*, x. 9.

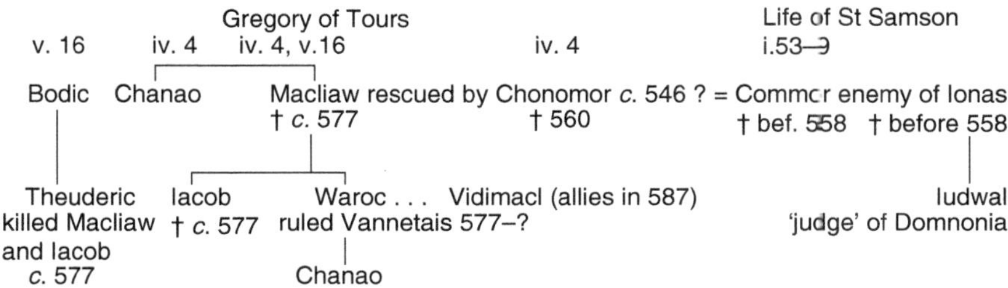

Figure 1.2. Breton rulers in the sixth century

Ebrachar then advanced to Vannes and was there led into the town by Bishop Regalis and his clergy. Waroc came to sue for peace, but then sent his son, Canao, to attack the rearguard of the Frankish army as it was trying to cross the Vilaine on its way home. When Ebrachar reached King Guntram he was accused of having been bribed by Waroc.

Several things emerge from the story of this campaign. First, the River Vilaine appears to have marked the frontier. However, Regalis, the bishop of Vannes, was not Breton and claimed only to do what Waroc told him because he had no other choice. Waroc may have controlled Vannes, but its sympathies may have been more Frankish than Breton. The impression is, as we have seen, that the Breton settlement was stronger in the countryside than in the city. Secondly, the Frankish attack was led by two dukes owing allegiance to Guntram, not to Chlothar II. Indeed, Beppolen was on particularly poor terms with the queen-mother, Fredegund. Their relations had become so bad that four years earlier, in 586, he had abandoned Fredegund and her son, Chlothar II, and had gone over to King Guntram, whereupon he 'was made duke of the cities which belonged to Chlothar', including Rennes; however, the citizens, loyal to Chlothar, had refused to allow him into their town.[138]

King Guntram himself had perhaps caused the failure of his army. This can be seen by contrasting the failure of 590 with an encounter with the Bretons three years earlier, in 587.[139] The Bretons had attacked the territory of Nantes. Guntram sent envoys to demand reparations. Duke Beppolen, Queen Fredegund's enemy, was not one of them, but instead they were headed by two bishops, of Orléans and Le Mans. 'There were also present magnates from the kingdom of Chlothar, King Chilperic's son.' King Guntram took the initiative but the approach was, in terms of relations between him and Chlothar II's supporters, bipartisan.

On the other hand, when, in 587, the Frankish envoys met the Breton leaders Waroc and Vidimacl in the territory of Nantes, the Bretons declared, according to Gregory, 'We also know that these *civitates* belong to the sons of King Chlothar.' This may not have been an entirely innocent remark. The King Chlothar to whom they referred was Chlothar I, the youngest of Clovis's sons, who had died in 561.

[138] Gregory of Tours, *Hist.*, viii. 42. [139] Gregory of Tours, *Hist.*, ix. 18.

Of his sons, only Guntram remained alive; the other Frankish kings were Guntram's nephews. As their uncle, Guntram had assumed a position of leadership, which he was determined to uphold in spite of considerable opposition in the kingdoms of both nephews; and, because Chlothar II's mother, Queen Fredegund, was bitterly hated by Childebert II's mother, Queen Brunhild, Guntram had little fear that his opponents would make common cause.[140] In any case, Guntram and his allies ensured that his leading enemies among the Eastern Franks were either killed or, in the case of Egidius, bishop of Rheims, driven into exile.[141] To Childebert II he promised that the latter would inherit all the *civitates* that he, Guntram, possessed. Yet he also protected Chlothar II. To Childebert II's envoys in 588, one of whom was Gregory himself, he declared:[142]

> If I do recognize Chlothar as my nephew, I will give him two or three cities in some part or other of my dominions, so that he may not feel that he is disinherited from my kingdom. Childebert has no reason to take offence if I make these gifts to Chlothar.

Any such utterance was disingenuous: earlier, namely in 585, not long after his brother Chilperic's assassination and in the midst of the Gundovald rebellion, Guntram had made Childebert II his heir for all his cities: 'As a result of sin, no one remains of my kindred except for you alone, you who are my brother's son. For you are to succeed to my whole kingdom, others having been disinherited.'[143] This excluded Chlothar II from the succession, promising everything to Childebert II.

Moreover, it seems that Queen Fredegund and the supporters of Chlothar II were not sure whether the boy was safe in the hands of Guntram. True, when, the previous autumn, 584, he was in Paris, a city loyal to Chilperic and his son Chlothar II, he had described both his nephews, Chlothar as well as Childebert, as 'his adopted sons'. That was immediately after the assassination of his brother, Chilperic; yet, now, when the crisis of Gundovald's bid for the kingship was reaching its height, Guntram took a very different line: the others who were not to be considered heirs certainly included Gundovald the Pretender, the current threat, but Chlothar II was hardly safe from exclusion. In 585, Guntram complained that successive arrangements for him to act as godfather at Chlothar's baptism had come to nothing;[144] and, as we have seen, Guntram did not sponsor Chlothar until 591; and, when he did so, it was to the intense annoyance of Childebert II.

These divisions were there to be exploited by the Breton ruler, Waroc. He himself was said to be a friend of Queen Fredegund; and he had succeeded in killing her particular enemy, Beppolen. When the boy, Chlothar II, became gravely ill, Fredegund vowed rich gifts to St Martin 'and so the boy appeared to get better'; but, to make sure, she sent messengers to Waroc to ask him to free the Frankish

140 Cf. what Gregory reports as his own words to Guntram, *Hist.* ix. 20, after the text of the Treaty of Andelot had been read out.

141 Ibid. ix. 8–12, 14; x. 19.

142 Ibid.; trans. Thorpe, *Gregory of Tours*, 509.

143 Gregory of Tours, *Hist.*, vii. 33.

144 Ibid. viii. 9.

captives he still retained.[145] Yet, Waroc's reply to the Frankish envoys in 587 had suggested that he entirely accepted that the *civitates* along the Breton border, and indeed the Bretons themselves, should be subject to the one remaining son of Chlothar I, namely Guntram. The ambiguities of Waroc's stance—a friend of Fredegund, the mother of Chlothar II, and yet prepared on occasion to acknowledge Guntram's right to take under his control the *civitates* along the Breton frontier—closely reflected the ambiguities of Guntram's policy towards his two nephews.

Earlier, there were two periods of conflict recorded by Gregory. The first again arose out of Frankish divisions. After the death of Theudebald, king of the Eastern Franks, in 555, Chramn, son of Chlothar I, had been established as a sub-ruler in those lands south of the Loire subject to Chlothar I. The other Frankish king with territory in the south was Childebert I, elder brother of Chlothar I. Childebert I would die in 558, Chlothar I in 561, so the period in which the tragedy of Chramn occurred was the last six years of the sons of Clovis, a period in which the issue of the succession, first, to Childebert I, who had no surviving sons, and then to the last surviving son of Clovis, Chlothar I, was critical. Relations between Chramn and his father, Chlothar I, were fatally damaged when the son allied himself with his uncle, Childebert I. Childebert was, at the time, seeking to take territory from Chlothar, while the latter was fully engaged with a Saxon revolt. When Childebert died in 558, Chramn was left without his patron and was compelled to submit to his father; but in 560 relations again worsened and he fled to Chonobor, 'count of the Britons'.[146] Chlothar pursued his son with an army; Chonobor was killed in battle, and Chramn fled. He was caught, detained with his wife and daughters in a peasant's hut, strangled, and then the hut and its occupants were burnt.[147] Chlothar, says Gregory, died exactly a year later.

Chramn's Breton support is likely to have been a legacy of the reign of Childebert I, Chramn's former ally. Between the death of Chlodomer in 524 and his own death in 558 Childebert had ruled over all of north-western Gaul. It is not, therefore, surprising that in Breton hagiography the Frankish king par excellence was Childebert.[148] Indirect evidence for his effectiveness in this role is the absence of any recorded attacks on the border *civitates* of Nantes, Redon, and Avranches during his reign, though, admittedly, Gregory of Tours might well not have known of such raids before he became bishop of Tours in 573. Chramn is unlikely to have

[145] Gregory of Tours, *Hist.*, x. 11.

[146] Gregory of Tours, *Hist.*, iv. 20. The forms of the name as given in the edition of Krusch and Levison (likewise Buchner) are: (1) (ablative) *Chonoobro*, (2) (nominative) *Chonoober*; in what follows, it will be argued that this is probably the same person as the *Chonomorem* (accusative) of iv. 4, with alternative spellings of *b* and *m* for the sound /v/. The *Chonoo* mentioned by French and Breton historians derives via the edition of Omont and Collon from MS B 5's version of iv. 20; in the English translations by Dalton and Thorpe, this was equated with the *Chanao* of iv. 4 (but Gregory treated the latter as an *n*-stem, ablative *Chanaone*, so the equation is scarcely possible).

[147] The outline of the story, but without the name of the Breton count, is in Marius of Avenches, *Chronica*, *s.a.* 560, ed. Mommsen, 237.

[148] F. Duine, *Mémento des sources hagiographiques de l'histoire de Bretagne. I. Les fondateurs et les primitifs* (Rennes, 1918), 175.

made the contacts with the Bretons that would allow him to take refuge among them at any other stage of his career apart from when he was in the company of Childebert. Before then he was either in his father's kingdom of Soissons (up to 555) or in the south of Gaul (from 555 to 556 or 557).

The link between Brittany and the former kingdom of Childebert outlived the death of the king in 558. One piece of evidence is the career of St Samson of Dol. The account in the First Life (which I would date to the seventh century) of the relationship between the saint and the king contains a standard element of Frankish political rhetoric, the wicked queen, and a characteristic element of Samson's hagiographical persona, the holy man victorious over serpents.[149] The story is designed to achieve two ends: the first was to demonstrate that the saint was responsible for the political triumph of Iudwal son of Ionas as ruler of Domnonia; the second was to show that the saint's church at *Penetale*, namely, St-Samson-sur-Risle, near the mouth of the Seine, was conferred on him by King Childebert.

In the Life, it appears as if the only Frankish king with whom St Samson had dealings was Childebert. But that is hardly correct: first, Samson attended the Council of Paris held between 556 and 573. It has been dated more closely either to 561–562 or to a date between 567 and 573.[150] The first date would indicate that St Samson remained active in Francia in the reign of Charibert, 561–567, the second that he was active in Francia in the reign of Chilperic, whose kingdom included Rennes between 567 and 584 and probably Avranches after Sigibert I's death in 575. Chilperic, moreover, named one of his sons Samson, which was an unparalleled act on his part.[151] Otherwise Merovingians were given one of a range of names proper to the dynasty; it may be that the Old Testament hero, notoriously long-haired, appealed to Chilperic as a model for a dynasty of 'long-haired kings', *reges criniti*, but the particular circumstances at the time of his birth may also have been crucial.[152] According to Gregory, Samson was born to Fredegund during the siege of Tournai in 575, when it appeared that Chilperic would be captured and killed by his brother Sigibert. Fredegund, in terror of death, rejected the child and wished to have him destroyed; but, having been rebuked by Chilperic, she ordered him to be baptized. 'He was baptized and was received from the font by the bishop himself.'[153] Gregory does not name the bishop who thus became the godfather of the child Samson and co-father, *compater*, with King Chilperic. We are clearly intended

[149] *Vita I S. Samsonis*, i. 53–9, ed. and trans. Flobert, 224–33, trans. Taylor, 53–8. For the date assigned to the Life, see below, 238–9 and n. 58.

[150] *Les Canons des conciles mérovingiens*, ed. and trans. Gaudemet and Basdevant, ii. 410, 424.

[151] Gregory of Tours, *Hist.*, v. 22; cf. I. N. Wood, 'Britain and the Continent in the Fifth and Sixth Centuries: The Evidence of Ninian', in J. Murray (ed.), *St Ninian and the Earliest Christianity in Scotland*, BAR Brit. Ser. 483 (Oxford, 2009), 77. A parallel has been suggested by Giot, Guigon, and Merdrignac, *The British Settlement of Brittany*, 143, namely a supposed Daniel, son of Chilperic; but this is a mere confusion with the Daniel who became king as Chilperic III; moreover, the latter was in the early eighth century; and Daniel was the name he had as a cleric, whereas Chilperic was the name he bore as a Merovingian king.

[152] E. Ewig, 'Die Namengebung bei den ältesten Frankenkönigen und im merowingischen Königshaus', *Francia*, 18/1 (1991), 21–69, at 28. On biblical names among the Britons, see R. Sharpe, 'The Naming of Bishop Ithamar', *English Historical Review*, 17 (2002), 889–94.

[153] Gregory of Tours, v. 22.

to infer his identity from the context. This might mean either that it was the bishop of Tournai or that the bishop was himself named Samson. If it was the bishop of Tournai, this was the only reference to such a bishop in Gregory, although a bishop of Tournai appeared once via his representative at a church council, Orléans 549. Given the exceptional name, however, there is at least an outside chance that the second is the correct explanation, and that Bishop Samson was the godfather of Samson, the son of Chilperic and Fredegund. Yet, even if the godfather was the bishop of Tournai, it is remarkable that the child should have been given such a name at such a time. It suggests that St Samson, whether still alive or recently dead, was held in high reverence by the king and the queen, even as they faced the imminent prospect of violent death.

That the relationship between Brittany and Childebert outlived the latter's death would make it easier to account for the evidence of Gregory on the death of Chramn and that of the Life of St Samson on the triumph of Iudwal son of Ionas. Gregory's *Chonomoris* was the Breton ruler who came to the aid of Macliaw, father of Waroc, *c*. 546; *Chonoober* was the Breton ruler who supported Chramn in 560 and was killed in battle as a result; in the Life of St Samson, *Commorus* was the 'unjust and unprincipled stranger' who had, before 558, 'come to be judge over the land; and their ruler, Ionas by name, who holds their land by hereditary custom, has been handed over to death as the result of wicked bribes wickedly given into the hands of the king and of the queen, his greatest bane'.[154] The death of *Commorus* in battle at the hands of Iudwal son of Ionas is represented as having occurred before the death of Childebert I in 558. We have, therefore:

Chonomoris	active *c*. 546
Chonoober	killed supporting Chramn in 560
Commorus	killed in battle against Iudwal son of Ionas no later than 558

There is a good chance that all three names refer to the same person, his identity obscured by different outcomes of contacts between British and Late Latin speakers.[155] First, the initial *ch*- is due to the numerous Frankish names with initial *ch*-; the British form has an initial *c* (a plosive *k*). The first element in *Chonomoris* and *Chonoober* is likely to be older *Cuno*-, with *o* for *u* in south-western British.[156] The name is attested in Old Welsh as *Conmor*, *Convor*, and *Cinvor*.[157] *Commorus* is likely to be a slightly later form, with syncope of the composition vowel and also influenced by Latin, and hence with *com*- for *con*-. As for *Chonoober*, since *b* and *m*

154 *Vita I S. Samsonis*, i. 53, trans. Taylor, 53; cf. i. 59 for the name.

155 For different views, see reviews of A. de la Borderie, *Histoire de Bretagne*, i, by J. Loth, *RC* 22 (1901), 112, and L. Duchesne, *Revue historique*, 66 (1898), 190; Mommsen, *Chronica Minora*, iii, MGH AA xiii, 5 n. 2; N. K. Chadwick, *Early Brittany* (Cardiff, 1969), 227 n. 4.

156 *LHEB*, § 5, p. 274 and n. 2.

157 *LL* 394.

between vowels were pronounced as varieties of *v*, this may also be a representation of **Conovor*.[158]

One may reasonably object that *Commorus*, killed no later than 558 during the reign of Childebert I, cannot be the same person as *Chonoober*, killed in 560 during the reign of Chlothar I, although he could well be the same person as the *Chonomoris* of *c.* 546. Yet, we need to remember that *Chonoober* is recorded in a near-contemporary source, Gregory's *Histories*, whereas *Commorus* appears in a saint's Life written no earlier than the seventh century and, in any case, heavily stylized. The stylization, moreover, is likely to have included making Childebert the Frankish king approached by Samson—Breton saints' Lives tended to have Childebert as their Frankish king, as we have seen, no doubt because he actually was the most long-lasting ruler of north-western Gaul in the sixth century;[159] and, as we have also seen, the most likely reason why *Chonoober* supported Chramn was the latter's alliance with Childebert.

It is at least worth considering the implications if these names all refer to the one person, whom I shall call Conomor. He is described in the Life of St Samson as ruler of Domnonia; but the inhabitants, apparently of the area around Dol, regarded him as an outsider. This would not mean that he was a Gallo-Roman, as has been argued, merely that his origins lay outside eastern Domnonia, the region around Dol.[160] Moreover, whatever his origins, he would have ruled at least from *c.* 546 to 560. The dynasty of Ionas and his son, Iudwal, on the other hand, appears to have ruled Domnonia, with interruptions from rivals, from 560 well into the seventh century.[161] Conomor was the Breton ruler during much of Childebert I's reign; Iudwal, on the other hand, established a dynasty that came to power in the aftermath of Childebert I's death. Change in Brittany followed change in Francia (see Map 7). The Domnonia ruled by Conomor and, later, Iudwal, was distinct from the kingdoms ruled by Chanao, Macliaw, Bodic, and, later, Macliaw's son, Waroc.[162] The kingdoms held by Waroc son of Macliaw and Theuderic son of Bodic were neighbours (they had both been parts of the kingdom held before 577 by Macliaw); and, since Waroc's kingdom included the Vannetais, it is quite likely that Theuderic's kingdom lay further west, in the area of Cornouaille (a name first attested in the Carolingian period).[163] We thus have evidence for at least three Breton *regna*: one in the north, Domnonia, two along the south coast, that of Theuderic in the west and that of Waroc further east. One *pagus* within Domnonia was Tréguier, from *Trecorii*, echoing the *Tricurius*, Trigg, of a Cornwall that still lay within Dumnonia north of the Channel.

158 In Gallo-Romance intervocalic /b/ became /v/ (*avoir* < *habere*) but intervocalic /m/ did not (*aimer* < *amare*, *nom* < *nomen*), whereas British had /b/ > /v/ and /m/ > a nasalized /v/ usually represented by /μ/. A British *Conomor* might well be understood by a Gallo-Roman as *Conobor*.

159 Fleuriot, *Les Origines*, 185–8.

160 Chadwick, *Early Brittany*, 223.

161 The evidence that Iudicael was son of Iudhail son of Iudwal is a later genealogy of uncertain value: L. Fleuriot, 'Old Breton Genealogies and Early British Tradition', *BBCS* 26 (1976), 1, 4.

162 Gregory of Tours, *Hist.*, iv. 4; v. 16.

163 Giot, Guigon, and Merdrignac, *The British Settlement of Brittany*, 146–7. Cf. *LL* 131, *cerniu budic* referring to Cornouaille by the name attested in Gregory as Bodic.

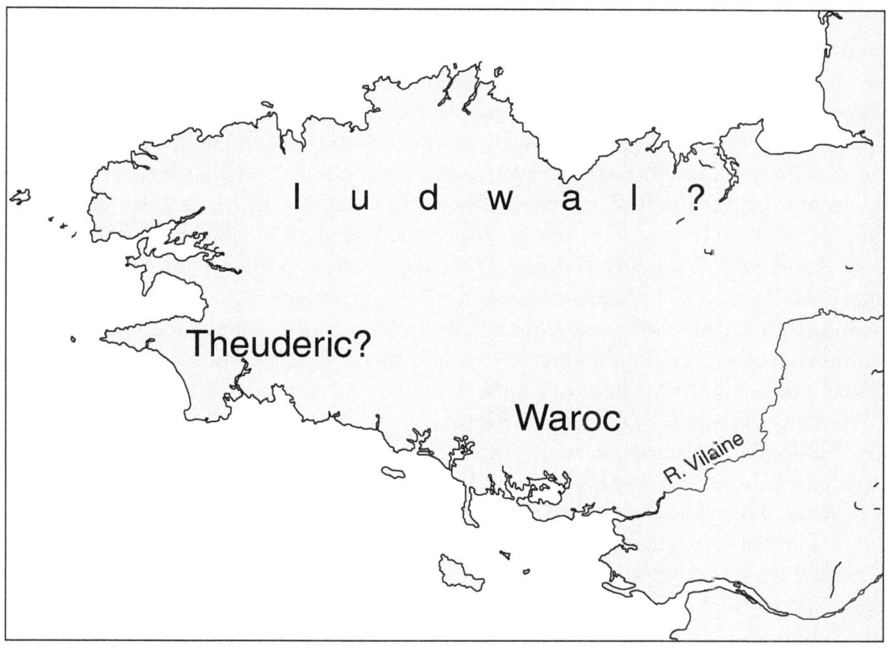

Map 7. The Kingdoms of Brittany, *c.* 580
Waroc is much the best attested of these kings, since he played a significant role in Frankish politics and thus in Gregory of Tours's *Histories*. Theuderic was mentioned by Gregory, Iudwal only by later sources. The River Vilaine, for part of its course, appears to have been the frontier between the Vannetais, ruled by Waroc, and the territory of Nantes, still under regular Frankish control.

Conflict between the Bretons and the Franks in the reign of Chilperic followed internal dynastic conflict in the southern Breton kingdoms. In the years running up to 577, Macliaw had controlled both his own kingdom and that of his former ally, Bodic; Bodic's son Theuderic had been driven into an exile that lasted 'for a considerable period'.[164] In 577, however, Theuderic, having collected a force *a Brittania*, 'from Britain', attacked Macliaw and slew both him and his son Iacob in battle. He then allowed another son of Macliaw, Waroc, to inherit that portion of Macliaw's kingdom that had originally been the father's before he usurped Bodic's *regnum*. Translators render *uiris a Brittania* as 'a band of Bretons' or 'bretonische Männer'.[165] They prefer, that is, one sense of *Brittania* in Gregory's *Histories*, namely 'Brittany', to the other, namely 'Britain'. They may well be wrong.[166]

164 Gregory of Tours, *Hist.*, v. 16.

165 Thorpe, *Gregory of Tours*, 273; Buchner, *Fränkische Geschichte*, 309.

166 It is possible that the Life of Oudoceus (Euddogwy), *LL* 130–1, in regarding *Budic* as exiled from Cornouaille to Dyfed, has transferred the actual experience of the son to the father.

Waroc, therefore, only held part of the kingdom ruled by his father. In the next year, 578, Chilperic sent an army against Waroc—not against the Bretons as a whole, but solely against the ruler whose father and brother had been killed the year before, and whose kingdom had been considerably reduced.[167] The named contingents of the army came from western *civitates*: Poitou, Touraine, the Bessin, Maine, and Anjou. Although Gregory adds 'with many others', it is striking that his list does not include the Redones or the Namnetici, namely the men of the neighbouring *civitates* of Rennes and Nantes. Waroc made a night attack on the Saxons from the Bessin and slew many of them. Three days later, however, he came to terms: he gave his son as a hostage to guarantee an agreement by which he would be Chilperic's faithful follower and that he would restore Vannes to Chilperic 'on condition that if he should deserve to rule it by the king's command, he would pay every year, without further notice, the tributes and everything that was due from it'. The army departed, Waroc forgot his promise, and sent Eunius, bishop of Vannes, to Chilperic, presumably to negotiate better terms. Effectively, Chilperic had gained nothing by his expedition. The next year, 579, the Bretons (presumably those ruled by Waroc), attacked the territory of Rennes, getting as far as Corps-Nuds, 16.5 kilometres south-south-east of the city.[168] Duke Beppolen was sent to punish the Bretons by raiding their territory, 'but this only led to greater madness'—referring perhaps to further Breton raids later the same year 'around the cities of Nantes and Rennes'.[169] Felix, bishop of Nantes, sent envoys to negotiate, and the Bretons promised compensation, but 'they wished to fulful none of their promises'. Felix, however, may have been more successful than Gregory allows (the two bishops were not on the best of terms). Gregory did not record any further trouble on the frontier until after Chilperic's death; and then, as we have seen, the context was tension between Frankish kingdoms. Chilperic, then, had attempted to take advantage of Waroc's difficulties at the beginning of the latter's period of power; he had failed to achieve anything lasting; the consequent violence was not helped by Duke Beppolen's counter-raid; but peace was restored by some diplomatic self-help by the bishop of Nantes.

The normal relationship between Bretons and Franks in the sixth century was peace not war. In every case of violence that has been examined special reasons explain why the norm did not prevail. These special reasons had, on the whole, more to do with the policies of Frankish kings than with those of Breton rulers, whether it was the failed opportunism of Chilperic or the tensions between Guntram and his nephews. The conditions underlying the normal peace were that the Bretons acknowledged Frankish supremacy; and for the Franks, at least, that meant that Breton rulers were counts, not kings.[170] Yet, they were not counts just like the ordinary counts of the Frankish kingdoms: the latter were appointed by kings as royal agents within the *civitates*. They operated in a context in which the bishops of the same *civitates* were also royal appointments and enjoyed a greater job security than the counts. Moreover, dukes were sometimes appointed

[167] Gregory of Tours, *Hist.*, v. 26. [168] Ibid. v. 29.
[169] Ibid. v. 31. [170] Ibid. iv. 4.

with authority over an area, an authority that sat uneasily with that of the counts and bishops.[171] Normal counts were responsible for ensuring that tributes were paid to the fisc; this is what Waroc promised to do for Vannes, but it was evidently an offer made under duress, to which he did not adhere.[172] Breton rulers, though they might be called counts, were not royal appointees; similarly, it is unlikely that appointments of bishops within the Breton lands required the royal *praeceptum* before they could be consecrated. The corollary of this relative independence was that Breton rulers did not form part of the governing elite of the Frankish kingdoms. No Breton became a duke, as did Chulderic the Saxon, who was made duke of Childebert II's *civitates* beyond the Garonne, or the Gallo-Roman Gundulf, Gregory's great-uncle.[173] Isolation was the price of independence.

It has been proposed that the normal relationship between Bretons and Franks was created by a treaty; and the treaty has even been given a date, 497.[174] The point is that this is the traditional date of the baptism of Clovis: a Frankish king had decided to prefer what his Gothic neighbours called 'the Roman religion' to the Arianism prevalent among the Germanic kingdoms further south; and, on this basis, he made an agreement, in the first place with the Gallo-Romans of Armorica and, secondarily, with the Bretons. The evidence adduced for this treaty consists of some brief passages in Procopius's *History of the Wars* (Persian, Vandal, and Gothic wars) and a chapter of Gregory of Tours. The first is from that point in the *Gothic War* at which the role of the Franks became important for the war in Italy. Procopius, therefore, set out to explain who the Franks were and why they were so powerful.[175] He located, correctly, the earlier settlements of the Franks along the lower Rhine. 'Next to the Franks lived the *Arboruchoi* who, together with all the rest of Gaul and, indeed, Spain, had from ancient times been subjects of the Romans.' The Franks attempted to conquer the *Arboruchoi*, who 'had changed their form of government, which they had long had' (probably referring to their acquiring their own rulers, separate from the emperor).

> But the *Arboruchoi* showed their valour and their good will towards the Romans and acted bravely in this war; and when the Franks were not in a position to force them into submission, they decided to make them their companions and relations by marriage. This proposal the *Arboruchoi* accepted not unwillingly, for both were Christians, and thus they came together as one people and acquired great power.

It has long been recognized that Procopius's *Arboruchoi* were the Armorici or inhabitants of Armorica of north-west Gaul (with an interchange of *b* and *m* similar

[171] For difficulties between these different figures, see, for example, ibid. v. 48, 49 (Gregory with Count Leudast and with Duke Berulf and Count Eunomius).

[172] Cf. ibid. vi. 22.

[173] Ibid. vi. 11; viii. 18.

[174] Fleuriot, *Les Origines*, 180–3, following S. Reinach, 'Francs et Bretons armoricaines', *Revue archéologique*, 5th Ser. 27 (1928), 246–53, whose argument is based on the evidence of Procopius discussed below.

[175] Procopius, *History of the Wars*, V. xii. 8–15, ed. and trans. H. B. Dewing, Loeb Classical Library (Cambridge, Mass., 1919), iii. 118–21.

to that in *Chonomoris* and *Chonoober*). Procopius, therefore, was referring to the Gallo-Romans north of the Loire and from the Seine valley westwards.

There is some exaggeration but much essential truth in Procopius's description. This is hardly surprising, since the Franks mattered greatly for the war in Italy. The exaggeration comes in the notion that the Franks did not conquer Gaul north of the Loire. The truth, however, is that the ruling elite of the Frankish kingdom embraced both Franks and Gallo-Romans (and also Burgundians) under the acknowledged authority of the Merovingian dynasty. And, as for the notion that the two peoples became one, that was not so much an untruth as an anticipation of what would happen in the seventh century, when the Gallo-Romans north of the Loire indeed became Franks, whereas those south of the Loire did not. Yet, if we understand it in this way, the implication is that the Bretons were not parties to this supposed treaty, even if they were settled within Armorica; for, as we have seen, the Bretons, unlike the Franks, the Gallo-Romans, and the Burgundians, did not become part of the ruling elite of Gaul.

The date provided by the baptism of Clovis is, however, very uncertain, and not just because Clovis may well have been baptized as late as 508: the link between Clovis and the Gallo-Romans of northern Gaul went back well before his baptism, as shown by the letter of Remigius, bishop of Rheims, welcoming his succession to his father and giving advice: 'Also your achievement should be without taint and honourable, and you should discuss matters with your bishops and always seek their advice, because, if you are on good terms with them, your province can be the better for it.'[176]

At this point in the argument, the chapter of Gregory of Tours becomes crucial, in which he says that from the time of Clovis the Breton rulers ceased to be called kings but were merely counts, subjects of the Franks.[177] The suggestion is that their change of political status was something that they themselves accepted as part of a settlement between them and the newly dominant power in northern Gaul, the Franks. This may well be the case, even though we have no explicit contemporary or near-contemporary evidence other than Gregory's all-too-brief statement; and there are other cases, admittedly later, when the Franks described someone as a count whom impartial contemporaries knew as a king.[178] What is far from clear is whether this settlement was part of that other agreement described by Procopius, between the Gallo-Romans north of the Loire and the Franks. Moreover, while it is doubtless true that ultimately the bond between Gallo-Romans and Franks was facilitated by the conversion of Clovis to Catholic Christianity, his collaboration with Gallo-Roman bishops began well before his baptism.[179] Yet, while we cannot date any agreement between the Franks and the Bretons, the argument that, in their relations, peace was normal, violence exceptional, suggests that there was some such

[176] *Epistolae Austrasicae*, ed. Gundlach, no. 2.
[177] Gregory of Tours, *Hist.*, iv. 4.
[178] The Frisian ruler Radbod: Continuation of Fredegar, cc. 6–9; Bede, *HE* v. 9–10.
[179] *Epistolae Austrasicae*, ed. Gundlach, no. 2.

agreement. It may well have arisen out of a common hostility to the Visigoths dating back to the 460s.

A plausible summary account of the settlement of Brittany may, therefore, run as follows. The first secure attestation of the presence of a sizeable British element in Armorica belongs to the 460s, the time of Mansuetus, bishop of the Britons, and of Riothamus, a king and leader of a British army allied to the Emperor Anthemius. A settlement of this period would probably have been with imperial authority. Even in the late sixth century, Breton control of the Vannetais was incomplete, while the territories of Nantes and Rennes were beyond Breton control though raided by them. One may, therefore, draw a contrast between the lands of the Osismi and the Coriosolites, probably settled peacefully and with Roman authority in the fifth century, and those of the Veneti, gradually taken by force in the sixth.[180] There probably was some kind of settlement between the Bretons and the Franks, although it cannot be dated to 497. Relations between Bretons and Franks in the sixth century appear to have been peaceful until the death of Childebert I in 558; and subsequent serious hostilities were spasmodic and arose mainly from the Frankish side. The understanding between Franks and Bretons in the sixth century is likely to have ensured that migration from Britain was directed towards existing Breton territory: the 'Britons of the dispersal' belonged to an earlier phase. Links between Brittany and Britain remained active: the *Brittania* from which Theuderic, a Breton ruler though bearing a Merovingian royal name, brought an army in 577 and re-established himself in his father's kingdom is quite likely to have been Britain. Ecclesiastical migration was probably common in this period, as illustrated by the career of St Samson of Dol. His is the best attested case, but the numerous Breton saints who established churches and monasteries may well belong to this phase, the one termed by Fleuriot 'the second migration' and dated by him to the period after the agreement between the Bretons and the Franks.[181] Gildas refers with disdain to aspirants to the priesthood or episcopate, unable to satisfy their ambition, even by bribery, in Britain, taking 'a positive pleasure in sailing across seas and traversing wide lands in order to attain at last such a glory'.[182] Some of these clerics, at least, 'with great pomp and great show' 'return home'. Brittany may well have been their main destination, though Ireland should certainly not be excluded; it is, in any case, interesting that the movements went in both directions. By the end of the sixth century the religious landscape of Brittany probably already had that character, so reminiscent of Celtic Britain and Ireland, that is later visible in Breton saints' lives, even though nearly all of them date from the Carolingian period or later.

The emergence of Brittany has implications for the history of the parent island. What is evident from the place-names and the broader history of the Breton language is that the dominant language among the settlers west of the River Vilaine was British. Yet, it will be argued in Chapter 2 that Latin survived in Wales and Cornwall as a normal spoken language, learnt in infancy, into the seventh century.

[180] Fleuriot, *Les Origines*, 206. [181] Ibid. 207.
[182] Gildas, *De Excidio*, c. 67.

In the fourth century, Latin appears to have been a normal means of communication in much of the diocese of 'the Britains'. One possible explanation is that the initial major settlement of Brittany came from the less Romanized west of the island because that was the zone of Irish raiding and conquest.[183] Another might be that essential to the establishment of Brittany was a military settlement, perhaps exemplified by the history of the army led by Riothamus, king of the Britons; and that the army or armies in question were recruited predominantly from the less Romanized and more British-speaking west of the island—as it were the Highland regiments of fifth-century Britain, comparable with those other highland troops of the late Roman state, the Isaurians of Anatolia. These two explanations could well both be true. Once the settlement was made, the closest links of the new Britain south of the Channel were with the south-west of Britain, and hence the appearance of a Breton *Domnonia* and *Tricorii* to match their insular counterparts and the near identity, at this period, of the Breton and Cornish dialects of British. The linguistic Britishness of western Brittany in the sixth century should not, however, be overemphasized. Fleuriot demonstrated the extent of Romance elements even in the west alongside islands of Breton-speakers in the east; and the triumph of Breton in the west, of Romance in the east, may be part of that process of consolidation of ethnic identity found right across Gaul in the seventh century. There is no need, therefore, to restrict the British immigration into Armorica to those fleeing from the Irish or to those fleeing from the English. The assumption of Breton hagiography, beginning with the First Life of St Samson, that their saints were likely to have been incomers from the island of Britain is a clue to a much wider migration in the sixth and seventh centuries in the wake of the military settlement of the fifth.[184] The success of the new Britain in Armorica made it a magnet as well as a refuge.

As we shall see in Chapter 6, the relative isolation of the Bretons within Gaul would have far-reaching consequences for all the Britons, north as well as south of the Channel. This isolation would strengthen, first, as a result of the Gallic Church's adherence to the Easter limits of Victorius of Aquitaine, something the Britons rejected;[185] secondly, because of the seventh-century process by which the Gallo-Romans north of the Loire—and presumably also the 'Britons of the dispersal' settled among them—were assimilated into a single Frankish people; and, thirdly, because of the growing importance of Frankish connections with the English of eastern Britain, especially after Gregory the Great initiated the mission that landed in Kent in 597.

[183] N. K. Chadwick, 'The Colonization of Brittany from Celtic Britain', *Proceedings of the British Academy*, 51 (1965), 262–70; ead. *Early Brittany*, 172–92.

[184] Fleuriot, *Les Origines*, ch. 11.

[185] Orléans 541, c. 1, ed. and trans. Gaudemet and Basdevant, *Les Canons des conciles mérovingiens*, i. 266–7; D. McCarthy, 'The Origins of the *Latercus* Paschal Cycle of the Insular Celtic Churches', *CMCS* 28 (Winter 1994), 25–49; Charles-Edwards, *Early Christian Ireland*, 406–7.

2

The Britons and their Languages

The period 400–1100 saw the emergence of Welsh from its parent language, British. By the end of the first three centuries of this period, by 700, what language one spoke had become the principal mark of national identity in Britain as a whole, not just for the Britons.[1] That was not so in 400: many Britons then spoke Latin, though many of them would also have been able to speak British (or British Celtic when distinguishing it from British Latin). In the sixth century, Gildas referred to Latin as 'our language', contrasting it with the Germanic of the Anglo-Saxon settlers.[2] But by about 700, British Latin had died out as a normal spoken language. For the inhabitants of Wales, their identity was, in 700, still British; but now a single language bound them all to their compatriots in what is now Strathclyde, the Isle of Man, Cornwall, and Brittany. They were all Britons as distinct from their neighbours to the north, the Picts, to the west, the Irish, and to the east, the English—or, for the Bretons, the Franks. The modern Welsh name for their language, Cymraeg, meant 'British' in 700; and the Cymry, the people, were the Britons, not just the Welsh.[3] The emergence of a separate Welsh identity was, therefore, a slow process, not completed until the twelfth century, after the end of the period covered by this book.[4] Similarly, the distinction between Briton and Breton is modern; and the Celtic language of Brittany is still Brezhoneg, Brittonic.

The development of the language in this period has, however, another historical interest. British underwent major changes between the fourth and the eighth century, changes which transformed it from being a language similar in type to Greek, Latin, and other old Indo-European languages, into a language most closely similar to French, on the one hand, and Irish on the other. The kinship with Irish was ancient—both were Celtic languages—but the similarity with French was the outcome of a shared historical experience within the Roman Empire. We may, therefore, divide the emergence of Welsh into two separate issues: first, the transformation of British in the late Roman and post-Roman periods from an ancient Indo-European language into a language of the type characteristic of

[1] Bede, *HE* i. 1: 'Haec (sc. insula) . . . quinque gentium linguis, unam eandemque summae ueritatis et uerae sublimitatis scientiam scrutatur, et confitetur, Anglorum uidelicet, Brettonum, Scottorum, Pictorum . . . .' Cf. iii. 6.

[2] Gildas, *De Excidio Britanniae*, 23. 3.

[3] T. M. Charles-Edwards, 'Language and Society among the Insular Celts', 711, discussing *Sanas Cormaic* (YBL), ed. K. Meyer (Halle, 1912), nos. 124, 206, 239, 883.

[4] H. Pryce, 'British or Welsh? National Identity in Twelfth-Century Wales', *EHR* 116 (2001), 775–801.

medieval western Europe; and, secondly, the process by which Welsh, at first merely a group of dialects of British, came to be separated from Cornish, Breton, and Cumbric (a term I shall use for the Brittonic language of Cumbria or Strathclyde). Because the final emergence of Welsh as a separate language occurred later than the changes that transformed western European languages, I shall adopt the following terminology: Old British is the language before the loss of nominal inflexion; Late British is the language after this change and before the emergence of Welsh as a distinct language. Late British included a range of dialects from Brittany to the kingdom of Dumbarton; even what is now Wales already included more than one British dialect.[5]

There is a particular reason why the languages of Britain need to be discussed at this point. An understanding of the linguistic situation of western and northern Britain is required before the evidence of the inscriptions can be exploited. As a whole, they constitute perhaps the richest source for the Britons in the post-Roman period; and the contrast between the post-Roman inscriptions and those of later centuries is of very great importance for anyone trying to appreciate the cultural and religious changes in early medieval Wales.

1. BRITISH 400–700

Welsh is a Celtic language, but its parent, British, was also deeply affected by Latin, so deeply that in some ways Welsh is akin to the Romance languages descended from Latin. These two aspects of Welsh evoke different ways of comparing and classifying languages.

To describe Welsh as a Celtic language is to see it as a twig at the summit of a tree of languages. Welsh is closely related to Cornish and Breton, all three being twigs from the same branch, British, the Celtic language spoken in pre-Roman, Roman, and post-Roman Britain. Twigs from another branch are Irish, Manx, and Scottish Gaelic. Others were the Continental Celtic languages of Antiquity: Gaulish, Lepontic, Celtiberian, and Galatian. All these, both Continental and Insular Celtic languages, came from an ancestral Celtic language. This 'Proto-Celtic' was in turn part of a further, more extended family of languages termed 'Indo-European' because descended from a single 'Proto-Indo-European' and because members of the family ended up scattered from India to Ireland. To classify languages according to their descent from ancestral languages—as French, Italian, and the other Romance languages are descended from Latin—is the genetic approach.

The other approach concerns itself with comparisons between languages at a given period, and also with contacts between languages—languages which may, or may not, be genetically related. To take one example, the English invasion of Ireland in the twelfth century, together with subsequent reinforcements,

[5] This is illustrated by a gloss in 'St Dunstan's Classbook', Oxford, Bodleian Library, Auct. F. IV. 32, fo. 38r, line 4, on *patruelibus*, *ceintiru*, which is distinctively South Welsh: T. M. Charles-Edwards, 'Some Celtic Kinship Terms', *BBCS* 24 (1970–2), 107–8.

established English as a language spoken in Ireland alongside Irish (and, for a time, French). In the nineteenth century, English became the sole spoken language over much of Ireland. The prolonged contact between the two languages is detectable, especially by examining, first, the influence of English upon Irish, in particular the numerous words borrowed from the politically dominant language, English, and, secondly, by examining the influence of Irish upon the forms of English spoken in Ireland. When sections of the Irish population switched from being monolingual speakers of Irish to bilingualism, and then to being monolingual speakers of English, they brought to their English some characteristics of Irish. For example, Modern Irish has no voiceless *th* sound (the *th* of *thin*, for which I shall use the Greek letter /*θ*/ to distinguish it from the voiced *th* of *the* and *than*, represented by /ð/).[6] On the other hand, Irish does distinguish, unlike English, between a 'broad' *t* and a 'slender' *t*: the broad *t* is articulated with the tongue touching the top teeth, while for the slender *t* it touches the ridge behind the top teeth. Irish people speaking English therefore tended to use their 'broad' *t* in place of standard English /*θ*/ and they kept their slender *t* for English *t*. In this way a trace of the contrast between broad and slender consonants—a crucial feature of the Irish sound system—was preserved in Hiberno-English.

Similar traces of a former language can be detected in Welsh. The former language in this instance was the Latin spoken in Britain from the first century AD until, very approximately, 700. Whereas Latin displaced Gaulish in what is now France, it failed to displace British in Britain; and yet it was spoken for centuries and was unquestionably the language of higher social and political prestige; many Britons were bilingual in Latin and British; and some areas of the island, especially those towards the south-east, may have been, for a time, largely Latin-speaking.[7] In the days of its dominance Latin bequeathed many words to British; and, as British Latin gradually died as a spoken language in the post-Roman period, it also bequeathed characteristics to the various Brittonic dialects (using 'Brittonic' for the family comprised of British and its daughter-languages, including Welsh, the 'Cumbric' of what is now northern England and southern Scotland, Cornish, and Breton). One example is the position of the stress accent in British by the fourth century. Whereas there is reason to believe that at an earlier period British had a stress on the first syllable of the word, by the late Empire it was penultimate—on the last but one syllable—except, of course, for monosyllabic words and unstressed words.[8] This is not precisely the same as Late Latin accentuation, but it is close enough to suggest some influence of Latin on British; both Old Irish and Old

[6] The forward slash, /, is placed either side of a letter or phonetic symbol when it represents a distinctive sound in the language. It is, for example, an essential means to cope with the vagaries of spelling, as with the initial *c* of English *cell* as opposed to the initial *c* of *car*: /s/ as opposed to /k/.

[7] P. Schrijver, 'The Rise and Fall of British Latin: The Evidence from English and Brittonic', in M. Filppula, J. Klemola, and H. Pitkänen (eds.), *The Celtic Roots of English* (Joensuu, 2002), 87–110; id., 'What Britons spoke around 400 AD', in N. J. Higham (ed.), *Britons in Anglo-Saxon England* (Woodbridge, 2007), 165–71.

[8] P. Schrijver, *Studies in British Celtic Historical Phonology* (Amsterdam, 1995), 16–22; id. 'What Britons spoke around 400 AD', 166–7.

English had initial stress. Another example is the creation of a pluperfect tense in British (as in Middle Welsh *hwy a athoedynt adref* 'they had gone home'): Irish has never had one; and it is far more likely that a new pluperfect was created in British on the model of Latin than that an old pluperfect was lost in the prehistoric period of Irish.[9]

Genetic and language-contact relationships can overlap; and sometimes they are difficult to disentangle. An important case in point is perhaps the most distinctive feature of Welsh and the other Brittonic languages, as well as Irish, Manx, and Scottish Gaelic: the 'mutations', namely the changes made at the beginning of a word to signify a grammatical relationship. The most important of these is the so-called 'soft mutation', also known as 'lenition'. To begin with—that is to say, back in late Roman Britain—this was a simple phonetic change, a form of assimilation principally of 'stop consonants' (or 'stops' or 'plosives') to vowels. To understand what was involved we need to bear in mind three distinctions between types of consonant as well as the broader contrast between all consonants and vowels. These three distinctions are between stops and fricatives, between geminate (double) and single consonants, and between voiced and voiceless consonants. A stop consonant is articulated by, very briefly, stopping the flow of air through the 'vocal tract' from the throat, through the mouth, and out by the lips; examples are /t/ and /d/ (stops) as opposed to /θ/ and /ð/ (both the *th* of *thin* and the *th* of *than*), which are fricatives. The latter sounds are made by the friction, hence 'fricative', as opposed to the stopping, of the airflow. Both the stop /t/ and the fricative /θ/ are voiceless consonants by contrast with their voiced counterparts, /d/ and /ð/. Just as geminate or strong consonants play a major role in Modern Italian, they also played an important part in British: British **kattos*, 'male cat', was distinguished from **katus* 'battle' not just by the ending (*-os* as against *-us*) but by the contrast between a geminate *-tt-* and a single *-t-*. With these three distinctions, one can establish part of a network of consonants.

Just as a fricative is articulated not by stopping the airflow but by impeding it, so as to produce the friction implicit in the name 'fricative', so also vowels do not stop

Table 2.1. A network of dental consonants

	Voiceless	Voiced
Geminate stop	tt	(dd was very rare)
Stop	t	d
Fricative	θ	ð

[9] P. Mac Cana, 'Latin Influence on British: The Pluperfect', in J. J. O'Meara and B. Naumann (eds.), *Latin Script and Letters* AD *400–900: A Festschrift presented to Ludwig Bieler* (Leiden, 1976), 194–203. P. Russell, 'Latin and British in Roman and Post-Roman Britain: Methodology and Morphology', in S. Laker and P. Russell (eds.), 'Special Issue: Languages of Early Britain', *Transactions of the Philological Society*, 109: 2 (2011), 138–7 offers some caveats.

Table 2.2. Stops, fricatives, and lenition

Voiceless geminate stop	voiceless single stop and voiceless fricative	voiced single stop and voiced fricative	vowels
tt	t	d	
	θ	ð	
			a, e, i, o, u
			ā, ē, ī, ō, ū

the airflow. In this respect the contrast between vowels and fricatives is less complete than between vowels and stops. Similarly vowels are voiced sounds, and voiced consonants are thus less sharply opposed to vowels than are unvoiced consonants. Single stops were also less sharply opposed to vowels than were geminates. For British, therefore, we can line up our consonants according to how sharply they were distinguished from vowels, taking the dentals (*tt*, *t*, *d*, *θ*, *ð*) as examples. In Table 2.2 above, the most sharply distinguished are on the top line and on the left:

The process known as lenition (or soft mutation) consists of movement of consonants from left to right and from top to bottom—in other words an approximation to the vowels which have been placed, for this reason, in the bottom right of the table. What happened in British was that, between vowels, voiced stops became voiced fricatives, voiceless stops became voiced stops and geminate stops became single stops. The broad nature of these changes can be described as an assimilation of consonants between vowels, 'intervocalic' consonants to surrounding vowels; that the changes primarily affected intervocalic stops indicates that assimilation was indeed the underlying process. Lenition, however, was a process of assimilation, not identification: a fricative such as /ð/ did not become a vowel. The velar fricative /γ/, lenited from /g/, later became zero, so that the lenited form of *genau* 'mouth' became *enau*, as in Modern Welsh *ei enau* 'his mouth'; but this was a subsequent change, not part of the original lenition. So, if we represent any vowel by V, a voiceless stop by T, a geminate voiceless stop by TT, a voiced stop by D, an unvoiced fricative by *Θ*, and a voiced fricative by Đ, the changes involved in lenition proceeded as follows:

1.	VDV > VĐV
2.	VTV > VDV
3.	VTTV > VTV

As can be seen, there was no change of VΘV > VĐV. At this stage there were no intervocalic voiceless fricatives in British, apart from *s*, which pursued its own path. Indeed, part of the background to lenition was precisely the poverty of fricatives in

British: there was plenty of phonological space to fill. It will also be apparent that the second change, the voicing of voiceless stops, VTV > VDV, must have taken place either at the same time as the first, VDV > VĐV, or later. If it had occurred earlier, so that an old T fell together with an old D, there would have been a double change: T > D > Đ. Yet this did not happen.[10] The same point applies to the third change in relation to the second.

Similar changes took place, at much the same time, in the western Romance dialects, those from which French, Occitan, Sard, Catalan, Spanish, Galician, and Portuguese are descended.[11] They did not affect southern and central Italian or Rumanian: hence Spanish Pedro but early Italian Petro (later Pietro) 'Peter', standard Italian *ripa* but Provençal, Catalan, and Portuguese *riba* (with a yet further assimilation in French *rive* and northern Italian *riva*). One particular feature, however, distinguishes the Insular Celtic languages from their western Romance neighbours. In all of them, both Celtic and western Romance, this partial assimilation of consonants to vowels occurred when the consonant was single and intervocalic: for example, in British **catus* became **cadus* (Welsh *cad* 'battle') but **cattā* '(female) cat', with double /tt/, retained a single voiceless /t/ (which later developed into a voiceless fricative /θ/): **cattā* > **catā* (as part of lenition) > *cath*, with 'spirantization', namely the change from a stop to a fricative or 'spirant', as well as the slightly earlier loss of the ending *-ā*.[12]

In the Insular Celtic languages, however, lenition happened, not just within a word, but across the boundary between one word and another within a single phrase. In western Romance, voicing of intervocalic voiceless stops occurred only in the interior of a word. Because of this difference, phonetic lenition gave rise to grammatical lenition in Insular Celtic but not in western Romance. To take an example, the Modern Welsh word for 'father' is *tad*, in origin an affectionate 'daddy'-type word as opposed to the more formal 'father'. 'His father', in the British spoken when Julius Caesar invaded the island, was **esio tatos*. Both the initial *t-* and the medial *-t-* of **tatos* were treated as intervocalic: the word boundary between **esio* and **tatos* made, in this respect, no difference. Whereas 'father' on its own in modern Welsh is *tad*, 'his father' is *ei dad*: both the initial and the medial *t* of **tatos* were voiced. The originally purely phonetic lenition of initial, but intervocalic, consonants gave rise to the grammatical system of lenition as found in

[10] For 'push' or a combination of push and 'drag', see A. Martinet, 'Celtic Lenition and Western Romance Consonants', *Language*, 28 (1952), 192–217; a revised version is chapter 11 of *Économie des changements phonétiques: traité de phonologie diachronique*, 2nd edn. (Berne, 1964); for theories based on 'drag' see P. Sims-Williams, 'Dating the Transition to Neo-Brittonic: Phonology and History, 400–600', in *Britain 400–600: Language and History*, eds. A. Bammersberger and A. Wollmann (Heidelberg, 1990), 232–6, and P. W. Thomas, 'The Brythonic Consonant Shift and the Development of Consonant Mutation', *BBCS* 37 (1990), 1–42.

[11] J. Herman, *Vulgar Latin* (Univ. Park, Pennsylvania, 2000), 46–7 (who notes, however, that the first definite examples are sixth century); Schrijver, 'The Rise and Fall of British Latin', 93–4, argues that, if they are related, western Romance voicing is more likely to have helped to trigger British (and, perhaps, Gaulish) voicing than the other way round.

[12] Following D. Greene, 'The Spirant Mutation in Brythonic', *Celtica*, 7 (1966), 116–19; A. Harvey, 'Aspects of Lenition and Spirantization', *CMCS* 8 (Winter 1984), 87–100; P. Russell, 'A Footnote to Spirantization', *CMCS* 10 (Winter 1985), 53–6, as against *LHEB* §§ 131–2.

medieval and modern Welsh; the lenition of internal single intervocalic stops, on the other hand, remained a mere phonological change. The same distinction can be made between the 'spirant mutation' of some initial consonants and a corresponding change in the interior of a word. Thus **tatos*, **esio tatos*, 'his father', and (with the feminine form of the possessive pronoun **esiās*) **esiās tatos*, 'her father', gave *tad*, *ei dad*, and *ei thad* in modern Welsh, where the initial *t-* changes to fit the grammatical context; the medial *t* of **tatos*, however, simply yields a *d* throughout. Similarly, **cattā* 'cat', by itself and prefixed by **esio* and **esiās*, gave *cath*, *ei gath*, and *ei chath* for 'cat', 'his cat', and 'her cat'. The *ch* of *ei chath* was part of the grammatical system of the mutations, but the corresponding internal change of /tt/ to /θ/ was simply a phonological change.

Another example is the lenition of adjectives following a feminine noun, as in *mam dda* 'good mother' (where *dd* is a spelling for the voiced fricative /ð/). *Mam*, again in origin an affectionate or informal 'mummy' word, comes from a British **mammā*.[13] Here *m* is a 'nasal' consonant rather than a stop or fricative, but the same principles apply: if it is single and intervocalic, it is lenited and becomes a fricative /v/ (probably originally a nasalized /v/). In **mammā* the first *m* is single, but the second is a double *-mm-*. Whereas the second *t* of **tatos* was single and was lenited to *d* in *tad*, the double *mm* of **mammā* yielded the final *-m* of *mam*. On the other hand, **mammā* ended with a vowel, so that the initial *d-* of the following adjective **dagā* 'good' was intervocalic; **mammā dagā* therefore gave Modern Welsh *mam dda* 'good mother', /mam ða/. Similarly 'the good mother', **sindā mammā dagā*, is *y fam dda* in Modern Welsh (where *f* is a spelling for the voiced fricative /v/). In *y fam dda*, therefore, the initial single *m* has been lenited to a fricative, whereas the medial double (or 'geminate') /mm/ remains as a single /m/.[14]

The Brittonic languages exhibit two affinities in their system of lenition: with the western Romance languages in some of the phonetic detail, but with Irish in the much more important fact that from a phonetic change emerged a grammatical device. The detail shared with western Romance was that a lenited voiceless stop was voiced rather than, as in Irish, becoming a voiceless fricative. What tied British to Irish, however, was the crucial importance in phonology of the phrase rather than merely the single word. Celtic lenition worked within phrases, such as **sindā mammā dagā*, just as it did within a single word. It crossed the boundary between words, but it did not (at this stage) cross the boundary of a phrase. The same importance of the phrase can be seen in the way scribes wrote Old Irish and Old Welsh: often they used gaps to separate phrases rather than words.

Once British final syllables had been lost (**mammā* > *mam*), the effect of being a single intervocalic stop, namely the following lenited *ð* of **ðagā* > *dda*, remained even when the cause had been removed: in *mam dda* the *dd* is no longer intervocalic. In British the agreement of the endings in *-ā* in **sindā mammā dagā* expressed the unity of the phrase; once the endings had been lost, this way in which the shape of the words revealed their role in the phrase was at an end.

[13] A relic of the more formal Celtic **mātīr* survives in the derivative *modryb* 'aunt'.

[14] Unless one counts the change from double *mm* to single *m* as part of lenition.

Lenition was now no longer merely phonetic but 'phonological' in that the difference had become significant and not just an effect of the consonant's environment. Moreover, it also assumed a major importance in the grammar of the language: the link between feminine noun and adjective was expressed by lenition rather than the agreement of endings. Changes at the beginning of words took over some functions previously performed by changes at the end.

Typologically, therefore, Irish and British were linked by lenition, itself the major element in a system of 'initial mutations'. Yet this link has a paradoxical aspect: Irish and British were indeed both Celtic languages, both descended from Proto-Celtic, but this connexion, in that both had initial mutations, was a novel development of the late Roman or immediately post-Roman period, several centuries after British and Irish had become separate languages. Admittedly it was based in part on something which may have been much older, the phonological shape of the phrase, but as a grammatical device it only acquired its significance after the loss of final endings. It was part of a whole pattern of change which turned the western European languages away from the grammar characteristic of Antiquity (in which agreement denoted by endings was crucial) into something very different. But this 'very different' was also, for British and Irish, shared and distinctive, a new typological Celticity. At the end of this turbulent period, not only was Latin well on its way to becoming one or other of the Romance languages, but British was on the road towards Welsh, Cumbric, Cornish, and Breton. For contemporaries, however, it long remained a single British language with local varieties.

British was in the centre of the linguistic turbulence of western Europe in the late Roman and post-Roman periods. It shared some major developments with Romance and others with what I shall call 'the languages of the northern seas'—the coastal languages from Scandinavia to northern Gaul, including the British Isles. This centrality explains why, in some respects, it resembles French and, in others, Irish. A principal change that came to distinguish western Europe as a whole, where it prevailed, from central and, even more so, eastern Europe, where it did not, was the decay of inflexion of the noun, pronoun, and adjective for case (for which I shall use the term 'declension'). Verbal inflexion was much more conservative among the Romance languages and in British. In Modern English declension only survives in a few relics, such as the personal pronoun—for example, *he, him, his*. Case is a device by which a noun, pronoun, or adjective is modified according to its role in the syntax of the sentence, a role often defined by its relationship with the verb, but sometimes by its relationship to another noun. An example is English 'He supported him', where *he* is the subject and *him* the object of the verb *supported*. In eastern Europe, among the Slavonic and Baltic languages, and to a somewhat lesser extent in central Europe, in German, a complex pattern of declension survives; in western Europe it does not. Italian, for example, has relics of a case system in the pronoun, but for the noun and adjective it distinguishes only singular from plural and masculine from feminine, as does Welsh. What happened was that, whereas Latin had six cases, they were ultimately lost altogether.[15]

[15] V. Väänänen, *Introduction au latin vulgaire*, 2nd edn. (Paris, 1967), 117–24, §§ 242–57.

This happened at different dates in the various Romance languages. Old French, Old Provençal, and Rumanian kept vestiges of the Latin declension: French, for example, retained two cases until the late medieval period. Elsewhere, however, as in Italian or Spanish, the case system, except in the pronoun, disappeared very rapidly. On this point, British agreed with Italian rather than with French. In Modern Welsh there remain one or two relics of case, as in *erbyn* 'against' from Old British **ari pennī* (literally 'facing a head') as against *pen* 'head' from British **pennos*, and in the early form of Caerdydd 'Cardiff', Caerdyf, 'The Fort of the Taf', Taf being the river that flows past the old Roman fort (contrast Llandaf, where there is no relic of case).[16] In Old Welsh there may have been one or two more such relics, as in a phrase in the *Gododdin*, *gwas nym* (= *nyf*) 'the resting place of heaven', but normal *nef* 'heaven'.[17] The existence of just a few such relics indicates that British may well have had a phase corresponding to Old French, but that it lasted only for a short period.

Italian accomplished this loss of declension without the loss of final syllables which occurred in the languages of the northern seas. Its word for 'man', *uomo*, plural *uomini*, retains the syllables of Latin *homo, homines*, whereas the French *homme, hommes*, does not. Neither do Welsh *gŵr* and Old Irish *fer*, 'man', retain the final syllable of Celtic **wiros* nor does English *man* retain the final syllable of Germanic **mannaz*. This loss of final syllables—or 'apocope' to give it a more succinct name—distinguishes north-western Europe both from eastern Europe and from the languages of the Mediterranean. Yet the loss of declension, as we have seen, was more complete in southern Europe than in the north-west. It cannot, therefore, have been a mere by-product of apocope, since the latter was confined to the north-west, and even in Gallo-Romance was later than in British and by no means as complete; in Gallo-Romance there was often a reduction of vowels to a single murmer vowel rather than total loss of the syllable.[18] This is important, since the opposite—that apocope both preceded and caused loss of declension—is easily presumed, arguing incorrectly from the correct starting point that the lost final syllables had played a crucial role in declension. A conclusive demonstration of the independence of the two developments—apocope and the loss of declension—comes from Old Irish, which, as a language of the northern seas, underwent apocope, but which nevertheless retained a rich declension. New means were employed to express an old grammar.[19]

[16] Caerdyf is the form reflected by the English Cardiff, but with the characteristic English devoicing of a final Welsh voiced consonant, as in the name of the river, Taff as opposed to Welsh Taf, /tav/. The Modern Welsh Caerdydd is an example of the sporadic interchange of /v/ and /ð'. By the Late Old Welsh period, a normal pronunciation was without the final consonant, as in *LL*: *Kardi*, 17. 8; 28. 7, 21, 26, *Kairdi* 28. 29; *Kairti* 93.

[17] *CA*, line 233; Jarman, *Gododdin*, line 238.

[18] See the Strasburg oaths in Nithard, *Histoire des fils de Louis le Pieux*, ed. Ph. Lauer (Paris, 1926), 104–7, e.g. *amur* < *amorem*, but *poblo* < *populum*, the latter with syncope rather than apocope; M. K. Pope, *From Latin to Modern French* (Manchester, 1934), §§ 251–60.

[19] J. T. Koch, 'The Loss of Final Syllables and the Loss of Declension in Brittonic', *BBCS* 30 (1983), 201–33. The means used in Irish included, among others, the initial mutations and the distinction between broad and slender consonants (neutral and palatalized).

British was particularly subject to linguistic turbulence, because it participated both in the changes that transformed Romance and those which affected the languages of the northern seas. Its history in the late Roman and post-Roman periods marked it out as a member of two clubs, of the predominantly Latin-speaking western Roman Empire (and the latter's successor states) and this new grouping in the north-west. Both clubs contained languages from different genetic families: British, a Celtic language, was part of the Romance group, while the north-western group, to which British also belonged, included both languages from the Germanic family and also the Romance of northern Gaul, the forerunner of French. Both these groupings underwent major changes: British and, as we shall see, British Latin experienced them all.

The role played by British in these two clubs was, however, distinct. In the Romance group it appears usually to have been a follower, but in the north-western group it was a leader. For example, a major phonological change in the Romance group was the loss of the distinction between long and short vowels.[20] A by-product of this change was confusion in Late Latin metrics, since in classical Latin verse the opposition between long and short syllables, in which vowel length played a major role, was crucial. The loss of distinctive vowel length, because it was of such cultural significance, attracted contemporary comment. Sporadic examples occur as early as the inscriptions of Pompeii (buried by the eruption of Mount Vesuvius in AD 79); but it seems to have become general in the Mediterranean Latin-speaking provinces by the fourth century.[21] Augustine noted that 'African ears do not distinguish short or long vowels'; the loss of distinctive vowel length reached British no earlier than the second half of the sixth century.[22] The change thus appears to have begun in the south and to have spread gradually northwards over a period of about two centuries. The non-Romance neighbours of British, Old Irish to the west and Old English to the east, retained the distinction between long and short vowels in stressed syllables.

In the north-western group of languages, however, British appears to have been in the vanguard. These languages share two features: syllabic loss (both final, 'apocope', and internal, 'syncope') and the shift of distinctive features away from the end of a word. The two processes mostly went together, so that distinctions initially expressed by the final syllable shifted to the preceding syllable or syllables, and the final syllable was then lost. In English *man*, the plural *men* has lost the final syllable of the Germanic plural **manniz*, but the final *-iz* of the plural ending 'affected' the *a* of the preceding syllable and changed it to an *e*. When the final *-iz* was lost, therefore, the distinction between singular and plural was expressed by the alternation of the internal vowels, *a* for the singular, *e* for the plural: *man, men* (OE *mann, menn*). Essentially the same process distinguished Welsh *gŵr* 'man' from *gwŷr* 'men', Old Irish *fer* (singular) from *fir* (plural), Celtic **wiros*, **wirī*. Chronology suggests that British underwent these changes relatively early. The usual date

[20] Schrijver, 'The Rise and Fall of British Latin', 92–3.

[21] Väänänen, *Introduction au latin vulgaire*, 29–32.

[22] St Augustine, *De Doctina Christiana*, IV. x (24) (ed. J. Martin, CCSL xxxii, 1962, p. 133); *LHEB*, § 35.

for British apocope is that it began in the late fifth century and was complete by the second half of the sixth.[23] Any modification is likely to see this date moved earlier rather than later.[24] In Scandinavian, however, it began in the late sixth century and continued through the seventh and eighth.[25]

The inner nature of the changes that all these languages underwent was clearly defined by the great French linguist, Meillet—writing about Germanic, but his words would do equally well for British, Irish, or, indeed, French:[26]

> Each vowel of an Indo-European word is, so to speak, autonomous, and the vocalic element of the syllable does not in any way depend on neighbouring consonants or vowels. In Germanic, however, the quality of the vowels—first the short vowels, and then, later, even the long vowels—is dictated by their position in the word and by the consonants and vowels which follow them in the same word.

What occurred was a change in the whole phonological style of a group of neighbouring languages.

One example will illustrate both the loss of declension, shared by British with Italian, Spanish, and Catalan, and the loss of syllables, shared with Old Irish, Old English, French, and Scandinavian. In his *De Excidio Britanniae* Gildas, writing of course in Latin, addressed the king of Gwynedd as *Maglocune*, 'O Maglocunus'. The medieval and modern form of the name is Maelgwn, and the object of Gildas's denunciation was later known as Maelgwn Gwynedd, 'Maelgwn of Gwynedd'. But there is another Welsh form of the underlying British name, namely Meilyg. The explanation of this pair, Meilyg and Maelgwn, requires us to posit a development through several stages. First, we have to begin in British before the loss of declension, and also before the confusion of different declensional types which preceded that loss. At this stage the nominative and accusative of a single name, meaning something like 'princely hound', took the form **Maglocū, *Maglocunen.* The name was a compound of two words, **maglos* (cognate with Old Irish *mál*), 'prince, ruler', and **cū* (Old Irish *cú*, Welsh *ci*, 'dog, hound').[27] It was characteristic

[23] *LHEB*, §§ 177–82.

[24] Cf. Sims-Williams, 'Dating the Transition to Neo-Brittonic', 260, who suggests that Jackson's dates may be at least half a century too late.

[25] A. Noreen, *Geschichte der nordischen Sprachen*, 3rd edn. (Strasburg, 1913), 83–7 (§§ 50 (b), § 51); S. Gutenbrunner, *Historische Laut- und Formenlehre des Altisländischen* (Heidelberg, 1951), 42–3, §§ 33, 34.

[26] A. Meillet, *Caractères generaux des langues germaniques*, 3rd edn. (Paris, 1926), 61–2: Chaque voyelle du mot indo-européen a pour ainsi dire son autonomie, et l'élément vocalique de la syllabe ne dépend à aucun degré des consonnes ou des voyelles voisines. En germanique, au contraire, le timbre des voyelles, d'abord des voyelles brèves, et, plus tard, même des voyelles longues, est commandé par leur place dans le mot et par les éléments consonantiques et vocaliques qui les suivent dans le même mot.

[27] D. Ellis Evans, 'A Comparison of the Formation of Some Continental and Early Insular Celtic Personal Names', *BBCS* 24 (1970–2), 415–34, at 420; Sims-Williams, *The Celtic Inscriptions of Britain*, 71, notes that some pairs may be due to a late reformation rather than to derivation from both the nominative and the oblique stem, but this does not apply to Meilyg/Maelgwn. On the complicated history of Welsh *ci*, Irish *cú*, see L. Joseph, 'Old Irish *cú*: A Naïve Reinterpretation', in A. T. E. Matonis and D. F. Melia (eds.), *Celtic Language, Celtic Culture: A Festschrift for Eric P. Hamp* (Van Nuys, CA, 1990), 110–30.

of this particular declension that, in cases other than the nominative **cū*, the *u* was short rather than long and was followed by *n* and then a further syllable: **Maglocunen* was the accusative case, **Maglocunos* the genitive.[28] In both, *-un-* with a short *u* was followed by a case-ending, *-en* for the accusative and *-os* for the genitive (compare English *his* with final *-s* for the genitive, as in 'his boat'). This contrast between the nominative **Maglocū*, with long *ū*, and the 'oblique stem' **Maglocun-* in **Maglocunen* and **Maglocunos* is what will ultimately account for the pair *Meilyg* and *Maelgwn*.[29]

The first change was phonological: a final *-ū* changed to *-ī*. This was part of a wider pattern by which the British long vowels played a form of 'follow-my-leader': *ū* changed to *ī*, final *-ō* to *ū*, and *ā* to *ō*.[30] These movements only affected the long vowels, so that the short *u* of **Maglocunen* and **Maglocunos* was unchanged. The second stage included two more or less contemporaneous changes. First, lenition changed *g* into a fricative *γ* and the voiceless *c* (standing for /k/) to the voiced *g*.[31] This affected both **Maglocī* and **Maglocunen*, changing them into **Maγlogī* and **Maγlogunen*. Secondly, the final *-ī* of **Maγlogī* 'affected' the vowel of the preceding syllable: the *o* became a central *ï*, the 'clear *y*' of Middle and Modern Welsh, so that **Maγlogī* became **Maγlïgī*. The next stage was the loss of final syllables, 'apocope': **Maγlïgī* became **Maγlïg*, while **Maγlogunen* became **Maγlogun*. Subsequently *-aγl-* changed to *-ail-* (*γ* to *i*). The fourth stage also entailed another syllabic loss, but now of a middle syllable, called 'syncope' to distinguish it from apocope, the earlier loss of the final syllable: the three-syllable **Mailogun* underwent the loss of the middle syllable giving **Mailgun*, spelt Maelgwn in Modern Welsh (the two-syllable **Mailïg* was unaffected, since it had no middle syllable). The fifth and final stage involved another form of vowel affection: by 'internal *i*-affection' **Mailïg* became **Meilïg*, spelt Meilyg in Welsh. Summarized in the form of a table (and using > for 'gave' or 'became'), the changes by which the two forms of the name parted company were as follows:

Table 2.3. Meilyg and Maelgwn

	-ū > *-ī*	final *i*-affection + lenition	apocope	*aγl* > *ail*	syncope + internal *i*-affection
*Maglocū	> *Maglocī	> *Maγlïgī	> *Maγlïg	> *Mailïg	> Meilïg (Meilyg)
*Maglocunen		>*Maγlogunen	> *Maγlogun	> *Mailogun	> Mailgun (Maelgwn)

28 For the short *-ŭ-* see P. Schrijver, *Studies in British Celtic Historical Phonology*, 50–1.

29 The accusative may have been the main source of forms reflecting the oblique stem, since it was also prevalent in Romance: Väänänen, *Introduction au latin vulgaire*, §§ 245–7.

30 K. McCone, *Towards a Relative Chronology of Ancient and Medieval Celtic Sound Change* (Maynooth, 1996), 145–65.

31 According to Jackson, *LHEB*, § 142, these two changes involved in lenition were contemporaneous; according to Sims-Williams, 'Dating the Transition to Neo-Brittonic', 223–36, the change of voiced stop to voiced fricative came first and was followed, after an interval, by the voicing of voiceless stops.

Gildas's *Maglocune* (leaving aside the Latin vocative ending *-e*) is probably an old-fashioned spelling for the stage reached by the oblique stem, *Maglocun-* after apocope, **Maɣlogun*. By this stage it was natural to create a Latin *Maglocunus* with a vocative *Maglocune*.

The form used by Gildas indicates that the change in British (and presumably the spoken form of British Latin) shared with Italian, Spanish, and other Romance languages, namely the loss of declension, had already occurred. Otherwise, instead of *Maglocune*, he should have used as his Latin form a vocative **Maglocō*, on the pattern of *latrō*, *latrones* giving Welsh *lleidr*, *lladron*. As in Gallo-Romance, there appear to have been two stages: first, there was a reduction to just two cases; subsequently even this distinction was lost. In the case of British, the two-case phase appears to have been brief, leaving just a few relics, such as nominative **brāwū* 'quern' giving Breton *breo*, but the oblique **brāwon-* giving Welsh *breuan*.[32] It likewise helps to explain the two forms taken in Welsh by a single Latin word *dracō*: nominative *dracō* > **dracī* > **dreigī* > Middle Welsh *dreig*, Modern Welsh *draig*; but accusative *draconem* > *dragon*), as well as such pairs of names as Meilyg and Maelgwn. With the complete loss of declension, however, the two forms of what had been one name parted company; this separation explains why, in Middle Welsh verse, one may have a singular *dragon* alongside a singular *dreic* (modern *draig*), as well as a plural *dragon* (from **dracī*, **draconem*, **dracones*). This must have happened in British by the sixth century, much earlier than in Gallo-Romance. Hence it would not have occurred to Gildas that he was doing anything odd in using what had originally been the oblique stem as the basis for his Latinized form. When the same king was mentioned in the *Historia Brittonum* of 829 × 830—about three hundred years after Gildas—he was called *Mailcun*, an Old Welsh spelling for *Mailgun*, Maelgwn. All the changes shared with the other languages of the north-west had now occurred: final *i*-affection, apocope, and syncope, to name only the most important. We may add lenition (not a general north-western sound change, but one for which a partially comparable development can be found in western Romance). Together they transformed a name which still just about belonged to Ancient Celtic into a form which it retained throughout the medieval and modern periods. As this example illustrates, the loss of declension, shared with Romance, came first, while the changes which had their counterparts either, as with lenition, only in western Romance or, as with *i*-affection, apocope, and syncope, in the north-western group, came later. British began by behaving as a citizen of the western (and increasingly Latin-speaking) Roman Empire; in the intervening period it partially shared a change with western Romance and with its Celtic neighbour, Irish; it ended by leading a maritime group that straddled the former frontier of Rome.

The effect of Latin upon British has extensive historical implications. It provides confirmation of other evidence suggesting that, by the fourth century, Latin may well have been the most widely spoken language in much of south-eastern Britain. It was not, that is, merely the language of the elite, the government, and the army. Even

32 Schrijver, 'The Rise and Fall of British Latin', 96–7, uses this example to argue that there were at least two cases in British immediately before the separation of Welsh and Breton.

graffiti were almost all in Latin. A further implication is that Germanic settlers in south-eastern Britain may not have been confronted by an existing population most of whom spoke British. Latin may well have been the language of the majority in the areas in which the Anglo-Saxons first settled. In turn, this will help to account for the paucity of British loanwords in Old English, other than place-names. The principal contact with British will have occurred later and also further west and north, as the Anglo-Saxons extended their territory beyond the earliest settlements.

A further implication is a parting of the ways between Britain and northern Gaul (east of the Breton frontier). During the period of Roman rule in Britain, the proportion of the population speaking Latin grew, just as it did in Gaul, even if not so fast. There is no reason to suspect a reversal of the trend towards Latin before 400. In the fifth, sixth, and seventh centuries, however, this process went into reverse in Britain, whereas in Gaul it continued. Indeed, by the late sixth century, the period of Gregory of Tours, Gaulish may have been extinct, whereas in Britain, in those parts which were not English-speaking, British Latin was in terminal decline, becoming extinct probably by 700. Those parts of Britain that, in 400, were probably most prone to speak Latin were, by 700, all English-speaking. In 400 the languages spoken on either side of the Channel were moving in the same direction carried along by the huge power of Latin; by 700 the linguistic situation on either side of the Channel was completely different. The one exception in 700 was Brittany, south of the Channel and yet containing a form of British which showed no sign that it would be swept away by Romance. North of the Channel, British Latin, on its way to a British Romance, had suffered a premature death at the hands of the English.

Some problems about Old English and its relationship to British Latin and Celtic British may be easier to resolve in the light of the chronology of these changes and the likely linguistic geography of Britain in AD 400.[33] As we have seen, British Latin and Celtic British travelled in very much the same direction in this period: the loss of distinctive vowel length affected both, probably at much the same date; British Latin seems to have been pronounced in a distinctively British way, influenced by the proportion of the population of Roman Britain bilingual in British and Latin. The first problem, that of the paucity of loanwords from British into Old English, is rendered much easier to understand if much of the area settled by Germanic speakers was in the south-eastern portion of the island, where Latin may well have been the dominant language in AD 400, although British is likely to have survived even there.[34] The second is the relationship of Old English to the Germanic languages of the Continent along the North Sea coast. Broadly, the

[33] The following argument is indebted to J. Hines, 'The Becoming of the English: Identity, Material Culture and Language in Early Anglo-Saxon England', in W. Filmer-Sankey and D. Griffiths (eds.), *Anglo-Saxon Studies in Archaeology and History*, 7 (1994), 49–59; id., 'Focus and Boundary in Linguistic Varieties in the North-West Germanic Continuum', in V. F. Faltings, A. G. H. Walker, and O. Wilts (eds.), *Friesische Studien*, ii (Odense, 1995), 35–62; id., 'Welsh and English: Mutual Origins in Post-Roman Britain?', *Studia Celtica*, 34 (2000), 81–104.

[34] M. Förster, *Keltisches Wortgut im Englischen* (Halle [Saale], 1921), 6–27; for a recent survey of the evidence, especially from place-names, see D. N. Parsons, 'Sabrina in the Thorns: Place-Names as Evidence for British and Latin in Roman Britain', in S. Laker and P. Russell (eds.), 'Special Issue: Languages of Early Britain', *Transactions of the Philological Society*, 109: 2 (2011), 113–37.

closer to the lower Rhine these languages were, the more rapidly they progressed along the linguistic road common to them all—and also to British and Gallo-Romance. The continental Germanic languages spoken by the ancestors of the Anglo-Saxon population were at different stages on this road, quite apart from other dialect differences; and yet these differences appear not to have played any significant role in shaping the dialect differences within Old English that certainly existed by the eighth century and were evident to contemporaries, such as Bede.[35] It is as if Old English were derived from a single form of the language. Moreover, that form of the language, if placed on the linguistic road being travelled by all the Germanic languages of the North-Sea area, was ahead of the rest. It was a colonial form of Germanic marked by exceptionally advanced progress along their common road. So far as language is concerned, this colonial form of Germanic was probably the first mark of an English identity.

If we assume that the nascent English of the fifth and sixth centuries, although sustained by a major migration across the North Sea, had also become the language of numerous former speakers of both British Latin and British Celtic, the origins of Old English become more intelligible. First, these languages had been travelling on a parallel road: they also were part of the North-Sea zone. They may have been further along that road than were the Germanic languages within the same zone. Secondly, we may assume that the form of Germanic that these British and British Latin speakers learnt was the most progressive, the colonial norm. They learnt the Germanic that was distinctively British as opposed to any one of the varieties brought by Germanic speakers from the Continent. The Anglo-Saxon settlement may also have ensured that by *c.* 700 the Britons spoke Celtic British rather than a British Romance descended from the Latin of Roman Britain: the Anglo-Saxons had conquered the main areas of strength of British Latin. On the other hand, however, those Britons who, over a few generations, abandoned their former language, whether British Latin or British Celtic, in favour of the language of their conquerors may have helped to ensure that the language of the Anglo-Saxons was English and not a medley of Anglian, Saxon, Jutish, and Frisian.

2. WELSH, THE OTHER BRITTONIC LANGUAGES, BRITISH LATIN, AND IRISH IN BRITAIN

A further problem which can be clarified by considering the impact of Latin on British is the emergence of a Pictish people. As we saw in the previous chapter, in the early Romano-British period the population of Britain beyond the frontier was considered to be no less British than the peoples to the south. From the end of the third century this changed. The different peoples beyond the frontier, Caledonians, Maeatae, Verturiones, Venicones, and others, were now considered to belong to a

[35] *HE* ii. 5, on Caelin and Ceaulin.

larger entity, the Picts;[36] and the Picts were not Britons—indeed, they were among the principal enemies of the Britons.

Comparison with the Rhine frontier indicated that the emergence of the Picts was in accord with a more general trend towards the creation of confederations of peoples on the barbarian side of the frontier. On the far side of the Rhine from the Roman province of Germania Inferior several small peoples became part of the Franks, and yet retained their separate identities as Chamavi, Bructeri or Ampsivarii. Similarly among the Picts, someone might be king of Atholl or Fortriu even though the rulers who gained most attention from annalists were kings of the Picts as a whole.[37]

What was remarkable about the situation in north Britain is that the dividing line between Picts and Britons came to be drawn approximately on the Forth–Clyde line, where the Antonine Wall was built, rather than on the much more long-lasting Hadrian's Wall, the Tyne–Solway line. The Votadini (later Gododdin) occupied territory on the North Sea coast, including Lothian, facing across the Firth of Forth towards Pictish Fife; yet there was never any question but that they were Britons. The frontier between Picts and Britons, and later on the east side between Picts and Northumbrians, fluctuated; but the distinct identities of Picts and Britons were firmly established. Even a writer as early as Gildas was so convinced that the Island of Britain was the original territory of the Britons, and yet also that the Picts were a separate people, that he perceived them as intruders by sea. They, like the Irish, were a 'transmarine nation' who came 'from the north'.[38]

For Bede the different nations of Britain, the Picts among them, were primarily distinguished by language: they spoke 'languages of nations'.[39] He evidently thought that they only spoke one language. It has been argued that some Picts spoke a non-Indo-European language; whether this is so has not been finally determined, but there is no doubt that they had a language closely allied with Late British; and this is the language which will be termed Pictish here.[40] By the eighth century, Pictish, even from the scanty remains we have, can be seen to have been distinct from British. We cannot say much about the grammar of the language, but it does not appear as if it possessed a full declension as did Old Irish.[41] The deficiencies of the evidence prevent anything more than the odd observation about Pictish lenition, but its treatment of /g/ accords with British

36 A. L. F. Rivet and C. Smith, *The Place-Names of Roman Britain*, 288–91 (Calidonia, Calidonii), 404 (Maeatae), 438–40 (Picti), 496–7 (Verturiones).

37 King of Fortriu, AU 693. 1, 763. 10; king of Atholl, AU 739. 7.

38 Gildas, *De Excidio Britanniae*, c. 14; N. Wright, 'Gildas's Geographical Perspective', in M. Lapidge and D. N. Dumville, *Gildas: New Approaches* (Woodbridge, 1984), 88–92.

39 Bede, *HE* i. 1, *quinque gentium linguis*.

40 In favour of a second, non-Indo-European, Pictish language, K. H. Jackson, 'The Pictish Language', in F. T. Wainwright, *The Problem of the Picts* (Edinburgh, 1955; repr. Perth, 1980), 129–66; against it, K. Forsyth, *Language in Pictland*, Studia Hameliana, 2 (Utrecht, 1997).

41 It is possible that it had a nominative and an oblique case as did Old French and Provençal, and as British had probably briefly possessed also: compare, in the A and B versions of the Pictish king-list, *Wrad*, Anderson, *Kings and Kingship*, 249. 10, *Uurad*, 263. 11, with *filius Wroid*, 249. 3, *filius Uuroid*, 263. 5; Jackson, 'The Pictish Language', Appendix, 166. On the other hand, if *Unuist* was originally a genitive of *Unust*, it did not retain the original *u*-stem inflexion of **Oinogustus*.

Table 2.4. *Oinogustus, Óengus, and Unwst

Celtic **Oinogustus*	>	Irish *Oíngus*	British *Unwst*	Pictish *Unust, Unuist*
Oí- ~ ü ~ u		retains *oi*	*oi* > /ü:/ > /ü/	*oi* > *u* (/u:/?)
Oín(o)-, Un(o)-		syncope of *o*	syncope of *o*	syncope of *o*
-γ-, zero		lenited *g* > /γ/	lenited *g* > /γ/ > zero	lenited *g* > /γ/ > zero
-guss ~ -wst, -ust		*st* > *ss*	*st* retained	*st* retained
-gust(us)		apocope	apocope	apocope

rather than with Irish.[42] Some features of British which had analogues in Romance may have been present in Pictish, but it is uncertain, for example, whether it voiced unvoiced stops, like British, or changed them into voiceless fricatives, like Irish.[43] Nor can we say that distinctive vowel length was lost in Pictish, as in British, or retained, as in Old Irish and Old English. On the other hand, two major developments which characterize the north-western group of languages, apocope and syncope, the two forms of syllabic loss, also occurred in Pictish. A good example is the name of the powerful Pictish king of the mid-eighth century known to the Durham *Liber Vitae* by his Pictish name as Unust, to the Britons as Unwst, but to the Irish as Óengus or Oíngus, all from Celtic **Oinogustus*, 'unique choice'.[44]

As this example illustrates, Pictish had more in common with British than with Irish, but it had started to strike out on its own path.

This new-found independence of Pictish is confirmed by the name *Alpin*, which corresponds to Welsh *Elffin*.[45] Two innovations separate the Welsh from the Pictish form. First, *Alpin* retains the original *-p-* which, after *l*, was changed to /f/, spelt *ff*, in British in the sixth century. Secondly, *Alpin* retains the original initial vowel *a-*, which in Welsh was changed to *e* by 'internal *i*-affection', namely an assimilation of the vowel to the *i* of the next syllable. Internal *i*-affection has been dated to the seventh century. These changes, therefore, *Alpin(us)* > **Alffin* > *Elffin*, were both innovations by British, and both occurred long after the Picts had become a confederation, while the second happened after Gildas had treated them as a 'transmarine nation', intruders 'from the north' on the soil of Britain. As this example illustrates, Pictish evolved as a language separate from British only after the Picts themselves had evolved into a separate people. Indeed, if it had not been for the emergence of a separate kingdom and people, it is entirely possible that the language spoken north of the Forth would have been regarded as just another dialect or group

[42] Jackson, 'The Pictish Language', Appendix, 163–4.

[43] The A King-List has Wredech, but the B King-List Uuredeg, Anderson, *Kings and Kingship*, 249. 3; 263. 3. Bede, *HE* iii. 4, has *Meilochon*, with lenited *-ch-* for old *-k-*, but the A and B King-Lists have *Mailcon* and *Melcon*, Anderson, *Kings and Kingship*, 248. 3; 262. 20, reminiscent of Old Welsh *Mailcun*, where *-c-* stands for *-g-*.

[44] P. Russell, 'The Names of Celtic Origin', in D. Rollason and L. Rollason (eds.), *The Durham* Liber Vitae: *London, British Library, MS Cotton Domitian A. VII*, 3 vols. (London, 2007), ii. 7.

[45] Jackson, 'The Pictish Language', 162; he explains the alternative form E(i)lpin as influenced by British.

of dialects of British. This should not lead us, however, to minimize the differences. Before Pictish separated from British it may have shared in some of the developments which caused British to resemble the Romance languages, such as the decay of declension, but it is very unlikely to have been so deeply affected by Latin as its southern neighbour. However, it certainly belonged with the north-western group even after it had begun to evolve independently.

The emergence of Welsh as a language separate from Cornish and Breton occurred over a long period. In 600, when British was spoken in a long strip from Stirling to the Loire, it was already subject to dialect differences. Some of them distinguished the British of the south-west, what would become Cornish and Breton, from the British of Wales; yet the most important change distinguishing early from later Old Welsh (and also Middle and Modern Welsh—the shift of the stress from the final to the penultimate syllable—occurred at much the same time in Welsh, Cornish, and Breton. Moreover, it did so as late as the ninth century.[46] This example points to a major difficulty in terminology and interpretation. Dialects come to be distinct when some sound-changes affect only one area or group within the territory and population of the language. Some changes might still affect the whole area or population, and the unity of the language would then remain clear, in spite of the appearance of dialects. But the date at which changes ceased to spread from one area or group to another ought also be a major turning point marking the division into separate languages; and yet, such is the potential for languages which have evolved from one base to go on developing in the same direction even independently, this second turning-point is difficult to determine. Moreover, as typological affinities between unrelated languages indicate, some changes may spread even after the languages have become quite distinct. One possible view is that there was no direct connection between the accent shift in Welsh, Cornish, and Breton. It is perhaps safer to rely on evidence about what contemporaries thought—whether the Britons thought they spoke varieties of the same language or different languages and whether contemporary Irish or English speakers took the same view. If we adopt this approach, the answer will be that the varieties of British remained dialects rather than independent languages until the twelfth century.

It is natural to suppose that territorial separation between the Britons of the south-west and their compatriots in Wales would lead to a linguistic divergence. On this assumption the divergence between Welsh and Cornish—or rather the British of the south-west as a whole—stemmed from the Anglo-Saxon conquest of

[46] The date given by Jackson, *LHEB*, §§ 13, 207, is even later, in the eleventh century. T. A. Watkins, 'The Accent in Old Welsh—its Quality and its Development', *BBCS* 25 (1972–4), 1–11; id., 'The Accent-Shift in Old Welsh', in H. Pilch and J. Thurow (eds.), *Indo-Celtica: Gedächtnisschrift für Alf Sommerfelt* (Munich, 1972), 201–5; id., 'Cyfnewidiadau Seinegol sy'n Gysylltiedig â'r "Acen" Gymraeg', *BBCS* 26 (1974–6), 399–405, prefers an earlier date; K. H. Jackson, 'The Date of the Old Welsh Accent Shift', *Studia Celtica*, 10/11 (1975–6), 40–53, maintains his earlier view; Koch, *Gododdin*, pp. cxxxvii–cxxxviii, has his own theory; P. Schrijver, 'Geminate Spellings in the Old Welsh Glosses to Martianus Capella', *Études Celtiques*, 34 (1998–2000), 147–60, at 147–55, argues for a date no later than the ninth century; Sims-Williams, *CIB*, 289, follows Schrijver.

the lower Severn valley. Once Gloucestershire was English territory, it might be supposed, the west British of Wales would be parted from the south-western British of Somerset, Dorset, Devon, and Cornwall. The territorial break was part of the evidence which led Kenneth Jackson to propose *c.* 600 or, slightly more elastically, the generation after the battle of Dyrham (AD 577 in the Anglo-Saxon Chronicle) as the parting of the ways.[47]

There are two grounds for hesitation over this proposal. First, and most simply, acquisition of political control is not the same things as a change of population or of language. On the evidence of Bede about Augustine of Canterbury's dealings with the Britons, the kingdom of the Hwicce had been founded by *c.* 600. The origins of that kingdom may have lain in the Cotswolds, but it would eventually encompass Worcestershire and Gloucestershire, and also the western fringes of Oxfordshire.[48] This kingdom is likely, however, to have retained a considerable British-speaking population at least during the seventh century. The territorial break between western and south-western British has to be placed, therefore, not at the creation of the kingdom of the Hwicce but at the date at which its population became overwhelmingly English-speaking.

Even when that had occurred, however, the linguistic separation was far from complete. The initial assumptions lying behind Jackson's proposal gave a far greater weight to territorial contiguity than to connections by sea. Yet the very nature of the Brittonic areas, from northern to south-western Britain, then to Brittany, and beyond to the Britonia of Galicia, from where a British bishop, Mailoc, attended the Council of Braga in 572, demonstrates the importance of connections by sea.[49] When discussing relationships between south-western Britain and Brittany, Jackson argued for a succession of migrations, of which much the greatest, according to him, was the last, in the late sixth century. This was a phase in which connections by sea were undeniably crucial. The burden of proof is upon the scholar who would argue that communications by sea, having once created populations on either side of the English Channel who long remained united in thinking themselves one people, speaking the same language, then became insignificant.

The conception of linguistic relationship which gives pride of place to territorial contiguity on land is appropriate when dealing with purely agricultural populations. It is not so appropriate for those who live partly off the sea; and it is inappropriate for trading communities and for the elite. Long after 600 contacts between Bretons, Cornishmen, and the Welsh can be traced in the few manuscripts which survive from Brittonic-speaking areas before 1100. The ninth-century manuscript of Juvencus's verse rendering of the gospels, now in Cambridge, with

47 *LHEB*, pp. 18–19, 24–7.

48 S. Bassett, 'In Search of the Origins of Anglo-Saxon Kingdoms', in id. (ed.), *The Origins of Anglo-Saxon Kingdoms* (London, 1989), 6–17.

49 B. Cunliffe, *Facing the Ocean: The Atlantic and Its Peoples, 8000 BC–AD 1500* (Oxford, 2001), ch. 10; E. G. Bowen, *Saints, Seaways and Settlements* (Cardiff, 1977), ch. 5; J. Wooding, *Communication and Commerce along the Western Sea Lanes AD 400–800* (Oxford, 1996); E. A. Thompson, 'Britonia', in M. W. Barley and R. P. C. Hanson (eds.), *Christianity in Britain, 300–700* (Leicester, 1968), 201–5.

its glosses, reveals, as we shall see, links between Wales and Brittany, as well as between Wales and Ireland. A ninth-century manuscript of Priscian's Latin grammar, now in Paris, has Old Welsh alongside Old Breton and Old Irish glosses.[50] Another ninth-century manuscript, now in Oxford, contains a Latin colloquy glossed in a mixture of Welsh and Cornish.[51] These glossed texts come from scholarly and clerical circles which accepted mobility as something normal. The sources will not extend far enough to reveal whether lay children of high status were fostered at a distance from home, just as their clerical kinsmen might go to school far from home, but such connections between Wales, Cornwall, and Brittany are a serious possibility.

The remains of Cumbric, the Brittonic language of southern Scotland and northern England, are too scanty to permit a full linguistic comparison with Welsh, Cornish, and Breton. It is, however, possible that its history was different from the next surviving Brittonic dialect to the south, Welsh.[52] The contrast between Cumbric and Welsh points to a further issue of interpretation. With a genetic approach to languages it is only natural to speak of two varieties of one language as separate languages once they have started down distinct paths towards full separation. The divide between the paths is, for this approach, more important than the distance between them once they have divided. Once the genetic approach is qualified by more typological considerations, the division between languages assumes a different aspect. Now it will be the contemporary situation rather than the ultimate destination which is crucial—the distance between the paths rather than the bare fact that they have become separate or that the paths would eventually lead to different destinations. If we then add a further consideration, namely the historical conditions which influenced the use of the language, a further set of issues arise. However, these latter approaches as opposed to the genetic one are appropriate to the early medieval historian: ultimate destinations or origins are not his prime concern.

In comparing Cumbric and Welsh we cannot, in general, pursue the more strictly linguistic lines of enquiry. Cumbric may not have survived beyond the twelfth century, so that we cannot know whether it would have become, like Cornish and Breton, a language quite distinct from Welsh.[53] Too little is known about it to determine how far the paths of Cumbric and Welsh had diverged either

[50] P.-Y. Lambert on the Priscian glosses: 'Les gloses du manuscrit BN Lat. 10290', *Études Celtiques*, 19 (1982), 173–213 (p. 181 for the Welsh scribe).

[51] See below, 647–8; ed. W. H. Stevenson, *Early Scholastic Colloquies* (Oxford, 1929), 1–11.

[52] As with the admittedly very minor difference between Cumbric *gos* as well as *gwas* 'servant' and Welsh with only a single form *gwas*, as in the anglicized Cumbric name Gospatric alongside Welsh Gwas Padrig: F. L. Edmonds, 'Personal Names and the Cult of Patrick in Eleventh-Century Strathclyde and Northumbria', in S. Boardman et al. (eds.), *Saints' Cults in the Celtic World* (Woodbridge, 2009), 49–51.

[53] For evidence that it survived in Ayrshire into the twelfth century, see W. J. Watson, *History of the Celtic Place-Names of Scotland*, 190–1. For similarly late survival in Cumberland, see K. Jackson, 'Angles and Britons in Northumbria and Cumbria', in J. R. R. Tolkien et al., *Angles and Britons: O'Donnell Lectures* (Cardiff, 1963), 82–3.

by 700 or by 1100. What can be said, however, is that the historical conditions affecting these two varieties of British were markedly different.

In 500, three languages were widely spoken in Wales: British, Latin, and Irish. By 900 British—on its way to Welsh—was the sole language of all but a few. There were English speakers, especially on the eastern borders; in some coastal areas, especially perhaps in Anglesey, there were Norse-speakers who were probably themselves often bilingual in Norse and Irish and, moreover, were accompanied by Irish speakers; but, by and large, the Britons of Wales spoke Welsh. A trilingual population had become a largely monolingual population. In northern Britain, however, the later period was the more multilingual. In the tenth century the British kingdom of Strathclyde (Ystrad Glud) expanded south-east across the southern uplands, down the valleys of the Nith and the Annan, and into what is now the county of Cumbria in England.[54] It thereby came to incorporate territory populated by a mixture of English and Norse speakers; its neighbour to the south-west, Galloway, was, by the twelfth century, predominantly Gaelic-speaking as was the kingdom of Alba to the north and Argyll to the west. Strathclyde itself probably contained a significant Gaelic-speaking element. A kingdom of several languages—Cumbric, English, Gaelic, and Norse—was the outcome of political expansion. The earliest document to survive from twelfth-century Glasgow contains a historical retrospect combined with a declaration of the nature of the kingdom: Strathclyde might have suffered grievously from Norse attacks but it had rebuilt itself while accepting that it was a people made up of different nations.[55] The stance it adopted, accepting a polyethnic and multilingual community, was the basis of Strathclyde's success in the late ninth and tenth centuries as it would be of the kingdom of Alba in the eleventh and twelfth.

In the post-Roman period, however, the earlier kingdom of Alclud or Allt Glud, so called after its royal centre and principal fortress at Dumbarton, is likely to have been largely monolingual. It lay beyond the former frontier on Hadrian's Wall; here, if anywhere in British territory, the British language should have remained the normal speech of the population, with Latin being a language known only to a few. Further south, in the area which would become Wales, the situation was quite different. Although the latter might have been a relatively unRomanized part of Britain before 400, there is clear evidence that Latin was a spoken language in the fifth and sixth centuries, and probably some way into the seventh.[56] Even though Latin was almost certainly less widely spoken in the west of Britain than in the south-east, features characteristic of the spoken language are widely attested.

It is characteristic of the spoken Latin of late Antiquity that the quantitative distinction between long and short vowels, to which differences in the point of

[54] See below, 481–2.

[55] *Early Scottish Charters Prior to 1153*, ed. A. C. Lawrie (Glasgow, 1905), no. 50: Sic omnibus bonis exterminatis, magnis temporum intervallo [*sic*] transactis, diverse tribus diversarum nationum ex diversis partibus affluentes desertam regionem praefatam [sc. Cumbrensem] habitaverunt: sed dispari genere et dissimili lingua et vario more viventes haud facile [inter] sese consentientes gentilitatem potius quam fidei cultum tenuere.

[56] *LHEB*, pp. 117–21, 123–4.

articulation were ancillary, disappeared. Instead, differences in the point of articulation, formerly secondary, were now crucial. So *vīvo* gives Italian *vivo*, but *bibo* gives Italian *bevo*, because a Latin short *i* was more open than a long *ī*, and hence short *i* > *e*, but long *ī* > *i*.[57] The details of the process might vary between the individual Romance languages, but the direction of change was the same. At an earlier period the diphthongs, *ae*, *oe*, had become simple long vowels; and this enabled, for example, *ae* to be written for *e* as well as *e* for *ae*.[58] Among the changes to consonants was the disappearance of final *-m* (early) and *-s* (late and only in some areas of Romance, including British Latin).[59] The consequences for the grammar were far-reaching: there was no distinction between, for example, *Petrus*, *Petrum*, *Petrō* (in British Latin all > *Pedro*, but in Italian > *Petro* > *Pietro*).

All these changes are attested in the British Latin inscriptions of the fifth and sixth centuries.[60] The texts of these inscriptions consist almost always of brief memorials of single persons; the few longer inscriptions are of considerable interest in themselves but are quite untypical. That they are normally memorials of the dead in the place of burial is indicated by one of the formulae used, 'Here lies X' (*Hic iacit X*);[61] but even when other formulae are adopted, more indirect evidence suggests that such inscriptions often had the very same primary purpose; this primary purpose, however, did not exclude other functions. Those under discussion initially are Latin inscriptions whose base letterform was the roman capital together with the inscriptions in the ogham alphabet and in an early form of Irish. Most are just in Latin (but often with Celtic names), but some are bilingual, Latin and Irish, while a few are purely in Irish. Other, almost certainly later, inscriptions will be discussed subsequently.

[57] Väänänen, *Introduction au latin vulgaire*, §§ 42–6.

[58] Ibid. § 59; Herman, *Vulgar Latin*, 31–4.

[59] Väänänen, *Introduction au latin vulgaire*, §§ 127–9; cf. C. Smith, 'Vulgar Latin in Roman Britain: Epigraphic and Other Evidence', in H. Temporini and W. Haase, *Aufstieg und Niedergang des römischen Welt*. II. *Prinzipat*, 29.2, *Sprache und Literatur*, ed. W. Haase (Berlin, 1983), 925–6.

[60] For the corpora of inscriptions see the bibliography. They are here cited by the system used in *CIB* for two reasons: this allows the reader who has access to any one corpus to consult its reading and it allows the reader who has access to all, or even just two, of them to compare their treatments of an individual inscription. An example is Llanboidy 1, which is 365/149/Gso-23/CM13. The order is by date of publication beginning with Macalister's *Corpus Inscriptionum Insularum Celticarum*. His no. 365 is followed by Nash-Williams's no. 149; their references are simply numerical; Tedeschi's, in his *Congeries Lapidum*, have a more complex form indicating first the region (Gso is south-west Wales) and then giving the number, as in Gso-23; the references in the volumes of the *Corpus of Early Medieval Inscribed Stones and Stone Sculpture in Wales* (vol. i, Redknap and Lewis; vols. ii and iii, Edwards) begin with an indication of the county and then give the number. CM13 is thus no. 13 in the Carmarthenshire section of Edwards, *Corpus*, ii. The collections of Nash-Williams and the new *Corpus* only cover Wales, unlike Macalister, who included all the Celtic countries except Brittany, or Tedeschi, who includes all the British inscriptions, also except for Brittany. For southern Scotland and the far north of England, the numbers of Thomas, 'The Early Christian Inscriptions of Southern Scotland' are used, prefixed by Scot. Thus the Yarrow inscription is 515/Scot9/S-10 (Macalister/Thomas/Tedeschi). For south-western England, Okasha's *Corpus* is cited in the form Ok + No. Thus Lewannick 1 is 466/Ok23/C-13 (Macalister/Okasha/Tedeschi). A conspectus is given in the Appendix. In the transcriptions underlining is used to denote ligatured letters.

[61] J. D. Bu'lock, 'Early Christian Memorial Formulae', *Archaeologia Cambrensis*, 105 (1956), 133–41.

The following are a few illustrative examples from North Wales which illustrate the divergence of the Latin of the inscriptions from the standard Latin of the grammars, both ancient and modern:

325/33/Gn-6, Llantrisant 1, Anglesey: VASSO for *vassus*, ADQUAE for *atque*[62]
393/101/Gn-31, Penmachno 4, Caern.: CONGERIES for *congerie*
394/103/Gn-32, Ffestiniog 1: CIVE for *civis*, CONSOBRINO for *consobrinus*
391/78/Gn-1, Aberdaron 2, Caern.: MULTITVDINEM for *multitudine*

As we shall see, these are representative of the British Latin inscriptions as a whole between 400 and 600.

The genitive singular ending of the 2nd Declension in *-i* was often used without any attention being paid to the syntax. This has, however, been a matter of dispute between the two leading experts of the twentieth century on early Welsh, Sir Ifor Williams and Kenneth Jackson, and more recently Dr J. N. Adams has taken yet another view, so the arguments need to be considered in detail. The debate arose from an article by Williams on a Cardiganshire inscription:

352A/122/Gso-4/CD22, Llangwyryfon: DOMNICI / IACIT FILIVS / BRAVECCI

Williams had a clear theory of the changes lying behind this inscription.[63] He distinguished two periods. In the first the distinction of case was preserved, but in the second it was not. In the earlier period, he thought that two formulae were both in use:

(a) DOMNICI FILI BRAVECCI, '(The stone) of Domnicus son of Braveccus'.
(b) DOMNICVS FILIVS BRAVECCI (HIC) IACIT, 'D. son of B. lies here'

In the later period a formula conflated from both (a) and (b) came into use as in the actual inscription:

DOMNICI IACIT FILIVS BRAVECCI

On this he observed that 'he (the person who composed the text of this inscription) lived in a period when the difference between the nominative and genitive cases had been forgotten.'[64]

Jackson's reply was part of a discussion of apocope, the loss of final syllables.[65] In the background, however, lie issues about the relationship of British Latin to British Celtic: if, for example, they were evolving in parallel, evidence for the decay of case distinctions in one might be relevant for the other. Also in the background is the distinction between the decay of inflexion by case, on the one hand, and apocope on the other: as we have seen, medieval Italian had lost case to a greater degree than

62 Cf. Smith, 'Vulgar Latin in Roman Britain', 911–12.

63 I. Williams, 'II. The Epigraphy of the Inscription', in C. Fox et al., 'The Domnic Inscribed Slab, Llangwyryfon, Cardiganshire', *Archaeologia Cambrensis*, 97 (1943), 205–12.

64 The issue throughout this section is the text of an inscription; for the distinction between (a) the author of the text, (b) the *ordinator*, who set out the text on the stone, and (c) the person, sometimes called the lapidary, who incised the inscription on the stone, see the next chapter.

65 *LHEB*, § 179 (pp. 622–4).

Old French, but loss of syllables was much more marked in Old French than in Italian. Koch has argued persuasively that the decay of case in British preceded the loss of final endings (apocope); moreover, the loss of case was preceded by a simplification of the declensions, so that among masculine nouns, for example, some declensions were abandoned in favour of the *o*-stem type, with its genitive in *-i*.[66]

Jackson's first point in his reply to Williams was to draw a parallel with the use in Irish ogham inscriptions of the genitive case (and here one must remember that Irish retained case distinctions right down to Modern Irish). The explicit reference to a memorial is relatively rare but is illustrated by a bilingual inscription from south-west Britain (bold is here used for the ogham):

> 466/Ok23/C-13, Lewannick I: INGENVI MEMORIA, **IGENVI MEMOR**, 'The memorial of Ingenuus'

Here INGENVI in the Latin and **IGENVI** in the Irish both appear in the genitive because they depend on *memoria* or **memor.**[67] Usually, however, Irish ogham inscriptions left the term for the memorial itself to be understood as in 446/353/Gso-40/P70, Nevern 1:

> Ogham: MAGLICUNAS MAQI CLUTA[RIGAS (?)[68]
> '(The memorial) of *Maglicu* son of *Clutari-*'
> Latin: MAGLOCVN FILI CLVTORI

The Latin version has its own problems into which we do not need to go.[69]

As Williams noted, some Latin inscriptions do seem to follow the same pattern as the ogham. Thus a Carmarthenshire inscription, 374/172/Gso-10/CM37, has simply:

> CVNEGNI '(The memorial) of Cunegnus'

In the Ingenuus inscription, explicitly, and perhaps also in the Cunegnus inscription, implicitly, the memorial stone refers to itself. Jackson maintained that the same interpretation could be applied to British Latin inscriptions using the formula *hic iacit*, 'here lies'. Thus he interpreted 431/308/Gso-17/P15, CVNOGVSI HIC IACIT, as equivalent to (CORPVS) CVNOGVSI HIC IACIT, '(The body) of Cunogusus lies here'. As a corollary of this argument, he maintained that an inscription such as that commemorating Cunogusus was evidence of Irish influence, whereas 'the more roman type of memorial . . . usually keeps the nominative', as in 323/32/Gn-30, HIC BEATVS SATVRNINVS SE[PVLTVS I]ACIT, 'Here the blessed Saturninus lies buried'.[70]

[66] J. T. Koch, 'The Loss of Final Syllables, 201–33.

[67] In Irish, *lie* 'stone' could be used, as in *CIIC*, no. 1 (but this is no earlier than the seventh century and is not in ogham).

[68] The end of the ogham inscription has been lost, including what was probably the last stroke of the **R.**

[69] See the discussion in Edwards, *Corpus*, ii, under P70, Nevern 1.

[70] *LHEB*, p. 622.

Williams allowed that one of his two original types had an implicit reference to the memorial or stone of the person commemorated, but, given that assumption, his postulated DOMNICI FILII BRAVECCI adhered to Latin syntax, since FILII agrees with DOMNICI. What makes the actual inscription, DOMNICI IACIT FILIVS BRAVECCI so puzzling is, first, that DOMNICI is not in the right case to act as subject of the verb IACIT, and, secondly, that FILIVS does not agree with DOMNICI. Jackson's second argument was designed to meet these two problems. He proposed that the inscription should be broken up into two sentences: *(corpus) Domnici iacit*, 'the body of Domnicus lies (here)', and *filivs Bravecci (fuit)*, 'he was the son of Braveccus'. An even more elaborate example is 342/70/Gse-17/B45:

CVNOCENNI FILIVS / CVNOGENI HIC IACIT

For this he proposed to fill out the presumed gaps as follows:

(corpus) Cunocenni—filius Cunogeni (fuit)—hic iacit
'(the body) of Cunocennus—(he was) the son of Cunogenus—lies here'

On this interpretation, the sentence naming the father of the person commemorated breaks the main sentence into two separate parts.

If one is prepared to accept this theory, there is yet another difficulty to face. In inscriptions such as the following two what is difficult is not a genitive where one might expect a nominative, but the reverse, a nominative where one ought to have a genitive:

334/54/Gse-6/B21: CATACVS HIC IACIT FILIVS TEGERNACVS
407/258/Gse-11/G92: HIC IACIT CANTVSVS PATER PAVLINVS

Here Jackson was ready to concede that 'there does seem to be a gross confusion of cases';[71] but such examples were argued to be in relatively late inscriptions and thus not decisive. A third argument, therefore, turned on date: late inscriptions—no earlier than the late sixth century—could be admitted to exhibit a confusion of case such as would justify Williams's conclusion; earlier inscriptions could not. The reason why Jackson took this position was, at least in part, that the late sixth century lay after his date for apocope in British, completed by the middle of the sixth century, and, for him, loss of case was tied to apocope. In addition, he must have thought that, in general, British and British Latin were undergoing parallel changes; and, for that reason, he was reluctant to admit that confusion of cases in British Latin occurred before apocope in British.

Later, however, Jackson modified his position: when writing about the Yarrow stone in Selkirkshire he introduced the notion of 'epigraphic -I'.[72] 'There is reason to think, however, that it [namely -I] came to be regarded at this time as an all-purpose termination for names in inscriptions, even where syntax demanded the nominative.' The examples he gave indicated that such inscriptions could not all be

[71] *LHEB*, p. 623.
[72] RCAHMS, *An Inventory of the Ancient and Historical Monuments of Selkirkshire* (Edinburgh, 1957), referring to the Yarrow inscription, no. 174 (515/Scot9/S-10).

relegated to the late sixth century or later. He then noted that 'This has been regarded as evidence that the British case-system was in full decay, and that the declensions had ceased to be properly distinguished.'[73]

In order to come to a firm conclusion it is necessary to classify the inscriptions according to the formulae they used. The dates given in parentheses are those of Tedeschi on epigraphic evidence (VI^{1} = first half of the sixth century, VI^{2} = second half of the sixth century, VI^{in} = the beginning of the sixth century, VI^{med} = the middle of the sixth century).[74] They are given so that one may judge whether or not there is a chronological shift from one formula to another. The main divisions are as follows:

A. Introduced by a word for the memorial or inscription itself.

B. No word for the memorial or inscription and no use of HIC IACIT: (a) without a patronymic, (b) with a patronymic.

C. No word for the memorial or inscription but with HIC IACIT.
   (i) HIC IACIT first: (a) with no patronymic, (b) with a patronymic (HIC IACIT X son/daughter of Y.
   (ii) HIC IACIT immediately after the first name but before a patronymic if there is one: (a) with no patronymic, (b) with a patronymic (X HIC IACIT son/daughter of Y).
   (iii) HIC IACIT in final position after a patronymic: X son/daughter of Y HIC IACIT.

The subdivisions in C have been made because significant differences might have accompanied distinctions of word order. Within these categories, examples are divided according to the distribution of endings in masculine -VS (or -O) and -I, feminine -A and -E.

Box 2.1(a). A classification of British inscriptions, 400–600

A. With *monumentum/memoria*[75]*/nomen*

358/138/Gso-8/CM4 (V^{2}–VI^{in})
MEMORIA VOTEPORIGIS PROTICTORIS
'The memorial of Voteporix Protector'
466/Ok23/C-13 (V) INGENVI MEMORIA, ogham IGENAVI MEMOR
505/IOM-2 (VII) AVITI MONOMENTI
'The memorial/grave of Avitus'

(continued)

[73] In his footnote to this sentence he refers to *LHEB*, § 182, where he made no such admission, rather than to Williams, who did.

[74] For problems of dating see the next chapter.

[75] 476/Ok45/C-33, BONEMIMORI (F)ILLI TRIBVNI, might be an example if Macalister were right in his interpretation: *mimori(a)* of Bona *fili(a)* of Tribunus. But it is more likely to be a name, *Bonemimorius*, derived from the formula *bonae memoriae*, as suggested by several scholars: see Tedeschi, *Congeries*, i. 266, on C-33; cf. *CIB* 272–3.

Box 2.1(a). continued

The third example, from the Isle of Man, is evidently a case of 'epigraphic -I', since otherwise the term for the grave itself would have to be in the genitive; but it may well be seventh century and thus, again, not decisive evidence.[76] In the following more complex inscription (the one that elicited Jackson's phrase 'epigraphic -I'), MEMORIA and IACENT occur together, uniquely, but in two separate sentences:[77]

515/Scot9/S-10 (VI[2]), Yarrow Stone:
HIC MEMORIA PE(rp)ETV(a) / IN LOCO INSIGNISIMI PRINCI/PES NVDI / ET DVMNOGENI HIC IACENT / IN TVMVLO DVO FILII / LIBERALI(S?)
'Here in this place (is) a perpetual memorial. The most distinguished leaders, *Nudi* and *Dumnogeni* lie here in a tomb, two sons of Liberalis.'

It is thus hardly surprising that Jackson should, by this stage, have refrained from attempting to break up the sentence so as to make NVDI and DVMNOGENI true genitives.

What may be a comparable formula uses *nomen* 'name':[78]
416/279/Gn-18 (V/VI[1]) EQVESTRI NOMINE
448/370/Gso-14/P107 (V) RINACI NOMENA

The two forms of *nomen* suggest that British Latin had lost the neuter gender; that *nomen* had been assimilated to feminine nouns in *-a*; and that NOMINE was a genitive of a new nominative **nomina*. If so, NOMINE is comparable with MONOMENTI, a genitive used where only a nominative would have been appropriate; and, moreover, it is considerably earlier.

Box 2.1(b). Inscriptions with no word for the memorial and no use of HIC IACIT

With no explicit reference to a memorial and without HIC IACIT. This category and the next are subdivided on the basis of the distribution of nominative (-US) and genitive (-I) endings (only representative examples together with some unusual ones are given).

(a) Without patronymic

1. X-us	392/77/Gn-2 (VI[med]) VERACIVS / P*RES*B*YTE*R
2. X-i	2027/Gn-7 (V/VI[1]) ERCAGNI
	445/354/Gso-39 VITALIANI / EMERETO

(*continued*)

[76] Tedeschi, *Congeries*, 302, on IOM-2.
[77] Underlining denotes ligatured letters.
[78] Tedeschi, *Congeries*, in his comment on Gso-14, gives several parallels from the Rhineland: W. Boppert, *Die frühchristlichen Inschriften des Mittelrheingebietes* (Mainz, 1971), 69, 94, 105, 159, 164–7, 169. But these are all of the form illustrated by the first of those cited: ☧ *In hunc / tumulum re/quiiscit / puella nu/mine Mune/trudis / qui vixsit / annus xxi*, and it is not an adequate parallel.

Box 2.1(b). continued

(b) With patronymic

1. X-i fili Y-i (representative examples):

364/144/Gso-21/CM9 (VI²) QVENVENDANI / FILI BARCVNI
400/177/Gn-11 (VI¹) VINNEMAGLI FILI SENEMAGLI
Extended variant: 454/402/Gso-43/P135 (VI¹) (reading of Edwards, *Corpus*) EVALI FILI DENOVI / CVNIOVENDE / MATER EIVS

The first line of this last inscription is a normal example of this type; the second line is an example of what purports to be a genitive form of a feminine name with *-e* for earlier Latin *-ae*; but, if that were so, the nominative *mater* in the third line would be in apposition to the genitive *Cuniouende*.

2. X-us/-a filius/-a Y-i — 362/142/Gso-20/CM7 (V)
Latin: AVITORIA / FILIA CVNIGNI
Ogham: INIGENA CUNIGNI AUITTORIGES

3. X-us filius Y-us — No examples

4. X-us fili Y-i
328/44/Gse-5/B4 (V/VI¹) . . . R]VGNIATIO / [FI]LI VENDONI

5. X-i filius Y-i
376/174/Gso-33/CM40 (VI¹) VENNISETLI / FILIVS ERCAGNI
(+ 339/68/Gse-2/B35 (VI¹) NAMINI FILIVS VICTORINI
380/84/Gn-8 (V) Ogham: ICORIGAS
Latin: ICORI FILIVS / POTENT/INI

(Placing this inscription here assumes that the Latinized form of the name was, at this period, nominative *Icorius*, genitive *Icori*. If one were to take *Icori* as a nominative, it would go under B (b) 2 above.)[79]

429/307/Gso-19/P13 (VI^{med}) SOLINI / FILIVS VENDONI)

6. X-i fili Y-us
430/306/Gso-18/P14 (VI^{med}) Ogham: ETTERN[I / MAQI /VIC]TOR
Latin: ETTERNI FILI VICTOR

Victor is a very common name in the fifth and sixth centuries; the genitive would be *Victoris*.

Box 2.1(c). Inscriptions with no word for the memorial but which use HIC IACIT

With no explicit reference to a memorial but with HIC IACIT (these examples are, it is hoped, complete, not just representative, except that some inscriptions the readings of which are uncertain have been excluded)

(*continued*)

[79] *CIB* 31–2, 54.

Box 2.1(c). continued

The classification is established on the basis of the position of HIC IACIT: (i) HIC IACIT + name (+ patronymic) as opposed to (ii) first name + HIC IACIT (+/– patronymic) and (iii) first name and patronymic + HIC IACIT, in other words HIC IACIT is (i) at the beginning, (ii) in medial position or at least after the first name, or (iii) at the end, after first name and patronymic. The position of HIC IACIT ought not to make any difference; the distinction between initial, medial, and final is made to demonstrate that any such possibility should be rejected.

(i) HIC IACIT first:

(a) With no patronymic

1. X-i:
   467/Ok24/C-12 (V/VI^{in})
   Latin: [HI]C IACIT VLCAGNI
   Ogham: ULCAGNI
2. X-us
   516/Scot1/S-4 (VI^{2}). — A ET Ω / HIC IACENT / SanCtI ET PRAE/CIPVI SACER/DOTES ID EST / VIVENTIVS ET MAVORIUS

(b) With a patronymic

1. X-i fili Y-I — 514/Scot8/S-2 (V/VI^{1})
   HIC IACIT / CARANTI FILI / CVPITIANI
2. X-i fili Y-us — No examples
3. X-i/-e filius/-a Y-I — 421/294/Gn-20 (V)
   HIC [IN] / TVM[V]LO IA/CIT . R[U]STE/CE . FILIA . PA/TERNINI . / ANI XIII . IN PA(ce)
   Tedeschi's reading.
4. X-us filius Y-i — 369/153/CM18 (lost)
   [HIC?] IACET CVRCAGNVS / [ ]VRIVI FILIVS
   370/157/Gso-30/CM22 (VI^{1})
   HIC IACIT / VLCAGNVS FI<LI>VS SENOMAGLI
5. X-us fili Y-i — No examples
6. X-us filius Y-us — Cf. 407/258/Gse-11/G92 (VI^{med})
   HIC IACIT CANTVSVS PATER PAVLINVS[80]
7. X-i filius Y-us — No examples
8. X-i filius Y-I — No examples

(ii) HIC IACIT after the first name: X hic iacit (filius Y)

(a) With no patronymic

(continued)

[80] Redknap and Lewis, *Corpus*, G92, translate, following Jackson's lead, 'Here lies Cantusus. His father was Paulinus'. This is entirely possible; but if one rejects in general Jackson's approach, namely splitting up these texts into separate sentences, it will become less attractive than 'Here lies Cantusus, father of Paulinus'.

Box 2.1(c). continued

1. X-i	319/9/Gn-21 (V/VI^{1}) CVNOGVSI HIC IACIT 412/277 (lost) FERRVCI HIC IACIT 1028/214/Gse-7/G119 (VII) VENDVMAGLI HIC IACIT 354/126/Gso-41/CD28 (VI^{1}) CORBALENGI IACIT / ORDOVS 388/94, DERVORI HIC IACIT[81] Probably also 318/6/Gn-5 (VI^{med})
An extended version:	
	401/183/Gn-37 (VI^{med}) BROHOMAGLI / IATTI IC IACIT / ET VXOR EIUS CAVNE
2. X-us	392/77/Gn-2 (VI^{med}) VERACIVS P*RES*B*ITE*R HIC IACIT 381/87/Gn-15 (VI^{med}) ALIORTVS ELMETIACO / HIC IACET[82] 355/128/Gso-42/CD29 (VI^{1}) SI[L]BANDVS IACIT 483/Ok51/C-27 (V/VI^{1}) (Tedeschi's reading) SENILVS IC IACIT
Extended versions:	
	391/78/Gn-1 (VI^{med}) SENACVS / PR*ESBYTER* / HIC IACIT / CVM MVLTITVDINEM / FRATRVM // PRESB[IT]E[R] 393/101/Gn-31 (V) CARAVSIVS / HIC IACIT / IN HOC CONGERIES LA/PIDVM 420/289/Gn-10 (V) PORIVS / HIC IN TVMVLO IACIT / HOMO PLANVS FVIT
(b) With a patronymic: i. X-i HIC IACIT fili Y-i	
	457/Ok18/Tedeschi, C-10 (VI^{med}) (Tedeschi's reading): DVNOCATI HIC IACIT FILI MESCAGNI 478/Ok48/C-24 (assuming that the second line contained a patronymic, X FILI) BROCAGNI IHC IACIT CIA[. . .]T[.] F[. . .] 327/43/Gse-1/B2 (VI^{1}): Ogham: TURPIL[LI MAQI(?) TRIL]LUNI

(continued)

[81] On the assumption that this is to be analysed in the same way as ICORI above, under B (b) 5.

[82] ELMETIACO is an indication that the person in question came from Elmet or Elfed (compare ORDOVS above, ii (a) 1, 'an Ordovician'); the ending -O is Late Latin for earlier -VS.

Box 2.1(c). continued

Latin: TVRPILLI IC IA/CIT PVVERI TRILVNI dVNOCATI
433/313/Gso 36/P22 (VI¹):
Ogham: [A]NDAGELLI MACU CAV[ETI(?)]
Latin: ANDAGELLI IACIT / FILI CAVETI
Llandanwg 3: GERONTI HIC IACIT / fiLI sPECTATI.[83]

ii. X-us filius Y-i

353/127/Gso-6/CD26 (VI¹)
Ogham: TRENACATTLO
Latin: TRENACATVS / IC IACIT FILIVS / MAGLAGNI
487/Ok10/C-6 (VI^med) (Tedeschi's reading):
DRVST[- - -]S HIC IACIT / CVNOMORI FILIVS

iii. X-us filius Y-us

334/54/Gse-6/B21 (VII) CATACVS HIC IACIT / FILIVS TEGERNACVS

iv. X-i fili(us) Y-us — No examples

v. X-i filius Y-i

352A/122/Gso-4/CD22 (VI¹/VI^med) DOMNICI / IACIT FILIVS / BRAVECCI
408/229/Gse-13/G77 (VI²) BODVOCI HIC IACIT / FILIVS CATOTIGIRNI / PRONEPUS ETERNALI / VEDOMAVI
470/Ok78/C-1 (VI²) LATINI IC IACIT / FILIVS MACARI

Exceptionally HIC IACIT separates the two elements of the patronymic:

331/41/Gse-15/B46 (VI²) [A?]NNICCI FILIVS [H] IC IACIT TECVRI IN HOC TVMVLO

(iii) HIC IACIT in final position

i. X-i fili Y-i

389/97/Gn-17 (VI¹)
IOVENALI FILI / ETERNI HIC IACIT
386/92/Gn-27 (V/VI^in)
MELI MEDICI / FILI MARTINI / I[A]CIT
387/95/Gn-28 (VI²)
FIGVLINI FILI / LOCVLITI / HIC IACIT
428/305/Gso-16/P12 (VI²)

(continued)

[83] A. Davidson, 'Two Early Medieval Stones from Llandanwg', *Archaeology in Wales*, 48 (2008), 73–5 (with cursive letters transcribed in lower case).

Box 2.1(c). continued

	Ogham: TRENAGUSU MAQI MAQITRENI Latin: TRENEGUSSI FILI / MACUTRENI HIC IACIT
	436/316/Gso-26/P26 (VI^{2}) EVOLENGGI / FILI / LITOGENI / HIC IACIT
ii. X-us filius Y-I	No examples
iii. X-us filius Y-us	No examples
iv. X-i filius Y-us	No examples
v. X-i filius Y-I	
	342/70/Gse-17/B45 (VI^{1}) CVNOCENNI FILIVS / CVNOGENI HIC IACIT 344/73/Gse-10/B50 (VI^{1}) DERVACI FILIVS IVSTI IC IACIT 451/401/Gso-48/P133 (VI^{med}) TVNCCETACE VX/SOR DAARI HIC IA/CIT 500/IOM-1 (V/VI^{1}) AMMECATI / FILIVS ROCAT[I] / HIC IACIT (bilingual, with an ogham counterpart)
Exceptional example	
	329/42/B41 CANNTIANI ET / PATER ILLIVS MACCV/TRENI HIC IA/CIVNT[84]

It is important to begin by asking what is the word left implicit, when an inscription is understood as '(memorial, body?) of Y'. Two main suggestions have been made: first, that it is some term for the memorial, such as *memoria* or *monumentum*, and, secondly, that it is a term for the body of the deceased, such as *corpus*. There is good evidence for the first but not for the second. This is somewhat awkward for Jackson's case, since his interpretation requires wide use of *corpus* or some equivalent as the implicit item on which the name in the genitive is supposed to depend. The typical *memoria* is a pillar-stone and is not lying anywhere.

The problem in interpreting the syntax of such inscriptions as the Llangwyryfon one by breaking up the text in the way proposed by Jackson is clear when one considers parallels from Gaul, for example, HIC IACET / SANCTVLVS / FAMVLVS DEI / ANNO- III ET MESE / SES IIII / PAVSAT DTE (= DIE) / MERCVRI ASTO/RIO- VC- CONS-.[85] Examples such as this, which is similar in construction to Kirkmadrine 1 from Galloway, argue strongly that the subject of

[84] Except for ET in place of ETI, I have preferred the reading in Redknap and Lewis, *Corpus*, to the one followed by Adams. The date in the *Corpus* is V/VI^{1}.

[85] E. Le Blant, *Inscriptions chrétiennes de la Gaule antérieures au VIIIe siècle*, 2 vols. (Paris, 1856, 1865), ii. 554, no. 667 (Lyons).

IACIT/IACET was the name of the deceased. When, therefore, Jackson interprets inscriptions using HIC IACIT by positing a term such as *corpus* as the subject of IACIT, he is implying a change to the traditional formula. Similarly, it is evident that a very common way of identifying a person in Celtic languages, from this date until the modern period, is to use name and patronymic, X son of Y. Jackson's interpretation requires him to break, when necessary, the syntactical connection between the name and the patronymic, placing them in separate sentences: first *(corpus) Domnici iacit* and then *filius Bravecci (fuit)*. Very occasionally an inscription does contain two sentences, as in 420/289/Gn-10 PORIVS / HIC IN TVMVLO IACIT / HOMO CHRISTIANVS FVIT; but even this example does not place the patronymic in a separate sentence from the first name. The interpretation thus succeeds in going against the grain both of the continental parallels and of the standard medieval Celtic use of first name + patronymic.

Jackson maintained that spoken British Latin endured into the seventh century; and, at least in *Language and History in Early Britain*, argued that the inscriptions still showed a knowledge of the Latin case-system. Later, when commenting on the Yarrow inscription, he moved towards the position adopted here, namely that the inscriptions show extensive confusion of cases and declensions. A recent brief survey of the post-Roman British inscriptions by Dr J. N. Adams has, however, concluded the exact opposite of Jackson's earlier position, namely that what the inscriptions show is not the survival of spoken Latin in western Britain after the departure of the legions but 'the work of writers who were not adept at using Latin and were copying epitaphs of limited type without displaying a creative ability to use the Latin language'.[86] The contention is that those who composed the inscriptions were largely ignorant of Latin, both spoken and written, and were using what, for them, was a dead language out of a sense that Latin was appropriate for funerary inscriptions.

Some elements in Adams's position are familiar. The frequent use of genitive forms for names is explained by invoking the use of the genitive in the ogham inscriptions. So far as the explanation by means of the ogham parallel goes, there is nothing here that was not in Jackson's account—and indeed in those of other scholars. Where Adams differs fundamentally from Jackson is in his assessment of what lay behind those inscriptions that use the phrase HIC IACIT. We therefore need to consider more closely what is supposed to have happened beginning with the relationship between Latin and ogham inscriptions and then considering the inscriptions with HIC IACIT. The Irish of the ogham inscriptions was a language in which distinctions of case were preserved, in forms such as the genitive in *-i* as opposed to a nominative in *-as* that were similar to the corresponding distinction between nominative and genitive in Latin. Adams cites the bilingual inscription, St Dogmael's 1 (449/384/Gso-44/P110):

Ogham: SAGRAGNI MAQI CUNATAMI
Latin: SAGRANI FILI CVNOTAMI

[86] J. N. Adams, *The Regional Diversification of Latin 200 BC–AD 600* (Cambridge, 2007), 616–20 (the quotation is from p. 619).

In addition to the exact correspondence here in the endings, he deploys a further argument for the dependence of the Latin on the ogham:

> In Latin filiations of all areas and periods *filius* almost invariably follows the name of the father. Its placement here before the name is based on that of *maqi* in the Celtic.

He has, however, forgotten one important counter-example to his rule about the word order of filiations: the Latin Bible. The new Irish and British Christians of the fifth century believed that their saviour was *Iesus filius Ioseph* (Luke 3:23, 4:22);[87] Patrick could have claimed scriptural authority when he referred to his father *Calpornius quidam filius Potiti*. Moreover, Continental Celtic had different forms of filiation from those found among the Britons and the Irish from the fifth century: two examples are ICCAVOS OPPIANICNOS 'Iccauos son of Oppianos', where filiation is denoted by the suffix *-ikn-*, and MARTIALIS DANNOTALI 'Martialis (son) of Dannotalos', where it is denoted by using the genitive.[88] Hence, the form of filiation found from this period onwards among the Irish and the Britons may well have been a recent innovation, although an example is found among the Bath curse tablets.[89]

Let us assume, however, for the moment that the Latin in this and similar examples is shaped by its ogham counterpart. In ogham inscriptions it is understood that the genitive is used for the first name because there is something understood that belongs to the person named: in this example, there is something 'of Sagragnas'.[90] It is not clear whether Adams thinks that the same applies to the accompanying Latin inscription: was it a mechanical copying of a model or was it, allowing for the unstated something that belonged to Sagragnas/Sagranus, correct? The spelling of the names in the Latin, when compared with the Irish, suggests that it was not merely mechanical copying: SAGRANI shows one sound-change (*-agn-* > *-ān-*) that is not shown in the ogham version.

Adams then gives six examples illustrating five types. In terms of the classification given above, these are:

1. X-us HIC IACIT filius Y-us
   334/54/Gse-6/B21 (VII) CATACVS HIC IACIT / FILIVS TEGERNACVS
2. X-i fili Y-i HIC IACIT
   387/95/Gn-28 (VI^{2}) FIGVLINI FILI / LOCVLITI / HIC IACIT
3. X-i filius Y-i HIC IACIT
   344/73/Gse-10/B50 (VI^{1}) DERVACI FILIVS IVSTI IC IACIT
4. HIC IACIT X-us filius Y-i
   370/157/Gso-30/CM22 (VI^{1}) HIC IACIT / VLCAGNVS FI<LI>VS SENOMAGLI

[87] Similarly in the Old Testament, Gen. 36:31–9.

[88] M. Lejeune, *Recueil des inscriptions Gauloises*, ii: 1, *Textes gallo-latins sur pierre* (Paris, 1988), L-9, L-13; P.-Y. Lambert, *La langue gauloise* (Paris, 1995), 96, 98–9.

[89] D. McManus, *A Guide to Ogam* (Maynooth, 1991), 51; R. S. O. Tomlin, *Tabellae Sulis: Roman Inscribed Tablets of Tin and Lead from the Sacred Spring at Bath* (Oxford, 1988), no. 30, has one example of X *filius* Y, but, exceptionally, the name given for Y is the mother's rather than the father's. It also has several examples of the father's name being given in the genitive.

[90] McManus, *Guide to Ogam*, 51; for some exceptions, see ibid. 117.

Two Longer texts:

5. 329/42/B41 CANNTIANI ET / PATER ILLIVS MACCV/TRENI HIC IA/CIVNT[91]
6. 401/183/Gn-37 (VI^{med}) BROHOMAGLI / IATTI IC IACIT / ET VXOR EIUS CAVNE

These six inscriptions all contain HIC IACIT (or IACIVNT) and thus raise the issue of agreement between verb and subject. Adams does not accept the idea that one should break up the syntax in the manner proposed by Jackson in *Language and History in Early Britain*. No. 4 illustrates the occasional correct use of cases. No. 1 uses only *-us* even for the name of the father, TEGERNACVS. No. 2, by contrast, uses only *-i* even for the name of the person said to 'lie here'. Adams proposes the same explanation as that put forward by Williams, namely that the error arises from conflating the type without HIC IACIT and following the ogham model (as in SAGRANI FILI CVNOTAMI) with the HIC IACIT type, as represented by no. 4. No. 3 exhibits a failure to make FILIVS agree with DERVACI. In the examples given under nos. 5 and 6 everything works reasonably correctly except for the names, which are all in the genitive.

The argument, therefore, starts from the evident incomprehension shown by these texts, except for no. 4, of the morphology of the noun in Latin and the associated rules of agreement between noun and verb and between noun and noun; and it concludes that they are 'not consistent with knowledge of Latin as a living language'. If by Latin we mean that stage of the language in which the declensions survived approximately as in the classical language, this is evidently true. If, however, it is intended to assert that the writers of these texts cannot have had a command of any form of the language and must have been British (or, at least, Celtic) speakers with only some half-understood Latin formulae imitated from other inscriptions, the argument does not follow. The examples cited by Adams are equally explicable on the premiss that British Latin survived into the fifth and sixth centuries, but in a form without distinctions of case. This is an economical assumption, since we know that British (Celtic) was losing distinctions of case at this very period; it is likely that the two languages spoken by the Britons, Latin and British, progressed in parallel. Moreover, Adams's examples and his reasoning are restricted to morphology and the syntax of agreement. He has taken no account of those inscriptions that show an evolution of the phonology of Latin identical with that found in Vulgar Latin on the Continent. To take one example, a bilingual inscription, probably of the fifth century:[92]

445/354/Gso-39/P71. Nevern 2.
Ogam: VITALIANI
Latin: VITALIANI / EMERETO

[91] Except for ET in place of ETI, I have preferred the reading in Redknap and Lewis, *Corpus*, to the one followed by Adams. The date in the *Corpus* is V/VI^{1}.

[92] *LHEB*, p. 183; Tedeschi, *Congeries*, 157.

The term *emeritus* may well be a cognomen.[93] This example shows a disregard of the normal rule of agreement: if the Latin VITALIANI is following the genitive case of the ogham, it should have been followed by EMERITI. So far, it fits Adams's argument entirely. But one should also consider the form EMERETO as opposed to *emeritus*: the confusion of short *i* and *e* and short *u* and *o* is characteristic of Late Latin. The phonology of the inscriptions, as we have seen, often indicates a spoken form of the language, whereas the morphology only shows that the writers of the texts did not know a form of Latin in which case distinctions were preserved.

Furthermore, Adams has not considered a further powerful argument that Latin remained a spoken language in western Britain during the fifth and sixth centuries, namely the character of the loanwords from British Latin into Irish. These admittedly included words of a distinctively ecclesiastical character, but they were not limited to such vocabulary.[94] The appearance in Old Irish of many words of a secular character, borrowed directly from British Latin rather than via British Celtic, and yet pronounced in a distinctively British manner, is a pointer to the survival of Latin as a spoken language in western Britain in the fifth and sixth centuries. Adams's argument is only persuasive if one is prepared to accept that the evidence should be restricted to what he has been prepared to discuss.

One of the premisses of Adams's argument was that the prevalence of genitive forms in Latin inscriptions in Britain was to be explained by the influence of ogham. Here he was following earlier scholars such as Williams and Jackson. However, although it is entirely plausible in such cases as the Nevern stone just cited, it is by no means so plausible in southern Scotland, as in the Yarrow inscription cited earlier or in the Liddel Water inscription.[95] That was not an area of Irish settlement: there are no confirmed bilingual inscriptions in the British areas of what is now Scotland and the north of England. 'Epigraphic -I' is also attested in Brittany, another area where ogham inscriptions are not found.[96] Moreover, the prevalence of final -I is part of a wider phenomenon: there is also the use of final -E in women's names, as in CAVNE cited by Adams under his no. 5. This is best explained as the Latin genitive of an *ā*-stem (classical Latin *-ae*): the genitive of Primitive Irish *ā*-stems as attested in the ogham inscriptions would not provide a model.[97] Then there is the confusion of declensions (not just cases) as in the following bilingual inscription from the Isle of Man, which conforms to Adams's type 3:

500/IOM-1. Andreas, Knock e Dooney.
Latin: AMMECATI FILIVS ROCATI HIC IACIT
Ogham: [AM]B[I]CATOS M[A]QI ROC[A]T[O]S[98]

93 See below, 188.
94 *LHEB*, ch. 4; D. McManus, 'The Chronology of Latin Loan-Words', *Ériu*, 34 (1983), 21–71.
95 See above, 147, and 514/Scot8/S-2.
96 W. Davies et al. *The Inscriptions of Early Medieval Brittany* (Oakville, Conn. 2000), F5, C1.
97 *LHEB*, p. 188; McManus, *Guide to Ogam*, 115–16.
98 *LHEB*, p. 173 n. 1: [AM]B[I]CATOS ('there is hardly room for I').

The Irish inscription contains a pair of genitives, but they are *u*-stem genitives in *-ōs* and thus provide no basis for the -I found in both names in the Latin. Only if we assume that the author of the Latin inscription knew enough Irish to appreciate that they were genitives could his endings in -I have followed their endings in *-ōs*; but if he did know that, why did he have FILIVS in the nominative as the counterpart of M[A]QI in the Irish? When we find that the Latin word *filius* 'son' appears in the nominative, even though the Irish counterpart MAQI is correctly in the genitive, it seems plain enough that the Latin case-system has broken down, even though the Irish one had not. Also, it is likely, to judge by the Middle-Welsh plural form *cadeu*, that in British **catus* had been a *u*-stem as in Irish, but here it is treated as if it were an *o*-stem.[99] The implication is that, on the Isle of Man as in Wales, such bilingual inscriptions were not just composed by Irishmen who also used Latin. Since the Irish native case-system remained intact, they could be expected to preserve the Latin one, if the Latin with which they were familiar still had a fully functioning system of declension. Instead, an inscription of this kind represents the meeting of three languages, Irish, British Latin, and British Celtic, of which two, British Latin and British Celtic, had lost their case-systems.

If the influence of Irish is not the explanation of 'epigraphic -I', the answer may lie in a combination of what was happening to British and British Latin together with an element of convention. As we saw earlier with Gildas's *Maglocune*, some British names—those that had been consonantal stems—had already by the sixth century begun to take two forms, one descended from the old nominative and the other from the oblique stem. In this name the use of the oblique stem is attested in an inscription from Nevern in Pembrokeshire:

446/353/Gso-40/P70. Nevern 1.
Ogam: MAGLICUNAS MAQI CLUTA[RIGAS (?)
Latin: MAGLOCVN FILI CLVTORI

The final -N of MAGLOCVN was done with the diagonal reversed, so that it goes from low left to high right; if this was done in order to get a ligatured NI, this could be read as MAGLOCVNI, but in Nevern 2, 445/354/Gso-39/P71, quoted above, the N is also reversed and yet a separate I is included. The great majority of inscriptions, however, use a genitive in -I, even though we have no reason to suppose that the Late British names derived from the earlier oblique stem were derived from the genitive rather than the accusative. What we need, therefore, is a reason why the genitive in -I (and feminine -E) should have become a standard convention that applied above all to personal names. The most likely explanation is that, at the stage when distinctions of case were going out of use, the ending -I was already standard in the patronymics, and similarly -E for feminine names. These endings were then generalized for all names as a pure convention among those who composed the texts of inscriptions. This will explain why, when other parts of an inscription were often reasonably correct, personal names showed 'epigraphic -I' (or -E).

[99] *LHEB*, pp. 187–8.

Late British Latin must have been in the same situation as the one we find in Modern Italian: *-i* is the mark of the plural of nouns continuing the Latin second declension, but no longer of the genitive singular, since there is no such case. British, by the fifth century, was in the same position. This is what explains the numerous relics of the plural in *-i* (for example, early Welsh *meip* from British **mapī*) as opposed to the very few relics of the genitive singular in *-i*. We may contrast this linguistic situation with that of a man who learnt his Latin from grammars, for example the Anglo-Saxon Bede or the Irishman Tírechán. The former writes much better Latin than the second, but both have learnt in the same way. The kind of mistakes made by Tírechán are of two types: one is familiar to all those who have had to learn a second language after childhood—he makes simple grammatical errors;[100] the second is more interesting—he writes a Latin in which Irish constructions or idioms prevail over their Latin counterparts.[101] Tírechán, however, was perfectly well aware of the distinction between Latin cases, even if he makes mistakes. Many of those who were responsible for the texts of the inscriptions were unaware of any case-system at all. They had not learnt their Latin from grammars. Latin was, therefore, in the fifth and sixth centuries, a spoken language, alongside Welsh and, as I shall argue, Irish.

Patrick Sims-Williams has shown that a considerably higher proportion than previously realized of the personal names in inscriptions from Wales and the Marches, 400–1100, have definite Irish connections.[102] This extends the evidence provided by the inscriptions in the ogham alphabet and in early forms of Irish, since the great majority of the 228 inscriptions of the period are in Latin, with only the names to indicate the affiliation of those commemorated. The inscriptions with Irish connections mainly belong to the early period, 400 – *c.* 600, and to the south, especially the south-west, and the north-west.

Good evidence that Irish was a spoken language in Wales comes from Kenfig in Glamorgan, many miles to the east of the main Irish settlements in Dyfed. A bilingual inscription runs as follows:[103]

Ogham: P[.]P[IA ?] / / ROL[..]N M[AQ]I LL[E]NA
Latin: PVMPEIVS / CARANTORIVS

[100] For example, Tírechán, *Collectanea*, 6. 1, ed. L. Bieler, *The Patrician Texts in the Book of Armagh* (Dublin, 1979), 126, *possimus* for *possumus*, *acciperunt* for *acceperant*.

[101] For example, 24. 1 (p. 140), *quae tenuit pallium apud Patricium et Rodanum* = *gaibes caille la Pátraic 7 Ródán*.

[102] P. Sims-Williams, 'The Five Languages of Wales in the Pre-Norman Inscriptions', *CMCS* 44 (Winter 2002), 1–36.

[103] 409/198/Gse-12/G86 now in the Margam Museum; the stone is damaged and the reading of the vowels is a matter of judgement. Nash-Williams's reading, restoring POPIA, is a distinct improvement on that of Macalister, *CIIC*, no. 409. See also McManus, *A Guide to Ogam*, § 6.20, who confirms P[.]P[, and The Royal Commission on Ancient and Historical Monuments in Wales, *An Inventory of the Ancient Monuments in Glamorgan*, i. 3, *The Early Christian Period* (Cardiff, 1976), 38, no. 849, which reads P[O or A]P[. . .]. On the form of ogham used for /p/ see P. Sims-Williams, 'The Additional Letters of the Ōgham Alphabet', *CMCS* 23 (1992), 39–44, esp. 42.

The Latin inscription is in square capitals. There is nothing in the form of the inscription to suggest that Pumpeius and Carantorius are different persons. The ogham inscription, however, appears to be in two parts: one, on the left of the Latin inscription, reading upwards; the other, on the right, reading downwards; in the transcription they are separated by a double / /. Only the left-hand ogham text corresponds to the Latin. The other may be quite separate and may have been cut at a different time. PVMPEIVS shows, in the first syllable, the Late Latin confusion of *u* and *o*. Like CARANTORIVS it is in the nominative case. POPIA would be an Irish form of the same name but assimilated both to the phonology and the morphology of Primitive Irish; and for this reason the lost vowels can be reconstructed with a high degree of probability.[104]

In the next major kingdom to the north, Brycheiniog in the centre of South Wales, two inscriptions, about five miles apart, each of which is bilingual, are of particular interest.

Trallwng[105]	Ogham:	CUNACENNI [A]VI ILVVETO
	Latin:	CVNOCENNI FILIVS / CVNOGENI HIC IACIT
Trecastle[106]	Ogham:	MAQITRENI SALICIDUNI
	Latin:	MACCVTRENI † SALICIDVNI

In the Trallwng ogham inscription the text is quite independent of the Latin. First, the ogham text identifies the person by descent from his grandfather, as in the use of Old Irish *aue*, rather than by his filiation, as in the Latin. Secondly, the initial CUNA- shows, by his choice of -A- rather than -O- (namely CUNA- rather than CVNO-), the development of Irish whereby the link vowel *-o-* was lowered and unrounded to *-a-*; this *-a-* subsequently lowered the preceding *-u-* to *-o-* and was itself lost (**cuno-* > **cuna-* > **cona-* > *con-*).[107] This independence of the ogham-cutter vis-à-vis the Latin suggests that Irish was for him a spoken language. On the other hand, on the Llywel inscription a few miles further west, the form of the name in the ogham inscription, MAQITRENI, is more archaic then the Latin MACCVTRENI, since it preserves the old *q* and *i* as against the later *c(c)* and *u*.[108] Here the Latin form of the name—still, of course, an Irish name even though in a Latin inscription—is closer to the probable pronunciation at the time. In this inscription, therefore, we have evidence in the ogham of a conservative Irish

[104] It shows *-omp-* > *-ōb-*; the restored last syllable [*-IA*] is a likely spelling for *-ijah*, the Primitive Irish nominative singular of a *io*-stem. Note that the use of *p* for /b/ is characteristic of Old Irish but not of ogham, and may be ascribed to Brittonic influence.

[105] Trallwng, 342/70/Gse-17/B45, situated in the church at SN 965 295. For the ogham Nash-Williams reads CVNACENNIVI, following Macalister, *CIIC*, no. 342, but the first V is merely a slip for U. Jackson, *Language and History in Early Britain*, p. 185, suggests *CUNACENNI [A]VI ILVVETO* and he is followed by McManus, *A Guide to Ogham*, § 4.11 (p. 62), Tedeschi, and Redknap and Lewis, *Corpus*.

[106] Llywel (Pentre Poeth) 341/71/Gse-9/B42. Nash-Williams reads MAQUTRENI but the U is a slip for I, as shown by the drawing. The stone is now in the British Museum.

[107] McManus, *A Guide to Ogham*, § 5.23.

[108] Ibid.; §§ 5.32, 5.33.

orthographical tradition surviving in Brycheiniog independently both of the Latin tradition and of the pronunciation of Irish at that period.

In the sixth century, therefore, both Latin and Irish were spoken languages in Wales. Brycheiniog as well as Dyfed was a kingdom of three languages. Both Latin and Irish enjoyed a higher social status than did British. By the ninth century, however, neither Latin nor Irish were normal spoken languages used for all purposes. Latin was a language of liturgy and learning; Irish was probably not spoken at all apart from the occasional immigrant or the churchman who had studied in Ireland: the epigraphic evidence for the death of normal spoken Latin in Britain will be pursued later, in Chapter 19. The best indication of the relationship of the three languages is the eighth- and ninth-century Juvencus manuscript (Cambridge University Library Ff.4.42).[109] This reveals the existence of a group of scholars, including Irishmen as well as Britons (including, very probably, one Breton glossator), whose primary language for scholarly purposes was Latin, but who accepted the Old Welsh form of British as a written language, at least for the purpose of glossing and entering marginalia.[110] The latter include the Juvencus *englynion*, the earliest Welsh verse to survive in a manuscript close to the date of composition. Another, perhaps overlapping, group of scholars was patronized by Merfyn Frych, king of Gwynedd, whose family probably came, as we have seen, from the Isle of Man, where Irishman and Briton may have lived side by side for centuries.[111] A further symptom of the status of Latin solely as a learned language is the relatively good grammar and innocence of Late Latin rhetorical preciosity shown by the two main Welsh writers of the ninth century. The *Historia Brittonum* from the first half of the century and Asser from the second both show a good command of Latin, considerably superior to many of their English contemporaries.[112]

The linguistic situation of Wales, Cornwall, and Brittany thus changed fundamentally between the fifth and the eighth centuries. In Wales and Cornwall three languages were spoken in the fifth century, British, Latin, and Irish; in Brittany two, British and Latin. The process by which Wales and Cornwall became, by 700, monolingual can be paralleled in part in northern Gaul. In the sixth century, Franks and Romans were intermingled, with separate languages, separate laws, and separate identities; by the eighth century they were all Franks. Ethnicity was, however, not shown in Gaul by what language one spoke: most Franks in the west spoke Gallo-Romance, even if they showed a preference for Frankish personal names.

[109] *Juvencus: Codex Cantabrigiensis Ff.4.42*, ed. H. McKee (Aberystwyth, 2000); *Juvencus: Text and Commentary*, ed. H. McKee (Aberystwyth, 2000).; also ead. 'Scribes and Glosses from Dark Age Wales: The Cambridge Juvencus Manuscript', *CMCS* 39 (Summer 2000), 1–22.

[110] M. Lapidge, 'Latin Learning in Dark Age Wales: Some Prolegomena', in D. Ellis Evans et al. (eds.), *Proceedings of the Seventh International Congress of Celtic Studies, Oxford, 1983* (Oxford, 1986), 97–101; A. Harvey, 'The Cambridge Juvencus Glosses—Evidence of Hiberno-Welsh Interaction', in P. Sture Ureland and G. Broderick (eds.), *Proceedings of the Eighth International Symposium on Language Contact in Europe, Douglas, Isle of Man, 1988* (Tübingen, 1991), 181–98, esp. 190–4.

[111] Lapidge, 'Latin Learning in Dark Age Wales', 92; N. K. Chadwick, 'Early Culture and Learning in North Wales', 94–103.

[112] See N. P. Brooks, *The Early History of the Church of Canterbury* (Leicester, 1984), 171–4, on the quality of Latin in use at Canterbury in the early ninth century.

What was the same on both sides of the Channel was the consolidation of linguistically divergent communities into monolingual peoples. Brittany was different from Cornwall and Wales and in some ways more like Francia: the islets of Latin-speakers in the west and of Breton-speakers in the east died out, but Brittany as a whole contained a large swathe of territory in the east that used Gallo-Romance. It came to resemble what might have happened if Britain had been free of English settlement and the more Latin-speaking east had developed undisturbed from the Roman period. Only in north Britain is there likely to have been a largely monolingual British community from the fifth up to the eighth century; but this formed a complete contrast with the Viking period, when Strathclyde expanded southwards and became a multilingual society. Now that we have an idea of the linguistic situation in Britain in the post-Roman period, it will become easier to handle the evidence of the inscriptions, most of which belong to the period 400–600.

3
Inscriptions

The post-Roman inscriptions of Celtic Britain attest both its cultural unity and its local variety, its continuity with Roman Britain and also the widespread impact of Irish settlement. Although the inscriptions are brief, they offer crucial evidence on several major issues. They have been central to debates over the relationship of Romano-British Christianity to that of post-Roman Britain. One school of thought has claimed their support for the proposition that post-Roman British Christianity was not an inheritance from Roman Britain but a reintroduction from Gaul; but other scholars have detected in the same inscriptions signs of Christian continuity within the island.[1] More generally, the inscriptions illuminate cultural and even political continuity from Roman Britain as well as the way Irish settlers sought to establish their position within a post-Roman world. Although the primary purpose of almost all inscriptions was commemorative, some, perhaps many, may have had other functions as well: as boundary markers or, more widely, as assertions of control over territory, as links with the past, either by reuse of Roman or prehistoric monuments (as with the Breton use of Iron-Age stelae)[2] or by echoing their appearance. In spite of the brevity of their texts, therefore, the inscriptions have a bearing on many aspects of post-Roman Britain. This chapter will be devoted to the inscriptions themselves so as to establish a firm foundation on which to rest subsequent arguments.[3]

1. LETTERFORMS: THEIR CONSTRUCTION AND TYPOLOGY

There is little direct evidence on how post-Roman British inscriptions were produced. This makes it all the more important to be alive to the possibilities and, in particular, to what can be deduced from the stones themselves. Most of the stone used was local, but not every stone was suitable.[4] For example, the

[1] For discontinuity: Nash-Williams, *ECMW*, pp. 1, 4; C. A. Ralegh Radford, 'Christian Origins in Britain', *Medieval Archaeology*, 15 (1971), 1–12. For continuity: C. Tedeschi, 'Osservazioni sulla palaeografia delle iscrizioni britanniche palaeocristiane (V–VII sec.). Contributo allo studio dell'origine delle scritture insulari', *Scrittura e civiltà*, 19 (1995), 66–121.

[2] W. Davies et al., *The Inscriptions of Early Medieval Brittany/Les inscriptions de la Bretagne du Haut Moyen Âge* (Oakville CT and Aberystwyth, 2000), 23.

[3] J. K. Knight, *The End of Antiquity: Archaeology, Society and Religion in Early Medieval Western Europe 235–700* (Stroud, 1999), 136–42, is a helpful introductory survey.

[4] See Redknap and Lewis, *Corpus*, i. 47–58 (the mudstones of Radnorshire are, for example, unsuitable: ibid. 47–9); Edwards, *Corpus*, ii. 19–29.

Table 3.1. The ogham alphabet

	1	2	3	4	5	*number of strokes*
b-row	B	L	F	S	N	
						strokes to right/below
'h' row	J?	D	T	C	Q	
						strokes to left/above
	M	G	G^{W}	ST?	R	
m-row						*strokes across stemline*
a-row	A	O	U	E	I	
						notches on stemline

Irish-language inscriptions in the ogham alphabet (see Table 3.1) were normally produced by making a variety of incisions on and across the angle or 'arris' of the stone. For this there needed to be such an arris and, in addition, the stone needed to be sufficiently hard and stable to allow incision on the angle without flaking.[5] Many inscriptions have indeed suffered from damage to the arris. Some ogham inscriptions start on the left-hand arris, go upwards, round the top and down the right-hand arris, but the value of the letter is determined by whether it is just a notch on the line of the arris (the 'stemline'), as with the vowels, or to the right or left or across, as in the four groups of consonant symbols (for convenience, the arris is represented by a horizontal line in the diagram, but it was usually vertical).[6]

Two considerations—that stone normally needed to be available locally and that only some stone was suitable—imply that the distribution of inscriptions may have been determined by the availability of suitable stone as much as by the strength of the inducements within a local community to commemorate a dead person on a permanent monument.

In the post-Roman period, unlike Roman Britain, and also unlike the Viking period, stones were not normally carefully shaped. It was more usual to choose naturally occurring pillar-stones or slabs, but even boulders might be used. Other than transport, therefore, there was no major stage between the quarrying of the stone and the preparation of the inscription itself.

Three distinct stages, however, need to be distinguished within the process of putting a Latin inscription on a stone:[7] first, the composition of the text; secondly, laying out the text on the stone by paint or other means; and, thirdly, the cutting or

5 In some cases such flaking has occurred, as in Margam (Eglwys Nynnid) 1, 409/198/Gse-12/G86.

6 D. McManus, *A Guide to Ogam* (Maynooth, 1997), 47. The table adopts the suggestions made for the value of H1, M3 and M4 by McManus, ibid., 36–8.

7 J. Mallon, *La Paléographie romaine*, Monumenta et Studia 3 (Madrid, 1952), 58–60.

picking of the inscription itself. 'Incision' will be used as a generic term for any letter shape formed by cutting into the stone; 'chiselling' for holding a chisel at an angle and hammering it to produce a continuous groove; 'picking' will be used for holding a chisel or punch more or less vertically and making a series of points which are then linked to make the line. There is no reason to think that any one of the three processes was carried out by specialists in epigraphic lettering; it is much more likely that there were too few inscriptions made to sustain specialization, and hence that these processes were the concern of persons whose main activity lay elsewhere. Tools used to make a linear cut in the stone were a chisel with a rectangular end and a punch with a blunt point; the incision may well have been carried out by smiths.[8] Laying out the text on the stone—the function called *ordinatio*—might be done by a professional painter in the Roman world, part of whose duties might be to put text as well as images and decoration on such surfaces as a wall; but in post-Roman Britain it is quite likely that one and the same person composed the text and laid it out on the stone. This is not necessarily the case, however: we know too little about the interior decoration of wooden buildings in the period to assert that no counterpart to the Roman professional painter can have existed. On the whole, it is best to keep a firm hold on the distinction between the three functions, in spite of uncertainties as to who might have performed the different tasks. The person who composed the text might have no familiarity with the letterforms used in epigraphy; the person who incised the letters may have been entirely illiterate.

In one relatively late inscription, from the ninth century, the Pillar of Eliseg, we have possible evidence for the second stage, *ordinatio*. Here someone names himself as Cynfarch and as having 'painted this handwriting at the request of Cyngen, his king'.[9] The prominence given to Cynfarch argues strongly against his function having been restricted to painting the letters after they were cut. He may well have had the function of composing the inscription as well as painting it on to the stone: the verb *pinxit*, 'painted', can be compared with scribal colophons using the related verb *depinxit* simply for writing, but it is quite likely that he both composed the text and laid out the inscription on the stone by paint. Cynfarch, therefore, is likely to have had the second function, that of the *ordinator*, although he may well also have had the first.

In considering the letterforms in British inscriptions we need to bear in mind the second and third functions or stages, the *ordinatio* and the incision. Although the incision may have been done by someone whose normal activities required no literate skills, the tools used, as well as the kind of stone on which they were used,

[8] Redknap and Lewis, *Corpus*, i, 122–4. The use of a punch is also sometimes very obvious in inscriptions in the Roman period, as in *RIB* 1564, 1624.

[9] + CONMARCH PINXIT HOC / CHIROGRAFU*M* REGE SUO POSCENTE / CONCENN, *EWGT* 2 (adapted to correspond to Lhuyd's transcript, ibid., photograph before p. 1); N. Edwards, 'Rethinking the Pillar of Eliseg', *The Antiquaries Journal*, 89 (2009), 25. On *pinxit* and *depinxit* see also J. Higgitt, 'The Stone-Cutter and the Scriptorium': Early Medieval Inscriptions in Britain and Ireland', in W. Koch (ed.), *Epigraphik 1988*, Veröffentlichungen der Kommission für die Herausgabe der Inschriften des Deutschen Mittalters, 2 (Vienna, 1990), 151.

would have affected the result. With that qualification, we may begin by considering the previous stage, the *ordinatio*. It was then that decisions were taken about the form of letters to be used. Throughout the post-Roman period, approximately from 400 to 600, the standard form of letter used in epigraphy was the roman capital. This has immediate implications, for this was not the form of letter normally used in contemporary book production or in less formal writing. To see the place of epigraphy within the totality of script, we need to place the roman capitals of epigraphy alongside the Insular half-uncial and minuscule of books and the cursive of less formal as well as of documentary writing.

Script, like spoken language, varied according to register and style. To see the analogy we may compare the forms of language used in liturgy and the law. Both these activities occasion relatively formal styles of language, but they differ because the nature of the activities and the traditions of language use which grow up among the two sets of specialists draw them apart. Law and liturgy thus engender distinct linguistic registers, although in terms of style both require a high degree of formality. To these two kinds of variation we may add the distinction between one language and another: most people in Celtic Britain in the sixth century spoke British (on its way to Cornish, Welsh, Cumbric and other, more short-lived varieties), some spoke Latin, probably in addition to British, but the liturgy was always in Latin.

Similar differences affected script. First, there was the difference of language: text in Latin was incised in roman capitals, but for Irish the ogham script was used. Ogham is first securely attested in Ireland in the first half of the fourth century.[10] Although it may well have been influenced by Latin, it was specifically designed to fit an early form of Irish (the one called Primitive Irish). In Britain, ogham was mostly used in bilingual inscriptions, ogham for Irish alongside roman capitals for Latin, whereas back home in Ireland it was used on its own, since the inscriptions there were almost always in Irish only.[11] Secondly, there is the difference of register: as we have seen roman capitals were used for epigraphy but Insular half-uncial and minuscule for formal book script, and cursive probably for documents and less formal writing. Thirdly, there is the difference of style: a trained scribe would use half-uncial for grand books, minuscule for more ordinary productions, and, when he was writing informally, cursive. The least well attested of these is cursive, although at the time it was the most widely used: the 'foundational script' taught to those learning to write was a simplified New Roman cursive.[12] Its influence, however, can be detected in the development of

[10] I am indebted to an unpublished paper by R. Ó Floinn on the Newgrange material dated to the first half of the fourth century by a medallion of Constantine I. McManus, *A Guide to Ogam*; S. Ziegler, *Die Sprache der altirischen Ogam-Inschriften* (Göttingen, 1994).

[11] An apparent exception is a stone at Cillín Cormaic, Colbinstown, Co. Kildare, *CIIC* 19, but this seems to have two separate inscriptions, one in ogham, OVANOS AVI IVACATTOS, and the other in Roman capitals IVVE[?]EDRVVIDES. It is not a bilingual inscription such as those found in Britain.

[12] R. S. O. Tomlin, *Tabellae Sulis: Roman Inscribed Tablets of Tin and Lead from the Sacred Spring at Bath* (Oxford, 1988), nos. 94–111 (also published as Part 4 of B. Cunliffe (ed.), *The Temple of Sulis Minerva at Bath, II: Finds from the Sacred Spring* (Oxford, 1988)); A. Petrucci, *Writers and Readers in Medieval Italy* (New Haven, 1995), 61.

Insular book scripts, and individual cursive letters that are sometimes used in inscriptions. That it was probably the script for documents as well as for informal writing can be inferred from three facts: first, that it survived in post-Roman Britain (as the epigraphic evidence demonstrates); secondly, that 'New Roman cursive' ('New' because it replaced Old Roman cursive by the early fourth century) became the normal documentary script for Latin in the late Empire, and thirdly, that, as can be deduced from the work of Gildas, Roman-style government survived sufficiently in Britain, as it did in Gaul, to encourage the corresponding survival of a documentary script. The post-Roman phase in British epigraphy is one in which roman capitals continued to be the normal script for inscriptions, although occasionally cursive intruded into a context in which it was substandard both because of register (capitals, not cursive, were the norm for epigraphy) and because of style (epigraphy deserving a more formal and permanent variety of script).

One other variety of script intruded into territory that was the normal preserve of roman capitals, but its origins and significance are more obscure. In most of the great Insular gospel books a type of letter called 'Insular display capitals' is used in very grand contexts, such as the opening words of a gospel. The famous Ardagh chalice from south-west Ireland provides an example of such letters in metalwork. Among Insular display capitals there are two subtypes, of which one is determined by a policy of replacing curves by straight lines and angles, while the other is curvilinear. Typical of the angular subtype is an **S** consisting of one vertical line with one short horizontal projecting to the right from the top of the vertical and one short horizontal projecting to the left from the bottom. Another letter of the same subtype is an **M** with three vertical stokes and a single cross-stroke about halfway down the verticals—the result resembles a gate and it can thus be called a 'gate-**M**'. I shall call this subtype of angular display capitals the 'geometric capital'.[13] Its intrusion into the domain of normal roman capitals was rarer than was that of cursive. For example, out of fifty-four post-Roman Latin inscriptions (of the fifth and sixth centuries) in the old counties of Pembroke and Carmarthen, roughly early medieval Dyfed (including Ystrad Tywi), about forty are purely in roman capitals, at least eleven have cursive intrusions, while only three have 'geometrical' intrusions.[14]

To understand the post-Roman inscriptions of Celtic Britain an essential first step is to establish the relationship between cursive, the source of most intrusive letterforms, and other forms of writing. Once that has been appreciated, it may be possible to understand why there are cursive intrusions into the capital letterforms used for epigraphy.

[13] Following N. Gray, *Lettering as Drawing: Contour and Silhouette* (Oxford, 1970), 22–7.

[14] The three are Llanboidy 1, 365/149/Gso-23/CM13, Llansadyrnin, 375/166/Gso-32/CM32, Llandeilo 1, 434/314/Gso-35/P21; the later Ramsey Island inscription 2005/P99, E. Okasha, 'A New Inscription from Ramsey Island', *AC* 119 (1970), 68–70, is entirely in geometrical display letters. The uncertainty over classifying inscriptions as purely in capitals or in capitals with cursive intrusions is largely accounted for by the numbers of lost inscriptions.

A trained scribe writing a book in an Insular book script—half-uncial for the grander text, minuscule for ordinary text—used a quill pen cut to produce a broad nib, akin to the calligraphic pen of today. Such a pen naturally produced a rhythm of thick and thin strokes. It could also be used to make the triangular serifs that became, by the mid-seventh century, characteristic of Insular book hands; these started life as a practical means of getting the ink to flow on rough Insular parchment, but they developed in the course of the seventh century into a decorative feature.[15]

A trained scribe did not first learn to write by acquiring a book hand or by using a broad-edged pen. That was a later stage reserved for the skilled practitioner. The first steps, moreover, were almost certainly not taken using a pen of any kind on parchment, but rather by using a pointed stylus and a wax tablet or a slate.[16] The tablet was a flat rectangular piece of wood, which was hollowed out on one side to receive wax; this then hardened and became suitable as a surface for writing. In one way, writing with a stylus on a wax tablet was more akin to incising an inscription than to writing with a pen: it used a sharp instrument to make a groove on the surface, whereas the broad-edged pen put down a layer of ink on top of the parchment—one surface on top of another. This is still more obvious for writing on a slate. Writing with a stylus did not produce the thicks and thins of the broad pen, nor such associated features as serifs. Moreover, the letterforms at which the complete beginner was aiming were not those of the book scripts but a simple version of what we know as New Roman cursive, to which originally belonged, for example, the Insular **g**.

Admittedly this form of writing, New Roman cursive, was also used by trained scribes for writing documents: their productions could be highly calligraphic in themselves, but they were not written with a broad pen on parchment but with a narrower nib, and traditionally on papyrus. Cursive letterforms were thus used, at one end of the spectrum, by trained scribes writing documents, and, at the other end, by beginners. The trained scribe wrote a flowing 'joined-up' script with many ligatures; the beginner wrote an 'unjoined-up' version, in which the different strokes of the pen were made separately, even within a single letter; similarly, such beginners were not yet able to join one letter with another. The 'unjoined-up' character of a beginner's script should be distinguished sharply from the extent to which the trained scribe writing a book script linked stroke to stroke and letter to

15 The calligraphic serif, a triangle on the left side only of an upright stroke, is to be distinguished from the roman epigraphic serif, which formed an equilateral triangle projecting on both sides. The calligraphic serif is found on numerous Irish inscriptions, including the dated Kilnasaggart inscription of *c.* 700, *CIIC* ii, no. 946. This is, however, a secondary 'carryover' from book hand to epigraphy and is very rarely found in Welsh inscriptions, as in 978/49/B16, Llandyfaelog Fach, SO 034 324, +BRIAMAIL / FLOU, and in Llantwit Major 3, 1012/223/G65, an inscription dated to the eighth or ninth century (in the **d** of *dī* for *dei*).

16 For the use of slates, see the examples found on Inchmarnock, on the west side of Bute: C. Lowe, *Inchmarnock: An Early Historic Island Monastery and its Archaeological Landscape* (Edinburgh, 2008), 128–49.

letter: for the latter the more links were made the more rapid and the less formal the script.

Changes in the material available for writing also probably made a significant difference. When Gregory, bishop of Tours, wrote about 590 in his *Histories* about the unpleasant accusations of a neighbouring bishop, Felix of Nantes, he remarked ironically how sad it was that Felix was not bishop of Marseilles, the principal Mediterranean port for Francia, for Felix would then have had more than ample supplies of papyrus on which to write letters slandering honest folk.[17] This offhand observation shows, first, that papyrus was still being imported into post-Roman Gaul, but that it was not so easy to come by in Nantes, at the mouth of the Loire, as it was in Marseilles, the great port of Provence. Nantes, however, appears to have been a port for trade with Ireland and western Britain; and so the papyrus which was in short supply in Nantes is unlikely to have been plentiful in Britain.[18] Papyrus, then, may still have been imported into post-Roman Britain, but not in such quantities as to allow it to be the normal material on which Gildas could write his letters to Vinnian. In post-Roman Britain, therefore, it is best to think of both the novice and the trained scribe, when he was writing less permanent texts, such as drafts of books, as using wax tablets.[19] For documents the trained scribe may also sometimes have used wax tablets—for example, for letters—but at other times he is likely to have used single sheets of parchment, namely the normal material for books. In fourth-century Britain, parchment and wax tablet probably coexisted with papyrus; but in post-Roman Britain the domain of papyrus is likely to have been progressively shared out between wax tablet and parchment.

This change in the range of materials available may have encouraged a tendency which, in any case, was already there. Since a trained scribe, who habitually used book hands to write on parchment, would have first learnt cursive, before he ever rose to the status of trained scribe, and would have continued to use it on wax tablets, it was easy for one set of letters to influence the other. This tendency was evidently influential in the development of the Insular book scripts of post-Roman Britain, since such Insular letterforms as those of **s** and **r**, as well as of **g**, already mentioned, derived from New Roman cursive. If the usual late Roman allocation of materials—one for books, another for documents, and yet another for drafting texts—had to be rearranged, that could well have encouraged the crossover of letterforms from one type of script to another.[20] The letterform may have followed its appropriate type of text on to a new material, for example cursive forms

[17] Gregory of Tours, *Hist.*, v. 3.

[18] E. James, 'Ireland and Western Gaul in the Merovingian Period', in D. Whitelock et al. (eds.), *Ireland in Early Medieval Europe: Studies in Memory of Kathleen Hughes* (Cambridge, 1982), 376–7.

[19] Adomnán, *De Locis Sanctis*, Praef. and ii. 2 (ed. and trans. D. Meehan, *Adamnan's* De locis sanctis [Dublin, 1958], 36 and 42).

[20] Some books were still written on parchment even in Frankish Gaul, for example, *CLA* v, No. 573 (Avitus); the division made in the text only seeks to represent the norm, not a universal rule.

accompanying correspondence in a shift from papyrus on to parchment. The intrusion of cursive letterforms into epigraphy thus belongs within a broader pattern of crossovers, by which one script bequeathed one or more letterforms to another.

A corollary of this pattern of crossovers is that it can be difficult to decide whether a particular intrusive letterform in an inscription using roman capitals derived from cursive or from an Insular book script. To take one example, the characteristic Insular **s** was derived from New Roman cursive. What one needs in order to make a certain classification is a letterform in Insular script which was not derived from cursive, such as the 'oc **a**' characteristic of half-uncial, so-called because it resembles an *oc* run together into a single letter (see Illustration 3.1). Several considerations, however, make it likely that intrusive letters in the post-Roman period, 400–600, were more likely to be derived from cursive than from an Insular book script. First, the most common intrusive letters are **f** and **s**; **f** occurs most often in *filius* 'son' (typically in the genitive singular *fili*) frequently in a ligature with the following **i**; its use in what may, in the context of post-Roman British epigraphy, be called a formula word and in a ligature make it more likely that it derives from cursive than from the high-grade book script, half-uncial. An intrusive **s** often occurs at the end of a word, especially when space is being saved. This, similarly, makes it unlikely that it derives from a high-grade script. Moreover, similar intrusive letters are well attested in Roman Britain in such less grand inscriptions as those on building stones; at that period and in that category of stone an intrusion from half-uncial is scarcely conceivable.[21]

The cursive letterforms intruded into roman capitals have usually in the past been termed 'half-uncials';[22] but for further reasons this is unlikely to be correct. The half-uncial script, as we have seen, was the grand book script of post-Roman Britain and Ireland (and, later, many Anglo-Saxon scribes as well). Even though, in its Insular form, it has special characteristics, it is nevertheless quite plainly a local variety of the half-uncial which became an important book script in the late Empire (it has been claimed that it derived from Africa).[23] This was the script which, in its fully developed form, was to be employed for such calligraphic masterpieces as the Book of Kells and the Lindisfarne and Lichfield Gospels. It is securely attested in Welsh book production in the *Liber Commonei*, written 817 × 835. In later Welsh inscriptions, notably many of those from Glamorgan, dating to the period 750–1100, this half-uncial script was undoubtedly used, as one can tell from the distinctive *oc* form of **a**.

It is essential, however, to distinguish the historical context of these later inscriptions from the context of their post-Roman predecessors. By the ninth

[21] Examples are: *RIB* 1817 (cursive **A** and **F**), 1821 (**s**).

[22] As by Nash-Williams, *ECMW*, *passim*, and by Jackson, *LHEB*, 159, although both also noted the presence of 'Roman cursive', *ECMW* 10, or 'vulgar and cursive forms', *LHEB* 159. Yet, once noted, cursive was hardly mentioned thereafter.

[23] B. Bischoff, *Mittelalterliche Studien*, 3 vols. (Stuttgart, 1966–81), i. 1–4.

Illustration 3.1. Llantwit Major 3, possibly to be dated to the third quarter of the eighth century (see below, 138), with a basis of half-uncial letterforms (note the characteristic **oc** form of **a** in lines 5 and 6), and with the geometrical 'gate-**M**' in line 3 alongside the half-uncial form of the same letter. © The National Museum of Wales.

and tenth centuries it was becoming increasingly common for lay people to be buried in ecclesiastical cemeteries—in the forerunners of the churchyards of today. Most of these later inscriptions are associated with churches, some of them with major churches, such as the elaborately decorated cross with accompanying inscription erected by Abbot Samson at Llanilltud Fawr to commemorate himself and King Ithel.[24] At this period, Llanilltud Fawr may have been the normal royal cemetery-church for the dynasty of Gwent and Glywysing. It is thus not in the least surprising to find epigraphic evidence for a grand book script at such a church as Llanilltud Fawr. Similarly, in Ireland, from no later than *c*.700, there were inscriptions which also employed half-uncial. Indeed, there one can see plenty of examples in which even the serifs of Insular book scripts have been imitated in inscriptions, something which was not normal in Wales.[25] Again, these inscriptions, unlike most Irish ogham inscriptions of the earlier period, were usually erected at churches, the great majority at a single monastery, Clonmacnois.

The context of the early British inscriptions was quite different, for the post-Roman period was one in which lay people, unlike monks and clerics, were not yet normally buried in church cemeteries.[26] True, in Dyfed about 70 per cent of inscriptions ended up by being associated with churches, whereas only 40 per cent did so in the north-west, roughly Gwynedd.[27] But this high proportion in Dyfed is probably best explained by supposing that, in that area, old lay cemeteries were later sanctified by having a church built on the site: the church came, secondarily, to the cemetery; the cemetery was not attached to a church from the start.[28] In the post-Roman period epigraphic letterforms were more likely to have been affected by cursive, which was relatively widely used, rather than the book script, half-uncial, used only for special texts and written by the trained scribe, most often to be found in important churches.

One reason why it was natural to think of half-uncial as the source of these intrusive letterforms was precisely that half-uncial was the grandest Insular book script. It was at the top of the hierarchy of scripts deployed by the trained scribe. Memorial inscriptions on stone were similarly grand affairs, designed to preserve the fame of eminent persons. So much is obvious for King Ithel, commemorated by Abbot Samson; but one good reason why so many of the post-Roman inscriptions have Irish connections is that the Irish settlers formed a dominant minority anxious to proclaim their dominance in a traditional Roman military fashion, by epigraphy on stone, over a corner of an old Roman province. Hence it was reasonable to think that the source of the intrusive letters should have been the grandest book script, especially because, as we have seen, it was half-uncial rather than the humbler minuscule that was normally used for inscriptions from the eighth to the end of the eleventh century.

[24] Llantwit Major 3, 1012/223/G65. [25] See n. 15 above.

[26] See below 598–9. [27] Edwards, *Corpus*, ii, p. 33.

[28] [A.] C. Thomas, *The Early Christian Archaeology of North Britain* (London, 1971), 67–8.

The history of one unusual letterform illustrates both why scholars might perceive half-uncial as the source of most intrusive letters and also why this is unlikely to be correct. In both Old and New Roman cursive a possible form of **n** looks like a minuscule **h** turned upside down so that the long vertical stroke remains on the left but the right-hand stroke goes upwards rather than downwards.[29] This appears in a roman capital inscription, dated to the sixth century, Llanychâr 1, 440/335/P48, for which we depend on a drawing by Lhuyd. It also occurs in a later inscription, Tregaron 2, 995/133/CD33, dated to the ninth century. Finally, it was used, again in the ninth century, on the Pillar of Eliseg, Llantysilio-yn-Iâl 1. By the ninth century this cursive letter had thus been accepted among the letterforms of Welsh half-uncial. The issue can then be stated simply: at what point in its progression from Roman cursive to Welsh half-uncial did the normal home of this letter in the eyes of contemporaries cease to be cursive and become half-uncial? For the traditional view to be correct, this must already have happened by the sixth century; yet it would be easier to suppose that it happened in the seventh century when the old distinctions between roman capitals for epigraphy, cursive for documents, and half-uncial for the grander form of book broke down.

However natural it may be to see half-uncial as the source of intrusive letters in inscriptions using roman capitals as their base, the temptation should be resisted. First, the diagnostic half-uncial *oc* **a** is not among the intrusive letters. Although some intrusive letterforms, such as **g**, **d**, and **t**, do resemble half-uncial letters, they also occur in cursive scripts and are thus non-diagnostic. There is no evidence until the ninth or tenth century of any attempt to render in British epigraphy the specific traits of Insular book scripts, such as the serifs—which do, however, appear in Irish epigraphy from the early eighth century onwards.[30] Moreover, if we consider the context, burial in non-ecclesiastical cemeteries, it is probable, as we have seen, that the more widely used cursive was the source rather than the specialized half-uncial. It is also helpful to remember the three stages of an inscription's production: composition of the text, *ordinatio* (laying out, by paint or charcoal the text upon the stone), and the final incision of the letters. Composition of a text for epigraphy, like other draft texts, is likely to have been in cursive script upon a wax tablet. Only at the stage of *ordinatio* would it be appropriate to shift to the distinctively epigraphic letterforms, roman capitals. The process of production was thus one in which it would not be surprising if cursive forms from the first stage occasionally intruded themselves into the second stage, *ordinatio*, and then into the final stage, the incision of the letters in the stone. When we turn from epigraphy to scribes writing on parchment, an analogous transfer may well account for the intrusion

29 A good example is the second letter of E. M. Thompson, *An Introduction to Greek and Latin Palaeography* (Oxford, 1912), 328, Plate 111, and see the table, pp. 336–7. Angular forms which show its derivation from a cursive form of a roman capital **N** are found in Tedeschi, *Congeries*, C-30, S-6, and IOM-2.

30 An inscription on a pillar-stone, *CIIC* ii, no. 946 (Kilnasaggart, barony of Upper Orior, Co. Armagh, grid ref. J 062 148) appears to name someone whose obit is in the Annals of Tigernach, *s.a.* 715 = 716. This is in half-uncial with serifs.

of cursive forms into Insular book scripts, since any new text finally written in half-uncial or minuscule on parchment is likely first to have been drafted in cursive on wax tablet.

The explanation of the other type of intrusive letter, 'geometrical capitals', is less certain. In a few later inscriptions in Ireland and Northumbria, they formed the base letterforms, and not just intrusions; but this only once happened in Wales.[31] There, the geometrical capital was always an intrusive form on stone; moreover it continued to be so even in the later period, when half-uncial was the base script for epigraphy.[32] Another possible clue is that, when they were used among the 'decorative capitals' of Insular gospel books, they were not letters formed by writing with a pen but were drawn and then decorated. There is no sign that they ever had a home among book scripts formed by writing with a broad-edged pen. Finally, they were constructed according to two principles: first, and most importantly, the substititution of straight lines and angles in place of curves; and, secondly, the avoidance of acute angles such as those found in a standard roman capital **M**. These clues point towards a form of lettering in which, for technical reasons, these two principles would sensibly be followed. This cannot have been a book script on parchment; nor can it have been a form of lettering which had its home on stone, since the incised geometrical capitals in Welsh inscriptions were an intrusive form.[33] This indicates by a process of exclusion that either metal or wood is likely to have been the starting place.

Here we meet a formidable difficulty. We have a metal object—the Ardagh Chalice from south-west Ireland—on which display capitals were used, both geometrical and curvilinear forms; but, because wood survives so much less well, we do not have a range of examples of lettering on wood which can be examined to see what letterforms were employed: in the British Isles there is little other than the lettering on St Cuthbert's coffin and portable altar.[34] There is an analogous problem over the history of the Insular free-standing cross. Textual evidence suggests that such crosses are likely to have been in wood; and a feature in the design of some stone crosses has attractively been explained as a carryover from the construction of wooden crosses.[35] A similar argument can be used to identify the origin of geometrical capitals. The display letters on metal used both curvilinear and geometrical forms: metal, therefore, was not the material which induced the adoption of the two principles of the geometrical letter—straight lines and angles in

[31] The SATVRNBIV inscription on Ramsey Island: *Corpus*, St Davids 10, P99.

[32] As on the Caldey Island inscription, 427/301/P6; note that the ogham inscription, although on the same stone, is quite separate.

[33] *Pace* M. P. Brown, *The Lindisfarne Gospels: Society, Spirituality and the Scribe* (London, 2003), 229; J. Higgitt, 'The Display Script of the Book of Kells and the Tradition of Insular Decorated Capitals', in F. O'Mahony (ed.), *The Book of Kells* (Aldershot, 1994), 217.

[34] B. Dickins, 'The Inscriptions upon the Coffin', and C. A. Ralegh Radford, 'The Portable Altar of Saint Cuthbert', in C. F. Battiscombe (ed.), *The Relics of Saint Cuthbert* (Oxford, 1956), 305–7, 326–34. For the Roman period, see *RIB* ii, fasc. 4, 1–27.

[35] Tírechán, *Collectanea*, c. 41, ed. L. Bieler, *The Patrician Texts in the Book of Armagh* (Dublin, 1979), 154–6; D. Kelly, 'The Heart of the Matter: Models for Irish High Crosses', *JRSAI* 121 (1991), 105–45.

place of curves and the avoidance of acute angles. Wood, however, is much more promising, because its grain could well have made it considerably easier and safer to prefer straight lines to curves. It is likely that planks were used which were cut from the central part of a trunk downwards, so that the lines of the grain would run vertically up and down the plank. Modern letterers on wood tend to prefer surfaces from across the top of a section of trunk, so as to avoid the vertical lines of the grain; but such pieces are only appropriate for indoors. The grain of the wood thus accounts for the first principle, straight lines in place of curves; but it also explains the second, the avoidance of acute angles, since the wood inside such an acute angle was liable to lift. For practical reasons, therefore, the home of the geometrical capital is very likely to have been in wood. Intrusions in lettering on stone were a carryover from one medium to another. The coexistence in inscriptions of the intruded geometrical letters side by side with curvilinear letters from the normal repertoire of roman capitals is likely to lie behind the later coexistence in Insular display capitals of geometrical and curvilinear forms, the latter being principally derived from half-uncial.[36]

The intrusions from cursive could be explained in part by remembering the three stages of production: composition of the text, *ordinatio*, and incision on the stone. The carryover of cursive letterforms worked in the same direction: from the cursive draft on the wax tablet to the *ordinatio* on the stone, and then to the third stage, the incision. For geometrical intrusions, however, it must have worked differently. Here the second stage is likely to have been crucial, provided we may make an assumption that the *ordinator* was accustomed to laying out lettering on wood as well as on stone. The third stage is less likely to have been relevant, since a standard technique used in Welsh inscriptions to make incisions on stone was to punch out the groove: the punch marks are quite often still visible, in spite of weathering.[37] Use of a punch, however, suggests a smith rather than a wright. Moreover, the alliance of *ordinator* and smith will readily explain why geometrical letterforms were also adopted in metalwork.

The implication of the inscriptions is that there was a vast difference between the world of post-Roman Britain and the Wales of the ninth and tenth centuries, between the Britain of Gildas and the Wales of Asser. In post-Roman Britain, literacy still existed widely beyond the Church; similarly, lay burials were not yet normally in churchyards. Epigraphy still continued in the traditional roman capitals with occasional intrusions from the cursive which was the 'common script' as well as the documentary hand of late Antiquity. In the ninth and tenth centuries, epigraphy, where it still persisted (mainly in the major churches of the south), was a concern of churchmen and their patrons. To pursue the contrast, however, we need to consider the inscriptions in the light of what could be concluded in the previous

36 So, for example, in the bottom line of the *Christi autem generatio* page in the Lindisfarne Gospels, f. 29r, the **a** of *mater* is the *oc* type from half-uncial, while the first **a** of *Maria* is from roman capitals and the second **a** again from half-uncial.

37 Redknap and Lewis, *Corpus*, 123; good examples include 986/62/B34, 1011/220/G63, 1013/222G66, 1024/255/G117.

chapter on the nature of British Latin. The case advanced there was that British Latin was a spoken language in the period of the Class I inscriptions, but that it had ceased to be a language learnt in infancy by the time of the half-uncial inscriptions. That argument, however, raises the difficult issue of dating the inscriptions.

2. DATING

So far I have assumed that the inscriptions in roman capitals belong to the post-Roman period, roughly 400–600, and that the half-uncial inscriptions are later. This now needs to be justified and, if necessary, refined. I shall exclude the revival of capitals which has been assigned to the late eleventh and twelfth centuries, since that is beyond our period.[38]

What has until recently existed is a pair of typologies for monuments as a whole, those of Nash-Williams and W. G. Thomas.[39] To their work has recently been added a discussion of the dating of the early inscriptions on palaeographical grounds by Tedeschi and of the dating on linguistic grounds of the Celtic elements in the inscriptions as a whole, both early and late, by Sims-Williams.[40] To a large extent, the typologies of Nash-Williams and Thomas have the same function, essentially classifying the monuments into groups; any chronological implication comes later. Tedeschi and Sims-Williams, however, have both proposed relative datings, the one epigraphic and the other linguistic. For Tedeschi, some letterforms are earlier than others: they cannot, by this method, be given absolute dates, but they can be sorted into groups, which have a chronological relationship with each other. Similarly, with Sims-Williams: he operates with a sequence of sound changes which can, in general, be dated one relative to the other. Again, any absolute chronology comes later, on the basis of those few monuments for which an absolute date is available, coupled with some general historical probabilities—for example, that the ogham inscription from Wroxeter and the Latin inscriptions from Wareham in Dorset are unlikely to be later than the seventh century, since, in the eighth century, those places were less likely to contain Irish or British elements.[41]

The typologies of Nash-Williams and Thomas are as follows on Table 3.2 (I place them in parallel since Thomas's system was explicitly intended as a refinement of Nash-Williams; it is largely followed by Redknap and Lewis, *Corpus*).[42]

Broadly, at least, these are helpful classifications. Inevitably there are problems of classification, some arising from stones that have both an inscription of Group I and a cross of Group II, others arising from uncertainties over the original position of a stone. Some of Thomas's Class C may not, in origin, have been recumbent, but

[38] For the revived use of capitals, see e.g. W. Davies et al., *The Inscriptions of Early Medieval Brittany*, 248–57 (M9 and M10, Saint-Gildas-de-Rhuys).

[39] Nash-Williams in *ECMW* 1–49; Thomas in RCAHMW, *An Inventory of the Ancient Monuments in Glamorgan*, i, Part 3, *The Early Christian Period* (Cardiff, 1976), 18–34.

[40] Tedeschi, 'Osservazioni', and *Congeries*, 3–81; Sims-Williams, *CIB*.

[41] 1061/DSD-15; and see below 189.

[42] Redknap and Lewis, *Corpus*, 59–67; cf. Edwards, *Corpus*, 49–54.

Table 3.2. The typologies of Nash-Williams and Thomas

Nash-Williams	Thomas
Group I: unshaped or roughly shaped stones with Latin and/or ogham inscriptions	Class A: corresponds to Nash-Williams' Group I
Group II: unshaped or roughly shaped stones with an incised or lightly carved cross; normally uninscribed	Class B: pillar-stones with incised cross Class C: recumbent grave slabs with incised cross
Group III: crosses, either free-standing or carved in relief on shaped slabs; some have inscriptions	Class D: standing sculptured slabs Class E: pillar-crosses, usually composite Class F: other decorated stones (usually placed here because difficult to classify)

rather vertical monuments; the slablike shape may sometimes be explained as much by the nature of the stone, and thus how it could best be quarried, rather than its ultimate function.

Some chronological implications have been seen in the nature of the monuments themselves, without adducing external evidence. It was important to Nash-Williams's argument that some crosses on stones bearing inscriptions of Group I were clearly added later than the inscriptions; but, on a number of stones, the cross and inscription may be contemporaneous. Again, Nash-Williams evidently saw his Group III as the culmination of the early Welsh incised cross: there was a real progression from Group II to Group III. Against this is the possibility that the distinction between these two groups may have had more to do with the wealth of the patron who could muster the resources to put up a more elaborate cross than with any chronological progression from simple beginnings to more elaborate and developed forms. Or, again, both of these interpretations might be true, in that a good many Group II monuments were earlier than those in Group III, but others were contemporaneous with them—the poor relations of grander crosses. It seems impossible to prove that Group II did not begin during the period of Group I and persist into the period of Group III.[43]

Sims-Williams's dating works by establishing a sequence of phonological change in British and then marking when a given change is reflected in the spelling used in an inscription. This confirms the broad shape of the chronology established from epigraphy. Where it is less conclusive is in closer dating of the numerous inscriptions belonging to the post-Roman phase, 400–600. The difficulties in the way of putting the inscriptions into a relative chronology are formidable. First and

[43] Compare the similar dating problems over the linear incised crosses of the West Highlands and the Hebrides: I. Fisher, *Early Medieval Sculpture in the West Highlands and Islands* (Edinburgh, 2001), 12–13.

foremost is the complex relationship between phonological change and changes in spelling. Most obviously, there is the possibility that traditional spellings may endure long after they have ceased to reflect any form of the spoken language. An example is the ogham version of the VOTEPORIX inscription, which retains a final -S (it should be before no. 21 in Sims-Williams's sequence of sound-changes) but already has Q > C before /o/ (it should be after no. 28): the retention of the final -S is probably a case of archaic spelling.[44] This is made worse by the likelihood that most of the inscriptions belong to a comparatively narrow time band, the two post-Roman centuries, 400–600, rather than being spread out more evenly across the entire period of Sims-Williams's enquiry, 400–1200. More fundamentally, what matters in dating an inscription is not, in fact, the date of a sound-change, but the date at which that sound-change begins to be represented in the spelling used in inscriptions. The sequence of sound-changes established by internal phonological logic will not necessarily match the sequence in which those changes emerged in epigraphic orthography. Hence, a sound-change A which, for reasons of phonological logic, has to occur before sound-change B may, nonetheless, be reflected in spelling later than B. Again, whereas there are no problems of logical circularity in arguing from the sequence of sound-changes, since the sequence is largely independent of epigraphic evidence, the situation is quite different for the sequence in which those changes emerged in spelling. A change in spelling will evidently be no earlier than a change in sound, but how much later it may be has to be established from somewhere; and for much of the period covered that has to be from the inscriptions. For some names, it is difficult if not impossible to decide whether they are Brittonic or Irish—or, indeed, Irish affected by the spelling conventions of British Latin. An inscription might, for example, commemorate an Irishman but be directed at a British readership; it might be designed by a speaker of Brittonic or of a Latin affected by Brittonic. One of the most important conclusions, after all, to which a study of the inscriptions leads is that three spoken languages existed side by side in post-Roman Celtic Britain: British, Latin, and Irish. These difficulties are what makes Sims-Williams's sifting of the possibilities so valuable, irritating though it may be to the reader who looks for quick answers. As for the proposed dating of the inscriptions, the problems noted by Sims-Williams and summarized above are less acute when there are several chronological symptoms within a single inscription. Often, however, all that one has to argue from is a single Celtic personal name.

Tedeschi's dating of inscriptions by epigraphy worked by first establishing two opposed types: one consists of inscriptions closely resembling third- and fourth-century Romano-British epigraphy and the other of inscriptions with letterforms which either are Insular or clearly prefigure Insular letters.[45] Other inscriptions are

[44] *CIB* 305, 307.

[45] Tedeschi, 'Osservazioni', 82. The early inscriptions are: Llangefni 1, 320/26/Gn-26; Penmachno 1, 393/101/Gn-31; Llanerfyl, 421/294/Gn-20; Whithorn 1, 520/Scot5/S-8; Hayle, 479/Ok16/C-8; the late ones are: Llangadwaladr, 970/13/Gn-25; Llanfihangel Cwmdu, 334/54/Gse-6/B21; St Fagans with Llanilltern, 1028/214/Gse-7/G119.

then placed in between these two extremes. There are thus two critical connexions in his arguments and one further, equally critical proposition. The two connexions are the link between his early type and Romano-British epigraphy and the link between his later type and Insular letterforms. The further proposition is that the inscriptions placed in between can be interpreted as a progression from one to the other, from the Romano-British type to the Insular type. In essence, this third element in his argument is close to Nash-Williams's method of dating the early inscriptions.[46] So also Tedeschi's late type resembles what Nash-Williams called 'mixed' inscriptions, although the latter included more examples.[47] A potential weak point for both Nash-Williams and Tedeschi is that there may have been no gradual progression from one type to another, but rather a fundamental switch from one type, roman capitals, to another, Insular. The extent to which cursive intrusions were admitted into inscriptions in capitals may have been as much a matter of local preference as of date. The three crucial elements in the argument will, therefore, be examined in turn: the link of the earlier type with Roman Britain, of the late type with Insular scripts, and the notion of a progression from one to the other.

The link between the earlier type and late Romano-British epigraphy is convincingly established. Tedeschi finds numerous letterforms on late Roman stones which anticipate those of post-Roman Christian epigraphy in Britain. Perhaps his most important contribution has been to show that post-Roman epigraphy is not a tradition imported from Gaul in the fifth century, as Nash-Williams was inclined to think, but rather a continuation of the Roman past within Britain. He does this by distinguishing features characteristic of late Romano-British epigraphy from features common to the epigraphy of the western provinces. The former, as well as the latter, continue into the post-Roman period; and hence there was a continuous British epigraphic tradition.

The second link is between his late type and Insular script. The examples cited are the Catamanus stone at Llangadwaladr in Anglesey (see Illustration 3.2), an inscription at Llanfihangel Cwm Du in Brycheiniog, and a third from Llanilltern near Cardiff.[48] The distribution—including one from the north-west and two from different parts of the south-east—is helpful; and it is crucial that the Catamanus stone has an approximate absolute date on the basis of more than one early historical source, provided we can accept that he was the father of the Cadwallon who was killed in battle in the autumn or winter of 634 and that the stone was inscribed soon after his death.[49] These three inscriptions belong to a small group which Nash-Williams called 'mixed-alphabet inscriptions', but which I shall call

[46] *ECMW*, pp. 12–13, and Appendix 1.

[47] *ECMW*, p. 12 n. 4.

[48] Llangadwaladr, 970/13/Gn-25; Llanfihangel Cwmdu, 334/54/Gse-6/B21; (St Fagan's with Llanilltern), 1028/214/Gse-7/G119.

[49] Bede, *HE* ii. 20; iii. 1; *Chronicle of Ireland*, 631. 1; 632. 1; *Annales Cambriae*, 613 (the obit of his father, Iago ap Beli in the same year as the Battle of Chester, which may have been slightly later, in 615: see note to *Chronicle of Ireland*, *s.a.* 613); *Early Welsh Genealogical Tracts*, ed. Bartrum, p. 9, Harl. Gen. § 1.

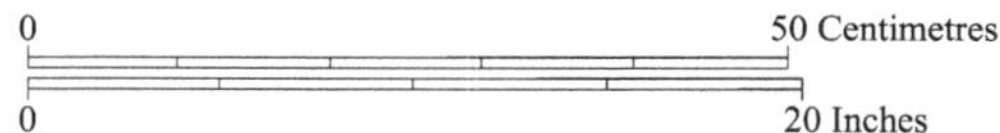

Illustration 3.2. Llangadwaladr, Anglesey, built into the north wall of the church; it commemorates Cadfan ab Iago, king of Gwynedd, and is therefore probably to be dated *c.* 625. It is the principal North Welsh example of an inscription with eclectic letterforms. The highly unusual form of **A** is attested in the 'Cathach', a psalter traditionally said to have been written by St Columba of Iona (d. 597). © Crown copyright: Royal Commission on the Ancient and Historical Monuments of Wales.

'eclectic' inscriptions, so as to distinguish them more clearly from inscriptions with intrusive letters. The vast majority of British inscriptions, early and late, had a basic script, into which some, as we have seen, intruded letterforms from elsewhere. What distinguishes eclectic inscriptions is that they had no identifiable base. Because they had no base, none of the letterforms can be described as having been intruded.

Illustration 3.3. This is an inscription from South-East Wales using eclectic letterforms; it is likely to be of the seventh century, and is now in the chapel of Llanilltern, but probably originally from slightly further south, close to what is now the Cardiff West service station on the M4: the letterforms include roman capitals, **V**, **N**, and 'angle-bar' **A**; **D**, **H**, **L**, and **T** have serifs, and, although they are different in construction, they are likely to be from half-uncial; the **G** is Insular (half-uncial or minuscule); the highly unusual **M** has a parallel in the Santon inscription on the Isle of Man. © Crown copyright: Royal Commission on the Ancient and Historical Monuments of Wales.

The CATAMANUS inscription is a complex case because it changes size in the middle and because it has an eccentric, and dominating, form of **A**. Inasmuch as it uses letters of different sizes, there may be something akin to the 'diminuendo effect' of Insular manuscripts, when a large initial is followed by a series of letters in decreasing size until the normal dimensions of the script are reached.

The first line is in a large size until, and including, the third **A**; similarly, the second line until the **P** of SAPIENTISIMUS. On the other hand, the eccentric **A** is always large; the best comparison for its form (which is not, in detail, consistent in all five examples) is an exceptional majuscule **A** resembling an uncial **A**, used as an initial or in diminuendo effects in some Insular manuscripts, beginning with the Cathach, roughly contemporary with this inscription. Because of the use of this **A**, there was no room for the distinctively half-uncial *oc* **a**. There is a tendency for some letter shapes to change with the change of size: the **M** and **N** in the first line are geometrical capitals (of the 'gate-**M**' type). In OMNIUM in the fourth line, they are quite differently formed, more like cursive. Because there are clear examples of geometrical capitals in the inscription, it may also be the case that the relatively square-shaped **U** is also derived from that alphabet, but this is not certain.

Non-diagnostic: **C**, **U**(?), **X**, **P**, **I**, **O**
Roman capital: **N** is a normal capital in line 2, although capital **N** occurs in half-uncial MSS
Cursive or Insular: **t**, **s**, **r**, **e**, **g**, **m**, and **n** in OMNIUM in line 4
Geometrical: **M** in line 1, beginning and end of line 3, **N** in line 1, **U** (if its square shape is significant)
Eccentric, possibly originally uncial, **A**

In the inscription from Llanfihangel Cwm Du the eclectic mixture is different: apart from non-diagnostic **I**, (1) cursive or Insular **T**, **G** and **F**; (2) geometrical **C** and **N**; (3) capital **E**, **S**, and a 'wigwam' angle-bar **A**. The inscription from Llanilltern is yet another mixture: apart from non-diagnostic **C**, (1) Insular **D**, **H**, **L**, and **T**, best classified as half-uncial since they have serifs, normal Insular or cursive **G**; (2) capitals, **V**, **N**, angle-bar **A**; (3) unusual **M** (see Illustration 3.3 above).

In none of these inscriptions is the **A** of the distinctively half-uncial *oc* form. In all these inscriptions it appears that there is no fixed standard set of letterforms, but that forms are being taken from at least three types. Because there is no norm, and they are not consistent in which letters they take from which script, apart from Insular or cursive **t** and **g**, they do not resemble each other in any other way than in their heterogeneous character. It is difficult to see how they can represent a single type towards which other inscriptions might be seen to progress. The inscriptions of the eclectic type are best seen as representing the collapse of one epigraphic tradition, that based on the roman capital, before it was replaced by another, based on book scripts, in particular half-uncial. On the other hand, the eclectic inscriptions cannot be regarded as constituting merely a brief transitional phase. On the one hand, the CATAMANUS inscription may be dated to *c.* 625, but, on the other, the inscription mentioning St David at Llanddewi Brefi[50] uses the form IDNERT that can hardly be placed earlier than the ninth century.[51] By this date epigraphically active churches in South Wales had, in general, been using half-uncial for their inscriptions for a century. Llanddewi Brefi was thus exceptionally conservative.

In order to test the notion of a progression, I shall examine selected inscriptions assigned to the fifth century by Tedeschi, but which are outside his select early group, and compare them with two other groups, one which he places in the first half of the sixth century and one in the second half of the sixth century. The select early group which Tedeschi used as his model for early inscriptions consisted of five horizontal inscriptions in roman capitals, without any intrusions.[52] There were either no ligatures or only one; some had formulae which could readily be paralleled in early Christian epigraphy outside Britain.[53] The specimen group of inscriptions assigned to the fifth century by Tedeschi is as follows:

Bryncir, 380/84/Gn-8, ICORI: Latin-ogham, but the Latin is horizontal; the final S of FILIVS cannot be a capital and would appear to be cursive ('rough pillar-stone', Nash-Williams, but actually wider than it is high).

Castell Dwyran, 358/138/Gso-8/CM3, Latin-ogham but the Latin is horizontal; no ligatures ('rough pillar-stone', Nash-Williams, but relatively broad and could be classified as a boulder).

Clocaenog, 399/176/Gn-9, SIMILINI: Latin-ogham, but the Latin is horizontal, no ligatures ('rough pillar-stone', Nash-Williams, but relatively wide, similar dimensions to the Voteporix stone).

Clydai 3, 431/308/Gso-17/P15, Clydai, DOBITVCI: Latin-ogham, the Latin inscription vertical; there is a change of size (line 1 large, line 2 smaller); reversed Z form of **S**. No cursive appears in the smaller size (contrast Cilgerran, 428/305/Gso-16/P12, and Jordanston, 432/312Gso-22/P20) ('rough pillar-stone', Nash-Williams, and relatively narrow).

[50] R. G. Gruffydd and H. P. Owen, 'The Earliest Mention of St. David?', *BBCS* 17 (1958), 185–93; eid., 'The Earliest Mention of St. David: An Addendum', *BBCS* 19 (1962), 231–2.

[51] *CIB* 274, and see below, 165.

[52] Tedeschi, 'Osservazioni', 82. The early inscriptions are listed above n. 45.

[53] As in Penmachno 4, 393/101/Gn-31; Llanerfyl, 421/294/Gn-20, and the Latinus stone at Whithorn 520/Scot5/S-8.

What is clear about this group is the significance attached to an inscription being horizontal as opposed to vertical, there being relatively few ligatured letters, and at most one intrusive letter.

The group placed in the first half of the sixth century includes the following:

> Llanddewi Brefi 1, 351/115/Gso-25/CD8: DALLVS DVMELVS; vertical; roman capitals with cursive **s** at the ends of both names (also found in Romano-British epigraphy, *RIB* 1821; curvilinear **M** (snakelike) = the second **M** in Tedeschi, 'Osservazioni', 81, Fig. 2, and compare Tedeschi, *Congeries*, i. 70, namely forms found in Roman Britain; one ligature.
>
> Penbryn 1, 354/126/Gso-41/CD28: CORBALENGI (see Illustration 3.4); vertical; roman capitals with no ligatures and no intrusive letters; the **R** is open-bowed and the diagonal stroke does not reach the lower line (the third shape in Tedeschi's reconstructed development, 'Osservazioni', p. 91).
>
> Pentrefoelas, 401/183/Gn-37: BROHOMAGLI; roman capitals with a cursive **s** at the end of EIVS; three ligatures.
>
> Llanfor, 417/282/Gn-24: CAVO SENIARGII; vertical; very possibly incomplete at the beginning; roman caps.; no intrusive letters. **C** conjoined with **AV**. The **R** is of the open-bowed type with the right-hand diagonal not coming down to the bottom line.

Here the inscriptions are set out vertically on the stone, unlike the predominantly horizontal inscriptions assigned to the fifth century. Where there are intrusive letters, they are cursive rather than geometrical and are also attested in Romano-British inscriptions.

The group assigned to the second half of the sixth century is represented by the following:

> Llantrisant, 325/33/Gn-6: horizontal; ligatures; cursive **q** and **d**; open-bowed **R** ('rough pillar-stone', Nash-Williams, but clearly a boulder).
>
> Mynydd Margam, 408/229/Gse-13/G77, BODVOCI: vertical; ligatures; **R** with horizontal right stroke (not all); upside-down angle-bar **A**; cursive **h** and **g** (a relatively narrow roughly quadrangular pillar-stone).
>
> Brithdir (Tirphil), 404/270/Gse-3/G28: vertical; eclectic (cap. **T**, **E**, **H**; geometrical **N**; cursive/Insular **g**, **r**, **s**, **m**).
>
> Cilgerran, 428/305/Gso-16/P12, Latin-ogham; Latin downwards; no ligatures; a change of size within the inscription; the smaller size has more cursive: **g**, **f**, **s**, **h**, **t** (beginning of lines large, end of lines small).
>
> Llandeilo 1, 434/314/Gso-35/P2, COIMAGNI; vertical, ligatured LI, cursive **m**, **g** (S form).

I here give a list of those monuments which Nash-Williams thought could be dated from textual sources,[54] together with one addition, the Ramsey Island inscription discovered since Nash-Williams published his work,[55] one redating of a monument

[54] Listed in *ECMW*, p. 1 n. 3; cf. Nash-Williams, 'Some Dated Monuments of the "Dark Ages" in Wales', *AC* 93 (1938), 31–56.

[55] E. Okasha, 'A New Inscription from Ramsey Island', 68–70.

Illustration 3.4. Penbryn 1. This inscription, in roman capitals and dated to the fifth or early sixth century, is situated near the coast north of Cardigan, on top of an earlier burial, which itself crowns a slight eminence commanding the immediate area. It is thus likely to be in its original site. The inscription includes the last mention of a people called the Ordouices by Tacitus. It is particularly striking because the personal name, Corbalengi, is Irish; it suggests that someone of Irish extraction could be considered to belong to a British people; he was probably described as an Ordovician because he was not buried in their territory. © Crown copyright: Royal Commission on the Ancient and Historical Monuments of Wales.

he thought was later, one addition from the Isle of Man, the GURIAT stone, and one from Cornwall, the DONIERT stone; information on these additional monuments is in square brackets. I have also removed one twelfth-century monument, *ECMW* 281, since it is far beyond the period of this book.

The reasonably probable datings can be reduced to those in Table 3.4 (it should be noted, however, that the degree of probability varies from case to case). These dated inscriptions cluster both geographically and chronologically: in the old kingdom of Gwent—and more specifically in Glywysing—and in the hundred

Table 3.3. The dating of inscriptions

Nash-Williams's dated monuments	Later revisions
Llansadwrn 1, 323/32/Gn-30, *c.* 530	Rejected because based on much later sources
Penmachno 3, 396/104/Gn-33, 540	There are problems with the interpretation of this fragmentary inscription; I have suggested a date 567 × 575.[56]
Castell Dwyran, 358/138/Gso-8/CM3, 540–50	The identification with Gildas's Vortiporius is very doubtful, but it has been suggested that Voteporix was an earlier member of the same dynasty, thus giving a *terminus ante quem*.
Cynwyl Gaeo, Maes Llanwrthwl 360/139/Gso-7/CM5, *c.* 550	Rejected because based on much later sources.
Llannor 2 390/96, ?6th century	Rejected because based on much later sources.
Llantrisant 1, 325/33/Gn-6, mid- to late-6th century	Rejected because based on much later sources.
Llangadwaladr 1, 970/13/Gn-25, *c.* 625	Some scholars accept this date; others, wrongly in my opinion, place the inscription later in the seventh century.
Llantwit Major 4, 1013/222/G66	If the Samson of this inscription is the same as the one in G65 (the next item), this one is also dated.
Llantwit Major 3, 1012/223/G65	Radford proposed an identification with the father of a *Fernmail filius Iudhail*, namely of the *Fernmail* who died in 775 (*AC*); this would suggest a mid-eighth-century date and Sims-Williams has adduced further evidence in its favour.[57] Thomas, however, proposed an identification with *Iudhail*, king of Gwent, who was killed in 848.[58]
[From outside Wales, one may add: Maughold, Isle of Man, 1066/Kermode, No. 48	The identification of GURIAT with the father of Merfyn Frych, who died in 844 is by no means certain but is generally accepted as probable.]
[St Davids 10 (Ramsey Island), 2005/P99	The SATVRNBIV of this inscription has been identified with a bishop who died in 831; this is no more than an attractive possibility.]
Llantysilio-yn-Iâl 1, 1000/182, mid-9th century	This dating of the Pillar of Eliseg is generally accepted.[59]
Llantwit Major 1, 1011/220/G63, mid-9th century	It is generally accepted that the person who had this monument erected to commemorate his father was Hywel ap Rhys, king of Glywysing, who died in 886.
[Redgate, Cornwall, 1054/Ok43	DONIERT is probably the *Dungarth rex Cerniu* of *AC s.a.* 875 = 876.]

56 See below, 235–8

57 C. A. Ralegh Radford, 'Two Datable Cross Shafts at Llantwit Major', *AC*, 132 (1983), 107–15, dated the epigraphy to before 800, making it possible that IUTHAHEL was Ithel, the father of *Fernmail filius Iudhail*, *ob.* 775; this would also allow an attractive identification of Abbot Samson and also ARTMALI: *CIB* 277–8.

58 RCAHMW, *Glamorgan*, i: 3, no. 933.

59 See below, 414–15.

Carew 1, 1035/303/P9, 1033–5	Radford's reading of this inscription, accepted by Nash-Williams, has been rejected more recently.[60]
St Davids 8, 1039/382/P97, 1078–80	This has to be dated in or after 1078, since it refers to Abraham as bishop, and he became bishop of St Davids in 1078. He died in 1080, but the inscription also refers to his sons and may, therefore, have been erected after his death. It is, however, unlikely to be much later than 1100.

years from the mid-eighth to the mid-ninth century. They do not help with one of the main problems, namely how to distinguish fifth- from sixth-century inscriptions.

The general considerations addressed so far will now be set alongside a series of sketches of the epigraphy of different British regions, with accompanying maps, beginning in the north, in southern Scotland, and moving southwards.

3. NORTH BRITAIN BETWEEN THE FORTH AND THE TYNE AND ALSO THE ISLE OF MAN[61]

In most of the other areas of post-Roman epigraphy in Britain the influence of Irish settlers is evident, partly in the presence of ogham inscriptions and partly in the widespread attestation of Irish personal names. North Britain (see Map 8) from the Firth of Forth south to the Cumbrian mountains, however, stands apart. The density of inscriptions is much less than in south-west or north-west Wales or Cornwall. There is no good evidence for Irish settlements at this period, even in Galloway, just across the North Channel from Ulster.[62] The Isle of Man, even though it is very close to Galloway, is strikingly different: the Irish presence is apparent, even though the island as a whole was regarded as British by Bede. In the south-west of the island there is a small group of purely ogham, and thus Irish-language, inscriptions, but not far away to the east is the Latin inscription at Santon; at the other end, in the north, there is a pair of stones containing both ogam and roman-letter inscriptions. They are, however,

[60] Edwards, *Corpus*, Carew 1, P9.

[61] This section depends heavily on K. Forsyth, '*Hic Memoria Perpetua*: The Early Inscribed Stones of Southern Scotland in Context', in S. M. Foster and M. Cross (eds.), *Able Minds and Practised Hands: Scotland's Early Medieval Sculpture in the 21st Century*, The Society of Medieval Archaeology Monograph, 23 (Leeds, 2005), 113–34.

[62] I accept the arguments of S. Taylor, 'The Element *Sliabh* and the Rhinns of Galloway', *History Scotland*, November/December (2002), 49–52, and id., '*Sliabh* in Scottish Place-Names: Its Chronology and Meaning', *Journal of Scottish Name Studies*, 1 (2007), 99–136, against the case put by J. MacQueen, 'Welsh and Gaelic in Galloway', *Transactions of the Dumfries and Galloway Natural History and Archaeology Society*, 32 (1955), 91–2; W. F. H. Nicolaisen, 'Scottish Place Names: 24. *Slew-* and *Sliabh*', *Scottish Studies*, 9 (1965), 91–106. Nicolaisen, 'Gaelic *Sliabh* Revisited', in S. Arbuthnot and K. Hollo (eds.), *Fuil súil nglais: A Grey Eye Looks Back* (Ceann Drochaid, 2007), 175–86, attempts to answer Taylor, but, in my judgement, unpersuasively.

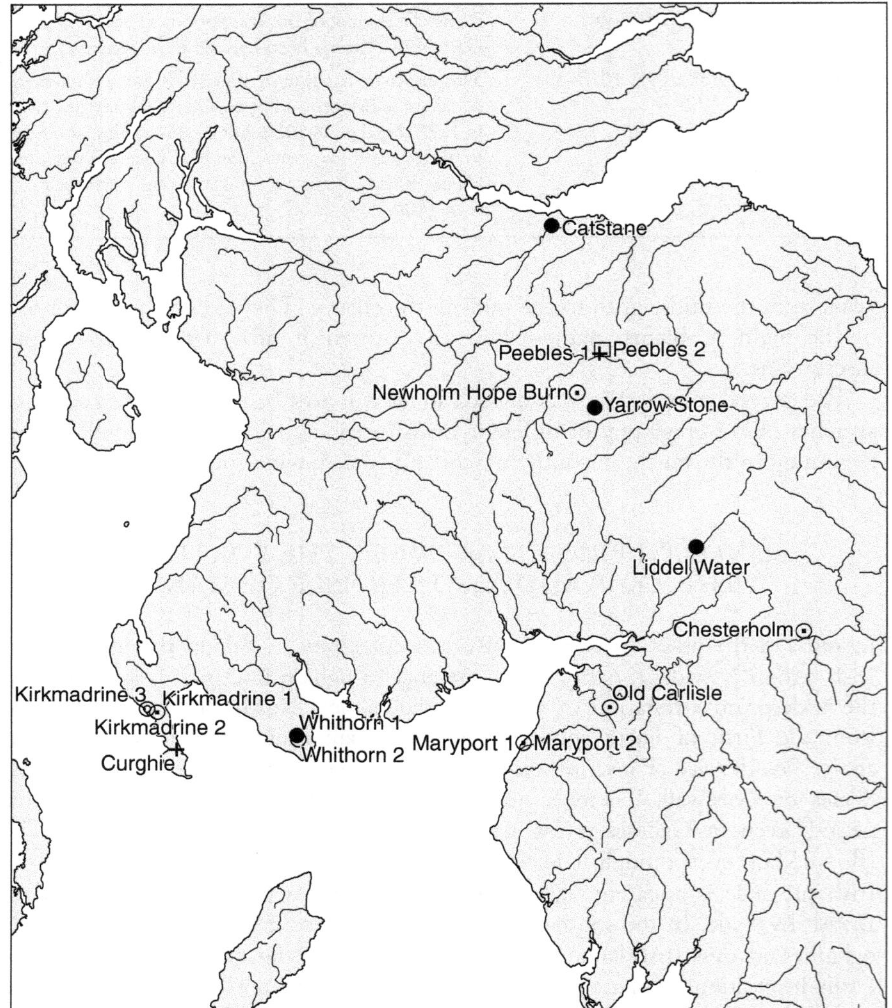

Map 8. North Britain

The epigraphy of Britain 'between the walls' is likely to owe a debt to that of the Carlisle area, at the western end of Hadrian's Wall (Maryport, Old Carlisle, and Chesterholm). From there it spread in two directions, west to the Rhinns of Galloway, and north to the Forth, the boundary between the Gododdin and the Picts.

of very different character: at Knock-e-Dooney there is an early bilingual inscription of the type found in Wales and Dumnonia; at Ballavarkish on the east coast, however, a cross-slab was inscribed with several names, one of which is in ogham, the others being in Insular letters (the names are both Irish and British).[63] Since the ogham inscription is on the left arm of the cross-slab (from the spectator's point of view), it can hardly be early, even though the form of the name, taken on its own, could be taken to be no later than the sixth century.[64] One of the names in the roman alphabet is in geometrical letters, while others are in minuscule; they may well be of different dates. The presence of a *Malbren scriba* commemorates a scholar, very probably attached to a church, whose name is apparently Irish.

In the middle of the island, concentrated around Maughold on the east coast, are the inscriptions that have no Irish connections, whereas they do betray an Anglo-Saxon as well as a British presence. The central east-coast group is also, like the Ballavarkish stone further north, on the whole later: for example the inscription commemorating a Gwriad who may well be the father of Merfyn Frych, later king of Gwynedd *c.* 825–844, is in half-uncial, not roman capitals.

The distribution of the British inscriptions of southern Scotland and the north of England resembles two arms extending westwards and northwards from the area around Carlisle and the western half of Hadrian's Wall. The first, the westward arm, stretches from Maryport, a Roman naval base on the coast of Cumbria, and Old Carlisle to Galloway, to Whithorn and Kirkmadrine. The second, the northern arm, goes up the Liddel Water, across the Southern Uplands, by the valley of the Yarrow, north to Peebles and to the Catstane (now in the precincts of Edinburgh airport, but not far from the Roman fort at Cramond on the Forth). The likelihood is that the area of the Wall was the starting point: first, Romano-British inscriptions are preponderantly associated with military centres, and the area of the Wall thus saw a major concentration; and, secondly, there are epigraphical links between the inscriptions of the Wall and those further west and north.

The context of some inscriptions is ecclesiastical, but most appear to be secular. The most clearly ecclesiastical is the group furthest west, at Kirkmadrine in the Rhinns of Galloway.[65] What may be the first in the series commemorates two churchmen, one with a Latin name, Viventius, the other with a British name but given a Latin ending, Mavorius.[66] They are called *sancti et praecipui sacerdotes*, 'holy and outstanding bishops/priests' (*sacerdos* was often used for a bishop as well as for a priest).[67] Similarly the *INITIUM ET FINIS* 'the beginning and the end' of the third inscription is unambiguously ecclesiastical.[68] The provenance of the

63 Kermode, *Manx Crosses* (1994), Appendices, pp. 15–16, *CIIC* 1068 (but 1069 in the plates), *CIB* 348.

64 *CIB* 84 (and n. 410), 129–30, 204, 307, 320.

65 *CIIC* 516–18, Tedeschi, *Congeries*, S-4, S-5, and S-6; D. Craig, 'The Provenance of the Early Christian Inscriptions of Galloway', in Peter Hill, *Whithorn and St Ninian: The Excavation of a Monastic Town 1984–91* (Stroud, 1997), 614–19 at 617–18.

66 *CIB* 33.

67 Compare *Collectio Canonum Hibernensis*, ed. Wasserschleben / ed. R. Flechner, i. 1.

68 Cf. Apoc. 1: 8.

inscriptions is the churchyard; and, if one takes together the provenance and the nature of the texts, it becomes very likely that Kirkmadrine lies on the site of an important post-Roman church of episcopal status.[69] The lost Curghie inscription further south in the Rhinns commemorates a *Ventidius subdiaconus*; here too the content of the inscription marks it out as ecclesiastical.[70]

Whithorn, further east in the Machars, is the site of one early inscription, the 'Latinus stone', with another a short distance to the south.[71] Some time after the Northumbrian conquest, Whithorn became the site of a bishopric. Bede's account makes it clear that the bishop in 731 was the first English bishop and had only relatively recently been consecrated.[72] The view of the past of the church communicated to Bede, very probably by the first bishop, Pehthelm, envisaged an earlier British episcopal church on the site, and claimed that it was the base from which Bishop Ninian converted the southern Picts between the Forth and the Mounth.[73] According to Bede, Whithorn, *Candida Casa*, was the burial place of Ninian 'where he himself and very many holy men rest in the body'. The Bernician church of Whithorn was thus held to be sanctified by the graves of holy Britons—a unique claim in Bede's *Historia Ecclesiastica*. Finally, Bede asserts that Ninian's Christianity was entirely Roman in character: 'at Rome he was correctly taught the faith and mysteries of the truth'. He was quite unlike the Britons of his own day.[74]

Excavation has demonstrated that Whithorn was an important settlement before the Northumbrian acquisition of the site.[75] How far the archaeology has vindicated Bede's account remains uncertain. For one thing, only part of the site was excavated; and, for another, the epigraphic evidence does not attest its ecclesiastical character in the way that the inscriptions at Kirkmadrine certainly do for that church. Two British inscriptions are critical: the one found on the site is relatively early, but not evidently ecclesiastical in nature, while the other, although undoubtedly ecclesiastical, is a little way to the south of Whithorn and is likely to be later.

The early inscription on 'the Latinus stone' is now thought not to have had a chi-rho above it, as has been asserted;[76] the text is arranged in horizontal lines as follows:[77]

[69] On the name see Watson, *History of the Celtic Place-Names of Scotland*, 162–3.

[70] 2023/Scot4; NX 127 382. The name is Latin: M. Handley, 'The Origins of Christian Commemoration in Late Antique Britain', *Early Medieval Europe*, 10 (2001), 177–99, at 194 n. 132.

[71] *CIIC* 520 and 519, Tedeschi, *Congeries*, S-8 and S-9.

[72] *HE* v. 23.

[73] *HE* iii. 4; Pehthelm is cited as a source in v. 13 and 18. Bede has ablative Nynia, Alcuin genitive Nynia and Nyniga, the latter an Old English spelling, *Epp*. 273, MGH Epp. iv. 431–2; the *Miracula Nynie Episcopi*, ed. K. Strecker, MGH, Poetae Latini Medii Aevi, iv. 943–61, has nom. Ninia (l. 18), Nyniau, ll. 171, 402; the *Hymnus*, ibid. 961–2, Nynia (l. 11) and acc. Nyniam (l. 24).

[74] I. N. Wood, 'Britain and the Continent in the Fifth and Sixth Centuries: The Evidence of Ninian', in J. Murray (ed.), *St Ninian and the Earliest Christianity in Scotland*, BAR, Brit. Ser. 483 (Oxford, 2009), 77, notes the parallel of the *Vita Prima S. Samsonis*, i. 37, where the saint, then abbot of Ynys Bŷr, met Irish scholars, coming from Rome on their way back to Ireland.

[75] P. Hill, *Whithorn and St Ninian: The Excavation of a Monastic Town 1984–91* (Stroud, 1997), 26–40.

[76] K. Forsyth, 'The Latinus Stone: Whithorn's Earliest Christian Monument', in Murray (ed.), *St Ninian and the Earliest Christianity in Scotland*, 23; for the contrary opinion see, e.g., D. Craig, 'The Provenance', in Hill, *Whithorn and St Ninian*, 615.

[77] *CIIC* 520/S-8; NX 443 404.

TE [DOMIN]VM / LAVDAMV[s] / LATINV[s] / ANN[OR]VM / XXXV ET / fILIA SVA / ANNI V / IC sINVM / FECERVT[N?] / NEPVS / BARROVA/DI

The translation of everything except the last four lines is clear:

> We praise you, the Lord. Latinus aged thirty-five years and his daughter aged five.

This section, therefore, falls into two parts: the first, 'We praise you, the Lord', looks as if it might be from a hymn with seven-syllable lines; the second, with the indications of the ages of Latinus and his daughter, belongs to a standard type of late Roman memorial also attested at Llanerfyl in Montgomeryshire and St Erth, Hayle, in Cornwall; the Llanerfyl and Hayle inscriptions appear to be secular.[78] Comparable examples also include late Romano-British as well as continental inscriptions which give the age of the deceased in the same manner, as, for example, in some inscriptions from near Carlisle.[79] The latter, indeed, suggest that the most likely models for the Whithorn inscription were probably from the area around the western end of Hadrian's Wall; and they also suggest the likelihood of a fifth-century date for the Latinus stone.[80] Admittedly the normal phrase is *vixit* [.] *annos* 'lived for so many years', but the use of the genitive *annorum* without *vixit* is unlikely to mark a difference of function.[81]

The difficult section is *ic sinum fecerut(n?) nepus Barrouadi*. At least, however, we can begin to interpret it with the assurance that the inscription as a whole is a memorial to Latinus and his daughter. *Ic* can be taken to be *hic* here'; that seems the easiest solution even though British Latin of the fifth century may well have lost the neuter gender and final *-m*, so that *ic* could be 'this' and agree with *sinu(m)*. The latter possibility is by no means to be ruled out; yet, if this were the case, [*h*]*ic* rather than *hunc* would suggest that *sinum* was nominative and was not the object of the verb. *Sinum* has generally been interpreted as a spelling of *signum* 'sign' with the loss of *g* before *n*.[82] The verb is shown as *fecerut*[*n?*] because some scholars have detected a smaller size N ligatured with a preceding T;[83] but the most recent reading, by Tedeschi, merely has FECERVT.[84] If the intended form of the verb was *fecerunt*, as seems likely, it was third plural perfect, 'they made' or 'they have made'; and that ought to rule out taking *nepus Barrouadi*, 'the grandson of Barrovadus', as the subject. Only, therefore, if we disregard the plural form of the verb would a translation 'Here the grandson of Barrovadus made a sign' become possible.

78 Forsyth, '*Hic Memoria Perpetua*', 116.

79 *RIB* 856, 862, 863, 908. For this reason, Tedeschi, *Congeries*, i. 296, rejects the argument advanced by C. Thomas, *Whithorn's Christian Beginnings*, First Whithorn Lecture (Whithorn, 1992), 5–6, and id., *Christian Celts: Messages and Images* (Stroud, 1998), 106, that the stone is not a memorial.

80 Llanerfyl 421/294/Gn-20; Saint Erth, Hayle 479/Ok 16/C-8.

81 As argued by Thomas, *Whithorn's Christian Beginnings*, 5. The Llanerfyl stone in Wales, 421/294/Gn-20, also does not use *vixit*.

82 For this sound-change in British see *LHEB* § 86; Jackson dates it to 450 × 500; his initial date of 450 depends on his dating of the lenition of voiced fricatives, which may be too late; in any case, it does not rule out a fifth-century date for the inscription if *sinum* < *signum*.

83 *CIIC* 520; Thomas, *Whithorn's Beginnings*, 4, fig. 3.

84 Tedeschi, *Congeries*, i. 295–6.

If we accept that the verb is plural, there seem to be two possible approaches: either the singular *nepus* for *nepos* is an error for the plural *nepotes* or those who made the sign were Latinus and his daughter.[85] Both interpretations are difficult: to take *nepus* as an error for *nepotes* is a counsel of despair, an explanation that ought only to be accepted if all else fails. Although British and British Latin were losing distinctions of case, they were not losing the distinction between singular and plural. Yet it is also difficult to think of his five-year-old daughter being joined with Latinus as the subject of the verb *fecerunt*, especially if *sinum* refers to the monument. It has been suggested that the word is not a form of *signum* but merely *sinus*, 'fold, lap, bay' in the special sense of 'refuge'.[86] But no examples have been given to show that Insular Latin gave a meaning to *sinus* such that it was applied to places of refuge or sanctuary. The standard term for that was *refugium*.[87] Moreover, it has been pointed out that reference to the ages of the persons commemorated is a sure indication that the stone is a memorial of the dead. The best course, therefore, is to take the verb as plural, referring to Latinus and his daughter, and to look for an interpretation of *si(g)num* which would make it possible to say that the two dead persons, Latinus and his daughter, 'made a/the *signum*'.

Three parallels have been noted to the use of *signum* referring to a stone memorial: one Roman, one early second-century Romano-British inscription from Cirencester; and one Old English, with *sign* as a unique loanword, from Yarm.[88] All three are, in different ways, exceptional: the inscription from Cirencester is metrical and the choice of *signum* may have been influenced by the requirements of the metre; the Roman example is the only one cited by Diehl; the Old English stone is later and behind *sign* may lie some such Old English word as *beacen*. The parallels help to confirm that the word in the Latinus inscription is indeed *signum*; the Roman stone even shows the same loss of *g*. It would, however, be helpful if one could think of a particular reason why the word might be used in a post-Roman British inscription.

One clue to the meaning of *signum* in British Latin is offered by the loans from *signum* in Welsh and Irish. Two quite distinct meanings are attested: the first is 'sign' in the sense, inherited from Roman paganism, of an omen or augury; the second is Christian, 'blessing'.[89] An example of *swyn* in a thirteenth-century Welsh lawbook, *Llyfr Iorwerth*, may give a hint (given the date of the text it can be no more than a hint). The issue at stake is the paternity of a child: the mother proposes to swear a solemn oath affiliating her child to a man, whom she will name. The lawbook requires her to swear the oath in the man's church. The church is identified slightly differently

[85] The first view, that *nepus* was for a plural *nepotes*, is implied by the translation in J. R. Allen and J. Anderson, *The Early Christian Monuments of Scotland* (Edinburgh, 1903; repr. Balgavies, 1993), ii. 497.

[86] Thomas, *Christian Celts*, 106.

[87] Lifris, *Vita S. Cadoci*, § 25, ed. and trans. A. W. Wade-Evans, *Vitae Sanctorum Britanniae et Genealogiae* (Cardiff, 1944), 78–81.

[88] Forsyth, 'The Latinus Stone', 28–9, notes *RIB*, no. 103 (Cirencester); E. Diehl, *Inscriptiones Latinae Christianae Veteres*, 3 vols. (Berlin, 1927), ii. 248, no. 3630; E. Okasha, *Hand-List of Anglo-Saxon Non-Runic Inscriptions* (Cambridge, 1971), 130, no. 145 (from Yarm, N. Yorks.).

[89] An early example of *sén* 'blessing' is from Colmán's Hymn to Brigit, which begins *Sén Dé* 'God's blessing'; *Thesaurus Palaeohibernicus*, ed. W. Stokes and J. Strachan (2 vols., Cambridge, 1901–3; repr. Dublin, 1975), ii. 299.

depending on whether the man is a native or an alien: if he is a native, 'she and the son come to the church where his burial is' (namely, since he is evidently alive, where his family is buried); if the man is an alien, he will not have a family burial church within Gwynedd, so that she will, literally, 'come to the church in which is his sign-water', *dwfr swyn*, 'and where he takes communion'.[90] This indicates that in medieval Wales allegiance to a church is bound up with three things: where one's family or kindred was buried, where one made the sign of the cross with holy water, and where one received communion. The assumption is likely to have been that all three would, for the native, usually identify the same church. It may then be suggested that a similar set of linked ideas lies behind the phrase *fecerunt si(g)num*, namely that 'here they made the sign', because 'here' was their family burial church. 'Making the sign' was something one was expected to do in one's family burial church.

If this is what lies behind the phrase, it will help to explain the context of the inscription. First, it implies that at Whithorn there was a church cemetery, in which at least one family or kindred was buried. Secondly, because the fifth century lay far back into the period in which lay people were, in general, still buried in kindred cemeteries, not in churchyards, whereas monks and clergy were buried in ecclesiastical cemeteries, Latinus is likely to have been a churchman (presumably not a monk in the sense of someone who had taken vows of poverty, and chastity, since he had a young daughter). Finally, one of the oddities of the inscription (assuming that *nepus* is singular) is the placing of 'the grandson of Barrovadus' at the end, apparently isolated. If, however, the understanding is that 'here' is the church to which Latinus belongs as a churchman, the placing of *nepus Barrouadi* immediately after *(h)ic si(g)num feceru(n)t* 'here they made the sign' will make sense: in this period, the usual pattern was for churchmen to belong to ecclesiastical kindreds, as the First Council of Orléans (AD 511), c. 4, assumes for Gaul:[91]

> We have decreed, with regard to the ordination of clerics, that no layman shall presume to the clerical office, unless either by command of the King, or with the consent of the [local] judge, [but] the sons of clerics, that is, the sons, grandsons, and great-grandsons, who are bound to follow the order of their parents, shall be in the power and control of the bishops.

The descendants of Barrovadus were probably just such a clerical kindred as was envisaged by this council. A full translation along these lines would be:

> We praise you, the Lord. Latinus, aged thirty-five years, and his daughter, aged five, made the sign here, (he being) the grandson of Barrovadus.

Interpreted in this way, the inscription reveals something of the social context of the church.[92]

90 D. Jenkins, *The Law of Hywel Dda: Law Texts from Medieval Wales* (Llandysul, 1986), 132–4, translating *Llyfr Iorwerth*, ed. A. Rh. Wiliam (Cardiff, 1960), § 100/2–4. The second, more literal, translation is my own.

91 *Concilia Galliae A. 511–A. 695*, ed. C. de Clercq, CCSL 148A (Turnhout, 1963), 6.

92 For a different view, which interprets Whithorn as a secular site, see Forsyth, '*Hic Memoria Perpetua*', 116; ead., 'Latinus Stone', 37.

The second inscription was first attested as being on the land of High Mains farm, about half a mile south-south-east of the excavated site at Whithorn, probably on the old route towards the Isle of Whithorn.[93] It is attached to a cross of arcs supported on a stem that widens out at the base:[94]

[L]OCI / PETRI APV/STOLI 'The place of the Apostle Peter'

The first line of the inscription is arranged on either side of the stem, but the rest, *Petri apustoli*, is below it. Whereas the Latinus stone, by its reference to the ages of the deceased, looks eastwards towards Hadrian's Wall, this one looks across the Irish Sea—its distinctive 'fishtail' serifs, highly unusual in the context of post-Roman British epigraphy, take us southwards to an inscription at the end of the Lleyn Peninsula, and the combination of *locus* and St Peter find their closest parallel in Ireland, in an inscription dated to *c.* 700 and composed in Irish at Kilnasaggart in the borderland between the Airgialla and Conailli Muirthemne.[95] *Locus* 'place' may be used for a church or monastery, as in Welsh *mynachlog* 'monastery' and *loc* in Breton place-names; another example is on a lost inscription from Peebles.[96] The inscription south of Whithorn is, however, unique in British epigraphy of 400–700 in that it is clearly not a memorial.[97] One possibility is that it was erected on or close to an outer enclosure of the church at Whithorn, but it is also conceivable that the *locus* was quite distinct from the settlement at Whithorn.[98] The fishtail serifs derive from a type attested in Rome itself in the late fifth century.[99] The epigraphy and the text, taken together, show that the inscription belongs to a British monumental tradition, but of an unusual variety. A sixth-century date is plausible, although it has been dated to the seventh; it belongs to a British epigraphic tradition and is unlikely to be as late as the Northumbrian acquisition of the Machars (no later than *c.* 700).[100] The inscription, because it associates the *locus* with St Peter, may have given Bede's

[93] Craig, 'The Provenance', 616–17.

[94] *CIIC* 519/S-9; NX 446 395.

[95] Aberdaron 1, 392/77/Gn-2; Kilnasaggart, *CIIC* 946 (the donor died in 716: Charles-Edwards, *The Chronicle of Ireland, s.a.*).

[96] 2024/Scot 11; the place-name use is likely to be later and is almost entirely confined to Brittany: Padel, *Cornish Place-Name Elements*, 151–2.

[97] Tedeschi, *Congeries*, i. 298.

[98] See map 1. 4 in Hill, *Whithorn and St Ninian*, 6; the argument put forward by Craig, 'The Provenance', 616–17, that because this inscription is comparable with that at Kilnasaggart and because the latter probably marked a cemetery, therefore it did not function as a boundary marker, is incorrect: it may very well have done both, *EIWK* 259–67.

[99] A. E. Gordon, *An Illustrated Introduction to Latin Epigraphy* (Berkeley and Los Angeles, 1983), 184, Plate 64, no. 99 (AD 471).

[100] Forsyth, '*Hic Memoria Perpetua*', 127–30, inclines towards a sixth-century dating, Tedeschi, *Congeries*, i. 298, dates it to the seventh; Hill, *Whithorn and St Ninian*, 38, to the eighth, but Hill's reasoning fits uneasily with the associations with the Isle of Man and north-eastern Ireland noted by Craig, 'The Provenance', 616–17; there is no necessary inference from the known enthusiasm for St Peter shown by the Northumbrian church after 664 to the conclusion that other traditions did not revere the prince of the apostles.

informant, Pehthelm, the notion that Ninian was much more Roman in his attitudes than were, in Bede's eyes, most British churchmen.[101]

The British inscriptions of North Britain appeared, as we have seen, to form two arms going out from a centre near Carlisle. It now appears that the western arm was unusually ecclesiastical in context. This is not true, however, of the northern arm running up to the Forth, as well as of the inscriptions near Carlisle itself. We may take two examples. The first is in the valley of the Yarrow, one of the tributaries of the upper Tweed.[102] The letters are lightly incised making it impossible to read just with the naked eye. The text is a memorial, but of unusual length and phrasing (cursive letters in the inscription are here represented by lower-case letters in the transcription):

> HIC MEMORIA P*ER*(P)ETV(A) / (I)N LO\CO/ INsIgNIsIMI PRINCI/PEs NVdI / (ET) dVMNOGENI HIC IACENT / IN TVMVLO dVO FILII / LIBERALI
>
> 'Here in the place is a perpetual memorial. The most noble rulers Nudus and Dumnogenus lie here in the grave, two sons of Liberalis.'

The cursive letters (**d**, **g**, and **s**) and the scribal abbreviation for *per* indicate a background of Latin literacy. The two *principes* both have British names, but their father, Liberalis, has a Latin name. *Nudi* and *Dumnogeni* are examples of what appears to be Latin genitive forms used where the nominative would be required; moreover, if *Nudi* is, as seems likely, a later form of the Nodons attested as a god in the temple at Lydney, Gloucestershire, a name that became Middle Welsh Nudd, it has the wrong Latin declension.[103] This all reflects the collapse of the British and British Latin declensions. It is dated by Tedeschi to the second half of the sixth century.[104] That would mean that it belongs to a period within which the English of Bernicia established control over the area further east, around Bamburgh and Lindisfarne.

The second example is from further north, a tiny cross-slab at Peebles, probably from the site of the Cross Kirk:[105]

> NEITANO / SACERDOS 'The priest/bishop Neitanus'

The base letterforms are no longer roman capitals; chronologically it is appreciably later than the other northern British inscriptions. Steer saw the letterforms as half-uncial 'with the addition of a few roman capital forms as in contemporary manuscripts'. Broadly this is correct, but the **A** of NEITANO is one found in display letters,[106] not in half-uncial, whereas the **d** of SACERDOS is a minuscule form of cursive origin. The inscription is thus inconsistent in terms of the

[101] Compare Bede's readiness to use epigraphic evidence in *HE* i. 15.

[102] *CIIC* 515/Scot9/S-10, Yarrow Stone; RCAHMS, *An Inventory of the Ancient and Historical Monuments of Selkirkshire* (Edinburgh, 1957), no. 174. NT 3481 2744. I follow Tedeschi, *Congeries*, i. 298–9, in interpreting P*ER* in P*ER*(P)ETV(A) as an abbreviation.

[103] *CIB* 97 n. 506. Cf. NV[D]INTI, Cynwyl Gaeo, 359/141/Gso-3/CM4.

[104] Tedeschi, *Congeries*, i. 298–9.

[105] K. H. Steer, 'Two Unrecorded Early Christian Stones', *PSAS* 101 (1968–9), 127–8.

[106] As, for example, in the lettering accompanying the symbols of the evangelists in the Echternach Gospels.

Insular hierarchy of scripts: it ranges from the top grade most of the way to the bottom. To that extent, it might be associated with the group employing eclectic letter forms, of which the CATAMANVS inscription at Llangadwaladr in Anglesey, dated to *c.* 625, is the best known, but it is closer to contemporary book scripts.

The name is Celtic, with a Vulgar Latin ending *-o* in place of classical *-us*; it may be compared with Middle Welsh Nwython, but it also corresponds to the name of the Pictish king as spelt by Bede, *Naiton*, in Gaelicized form *Nechtan*; the Pictish comparison is the more likely, although it should be noted that in northern British genealogies the name occurs in a form likely to have been influenced by Pictish.[107] The late seventh- or early eighth-century date proposed by Steer is persuasive. The memorial may thus be dated after the final conquest of the Gododdin by the Bernician English and after the arrival of Aidan in Northumbria; and, in that case, it is vital evidence for the survival of churchmen who were not themselves either English or Irish under Bernician rule. It is an inscription with a Pictish name given a Vulgar Latin ending *-o*, as in British inscriptions, and with letterforms that echo the full range of Insular scripts from display letters down to cursive minuscule. This area, to the west of the great forest around Selkirk, is the part of the Tweed basin where evidence for British survival is strongest.[108]

The epigraphic evidence is thus important in showing that, in the post-Roman period, the northern Britons beyond Hadrian's Wall shared in the Latin culture bequeathed by the Empire. Latin was not merely the liturgical language of the Church, for it was also used to commemorate lay nobles, such as Nudus and Dumnogenus. In the far south-west, in Galloway, however, the surviving inscriptions are, uniquely for this early period, exclusively ecclesiastical. Northern Britain between Forth and Solway is also important in that it displays British epigraphy in an area much less subject to Irish influence than were most British territories further south.

The Isle of Man (see Map 9) offers one major contrast with the area between the Solway and the Forth–Clyde line: it has several ogham inscriptions, including both monolingual and bilingual examples, attesting the presence of Irish speakers. One inscription from southern Scotland may contain an Irish name (although this is disputed), but there are no examples using the ogham script.[109] Moreover, the distribution in the Isle of Man is straightfoward: the pure ogham inscriptions are in the south-west, the bilingual ones in the north; and between them, on the east coast, are all the non-Irish inscriptions. The fifth-century Spanish historian Orosius regarded the Isle of Man as Irish;[110] and this seems very likely to be true, since from the late fourth through much of the fifth century the Irish seem to have

[107] *CIB*, 179. The northern British form, Neithon, has, however, British *-th-*.

[108] See Map 2 in C. Stancliffe, *Bede and the Britons*, Fourteenth Whithorn Lecture (Whithorn, 2007), 26–7.

[109] 511/Scot10/S-7. Newholm Hope Burn, Manor Water, now in Peebles Museum, NT 192 307 (St Gordian's); RCAHMS, *Peeblesshire* (1967), i, no. 376; *CIB* 155–6 n. 922 (which notes that Jackson regarded it as British), 190, 310, 317. BARROUADI in the earlier Whithorn inscription might be Irish but there is a perfectly viable British etymology, *CIB* 120 n. 664, 320.

[110] Orosius, *Libri Historiarum aduersum Paganos*, ed. C. Zangemeister, CSEL 5 (Vienna, 1882), 1. 2. 82 (p. 30).

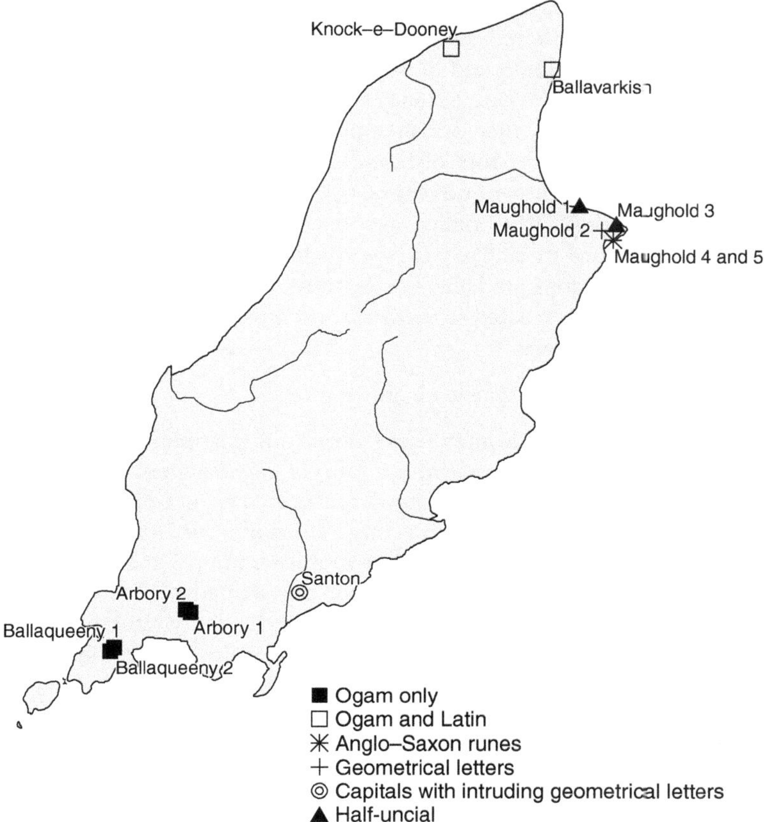

Map 9. The Isle of Man
The Isle of Man, of all the British regions, has the clearest differences in epigraphy between areas: the south-west is the area of pure ogham inscriptions, the north of bilingual inscriptions, Irish and Latin (and ogham and Roman letterforms); the intervening area has everything else, including all the later inscriptions.

had control of the sea separating them from Britain. Bede, however, who knew Orosius's work well and clearly used it here, changed the ethnic attribution of the island to British;[111] and this, too, is likely to be correct, since, as we shall see, the dynasty of Gwynedd from *c.* 825 until (with some interrruptions) 1282–1283 appears to have derived from the Isle of Man. Ultimately, after the Viking period, the Isle of Man would emerge speaking its own dialect of Gaelic, which it may well have shared with the Gaelic speakers of Galloway, only a few miles to the north.

Two possible stories can be told to account for the epigraphic and other historical evidence. First, the distribution of the ogham inscriptions makes it possible to

[111] Bede, *HE* ii. 9; the form of the name *Meuania* derives from Orosius (presumably for something like *Manauia*, later Manaw).

suppose that the island had always, in the pre-Viking period, had speakers of both British and Irish. The inscriptions suggest that, before the Vikings, the British and Irish may have been concentrated in different parts of the island; and the broader distribution of power in the Irish Sea may have decided which group was dominant.

The other possibility is that British supplanted Irish (Gaelic) only to be supplanted in its turn by a mixture of Scandinavian and Irish from about 900. In favour of the latter interpretation is the comparison with Galloway, where there is no good reason to think that Gaelic was spoken before the Vikings.[112] Moreover, the ogham inscriptions are all likely to be early, fifth or sixth century, whereas some of the British inscriptions are later. For example, an inscription at Santon in the south-east of the island, is dated to the seventh century by Tedeschi.[113] The text of the inscription is as follows:

AVITI MONOMENTI 'The tomb of Avitus'

Avitus is a well-known late Roman name, borne, for example, by an emperor from Gaul in the fifth century; *monomenti* is a form of *monumentum* 'memorial, tomb', the Latin word which gave Welsh *mynwent* 'cemetery, graveyard'.[114] Here it is clearly in one of the original Latin senses, 'memorial' or 'tomb'. Yet, although Welsh *mynwent* is some kind of parallel, the formula is unique in post-Roman British epigraphy, although it can be paralleled from continental and North African early Christian epigraphy.[115] Moreover the inscription is also very unusual in that it has epigraphic serifs. Serifs of any kind are very rare in British inscriptions; in Ireland scribal serifs are common in inscriptions from *c.* 700; but, because they are scribal in origin, they do not offer a parallel to this inscription.[116] The fishtail serifs attested in the later Whithorn inscription (LOCI PETRI APUSTOLI) and at Capel Anelog, Aberdaron, also had a clear continental derivation; and, like the Santon inscription, they indicated links between the Continent and the coastlands of the Irish Sea. The first **M** of MONOMENTI, however, is distinctively Insular, and is paralleled in an inscription at Capel Llanilltern, Glamorgan; the latter is also unusual in having epigraphic serifs.[117] Both the Santon and the Llanilltern inscriptions appear to reflect an external influence from the Continent at much the same date and also the influence of Insular scribal practice, probably in the seventh century.

A still later British inscription is from the coast between Maughold and Ramsey:[118]

112 See above, nn. 61–2.

113 *CIIC* 505/IOM-2. Santon. NGR SC 311 712. Kermode, *Manx Crosses*, no. 34 (p. 114) and Appendix A; *Manx Archaeological Survey, 5th Report* (1935), 21. Dug up when the present church was built in 1782.

114 For the linguistic issues raised by the inscription, see *CIB* 53 (and n. 202), 90, 96, 185, 198, 272.

115 Tedeschi, *Congeries*, i. 302.

116 For the distinction, see n. 15 above.

117 St Fagan's with Llanilltern, 1028/214/Gse-7/G119.

118 Port e Vullen, SC 473 928; P. M. C. Kermode, 'A Welsh Inscription in the Isle of Man', *ZCP* 1 (1897), 48–51; id., *Manx Crosses*, no. 48, and Appendix A to the reprint. Of the same half-uncial phase is Maughold 3, churchyard, SC 493 917: A. M. Cubbon, 'The Early Church in the Isle of Man', in S. M. Pearce (ed.), *The Early Church in Western Britain and Ireland*, BAR, Brit. Ser. 102 (Oxford, 1982), 256–82 at 262: IHS XPS BRANHUI HUC AQUA DIRIVAVIT (with the characteristic oc **a**).

CRUX GURIAT 'The cross of Gwriad'

This is entirely in half-uncial and thus belongs to the phase of British epigraphy after the seventh century, when the old epigraphic letterforms had been generally abandoned in favour of a carryover from book script. The name GURIAT has entirely lost its final syllable and an initial /w/ has developed to /gw/, an eighth-century change according to Jackson.[119] If the identification with the father of Merfyn Frych is correct—and there is no epigraphic difficulty—it is to be dated *c.* 800 at the opening of the Viking period. The name is unambiguously British.

If we were to keep to the evidence of the monolingual inscriptions, it would seem likely that an Irish phase was followed by a British phase, and that the Irish phase belonged to the fifth and part, at least, of the sixth century, while the British phase covered the seventh and eighth. The northern part of the island, however, was the home of the bilingual Latin and Irish inscriptions of the kind familiar from parts of Wales and Cornwall. A particularly interesting stone was found in 1911 in an excavation in the keeil of Knock e Dooney:[120]

Latin: AMMECATI FILIVS ROCATI HIC IACIT
Ogham: [AM?]B[I]CATOS M[A]QI ROC[A]T[O]S

What is important about this inscription is that the Irish and Latin versions are independent of each other: although they contain the same names and so commemorate the same person, they are addressed to quite different readers. The ogham inscription works according to the standard rules: it is in Irish, still a fully inflected language; the names are in the genitive case, and so also is MAQI 'son'. It can be translated 'of Ambicatus son of Rocatus'. The Latin inscription, however, works according to the normal pattern for British Latin inscriptions of the post-Roman period: the names are adapted to the phonology of British Latin; and, while the names themselves purport to be in the genitive, FILIVS appears to be in the nominative; moreover, at the end we have the standard phrase 'lies here', which has no counterpart in the ogham. The grammar and formulae of the Latin version are adapted to suit readers speaking a late British Latin which, in spite of initial appearances, lacked distinctions of case. In the south-west of the island pure Irish inscriptions in the ogham alphabet assumed Irish-speaking readers; in the north of the island both communities were present, an Irish one and one using both Latin and British. This inscription, however, appears to be early: there is no reason here to think that an Irish presence on the island was replaced by a British one; both coexisted. The likelihood, therefore, is that both languages were present on the island throughout the period from 400 until the Viking conquest, which may, as

[119] *LHEB*, § 49.

[120] 500/IOM-1, NX 404 021; now in the Manx Museum, Douglas; Kermode, *Manx Crosses*, Appendix A. According to Jackson, *LHEB*, 173 n. 1, there is not enough room for an initial I-, the expected form. It is not obvious from Kermode's drawing, *Manx Crosses*, Appendix A, 8, that this is correct.

Table 3.4. Dated inscriptions

Dated inscriptions in Roman capitals	
Castell Dwyran	Probably before *c.* 550, Carmarthenshire / Dyfed
Penmachno 3	Perhaps 567 × 575, Caernarvonshire / Gwynedd
An eclectic inscription	
Llangadwaladr	*c.* 625, Anglesey / Gwynedd
Inscriptions In half-uncial	
Llantwit Major 4	mid-eighth century, Glamorgan / Gwent (Glywysing)
Llantwit Major 3	mid-eighth century, Glamorgan / Gwent (Glywysing)
CIIC 1066	*c.* 800, Isle of Man
Llantysilio-yn-Iâl	mid-ninth century, Denbighshire / Powys
Llantwit Major 1	mid-ninth century, Glamorgan / Gwent (Glywysing)
1054/Ok43	DONIERT is probably the *Dungarth rex Cerniu* of AC *s.a.* 875 = 876
Inscription in Insular minuscule	
St Davids 8	1078–1100, Pembrokeshire ← Dyfed

we shall see, have been as late as 902. Which language was dominant was decided by the balance of power in the Irish Sea.

4. GWYNEDD

In Wales, most inscriptions belong to the west rather than to the east, to Gwynedd (see Map 10) west of the Conwy, to Dyfed (including Ystrad Tywi and the south of Ceredigion), and to the west of Gwent (including Glywysing). Only in Brycheiniog did a region well stocked with inscriptions come close to the English border as the latter emerged in the seventh century. In one way, Gwynedd is epigraphically like Scotland, but South Wales, especially Dyfed, is more like the Isle of Man. In Wales as a whole, there are three epigraphical phases: the first covers the majority of inscriptions, those in which the base letterforms were roman capitals; the second comprises inscriptions of no single set of underlying letterforms, but instead an eclectic mix; the third consists of inscriptions using book scripts, Insular half-uncial or (occasionally) Insular minuscule. Of these three phases, the first, that of the roman capital, is well represented both in north-west Wales and in the south; the second is found in Gwynedd only in two inscriptions in Anglesey,[121] and

[121] For Anglesey, see N. Edwards, 'Anglesey in the Early Middle Ages: The Archaeological Evidence', *Trans. Anglesey Antiquarian Society and Field Club* (1986), 21–4.

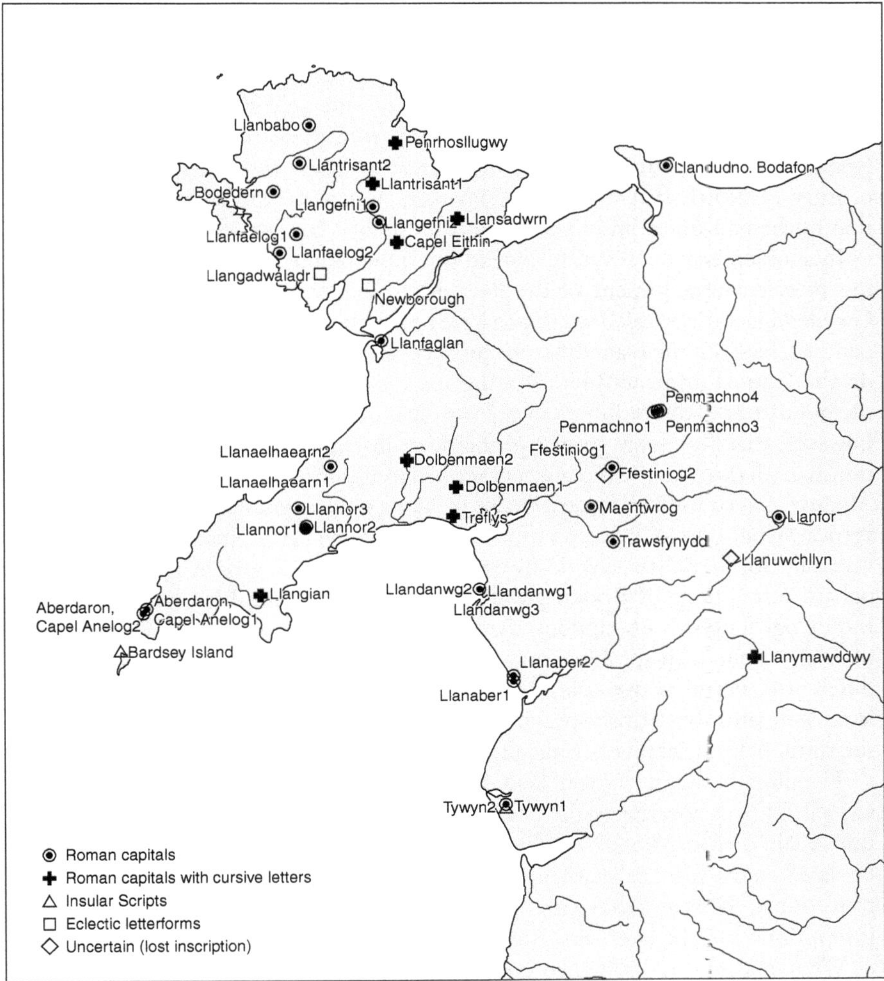

Map 10. Gwynedd inscriptions
The map suggests different local preferences: western Anglesey has pure roman capitals, but eastern Anglesey allows cursive intrusions; inscriptions in the northern part of Llŷn are nearly all in pure roman capitals, from Capel Anelog to Llanelhaearn just into Arfon; the southern part of Llŷn is an extension of Eifionydd with cursive intrusions into a capital base; the interior prefers pure capitals except for Llanymawddwy.

occasionally, in a much more scattered distribution, in the south; the third is barely represented at all in Gwynedd, on Bardsey off the tip of the Llŷn peninsula and at Tywyn in Meirionydd, but it is well represented in the south.

Any continuous tradition of epigraphy on stone cannot be traced in Gwynedd after *c.* 625, namely after the CATAMANUS stone at Llangadwaladr, not far from Aberffraw. It, like the Newborough stone nearby, very probably laid out by the same *ordinator*, belongs to the second phase, that of the eclectic letterforms. In Gwynedd, therefore, it appears that the shift from roman capitals to eclectic forms was part of the decline and death of post-Roman epigraphy on stone in the north-west. The two later inscriptions, on Bardsey and at Tywyn, look like isolated revivals with no direct link connecting them with the earlier tradition. The post-Roman British epigraphic tradition, therefore, came to an end in the seventh century in North Britain and in Gwynedd, but it continued into a new phase, that of the half-uncial inscriptions, on the Isle of Man and in South Wales.

In another, way, however, Gwynedd was quite unlike North Britain. In the latter, the prevalent arrangement of the inscription on the stone was horizontal; but in Gwynedd it was vertical. Two things have reasonably governed interpretations of this contrast. First, on the Llanerfyl stone in Wales and on the Hayle stone in Cornwall, as on the Latinus stone at Whithorn, the specification of the age of the person commemorated is a direct inheritance from late Roman practice.[122] It is a practice, however, that was soon given up, for these inscriptions are, in that respect, very unusual. All three may reasonably be ascribed to the fifth rather than the sixth century. All three also continue Roman practice in laying out the inscription horizontally. The vertical layout thus looks like an innovation. Secondly, ogham inscriptions are laid out vertically, for they characteristically use the vertical angle or arris of a pillar-stone. The ogham inscriptions of Britain are in an early form of the Irish language, so that monolingual ogham inscriptions are directed, as we have seen in the case of the Isle of Man, at an Irish-speaking readership, while bilingual inscriptions look to two different readerships, one using Irish and the other using British Latin (though the latter were probably British-speaking or bilingual in British and Latin). Inscriptions in the third, half-uncial phase, generally revert to a horizontal layout.

The link between vertical layout and Irish influence is not automatic. The Castell Dwyran inscription in Carmarthenshire is bilingual but the Latin inscription is laid out horizontally.[123] For that reason it is possible to argue that it should be dated to the fifth rather than to the sixth century;[124] and it can thus be seen as transitional, between the early, more purely post-Roman and thus horizontal inscriptions and the later, consistently vertical layout.

What makes Irish influence on the layout especially plausible is that an Irish presence can be detected more widely than merely in areas that have ogham inscriptions. Many personal names in inscriptions that are otherwise solely in Latin are Irish. When these are mapped and compared with clearly British names, they clarify the picture derived from ogham inscriptions.[125] There are relatively few ogham inscriptions in North Wales compared with Dyfed, Brycheiniog, and the western part of the old Gwent (now Glamorgan). There is one at Llanfaelog, close to Aberffraw in Anglesey, one at Llystyn-gwyn in the parish of Dolbenmaen, close to

[122] e.g. *RIB* 356–60, 363, 365 (Caerleon), 523, 525–6 (Chester), 864–7 (Maryport).

[123] 358/138/Gso-8/CM3.

[124] No later than the beginning of the sixth century, Tedeschi, *Congeries*, i. 120; similarly *CIB* 346–7.

[125] P. Sims-Williams, 'The Five Languages of Wales in the Pre-Norman Inscriptions', *CMCS* 44 (Winter 2002), 1–36.

the northern boundary of Eifionydd and close also to the route southwards from Caernarfon, skirting the western edge of Snowdonia. The third is well to the east, at Clocaenog in Dyffryn Clwyd, the old Dogfeiling.[126] This inscription is of particular interest, since it is on a natural mound, subsequently called 'Bedd Emlyn', 'Emlyn's Grave', close to the source of the River Clwyd. It is on a hill, called Bryn-y-Beddau, 'The Hill of the Graves', where it is accompanied by another stone, without an inscription, on another natural mound close by. The mounds may already have been believed to be ancient graves when the stones were erected.

This scatter of ogham inscriptions is too thin, on its own, to form any clear impression. The Irish personal names on other inscriptions, however, indicate that the Irish presence was strongest on Anglesey, then Caernarfonshire, and finally Denbighshire, but absent from Merionethshire and Flintshire, as well as from Montgomeryshire further south.[127]

Merionethshire has a good collection of early inscriptions. Since it lies outside the area defined by personal names as subject to strong Irish influence, it offers a guide to epigraphic practice that can be compared with areas that were subject to strong Irish influence. Unfortunately, however, some early inscriptions are lost and known only from drawings that do not permit a definite conclusion about the arrangement of the text on the stone. Those parts of Merionethshire that have inscriptions consist of three distinct medieval units: Ardudwy between Afon Glaslyn by Porthmadog and Afon Mawddach, Meirionydd, and Penllyn. Of these, the early inscriptions in Meirionydd are all lost, Penllyn has just one, at Llanfor near Bala, and the rest (seven) all belong to Ardudwy.[128] Of these one is only a fragment of the original stone, but of the remaining six, half are arranged horizontally and half vertically. The three horizontal inscriptions have all been dated to the fifth century, while the vertical ones have been regarded as later, mainly sixth century.

In Anglesey, where there are four definite Irish personal names but no definite British ones, vertical inscriptions outnumber horizontal ones by 7 : 4. In Caernarfonshire, where the Irish personal names are slightly outnumbered by the British ones, 3 : 5, vertical inscriptions are still about twice as common as horizontal ones. There is, therefore, a broad agreement between Irish presence and a vertical layout. It is when one comes down to detail that the connection is less obvious. For example, there are three inscriptions in the cantref of Eifionydd, on the south-west side of Snowdonia, roughly from Cricieth to Porthmadog.[129] All three are in roman capitals with the odd intrusive cursive letter, and to that extent they form a distinctive group. But Dolbenmaen 2 (Llystyngwyn) has a horizontal layout

126 Clocaenog, 399/176/Gn-9; now in the National Museum of Wales, Cardiff, but first attested in letters by Edward Lhuyd as 'on the summit of Bryn y Beddau, upon a barrow popularly known under the name of Bedd Emlyn', W. W. E. Wynne, 'Letters of E. Lhwyd, *Archaeologia Cambrensis*, 3 (1948), 310; Westwood, *Lapidarium Walliae*, 203. The grid ref. is SJ 052 532.

127 Sims-Williams, 'The Five Languages', 29 (map 4).

128 413/272/Gn-12; 414/271/Gn-13; 416 (1)/278/Gn-19; 416 (2)/279/Gn-18; 417/282/Gn-24; 420/289/Gn-10/2019/Gn-4. For Llandanwg 3 see A. Davidson, 'Two Early Medieval Stones from Llandanwg', *Archaeology in Wales*, 48 (2008), 73–5.

129 Dolbenmaen 1 and 2, Treflys: 397/105/Gn-35; 380/84/Gn-8; 398/106/Gn-38.

whereas the other two are vertical; and, yet, the stone with a horizontal layout is also a bilingual stone, with Latin and ogham. Similarly, the Clocaenog stone from further east, in Denbighshire (in the cantref of Dyffryn Clwyd), is bilingual and yet has a horizontal layout. Thus two out of three northern ogham stones are of this type. As we have seen, two relatively late inscriptions on Anglesey, both of the seventh century, and both eclectic in their letterforms, were probably laid out by the same *ordinator*; yet, one is vertically arranged while the other has a horizontal layout.[130] Moreover, the horizontal inscription is on a pillar-stone, not a slab, so that the form of the stone can hardly be the explanation.

It is possible to tell a story that will take account of these facts. The first phase after the Irish presence made itself felt epigraphically retained the two traditions side by side: the Latin inscriptions horizontal and the ogham vertical: this will be the phase represented by Dolbenmaen 2 and, in the south, the Castell Dwyran stone. These inscriptions are dated to the fifth century by Tedeschi. Subsequently, the two traditions interacted, so that a vertical layout was introduced into the Latin tradition, but it never entirely superseded the horizontal arrangement. At the same period, the use of the ogham alphabet was fading out in Gwynedd; and that is why ogham inscriptions, because they were early, coexisted with horizontal layouts in two early Latin inscriptions.

Yet, one cannot simply regard the horizontal layout for Latin inscriptions as earlier than the vertical one: true, it was the form inherited from the Roman period, but it remained an option into the seventh century. Some room has to be left for local or even individual preference: the two Aberdaron (Capel Anelog) inscriptions at the western end of the Llŷn peninsula, which on other grounds seem to belong together, both have a horizontal layout; but those further east in Llŷn or just over the border, at Llanaelhaearn on the east side of Yr Eifl, all have a vertical layout.[131] On Anglesey, those in the western half of the island all have a vertical layout, while those in the eastern half are mixed but predominantly horizontal; the curious difference between the two seventh-century stones, noted above, follows this local divide, which clearly persisted over more than one generation. If we leave aside the two seventh-century inscriptions, with their eclectic letterforms, only the eastern half of the island has inscriptions with cursive letters intruding into a capital base. This difference, too, seems to be a matter of local preference rather than of date. The division between the west and the east of the island is later reproduced in the alliances of saints centred, respectively, on St Cybi in Caergybi and Seiriol and Iestin in Penmon.[132]

Gwynedd, therefore, gives us some clues as we move southwards. On the one hand, we have the broad picture: there was a relationship between an Irish presence and the flourishing of monumental commemoration on stone. First, north-west Wales was not an area in which there were many Romano-British inscriptions; a new Irish elite not only introduced their own ogham memorials but adopted and

[130] Llangadwaladr (the CATAMANUS stone) and Llangaffo 12: 970/13/Gn-25; and *ECMW* 35.

[131] Llangian, Llannor 1–3, Llanaelhaearn 1–2.

[132] *Bonedd y Saint*, § 76, ed, Bartrum, *EWGT* 65; *Vita S. Kebii*, ed. and trans. Wade-Evans, §§ 5, 16–17, *VSBG* 236, 244–6. Cf. Edwards, 'Anglesey in the Early Middle Ages', 24–7.

spread a Latin epigraphical tradition more widely than it ever had been spread under the Empire. One need only compare Montgomeryshire and Radnorshire, with no signs of an Irish presence, and only a single early inscription at Llanerfyl, with the much denser scatter in the north-west. And, secondly, as that Irish elite was assimilated to the local British culture, so the epigraphic habit faded. On the other hand, we have local variation in layout and in the choice of letterforms. Moreover, some differences that we might have thought likely to be chronological appear to be local. This suggests that it is right to be cautious about our ability to distinguish at all minutely between different phases in post-Roman British epigraphy: sometimes, as with the Whithorn Latinus inscription in the north or the Llanerfyl stone in Wales, there is very good reason to give an early date, but the chronology of the inscriptions is often difficult. We shall meet other examples illustrating the same point in the south.

5. SOUTH WALES: DYFED, BRYCHEINIOG, AND GWENT

In the south, also, the post-Roman popularity of commemorative monuments on stone is associated with an Irish presence. In Dyfed, indeed, even pure ogham inscriptions are preserved, as on the Isle of Man; yet their distribution is quite unlike that on Man (see Maps 11, 12, and 13). There, a neat division prevailed: in the

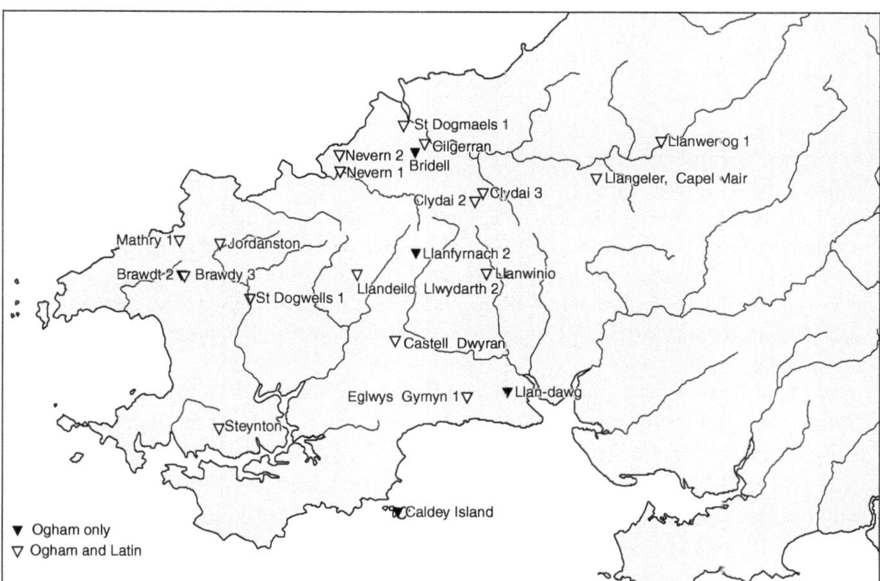

Map 11. Dyfed: ogham
Dyfed was the region with most ogham stones; most were bilingual but the pure oghams are widely distributed. The main concentration is around the Preseli mountains and extending north to the valley of the Teifi. The mainland of Penfro in the south has none.

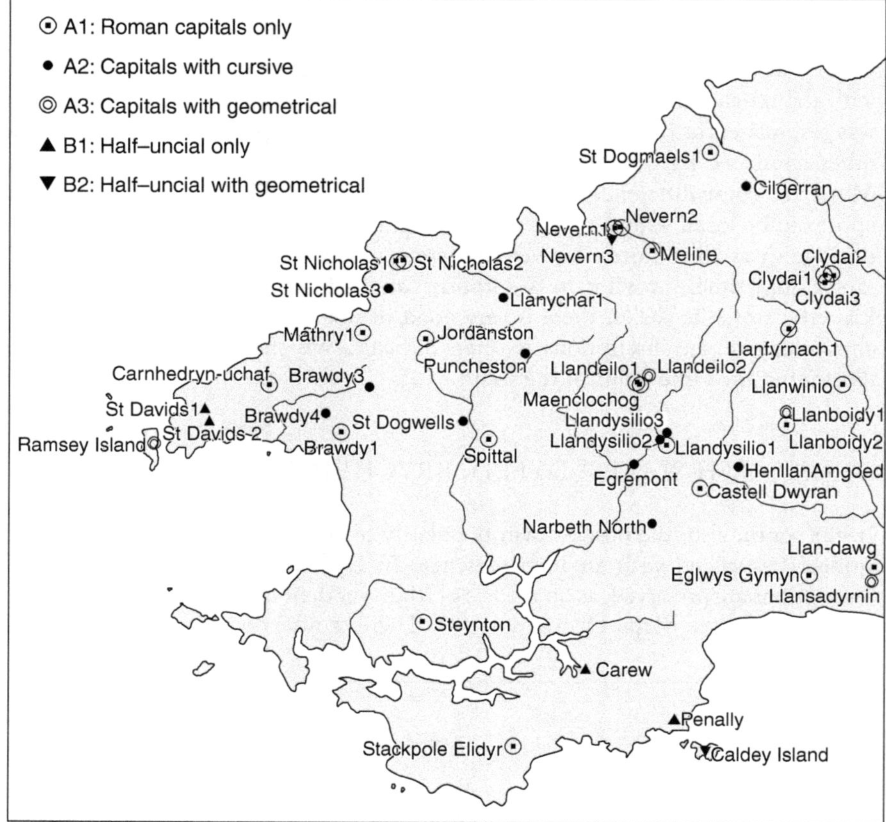

Map 12. West Dyfed: Latin inscriptions
The Latin inscriptions of Dyfed have a similar distribution to the oghams, concentrated in the northern half of Pembrokeshire and the neighbouring part of Carmarthenshire, but Penfro is not excluded. The pure capitals and capitals with cursive intrusions are more intermixed than in Gwynedd. The later, half-uncial inscriptions are much less densely distributed than the older ones in roman capitals and show a strong correlation with major churches.

south-west pure ogham inscriptions; in the north bilingual stones. In the Greater Dyfed, the six pure ogham inscriptions are well scattered: from Brawdy in the west, in Pebidiog, not far to the east of St Davids, to Llan-dawg by the estuary of the Pembrokeshire Taf, and finally, in the east, to Llwchwr (Loughor), also by an estuary; and, from Caldey Island off the southern coast of Penfro to Bridell not far from the River Teifi and the boundary with Ceredigion. The bilingual inscriptions were also well scattered, extending up the Teifi as far as Llanwenog, just into Ceredigion; and sometimes, as at Brawdy and at Bridell, they were close to pure ogham inscriptions. There was no such division as on the Isle of Man. Yet, if we take the post-Roman inscriptions as a whole what emerges is a much greater density in the northern part of Pembrokeshire and the adjacent part of Carmarthenshire, especially in the old *cantrefi* of Pebidiog, Cemais, and Emlyn. Yet, for agricultural purposes this was the less desirable area, lying on either side of the Preseli Mountains and running up to the Teifi. It coincides with what became the Welsh as opposed to the English part of Pembrokeshire, as in the brisk judgement of their relative fertility by George Owen of Henllys: 'This plow land in the welshe Contrey being the Barenest and worst parte of the shere was in old tyme rentid about xx^{s} a yere and in the English parte being the best land about xxvj^{s} 8^{d}.'[133]

The distinction that is clear in the south is between the post-Roman stones and those from the eighth century onwards. In Dyfed, the latter have a much more limited distribution: they are found around St Davids, in a rough line from Caldey Island to the head of the Daugleddau estuary, taking in Penally and Carew on the mainland, and, finally, at Nevern: there is a concentrated western group and a southern group, more strung out, while the Nevern inscription is isolated. Further east, in Ystrad Tywi, there is another more elongated group, from Llanarthne on the Tywi northwards via Llanfynydd to Llanllwni, not far from the Teifi. The earlier inscriptions are far more numerous, with the densest concentration in the land sloping southwards from the Preseli Mountains.

In Ceredigion, the distribution is different: whereas in the northernmost part, the medieval cantref of Penweddig, there were no early medieval inscriptions, the importance of Llanbadarn Fawr from about the ninth century is well attested by sculpture. The rest of Uwch Aeron—what became the commotes of Mefenydd, Anhuniog, and Pennardd—has the most inscriptions; and most of them are later, probably no earlier than the ninth century. The southern part of Ceredigion, Is Aeron, is transitional: the commotes of Is Coed and Gwynionydd, along the lower Teifi, appear more like a northern extension of Dyfed and Ystrad Tywi: roman capitals dominate, one of which is bilingual, Latin and ogham. Only in this southern zone is a definite Irish presence revealed in the early epigraphy, whereas two later stones further north have Irish names.[134] Slightly further north, in the commotes of Caerwedros and Mebwynion, however, there are two half-uncial inscriptions but only one in roman capitals.

In the Greater Gwent, inscriptions of all periods cluster in the west, between the Nedd and the Ogwr—between Baglan in the west and Merthyr Mawr near the mouth of the Ogwr. This is the area named *Margan* in the Life of St Cadog.[135] But, in the later period, one cluster exists east of the Ogwr, namely the inscriptions at Llanilltud Fawr; and this seems, in the ninth century, to have been a royal cemetery-church as well as a prominent monastery. In this later period, inscriptions in half-uncial also suggest the importance as churches of Merthyr Mawr on the Ogwr and a string of other churches in the thin coastal defile in the far west of the

133 *OP* ii. 367.

134 The earlier inscriptions are Penbryn 1, 354/126/Gso-41/CD28 (where the name is Irish), and Llanwenog 1, 353/127/Gso-6/CD26 (the bilingual inscription); the later inscriptions are Llanfihangel Ystrad 1 (Llanllŷr), 993/124/CD20, and Llanwnnws 1, 994/125/CD27.

135 *VSBG* 24.

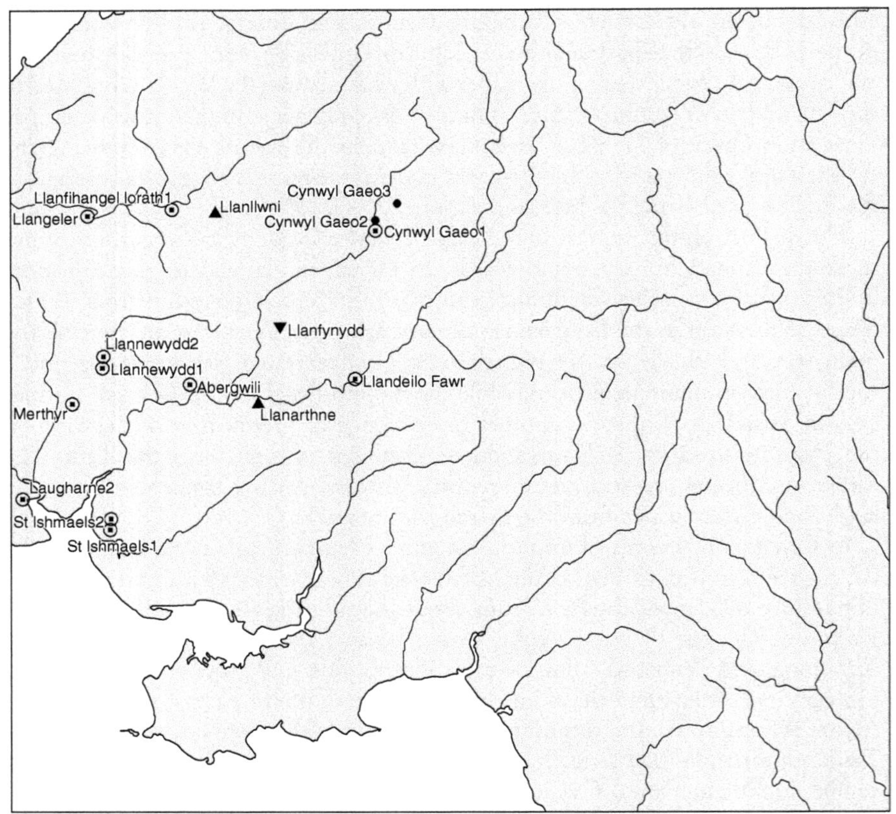

Map 13. East Dyfed: Latin inscriptions
The inscriptions thin out as soon as one goes east of the Tywi estuary.

kingdom, Baglan, that which is now Port Talbot and Aberafan, Margam, and Eglwys Nynnid.[136]

In Brycheiniog, the six ogham inscriptions are mainly strung out along the course of the Roman road from Crickhowell in the east to Llywel in the west, leaving one of the two pure ogham inscriptions, Ystradfellte, as an outlier. When the inscriptions in roman capitals are examined, the outlying area on the southern

[136] These western stones, both early and late, are well represented in the collection in the admirable Margam Stone Museum.

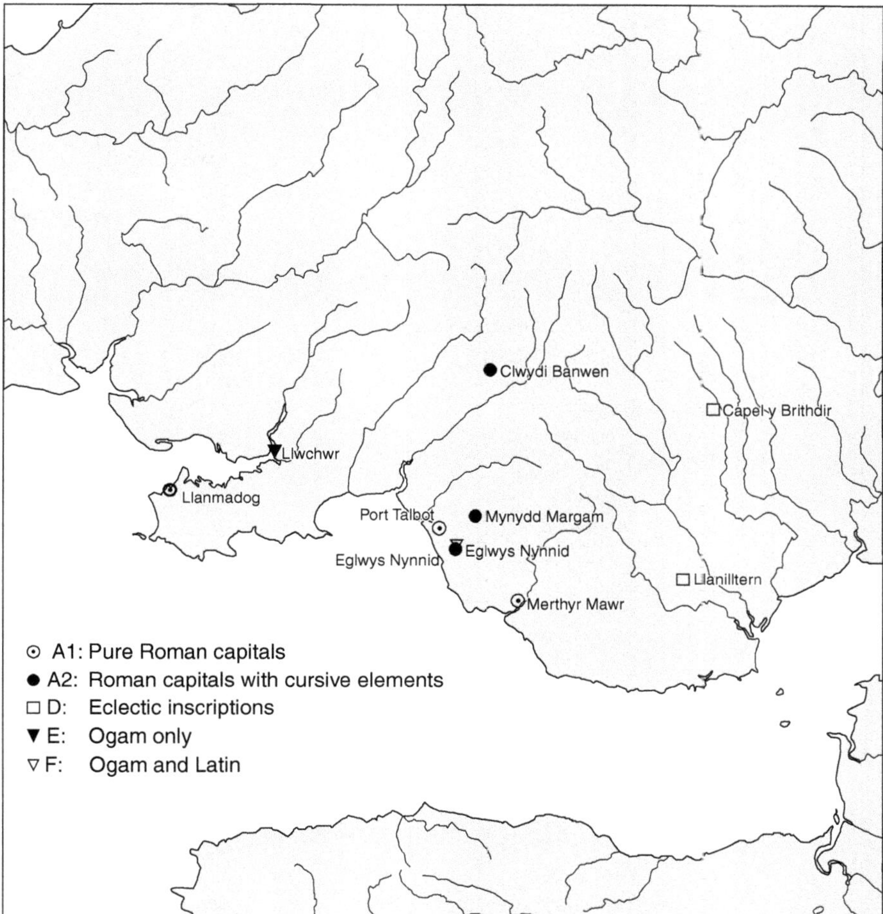

Map 14. Early Glamorgan
This map includes the old territories named as Gwent and Glywysing, and also Gŵyr, which usually belonged to Dyfed. Two ogham inscriptions suggest Irish settlement in the lands west of the Ogwr, and there are only two eclectic inscriptions east of Merthyr Mawr by the estuary of the Ogwr.

slopes of the Brecon Beacons becomes much more significant. In the later period, however, this outlying area is again reduced to a single inscription; the rest form a half-circle of churches around Llan-gors, the royal crannog of the ninth and early tenth century, itself with a half-uncial inscription at the nearby church of that name.

Two groups deserve special consideration: those in the upper part of the Teifi valley, and a probable family group on the south side of the Preseli Mountains. I shall take the second first, since it is, as a whole, relatively early.

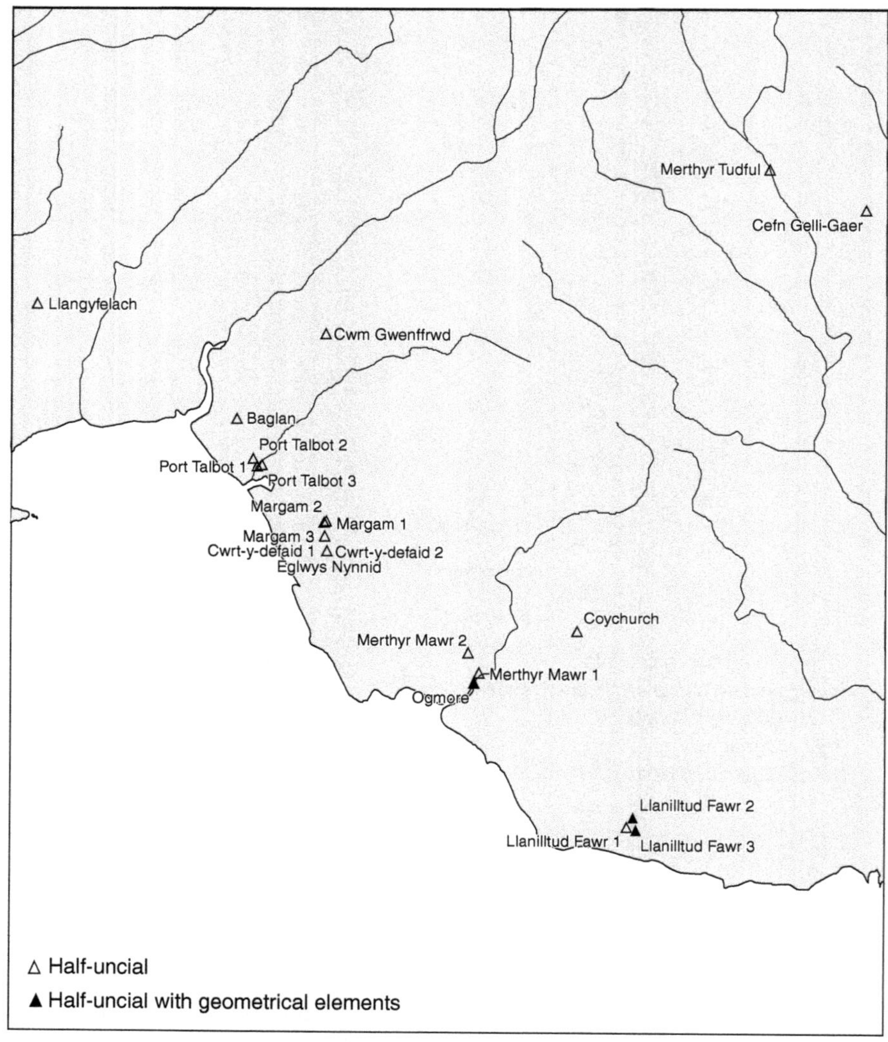

Map 15. Late Glamorgan
The later inscriptions on the whole preserve the same westerly distribution as the early ones, except for Llanilltud Fawr (Llantwit Major), a major monastery in which kings appear to have been buried in the eighth and ninth centuries.

The probable family group consists of three inscriptions. All three come from the old churchyard of Llandeilo Llwydarth or its immediate neighbourhood.[137] Llandeilo 2 is a bilingual inscription:

[137] Llandeilo 1, 434/314/Gso-35/P21; Llandeilo 2, 433/313/Gso-36/P22; Maenclochog 1, 441/345/Gso-15/P58. Llandeilo 1 and 2 are first recorded in the church or churchyard (Llandeilo 2 *c.* 1698);

Ogham: [A]NDAGELLI MACU CAV[ETI(?)]
'of Andagellas son of Cauetas'
Latin: ANDAGELLI IACIT / FILI CAVETI

The form MACU for earlier MAQI shows that it is not in the earliest stratum of ogham inscriptions.[138] The Latin version takes no account of the case ending necessary to provide a grammatical subject for the verb IACIT 'lies' and the usual HIC 'here' is omitted. Llandeilo 1 is only in Latin, but the names are again Irish:

COIMAGNI / FILI / CAVETI, 'Coimagn(us) son of Cauet(us)'

M and N are in angularized forms, early versions of the geometrical letters later used as ornamental drawn letters in the grandest Insular gospel books. For this reason, this inscription has been dated to the second half of the sixth century.[139] A third inscription, also just in Latin, is now in the churchyard at Cenarth on the Teifi, about twelve miles north-east of Llandeilo Llwydarth:

CVRCAGNI / FILI / ANDAGELLI 'Curcagn(us) son of Andagell(us)

The distance encouraged doubt over the identification of the two Andagelli; yet the Cenarth stone is known to have been moved in modern times from very close to Llandeilo church, and the geology of the three stones also indicates their common background. The fragment of genealogy proposed by Macalister for a family of Irish settlers was thus as follows (Latin nominative endings have been used), with the dates given to their inscriptions by Tedeschi:

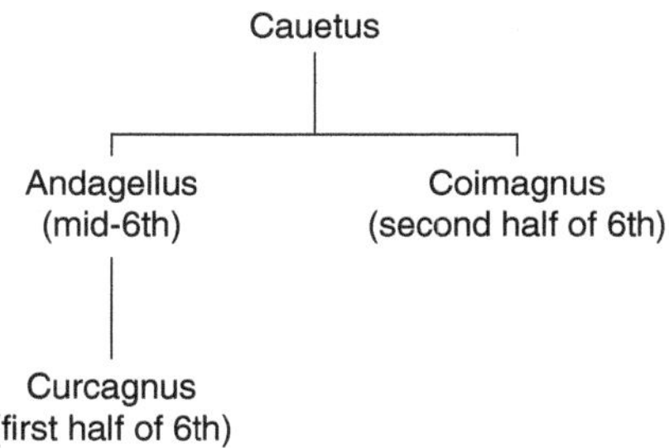

Kenneth Jackson, however, took issue with Macalister in his review: '[*CIIC*] 441 cannot belong to a son of 433, as it is epigraphically at least fifty years older'.[140] He wished to date the CVRCAGNI FILI ANDAGELLI inscription, now at Cenarth, to the fifth century. Even though Macalister had correctly indicated the history of how the stone came to move from near Llandeilo Llwydarth church to Cenarth,

Maenclochog 1 is first attested about a quarter of a mile to the north-west, but it is now at Cenarth on the Teifi. All three stones are dolerite, probably from the Preseli Mountains, but of varying coarseness (see *Corpus*).

[138] *CIB* 76, 167–8, 344–5, 359.

[139] 'Late sixth century', *LHEB* 312; second half of sixth century, Tedeschi, *Congeries*, i. 152.

[140] Review of *CIIC* i in *Speculum*, 21 (1946), 523.

Jackson was so confident of his epigraphical dating that he could dismiss Macalister's reconstruction out of hand. Admittedly, it might be the case that Curcagnus died young and that Coimagnus lived even longer than his brother Andagellus. Yet, if Curcagnus died before his father, it is remarkable that only the father had an ogham inscription. Perhaps a more likely view is that the epigrapher's dating bands are too narrow and their relative dating sometimes wrong. The close proximity of these inscriptions, once allowance is made for the movement of one of them to Cenarth, makes it very likely that, as Macalister maintained, we here have an important Irish family settled to the south of the Preseli Mountains. The churchyard at Llandeilo Llwydarth may originally have been the kindred cemetery of this family, and only later have acquired a church. Since it was later one of 'the seven bishop-houses of Dyfed', it would be interesting to know whether the later importance of the church continued an earlier importance of the descendants of Cauetus.

The group of inscriptions in the upper Teifi valley is quite different. They come from two centres: Llanddewi Brefi and Tregaron, both in the later commote of Pennardd. Both include an inscription of the post-Roman period together with one or, in the case of Llanddewi Brefi, two later inscriptions. Llanddewi Brefi lies on, and takes its second name from, the Brefi, a tributary of the Teifi, shortly before it joins the main river; this same tributary also gave its name to the Roman fort at Llanio on the other side of the Teifi, namely Bremia. In Rhigyfarch's Life of St David a site by the Teifi was remembered as the place where St David secured a great triumph against the Pelagians; and this story was told elsewhere, for Lifris's Life of St Cadog has an explanation of why it was David and not Cadog who led the orthodox to victory.[141] David, that is, was accepted in South Wales, at least by the late eleventh century, as the outstanding heir to St Germanus. One of the inscriptions shows that, by its time, there was already a link between the site and St David.

The earliest inscription, however, Llanddewi Brefi 1(see map 16), is much earlier and may be evidence of an Irish presence even here, far from the main concentration of Irish influence in western Dyfed, and some distance, too, over difficult mountain country, from the other main area of Irish settlement, Brycheiniog.[142] It is a rough pillar-stone with a vertical inscription in two lines, reading downwards, with one ligature:

D]ALLVs / DVMELVs

The inscription is in roman capitals with a cursive **s** at the ends of both names, a feature that is also found in Romano-British epigraphy;[143] the **M** of DVMELUS is curvilinear (snakelike) and is again a form inherited from Roman Britain.[144] The

[141] *Vita S. David*, §§ 49–53, *Vita S. Cadoci*, § 17, ed. Wade-Evans, *VSBG* 60–3, 164–6. The place is named as Llanddewi Brefi in the Welsh Life, *Buched Dewi o Lawysgrif Llanstephan 27*, ed. D. Simon Evans (Cardiff, 1965), 17, and as Brefi in the poem in honour of St David by Gwynfardd Brycheiniog, CBT II. 26, *passim* (also, probably, as Llanddewi, l. 73).

[142] 351/115/Gso-25/CD8.

[143] *RIB* 1821.

[144] It corresponds to the second **M** in Tedeschi, 'Osservazioni', 81, Fig. 2; cf. his *Congeries*, i. 52.

name *Dumelus* might be either Irish or Welsh: *Dallus Dumelus* appears to mean 'Blind Unfortunate'.[145]

The second inscription is fragmentary and can only be reconstructed with the aid of two drawings by Edward Lhuyd, of which the second was made in much better conditions.[146] It is eclectic in its letterforms: Insular **h**, **t**, **d**, **b**, **q** **m**, geometrical capitals **A**, **N**, but also several ordinary roman capitals, **R**, **F**, **V**, **L**, **S**, **P** and also **D** (alongside other forms of **d**) . For that reason, it was understandably originally dated to the seventh century by Jackson, even though he knew of one of two drawings by Edward Lhuyd.[147]

> (a) [+ hI]C IACEt (b) [I]dNERt FILIVS IA[CObI / qV]I OCCISVS [F]VIT PROPTER PR[EdAM (?) / SANCtI dAVID]
>
> 'Idnerth son of Iacobus lies here, who was slain on account of the plundering of St David'

The two drawings, taken together, make it very likely that the form of the name is *Idnert*, from an earlier **Iudnert*, and the form *Idnert* is unlikely to be earlier than the ninth century.[148]

Different specialists have given different dates to this inscription for very good reasons. On the one hand, there is the argument from letterforms: eclectic inscriptions are seen as transitional between the roman capitals characteristic of the fifth and sixth centuries and the inscriptional lettering based on Insular book scripts, half-uncial or minuscule, attested from the eighth century. The only dated eclectic inscription, the Catamanus inscription from Llangadwaladr in Anglesey, is consistent with this view: it belongs to the seventh century. On the other hand, the orthographical evidence makes it unlikely that the form *Idnert* could be as early as the seventh century: *iud-* remained the standard spelling in Old Welsh even after the change from *iud- to id-* had occurred. Conservative spelling is attested in this very inscription, since the *nert* of *Idnert* had changed to *nerth* in the sixth century. The best prospect for a resolution is likely to come from reconsidering the letterforms. Here two approaches may be adopted: first, it might be that, in this particular church, eclectic letterforms remained acceptable much later than elsewhere. What elsewhere might indeed be letterforms characteristic of the seventh century would here have lasted much longer. The second approach would be to

145 *CIB* 91 n. 464, 303; Sims-Williams, 'The Five Languages', 27.

146 Llanddewi Brefi 9, 350/116/CD9; R. G. Gruffydd and H. P. Owen, 'The Earliest Mention of St. David?', 185–93, and 'The Earliest Mention of St. David: An Addendum', *BBCS* 19 (1962), 231–2; it was read by Edward Lhuyd for the second time in 1699 but broken up for building stone after 1812. The fragments that remain are indicated by the text not enclosed in brackets.

147 *LHEB*, 346 n. 2 (seventh century), 620 (first half of seventh century).

148 Apart from the *Corpus*, see *CIB* 230, 274; *LHEB* 345–7 (§ 36 (2)); K. H. Jackson, 'The Idnert Inscription: Date, and Significance of Id-', *BBCS* 19 (1960–2), 232–4. *Iud-* > *Id-* is one of the changes which occurred before the shift of the stress accent in polysyllables to the penultimate; the latter is now dated to the ninth century (above, 92), so that the phonological change by which *iud* split between /ið/ in an old non-final and thus unstressed syllable and /ʉð/ in final syllables (including the monosyllable *udd*) cannot be later than the ninth century; *Iud-* remained the spelling in Old Welsh, so that the phonological change is unlikely to be much earlier than the ninth century.

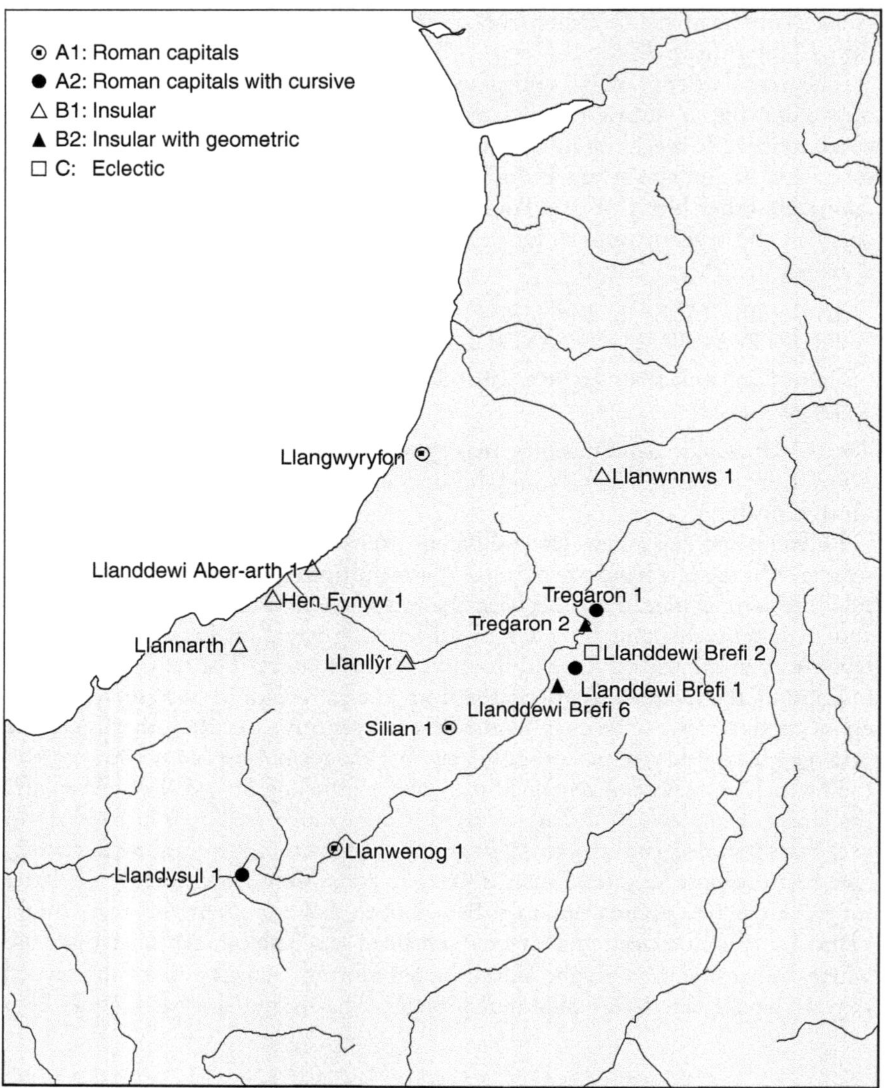

Map 16. Ceredigion: inscriptions

The distribution is largely southerly, with no surviving inscription north of the early one at Llangwyryfon, which is isolated, since the other early inscriptions are south of the Aeron. In the Aeron valley there is a cluster of inscriptions using Insular letterforms. The other, more varied cluster is in the upper Teifi, notably at Llanddewi Brefi.

posit a conscious revival of older letterforms, but not in a consistent manner. For example, the last word in the inscription is dAVID, with a final capital **D** but an initial straight half-uncial **d**.

At this point, a third inscription offers some help, Llanddewi Brefi 6.[149]

CENLISINI B(enedica)T D(eu)S
'May God bless Cennlisini'

This is in Insular half-uncial with strong geometrical influence. In other words, the base is a high-grade book script; and the geometrical influence can here confidently be ascribed to the wish to give it additional grandeur, since geometrical letters were used in manuscripts written in half-uncial for the beginnings of gospels and similarly exceptionally important text. If this gives us a reliable clue, the likely explanation for the IDNERT inscription is that the capitals, both roman and geometrical, were used to enhance the status of the monument. The geometrical capitals would come from grand manuscripts (of the same type as the Lichfield Gospels, which were at Llandeilo Fawr in the ninth century); roman capitals are used as part of a display script alongside geometrical capitals in some Anglo-Saxon books, for example, British Library, Royal 1. E. VI, fo. 44, dated to the late eighth century.[150] Alternatively, and more probably, the roman capitals, found in another late inscription in Ceredigion,[151] may have been imitated from much earlier inscriptions.

The coexistence of post-Roman and later inscriptions is also found a few miles further up the Teifi at Tregaron. The early inscription is a fragment in roman capitals with some intrusive cursive letters:[152]

POteNINA / MVLIIeR
'Potenina wife [of . . .]

The cursive influence is best seen in the **te** of POteNINA, where the **e** (shaped like a Greek epsilon, ϵ) has a medial horizontal stroke in line with the horizontal of the previous **t**. This is how this pair of letters is often written by scribes so as to make a ligature between the horizontals of the **t** and the **e**.

The later inscription, Tregaron 2, consists of a name in half-uncial within a rectangular frame, at the head of which is a cross and at the bottom a pattern of twelve small squares in three lines:[153]

ENEVIRI
'Eneuir(i)'

This inscription is 'expertly carved' with 'beautifully proportioned and distinctively constructed letters' showing the influence of geometrical lettering.[154] The upper

149 Llanddewi Brefi 6, 992/120/CD13; on the name see *CIB* 106.

150 J. J. G. Alexander, *Insular Manuscripts, 6th to the 9th Century* (London, 1978), Cat. no. 32, Plate 160.

151 Henfynyw 1, 990/108/CD2.

152 Tregaron 1, 356/132/CD32.

153 995/133/CD33. On the name, see *CIB* 72, 110–11.

154 Helen McKee *apud* Edwards, *Corpus*, ii. 195.

Teifi group, therefore, demonstrates a literacy that has endured across the divide between post-Roman and later epigraphy. The later inscriptions are of especial interest, at Tregaron because of the exceptional quality of the lettering, at Llanddewi Brefi because of the content of the text together with the effort to give a special status to the inscription.

6. SOUTH-WEST BRITAIN AND BRITTANY

In the territory of the *civitas* of the Dumnonii (see Maps 17 and 18) in the far south-west of Britain, no Roman inscriptions survive, and perhaps none was ever made. Post-Roman inscriptions are, however, quite numerous. The epigraphic habit, although ultimately of Roman derivation, only took hold after the Roman army and Roman tax-gatherers had left. In this respect, romanization advanced furthest after Rome had departed. As in Wales and the Isle of Man, this new advance of Roman epigraphy is also linked with Irish settlement. The six ogham inscriptions of Devon and Cornwall cluster either side of the Tamar, from near Camelford in the west to near Ivybridge in the east. There are, however, inscriptions only in Latin further west that contain Irish names.

Two sites illustrate the Irish presence. At Lewannick, not far from Launceston in east Cornwall, two bilingual inscriptions are now in the church. The first is unusual because, even in the ogham, there is a word for the memorial itself.[155]

Latin: INGEN/VI / MEM/ORIA
Ogham: IGENAVI MEMOR
'The memorial of Ingenuus / I(n)genavas'

The use of *memoria* in the Latin recalls the VOTEPORIX stone from Castell Dwyran in Dyfed. Here, however, a loan from Latin *memoria* has also been used in the ogham version, corresponding in form to Old Irish *mebuir* and Welsh *myfyr* but in meaning to Old Irish *memmrae* 'a memorial'.[156] The personal name is Latin, so that, were it not for the ogham, we should have no reason to suppose that the man commemorated was Irish.

The other bilingual stone at Lewannick is built into the wall of the church.[157]

Latin: [HI]C IACIT VLCAGNI
Ogham: ULCAGNI

The form of the text is much more typical than its fellow, with HIC IACIT 'lies here' in the Latin followed by an Irish name (Old Irish Olcán). The same Irish

[155] 466/Ok23/C-13. Lewannick 1, in the churchyard. SX 276 807. For place-name attestations of *memoria* > *myfyr*, see A. Breeze, 'Morville in Shropshire and Myfyr in Gwynedd', *Journal of Celtic Studies*, 4 (2004), 201–3.

[156] McManus, *Guide to Ogam*, 119 (§ 6.27).

[157] 467/Ok24/C-12.

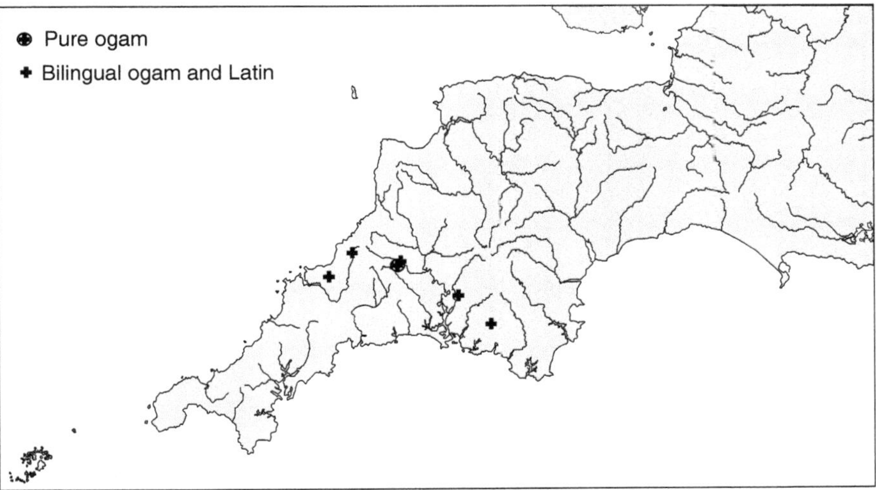

Map 17. Dumnonia: ogham
The ogham inscriptions of the south-west are in a band from Cornwall east of the Hayle to south-west Devon. Most are bilingual: Latin and Irish. This band is likely to indicate the area of the main Irish settlement.

name appears further west at a farm called Nanscow in the parish of St Breoc, south of the Camel estuary and south-west of Wadebridge.[158]

Tedeschi: VLCAGNI F[ILI]
SEVERI

The last part of FILI is buried in the ground. Here the son has an Irish name, but the father a Roman one. As the Irish presence is revealed in the personal names so also is the way romanization has spread from the native British population to the Irish settlers.

The epigraphy of Brittany demonstrates the link with Britain, but it is unlike that of most of the parent island in that it is free of Irish influence.[159] In that way, Brittany is like northern Britain: both show that, even though Irish influence encouraged the wider use of epigraphic commemoration on stone, there was an underlying British layer. This underlying stratum is most clearly revealed at the northern and southern ends of British territory, in what is now southern Scotland and in Brittany; it is also evident more locally in Wales, as in south Pembrokeshire as opposed to north Pembrokeshire.

The Breton inscriptions are also important in that they continued into the phase after roman capitals ceased to be the standard letterforms for epigraphy. The later inscriptions range from display capitals at the top of the range to minuscule.

158 472/Ok35/C-20, SW 969 708.

159 W. Davies *et al.*, *The Inscriptions of Early Medieval Brittany*. The inscriptions are catalogued by *département*, e.g. F1 is the first inscription from Finistère.

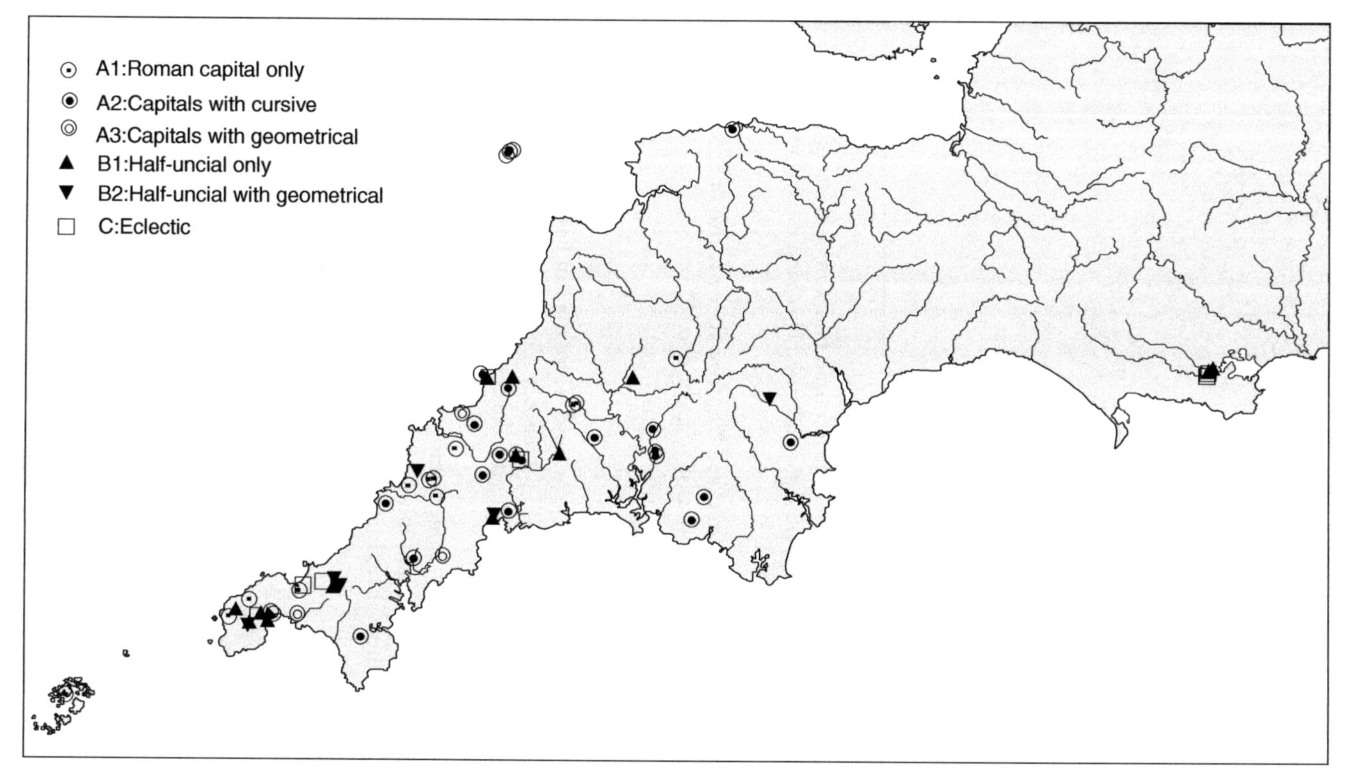

Map 18. Dumnonia: Latin inscriptions
The British inscriptions in Devon are mainly, as one would expect, early, but there are two later ones, as well as the isolated group at Wareham in Dorset. In Cornwall the Latin inscriptions are much more widely distributed than the ogham ones, extending even to the Scillies.

The Breton inscriptions thus exemplify both the post-Roman tradition, inherited from the Empire, when the letterforms of epigraphy were distinct from those of written texts, and the later tradition, when epigraphical letterforms were an offshoot of book scripts. Brittany, therefore, belongs with south-western Britain and South Wales in continuing to use inscriptions on stone after the seventh century, whereas North Wales did not. The later Breton stones demonstrate, first, that the full Insular hierarchy of scripts was used in Brittany (see Map 19), and, secondly, that the cultural link between Brittany and the British lands in Britain itself continued after the sixth century. The Bretons might be politically subject to the Franks, but in epigraphy the principal attachment to the other Britons remained.

The distribution of the Breton inscriptions is predominantly coastal, where the main population is likely to have been concentrated, but it is also linked with areas of granite. This type of stone was used for prehistoric stelae, and several of the early medieval inscriptions are on reused stelae. The distribution may, however, be skewed by different rates of loss. Some stones known to scholars in the early modern period have since gone missing, and others, not recorded, are likely to have suffered the same fate, especially in the more prosperous parts of the country. Even so, the density of inscriptions was probably always thinner than in the Irish-influenced parts of Britain.

The inscriptions of Finistère, in the diocese of Léon, form a small group in the far north-west.[160] The earliest is probably Plourin 3, F5, which for linguistic reasons can be dated no earlier than 550.[161] It is lost, but to judge by the drawing its base letterforms were capitals, while it also had cursive letters, the usual **s** and **f** in an **fi** ligature, but also **l**. An important inscription for the early medieval culture of this part of Brittany is Lanrivoaré, F2. The lettering consists of Insular display capitals, with clearly marked serifs. It has been dated to the late seventh or the eighth century on the grounds that the letterforms closely resemble the geometrical display letters found in the great Insular gospel books. It needs to be placed alongside other similar inscriptions, such as the one in geometrical display letters from Toureen Peakaun in Co. Tipperary or the Ramsay Island inscription close to St Davids. As opposed to the geometrical letterforms sometimes found among capitals, these belong to a period when the use of book scripts was normal in Insular epigraphy, and hence they indirectly attest an interest in *de luxe* manuscripts of the kind to use such letterforms. A more ordinary inscription, F1, is on the coast at the chapel of S. Gonvel in Landunvez. This is lost, but the drawing suggests a half-uncial inscription of the kind which, in Wales, is normally found in an ecclesiastical context. This one is no exception: it does not apparently commemorate a dead person, but simply declares that 'This cross, Abbot Budnoenus ordered it to be made'.

160 I have omitted F4, Plourin 2, which is lost and may well be too late to be part of an Insular tradition of epigraphy.

161 On the assumption that VENO- is from **windo-*: cf. *LHEB*, § 7.

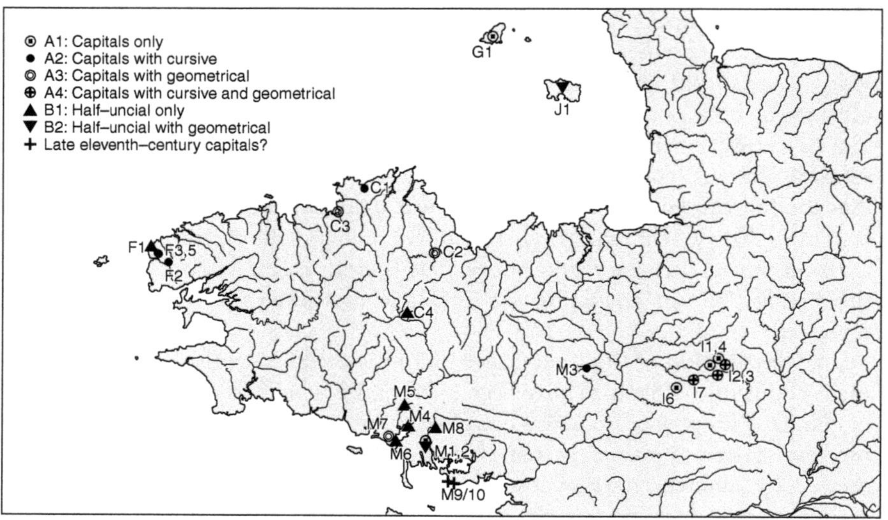

Map 19. Brittany: inscriptions
The Breton inscriptions are mostly near the sea in two clusters, one in the far west, the other in the Vannetais; the main exception to the seaward distribution is the cluster south-east of Rennes, in Ile-et-Vilaine. The Channel Islands appear to have been part of the British diaspora.

Further east, in the *département* of Côtes-d'Armor, the surviving inscriptions are much more scattered—more so, indeed, than in any other part of Brittany. C1, at Louannec on the north coast, is early, probably sixth century, but it has a cursive **g**. It is a classic example of the disregard for Latin morphology found in many Insular inscriptions of the post-Roman period: the name of the person being commemorated would be *Desiderius* in correct Latin but is here rendered DISIDERI as if it were in the genitive case, while the father's name BODOGNOVS, which ought to be in the genitive case, is instead in the nominative. Further east, in the diocese of St-Brieuc, C2, Plouagat, has an inscription still in capitals, but these are tending towards full Insular display lettering. It is dated to the late sixth or seventh century and illustrates how the route towards such display lettering was prepared in epigraphy before it ever appeared in manuscripts. An inscription further south, Sainte-Tréphine, C4, is unusual for being situated in the interior of Brittany.[162] It is later, dated between the eighth and the tenth century, is in Insular half-uncial, and declares itself to be 'the cross of Michael'.

The inscriptions of the Morbihan, in the Vannetais, are, taken in the round, different from those further north. The majority are of the later period, from the seventh century to the eleventh. One, Locoal-Mendon, M6, may even

[162] Davies et al., *The Inscriptions of Early Medieval Brittany*, suggest that it may have been moved.

commemorate a known person, Prostlon, the wife of the Breton ruler Pascweten, who died in 876, and the daughter of Salomon, who died in 874. The earlier, post-Roman inscriptions of the area are more scattered: one (M2) at Crac'h on the west side of the Morbihan itself, 'The Little Sea', another (M7) further west, at Locoal-Mendon by the estuary of the Etel, and the third (M3) well to the north-east at Guer. The later inscriptions of the area are clustered more closely around the Etel and the Auray rivers, with the exception of two, even later, probably eleventh-century inscriptions in revived capitals at Saint-Gildas-de-Rhuys, on the south side of the Morbihan.

The easternmost Breton inscriptions of the early medieval period come from an area to the south-east of Rennes, where we earlier saw Breton incursions of the late sixth century.[163] Four of them (I1–4) come from a single cemetery at Bourg Saint-Pair in the commune of Bais, dated to the end of the sixth or the beginning of the seventh century. The lettering of all four is very similar, and it is very likely that the date of the cemetery is also the date of the inscriptions. They are unlike the majority of Breton inscriptions in both material and the method of inscribing: they are on slate and I1 and I3–4 were made by drilling holes at the angles and then linking them, usually by straight lines. This is a technique that naturally produces angularized letterforms that foreshadow the geometrical display letters. I2 is very similar but with fewer drilled holes, more ligatured letters, and a cursive **r**. Inscriptions of this kind are not restricted to this one cemetery: at Retiers, about twelve kilometres south-west of Bais, an inscription (I6) is also on slate and used the same technique.

The previous chapter on the languages of the Britons and this one, on their inscriptions, show, with variations, one general pattern of change, from an epigraphy that evolved directly, as Tedeschi showed, from that of late Roman Britain, an epigraphy tied to the Latin language, still for some Britons a spoken language of the home, to an epigraphy that was much more ecclesiastical, closely tied to book scripts, and using a Latin now learnt in a school. In North Britain this development was cut short about 700 by Northumbrian expansion; in North Wales, epigraphy largely ended in the seventh century; but elsewhere, on the Isle of Man, in South Wales, Cornwall, and Brittany parallel developments occurred. One great advantage of inscriptions is that they make a bridge between material culture and the culture of the book and the Church. It is thus highly significant that one can tell a similar story over so many of the British lands. In the next chapter, however, we shall look more closely at the Irish impact on western Britain, an impact seen most particularly in the inscriptions of Cornwall, Wales, and the Isle of Man.

[163] Above, 70.

4

The Britons and the Irish, 350–800

1. IRISH RAIDS AND SETTLEMENTS IN BRITAIN

Irish raids on Britain began to be seriously damaging after the breaking of a treaty in 360. They reached an early climax in the 'barbarian conspiracy' of 367, when the Irish combined with the Picts and the Saxons to attack Britain. Irish raids were still continuing in the fifth century, as the experience of St Patrick makes plain. Good contemporary written evidence exists, therefore, to date Irish raids on western Britain: they appear to have lasted for the better part of the century after 360. More difficult to date is settlement of the kind attested by ogham inscriptions, Irish personal names in other inscriptions, and place-names.[1] The settlement of the Irish in western Britain did not require a mass migration, but it did need enough incomers to maintain an Irish-speaking elite for, perhaps, a minimum of two or three generations before it was assimilated to the British population—and such an assimilation appears to have happened by *c.* 600.

One clue to the date of the settlement is, as we have seen, Orosius's description of the Isle of Man as Irish, when compared with Bede's reference to it as British and the epigraphic evidence for the presence of both peoples on the island.[2] An Irish domination over the Irish Sea is likely to have issued in Irish control of the island, if only because of its strategic position. On this basis, we may suggest that Irish settlement was already under way by the early fifth century.

Some early ogham inscriptions, themselves vertical, coexisted with Latin inscriptions arranged horizontally on the stone in the Romano-British manner. These have been ascribed to the fifth century. An especially interesting example is the Castelldwyran stone first attested in the cemetery of that name, close to the route of the Roman road westwards from Carmarthen (it is now in Carmarthen Museum):[3]

Ogham: VOTECORIGAS (vertical; reading upwards on the left)
Latin: MEMORIA / VOTEPORIGIS / PROTICTORIS

[1] The conclusions of M. Richards, 'The Irish Settlements in South-West Wales: A Topographical Approach', *Journal of the Royal Society of Antiquaries of Ireland*, 90 (1960), 133–62, have been undermined, mainly for Ceredigion rather than for the core of Dyfed, by I. Wmffre, 'Post-Roman Irish Settlement in Wales: New Insights from a Recent Study of Cardiganshire Place-Names', in K. Jankulak and J. Wooding (eds.), *Ireland and Wales in the Middle Ages* (Dublin, 2007), 46–61.

[2] Above, 148–52.

[3] 358/138/Gso-8/CM3; SN 144 182.

The use of the title *protector* (with Late Latin confusion of short *i* and *e*) is intriguing since parallels are available elsewhere in the post-Roman world. Nash-Williams compared a fragmentary inscription from Toulouse, which recorded a lengthy period of service as *protector*.[4] In origin, it was used for elite household guards of the emperor—hence the emperor's 'protectors'—but in the late Empire it became, in addition, an honorary title. In Ostrogothic Italy, Cassiodorus preserved in his *Variae* the formal letter giving the title to someone who had retired from running the postal service.[5] Closer to Voteporix, however, is the case of Hariulf of the Burgundian royal family, who was termed 'household protector' on his memorial inscription.[6] The term was used, therefore, in the royal kindreds of the post-Roman west. Voteporix was long identified with the Vortiporius, the tyrant of the Demetae denounced by Gildas, in spite of the difference between the prefixed prepositions *wo-* 'under' and *wor-* 'over'; but the relatedness of the names and the Burgundian parallel encourage us to think of him as another member of the same dynasty.[7] This would allow us to retain the dating to the fifth century proposed on epigraphic grounds.[8] It has also been argued that the meaning of the first element in the name *Vo-tepo-rix* 'refuge-king' (Welsh *godeb*) would appropriately have been trumped by a later *Vor-tepo-rix*, with a first element *Vor-* meaning, in this context, something such as 'superior'.[9] If all this is correct, an Irish dynasty was established in Dyfed before the end of the fifth century; moreover, it showed an interest in stressing links with the Roman past in the titles it adopted as well as in the use of Roman epigraphy. In the sixth century, probably in the second quarter, Gildas's Vortiporius was evidently a Christian even if he was not a good one.[10]

In North Wales the issues are more complicated. When the Irish of *c.* 700 looked back on their past, they distinguished three leading peoples in Ireland: the Laigin or Leinstermen, the Ulaid or Ulstermen, and the Féni.[11] Up until *c.* 500, the Laigin held the eastern seaboard from the triple estuary of the Suir, Nore, and Barrow (near Waterford) north as far as the valley of the Boyne. Beyond the Boyne and the hills on its north side, the land subject to the Ulaid may have begun. The northern part of the Leinster coast, from the Wicklow Mountains north to include the Boyne, appears to have been the most important entry point for Roman goods into Ireland.[12] About 500, however, the Leinstermen lost their northern province, from the Liffey at Dublin

[4] E. Le Blant, *Inscriptions chrétiennes de la Gaule* (Paris, 1856), ii, no. 606 (Toulouse; fragmentary but including *a*NNOS XXXV . . . *milit*AVI(t) ANNOS XV . . . *pr*OTECTOR).

[5] Cassiodorus, *Variae*, xi. 31 (ed. Th. Mommsen, MGH, Auctores Antiquissimi, xii. 348); cf. A. H. M. Jones, *The Later Roman Empire* (Oxford, 1964), 53–4, 597, 636–40.

[6] E. Le Blant, *Nouveau recueil des inscriptions de la Gaule* (Paris, 1892), no. 38: HARIULFVS PROTECTOR DOMESITICVS EILIVS (for FILIVS) HANHAVALDI REGALIS GENTIS BVRGVNDIONVM . . . A good photograph is in A. Wieczorek et al., *Die Franken—Wegbereiter Europas, 5 bis 8. Jahrhundert n. Christ*, 2nd edn. (Mainz, 1996), ii. 842.

[7] *CIB* 346–7.

[8] Tedeschi, 'Osservazioni', 103–4, 115, id., *Congeries*, i. 120.

[9] *CIB* 347.

[10] For the dating of Gildas's *De Excidio Britanniae*, see below, 215–18.

[11] *ECI* 580, 583; for what follows, see ibid. 441–68.

[12] B. Raftery, *Pagan Celtic Ireland: The Enigma of the Irish Iron Age* (London, 1994), 207–19, especially the map on p. 214, on the basis of the material collected by J. D. Bateson, 'Roman Material

northwards, to the Féni, who had attacked them from the west. The Féni thus acquired an outlet to the Irish Sea, and with it one of the most fertile provinces of Ireland, Brega.

These events in Ireland may be of great significance for Wales. The name of the north-western peninsula pointing across the Irish Sea towards Leinster is Lleyn (later Llŷn); and this is likely to be a direct borrowing from the name of the Leinstermen, Laigin; a genitive plural form is likely to be contained in Dinllaen, 'fortress of the Laigin', on the northern coast of Lleyn close to Nefyn.[13] On the other hand, the name Gwynedd has been linked with the name of the new Irish presence in the Irish Sea, the Féni.[14] Yet Gwynedd was also a new creation of the post-Roman period. In the Roman period, as we saw in the Introduction, this was the land of the Ordovices.[15] Apart from one place-name of very doubtful etymology,[16] the sole evidence for them after 400 comes from an inscription at Penbryn near the coast of Ceredigion, about seven miles north-east of Cardigan.[17] It is a wide, roughly quadrangular pillar-stone, with an inscription reading vertically downwards:

> CORBALENGI IACIT / ORDOVS
> Corbaleng(us) lies (here), an Ordovician

It has been dated to the fifth century. The reason why Corbalengus was, most unusually, ascribed on his monument to a particular people, is likely to be that he was buried outside the territory of the Ordovices.[18] The site of the inscription, originally on top of an earlier cairn, is only a few miles north of the Teifi and is very likely to have been within the territory of the Demetae. What makes this inscription especially interesting, however, is that the name Corbalengus is Irish.[19] A very attractive explanation has been suggested, namely that Corbalengus's family was of Irish extraction but had been settled long enough among the Ordovices to ensure that he was perceived as an Ordovician even when he died among the Demetae.[20] The Irish settlements in Wales appear not to have undermined the old *civitates*: the densest Irish settlements were in North Pembrokeshire, but that area remained a core part of Dyfed.

from Ireland: A Reconsideration', *PRIA* 73, C (1973), 21–97; id. 'Further Finds of Roman Material from Ireland', *PRIA* 76, C (1976), 171–80; *ECI* 155–6.

[13] J. Lloyd-Jones, *Enwau Lleoedd Sir Caernarfon* (Cardiff, 1928), 6; Owen and Morgan, *Dictionary of the Place-Names of Wales*, 296, 396.

[14] Lloyd-Jones, *Enwau Lleoedd Sir Gaernarfon*, 5–6; id., 'Gwyrfai', *BBCS* 2 (1923–5), 111–12.

[15] Above, 20–1.

[16] Lloyd-Jones, *Enwau Lleoedd Sir Gaernarfon*, 4–5, is very hesitant; Owen and Morgan, *Dictionary of the Place-Names*, 125, regard the second element of Dinorwig as unclear.

[17] CD28 Penbryn 1, *ECMW* 126, Tedeschi, *Congeries*, Gso-41. NGR SN 289 514. See above, 137.

[18] P. Sims-Williams, 'The Five Languages of Wales in the Pre-Norman Inscriptions', *CMCS* 44 (Winter 2002), 1–36, at 26–7, and the commentary in Edwards, *Corpus*, ii. 185–7.

[19] For this reason, the scenario sketched by R. Geraint Gruffydd, 'Why Cors Fochno?', *THSC* N.S. 2 (1996), 19, namely that Corbalengus 'belonged to the first wave of Brittonic incursion south of the Dyfi and Ystwyth', is unlikely.

[20] Edwards, *Corpus*, ii. 187.

Illustration 4.1. This inscription, in roman capitals, perhaps to be dated to the first half of the sixth century, is now in the church of Penmachno but was brought there from Ffestiniog, a few miles to the south-west. It is the first attestation of the kingdom known as Gwynedd and the people known as Gwyndyd. It is also striking for its use of Roman political vocabulary but in Vulgar Latin.

Yet the Ordovices, unlike the Demetae, did not long survive the fifth century. An inscription, now kept in the church at Penmachno in Gwynedd, but earlier from Ffestiniog (see illustration 4.1), a few miles to the south-west, reveals the existence of a new *civitas* in the north-west:[21]

[21] Edwards, *Corpus*, iii, Ffestiniog 1, 394/103/Gn-32.

CANTIORI HIC IACIT / VENEDOTIS CIVE FVIT / [C]ONSOBRINO // MA[G]LI / MAGISTRATI

Cantiori lies here. He was a citizen of Gwynedd, a kinsman of Maglus the magistrate.

Cantiori bore a British name; and the way in which he was described, in Late Latin on its way to Romance, is redolent of a Roman political order: he was a *civis* of a named *civitas*, and his kinsman, Maglus, was a magistrate. Tedeschi dates it to the early sixth century.[22] By the time that Gildas was writing the *De Excidio Britanniae*, Gwynedd, under the rule of Maglocunus (Maelgwn), was the dominant kingdom in Wales.

Yet, there may be an odd difference between these two inscriptions. The personal name of the Ordovician was Irish, that of the citizen of Gwynedd British. Yet, in the opinion of most scholars, the very name of Gwynedd has Irish connections.[23] As we saw earlier, in the seventh century, Ireland was dominated by three 'noble races', the Leinstermen, the Ulstermen, and the Féni. The last-named, the Féni, were the rising power in the island: to them belonged the Uí Néill and other Connachta dynasties of the northern half and the Éoganachta of Munster. Part of their rise was the conquest of Brega north of the Liffey in the Irish midlands, adjacent to the Irish Sea, at the expense of Leinster. The Féni had been excluded from the Irish Sea, and thus from direct contact with Britain, by the other two 'noble races'. The evidence suggests that the Féni conquered Brega no earlier than *c.* 500. We have, therefore, a striking agreement of date: the Féni conquered the main outlet to the Irish Sea *c.* 500 and the replacement of the Ordovices by a new Gwynedd was also *c.* 500. The chronology of these changes gives weight to Lloyd-Jones's suggestion that Gwynedd was a borrowing from Irish Féni.[24] The usual view, however, has been that the name Gwynedd was cognate with Féni, a singular feminine **Wēnijā* giving Gwynedd alongside a plural masculine **Wēnijī* giving Féni; that is, allowing for the difference of gender and number, they are held to go back to a common original rather than one being borrowed from the other.

It is worth considering more fully the possible implications of these two inscriptions and the names they contain. They can be taken to suggest the following story. In the first half of the fifth century at least, the old *civitas* of north-west Wales, the Ordovices, remained intact. West of the Irish Sea, the area of greatest Roman contact with Ireland, namely Brega and the neighbouring region to the south of the Liffey, remained part of Leinster. In north-west Wales, links with this 'Greater Leinster' before 500 are attested by such place-names as Lleyn and Dinllaen, 'The Fortress of the Leinstermen'. The Irish settlement among the Ordovices, suggested

[22] Tedeschi, *Congeries*, Gn-32; cf. *CIB* 358; R. G. Gruffydd, 'From Gododdin to Gwynedd: Reflections on the Story of Cunedda', *Studia Celtica*, 24/25 (1989–90), 9, suggests that the Maglus of this inscription was Maelgwn Gwynedd, but see Sims-Williams, *CIB*, 158 n. 939.

[23] J. Morris-Jones, *Welsh Grammar* (Oxford, 1913), 46 (§ 38. ix), based on the *cynghanedd lusg* in *Dafydd ap Gwilym Apocrypha*, ed. and trans. H. Fulton (Llandysul, 1996), no. 15, line 1, *Y fun addwyn o Wynedd*; *LHEB* 655; E. P. Hamp, 'Notulae Etymologicae Cymricae', *BBCS* 28 (1978–80), 215, id., '*Goídil, Féni, Gŵynedd*', *Proceedings of the Harvard Celtic Colloquium*, 12 (1992), 43–50; id., 'Fian[L]', *Studia Celtica Japonica*, 8 (1996), 87–95; Sims-Williams, *CIB* 191.

[24] Lloyd-Jones, *Enwau Lleoedd Sir Gaernarfon*, 5; a suggestion also made by Koch, *Gododdin*, p. xcvii n., but doubted by me, *ECI* 160 n. 67, I now think wrongly.

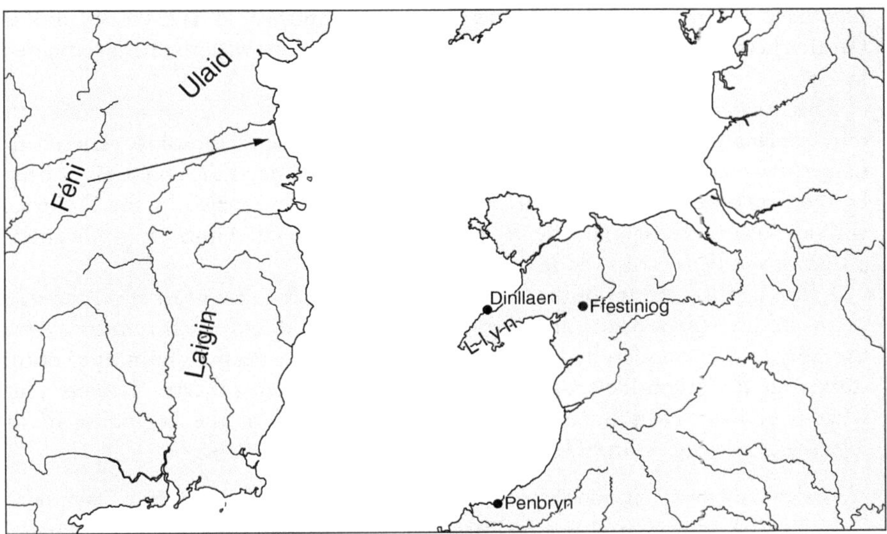

Map 20. Gwynedd, the Féni, and the Laigin
The map shows place-name evidence for links with the Laigin, the Leinstermen, in Llŷn and Dinllaen, and epigraphical evidence for Gwynedd (a name related to the Féni) replacing the Ordovices, still attested by the inscription at Penbryn.

by the personal name *Corbalengi* in the Penbryn inscription, should belong to this phase. About 500, however, the Féni conquered Brega and thus broke through to the Irish Sea. At much the same time, the Ordovices were replaced by Gwynedd, a kingdom, and the Gwyndyd, the people of Gwynedd. The close correspondence of date, *c.* 500, for the two changes may be taken as evidence that the appearance of the Féni (see Map 20) on one side of the Irish Sea and of Gwynedd on the other side were linked: Gwynedd might have been 'the land of the Féni', named after the new rulers of Brega.

The change might have been caused by an extension across the sea of the conquest of the Irish midlands; but it might also have come about more peacefully. We might assume that the Irish settlers in north-west Wales, such as Corbalengus's family, were predominantly connected with Brega, and that they switched allegiance to the new rulers of their native province in Ireland. The Irish settlers of north-west Wales, although sufficiently powerful to cause a change of political identity, shared power with the local British elite, to which Cantiori, with his evidently British name, probably belonged. Similarly, the Maelgwn or Maglocunus denounced by Gildas only about a generation after the replacement of the Ordovices by Gwynedd would appear to have been British. One may speculate a little further and suggest that the change of name was acceptable to the Britons of Gwynedd because it formed part of some alliance with the Féni, the new power in Ireland and in the Irish Sea. Such an alliance could have abated the Irish raids and even have played some part in changing the balance of power in the Irish Sea to the advantage of the Britons. The actual Irish settlement within Gwynedd would then have occurred no later than the fifth century and would have come from the Greater Leinster of that period. It could be contemporary with the Irish settlement in Dyfed.

This story is one possible explanation of the evidence; it is not necessarily the only explanation. Its strongest point is, if we accept the relationship between the names Gwynedd and Féni, the apparent closeness in time of the conquest of Brega by the Féni and the change from a north-west Wales dominated by the Ordovices with an Irish settlement already in place to one incorporated into a new Gwynedd, a land of the Féni across the sea.

Adopting this account of the creation of Gwynedd requires us to reject the story given, in different versions, in ninth-century Gwynedd and tenth-century Dyfed: the story of the conquest by Cunedda and his sons. The deeper significance of this story, even if one considers it to be fiction, will be considered in later chapters. Here what is at issue is its literal truth. A version is given at the beginning of the 'Northern History' in the *Historia Brittonum*, dated to 829–30:[25]

> Maelgwn, the great king, was reigning among the Britons, that is, in the land of Gwynedd; for his great-grandfather, that is, Cunedda, together with his sons, of whom there were eight, had earlier come from the north, that is, from the land which is called Manaw Gododdin, 146 years before Maelgwn was reigning, and with a very great slaughter they expelled the Irish from these lands, and they never came back again to settle there.

The context was that Maelgwn's reign overlapped with that of Ida of Bernicia, which was believed to have begun in 547.[26] Cunedda's migration was thus dated to somewhere approximately around 400: we do not know the year in which the *Historia Brittonum* believed Maelgwn to have begun his reign. The implication is, therefore, that the Irish settlement in Gwynedd came to an end about 400; and yet the Penbryn inscription shows that the Ordovices lasted through much of the fifth century and that they then included an Irish element.

The brief narrative translated above referred to Gwynedd as a *regio* but said that Cunedda and his sons expelled the Irish 'from these *regiones*' in the plural, *ab istis regionibus*. What they might have been is revealed by a much earlier passage in the *Historia Brittonum*, where it is attached to an origin legend of the settlement of Ireland:[27]

> Finally there came Damhoctor and lived there with all his people in Britain to this day. Istoreth, son of Istorinus, occupied Dalrieta with his people; Builc, however, with his, occupied the Isle of Man and others around about; the sons of Liethan, however, settled in the land of the Demeti and in other lands, that is, Gŵyr, Cedweli, until they were expelled by Cunedda and his sons from all the lands of the Britons.

These appear to be a string of Irish settlements in Britain. Where Damhoctor settled we are not told, but the others run from north to south, from what is now Argyll to the Isle of Man and finally to South Wales. This passage skips over Gwynedd, unless we are to understand that Damhoctor settled there, after which

[25] *HB* 62. [26] See below 343–4. [27] *HB* 14.

the text runs through less significant settlements from north to south. The only Irish people in this passage, which can be identified with an Irish kingdom and people in the historical period, is the one called 'the sons of Liethan', who are likely to be the Uí Liatháin of what is now the south-east of Co. Cork; yet in an Irish text of *c.* 900, Cormac's Glossary, they are said to have settled in Cornwall.[28]

Also in the Harleian manuscript, which contains the earliest version of the *Historia Brittonum*, but at the end of a collection of genealogies dating from the third quarter of the tenth century, is a further and very different version.[29] The number of sons has now risen to nine; the Irish are not mentioned; but we are told that the lands settled by the sons of Cunedda stretched from the Dee to the Teifi. The heartland of Dyfed, however, lay south of the Teifi, as did Gŵyr and Cedweli.

The story of Cunedda and his sons thus occurred in different versions already by 830. Although, as we shall see in Chapter 15, the earliest version of the *Historia Brittonum* was written during the reign of Merfyn Frych in Gwynedd—a king who had come from another Manaw, not Manaw Gododdin but Ynys Fanaw, the Isle of Man—the story was not invented as propaganda for Merfyn. The fit between their claims and any ambitions he may have held is not nearly exact enough; and the degree of variation in the different versions suggests that the story was already old by 830. That is not to say that, in its literal form, it has any chance of being true: the evidence of the ogham inscriptions and of the Irish personal names in other inscriptions shows that the Irish settlements retained their ethnic affiliation in the fifth century and probably well into the sixth. Gwynedd, Dyfed, and Brycheiniog are likely to have been partially Irish even in the days of Maelgwn Gwynedd, 'the great king', ancestor of the Maelgyning, the dynasty that, with its cousins of Rhos, ruled Gwynedd until the accession of Merfyn in 825.

2. THE BEGINNINGS OF IRISH CHRISTIANITY

We have it on the contemporary evidence of Prosper of Aquitaine that slave-raids by the barbarians, by introducing Christian slaves into the homes of the barbarians across the frontier, sometimes achieved the conversion of the raiders to Christianity.[30] The Irish, from the mid-fourth far into the fifth century, were avid slave-raiders. Patrick himself was taken as a slave in one of these raids, and, according to himself, the experience of living as a slave on the far western side of Ireland among a pagan people transformed him from a merely formal Christian into a someone who would, in spite of everything his kinsmen could say, return to Ireland in the hope of converting them to his faith.[31]

28 *Sanas Cormaic: An Old Irish Glossary*, ed. K. Meyer, Anecdota from Irish Manuscripts, ed. O. J. Bergin et al., 4 (Halle, 1912), 75, no. 883.

29 HG 32–3 in *EWGT* 13.

30 Prosper, *De Vocatione Omnium Gentium*, ii. 33 (ed. Migne, *PL* li. 717–18).

31 The standard edn. is by L. Bieler, *Libri Epistolarum S. Patricii Episcopi* (a) in *Classica et Medievalia*, 11 (1950), 1–150, and 12 (1951), 79–214; (b) reprinted Irish Manuscripts Commission (Dublin, 1952); (c) reprinted Royal Irish Academy (Dublin, 1993); a very useful edn.

In 429, a deacon called Palladius was sent to Pope Celestine to persuade him to give his authority to an attempt by Germanus, bishop of Auxerre, to fortify the orthodoxy of the British Church against 'the enemies of grace'. These 'enemies of grace', as the convinced Augustinian Prosper calls them, were followers of Pelagius; they had been exiled by a law of the emperor Honorius in 418 and had taken refuge in their native island, safe since the collapse of Constantine III's regime, from imperial officials.[32] In 431, the expedition of Germanus to Britain to combat the Pelagians had, however, an unexpected sequel. Prosper's contemporary chronicle is again the source: 'Palladius, having been ordained by Pope Celestine, is sent, as their first bishop, to the Irish who believe in Christ.'[33] The connection between the Pelagian controversy in Britain and an interest in the Irish Christians is indicated by another reference by Prosper to the mission in a work written in the 430s:

> He (Celestine) has been, however, no less energetic in freeing the British provinces from this same disease (the Pelagian heresy): he removed from that hiding-place certain enemies of grace who had occupied the land of their origin; also, having ordained a bishop for the Irish, while he labours to keep the Roman island catholic, he has also made the barbarian island Christian. (Prosper, *Contra Collatorem*, c. 21)[34]

Celestine was not, in fact, the prime mover: that was Germanus, but the pope gave his authority both to Germanus's expedition to Britain and to the sequel, the ordination of Palladius as the first bishop for the Irish. Celestine, however, was also the pope who, a few years earlier, had given the ruling that 'No bishop may be given to people unwilling (to receive him). The consent and wishes of the clergy, the laity, and (secular) authority are required.'[35] The likelihood is that a request from some Irish kingdom had reached Germanus's group, either when they were in Britain or via their allies in Britain soon after they had returned to Gaul. They then sought papal authority and Palladius was consecrated bishop for this Irish Christian community.

The emergence of a Christian community in Ireland in the early fifth century was contemporary with the Irish raids and settlements in Britain. It cannot, however, have consisted merely of British slaves taken by Irish raiders, provided we can take seriously Pope Celestine's reference to 'the clergy, the laity, and (secular) authority'. The term translated '(secular) authority' is *ordo*, sometimes used for the *ordo* of a *civitas*; and that is probably the kind of body that Celestine was thinking of—the local aristocracy of a distinct political community. We should think more of the connections across the Irish Sea begun by trade but extended by settlement. If we then ask which part of Ireland is most likely to have been involved,

is that by R. P. C. Hanson and C. Blanc, *Saint Patrick: Confession et Lettre à Coroticus*, Sources chrétiennes, no. 249 (Paris, 1978); for the structure of Patrick's works see the edn. by D. R. Howlett, *The Book of Letters of Saint Patrick the Bishop* (Blackrock, Co. Dublin, 1994).

32 *PL* li. 271.

33 Prosper, Chronicle, *s.a.* 431, ed. Th. Mommsen, *Chronica Minora saec. IV. V. VI. VII*, 3 vols, MGH AA 9 (Berlin, 1892), i. 473.

34 *PL* li. 271.

35 Celestine, *Ep.* iv (ed. Migne, *PL* l. 434).

the answer must be the Greater Leinster as it existed before *c.* 500: it included the area in which most Roman material of the fourth century has been found, and it is in this area that later evidence would place the earliest mission.[36] About Patrick, however, the one secure topographical detail we have places his work on the west coast of Ireland, and in particular in the north of Co. Mayo, in the kingdom that in the seventh century and later was ruled by the Uí Amolngada. Principally for this reason it is highly likely that Patrick's activity in Ireland was a generation later than the mission of Palladius and should thus be dated to the second half of the fifth century. Palladius was very probably from Gaul, although his involvement with the Irish was almost certainly a consequence of Germanus's first expedition to Britain. Patrick, however, was a Briton and his writings were directed in large part to Britons.

Patrick was active in the west, a part of Ireland likely to have been dominated by the Féni, and in the half-century before they conquered most of the Irish midlands, Mide and Brega. His own account in the *Confessio* shows that he was far from securing a rapid triumph signalled by the conversion of the principal kings: he was apparently more successful with the young than with the old, and perhaps with women rather than with men.[37] By the date of St Columba's birth *c.* 520 to a branch of the Uí Néill based in the far north-west, Christianity had a grip on the ruling dynasties of a part of Ireland most remote from Leinster. It is not surprising, therefore, that the memory of Patrick, the apostle of the Féni, should prevail over that of Palladius, the apostle of Leinster; and yet, in order to construct the seventh-century account of a Patrick who converted the whole of Ireland, it was necessary to borrow several elements from the story of Palladius, such as the link with St Germanus of Auxerre. Moreover, the removal of Palladius from the limelight did not occur rapidly as an immediate consequence of the triumph of the Féni: Columbanus of Luxeuil and Bobbio, himself from Leinster, recalled Palladius as the apostle of the Irish.[38] By the middle of the seventh century, however, the reputation of Patrick as 'the *papa* of the Irish' was secure.[39]

In one way, at least, the Patrician legend as it grew up in the sixth and seventh centuries expressed a truth: after the initial impetus from the circle of Germanus and from Pope Celestine the main work of Christianizing Ireland was carried forward by Britons. This is implied by the history of Latin words borrowed into Irish.[40] They are numerous and continue in a single unbroken sequence through into the period when Ireland was Christian. When distinctive sound-changes had occurred in the parent

[36] *ECI* 233–40.

[37] *Confessio*, §§ 41–2, 49–56.

[38] Columbanus, *Ep.* v. 3 (ed. G. S. M. Walker, *Sancti Columbani Opera* (Dublin, 1947), 38.

[39] Cummian, *De Controversia Paschali*, ed. and trans. M. Walsh and D. Ó Cróinín, *Cummian's Letter De Controversia Paschali and the De Ratione Computandi* (Toronto, 1988), 84, l. 208, 'sanctus Patricius papa noster'.

[40] D. McManus, 'The Chronology of Latin Loan-Words', *Ériu*, 34 (1983), 21–71; id. 'The so-called *Cothrige* and *Pátraic* Strata of Latin Loan-Words in Early Irish', in P. Ní Chatháin and M. Richter (eds.), *Irland und Europa: Die Kirche im Frühmittelalter / Ireland and Europe: The Early Church*, Veröffentlichungen des Europa Zentrums Tübingen, Kulturwissentschaftliche Reihe (Stuttgart, 1984), 179–96.

British Latin (often influenced by British Celtic), they were reflected in the words borrowed into Irish; similarly, the borrowing will have occurred at a particular point in the sequence of Irish sound-changes, so that changes occurring after that date will affect the borrowed word. These Latin loanwords in Irish show, among other things, that British clergy active in Irish circles pronounced their Latin more or less as if it were British—a British that, by this time, was heavily influenced by Latin.

The context of Patrick's *Confessio* may also indicate that a British synod still had responsibility in his day for the nascent Irish Church. Patrick wrote the *Confessio* in large part to rebut two accusations made against him in a synod held in Britain. The first was that he had been shown to have received episcopal consecration unworthily: he had committed a sin as an adolescent and had revealed it in confidence to a close friend; but apparently he had not declared it before he was consecrated; now, however, when he had been working as bishop for several years, it had been made public by the friend. The second was that he was making a profit out of his work as a missionary. As I read his text, Patrick had not been condemned by the synod as worthy to be degraded from his episcopal office, yet his reputation was seriously threatened among his British collaborators and his Irish flock.

Once, however, the kings of the Irish had almost all become Christian, the formal ties between the British and Irish Churches would naturally have come to an end; and this is most likely to have happened in the early sixth century. The period of the closest connection between Irish and British Christianity overlaps, therefore, with the period to which epigraphers have dated the British inscriptions revealing an Irish presence in Britain. Formulae used in many of these inscriptions, such as *Hic iacit* 'here lies', are Christian; and this is enough to show that, in the overall history of the Christianization of the Irish, the adoption of the new religion by the Irish settled in Britain must be given its proper place. Both Corbaleng(i) the Ordovician and Cantiori the citizen of Gwynedd were commemorated using versions of a Christian formula, *Hic iacit*.

The Irish settlers must also be given their proper place in the history of the Christianization of Britain. In 400 Celtic paganism remained a powerful presence in Britain.[41] On the one hand, the skimpy evidence is just enough to reveal a British Church organized along the lines prescribed by the Council of Nicaea in 325: *civitas* capitals were to have bishops who were to be responsible for pastoral care in the territories of the *civitates*. As the Church developed under imperial favour during the fourth century, imperial provinces were to have their counterparts in the Church and provincial synods were to meet regularly under the presidency of a metropolitan bishop. Britain was also beginning to share in the new enthusiasm for the cult of saints, especially martyrs, as at St Albans and at Caerleon.[42] On the other hand, in the second half of the fourth century the shrine of Nodons at Lydney in

[41] P. Salway, *Roman Britain*, 737–9; D. J. Watts, *Religion in Late Roman Britain: Forces of Change* (London, 1998).

[42] R. Sharpe, 'The Late Antique Passion of St Alban', in M. Henig and P. Lindley (eds.), *Alban and St Albans: Roman and Medieval Architecture, Art and Archaeology*, British Archaeological Association Conference Transactions 24 (Leeds, 2001), 30–7; id., 'Martyrs and Local Saints in Late Antique Britain' in Thacker and Sharpe (eds.), *Local Saints and Local Churches*, 75–154.

Gloucestershire, on the west side of the Severn, attracted a level of support that indicates aristocratic patronage. Yet, by the date of Germanus's first visit to Britain the rich and noble appear to have been Christian. The decisive period in the Christianization of the aristocracy in late Roman Britain is unlikely to have been very different from that of the Christianization of the Roman senatorial aristocracy or the aristocracy of Gaul.[43] When the leaders of the Irish settlement in western Britain welcomed *Romanitas* in the fifth century, often using Roman names and sometimes Roman titles, such as *protector*, they adopted it in a Christian form. In the fourth century the main strength of Christianity is likely to have been in eastern Britain: of the three British bishops that attended the Council of Arles in 314, two were bishops of major cities, capitals of provinces, York and London, and the third was probably from Lincoln, also in the east and a provincial capital.[44] The Christianization of the Irish in the far west of Britain by *c.* 500 at the latest and in the far north-west of Ireland by *c.* 525 indicates that Christianization was a long process with a geographical direction from east to west. The presence of the Irish on both sides of the sea facilitated that westwards movement.

3. THE SIXTH CENTURY AND THE SHIFT OF GRAVITY

After the fifth century there is no reason to believe that the Irish Church was formally attached to its British counterpart. The sixth century saw the flourishing of monasticism in Ireland and western Britain; it also saw the early maturity of Christian learning in Ireland, evident in the writings of Columbanus and in his confidence in the scholarship of his native land.[45] Irish and British monasticism were linked, as is shown by the textual tradition of the penitentials, which were originally primarily monastic; but ever since the days of Faustus of Riez and, later, St Patrick, the monasticism of Gaul had also been influential in Britain and Ireland.[46] Knowledge of another major monastic writer, Cassian of Marseilles, came to Ireland through Britain, as shown by the distinctively British form of his name in Irish, Cassión.[47]

One critical issue in Insular monasticism provoked an open dispute with echoes on both sides of the Irish Sea: poverty and the plough team. In contemporary

[43] P. R. L. Brown, 'Aspects of the Christianization of the Roman Aristocracy', *Journal of Roman Studies*, 51 (1961), 1–11, repr. in his *Religion and Society in the Age of St Augustine* (London, 1972), 161–82; R. Van Dam, *Leadership and Community in Late Antique Gaul* (Berkeley, Cal., 1985), 141–76.

[44] C. Thomas, *Christianity in Roman Britain to AD 500* (London, 1981), 133, 197.

[45] Columbanus, *Ep.* i. 4, ed. Walker, *Sancti Columbani Opera* (Dublin, 1957), 6; cf. Jonas, *Vita S. Columbani*, cc. 2 and 5.

[46] Patrick, *Confessio*, c. 43; M. W. Herren, 'Mission and Monasticism in the *Confessio* of Patrick', in D. Ó Corráin et al. (eds.), *Sages, Saints and Storytellers: Celtic Studies in Honour of Professor James Carney* (Maynooth, 1989), 76–85. For Faustus, see below, 199–202.

[47] The form *Cassión*, attested in a text of *c.* 597, in the *Amrae Choluimb Chille*, ed. and trans. W. Stokes, 'The Bodleian Amra Choluimb Chille', *Revue Celtique*, 20 (1899), 254 (§ 55), ed. and trans. T. O. Clancy and G. Márkus, *Iona: The Earliest Poetry of a Celtic Monastery* (Edinburgh, 1995), 108–9, betrays a British intermediary by its use of *ō* for *ā*.

farming the most obvious dividing line between the poor and the relatively well off was possession of a plough team or, at least, a share in a plough team. Monks, however, were supposed to embrace a life of poverty; and, so, it seemed clear to some that they should do without plough oxen and cultivate the land by dragging ploughs themselves or digging, like the poor. Gildas, however, thought that this was going too far. The issue at stake in a fragment of one of his letters is when should one abbot accept a monk who has left another abbot:[48]

> Still less should we welcome those who come from holy abbots who are under suspicion only because they possess animals and vehicles because it is the custom of their country or because of their weakness: these are things that do less harm to their owners, if they are possessed in humility and patience, than is done to those who drag ploughs and plunge spades in the ground in presumption and pride.

It has been observed that this passage makes it very likely that, in his Life of St David, Rhigyfarch had some good source for St David's form of monastic life, for it reveals St David as just such a rigorous ascetic as was here criticized by Gildas.[49] An Irish counterpart to St David was Fintan of Clonenagh, whose Life, probably of the eighth century, has a story of the saint resisting a deputation of his brother saints, led by St Cainnech, who asked that he should relax the austerity of his rule: the difference between Cainnech and Fintan reproduces that between Gildas and, so we may infer, St David.[50]

The similarities between the Irish and British Churches were sustained by personal ties rather than by institutional links. Columbanus records correspondence between Gildas and Vinnian, perhaps the Vinniau or Findbarr who was Columba's teacher and bishop of Movilla and thus a close neighbour to Columbanus's former monastery of Bangor (Co. Down).[51] When Columbanus left Bangor for Francia, he appears to have landed in Brittany. He was certainly aided in his early years in Burgundy by a neighbouring abbot with a British name, Carantoc, and his own community contained Britons as well as Irish, Franks, Gallo-Romans, and Burgundians. The seventh-century Life of St Samson, who came from South Wales but migrated to Dol in north-eastern Brittany, describes the saint as spending some time in Ireland and then returning from Howth, now a suburb of Dublin.[52] A younger contemporary, Fintan mac Tailcháin, alias Munnu, founded the monastery of Taghmon, Tech Munnu, in Co. Wexford. The early ninth-century Martyrology of Tallaght preserves what may be a fragment of a *Liber Memorialis* of Taghmon, and the names include several that are British.[53]

[48] Gildas, Fragment no. 4, trans. Winterbottom, *Gildas: The Ruin of Britain*, 81.

[49] J. Morris, 'The Dates of the Celtic Saints', *Journal of Theological Studies*, NS, 17 (1966), 349–50, 384–5; D. N. Dumville, *Saint David of Wales*, Kathleen Hughes Memorial Lectures, 1 (Cambridge, 2001), 12–14; reprinted in his *Celtic Essays, 2001–2007*, 44–7.

[50] *Vita S. Fintani de Cluain Edhnech*, §§ 4–5, ed. W. W. Heist, *Vitae Sanctorum Hiberniae* (Brussels, 1965), 147.

[51] Columbanus, *Ep.* i. 7 (ed. Walker, *S. Columbani Opera*, 8–9).

[52] *Vita Prior S. Samsonis*, i. 37–8 (ed. Flobert, *La Vie ancienne*, 200–2).

[53] T. M. Charles-Edwards, 'Britons in Ireland, *c.* 550–800', in J. Carey, J. T. Koch, and P.-Y. Lambert (eds.), *Ildánach Ildírech: A Festschrift for Proinsias Mac Cana* (Andover, Mass., 1999), 23–5.

More compelling as evidence for the shared ecclesiastical culture of the Britons and the Irish at this period and for several centuries is that they not only used the same scripts but that Insular script continued to develop in the same direction on both sides of the Irish Sea at least as far as the mid-ninth century when shared innovations were occurring at much the same time.[54] On the other hand, in epigraphy the paths diverged *c.* 700;[55] and the numerous inscriptions at Clonmacnois are quite unlike Welsh ones of the same date. The spelling of Old Irish has a distinctively British aspect, unlike the orthography of the ogham inscriptions in Ireland. Yet this 'Brittonicization' of the way Irish was written was a long process: we can see the first signs of it in ogham inscriptions in Wales but it was not complete even by *c.* 700.[56] The close ties between western Britain and Ireland that began in violence subsequently formed the first basis of an Insular culture that would spread to northern Britain, including Northumbria. One of its prime characteristics was already seen in the bilingual inscriptions of the fifth and sixth centuries: the willingness to give a similar honour to Latin and to the vernacular. For the Irish, but not initially for the Britons, both were worthy to be used to commemorate great men on stone.

Although it is right to see the culture of Celtic Britain and Ireland in the pre-Norman period as largely a shared one, two cautionary notes are in place. First, the centre of gravity of that culture shifted west during the sixth century, from Britain to Ireland. In Britain, Gildas recorded the destruction of the cities, the old centres of Romanization. Although one or two centres of British Christianity may have survived in the east—St Albans is the best example—they were cut off from other Britons by Gildas's day. At a period when Irish Christianity was beginning to flourish, British Christianity was fragmented and in retreat. Secondly, the close ties between western Britain and Ireland did not issue in a 'Celtic Church' but rather in distinct Churches within a single cultural zone. Even the term 'Celtic Christianity' is unacceptable, since it suggests a contrast between 'Celtic' and 'Roman', a contrast that is too close to the viewpoints of its enemies in seventh-century England, who would condemn 'the schismatics of Britain and Ireland'.[57] In opposing Celtic and Roman it is both anachronistic (contemporaries did not use the term 'Celtic') and redolent also—because 'Celtic' in this context has often been used in contrast to 'Roman'—of the Protestant search for some ancient non-Roman form of Christianity in these islands which began as soon as Henry VIII decided to break with Rome.[58]

[54] D. N. Dumville, *A Palaeographer's Review: The Insular System of Scripts in the Early Middle Ages*, i (Kansai, 1999), 125.

[55] As shown by the Kilnasaggart inscription from Co. Armagh, *CIIC*, no. 946 (the donor died in 716: Charles-Edwards, *The Chronicle of Ireland*, i. 191).

[56] 342/70/Gse-17/B45; 409/198/Gse-12/G86; A. Harvey, 'Some Significant Points of Early Insular Celtic Orthography', in D. Ó Corráin et al. (eds.), *Sages, Saints and Storytellers: Celtic Studies in Honour of Professor James Carney* (Maynooth, 1989), 56–66.

[57] *Vita S. Wilfridi*, c. 5 (ed. and trans. B. Colgrave, *The Life of Bishop Wilfrid by Eddius Stephanus* (Cambridge, 1927), 12/13), *scismatici Brittaniae et Hiberniae*; similarly, but in different terms, cc. 12, 47.

[58] D. E. Meek, *The Quest for Celtic Christianity* (Edinburgh, 2000); originally this took the form of asserting a non-Roman British Church: a classic example is the brilliant introduction by Richard Davies, bishop of St Davids, to the 1567 Welsh translation of the New Testament. *Rhagymadroddion,*

4. ETHNIC CONSOLIDATION

In the fifth century Corbalengus, someone of Irish descent, and perhaps also Irish speech, could be accepted in his exile as a member of an old British people, the Ordovices. He could be identified, that is, in good Roman manner by his *origo*, the *civitas* to which he belonged by virtue of the territory in which he was born. The Venedotes (Gwyndyd) of the new Gwynedd were *cives*, fellow-citizens, in their new kingdom, whether they were Britons or Irish. An inscription could be put up, probably in the fifth century, in both Latin and Irish at Nevern in the territory of the Demetae to commemorate a Vitalianus *emeritus*.[59] The name Vitalianus is Latin, and, in the ogham, is regularly in the genitive. The same genitive form is used in the Latin, where it is accompanied by a Late Latin form of *emeritus*, with *i* replaced by *e* and the ending *-us* by *-o*. The term *emeritus* has a long history in Latin, being used for a veteran who had served his time in the army, but also for others who had completed periods of service. It was used as a *cognomen*, additional name, in Roman Britain, as elsewhere.[60] In a Christian context it could imply that someone had died well, having served God well during life, and this is the interpretation preferred here by Tedeschi.[61] What is striking about this inscription is that only the use of ogham indicates that the person was Irish; everything else points to a Roman context. It and many other inscriptions like it point to a sharp contrast between the east and the west of Britain: the cultural attitudes of the Germanic settlers in the east could hardly have been more different from those of the Irish settlers in the west. In the east, even though there is good reason to think that it was more Romanized than the west, there are no fifth- and sixth-century bilingual inscriptions in Germanic and Latin, no Germanic leaders proudly claiming their place in a Roman world by such titles as *protector* or *tribunus*, and no adoption until the end of the sixth century of the Christianity that had been widespread in eastern Britain in 400. The contrast becomes all the sharper as soon as it is remembered that across the Channel the Frankish elite behaved like the Irish elite in Britain.

Both the Franks and the Irish partly assimilated themselves into the society within which they settled and partly assimilated that society to themselves. The effect was a contrast between the Frankish kingdom of Clovis or the western Britain of his day and the Francia or Britain of 700. By the death of Clovis in 511 the

1547–1659, ed. G. H. Hughes (Cardiff, 1951), 17–43; G. Williams, 'Some Protestant Views of Early British Church History', *Welsh Reformation Essays* (Cardiff, 1967), 207–19.

[59] Nevern 2, 445/354/Gso-39/P71. See also above, 109–10.

[60] Tedeschi, *Congeries*, i. 157 (Gso-39), compares *RIB* nos. 152 (Bath, a *serving* centurion), 892 (Old Carlisle fort, dedication of a share of spoils; therefore a serving soldier), 1716 (Chesterholm, Flavia Emerita, a woman). Edwards, *Corpus*, P71, suggests tentatively that there were two inscriptions: (i) the ogham; (ii) the Latin for the son, Emeritus son of Vitalianus, comparing *CIIC* 488; but there *FILII* is used and the explanation is, in any case, unnecessary.

[61] The *Corpus* points out that the Latin could be translated 'Emeritus (son) of Vitalianus', comparing *CIIC* 488/Ok60/DSD-12 (Devon), where the Latin commemorates the son of the person commemorated in the ogham; yet, in that case, the son's relationship to his father was expressed in the normal way, 'X son of Y'. This translation is therefore unlikely to be correct.

Franks and Gallo-Romans had, broadly, learnt to live as partners within one polity. The Frankish kingdom of 511 contained two principal peoples, Franks mainly in the north and east, elsewhere Gallo-Romans; yet, at the same time, there were numerous ethnic pockets, Sarmatian, Saxon, and others, the Britons 'of the dispersal' among them. In western Brittany, even in the areas most solidly settled by the Britons, there were pockets of Gallo-Romans. True, broad distinctions also existed in northern Gaul, such as those implied by the Life of St Samson between Brittania, Romania, and Francia; but within the Romania of the Life also lived the Saxons of the Bessin, the territory around Bayeux.

Similarly, north of the Channel, there were British pockets even in English territory, such as the valleys of the Chilterns, including St Albans, or the Britons who seem still to have been preserving the cult of St Sixtus in Kent when Augustine arrived in 597.[62] In the west the Lleyn peninsula presumably had an Irish, and specifically Leinster, character not shared by all of Gwynedd; and in Dyfed the Irish settlement, to judge by the inscriptions, was densest between the southern slopes of the Preseli Mountains and the Teifi. Northern Gaul and southern Britain *c.* 550 were more like the eastern Europe of 1900, with its intermingled ethnicities, than the western Europe of today. The situation by 700 was changing fundamentally, but not at the same speed, over all the lands between the Loire and the Forth. By then it was possible for Bede to make the closest possible connection between language and nationality: for him, apart from Latin, four 'languages of nations' were spoken in Britain. After the Pippinids (later Carolingians) had taken power in northern Gaul, apart from Brittany, a Francia north of the Loire faced a Romania to the south. The mass of the population of the old Romania of the Life of St Samson, to the east of the Breton frontier as far as the Seine, were now simply Franks and declared their Frankishness in their personal names, even though they still spoke *lingua Romana*, what we call Gallo-Romance.[63] Here language did not have the same significance that it had for Bede, but the consolidation was nevertheless profound and lasting. In western Brittany there was a similar ethnic consolidation to that recorded by Bede, but now to the benefit of the Breton dialect of British and of a British identity. These consolidations, however, were achieved at different dates. Perhaps the earliest was the assimilation of the Irish of western Britain, south of the Clyde, to the Britons among whom they lived; this may have occurred around 600, when the inscriptions become less numerous. On the other side, with the prolonged advance of English political control westwards, some pockets of Britons remained in English territory even in 700, as shown by the inscriptions at Wareham in eastern Dorset.[64] The final hardening of the Welsh frontier with Mercia would not come until the eighth century and the reign of Offa. By 700,

[62] R. Sharpe, 'Martyrs and Local Saints in Late Antique Britain', in A. Thacker and R. Sharpe (eds.), *Local Saints and Local Churches in the Early Medieval West* (Oxford, 2002), 118, 123–5; C. Stancliffe, 'The British Church and the Mission of Augustine', in R. Gameson (ed.), *St Augustine and the Conversion of England* (Stroud, 1999), 121–2.

[63] For other terms, see A. Blom, '*Lingua Gallica, Lingua Celtica*: Gaulish, Gallo-Latin, or Gallo-Romance?', *Keltische Forschungen*, 4 (2009), 7–54.

[64] Above, 129.

also, it is likely that British Latin had ceased to be a spoken language of the home: speaking British could now be the crucial mark of Britishness in a way that could not have been the case in the Britain of Gildas.

In this period of ethnic consolidation may be placed the legend that Cunedda and his sons came from Manaw Gododdin, expelled the Irish from much of Wales, and founded the dynasty of Gwynedd.[65] It is much more likely, as contemporary inscriptions indicate, that Gwynedd was founded by the Irish, or at least in a very close alliance with them. In this respect, therefore, the legend tells the opposite of the truth. Its story, however, is one of British unity and national purity: of the Britishness of Wales rescued by the Britons of the far north, on the borders of Pictland, and of Irish expelled not assimilated. Even in the tenth century, in *Armes Prydein*, the lands of the Britons were conceived as stretching from Manaw to Llydaw, from Manaw Gododdin in the north to Brittany in the south.

By 700 the relationship between Britain and Ireland was completely different. Alongside the shift of an intellectual primacy across the sea to Ireland, a relative peace prevailed between the two peoples. By then the Isle of Man was regarded as British: a failed attempt by the Ulstermen to regain control may be behind two concise entries in the Chronicle of Ireland in 577 and 578. In the years either side of 700 there was a flurry of British military activity in eastern Ireland. The defeat of the Cruithni by Britons in 682 in a battle at their principal stronghold at Ráith Mór Maige Line (now on the eastern outskirts of Antrim Town) may have had Isle of Man connections.[66] In 697 Britons and Ulstermen combined to lay waste Mag Muirthemne (in Co. Louth).[67] Further south, Britons slew Írgalach son of Conaing, of the ruling dynasty of Brega, at Inis Mac Nesán, Ireland's Eye.[68] So far there is more than a hint that Britons were acting in alliance with the Ulaid, the Ulstermen proper: first, in 682, against their rivals within the province, the Cruithni, then further south in Mag Muirthemne in an alliance acknowledged by the annalist; and then further south again, off the coast of Brega. But in 703, the year after the killing of Írgalach, we have something different: 'The battle of Mag Culind in Ardd Ua nEchdach between the Ulaid and the Britons, in which fell the son of Radgann, the adversary of the churches of God. The Ulaith were the victors.'[69] We are now back in the north-east, not in the lands of the Cruithni but in the Ards peninsula, within the territory of the Ulaid proper. Where the Ards peninsula separates from the mainland were two major monasteries: Bangor and Movilla. Across Strangford Lough lay another, Nendrum. For an 'adversary of the churches of God' there were rich pickings in the coastland of Ulster. These events, it may be remembered, all lie in the twenty years after the attack by the Northumbrians on Brega, an attack which presupposed a new English power in the Irish Sea, one that Bede recalled as having first been won by Edwin of Northumbria when he briefly gained control of Anglesey and Man. By *c.* 700, also, the Northumbrians are likely to have conquered what is now south-western Scotland. Yet, although, before

[65] *HB*, caps. 14, 62; HG 32, ed. Bartrum, *EWGT* 13; *VSBG* 148.
[66] AU, *CI* 682. 2. [67] AU, *CI* 697. 10.
[68] AU, *CI* 702. 2. [69] AU, *CI* 703. 1.

their great defeat at Nechtanesmere in 685, the Northumbrians threatened the stability of the Irish Sea region, the norm in relations between Britons and Irish was peace. More typical of eighth-century relations between Britons and Irish was Colmán son of Fáelán (two good Irish names) 'of the Britons', abbot of Slane on the Boyne, one of the most important monasteries of Brega, and himself the founder of one of the main clerical dynasties of the area.[70]

[70] *CI* 751. 9; K. Hughes, *The Church in Early Irish Society* (London, 1966), 163.

5

From Pelagius to Gildas

The inscriptions revealed a spoken British Latin on its way to Romance, in decline but still surviving up to the seventh century alongside an increasingly dominant British. Both languages, British Celtic and British Latin, tended to change in parallel, as one would expect if there were many bilingual speakers. In this chapter the discussion will shift from the generality of the British population to a very small intellectual elite, those Britons whose writings revealed them as the peers of the best minds in Latin Christendom.

In the first centuries of the Roman Empire a non-Italian wishing to make a reputation as a poet or prose writer in Latin had to go to Rome. By the late fourth century, however, Ausonius from Aquitaine could attain both political influence and fame as a poet without making his permanent home south of the Alps. Since the western emperor was often at Trier, men who had the requisite education could pursue a career at court outside Italy;[1] and even when the emperor was at Milan, he was still in Cisalpine Gaul. From the fifth century the most successful careers might take two directions: in the service of the state, whether emperor or barbarian king, or in the Church. Hence St Germanus of Auxerre was first a provincial governor and then a bishop; and he lost nothing of his power to influence events outside the territory of Auxerre by his change of office.[2] On the other side, the most distinguished legal writing of the fifth century was the Code of the Visigothic king Euric for his Gothic subjects, thought to have been written by a Roman jurist, Leo of Narbonne.[3] According to Levy, 'it may safely be called the best legislative work of the fifth century... superior to the Code of Theodosius, which was a mere anthology, superior to the contemporary imperial decrees with their obscure verbosity.'[4]

There was, therefore, a cultural movement from the centre to the provinces in the late Empire, a movement that continued as the western Empire itself fell apart. This movement occurred in two stages: first, when the imperial court itself was normally to be found in a major provincial centre not too far from the frontier; and, secondly, when barbarian kings became the masters of provinces but wished to rule, to some degree, like emperors, and when bishops, whose primary concerns were with their own cities, became central figures in late Roman culture. Britain, however, was only

[1] As did the Ponticianus of Augustine, *Confessions*, VIII. vi. 14–15.

[2] For Germanus as governor, Constantius, *Vita Germani*, § 1; cf. R. Van Dam, *Leadership and Community in Late Antique Gaul* (Berkeley, 1985), 142.

[3] On the basis of Sidonius Apollinaris, *Epp*. viii. 3.

[4] E. Levy,'Reflections on the First "Reception" of Roman law in Germanic States', in his *Gesammelte Schriften* (Cologne, 1963), i. 209.

occasionally the beneficiary of these changes. The major imperial centre for the north-western dioceses, those included in the Prefecture of the Gauls, was Trier; even though the Caesar Constantius I may have died at York and his son, Constantine the Great, have thus been proclaimed his successor there, the latter had to pursue his ambitions across the Channel. Even into the fifth century known British writers had already left Britain before they acquired a wide reputation. It is not until the sixth century, with Gildas, that we have a text of high intellectual aspiration written by someone who did not leave British territory.[5] Moreover, the Germanic invaders of Britain threw up no Euric to patronize Roman culture even for his barbarian followers. Not until the beginning of the seventh century would an English king sponsor written law; and then it came in the wake of Æthelberht of Kent's conversion to a Christianity introduced from Rome, and the text itself was simple in form and English in language.[6]

On the other hand, Britain was unusually favoured by a third stage in the spread of Mediterranean culture. In sixth-century Gaul, Gregory of Tours still thought of the Rhine as a frontier between a more or less civilized world and a barbarian hinterland.[7] The culture he exemplified had made little progress east of the Rhine and north of the Danube in spite of the Frankish hegemony over large parts of what is now Germany. The English parts of Britain thus fitted into this pattern: although, like Saxony and Frisia, they belonged to a part of the world dominated by the Franks, they did not espouse the religion adopted by the Frankish kings. To the west, however, the limits of the former Roman Empire were transcended, so that by the second half of the sixth century Ireland was extensively Christianized, with an elite that had embraced the Latin culture of its neighbour, Britain.

This change—from a complete intellectual dominance enjoyed by the lands around the Mediterranean to a greater independence of the north-western provinces—can be followed in the careers of three Britons: Pelagius, Faustus, and Gildas.

1. PELAGIUS

Pelagius first appears in the historical record when he was already at Rome, where he is likely to have gone as a young man. If he was the unnamed monk, an ex-lawyer, to whom Jerome referred, he was there in 393 or 394.[8] The difficulty, however,

[5] His eleventh-century Breton Life claims that he left the island of Britain for Brittany via Rome and Ravenna, ed. and trans. H. Williams, *Gildae De Excidio Britanniae* (London, 1899), §§ 13–16; whether or not this has any foundation in fact, he remained ultimately within the lands of the Britons.

[6] P. Wormald, *The Making of English Law: King Alfred to the Twelfth Century* (Oxford, 1999), i. 93–101.

[7] Gregory of Tours, *Hist.*, iv. 49 ('the savagery of the *gentes* who live across the Rhine'); cf. *Epp. Austrasicae*, ed. Gundlach, no. 9, pp. 122–4 (Germanus, bishop of Paris, to Brunhild).

[8] Jerome, *Letters*, 50. 2 (CSEL 54, 388–95). The identification was upheld by G. de Plinval, *Pélage, ses écrits, sa vie et son reforme* (Lausanne, 1943), 50–63, R. F. Evans, *Pelagius: Inquiries and Reappraisals* (London, 1968), 31–7, but opposed by Y.-M. Duval, 'Pélage est-il le censeur inconnu de l'*Adversus Iovinianum* à Rome en 393? ou 'Du "Portrait-Robot" de l'hérétique chez S. Jérome', *Revue d'histoire ecclesiastique*, 75 (1980), 530–40. B. R. Rees, *Pelagius: A Reluctant Heretic* (Woodbridge, 1988), 4–5, comes down in favour of the identification.

with Jerome's references to his opponents is that they were chosen for their mud-slinging potency rather than with a strict regard for truth; for example, he says that Pelagius was 'a porridge-sodden Irishman', whereas other sources regard him as a Briton.[9] Pelagius himself rejected the designation of 'monk', but in terms that showed that he regarded the monk as essentially a solitary, a hermit.[10] He was evidently, to judge by his writings, an ascetic; and, at that period, the divide between monks and other ascetics was much less clear-cut than it later became.

The Pelagian network—for that is what it was, rather than a party or sect—was beginning to form in the 390s, when Pelagius is likely to have met Caelestius and Rufinus the Syrian, and when he was establishing himself as a spiritual guide for members of the senatorial aristocracy.[11] The first text written by Pelagius of which we know is his commentary on the Epistles of St Paul, composed in Rome between *c.* 406 and 410. His other surviving works were written after he, in the company of many others, had left Rome in the face of Alaric's approach; he then went first to Africa and shortly afterwards to Palestine. His emergence as the target of attacks by Jerome and Augustine dates from his stay in the east; and it is likely to have been while he was in the east that the growing gravity of the controversy drove both sides to take more extreme positions.[12] In 415 Pelagius was acquitted by the Synod of Diospolis, but Augustine's hostility to his teaching deepened.

In 418 Pelagius was condemned first by the Emperor Honorius and then by Pope Zosimus.[13] As a result he was expelled from Jerusalem, where he had earlier been protected by the bishop, John. Nothing further is known of him, but he may have left for Egypt and perhaps died not much later. The imperial condemnation of 418 required adherents of Pelagius's views to be tried and sent into exile. Prosper of Aquitaine, a staunch opponent of all views Pelagian, wrote in his Chronicle that the strength of British Pelagianism owed much to a group, led by one Agricola, himself the son of a Bishop Severianus;[14] it may well be that they had been exiled from the Empire and had taken refuge in their native country, Britain.[15] It is easy and probably correct to make the connection and claim that the strength of British Pelagianism was an unintended result of sentences of exile under the terms of the law of 418. By 429, the date of Germanus's first journey to Britain, a party labelled by its opponents as Pelagian was well established in Britain. Thereafter British and also Irish Christianity was liable to be reproached with adherence to Pelagian

[9] *Commmentary on Jeremiah*, iii, Pref. (CSEL 59, 151); Rees *Pelagius*, xiii.

[10] In *On the Divine Law*, c. 9, PL xxx. 115, Pelagius (if he was the author of the letter) describes the description of someone as a monk as a *nomen alienum*. Rees, *Pelagius*, xiv and n. 24; Rees, *The Letters of Pelagius*, 102.

[11] P. R. L. Brown, 'Aspects of the Christianization of the Roman Aristocracy'; id., 'Pelagius and his Supporters: Aims and Environment', *Journal of Theological Studies*, New Ser., 19 (1968), 93–114, reprinted *Religion and Society*, 183–207.

[12] T. De Bruyn (trans.), *Pelagius's Commentary on St Paul's Epistle to the Romans*, Oxford Early Christian Studies (Oxford, 1993), 27, on the more extreme revision of the commentary, perhaps by Caelestius.

[13] *PL* lvi. 492.

[14] Prosper, *Epitoma Chronicon*, *s.a.* 429, ed. Mommsen, *Chronica Minora*, i. 472; R. A. Markus, 'Pelagianism: Britain and the Continent', *Journal of Ecclesiastical History*, 37 (1986), 200–4.

[15] So H. Williams, *Christianity in Early Britain*, 209–10.

views.[16] Not only was Pelagius himself a Briton but a classic of western hagiography demonstrated to later generations the power of Pelagianism in his native country.[17]

The context of the Pelagian affair was shaped by two threats to the Catholic Church: one, Manicheism, was widespread in the Roman Empire and extended far outside its bounds, even into China; the other, Donatism, was a problem for North Africa, and therefore for the greatest Latin theologian of the time, Augustine, bishop of Hippo.

Manicheism raised, in a fundamental form, the problem of evil. Christianity asserted that even the most secret thoughts and impulses were transparent to God; and God was almighty, utterly good, and the creator of the entire universe. Yet, a person of any sensitivity was aware of his own evil impulses and the egotism of his will and mind. Moreover, suffering seemed to be part of the composition of the world: the lamb and the wolf did not lie down in peace together. The material world might have its attractions but it worked by change, decay, and death. For the Manichees, the good God was not all-powerful: he was opposed by an evil principle of equal power who had invaded his creation and made the material world his dominion. Moreover, the good God's very nature made him unfit for a violent struggle with the evil principle. The individual person reproduced this dualism: his material body was the seat of evil passions, but the true person, the spirit, stood apart.

Donatism was born out of the last great persecution of Christians. Many Christians in North Africa had failed in the face of torture and execution to stand firm by their faith. Bishops had handed over the books of the Holy Scriptures to the persecutors, an act that corrupted their office. For the Donatists, the Church was holy and could not tolerate such treachery, above all in its bishops. Two rival African churches emerged: one that claimed the status of heroic holiness and rejected the backsliders, and the other prepared to embrace the sinner.

Augustine was himself an ex-Manichee (something his opponents would never forget); but, as a bishop in the Catholic Church in Africa, he was threatened more acutely by the Donatists. He therefore suspected anything that smacked of a spiritual elitism over against the mass of Christians. Pelagius, in Rome, was concerned above all with the Manichees. The latter were fond of citing the authority of St Paul's Epistle to the Romans, chapter 7:[18]

> For we know that the law is spiritual: but I am carnal, sold under sin. For that which I do I allow not: for what I would, that do I not; but what I hate, that I do . . . For I know that in me (that is, in my flesh) dwelleth no good thing . . . For I delight in the law after the inward man: but I see another law in my members, warring against the law of my mind, and bringing me into captivity to the law of sin which is in my members.

[16] For example, Bede, *HE* ii. 19 (on the Irish Church); Rhigyfarch, *Vita S. Davidis*, §§ 49–52, ed. and trans. Sharpe and Davies, pp. 142–7, by implication a defence of the Christianity of the Britons from the late eleventh century.

[17] Bede, *HE* i. 10 (based on Prosper) and 17 (almost entirely derived from Constantius's Life of Germanus).

[18] Verses 14–15, 18–19, 21–3 (Authorized Version).

Pelagius, in his commentary on this epistle, is careful to assert the original freedom of the will. So, on 'but I am carnal, sold under sin', he comments:[19]

> [Sold as if] I were resolved upon sin, so that, should I accept its advice, I make myself its slave, I of my own accord subjecting myself to it; and now, as if drunk with the habit of sins, I do not know what I do.

Slavery to 'the law of the members', to flesh, was a secondary consequence of a free choice, for the power of sin was a consequence of sin itself, freely chosen, and of the way it formed habits and so led mind and will, as if bound, along the paths of iniquity: 'it is not the case, as the Manichaeans say, that it was the nature of the body to have sin mixed in'.[20]

We see Pelagius in his other surviving writings as above all a spiritual guide to the aristocracy.[21] His letter to Demetrias is fortunately both one of his unquestionably authentic writings and explicit in relating moral advice to theological understanding. It was addressed to a girl from a family of exceptional nobility, the Anicii. She had refused the marriage arranged for her and had taken a vow of virginity. Pelagius warmly encouraged her to stand firm. He did so in a way that made a link between the nobility of her birth and the nobility of her soul:[22]

> Let all that dignity which you derive from your famous family and the illustrious honour of the Anician blood be transferred to your soul. Let that man be counted famous, lofty and noble, let that man be counted as guarding his nobility and keeping it intact, who thinks it beneath him to become a slave to vices and to be overcome by them.

The noble Christian had to preserve that original freedom of the soul.

Two argumentative strategies mingled in this letter. On the one hand, Pelagius asserts a link between freedom as a status and freedom as a condition of the will; on the other hand, he argues that someone such as Demetrias, who has embraced asceticism, has adopted a heroic sanctity nobler than the ordinary obligations of normal Christians: Demetrias, an aristocrat of Christianity, rightly aspires to an ideal above 'this common, mediocre kind of life of ours', one that will prevent her from 'being cheapened by mere association with the majority'.[23]

This might seem a mere appeal to a young girl's pride in her noble blood, but there is more to it than that. Pelagius distinguishes four moral qualities of action: what is forbidden, what is permitted, what is commanded, and what is advised:[24]

> Certain things are forbidden, some are allowed, some are advised: evil things are forbidden, good things are enjoined; intermediate things are allowed, perfect things are advised . . . For

[19] *Expositiones XIII Epistularum Pauli*, ed. A. Souter, *Pelagius's Expositions of the Thirteen Epistles of St. Paul* (Cambridge, 1922–31), ii. 58; de Bruyn, *Pelagius's Commentary on St Paul's Epistle*, 103–4.

[20] Souter, *Pelagius's Expositions*, ii. 53; de Bruyn, *Pelagius's Commentary*, 99, on Romans 6:19.

[21] P. R. L. Brown, 'Pelagius and his Supporters'.

[22] *Letter to Demetrias*, 22. 2, *PL* xxx. 37, trans. B. R. Rees, *The Letters of Pelagius and his Followers* (Woodbridge, 1991), 60.

[23] Ibid., 1. 2 (*PL* xxx. xxx. 16), trans. Rees, *Letters*, 36. Cf. R. A. Markus, *The End of Ancient Christianity* (Cambridge, 1990), 63–83.

[24] *Letter to Demetrias*, 9. 2 (*PL* xxx. 24), trans. Rees, *Letters*, 45.

righteousness is enjoined on everyone without exception... Marriage is allowed, so is the use of meat and wine, but abstinence from all three is advised by more perfect counsel.

He distinguishes, therefore, the realm of obligation—to refrain from doing evil things and to do the good things required of a Christian—from what is morally indifferent and thus permitted, and also from the realm of the ideal, 'the perfect things' that are merely 'advised', not 'enjoined on everyone'. The Christian is commanded to observe the moral law but also called to an ascetic ideal.

Pelagius's praise of human freedom, the freedom of choice, was both a way of encouraging people in their spiritual aspirations and his answer to the Manichees. Human love of God was inherently nobler because freely given; any gift of grace, therefore, could not constrain the will:[25]

Man's status is better and higher for the very reason for which it is thought to be inferior: it is on this choice between two ways, on this freedom to choose either alternative, that the glory of the rational mind is based.

Here Pelagius takes up a position reminiscent of the early Augustine of the *De Libero Arbitrio* and turns it into an explanation of how a creator God who is wholly good can coexist with evil in His creation.[26] The possibility of evil is inherent in the freedom of moral choice; yet, not to allow that freedom to exist would impoverish creation, for it would preclude love freely given.

Pelagius, however, used the one pattern of argument for Adam, the father of the human race, and for Demetrias, a Christian in the early fifth century. The latter, the heir of Adam's fall, still retained the ability to distinguish good and evil and to choose between them by the light of her own mind. Pelagius is here the Christian heir of the Late-Antique philosopher, offering rational arguments to promote spiritual elevation in the mind of the disciple:[27]

There is, I maintain, a sort of natural sanctity in our minds which, presiding as it were in the mind's citadel, administers judgement equally on the evil and the good and, just as it favours honourable and upright actions, so too it condemns wrong deeds and, on the evidence of conscience, distinguishes the one side from the other by a kind of inner law.

Yet, what was perhaps acceptable as exhortation to an aspirant ascetic became much more controversial when advanced as a theology of the human condition. What was likely to prove controversial was the notion that whatever sanctity lay in the interior of the mind was natural, not a consequence of supernatural grace. The implications for any understanding of human evil and the 'Fall of Adam' were far-reaching.

Pelagius's understanding of the Fall emerges from his commentary on the Epistle to the Romans. We have already met him, in this commentary, asserting that slavery to sin was, in the individual Christian, a consequence of a free choice to

25 Ibid., 3. 1 (*PL* xxx. 17), trans. Rees, *Letters*, 38.

26 Brown, *Augustine of Hippo*, 148–9, and Augustine, *De Libero Arbitrio*, II. 5–7, ed. W. Green, CSEL 74 (Vienna, 1956), 38–9.

27 *Letter to Demetrias*, 4. 2 (*PL* xxx. 19), trans. Rees, *Letters*, 40; W. Löhr, *Pelagius—Portrait of a Christian Teacher in Late Antiquity*, The Alexander Souter Memorial Lectures on Late Antiquity 1 (Aberdeen, 2007), 16–18.

commit sin. It was, like slavery to nicotine, a result of a choice made when still free. Pelagius did not deny the corruption of the will, but only claimed that corruption followed a choice made when still incorrupt. The corruption, the slavery, was not, therefore, a biological inheritance from Adam. Commenting on St Paul's 'Therefore, as by one man sin entered into the world, and death by sin', he says:[28]

> By example or by pattern. Just as through Adam sin came at a time when it did not yet exist, so in the same way through Christ righteousness was recovered at a time when it survived in almost no one.

Adam's sin was an example or pattern that later generations chose to follow. As he writes later in the commentary: 'Adam became only the model for transgression, but Christ [both] forgave sins freely and gave an example of righteousness.'[29] There is a great gulf between this and the famous passage in Augustine's *Confessions* on the jealousy of an unweaned infant:[30]

> I have personally watched and studied a jealous baby. He could not speak and, pale with jealousy and bitterness, glared at his brother sharing his mother's milk. Who is unaware of this fact of existence?

When, however, Pelagius in his Commentary on Romans, confronts the claim that sin is inherited physically from parents, he summarizes the arguments of the opponents of the idea, omitting the counter-arguments of its supporters.[31]

The implication was that baptism forgave past personal sins, not any sin derived from Adam. Unbaptized children who died before the age of responsibility had not committed personal sins; and there was thus no reason why they should be punished. Baptism inaugurated an obligation to a specifically Christian standard of virtue, but it did not make a fundamental change to the moral nature of the individual. Moreover, if moral corruption derived from freely chosen sin, it was logically evident that there might be individuals who had not chosen to sin and were thus free from corruption, from the slavery to sin that flowed from sin. Pelagius appealed to the examples of Melchisedek and Job in the Old Testament; Job, for example, was not a Jew and yet was someone of recognized holiness.[32] If one were to extrapolate from such examples to the period of the New Testament, it might seem that, at the very least, there might be good men and women beyond the range of any preaching of the Christian gospel whose lives merited heaven rather than hell.

Yet, for Pelagius, baptism made a fundamental change: 'He wants one who has been baptized to be as perfect [as one who in a way cannot sin].'[33] 'So also, "one who is born of God does not sin" (John 3: 9): for, because he has been crucified, and all his members are filled with sorrow, he will hardly be able to sin.'[34] By

[28] Souter, *Pelagius's Expositions*, ii. 45 (on 5: 12); de Bruyn, *Pelagius's Commentary*, 92.
[29] Souter, *Pelagius's Expositions*, ii. 48 (on 5: 19); de Bruyn, *Pelagius's Commentary*, 95.
[30] Saint Augustine, *Confessions*, I. vii. 11, trans. H. Chadwick (Oxford, 1991), 9.
[31] Souter, *Pelagius's Expositions*, ii. 46–7 (on 5: 15); de Bruyn, *Pelagius's Commentary*, 94.
[32] Pelagius's Letter to Demetrias, 5–6 (*PL* xxx. 20–2).
[33] Souter, *Pelagius's Expositions*, ii. 49 (on 6: 1); de Bruyn, *Pelagius's Commentary*, 96.
[34] Souter, *Pelagius's Expositions*, ii. 50 (on 6: 7); de Bruyn, *Pelagius's Commentary*, 97.

baptism past sins are forgiven; but by baptism, also, someone commits himself for the future to a sinless life in Christ; and, moreover, sinlessness, for the baptized, is possible. Christ died to effect this transformation: to assure forgiveness for past sin and to give an example of perfection for the future. The example given by Christ would work, for the baptized Christian, in alliance with conscience, that 'inner sanctity in our minds'. It would have a power even greater than the example given by Adam, which began the enslavement to habits of sin. Precisely because the power of example and of habit was so great, it was essential that the baptized Christian must not begin again to travel Adam's path to enslavement. Those who, unlike Pelagius, believed that sinfulness was a condition inherited physically from one's parents could accept that, in this life, even a baptized Christian would never be wholly free from the power of sin. But, for Pelagius, there was no such explanation: in baptism the Christian had died to sin, and that should be the end of the matter:[35]

> just as [the Father] is glorified in the resurrection of the Son, so too on account of the newness of our way of life he is glorified by all, provided that not even the signs of the old self are recognizable in us. For we ought not to want or desire anything that those who are not yet baptized, and all those who are still entangled in the errors of the old life, want or desire.

The crucial thing about Pelagius is that this was not just an aspiration but a requirement—a requirement necessitated by his theology.

2. FAUSTUS OF RIEZ

Faustus was born in Britain in the last decade of direct Roman rule, 400 × 410.[36] Like Pelagius, he left his homeland as a young man, but, unlike Pelagius, he can be shown to have maintained his links with Britain even as an old man. The first definite event in his life was in 433 or 434 when he succeeded Maximus as abbot of Lérins, a small island off the coast of Provence, where Honoratus had founded a monastery early in the fifth century.[37] Lérins soon became the principal monastery of Provence, extending its influence over much, though not all, of Gaul: Lupus, bishop of Troyes, who accompanied Germanus of Auxerre to Britain in 429, was a former monk of Lérins.[38] Since Faustus became abbot in 433 or 434, it is likely that he had already become a monk at Lérins before the founder and first abbot, Honoratus, left the monastery in 426 or 427

[35] Souter, *Pelagius's Expositions*, ii. 49 (on 6: 4); de Bruyn, Pelagius's *Commentary*, 96–7.

[36] Sidonius, *Epp.* ix. 9; Avitus, *Ep.* 4, *De subitanea paenitentia*, to King Gundobad (ed. Peiper, pp. 29–30). For a survey of Faustus's career and a bibliography, see C. Stancliffe, 'Faustus (400 × *c.* 490)', H. C. G. Matthew and B. Harrison (eds.), *Oxford Dictionary of National Biography* (Oxford, 2004), xix. 161–3. His writings were ed. A. Engelbrecht, *Fausti Reiensis praeter Sermones Pseudo-Eusebianos Opera*, CSEL 21 (Vienna, 1891).

[37] Sidonius, *Carmina*, xvi. 112; S. Pricoco, *L'isola dei santi: il cenobio di Lerino e le origini del monachesimo gallico* (Rome, 1978), 55–6.

[38] F. Prinz, *Frühes Mönchtum im Frankenreich*, 2nd edn. (Darmstadt, 1988), maps II and III.

to succeed Patroclus as bishop of Arles.[39] And since he survived into the second half of the 480s, it is probable that he came to Lérins as a very young man in his late teens or early twenties; and on that basis we can also fix the approximate date of his birth in Britain. It is clear, at all events, that he came to Lérins having already acquired a considerable Latin culture, including study of pagan Latin texts.[40]

Faustus did not remain at Lérins for the rest of his life: by 462 at the latest he had succeeded Maximus as bishop of Riez. In 473–4, and thus when already a bishop, he wrote his main theological work, *De Gratia*, for Leontius, bishop of Arles. In 475, he was one of four bishops who negotiated a treaty with Euric, king of the Visigoths; but in 477, in spite of the terms of the treaty, Riez was taken by Euric's forces and Faustus was sent into exile. He was to return from exile, probably when Euric died in 485, but that is the last date in his career which can be determined. The span of his life thus stretches from a date of birth close to the time when Constantine III took the army of Britain to Gaul, past the great Saxon victories of the 440s, past not just the sending of Palladius to Ireland in 431 as the first bishop for the Irish but also the major part of St Patrick's mission; and it would end after barbarian kings had conquered all of Gaul but when the Britons were recovering some of the territory they had lost to the Saxons. It has even been suggested that Faustus was the author of the 'Chronicle of 452', which recorded the major Saxon conquest early in the 440s.[41]

In 429, when Faustus was still just an ordinary monk of Lérins, Germanus of Auxerre and Lupus of Troyes were sent to confront a Pelagian party in Britain, a party probably created when, in 418, the emperor exiled Pelagians and they took refuge in Britain, beyond the limits of his power. When Faustus became abbot in 433/4, Augustine had recently died at Hippo and his predestinarian views had already stimulated theological controversy in Provence. Cassian of Marseilles had devoted the thirteenth book of his *Conferences* to an argument against the view that human nature was hopelessly corrupted by Adam's fall, and against the idea that Christ did not die for all but only for the elect. Cassian in his turn was attacked by Prosper of Aquitaine, the ablest follower of Augustine in the next generation. More than forty years later, in 473–4, Leontius, bishop of Arles, finding himself troubled by an adherent of Augustinian predestinarianism, commissioned Faustus to set out the case for the views then dominant in Provence—views close to those defended by Cassian. Faustus's response was *De Gratia*. The Provençal phase of this long debate, which has troubled Christian theology ever since, continued until 529. In that year, the Second Council of Orange, under the presidency of Caesarius, bishop of Arles, another former monk of Lérins, came down in favour of a moderate Augustinian view, one which did not include 'double predestination', namely the theory that

[39] Prosper, *Chronicon*, s.a. 426 ed. Mommsen, *Chronica Minora*; i. 471, § 1292; A. Engelbrecht, *Studien über die Schriften des Bischofes von Reii Faustus* (Vienna, 1889), 65.

[40] P. Courcelle, 'Nouveaux aspects de la culture lérinienne', *Revue des études latines*, 46 (1968), 399–409.

[41] I. N. Wood, 'Continuity or Calamity: The Constraints of Literary Models', in Drinkwater and Elton (eds.), *Fifth-Century Gaul*, 16–17.

God predestined not just the elect to heaven but also the damned to hell.[42] Caesarius sent the decrees of the council to Pope Boniface II, who replied affirming their orthodoxy. In the aftermath of this council, Faustus's teachings came under a cloud, but it is significant that no such dimming of his fame, or that of Cassian, seems to have extended to Britain. To judge by Columbanus's high opinion of Faustus *c.* 600, his reputation remained high among Insular Christians; similarly, Cassian (in the British form of his name, Cassión) was cited approvingly in the lament on the death of Columba of Iona, 597.[43] By the time of the *Historia Brittonum* of 829–830, Faustus had become a figure of hagiographical legend, the son of Vortigern by an incestuous union with his own daughter, a saint and himself the subject of a miracle by St Germanus, who baptized him, brought him up, and provided him with a great monastery on the banks of the Rhine (probably a confusion with the name of his diocese, Riez).[44]

In the *De Gratia*, Faustus picked his way with care through the theological minefield left by his predecessors. The development of the controversy had, in the lifetimes of Pelagius and Augustine, widened the gap between them. Instead of a network of like-minded persons, Pelagianism was given a new image by its opponents, as a heretical movement with a named head, Pelagius. As a result of this impulse to extreme opposition, many who would not have agreed with Pelagius were reluctant to follow Augustine all the way; and yet, for Augustine's most vocal supporters, any such reluctance was liable to be interpreted as covert support for his opponents. Faustus began, therefore, with a strong condemnation of Pelagius, the *pestifer doctor* (the other members of his network had passed from the limelight). In the course of this condemnation, Faustus made it clear that he agreed with Augustine's theory of original sin: Adam and Eve's disobedience to God caused an inner disobedience in their own human natures: desire rebelled against reason, and sexual intercourse ungoverned by reason passed down to the next generation the same psycho-sexual disorder in which, from that time on, every generation was conceived.[45]

After this opening salvo against Pelagius, however, Faustus spent the rest of the work arguing against the followers of Augustine. In large part his methods of argument resemble those of Cassian: numerous quotations from scripture, stored up in the mind through a monk's reading and meditation upon the Bible, were deployed to support each proposition. Yet, Faustus's choice of words and his

[42] *Les Canons des conciles mérovingiens (VIe–VIIe siècles)*, ed. and trans. J. Gaudemet and B. Basdevant, Sources chrétiennes, nos. 353–4 (Paris, 1989), i. 154–85. The numerous citations of Prosper indicate its stance.

[43] *Sancti Columbani Opera*, ed. and trans. G. S. M. Walker (Dublin, 1957), 68; C. Stancliffe, 'The Thirteen Sermons attributed to Columbanus and the Question of their Authorship', in M. Lapidge (ed.), *Columbanus: Studies on the Latin Writings* (Woodbridge, 1997), 93–202, esp. 197–9; *Amra Choluim Chille*, ed. W. Stokes, 'The Bodleian Amra Choluim Chille', *Revue Celtique*, 20 (1899), 254, § 55.

[44] *HB*, c. 48 (and cf. c. 39; on the Pillar of Eliseg, however, the child born to Vortigern and blessed by Germanus is Britu, not Faustus; and the mother was not Vortigern's own daughter, but the daughter of the emperor Magnus Maximus).

[45] 'Unde autem ueniat nexus iste, qui posteros trahit, si requiras: sine dubio per incentiuum maledictae generationis ardorem et per inlecebrosum utriusque parentis amplexum', *De Gratia*, i. 2 (ed. Engelbrecht, 13. 2–5).

definition of the positions he proposed to defend were more careful than Cassian's. The latter might be understood—as he was by Prosper—as claiming that, for some, salvation began with a movement of the will unaided as yet by divine grace.[46] Faustus, however, used a striking metaphor: God from the start drew each human being to himself, but the God who sought out each person required of him that he should keep His commandments, so that 'the one who was called could be caught and pulled by a little handle of the will'.[47] Grace worked within the individual will; God drew the human will to himself as a lover draws his beloved.

Faustus's methods of reasoning were not confined to the accumulation of quotations. He was also able to offer a logical analysis. Like Cassian, he has an argument against those who claim that Christ did not die for all but only for the elect.[48] His first supporting quotation was from the First Epistle to the Corinthians: 'For as in Adam all die, even so in Christ shall all be made alive.' He then goes on to point out that his opponent cannot argue that this is an example of the figure of speech, *pro parte totum*, 'the whole standing for a part', since 'all' occurs twice, once in the first part of the sentence, 'in Adam all die', and once in the second, 'in Christ shall all be made alive'. Since it is evident that all men without exception do 'die in Adam', so 'all' must equally be without exception in the second part. True, some will reject Christ, yet they too will be brought to life on the last day. The wicked will rise again by virtue of Christ's resurrection, but they will rise to be punished, not vindicated, by the divine judge. Here Faustus shows the skills of a well-educated man: he can handle the terms of literary analysis and he can argue like a good logician. Faustus was also an outstanding preacher, praised by Sidonius for his eloquence. His sermons would form part, perhaps the major part, of the collection that passed under the name of Eusebius 'Gallicanus'.[49]

The significance of Faustus's career for the history of Britain is twofold: first, like Pelagius, he illustrates the ability of Britain *c.* 400 to produce figures who would subsequently be among the most influential Latin theologians in the lands around the Mediterranean. Secondly, his ability to maintain links with Britain and his subsequent reputation in Britain and Ireland showed that, even though Britain had slipped out of the reach of imperial power, it was not cut off from Provence, the most deeply Romanized part of Gaul and a major centre of the growing monastic movement in the West.

3. GILDAS

Gildas is the sole British writer from the sixth century whose work survives, at least in part. As such he is a unique witness to the high culture of the Britons in that

46 Cassian, *Conferences*, xiii. 11–12.

47 *De Gratia*, i. 16 (ed. Engelbrecht, 53. 4–6).

48 Cassian, *Conferences*, xiii. 7; Faustus, *De Gratia*, i. 16 (ed. Engelbrecht, 48–9).

49 Eusebius 'Gallicanus', *Collectio Homiliarum*, ed. F. Glorié, 3 vols., CCSL 101, 101A, 101B (Turnhout, 1970–1); C. Stancliffe, 'The Thirteen Sermons', 118–26.

century.[50] He is also a principal source for relations between the Britons and their neighbours.[51] For events up to the end of the fifth century, as we have seen, Gildas is often more interesting for his misconceptions than for any reliable information that he offers, but for his own generation and that of his parents his open letter to contemporary kings, judges, bishops, priests, and other clergy is a crucial source. It is, however, best understood in the context of his other work, even though much of the latter survives only in fragments.

The usual title given to his open letter is *De Excidio Britanniae*, 'On the Ruin of Britain'.[52] It derives from the title given in Smith's catalogue of the Cottonian library when the principal manuscript, Cotton, Vitellius, A. VI was still undamaged.[53] This describes very well what later writers, from Bede onwards, considered to be the message of the text. It also accords well with a central comparison made by Gildas, by which he saw himself as a latter-day Jeremiah lamenting over the fall of Jerusalem and the exile of its people in Babylon: Britain was his Jerusalem and he feared that the Saxons might prove to be the new Babylonians; already, because of 'the unhappy partition with the barbarians', 'our citizens' were unable to visit many of the graves where God 'lit for us the brilliant lamps of holy martyrs'.[54] Yet Gildas wrote to persuade the leaders of his people of their sins and thus to avert disaster. Later writers knew that the Saxons (or English) did in the end succeed in conquering most of Britain, but such hindsight should be avoided in interpreting the text: for Gildas, the disaster of a more complete Saxon conquest threatens, but it has yet to happen.[55]

Gildas himself describes his open letter as an *historia*, but modern critics usually reject this description, perhaps somewhat too brusquely.[56] Gildas, they say quite correctly, was a prophet; and they infer from this, less securely, that he was not an historian. Yet, he thought of himself as both prophet and historian; and it is his understanding of his own work that must be our starting point, both because it is illuminating in its own right and because it is a necessary preliminary before any inferences are drawn from his text about the history of his time. It will also be

50 F. Kerlouégan, *Le* De Excidio Britanniae *de Gildas. Les destinées de la culture latine dans l'île de Bretagne au VIe siècle* (Paris, 1987). The unity and authenticity of the *De Excidio* was also convincingly supported by T. D. O'Sullivan, *The 'De Excidio' of Gildas: Its Authenticity and Date* (Leiden, 1978), chs. 1–3.

51 See, in particular, P. Sims-Williams, 'Gildas and the Anglo-Saxons', *CMCS* 6 (Winter 1983), 1–30.

52 I have used the text and translation of M. Winterbottom, *Gildas: The Ruin of Britain and Other Documents* (London and Chichester, 1978), following the traditional chapter divisions used by him and the numbered sub-sections which he provides; he uses, in his Latin text, a variant of the usual title, namely *De Excidio Britonum*, but the usual form reflects Gildas's own preference for writing about *Britannia*; the *Britanni* as such appear only in a proverb, 6. 2, and in a quoted phrase, 20. 1, *Britones* never. Also to be noted is the edition by Th. Mommsen, *Chronica Minora Saec. IV. V. VI. VII*, iii, MGH AA xiii (Berlin, 1898), 1–85.

53 Mommsen, *Chronica Minora*, iii. 10, 13.

54 *De Excidio*, 10. For the importance of the Lamentations of Jeremiah, see K. George, *Gildas's* De Excidio Britonum *and the Early British Church* (Woodbridge, 2009), 20–1, 29–41.

55 e.g. Bede, *HE*, i, caps. 7, 12–16, 22 Alcuin, *Epp.* nos. 17, 129; for others, see D. Howlett, *Cambro-Latin Compositions* (Dublin, 1998), 52–4.

56 *De Excidio*, 37. 1; for example, *EHD* i. 588, 2nd edn. 640: 'This is not a history, but a denunciation of the sins of his countrymen'.

helpful, first, to compare Gildas with his contemporaries and immediate predecessors on the Continent, Cassiodorus, Salvian, and the writers of the *Epistolae Austrasicae*, and then to see what his first known imitators, the Irishmen Columbanus and Cummian, made of his work.

When Gildas thought of prophecy, this was not what we usually mean by the term, namely prediction of future events. His was fundamentally an Old Testament conception of a prophet, someone who, guided by God, declared to his people their current spiritual state. To quote Gildas himself, 'Favouring the good and forbidding men the bad, they were in a sense the mouth of God and the instrument of the Holy Spirit'.[57] The only reason why the future was relevant at all was that God's judgement might visit future reward or punishment on present virtue or sin. The present was the primary concern of the prophet, but informed by a belief in a divine judgement that expressed itself within history, not just at the end of time. In one way, however, Gildas's prophecy differs from his Old Testament models. His duty to speak out was the outcome of scriptural learning. His understanding of his people's condition and what should be said about it came from two kinds of knowledge: knowledge of the current condition of his people and knowledge of scripture. The latter shaped the former.

The prophets cited by Gildas were not just those in the prophetic books of the Old Testament. Almost as important were prophets whose deeds formed part of the historical books: Samuel, Elijah, and Elishah. As a consequence there was, for him, no gap in the Old Testament between history and prophecy: history could properly be combined with prophecy, because in the historical books prophecies were themselves historical events and revealed the significance of other historical events. Moreover, prophecy that revealed the significance of current events was especially appropriate in a history of contemporary and recent times. In his own terms, Gildas was rightly both prophet and historian.

Moreover, history might be found in books of the Old Testament that seem far removed from any such genre. Of the destruction of towns and countryside by the Saxon onslaught Gildas wrote:[58]

> So it was that in this assault, comparable to that of the Assyrians of old upon Judaea, there was fulfilled according to history for us also what the prophet said in his lament: 'They have burned with fire your sanctuary on the ground, they have polluted the dwelling-place of your name.'

The prophet cited is, in fact, Psalm 73. The sense of 'history' here is closely allied with the use of the term in exegesis. Later in the text Gildas wrote, 'I should certainly like, so far as my feeble talents allow, to interpret, in the historical and moral senses, all these testimonies from holy scripture'.[59] Here, 'the historical sense' means the literal sense of the biblical text. Similarly, what Gildas is saying about Psalm 73 is that its prophecy found a literal fulfilment in the disasters that befell Britain: Britain fulfilled in history, actual historical events, what the psalmist lamented. Gildas is arguing that the Old Testament assault on Judaea by the

[57] *De Excidio*, 37. 3. [58] *De Excidio*, 24. 2. [59] *De Excidio*, 93. 4.

Assyrians, and the Saxon onslaught on Britain, can be combined as two fulfilments of the one prophecy contained in the psalm.

The *De Excidio* consists of a preface followed by three sections: on the past history of Britain, on contemporary kings and judges, and on contemporary churchmen. Although these sections are not laid out as distinct 'books' in the standard editions, they were divisions intended by the author to be apparent to his readers.[60] We can tell this from two kinds of evidence. At the end of the Preface (chapters 1–2), Gildas lists the topics he will cover in the first of the three sections, namely that on the past history of Britain (chapters 3–26; here the traditional chapters of the editions broadly correspond to Gildas's listed topics and are, to the extent that they do correspond, authorial). Gildas lists these topics of the first section although his primary intention was to discharge 'the debt so long incurred' by speaking out against the wickedness of kings, judges, priests, and others in authority—and that was what he did in the second and third sections. For Gildas, the past history of Britain was a preliminary to what he had to write about its present; and his list defines what he wishes to cover in the preliminary first section.

The second and third sections are separated by stylistic parallelism and by authorial asides. The second (chapters 27–65) begins with an almost incantatory passage, based on antithesis:

> Britain has kings, but they are tyrants; she has judges, but they are wicked. They often plunder and terrorize—the innocent; they defend and protect—the guilty and thieving; they have many wives—whores and adulteresses . . .

The third (chapters 66–110) begins in just the same manner:

> Britain has priests, but they are fools; very many ministers, but they are shameless; clerics, but they are treacherous grabbers. They are called shepherds, but they are wolves all ready to slaughter souls . . .

The end of the second section also contains an explicitly transitional passage:[61]

> So far I have addressed the kings of my country both in my own words and in the oracles of the prophets . . . How glad I should be to let modesty step in and to rest here, like one tossed on the sea-waves and at last carried by his oars to the longed-for haven: if I did not see such great mountains of wickedness raised against heaven by bishops and other priests and clerics of my order also.

This transition reveals, in passing, that Gildas was a cleric of an 'order' or rank below that of the priesthood: deacons and lesser clerics would also be the target of his indignation, not just bishops and priests.[62]

The preface contains Gildas's explanation of his intentions in writing the *De Excidio*.[63] In part, it is a traditional expression of modesty and of good intentions,

[60] *Gildas: New Approaches*, xii; Mommsen's preface to his edn., *Chronica Minora*, iii, p. xv, on Avranches 162.

[61] *De Excidio*, 64–5.

[62] *De Excidio*, 109. 2.

[63] M. Winterbottom, 'The Preface of Gildas's *De Excidio*', *THSC* (1974–5), 277–87.

designed to forestall likely criticism of text and author. The opening words—'In this letter I shall deplore rather than denounce; my style may be worthless; but my intentions are kindly'—offer a taste; and it is significant that Gildas will, in fact, both deplore and denounce, with vigour. As a part of this defensive role of the preface, Gildas revealed that he had been meditating some such letter for at least ten years:[64]

> I had decided to speak of the dangers run not by brave soldiers in the stress of war but by the lazy. And it was, I confess, with unmeasured grief at heart that I kept silent (the Lord, scanner of consciences, is my witness) as the space of ten years or more passed by. Then, as now, my inexperience and my worthlessness restrained me from writing any warning, however modest.

In a passing remark Gildas revealed that when he was writing it was forty-three years and one month since he was born.[65] The implication is that Gildas first conceived the idea of writing an open letter when he was in his early thirties, when he would already have been old enough to be ordained a priest, but he was still unordained ten years or more later. Gildas was therefore writing as one in a subordinate grade in the Church to deplore and denounce the wickedness and idleness of his superiors as well as his equals.

Yet he also thought that he was repaying a debt in writing his letter. The debt seems to have arisen from his learning. Admittedly he is modest about that too: 'What, you wretch (I say to myself), have you, like some important and eminent teacher (*doctor*), been given the task of standing up against the blows of so violent a torrent.'[66] We may perhaps infer that, even though it was proper to be modest about his attainments as a teacher, that was what he thought he was, a *doctor*. As we shall see later, one of the unusual characteristics of the British Church by the end of the sixth century was that a distinct order of teachers or scholars had the right to participate in synods together with bishops and leading abbots.[67] If this was already true in Gildas's time—and because the early Irish Church had the same characteristic it probably was already true—this special authority would have been enough to give Gildas the obligation to speak out. Any Christian has the obligation to warn the sinner, but the obligation of a *doctor* is especially grave.

Support for such an interpretation comes from the preface itself. After saying that he had kept silent for ten years and more, Gildas explains why he decided to write his letter. What we then get is a series of clauses introduced by *legebam* 'I was reading', and each clause offers an example from the Old Testament of disaster justly visited upon sinners. The series ends with the Lamentations of Jeremiah: 'I read how, because of the sins of men, the voice of the holy prophets rose in complaint, especially Jeremiah's, as he bewailed the ruin of his city in four alphabetic songs.' The clauses introduced by *legebam* are succeeded by another

[64] *De Excidio*, 1. 2.

[65] *De Excidio*, 26. 1. The translation of this passage has caused difficulty (Wood, 'The End of Roman Britain', 22–3); I follow Winterbottom.

[66] *De Excidio*, 1. 14.

[67] See below 589–90.

series introduced by *videbam* 'I was seeing' (repeatedly). These set out the misfortunes of the Church of Gildas's time and the sins of British Christians, but each of them is set in apposition to an Old Testament counterpart: 'I saw that "the sons of Sion" (that is of the holy mother Church), "once glorious and clad in fine gold, had embraced dung".' Here Gildas is quoting the Lamentations of Jeremiah and interpreting them as referring to his homeland, his *patria*, Britain. He then explains the method behind these sentences: 'I gazed on these things and many others in the Old Testament as though on a mirror reflecting our own life.' He then did the same, only more surely, for the New Testament: we thus get a new series of sentences beginning *legebam*, varied by *audiebam*, each giving a text from the New Testament.

What Gildas was doing, therefore, was first giving a sequence of examples or instances, *exempla*, from the Old Testament; then a statement of his method; and finally a sequence of quotations, *testimonia*, from the New Testament; he regarded the New Testament quotations as superior in authority to the Old Testament examples.[68] The first *legebam* series is devoted to *exempla*; the *videbam* series to contemporary British phenomena seen as counterparts of Old Testament equivalents; and the second *legebam* series to New Testament *testimonia*. Another example of the technique of piling up biblical *exempla* may be seen in the first of the fragments of Gildas's other works.[69]

In the Preface, Gildas was almost in what one might term autobiographical mode. He tells us the history of his thoughts and of his text: how it was ten years since he had concluded that someone should deplore publicly the sins of his countrymen; and how he kept silent because of his *imperitia*, his lack of expertise. Yet, even during his ten years of silence, he studied the scriptures; and what he read there made him fear for his country and fear for his own salvation if he did not speak out. The resolution of this conflict between *imperitia* and the obligation of speaking out, on pain of damnation, was a biblical *exemplum*, the story of Balaam's ass: Balaam the prophet might be ever so much more learned than his ass, but it was the ass who saw and pointed out the angel of the Lord standing in the way, when his master saw nothing and only belaboured the poor ass. All this was an elegant way to forestall criticism, a testament to a rhetorical training. Yet, what the profession of lack of expertise, *imperitia*, cannot conceal is that the reason why Gildas felt especially obliged to speak out was his *peritia*, his knowledge of the law contained in the scriptures. Even if, in his early thirties, he had felt inexpert, the subsequent ten years had seen an anxious study of the Bible. His ten years of silence had made him a master of the authoritative text.

What Gildas was doing was what his successors would also do, and a rich selection of their prophetic exegesis is preserved in the early eighth-century *Collectio Canonum Hibernensis*, of which Gildas himself was a major source.[70] The

68 *De Excidio*, 1.7, *legebam clarius*.

69 *Fragmenta Gildae*, ed. Winterbottom, *Gildas*, 143, § 1, trans. 80.

70 R. Sharpe, 'Gildas as Father of the Church', in Lapidge and Dumville (eds.), *Gildas: New Approaches*, 191–205.

Hibernensis also relied upon scriptural *exempla* and *testimonia* as the two principal categories of support for the rules it propounded.[71] As Gildas in the *De Excidio* usually took his *exempla* and *testimonia* in the order of the books of the Bible, so also did the *Hibernensis*. As the scholars—*sapientes* and *scribae*—whose work was collected in the *Hibernensis* applied the Old and New Testaments to contemporary society, so also did Gildas. The way to come to a correct judgement was stated as follows in the *Hibernensis*:[72]

> scriba interroget scripturam; inde ait Faustinus: Scrutatus sum et interrogavi et constitui judicium. 'Let a *scriba* interrogate Scripture; of this Faustinus says: "I have examined and I have interrogated and I have made a judgement".'

The *scriba* of early Irish sources was an expert in a biblically-based law. As one would expect from an impersonal legal text, the *Hibernensis* was not afraid to regard its experts as *periti*. There was no modest profession of *imperitia* in the *Hibernensis*.

A bridge between Gildas and the *Hibernensis*—apart from the one offered by the latter's use of Gildas—is provided by Cummian's letter of *c*. 633.[73] Here we have the same intellectual procedures as in Gildas's *De Excidio*, and even verbal echoes of the text. Cummian's Letter was, however, unlike Gildas's in one respect: it was addressed to two named persons, Ségéne, abbot of Iona, and Béccán, probably a well-known hermit living on the Island of Rhum in the Hebrides. Cummian's letter is also of admonition; he also opens by explaining that he has delayed and hesitated before writing the letter; he also follows the same procedure of working through the Bible, the Old Testament preceding the New, and then other authoritative texts, to find evidence for his judgement on the issue at stake. Just as Gildas's Preface has an autobiographical tinge to it, in that the texts and examples he has assembled are presented as things that 'I have read' or 'seen' while meditating anxiously on the state of Britain, so Cummian presents his collection of evidence as material that 'I have found'. As Michael Winterbottom noted, Cummian's Letter was organized on the model of Gildas's Preface rather than the main text. As Gildas expressed his fear arising from his reading, so also did Cummian. There are differences between Gildas and Cummian, but they generally stem from the different situation each encountered. Cummian's letter was a challenge to other scholars, Ségéne and Béccán, that they should either accept his judgement on the right Easter limits or offer better texts to refute him. He envisages a clash of scholars rather than a prophetic indictment of the morals of a nation. For that reason, whereas Gildas, and likewise the *Hibernensis*, were concerned with the moral sense of scripture, Cummian was not. He was more prone to combine a scriptural text with a patristic interpretation of the same text, something that recurs quite often in the *Hibernensis*. Gildas says that he would have wished to do the same, but in the

[71] T. M. Charles-Edwards, 'The Construction of the *Hibernensis*', *Peritia*, 12 (1998), 209–37.

[72] *Hib*. xxi. 1.

[73] Cummian, *De Controversia Paschali*, ed. and trans. M. Walsh and D. Ó Cróinín, *Cummian's Letter De Controversia Paschali and the De Ratione Computandi* (Toronto, 1988), 1–112.

interests of brevity he refrained. Yet these differences only, in the end, highlight the fundamental agreement in their intellectual method.

Columbanus's Letter 5, to Pope Boniface IV—like the *De Excidio* a letter of warning and urging to action written by someone inferior in terms of the grades of the Church to a superior—has been shown by Michael Winterbottom to echo Gildas's text.[74] What these examples, Columbanus's Letter 5 and Cummian's Letter to Ségéne and Béccán, demonstrate is that the early reception of Gildas's work in Ireland was such as to betray a good understanding of what he was attempting to achieve. Just as Gildas's penitential forms part of a tradition extending from Britain to Ireland, and from the sixth century to the seventh and eighth, so also the approach he used in the *De Excidio* was part of a continuum embracing Ireland as well as Britain and extending into the eighth century. It is even possible that the popularity of his methodology among Insular writers owed much to the authority of his name, to which Columbanus explicitly appealed.[75]

A notable feature of the structure of the *De Excidio*, is the combination of history of the past in what I shall call Book I with prophetic warnings about the present directed at what Gildas describes as the different orders of British society in Books II and III. The division between Book I and II does not, however, coincide with the move from Gildas's own words to *exempla* and *testimonia* from scripture. The first part of Book II, on kings and judges, is occupied by denunciations of five kings. As Gildas writes later, 'So far I have addressed the kings of my country both in my own words and in the oracles of the prophets.'[76] The denunciations of the five kings are what he here describes as 'my own words'. The shift to 'the oracles of the prophets' occurs about a third of the way through Book II.

The scope of the *De Excidio* purports to be the island of Britain, also described as Gildas's *patria*, homeland.[77] Here, however, we must distinguish between the intended range of the work and the portion of Britain about which Gildas was well informed. In principle, it might be true, as some have argued, that Gildas was well informed only about northern Britain, but he would still regard himself as writing about the whole island.[78] For Gildas, then, 'Britain' is the entire island, but it is also a figure for the British people, so that 'Ever since it was first inhabited, Britain has been ungratefully rebelling, stiff-necked and haughty'.[79] Even though Britain already contained peoples other than the Britons, Gildas took his

[74] M. Winterbottom, 'Columbanus and Gildas', *Vigiliae Christianae*, 30 (1976), 310–17.

[75] Columbanus, *Ep*. i. 7, ed. and trans. G. S. M. Walker, *Sancti Columbani Opera* (Dublin, 1957), 8–9.

[76] *De Excidio*, 64. 1.

[77] *Patria, De Excidio*, 1. 1; 21. 5; the island of Britain, ibid., 3. 1; 8. 1. Britain is a province, however, in a quotation cited as if from Porphyry, but actually from Jerome (*Ep*. 133. 9), 4. 3.

[78] A northern focus is best defended by E. A. Thompson, 'Gildas and the History of Britain', *Britannia*, 10 (1979), 214–20; that the scope is the island of Britain is argued by N. Wright, 'Gildas's Geographical Perspective: Some Problems', in Lapidge and Dumville (eds.), *Gildas: New Approaches*, 85–105. C. Daniell, 'The Geographical Perspective of Gildas', *Britannia*, 25 (1994), 213–16, analyses relevant terms, such as *Britannia, insula, patria*, and *regio*; N. J. Higham, *The English Conquest: Gildas and Britain in the Fifth Century* (Manchester, 1994), ch. 4.

[79] *De Excidio*, 4. 1.

identification of the island with his own people seriously. He did not only regard the Saxons and the Irish as coming from beyond the sea, but the Picts also were described as a 'transmarine people' coming 'from the north'.[80] This is so even though Gildas also writes of a wall being constructed across the island to keep the Picts and the Irish at bay.[81] The answer may be that, as argued elsewhere, the Picts were in origin a confederation of British peoples formed in the third century beyond the Antonine Wall, who were thus not under Roman rule.[82] From that confederation a new people eventually emerged. For Gildas and, later, for Bede the Picts were not Britons; and yet, as Picts, they were a new arrival on the ethnic map of Britain. It may thus have been easy to think that they, like the Irish and the Saxons, were invaders from beyond the sea.

A further problem arises from the limitation of his denunciation of kings to five named rulers, 'these five mad and debauched horses from the retinue of Pharaoh which actively lure his army to its ruin in the Red Sea'.[83] These kings were as follows, with their kingdoms, if named:[84]

Constantinus	Damnoniae tyrannus
Aurelius Caninus	?
Vortiporius	Demetarum tyrannus
Cuneglasus	Rhos?[85]
Maglocunus	?

Maglocunus, later Maelgwn, was described in the *Historia Britonum*, of 829/30, as ruling 'in the land of Gwynedd'; and his name also appears in the genealogies of the kings of Gwynedd.[86] We know from an early inscription, probably of the first half of the sixth century, that Gwynedd was a political entity at the period;[87] and an inscription in Anglesey is likely to commemorate Maelgwn's great-great-grandson.[88] The phrase used of him by Gildas, *insularis draco*, 'island dragon', might refer to Anglesey, but it might also refer to the island of Britain as a whole. If, however, we accept that Maglocunus was the ruler of Gwynedd, it looks as though Gildas was following a geographical sequence, beginning in the south-west, going round the Severn estuary, and then further north, ending in north-west Wales. In terms of late Roman political divisions, all these kings would then belong to the province of *Britannia Prima*, which had its capital at Cirencester. Whether such

[80] *De Excidio*, 14. That the Irish were also a *transmarina gens* makes the explanation given by Sir Ifor Williams (following Bede), *CA*, note to 1209, that the Picts were beyond *Merin Iddew*, the Firth of Forth, less likely.

[81] *De Excidio*, 15. 3.

[82] Above, 34–6.

[83] *De Excidio*, 37. 2.

[84] K. H. Jackson, 'Varia : 2. Gildas and the Names of the British Princes', *CMCS* 3 (Summer 1982), 30–40.

[85] For the likely association with Rhos, see D. E. Thornton, *Kings, Chronologies, and Genealogies* (Oxford, 2003), 80–2.

[86] *Historia Brittonum*, c. 62; *EWGT* 9 (HG 1), 36, 38, 47 (JC 22), 95 (ABT 1).

[87] Ffestiniog 1: 394/103/Gn-32.

[88] Llangadwaladr 1: 970/13/Gn-25.

provinces had any political significance in sixth-century Britain is very doubtful, but their Gaulish equivalents survived in the ecclesiastical sphere: each province had its metropolitan bishop. There is, then, a possible disjunction between the way Gildas took the entire island as his target and the limitation of his named kings to one former province. On the other hand, Gildas does not seem to have been addressing all the kings in the former *Britannia Prima*, since there is no room for both Gwent and Brycheiniog.[89]

It is difficult to accept that royal wickedness was confined to one province; but it may be that other kings, closer to the English or the Picts, fell in Gildas's mind more into the category of 'brave soldiers in the stress of war'.[90] One of the possible fragments of his lost work concludes, 'We should be afraid of this fate [the leprosy suffered by Miriam in Numbers 12] when we disparage good princes for trifling faults.'[91] Moreover, Gildas later rebukes contemporary priests by comparing them with Melchisedek, priest and king of the Book of Genesis:[92]

> Which [of the contemporary priests in the sixth century] like Melchizedek offered sacrifice and gave blessing to the victors only when they had, to the number of three hundred (that is, the mystery of the Trinity) freed a just man and defeated the dire armies of five kings?

The five kings in question were those of Genesis 14: 8, who included the kings of Sodom and Gomorrah. The choice of five principal targets may derive from this biblical *exemplum*. In any case, the location of the five kings—in some cases certain, in others probable or even merely conjectural—argues against any notion that Gildas's knowledge was largely confined to northern Britain.

Even though Gildas addresses the five kings in the second person, his letter was an open one. The churchmen denounced in Book III are not named; moreover the preface envisages his readers as both 'noble soldiers of Christ' and 'foolish rebels'.[93] Gildas has not sent it only to specific persons, those whom he thought especially worthy of moral admonition. What we may presume to have happened is that, after his ten or more years of cogitation, when he felt he must 'pay the debt so long ago incurred', Gildas released at least one fair copy of his letter for further copying by anyone who wished to have the text.[94] At this period, that was the equivalent of publication.[95]

That the letter was an open one immediately poses problems arising from a comparison with Gildas's younger contemporary, Gregory of Tours. In the preface to the *Miracles of St Martin*, Gregory quotes his mother's comforting remarks on the rusticity of his style: 'Do you not know that, because of people's ignorance, the manner in which you speak is considered to be more comprehensible to us?

[89] A. Woolf, 'The Britons: From Romans to Barbarians', 360, notes a rough coincidence of the five kingdoms with the areas in which Class I inscribed stones are concentrated. These were also areas of strong Irish influence (see above, 154–64, 168–9).

[90] *De Excidio*, 1. 2

[91] *Fragmenta Gildae*, 9, ed. Winterbottom, *Gildas*, 145, trans. 82.

[92] *De Excidio*, 69. 3.

[93] *De Excidio*, 1. 16.

[94] Ibid.

[95] Compare Bede, *HE*, Pref. and Wallace-Hadrill, *Commentary*, 207.

Therefore do not hesitate and do not stop recording these events, because you would commit a crime if you were silent about them.'[96] Gregory's mother was quite right: his Latin, though indubitably rustic, is lively and approachable. Gildas's Latin is also lively, but far less easy of access. As has been shown, Gildas writes in a high style which borrows adornments from poetry.[97] His style is not merely lofty but mannered; and the devices he uses include some which make it more difficult to read his text. He makes it necessary to read his sentences more than once and so disentangle their construction. Yet his intended readership included kings and secular judges as well as churchmen. What makes the problem more acute is that Gildas's high style is often very effective in giving weight and urgency to his message, as in the series of rhetorical questions in Book III; they use a series of *exempla* from the Bible starting with Genesis, and also from Rufinus's translation and continuation of Eusebius's *Ecclesiastical History*.[98] He apparently thought that his style would make his warnings more likely to come home to their intended targets. This is important because medieval writings were as likely to be heard being read out aloud as read in private; and one might wonder whether someone reading a text out aloud might simplify or even, on occasion, translate. Any such change, however, would nullify the effect for which Gildas is striving. He cannot, therefore, have desired any such simplification.

One can see the tension between high style and literary capacity in the writings of sixth-century churchmen and royal officials from Gaul, men who did not take the route adopted by Gregory of Tours. Letters of Remigius, bishop of Reims, Nicetius, bishop of Trier, and Germanus, bishop of Paris, are preserved in the Austrasian letter collection, compiled at the end of the century, together with letters by Gogo, tutor of the boy-king, Childebert II, as well as letters written in the names of various kings, Theudebert I, Theudebald I, and Childebert II. The collection is especially useful in exemplifying the letter-writing skills of laymen as well as churchmen. Gogo revealed that he saw himself as pupil of the aristocratic administrator Parthenius, nephew of a fifth-century emperor:[99]

> But this irrigating current [of his correspondent's eloquence] elicits a response in an untaught mind and imposes order on a barbarous writer who has rather learnt, with Dodorenus, the languages of barbarian tribes than, from Parthenius of good memory, to master rhetorical composition.

For a Frank it was proper to apologize in good traditional style for one's lack of eloquence by claiming to belong more to a barbarian than to a Roman culture; yet both the apology and the style of the letter show a training in how to write elevated Latin. Even at the end of the sixth century, the example of Asclepiodotus, who held

[96] Gregory of Tours, *Libri de Virtutibus Sancti Martini Episcopi*, I. Pref. ed. Krusch, MGH SRM i.2, 136, trans. R. Van Dam, *Saints and their Miracles in Late Antique Gaul* (Princeton, NJ, 1993), 200.

[97] Kerlouégan, *Le De Excidio Britanniae de Gildas*, 239–51, 258, 272; Winterbottom, *Gildas*, 7–9.

[98] *De Excidio*, 69–75.

[99] *Epp. Austras.*, xvi. 4. For Parthenius, see J. R. Martindale, *Prosopography of the Later Roman Empire*, ii. 833–4, Parthenius 3; K. F. Stroheker, *Der senatorische Adel im spätantiken Gallien* (Tübingen, 1948), 199, no. 283.

high office under Guntram and Childebert II, demonstrates that it was still possible in Gaul for someone of Roman background to pursue a career in royal administration and so acquire high rank and power.[100] All these writers in the Austrasian collection from the eastern part of Frankish Gaul had literary ambition; but none of them had the easy command of good grammatical Latin enjoyed by Gildas.

As was argued in Chapter 2, the Latin of the fifth- and sixth-century British inscriptions shows a collapse of the declensions accompanying a falling together of short *i* and *e*, *u* and *o*. This showed that spoken British Latin shared in some of the principal changes which transformed Latin into Romance; in that sense, by 500 a Romance dialect was spoken in Britain, a sister to the Gallo-Romance of northern Gaul. In the work of Gregory of Tours, it is sometimes possible to see examples of these changes from Late Latin to early Romance;[101] in the seventh-century chronicle of Fredegar they are still more obvious.[102] Yet in Gildas's Latin they do not appear: his Latin is untainted by the Romance spoken in Britain in his day, even though his forms of names sometimes reveal the influence of Late British Latin pronunciation.[103] The names reveal that the changes had occurred, but, with that very minor qualification, Gildas's Latin is remarkably correct. The implication is that one of his British contemporaries, whether he was brought up as a speaker of British or of Latin, would have had to learn standard Latin at school, as we must, before he could read the *De Excidio*. There is no difficulty in supposing that churchmen could receive such an education: it is apparent, for example, that the Irishman Columbanus, later in the same century, both read Gildas and appreciated his style. Many British churchmen would, by this date, have been born into monolingual British-speaking families and would have had the same need to learn Latin as had Columbanus. The difficulty is over kings and judges. True, Gildas said of Maelgwn that 'you have had as your teacher the refined master of almost all Britain';[104] but Maelgwn may well have been unusually learned for a king.

By implication, therefore, Gildas's *De Excidio* raises major questions about the nature of culture and education in sixth-century Britain. These may best be approached via arguments put forward by François Kerlouégan, Michael Winterbottom, and Michael Lapidge.[105] They demonstrated that the *De Excidio* needs to be understood in terms of the techniques of Latin forensic oratory taught by rhetors, that is by the more advanced teachers, whose schools were attended typically in one's late teens, after one had been to the school of a grammarian.

[100] Martindale, *Prosopography*, iii. 134–5 (Asclepiodotus 3 and 4); Stroheker, *Der senatorische Adel im spätantiken Gallien*, 149, no. 38.

[101] M. Bonnet, *Le Latin de Grégoire de Tours* (Paris, 1890).

[102] *Quellen zur Geschichte des 7. und 8. Jahrhunderts*, ed. and trans. H. Wolfram, A. Kusternig and H. Haupt (Darmstadt, 1982), 18–33; O. Haag, 'Die Latinität Fredegars', *Romanische Forschungen*, 10 (1899), 835–932.

[103] As in *Vortipori*, *De Excidio*, 31. 1, for *Vortepori* and an earlier *Vorteporix*. In a Latin name a late spelling is attested in *Agitius* (*Agitio, Agitium*, 20. 1), if that is for Aëtius (see above, 38 n. 38).

[104] *De Excidio*, 36. 1.

[105] *De Excidio*, 470–5; M. Lapidge, 'Gildas's Education and the Latin Culture of Sub-Roman Britain', in Lapidge and Dumville (eds.), *Gildas: New Approaches*, 27–50; M. Winterbottom. 'The Preface of Gildas' *De Excidio*', *THSC*, 1974–5, 277–87.

The grammarian taught his pupils both correct Latin and the close reading of major school texts, above all Virgil. In the fourth century someone might attend municipal schools run by such grammarians and rhetors, but with the decline of the Empire in the late fifth century, in Gaul and presumably no later in Britain, they died out. On the other hand, it was possible even then to secure the same education from private tutors. However, such an education was not undertaken for purely intellectual profit: especially when it was crowned by training in forensic rhetoric, the purpose was to equip the pupil to plead in the law courts and also to make him fit to become an administrator in the imperial bureaucracy.

Lapidge contrasts this education, whether in the municipal schools of the fourth century or the private tuition of the fifth, with what fifth- and sixth-century monastic and episcopal schools had to offer. Their education was also utilitarian, but with quite different aims: they wished to equip monks to read the Bible and to sing the office; similarly clerics in an episcopal school would read ecclesiastical rather than secular texts.[106] Neither were concerned with the techniques of pleading in a secular law court. We may take one example, Cassian, who is of special interest for Britain, since the Irish form of his name (*Cassión*) indicates that his extensive influence on early Irish Christianity was mediated via Britain.[107] In his view, to be accomplished in rhetoric implied the sin of vainglory, and 'the syllogisms of dialectic and Ciceronian eloquence are unworthy of the simple truths of faith'.[108] For Lapidge, therefore, Gildas must have received an education from a private rhetor in the expectation that he might use his training 'in some facsimile of Roman government'.[109] Moreover, enough of the leaders in British society must have received the same education for Gildas to assume an understanding of his Latin and his rhetorical approach in his readers (and any audience when it was read out aloud). For Lapidge, Gildas can be understood by setting him in the context of other late Latin writers who used the same rhetorical skills. His culture looked to the late Antique past not to the medieval future.

His case may need some qualifications. I have already argued that the way he uses the Bible, with *exempla* accompanied by *testimonia*, anticipates the same approach in early Irish writers such as Cummian and in the *Collectio Canonum Hibernensis*. To that extent his intellectual methods look forward to later Insular culture. Lapidge, on the other hand, illuminatingly compares the way Gildas marshals the evidence of the prophets with a Roman pleader deploying the jurisconsults, experts in Roman law. As he begins to cite scriptural witness against the wicked kings, Gildas declares, 'Now, as before, therefore, let the holy prophets reply (*respondeant*) in my stead'.[110] Lapidge argues that by *respondeant* Gildas meant something more than merely 'reply'.[111] In Roman law the pleader was an expert in argument but not an authority on the details of the law; he therefore summoned a jurisconsult as an expert witness. Gildas thus

106 Gregory of Tours, *Vita Patrum*, § 2, Preface; *Hist.*, i, Preface.

107 Above, 185 n. 47.

108 *Institutiones*, v. 1, 4; xii. 19; quoted by Lapidge, 'Gildas's Education', 30.

109 Lapidge, 'Gildas's Education', 49.

110 *De Excidio*, 37. 3.

111 Lapidge, 'Gildas's Education', 46–7.

puts himself into the role of the pleader and invokes his expert witnesses, the prophets. The first of these experts was Samuel, whom Gildas also describes as an *adstipulator*, again a legal term for one who participates in a contract, a *stipulatio*: the *De Excidio*, as we have seen, was described by Gildas as the discharge of a contractual debt.[112] Two legal parallels thus jostle together in this one passage.

On the one hand, therefore, Gildas's *modus operandi* looks forward to early Irish canon law, and, on the other, it looks backwards to the law courts and the jurisconsults of the Empire. Similarly, his style and the education that lay behind it look backwards to the schools and the bureaucracy of the late Empire; and yet his style found able imitators among the Irish. The problem can be made easier if we accept, first, that the ecclesiastical and monastic schools to be found among the Britons and the Irish did not have the disdain for rhetoric professed by some of their continental equivalents, and, secondly, that the custom of fosterage was adapted to ecclesiastical education. The private tutor that Lapidge detects behind Gildas's education may have passed into the foster father attested as the teacher of Columba.[113] This still leaves us, however, with the problem that the education undergone by Gildas was for a purpose, namely to fit men for positions in the imperial bureaucracy; hence Lapidge's conclusion that some 'facsimile' of imperial government survived in subRoman Britain. Although Maelgwn had for a period been a monk, that interlude appears to have had nothing to do with his time as a pupil of 'the refined master of almost all Britain'. The two are kept separate in Gildas's text.[114] Maelgwn's education, therefore, might have been intended to further a secular career. The probable conclusion is that there was some form of Roman administration surviving in Britain approximately about 500, as it survived in Frankish Gaul even in the sixth, but that the education which sustained it was also put to good use by the Church, both in Britain itself and in the Irish mission field. Since Ireland had no 'facsimile of Roman government', the latter cannot have been presumed by the form of culture that Gildas and his like passed on to the Irish. What was passed on was a certain conception of the role of biblical scholarship in the synods of the Church, and therefore in the making of law for a Christian society.

So far we have been content with a rough date for Gildas's *De Excidio*, namely the first half of the sixth century. Attempts to obtain a closer date have depended in the main upon the internal evidence of his text. There is, however, an obit for Gildas in an annal for 570, which is of uncertain authority but deserves more respect than it has received.[115] It can be assigned to the Chronicle of Ireland, an ancestor text for the various Irish annals which ran up to 911, because it appears in the Annals of Ulster and at least one of the Clonmacnois group of chronicles.[116]

[112] *De Excidio*, 39. 1; but the word can be used more loosely just for a witness and is so understood by *Thesaurus Linguae Latinae*, *s.v. astipulator*.

[113] Adomnán, *Vita S. Columbae*, iii. 2.

[114] *De Excidio*, 34; 36. 1.

[115] Sims-Williams, 'Gildas and the Anglo-Saxons', 3, is sceptical, but see Stancliffe, 'The Thirteen Sermons', 179–80.

[116] A doublet is in the second hand at 577. 6; it is in the Annals of Tigernach in an annal corresponding to AU 570, and also in the Annals of Inisfallen, *s.a.* 567. The corresponding entry in

For the period between *c.* 560 and *c.* 740, the Chronicle of Ireland derived nearly all its material from an earlier text, a set of annals kept on Iona, which itself appears to have used more than one set of annals from Columban churches. If the obit for Gildas was entered in a Columban text in the second half of the sixth century, it would deserve to be accepted as very likely to be reasonably accurate.[117] On the one hand, some annal entries for famous churchmen of the sixth century were plainly later additions, notably dates for their births; and Gildas was probably famous enough in Ireland to merit such treatment. However, Irish interest in Gildas is attested very early, in a letter of Columbanus which records that Gildas corresponded with *Vennianus*: this person may be the Vinnian to whom a penitential is attributed; and both *Vennianus* and Vinnian may be identified as Findbarr of Movilla.[118] He, however, is likely to have been one of Columba's teachers. A short chain of personal connections may, therefore, link the founder and patron saint of Iona, Columba, with Gildas; and such a link would make it more likely that the obit was contemporary. The obit, then, is worthy of attention, but it is not conclusive evidence.

A strong argument for placing the *De Excidio* no later than about 545 is that Gildas does not mention the major pandemic of plague which struck the Roman world in the 540s, spreading west and north from Egypt. Gaul suffered severely from this plague, which makes it very unlikely that Britain escaped.[119] One would have expected the plague to be cited as punishment for the manifold sins of Gildas's contemporaries, if it had already reached Britain.[120]

The internal evidence derives from the impression that Gildas gives of the distance of time between the date of publication of the *De Excidio* and an event of the fifth century, the letter of the Britons to *Agitius* 'thrice-consul', who is very probably Aëtius, who did indeed receive the quite exceptional honour of being consul three times.[121] If we assume that the letter was genuinely sent by the Britons to Aëtius after he became consul for the third time and before he was assassinated, that gives us a date-range 446 × 454. The rest is simply what Gildas thought was the sequence of events; it is not implied that he got it right, although we have to assume that his sense of the overall passage of time was consistent with what he says about the intervening events. The historical sequence as presented in Gildas's text can be set out as follows:

the *Annales Cambriae* very probably derives from the Chronicle of Ireland: see D. N. Dumville, 'When was the "Clonmacnoise Chronicle" created? The Evidence of the Welsh Annals', in K. Grabowski and D. N. Dumville, *Chronicles and Annals of Mediaeval Ireland and Wales* (Woodbridge, 1984), 209–26.

117 For complications arising from the fact that the Iona annals themselves derived from more than one source, see T. M. Charles-Edwards, *The Chronicle of Ireland* (Liverpool, 2006), i. 35–51. Any entry for this period may well be two to three years too early.

118 *ECI* 291–3.

119 Gregory of Tours, *Hist.*, iv. 5 (*lues illa quam inguinariam vocant*); vi. 14 may refer to bubonic plague (*inguinarium morbum*) in Narbonne in 582; ix. 21 refers to what appears to be bubonic plague in Marseilles, spreading north as far as Lyons, in 588.

120 Stancliffe, 'The Thirteen Sermons', 180.

121 What follows is a simplified version of D. N. Dumville's proposed chronological sequence, *Gildas: New Approaches*, 83.

446 × 454	Letter of the Britons to Aëtius, the leading Roman general: 'The barbarians push us back to the sea, the sea pushes us back to the barbarians', 20. 1.
	Famine and victories against *hostes*; Irish withdraw and Picts quiescent: 20. 2 – 23. 1
	Luxuria, 'moral excess', in peace, 21. 2–6
	Warnings of another attack by Picts and Irish leads to the convening of a council by the 'proud tyrant', *superbus tyrannus* 22.
	An invitation to the Saxons who, on the orders of the proud tyrant, are settled 'at first in the eastern part of the island', *primum in orientali parte insulae*, 23.
	The arrival of more Saxons, 23. 4.
	The Saxons ask for 'food supplies', *annonae*, which, when delivered, silence their demands 'for a considerable period', *multo tempore*, 23. 5.
	Complaints by the federated Saxons that the food supplies are not forthcoming on an ample enough scale; they demand more declaring that, if they are not handed over, they will break the treaty, *foedus*; shortly afterwards they put their threats into action, 23. 5.
	War spreads from sea to sea; cities are besieged, ravaged, and left deserted, 24.
	Some Britons submit, some go into exile, and some take refuge in the mountains, 25. 1.
	The Saxons go home (*cum recessissent domum*), presumably to their base in Britain; and, after a time (*tempore igitur interveniente aliquanto*), the 'remnants', *reliquiae*, of the Britons come together and, under the leadership of Ambrosius Aurelianus, challenge the Saxons to battle and win a victory, 25. 2–3.
	'From then on victory went now to our countrymen, now to their enemies', *Ex eo tempore nunc ciues, nunc hostes, uincebant*, 26. 1.
?480s/490s	Battle of Mount Badon; birth of Gildas, 26. 1.
c. 530 × 545	Gildas wrote his book *On the Ruin of Britain*, in the forty-fourth year since his birth, which was also the date of the battle of Mount Badon.[122]
540s	Plague crosses the Near East and Europe.[123]

Especially because of the phrase *multo tempore* it is apparent that the sequence up to the Battle of Mount Badon would fit more comfortably into a period of no less than a generation. If one then adds the forty-four years since Mount Badon and the birth

[122] 'The year of the the siege of Mount Badon' in *De Excidio* is also the forty-fourth year (counting backwards from the present), and is also the year of Gildas's birth (the relative pronouns, *quique . . . qui et . . .* have *annum obsessionis Badonici montis* as their antecedent. This, together with the *iam* of *mense iam uno emenso*, makes it difficult to translate the sentence in any other way than does Winterbottom, although I. N. Wood, 'The End of Roman Britain', 23, proposes to take the forty-fourth year as pertaining to the interval between the initial victory of Ambrosius Aurelianus and the siege of Mount Badon.

[123] Gregory of Tours, *Hist.*, iv. 5, places the arrival of the plague in the Auvergne eight years before the death of St Gall, which occurred in 551; his date, therefore, was 543.

of Gildas, a date no earlier than about 530 becomes probable. This, then, is a *terminus post quem*; and the *terminus ante quem* is supplied by the pandemic of plague. If one thinks the annalistic obit for Gildas is at all weighty evidence, that will incline one to prefer the later part of the period *c.* 530 – 545 and thus to maintain the traditional date *c.* 540.

A real difficulty, however, has been pointed out by Sims-Williams.[124] This is, first, that the letter to Aëtius may well have been occasioned by Saxon rather than Irish and Pictish attacks; and, secondly, serious Irish and Pictish attacks may have ended earlier; and therefore we cannot tell whether to begin the chronological sequence with the letter to Aëtius or with the earlier Irish and Pictish attacks. Gildas's sense of the passage of time might have more to do with the interval since the latter rather than the former, that is to say, he might have put the appeal to Aëtius too early rather than merely dating the Irish and Pictish attacks too late. There is, therefore, no conclusive dating for Gildas, although the balance of the evidence inclines towards the period 530 × 545.

The significance of Gildas's *De Excidio Britanniae* lies partly in the way it allows us to see the cultural connections between late Roman Britain and Britain and Ireland in the seventh and eighth centuries. Because of the assumptions that Gildas must have made about his readership, it shows that a late Antique rhetorical education persisted into the sixth century for laymen as well as for clerics. As well as revealing the training of a rhetor, however, Gildas's text is also penetrated through and through by a biblical culture. This is more than just familiarity with the scriptural texts; Gildas asserts that it is right to take the Britons as 'a latter-day Israel', a counterpart in the new covenant to the Jewish people under the old covenant, a people of whom 'the Lord could make trial . . . to see whether it loves him or not'.[125] The Britons are a people to whom the Old Testament prophets speak directly, collectively as well as individually, calling them to repentance, because the British people sins collectively and will therefore be judged collectively, as was Israel. His deployment of scriptural examples and texts looks forward to Cummian and the other Irish scholars whose work lies behind the *Collectio Canonum Hibernensis* of 716 × 725. His declaration, 'Let the holy prophets reply in my stead', probably looks back to the jurisconsults brought as expert witnesses into the court of Roman law, but it also looks forward to the *testimonia* of the Irish canon lawyer. The correctness of his Latin and the sure confidence with which he handles his rhetoric compare exceedingly well with the Latin written by Gallo-Romans in the sixth century.[126] Because grammatical correctness and rhetorical confidence was transmitted from Britain to Ireland in the fifth and sixth centuries, it is most unlikely that Gildas was exceptional. The use of Latin as a spoken language was on the retreat in Britain but was now general in most of Gaul; and yet the standard written Latin of Britain survived much better than its counterpart in Gaul.

124 Sims-Williams, 'The Settlement of England in Bede and the *Chronicle*', 6–15.
125 *De Excidio*, 26.
126 I here exclude Venantius Fortunatus, who, though he settled in Gaul, was educated at Ravenna.

Gildas's culture is inexplicable except as an inheritance from the Roman past; and yet he was clear that the Britons were not Romans. His testimony will be vital in the next chapter, in which two relationships of Britons to Rome will be explored: first, the rapid shift away from the material conditions of fourth-century Roman Britain and, secondly, the extent to which, and the ways in which, Britons and others associated the Britons with Rome or separated them from Rome.

6

Rome and the Britons, 400–664

The end of Alfred Duggan's historical novel *The Conscience of the King* has Cerdic as a former citizen of Roman Britain, subsequently founder of the West-Saxon dynasty and ancestor of kings of England, reflecting on a successful life punctuated by the 'misfortunes' he had inflicted on his brother, his father, and his wife:[1]

> One can get used to filth, and I no longer mind very much when I see a louse swimming in the stew on my table (most of my followers eat on the floor). I am resigned to hearing every night the raucous songs of drunken warriors, and to listening patiently to long and badly-expressed speeches before taking the simplest decision. I sleep on straw, and when it rains I get wet. But I would like to talk to a well-educated and intelligent man before I die, and I know that is quite impossible.
>
> There is one other thing that worries me, especially when I lie awake at night. Suppose all that nonsense that my brother Paul used to preach is true after all? In that case I shall certainly burn in Hell for ever and ever. But it was fun while it lasted.

Parallels can be cited from the fifth and sixth centuries for much that is here said to have passed through Cerdic's mind. Cerdic is rightly made to combine material and intellectual culture in indicating the gulf between a well-to-do Roman's life and that of an English barbarian, as well as the gulf between late Roman Christianity and the religion of the Anglo-Saxons. In one way, however, Duggan's evocation of the transition misleads: what it does not point out is that the gap in material culture between the Roman past and the post-Roman present might be even greater for the Britons than it was for the English. There is no reason to think that an English warlord of the fifth century had to make do with a leaking roof or that his followers ate on the floor. Moreover, the English retained both the making and the use of pottery; and, whereas the British elite might use imported wares, the Britons did not themselves manufacture it: in Celtic Britain pottery was made for a time in Cornwall, and across the Irish Sea also in north-east Ireland, but not in Wales.[2] Historians who have described the transition from Roman Britain to Anglo-Saxon England have usually been less all-embracing than the historical novelist, preferring

[1] A. Duggan, *The Conscience of the King* (London, 1951), 244. Part of this chapter is a revised version of T. M. Charles-Edwards, 'Rome and the Britons, 400–664', in T. M. Charles-Edwards and R. J. W. Evans (eds.), *Wales and the Wider World: Welsh History in an International Context* (Donington, 2010), 9–27.

[2] G. Hutchinson, 'The Bar-Lug Pottery of Cornwall', *Cornish Archaeology*, 18 (1979), 81–103 (p. 89 for dating), and M. Ryan, 'Native Pottery in Early Historic Ireland', *PRIA* 73 C (1973), 619–45 (623–7 for dating, map 645), on Ulster souterrain ware.

to concentrate on material or other aspects of culture as they wished. I shall begin with the issue of the steep decline of British material culture and then turn to the question how far the Britons retained a Roman identity after they ceased to be subject to Roman government.

1. MATERIAL CULTURE

In AD 40, the British rulers of southern Britain had a coinage, were part of a trading system that revolved round the Empire, and had the ability to organize the building of great hill forts. In AD 450, the surviving Britons had no coinage of their own and Britain was no longer issued with imperial coins; the neighbouring parts of the Empire were disrupted by war and civil strife; and the British elite had deserted Roman-style country estates for hill forts that were modest by comparison with those of AD 40. In material terms, the Roman period may have brought exceptional prosperity to Britain, but the Britons had a lower standard of living after Rome than they had had before Rome. It has been suggested that the inclusion of Britain within a long-distance commerce that saw its products reach even the houses of ordinary farmers was the reason why the decline of the fifth century was so precipitous.[3] The local skills and exchange networks that had sustained the British prosperity of AD 40 were undermined by mass production and wide-ranging distribution. When the latter was made impossible by war and political fragmentation, the local skills were not there to replace them. A related point is that the area of Roman Britain that would become Wales was an importer of traded goods from further east within Britain and by sea from abroad: when these sources of supply were cut off by war, there was no equivalent source in western Britain that could take their place.[4] In 400, New Forest Ware was still traded over much of southern Britain and parts of northern Gaul; by 450 the Britons were entering a period in which pottery was no longer produced within their kingdoms but only imported by sea.

This bleak picture of the fifth century is true but needs to be qualified. The contrast between AD 40 and AD 450 works best by comparing the south-eastern Britain of the period before the Claudian conquest with the western and northern Britain of the period after the major Saxon conquests of the 440s. Yet western Britain was very imperfectly Romanized even in the fourth century: although the Dumnonii of the south-west peninsula, and the Silures and Demetae of what would become south Wales had *civitas* status and thus *civitas* capitals—Exeter, Caerwent, and Carmarthen—there is no evidence of any such capitals in the rest of what became Wales. North Wales remained a militarized region with forts such as Caernarfon and Holyhead, but probably no *civitates* and no villas. The northern Britons on both sides of Hadrian's Wall were in an even more military zone. Only after 400 would Roman-style epigraphy reach the Dumnonii; and only after 400 do we have evidence

[3] B. Ward-Perkins, *The Fall of Rome and the End of Civilization* (Oxford, 2005), 136–7.
[4] C. J. Arnold and J. L. Davies, *Roman and Early Medieval Wales* (Stroud, 2000), 95.

of a *civitas* in the north-west of Wales—a *civitas* in the eyes of its own elite, not, of course, in the eyes of a Roman government now without any control over the government of Britain.[5] Even in Provence the elite had retreated to hill forts in the face of Germanic invasions in the third century: Britain was not unique.[6]

Between *c.* 475 and *c.* 550 'Phocaean Red Slipware' was imported into south-western Britain from the eastern Mediterranean.[7] It is a fine tableware with a burnished finish produced in what is now western Turkey. The version imported into Britain was produced mainly in the years 475 to 525 with fewer imports from 525 to 550. What distinguishes its distribution from earlier wares in the same tradition is that it was very much an elite item and was largely confined to the south-west, Cornwall and south Wales. Almost half the excavated examples come from one site, Tintagel on the north coast of Cornwall. Tintagel used to be regarded as a monastic site, but that has been abandoned in favour of seeing it as a secular site of high status, probably royal.[8] In the later part of this period, 525–550, when finds of Phocaean Red Slipware tail off, there is a brief period in which another Mediterranean ware of similar quality, African Red Slipware, was imported into western Britain. This is again mainly found in the south-west, but it reached up the Irish Sea as far as Whithorn and Iona.

Western Turkey was, in the fifth and sixth centuries, part of the East Roman Empire. After Justinian's reconquest of Africa in 533, the southern shores of the Mediterranean were also again part of the Empire. What these finds reveal, therefore, is a trade between the Empire and south-western Britain. What is particularly intriguing about this trade, however, is that finds of Phocaean Red Slipware barely exist in western Gaul. Even in southern Spain there is no such concentration of finds as in the territory of the Dumnonii in south-western Britain. At the same period as these imports of tableware, amphorae are found, impossible to date directly but associated with the tableware and thus dated indirectly. What the amphorae carried cannot, in general, be proved, but oil and wine are very probable. Wine from the eastern Mediterranean was highly valued in sixth-century Gaul.[9]

What remains unclear is what was exchanged for the fine tableware and for the wine or oil carried in the associated amphorae. One possibility is tin, though precious furs have also been suggested.[10] An associated issue is how the trade was

[5] 394/103/Gn-32, Ffestiniog 1 (now kept at Penmachno).

[6] W. E. Klingshirn, *Caesarius of Arles: The Making of a Christian Community in Late Antique Gaul* (Cambridge, 1994), 162.

[7] What follows is based on E. Campbell, *Continental and Mediterranean Imports to Atlantic Britain and Ireland, AD 400–800*, CBA Research Report 157 (York, 2007), 14–18, and J. M. Wooding, *Communication and Commerce along the Western Seaways, AD 400–899*, Brit. Arch. Rep. Int. Ser. 654 (Oxford, 1996), 64–92, for textual evidence.

[8] The change of interpretation goes back to O. J. Padel, 'Appendix II: Tintagel—An Alternative View', in C. Thomas, *A Provisional List of Imported Pottery in Post-Roman Western Britain and Ireland* (Redruth, 1981).

[9] Gregory of Tours, *Hist.*, vii. 29 (wine from Gaza, from an area which was, however, not associated with the trade to Britain).

[10] L. Alcock and E. A. Alcock, 'Reconnaissance Excavations on Early Historic Fortifications and Other Royal Sites: 4, Excavations at Alt Clut, Clyde Rock, Strathclyde, 1974–75', *Proceedings of the Society of Antiquaries of Scotland*, 120 (1990), 128.

organized at the British end. Tintagel is not a place which any sensible seaman would consider a good place to land cargoes. It was not prominent in the trade because it had a good harbour or because it was a natural landing place for goods coming from the south. What distinguished it was presumably political power. It would have been easier for ships from the eastern Mediterranean to land their cargoes in one or more of the much better harbours on the south coast of Cornwall, from where it would have been transported to Tintagel. A corollary of this interpretation is that whatever power controlled Tintagel also controlled the trade in tin, if that is what was exported. Moreover, if the key to the rich accumulation of Mediterranean pottery at Tintagel is the power of the Dumnonian ruler rather than the safety of the harbour, that power may have compelled Dumnonians to bring imports from the south coast to Tintagel, just as it controlled the tin, rather than compelling East-Roman merchant ships to make the dangerous voyage round Land's End.

A further corollary of the explanation of the trade in terms of tin concerns the other sites where these goods from the Empire are found. These include Dinas Powys in south-east Wales and Longbury Bank in the south-west, as well as Garranes, an important ring fort in what is now Co. Cork and may have been within the kingdom of Éoganacht Raithlinn from the sixth century.[11] These sites were not participants in this pattern of exchange by virtue of controlling any sources of tin; and yet they were all important secular sites—Dinas Powys within the kingdom of Gwent, Longbury Bank within Dyfed. A possibility is that these received goods from Tintagel as gifts rather than as trade. In that case, the trade would have facilitated a network of alliances between kingdoms. Yet a note of caution should be struck: the nature of the site at Longbury Bank is uncertain. No structures were found, but the excavators were reluctant to see it as an undefended trading site, preferring to think that a hall existed but had, by chance, not been uncovered. If, however, Longbury Bank was a trading site associated with a nearby royal centre at Tenby, it is not obvious why diplomatic gifts should end up at the trading site rather than at the royal centre unless we assume a mixture of trade and gift. This would be natural if merchants worked for rulers.

The chronology of this trade, approximately between 475 and 550, is significant. The starting date is close to the time when a British army, led by Riothamus, was part of an imperial alliance involving the eastern emperor, Leo, his client as western emperor, Anthemius, and the Burgundians.[12] The end date is close to the Justinianic plague and to a break in relations between the emperor and western Christians over 'the Three Chapters'. We shall see later that Justinian's successor, Justin II, made efforts to repair this break and that these efforts were welcomed in Britain as well as in Gaul. The period 475–550 also included much of Gildas's lifetime and was described by him as, first, a time of British military recovery and then of relative peace. These considerations do not allow us to be certain about the context of the trade, but it is possible to sense what that context might have been.

[11] For the context and importance of Longbury Bank, see also below, 659–61.
[12] See above 59–60.

The mid-sixth century did not see a complete end to trade coming from the south into the Irish Sea, but the source and content of subsequent shipments were quite different. D ware, *Dérivées sigillées paléochrétiennes* of the Atlantic group (DSPA), was probably produced in the Bordeaux area and perhaps on the Loire; the former recalls the perception that Old Irish *bordgal*, borrowed from the name of Bordeaux, *Burdigala*, and meaning an assembly place, indicates a trade from the Gironde to Ireland.[13] These imports were thus coming from the Atlantic seaboard and not from the Mediterranean. Yet they overlap chronologically the Mediterranean imports in the south-west, whereas they overlap the later E ware, which starts from the second half of the sixth century, in North Britain, with South Wales showing both associations. The earlier DSPA may have been taken on board by Mediterranean ships. Perhaps the most interesting subcategory of DSPA was of the 'mortaria' traditionally used for making fruit and vegetable purées in the Roman manner.

E ware appears to have been imported from the second half of the sixth century, and throughout the seventh, with, perhaps, some reduced imports in the eighth.[14] In the early medieval province of Ulster (which lay east of the Bann) imports of E ware were followed from the eighth century to the twelfth by 'souterrain ware', which was locally produced. Remarkably, although this has a relatively dense distribution across Ulster, it is rarely found outside the province. The distribution of E ware was, however, much wider than that of the earlier Mediterranean wares and of souterrain ware. In Britain find-sites are almost all coastal, but in Ireland it is even found on an inland 'seat of kingship', at Clogher, Co. Tyrone. It is not, however, found widely in excavated 'raths' or 'ring forts', far the most common Irish secular settlement site. The trade, therefore, was a luxury one, not to be compared with imports of the Roman period, which reached even relatively humble British farms as at Cefn Graeanog.[15] Several types of vessel were imported, with jars the most common. Although it is a coarse rather than a fine ware, the consistency and quality of production suggest that it came from a single area and was not a domestic product. Unfortunately, the area of production is not known, but it is likely to have been between the Loire and the Gironde, with the Saintonge area an attractive candidate. Its ceramic pedigree, however, is not from the late Roman pottery of the area between the Loire and the Gironde but from Frankish wares further east and north.

The association with royal sites might suggest that E ware was itself a high-value product, but this is very probably deceptive. First, its most likely function was for

[13] K. Meyer, *Miscellanea Hibernica*, University of Illinois Studies in Language and Literature, 2: 4 (Urbana, 1917), 34; but the claim of H. Zimmer, 'Über direkte Handelsverbindungen Westgalliens mit Irland im Altertum und frühen Mittelalter', *Sitzungsberichte der königlichen Preussischen Akademie der Wissenschaften* (1909), 363–400, 430–76, 543–613; (1910), 1031–119, that there was a flourishing trade bringing wine to Ireland from south-western Gaul before AD 600, has been undermined by J. M. Wooding, *Communication and Commerce*, 32–4.

[14] The terminal date, in so far as it is affected by one important site, Whithorn, may have been skewed by the Northumbrian conquest of what is now Galloway.

[15] P. J. Fasham et al., *The Graeanog Ridge: The Evolution of a Farming Landscape and its Settlements in North-West Wales*, Cambrian Archaeological Monographs, no. 6 (Aberystwyth, 1998), 142–6.

transport and storage. Since it is a coarse ware, what was of high value was hardly the pottery itself but rather what it carried. In general this is not known, but exotic dyes are likely to be one commodity carried in E-ware jars. Similarly, it is not known what was exchanged for the goods carried in E ware, but leather shoes have been suggested as one possibility. If the chronology is correct, namely that the trade began in the second half of the sixth century, reached its maximum in the first half of the seventh century, and then tailed off gradually, it roughly coincides with the development of Frankish power. This reached its peak after conquests during the 530s and only declined in the second half of the seventh century. What is clear is that the E-ware trade probably came from the area called Aquitania at the time, an area of only modest Frankish settlement but one dominated by Frankish kings up to the late seventh century.

Glass finds in western Britain indicate a pattern of trade similar to the pottery, namely an external origin with the earliest group (A) associated with late Roman products from the Mediterranean, and intermediate categories (C and D) overlapping the Mediterranean and Frankish sequences of pottery imports. There are, however, important differences: the E group of glassware may have been produced in the area of Whithorn in the late sixth and early seventh centuries, while the B group (characterized by a deep blue colour and probably of high value) is likely to have been produced in Kent. It only reached south-east Wales, although it also reached both British and Pictish areas of North Britain.[16]

Hanging-bowls, a form of thin copper-alloy bowl designed to be suspended from three or four hooks, provide evidence for a quite different pattern of exchange. They usually have Celtic decoration but are mainly found in Anglo-Saxon graves of the period 550–650. When they have been repaired locally in the area in which they are found, the craftsmanship of the repairs is sufficiently different from that of the original manufacture to show that they were imports from somewhere else.[17] They were not made by Celtic craftsmen working for Anglo-Saxon employers in eastern Britain; and thus the Celtic form of decoration is the best guide to their place of origin. Unfortunately it is not known from where in Celtic Britain or Ireland they were imported into Anglo-Saxon England. This uncertainty is itself, however, a symptom of the shared material culture on either side of the Irish Sea and reaching up into the Hebrides.

That shared material culture began to emerge in the fifth century, as shown by the development of one fourth-century British type of brooch into the standard form, the penannular brooch, class 1, in both Celtic Britain and Ireland and at very much the same date.[18] Although there are two main concentrations of the fourth-century forerunner, on Hadrian's Wall together with the territory of the Votadini

[16] See the map, fig. 48, in Campbell, *Continental and Mediterranean Imports*, 73.

[17] S. Youngs, 'Fine Metalwork to *c.* 650', in S. Youngs (ed.), *'The Work of Angels': Masterpieces of Celtic Metalwork, 6th–9th Centuries AD* (London, 1989), 47.

[18] R. Ó Floinn, 'Patrons and Politics: Art, Artefact and Methodology', in M. Redknap et al. (eds.), *Pattern and Purpose in Insular Art* (Oxford, 2001), 1–14 (1–8 on brooches); S. Youngs, 'Britain, Wales and Ireland: Holding Things together', in Jankulak and Wooding (eds.), *Ireland and Wales in the Middle Ages* (Dublin, 2007), 80–101.

and in the south-west from the upper Thames valley to the lower Severn, details of the decoration make it likely that the latter was the source of the Irish brooches. That is to say, some brooches, probably from the lower Severn area were taken to Ireland and were there imitated. The effect was that these brooches, very probably an important symbol of rank, became a shared language of status on both sides of the Irish Sea. The distribution of these brooches thus formed one part of a complex of ways in which old barriers between Roman Britain and barbarian Ireland were broken down, beginning in the fourth century and gaining its full effect in the fifth with the Christianization of Ireland.

A distinction is therefore necessary between the geographical extent and the social penetration of the culture bequeathed by the western Roman Empire, now Christian, as its military power faded. So far as the geographical extent is concerned, everything seems positive: the collapse of the military barrier between Britain and Ireland leads more to the Romanization of the Irish than to the barbarizing of the Britons. Yet, in Britain itself, the social reach of Roman material culture is very much weaker: the courts of British rulers might consume purées of fruit and vegetables in the Roman manner; Latin might be heard as well as British; yet the mass of the population was increasingly composed of monoglot British-speakers who never used ceramic vessels of any kind. Urban living was a thing of the past; in the last echoes of the cities of Roman Britain, as at Wroxeter, there might be grand buildings, but they were now of wood not stone.[19] The corner had been turned that enabled Bede to say of the seventh-century Britons that they built in wood, not in the Roman manner, in stone.[20]

2. BRITONS: ROMANS OR BARBARIANS?

By the sixth century it was already several generations since the emperor last exercised any direct military and administrative control over Britain; yet, the Britons were still sometimes described as *cives*, 'fellow-citizens', of those who remained within the Roman Empire. Ever since the reign of Caracalla early in the third century all free Britons, other than those beyond the frontier, had been part of the community of citizens which the Roman Empire had created; and the effect outlasted the cause. Also in the sixth century, however, they were sometimes regarded as barbarians, outside that community of fellow-citizens. First it is necessary to investigate this contrast: to see who considered them to be citizens and who thought of them as barbarians; this will then make it easier to understand why there should be these two incompatible views; and whether there was a progression over time from an acceptance of Britons as fellow-citizens to a view of them as one among the many barbarian peoples of north-western Europe.

As was pointed out in Chapter 1, the distinction between acknowledgement of imperial authority and a wish to be directly subject to imperial power is vital for the

[19] R. White and P. Barker, *Wroxeter: Life and Death of a Roman City* (Stroud, 1998), 118–36.
[20] Bede, *HE* iii. 4 (on Candida Casa, Whithorn).

fifth and sixth centuries. In the first decade of the fifth century, Britain ceased to be directly subject to imperial power. The reason was that the Empire ceased to have the power to rule Britain. Yet, in the fifth century the Britons were not alone in assuming that they still adhered to Rome. The contrast made between Britain and Ireland by Prosper of Aquitaine, writing in the 430s, makes the point succinctly:[21]

> He (Celestine) has been, however, no less energetic in freeing the British provinces from this same disease (the Pelagian heresy): he removed from that hiding-place in the Ocean certain enemies of grace who had occupied the land of their origin; also, having ordained a bishop for the Irish, while he labours to keep the Roman island catholic, he has also made the barbarian island Christian.

Britain is Roman and must be kept Catholic; Ireland is barbarian and must be made Christian. There is no expectation that Ireland, by becoming Christian, will become Roman; and, equally, there is no expectation that Britain, because it no longer pays taxes to the emperor and is no longer protected by the emperor's armies, must therefore lose the title of Roman.

In the second half of the fifth century Patrick has similar assumptions, only these are conveyed, as they would be by Gildas in the sixth, more by the term *civis*, 'fellow-citizen', than by *Romanus*, 'Roman'. His *Letter to the Soldiers of Coroticus* was written to the Christian and British soldiers of a Christian and British king, who might have expected to be considered fellow-citizens by Patrick. This assumption is what gives a sharp edge to Patrick's words:[22]

> I have composed and written these words with my own hand to be conveyed and handed over, sent to the soldiers of Coroticus—I do not say 'to my fellow-citizens' nor 'to fellow-citizens of saintly Romans', but, on account of their evil deeds, 'to fellow-citizens of the demons'.

Coroticus's Britons might claim that they were fellow-citizens of the Romans; but what Patrick considered crucial was whether they were fellow-citizens of 'saintly Romans'. Rome was now not just imperial: it was Christian.

Patrick is also very interesting in a later section of the *Letter* for the way in which he refers to the Gallo-Romans. Indeed, so far as I know, he is the only ancient author who has a more or less direct counterpart to the modern term 'Gallo-Roman', namely *Romanus Gallus*:[23]

[21] Prosper, *Contra Collatorem*, c. 21, ed. Migne, PL li. 271: Nec uero segniore cura ab hoc eodem morbo Britannias liberauit, quando, quosdam inimicos gratiae solum suae originis occupantes etiam ab illo secreto exclusit Oceani, et ordinato Scotis episcopo, dum Romanam insulam studet seruare catholicam, fecit etiam barbaram christianam.

[22] Patrick, *Epistola*, § 2, ed. L. Bieler, *Libri Epistolarum Sancti Patricii Episcopi*, 2 vols. (Irish Manuscripts Commission; Dublin, 1952; repr. Dublin, 1993): Manu mea scripsi atque condidi uerba ista danda et tradenda, militibus mittenda Corotici, non dico ciuibus meis neque ciuibus sanctorum Romanorum, sed ciuibus daemoniorum, ob mala opera ipsorum.

[23] Ibid. § 14: Consuetudo Romanorum Gallorum Christianorum: mittunt uiros sanctos idoneos ad Francos et ceteras gentes cum tot milia solidorum ad redimendos captiuos baptizatos. Tu potius interficis et uendis illos genti exterae ignoranti Deum; quasi in lupanar tradis *membra Christi*.

> The habit of the Gallo-Roman Christians (is this): they send saintly and suitable men to the Franks and other pagan peoples with very many thousand *solidi* to ransom baptized captives. You, however, kill them and sell them to a foreign people ignorant of God; it is as if you were entrusting Christ's limbs to a brothel.

This passage has the contrast between Romans and Christians, on the one hand, and *gentes*, non-Roman and non-Christian peoples on the other. It combines the *gentes* of Roman political discourse (barbarian peoples as contrasted with Roman citizens) with the *gentes*, namely Gentiles, of the Old and New Testaments. Gildas is, in his use of *gens*, less conservative: it is one of the most remarkable features of his political vocabulary in the next century that he is quite happy to write of the Romans as a *gens*, just as he is quite happy to term the emperors *reges*, kings.[24] The traditional distinctions between the Roman people (*populus Romanus*) and barbarian nations (*gentes*) and between the Christian people and the Gentiles have been abandoned or forgotten; so, too, the distinction between a Roman emperor and barbarian kings. Patrick is thus on the route towards Gildas's political vocabulary, but he seems to be more closely attached to the assumptions of the late Empire.

The religious aspect of *Romanitas* was now becoming stronger. The name of the Roman Empire was sometimes given as the *sacratissima res publica*, 'the most holy state';[25] it was holy because it already saw itself as the earthly expression of divine authority. In the west, in the fifth century, Patrick's *Letter to the Soldiers of Coroticus* gained force because unChristian acts could be assumed to be acts which one *civis* should not commit against another. To carry off Christian captives was to be unworthy of the name of 'fellow-citizen'.

The fifth-century situation was thus complex and unstable. On the one hand, Britain was generally thought to have remained Roman even if the officials and army of the central government were no longer found north of the Channel. On the other hand, by the end of the century it was easier to think of the *Galli* as *Romani* but of the Britons—or, at least, those who behaved as good Christians and did not ally themselves with barbarian Irish and Picts—as *cives* of those same *Romani Galli* rather than as themselves *Romani*. At least part of the reason was the British settlement in north-west Armorica, for the Britons of Gaul appear never to have been thought by the *Galli* as simply another set of Romans.

3. THE SIXTH CENTURY

In Gaul a distinction must be made between the different standpoints of the Franks, the Bretons, and the Gallo-Romans (by 'Bretons' I mean merely Britons settled in Armorica; at the time they were known simply as Britons, and in

[24] Cf. G. Tugène, *L'Idée de nation chez Bède le Vénérable*, Études Augustiniennes (Paris, 2001), 53–8, on 'la "gentilisation" des Romains dans l'historiographie médiévale'.

[25] *Epistolae Austrasicae*, ed. W. Gundlach, no. 42, in *Epistolae Merowingici et Karolini Aevi*, ed. E. Dümmler, MGH (Berlin, 1892), 148; similarly the emperor might be termed 'sacratissimus pater noster imperator', ibid., p. 152 no. 47.

translating contemporary texts about the Bretons I shall therefore refer to them as Britons). In the early Breton legal text known in several manuscripts of the A version as 'Excerpts from books of the Romans and the Franks' one rule goes as follows:[26]

> If any Catholic lets his hair grow in the fashion of the barbarians, he shall be held an alien from the Church of God and from the table of every Christian until he makes amends for his offence.

This text has plausibly been dated to the sixth century by Fleuriot.[27] The background is partly illuminated by an event of the year 590 recounted by Gregory of Tours.[28] Guntram, then the senior Frankish king, had sent an army to punish the Bretons for raids in the border territories of Rennes and Nantes. Fredegund, the widowed mother of another Frankish king, Chlothar II, secretly sent a contingent from the Saxons settled around Bayeux to aid the Bretons against the Frankish army. The Saxons were to cut their hair in the Breton way and so pass themselves off as Bretons. When they had done so, these Bretons in disguise would probably also have been distinct from the Franks. They too seem to have worn their hair long, though not as long as did their kings or boys up to the age of twelve.[29]

This Breton legal text therefore makes an odd contrast, 'Catholic' against 'barbarian'. (The usual contrast was between 'Catholic' and 'heretic' or between 'Catholic' and 'pagan'; 'Roman' was the term regularly opposed to 'barbarian'.) By implication, then, the Bretons were Catholics and their long-haired enemies were the barbarians; it was a Catholic duty for the Bretons not to compromise their identity. The contrast between Christians and barbarians can be paralleled in a British penitential text, which has been dated to the early sixth century; and the Bretons had to face, as well as Franks, the Saxons, not just of the Bessin but of the lower Loire.[30] Yet, who were these barbarians to be contrasted with Catholics? The mention of long hair suggests the Franks and the Saxons; and, yet, this legal text is not usually dated to a period before the conversion of Clovis to Catholic Christianity, after which Franks were slowly but increasingly Christianized. Admittedly, until the second half of the seventh century the Franks, though Christian, remained happy to be regarded as a barbarian nation.[31] Yet, on the other hand, the Catholicity of the Frankish rulers after Clovis was not in question. Perhaps, then, the text should be dated to the late fifth or early sixth century, before the Franks

[26] *Canones Wallici*, Version A, § 61, ed. L. Bieler, *The Irish Penitentials* (Dublin, 1963), 148/9.

[27] L. Fleuriot, 'Un fragment en Latin de très anciennes lois bretonnes armoricaines du VIe siècle', *Annales de Bretagne*, 78 (1971), 601–60; cf. D. N. Dumville, 'On the Dating of the Early Breton Lawcodes', *Études Celtiques*, 21 (1984), 207–21, who is more sceptical.

[28] Gregory of Tours, *Hist.*, x. 9.

[29] *Pactus Legis Salicae*, ed. K. A. Eckhardt, MGH, Legum Sectio I, iv. 1 (Hanover, 1962), §§ 24. 2–4; 97. 1–2; 104. 1–3; Gregory of Tours, *Hist.*, ii. 41; vi. 24 (the last of which shows that the kings wore their hair down their backs: *crinium flagellis per terga dimissis*).

[30] 'The Synod of the Grove of Victory', § 4, ed. and trans. Bieler, *The Irish Penitentials*, 68–9; L. Fleuriot, *Les Origines de la Bretagne* (Paris, 1980), 199–202.

[31] E. Ewig, 'Volkstum und Volksbewusstsein im Frankenreich', *Settimane*, 5 (1958), 614–22, repr. E. Ewig, *Spätantikes und fränkisches Gallien* (Zürich and Munich, 1976), i. 249–55.

began to be regarded as fully Christian and when Breton territory lay not far from the Visigoths, Arian heretics.

The latter relationship, between Bretons and Visigoths, is worth considering more closely. For one thing, the major recorded British military presence in Gaul in the second half of the fifth century had been to counter the Visigothic threat on behalf of Emperor Anthemius. For another, we know from Gregory of Tours that the Visigothic Arians contrasted themselves as orthodox Christians with 'the Romans'; for them being 'Roman' included being wrong on the nature of the Trinity.[32] Such a contrast between orthodox Visigoth and heretical Roman appears to be the mirror image of the contrast made by the Breton legal text, between Catholic and barbarian. In both cases the old opposition between Roman and barbarian has taken a new colour from the contrast between orthodoxy and heresy or paganism.

Alongside this Breton legal text can be set the *Pactus Legis Salicae* of the Franks. The date of the first surviving recension of the Salic Law is controversial but it is most unlikely to be later than the reign of Clovis, who died in 511.[33] A comparison of two rules is instructive:[34]

XLI. 1 But if anyone kills a free Frank or [any] barbarian who is living in accordance with the Salic law, and it can be proven that he did this, let him be held liable for 8000 denarii, which make 200 solidi (known in the malberg as *leodi*).

XLI. 9 But if a Roman landlord (who has not been a table-companion of the king [MS A1 only]) is killed, let him who is proved to have killed him be held liable for 4000 denarii, which make 100 solidi (known in the malberg as *uualaleodi*).

These two clauses show a contrast between barbarian and Roman: there is a readiness to allow that barbarians other than the Franks themselves may choose to live by Salic Law and will be assigned the same relatively high wergild (the wergild for a freeman was known in Frankish as *leodi*); the corresponding Roman is not just given a wergild worth only half as much, but this lesser wergild was known as *uualaleodi*. The opposition between *leodi* and *uualaleodi* was between the wergild assigned to Franks and other barbarians living by Salic Law, on the one side, and that assigned to the Romans, who were known to the Franks as *Walas*, on the other. The same wergild of half the value of the corresponding barbarian (non-Roman)

[32] Gregory of Tours, *Liber in Gloria Martyrum*, cc. 24, 79, MGH SRM i. 2, pp. 502, 541.

[33] It predates the *Pactus pro Tenore Pacis*, promulgated by two of Clovis's sons, Childebert I and Chlothar I, and the absence, in the A version, of any reference to Christianity accords with the assumption of the Breton *Excerpta* that Germanic barbarians are not Catholic Christians; the *Lex Salica* contrasts with the emphatically Christian edict of Childebert I: *Capitularia Regum Francorum*, I. i, ed. A. Boretius, MGH, Capit. (Hanover, 1881), no. 2, *Childeberti I Regis Praeceptum* (pp. 2–3). For a discussion of the dating, see T. M. Charles-Edwards, 'Law in the Western Kingdoms between the Fifth and the Seventh Century', in A. Cameron, B. Ward-Perkins and M. Whitby (eds.), *The Cambridge Ancient History*, xiv, *Late Antiquity: Empire and Successors, A.D. 425–600* (Cambridge, 2000), 271–5.

[34] *Pactus Legis Salicae*, ed. Eckhardt, xli. 1 and 9; trans. T. J. Rivers, *Laws of the Salian and Ripuarian Franks* (New York, 1986), 86–7 (I have modified the translation of c. 9).

and the same designation of them as *Walas* or *Wealas* recurred some two centuries later in the West Saxon laws of Ine (promulgated *c.* 690). The term is the origin of the modern 'Wales'; and the adjective derived from *Walas*, *wilisc*, is the origin of 'Welsh'.[35] At this stage, however, *Walas* meant, to a Frank who remembered that his forefathers came from across the Roman frontier, the descendants of the former citizens of the Roman Empire. The term united, therefore, the Britons of late seventh-century Britain with the Romans of Gaul of the post-Roman period. It is probably fair to deduce that the Franks of Clovis's reign would have regarded the Britons settled in Gaul just as much as *Walas* as were the Gallo-Romans, for they, too, had been citizens of the Empire.

Considerable changes had occurred in the century or so between Prosper of Aquitaine writing in the 430s of Britain as 'the Roman island' and Gildas in the first half of the sixth with his Roman *gens* from whom the Britons were quite distinct. Not just had the Saxons conquered much of Britain and thus rendered it unquestionably barbarian territory, but the distinctness of the Britons of Gaul—the Bretons—from the Romans of Gaul exerted a powerful and constant pressure towards separation of all Britons from all Romans. Patrick's *Romani Galli* indicates that the Gauls were now being seen as Romans in a way that the Britons were not. Yet, from a Frankish viewpoint, Britons are likely to have been seen as *Walas* as much as were the Gallo-Romans.

In the second half of the sixth century a rhetorician and poet from Ravenna, Venantius Fortunatus, settled in Francia. He arrived about 565, when he praised several Frankish kings, moved to Poitiers, and became a friend of Gregory of Tours.[36] One of his patrons was Felix, bishop of Nantes and therefore, as bishop of a city on the border of Breton territory, deeply concerned with relations between Franks, Gallo-Romans, and Bretons. Fortunatus is a valuable guide to those relations from the Gallo-Roman side: Felix was of an aristocratic family from Aquitaine, one which had a hold on the bishopric of Nantes, just as Gregory's family had on the bishopric of Tours.[37] It is most unlikely that the poet from Ravenna would have had views on the Bretons other than those of the bishop of Nantes. For Fortunatus on Felix, the Bretons were very much not Catholics confronting long-haired barbarians. He describes Felix as:[38]

> An apostolic shepherd who prevails over the claims (*iura*) of the Britons, secure in the face of adversity, you put arms to flight by hope in the cross.

[35] Ine, cc. 23, 24, 32, 33; M. L. Faull, 'The Semantic Development of Old English *wealh*', *Leeds Studies in English*, 8 (1975), 20–44, esp. 20–3. Faull cites the evidence of the *Pactus Legis Salicae* for the Romans being given a lower wergild than the Franks, but seems not to have noticed that the Malberg gloss uses *Walas* for the Romans. This may be because she is wedded to the idea that when the Anglo-Saxons settled in Britain *Walas* meant 'Celts'. For the place-name evidence, see K. Cameron, 'The Meaning and Significance of Old English *walh* in English Place-Names', *Journal of the English Place-Name Society*, 12 (1980), 1–53.

[36] J. W. George, *Venantius Fortunatus: A Poet in Merovingian Gaul* (Oxford, 1992), 22–34.

[37] J. R. Martindale, *Prosopography of the Later Roman Empire* (Cambridge, 1992), iii A, under 'Felix 5'.

[38] Venantius Fortunatus, *Opera Poetica*, ed. F. Leo, MGH AA. iv. 1 (Berlin, 1881), iii. 5: Actor apostolicus, qui iura Britannica uincens, / Tutus in aduersis, spe crucis arma fugas.

This hostility to the Bretons went together with an understanding that they were barbarians, and this perception is all the more telling because it emerges most clearly in a text in which the Britons (here certainly not just Bretons) were perceived in a favourable context. Fortunatus's royal friend Radegund was seeking a relic of the True Cross from Constantinople. To help her he composed a poem addressed to the Emperor Justin II (565–579) and the Empress Sophia. This praised them for healing the rift with the western Churches caused by Justinian's drive to have the so-called Three Chapters condemned:[39]

> [On Justin] The happy tale of the faith runs to the furthest nations; and across the Ocean, the British land approves. . . . [On Sophia] On one side the Roman offers praises, on the other even the barbarian—German, Batavian, Basque, Briton.

Here, then, the Briton, like the Basque, appears unambiguously among the barbarians rather than as a fellow-citizen of the Romans. Fortunatus thus goes further than the Council of Tours in 567, where the Britons are simply distinguished from the Romans:[40]

> We also add that no-one should be so bold as to ordain a Briton or a Roman in Armoricum without the consent of the metropolitan or of the bishops of the same province or letters [of authorization].

As the texts illustrate, *Galli* and *Brittones* were not two equal constituent parts of a larger body, the Romans, for, by the sixth century, the *Galli* had been swallowed up in the *Romani*, something that never happened to the Britons: Gregory of Tours wrote of *Galliae* 'the Gauls', but not of *Galli*; yet he was happy to describe people as Britons. The distinctness of the Britons from the Gallo-Romans in Gaul can be followed back into the fifth century, since an earlier Council of Tours, in 461, included among the bishops who subscribed, 'Mansuetus, bishop of the Britons'.[41] Proper Gallic bishops were leaders of a city and its territory, not of an ethnic group. The Britons were different.

In the late sixth century the difference was especially acute in the border zone, both in areas still subject to the Franks and those subject to Breton rulers. As we saw in Chapter 1, Gregory of Tours presents Regalis, bishop of Vannes, as speaking on

[39] Fortunatus, *Opera Poetica*, Appendix, 2. Ad Iustinum et Sophiam Augustos, 565 × 575: Currit ad extremas fidei pia fabula gentes, / Et trans Oceanum terra Britannica fauet. . . . Illinc Romanus, hinc laudes barbarus ipse, / Germanus, Batauus, Vasco, Britannus agit. A translation, very slightly different from the one given here, is in Judith George, *Venantius Fortunatus: Personal and Political Poems*, Liverpool Translated Texts (Liverpool, 1995), 113, 115. Compare the similar list of peoples, including Britons, said by Fortunatus to have been terrified by Chilperic, *Opera Poetica*, ix. 1.

[40] *Concilia Galliae, A. 511–A. 695*, ed. C. de Clercq, CCSL 148 A (Turnhout, 1963), Council of Tours, AD 567, c. 9: Adicimus etiam, ne quis Brittanum aut Romanum in Armorico sine metropolis aut comprouincialium uoluntate uel literis episcopum ordinare praesumat.

[41] *Concilia Galliae, A. 314–A. 506*, ed. C. Munier, CCSL 148 (Turnhout, 1963), 148: *Mansuetus episcopus Britannorum*. It is important that Mansuetus appeared at a council at Tours, since this indicates that his Britons were, as was Brittany later, within the metropolitan province headed by the bishop of Tours.

behalf of the clergy and country people of the Vannetais, when he declared to the Frankish dukes sent by King Guntram to bring the Bretons to heel:[42]

> We are innocent of any charge in our relations with our lords, the kings, nor have we displayed any contumacious disregard of their interests, but since we are placed in captivity to the Britons, we have been subjected to a heavy yoke.

By implication, those on behalf of whom Bishop Regalis spoke were Romans subject to the Bretons though still claiming to preserve a direct allegiance to the Frankish kings. In the neighbouring territories of Rennes and Nantes, still 'Roman' and normally subject to the Franks, the Bretons were prone to raid, especially at the time of the grape harvest.

In late fifth- and sixth-century Gaul, therefore, Britons and Romans were distinct; but it was only in the late sixth century that the Britons were unambiguously detached from the community of fellow-citizens and placed among the barbarians; and even then—and even among the Gallo-Romans—that detachment was not complete. In a poem to Lupus, duke of Champagne, Venantius Fortunatus declared:[43]

> But let the rest on my behalf compete to render you praises, and let each celebrate you, with petition, with song, as best he may; let the Roman applaud you with the lute, the barbarian with the harp, the Greek with the lyre of Achilles, the Briton with the crowd (*crotta*). . . . Let me offer you my humble little verses, let the barbarian songs offer lays (*leudos*). So, in different modes, may a single praise ring out to a man.

The Briton here is neither a Roman nor a barbarian, for, as the contrast between the Roman and the Greek shows, 'Roman' is here applied to a more limited group than the citizens of the former Empire. The Roman in this passage is likely to be a Latin-speaker as opposed to speakers of Greek and Germanic; if that is so, the Britons were probably also being identified by speaking a language other than Latin, while the *Galli*, now Latin-speakers, were subsumed under the term *Romani*. The poem is displaying the consensus of different linguistic groups in praise of Lupus, just as those assembled to sing the praises of King Guntram as he made his ceremonial entry into Orléans in 585 were separated into distinct linguistic groups.[44]

As we have seen, in the Salic Law, no later than 511, the *Walas* probably comprised Britons as much as Romans. This failure to distinguish was not a consequence of any remoteness. As the authority of Rignomer, one of Clovis's rival Frankish kings, over Le Mans shows, the Franks already exercized power on

[42] Gregory of Tours, *Hist.*, x. 9.

[43] *Opera Poetica*, vii. 8: To Duke Lupus (duke of Champagne):

> Sed pro me reliqui laudes tibi reddere certent,
> Et qua quisque ualet te prece, uoce, sonet,
> Romanusque lyra, plaudat tibi barbarus harpa,
> Graecus Achilliaca, crotta Britanna canat. . . .
> Nos tibi uersiculos, dent barbara carmina leudos,
> Sic uariante tropo laus sonet una uiro.

Cf. George, *Venantius Fortunatus: Personal and Political Poems*, 64.

[44] Gregory of Tours, *Hist.*, viii. 1.

the borders of what was becoming Brittany.[45] The Salic Law dates, however, from before the alliance of Franks and Gallo-Romans had its full effect. In the late sixth century, in the lifetime of Venantius Fortunatus and Gregory of Tours, the elite of the Frankish kingdoms was formed by Gallo-Romans and Burgundians as well as by Franks; and this becomes yet clearer in the early seventh century.[46] Because, by then, Gallo-Romans tended to regard the Britons as barbarians, this attitude naturally spread to the Franks: a standard theme of Fortunatus's poems addressed to Franks is the bond between Romans and Franks, fortified by a Frankish readiness to share in the culture of the Romans.[47] Moreover, the same ambition to display both cultures is attested in the rare texts written by eminent Franks.[48]

When Gregory of Tours wrote of Breton dynastic struggles, he described the constituent political territories of Brittany as *regna*, kingdoms; yet he immediately went on to qualify this term, 'For since the death of Clovis the Britons have always been under the power of the Franks, and they have been called counts, not kings.'[49] No doubt this statement reflected what the Franks themselves claimed; but, whereas in their own *regna* Frankish kings appointed counts, it seems from Gregory's narrative that they had no such authority in Brittany. Because the Bretons were only half-subject satellites of the Franks, they could not gain a place within the leadership of the Frankish kingdoms. Gregory of Tours offers not a single example of a Frankish king appointing someone as bishop or count within Brittany; and Gregory's evidence is telling, since Brittany lay within the province of which he was metropolitan bishop: the two-way traffic of recruitment and promotion between leading figures in the *civitates*, ambitious for office, and the courts of the Frankish kings, through whom advancement came, a traffic so important for the cohesion of the Frankish *regna*, did not operate in Brittany. A political division between the Romans of Gaul, who were full partners in the Frankish kingdoms, and the Bretons, who were not, accentuated the existing opposition between Roman and Briton. Although the Franks may have continued to regard the Bretons as much as the Gallo-Romans as *Walas*, the Gallo-Romans themselves appear to have disowned the link. Moreover, in the seventh century it was becoming more difficult to regard the Franks as *barbari*, and thus the way was prepared for the Franks and Romans of northern Gaul to become one people, called Franks but now embracing all the inhabitants of the Frankish core territory between the Rhine and the Loire—with the exception of the Bretons.[50]

The evidence for any detachment of the Britons from Rome comes from the Gallo-Roman side, the principal drivers being conflict between Bretons and their neighbours and the nature of the elite in the Frankish *regna*; what the Britons of the late sixth century thought remains to be discussed. One of the Penmachno

[45] Gregory of Tours, *Hist.*, ii. 42.
[46] Ewig, *Spätantikes und fränkisches Gallien*, i. 254–5.
[47] Fortunatus, *Opera Poetica*, vi. 2, vii. 7 and 8.
[48] For example, the letter of Gogo in *Epp. Austras.*, ed. Gundlach, no. 16.
[49] Gregory of Tours, *Hist.*, iv. 4.
[50] Ewig, *Spätantikes und fränkisches Gallien*, i. 252–4.

Illustration 6.1. This inscription, found near the Eagles Hotel, Penmachno, and now in the church, may attest British loyalty to the Emperor Justin during the period of his successive consulships, 567–579. Its interpretation is rendered difficult by its fragmentary condition: the stone is slate and it has split along the vertical line. Very unusually, the text is partly horizontal and partly vertical.

inscriptions (see Illustration 6.1 above) in North Wales, very helpfully discussed by Jeremy Knight, may give us a clue.[51]

Vertical section:	] FILI AVITORI
Horizontal section:	
Nash-Williams:	IN TE(m)PO[RE] / IVSTI[NI] CON[SVLI]
Knight:	IN TE(m)PO[RE] / IVSTI[NI P(ost)] / CON(sulatum) [XXV]

There are three particular problems with this inscription: first, it is fragmentary, having split along the vertical plane of a slatey stone; secondly, the text is in two parts, one vertical, running in the same direction as the split, and the second horizontal, running across the split. The beginning of the vertical section is lost and the right-hand parts of the horizontal section. The lost first line of the vertical section has been conjectured, very reasonably, to consist of something such as HIC IACIT 'here lies' followed by the first name of the person concerned. The nastier problems arise over the interpretation of the fragmentary horizontal section. The crucial difficulty, one which was noted by Jeremy Knight, is what to make of the phrase IN TE(m)PO[RE] IVSTI[NI]. The usual line taken on the inscription as a whole is that it is an example of a system of dating used in the mid- and late sixth century, by which particular years were specified by saying that they were so many years after the consulate of either Iustinus (540) or Basilius (541). An example is the following, from Lyons:[52]

> Christ, Stephen, God's servant, *primicerius* of the School of Readers serving the church of Lyons rests in this place. He lived for 66 years. He died on the eighth day before the Kalends of December twelve years after the consulship of Justin, the fifteenth indiction.

XR IN HOC LOCO . REQVIESCIT
FAMOLVS D(e)I STEFANVS PRIMICIRIVS
SCOLAE LECTORVM SERVIENS ECL(esiae)
LVGDVNINSI VIXIT ANNOS LXVI
OBIIT VIIII K(a)L. DECEMBRIS DVODECIES P(ost) C(onsulatum)
IVSTINI INDICTIONE XV

Jeremy Knight's reconstruction is the best to date working to this assumption. The problem is, however, that, if the Penmachno inscription is an example of the so-called 'post-consular' dating, the phrase 'in the time of Justin' is misplaced: such a phrase situates an event during a period, typically the reign of a king or emperor. It does not specify the particular year within that period; but the post-consular dating system, on the other hand, was designed to specify the year; hence Knight's

[51] Penmachno 3, 396/104/Gn-33; J. K. Knight, 'Penmachno Revisited: The Consular Inscription and its Context', *CMCS* 29 (Summer 1995), 1–10. It is also discussed by M. A. Handley, 'The Origins of Christian Commemoration in Late Antique Britain', *Early Medieval Europe*, 10/2 (2001), 192–4; id., *Death, Society and Culture: Inscriptions and Epitaphs in Gaul and Spain, AD 300–750*, BAR International Ser. 1135 (Oxford, 2003), 130.

[52] E. Le Blant, *Inscriptions chrétiennes de la Gaule antérieures aux VIIIe siècles*, 2 vols. (Paris, 1856–65), no. 667A.

reconstruction, according to which the inscription, before it was damaged, would have read 'in the time of Justin, [.] years after (his) consulship'. Yet this still couples two distinct dating systems, that to an undefined year within an emperor's reign with that to a specific year after a consulship of 540.

The suggestion which I shall make is based on the Chronicle of Marius of Avenches, one of the most important sources for Burgundian and Frankish history in the sixth century. This chronicle uses post-consular dating from Basil (consul 541) in the period from 542 to 566, but then Iustinus Minor (that is, Emperor Justin II), not from the beginning of his reign but in the period of his successive consulships 567–579.[53] It then continues with Tiberius Constantinus (Tiberius II) from 580 to 581, where the chronicle ends. This means that IN TEMPORE IUSTI[NI] CON could refer to Emperor Justin II, who was also a consul for much of his reign, 567–579, rather than to the consul Justin of 540. The advantage of this interpretation is that it allows for the phrase 'in the time of the consul Justin' and explains how such an intrusion from an apparently alien method of dating into the post-consular system could occur. It enables us to have our cake and eat it, to see that it is attached to the post-consular tradition (as in the chronicle of Marius of Avenches) and yet allow for *in tempore*; we can keep the relatively conservative reconstruction of Nash-Williams; and it also supplies a reasonable date for the inscription, namely in the period 567 × 579.

This emperor, Justin II, was also, as we saw earlier, the one lauded by Fortunatus because he had healed the rift between east and west over the Three Chapters: he was the emperor whose orthodoxy was the subject of celebration even among the distant Britons beyond the Ocean. In the early sixth century, the Franks had recognized the ultimate authority of the emperor even while, as with Theudebert I, they pursued policies largely hostile to the Empire's interests. What made a formal break was the Three Chapters affair, an attempt to promote theological unity in the East which met with general condemnation from those Latin Christians living beyond the reach of imperial power in the West. Hence, in the last fifteen years of Justinian's reign, relations were much cooler: Theudebert's son, Theudebald (547–555) did not salute Justinian as his 'father', as did Theudebert, a significant point of diplomatic protocol.[54] Moreover, the antipathy to Justinian's religious policies was not peculiar to the Franks and Gallo-Romans but general in the West, including, for example, those Italians subject to Lombard rulers. By the time of the late sixth-century correspondence between the Frankish kings and the emperor Maurice, however, the Frankish king, Childebert II, was once more acknowledging some form of duty to his 'father'.[55] Justin II's diplomacy had thus largely won over the West (apart from the Catholics ruled by the Lombards). This was the change signalled by Marius's shift from a strict post-consular dating to

[53] *Marii Episcopi Aventicensis Chronica*, ed. Th. Mommsen, *Chronica Minora*, ii, MGH AA xi (1894), 238–9.

[54] *Epistolae Austrasicae*, ed. Gundlach, pp. 131–3 nos. 18, 19, 20,.

[55] Ibid., p. 138 no. 25.

dating by the consulships of Justin II; and since the change was welcomed even in distant Britain, it is not improbable that it was recognized in the same way.

Responses to the western diplomacy of the emperors of the sixth century demonstrate again the need to make a distinction, between acknowledgement of authority and a wish to be subjected to power. The Frankish king who acknowledged the authority of the emperor accepted an alliance in which he was the junior partner, in power as well as in prestige. Because he was the junior partner, he accepted that the emperor would set the pace, and that he would normally have to align himself with imperial policy rather than the emperor having to align himself with a mere 'son'. Even if he were to pursue policies opposed to imperial interests, as did Theudebert I, he would attempt to appear as if he were doing nothing of the kind. The significance of this stance is evident if one considers what happened when it changed, as when Alboin, king of the Lombards, abandoned an imperial alliance and declared himself an Arian before his invasion of Italy in 568–569. That change altered the shape of the Mediterranean world for good.

The Lombards and the Franks mattered to the Empire because of Italy. If Emperor Justin II received Fortunatus's poem in praise of him and the empress, he may have smiled to think that he was honoured even in far-off Britain, but it will have been no more than a small addition to imperial prestige. For the Britons, however, it would have been of greater consequence, for to date one's public monuments by the consulships of an emperor in Constantinople was as eloquent a way as could be found of affirming that one still belonged to the far-flung and loose-knit community of citizens of which he was the head. And it was not a merely symbolic matter: western rulers could still, after all, think as late as the winter of 668 that imperial diplomacy might be seriously dangerous, as we know from Ebroin's imprisonment of Abbot Hadrian on his way to England, 'because he was suspicious that he might have undertaken an embassy from the emperor to the kings of Britain, an embassy hostile to the kingdom for which at that time he had the chief responsibility'.[56]

4. THE SEVENTH CENTURY

The Breton *Excerpta de libris Romanorum et Francorum*, as we have seen, opposed barbarian to Catholic rather than barbarian to Roman. In the seventh century, Bretons appear to have contrasted themselves with the Romans of Gaul. In the older Life of St Samson of Dol, the saint's foundation at *Pennetale*, on the south bank of the Seine close to its mouth, was said to lie in *Romania*:[57] the south side of the English Channel was divided between *Brittania* to the west, a *Romania* that included what is now Normandy west of the Seine, and, one may presume, a

[56] Bede, *HE* iv. 2.

[57] For the situation of *Pennetale*, see J. Malco, 'Ermitages et monastères bretons dans la province de Rouen au haut Moyen Âge', in J. Quaghebeur and B. Merdrignac (eds.), *Bretons et Normands au Moyen Âge* (Rennes, 2008), 75, fig. 3; for *Romania*, B. Merdrignac, 'La Neustrie / Normandie dans les vies de saints bretons', ibid. 39–43.

Francia further east.[58] This usage would hardly be possible after the seventh century; in the Carolingian *Vita Secunda* of St Samson (of the ninth century) all references to *Romania* have disappeared; the north of Gaul was divided merely between *Britannia* in the west and *Francia* in the east.[59] In the sixth century some texts, such as the Treaty of Andelot of 587, had used *Francia* for all the territories ruled by Frankish kings; but Gregory of Tours himself used *Francia* for the eastern kingdom—what would become Austrasia—and probably also for what would become the part of Neustria east of the Seine.[60] This usage left the lands immediately to the east of Brittany as a territory that was neither *Francia* nor *Brittania*; and although the term is not in Gregory, it may well be that he also would have recognized it as *Romania*. From the late seventh century, however, *Francia* always included all northern France as far west as the Breton frontier and as far south as the Loire as well as the lands further east. *Romania* was then restricted to the lands south of the Loire, increasingly independent of the Franks until reconquered by Charles Martel and his sons, Carloman and Pippin.[61]

The shift to a more strongly religious conception of what made a Roman and a citizen exposed the Britons in the seventh century to a damaging charge. The true *Romani* were now those who obeyed the decisions of the bishop of Rome and the Christian world at large on such issues as Easter and the tonsure.[62] In 541, the Church of Gaul had agreed on an Easter calculation which was not accepted by the Britons.[63] Yet, as we have seen, the Britons remained part of the Christian community of the

[58] *La Vie ancienne de Saint Samson de Dol*, ed. and trans. P. Flobert (Paris, 1997), Prol. 2; i. 60, 61. For this reason I cannot accept the eighth-century date proposed by the editor on the basis of what, as far as I can see, are (1) quite uncertain echoes of Bede (pp. 98–9); (2) a misconceived argument about British attitudes to Gregory the Great (pp. 30, 93: he takes no account of the British element in Columbanus's community, although he is aware of Columbanus's interest in the works of Gregory); and (3) the supposed influence of the Insular culture of the age of Bede (pp. 34–5: this takes no account of the evidence for British and Irish culture as early as the sixth century). J.-C. Poulin, 'Hagiographie et politique: La première Vie de Saint Samson de Dol', *Francia*, 5 (1977), 1–26, argues for a ninth-century date on the grounds that the Life is deeply influenced by Sulpicius Severus's Life of St Martin and was thus attempting to make St Samson an equal of St Martin; this was then supposed to require it to be placed in the context of the attempt to make Dol into an archbishopric independent of Tours. As can readily be seen, Poulin offered a contextualization of the Life which might be attractive if one already knew that it belonged to the ninth century. Otherwise the influence of the Life of St Martin on later hagiography was too widespread to justify any such inference. See now R. Sowerby, 'The Lives of St Samson', *Francia*, 38 (2011), 1–31.

[59] *Vita Secunda S. Samsonis*, ii. 3, 12, 20, ed. F. B. Plaine, 'Vita Antiqua S. Samsonis Dolensis Episcopi', *Analecta Bollandiana*, 6 (1887), 122–3, 134, 142.

[60] Gregory of Tours, *Hist.* iv. 14; ix. 20; Ewig, *Spätantikes und fränkisches Gallien*, . 156, 158–60, 262.

[61] Continuation to Fredegar, *Chronica*, c. 25, in *Chronicarum quae dicuntur Fredegarii Scholastici Libri IV cum Continuationibus*, ed. B. Krusch, MGH SRM ii (1888), 180; from the beginning of Book IV ed. and trans. J. M. Wallace-Hadrill, *The Fourth Book of the Chronicle of Fredegar with its Continuations*, Nelson Medieval Classics (London, 1960), 98: Carlomannus atque Pippinus germani principes, congregato exercito, Liger alveum Aurilianis urbem [Orléans] transeunt, Romanos proterunt, usque Beturgas urbem [Bourges] accedunt.

[62] K. Hughes, *The Church in Early Irish Society* (London, 1966), 103–10: from *c.* 632 there were Irish *Romani* who contrasted themselves with unRoman Britons echoing the contrast between *Romani* and *Brittones* in Gaul.

[63] Orléans 541, c. 1, in *Concilia Galliae, A. 511–A. 695*, ed. C. de Clercq, CCSL 148A (Turnhout, 1963), 132.

West that welcomed Justin's overtures. The conflict, however, was sharpened when the Gregorian missionaries arrived in Britain, for they came via Francia and relied on Frankish help. Their view of the Britons could hardly but be influenced by Frankish and Gallo-Roman views of the Bretons. Moreover, tensions within Frankish Gaul reacted on the new missionaries' perceptions of their British and Irish neighbours, as one can see from the letter of Laurence, bishop of Canterbury, given by Bede, in which Columbanus, the Irish abbot of Luxeuil, was condemned.[64] When Columbanus was expelled by Theuderic II in 610, Irishmen and Britons were allowed by the king to accompany him into exile; natives of Gaul were ordered to remain.[65] Those who refused to conform to the Roman Easter could, by 632/3, be portrayed by Cummian as 'an insignificant group of Britons and Irish who are almost at the end of the world, and, if I may say so, but pimples on the face of the earth'.[66] In the middle of the seventh century, Wilfrid, later to be the spokesman of the Roman party at the Synod of Whitby in 664, learnt from the archdeacon Boniface at Rome 'the calculation of Easter, of which the schismatics of Britain and Ireland were ignorant'.[67] In the early eighth-century Irish *Collectio Canonum Hibernensis*, the Britons are 'opposed to everyone and cut themselves off from Roman custom and from the unity of the Church'.[68]

In the period around 600, there began among the English a movement towards Rome, visible in the archaeology of the conversion period,[69] and culminating in the attitudes of men such as Wilfrid. For the latter, and for his supporter, Agilbert, bishop of Paris, the Britons were emphatically not Roman; rather they were schismatics and heretics, enemies of papal Rome. Wilfrid's plan as bishop of York was to promote an architecture, script, and monastic rule that would render Northumbria more Roman than it ever was in the days when British kings ruled there or when Irish monks preached to the pagan English. Just as Patrick excluded King Coroticus and his soldiers from the community of fellow-citizens because of the savagery of their actions, so Bede wrote of the British king Cadwallon that 'because he was a barbarian, he was even more savage than the pagan [Penda of the Mercians]'.[70]

Religious differences also affected the Bretons. Fredegar has a significant story about an effort by Dagobert, king of the Franks (629–639) to bring the Bretons into subjection.[71] For Fredegar, there was no difficulty about calling Iudicael king, not just count, of the Bretons: whereas Gregory denied Breton rulers the title of

[64] Bede, *HE* ii. 4.

[65] Jonas, *Vita S. Columbani*, ed. B. Krusch, *Ionae Vitae Sanctorum Columbani, Vedastis, Iohannis*, MGH SRG (Hanover, 1905), i. 20.

[66] Cummian, *De Controversia Paschali*, ed. and trans. M. Walsh and D. Ó Cróinín, *Cummian's Letter De Controversia Paschali and the De Ratione Computandi* (Toronto, 1988), 109–10.

[67] Stephen, *Vita S. Wilfridi*, ed. and trans. B. Colgrave, *The Life of Bishop Wilfrid by Eddius Stephanus* (Cambridge, 1927), ch. 5.

[68] *Collectio Canonum Hibernensis*, ed. H. Wasserschleben, *Die irische Kanonensammlung* 2nd edn. (Leipzig, 1885), xx. 6.

[69] H. Geake, *The Use of Grave-Goods in Conversion-Period England, c.600–c.850*, BAR Brit. Ser. 261 (Oxford, 1997).

[70] Bede, *HE* ii. 20.

[71] Fredegar, *Chronica*, iv. 78.

king, Fredegar allowed Iudicael to be king even though he was subject to the Franks. What happened was that a Frankish army was returning from a campaign against the Basques. Dagobert sent messengers to the Bretons to say that the army would be sent into Brittany unless the Bretons made amends for offences against vassals of the Frankish kings. Iudicael immediately made for Dagobert's court, where he offered satisfactory submission; yet he refused to partake of Dagobert's hospitality by eating at his table, 'because Iudicael was a devout man and greatly feared God'. Instead, he went to eat with Dado, Dagobert's referendary, 'whom he knew to be an adherent of holy religion'.[72] Admittedly one reason why Fredegar was interested in this conscientious Breton king was that he himself had strongly criticized the morality of Dagobert's court, once he had become king in Neustria.[73] Iudicael was not refusing to value any Frankish religious practice. Yet, his attitude is reminiscent of that shown by Britons to Laurence, bishop of Canterbury, and that followed towards English Christians, so Aldhelm complained, by the Britons of Dyfed.[74] The Gallo-Romans and the English were not alone in sharpening ethnic distinctions by invoking religious differences, and yet the main pressure was directed by them against the Britons, partly because Gallo-Romans and later the English were able to align themselves with the Church at large and Rome in particular. Increasingly from the fifth to the seventh century, therefore, as the meaning of 'Roman' shifted, the Britons seemed to their neighbours increasingly unRoman. It may seem odd that seventh-century Englishmen could portray themselves as the true *Romani* by contrast with those former inhabitants of the Empire, the Britons. They could do so, however, because of the earlier division between Romans and Britons in Gaul, because the Gallo-Romans, unlike the Bretons, were conjoined with the Franks in a single political system, and because the term 'Roman' acquired a strongly religious connotation.

The Britons, then, never left the Roman Empire. That is, they may have rebelled against particular emperors, but they never finally renounced imperial authority. Unlike their neighbours across the Channel and across the Breton frontier, former *Galli*, now *Romani*, they continued to regard themselves as Britons, not Romans. But, over a long period, from the fifth to the seventh century, they were pushed out, not by the Empire itself, but by neighbours in the West, principally Gallo-Romans, then the Franks, and, finally, the English. From being the fellow-citizens of the *Galli* they became linked in waywardness—and, according to some, in outright heresy—with the unquestionably barbarian Irish. This parting of the ways marks the end of the post-Roman phase in the history of the Britons and thus the end of the first part of this book.

[72] Cf. *Vita Eligii*, i. 13, ed. B. Krusch, MGH SRM iv. 680, on the role of Eligius as ambassador to the Breton king, not named but presumably Iudicael.

[73] Fredegar, *Chronica*, iv. 60.

[74] Bede, *HE* ii. 4: Laurence complained that the Irishman, Dagán, in refusing to eat with the Gregorian missionaries, was agreeing with the Britons; Aldhelm, Letter IV, ed. R Ehwald, *Aldhelmi Opera Omnia*, MGH AA xv (Berlin, 1919), 481, 484, trans. M. Lapidge and M. Herren, *Aldhelm: The Prose Works* (Ipswich, 1979), 155, 158.

PART II

EARLY WELSH SOCIETY

7

Charters and Laws

1. THE BOOK OF LLANDAFF

The history of early medieval Wales often has to be written from the twelfth century backwards, since most of our sources survive from collections of texts assembled after the Norman Conquest. An outstanding example of this truth is the manuscript known as the Book of Llandaff or *Liber Landavensis*, written before the death of Urban, bishop of Llandaff, in 1134. This manuscript is perhaps the most controversial of all sources for early Welsh history, but its collection of charters, the linked Llancarfan collection, and the very small collection from Llandeilo Fawr are essential sources for anyone who would attempt to understand Welsh society between *c.* 600 and 1064.[1] Although the Llandeilo collection is the smallest, it has the great advantage that the documents were written into the Lichfield Gospels, then at Llandeilo, before that manuscript was taken to Lichfield in the tenth century.[2] The next collection in terms of size is from Llancarfan. In Chapter 8 we shall discover that its evidence is essential to understanding what form of society was presupposed by the Llandaff charters. The Llandaff collection is, however, by far the largest and will be discussed first.

The Book of Llandaff is a mixture of elements that, to a modern mind, do not naturally go together.[3] In its original form, it began with a copy of St Matthew's Gospel. This was followed by two Saints' Lives, those of St Elgar and St Samson. Then came texts pertaining to the campaign mounted by Urban, bishop of Llandaff, to extend (or, as he put it, to defend) the boundaries of the diocese, in opposition to the bishops of St Davids and Hereford. The documents belong to the period 1126–32.

Next came a further combination of Saints' Lives and documents, only now the saints in question were those claimed, in the Book of Llandaff itself, to have been the first three bishops of the see: Dyfrig, Teilo, and Euddogwy. In yet another

[1] The Book of Llandaff, ed. J. G. Evans and J. Rhŷs, *The Text of the Book of Llan Dâv* (Oxford, 1893), of which pp. xliii–xlviii contain an edition of the marginalia from the Lichfield Gospels; the Llancarfan charters are §§ 55–68 of *Vita S. Cadoci*, ed. A. W. Wade-Evans, *Vitae Sanctorum Britanniae et Genealogiae* (Cardiff, 1944), 124–36; cf. A. W. Wade-Evans, 'The Llancarfan Charters', *Archaeologia Cambrensis*, 87 (1932), 151–65.

[2] D. Jenkins and M. E. Owen, 'The Welsh Marginalia in the Lichfield Gospels. Part I', *CMCS* 5 (1983), 37–66, and 'The Welsh Marginalia in the Lichfield Gospels. Part II: The "Surexit" Memorandum', *Cambridge Medieval Celtic Studies*, 7 (Summer 1984), 91–120.

[3] D. Huws, 'The Making of *Liber Landavensis*', in his *Medieval Welsh Manuscripts* (Cardiff, 2000), 123–57, originally in *National Library of Wales Journal*, 25 (1987–8), 133–60.

complication, the hagiographical material on Dyfrig (Dubricius) acted as a sandwich containing within itself a group of charters in which Dyfrig was the beneficiary. This Dyfrig sandwich was then followed by further texts: an account of Bishop Urban's discovery of Dyfrig's grave on Bardsey Island and his translation of the relics to Llandaff, and documents concerning the prosecution of Llandaff's interests during the pontificate of Calixtus II (1119–1124).

The section on the second saint of the three, Teilo, is complicated in a different way. The Life of the Saint is followed by a text, in Latin and in Welsh, setting out the *braint*, status, of the saint and his church; and this text is itself followed by charters in which Teilo is presented as the beneficiary. *Braint Teilo* has its less elaborate counterparts in the Dyfrig and Euddogwy material; but it was written, unlike them, on an inserted leaf. The scribe is likely to have been the editor of the whole book, plausibly identified with Urban himself.[4] Yet it may well be the fruit of second thoughts. In its present form, at least, it was not part of the original plan.

The last Life among the trio, that of Euddogwy (Oudoceus), is followed immediately by charters: in this case, the statement of the privileges of his churches, the counterpart to *Braint Teilo*, was contained within the framework of the Life. After the charters in which Euddogwy was the beneficiary, there follows a grand sequence of further charters arranged according to the compilers' notion of episcopal succession at Llandaff. This is taken to the point at which three bishops are included for whom there were no charters: *Eluogus*, Nobis, and Marchlwyth.[5]

The Book of Llandaff is, therefore, a combination of three elements: a gospel, saints' Lives, and finally documents, principally charters. Similar combinations are known from all parts of the British Isles.[6] In Ireland, the Book of Armagh, written in 807, included the gospels, Lives of St Martin of Tours and of St Patrick, and a collection of documents of concern to the community of Patrick, whose principal church was Armagh.[7] In Scotland, the Book of Deer is a ninth-century gospel book with a small collection of charters.[8] In England, the Sherborne Cartulary includes gospels and collects for liturgical use.[9] In Wales there are two important parallels: the Lichfield Gospels were kept at Llandeilo Fawr in the ninth century, when documents were added in the margins and other vacant spaces;[10] the Life of St Cadog, contained in a manuscript probably written at Monmouth Priory in

[4] J. R. Davies, '*Liber Landavensis*: Its Date and the Identity of its Editor', *CMCS* 35 (1998), 1–11; on the other hand, Davies, *The Book of Llandaf*, 132–42, now argues that Caradog of Llancarfan was the author of the whole book.

[5] *LL* 206, 217, 246.

[6] Davies, *Book of Llandaf*, 143–7.

[7] R. Sharpe, 'Palaeographical Considerations in the Study of the Patrician Documents in the Book of Armagh', *Scriptorium*, 36 (1982), 3–28.

[8] K. Forsyth (ed.), *Studies on the Book of Deer* (Dublin, 2008); K. H. Jackson, *The Gaelic Notes in the Book of Deer* (Cambridge, 1972).

[9] F. Wormald, 'The Sherborne "Cartulary"', in D. J. Gordon (ed.), *Fritz Saxl: A Volume of Memorial Essays* (London, 1957), 101–19; *Charters of Sherborne Abbey*, ed. M. A. Donovan (Oxford, 1988), pp. xvi–xvii.

[10] Jenkins and Owen, 'The Welsh Marginalia in the Lichfield Gospels. 37–66. *The Text of the Book of Llan Dâv*, ed. Evans and Rhŷs, pp. xliii–xlviii, contain an edition of the marginalia from the Lichfield Gospels.

the early thirteenth century, is accompanied by an appendix. This is probably of somewhat earlier date than the Life itself, and it includes a collection of fourteen charters alongside hagiographical anecdotes and details on the property and revenues of the canons.[11]

The combination of gospels, Lives, and charters is thus widely attested in the British Isles; some examples can also be cited from the Continent.[12] The reason why these apparently disparate genres of text were thought appropriate companions emerges from the Welsh examples. The fifth among the documents in the Lichfield Gospels is a manumission of a slave and his family:

> It is necessary to write a text [showing] that the four sons of Bleddri—Gwrtheyrn, Cyfwlch, Ed[...], Arthwys—granted freedom to Bleiddudd son of Sulien and his descendants for ever, in exchange for a price. And this is the confirmation that he gave for his freedom four pounds and eight ounces [of silver] before the following appropriate witnesses: of the laity, Rhiwallon son of Cyffro, Gwen[...] son of [...]r, *Guoluic* [son of...]*dan*, *Ov*[...] son of *Gurcinnim*, Merchwyn son of *Salus*, Arthan son of Cyfwlch, Idri son of Idnerth; of the clergy, Nobis, bishop of Teilo, Sadyrnwydd, *sacerdos* of Teilo, Dyfrin and Cuhelyn, son of the bishop, Sadyrnfyw, *Camibiau*, and Sulien the scholar, who accurately wrote [it down]. Let the person who has maintained this decree of freedom for Bleiddudd and his offspring be blessed; but let the person who has not maintained it be cursed by God and by Teilo in whose Gospel Book it has been written; and let the whole people say, 'Let it be so, let it be so.'

The text of the manumission of Bleiddudd is enmeshed in ceremony. First, there is the legal ritual of an exchange: Bleiddudd hands over, in front of witnesses, both clergy and laity, the agreed price of his freedom and that of his descendants.[13] The sons of Bleddri accept the silver before the same witnesses. The first two witnesses named among the clergy are Nobis, bishop of Teilo, and Sadyrnwydd, *sacerdos* of Teilo (the *sacerdos* was probably the person within the community responsible for its liturgical services). Secondly, the text is written in the margin of 'the gospel book of Teilo'. Thirdly, a prayer is uttered that God and His saint, Teilo, will bless anyone who maintains 'the decree of freedom' and that they will curse anyone who does not maintain it. Since the people are then presented as saying '*Fiat, fiat*', 'Let it be so, let it be so', we may infer that the prayer was uttered, perhaps by Bishop Nobis, after the exchange was made, and that 'the people' were those present in a public assembly (perhaps also acting as the congregation within the church). The presence of the people at an assembly will help to explain why the manumission was perceived as a decree and not just a private contract of exchange.[14]

[11] See appendix to *Vita S. Cadoci*, §§ 45–70, *VSBG* 116–41; the end of § 44 is a colophon for the main Life.

[12] D. Jenkins, 'From Wales to Weltenburg? Some Considerations on the Origins of the Use of Sacred Books for the Preservation of Secular Records', in N. Brieskorn et al. (eds.), *Vom mittelalterlichen Recht zur neuzeitlichen Rechtswissenschaft: Bedingungen, Wege und Probleme der europäischen Rechtsgeschichte* (Paderborn, 1994), 75–88.

[13] O. J. Padel, *Slavery in Saxon Cornwall: The Bodmin Manumissions*, Kathleen Hughes Memorial Lectures, 7 (Cambridge, 2009), 23, notes that the sum is remarkably high and makes the attractive suggestion that they may have been paying to avoid enslavement after committing an offence.

[14] Cf. *LL* 205, which presents the sanction as having been recited during a perambulation.

If the people were present in an assembly, so also were God and His saint, Teilo. Nobis was Teilo's bishop; the book in which the text was written was Teilo's gospel book; and Teilo was invoked in prayer. In another document in the Lichfield Gospels the first clerical witness named was the saint himself, *Teliau testis*, and at the end of the clerical witness list the scribe wrote, 'and the whole community (*familia*) of Teilo'.[15] The saint and his community witnessed together. Yet the saint was the servant of a God no less involved: in two other documents in the same series, God heads the list of clerical witnesses.[16] The gospel book was the narrative of the Word made flesh; and thus there was a coincidence of the words of manumission (or grant or reconciliation) shaped upon the parchment skin and the Word expressed in gospels upon parchment skins in the very same book: as the words of the gospels were secured by the authority of God, so the words of manumission, in marginal dependence upon the gospel, were secured by the power of the same God to witness, to bless, and to curse.[17]

This conjunction of God, saint, community, book, and ritual action offers a rationale for what we see in the Book of Llandaff, namely a parallel conjunction of gospel narrative about God made flesh, narrative about saints, holy in the image of the same God made flesh, and of legal documents concerning the good health of the community, churches and people belonging to three saints, Dyfrig, Teilo, and Euddogwy. The Book of Llandaff is the most complete expression of this conjunction of text and ritual action, heaven and earth, saint and community, since it combined the three elements of gospel, saint's Life and document. The Lichfield Gospels do not contain a saint's Life, while the Life of St Cadog was not, so far as we know, combined with a gospel book. Other examples have probably perished: in 1538 the Protestant bishop of St Davids, William Barlow, wrote to Thomas Cromwell that, in spite of popular devotion to the relics of St David, he had 'caused to be sequestred and taken awaye . . . a worm eaten boke covered with sylver plate.'[18] An isolated charter from Clynnog survives in a late medieval *inspeximus*; this may well have come from a gospel book of St Beuno's church at Clynnog.[19]

In what follows we shall be mainly concerned with one element in the Book of Llandaff, the charters, but it will be necessary to bear in mind the combination of ritual and text, both guaranteed by God and by saint. For example, since the authenticity of the Llandaff charters is a hotly contested issue, it is useful to remember one possible definition of inauthenticity in charters of this kind, namely

[15] Chad 2.

[16] Chad 3 and 4.

[17] Cf. . . . *a deo*, Chad 3, 5 and very probably 4 (where the final legible letters, *er[* . . . are sufficient evidence for supplying *er[it a deo]*).

[18] J. Wyn Evans, 'The Reformation and St Davids Cathedral', *Journal of Welsh Ecclesiastical History*, 7 (1990), 5, on Bishop Barlow and the ancient book at St Davids.

[19] It is not known what was the exemplar from which the copy in Harley 696 was taken (the *inspeximus* is in a different hand from the rest; and it is not in the source for most of the text, Bangor University, Baron Hill MS 6714): P. Sims-Williams, 'Edward IV's Confirmation Charter for Clynnog Fawr' in C. Richmond and I. Harvey (eds.), *Recognitions: Essays presented to Edmund Fryde* (Aberystwyth, 1996), 229–41, at 229–30. But the ultimate source appears to have been a 'Book of St Beuno', ibid. 235.

Table 7.1. The construction of the Book of Llandaff

Text	Scribe	Quiring	Printed edn. (pp.)
A. St Matthew's Gospel	Scribe *Y*	2–4	–
B. Lives of Elgar and Samson	Scribe *B*	5	1–25
C. Urban documents, 1126–32	Scribe *B*	6	27–67
D. Lives of Dyfrig (including charters) Urban documents to 1120 Life of Teilo + *Braint Teilo* + charters Life of Euddogwy + charters Charters for 22 out of 25 named bishops	Scribe *A* rubricated by *B* (*Braint Teilo* inserted by *B*)	7–14	68–280

that a charter is inauthentic when no ritual action corresponding to the text ever took place.[20] Also, the Lives are valuable indications, not just of the purposes of the compilers of the Book of Llandaff, but of the difficulties they faced. Everyone agrees that the book was planned in association with Bishop Urban's campaign on behalf of his see. There were three main scribes, all of the middle third of the twelfth century, known as *Y* (who wrote the surviving original part of the gospel), *A* (who wrote the Lives of Dyfrig, Teilo, and Euddogwy together with the associated Urban documents and the charters), and *B* (who rubricated *A*'s section and also wrote the Lives of Elgar and Samson and the Urban documents relating to the period 1126–1132). The book was thus laid out as in Table 7.1 (disregarding the first quire, which was not part of the original text). Scribe *B* has been seen as the editor of the whole book, and he has been identified with Bishop Urban himself.[21]

An essential element in the plan was to present Urban's campaigns alongside a seamless succession of bishops running all the way from Dyfrig to Urban's predecessor, Herewald. All were claimed to be bishops of Llandaff. Moreover, in spite of the supposed antiquity of the see, going back before Gregory the Great sent Augustine of Canterbury to convert the English, and in spite of the claim that Dyfrig and Teilo were archbishops, the Book of Llandaff was pointedly loyal to Canterbury.[22] Its most recent bishops were said to have been consecrated by the archbishop;[23] and this position was traced back to the third patron saint, Euddogwy.[24] It is likely that the care taken to present such a picture of loyalty to

20 Charters in this tradition do not themselves perform a grant, exchange, or manumission, but recall it just as the gospel recalls the life and sayings of Christ.

21 J. R. Davies, '*Liber Landavensis*', 3–7.

22 Cf. *LL* 88, 132, 240.

23 *LL* 252a, 252b., 266; only the consecration of Gwgon, 963 × 972, is judged to have been at all likely to have been by the Archbishop of Canterbury: W. Davies, 'The Consecration of the Bishops of Llandaff in the Tenth and Eleventh Centuries', *BBCS* 26 (1974–6), 68, 69.

24 *LL* 132.

Canterbury stemmed from a mixture of motives: from the truth that one or two bishops had indeed been consecrated by English archbishops, either by the archbishop of Canterbury or by the archbishop of York;[25] from the realization that, with Glamorgan under the control of Robert of Gloucester, Henry I's powerful illegitimate son, the future lay within an English ecclesiastical framework; and, finally, from a desire to withstand the claims of St Davids.[26]

Two views of the Llandaff charters have been advanced. According to one, while the compilation as a whole was concerned to maintain a false view of an unbroken series of bishops at Llandaff, the charters themselves were not, in general, twelfth-century forgeries but versions of genuine documents edited to support the claims of Llandaff. This is the position supported by Wendy Davies in two books and in a series of articles.[27] According to the other view, argued by Christopher Brooke and others, the degree of editorial interference with whatever earlier texts may have been available makes it impossible to identify reliable texts for the period before *c.* 1050.[28] Which of these views is correct is an issue that no history of early medieval Wales can evade.

The case for the defence has been presented on several levels, from relatively minor miscopyings of older texts all the way to a comprehensive view of the evolution of charters in the Celtic countries. The first can largely be neglected. After all, it is unlikely, even if the charters were forged *de novo* in the twelfth century, that draft texts were not written before the extant fair copies; and where personal names of kings and bishops are in question, any forger worth his salt would make use of any lists or genealogies available, and these could be miscopied. The main substance of the case for the defence can, however, be placed under five headings: the diplomatic study of the charters (namely of the standard formulae employed in such documents and the internal organization of the text); the composition of the witness lists; details of the contents suggesting an origin going back before the twelfth century; the topography of the charters, indicating different locations for the archives from which the texts came (namely not just Llandaff); and, finally, linguistic evidence for the dates of charters.

The arrangement of the charters in the Book of Llandaff was based upon a sequence of twenty-nine bishops from Dyfrig in the sixth century to Herewald in the late eleventh, all of whom were claimed to be bishops of Llandaff.[29] Not far below the surface of the final collection, however, there are clear indications that this sequence was largely false, in the sense that most of the bishops were not of

25 Davies, 'The Consecration of the Bishops of Llandaff', 64–7.

26 J. R. Davies, *Book of Llandaf*, 46–53, 66–7; J. Conway Davies, *Episcopal Acts and Cognate Documents relating to Welsh Dioceses*, 2 vols. (Cardiff, 1946–8), i. 147–90.

27 W. Davies, *An Early Welsh Microcosm: Studies in the Llandaff Charters* (London, 1978); ead. *The Llandaff Charters* (Aberystwyth, 1979).

28 C. N. L. Brooke, *The Church and the Welsh Border in the Central Middle Ages* (Woodbridge, 1986), 44–8.

29 Dyfrig's *floruit* is deduced from that of St Samson, who attended a council in Paris between 556 and 573, perhaps in 561–2; *Concilia Galliae*, ed. de Clercq, 210; *Les Canons des conciles mérovingiens*, ed. and trans. Gaudemet and Basdevant, ii. 410, 424; *Vita Prima S. Samsonis*, i. 13. The second-last bishop is entitled 'Teilo's bishop' in his obit in 1045 (*Brut*); Herewald died in 1104.

Llandaff; instead they belonged to churches in Ergyng and Gwent. The official list is headed by three patron-saints claimed by Llandaff, Dyfrig, Teilo, and Euddogwy. Hence the standard charter in the Book of Llandaff records a grant 'to God and to Saints Dyfrig, Teilo, and Euddogwy and in the hand of Bishop X and his successors in the church of Llandaff for ever'. However, in the charters assigned to nos. 4–13 in the official list, Euddogwy is regularly left out, and so also, sometimes, is Teilo. In 163a all three saints were omitted. A further indication is that, in 165, *Comeregius*, eighth in the official list, is described as a disciple of St Dyfrig, which should have made him a contemporary of St Teilo, no. 2 in the list. On the other hand, Berthwyn, no. 14 in the list, is described in 180b, as Euddogwy's successor, while Berthwyn's successor, Trychan, is well attested as a witness to his predecessor's charters.

At the very least, therefore, there should have been two parallel episcopal successions, one attached to Dyfrig and the other to Euddogwy. In the official list these are 1 + 4–13 and 3 + 14–18 (but no. 16 was not assigned any charters). The division between the two successions is confirmed by the witness lists, since those of no. 3, Euddogwy, are continued by those of no. 14, Berthwyn. It is further strenghtened by the situation of the estates granted: the Dyfrig collection (1 + 4–13) is concentrated in Ergyng, the Euddogwy collection (3 + 14–18) in Gwent. Neither collection shows any sign, other than the re-editing necessary to produce the official succession, of any connection with Llandaff.

By examining the chronology of the charters further progress can be made. The Dyfrig or Ergyng charters (ascribed to nos. 1 + 4–13 in the episcopal list) can be further divided. In the witness lists there is a break between 166 and 167, between Bishops Arwystl and Gwrfan. Those between 160 and 166 are associated with early kings of Ergyng; the only royal witness to charters 167–174a was Meurig ab Arthfael, father of two kings of Gwent named by Asser as active in the 880s. This small group of charters may thus be assigned to the ninth century. Among the Ergyng charters, therefore, there is an early group, 160–6, and a late group, 167–74a, separated by about two centuries. This division is further supported by linguistic arguments: the early group exhibits features of archaic Old Welsh, the names in the late group are fundamentally standard Old Welsh, both groups having occasional modernizations in the direction of the late Old Welsh contemporary with the final compilation of the Book of Llandaff.[30]

Later in the sequence, there is a chronological break in the succession to Berthwyn: he is followed seamlessly by Bishops Trychan (Turchan), who was previously his *lector*, namely teacher in his church, and Cadwared; but the next bishop, Cerennyr, belongs to the mid-ninth century. His clerical household was continuous, not with the next bishop in the official sequence, Pater, but with Bishop Nudd, who was himself a member of Cerennyr's entourage; Pater's household was continued by that of Gwgon, although there are four bishops in between according to the official sequence.

30 On the linguistic evidence, see P. Sims-Williams, 'The Emergence of Old Welsh, Cornish and Breton Orthography, 600–800: The Evidence of Archaic Old Welsh', *BBCS* 38 (1991), 20–86.

Table 7.2. Collections of archives

Stage 1:	A (Dyfrig), B (Teilo churches), C, D, E, F
Stage 2 (after 872):	D+E (Ergyng) C+F G, H (Gwent and Ergyng)
Stage 3 (after 872):	DE+CF (combined at Llancarfan)
Stage 4 (after 975):	G+H augmented by J (Gwent)
Stage 5 (*c.*1022–46):	DECF+GHJ (J still expanding)
Stage 6 (*c.*1107–28):	minor glossing influenced by Worcester practice
Stage 7 (*c.*1124–8):	AB+DECFGHJ

Wendy Davies used a range of such arguments to show that the charters fall into nine groups, which she labelled A–J.[31] She has further argued that these groups were combined into larger collections in successive stages.

What purport to be the earliest charters (those in A and B) appear to have come from separate sources and were the last to be added to the main collection, namely at Llandaff in the twelfth century. A check on the chronological sequence of the charters can also be obtained by placing the charters in a sequence offered by the genealogy of the principal dynasty of Gwent (and Glywysing) and some minor dynasties, as in Figure 7.1. The genealogy is largely constructed from the charters themselves, but with the aid of two pedigrees in the Harleian Genealogies and one pedigree in Jesus College MS 20.[32] Where a reference to a charter occurs next to a line of descent, the charter itself attests the link.

As for the diplomatic, Wendy Davies argued that there was a distinct tradition governing the writing of charters in the Celtic countries.[33] Consider the following two texts written into the Book of Deer, a gospel book from Old Deer in Aberdeenshire. The first is written in a local variant of Middle Irish, the second in Latin:[34]

(1) Gartnait and the daughter of Gille Mícael gave *Ball Domin* in Pitfour to Christ and to Colum Cille and to Drostán. With Gille Callíne, priest, and Feradac son of Mal Bricín and Mal Girc son of Trálín as witnesses.

(2) David, king of Scots, to all his good men, greetings. You should know that the clergy of Deer are to be quit and immune from all lay service and undue exaction, as it has been written in their book, and as they proved by argument at Banff and swore at Aberdeen. Therefore I firmly command that nobody should dare to inflict any injury on them or on their goods. By the witness of Gregory, bishop of Dunkeld; by the witness of Andrew, bishop of Caithness; by the witness of Samson, bishop of

[31] F can also be divided into F (i) and F (ii) because of the chronological break between Bishops Cadwared and Cerennyr.

[32] HG 28 and 29, JC 9 in *EWGT* 12, 45 (but note that Bartrum subsequently came to the view that the additions in italics in HG 29 were wrong: P. C. Bartrum, 'Corrections to *Early Welsh Genealogical Tracts*', *BBCS* 40 (1993), 171–2). For an earlier investigation along similar lines, see E. D. Jones, 'The Book of Llandaff', *National Library of Wales Journal*, 4 (1945–6), 141.

[33] W. Davies, 'The Latin Charter Tradition in Western Britain, Brittany and Ireland in the Early Mediaeval Period', in D. Whitelock et al., *Ireland in Mediaeval Europe* (Cambridge, 1982), 258–80.

[34] Forsyth (ed.), *Studies on the Book of Deer*, 140, 142; Jackson, *Gaelic Notes*, 31, 32 (nos. IV and VII); the translations are mine.

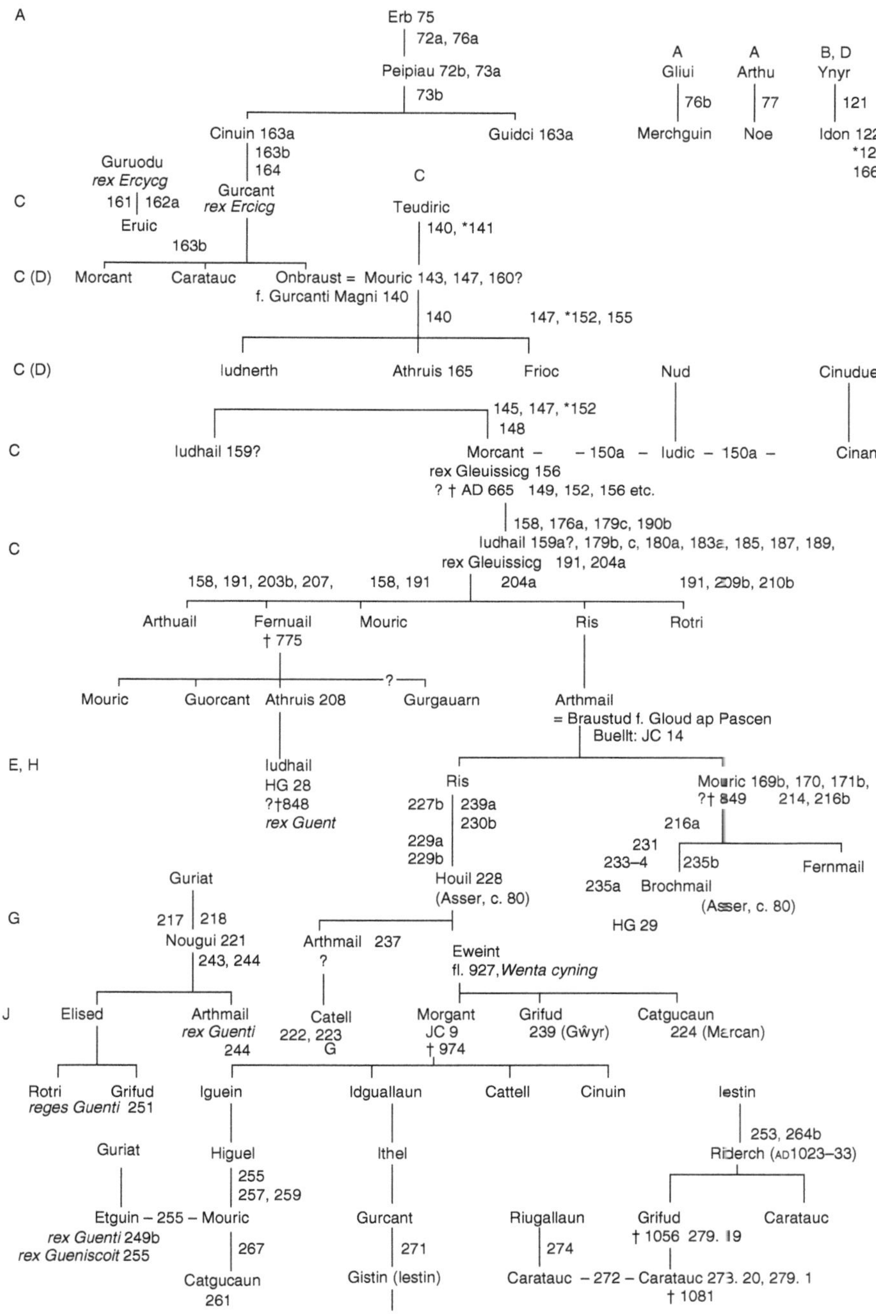

Figure 7.1. The kings of Gwent and the Llandaff charters

Note: † = obit, * marks charters in any way especially dubious

> Brechin; by the witness of Donnchad, earl of Fife and Mal Mori of Atholl, and Gilla Bríte of Éngus, and Gilla Comded son of Áed, and Brocín and Cormac, abbot of Turriff, and Adam son of Ferdomnach and Gille Aindrías son of Matne, at Aberdeen.

The first is a bare narrative of something that happened in the past; it is written in the third person and in the past tense. The second is in the form of a letter written by the king, in the first person, to his subjects and especially to his servants. It records past events—indeed there is a narrative sandwiched inside the text—but the immediate purpose of the letter is to give orders, not to tell a story. In both documents the final element is a list of witnesses. In the first text the witnesses are named as persons who could testify that Gartnait and the daughter of Gilla Mícael did indeed give *Ball Domin*. The gift, therefore, will have been made by some public act capable of being witnessed. In the second text, the role of the witnesses is rather more oblique: they were witnessing both David I's letter in itself and the events recounted in the narrative within the letter. The first is an example of a 'Celtic charter'; the second of the 'writ-charter' (namely letter-charter) favoured by the Anglo-Normans after the conquest of England. Here we see it reaching the north-east of Scotland. By the time of Urban, bishop of Llandaff, this writ-charter was the standard form in Henry I's kingdom; and since Urban had thrown in his lot with Anglo-Norman authority, one might have expected him to cast his charters in the current form. In fact, however, the documents in the Book of Llandaff followed the model of the Celtic charter.

This is all the more notable since there was a third possibility, namely the solemn diploma, which had been the norm in Anglo-Saxon England. The following are two versions of a single charter, of importance for the ecclesiastical history of south-east Wales. They are preserved in two cartularies from Worcester, of which that in the British Library Cotton MS Tiberius A. xiii is earlier than that in British Library Cotton MS Nero E. i.[35]

The Tiberius version:

> Our Lord Jesus Christ reigning for ever over the surface of the world, which is surrounded by water on four sides, in the year of His Incarnation, 1005, in the third indiction, I Æthelred, king of the English, with the consent of the bishops and leaders of the same people, for the salvation of our souls and also for the good health of our kingdom, with full devotion of mind, shall give as a perpetual inheritance a certain portion of land, that is of [. . .] hides at Over, to the episcopal see which is called Dewistow ['St David's place']. For those who maintain and preserve this our donation let there be peace, but for those who oppose it damnation, unless they have previously done penance. I, Æthelred, king of the English, shall confirm this my alms with my own hand.

The Nero version:

> Our Lord Jesus Christ reigning for ever, in the year of His Incarnation, 1005, I, Æthelred, king of the English, with the consent of the bishops and leaders of the same people, for the

[35] N. R. Ker, 'Hemming's Cartulary', in R. W. Hunt et al. (eds.), *Studies presented to F. M. Powicke* (Oxford, 1948), 73–4; cf. A. Scharer, *Die angelsächsische Königsurkunde im 7. und 8. Jahrhundert* (Vienna, 1982), 281–4.

> redemption of my soul, grant a certain parcel of land at Over to the episcopal see at Dewistow, for a period of three lives—when these are over, let it be restored to the church of Worcester—but on this condition, that he who presides over the aforesaid bishopric is to be subject in all things to the pastor of the church of Worcester.

The language in this type of charter is altogether grander than in either of those illustrated so far. Like the writ-charter, it is in the first person. Whereas the Deer documents acquired their force largely from the sacredness of the gospel book in which they were written, this one creates its own solemnity. As the opening phrases show, it is, in itself, a religious text. The grant itself is portrayed as alms given for the salvation of the king's soul and the prosperity of his people.

What this charter, in its two versions, illustrates is that there is not a clear-cut choice between authenticity and forgery. As far as we can tell, the Tiberius version is an accurate representation, in solemn and traditionally sanctified language, of an equally solemn and traditionally sanctified act, namely a grant in public assembly to a church. This version, therefore, is likely to be entirely authentic. The Nero version, however, plainly relates to the same royal grant: it has the same date, donor, and beneficiary; it refers to the same land. Yet it adds qualifications that change the nature of the legal act performed by the king. Whereas the Tiberius text had Æthelred make a perpetual grant to Dewistow, the Nero text has him make a grant to last only for three lives, after which the land was to be 'restored to the church of Worcester'. Moreover, the grant was subject to yet another condition, namely that the person presiding over Dewistow should, in all things, be subject to the bishop of Worcester. The implication of this version was, perhaps, that the land at Over belonged by right to Worcester, and that the bishop of Worcester had been brought to consent to a lease of Worcester land for three lifetimes in exchange for a promise of obedience on the part of the bishop of Dewistow. We shall see later quite what made such extravagant-sounding claims to authority over another bishop plausible. What is important here is the relationship of this text to the earlier Tiberius version and to the act performed by Æthelred in 1005.

A marginal note to the earlier version throws further light. Written sideways is the further clause, only partially legible:

> with this condition, however, that in all things he be a humble and devoted servant, together with his community, to the bishop . . . and . . . after [three life-]times. . . .

In somewhat different language, this marginal note seems to contain what distinguished the later Nero version from the Tiberius text. Perhaps Worcester always had a claim to the land at Over, and this was why the original charter was copied into the Tiberius cartulary. The Nero cartulary, however, probably contained the official position of the church of Worcester by the late eleventh century, by which time the period of three lives was either over or close to its end. By a mildly roundabout route, a charter intended to benefit Dewistow 'in perpetuity' could be made to constitute evidence for Worcester's claim to Over that was all the more telling because it did not, in the first place, benefit Worcester but rather Dewistow. This specimen example demonstrates, therefore, what could be accomplished by edition rather than by outright forgery. Why tell an outright lie when a half-truth was much more effective? The text once edited looked authentic, because it was indeed largely authentic; yet it sealed off any claim on behalf of Dewistow by confining the latter's rights to the past—to the period of three lives.

Part of Wendy Davies's argument is that the editing of the Llandaff collection was influenced by Worcester practice in the late eleventh century.[36] Yet there was no attempt to recast the Llandaff charters either in the mould of the Anglo-Saxon diploma or the Anglo-Norman writ-charter. Instead, the Llandaff scribes worked within the Celtic charter tradition, even though this archaic mode of writing charters was hardly calculated to impress men such as Robert of Gloucester, lord of Glamorgan. Their faithfulness to older traditions is thrown into clear relief by one exception: charter 243 follows the form of the diploma and contains some stylistic features characteristic of English charters of the mid-tenth century.[37] This charter claims that Bishop Gwgon was also, by hereditary right, abbot of Llancarfan, and the unique form of the document may derive from experiments made at that house—all the more interesting because there is no trace of any such thing in the charters appended to the Life of St Cadog, which are earlier in date.

2. THE SIGNIFICANCE OF THE DOUBLETS

The crucial step in the argument that the Llandaff charters are usable historical documents for the periods from which they purport to derive is this: the Llandaff scribes admittedly edited their charters, but they did so by addition rather than by wholesale rewriting. When these additions have been peeled away, so it is claimed, what remains is syntactically coherent text. Up to a point such a *modus operandi* is also illustrated by the Worcester charters, as the marginal additions in the Tiberius cartulary illustrate. Nevertheless, the Nero version had to omit an essential phrase in the words describing the grant to Dewistow: if they had included the phrase *in sempiternam hereditatem*, 'as a perpetual inheritance', it would have flatly contradicted the crucial claim that the grant was only for three lives.

Equally significant changes were not beyond the reach of those responsible for the Llandaff charters as we have them, whether or not the changes were made by the compilers of the *Liber Landavensis* or by earlier editors. This can be shown by examining those charters for which we possess more than one version (see below).[38] Most of these are doublets within *Liber Landavensis* itself—a circumstance that suggests the influence of earlier editors—but in two cases there is a version in the Llancarfan collection to set alongside a text from Llandaff. These texts were important to the case made by Christopher Brooke for seeing through-going forgery behind the Llandaff charters: for him, the Llandaff versions were made

[36] W. Davies, 'Saint Mary's Worcester and the *Liber Landavensis*', *Journal of the Society of Archivists*, 4 (1970–3), 459–85; but for a different view see J. R. Davies, *The Book of Llandaf*, 98–105.

[37] Davies, *Llandaff Charters*, 125.

[38] The usefulness of the doublets was pointed out by P. Sims-Williams, 'Review', 127. His list is: 73b/163a; 74/171b; 175/186b; 176a/190b; 179a/188b; 179b/191; *LL* 180b/*VSCad*, § 67, *LL* 210b/§66.

from the Llancarfan charters; and the degree of forgery could thus be gauged from the differences between the texts.[39]

Life of St Cadog, § 66

It ought to be known that *Conbelin* gave an estate called *Lisdin Borrion* in order to earn a profit in the heavenly kingdom, together with his body, to God and to Saint Cadog, and that every year this was to pay him [Cadog] six *modii* of ale together with bread and meat and honey.

The witness is *Conigc*, who upon his hand [held what] *Concuun* wrote, that is, a chirograph.

LL 210b. Din Birrion

Cinuelin son of *Conuc* sacrificed *Din Birrion* to God and to Saints Dyfrig, Teilo and Euddogwy, and [placed it] in the hand of Bishop Cadwared and all the bishops of Llandaff, by the word and consent of the king, Rhodri son of Ithael, together with three *modii* of land and with its entire privilege and every common right in field and in woods, in water and in pastures.

From the clergy the witnesses are: Bishop Cadwared, *Guodel, Lulic, Guorapui.*

The first charter appended to the Life of St Cadog to be discussed records a grant by a man called Cynfelyn (*Conbelin*) of an estate called Llystin Byrrion (*Lisdin Borrion*) to God and to St Cadog. Cynfelyn had apparently taken to heart the gospel saying that someone should lay up treasure in heaven: his grant was made *pro commercio regni caelestis*, to earn a return in the heavenly kingdom. Not only did he give the estate, but he also gave his own body; in this context, that is likely to mean that he gave his body to be buried in Cadog's cemetery, not merely holy ground but also under the special patronage of the saint. The estate meanwhile was to supply a food-render of six *modii* of ale every year to Cadog, accompanied by bread, meat, and honey in due proportion. Of course, Cadog himself, long since dead, had no need of ale, bread, meat, and honey, but his earthly household certainly did. Their lord was Cadog, and food given to the saint might appropriately be consumed by his household. Only a single witness is named, *Conigc*; he was the abbot of Llancarfan (earlier Nant Carfan); his action in receiving into his hand the chirograph that recorded the grant presents him as the principal earthly representative of St Cadog.[40]

The corresponding grant in the Book of Llandaff was also made by Cynfelyn, whose father, Cynwg, is here recorded. Instead of Llystin Byrrion, the estate itself is called simply *Din Byrrion* (Llystin appears to be *llys* prefixed to *din* 'fort', so the difference is not as great as might appear).[41] Everything else, apart from donor and estate, is different. These are matters of both form and substance. The Llancarfan charter begins with a 'Notification', 'It ought to be known'; the Llandaff version does not. Instead of a render of six *modii* of ale, together with bread, meat, and honey, the Llandaff text defines the land attached to Din Byrrion as 'three *modii* of

[39] The translations in what follows are mine.

[40] The approximate date of the Llancarfan charter is only known through the doublet in the Book of Llandaf, but the Llancarfan charter then serves to date the B collection of Llancarfan charters to the second half of the eighth century: see appendix. For Nant Carfan (Latin *Carbani uallis*), see *LL* 145, 147, *Vita S. Cadoci*, § 18, ed. Wade-Evans, *VSBG* 62.

[41] Cf. Lis Castell, *LL* 125b.

land'; a *modius* is here a measure of land rather than of ale. The grant is made 'by the word and consent' of the king, Rhodri son of Ithael, whereas no king was even mentioned, let alone said to have consented to the grant made to St Cadog. The land enjoys various rights described by a formula, 'with its entire privilege . . . and in pastures', reminiscent of *Braint Teilo*, 'The Privilege of Teilo'. The recipients were God and the three saints claimed as patrons of Llandaff, Dyfrig, Teilo, and Euddogwy. Finally, the witnesses are different. Although only clerical witnesses are listed, instead of the usual combination of clerical and lay witnesses, there are at least four of them, as opposed to the single witness in the Llancarfan charter. This pair of texts, proximately derived from Llancarfan and Llandaff, raise some very awkward problems: to put it bluntly, if the two texts are about the same transaction, what secure information can be extracted from such a string of contradictions?

Before we make any attempt to confront this problem, we may take a look at the second charter attached to the Life of St Cadog and its counterpart in the Book of Llandaff.[42] This provided the most striking evidence for the prosecution put forward by Christopher Brooke.[43]

VITA S. CADOCI, § 67, AND *LL* 180B. LLANGADWALADR TRE'R ESCOB / BISHTON, GWENT IS COED, ST 387 873.[44]

Vita S. Cadoci, § 67.

Later generations should be informed that *Guoidnerth* gave Llangadwaladr to God and to St Cadog, so that every year a vat of three *modii* of beer should be rendered to him with all dues on account of the kinslaying of his brother *Merchiun*. And he gave as many renders to Dogunni.

For this the witnesses were: Bishop Berthwyn, *Conmil*, *Terchan* and his community, Sulien, abbot of Llancarfan, *Lumbiu* the priest, *Biuonoi*, *Iacob* and the community of St Cadog; Sadwrn, *princeps* of the altar of Dogunni, *Marcant*, *Guoidnerth*. Whoever shall have preserved [this grant], he shall be blessed; and whoever shall have injured it, he shall be cursed by God.

***LL* 180b.**

You should know, dearest brethren, that in the time of Bishop Euddogwy, at the prompting of the devil, *Guidnerth* killed his brother *Merchion* on account of a struggle for the kingship . . . [account of a synod and the pilgrimage of *Guidnerth*] . . . Subsequently *Guidnerth* gave to God and to Saints Dyfrig, Teilo, and Euddogwy and into the hand of Bishop Berthwyn, and all his successors of Llandaff, Llangadwaladr with all its land, with wood and with maritime rights and with all its liberty, without any tribute to earthly man, but only to the church of Llandaff and its shepherds, and with its [rights of] sanctuary in perpetuity.

[42] The Llancarfan charter belongs to the A collection (see appendix), which is dated by some of the witnesses to the seventh century.

[43] Brooke, *The Church and the Welsh Border*, 32–3.

[44] Parish of Llangadwaladr or Bishopston, deanery of Netherwent, *PW* 78, which includes *Ecclesia S Ciuiu* = *LL* 31 (*uillam Lann gatualatir cum ecclesia sancti ciuiu*), and similarly *LL* 43 and 90.

From the clergy the witnesses are: Bishop Berthwyn, *Gunuiu* the *lector*, *Confur*, *Conguarui*, *Torchan*. From the laity: King Morgan, *Guednerth*, Iddig son of Nudd, Iago son of *Mabsu*, *Guengarth*, *Elioc*, *Gabran*, Elffin, Samuel.

Whoever shall have preserved [this grant], let him be blessed; but whoever shall have violated it, let him be cursed. AMEN.

Its boundary is: Aber Nant Alun in the marsh . . . to Aber Nant Alun where it began.

In the charter attached to the Life of St Cadog a man called Gwyddnerth (*Guoidnerth*) is said to have killed his brother. The killing of a kinsman was an act peculiarly unamenable to worldly justice; however, a solution might perhaps be sought through the Church.[45] The giving of alms was part of the penitential regime for sinners, whether they were given to the poor or the Church. The charter declares, on the one hand, that Gwyddnerth gave Llangadwaladr to God and to St Cadog, and, on the other, it says that he subsequently gave renders to Doguinni, the saint of Llandough (Llandochau) on the south-western edge of modern Cardiff.[46] This could be a mere aside, having nothing to do with Llangadwaladr; the renders to Doguinni would then be due from some other estate, unnamed. Yet it might not be an aside at all, provided that the renders to Doguinni were also due from Llangadwaladr. In that case, one estate, attached to a church, Llangadwaladr, would have supplied six *modii* of ale and the appropriate bread and meat to the *familia* of St Cadog and similar renders to the *familia* of Docguinni.

But then what should one make of the sentence in the charter saying that Gwyddnerth gave Llangadwaladr to God and to St Cadog? It would seem, on the face of things, unlikely that an estate given to St Cadog should then be obliged to give renders to St Docguinni. Perhaps a more complicated interpretation is the only way of making a connection between the grant to St Cadog and the grant to St Docguinni. On this view, there were two elements in the gift: first, Gwyddnerth gave the local church, Llangadwaladr, to St Cadog; secondly, he gave an annual food-render, also to St Cadog, from the land hitherto attached to the church but still in his possession. To Docguinni he gave the same food-render, but no church. The grant of the church would be outright, conveying ownership; but the rest would signify just two contracts to

[45] *The Legal Triads of Medieval Wales*, ed. and trans. S. E. Roberts (Cardiff, 2007), 86, *Mk* 93, Adomnán, *Life of St Columba*, i. 22, *Beowulf*, 2435–71, and D. Whitelock, *The Audience of Beowulf* (Oxford, 1951), 18.

[46] The text would flow better if, in place of *tandem*, it had *totidem*, 'as many renders'. Wade-Evans translated *redditus* by 'the returns' as if the *redditus* were those previously granted to Llancarfan; this is unlikely, if only because the charter was preserved in the archive of Llancarfan.

deliver food-renders to two different churches from an estate that remained the property of Gwyddnerth.

With this interpretation of the Llancarfan charter in mind we may turn to consider its counterpart in the Book of Llandaff. This was written as a memorandum to the community of Llandaff to remind them of what had happened in the time of St Euddogwy and of his purported successor, Berthwyn.[47] It has an extensive narrative of the fratricide, of the ensuing synod, and of a penitential pilgrimage undertaken by Gwyddnerth; neither synod nor pilgrimage received any mention in the Llancarfan charter. The grant itself was of 'Llangadwaladr with all its land . . . without tribute to any earthly man, but only to the church of Llandaff'. The phraseology emphatically excludes any such interpretation as the one I have offered for the Llancarfan charter. The land is chained to the church and the possibility of any further render is explicitly excluded. Yet perhaps the text protests too much. The two charters may even be two sides of a legal argument. The Llancarfan charter might, then, have been willing to admit the claims of St Docguinni precisely because the Llandaff charter claimed an exclusive right to Llangadwaladr: two major communities would then have been yoked together in opposition to the claims of Llandaff. Similarly, the Llancarfan witness list includes three communities, that ruled by Tyrchan (Terchan, Turchan, Trychan), Llancarfan itself, namely the monastery of St Cadog, and the community of St Docguinni: the Llancarfan text may descend from one belonging to the community headed by Terchan. Allied with other communities Llancarfan might hope to repel the more aggressive claims of Llandaff or, rather, its predecessor. The Llandaff charter fails to mention any other monastery.

We may now return to the earlier Llancarfan charter and to the contradictions between it and its Llandaff counterpart. Instead of six *modii* in the Llancarfan charter there were three *modii* in the Llandaff text; the recipients were different and so were the witnesses. Admittedly there is an easy explanation for the six as against three *modii*, since a scribal confusion between *ui* and *iii* would be unremarkable; but otherwise the Llandaff charter might be a rewritten version of the Llancarfan charter as Brooke suggested. Yet the difference between the witnesses also makes it possible that a less simple explanation may be involved. A possibility is that there was a similar situation behind this first pair of charters as there may have been behind the second pair. On this interpretation, Cynfelyn gave a render of six *modii* to Cadog and a render of three *modii* to the community headed by Tyrchan. The two gifts were separate transactions and could thus have different witnesses without any difficulty. True, it remains a difficulty that both charters make Cynfelyn grant to their respective churches the estate-centre, Llystin Byrrion or Din Byrrion. Yet it will always have been a temptation for churches to try to convert the right to a render from an estate into outright ownership of that estate. Whether this whole interpretation is true for either or both of these pairs of charters, it has underlined the need to

[47] Although Berthwyn was not Euddogwy's successor according to the final scheme in the Book of Llandaff (a single line of succession from Dyfrig to Herewald), he is evidently just that in the narrative in 180b (which indicates that the narrative was not composed by Bishop Urban or his collaborators).

make a clear distinction between a contractual right to a render and outright ownership. We shall explore the implications of this distinction further later.

In the section of the Book of Llandaff devoted to Bishop Berthwyn there are several doublets, pairs of charters which, like those already considered, seem to refer to the same occasion, with the same donors and the same estate. The existence of such doublets within the collection is a strong argument that Bishop Urban and his collaborators were, at least in part, assembling and editing existing texts rather than composing charters *de novo*. The broad trend behind the Book of Llandaff is that earlier archives of churches originally independent of Llandaff were acquired by Llandaff as part of its drive to extend its jurisdiction over as much of South Wales as possible. Doublets would then be produced in two ways: when two churches subsequently subject to Llandaff each had a claim to the one piece of land; and also when one church made two different collections of its charters, perhaps in order to update its archive. A variant of this second way would arise when one church became subject to a second church (neither of them being Llandaff) and the second acquired the archive belonging to the first and made a new collection of charters. This would then be repeated when Llandaff acquired the new combined collection and added it to those already in its archive.

The two pairs of charters we shall consider are a selection to be set alongside the two pairs from different archives already discussed.

LL 175	*LL* 186b
It ought to be known to us that *Ilias* gave a church with four *modii* of land around it, together with its entire render, both great and small, to God and to Dyfrig and Teilo and Bishop Berthwyn and all his successors in the church of Llandaff in perpetuity.	*Ilias*, for the sake of his soul and for the writing of his name in the Book of Life, gave a church in the midst of Aber Mynwy, with four *modii* of land around it, by the word and consent of King Ithael and of his sons, *Fernuail* and Meurig, and with its entire render, from great to small, to Saints Dyfrig, Teilo and Euddogwy, and [placed it] in the hand of Bishop Berthwyn and all his successors in the church of Llandaff, and with every privilege and its entire common right in field and in woods, in water and in pastures.
This grant in alms was made at Aber Mynwy by the word and consent of Ithael, the father, and of the sons, *Fernuail* and Meurig, and with its entire common right in field and woods, in water and in pastures, and with three abbots as witnesses, *Dagan*, abbot of Nant Carfan, Sadwrn, abbot of [Saint] *Dogunni*, *Eluoed* abbot of [Saint] Illtud, Trychan the *lector*. Of the laity there are: King Ithael with his sons, *Fernuail* and Meurig, *Ilias, Elcun, Mabsu*, Idnerth son of Idwallon, *Dounerth* son of Iddig, *Ceriau, Iudnoe*.	Of the clergy the witnesses are: Bishop Berthwyn, *Turchan, Dagan*, abbot of Nant Carfan, *Elguoid* abbot of [Saint] Illtud, Sadwrn abbot of [Saint] *Docunni*. Of the laity: King Ithael, *Fernuail* and Meurig his sons, *Ilias*, Elffin, *Mabsu*, Idnerth son of Idwallon, *Duinerth* son of Iddig, *Ceriau, Guoruodu, Conhae, Iudnoe*.
Whoever should preserve [this grant], let him be blessed; whoever, on the other hand, should violate it, let him be cursed.	Whoever should have preserved [this grant] may God preserve him; whoever should have parted it from the church of Llandaff, let him be anathema.

There is one particular difficulty to be faced at the outset. In 186b it is made quite clear that the church granted was in Aber Mynwy (the modern Monmouth, where the River Mynwy or Monnow flows out into the Wye). In 175, however, it appears as if Aber Mynwy was the place where the grant was made in the presence of King Ithael and his two sons rather than the place where the church was situated.[48] Since, in 175, the church granted by *Ilias* was otherwise unidentified, it may have been assumed that the grant was deliberately made on site, rather as in later Welsh law a case over land was heard before the king on the land in dispute;[49] yet, that, if true, was only implicit. If we can accept this explanation, there is then no reason for doubting that this pair of charters is a true doublet. The witness list in 186b has two extra names among the laymen; and either *Elcun* in 175 or *Elfin* in 186b must be miscopied; otherwise the lists are essentially the same and, with one exception, in the same order.

Leaving aside the witness lists, the rest of the charter appears in two very different arrangements. For the elements out of which it is composed I shall use non-technical descriptive terms, except that 'Notification' is a technical term for such clauses as 'It ought to be known to us', and I shall use 'Motive' for a clause such as 'for the sake of his soul and for the writing of his name in the Book of Life', and *Braint* ('privilege, status') is used for set phrases taken in all probability from *Braint Teilo* or its sister saintly privileges.

175	**186b**
Notification	——
——	Motive
grant	grant
render	royal consent
God & saints as recipients	render
Berthwyn as worldly recipient	saintly recipients
place & royal consent	placing in Berthwyn's hand
braint	*braint*

The striking differences are the absence of a Notification in 186b, of a Motive in 175; and the positioning of the royal consent. But there are other, more minor, differences: God heads the saintly recipients in 175 but is omitted in 186b; in 186b Euddogwy is included among the saintly recipients but in 175 he is omitted; in 175 Bishop Berthwyn and his successors immediately follow the saintly recipients as part of the same list, but 186b refers to a distinct ceremony by which some symbol of the land granted (such as the gospel book containing a text of the charter) was placed in Bishop Berthwyn's hand; in 175, unusually, the witness list is attached syntactically to the *braint*; in 186b it is quite separate. The two texts are, therefore,

[48] An associated problem is the blank left in the MS after *podium*.
[49] *Llyfr Iorwerth*, ed. A. Rh. Wiliam (Cardiff, 1960), § 73, *LTMW* 84–5.

only approximately in the same order; and the elements of which they are composed are not always the same.

On the other hand, there is a small core which is phrased almost identically in the two texts:

175	186b
Ilias gave a church with four *modii* of land around it, together with its entire render, both great and small, to . . . Dedit Ilias podum quattuor modiorum agri circa se, cum omni censu suo, magno uel modico . . .	*Ilias* gave a church with four *modii* of land around it, and with its entire render, from great to small to . . . Ilias dedit podium cum agro quattuor modiorum circa se, & cum omni censu, a magno usque ad modicum . . .

The close resemblance in this core suggests that there is a textual connection between the two charters. Otherwise one might have supposed that a single ceremony of donation, in public assembly and with particular witnesses, was separately recorded in two churches. In that case, the only connection would have been non-textual—the event itself. However, the core suggests a single recording with two 'daughter-texts'.

One reaction to the connection between the two texts might be to say that the core alone was genuinely early and that everything else was later addition. To some extent this is true: the section I have called *braint*, because its phraseology was probably taken from *Braint Teilo* or one of the other two *braint* sections, is very likely to be just such an addition. Yet some other elements should not be dismissed. Notifications are normal among the Llancarfan charters and also among those in the Lichfield Gospels.[50] It is hard to say whether 175, with a Notification, or 186b, without, reflects the original better. Similarly, the reference in 186b to 'the hand of Bishop Berthwyn' may be to a ceremony mentioned in the Llancarfan charters, for example § 56: 'Bronwydd and his three sons . . . held the written text of a *graphium* on the hand of Conigc, *princeps* of the altar of Cadog'.[51] The term *graphium* for a charter can be paralleled in Asser's Life of King Alfred and in an early Glamorgan inscription.[52]

A better view is that the core, as I have termed it, was relatively fixed but that other parts of the charter were more fluid. By 'fluid' I mean that a scribe who copied the charter was not prohibited from changing the wording to suit his notion of how the narrative might best be expressed. This phenomenon is evident in several later

[50] Only § 57 in the Llancarfan collection, a text otherwise suspicious, lacks a Notification; Chad 1, 3, 4, 5, 6 have Notifications.

[51] Part of the B group of the late eighth century: see Appendix.

[52] Asser, *Life of King Alfred*, ed. W. H. Stevenson (Oxford, 1959), § 11; Merthyr Mawr 2, 1022/240/G99; the Old Welsh *grefiat* appears in Chad 2, *LL* xliii.

Welsh texts, both Latin and vernacular.[53] In most diplomatic traditions the scribes followed a certain more or less fixed path when writing a charter for a particular donor: particular formulae were chosen from among the range of possibilities, and in that way those who knew the conventions could tell whether a particular charter was genuine or not. Suggestions have also been made that a charter could use a numerical pattern to demonstrate its authenticity.[54] Here again the presupposition was that a specialized group of experts knew the rules and could recognize the bumbling efforts of ignorant forgers. For, if everyone knows how to authenticate a charter, no charter can be authenticated.

Our charters, however, appear to be authenticated by another route, namely by being written into a gospel book.[55] Those named in the witness list not only witnessed the transaction itself but might also authorize the writing of a charter in the gospel book. At the end of a record of a law suit in the shire court of Herefordshire, a text written into the Hereford Gospels, it is stated: 'And Thurkil rode then with the permission and witness of all the people to St Ethelbert's minster, and had it entered in a gospel book'.[56] They might further witness the placing of the gospel book containing the charter in the hands of the earthly recipient.[57] The assumption here is that only by public authority, whether of king, bishop, abbot, assembly—or various dignitaries in an assembly—was it permissible for a text to be written in a gospel book. Once in a gospel book it could readily be copied into another gospel book (for example into the Book of Llandaff itself); and, during copying, the text was fluid provided that the nature of the transaction was still accurately expressed. A particular set way of describing the grant was not necessary; the core of the charter was only relatively fixed because it set out the essentials of the transaction. Even there, I have not, in discussing this pair of texts, included within the core the recipients or beneficiaries, partly because the two texts express Berthwyn's role very differently, partly because the saintly trio of Dyfrig, Teilo, and Euddogwy was one of the latest elements in the history of the texts, part of the effort to make Llandaff into the premier church of south-eastern Wales. Yet recipients ought to have been part of the core of the text, as shown by syntax and common sense.

The final pair of texts concern an estate by the River Ewenni, not far from the modern Bridgend in Glamorgan (Pen-y-Bont ar Ogwr).

[53] T. M. Charles-Edwards, 'The Textual Tradition of Medieval Welsh Prose Tales and the Problem of Dating', in B. Maier and St. Zimmer (eds.), *150 Jahre "Mabinogion"—deutsch-walische Kulturbeziehungen*, Buchreihe der *Zeitschrift für celtische Philologie*, 19 (Tübingen, 2001), 28–31; id., *The Welsh Laws* (Cardiff, 1989), 33–4.

[54] D. Howlett, *Sealed from Within: Self-Authenticating Insular Charters* (Dublin, 1999).

[55] Cf. D. Broun, *The Charters of Gaelic Scotland and Ireland in the Early and Central Middle Ages* (Cambridge, 1995), 36–7 on textual fluidity, 42 on authentication by being written into a gospel book.

[56] *EHD* i, no. 135.

[57] The examples of *in manu episcopi* in *LL* are mainly in texts relating to the period *c.* 800–910 and may derive from the originals: Davies, *The Llandaff Charters*, 143. In the text of Chad 1, the donor is said to have placed the gospel book on the altar of St Teilo's church.

LL 176a: The township (*villa*) of Cynwg

It ought to be known that *Conuilius* son of *Gurceniu*, by the word of Morgan and his son Ithael, gave a township in which lies the tomb of *Gurai*, namely the township of Cynwg, to God and to the three saints, Dyfrig, Teilo and Euddogwy, together with its entire privilege and its whole common right in field and in waters, in wood and in pastures, [and] to Bishop Berthwyn and all the bishops of Llandaff in perpetuity. And together with the alms he had given, *Cormil* ordered his son Cynwg and his sons, from generation to generation, that they should always serve the altar of Llandaff from the aforesaid land.

Its boundary is from the summit of the mountain of *Gurai* as far as the river Ewenni. Its width, however, is from the great ditch as far as the ditch by the sea.

Of the clergy the witnesses are: Bishop Berthwyn, Sulien, abbot of Nant Carfan, Sadwrn, abbot of [Saint] *Docguinni*, *Gurhaual*, abbot of [Saint] Illtud. Of the laity: King Morgan and his son Ithael, *Conuil, Iunet, Condiuit, Concuman, Mabsu, Gurhitir*, Samuel, Iddig, *Guednerth*, Morgan's brother.

Whoever shall have preserved [this grant], may God preserve him. But whoever shall have parted [it] from the church of Llandaff, let him be anathema.

LL* 190b, *Maerun

Conuilius son of *Gurceniu* bought an estate, that is, the township in which lies the tomb of *Gurai*, from King Morgan and from his son Ithael, and from his wife *Ricceneth*, and having bought that township by the word of the king and with his consent, he granted it in alms to God and to saints Dyfrig, Teilo and Euddogwy, and to Bishop Berthwyn and all his successors in the church of Llandaff in perpetuity, together with its entire privilege, and with wood and maritime rights, and with every common right in water and in woods, in field and in pastures.

From the clergy the witnesses are: Bishop Berthwyn, *Conuor, Guelerion*, Gwrfoddw, Heini, *Eudem, Morheb*, abbot of the Church of Dewi, Daniel, *Elhauaid, Gurcu*. From the laity: King Ithael and his son Meurig.

Whoever shall have preserved [this grant], may God preserve him. But whoever has violated it, let him be anathema.

If we divide both of the texts at a point immediately after the grant of the land, the version at 190b is fuller up to that point, while the other version, the one at 176a, is fuller thereafter. In 190b it is said that Cynfyl (Conuilius) bought the estate from the king, his son and his wife, and only then, with the king's consent, gave it to Llandaff. The purchase was strictly inessential information: the royal consent was a separate issue from the purchase, since only the king consented while the land was also bought from his son and his wife. At this period, so it seems, all transfers of land, or at least transfers to the Church, required royal consent irrespective of whether the land had been bought from the king.[58]

In 176a the second part of the charter, after the grant, has a crucial sentence which is not found in 190b. It says that the donor, Cynfyl, ordered his son Cynwg and the latter's descendants to serve 'the altar of Llandaff from the aforesaid land'.

[58] W. Davies, *An Early Welsh Microcosm*, 50: charters without explicit reference to the consent of the king start *c.* 738. This charter is probably earlier, ibid. 173.

On the other hand 176a has a boundary clause, while 190b does not. Some, but not all, boundary clauses in the Book of Llandaff are likely to be later additions;[59] but the designation of one son as both heir to the land given to a church and, at the same time, as one bound to serve the altar of that church has good parallels both in the Llancarfan charters and in early Irish texts.[60] It is more likely to have been omitted in 190b than added in 176a.

The two witness lists are also very different. The 'three abbots' in 176a (of Nant Carfan, Llandough, and Llanilltud) are not found in 190b; the abbot of the church of Dewi of 190b is not in 176a. The lay witness list in 190b is restricted to royalty, excluding even the donor, who, in 176a, immediately follows the king and his son. The process of change is as much through omission of primary text as through addition of new phrases and clauses: the three abbots may well be an addition in 176a; its lay witness list, however, is likely to preserve names omitted in 190b. A charter of this kind was evidently not a new concoction in the early twelfth century: both versions appear to have had separate and independent histories. Those who copied and preserved them seem not to have thought it necessary to keep, or even to pretend to keep, the precise wording of the original texts. What was expected was the preservation of the essential content of a charter. Such a relaxed approach to the writing and copying of charters made it easier to edit a text so as to make it grant more rights than had the original, and also to update the saintly beneficiaries of a grant to suggest that all were made directly to Llandaff rather than to churches whose heirs Llandaff had become, or claimed to be, via the inheritance of their archives. These texts cannot be understood as fixed title deeds but only as texts evolving as part of a similarly evolving process of ecclesiastical landownership with all the disputes and contentious claims such a process is bound to have included.

We began by comparing the Llandaff charters to the Old English diploma and to the Anglo-Norman writ-charter. In those traditions there was much use of relatively fixed formulae; as a result a charter might be exposed as a forgery because it made use of anachronistic formulae. In the tradition to which the Llandaff and Llancarfan charters belonged, textual fluidity was the norm, not fixed formulae. There were some formulae, such as that claiming 'its entire privilege in field and in woods, in water and in pastures', but these are likely to be late additions: they have a suspicious relationship to the 'privileges' attached to the Lives of the three saints, Dyfrig, Teilo, and Euddogwy. These three saints were almost always attached to God himself as the three heavenly beneficiaries of a grant; here again the language was relatively formulaic and correspondingly suspicious. In the official theory embodied in the Book of Llandaff, a single sequence of bishops of Llandaff was headed by the first three saintly figures of Dyfrig, Teilo, and Euddogwy, and they were followed in order by Ufelfyw, Aeddan, Elwystl, Inabwy, *Comeregius*, Gwrfan,

[59] Davies, *The Llandaff Charters*, 143; J. Coe, 'Dating the Boundary Clauses in the Book of Llandaf', *CMCS* 48 (Winter 2004), 1–43.

[60] Llancarfan, § 59 (of the B group); cf. § 58 (an unreliable text of the C group); Tírechán, *Collectanea*, § 15. 2 (ed. Bieler, *The Patrician Texts in the Book of Armagh*, 134).

and *Grecielis*; yet within the text of one charter Euddogwy is said to have been succeeded by Berthwyn, officially the eleventh bishop.[61] Between Euddogwy and Berthwyn the charters regularly omit Euddogwy from the beneficiaries and sometimes even Teilo; in one or two all saintly beneficiaries were left out.[62]

We began with two contrasting views of the Llandaff charters, as forgeries or as genuine documents with later additions that can be identified. As documents claiming that Llandaff was the beneficiary of the grants, the charters are admittedly forgeries; but the argument that genuine grants to churches other than Llandaff underlie most texts is persuasive. What remains relatively trustworthy is the core of the charter, excluding, in general, the saintly beneficiaries. Its text is often fluid, as the doublets demonstrate. From the same evidence, we can see that there were also more and less complete versions of the core. Yet they differed in how much they said rather than in the substance of what they both said. We cannot use the Llandaff charters as evidence for the entire estates of its predecessors at any one time; what we can do, however, is use them for changes in the way particular units of land and the rights attached to them were described. These changes, as we have seen, were both chronological and geographical.

3. THE LAW OF HYWEL DDA

Welsh vernacular manuscripts only survive from the middle of the thirteenth century. Among the earliest and also, taking the period 1250–1500 as a whole, perhaps the most numerous are manuscripts containing texts of *Cyfraith Hywel*, the Law of Hywel.[63] The Hywel in question was Hywel Dda, son of Cadell ap Rhodri Mawr and the most powerful Welsh king of the first half of the tenth century as well as a crucial ally of successive kings of the English. In J. E. Lloyd's *History of Wales*, an admirable summary of the principal contents of the Law of Hywel thus took its place in his first volume, on Wales before the Normans. This approach was challenged by J. G. Edwards in a lecture given in 1928 as part of millenary celebrations to recall Hywel's pilgrimage to Rome in 928, a pilgrimage recorded in *Annales Cambriae*.[64] The principal, although not the only, witnesses to the belief that Hywel was responsible for a major reform of Welsh law are the prologues to the texts preserved in lawbooks from *c.* 1250 onwards. It was on them that Edwards concentrated his critical attention. He was able to show that they differed among themselves and that some details were pious embroideries. For example, the reason for celebrating not just Hywel but Hywel's law in 1928 was a story in one branch of the text of *Llyfr Iorwerth*, itself a lawbook of the first half of the thirteenth century, recounting how Hywel,

61 180b.

62 e.g. 163a.

63 D. Huws, *Medieval Welsh Manuscripts* (Cardiff, 2000), 57–64.

64 J. G. Edwards, *Hywel Dda and the Welsh Lawbooks* (Bangor, 1929), reprinted in D. Jenkins (ed.), *Celtic Law Papers Introductory to Welsh Medieval Law and Government* (Brussels, 1973), 137–60.

accompanied by the bishops of St Davids, Bangor, and St Asaph, went to Rome to obtain papal authority for the laws which they had just revised.[65] Although the author of this tale, who probably lived in the late thirteenth century, knew that Hywel had gone to Rome and knew also enough about Hywel not to include the bishop of Llandaff in the party, the identity of the other bishops reveals the conditions of the author's time, not that of Hywel.[66] More generally, Edwards argued that behind the prologues lay notions of government proper to the twelfth and thirteenth centuries, especially the royal inquest. Since Edwards gave his lecture, the prologues have been submitted to closer scrutiny by Huw Pryce, who has demonstrated how small details reveal the conditions of the twelfth and thirteenth centuries.[67]

From 1928 onwards there have been two schools of thought about Hywel Dda and Welsh law: the first, in the tradition of J. E. Lloyd, has continued to maintain that the attribution is likely to be correct;[68] the second, in the tradition of J. G. Edwards, has seen the attribution as belonging to a wider European pattern by which lawbooks of the twelfth or thirteenth centuries were attributed to authoritative figures of the past, such as Edward the Confessor.[69] In that case, the attribution to Hywel Dda would be an important fact about twelfth- and thirteenth-century Wales, not a reason for using the lawbooks as evidence for pre-Norman Wales.

Here a distinction must be made. No one has denied that parts of Welsh law have every appearance of an antiquity going back long before the twelfth century. It is not just that, to take one example, the law of marriage is very remote from the conception of marriage enshrined in the canon law current when the lawbooks were written; it is also that it is often possible to elucidate the likely development of Welsh law by comparing it with Irish law, a legal tradition extensively attested in texts of the seventh and eighth centuries.[70] That, however, is a judgement on the content of Welsh law, not on the descent of Welsh lawbooks from some lost text of the tenth century.

One example will illustrate the point. Some versions of the Law of Hywel contain a text called 'The Seven Bishop-Houses of Dyfed'. This has every appearance of dating from a period before the Norman invasion of Dyfed in 1093. Yet there is no good reason to think that it was part of a text stemming immediately

[65] For a critical edition and translation of the text see T. M. Charles-Edwards and P. Russell (eds.), *Tair Colofn Cyfraith. The Three Columns of Law in Medieval Wales: Homicide, Theft and Fire* (Bangor, [2007]), 260–3.

[66] *AC*, ed. Dumville, *s.a.* 928; cf. *Brut*, *s.a.* 929.

[67] H. Pryce, 'The Prologues to the Welsh Lawbooks', *BBCS* 33 (1986), 151–87.

[68] For example, D. A. Binchy, *Celtic and Anglo-Saxon Kingship* (Oxford, 1970), 21–3, 27–30; T. M. Charles-Edwards, *The Welsh Laws* (Cardiff, 1989), 68–86.

[69] R. R. Davies, 'The Peoples of Britain and Ireland, 1100–1400. III. Laws and Customs', *TRHS*, 6th Ser., 6 (1996), 8; H. Pryce, 'Lawbooks and Literacy in Medieval Wales', *Speculum*, 75 (2000), 29–68; id., 'The Context and Purpose of the Earliest Welsh Lawbooks', *Cambrian Medieval Celtic Studies*, 39 (Summer 2000), 39–63.

[70] F. Kelly, *A Guide to Early Irish Law* (Dublin, 1988), on the contents of the Irish legal texts; D. A. Binchy, 'Some Celtic Legal Terms', *Celtica*, 3 (1956), showed the fruitfulness of comparison; the method is further pursued in *EIWK*.

from a supposed initiative on the part of Hywel to reform Welsh law. The most fundamental division in the textual history of the Welsh laws is between one tradition associated with Gwynedd and another associated with Deheubarth. The former is represented by *Llyfr Iorwerth*, attributed to Iorwerth ap Madog ap Rhawd, and there is good reason to think, first, that Iorwerth really was the author of the text in the form we have it, and, secondly, that he himself belonged to a kindred of lawyers and poets in Arfon and that his *floruit* belongs to the first half of the thirteenth century.[71] The second tradition is represented by several distinct textual families, by *Llyfr Cyfnerth*, the Latin redactions of Welsh law, and by a Welsh offshoot of the Latin tradition, *Llyfr Blegywryd*. (In the cases of *Llyfr Cyfnerth* and *Llyfr Blegywryd* the ascriptions to named persons are found within the texts but have little or no authority, unlike the ascription of the principal northern lawbook to Iorwerth ap Madog; never the less they remain useful titles.) So far as texts are concerned, if a particular 'tractate' is found both in *Llyfr Iorwerth* and in the southern lawbooks, it passes the first test for supposing that an earlier form of the text may go back to a pre-Norman lawbook that might possibly be the outcome of Hywel's reform. The Seven Bishop-Houses of Dyfed fails this first test: it is confined to southern lawbooks. It is still likely that it is pre-Norman, but it is likely to have been added to southern versions of Hywel's law at a later date. Not only legal content may be old but even texts may be old without implying anything about the relationship of Hywel to *Cyfraith Hywel*.

The argument that there was a relationship between Hywel and a text describing Welsh law compiled in the tenth century has two principal elements. First, *Llyfr Iorwerth* is likely to have been reshaped by Iorwerth starting from an earlier lawbook, now lost, which had an arrangement very similar to that preserved in most of the manuscripts of *Llyfr Cyfnerth*; and, yet, that earlier lawbook used by Iorwerth was not itself a copy of *Llyfr Cyfnerth*. *Llyfr Iorwerth* sometimes contains legal ideas and procedures in an earlier form than those preserved in *Llyfr Cyfnerth*, and thus the tradition behind its text appears to be independent of the southern lawbooks. The different copies of *Llyfr Cyfnerth*, however, are likely to go back to an original compiled during the reign of the Lord Rhys in Deheubarth, that is, in the second half of the twelfth century.[72] By the time of Rhys ap Gruffudd's death in 1197, there were already independent written traditions of Welsh law in Gwynedd and Deheubarth, which nonetheless have so close a similarity in their organizaton as texts that both are likely to go back to a single earlier 'model-lawbook'.

The second element in the argument has to do with the most likely date for this hypothetical model lawbook. Students of Irish law are impressed by two aspects of Welsh lawbooks. The first is that they have the same general character as the main Irish lawbook, the *Senchas Már*. That is, they are manuals written to instruct those who are learning the law. They arrange the material into tracts or tractates, sometimes bearing titles but always attempting to explain the law on a particular topic. They are texts internal to a legal profession, written by lawyers

[71] D. Jenkins, 'A Family of Medieval Welsh Lawyers', in Jenkins (ed.), *Celtic Law Papers*, 123–33.
[72] Pryce, 'The Prologues', 152–5.

for lawyers. They are not collections of royal edicts, and they therefore resemble each other much more than either resembles Anglo-Saxon or continental Germanic law. Secondly, when compared with Irish law, they are much more royalist: not only do they open with a long tract on the king and his court, but when discussing *galanas*, feud, they concentrate on the king's rights to fines from those who abet homicide—in principle a quite secondary issue. Within these royalist sections of the law are symptoms of Anglo-Saxon influence.[73] These appear in the names of important figures within the court: *distein* borrowed from Old English *discþegn* 'dish-thegn' and *edling* borrowed from Old English *æþeling* 'noble, prince', but given a new meaning, 'heir-apparent', derived from older words for the same position, *gwrthrych* and *gwrthrychiad*.[74] In the law of *galanas* there are signs of English influence in the distribution of the compensation for a killing. If we then look for a powerful Welsh king with close links with English kings—a king whose authority over most of Wales might give a royalist shape to the texts of Welsh law both northern and southern—Hywel Dda would be much the most promising candidate, even if no prologue associated him with the law and that law was never called 'The Law of Hywel'. Gruffudd ap Llywelyn in the eleventh century exercised an even wider power, but his relations with the English court were hostile and that court was less concerned with lawmaking than it had been in the tenth century. The English kings with whom Hywel was allied and whose courts he attended were active legislators in areas of the law where English influence is detectable in the Welsh lawbooks, and their edicts were added to an existing text, King Alfred's *domboc* 'book of edicts'. The tradition of English legal writing in the tenth century proclaimed the authority of a new English royal dynasty; the Britons were not immune from the geographical scope of their laws.[75]

The issue as to whether the concept of 'The Law of Hywel' rests on historical fact or a highly successful fiction is important for the history of Welsh legal writing and for the relationship between Hywel and the kings of the English. The following will give some idea of the shape of the 'model lawbook' and the sections that are likely to preserve pre-Norman Welsh law. When there are important parallels in Irish law of the seventh and eighth centuries, especially if this is conjoined with a linked vocabulary, it suggests that the surviving content of that part of the law is the outcome of a long development, very probably older than the tenth century. The comparison with early Irish law may indicate the nature of the development; and it

[73] M. E. Harris, 'Compensation for Injury: A Point of Contact between Early Welsh and Germanic Law?', in T. G. Watkin (ed.), *The Trial of Dic Penderyn and Other Essays* (Cardiff, 2002), 39–76. Also the law of theft: Charles-Edwards and Russell (eds.), *Tair Colofn Cyfraith*, 40–53.

[74] Binchy, *Celtic and Anglo-Saxon Kingship*, 27–30, but with the correction given by D. N. Dumville, 'The Ætheling: A Study in Anglo-Saxon Constitutional History', *Anglo-Saxon England*, 8 (1979), 1–33, who shows that *æþeling* did not mean 'designated successor' although some successors were designated.

[75] P. Wormald, *The Making of English Law: King Alfred to the Twelfth Century*, i, *Legislation and its Limits* (Oxford, 1999), esp. 264–312; for Britons and tenth-century English royal law, see IV Edgar 2. 2 (*EHD* i, no. 41).

would thus justify using the texts as evidence for the history of pre-Norman Wales even if the ascription to Hywel were mere fiction.

I.	Prologue	The form is as likely to be shaped by the 'Celtic charter' as by post-Norman Conquest English inquests. One prologue, that in Latin Redaction A, still has *Britannia* for Wales.[76]
II.	Laws of Court	As a whole this section is one of the most likely to have been written or rewritten in the tenth century. It contains some elements going back to a still earlier period, such as the concept of the heir-apparent as 'the expected one' or the right of the *pencerdd* to a *cyfarws neithior*, a gift from a bride when she is first married.[77] But other parts are unlikely to go back any further than the tenth century, such as the privileged position of the chief falconer.[78]
III.	Laws of Country Four lists of nine: the Three Columns of Law and the Nine Tongued-ones.[79]	Much of this bears the imprint of Anglo-Saxon influence and may be ascribed to the tenth century. The Welsh king was deeply involved in the feuds of his subjects, partly to encourage peace-making, partly as a means of exacting financial dues and penalties. There is no way of knowing whether such a deep involvement goes back beyond the tenth century.
	Land	The long section on the procedure of claims to land in *Llyfr Iorwerth* is very likely to belong to the thirteenth century. The sections on the division of the patrimony and on *dadannudd*, a special procedure for claiming land, are likely to be very old.[80]
	The value of wild and tame	This is almost certainly, as we have it, twelfth and thirteenth century.
	Corn-damage	Nothing to suggest great antiquity.[81]
	Joint-ploughing	Probable parallels in early Irish law.[82]

[76] *The Latin Texts of the Welsh Laws*, ed. H. D. Emanuel (Cardiff, 1967), 109.

[77] D. A. Binchy, 'Some Celtic Legal Terms', *Celtica*, 3 (1956), 221–31; P. Mac Cana, 'Elfennau Cyn-Cristnogol yn y Gyfreithiau', *BBCS* 23 (1968–70), 316–20.

[78] D. Jenkins, 'Hawk and Hound: Hunting in the Laws of Court', in Charles-Edwards et al. (eds.), *The Welsh King and his Court*, 255–80, esp. 261.

[79] For this section see Charles-Edwards and Russell (eds.), *Tair Colofn Cyfraith*, *passim*.

[80] *EIWK* 211–15, 274–303, 520–7.

[81] Ibid. 456–9.

[82] Ibid. 446–56.

Suretyship	The most conservative version of the law of suretyship and contract is in *Llyfr Iorwerth*. It shows clear parallels with early Irish law.[83]
Women	Much of this material is likely to descend from before Hywel's time. The way divorce is described has been influenced by church reformers in the twelfth century.[84]
Value of houses, trees, and equipment	Nothing to suggest great antiquity.

Some sections, therefore, are likely to offer valuable hints on what the law may have been in the pre-Norman period, others are not.

There are, then, major problems with the principal categories of written evidence for early Welsh society. Among the charters, the most dependable texts form the smallest collection, that written into the Lichfield Gospels when they were at Llandeilo Fawr. The Llancarfan collection is larger than the Llandeilo one and is likely to have been less radically edited than the charters in the Book of Llandaff. In the next chapter we shall see how the Llancarfan collection, when analysed with the help of the laws, holds the principal key to understanding the long-term development of relations between lords and peasants in early medieval Wales. With this key it will be possible to open some of the doors that seemed to bar the way to anyone seeking to make reliable inferences from the Llandaff charters.

Appendix: The Llancarfan Charters

The Llancarfan charters can be linked by common witnesses both to each other and, sometimes, to charters in the Llandaff collection. In addition, as we have seen, we have doublets where the charter itself is linked to a twin. Links between witnesses establish three groups, A, B, and C.

GROUPS OF LLANCARFAN CHARTERS

55 linked with 56, 59, 61, 66	B group
57 linked with 58, 63 (Cadog), ??68 (Eutegyrn)	C group
60 (no links)	

[83] R. Chapman Stacey, 'The Archaic Core of Llyfr Iorwerth', in Charles-Edwards et al. (eds.), *Lawyers and Laymen: Studies in the History of Law presented to Professor Dafydd Jenkins* (Cardiff, 1986), 15–46; ead. *The Road to Judgment: From Custom to Court in Medieval Ireland and Wales* (Philadelphia, 1994), ch. 6; H. Pryce, *Native Law and the Church in Medieval Wales* (Oxford, 1993), 53–65.

[84] D. Jenkins, and M. E. Owen (eds.), *The Welsh Law of Women: Studies presented to Professor Daniel A. Binchy on his Eightieth Birthday, 3 June 1980* (Cardiff, 1980); D. B. Walters, *The Comparative Legal Method: Marriage, Divorce and the Spouses' Property Rights in Early Medieval European Law and Cyfraith Hywel* (Aberystwyth, 1982); R. Chapman Stacey, 'Divorce, Medieval Welsh Style', *Speculum*, 77 (2002), 1107–27.

62 linked with 64, 65, 67, 68	A group
Of these:	
65, 68	Early A group (Meurig king)
62, 64, 67	Late A group (Morgan king)

Of these C is the least trustworthy, since it purports to belong to the time of St Cadog himself.[85] Leaving that aside, therefore, there are two remaining groups. A is the earlier, since there is a strong overlap between the witnesses to these Llancarfan charters and *LL* 144 and to a slightly lesser extent with 140 and 143, namely with the beginning of Wendy Davies's 'second sequence' of witnesses.[86] In terms of her dating, this would place the A group in the seventh century. For the B group the witness lists do not provide an external dating: the abbots of Llancarfan named, Conigc and Paul, do not appear in the Llandaff charters. Fortunately, however, one of the doublets noted above, Llancarfan 66 and *LL* 210b, enables us to date the B group to the second half of the eighth century.[87]

85 So Brooke, *The Church and the Welsh Border*, 32 n. 68.
86 Davies, *Llandaff Charters*, 41.
87 Ibid. 118.

8

Lords, Food-Renders, and Peasants

The principal evidence for early Welsh society can be divided between the charters and the laws. On the basis of their evidence, discussed in the previous chapter, it will be possible in the next three chapters to offer a tentative picture of early medieval Welsh lordship, kinship, and kingship. Some understanding of these social institutions will then form an essential background to the narrative chapters (12–17), which pursue the history of the Britons from the mid-sixth century down to 1064.

As we have seen there are critical problems affecting much of the charter evidence. Fortunately, however, the elements most likely to have been added later are, first, the relatively fixed and formulaic phrases outside the core of the charter; and, secondly, within the core, the saintly beneficiaries: Dyfrig, Teilo, and Euddogwy. Admittedly, even the core can be textually fluid, but in this tradition the more fixed elements are often the least trustworthy. The difficulty with the extant texts of the laws is that they are later than our period: the earliest family of texts, that known as *Llyfr Cyfnerth* (abbreviated Cyfn), appears to stem from an original lawbook compiled in the second half of the twelfth century.[1] Yet, by comparing different texts, by paying careful attention to the terminology, and by relating the laws to other evidence, it is possible to make adequately reliable judgements on which elements date from the pre-Norman period. The charters, however, will be our starting point, developing the argument from the point reached in the last chapter.

1. *UNCIAE* AND *MODII*: FOOD-RENDERS AND ESTATES

With one or two exceptions the charters in the Book of Llandaff purport to be grants of land.[2] In discussing the two charters which are in both the Llandaff and the Llancarfan collections, the question has been raised whether some grants were not of food-renders rather than of the land itself. This issue is, however, entwined with a further contrast between the two collections. The core of a Llandaff charter is typically expressed in one of the following ways:

[1] H. Pryce, 'The Prologues to the Welsh Lawbooks', *BBCS* 33 (1986), 152–5.
[2] 236 is a grant of people not land.

(a) X gave so many *unciae/modii* of land to God etc.
158: King Ithael son of Morgan and his sons Ffernfael and Meurig gave three *unciae* of land, namely *Emricorua* . . . to God etc.

(b) X gave the church of Y to God etc. with so many *unciae/modii*
164: King Gwrgan son of Cynfyn . . . gave to God etc., and in the hand of Bishop Inabwy, the church of St Buddwalan with two *unciae* and a half *uncia* around the church . . .

(c) X gave land of so many *modii* at Y to God etc.
178: *Conblus* son of Iago granted the land of three *modii* on the River Wye . . . to God etc.

The text does not suggest that there was any great difference of meaning between these three, except that (b) is common when the object of the verb 'gave' was a named estate-centre, such as a church. An example of an estate that was granted by mode (a) and only subsequently came to resemble one usually granted by mode (b) is 162a. Gwrfoddw, king of Ergyng gave an *uncia* of land, in which a church was then founded. The first priest of the church was named *Guorboe*; and hence the church, with its appendant estate, came to be known as *Lann Guorboe*, the modern Garway.[3]

All three of these methods of expressing the object of the grant may be contrasted with the way the Llancarfan charters express similar grants of land:[4]

> § 61: *Temit* gave land, namely from the estate of *Crucin* . . . which should pay six *modii* of ale every year, together with loaves and carcases to the *familia* of Cadog . . .

In the Book of Llandaff the *uncia* and the *modius* almost always appear to be units of land; in the Llancarfan charters only the *modius* is used and it is a unit of ale, the leading component in the food-render. Similarly, one of the charters in the Lichfield Gospels declares that

> Rhys and the kindred of Grethi gave Tref Wyddog as the experts may conduct [those making a perambulation?]. This is its render . . .[5]

In these charters an estate is associated with its render; it is defined by bounds or by a render, or by both.

The distribution of the *uncia* is early and eastern.[6] Only one example appears to postdate *c.* 800; and the *uncia* is used, together with the *modius*, for estates in Ergyng (south-west Herefordshire) and Gwent (Monmouthshire). Further west, in Glamorgan, Brycheiniog, and Gŵyr, the sole unit employed is the *modius*. Hence it is unsurprising that Llancarfan, situated in Glamorgan, used only the *modius*. There is a further characteristic of the *uncia*: it is relatively large. In the Book of Llandaff

[3] Grid ref. of Garway, SO 455 225.

[4] This charter belongs to the B group of the second half of the eighth century: see Appendix, 272–3.

[5] Chad 3; cf. D. Jenkins and M. E. Owen, 'The Welsh Marginalia in the Lichfield Gospels. Part I', *CMCS* 5 (Summer 1983), 53–4.

[6] For what follows see W. Davies, '*Uncia: Land Measurement in the* Liber Landauensis', *Agricultural History Review*, 21 (1973), 111–21.

itself it is twice defined as equivalent to twelve *modii*.[7] From the few examples when a charter used the *uncia* and also had bounds, Wendy Davies estimated that it was employed for an area in the order of 500 acres. She argued that, as a unit, it descended from the Romano-British period in the particular sense of the inheritance of one man.[8] Given its approximate size, the heir in question must have been of noble status. In the Book of Llandaff most donors of *unciae* were kings.

Although the *uncia* was described as a measurement, *mensura*, one should not jump to the conclusion that is was an abstract spatial unit, such as a hectare.[9] Medieval measures of land regularly arose from some process used in relation to the land: some began life as units of cultivation, such as the acre, which comes from ploughing; some might be derived from divisions of the inheritance, as Wendy Davies argued was the case with the *uncia*. The other unit employed in south-eastern Wales, the *modius*, was used in the Roman period for a quantity of grain and thus for the area of arable land for which a *modius* of seed would be appropriate. In one charter in the Book of Llandaff, it was used for a quantity of wheat.[10] The *modius* of the Llancarfan charters, however, was not a unit arising from sowing, but instead was used of the grain element in a food-render, and, moreover, almost always of one part of the grain element, the ale (made from malted barley) as opposed to the loaves of bread. Such an element in a food-render was described as so many *modii* of ale; one may compare eighth-century Ireland where the *míach* of malted barley was a principal element in a standard food-render.[11] A further comparison is with some isolated references in Domesday Book for Cornwall: in Helston there were, apart from the usual *uillani*, *bordarii*, and *serui*, forty *ceruisarii* 'ale-men'; and a single hide of land taken from St German's by the Conqueror's half-brother, the Count of Mortain, had rendered a barrel of ale and thirty pence in 1066.[12] Hence the process of making ale from malted barley, and malted barley from ordinary barley grain, must have been the reason why a *modius* could be used in the same breath of land and wheat in the Book of Llandaff, 216b:

> *Aguod* son of Ieuaf... sacrificed to God, together with the word of Meurig, king of Morgannwg, the township of *Penn Onn* together with its church, *lann Tilull*, [and] together with three *modii* of land and with six *modii* of wheat.

The likeliest explanation of this odd turn of phrase is that three *modii* of land constituted the area which would, under local conditions, be expected to deliver three *modii* of ale to the lord. This estate would thus have been required to supply twice as much wheat as barley. Three *modii* of land owed more than just three *modii* of ale: the ale was merely the leading item in the total render, not necessarily the largest item.

[7] 200, 216a.

[8] For another use, common in Ireland as well as in Wales, namely the *uncia* as an ounce of silver, see 204b.

[9] 161: *mensuram trium unciarum*.

[10] 216b.

[11] *Cáin Aicillne*, ed. and trans. R. Thurneysen, *ZCP* 14 (1923), § 8 = *CIH* ii. 481. 26–30; F. Kelly, *Early Irish Farming* (Dublin, 1998), 246–7.

[12] DB 120a, d.

Another way in which the unit of measurement derived from a process of agricultural production is revealed by two Llancarfan charters: in § 57 the land is to provide 'two vats of six *modii* of ale', in § 67 'a vat of three *modii* of ale'. It is then to be noted that, in the Llancarfan charters, *modii* came in units divisible by three: three, six, nine and twelve.[13] This was presumably because, as the same collection shows, one standard *uas* or vat contained three *modii*.[14] These two units, the vat and the *modius*, derived from two different stages in the one process of production: the *modius* was originally a unit of grain (in this instance barley), while the vat was a unit designed for the final stage, the ale itself.

In the Book of Llandaff, as we have seen, the habit was to speak of so many *modii* of land or, alternatively, of the land of so many *modii*. The second could readily be an abbreviated way of stating the same relationship between land, crop, and final product used in a food-render as in the Llancarfan charters. One complex transaction of the second half of the eighth century strongly suggests that this was indeed the case:[15]

> King Athrwys son of Ffernfael sacrificed *Ca[i]r Riou* together with an *uncia* of land to God etc.... and in the hand of Cadwared; and Lleufryd, *hereditarius*, received the land from Bishop Cadwared and the clergy of Llandaff, being required to give every year six *modii* of ale together with its entire due in bread and in meat, together with a sester of honey. And at the will of the bishop, whenever it might please him and his chapter, he was to quitclaim it from himself and from his descendants for ever.

Cadwared, therefore, received an estate of one *uncia* (= twelve *modii*) from the king and gave the land (or just 'land'—the Latin does not show which) to Lleufryd, *hereditarius*. There are two ways to interpret the relationship envisaged between Cadwared and Lleufryd. The first is that the bishop handed over the whole estate of one *uncia* to Lleufryd on the basis that the latter was to be a tenant-at-will and was to owe Cadwared and his community half the possible render due for an *uncia* of land. The second is that the *ager* handed over to Lleufryd was defined exactly as it would have been in the Llancarfan charters—by means of the render payable to Cadwared and his community. In that case, what was handed over to Lleufryd was not the whole estate of one *uncia* or twelve *modii*, but just half of it, namely an *ager* owing six *modii* of ale and the accompanying renders of bread and meat. Lleufryd, we may suppose, was resident on the estate before it was given by the king to Llancarfan. On the first view, he ended up in full but potentially temporary and

[13] § 57 belongs to the C group, of indeterminate date and uncertain authenticity; but § 67 belongs to the seventh-century A group: see Appendix to the previous chapter. § 57 records two grants; the second was made by Meirchion and the render in that case is of 'three vats, which contained six *modii*' rather than the two vats of the other grant. Either this was a vat of a special size or there was a scribal error confusing '.ii.' and '.iii.'

[14] This equation does not hold for all districts and all periods: in Latin Redaction A of the laws four *modii* were equated with a vat: *The Latin Texts of the Welsh Laws*, ed. H. D. Emanuel (Cardiff, 1967), 135. 40–136. 1. The land of one *modius* was also defined in the same text, 136. 3–4, as 312 acres, a larger area than that deduced by Wendy Davies for the *modius* of the Book of Llandaff; that may well be a consequence of the relative richness of most of the land granted in the Llandaff charters.

[15] 210a.

certainly conditional possession of the entire *ager* of one *uncia*; on the second view, he ended up in equally conditional and potentially temporary possession of only half the estate. It is an important qualification, to which we shall return, that Lleufryd would himself have been of lordly condition: he could not have cultivated either twelve or six *modii* on his own. On the first view, therefore, the estate would have sustained Cadwared and his community by delivering six annual *modii* of ale, together with bread, meat, and honey, while, implicitly, it also maintained, or helped to maintain, Lleufryd in a style appropriate to his rank. According to Cadwared and his community, Lleufryd was a tenant-at-will, in charge of the estate only for so long as they wished; Lleufryd may have had other ideas.

Another probable implication of the situation faced by Lleufryd, on the first interpretation, is that, so far as Bishop Cadwared was concerned, Lleufryd undertook the risks that flowed from variable harvests. A difficulty inherent in a regime of food-renders was that, while the obligation might be fixed, the wherewithal to discharge the obligation was variable: it depended on the weather and on the incidence of disease. Yet, if Cadwared and his community fixed the render payable by Lleufryd at the level of six *modii* for an estate assessed at one *uncia* (and thus twelve *modii*), they might well have been able to shift most of the risk onto Lleufryd's shoulders. In good years he would have done well; but in bad years it would be his barns that would have been emptied and his livestock depleted.

Yet another method of coping with the inflexibility of food-renders was to allow substitution of one commodity in place of another. Such an option was explicitly allowed in some later lawbooks;[16] but it is also glimpsed in one of the seventh-century Llancarfan charters (§ 64). An estate called *lecguoidel* (Llech Wyddel) was granted to Llancarfan; its render was to be three *modii* of ale, with bread and meat; but then the charter adds: 'and if by chance there should be a lack of ale, let it render four *modii* of wheat or a white cloak'.

In the Llancarfan charters, as we have seen, *modii* came in groups of three for the good reason that a vat of ale contained three *modii*. If, then, the *modius* of the Book of Llandaff was also a measurement of the ale element in a food-render, we should expect the majority of examples of the unit to be divisible by three. This is indeed the case: there are forty-four examples of *modii* divisible by three as against fifteen which were not thus divisible. The strong probability is, therefore, that the Llandaff measurements expressed in *modii* were just like those in the Llancarfan charters: they primarily expressed the ale element in a standard food-render and only secondarily the land that would produce such a render.

Since the Book of Llandaff twice states an equation by which twelve *modii* constituted one *uncia*, we may go on to infer that those estates described in terms of *unciae* belonged to the same regime of food-renders as those described in terms of *modii*. This inference, however, poses two further problems: if estates measured in *unciae* were not different, except usually in size, from estates measured in *modii*, why did *unciae* have the special distribution revealed by Wendy Davies? They

[16] *EIWK* 370–1, 389–90.

belonged, it will be remembered, to Ergyng and Gwent, not to other parts of the south-east; and they were also predominantly early. Secondly, why were both *unciae* and *modii* used in the Book of Llandaff as if they were units of land rather than of renders (as were the *modii* in the Llancarfan charters)?

A possible answer to these two questions starts from the nature of the *uncia*, defined by Wendy Davies as 'an heir's portion', and thus primarily a measure of land rather than of food-renders; one might compare the *pett* of Pictish Scotland (*pett* is cognate with Irish *cuit* 'share' and Welsh *peth* 'thing'). On the other hand, the *modius*, as we have seen, was primarily a unit of food and only secondarily of land. Hence, when *unciae* and *modii* were brought into a single system by means of the equation by which twelve *modii* constitute one *uncia*, two quite different processes were combined: the division of inherited land (*uncia*) and the supply of food-renders, as defined by their leading component, ale (*modius*). The implication of making the equation at such a level (one *uncia* being of the order of 500 acres) was, as we have noted, that the standard heir's portion denoted by the *uncia* of twelve *modii* was an aristocratic inheritance. If, as Wendy Davies argued, the *uncia* of Gwent and Ergyng descended from late Roman Britain, we may hazard a guess that the person expected to inherit an *uncia* was a *curialis*, one of the local nobility of a *ciuitas* such as the Silures: St Patrick's family was of this rank.

In this system, the *modius* was linked to the *uncia* by means of the equation; and since the *uncia* was inherently a unit of land, the *modius* was readily understood as the land, which was one-twelfth of an *uncia*. The *uncia* attracted to itself the *modius* and so made it a measure of land as much as a measure of food. The whole system reveals many of the agricultural and social arrangements of the south-east: the relationship between peasant and lord, respectively producer and receiver of food-renders; the kind of mixed agriculture presupposed by the food-renders; and the nature of the aristocracy, largely constituted by what might be described as a local gentry.

The *uncia* was early rather than late, probably because social change rendered the particular standard of landed inheritance for a noble (one *uncia*) obsolete. The isolated example after 800 may be explained as the use of an archaic unit, now simply twelve *modii* and nothing more. More difficult is the question why the distribution is eastern. Ergyng is an early region, the surviving Welsh portion of a district attached to Ariconium, Weston-under-Penyard, just to the south of Ross-on-Wye. Gwent, on the other hand, in the sense in which it was roughly equivalent to Monmouthshire and thus excluded Glamorgan, was not an early unit. The old Gwent included most of Glamorgan (not Gŵyr, Gower). It was the descendant of the Romano-British *ciuitas* of the Silures, of which the capital was Venta Silurum, Caerwent. It may be argued that Gwent and Ergyng, being further east, retained the element of *Romanitas* in the local organization of estates implied by the term *uncia*. But Roman *villae* extended into the Vale of Glamorgan, so that this argument seems questionable. It may be that surviving aristocratic estates of the size to allow use of the term *uncia* were concentrated close to the *ciuitas* capital of the Silures at Caerwent and in the local *pagus* attached to Ariconium. This receives some support from the dominance of Gwent (in the narrow sense) within Gwent (in the wider sense) even in the early medieval period.

A further related problem is why the equation was established as one *uncia* comprising twelve *modii*. An initially attractive answer is that the annual food-render for one *uncia* was divided into twelve *modii* because that allowed for the delivery of one *modius* every month.[17] Yet this is improbable, if only because there is no sign in the Llancarfan or Llandaff charters of any division between winter and summer renders (as in Chad 3 in the Lichfield Gospels and in many post-Norman versions of the laws), let alone of renders according to the month.

The combined evidence of the Llandaff and Llancarfan charters indicates that there was a single standard regime of food-renders throughout the wider Gwent, heir to the old territory of the Silures. Other evidence, either slighter or later, in the Lichfield Gospels and in the laws, indicates that something broadly similar operated throughout early medieval Wales, but that the details were different.

The three main categories of the early medieval diet in north-western Europe were bread, the accompaniment to bread (varying according to the season and according to a person's wealth), and drink. In Welsh these three were *bara*, *enllyn*, and *llyn*, in Latin usually *panes* (in the plural and thus meaning 'loaves'), *companaticum, companagium*, or *pulmentum* for the accompaniment to bread, and *potus*. The three categories and the terms for them are, therefore, as follows:

	Welsh	Latin
Bread/loaves	*bara*	*panes*
Accompaniment	*enllyn*	*companaticum* etc.
Drink	*llyn*	*potus*

I have set them out in the order which one would expect and which is followed by the Latin terms. Since bread is accompanied by a *companaticum* it comes first, followed by the accompaniment, while *potus*, 'drink', comes third.

The terms for an accompaniment to bread were, however, strikingly different in Latin and Welsh. The Latin term *companaticum* or *companagium* proclaims its function in relationship to bread: what is eaten together with (*com-*) bread (the *pan-* in *panis, panes*).[18] Rather less obvious, but just as significant, is the Welsh word *enllyn*. This is, literally, 'something related to (*en-*) drink (*llyn*)'. The Latin word *companaticum* looks towards bread, *panis*; but the Welsh word *enllyn* looks towards drink, *llyn*. This is puzzling, since an accompaniment was eaten together with bread, and eating was distinct in early Welsh as in other European languages from drinking.[19] The natural connection was, therefore, as in the Latin terms. The whole reason for this particular classification of the diet was that bread was normally a constant element in the diet, whereas what accompanied the bread was variable, including more meat in winter, more dairy products in summer. The *companaticum* of November would not be the same as the *companaticum* of May.

[17] Compare the organization of the late Anglo-Saxon estates of Bury St Edmunds in A. J. Robertson, *Anglo-Saxon Charters* (Cambridge, 1939), 194. 28–196. 6.

[18] Similar, but slighly different, is the 'company', those who share *panis* 'bread'.

[19] Thus, in the feasts of Middle Welsh literature, *cyfeddach*, drinking, follows the eating: *PKM* 13. 25; 25. 25–6.

The Welsh term *enllyn* is, therefore, something of a puzzle. Yet the conundrum is satisfactorily solved by the evidence of the Llancarfan and Llandaff charters; moreover, it is hard to see what other explanation there could be. In these charters from south-eastern Wales, explicitly in the Llancarfan material, implicitly in those from the Book of Llandaff, the standard render included the following elements (in order): ale + bread + carcases of meat (+ honey). I have bracketed the honey element because that is not always specified; also, it was special in that it could be made into mead, and thus form part of the drink element, or it could be used in its original form and would then form part of the accompaniment. Leaving honey aside, this scheme may be compared with our tripartite division of the diet:

Drink	*llyn*	ale
Bread	*bara*	loaves
Accompaniment	*enllyn*	carcases

The Llancarfan charters specified how much ale was due and this defined what had to be supplied in both of the other categories. It was not necessary to specify them independently: *llyn* defined the entire render. For that reason estates could be defined in terms of *modii*, units of ale, namely the form of drink that, in the later laws, was rendered by non-noble townships.[20] The leading role of the drink element is also expressed by the term *enllyn*: the quantity of *enllyn* was determined by the quantity of *llyn*. The sequence of renders in the Llancarfan charters included both the natural association between bread and accompaniment (loaves are followed immediately by carcases) and the one created by the leading role of the drink element in the entire render: *enllyn* was determined by *llyn*. The two related words, *llyn* and *enllyn*, enveloped within them the third element, bread. Admittedly the sequence in the specification of a render suggested by the two terms *llyn* and *enllyn* might have been *llyn* + *enllyn* + bread as well as *llyn* + bread + *enllyn*, but the leading role of *llyn* is required to explain the *modii* of the Llandaff charters as well as being explicitly expressed in the smaller Llancarfan collection. The explanation for the pair of terms, *llyn* and *enllyn* is thus given by the charters from south-eastern Wales.

A further crucial aspect of the evidence provided by this pair of terms is that Welsh *enllyn* has a cognate in Irish *annland* and thus appears already to have been of considerable antiquity before the first of the Llandaff charters was written.[21] The linguistic evidence, taken together with that of the charters, reveals an ancient agrarian organization: if one were to ask what was the relationship between lords and peasants in the less Romanized parts of Roman Britain, this evidence would provide much of the answer.

Yet the priority of the drink element in a food-render was acknowledged neither in the two pertinent charters in the Lichfield Gospels, Chad 3 and 4, nor in the later laws. In Chad 3 the render was divided into a summer render and a winter render.

[20] *WML* 56.12–13.

[21] Vendryes, *Lexique*, A-76 reports the view of Holger Pedersen, *Vergleichende Grammatik der Keltischen Sprachen*, i. 115 (because of *and-* rather than *ind-*); but see M. Dillon, 'The Negative and Intensive Prefixes in Irish and the Origin of Modern Irish *an* "very, great"', *Transactions of the Philological Society*, 1944, 103; *GPC* 1218 *s.v.*

To that extent the information was at a more detailed level than in the Llancarfan charters. The summer render had the structure, bread + accompaniment, *bara* + *enllyn*; drink, *llyn*, was simply omitted. In the winter the structure was the same, except that a final element may have been added, namely *ebran*, horse-fodder.[22] In Chad 4 a summer render consisted of *bara* + *enllyn* (the latter comprising meat, as in winter, and dairy products). These two charters concern estates close to Llandeilo Fawr in Ystrad Tywi, further west than almost all the estates recorded in the Llandaff charters. One reason might be regional variation of custom; a simpler one might be that the community of Llandeilo Fawr was suffiently ascetic to avoid alcoholic drink, a mark of the stricter form of early Welsh monasticism.[23] In that case ale would not have formed part of the render if it was destined for the monks themselves rather than other elements of the *familia*.

The later laws suggest that by the twelfth and thirteenth centuries there were considerable local differences. In the vernacular versions of the laws the tendency was to put first the variable element in the render, the *enllyn*. Cyfn, for example, has the sequence *enllyn* + *bara* + *llyn*, namely the reverse of that in the Llancarfan charters.[24] One distant echo of the old system is that the standard render was due from land that provided one vat of ale, equivalent to three *modii* in the Llancarfan charters. The advantage of the later evidence is that it supplies greater detail about the constituent elements of the renders; but what the charter evidence gives us is the earlier system by which the principal elements of the food-renders were related to each other and to the land—namely the leading role of the drink element within the render and therefore in defining units of land. In conjunction they enable us to understand the crucial threefold relationship between land, the peasantry, and their lords.

2. THE RURAL LANDSCAPE

By the time the Book of Llandaff was compiled, and already in the ninth century to judge by the documents from Llandeilo Fawr in the Lichfield Gospels, an estate might be conceived as comprising an entire *mainaur* (Middle Welsh *maenawr* or, in North Wales, *maenawl*)[25] or solely a *uilla* (in Welsh *tref*). Both the *maenawr* and the *tref* are also attested in prose literature and in the laws. The *tref* was a unit which had existed by that name throughout the period covered by the Llandaff charters;[26] for the *maenawr*, however, there is no good evidence to suggest that, as a concept, it goes back before the tenth century. That is not to say that a particular *maenawr* may not be earlier than 900, simply that we have no evidence that, if it was, it was then

22 Depending on the significance of *mannuclenn*. Cf. A. Falileyev, *Etymological Glossary of Old Welsh* (Tübingen, 2000), 109.

23 Cf. Rhigyfarch, *Vita S. Davidis*, ed. and trans. Sharpe and Davies, § 25.

24 *WML* 56.17–57.9.

25 The base of *maenawr* would appear to be *maen* 'stone': *GPC s.v. maenor* is non-committal on the suffix *-awr*.

26 Cf. Ir. *treb*.

known as a *maenawr*.[27] The term is used in 72a, which purports to be from the lifetime of St Dyfrig but is probably a story about the foundation of Welsh Bicknor put into the form of a charter in the ninth or tenth century.[28] *Maenawr* is also used in 125a and in 165, which appear to have been rewritten later;[29] 165, however, offers one useful piece of evidence in that it uses the term *territorium* as a Latin equivalent for *maenawr*. Finally, *maenawr* also appears in the titles of some charters (123b, 180a, and 263), but again titles are likely to be later, perhaps much later, than the charters themselves. It may be significant that the area in which the *uncia* is attested in the Book of Llandaff—Gwent and Ergyng—does not overlap with the area in which the *maenawr* is attested, Dyfed.[30]

Two intertwined problems therefore arise from this evidence: the first is that of change over time, while the second is of variation according to district. The contrast between an early regime of *unciae* and a later regime of *maenorau* and *trefi* seems also to be a contrast between an eastern form of estate organization, proper to Gwent and Ergyng, and a western form. We can pursue these problems by examining the evidence for the *maenawr* and then taking, in turn, groups of charters, beginning with an early one and going on to later texts.

In the laws, and by implication also in prose literature, a number of contiguous *trefi* made up a *maenawr*.[31] The number of *trefi* required to make a *maenawr* varied in the laws from one text to another, whether a *maenawr* belonged to the lowlands or the uplands, and also according to the status of the *tref* in question, especially whether it was free or unfree. In the laws and in late surviving *maenorau*, such as the *maenol* attached to the cathedral church of Bangor, the *maenawr* appears more as an administrative unit than as an estate.

The fullest evidence in the Book of Llandaff comes from 253, ascribed to the time of Bishop Joseph, early in the eleventh century, but its use of *Gualia* for Wales stamps it as a twelfth-century text, or at least as one rewritten in the twelfth century. As an appendix to the main narrative in the charter, it includes a list of churches and estates in the diocese of St Davids which belonged, so it was claimed, to Llandaff.[32] This list resembles 165 in that *territorium* is used as an equivalent to *maenawr*,

27 An interesting example is Manorbier, Middle Welsh Maenawr Byr, which looks as though it may have been the mainland estate attached to the island monastery known after the founding saint, Pŷr, as Ynys Bŷr, Caldey Island. This monastery is well attested in the Life of St Samson as one well blessed with material affluence (*Vita S. Samsonis*, ed. Flobert, i. 36), but it is a matter for guesswork when it acquired Maenawr Bŷr. For the later fortunes of the *maenawr* see *EIWK* 445–6.

28 Davies, *Llandaff Charters*, 92–3.

29 Ibid. 96, 105–6.

30 Outside Dyfed, later evidence shows that it also existed in Gwynedd.

31 Hence in *Math* the army of Gwynedd awaited the forces of Pryderi *yghymherued y dwy uaynawr*, namely *Maynawr Bennard a maynawr Coet Alun*, *PKM* 72. 10–12, but the pigs were put in a sty in 'the highest *tref* in Arllechwoed', namely *yn y cantref arall issot* (as seen from Arfon), ibid. 71. 14. For an attractive argument that this reflects local knowledge derived from Clynnog Fawr, see P. Sims-Williams, 'Clas Beuno and the Four Branches of the Mabinogi', in B. Maier and S. Zimmer (eds.), *150 "Mabinogion"—Deutsche-walische Kulturbeziehungen* (Tübingen, 2001), 111–27.

32 Part of the list also occurs in 123; J. R. Davies, *The Book of Llandaf and the Norman Church in Wales*, 88–9, and cf. his Appendix 4.

alongside *uilla*, which was always the counterpart to Welsh *tref*. The distinction between *maenawr* and *tref* is exemplified by the following:

(i) *Pull Arda* by *Mainaur Pir*: only a *uilla*.
(ii) Tref Carn: just a *uilla* without a church.[33]
(iii) Llandeilo *Luin Guaidan*: just a *uilla* in Efelfre.
(iv) Llandeilo Fawr with its two *territoria*.[34]
(v) Llan Gronwern with the three *territoria* of Amrath (Amroth, Pemb.).
(vi) *Lan Issan*, a *mainaur* in *Amithieil*.
(vii) *Mainaur Mathru* (Mathry, Pemb.).

The earliest evidence may be in a charter which belongs to the late ninth or early tenth century, 235a. This is a grant of *Villa Cyuiu*, an estate of three *modii*. It is described as a member of the *territorium Merthir Teudiric* (Mathern, Monm.) A priest of *Merthir Teudiric* is attested in a late eleventh-century charter (274); and in the papal bulls addressed to Bishop Urban it is listed as '*Merthir Teudiric* together with [its] churches'.[35] By the twelfth century, therefore, *Merthir Teudiric* appears to have been a principal church with other churches dependent on it. The earlier charter about *Villa Cyuiu* has to do with estate structure rather than any ecclesiastical organization; but a similar pattern of subordinate settlements dependent on *Merthir Teudiric* is implied; and, finally, there is a reasonable chance that, behind the Latin word *territorium* in the phrase *territorium Merthir Teudiric* lay the Old Welsh *mainaur*. *Merthir Teudiric*, with three possible functions, as a complex estate, as a combination of principal and subordinate churches, and perhaps also as a unit of royal administration, may be a good example of what has variously been termed a 'multiple estate' and a 'small shire'.[36]

Another good example may be *Mainaur Crucmarchan*. According to the heading of a charter (163) belonging to the episcopate of Joseph (d. 1045), and probably dating to a time after his move to Llandaff, Llansanffraid-ar-Elái (St Bride's-super-Ely) was 'in Maenor Crugmarchan'. Melville Richards included Peterston-super-Ely and Llanilltern within Maenor Crugmarchan, and thus a block of land on the northern side of the River Ely.[37] If this is correct, it should also have included *Lann Tilull*, namely Saint-y-Nyll (216b), which lies just to the north of Llansanffraid-ar-Elái and between it and Llanilltern.

A further contrast between early and late charters is in their use of the terms *ager*, either 'estate' or, more generally, 'land', and *uilla* (Welsh *tref*), 'farm', 'township',

[33] For possible implications of being a *tref* without a church see *WML* 51. 15–18; 128. 14–17.

[34] Including Maenordeilo and Meddyfnych; G. R. J. Jones, 'Post-Roman Wales', in *The Agrarian History of England and Wales*, i, part ii, A.D. 43–1042, ed. H. P. R. Finberg (Cambridge, 1972), 308–20. The bounds are in *LL* 77.

[35] *LL* 31, 43.

[36] G. R. J. Jones, 'Multiple Estates and Early Settlement', in P. Sawyer (ed.), *Medieval Settlement* (London, 1976), 15–40; cf. G. W. S. Barrow, *The Kingdom of the Scots*, ch. 1, 'Pre-feudal Scotland: Shires and Thanes', ch. 11, 'Rural Settlement in Central and Eastern Scotland', 233–49.

[37] *WATU* 149.

'townland'. A seventh-century group of relatively trustworthy charters is D, a collection of nine texts from Ergyng. It consists mainly of large grants, all royal, including four of three *unciae*, equivalent to thirty-six *modii*. The double significance of *ager* as, on the one hand, a particular estate and, on the other, land in general is brought out by 162a, in which Gwrfoddw, king of Ergyng, gave, in addition to the grant in 161, 'another *ager*/estate, namely an *uncia* of *ager*/land'. Apart from grants of existing churches, as opposed to grants of land to churches or to found churches, *ager* was the only term used for what was given, never *uilla*; moreover *uncia* was the only unit used in this collection to express the size of a grant. Grants of churches were somewhat different: the *uncia* was still used, but the grant was phrased to make a definite distinction between the land given and the church itself. So Gwrgan son of Cynfyn, king of Ergyng, gave the church of *Loudeu* with three *unciae* of land; he also 'gave the church of St *Budgualan* with two *unciae* and a half-*uncia* around the church'.[38] The conception of a grant of a church together with land surrounding it is common even in the tenth century, although by then the extent of the land given is much smaller.[39] In the early grants of churches with land the term *ager* is not used. There is a concern to present the primary object of the grant as the church and the surrounding land as secondary and even as physically surrounding the church itself. The church thus appears as the centre of an estate. In the other charters, the *ager* is not conceived as the centre of an estate but as the estate as a whole, and there is no other term which refers to a central settlement or building within the estate.

The next collection of charters, E, was also from Ergyng, but ninth century and so some two centuries later than D, from a period when Ergyng seems no longer to have had its own king, but was loosely dependent on Gwent.[40] This collection includes no royal grant and the average size of grant is much smaller than in D. The term *uilla* makes its appearance in 168: *Cuchein* son of Gloyw 'gave the *uilla* of the (long) valley, with its three *modii*'.[41] This is an example of the commonest size of *uilla*, the *tref* owing three *modii*, namely a single vat of ale. In other words, it was a quarter of one *uncia*. The grant is phrased more like the earlier grants of churches than the grants of *ager*: there appears to be an estate-centre 'with its three *modii*', where 'its' indicates that the land belongs to the *uilla*. This accords with the earliest meaning of Welsh *tref*, a farmhouse together with its land; the double sense (farmhouse(s) + land) persisted even when the central settlement consisted of several houses.[42]

In E, however, *ager* remained the usual term even for small estates, although in 171a the grant is phrased, exceptionally, as if the *ager* might have been an estate-centre: '*Gulferi* and *Cinuin* and *Nir*, sons of Gwrgan, and *Bonus* together with his sons gave an *ager* in uncultivated land . . . with its two *modii*.' The father of *Gulferi*,

[38] 163b, 164.

[39] 228, 230a, 231.

[40] Meurig attests 169b, a grant of Kilpeck, and 170; he is probably Meurig ab Arthfael, father of the kings of Gwent mentioned by Asser, *Life of Alfred*, c. 80.

[41] 'Long' is only in the Welsh version in the title, *Hirpant (Hirbant)*.

[42] For the fortunes of the *tref* in the twelfth and thirteenth centuries, see *EIWK* 444–6.

Cinuin, and *Nir*, namely Gwrgan, together with the same *Bonus*, made other grants in 169a: 'Gwrgan gave the part of an *ager* across the road.... And Bonus gave another *ager* from his *uncia* just as Gwrgan gave (his gift).' In both of these charters it is explicitly stated that the donors gave parts of estates.[43] Gwrgan, *Bonus* and their sons may well have been part of a kindred: the phrase 'from his *uncia*' was what suggested to Wendy Davies that *uncia* meant 'inheritance'.[44]

A still later collection is G, from Gwent and containing charters belonging to the late ninth and early tenth centuries. In this collection *ager* only occurs in the more general sense of 'land'. The standard form is exemplified by 223: 'Asser, together with his father, Marchudd, granted ... *uilla Segan* with nine *modii* of *ager*/land.' As in 168, the *uilla* appears as an estate-centre, with the land attached. The nearest approach to older forms of expression is for the largest grant in the group, 221: '*Bledruis* son of *Guollguin*, lying in a sickness which was taking him to his death, granted in honour of his burial *Cairnonui* with an *uncia* of *ager*/land and half an *uncia*, namely a half of the entire *ager* of *Cairnonui*.' Here there was an estate-centre consisting—quite exceptionally for the Llandaff charters—of a fortress, *caer*; and apparently this went with a larger appendant estate and perhaps with an unusually conservative perception of the estate. Yet, it should be remembered that, in Brittany, there are numerous examples of *ker* used for ordinary farmsteads, and, in Cornwall, for enclosed farmsteads, called 'rounds'.[45] Old Welsh *cair* is also attested among the list of prebends attached to the Life of St Cadog, where it cannot mean 'fortress', for example *Cayr i coc*, 'The Cook's *Caer*'.[46]

The late collection from Ergyng, E, may have been generally conservative in its phrasing. The period of transition in Gwent can be illustrated by eighth-century charters from the very large and long-enduring collection F. In 201 '*Conuus* son of *Iacoi* bought the church of *Gurthebiriuc* together with an *uncia* of *ager*/land and a half-*uncia* around it from King Ffernfael son of Ithael in return for an excellent horse worth eleven cows and a falcon worth twelve cows' (and various other items). The phraseology here is the same as that used for a grant of a church and land in the early collection from Ergyng, D. In 202:

> Cynwg son of *Conuil* bought the *uilla Breican* from King Ithael son of Morgan, which is known by another name as the *uilla* of *Ellgnou*, for two horses, one worth eight cows, the other worth three cows, and a sword worth twelve cows, and a (drinking) horn worth ten cows, and another worth fourteen cows.

In the bounds (given in Latin and perhaps contemporary with the grant) other, immediately adjacent, *villae* were mentioned: the *uilla* of *Guoidhearn*, the *uilla* of *Conguint*, the *uilla* of *Conlipan*, and the *uilla* of *Marchleu*. The *uilla Breican* or *uilla* of *Ellgnou* lay at the centre of a block of five *uillae*, four of which were only described as the *uilla* of a named person, while the fifth had alternative names, one

[43] When an entire estate was granted this could be stated by using the phrase *ager plenus*, 'full *ager*', as in 158 and 179c; similarly a *uilla* could be *plena*, as in 186a.

[44] See above, 276.

[45] Padel, *Cornish Place-Name Elements*, 50–4.

[46] *VSBG* § 49. See below, 605–6, for further discussion.

of which contained a personal name. A land of *uillae* is revealed in a different way in 203a, also recording both a purchase and a subsequent grant: '*Bricon* son of *Guincon* bought an *ager*/estate of three *unciae*, that is, the *uilla* of *Tancur* son of *Condu* and the *uilla* of Dewi son of *Iust* and the *uilla* of *Iliman* son of Samson' in return for (together with various horses) 'the entire clothing of one man worth fourteen cows'. An *ager* of these dimensions (equivalent to thirty-six *modii*) did not have a single named centre but was made up of *uillae*. In this example, moreover, an *uncia* was also described as a *villa*: the three *unciae* turned out to be the three *villae* of the named men.

This small group of eighth-century land purchases, including also 203b, and the seventh-century text, Llancarfan § 65, reveal several aspects of the economy as well as the society of south-eastern Wales at the time. Most evidently, there was some sort of land market, in which men of high status could buy estates from the king; but royal consent was still required for the subsequent grant, so the charters most certainly do not demonstrate a free market in land.[47] What one can say is that the king could provide a land market for his leading men: that was one source of his power. Secondly, although a range of high-value goods were used to make the purchases, they were all valued in terms of cows, something which was generally true in Wales up to the twelfth century. Whereas land was generally valued in terms of its renders, such precious goods as horses, swords, good-quality clothing, and drinking horns, the accoutrements of an aristocratic mode of life, were valued in cows. The linen garment recovered by the excavation of the royal crannog on Llangors lake would thus have been worth so many cows.[48] Cows, however, were not the only unit of exchange: we have already met silver (in so many *scripuli* or *unciae*, both units of weight); but probably cows were the most common. Gifts of garments or horses, valued in cows, might be given to secure the agreement of kinsmen and others to a purchase of land, as shown most clearly by Llancarfan § 65:

> It should be known that Gorgynnif bought Tref Rhaeadr from Meurig to be his own inheritance in exchange for a sword, the hilt of which was gilded and was worth twenty-five cows. He also bestowed on Cyngen son of Paul a horse valued at four cows, together with the value of three ounces [of silver] of clothing, and to Cynfor the son of Cyngen an excellent horse; and to *Andres* the son of Morgan a sword of the value of four cows. Likewise the same [Gorgynnif] gave the value of four cows to Idnerth son of Meurig, and one ox to Cornofan, his foster-father, and another cow to the king's steward, Gwenarth. After this purchase, therefore, Meurig and Cyngen held a document consisting of a charter on Gorgynnif's hand as a perpetual inheritance for him and for his offspring. Gorgynnif, for his part, gave this township to the church of St Cadog as a perpetual possession till the Day of Judgement, and he held the chirograph of the gift on the hand of Jacob, abbot of Nant Carfan, for the commemoration of this alms-giving in the presence of suitable witnesses, whose names are written below: Bishop Euddogwy . . . Of the laity, Meurig and

[47] Davies, *An Early Welsh Microcosm*, 51–4.

[48] H. Granger-Taylor and F. Pritchard, 'A Fine Quality Insular Embroidery from Llan-gors Crannóg, near Brecon', in M. Redknap et al., *Pattern and Purpose in Insular Art* (Oxford, 2001), 91–9.

> his sons . . . For the aforementioned Tref Rhaeadr belonged to *Mesioc* by hereditary right, and to him Gorgynnif gave a horse worth three cows, so that he might agree to this grant. Whoever should violate this, he will be cursed by God.

Meurig was probably the king of that name (he appears in § 68, where several of the same names recur), but he was far from the only person whose consent had to be bought. *Mesioc* was probably of lesser status, the actual cultivator of the land, which he had inherited, but together with subjection to men closer to the king. Gorgynnif, who appears as a witness in § 68, was probably a leading noble in the company of the king.

Part of what was involved in the change in the texts from the *ager* to the *uilla* was a shift from very large to smaller grants;[49] but this was not the only reason, as shown by the late Ergyng collection, E, in which the grants were smaller than in the earlier D group but still remained loyal to the old terminology of *uncia* and *ager*. Where *ager* appears in charters after the mid-ninth century, it tends to be for special reasons, as in 227a of the late ninth century. Here the title is *Villa Eliau*, but the text of the charter runs: '*Eliav* son of *Acheru* sacrificed an *ager* of one *modius*.' The *uilla* took its name from the donor. It may previously have formed part of a larger unit rather than forming an *ager* in the sense of an estate; at any event, in the charter it was an anonymous piece of land. In the previous chapter we met 176a with its doublet among the Llandaff charters. In one Llandaff version the *uilla* was successively described as 'the *uilla* in which is the grave of *Gurai*' and as *uilla Conuc*. The later name arose because the donor, *Conuil* son of *Gurceniu*, attached to his grant a command addressed to his son *Conuc*, namely that he and his heirs should serve the altar 'from generation to generation from that land'. This *uilla* can only have received its new name after the date of the original grant. The names of *uillae* frequently described them as 'the *uilla*/*tref* of X' where X was a named person; but they were also prone to change their names when they ceased to be significant. *Uilla Conuc* would remain significant both while he himself occupied the land and while his lineage continued to discharge their obligations from the *uilla*. An extreme case is 151a, an early charter in which a *uilla* called *uilla Gregurii*, the *uilla* of Gregorius, is also called 'The Ferry on the River Taf' or 'The Ferry at the head of the port' or 'The *uilla* of the five sons of *Ourdeueint*'.[50] A *uilla* was not necessarily a single farm currently occupied by the person whose name also served to name the *uilla*.

An *ager*, however, unlike a *uilla*, was not normally named after an individual person, whether donor, current occupant, or ancestor of a lineage in occupation.[51] It often consisted of *unciae*, a unit which itself, like the *ager*, went out of use in the ninth century. The same century may have seen the appearance of a new grouping

[49] Davies, *An Early Welsh Microcosm*, 57–8.

[50] Gregurius is a form of Gregorius with the expected *u* in place of *o*. It is not a name otherwise found in the Book of Llandaff and it may have been preserved from a period when such a Roman name was still in current use.

[51] An exception may be 176b, recording the grant of *Ager Helic* and *Ager Tencu*; the first is named after a natural feature, 'Willow Estate', but *Tencu* looks as though it is a personal name.

of *uillae*, the *maenawr*. The use of the term *uillae* or *trefi* was loosely associated with a shift to smaller grants, although not all districts changed their terminology in line with the change to smaller estates. *Uillae* were normally measured in *modii* rather than in *unciae*; and most of those so measured owed three *modii*, namely a single vat of ale. A *uilla* owing only one vat of ale was, however, essentially the *tref* of the later laws. Initially it looks, therefore, as though the most important change in the organization of estates occurred around the ninth century.

Yet these changes of terminology occurred alongside a pattern for the payment of food-renders that may already have been ancient by the time it first appears in the Llancarfan charters. The *tref* or *villa* cannot be an innovation replacing the *ager* and the *uncia*, for it was already an ancient term at the beginning of our period, as shown by comparison with Irish *treb*. The combination of changes in terminology with the continuity of the *tref* poses a problem: whether the changes of terminology were no more than that or were, perhaps, changes in the way the payment of food-renders were organized at a higher level than the single *tref* or *villa*. These questions are closely related to the topic of 'the multiple estate'. If the *maenawr*, discussed above as a grouping of *trefi*, was a multiple estate, as has been claimed, did its absence from the record before the ninth century mean that the multiple estate itself was not part of Welsh agrarian life before the ninth century?

The concept of a multiple estate embraces several characteristics, not all of which need occur together; and therefore they will not all occur together in every case. One of the main accounts of the theory presented a model of a multiple estate derived from a thirteenth-century Welsh lawbook, *Llyfr Iorwerth*, and then went on to give examples both from Wales and from England.[52] The argument maintained that something approximating to the model existed before the Anglo-Saxon settlement and was inherited by the settlers. Much further detail has been provided for England, and occasionally for Cornwall, by Rosamond Faith.[53] The description that follows seeks to include all the main characteristics in terms of, first, settlement patterns; secondly, the obligations of the population and their social status; and, thirdly, the relationship between the estate and higher political authorities.

In terms of settlement, a multiple estate has a principal centre but also satellite settlements. The satellite settlements may have specialized functions, for example in growing barley or as summer and autumn dwellings when, as commonly in Wales, herds and flocks were moved to summer pastures on 1 May and brought back to winter pastures on 1 November. This was the practice of transhumance, whose former ubiquity is revealed by place-names for 'summer-houses' and the equivalent, *hafod*, *hafoty*, *lluest*.[54] Secondly, in terms of the obligations of the population of the estate and their social status, it is commonly the case that obligations are heavier and social status lower for those housed close to the centre. Slaves are most likely to

52 Jones, 'Multiple Estates and Early Settlement'.

53 R. J. Faith, *The English Peasantry and the Growth of Lordship* (London, 1997).

54 M. Richards, '*Hafod* and *Hafoty* in Welsh Place-Names: A Semantic Study' *Montgomeryshire Collections*, 56:1 (1959), 13–20; id. '*Meifod, Lluest, Cynaeafdy* and *Hendre* in Welsh Place-Names', *Montgomeryshire Collections*, 56:2 (1960), 177–87.

exist in any numbers at or near the centre, while the periphery tends to be the home of freedom. In the latter the peasants may only owe renders of the kind we have seen most clearly in the Llancarfan charters, whereas those close to the centre, even if they were not slaves, were obliged to perform labour services. If the Welsh lord of a multiple estate had demesne land, it would be what was later called 'mensal land', *tir bwrdd*, land adjacent to the centre and devoted to supplying the lord's table with food and sometimes drink on demand, as opposed to the fixed food-renders from free peasants.[55] Thirdly, kings might alienate whole multiple estates and might expect hospitality at their centres, even when they had been alienated. The theory of the multiple estate was also linked to another argument, about 'the small shire'.[56] According to this, Britain from the Highland Line in Scotland to the English Channnel was divided into areas, often called in Latin sources *regiones*, that were smaller than the shires of late Anglo-Saxon England or the provinces of Scotland. These were the territorial units out of which kingdoms were constructed.

Welsh documents from before 1064 are not sufficient to attest all these features. That multiple estates existed in Wales is clear. One good example emerges from bounds given in Chad 6 in the Lichfield Gospels and was elucidated by Glanville Jones.[57] The territory in question is called *mainaur med diminih*, and the place-name has been identified as Meddyfnych, now Myddynfych, a farm that has recently been swallowed up by the northern suburb of the town of Ammanford.[58] Ammanford itself is a recent town, named from the ford over the River Aman. From this river northwards, for nearly five miles to the watershed before the land slopes down towards Llandeilo and the River Tywi, the land belonged to the parish of Llandybïe; and it appears that the *Maenawr Meddyfnych* embraced an area very similar to the parish. Yet the centre of the *maenawr*, namely Meddyfnych, was two and a half miles to the south of the later parish church of Llandybïe: the ecclesiastical and secular units were distinct in terms of their centres, even though they largely coincided in their boundaries. By the twelfth century, the area of *Maenawr Meddyfnych* was part of the commote of Is Cennen, the land this side of the River Cennen, one of the three commotes of Cantref Bychan, 'The Small Cantref' as distinct from Cantref Mawr, 'The Large Cantref', both *cantrefi* being part of Ystrad Tywi. The hierarchy of *tref*, *maenawr*, commote (*cwmwd*), and cantref, as set out in the thirteenth-century lawbook *Llyfr Iorwerth*, cannot be shown to go back before the eleventh century.[59] What is clear, however, is that the *maenawr* was intermediate between the *tref* or 'township' and the larger territories named in early sources, that were, by the twelfth century, either commotes or cantrefs.

A unit at this level, between *tref* and commote, might, from an early period, have its counterpart in the organization of the Church. An example is the church of Basaleg, near Newport. The name Basaleg is derived from Latin *basilica*, in Gaul a

[55] For *tir bwrdd*, see *Llyfr Iorwerth*, ed. Wiliam, 94/6, *LTMW* 125; for services and renders on demand, *Llyfr Iorwerth*, 94/9, *LTMW* 125–6.

[56] Barrow, 'Pre-Feudal Scotland: Shires and Thegns'.

[57] G. R. J. Jones, 'Post-Roman Wales', 308–11.

[58] NGR SN 629 132.

[59] *Llyfr Iorwerth*, ed. Wiliam, § 90, *LTMW* 120–2.

standard late-Roman term for a church of some importance which was not an episcopal see. Basaleg by Newport is its only appearance in Wales, and similarly Baislec in Co. Roscommon, also an early church, was its only appearance in Ireland.[60] In the thirteenth century, Basaleg was the mother-church of a large portion of the cantref of Gwynllŵg including the chapelries of St Brides Wentloog (Gwynllŵg), Coedcernyw, Machen, Bedwas, Rhisga, Henllys, and Mynyddislwyn.[61] On this basis it has been persuasively argued that Basaleg was the major church of Gwynllŵg before the rise of St Woolloos, Newport (*egglis Guunliu*, 'the church of St Gwynllyw').[62]

One difficulty with the theory is that the units of land encompassing a multiple estate seem to vary widely. At one end of the scale, the entire cantref centred on the royal court of Aberffraw in Anglesey, and divided into the two commotes of Llifon and Malltraeth, was the territorial framework for services and renders to Aberffraw itself.[63] At the other end we may place the *maenawr* of Meddyfnych, roughly one later parish within one of three commotes making up Cantref Bychan.[64] Different lordships, with the king of Gwynedd at one end of the scale and an ordinary *uchelwr* at the other end, are always likely to have engendered different geographical patterns of render and service. This difficulty has also been urged by historians of Anglo-Saxon England against the concept of 'the multiple estate' in the form in which it was developed by Jones.[65]

Another difficulty is the likelihood that many such lordships were very short-lived. If partible inheritance applied in our period to the grants made by kings to their favoured supporters, as it clearly did in the twelfth and thirteenth centuries, a lay lordship of this kind would only have lasted in its original form for a single generation.[66] Much more stable, however, would have been the lordships of the Church; and it may, therefore, be no coincidence that the good early evidence comes from such churches as Llandeilo Fawr.

Finally, too much reliance on the evidence of a thirteenth-century text, *Llyfr Iorwerth*, to provide a model then deemed to apply as much to the pre-Norman period as to the date of the text itself exposes the argument to the criticism that the territorial articulation of lordship is unlikely to have remained constant over so many centuries.[67]

The concept of the multiple estate can be defended, however, if, first, we accept that there was a pattern by which a central place with less freedom was accompanied by satellite settlements with more freedom; and, secondly, if this pattern was replicated both at the level of *regiones*, such as Arfon and Llŷn, and in the smaller

[60] C. Doherty, 'The Basilica in Early Ireland', *Peritia*, 3 (1984), 303–15.

[61] *Calendar of Patent Rolls, 1327–1330*, 507–8.

[62] J. K. Knight, 'The Early Church in Gwent, II: The Early Medieval Church', *Monmouthshire Antiquary*, 9 (1993), 9–10 and map 3; Lifris, *Vita S. Cadoci*, c. 28, ed. Wade-Evans, *VSBG* 90.

[63] Jones, 'Multiple Estates and Early Settlement', 19–24.

[64] Jones, 'Post-Roman Wales', 308–11.

[65] J. Blair, 'Frithuwold's Kingdom and the Origins of Surrey', in S. Bassett (ed.), *The Origins of Anglo-Saxon Kingdoms* (London, 1989), 104–5.

[66] *EIWK* 250–1.

[67] W. Davies, *Wales in the Early Middle Ages*, 44–6.

unit of the *maenawr*. The evidence of the documents written in the margins of the Lichfield Gospels suggests that it was.[68] A more general consideration arises from the antiquity of the food-render paid by the free: a fixed render was complemented by the variable demands that a lord could make upon more servile peasants at the centre. The agricultural use of slaves, ubiquitous in the early Middle Ages, complemented the fixed dues of the free. The word *maenawr* may not be attested before the ninth century, but such territorial units are likely to have been older. This defence, however, has conceded to the critics that the theory needs to be stated in very general terms—of the complementarity of the more extensive lordship over the free and the more intensive lordship over the unfree and of the association of the unfree with the central settlement and of the free with satellite settlements. In this form it does not assert that the pattern found in *Llyfr Iorwerth* can be applied directly to the ninth century, and it does not assert that such units as the *maenawr* were immutable.

The evidence on which to base a picture of Welsh society in the early medieval period is patchy and difficult. It is concentrated in the south and, where it relies on the Llandaff charters, it depends on texts that are demonstrably fluid and derive from the archives of churches that cannot be identified with any certainty. Yet the precious evidence of the Llancarfan charters, allied with a linguistic analysis of the terms used in the laws, is very likely to give us the key to understand how lordship over the free functioned and had functioned for many centuries. We are, however, much less well informed on lordship over the unfree.

[68] A more recent study of the *maenawr* in the Teifi valley has offered further support: J. Bezant, *Medieval Welsh Settlement and Territory: Archaeological Evidence from a Teifi Valley Landscape*, BAR, Brit. Ser. 487 (Oxford, 2009).

9

Kinship and Status

The charters in the Book of Llandaff and those appended to the Life of Cadog do not supply a sustained view of kinship but instead glimpses, some of them sources of puzzlement as much as of knowledge. The later laws offer a more rounded view, backed up by hagiography and narrative literature, none of which is earlier than the late eleventh century with the probable exception of the prose tale *Culhwch and Olwen*.[1] On the other hand the charters need to be interpreted in the light of an understanding of early Welsh kinship. The *uncia*, to take one example, has been understood to have meant, at an early stage, 'an heir's portion',[2] but that does not reveal the pattern of inheritance by which land was transmitted down the generations. Similarly, the fortunes of both the *ager*, 'estate', and the *uilla* or *tref* were determined by inheritance: *Conloc*'s estate, the *ager Conloc* of four *unciae*, was granted by Peibio son of Erb, king of Ergyng; among the lay witnesses were '*Conloc*'s heirs', *heredes Conloc*.[3] Again, however, such a charter did not need to state the rules by which it was determined that one person was *Conloc*'s heir and another was not.

It is risky to interpret the fragmentary but mostly early evidence of the charters with the help of the more forthcoming laws and hagiography, for they may be up to five centuries later in date. The risk is that such a strategy will lead us to underestimate the importance of the changes that occurred in the meantime. Yet the danger can be lessened by seeking those elements in the later evidence that can reasonably be argued to be early.

1. THE GENERAL CHARACTER OF EARLY WELSH KINSHIP

The broad picture that the later evidence suggests can be defined by two contrasts: first, between the kinship of inheritance and the kinship of status and alliance; and secondly between the 'co-heirs', an agnatic lineage of only four generations in depth, and the larger and deeper lineage known as the *cenedl*. By 'deeper' is meant 'containing more generations' (for example, the descendants in the male line of a great-great-great-grandfather would form a deeper lineage than the descendants of a great-grandfather). The crucial starting point implied by the first contrast is that there was no single pattern of kinship that obtained for all aspects of life. The

[1] See below, 654. [2] Davies, '*Unciae*', 119. [3] *LL* 76a.

kinship that influenced the choice of allies was not the same kinship that determined the rules of inheritance. Anyone, therefore, who seeks to discover a single Welsh kinship system has already been diverted on to a road that leads only to confusion and oversimplification. If the truth is that there were several kinships rather than a single kinship, an attempt to find the one Welsh kinship system will encourage an undue prominence to be given to that one form at the expense of the others.

The kinship of inheritance is intimately connected with one term of the other contrast, the co-heirs as opposed to the wider *cenedl*.[4] I have described the co-heirs as a shallow agnatic lineage of four generations; by that I mean that the descendants, through males (and thus 'agnatic'), of a single man as far as his great-grandsons were the co-heirs. The lineage was named after the single common ancestor (the first generation) and comprised his sons (the second generation), grandsons (the third), and finally great-grandsons (the fourth). For the purposes of inheritance it worked in generations. First, the sons shared the inheritance of their father equally; then, if they so wished, the grandsons reshared; and, finally, again if they so wished, so did the great-grandsons. If a man died before the sharing in his generation took place, his sons stepped into his shoes. On the one hand, therefore, there was the regular partition among the sons; and, on the other, the optional resharing by grandsons and great-grandsons. The sharing that was both more common and more noticed was the regular sharing by the sons. Because it had this strongly generational character, the group of co-heirs only lasted for one generation in its original shape.

The *cenedl*, however, was a deeper lineage, again agnatic, but now existing for the discharge of hereditary obligations, the enjoyment of hereditary privileges and entitlements, for mutual support and political weight, rather than for sharing the inheritance. It had a *pencenedl*, 'chief of kindred', who had the right to discipline his kinsmen and enjoyed exceptionally high status.[5] The *cenedl*, like the co-heirs, was an agnatic lineage, since the issue of whether someone belonged to it turned on paternity. Only sometimes, in special circumstances, could the son of a woman of the *cenedl* be admitted. Moreover, since paternity decided membership, it also decided who was and who was not a member of the shallower lineage of four generations, the co-heirs. A person whose putative father successfully denied his paternity would be member of neither the father's *cenedl* nor his group of co-heirs, for the one test—is this boy the child of this father?—would decide both questions. The co-heirs seem to have been conceived as a land-sharing group within the *cenedl* rather than anything wholly different.

An informative hagiographical view of the *cenedl* and the *pencenedl* is offered by an anecdote appended to the Life of St Cadog (it comes after the charters and it is separated from the last charter by a gap).[6] A briefer version of the story is given in

[4] For the evidence for the co-heirs see *EIWK* 211–15.

[5] There is a suggestion that the *cenedl* may have had other officers, or perhaps merely recognized roles, in a triad in two Cyfn MSS: 'Three indispensable persons of the *cenedl*: the *pencenedl* and its avenger and its representative in pleadings' (*Mk* 81 = *U* 48), *The Legal Triads*, ed. Roberts, 86–7.

[6] Life of Cadog, § 69. H. D. Emanuel, 'An Analysis of the Composition of the "Vita Cadoci"', *National Library of Wales Journal*, 7 (1951-2), 221–2, regards this version in § 69 as later, on what

the Life itself:[7] the anecdote itself may not be older than Lifris's Life, although it could well be the source of the version of the story in the Life; in that case the substance of the tale was older. The main Life has stories about Arthur, Maelgwn, and Rhun, all designed to show the saint's power over even the greatest of kings. In particular they demonstrated the authority of Cadog's sanctuary or 'place of protection', *noddfa*, confirmed even by such warlords from Gwynedd and further afield, far from Llancarfan. To understand the story we must bear in mind that St Cadog's father was Gwynllyw, who gave his name to Gwynllŵg (older Gwynllywg), the *cantref* stretching back from the sea between Cardiff and Newport, between the Taf, the Usk, its tributary, the Ebbw, and the ridge on the east side of Glyn Ebbw. Cadog's grandfather was Glywys, thought to have given his name to Glywysing, sometimes an old name of Glamorgan, but also sometimes a dynastic name for Gwent in the sense by which it also embraced Glamorgan. Gwynllyw was the eldest son of Glywys and so gave his name to the leading region or *cantref* in Glamorgan, namely Gwynllŵg; he was king of all Glamorgan but allowed his younger brothers sub-kingships or lordships in the other *cantrefi*. One of them, for example, was the *Gurai* believed to have given his name to the cantref of Gwrinydd (*Guorinid*) and it was his tomb that was commemorated in *LL* 176 and its doublet, 190b, as well as being linked in 176 with the name of a hill, *mons Gurai*.

According to the story, Maelgwn, king of Gwynedd and overlord of all Wales, imposed by force a tribute of a hundred cows and a hundred calves on every district. His tribute-gatherers, *exactores*, arrived to gather the tribute from Gwynllŵg but were distracted from their task by the spectacle of a most beautiful girl, whom they promptly bore off. Her kinsfolk, however, avenged the deed by catching up with them and killing three hundred, leaving only one survivor to take the news to Maelgwn.[8] He sent his messenger to demand from Cadog the wergild for the slain tribute-gatherers. Cadog replied that he would pay nothing under threat, but only after proper judgement. The king refused to submit to judgement, in spite of warnings from St Meugan, was miraculously blinded, and forced to negotiate terms with St Cadog.

For us the terms are what is interesting. Cadog demanded, first, a *refugium*, 'refuge' in the technical sense of a *noddfa*, area of protection or sanctuary, for the *ciuitas*, 'city', of Gwynllŵg—'city' referring, as commonly in early Irish sources, to a major monastery.[9] As in the Irish examples, the concept of a *ciuitas refugii* was taken from the Old Testament.[10] The *noddfa* was to be as good as that enjoyed by

grounds is unclear to me; cf. J. K. Knight, 'Sources for the Early History of Morgannwg', in H. N. Savory *Glamorgan County History*, gen. ed. G. Williams, ii, *Early Glamorgan* (Cardiff, 1984), 385–9.

[7] Life of Cadog, § 23.

[8] Cf. A. O. H. Jarman, *Gododdin*, ll. 243, 245, 551–2, 865–78.

[9] On ecclesiastical sanctuary in Wales, see H. Pryce, *Native Law and the Church in Medieval Wales* (Oxford, 1993), 163–203, especially 168–74, and below, 601–3.

[10] C. Doherty, 'The Monastic Town in Early Medieval Ireland', in H. B. Clarke and Anngret Simms (eds.), *The Comparative History of Urban Origins in Non-Roman Europe*, BAR International Ser. 255 (Oxford, 1985), 45–75, esp. 57–60.

St David's monastery at Mynyw: the implication was that the *noddfa* of Mynyw was so extensive and well protected as to supply a standard to which others would aspire. Maelgwn then made an agreement of mutual support between his lineage and Cadog's kindred of Gwynllŵg. Cadog's response was to declare to Maelgwn his 'tradition', namely that every noble of his kindred should have a wergild of 450 cows (an outrageously high figure). Among the other demands made by Cadog were three concerning the chief of his kindred, the *pencenedl*:

(1) If anyone of my lineage should have been arrested without the consent of his chief of kindred, let him (the arrester) release him unharmed together with his property. If, however, he is arrested with the consent of his chief of kindred, let him be held in custody, until he (the chief of kindred) has released him.

(2) Let no tribute be paid to the king from my lineage, except for a contribution of livestock after the end of seven years;[11] and let the chief of kindred keep for himself a third part, and let him deliver to the king the other two parts.

(3) If anyone should have injured the chief of kindred of Gwynllŵg, or if he has shed his blood, let no compensation be paid except in land and gold and animals.

Whoever wrote this story was concerned to claim special exemptions from tribute for Gwynllŵg: no annual tax and no *exactores*, but instead an aid or contribution every seven years to be delivered by the chief of kindred. He was also concerned, however, to exalt the office of chief of kindred as well as the status of the nobles of the kindred.

The kindred of this story is evidently the wider kindred, the *cenedl*, headed by the *pencenedl*. It is identified as Gwynllŵg, the lineage of Gwynllyw, Cadog's father; Cadog himself was celibate and had no descendants, but the saint was so far identified with his father's offspring that he could be made to speak unhesitatingly of Gwynllŵg as his own lineage, as if it were descended from him. Although the story purports to be about Cadog and thus about the generation of Gwynllyw's children, in reality it is about a later period when there was a *cenedl* descended from Gwynllyw, which in Cadog's day there was not. This later period was one in which Gwynllŵg was both a *cenedl* with a *pencenedl* and also a district, *pagus*, with defined boundaries. The two were combined: if a member of Gwynllŵg, the lineage, were to buy land in Glywysing or Gwent outside the boundaries of Gwynllŵg, the district, he might hold it as a perpetual inheritance but was to pay the king the value of the land and render the normal tribute; within Gwynllŵg no tribute was due.[12] Llancarfan itself was in Penychen, not Gwynllŵg, and thus the people of Penychen

[11] This may be an extreme claim based on the customary due later known as *cymorth* (*commorth*), 'joint aid', which was common in much of South Wales and was often based on a three-year cycle: W. Rees, *South Wales and the March, 1284–1415: A Social and Agrarian Study* (Oxford, 1924), 229–33.

[12] Cf. Life of Cadog, § 25.

benefited from Cadog's agreement with Maelgwn.[13] Yet the *refugium*, the *noddfa*, was described as being preserved in the *graphium*, 'charter', of his (Cadog's) lineage, Gwynllŵg.[14] They also, and not just the people of Penychen, enjoyed Cadog's special protection. This identification of a *cenedl*, headed by a *pencenedl*, with a district is attested later in thirteenth-century Powys, where the *pencenedl* of Cegidfa (modern Guilsfield) presided over the Cadelling of Cegidfa, a kindred that claimed descent from the old ruling family of Powys.[15]

Both the *cenedl* and the co-heirs were kindreds of the land, the *cenedl* at a more political level, as the dominant lineage of a district, the co-heirs at the more local level of the lands shared out among sons, grandsons, and great-grandsons. In terms of the other contrast, the kinship of land as opposed to the kinship of status and alliance, the co-heirs stood at one extreme while the *cenedl*, because of its more political role, was nearer the centre. In terms of forms of kinship, however, both were contrasted with the kinship of alliance, as illustrated by one of Maelgwn's concessions to that hardest of bargainers, St Cadog:[16]

> King Maelgwn made an eternal agreement with St Cadog and with his successors (as abbots of Llancarfan), saying, 'If any members of my kindred should break this agreement, he shall be accursed. Everyone who remains of my kindred shall assist your kindred of Gwynllŵg like a uterine brother.'

Someone's uterine brother—half-brother by the same mother but with a different father—was not his co-heir; he was not a member of the same *cenedl*; he could not, therefore, be a competitor for any office attached to the *cenedl*; and, if he was of royal descent, he could not be a competitor for the same kingship. Yet his relationship was a form of kinship which promised alliance. The kinship of alliance was not, therefore, agnatic, like the kinship of land and inheritance, but bilateral, reckoned through both males and females.

The alliance between Maelgwn's kindred and that of Gwynllŵg was indeed between agnatic lineages, but it was to be as if they were uterine brothers, the closest possible relationship for men solely through women. A similar assumption about the bilateral kinship of alliance is betrayed at the beginning of the earliest Welsh prose tale, *Culhwch and Olwen*. Culhwch was the son of Celyddon, a king, and of Goleuddydd, 'Bright Day', herself the daughter of another king, Anflawdd. Her sister, Eigr, was mother to King Arthur. When Culhwch's stepmother fixed a fate upon Culhwch that his body would never touch a woman until he won Olwen, daughter of the giant Ysbaddaden, his father came to the rescue:[17] '"You can obtain that easily, my son," said his father to him. "Arthur is your first-cousin."' The kinship between Culhwch and Arthur was solely through females. Yet its function was slightly different from that of the relationship between Maelgwn's

13 Life, § 24. It may be important that Penychen, 'head of oxen', was not a name derived from a kindred.

14 Cf. Pryce, *Native Law and the Church*, 171.

15 *EIWK* 205–6.

16 *Vita S. Cadoci*, § 69.

17 *Culhwch and Olwen*, ed. R. Bromwich and D. Simon Evans (Cardiff, 1992), p. 3, ll. 56–8.

kindred and Gwynllŵg. There the alliance was between agnatic kindreds; here it helps one individual who can rely on the power of his mother's sister's son.

Marriage was one of the principal means by which an alliance might be created or reinforced between two kindreds. One of 'the three things common to a kindred' was 'the son of a woman given [in marriage] by gift of kin to their enemy. It is right for that child to be common between the two kindreds'.[18] The plot of *Branwen* concerns one such event, when Matholwch, king of Ireland, comes to Britain seeking the hand of Branwen, sister of Bendigeidfran, king of Britain, 'the Island of the Mighty', so as to *ymgyfathrachu*, 'mutually-inter-lineage', with Brân and thus 'bind the Island of the Mighty with Ireland so that they may be stronger'.[19] Marriage as a source of kinship may have taken more than one form, even when it was a union by betrothal and gift of kin. In Old Welsh *dauu* (*dawf* 'son-in-law') glosses *cliens*, 'client', and it is likely that it had a double meaning, both 'son-in-law' and 'client'.[20] This probably adds to the irony by which Ysbaddaden describes Culhwch as 'the material of my son-in-law' and subsequently as *anwar dawf* 'undutiful son-in-law'.[21] At least one form of marriage seems to have implied that the bridegroom would become the client of his father-in-law.

An extension of the kinship of alliance was fosterage; and here, too, there may have been a subordinating variety alongside another which had no such consequence.[22] Fosterage was by far the most important form of artifical kinship as opposed to natural kinship in the Celtic countries. In England and in Francia, on the other hand, god-parenthood, spiritual kinship, had already come to play a major role in the conversion period, the sixth and seventh centuries.[23] On the other hand, fosterage is much less prominent in early Welsh sources, especially the laws, than in their Irish counterparts. The reason may be that, in Ireland, fosterage belonged to the formal legal structure of society: it was governed by contract and it usually entailed a payment or payments by the natural parents to the foster-parents. Like other contractual pairs—lord and client, husband and wife—fosterage received an entire legal tract to itself.[24] In the Welsh laws there is only the occasional side-glimpse, as when we are told that, if a noble's son was put out to fosterage with a villein with the consent of the latter's lord, the noble's son was entitled to share in the division of that villein's inheritance with his natural sons.[25] This is evidently stated as an exception to a more general rule, namely that fosterage did not confer rights of inheritance.

[18] *WML* 140. 7–10.

[19] *PKM* 30.

[20] Among the Old Welsh glosses on Ovid, *Ars Amatoria*, Bk. 1, in 'St Dunstan's Classbook': J. C. Zeuss and H. Ebel, *Grammatica Celtica*, 2nd edn. (Berlin, 1871), 1055; *EIWK* 85.

[21] *Culhwch and Olwen*, ed. Bromwich and Evans, ll. 518, 525, 540, 553.

[22] P. Parkes, 'Celtic Fosterage', *Comparative Studies in Society and History*, 48: 2 (2006), 359–94.

[23] J. H. Lynch, *Godparents and Kinship in Early Medieval Europe* (Princeton, NJ, 1986).

[24] F. Kelly, *A Guide to Early Irish Law* (Dublin, 1988), 86–90, 270 (no. 19).

[25] *WML* 51. 19–22; Ior, 94/10; *LTMW* 126.

Enough evidence survives from the twelfth century to show that fosterage was then a widespread and politically influential form of artificial kinship.[26] It is evident, in particular, that the initial agreement made between foster-parents and natural parents usually engendered strong ties between foster-parents and foster-children and between all children, whether fosterlings or natural children, cared for by one couple. That the last relationship was of great antiquity, stretching back through the early medieval period and beyond, is confirmed by the semantic history of *aillt*, initially meaning 'someone fostered', and, more particularly, *cyfaill* 'friend' from earlier *cyfaillt* 'someone fostered together with someone else': my *cyfaillt* was someone fostered, *aillt*, along with me. It is difficult to know whether it had already acquired its secondary meaning of 'friend' by the eleventh century: an oath in *Culhwch and Olwen* might be sworn 'by the hand of my friend', *vyng kyueillt*, but it could also be translated 'by the hand of my fosterbrother'.[27] Similarly, the simple word *aillt* meant a client in the early poem, *Y Gododdin*, one 'mead-reared' in the hall of a king, but by the twelfth century could be equated with a villein, one of several examples from the language of early Welsh society of terms moving down the ladder of status.[28] In this way the compound, *cyfaillt* parted company with the simplex, *aillt*, so that by the twelfth century a Welsh speaker would probably have had difficulty in saying why a *cyfaill(t)* was a *cyf-aillt*. For our purposes, *cyfaill* has a double value: it confirms what one would in any case strongly suspect from twelfth-century Welsh evidence in conjunction with eighth-century Irish sources, that fosterage was widespread and influential in our period; but it also shows that fosterage was a sufficiently important source of alliances between individuals to give rise to the ordinary word for a friend by the eleventh century. The reason why fosterage was less prominent in Welsh than in Irish law cannot, therefore, be because it was less significant an institution; it may be, as has been suggested, because it belonged more to an informal sphere of social arrangements; it may also be for a more accidental reason, that Welsh law described suretyship in detail—the means by which formal contracts were made and established—but stopped there rather than, as in Irish law, going on to describe in equal detail the workings of particular human relationships established by contract.

Ecclesiastical sources add another dimension: the parallel between foster-father and foster-son, on the one hand, and teacher and pupil on the other. Again, it is not so evident in Welsh as in Irish sources that the relationship of master and pupil was seen as a form of fosterage, except that *athro* 'teacher' originally meant 'foster-father'.[29] In Ireland, as early as the seventh century, it was assumed that a cleric or monk might foster a child, especially but not exclusively a child destined for the

26 Gerald of Wales, *Descriptio Kambriae*, ii. 4, ed. J. F. Dymock, *Giraldi Cambrensis Opera*, vi, Rolls Series (London, 1868), 211–12.

27 *Culhwch and Olwen*, ed. Bromwich and Evans, ll. 134, 957.

28 Jarman, *Gododdin*, ll. 381 (= Williams, *Gododdin*, 397), 704 (= Williams, *Gododdin*, 918), 933 (= Williams, *Gododdin*, 1198). R. G. Gruffydd, *Edmyg Dinbych*, 16, 19, l. 24, and see below 664 (where 'yeomen' translates *eillon*, the plural of *aillt*).

29 This is more fully discussed below, 603.

priesthood or monastic life.[30] It was also assumed from the same date that the pre-Christian religious and learned role of druid had also, in the past, made men suitable to act as fosterers.[31] The same broad conception of the teacher as fosterer may well lie behind aspects of early Welsh education. The Lives of Welsh saints perceived education not so much as attending a school, though that is found in Wales as in Ireland, but as being put into the care of a particular teacher.[32] It was an arrangement between the teacher and the natural parents by which the child came to live with the teacher and received instruction. For children of high status it was probably understood in Wales as in Ireland that some children should have more than one set of foster-parents and thus more than one set of alliances engendered by fosterage: at the end of *Pwyll Pendefig Dyfed*, Pwyll says to Teyrnon, who has up till then cared for his son, Pryderi, that 'because you have reared him until now, we shall give him in fosterage to Pendaran Dyfed'.[33] The assumption hidden behind the conjunction 'because' must be that a royal child needed more than one alliance through fosterage, and that this was sufficiently important to override the considerable pain the parting entailed for Teyrnon and his wife. Teachers appear to have taken pupils from the age of seven onwards, so that they could well have gone to ordinary foster-parents before that age. Similarly, it was taken for granted in Wales, as in Ireland, that a pupil could go from one teacher to another. Multiple teachers could be seen as multiple fosterers.

A hagiographical story preserved in the ninth-century *Historia Brittonum* shows that there was another source of artificial kinship apart from fosterage; but it also offers an example of a teacher who was seen as a foster-parent.[34] This second form of artificial kinship was divided in liturgical texts of the period (not from Wales) into two forms: *capillatoria* 'hair-cutting' and *barbatoria* 'beard-cutting', namely of the first hair of the infant and the first beard of the adolescent.[35] Both rites were derived from the Roman Empire and are well attested in early medieval Francia and Italy but not in Ireland or England. They are symptoms of the Roman past shared by Wales with continental Europe west of the Rhine, but not with its neighbours within the British Isles.

In the *Historia Brittonum*, Vortigern, king of the Britons, was perceived not just as wicked, as the man who through lust for Hengest's daughter gave Kent to the English, but also as pagan.[36] A leading instance of his iniquity was that he committed incest with his own daughter and so fathered Faustus, subsequently a monk and a saint:[37]

30 Adomnán, *Life of Saint Columba*, ii. 1, 25; iii. 4; Tírechán, *Collectanea*, 14. 6; 18. 1; 48. 3.

31 Tírechán, *Collectanea*, 19. 1; 26. 17–19.

32 *Vita Prima S. Samsonis*, i. 7; *Vita S. Cadoci*, § 6; *Vita S. Dauid*, § 11.

33 *Pedeir Keinc y Mabinogi*, ed. I. Williams (Cardiff, 1932), 27; cf. Tírechán, *Collectanea*, 26. 5; *EIWK* 79–80.

34 *Historia Brittonum*, ed. Faral, c. 39, taken together with c. 48.

35 *EIWK* 180–1.

36 He had *magi*, *Historia Brittonum*, ed. Faral, cc. 40–2, and refused to be converted by St Germanus, ibid. c. 47.

37 Ibid. c. 39. For the real Faustus see above, 199–202.

> Adding yet another to all his iniquities, Vortigern took his own daughter as his wife, and she bore him a son. And when this was discovered by St Germanus, he came together with all the British clergy to rebuke him. When a great synod of clergy and laymen had been assembled in a single council, the king instructed his daughter beforehand that she should go to the meeting and should place her son in Germanus's lap and should say that he (Germanus) was the father of her son; and the woman did as she had been instructed. Germanus, however, received him (the child) kindly and began to speak: 'I shall be a father to you and I shall not send you away, unless a razor together with scissors and a comb be given to me and it be permitted to you to give them to your father according to the flesh.' And the boy heard him and went to his grandfather—his father according to the flesh—and said to him, 'You are my father: crop my head and the hair of my head.' And he (Vortigern) fell silent and kept his mouth shut and was unwilling to reply to the boy, but he got up in a great rage and fled from the sight of St Germanus; and he was accursed and condemned by St Germanus and by the entire council of the Britons.

Here St Germanus uses the razor, scissors, and comb to set up a miraculous, and also highly dramatic, condemnation of the wicked king. What Vortigern had intended was turned on its head. The premiss of the holy man's words was, however, that a natural father should, in the ordinary course of events, perform the ritual action of cutting the first hair of his child's head. Vortigern was not just convicted by the child's words but also by the child's actions. According to a later passage, St Germanus subsequently baptized the boy, Faustus, fostered him, and educated him.[38] He was the boy's godfather *qua* baptizer, his foster-father, and his teacher. Once Vortigern had refused to acknowledge his son by performing the rite of cutting the first hair of the newly born child, Germanus replaced him as father.

This passage needs to be compared with another, this time in *Culhwch and Olwen*. When Culhwch had arrived at Arthur's court on New Year's day, and had secured entry to the king's hall in spite of the initial refusal of the porter to admit him, he addressed to Arthur an extraordinarily bold and rhetorically assertive speech. Its purpose was to secure from Arthur a promise that he might have the special annual gift, *cyfarws*, granted in the laws to the king's *teulu*, but that he himself should specify what it should be.[39] What he wanted ultimately was that Arthur should promise to secure for him Olwen, daughter of Ysbaddaden Chief-Giant; but that was not what he asked for first. At the end of his speech, when he had already been promised the status of a royal heir-apparent in Arthur's court and had threatened to proclaim Arthur's dishonour as far as his fame had gone before, that is, to the four corners of the world, what he asked for was that Arthur should trim his hair.[40] Arthur took a golden comb and scissors with silver loops and began to comb the hair of his head; and Arthur said, 'My heart grows tender towards you. I know that you come of my blood. Say who you are.' One of the many humorous elements in this passage is that Culhwch should have identified himself long since.

[38] *Historia Brittonum*, ed. Faral, c. 48.

[39] For the *cyfarws*, see *WML* 10. 15, Ior § 6/15, Charles-Edwards, Owen, and Russell (eds.), *The Welsh King and His Court*, 564.

[40] *Culhwch and Olwen*, ed. Bromwich and Evans, pp. 6–7.

He had received such an extraordinarily deferential welcome in Arthur's court because of the sheer élan of his approach and because he was exceptionally handsome—more handsome than anyone the far-travelled and middle-aged porter, Glewlwyd Gafaelfawr, had ever seen. He had been accepted on his own valuation because of the externals of his appearance; but now Arthur sensed that he was his kinsman and Culhwch was finally induced to say who he was. By this strategy Culhwch confirmed Arthur's open-ended promise. Culhwch could now rely not just on the impact of appearances coupled with self-assertion but upon kinship and something more: Arthur had cut the hair of his head. The European parallels, together with the evidence of the *Historia Brittonum*, show that this was a rite which made a child or youth into the son of the person performing the rite—very much as if he were a foster-son, not entitled to inherit but otherwise with the right to every support. The rite had this effect because, as assumed by the *Historia Brittonum*, it was regularly performed by the natural father.

In these two passages there are enough clues to show that such cutting of the hair of a baby or a youth was a rite of passage as well as an assertion of paternity, natural or artificial. In one case, that of Faustus, the child was newly born; in the other, Culhwch was on the borders of young manhood and was newly anxious to marry. In the early medieval liturgical collections of blessings, there were two, one for the rite of passage of a child and the other for the youth: in *capillatoria* the first hair of an infant's head was cut, regularly by the natural father, occasionally by an artificial father; in *barbatoria* the newly grown beard (*barba*) of a youth was trimmed for the first time.[41] When the future emperor Nero underwent the old Roman form of the rite, the hair that had been cut from the beard was placed in a box and taken to the Capitol.[42] *Barbatoria* was a rite of passage which marked entry into adult sexuality; in Culhwch's case, the cutting of his hair by Arthur followed hard upon the awakening of his sexuality by the stepmother's fixing of his fate: 'The boy blushed and love of the girl entered into every limb of his body, although he had never seen her.'[43]

Yet it is far from clear that a Welsh audience of the eleventh century would have understood all the niceties of *barbatoria* and *capillatoria*. First, at Culhwch's stage of life, the correct rite should have been *barbatoria*, the cutting of the beard; and yet it is described as if it were *capillatoria*, the cutting of the hair of the head. Also, it is not entirely clear that it functioned to make Arthur a ritual father as opposed to being a way of claiming natural kinship and thus the duty of giving support that such kinship entailed. In the *Historia Brittonum* it is certain that Germanus became Faustus's artificial father, but it is quite uncertain whether that was because he baptized him, cut his hair, fostered him, or all three. It is even uncertain whether, when Vortigern fled from the council, Germanus proceeded to cut the child's hair

[41] J. Deshusses, *Le Sacramentaire Grégorien. Ses principales formes d'après les plus anciens manuscrits. Étude comparative*, Spicilegium Friburgense, xvi, xxiv, xxviii (Freiburg/Schw., 1971–82), i. 339–40; A. Franz, *Die kirklichen Benedictionen im Mittelalter* (Freiburg im Breisgau, 1990), ii. 245–52 (die Haarschur) and 253–7 (die Bartschur); *EIWK* 180.

[42] Suetonius, *Nero*, 12. 4.

[43] *Culhwch and Olwen*, ed. Bromwich and Evans, ll. 52–3.

because his natural father had refused to do so. Perhaps it is best to conclude that Germanus's relationship with Faustus appealed at one stage or another to all forms of artificial parenthood, even that of a teacher. At least there is quite enough to show that the two rites of cutting the hair of the head and cutting the hair of the beard were inherited by the Britons from the time when they were citizens of Rome, even if, by the eleventh century, it had become a vague memory.

Although this element of Welsh kinship was inherited from Rome, most of the rest was apparently Celtic. The evidence bears principally on the co-heirs, the agnatic lineage of four generations, which shared, and optionally reshared, the inheritance. The limit of four generations was not only decisive in the sphere of inheritance of land. In the later laws it was the point at which possession of land was converted into proprietorship, *priodolder*; for an alien, an *alltud*, who was attached to a lord, it was the point at which optional attachment was converted into permanently inheritable subjection. These aspects of the limit of four generations all hang together as aspects of inheritance. They tend to look at the kindred from the top down, from the common ancestor seen as the starting point down to his great-grandsons. With the great-grandsons, sharing of his inheritance came to an end; if he was a non-proprietor his great-grandson became a proprietor; if he and his descendants were aliens attached to a lord and his descendants, his great-grandson would become indissolubly attached to the first lord's great-grandson.

There was, however, another way of looking at the same lineage, from the point of view of one of the great-grandsons rather than of the common ancestor.[44] The person from whose standpoint we shall now look at his fellow co-heirs we shall call 'ego' (Latin for 'I'). His terms for his fellow co-heirs were as follows (putting Welsh first and comparing Welsh terms with those in Breton and Irish):[45]

Table 9.1. Terms for cousins

	1st cousin	2nd	3rd	4th
Welsh	*cefnderw*	*cyferderw*	*ceifn*	*gorcheifn*
Breton	*qenderv compès*	*qevenderv*	*qeffnyand*	*bugale ar gueffnyanded*
Irish	*derbfine*		*fine*	

The starting point of all the Welsh and Breton terms is represented by *ceifn*, which probably began by meaning 'joint grandson/descendant'. *Cefnderw* began as *ceifn* qualified by the adjective *derw*, 'certain, definite, true'. The Breton *qenderv* and *qevenderv* are forms cognate with *cefnderw*. In spite of the passage of time from the late Roman and post-Roman period when British settlers came to dominate north-

[44] For what follows, see *EIWK* 190–3.

[45] The Breton terms are taken from Grégoire de Rostreven, *Dictionnaire français–breton* (Rennes, 1732); the terms are given in his orthography, not in a modern standard spelling.

west Gaul until the time when all these terms are recorded (in Welsh in the thirteenth century, in Breton not until the eighteenth century), they reveal that the distinctions between first and second, and between third and fourth cousins are relatively recent. These distinctions are made in different ways in Welsh and Breton, whereas the distinction between first and second cousins taken together, and third and fourth cousins taken together, is the same in Welsh and Breton. In both cases it was a distinction (using Welsh words) between *ceifn derw* (> *cefnderw*) for the first and second cousins and plain *ceifn* for the third and fourth cousins. The adjective *derw* distinguished the closer cousins, first and second, from the more remote, third and fourth. In the Irish terms, *fine* means both 'kindred' and 'kinsman' or 'kinswoman', while *derb* is cognate with Welsh *derw*, Breton *derv*. The point at which a cousin ceases to be *derw* in Welsh or *derv* in Breton is the same as the point dividing a *derb* kinsman from a non-*derb* kinsman in Irish. In Irish, however, there was no distinction between first and second cousins, nor between third and fourth cousins. From this comparison it can be inferred that the limit marked by the word *derw* and its cognates had remained the same since remote pre-Roman antiquity. On the other hand, distinctions between cousins other than at the limit between the second and the third cousin may have been post-Roman: they can only have been earlier if the innovation by which each cousin as far as the fourth was given a separate name occurred when, in Roman Britain, a dialect distinction had grown up between southern or south-west British and west British.

Beyond the fourth cousin there cease to be any Breton cognates for terms found in the Welsh laws.[46] That limit also corresponds to the outer limit of recognized kinship in early Irish law. The extension of the outer limit to fifth and finally sixth cousin found only in Welsh may be due to three influences in combination: the extension, from the seventh to the tenth century, of those kin prohibited from marrying in canon law; the tendency in border areas, and subsequently more widely, for the wider kindred recognized for the payment of the wergild in Anglo-Saxon England to be acknowledged at least as a theoretical possibility in Welsh law; and finally the existence of the much deeper lineage, the *cenedl*, within which such wider collateral kin would be included. In one term there may be a borrowing from Old English. The evidence that exists, therefore, points to these changes as occurring in the period between the fourth and the eleventh century.

2. THE EVIDENCE OF THE CHARTERS

The usual purpose of the charters is to commemorate an individual's grant of land to a church. Any role of the kindred, whether of the donor or belonging to the church, was normally relegated to the background.[47] Nevertheless there is a fair spread of evidence scattered through the Book of Llandaff, and also, rather more densely, in the Cadog charters.

[46] For the basis for the arguments in this paragraph, see *EIWK* 191–4.
[47] Davies, *An Early Welsh Microcosm*, 55–6.

Where individual relatives appear, they were generally sons, brothers, or fathers.[48] To identify someone as 'son of X' is common, but it is not normal in the Llandaff witness lists. Occasionally, however, small groups of kinsmen are attested. In the second half of the eighth century, *Aguod* son of Ieuaf had a quarrel with Bishop Cerenhir.[49] The households of both men seemed to have joined in with gusto, even if they were not responsible for beginning the affair. Finally *Aguod* came to the door of the church, hurled stones against it in token of his anger, and departed in flight pursued by ecclesiastical anathemas. For this insult to a sacred building *Aguod* paid heavily: he was induced to grant the *uilla* of *Penn Onn* with its church, *Lann Tilull*, and with three *modii* of land and three *modii* of wheat. Among the witnesses were *Aguod*'s son, Idnerth, and his brother, Briafael.[50] Another son, Owain, appears as a witness in a slightly later charter.[51] The group thus revealed was as follows:

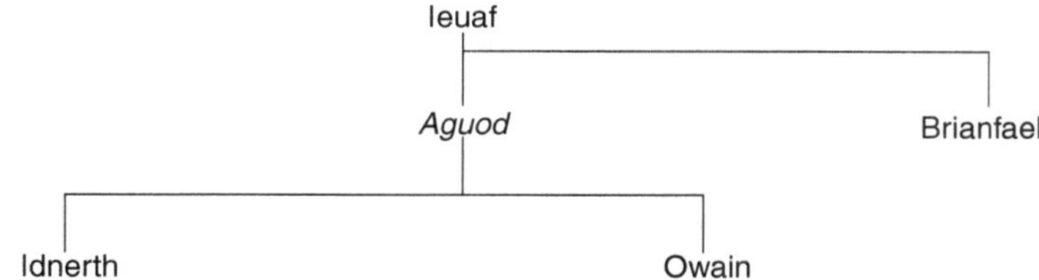

Figure 9.1. The kindred of Ieuaf

The same tendency of a man to be associated with brothers and sons, as well as a father, is found among kings. In 191, Iddon son of Ceirio bought a *uilla* from Ithael, king of Glywysing, and from his sons, Ffernfael, Meurig, and Rhodri. In the witness list, Ithael heads the laymen, followed by four of his sons, Arthfael, Meurig, Rhodri, and Rhys.

Any direct evidence for partible inheritance is confined to an undatable story about Merthyr Clydog, namely Clodock in Ewias. A reasonably straightforward charter concerning Merthyr Clydog, 195, is preceded and followed by hagiographical narratives, one (193) about the martyrdom of King Clydog, the place his body found a rest, and its refoundation, while the other (196) told a not very edifying tale on the embarrassing consequences of a married couple choosing to have open-air sex on a Sunday as they were on their way to hear divine service at Merthyr Clydog.[52]

[48] Ibid. 111.

[49] *LL* 216b. For the date, Davies, *Llandaff Charters*, 119–20.

[50] I take Briafael to have been *Aguod*'s brother not Idnerth's because of the phrasing of the text of the witness list, as indicated by my commas: 'auguod, iudnerth filius eius, et frater eius briauail'.

[51] *LL* 222.

[52] Davies, *Llandaff Charters*, 114–15, notes that this text would have been of no use for the compilers of the Book of Llandaff in the twelfth century: it explains that the man in question had unjustly taken the meadow in which he and his wife had sex from Merthyr Clydog and now returned it free of all lay service. Yet, it was not quite useless, since it gives the bounds of the land given to Merthyr Clydog. However, the king is said to be king of Morgannwg, which suggests an eleventh-century date.

In the first story, we are told that, some time after the martyrdom of Clydog, two brothers, exiled from Penychen because of a feud, came with their sister's son, Cynfwr, to the place where the martyr's body rested. The two brothers became hermits, but their sister's son himself had five sons; and that was why the land attached to the church always remained divided into five portions. The purpose of this part of the story was partly to explain the five portions, but also that the heirs of the church descended from a man who came from outside Ewias, namely from Penychen. The inhabitants of Ewias, in which Merthyr Clydog was situated, had no hereditary claim to any portion of the church's property.

The evidence of the charters is consistent with the rules of partible inheritance set out in the laws. There are, however, three charters which show women having a claim to land. In the last of the charters in the Cadog collection, King Meurig was recorded as giving three pieces of land to Llancarfan.[53] Two of these portions belong to *Gorbrith* and *Gassoc* and likwise to their sister, *Sule*. None of the three was included in the witness list; apparently they were granted by the king with the land and the livestock. In another charter, one of the two versions of a charter discussed among the doublets in the Book of Llandaff, the donor first buys a *uilla* 'from King Morgan and from his son Ithael, and from his wife, *Ricceneth*'.[54] Here we are at the other end of the social hierarchy from the peasants, *Gorbrith*, *Gassoc*, and *Sule*; and the woman in question was a wife and not a sister. *Ricceneth* may have possessed the *uilla*, in whole or in part, as her *cowyll* or maiden-fee.[55] A third charter records two gifts, one by King Ffernfael ab Ithael to his queen, Ceingaer, and a second by the queen herself to Bishop Cadwared.[56] These examples suggest a distinction: on the one hand, a queen may own land and be entitled to grant it to the Church. On the other, when land was granted with its peasant population—in other words, as inhabited and cultivated land—peasant women not just men might be understood to form part of the grant and to go with the land to the new owner. In between the queen and the peasant woman the charters offer no evidence that women had possession of land by inheritance. Some aristocratic women very probably did, since it was possible, as we have seen, to buy land from the king; and bought land was acquired rather than inherited. There is a good chance that acquired land could be alienated much more freely than inherited land, especially if that land had passed down for four generations within the one kindred.

Terms for a kindred, *progenies*, *generatio*, and *parentela*, are likely to reflect Welsh *cenedl* and thus the deeper lineage associated with hereditary obligations, privileges, and politics. We have met already the charter in which *Guallunir* gave to God and to St Cadog the estate of Pencarnau.[57] He also made a testament according to which the estate was to pass to one of his sons, *Iudnou*, so that 'he and his heirs were

[53] *Vita S. Cadoci*, § 68.

[54] *LL* 190b.

[55] D. Jenkins and M. E. Owen (eds.), *The Welsh Law of Women* (Cardiff, 1980), 76–8, 196.

[56] *LL* 207.

[57] *Vita S. Cadoci*, § 59. The name is probably continued in the singular as Pencarn, ST 287 841, just to the south-west of Newport. On the donor and his son Gwyddnerth, both of whom appear as donors in the Book of Llandaff, see Davies, *An Early Welsh Microcosm*, 119.

to serve the community of Cadog from the profits of this estate apart from themselves'. I take this to mean that the grant and accompanying testament were designed to enable *Iudnou* and his heirs to maintain themselves from this estate. *Guallunir* may have been the brother of King Morgan ab Athrwys, and another of his sons, Gwyddnerth, made a grant to Llandaff, or to Llancarfan and Llandochau, of Llangadwaladr, Bishton in Gwent is Coed.[58] This grant was made as penitential alms for Gwyddnerth's killing of his brother, Meirchion. If the witness list to 190b should read 'G[u]aidnerth filius Morcanti fratris', *Guallunir* was brother to King Morgan ab Athrwys. Hence the family may have included the following:

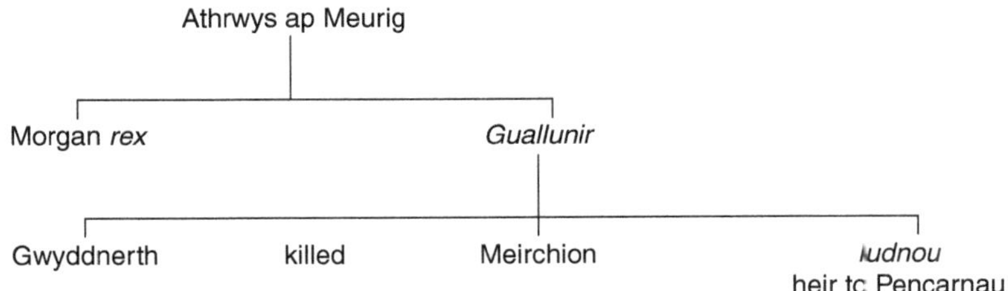

Figure 9.2. The kindred of Athrwys ap Meurig

This would then be a cadet branch of the royal house. The high status is consistent with the terms of the obligation placed upon *Iudnou*. The render due from the estate to the community of St Cadog was nine *modii* of ale with the accompanying loaves, carcases, and honey.[59] This was to be delivered to feed the community 'wherever Cadog's clergy should have chosen to eat and drink, namely in Basaleg or in Pencarnau'. Since Basaleg was later the mother-church of a large portion of Gwynllŵg and is almost certain to have been a church of importance from an early date, the phrase 'in Basaleg or in Pencarnau' may mean that Pencarnau was the secular centre of the region, while Basaleg was the ecclesiastical centre.[60] The nine *modii* and accompanying renders were not, therefore, merely the usual obligation of peasants to their lord. Initially, of course, they were just that, to be delivered to *Iudnou*; but what this charter is concerned with is not that stage or indeed that level of society but with the entertainment given by *Iudnou* and his heirs to the clergy of St Cadog. In the terms of the laws, the nine *modii* began as *dawnbwyd* from the peasants to *Iudnou* but then became *gwestfa* provided by *Iudnou* for Cadog's *familia*. *Iudnou* did not deliver the food to Llancarfan but entertained his clerical guests on his own land; for the land was indeed both Cadog's and *Iudnou*'s, so that the one might provide food and drink for the other's men.

[58] See above, 258–60 (on the doublet, Cadog § 67 = *LL* 180b).
[59] *Vita S. Cadoci*, § 59.
[60] Above, 290–1. *WATU* 172 under Pen-carn.

Guallunir, therefore, was able by his gift and his testament, namely a legal transaction closely comparable to the Irish *audacht*, oral testament or will, to impose obligations on one branch of his descendants.[61] The lineage descended from *Iudnou* would for evermore be distinct from the offspring of *Guallunir*'s other sons, because *Iudnou*'s descendants had a perpetual obligation arising from their inheritance of Pencarnau, whereas the descendants of the other sons did not. If, like similar Welsh lineages in the twelfth and thirteenth centuries, they partitioned and repartitioned their lands so that, in time, they too became peasants, the agnatic descendants of *Iudnou* may well have restricted any partitioning instead to co-heirs; but they would all have had the obligation to entertain the clergy of Llancarfan. The right to share might mark out the shallow, four-generation lineage, the co-heirs, but the obligation would still lie heavy on the entire lineage descended from *Iudnou*.

Such a definition of a lineage as a result of the act recorded in a charter was even more decisive when it involved a more complete subjection than that imposed on the royally connected *Iudnou*. A charter from Ergyng records a grant by *Cuchein* son of Gloyw of the *uilla Hirpant*, a small *tref* of three *modii*; he also granted *Guingal* together with his lineage to serve the church.[62] *Guingal* appeared in the lay witness list and was thus probably not of unfree status. Nevertheless, the reference to an obligation to serve suggests something rather more humbling than the aristocratic entertainment provided by *Iudnou*. One of the charters purporting to belong to the days of St Teilo himself has a more extreme example.[63] It would certainly not be safe to treat this as a text of the sixth century; the transaction cannot be authenticated or dated; what the charter does do, however, is to illustrate the kind of thing that, by the early twelfth century at least, was thought possible. A rich man called *Tutuc* had been so furious at trespass by pigs in his corn fields that he attacked the pigherd. In penance he subjected himself to St Teilo together with two *uillae* in perpetual servitude, and also together with his entire lineage. Talk of perpetual servitude suggests that he and his descendants would have become slaves.

3. HEIRS AND *HEREDITARII*

The Book of Llandaff uses two terms whose apparent literal translation is 'heir'. One is the usual Latin word, *heres*, the ultimate source of English 'heir'; the other is the longer—and, as a noun, most unusual—*hereditarius*. (As an adjective it is common and is the source of English 'hereditary'.) The usage in the Book of Llandaff is very much as if one were to call one set of people 'heirs' and the other set 'hereditaries': one man might be the heir of, say, Meurig, while another might be 'Rhodri, the hereditary'. Of the nine charters in which *hereditarius* is used, all but one belong to groups C and F and may be assigned to the period from the late

[61] On the testament in Welsh law, see Pryce, *Native Law and the Church*, 118–23; on the parallel *timnae* and *audacht* in Irish law, see Kelly, *Guide to Early Irish Law*, 122–3.

[62] 168.

[63] 127.

seventh to the late eighth century.[64] The one outlier is in group J and belongs to the first half of the eleventh century.

As we shall see later, these two sets, 'heirs' and 'hereditaries' partially overlap; yet their range of meanings remains distinct. One can see this, in the first place, from the way *hereditarius* is used and the ways in which it is not used. A wholly unsurprising use of *heres* 'heir' is 'the heirs of X', for example *heredes Conloc*, 'Conloc's heirs'.[65] Since partible inheritance was the rule, a particular ancestor, such as *Conloc*, would have a plurality of heirs. As we saw earlier, the *ager* of *Conloc*, 'land of *Conloc*', corresponded to 'the heirs of *Conloc*'; both were very much 'of Conloc'. *Hereditarius* was not used in that context: there are no examples of 'so-and-so's hereditaries' as an open-ended set of individuals. Usually it occurs as a virtual title attached to one named person: Iddig *hereditarius*, *Gurdocius hereditarius*, and Gafran *hereditarius*.[66] In three charters pairs of hereditaries appear, for example 'with the consent of the hereditaries, Ithael and Ffreudur'.[67] But there are never more than two hereditaries at a time.

Secondly, *hereditarius* was sometimes used of very grand personages. In one charter, 150a, Iddig son of Nudd, *hereditarius*, appeared as joint-donor, together with the king, of an estate called Porthcaseg, just to the north of Chepstow. In the next charter, 150b, Iddig is again a joint-donor, but both of them are described as kings. Even when Iddig was a *hereditarius* and before he became king, he not only participated in the grant but appeared immediately after the king in the witness list. The wording was: 'Of the laity, Morgan the king, Iddig the hereditary, son of Nudd'. The other witnesses had no titles or special descriptions. It is not surprising, therefore, that some hereditaries belonged to the select group of men who witnessed more than one charter. Gafran appears among the witnesses of 180a as 'Gafran *hereditarius*'; he also witnessed 158, 187, 189 and 204a, the last of these being a charter in which the donor was his son; another son witnessed 190b. The land granted in these charters included estates in both Gwent is Coed and Glamorgan, whereas most lay witnesses were confined to one district.[68] Another *hereditarius*, Gwrhydr, participated in the grant recorded in 148 and may well have been the person of the same name who witnessed one of the Cadog charters;[69] a possible son played a major role in a complex transaction recorded in another of the Cadog charters.[70]

The term *heres*, 'heir', was sometimes used in a way which did not suggest high rank. One example we have met already, *heredes Conloc*, 'Conloc's heirs'. Another appears casually in a boundary clause attached to an early tenth-century charter recording a grant of land in Gwent: 'as far as the estate of the sons of Grugog with its heirs, Boddwg and *Eimin*.' Sometimes, however, *heres* is used in a way

64 *LL* 148, 150a, 158 from group C; 179b, 180a, 195, 209a, 210a from group F; 264a from group J.
65 *LL* 76a.
66 *LL* 150a, 158, 180a.
67 *LL* 195.
68 Davies, *An Early Welsh Microcosm*, 114–17.
69 *Vita S. Cadoci*, § 62.
70 Ibid. § 55.

reminiscent of *hereditarius*. In 202 the donor was Cynwg son of *Conuil*, a member of a high-ranking family. In another charter, discussed earlier, his father granted an estate by the River Ewenni in Gwrinydd, 'from which Cynwg and his sons, from generation to generation, should serve the altar'—and hence the *uilla* became known as the *uilla* of Cynwg.[71] Here, however, Cynwg himself purchased another *uilla*, also in Gwrinydd, from King Morgan. Initially, the *uilla* was called *uilla Breican*, but it received another name as a result of the grant, *uilla Ellgnou*. The reason emerges from the lay witness list, which includes *Ellgnou heres*. It is a fair bet, although the charter gives no direct indication, that Cynwg did for *Ellgnou* what his own father, *Conuil* son of *Gurceniu*, had done for him in the very same district of Gwrinydd; and that it was this change of property relations which caused the change of name from *uilla Breican* to *uilla Ellgnou*. *Ellgnou* may have been Cynwg's son, or at least his kinsman.

This example belongs to the eighth century, but a pair of texts from the eleventh tells a similar story. During the episcopate of Joseph (d. 1045), Seisill son of *Gistlerth* gave land at Cegin Penrhos ar Wy, lying opposite Llangynfall on the other side of the Monnow just up from Monmouth.[72] The immediate beneficiary seems to have been Llangynfall, which was itself apparently subject to Llandaff. Among the lay witnesses were *Audi* and *Guilstan* sons of Sigilm, *hereditarii* (all three bearing English names). A twelfth-century list of churches in Ergyng was followed by details about arrangements under Bishop Herwald in the days of Edward the Confessor, Harold, and William the Conqueror; among those pertaining to the reign of Edward the Confessor was the following note:[73]

> In the time of Edward, king of England, and Gruffudd, king of Wales, Bishop Herwald consecrated Henllan Dyfrig and Llandeilo within the one cemetery; and he ordained Einion ap Cyngen as priest, while the heirs (*heredes*) of the land attached to those churches, remaining subject to Bishop Herwald, continued to be Moriddig son of *Cini*, Morfran son of *Audi* and his brother *Cinhi*, and *Marcguein* son of Elgu, and *Potin*.

Henllan Dyfrig and Llandeilo are now represented by Hentland, four miles west-by-north from Ross-on-Wye.[74] It is also worth noting that, after two generations of English names, *Audi* and *Sigilm*, Morfran bore a Welsh name.

These six named men were what, in Anglo-Norman England, were called *firmarii*, 'farmers', in the old sense of men who owed a *ferma* or *firma*, Old English *feorm*, namely a food-rent, later commuted to a money-rent. The *firmarius* was the lessee of an estate and was responsible for paying the food-rent prescribed in the lease to his lord. The Latin form, *ferma*, of the Old English *feorm* is what is used in this text. Great lords at that period—and this included churches—did not themselves run most of their estates directly but leased them out to men who were usually of good social standing. Morfran son of *Audi* is likely to have been son of the *Audi*, *hereditarius*, who witnessed the grant of land a few miles to the south earlier in the century. Morfran was not himself described as an *hereditarius* like his father but as one of the heirs of the lands belonging to the two churches in the same

[71] *LL* 176a/190b. [72] *LL* 264a. [73] *LL*, 274. [74] SO 543 264.

cemetery. Bishop Herwald's standard practice was to ordain the sons of priests to churches, after he had (re-)consecrated the churches themselves 'under the heir so-and-so'. Thus 'in the time of Harold' he 'in similar fashion consecrated Llanbedr under the heir, *Cidrych* son of *Gunncu*, and Cadien and his sons, *Gunna* and *Eutut*.[75] *Heres*, 'heir', appears to be the broader term, *hereditarius* the more specific; and they overlapped so that there were people to whom both could be applied.

This array of evidence does not, however, reveal precisely what an *hereditarius* was—why he was of high status and what it was to which he had an hereditary right. There is always the danger that the guises in which the *hereditarius* appears in the Book of Llandaff were not those which made him an *hereditarius*. It would be unfortunate if we committed the same error as someone who observed soldiers engaged in crowd control and concluded that the job of a soldier was just that.

One crucial issue is whether a person described as *hereditarius* in a charter is likely to have had some rights over the estate about which the charter was written. Even if, like Gafran *hereditarius*,[76] he only appears in the witness list, we cannot conclude that his status as an *hereditarius* had nothing to do with the transaction: the examination of the doublets in the Book of Llandaff has shown how unsafe it is to argue from silence. Lleufryd, *hereditarius*, who appears in a late eighth-century charter discussed in the previous chapter, offers a puzzling example.[77] He does not, like Gafran, receive his title in the witness list but in a sentence immediately following that recording the royal gift of *Cair Riou*:

> and Lleufryd, *hereditarius*, received the estate from Bishop Cadwared (and from the clergy of Llandaff), on the basis that he would give them every year six *modii* of ale with its whole due in bread and in meat and with a sester of honey.

One possibility is that the transaction worked as follows: before the king, Athrwys ap Ffernfael, made this grant, Lleufryd was the king's hereditary tenant for the estate: like an Anglo-Norman *firmarius* he ran the *ager* and ensured that the food-renders were paid. If one peasant could not deliver ale but could, instead, supply wheat, it would have to be agreed with Lleufryd. When King Athrwys decided to give *Cair Riou* to a church (perhaps Llandogo), an arrangement was made between king and church. *Cair Riou* went to the church, but the church, in its turn, then handed over the estate to Lleufryd. In other words, whatever Lleufryd's position was under King Athrwys, his rights and obligations in relation to the new ecclesiastical lord were not just a continuation of the old order when he was the tenant of the king. Instead they flowed from a new bargain made with the church.

In the charter, this new bargain was perceived from the church's standpoint. First, in terms of the food-render, Lleufryd was to deliver, as we saw earlier a render corresponding to half its assessed annual value, six *modii* in place of an *uncia*. That was a promise for the future, of what Lleufryd would deliver. Then the charter slips into the past tense, giving an historical statement about what had happened when

[75] *LL*, 276. Llanbedr is Peterstow, lying between Hentland and Ross-on-Wye at SO 563 249.
[76] *LL* 180a.
[77] *LL* 210a. See above, 277–8.

the bargain was made: 'and at the will of the bishop and for as long as it might be pleasing to him and to his chapter he (Lleufryd) was quitclaiming it from himself and from his offspring for ever.' The second word 'it' in the translation, referring to what Lleufryd quitclaimed, corresponds to a feminine adjective in the original text; it cannot refer back to the masculine *ager* but only to the vernacular *cair* 'fortress' in the name *Cair Riou*. This, however, was the centre of the estate and the entire complex was presumably intended. Hence, what this sentence indicates is that Lleufryd was renouncing, for himself and for his descendants, any hereditary right in the estate. It might *de facto* pass down from him to an heir, but it would never become, *de iure*, an inheritance within his family.

In a charter which describes Lleufryd as *hereditarius*, a principal concern was to deny that Lleufryd or his descendants would ever become heirs—that they had then, or would have in the future, any hereditary right to remain as lease-tenants of *Cair Riou* and the *uncia* of land which belonged to it. Admittedly the clause in which Lleufryd was said to have renounced any personal claims to *Cair Riou* other than the will of Cadwared appears not to be original in the form in which we have it. Those who had to agree to Lleufryd's continued control of *Cair Riou* were Bishop Cadwared and his chapter. This is, however, the terminology of the twelfth century: an earlier text should have said 'Cadwared and his community', 'community' standing for *familia*, literally 'household', the standard term for much, if not all, of the early Middle Ages. Just as almost all the charters were rephrased so as to suggest that the church (or chapter) of Llandaff was a beneficiary, so the term 'chapter' here stood for the canons of the cathedral, a terminology which probably came into Glamorgan in the late eleventh or early twelfth century.[78] Yet, although the terminology was updated, it does not follow that the clause as a whole was a late addition to the charter. Arrangements similar to Lleufryd's tenancy of *Cair Riou* are well attested in the Book of Llandaff and remained common, as we have seen, even after the Norman Conquest. In the account of Bishop Herwald's activities in the second half of the eleventh century, there was no reluctance to describe laymen in control of ecclesiastical property as 'heirs', *heredes*. The clause in this charter is unique in the Book of Llandaff. As long as it cannot, as a whole, be regarded as a later insertion, it stands against an intepretation of *hereditarius*, which understands it as a continuing hereditary tenancy.

If we look outside the immediate context of the examples of *hereditarius* given in the Book of Llandaff, informed speculation is the best we can achieve. A term used in the Four Branches of the Mabinogi for someone of high rank, but which is not current in the laws, is *dylyedog*, literally 'entitled', similar to *hereditarius* in that it began life as an adjective and was then used as a noun. Yet, again, the contexts in which it is used do not show what a *dylyedog* was entitled to receive or hold; and this comparison thus leads only to further speculation. One might argue that a regime of food-renders necessarily divides society into those who are entitled to receive and those who are obliged to deliver renders. The fundamental divide in society can be

[78] Compare *Vita S. Cadoci*, § 48, the *canonici* of Llancarfan; *familia*, ibid. §§ 55, 56, 59, 61, 63, 64, 65, *congregatio* § 67, *famulitio* § 68.

seen in terms of entitlements and obligations to one and the same thing, the delivery of food-renders. Such a situation might well, therefore, yield a term for a nobleman meaning 'someone entitled' (to receive food-renders). *Hereditarius* might then be a quasi-equivalent in Latin, expressive of hereditary right rather than, as with *dylyedog*, simple entitlement.

This speculation implies that the restricted number of *hereditarii* in the Book of Llandaff were just the few who happened to retain a title which many others could have claimed. This is not unlikely: for example, Iddon ap Ceirio was described as *hereditarius* in one doublet but not in the other.[79] On the other hand, there is another way of understanding *hereditarius* which would make it apply to a more restricted group than all those entitled to receive food-renders. One legal manuscript, Latin Redaction A, explains the Welsh term *swydd*, itself a borrowing from Latin *sēdēs*, 'seat', as meaning *hereditas*, 'inheritance'.[80] Offices that were the perquisite of a *cenedl* were allocated by the chief of kindred, the *pencenedl*.[81] Elsewhere in the laws, the nature of the drink element in the food-renders due from a township was dependent on its status; and this status included, as one possibility, being a township to which an office was attached.[82] In yet another lawbook, the landed nobility was separated into two classes: one possessing a *swydd* and another not.[83] On the basis of these fragments of evidence, one could understand *hereditarius* as 'one hereditarily entitled' to an office, while the ordinary *heres* remained as the heir of land.

Kinship was a pervasive influence on the lives of the Welsh in the early Middle Ages and it remained so as long as Welsh society continued to have a distinctive character. It pervaded the Church as much as the laity; only for the slave was its power slight, at least in terms of formal rights and duties. For the structure of politics and kingship it was critical, as we shall see in the next chapter; and, even for a political narrative, it is a major part of the background, essential if one is to gain a sense of the context of events. It is, however, also true that Welsh kinship was complex, taking radically different forms depending on what was at issue: the kinship of inheritance was not the same as the kinship of alliance or the kinship of status. A failure to appreciate the differences has, for example, caused historians to misunderstand the rise of the Merfynion, as we shall see in Chapter 15.

[79] He is in *LL* 179b, but not in 191.
[80] *LTWL* 146; *EIWK* 204.
[81] *LTWL* 139. 35–7; 239. 6-8; Bleg 83. 25–84. 1.
[82] *WML* 56. 10–11.
[83] *LTWL* 339. 30–9.

10
Kingship

Evidence for the kingship of the post-Roman Britons has two faces: one looks back to Roman Britain; the other looks across the Irish Sea. Early sources, especially Gildas and the early inscriptions, betray a political culture inherited from a Roman past; later sources, especially those from after our period, are more reminiscent of features of early Irish kingship. In some cases, there is a strong probability that aspects of the Welsh kingship of the twelfth century were also part of the kingship of the Britons in earlier centuries; it is merely that the richer sources of the twelfth century allow things to emerge that had been hidden in the sparse documentation of earlier centuries. At least two reactions are therefore possible: perhaps different sources merely offer different views of one and the same institution, largely unchanging; on the other hand, it may be that British kingship became more barbarian—that is, less Roman—after the sixth century. One reaction ascribes differences to the sources, the other to reality.

1. THE INHERITANCE FROM ROMAN BRITAIN

The early Roman Empire did not readily tolerate kings within its borders. By the end of the first century AD there were no kings left in Roman Britain. The *civitates*, local peoples, over whom kings had once ruled were still there. Indeed, they were a cornerstone of the Roman state; but they were governed by local aristocracies. An inscription attests the *ordo* of the Silures, that is, the governing aristocracy of the people of what would become south-east Wales.[1] On the other hand, beyond the frontier to the north there remained other British peoples. Those who ended up living approximately between the two walls, Hadrian's Wall and the Antonine Wall, continued to be considered Britons even after the Pictish federation formed to the north. For these peoples between the Walls, kingship probably remained a viable form of government, in spite of the periods during which they came under direct Roman rule. If the Coroticus denounced by St Patrick was king of Alclud, as claimed in the Book of Armagh, kings are at least attested in the north from the fifth century.[2] Even northern British rulers from the Firth of Forth and from Loch Lomond southwards to Hadrian's Wall remained, however, Britons rather than Picts; this is most likely to have been because they were normally clients of the

[1] *RIB* 311. [2] *The Patrician Texts in the Book of Armagh*, ed. Bieler, 66.

Empire.[3] Their identity was tied to the Roman inheritance even if, as Britons, they regarded themselves as quite distinct from the Romans.

In the fifth century, the Britons to the south of Hadrian's Wall acquired new kings. They also exported their kingship south of the Channel, in particular to what would become Brittany. According to Gregory of Tours, the early leaders of the Bretons were kings.[4] The same historian claimed that the Romans of northern Gaul also acquired a king, Syagrius 'king of the Romans', who was based at Soissons.[5] For Gregory, therefore, small kingships spread across northern Gaul and the Rhineland in the fifth century: until Clovis defeated Syagrius *c.* 587, there were not only several kings among the Franks, but also a king of the Romans and kings among the Bretons. Kingship was not confined to the barbarians; if Gregory was correct, kingship was also not confined to the Britons among the former citizens of the Empire. Small-scale kingship was a matter of geography rather than allegiance to Rome: in southern Gaul, south of the Loire, more powerful barbarian kings with wider territories—kings of the Visigoths and the Burgundians—ruled much of the former lands of the Empire, but in northern Gaul and in Britain small-scale kingships were the norm. Often they appear to have been based in a single *civitas*: the Frank Ragnachar was based in Cambrai, a relation, Rignomer, in Le Mans.[6] Clovis's father, Childeric, may have acquired authority over the entire province of Belgica Secunda, but his base was Tournai, where he was buried *c.* 482.[7] After Clovis, however, larger kingdoms were the norm among the Franks, even allowing for partition between Merovingian claimants. When, in 588, Guntram declared that he might allow his young nephew, Chlothar II, 'two or three *civitates* in some part of my kingdom', he was envisaging not merely close dependence of nephew on uncle but also what, in Frankish terms, was a very small kingdom.[8] Yet, in post-Roman Britain, kingdoms based on a single *civitas* became the norm: there were kingdoms of Dumnonia, of Demetia, and of Ventia, namely Gwent; Gwynedd was a *civitas*; and the kingdoms between the Walls—Gododdin and Alclud—were on the same scale.[9] The *superbus tyrannus*, Vortigern, may have ruled a wider area in the fifth century, but no evidence survives to show how extensive it was. In the second half of the fifth century, therefore, the boundary between *civitas* kingdoms and larger ones lay on the Loire, but by the date of Clovis's death, 511, it had withdrawn northwards to the Channel.

By the ninth century some Welsh kingdoms were on a yet smaller scale. The old Ventia (Gwent) was often divided between Glywysing to the west and Gwent to the east; as for Brycheiniog, if its territory had belonged to the *civitas* of the Silures under the Romans, it was now quite separate from the successor-state to the Silures,

[3] See above, 35–6.

[4] Gregory of Tours, *Hist.*, iv. 4.

[5] Ibid. ii. 27.

[6] Ibid. ii. 42.

[7] *Epistolae Austrasicae*, no. 2.

[8] Gregory of Tours, *Hist.*, ix. 20.

[9] *Vita Prima S. Samsonis*, ed. Flobert, i. 1: Nam pater eiusdem sancti Samsonis, sicut iam dixi, Demetiano ex genere, Amon nomine, et eius mater, de Ventia, prouintia proxima eiusdem Demetie.

Gwent. So also, at least intermittently, was the small territory of Erging, heir to a Romano-British *vicus*, Ariconium. The *Historia Brittonum* reveals the existence, *c.* 830, of a dynasty which ruled the two small territories of Buellt and Gwerthrynion.[10] In the north, the later cantref of Rhos may have had its own dynasty.[11] All these would have been, at the best, *pagi*, subdivisions of a *civitas* in the Roman period. A tension can thus be seen between two tendencies: on the one hand, it was natural to preserve the *civitas* as a kingdom; on the other, dynastic segmentation might well lead to a partitioning of the territory of a *civitas* between two or more smaller kingdoms. For one thing, the unity of the *civitas* was not as clear in the ecclesiastical domain as it was in Gaul: in the latter, bishops presided over *civitates*, but in Britain there might be a plurality of bishops within the one *civitas*.[12] Since episcopal authority was a powerful force in Gaul towards maintaining the cohesion of the *civitas*, it would not be surprising if, north of the Channel, that cohesion was sometimes undermined.[13] Even south of the Channel the *civitas* did not survive undivided in north-eastern Gaul.[14]

Post-Roman British kingship, as one might expect, owed much to its Roman inheritance. Yet, especially because there had, as far as we can tell, always been British kings beyond Hadrian's Wall, there was also a British tradition of kingship, largely unbroken since the Iron Age: only briefly had direct Roman rule extended over the land between the Walls. There was, therefore, a political tradition influenced by Rome and yet still retaining its native forms of rule; these may have been imitated by the new kingships south of the Wall. With the triumph of Christianity, there was yet another model of kingship in the Old Testament. When Gildas remarked, 'Kings were anointed, not in God's name, but as being crueller than the rest', he was alluding to the anointing of Saul and David by the prophet Samuel and using the comparison to accentuate the contrast between Christian profession and unchristian conduct.[15] Whether his contemporary kings were actually anointed at their inauguration is very doubtful; but he could be confident that his readers would recognize the allusion and appreciate its implications.

Gildas's assumptions about kingship and government quickly reveal both the links to the Roman past and the new order. As we have seen, he took it for granted that arrangements between barbarians and British rulers might follow Roman forms: there might be a formal alliance, *foedus*, and the barbarians would thus become *foederati*, allied troops.[16] As *foederati* these barbarian troops would be maintained by food supplies, *annonae*, that came from the taxes of the former Empire, taxes that, since the third century, had often been taken in kind.

[10] *HB* 49.

[11] *EWGT* 108, ABT § 25; cf. *EWGT* 10, HG § 3.

[12] See below 587–90.

[13] Even in Gaul, the ecclesiastical unity of the *civitas* was sometimes threatened, as in Châteaudun, Gregory, *Hist.*, vii. 17; in the far north-east it was undermined entirely, E. Ewig, *Spätantikes und fränkisches Gallien*, ii. 91–5.

[14] Ewig, *Spätantikes und fränkisches Gallien*, i. 506–7.

[15] Gildas, *De Excidio*, 21. 4.

[16] Ibid. 23. 5, *rupto foedere*.

Apparently they were to be delivered month by month, since Gildas also gave them the name *epimenia*, derived from Greek, and meaning 'monthly supplies'.[17] That Gildas could make such assumptions implies that, to some extent at least, the taxation system of the Empire survived north of the Channel in the fifth century as we know that it did in Gaul in the sixth.

Justice was administered by kings and by judges. The distinction between them is clear, even though they are sometimes lumped together. 'He turns his attention also to greedy judges: "Your princes [namely, leaders] are disloyal, they are thieves' accomplices".'[18] The late-Roman inheritance would lead one to suspect that bishops had a judicial role that overlapped that of secular judges: ever since Constantine I's reign, bishops had been given jurisdiction under Roman law. Gildas's principal judges, however, belonged with kings and were thus secular officials; the same link is suggested by the Welsh loanword from *iudex*, *udd*.[19] On the other hand, his choice of Old Testament quotations to use as ammunition against priests (*sacerdotes*, including bishops), indicates that some of them had a judicial role.[20] If, as is probable given the evidence from Gaul, British churchmen in the post-Roman period had a judicial competence, it would help to explain the emergence of a canon law in the missionary territory in Ireland that was administered by ecclesiastical judges who were also experts in the exegesis of scripture. On the other hand, this canon law was not an offshoot of Roman law, which would have had no purchase in Ireland, a country proud not to have been conquered by Rome:[21] it took the canons of the Church and the Bible as a basis and created a much extended system that was essentially something novel, the law set out in 'The Irish Collection of Canons', *Collectio Canonum Hibernensis*. To judge by Gildas's use of the Bible, this process began in Britain.[22]

Gildas uses the term 'tyrant' initially in the normal late Roman sense of someone who had seized imperial power by violence. In this sense, it referred to the way power was acquired rather than how it was exercized. Magnus Maximus adopted 'the imperial insignia, which he was never fit to bear: he had no legal claim to the title, but was raised to it like a tyrant by rebellious soldiery.'[23] Magnus Maximus was contrasted with 'legitimate emperors'.[24] On the other hand, when he denounced the five kings ('Britain has kings but they are tyrants'),[25] the term 'tyrant' referred more to the way they exercised power than to how they acquired it. Only

[17] Ibid. See above, 44, 53–4

[18] Ibid. 27; 43. 2.

[19] Thus Urfai, *udd Eidyn*, Jarman, *Gododdin*, 954, *CA* 1220, may well have had an authority subordinate to that of the ruler, although in *PT/CT* iii. 18, the meaning is 'ruler'. Cf. the *iudex* of *Vita I S. Samsonis*, i. 53, and P.-Y. Lambert, 'Gloses en vieux breton', *Études Celtiques*, 30 (1994), 221–8, no. 3 'A propos de Vbret. *Iud-* et *Iudic-*'.

[20] Gildas, *De Excidio*, 88. 1; 94. 2.

[21] Columbanus, *Ep.* v. 11 (ed. and trans. G. S. M. Walker, *S. Columbani Opera*, 48).

[22] See above, 207–9.

[23] Gildas, *De Excidio*, 13. 1.

[24] Ibid. 13. 2.

[25] Ibid. 27.

Maelgwn is said to have acquired power by force.[26] Moreover, it is striking that Gildas made no distinction between kings and emperors: those who ruled the Empire might be called 'kings of the Romans' as well as emperors.[27]

Although the legal terms used by Gildas imply a familiarity with the vocabulary associated with Roman law, it remains true that medieval Welsh law was not an offshoot of the Roman legal tradition. The Romans of Gaul, whom we call Gallo-Romans, adhered to Roman law, even when they lived under Burgundian, Visigothic, or Frankish kings. When, in the seventh and eighth centuries, those who lived north of the Loire adopted a Frankish identity and Frankish law, those south of the Loire continued to think of themselves as Romans and continued to live by Roman law. There have been attempts to detect inherited Roman elements in Welsh law, yet none of those suggested is above suspicion.[28] The likeliest area in which a Roman inheritance can be detected is in the 'Celtic charter', a device which was successfully transmitted from Britain to Ireland.[29]

2. THE NATIVE ELEMENT IN POST-ROMAN BRITISH KINGSHIP

The native as opposed to the Roman element in post-Roman British kingship appears first in the terms used for kings and heirs-apparent. Analysis of the terminology also reveals changes within the early medieval period; and, even though these changes cannot, in general, be dated at all closely, they need to be borne in mind when discussing the political history of the Britons.

A term used in the twelfth century to make the contrast between greater and lesser kings is *arbennig*. In one version of the thirteenth-century southern lawbook *Llyfr Blegywryd* it is said that 'Rhys ap Gruffudd, *arbennig* of Deheubarth, with the agreement of his kingdom, established valuation by oath for every animal'.[30] The use of this term *arbennig* for the ruler of a major kingdom, such as Deheubarth, corresponds with its use in the phrase *eisteddfa arbennig* 'principal seat', which was confined to the main courts of the leading kingdoms, such as Dinefwr in Deheubarth and Aberffraw in Gwynedd.[31] In the Latin the term used is *sedes principalis*; and this indicates that *arbennig Deheubarth* was equivalent to *princeps Sutwallie*, a well-attested title of Rhys ap Gruffudd.[32] Both Owain Gwynedd and Rhys ap

[26] Ibid. 33. 4.

[27] Ibid. 5. 1, *reges Romanorum* rule the *orbis imperium*, but they are emperors, 4. 4; 13. 2; the Empire is a *regnum*, 6. 1; their authority is *Romanum imperium*, 15. 1.

[28] P. Collinet, 'Droit celtique et droit romain', *Revue celtique*, 17 (1896), 321–36; *EIWK* 302–3.

[29] See above, 252, 254–6.

[30] DC II. xxxi. 9 = *Llyfr Blegywryd*, ed. Williams and Powell, p. 154 (variant to 93. 24); that some such sentence was in the original is indicated by *LTWL* 361.

[31] *Llyfr Blegywryd*, ed. Williams and Powell, 3. 27.

[32] *LTWL* 317; the Latin *sedes principalis* indicates that *arbennig* in *eisteddfa arbennig* was an adjective not a noun, but the nouns and adjectives (*arbennig* noun and adjective, *princeps* and *principalis*) are likely to have been linked; *Acts*, ed. Pryce, no. 28: 'Resus Sudwallie proprietarius princeps'; Benedict of Peterborough (= Roger of Howden), *Gesta Henrici Secundi*, i. 162.

Gruffudd adopted the title of *princeps*. Admittedly it is likely that the appearance of this title in Wales in the 1160s has everything to do with the particular conditions of the time, when Owain Gwynedd in North Wales and Rhys ap Gruffudd in the south emerged as principal kings in their parts of the country; but the use of *princeps* for someone having leading authority goes back several centuries, at least in an ecclesiastical context, since Wales shared with Ireland the use of *princeps* for the head of a church.[33] As a term for the overking of a *gwlad*, it is attested in the Life of St Gwynllyw, while the notion of a principal seat of kingship, *primaria sedes*, is also attested in the Life of St Cadog.[34] There is thus a possibility that *princeps* and *principalis* were already associated with a higher grade of kingship in the eleventh century. Finally, it is attested in a poem ascribed to Taliesin: Urien of Rheged was *arbennig teyrnedd*, 'chief of rulers'.[35] This earlier usage may, indeed, help to explain why *princeps* had the particular sense of 'principal king' for the Welsh in the 1160s, whereas David I of Scotland, before he became king, had been 'prince of Cumbria'—that is, a subordinate ruler with a title below that of king.[36] The critical aspect of the Welsh term was that it was attached to rule over the major kingdoms, such as Gwynedd or Glamorgan. The endurance of units corresponding roughly to the *civitates* of the Roman and pre-Roman periods, such as Dyfed from Demetae, alongside lesser kingships within such units, shows that the distinction between the principal king of a *gwlad* and lesser kings was an essential aspect of Welsh politics. In the case of *arbennig/princeps* we have a term which, in its Latin guise, looked back to Rome, but the distinction between *princeps* and lesser ruler referred to a long-standing aspect of native British society.

In the poetry of the twelfth-century poet Cynddelw, more of whose work survives than for any other Welsh poet before 1282, a distinction is implicit between two words both usually translated 'king', *brenin* and *rhi*.[37] *Brenin* is used of God and of major kings; *rhi* is used more widely, of lesser kings as well as greater ones. In prose of the twelfth and thirteenth centuries, *brenin* was the normal word for a king, whereas *rhi* was confined to poetry. There may, however, have been significant change between the twelfth and thirteenth centuries: English sources show that even minor Welsh rulers might be regarded as kings as late as the reign of Henry II; but in the next century the tendency was to restrict regality to the most powerful figures, notably to kings of Gwynedd or Deheubarth. It is quite likely that the minor Welsh kings who came to the Council of Oxford in 1177 in the train of their powerful patron Rhys ap Gruffudd would have been refused the title of *brenin* but readily called *rhiau*.[38]

33 *AC* 856 = 858.

34 *VSBG*, pp. 24 (applied to the *cantref* rather than to the *llys*), 172.

35 *PT* iii. 26; cf. 7 ('Ac ef yn arbennic, yn oruchel wledic').

36 *The Charters of David I*, ed. G. W. S. Barrow (Woodbridge, 1999), no. 15.

37 See Table 9. 1 in Charles-Edwards et al., *The Welsh King and his Court*, 214

38 Benedict of Peterborough (= Roger of Howden), *Gesta Henrici*, i. 162: Council at Oxford, held 'to hold talks with the kings and more powerful men of Wales, who had come there at his command to confer with him: namely Rhys ap Gruffudd, king of South Wales, and Dafydd ab Owain, king of North Wales, and Cadwallon, king of Elfael, and Owain of Cyfeiliog, and Gruffudd of Bromfield and Madog ab Iorwerth Goch, and many others of the more noble men of Wales'.

Of the two terms *brenin* and *rhi*, *rhi* has much the longer pedigree. It appears in a number of personal names that are likely to perpetuate old conceptions of kingship: *Tudyr* (*Tudur*) and *Tudri* exhibit the alternation between forms derived from the nominative case and those from the oblique stem. They should, therefore, be at least as old as the end of the Romano-British period.[39] Their literal meaning is 'king of a people' (*tud* 'people') and their formation recalls early Gaulish names such as Vercingetorix.[40] A close comparison is with Old Irish *rí túaithe*, 'king of a people'.[41] A word for a noble, used mainly in the legal texts from South Wales, is *breyr*, for which a direct cognate exists in the Galatian name Brogorix.[42] The literal meaning of this term is 'district-king' (*bro* 'district'); and it seems likely that this was once a synonym for *tudyr*. *Rhi* also has direct cognates outside Celtic, for example in Latin *rex*. For *brenin*, however, there is no such family of compounds preserved in personal names or elsewhere.[43]

One of Justinian's supporters among the Roman senatorial aristocracy during the reconquest of Italy bore the name Bregantinus or Bergantinus. In this name Late Latin confusion of short *i* and *e* has produced the *e* instead of the expected *i*: *Brigantinus* would be a correct Latinization of a Celtic **brigantīnos*, the ancestor of Welsh *brenin*.[44] Such names might well derive from a relatively exalted title or term of status, but this cannot be regarded as certain.[45] In Breton the cognate of *brenin* means 'free man', so that the meaning of Welsh *brenin* 'king' may well be an innovation, especially as Welsh *braint* 'privilege, status' (British **briganti*), from which **brigantīnos* was formed may be used of the rank of a freeman as much as of a king.[46] There is no certain example of *brenin* 'king' in the *Gododdin*.[47] As we shall see later, explanations have been suggested for Welsh *brenin* which have interesting historical implications; but for the time being it will be enough to acknowledge that, while the word itself almost certainly goes back to British, its meaning in Welsh is quite likely to be an innovation of the early medieval period. In particular, *brenin* seems to have leapt over *breyr*, moving from 'freeman' to 'leading king'.

39 See above, 85–7.

40 D. Ellis Evans, *Gaulish Personal Names*, 243–9.

41 *Críth Gablach*, ed. D. A. Binchy (Dublin, 1941), line 448.

42 Evans, *Gaulish Personal Names*, 246.

43 T. M. Charles-Edwards, 'Native Political Organization in Roman Britain and the Origins of Middle Welsh *Brenhin*', in M. Mayrhofer et al. (eds.), *Antiquitates Indogermanicae* (Innsbruck, 1974), 35–45; cf. E. P. Hamp, 'Varia 5. **brigantinos*', *Études Celtiques*, 23 (1986), 50–1.

44 *Epistolae Austrasicae*, ed. Gundlach, No. 19. Martindale, *Prosopography of the Later Roman Empire*, ii. 225, *s.v. Bergantinus*. Cassiodorus, *Variae*, viii. 23 (Bergantino *Viro Illustri* Comiti Patrimonii); ix. 3 (ditto); Procopius, *BG* 1. 26. 1–2 Βηργεντῖνός (Roman senator); 2. 21. 41 (ditto), ed. Dewing, *History of the Wars*, iii. 246, iv. 56. Possible Gaulish evidence for **brigantīnos* is scrutinized and found wanting by J. de Hoz, 'Did a **brigantīnos* exist in Continental Celtic?', in P. Anreiter and E. Jerem (eds.), *Studia Celtica et Indogermanica* (Budapest, 1999), 145–9.

45 Cf. Dagovassus and OE names in *Wealh-*.

46 *Llyfr Blegywryd*, ed. S. J. Williams and J. Enoch Powell (Cardiff, 1942), 5. 12: *Tri ryw dyn yssyd: brenhin, a breyr, a bilaen.*

47 It occurs only once, in the B version, *CA* 1095 (and Jarman, *Gododdin*, 851), but the A version has *teyrn*, 1072. Since a disyllabic word would fit better into the metre, *teyrn*, an old disyllable, is preferable to *brenin*, whose older trisyllabic form is attested even in early Middle Welsh.

Breyr, on the other hand, moved in the opposite direction, losing its regal significance and so coming to mean merely 'noble'.

A term for a ruler that appears to have previously merely meant 'lord' is *gwledig*. In the genealogies certain major ancestors, such as Cunedda, supposed ancestor of the early dynasty of Gwynedd, are sometimes given the title *gwledig*.[48] In the *Historia Brittonum*, Vortigern is made to ask the boy Ambrosius,

> 'What is your name?' He replied, 'I am called Ambrosius'—that is, he was seen to be *Embreis guletic*. And the king said, 'From what lineage were you born?' And he said, 'My father was one of the consuls of the Roman people.'[49]

Yet, in Cynddelw's poetry, *gwledig* is used for lesser rulers as readily as for major ones; it is an equivalent of *rhi* rather than of *brenin*. *Gwledig*, moreover, was formed from *gwlad*, and this term, too, seems to have changed in meaning during the early medieval period. In one of the poems ascribed to Taliesin, his patron, Urien of Rheged, is praised by comparison:[50]

> *gwacsa gwlat da wrth Urföen.*

In the context, this ought to mean, 'Useless is a good lord compared with Urien'.[51] Although in Middle and Modern Welsh *gwlad* means 'country', its Irish cognate, *flaith*, has a triple meaning, 'lordship; kingdom; lord'. This example makes it likely that in early Welsh, *gwlad* could have at least a double meaning, 'lord' and 'country'. *Gwledig*, then, was at first no more than an equivalent of *gwlad* in its rarer sense of 'lord'—a sense which included 'ruler' and might be equivalent to British Latin *consul*.[52] It may have gained status as *gwlad*, in its more common meaning, shifted from any territory over which a lord had authority to a major political unit, such as Gwynedd, Powys, Deheubarth, or Morgannwg; yet this change was not admitted to Cynddelw's deliberately archaic vocabulary.

A term for a ruler which seems not to have changed significantly in meaning is *teyrn*. It is attested in the pre-Roman British coins and is still one of the main words for a ruler in the tenth-century *Armes Prydein*.[53] A compound found in both Welsh and Breton, but in different senses, was Welsh *mechteyrn*, Breton *machtiern*. In Brittany he appears in the Redon charters of the ninth century as a very local leader

48 *EWGT* 38, 95, 111, *Kuneda wledic*, alongside *Cuneda vrenhin*, ibid. 36

49 *HB* c. 42.

50 *PT*/*CT*, vii. 53.

51 A further likely example is *Culhwch ac Olwen*, ed. Bromwich and Evans, lines 90–1, *mab brenhin gvlat teithiawc*, where the parallel in line 95, *mabyon gwladoed ereill*, makes it likely that *brenhin* here is presented as equivalent to *gvlat teithiawc* ('the son of a *brenin*, a *gwlad teithïog*) or, alternatively, is an embedded gloss; also, the adjective *teithiawc* should have been applied to a person, the *brenhin* rather than a country, *gwlad* in the normal later sense; compare *CA* 1095 (*a chan oed mab brenhin teithiauc*) and, similarly, in *Culhwch* itself, line 586. The *mabyon gwladoed ereill* were to be housed in the *yspyty*, whereas the *mab brenhin gvlat teithiawc* would be allowed through the gate so as to enter the hall: hence the *gwladoed ereill* would appear to be rulers of lesser rank than a *brenhin teithiauc*. This in turn makes it likely that *gvlat* in ll. 90–1 should not be taken in the later sense of 'major kingdom', such as Gwynedd or Powys.

52 *PT* ii. 2; iii. 8; *HB* c. 42 (*consul*).

53 *Armes Prydein*, ed. Williams, lines 14, 40, 180.

with a scope of activity restricted to one or two villages.[54] It looks as though the word is from *mach* 'surety' and *teyrn, tiern*. In the tenth-century Welsh poem *Armes Prydein*, however, the *mechteyrn* was the English overking, who was also called emperor of Britain.[55] The explanation of the difference between the Breton and Welsh meanings is difficult: a speculative answer relies on an Irish comparison, namely the practice by which 'base-client' rulers had to give hostages to guarantee subservience. It may be that a Welsh overlord would demand sureties, *meichiau*, to guarantee the payment of his tribute, *mechteyrnged*.[56] In such a relationship, the 'surety-ruler' might be taken to be the overlord or the client, and perhaps the one meaning was adopted in Breton and the other in Welsh.

In the tenth century, the *mechteyrn* was English and yet claimed to be emperor of Britain. In the thirteenth century, *mechteyrnged* would be claimed by the king of Gwynedd from other Welsh rulers—a bold demand, never fully realized.[57] In the early Middle Ages, also, there never was a single king of Wales, even though one or two came close to achieving such an ambition. Yet, in their conception of history, the Welsh thought of something even greater, a kingship of Britain or the Britons rather than of a kingship of the Welsh. An accident of miscopying in the *Liber Pontificalis*, the series of short biographies of the popes, meant that for Bede and for the *Historia Brittonum*, Roman conquest was thought to have allowed the continuance of a king of the Britons.[58] The Romans had indeed conquered Britain, but they had then demanded tribute and returned home. They returned only when the Britons rebelled against their overlordship or appealed for their help. The *Historia Brittonum* maintained that, in AD 167, the British king, Lucius, 'with all the sub-kings of the entire British people', had sent an embassy to Rome and had received the Christian faith 'from the emperors of the Romans and from the Roman pope, Eucharistus'.[59] Although this story was a legend, born of a simple error, it was authoritative from the eighth century onwards. The *Liber Pontificalis*, in its biography of Pope Eleuther (fl. *c.* 180) has the following brief sentence: 'He received a letter from Lucius, a British king, who wanted to become a Christian on his authority'.[60] It is very probable, as shown by Adolf Harnack, that this is the outcome of a confusion between Birtha, the castle of Edessa, and Britain; the

[54] W. Davies, 'On the Distribution of Political Power in Brittany in the Mid-Ninth Century', in M. Gibson and J. L. Nelson, *Charles the Bald: Court and Kingdom*, BAR, Int. Ser. 101 (Oxford, 1981), 87–107, and ead. *Small Worlds: The Village Community in Early Medieval Brittany* (London, 1988), ch. 7.

[55] *Armes Prydein*, ed. Williams, ll. 18, 100. Similarly, in the fourteenth-century legal manuscript *H*, the *mechdeyrn ddylyed* must be the 'overlord's entitlement' not the 'under-king's obligation': *AL* XIV. iv. 5. In *LTWL* 207 it might be either, although *dylyed* has the sense of 'entitlement' before it has that of 'obligation'.

[56] W. Davies, 'Suretyship in the *Cartulaire de Redon*', in T. M. Charles-Edwards et al. (eds.), *Lawyers and Laymen* (Cardiff, 1986), 82; R. Chapman Stacey, 'King, Queen and *Edling* in the Laws of Court', in Charles-Edwards et al. (eds.), *The Welsh King and his Court*, 42–4.

[57] R. R. Davies, *Conquest, Coexistence and Change*, 294.

[58] Bede, *HE* i. 4; *HB* 22; A. Harnack, 'Der Brief des britischen Königs Lucius an dem Papst Eleutherus', *Sitzungsberichte der königlich-preussischen Akademie der Wissenschaften* (1904), xxvii. 909–16.

[59] *HB*, c. 22.

[60] R. Davis, *The Book of Pontiffs (Liber Pontificalis)* (Liverpool, 1989), 6.

ruler of Edessa, Abgar IX (Lucius Aelius Septimius Megas Abgarus IX), was thus transformed into a British king. It is highly unlikely that there was any propagandist intent behind the error, since the sixth-century author of the early part of the *Liber Pontificalis* showed no interest in papal sponsorship of missions: the role of Celestine in authorizing the sending, as his representative, of Palladius as first bishop of the Irish is passed over.

The notion of a single kingship of the Britons is found elsewhere: the *Historia Brittonum* saw Julius Caesar's first invasion as directed against the British king, Bellinus son of Minocannus; the same term, *rex Britannicus*, later used for Lucius, was used here also.[61] Welsh scholars may have noted Suetonius, *De Vita Caesarum*, where he describes Cunobelinus as *rex Britannorum*, which a Welsh reader would probably have understood as 'the king of the Britons'.[62] The assumption may be that, as with Lucius and his sub-kings, a single British king was thought to have had under-kings subject to him. Julius Caesar's aims are portrayed in the *Historia Brittonum* in early medieval terms: he demanded hostages and tribute from the Britons.

One element in this conception of the past is already attested in Gildas's *De Excidio*. Once the Romans conquered Britain, they went back to Rome.[63] In the late Roman period, Britain appealed to Rome for help against her Irish and Pictish invaders; a legion was dispatched, was victorious, and then returned home; the Irish and Picts attacked again, the Britons again appealed for help, and again a Roman army was dispatched, only to return home.[64] It was hardly surprising that later writers understood this in terms of an overlord bringing aid to subject Britons.[65]

In *The Four Branches of the Mabinogi*—in its present form from after our period, but with a history which extends back into it—the conception of a kingship of Britain before the arrival of the Romans is taken for granted.[66] The events of the narrative were placed shortly before the Roman conquest: Caesar's enemy, Cassivellaunus, appears in the Second Branch as Caswallon, king of Britain.[67] The political vocabulary of *The Four Branches* envisages a single *brenin* of Britain (*alias* 'The Island of the Mighty'), who is also termed 'crowned *brenin* of London'.[68] A ruler of Gwynedd or Dyfed is termed an *arglwydd* 'lord'.[69] The conception of the political unity of Britain was not confined to the *Historia Brittonum*, with its single 'British king' with *reguli*, 'sub-kings', under him. It is possible that the *Historia Brittonum*'s opposition of *Britannicus rex* to *reguli* would have been understood in the vernacular as a contrast between *brenin* and *rhiau*, but

61 *HB*, c. 19.

62 Suetonius, *De Vita Caesarum*, Gaius Caligula, 44 (*C. Suetoni Tranquilli De Vita Caesarum Libri VIII*, ed. M. Ihm, Leipzig, 1907, 189).

63 Gildas, *De Excidio*, 6.

64 Ibid. 15–17.

65 *HB*, c. 30.

66 See below, 668, the discussion of *Echrys Ynys*.

67 *PKM* 45, 49.

68 *PKM* 29.

69 *PKM* 1, 67, 92.

that, by the time of our text of *The Four Branches*, the word *rhi* was restricted to poetry and so replaced by *arglwydd*.

A mixture of old and new may also be present in the phrase 'crowned *brenin* of London'. On the one hand, crowning as an attribute of a ruler of Britain betrays assumptions dating from the tenth-century empire of Britain;[70] but, on the other, the role of London is more easily understood as a reference to the Roman past than a late-Anglo-Saxon or Anglo-Norman present. From the time of Edward the Confessor, Westminster became a major royal centre where kings were crowned;[71] but, in contemporary eyes, Westminster was quite distinct from London. It seems, therefore, as if the conception of a political unity of Britain was already present in Gildas's *De Excidio* and was regularly reshaped to accord with contemporary conditions; and, yet, it never lost its links with a remote Roman and even pre-Roman past.

That remote past has been invoked to explain the special meaning of Welsh *brenin*. Two problems have already been raised: first, that Old Breton *brientin*, cognate with *brenin*, meant 'freeman';[72] and, secondly, that *brenin* as a term for 'king' was, in any case, a much more recent term than *rhi*. To resolve the second problem, D. A. Binchy proposed a connection with the name of the northern British people, the Brigantes.[73] He understood this connection as a British version of an idea well attested in Irish, the marriage of the king with the goddess of his realm.[74] In Irish literature the marriage took various forms over several centuries: it evidently became a literary motif which could be adapted to the needs of the story or of the propagandist. The best-known version presented the goddess as 'the Hag of Sovereignty' or 'the Loathly Lady'; the best-known attestation of this version belongs probably to the eleventh century and was employed to defend the threatened primacy of the Uí Néill dynasty. The idea was, however, double-edged: it could be invoked to justify deposing an unsatisfactory king—the goddess was all too prone to divorce an inadequate partner and find a more pleasing mate. A natural context for the idea was the lawyers' belief in a contract between king and people, a contract with obligations on both sides; failure to meet the obligations

[70] See below, 517–18.

[71] Westminster was consecrated on 28 December 1065 and was used for the coronation of William the Conqueror in 1066: ASC DE 1066.

[72] The plural *brientinion* glosses *ingenuis* in the Orléans glosses on the *Collectio Canonum Hibernensis*: W. Stokes, *The Breton Glosses at Orléans*, repr. separately from *Transactions of the Philological Society, 1885–7*, no. 183. The lemma is the title of xxxvi. 3 in Wasserschleben's edition, xxxv. 3 in Flechner's: *De captiuis ingenuis in eodem sabato liberandis*. This title re-applied the text in the body of the chapter (Jeremiah, 34: 13–14, which concerned the freeing of Hebrew slaves in the seventh year, the jubilee) to the freeing of slaves born free as opposed to born in slavery. *Brientinion* appears to have been intended as a translation of *ingenuis* in the sense of 'born free'.

[73] D. A. Binchy, *Celtic and Anglo-Saxon Kingship* (Oxford, 1970), 12–13.

[74] R. A. Breatnach, 'The Lady and the King: A Theme of Irish Literature', *Studies*, 42 (1953), 321–36; P. Mac Cana, 'Aspects of the Theme of King and Goddess in Irish Literature', *Études Celtiques*, 7 (1955–6), 76–114, 356–413; 8 (1958–9), 59–65; J. K. Bollard, 'Sovereignty and the Loathly Lady in English, Welsh and Irish', *Leeds Studies in English*, 17 (1986), 41–59. M. Herbert, 'Goddess and King: The Sacred Marriage in Early Ireland', in L. O. Fradenburg (ed.), *Women and Sovereignty* [= *Cosmos*, 7] (Edinburgh, 1992), 264–75.

could lead to the rescinding of the contract.[75] A further context was competition within a dynasty for the succession to the kingship: as claimants cultivated the favour of the people so they might be thought to woo the goddess. When the kingship in question was an over-kingship, more than one dynasty might be competing. The Irish parallels thus suggest an idea with ancient roots but one which, in the Christian period, was a traditional metaphor with a range of politically important messages attuned to particular contexts.

Binchy's theory invokes the ancient roots of the idea of the marriage between king and goddess of Sovereignty. A goddess well attested in inscriptions from West Yorkshire and Hadrian's Wall was Brigantia.[76] The distribution of these inscriptions permits the suggestion that she was the sovereignty goddess of the Brigantes, particularly worshipped in their core region and on their northern frontier.[77] Binchy's suggestion, therefore, was that the **brigantīnos* was the royal mate of the goddess Brigantia (in British probably **Brigantī*). The Welsh *brenin* 'king' was thus an inheritance from a British past; but it was not common to all the Britons, only to those with a special cult of the goddess Brigantia, namely the Brigantes. Place-name evidence, however, indicates that the cult of Brigantia extended more widely than the territory of the Brigantes.[78] To take only one example of particular significance, the name of the southernmost river of Anglesey, which goes into the sea just to the south-east of Newborough, and thus not far from the later royal seat of Gwynedd at Aberffraw, is Braint (from British **Brigantī*); and British river-names sometimes bear the names of goddesses (as in Aeron from **Agronā*, the goddess of slaughter and battle, *aer*).

Although Binchy's theory has had to be modified, it probably remains the best explanation for Welsh *brenin*. The metaphor of the king's marriage with the goddess of Sovereignty is well attested in Welsh poetry of the twelfth and thirteenth centuries.[79] It is important, however, that in the poems of Prydydd y Moch in the late twelfth century sovereignty appears in the form of a marriage between the king and Britain: the king is *gŵr priod Prydain*, 'the husband of Britain', as well as *priodor Prydain*, 'the rightful possessor of Britain'.[80] Even when the person is king of

[75] T. M. Charles-Edwards, 'A Contract between King and People in Early Medieval Ireland? *Críth Gablach* on Kingship', *Peritia*, 8 (1994), 107–19.

[76] *RIB*, Nos. 627 (AD 208), 628, 630 (all three W. Yorks.), 1053, 1131, 2066 (AD 212 × 217) (three on or near Hadrian's Wall), 2091 (Birrens fort); and one to Bregans, no. 623, W. Yorks. A. R. Burn, *The Romans in Britain: An Anthology of Inscriptions* (Oxford, 1969), no. 194, suggests that 'this personification of the North-Country becomes popular at this time', namely *c.* AD 208, the date of *RIB*, no. 627. Perhaps some time had to pass after the great rebellion of 155–7 before epigraphic acknowledgement of the cult would be uncontroversial.

[77] T. M. Charles-Edwards, 'Native Political Organization in Roman Britain and the Origins of Middle Welsh *Brenhin*', in M. Mayrhofer et al. (eds.), *Antiquitates Indogermanicae* (Innsbruck, 1974), 39.

[78] E. Ekwall, *English River-Names* (Oxford, 1928), 51–2; I. Williams, *Enwau Lleoedd* (Liverpool, 1945), 36.

[79] Rh. Andrews, 'Rhai Agweddau ar Sofraniaeth yng Ngherddi'r Gogynfeirdd', *BBCS* 27 (1976–8), 23–30, where enough of the examples are convincing to establish the conclusion.

[80] *Gwaith Llywarch ap Llywelyn 'Prydydd y Moch'*, ed. E. M. Jones and N. A. Jones, CBT v. 1. 9 (AD 1170 × 1194); 5. 59–60 (1175 or 1194?); 6. 1, 35 (1175 × 1195); 7. 7–8 (1175 × 1195); cf. *CA* 152–3, 'gwledic gwd gyngein / nef ynys brydein', 'Where can be found the lord of the heaven of the

Gwynedd, he is said to be the husband of Britain. Since such claims on the part of poets occurred alongside a recognition by Welsh lawyers—sometimes themselves kinsmen of the poets—that the king of Gwynedd owed tribute to 'the crowned king of London', it is likely that the conception of the king of Gwynedd as 'husband of Britain' stems from the belief, already there in Gildas's *De Excidio*, that the Britons were the rightful heirs of Britain, all other peoples within the island being intruders. It was a matter of enduring rights not contemporary fact. Furthermore, 'Britain' here is probably the Island of Britain rather than a term for Wales: the best examples in Welsh poetry come from a period after *Britannia* had ceased to be a term for Wales. Gildas, it may be remembered, hardly ever wrote directly about 'the Britons'; instead he used the name Britain, conceived as if she were a person. For him, this tied together Britain and the Britons, but it is worth remembering that, in the Romano-British period, Britannia also was a goddess with her own cult.[81] The metaphor of the marriage with the goddess of Sovereignty, in the form of a marriage between a king and Britain, would be enough to ensure that the *brenin* was the major king, not the minor *rhi* of a small kingdom, smaller even than the *civitas*.[82]

At this point it may be helpful to recall the various forms taken by early medieval overlordship, such as a *brenin* might exercize over a *rhi*. These differed in two ways: first, some were lighter than others; but, also, some differed in form rather than in heaviness. The mildest was to claim the position of being the focus of an alliance. Such an alliance aimed to bind the participants to share the same friends and enemies as the king who was the focus: the alliances and hostilities of the others were to be dependent upon his.[83] The point at which this form of overlordship was most likely to generate conflict was over the issue of harbouring exiles, illustrated by the letter of Wealdhere, a late seventh-century bishop of London, to Berhtwald, archbishop of Canterbury.[84] English exiles of a royal dynasty might take refuge among the Britons, as did St Guthlac in the days when he was a royal prince, probably with aspirations to rule the Mercians.[85] In the sixth century, the Breton ruler Macliaw was compelled to take refuge with another ruler, Chonomor.[86] The alliance focused on one participant was capable of being seen by contemporaries (as well as by modern historians) as either a simple alliance or an overlordship, since it partook of both. The second level of overlordship went a bit further: the overlord claimed the right to summon his clients, as I shall call them, to march in his armies,

Island of Britain?', Jarman, *Gododdin*, 162–3 (for the emendation of *gyfgein* to *gyngein*, see Sir Ifor Williams's note *ad loc.*).

81 *RIB*, nos. 643 (York), 2195 (Antonine Wall).

82 Cf. Gildas, *De Excidio*, 33. 2, where Maelgwn as *cunctis paene Brittaniae ducibus tam regno quam status liniamento editior* is compared with God as *rex regum*.

83 The undertaking to have the same allies and enemies was similar to the oath of fealty in *Swerian*, ed. Lieberman, *Die Gesetze der Angelsachsen*, i. 396, where the person becoming a lord's man swears: ic wille beon N. hold ⁊ getriwe ⁊ eal lufian ðæt he lufað ⁊ eal ascunian ðæt he ascunað, 'I will be faithful and true to N and love all that he loves and reject all that he rejects'.

84 *EHD* i, no. 164.

85 Felix, *Life of St Guthlac*, ed. and trans. B. Colgrave (Cambridge, 1956), c. 34; *EHD* i, no. 156.

86 Gregory of Tours, *Hist.*, iv. 4.

as, say, Cadafael of Gwynedd marched in Penda's army in 655. The third level included the first two but added another element, that hostages should be given by the client to the overlord, as Oswiu had given his son, Ecgfrith, as a hostage to Penda before the campaign that led to the Battle of the Winwaed in 655.[87] The fourth required the client-kings to attend their overlord's court on special occasions. In the tenth century, charter witness lists indicate that for part, at least, of Æthelstan's reign, the Welsh kings, Hywel Dda of Dyfed, Idwal of Gwynedd, and Morgan of Gwent, regularly performed this duty.[88] A fifth level of overlordship included the first four but added tribute; the first two levels were honourable forms of subjection, the third and fourth were less favourable, but the fifth was definitely considered to import a certain servility into the relationship.[89]

Yet another element, namely that the client-ruler was denied the status or, less severely, the full status of king might add a sixth level: he was a *dux* or perhaps a *subregulus*. This level, however, was capable of being seen differently by the overlord and his client: the Franks denied the rank of king to Breton rulers in the sixth century, but that does not mean that the Breton subjects of such 'counts' took the same view.[90] And it was also possible for this form of overlordship to exist without some or even most of the previous levels, as when the Frisian king, Radbod, a notably independent ruler of the early eighth century, was termed a *dux* in Frankish sources but a king elsewhere.[91] The late Merovingian overlordship relied heavily on titular supremacy: the leaders with most military power, dukes and mayors of the palace, were all the more willing to give their allegiance to a single Merovingian king, because that king was unlikely to threaten their control over their territories. In such a case denying kingship to a subordinate ruler was more a style or form of overlordship than a level. But when, for example, the ruler of the Hwicce ceased to be regarded as a king, that did indeed add another level to his subjection to Mercian overlordship.

In the seventh and final level, princes, officials, and perhaps also nobles of the overlord's kingdom gained land or authority within the client kingdom: this also happened, to the kingdom of the Hwicce in the eighth century.[92] There were, therefore, both different levels of overlordship, some lighter, some heavier, and different styles of overlordship—different ways of exercizing power over a client-king, ways which were alternative devices rather than different levels of power.

One natural context for deployment of the metaphor of the marriage with the goddess was, as we have noted, competition for the royal succession—a competition for the favours of the goddess. This is also a context in which we find other old

[87] Bede, *HE* iii. 24.

[88] For example S 413, 416, 417.

[89] Stephen, *Vita Wilfridi*, 20, 'non tam ad bellandum quam ad redigendum sub tributo servili animo', 'intending not merely to fight but to subject them to paying tribute in a servile spirit'; 'saoire Ua Neill o Sinainn go muir, gan cain gan cabhach', 'the freedom of the Uí Néill from the Shannon to the sea, without tributary servitude, without joint-debt', CS 978 = 980.

[90] Gregory of Tours, *Hist.*, iv. 4.

[91] *Liber Historiae Francorum*, cc. 51, 52; Fredegar, Cont. cc. 8, 9; Bede, *HE* v 9, 10.

[92] S 116 = *CS* 236.

terms, still present in the twelfth and thirteenth centuries, but with a lineage going back right through the early medieval period and beyond. For a small kingdom, the assumption by the ninth century was that a single kindred constituted the royal dynasty. This is implicit in the way the *Historia Brittonum* identified the minor territory of Gwerthrynion with the kindred descended from Gwrtheyrn (Vortigern): Gwerthrynion was first the kindred and secondarily the kingdom.[93] The same assumption is present on a grander scale in the brief narrative in the tenth-century Harleian genealogies about the origins of the early kings of Gwynedd and other parts of north and west Wales:[94]

> These are the names of the sons of Cunedda, of whom there were nine: Tybion, the first-born, who died in the land which is called Manaw Gododdin and did not come hither with his father and his aforementioned brothers; Meirion, his son, divided their possessions among his kinsmen; the second was Osfael; the third Rhufon; the fourth Dunod; the fifth Ceredig; the sixth Afloeg; the seventh Einion Yrth; the eighth Dogfael; the ninth Edern.
>
> This is their boundary: from the river which is called Dwfr Dwyw [Dee] as far as the other river, the Teifi. And they settled many lands in the western part of Britain.

An early medieval churchman, reading this account, would very probably be reminded of the story of Abraham, Isaac, and Jacob in the book of Genesis—of the voluntary exile undertaken by Abraham from the land of the Chaldees into Palestine, of God's promise that Abraham would be the father of a great nation, of the way his grandson, Jacob, gave his other name, Israel, to that nation, and how his twelve sons gave their names to the twelve tribes of Israel. Meirion, who stepped into his father's shoes and divided the lands among his uncles, gave his name to Meirionydd, Osfael to Osfeiling or Osfeilion, Rhufon to Rhufoniog, Dunod to Dunoding, Ceredig to Ceredigion, Dogfael to Dogfeiling, Edern to Edeirnion.[95] Elsewhere we are told that Afloeg gave his name to Aflogion or Afloegion, a more mysterious entity than the rest.[96] Einion Yrth was the ancestor, although this is not stated, of the kings of Gwynedd; his descendant was Maelgwn, who gave his name to the Maelgyning.[97] The text may well have been framed precisely in order to allude to Genesis and so adorn a political claim with hallowed scriptural language.

[93] *HB*, c. 49.

[94] *EWGT* 13, HG 32.

[95] Osfeilion was in Anglesey, as shown by AC 902: Igmunt in insula Mon uenit et tenuit Maes Osmeliaun. The district was near or around Llanfaes in Anglesey if we assume that the *maes* of Llanfaes was *Maes Osmeliaun*. This seems likely given the distribution of Viking-age findspots in Anglesey: M. Redknap, 'Viking-Age Settlement in Wales: Some Recent Advances', *THSC 2005*, NS 12 (2006), 17, fig. 5. For Dogfeiling, see *Marwnad Cynddylan*, lines 9 and 15, ed. R. G. Gruffydd, *Bardos*, 19, 23; ed. Rowlands, *EWSP* 174; *EWGT* 92 (By A 29. 8); but ibid. 45, JC 7, has *Docuayl yg Keueilyawc*; *WATU* 59 and Map 44: originally = Dyffryn Clwyd, then one of the commotes within that cantref.

[96] *EWGT* 45, JC 7, later Gaflogion, J. G. Evans, *Report on Welsh Manuscripts*, ii. 4 (London, 1910), 941, and Cafflogion, *WATU* 27 (both based on back-formations involving lenition); *WATU* map 66. On the formation of these names, see M. Richards, 'Early Welsh Territorial Suffixes', *Journal of the Royal Society of Antiquaries of Ireland*, 96 (1965), 205–12.

[97] *The Poems of Taliesin*, ed. I. Williams, xi. 36; *Book of Taliesin*, ed. Evans, 30. 17–18; CBT II. 28. 46; III. 24. 164; IV. 4. 271; IV. 12. 18.

The story of Cunedda and his sons also has, however, more particular messages. Meirion divided the lands as the son of the eldest son of Cunedda. This has a double implication: first, that, if a brother died before a partition of the inheritance could take place, his son or sons would act in his place; and, secondly, that in a royal dynasty the brother who partitioned the land was not, as usual with non-royal inheritance, the youngest son, but the eldest.[98] True, Meirion probably would have been younger than his co-sharers, namely his uncles; yet the text specified that he acted in the place of his father and thus his own age was probably irrelevant. Often, if the eldest son divided the inheritance, this would mean that the successor to the kingship divided the lands of his brothers and so could control the distribution of landed power in the dynasty. Yet the implication was not entirely straightforward: Einion Yrth, the son of Cunedda who was the ancestor of the later kings, was the seventh son, not the first.

The story therefore has a bearing on an issue over royal succession, on which scholars have taken different views. The problem arises from two themes in the evidence: on the one hand, the legal texts that discuss, at the beginning of the 'laws of court', the king and queen, also contain a section on the heir-apparent to the kingship.[99] The following is from MS *E* of *Llyfr Iorwerth*, a lawbook of the first half of the thirteenth century, with an italicized addition at the beginning from the other branch of the tradition represented by MSS *B* and *D*:[100]

> [1]*Gvrthdrych .i.* edlig, yu yr hun a dyly gwledychu gwedy y brenhin ac a dyly bot yn anrydedussaw wedy y brenhyn a'r vrenines. [2]Ew a dyly bot yn uab neu yn nei y'r brenhyn . . . . [5]Ny dyly ynteu rody dym o hynny heb gannyat y brenhin; a phan uo marv yr edlig, ew a dyly adau y ueirch a'y gun y'r brenhyn, cany dyly ew talu ebediu namyn hunnu. [6]Sew achaus nas dyly, urth y uot yn aylaut y'r brenin. [7]Sew yu aylodeu y brenhin, y ueibyon a'y neieint a'y gevyndyrv. [8]Rei a dyweyt bot yn edlig pob un o'r rei hyny. [9]Ereill a dyweit nad edlig neb namyn y neb a rodo y brenhyn ydau gobeith a gurthrychyat.
>
> *The expected one, that is,* the edling, is the one who ought to rule after the king and who ought to be the most honourable after the king and the queen. It is right that he should be a son or nephew to the king. . . . He is not entitled to give any of these things without the permission of the king. And when the edling dies, he should leave his horses and his hounds to the king, since he ought not to pay a death-due other than that. This is the reason why he ought not, because he is a 'king's limb'. These are the limbs of the king: his sons and his nephews and his first cousins. Some say that each one of those persons is an edling. Others say that only the one to whom the king gives hope and expectation is edling.

[98] *Llyfr Iorwerth*, ed. A. Rh. Wiliam, 82/6–7, trans. Jenkins, *LTMW* 99.

[99] On the character of the lawbooks' treatment of king, queen, and *edling*, see R. Chapman Stacey, 'King, Queen, and *Edling* in the Laws of Court', in Charles-Edwards et al. (eds.), *The Welsh King and his Court*, 29–62.

[100] Compare the text of MS *B* in *Llyfr Iorwerth*, ed. Wiliam (Cardiff, 1960), § 4, and trans. D. Jenkins, *The Law of Hywel Dda: Law Texts from Medieval Wales* (Llandysul, 1986), 6–7; *Latin Texts of the Welsh Laws*, ed. Emanuel, 277. 27–278. 10.

This passage begins with the principle that there is a single heir-apparent whose identity has already been settled by the current king.[101] The competition for the succession ought, therefore, to take place during the previous king's reign; and it ought to deliver a single agreed successor. This single heir-apparent has various names: *edling* is a loan from Old English *ætheling*, 'person of noble birth', 'prince'; *gwrthddrych*, however, is pure Welsh, 'the expected one', the person to whose kingship the people look forward; it has been compared with the way the early eighth-century Irish lawtract described the heir-apparent: 'The second to a king, why is he so called? Because the entire people looks forward to [his] kingship without contention against him'.[102] Elsewhere he is given the longer title, *gwrthrychiad*, although in the version given above *gwrthrychiad* is the expectation which the current king grants.[103] The passage also brings out into the open a disagreement over the meaning of *edling*. The alternative view, according to which the title *edling* applied to all 'the king's limbs', reflected the meaning of the Old English *ætheling* more accurately than did the normal use of *edling* for the heir-apparent;[104] but even this alternative view did not claim that there was not an heir-apparent. Presumably he would have been called *gwrthddrych* or *gwrthrychiad* and the equivalence stated by 'that is, the edling' would have been denied.

The view of the lawyers, therefore, both of North and South Wales, was that there was a single heir-apparent to the kingship. The existence of a recognized position of designated heir-apparent already in the ninth century is supported by Asser's reference to Alfred as his brother's *secundarius*, by which Asser meant 'heir-apparent' and not merely 'second in power' as in Stephen of Ripon's description of Berhtfrith as *secundus a rege*, 'second after the king'.[105] The ability of the current king to designate his heir, to give him 'hope and expectation', was an important lever of power to enable the king to control his close kinsmen; so, also, if he was the eldest son, was his right to allocate lands to his brothers. The first duty of a Welsh king was to rule his kindred; only if he succeeded with them would he succeed as a king of the whole people.

Yet, another theme was allied to this right to partition the lands of his brothers, since such lands would often consist of an entire *cantref* or commote over which the lord, *arglwydd*, would exercise a quasi-regalian authority. The beginning of the Life of St Gwynllyw contains a statement of a model relationship between royal brothers. St Gwynllyw was the eldest son of Glywys, 'king of the southern Britons' and eponymous ancestor of the Glywysing of south-east Wales. Gwynllyw 'was not

[101] J. B. Smith, 'Dynastic Succession in Medieval Wales', *BBCS* 33 (1986), 199–232; T. M. Charles-Edwards, 'Dynastic Succession in Early Medieval Wales', in R. A. Griffiths and P. Schofield (eds.), *Wales and the Welsh in the Early Middle* Ages (Cardiff, 2011), 70–88.

[102] *Críth Gablach*, ed. D. A. Binchy (Dublin, 1941), § 29, discussed by Binchy, 'Some Celtic Legal Terms', *Celtica*, 3 (1956), 221–8.

[103] Latin Recension C has both *gwrthrychiad* and *gwrthrych*: *Latin Text of the Welsh Laws*, 277. 27; 278. 4.

[104] D. N. Dumville, 'The Ætheling: A Study in Anglo-Saxon Constitutional History', *Anglo-Saxon England*, 8 (1979), 12–13.

[105] Stephen, *Life of St Wilfrid*, c. 60: *secundus a rege princeps.*

a suppressor, but a supporter of kinship'; 'being the eldest he might have kept the whole but he was unwilling to suppress his brothers', and thus he gave each of his six brothers one of the seven *cantrefi* of Glamorgan, reserving only Gwynllŵg for himself.[106] Gwynllyw, as we saw in the previous chapter, was seen as ancestor of a kindred, Gwynllŵg—a kindred whose inheritance consisted of the *cantref* also called Gwynllŵg. Inheritance and kindred were virtually one and the same thing. The ideal, as presented in this early twelfth-century Life, was that a new king should seek to endow all of his brothers with lordship—a plan which has been compared with the apanages granted by Capetian kings to their brothers.[107] What is notable in the Life of St Gwynllyw is that the person who allows a partition of lands is the eldest brother, not the father. Glywys did not decide that each of his sons should receive a *cantref*; that was the prerogative of Gwynllyw as the eldest son. On this view, the choice of the heir-apparent should be made during the previous king's reign, but the division of land was made by the successor at the beginning of his reign. We shall return later to the question of what happened to the brothers' descendants.

Mere descent, however, did not qualify someone as a plausible contender for the kingship. Another term preserved in the twelfth-century poetry of Cynddelw is *deifniog rhi*, 'material of a king'. Cynddelw was lamenting the death of Iorwerth Goch, younger brother of Madog ap Maredudd, king of Powys. In the course of the lament he has the line, 'Haeddws deifniog rhi defnydd fy marddawd', 'the material of a king deserved the matter of my praise'.[108] The significance of the phrase 'material of a king' is partially revealed in the line itself, since *deifniog* was itself formed from *defnydd* at an early period before the latter acquired the final *-dd*.[109] There is highly significant wordplay in the line, of a type common in Cynddelw's poetry: 'The *deifniog* of a king deserved the *defnydd* of my praise.' The suggestion is that, as Iorwerth Goch deserved to be king, he also deserved the content of Cyndddelw's poem, that is, praise worthy of a king. In Irish the cognate *damnae ríg* was used for possible contenders for the succession; although they might not become king, such men were kingly; and, because they were acknowledged to be kingly, they sustained the kingly status of their branch of the dynasty.[110] In praising Iorwerth Goch, Cynddelw was not expressing any sentiment disloyal to Madog ap Maredudd, the brother who actually did become king of Powys and who had already died at this date. He was not claiming that Iorwerth Goch should have become king: to claim that Iorwerth Goch was of kingly worth did not imply for one moment that he was of even kinglier worth than Madog. Iorwerth met a

[106] *Vita S. Gundleii*, § 1, *VSBG* 172; cf. *Vita S. Cadoci*, Pref., *VSBG* 24.

[107] Smith, 'Dynastic Succession', 206–9, 216–18.

[108] CBT iii. 12. 5; Rh. M. Andrews and D. Stephenson, '*Draig Argoed*: Iorwerth Goch ap Maredudd, *c.* 1110–1171', *CMCS* 52 (2006), 81–2, take a different view, which, however, obliges one to suppose that Cynddelw was prepared to recognize Iorwerth Goch as a 'well-endowed' *rhi*, which does not seem to me probable.

[109] Dated by Jackson, *LHEB*, § 38 A. 3, to *c.* 400.

[110] *EIWK* 90–111.

standard; Madog prevailed in a competition. Here again, because of the relationship between *deifniog* and *defnydd* and the Irish cognate, *damnae ríg*, ideas preserved in the poetry of the twelfth and thirteenth centuries can be argued to have been inherited from the remote past; in this instance it is probable that the conception was already old when, in 410, the emperor Honorius told the British *civitates* to look to their own defences.

The process by which a prince became king was complex. For one thing it involved different players: the king might give 'hope and expectation' to one contender in particular and so make him *gwrthddrych*, but he would hardly favour anyone whom the influential section of his people did not already regard as 'material of a king'. Even in the early thirteenth century, and faced with as powerful a king as Llywelyn ab Iorwerth, the poets expressed a clear preference for the king's elder son, Gruffudd; but they did not claim that Dafydd, the king's designated heir, was unworthy to be king.[111] Once someone was recognized as 'material of a king', he entered a competition with the others similarly favoured. The laws give the decision as to who was the winner in this competition to the king, but one should not suppose that no one else sought to influence the outcome; according to Gerald of Wales, foster-parents of each of the various candidates would work hard to seek their particular foster-son's success.[112]

When the twelfth- and thirteenth-century laws laid out the position of *edling* or *gwrthddrych*, a king of Gwynedd might claim authority over other kings outside Gwynedd, but within his own kingdom there were no client-kings. After 1125 there was only one royal dynasty within Gwynedd.[113] For an earlier period, however, no such assumption can be made, even if it was sometimes true. This raises the question whether different dynasties might compete for the kingship of Gwynedd. Within their own smaller kingdoms, royal succession would presumably have been decided within the limits of a single royal kindred, but when it came to Gwynedd, the issues would have been quite different. This issue was critical in the eleventh century. In the tenth century, the descendants of Anarawd ap Rhodri monopolized the kingship of Gwynedd, except for eight years, 942–950, when Hywel Dda, a cousin, took Gwynedd in addition to Dyfed and Ceredigion. In the eleventh century, however, Anarawd's descendants only held the kingship for a few years, excluded notably by Llywelyn ap Seisyll (*ob.* 1023) and his son, Gruffudd ap Llywelyn (*ob.* 1064). The ancestry of Llywelyn ap Seisyll is unknown, probably because, once Anarawd's descendants returned to power, they were happy to see their rivals' pedigrees consigned to oblivion. Even after 1064 other lineages than the Merfynion competed for the kingship of Gwynedd, for example Trahaearn ap Caradog of Arwystli. Against such claims the Life of Gruffudd ap Cynan brings

[111] CBT v. 29 and 30, vi. 3.

[112] Gerald of Wales, *Descriptio Kambriae*, ii. 4.

[113] *Brut*, 1125: 'And a little after that, Cadwallon ap Gruffudd ap Cynan, the man who was mentioned above, slew his three uncles, namely, Goronwy and Rhiryd and Meilyr, sons of Owain ab Edwin.' This was the end of a dynasty associated with Tegeingl, possibly another branch of the Merfynion: P. C. Bartrum, *Welsh Genealogies* (Cardiff, 1974), i. [42], ii, *s.v.* EDWIN 1.

forward implicit arguments based on the law of inheritance: claimants other than the descendants of Anarawd ap Rhodri are seen as intruders.[114] If, however, we argue from the broad shape of events, it looks as though there were periods, such as the tenth century, when a single royal lineage monopolized the kingship of Gwynedd, and other periods when there was no single royal lineage in control: in the late eighth and early ninth century, the Maelgyning probably had to share the kingship of Gwynedd with the dynasty of Rhos.[115]

The role of the royal pedigree in claims to succession is less clear than its role once someone was king. Membership of a royal kindred that belonged to the kingdom in question was a necessary but not a sufficient qualification for any claim to get off the ground. It was a ticket to enter the race, but not a guarantee even that one would start. A candidate who was genealogically qualified might not be *deifniog rhi*. Once someone had become king, and even when he had been designated as *gwrthddrych*, such issues did not arise. One type of genealogy, however, seems to have played a significant role in establishing someone as *deifniog rhi*. In the eleventh century, as we have seen, the descendants of Anarawd ap Rhodri ap Merfyn, the Gwynedd branch of the Merfynion, were largely out of the kingship. Iago ab Idwal held the kingship of Gwynedd for a few years before his death in 1039, but after 1039 they were in exile in the kingdom of Dublin.[116] When Iago's grandson, Gruffudd ap Cynan, made his bid for the kingship, beginning in 1081, he needed every argument he could find to strengthen his case. This necessity probably explains the unusual elaboration of his genealogy at the beginning of his Life, composed in the reign of his son, Owain Gwynedd, and thus before 1170; a date 1137 ×1148 is likely.[117] The biographer's first step is to give Gruffudd's patriline back to Rhodri Mawr, and then via Rhodri's mother, Ethyllt, to the Maelgyning. He then gives his mother's patriline back to Harald Fairhair, namely his 'descent on his mother's side' or his 'descent on his mother's side according to his mother's father'. Thirdly he gives the pedigree of his mother's mother; then there is the descent of his mother's father's mother, and finally of his mother's father's father's mother. In effect, the biographer searches for king's daughters, Gruffudd's ancestresses, through whom he can attach Gruffudd to as many royal dynasties as possible and so demonstrate as much royal descent as possible. As it happens he finds them on his mother's side not on his father's; the latter is therefore represented only by the single patriline. The resulting picture of Gruffudd's descent is as follows:

[114] *Vita Griffini filii Conani*, ed. Russell, §§ 10, 12; the terms used in the medieval Welsh translation of the Life are also interesting, *Historia Gruffud vab Kenan*, ed. D. S. Evans (Cardiff, 1977), 6–8; *EIWK* 294–6.

[115] See below, 476–7.

[116] See below, 554–5.

[117] *Vita Griffini filii Conani*, ed. Russell, 46–7; D. Thornton, 'The Genealogy of Gruffudd ap Cynan', in K. L. Maund (ed.), *Gruffudd ap Cynan: A Collaborative Biography* (Woodbridge, 1997), 79–108; *EIWK* 220–4.

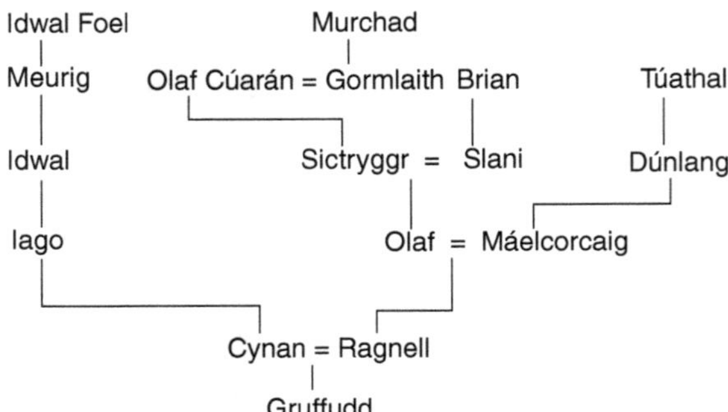

Figure 10.1. The ancestors of Gruffudd ap Cynan

The principle behind this genealogy was that, on the whole, men married women of a status equal to their own. Hence, if a man married into royalty, he would normally himself be royal. *Ymgyfathrachu* 'mutual-joint-inter-lineaging' began as a means to make alliances, but it ended by marking the status of children born of the alliance. His father's marriage into the dynasty of Dublin thus meant that Hiberno-Norse royalty sustained Gruffudd's claim to be of royal status. Paradoxically, it was his father's exile which was the reason for so many grand ancestresses; yet, because Cynan ab Iago was royal, even though he was not king, his marriage was royal and his son was royal. He was *deifniog rhi* in terms of his descent.

The impression created by such terms as *deifniog rhi* and *gwrthddrych*, taken together with their Irish counterparts, is that the pattern of royal succession was inherited from a remote Celtic past. Yet, most of the kingdoms of the Britons in the time of Gildas were either new creations or, at least, revivals. Moreover, at that time, so one might expect, the immediate Roman past would have bulked much larger in the Britons' political inheritance than a remote Iron Age. It is worth taking another look, therefore, at Gildas's kings.

Dynasties, in Gildas's *De Excidio*, appear primarily in two guises: as the theatre of kin-slaying and as another example of moral degradation. Constantine, king of Dumnonia, killed two royal youths; if one can argue by weight of parallels, the likelihood is that they were potential rivals for the kingship because they belonged to Constantine's own kindred. Certainly, Constantine was accused directly of parricide.[118] Maelgwn, the 'island dragon', killed to come to the throne: 'Did you not, in the first years of your youth, use sword and spear and flame in the cruel dispatch of the king your uncle and nearly all his bravest soldiers.'[119] Subsequently he took his brother's son's wife and went on to slay her husband.[120] Moral degradation was exemplified in the grandchildren of Ambrosius Aurelianus, himself the son of 'parents who had worn the purple': 'His descendants in our day have

[118] Gildas, *De Excidio*, 28. [119] Ibid. 33. 4. [120] Ibid. 35. 2.

become greatly inferior to their grandfather's excellence.'[121] Vortipor, 'tyrant of the Demetae', was 'the bad son of a good father'.[122] To judge by Gildas, then, royal dynasties were created in the fifth century and the same dynasties sometimes, at least, endured into the sixth. The example of Riothamus suggests that the same timescale applied to those Britons who had migrated to Gaul.

Gildas is also informative on the companions of kings: 'they despise the harmless and the humble, but exalt to the stars, so far as they can, their military companions, bloody, proud and murderous men, adulterers and enemies of God'.[123] As for Maelgwn:[124]

> Your excited ears hear not the praises of God from the sweet voices of the tuneful recruits of Christ, not the melodious music of the Church, but empty praises of yourself from the mouths of criminals who grate on the hearing like raving hucksters—mouths stuffed with lies and liable to bedew bystanders with their foaming phlegm.

This is usually, and probably correctly, taken to refer to bards—praise-poets—lauding Maelgwn in the vernacular. Gildas's younger contemporary, Venantius Fortunatus, mentions British bards and also a distinctively British instrument, the *crotta*, the *crwth*, a form of stringed instrument, a 'crowd'.[125] But, as Fortunatus's work exemplifies, sixth-century kings could be praised in Latin and within the conventions of imperial panegyric; for kings such as Chilperic, who had his own aspirations to write Latin verse as well as to lord it over his kinsmen, panegyric composed as if to an emperor would be especially flattering.[126] There is no reason to think that Gildas denounced those who praised Maelgwn because they sang in the vernacular; what mattered for him was that their praises were lies. Because Welsh literature has a strong tradition of panegyric it is reasonable to think that Gildas's *praecones*, translated 'hucksters' by Winterbottom, but used also for 'heralds' and even 'panegyricists', may have been British bards; but they may also have included panegyric poets using Latin.[127]

The two forms of companion, *commanipulares*, 'military companions', and *praecones*, perhaps 'panegyricists', were tied together in early Welsh poetry. The poet praised the warrior, and a great poem made the fame of both warrior and poet endure. Reputation was the pivot on which much of early Welsh political life seems

121 Ibid. 25. 4.

122 Ibid. 31. 1.

123 Ibid. 27.

124 Ibid. 34. 6 (note *praeconum ore ritu bacchantium concrepante*); on this I follow P. Sims-Williams, 'Gildas and Vernacular Poetry', in Lapidge and Dumville, *Gildas: New Approaches*, 174–6; cf. J. E. Caerwyn Williams, 'Gildas, Maelgwn and the Bards', in R. R. Davies et al. (eds.), *Welsh Society and Nationhood*, 22–7, who also discusses, 29–30, *De Excidio*, 66. 4, *ineptas saecularium hominum fabulas*, 'the foolish stories of worldly men'.

125 Venantius Fortunatus, *Opera Poetica*, ed. F. Leo, vii. 8; H. Moisl, 'A Sixth-Century Reference to the British *Bardd*', *BBCS* 29 (1980–2), 269–73, and Sims-Williams, 'Gildas and Vernacular Poetry', 179.

126 J. W. George, *Venantius Fortunatus: A Poet in Merovingian Gaul* (Oxford, 1992), 12–13, 48–57; Chilperic's poem for the feast day of St Medard is ed. K. Strecker, MGH Poetae iv. 2 (1923), 455–7.

127 The translation of *praecones* is discussed by Sims-Williams, 'Gildas and Vernacular Poetry', 175.

to have turned. Arthur's remark to Cai in *Culhwch and Olwen*, 'we are noble as long as men seek us out', reveals one side of a social contract that is normally implicit. The other side was that a noble needed access to the king's hall if his rank were to be confirmed. A warrior called Llifiau is praised in the *Gododdin* in that 'He was not excluded in the *cyntedd* from the mead-drink';[128] the *cyntedd* was the part of the hall in which the king and heir-apparent sat. The contractual linkage went further as another pair of lines in the *Gododdin* illustrate:

> He attacked in battle, in the forefront,
> In return for mead in the hall and drinking of wine.

The king's household was the core of his military force, so that there were very good reasons why Gildas's five kings would 'exalt to the stars, so far as they can, their military companions'.[129]

One of the curious features of early Welsh history is the close resemblance between the standard career of a Welsh *bonheddig*, according to the principal lawbook from Gwynedd, and the pattern which obtained in seventh-century Northumbria. When a *bonheddig* reaches the age of fourteen, 'it is right for the father to take his son to the lord and to commend him to him. And then it is right for him to do homage to the lord'.[130] At the end of this section two statuses are set out in terms of *galanas* and *sarhaed*: one is for the *bonheddig canhwynol*, an 'innate *bonheddig*', namely sixty-three kine for the *galanas* and three kine with sixty pence for the *sarhaed*. But if he is a *gŵr ar deulu*, 'a man of the bodyguard', the *galanas* will be eighty-four kine and the *sarhaed* four kine and eighty pence.[131] When he succeeds to his inheritance he will 'ascend' to the status of *uchelwr* or *marchog*, which entails a *galanas* of 126 kine and a *sarhaed* of six kine and 120 *d*. Although it may be tempting to translate *marchog* here by 'knight', because that is indeed the Welsh word used in the Welsh Arthurian Romances for a knight, the temptation should be resisted. This *marchog* gains his status not by dubbing but by inheritance; and this Welsh *marchog* has passed beyond the stage at which, as a *gŵr ar deulu* or *teuluwr*, he belongs to the military retinue of the king. Among the Welsh glosses on Ovid's *Ars Amatoria* (of the second half of the ninth century or early in the tenth), Latin *adulter* 'adulterer' is explained by giving an example, *guas marchauc*, 'servant of a *marchog*'.[132] Here *marchog* may well be a term of high status but he is also probably older than the *gwas*: the queen Pasiphae in Ovid's text is imagined as having an affair with the *gwas* rather than with the *marchog*.

As for the *gŵr ar deulu*, his status is well below that of the *uchelwr* but above that of the ordinary *bonheddig*. All young freemen, at the age of fourteen, seem to have been commended to the Lord or king, but only some were chosen to be recruited

[128] Jarman, *Gododdin*, l. 250; *CA*, l. 245.

[129] Gildas, *De Excidio*, 27.

[130] Jenkins, *LTMW* 131, translating *Llyfr Iorwerth*, ed. Wiliam, 98/5.

[131] For the *teulu*, literally 'house-host' of the king, see S. Davies, *Welsh Military Institutions, 633–1283* (Cardiff, 2004), ch. 1.

[132] *Saint Dunstan's Classbook from Glastonbury*, ed. R. W. Hunt, Umbrae Codocum Occidentalium, 4 (Amsterdam, 1961), fo. 41r, l. 22 = l. 309 of *Ars Amatoria*.

into his war band or *teulu*. A privileged section of the free population were thus brought into the life of the court in their teens. The implication of the higher status attached to the *uchelwyr* is that they would no longer have formed part of the *teulu*. Hence a desirable career would have taken a young *bonheddig* into the *teulu* after he was commended by his father, and he would have left the *teulu* at the very latest when he succeeded to his inheritance on his father's death. The *teulu* gave young men a status and a role within the kingdom independent of their father's authority and when they were between childhood and the adulthood of a farmer. All this is very like the *militia* of the seventh-century Northumbrian kings, to which a young noble might be recruited in his teens, as was St Benedict Biscop, the founder of Wearmouth. There, too, acquisition of land, possibly by a gift of land from the king as well as by inheritance, signalled the departure of a nobleman from the war band and his entry into the life of a local aristocrat. The parallel, as well as the way both the Briton and the Englishman might 'earn his mead' in the king's war band, suggest that the medieval Welsh *teulu* may have had a long history before it ever entered the pages of the lawbooks. Because of partible inheritance both the early English nobleman and his Welsh counterpart needed royal favour in the form of land-grants to maintain the wealth and influence of his father. The effect of this cycle of partition and, with good fortune, new gift of land is still visible in the Wales of the thirteenth century, but by then it was probably centuries old.[133]

Appendix. A regnal list: *Cyfoesi Myrddin a Gwenddydd ei Chwaer*[134]

Cyfoesi Myrddin a Gwenddydd ei Chwaer is a long prophetic poem in the form of a dialogue between Myrddin and his sister Gwenddydd.[135] Myrddin was already in the tenth century a standard poetic persona to whom prophetic poems could be ascribed. This is demonstrated by the opening of *Armes Prydain*, another prophecy ascribed to Myrddin: it is so phrased as to imply that Myrddin's prophetic role was already a recognized convention.[136] In *Cyfoesi*, however, the use of Myrddin's poetic persona is less formulaic than in *Armes Prydain*. Here there are references to his career as a wild man of the wood, to the battle of Arfderydd, and to his patron, Gwenddolau. Conventions of another kind are, however, evident: Gwenddydd, the sister, speaks as if she were Myrddin's disciple, eliciting his prophecies one by one by the questions she puts. This is the standard form, both in convention and reality, adopted by the teacher and his pupil; and Myrddin's prophecies are thus the knowledge passed down in

133 *EIWK* 238–9.

134 *Cyfoesi Myrddin a Gwenddydd ei Chwaer*, ed. M. B. Jenkins, 'Aspects of the Welsh Prophetic Tradition in the Middle Ages', unpublished Ph.D. thesis, University of Cambridge (1990), 33–90; for the date of the original version, see ibid. 40–1; *The Poetry in the Red Book of Hergest*, ed. J. G. Evans (Llanbedrog, 1911), 1–4, cols. 577–83. I am indebted to the help of Owain Wyn Jones with this text.

135 A. O. H. Jarman, 'The Merlin Legend and the Welsh Tradition of Prophecy', in R. Bromwich et al. (eds.), *The Arthur of the Welsh: The Arthurian Legend in Medieval Welsh Literature* (Cardiff, 1991), 119.

136 See below, 520, 534.

Table 10.1. The Regnal List in *Cyfoesi Myrddin a Gwenddydd ei Chwaer* compared with genealogies and annals

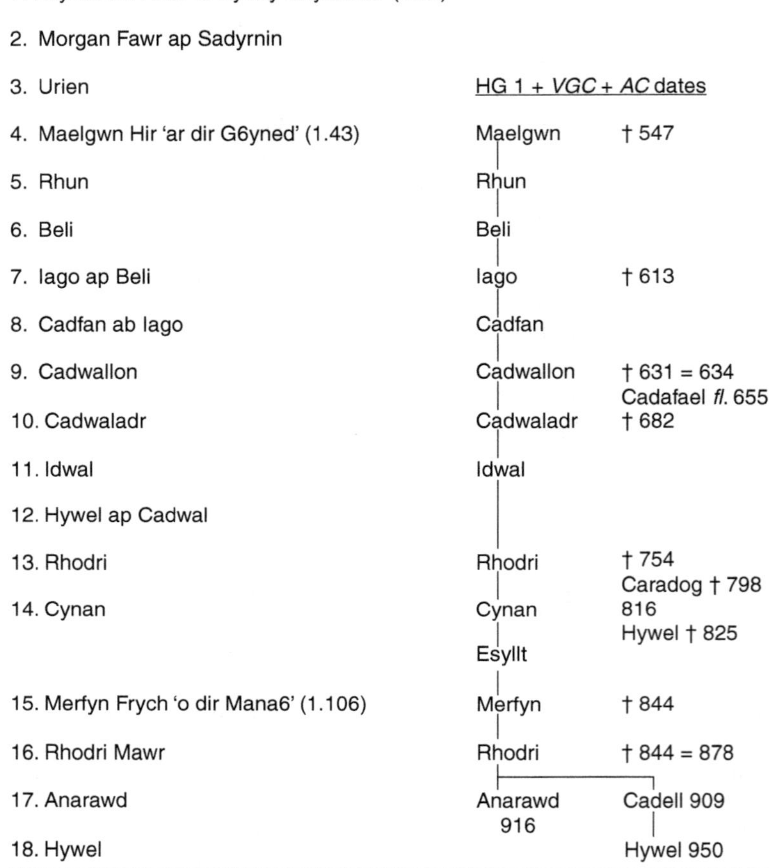

1. Rhydderch Hael 'a Cymry oll ydana6' (1.15)		
2. Morgan Fawr ap Sadyrnin		
3. Urien	HG 1 + *VGC* + *AC* dates	
4. Maelgwn Hir 'ar dir G6yned' (1.43)	Maelgwn	† 547
5. Rhun	Rhun	
6. Beli	Beli	
7. Iago ap Beli	Iago	† 613
8. Cadfan ab Iago	Cadfan	
9. Cadwallon	Cadwallon	† 631 = 634
		Cadafael *fl.* 655
10. Cadwaladr	Cadwaladr	† 682
11. Idwal	Idwal	
12. Hywel ap Cadwal		
13. Rhodri	Rhodri	† 754
		Caradog † 798
14. Cynan	Cynan	816
		Hywel † 825
	Esyllt	
15. Merfyn Frych 'o dir Mana6' (1.106)	Merfyn	† 844
16. Rhodri Mawr	Rhodri	† 844 = 878
17. Anarawd	Anarawd 916	Cadell 909
18. Hywel		Hywel 950

a tradition of learning. These features distinguish the form of the poem from the broadly comparable Irish prophecies, *Baile Chuinn* and *Baile in Scáil*.[137] Like them it contains a regnal list in the form of a prophecy; but, whereas in *Baile Chuinn* the prophet is the ancestor of most later kings of Tara, and in *Baile in Scáil* the spectre performs the same role, Myrddin's prophetic gifts belong more with the poets. They may be presented as having been called into existence by the terror of the battle of Arfderydd, but Myrddin's knowledge

[137] *Baile Chuinn*, ed. E. Bhreathnach and K. Murray in E. Bhreathnach (ed.), *The Kingship and Landscape of Tara* (Dublin, 2005), 73–94; *Baile in Scáil*, ed. K. Murray, Irish Texts Society 58 (London, 2004).

is also to become part of poetic tradition. In this poem, the teaching of the prophetic poet echoes the teaching of the Latin scholar, especially as it is presented in the colloquy texts.

Prophecies of this type can plausibly be dated by the kings whose reigns were foretold. A sequence taken from earlier lists and running down to a contemporary ruler is given poetic form; but it is followed by obscure prophecy. Past and contemporary kings can be readily identified, but, because it claims to be prophetic, the poem continues on beyond the reign in which it is composed; but from this point it necessarily becomes more obscure in style. A suggestion, therefore, is that the date of the poem belongs within the reign of the last clearly identified king. This poses a problem for *Cyfoesi*, which we can appreciate by following its sequence of kings. The earliest rulers named do not form a chronological sequence but are a roughly contemporaneous group of northern British kings: Gwenddolau, Myrddin's supposed patron, Rhydderch of Dumbarton, Gwenddolau's enemy, Morgan Fawr, and Urien. We then move back a generation to Maelgwn of Gwynedd, with whom the regnal list proper begins. The immediately following rulers are all Maelgwn's descendants and all are kings of Gwynedd. This part of the poem, then, is a regnal list of the Maelgyning, the lineage descended from Maelgwn. It does not include those kings, not of the Maelgyning, who appear to have belonged to the related line of Rhos (the identity of no. 12 is unknown).

The regnal list seems to be derived from a pedigree of the Maelgyning kings of Gwynedd in the form known from the Harleian Genealogies and later versions. The assumption is that a father is normally succeeded by one of his sons. It accords with the statements in the laws about the *edling*, except that it does not allow for the claim of a brother or a brother's son except in the case of the last named in the original sequence, Hywel Dda, who appears as if he succeeded directly to Anarawd, rather than, as happened in reality, through the death of Idwal Foel ab Anarawd. This makes it plausible to date the poem to the period when Hywel reigned over all the territory of the Merfynion.

PART III

THE BRITONS AND THE ENGLISH, 550–1064

11

The Britons and the Northumbrians, 547–685

The Evidence

The relationship between the Britons and the English reached by the end of Chapter 1 was the situation when Gildas wrote the *De Excidio*. The relationship between the Britons and the Roman past was pursued into the seventh century in Chapter 6. With this present chapter we shall begin to consider again the Britons and the English after the time of Gildas; and in subsequent chapters this relationship will be traced up to 1064. For the period after Gildas a new set of sources become critical, bringing new problems with them. This chapter considers some of the leading British sources for the second half of the sixth and most of the seventh century.

The Northumbrian regnal list of Bede's time and later began with Ida, first king of Anglian Bernicia.[1] In the summary of chronology in Book V, chapter 24, of the *Ecclesiastical History*, Bede placed this new start in 547: 'Ida began to reign, from whom the royal lineage of the Northumbrians takes its origin, and he remained in the kingship for twelve years.' The new kingdom bore a British name, as did its neighbour to the south, Deira;[2] and it remained for several reigns relatively small until the eighth king in the list, Æthelfrith, who reigned from 592 to 616. He, according to Bede, was 'a most powerful king and most desirous of glory, who, more than all the leaders of the English harried the people of the Britons.... No one among the nobles, no one among the kings made more of their lands either tributary to the people of the English or inhabitable by them, having exterminated or subjugated their inhabitants.'[3] By 'exterminated' Bede may have meant either 'expelled' or 'slain'.[4] Much of this expansion must have been within the lands between the Forth and the Tyne formerly occupied by the British people called the Gododdin. The Gododdin, however, also gave their name to one of the principal early Welsh poems. The poem, the *Gododdin*, may, if only we can interpret it

1 P. Hunter Blair, 'The *Moore Memoranda* on Northumbrian History', in C. Fox and B. Dickins (eds.), *The Early Cultures of North-Western Europe* (Cambridge, 1950), 246; repr. P. Hunter Blair, *Anglo-Saxon Northumbria*, ed. M. Lapidge and P. Hunter Blair (London, 1984), ch. VI; for later texts of the regnal list, see D. N. Dumville, 'The Anglian Collection of Royal Genealogies and Regnal Lists', *Anglo-Saxon England*, 5 (1976), 32, 35–6.

2 *LHEB*, pp. 419–20, 701–5.

3 Bede, *HE* i. 34.

4 F. Clark, 'The Northumbrian Frontiers *c.* 500–850', D.Phil. Thesis (Oxford, 2009), 133–5.

correctly, present a British view of the same struggle between the northern English and the Britons. Out of British territory the northern English were shaping what would become, until 685, an outstandingly successful military force.

Bede's statement about the origins of Northumbria is, however, problematic: it identifies the origins of the Northumbrian royal dynasty with the beginning of the reign of Ida in Bernicia; and yet Bernicia was only one component of what became Northumbria. To the south was the kingdom of Deira, roughly corresponding to the later Yorkshire; and archaeology makes it exceedingly likely that an Anglian kingdom was established in Deira well before Ida came to the throne of Bernicia.[5] Moreover, as early Bernicia grew at the expense of the Gododdin, so Deira had a British neighbour, Elmet (Elfed), whose name is still recalled in such names as Sherburn-in-Elmet.[6] Both components of the later Northumbria emerged in a British context; yet later Welsh texts, with few exceptions, gave most attention to Bernicia rather than to Deira and thus did little to correct Bede's Bernician perspective. Indeed, so much blood had been shed to construct Northumbria out of Bernicia and Deira that it was politic to suggest that unity came first and division second: for Bede, Bernicia and Deira were parts of an originally unified Northumbria;[7] and Ida, founder of the Bernician dynasty, was thus represented as the founder of the Northumbrian kingdom. It is likely that this view was shared by most of his readers, including Ceolwulf, the king to whom he sent his *Ecclesiastical History* to read before it was released for copying, even though a loyalty to Deira, and thus a very different view of the past, is attested in Bede's lifetime in the Whitby Life of Gregory the Great.[8] As the origins of Northumbria were obscured by later events that saw, first, a feud between the Bernician and Deiran dynasties, and so rival Bernician and Deiran views of their past, and, second, the triumph of the Bernicians and their history, so Bede's views of the Britons, as we shall see in the next chapter, were obscured by what happened to relations between the English and the Britons in the late seventh century.

As a background to a discussion of the sources, we need an outline chronology of events, which can be presented, in the plan favoured by the *Historia Brittonum*, according to the reigns of Northumbrian kings. The dates, however, are mainly derived from Bede and the Northumbrian regnal list.[9] 'In the year 547 Ida, from whom the royal kindred of the Northumbrians derives, began to reign, and his reign lasted for twelve years'.[10] His grandson, Æthelfrith, reigned from 592 until

[5] See below, 382.

[6] A. H. Smith, *The Place-Names of the West Riding of Yorkshire*, 8 vols. (Cambridge, 1961–3), iv. 1–3: Elmet is attested as an English district-name from Bede onwards; the place-names 'X-in-Elmet' from the fifteenth century.

[7] *HE* iii. 1, on which see J. M. Wallace-Hadrill, *Bede's Ecclesiastical History of the English People: A Historical Commentary* (Oxford, 1988), 87, 226–8.

[8] *The Earliest Life of Gregory the Great*, ed. B. Colgrave (Kansas, 1968; repr. Cambridge, 1985), ch. 16 on the tyranny of Æthelfrith; ch. 18, p. 102: 'coenobium famosissimum Aelflede, filię supradicte regine Eonflede, natę, ut supra diximus, Eduine, femina valde iam religiosa'.

[9] Bede, probably as part of his preparation of the *Ecclesiastical History*, drew up a list of dates, which he inserted at the end of the work, in Bk. 5, ch. 24.

[10] *HE* v. 24; Blair, 'The Moore Memoranda', 246.

his death in battle in 616. The latter's reign was divided into two halves: in 603, he defeated a major attack by the king of Dál Riata, Áedán mac Gabráin;[11] and in 604, according to the *Historia Brittonum*, he conquered his southern neighbour, Deira, and drove out Edwin, who belonged to the Deiran royal kindred.[12] Towards the end of his reign, probably in 615 or early in 616, he defeated and slew Selyf ap Cynan at the battle of Chester.[13] This was the first attested intervention of a Northumbrian king in what would become the borderland of Wales. This victory was soon followed by Æthelfrith's death in battle against Rædwald, king of the East Angles, the leading southern English king of the period and patron of Edwin of Deira.

Edwin now became king of Northumbria and imitated Æthelfrith in driving the latter's sons into exile. Probably early in his reign he conquered Elmet, the British kingdom in what is now West Yorkshire.[14] At Easter 627 Edwin was baptized a Christian.[15] Before the end of his reign, in 633, he had established a wide authority over Britons as well as English; this included Anglesey and the Isle of Man, thus securing a dominance in the Irish Sea.[16] His death in battle came about, as Bede described it, through a rebellion led by Cadwallon, king of the Britons, with the aid of Penda, of the Mercian royal kindred.[17] Cadwallon was briefly dominant in Northumbria from the autumn of 633 to the autumn or winter of 634, killing both Osric, who had become king of Deira, and Eanfrith, king of Bernicia; but he was in his turn slain by Eanfrith's brother, Oswald, son of Æthelfrith, in the battle of *Denisesburna*, close to Hexham, Old Welsh *Cantscaul*.[18] Early in Oswald's reign, Irish missionaries from Iona began the final conversion of Northumbria to Christianity, a conversion that had been gravely threatened by the death of Edwin. Oswald, like Edwin, was held to have exercised power over Britons as well as English, outside as well as inside Northumbria.[19] But in 642 he, again like Edwin, died in battle against an alliance of Mercians and Britons at *Maserfelth*, Old Welsh *Cocboy*, the modern Oswestry close to the modern border of Wales.[20]

His brother and successor, Oswiu, reigned until 670; but for the seven years 644–651 he lost control of Deira to Oswine, son of the Osric slain by Cadwallon in

[11] There is room for doubt over Bede's date: the Annals of Ulster give an obit for two of Áedán's sons, Bran and Domangart, in the annal for 596, which is likely to need correction to 599; Adomnán, *Vita S. Columbae*, i. 9, says that Columba prophesied Domangart's death *in Saxonia bellica in strage*, 'in a battle-slaughter in England'. This may have been *Degsastan*; but the date, even if it is 599, will still lie towards the middle of Æthelfrith's reign.

[12] *HE* i. 34; *HB*, c. 63; Blair, 'Moore Memoranda', 246.

[13] *HE* ii. 2; AU *s.a.* 613 (probably for 615 or 616), AT, CS; cf. T. M. Charles-Edwards, *The Chronicle of Ireland*, 2 vols. (Liverpool, 2006), i. 128.

[14] *HE* iv. 23/21 (referring back to the death of Hild's father, Hereric, in exile with 'the king of the Britons, Cerdic'); *HB*, c. 63.

[15] *HE* v. 24.

[16] *HE* ii. 5.

[17] *HE* ii. 20.

[18] *HE* iii. 1; *HB*, c. 64; On *Cantscaul* see I. Williams, 'Bellum Cantscaul', *BBCS* 6 (1931–3), 351–4; K. H. Jackson, 'On the Northern British Section in Nennius', in N. K. Chadwick (ed.), *Celt and Saxon: Studies in the Early British Border* (Cambridge, 1963), 34.

[19] *HE* ii. 5; iii. 6.

[20] *HE* iii. 9; *AC s.a.* 644. For the site, see below, 391–2.

634 (Oswine was the grandson of Edwin's paternal uncle, Ælfric).[21] In 651, however, Oswine was slain, and in 655, Oswiu also managed to defeat and kill Penda, king of the Mercians. His power in Britain reached its height in the three years after the battle; and he, like Edwin and Oswald, included Britons outside Northumbria among his subjects.[22] In 664, Oswiu presided over the Synod of Whitby, at which the Easter dating followed on Iona was abandoned in favour of the Roman Easter. The bishop of the Northumbrians, Colmán, returned home with some of his followers, both Irish and English, and the authority of Iona over the Northumbrian Church and its offshoots came to an end.

Oswiu died in his bed in 670 and was succeeded by his son, Ecgfrith. Ecgfrith achieved a dominance in Britain in the period 675–679 akin to that of his father in 655–658, but this came to an end in 679 with his defeat by the Mercians in the battle of the Trent.[23] Ecgfrith continued, however, with an expansionist policy in the north against the Picts, and even invaded Ireland in 684; but in the following year he was defeated and killed by the Picts during a campaign intended to reassert his overlordship.[24] This brought to an end any Northumbrian hopes of dominance in Britain. Bede acknowledged that the Picts, the Irish in Britain, and some of the Britons recovered their freedom from Northumbrian lordship in 685 'and they have retained it for about 46 years' (685–731).[25]

1. THE *ANNALES CAMBRIAE*, THE CHRONICLE OF IRELAND, AND THE *HISTORIA BRITTONUM*

A manuscript of *c.* 1100, Harley 3859, preserves the earliest version of the *Historia Brittonum*, dated to the fourth year of the reign of Merfyn Frych, probably 829–830.[26] Inserted into this manuscript's copy of that text, after the section concerned with the wars of the Northumbrians and the Britons, are two further texts, the *Annales Cambriae* and the collection of British genealogies known from this manuscript as 'the Harleian Genealogies'. All three texts were printed in the sequence of the manuscript by Edmond Faral.[27] The date of the collection in this manuscript can be fixed by two considerations: its version of *Annales Cambriae* comes to an end early in the reign of Owain ap Hywel, king of Dyfed from 950 until *c.* 970; the Harleian Genealogies open with two lines of descent both converging at Owain. The strong likelihood is, therefore, that the collection

21 *HE* iii. 1 and 14. In that sense, Oswine was *de stirpe regis Aeduini*, 'of the lineage of King Edwin', iii. 14.

22 *HE* ii. 5.

23 *HE* iv. 21/19; Stephen, *Vita S. Wilfridi*, c. 20.

24 *HE* iv. 26/24; Stephen, *Vita S. Wilfridi*, c. 44.

25 Ibid.

26 The place of writing of Harley 3959 is uncertain: *Annales Cambriae, A.D. 682–954: Texts A–C in Parallel*, ed. and trans. D. N. Dumville (Cambridge, 2002), vi. For the *Historia Brittonum* as a whole, see below, Ch. 14; here we are concerned solely with the relationship of one of its sections, the Northern History, to the *Annales Cambriae* and to the Chronicle of Ireland.

27 E. Faral, *La Légende arthurienne: études et documents*, 3 vols. (Paris, 1929), iii. 4–62.

belongs to the third quarter of the tenth century. The forms of the names in the manuscript are consistent with such a date.

The *Annales Cambriae*, the Harleian Genealogies, and the *Historia Brittonum* have a special value: for the history of the Britons between Gildas and the ninth century, they constitute most of the written evidence, other than poetry, that derives from the Britons themselves. Other sources, such as Bede's *Historia Ecclesiastica* and the Anglo-Saxon Chronicle, add much, but from a standpoint hostile to the Britons.[28] Yet, if arguments put forward by Kathleen Hughes are correct, two of these British sources, the *Annales Cambriae* and the *Historia Brittonum*, and also the main strand of information on the Britons in a further important source, the Chronicle of Ireland, all derived their information on this period from a single lost text emanating from the northern Britons.[29]

The point at which the *Historia Brittonum* comes into contact with the *Annales Cambriae* is in its section sometimes known as 'the Northern History'.[30] It was precisely after this section that, in the Harleian manuscript, the A version of *Annales Cambriae* and the unique copy of the Harleian Genealogies were inserted. The Northern History uses as its chronological framework a Northumbrian regnal list in the form which it took at the end of the eighth century, itself attached to a collection of English genealogies.[31] On the other hand, the material contained within the framework extends no later than the battle of Nechtanesmere, 685; and even then, the notice of Nechtanesmere is attached to a genealogy and is separated from the main body of material within the regnal list: taken together the inserted material—both that within the genealogies and the Northern History itself—runs from the days of Maelgwn Gwynedd, whom it places in the middle of the sixth century, up to the end of Northumbrian domination over the peoples of northern Britain. The main interest is in the relations between the Britons and the Bernician and Deiran kings of Northumbria.

A similar interest is also prominent in the seventh-century section of the *Annales Cambriae*.[32] Kathleen Hughes, however, took this observation further and argued that these two texts shared a common source; that this source derived from the lands of the northern Britons; and that it was a set of notes on northern history; they were not in annalistic form and were compiled well after the time of the events, not long before the date of the *Historia Brittonum*. In addition to this, she argued that this northern text was also the source used by the Chronicle of Ireland for its annal-entries on the northern Britons. (The Chronicle of Ireland does not survive as such but can, to a considerable extent, be reconstructed from its offspring, principally the Annals of Ulster, the Annals of Tigernach and

[28] Bede's evidence will be considered in the next chapter.

[29] K. Hughes, *Celtic Britain in the Early Middle Ages* (Woodbridge, 1980), 91–100.

[30] *HB*, cc. 61–5; the English genealogies are cc. 57–61.

[31] D. N. Dumville, 'The Anglian Collection of Royal Genealogies and Regnal Lists', 23–50; reprinted as no. V in his *Histories and Pseudo-Histories of the Insular Middle Ages* (Aldershot, 1990).

[32] In addition to Faral's edition, see E. Phillimore, 'The *Annales Cambriae* and the Old Welsh Genealogies from Harleian MS. 3859', *Y Cymmrodor*, 9 (1888), 141–83; *Annales Cambriae, A.D. 682–954: Texts A–C in Parallel*, ed. and trans. D. N. Dumville (Cambridge, 2002).

Chronicum Scottorum.)[33] Instead, therefore, of what might have seemed to be three independent texts, we have, on her argument, only three derivatives of the one text; and this was itself not a contemporary record but a less reliable retrospective account of the history of the northern Britons. This single retrospective source will not have included everything in the Chronicle of Ireland concerning Britons: entries on Britons active in Ireland, such as those under 697, 702, and 703, can be presumed to have entered the record in the same ways as other Irish events.[34]

A crucial element in Kathleen Hughes's argument was also present in her outstanding work on the Irish annals. This was a preference for explaining patterns of information in annals by positing textual relationships rather than oral links. A straightforward example is provided by the difference of opinion between her and Alfred Smyth over the Bangor element in the Chronicle of Ireland (itself, in one of its forms, a source for the *Annales Cambriae*).[35] She accepted that the main source for the Chronicle of Ireland up to *c.* 740 was an Iona chronicle, but because it also contained a full series of obits of abbots of Bangor for the seventh century, she posited a set of Bangor annals that were incorporated into the Iona chronicle and thence into the Chronicle of Ireland. Smyth, however, preferred to see the Bangor element as deriving from the close relations between Iona and Bangor attested in Adomnán's Life of Columba. Smyth's assumption was that an Iona annalist would have included obits of abbots of an important monastery allied to Iona and that the news of the deaths of these abbots would have arrived by word of mouth rather than in the form of annals. This conception of how information was gathered by Irish annalists works well for Bangor and Aghaboe, the principal monastery of St Cainnech, but very badly for another major ally of Iona, Taghmon in South Leinster, and also very badly for Durrow.[36] It is probably wise to allow for different modes of collecting information: not just through monastic alliances and dependencies but also through synods and other assemblies in which clergy and monks participated. An example would be the royal assembly of 851 at which two elements among those attending were 'Diarmait and Féthgna with the community of Patrick and Suairlech with the clergy of Mide'.[37] The 'Fair of Tailtiu' appears to have been an annual event and was attended by clerics and monks as well as laity.[38] It would have been an ideal occasion for a monastic annalist to gather information. As for British information in Irish chronicles, it is worth remembering the British

[33] K. Hughes, *Early Christian Ireland: Introduction to the Sources* (London, 1972), 100–7; T. M. Charles-Edwards, *The Chronicle of Ireland*, 44, sets out the evidence. D. P. McCarthy, *The Irish Annals: Their Genesis, Evolution and History* (Dublin, 2008), chs. 6 and 7, has a different theory but has been answered by N. Evans, *The Present and the Past in Medieval Irish Chronicles* (Woodbridge, 2010), ch. 3.

[34] AU *s.aa.* 697. 10; 702. 2; 703. 1; trans. Charles-Edwards, *The Chronicle of Ireland*, 697. 10; 702. 2; 703. 1.

[35] Hughes, *Early Christian Ireland*, 122–3; A. P. Smyth, 'The Earliest Irish Annals: Their First Contemporary Entries, and the Earliest Centres of Recording', *PRIA* 72 C (1972), 41. McCarthy, *The Irish Annals*, 168–85, argues, wrongly in my opinion, that the main source was annals kept at Clonmacnois.

[36] Charles-Edwards, *The Chronicle of Ireland*, i. 34–5.

[37] AU 851. 5.

[38] *ECI* 476–9, 556–9.

element in such monasteries as Iona as well as the Irish monks and clerics living in Britain and the specific concerns of Iona with Northumbria and Pictland.[39]

A second important element in Hughes's work was the distinction between ecclesiastical chronicles, such as the Chronicle of Ireland, and chronicles of a more secular outlook. In the Chronicle of Ireland clerical and monastic obits predominated; but in the *Annales Cambriae*, from 613 onwards, more attention was paid to the wars and deaths of kings than to the Church. When, therefore, a particular strand of information within the Chronicle of Ireland, let us say on northern Britain, was more secular than the Chronicle as a whole, Hughes saw a northern British text as responsible: secularity was a defining feature of the northern British source, ecclesiastical concerns of the destination in the Chronicle of Ireland. There is no doubt that the fundamental distinction between ecclesiastical and secular chronicles is helpful, but there is a serious difficulty with the particular use to which Hughes put it. If we consider the Northumbrian strand in the Iona chronicle, it is evident that it has a more secular character than the mainstream of Irish information. Yet this should not be ascribed to the existence of a Northumbrian source with an outlook different from that of the Iona chronicle. It is more likely that the Northumbrian strand in the Iona chronicle is due to Iona's own abiding interest in Northumbria and its kings throughout the seventh and early eighth centuries. The Iona chroniclers therefore had a rather different outlook on what, from their point of view, were foreign countries than they had on Ireland.

In Kathleen Hughes's view, then, the *Annales Cambriae* only began to be a contemporary Welsh record from the late eighth century, from which time several entries indicate that the chronicle was kept at St Davids. Before then she saw two other distinct sections of the text: the first was from the start in the mid-fifth century up to 613; the second ran from 614 up to 777, after which the St Davids annalist took over. The annals from the start in 445 up to 613 were largely a selection from the Chronicle of Ireland, while those from 614 to 777 were based on a northern British source. In other words, in her view the *Annales Cambriae* consisted of three discrete sections, the next section taking over from the one before. Here David Dumville's views are different: he offered evidence that some entries were taken from the Clonmacnois version of the Chronicle of Ireland right down to the end of the A-text of *Annales Cambriae*.[40] A high proportion, however, of such entries in Hughes's second period, 614–777, consists of notices of natural events, such as eclipses and earthquakes, and also visitations of plague. The implication, and this is of great importance, is that the text of *Annales Cambriae* was produced by a fierce abbreviation of one, at least, of its main sources, the Chronicle of Ireland in its Clonmacnois version. In this respect, the *Annales Cambriae* were like the Annals of Inisfallen, also a derivative of the tenth-century

[39] Adomnán, *Vita S. Columbae*, iii. 6; cf. the Englishman, Coeddi, bishop of Iona, AU 712. 1, and the probable Briton, Oan, *princeps* of Eigg, AU 725. 7; *ECI* 299–326.

[40] D. N. Dumville, 'When was the "Clonmacnoise Chronicle" created? The Evidence of the Welsh Annals', in K. Grabowski and D. N. Dumville, *Chronicles and Annals of Mediaeval Ireland and Wales* (Woodbridge, 1984), 211–12.

Clonmacnois Chronicle. What we see in the result of this abbreviation is more the interests of the abbreviator than of his source. This leads to a surprising fact: if we compare the *Annales Cambriae* with the Chronicle of Ireland, especially in its Clonmacnois version, it becomes clear that the Welsh abbreviator did not include as much British material as one would have expected.[41] This explains Hughes's view that his principal source for 614–777 was the supposed Northern British Chronicle: that is, the abbreviator was not looking out for British entries in the Clonmacnois Chronicle, because he had another preferred source. On the other hand, he did retain a scattering of eclipses and the like, perhaps because such things provided a chronological anchor and were part of the tradition of annal writing.

A further development in scholarly understanding of *Annales Cambriae* arises out of the chronicler's interest in the Easter question and Elfoddw, 'archbishop of Gwynedd'.[42] This suggests that the St Davids chronicle was derived from a North-Welsh chronicle, perhaps put together at Abergele, which was the subject of a unique entry at 856 (= 858), and where Elfoddw may have been buried.[43] This chronicle overlapped the change to the Roman Easter in 768, ascribed to Elfoddw, since there are symptoms of its use of an 84-year paschal table.

My main concern, however, is not just with the middle section, 614–777, in Kathleen Hughes's division of *Annales Cambriae,* but with her northern British source and its other alleged offspring in the Chronicle of Ireland and in *Historia Brittonum.* If we take first the Chronicle of Ireland, it is immediately apparent that the argument here is much more difficult than it is with the other proposed relationship between the *Annales Cambriae* and the *Historia Brittonum.* First, we have two possible explanations of any resemblances: the dependence of *Annales Cambriae* on the Clonmacnois Chronicle, itself a revision of the Chronicle of Ireland, and, secondly, the claimed dependence of both the Chronicle of Ireland and *Annales Cambriae* on the supposed Northern British Chronicle. These different paths by which the same information might appear in both *Annales Cambriae* and the Chronicle of Ireland are shown in Figure 11.1. (a and b).

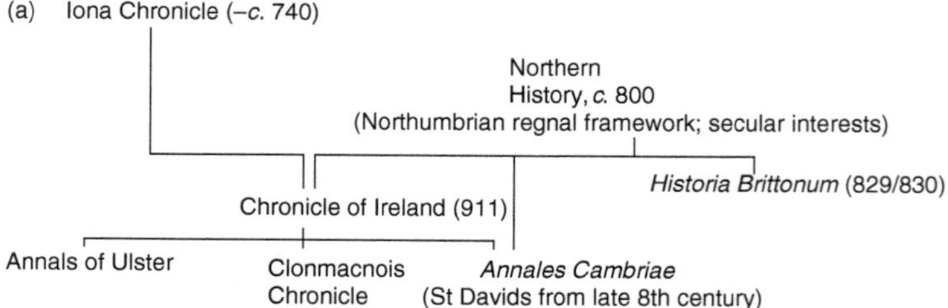

Figure 11.1(a). Kathleen Hughes's conception of the textual relationships of *Annales Cambriae*

[41] See *The Chronicle of Ireland,* under 632. 2; 638. 2; 642. 1, 4; 658. 3; 672. 6, 694. 6.

[42] D. N. Dumville, '*Annales Cambriae* and Easter', *The Medieval Chronicle*, 3 (2004), 40–50, reprinted in his *Celtic Essays, 2001–2007* (Aberdeen, 2007), 25–33.

[43] M. Miller, 'Final Stages in the Composition of the Harleian *Annales Cambriae*: The Evidence of the Framework', *Journal of Celtic Studies*, 4 (2004), 211; CBT i. 27. 93.

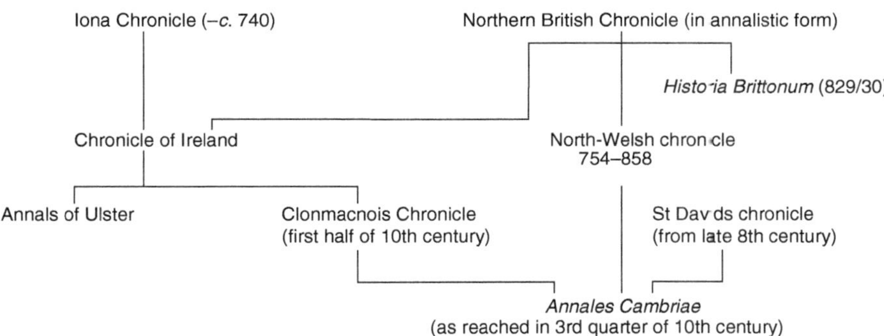

Figure 11.1(b). David Dumville's conception of the textual relationships of *Annales Cambriae*

A further complication is created by the annalists' conventions reporting events. Hughes used the difference between the Chronicle of Ireland and *Annales Cambriae* in their reporting of battles to argue against any direct dependence of one on the other. Take for example, the battle in which Cadwallon was killed (631 in *Annales Cambriae*, 632 in AU).

[630]	an.	1.	Guidgar uenit et non redit.
		2.	Kalendis Ianuariiis. **Gueith Meicen, et ibi interfectus est Etguin cum duobus filiis suis; Catguollaun autem uictor fuit.**
[631]	an.		**Bellum Cantscaul in quo Catguollaun corruit.** [AU 632.1: Bellum Cathloen, regis Britonum, 7 Anfrith.] [AT Cath la Cathlon 7 Anfraith qui decollatus est, in quo Osualt mac Etalfraith uictor erat et Catlon, rex Britonum, cecidit.]

The Irish annalist originally recorded this event using the convention by which the battle was named after the principal victim: it was 'the battle of Cathlon' because in it Cadwallon was defeated and killed. A process of abbreviation has made it look as though Eanfrith, killed by Cadwallon slightly earlier in the same year, was a victim in the same battle along with Cadwallon. This, together with a failure to comprehend the earlier convention, led to further misunderstanding found both in the Annals of Tigernach and the Annals of Clonmacnois—a misunderstanding which may well, therefore, go back to the Clonmacnois Chronicle of the tenth century. The *Annales Cambriae*, however, used a quite different convention, identifying the battle by the place, *Cantscaul*, a Welsh rendering of Hexham.[44] In this case, therefore, the *Annales Cambriae* were independent of the Clonmacnois Chronicle, not only because of the different way of recording the event but also because the

[44] See above, n. 18.

misunderstandings in the Clonmacnois Chronicle were not reproduced. On the other hand, the entry as it is in the Annals of Ulster could have been derived from an entry using the conventions found in *Annales Cambriae*, if we suppose that an Irish annalist translated it into his own conventions. Admittedly the detail about Eanfrith is not in the *Annales Cambriae*; but it could have been in a hypothetical Northern British chronicle. So what we are left with, if, and only if, we are determined to see a textual relationship between the Chronicle of Ireland and a supposed Northern British chronicle, is the supposition that, in this instance, a source for the Chronicle of Ireland was a Northern British chronicle.

Yet, because there are no verbal correspondences, there is very little evidence of any textual relationship at all. I have already dismissed the argument based on the secular character of the British strand in the Chronicle of Ireland. What we are left with is Hughes's observation that her northern British strand in the Chronicle of Ireland came to an end at very much the same date as her northern British phase in *Annales Cambriae*. The notice of the death of Abbot Cuthbert in 777 marks the end of the northern British phase in *Annales Cambriae*, since Hughes convincingly identified him with the abbot of Wearmouth-Jarrow who wrote the famous account of Bede's death. She then suggested that the notice of the burning of Dumbarton, on the 1st of January 780 according to AU, marked the end of the northern British strand in the Chronicle of Ireland. That is the kind of detail that would make a welcome supporting argument to a case that was already strong, but it will not carry much weight on its own. The plain fact is that there is rather too much British material in the Chronicle of Ireland that is not in *Annales Cambriae* (or the *Historia Brittonum*) and vice versa for Hughes's claim to stand up without detailed verbal correspondences; and, as we have already seen, no such correspondences are on offer. It is better to regard the British strand in the Chronicle of Ireland as independent of any Northern British chronicle used by *Annales Cambriae*.

Some supporting evidence for this conclusion is given in Table 11.1, where it is assumed that the Clonmacnois Chronicle shared the same chronological dislocations for the period up to *c.* 710 as can be seen in the Annals of Ulster.[45]

In the Chronicle of Ireland, there was, as I have argued elsewhere, a chronological dislocation about 640 caused by the Iona annalist splicing two sources.[46] Most events up to *c.* 640, ending with the death of Oswald of Northumbria in battle against Penda in 642, were dated two to three years too early. Beginning at least with the obit of Domnall mac Áeda in 640, another source produced a much more accurate chronology. In the *Annales Cambriae* some entries before 640, such as the obit for Columba and the baptism of Edwin, are dated too early, whereas the death of Oswald is two years too late. The former set of entries in *Annales Cambriae* probably derive from the Chronicle of Ireland, whereas the notice of the death of Oswald was independent. The general run of these entries suggests that most of them, even after 640, came from the Chronicle of Ireland.

[45] For discussion, see Charles-Edwards, *The Chronicle of Ireland*, i. 35–58.
[46] Charles-Edwards, *The Chronicle of Ireland*, 35–43.

Table 11.1. The chronology of *Annales Cambriae* compared with the Clonmacnois Chronicle and other sources

597 Bede, death of Columba		AC 595 Clonmacn. 595
627 Bede, baptism of Edwin		AC 626 Clonmacn. 625
633 Bede, death of Edwin		AC 630 Clonmacn. 631
634 Bede, death of Cadwallon		AC 631 Clonmacn. 632
642 Bede, death of Oswald		AC 644 Clonmacn. 639
655 Bede, Winwæd		AC 656 Clonmacn. 656
670 Bede, death of Oswiu		AC 669 Clonmacn. 671
676 Comet Bede 678		AC 676 Clonmacn. 677
	(Plague in Britain)	AC 682
	(Plague in Ireland)	AC 683 Clonmacn. 683
705 Bede, death of Aldfrith		AC 704 Clonmacn. 704
716 Bede, death of Osred		AC 717 Clonmacn. 716
Death of Beli ab Elffin		AC 722 Clonmacn. 722
Battle of *Monad Carno*		AC 729 AU 729 (–AT,CS here)
735 Cont. Bede, death of Bede		AC 735 Clonmacn. 735 (not AU)
750 Picts defeated by Britons		AC 750 Clonmacn. 750
750 Cont. Bede, death of Tewdwr ap Beli		AC 750 Clonmacn. 752 (AT)
775 Simeon of Durham, death of *Cynoth* k. of the Picts		AC 776 AU 775 (AT, CS lacking)
796 Simeon of Durham, death of Offa		AC 797 AU 796
867 ASC, battle of York		AC 866 Clonmacn. 867

The serious case for a Northern British chronicle rests on the comparison between the *Annales Cambriae* and the *Historia Brittonum.* It may be taken in two stages: first, the issue whether there was a common source; and, secondly, whether that source was from northern Britain. Kathleen Hughes noted the shared names of battles: *Gueith Meicen / Bellum Meicen, Bellum Cantscaul, Bellum Cocboy, Strages Gaii Campi.*[47] Then there was agreement on points of information: for example, both the *Annales Cambriae* and *Historia Brittonum* were agreed that two sons of Edwin were killed with their father.[48] The early date as against Bede suggests that the placing of the battle in the annalistic sequence was derived from the Clonmacnois Chronicle, but the information given is much closer to the *Historia Brittonum.*

[47] *AC s.aa.* 630, 631, 644, 656; *HB*, cc. 61, 64, 65.
[48] *AC* 630; *HB*, c. 61.

Historia Brittonum, § 61	AC
Duo filii Edguin erant, et cum ipso corruerunt in bello Meicen, at de origine eius numquam iteratum est regnum, quia non euasit unus de genere illius de isto bello, sed interfecti omnes sunt cum illo ab exercitu Catguollauni, regis Guendotae regionis.	Gueith Meicen; et ibi interfectus est Etguin cum duobus filiis suis; Catguollaun autem uictor fuit. AT: Cath Etuin maic Ailli regis Saxonum, qui totam Britanniam regnauit, in quo uictus est a C[athl]on rege Britonum et Panta Saxano.

The Annals of Tigernach, which here probably reproduce the Clonmacnois Chronicle, make no reference to Edwin's sons; they also add the clause 'who ruled the whole of Britain', a piece of information probably derived from Bede. The focus of the Annals of Tigernach and of *Annales Cambriae* is on the battle, as one would expect from chronicles. In the *Historia Brittonum* it is on the royal kindred to which Edwin belonged; but that is appropriate, since this passage comes from the paragraph on the Deiran royal dynasty. Once that difference is allowed for, the information given is largely the same. To move from the *Annales Cambriae* to the *Historia Brittonum* one needs only to make the assumption that the two sons killed with Edwin according to the *Annales Cambriae* were his only sons and that they left no sons of their own. This one might perhaps infer from the importance given to the information about Edwin's two sons in the annal. Bede, however, tells us that one son was killed in the battle, but that another was later killed by Penda.[49] It is true that none of Edwin's direct descendants attained the kingship; but Edwin was not the last of his dynasty, since that distinction was reserved to Oswine, king of Deira and friend of Bishop Aidan, whose death in 651 was recorded not just by Bede but by the Chronicle of Ireland.[50] So, although the *Historia Brittonum* was probably aware of Bede's *Historia Ecclesiastica*, it did not follow it here.[51]

Similarly, both the *Annales Cambriae* and the *Historia Brittonum* were agreed that Rhun ab Urien, not Paulinus, baptized Edwin.[52] The baptism was recorded by the Annals of Tigernach, but the role of Rhun ab Urien is found only in the two British sources.[53] The phrasing in the *Annales Cambriae* would permit one to suppose that the second half of the entry, 'and Rhun ab Urien baptized him', *et Run filius Urbgen baptizauit eum*, was a secondary addition to a brief entry derived from the Clonmacnois Chronicle; but this is uncertain since the succinct nature of the extant annal entries is due to the abbreviator quite as much or more than to the original text. In the *Historia Brittonum*, however, some of the detail about Edwin's daughter, Eanfled, looks as though it derives from a careless reading of Bede,

49 Bede, *HE* ii. 20.

50 Bede, *HE* iii. 14; the error might have arisen from a deduction made from the Northumbrian regnal list, since that did not include Oswine, who was only king of Deira.

51 *HB*, c. 63, Bede, *HE* ii. 9, 14, on the baptisms of Eanfled and Edwin, discussed below.

52 *AC* 626; *HB*, c. 63.

53 AT 626.

notably the 'twelfth day after Pentecost';[54] yet Eanfled was to be a major figure in Northumbria for much of the seventh century, Oswiu's queen and later presiding over Whitby along with Ælfflæd, her daughter, someone whose precedence in the adoption of Christianity might deserve to be fully recorded.[55]

The evidence for some textual connection between *Annales Cambriae* and *Historia Brittonum* is significant but not wholly conclusive. First, the names of the battles, such as *Bellum Cocboy*, may well have been widely used among the Britons: they might, quite simply, be the British names of the battles in question. Secondly, the claim that Rhun ab Urien baptized Edwin may also have been widespread among the Britons as a counter to the depreciation of their Christianity after the Synod of Whitby in 664. Even if it was false, that does not mean that the claim was confined to the supposed Northern British chronicle.[56] The textual history of *Annales Cambriae* was admittedly one of matching different sources of information: even if a source for the *Historia Brittonum* was also used by the *Annales Cambriae*, that does not oblige us to think that the bulk of the annal entries in the period 614–777 came from this one source. There is enough material in the period about the Britons, both northern and southern, to encourage the conclusion that there was a Chronicle of the Britons as a whole rather than just a Northern British chronicle.

If there is a particular interest shown by the Northern History, it was in two royal kindreds: those of Gwynedd and Rheged. The beginning of the Northern History synchronized Maelgwn Gwynedd with Ida, founder of the Bernician dynasty and the first name in the Northumbrian (initially Bernician) regnal list. Among Maelgwn's descendants, the Maelgyning, it records Cadwallon, Cadafael, and Cadwaladr. Urien of Rheged was described as being the most effective of all the British kings in the prosecution of war; his son, Rhun, was the British cleric who, so the Northern History claims, baptized Edwin. It makes no reference to the dynasty of Alclud (Dumbarton). The only reference to the Gododdin and their land is to one of its districts, Manaw, from which Maelgwn's great-grandfather, Cunedda, is said to have migrated to Gwynedd. In the *Annales Cambriae*, however, apart from Rhun ab Urien, the northern kingdom of concern was Alclud, not Rheged.[57] This is a strong argument for the independence of these two sources.

Finally, if we do accept the likelihood of a common source for the *Annales Cambriae* and the *Historia Brittonum*, was it, as Kathleen Hughes claimed, non-annalistic, a set of notes on northern history, or, as David Dumville would prefer, a set of northern annals? Put another way, Hughes maintained that the source most closely resembled the *Historia Brittonum*, Dumville that it was closer to the *Annales Cambriae*. One possible piece of evidence is the error in the *Historia Brittonum* over the obit for Cadwaladr, king of Gwynedd. In the *Annales Cambriae*, this is given as 682: 'There was a great plague in Britain, in which Cadwaladr son of Cadwallon died.' In the *Historia Brittonum*, however, Cadwaladr was made to die in an earlier

[54] See below, 446. [55] Bede, *HE* iii. 15; iv. 26/24.
[56] For further discussion, see below, 446.
[57] *AC s.aa.* 627, 722, 750, 760.

plague, namely the more famous one of 664: 'While he [Oswiu] was reigning, there came a plague of men, while Cadwaladr was reigning among the Britons after his father, and in it he perished. And he killed Penda on the field of Gai . . .'[58] It is difficult to decide from this passage on its own, whether it was Cadwaladr or Oswiu who died in the plague. Hughes inferred from the *Annales Cambriae* and from other evidence for the death of Oswiu that it must be Cadwaladr; but then the conflict in the date would indicate that neither could the *Annales Cambriae* have been drawn from the *Historia Brittonum* nor was the *Historia Brittonum* derived from *Annales Cambriae*; instead both were derived from a common source, one in which Cadwaladr's name was spelled *Catgualart*, with inversion of the normal *-tr*. Against this, as Dumville pointed out, is the fact that both examples of *Catgualart* are in the same manuscript, so that the spelling *Catgualart* could come from a relatively late stage in the textual transmission.[59] All we can say about the discrepancy in the date is that the *Annales Cambriae* are likely to be right, since the plague of 664 was much better known subsequently; it would, therefore, have been all too easy to suppose from the mention of plague that the date must be 664. And, if they are right, it is not easy to see how this correct dating could have been arrived at starting from 'a scholar's compilation made from scattered notes and memoranda, probably shortly before the writing of the *Historia Brittonum* early in the ninth century'.[60]

The second piece of evidence for Hughes's argument derived from the account of the *Strages Gaii Campi*, Bede's battle of the Winwaed in 655.[61] The *Annales Cambriae* recorded the death of Penda in the year after the battle, and a plundering expedition by Oswiu in the year after that (information not in the Harleian manuscript is given in square brackets):

[656]	an.	Strages Gaii campi.
[657]	an.	Pantha occisio.
[658]	an.	Osguid uenit et praedam duxit.
	[AU 658. 2: Mors Gureit regis Alo Cluathe.]	

The *Historia Brittonum*, however, had Oswiu slay Penda in the battle itself; moreover, it assumed an earlier plundering by Oswiu at the expense of the Britons, the plunder in question being returned by Oswiu, under Penda's pressure, to the kings of the Britons at the fortress of *Iudeu*. This, we must assume, was before the battle. Hughes maintained that it was the same sequence of events differently arranged: the plunder placed last in *Annales Cambriae* was actually the first; and

[58] *HB*, c. 64.

[59] See his note to Hughes, *Celtic Britain*, 94 n. 48. The same spelling is also reflected by a form in the genealogies in the same manuscript: HG 18 in *Early Welsh Genealogical Tracts*, ed. P. C. Bartrum (Cardiff, 1966), 11.

[60] Hughes, *Celtic Britain*, 99. The Chronicle of Ireland's references to a plague affecting children would not have been much help: AU 683. 4; 685. 1.

[61] Hughes, *Celtic Britain*, 92.

the notice of the death of Penda was wrongly made into a separate annal. All this would be easier, she claimed, if the source resembled the *Historia Brittonum* than if it was a set of annals. The significant point here concerns the plunder: the separate obit for Penda might easily be a later error made in the process of abbreviation, a mechanical insertion of an *an.* marking a new year. However, it seems to be a straight assumption that the plundering recorded in *Annales Cambriae* was the plundering assumed in *Historia Brittonum*. It is entirely probable that Oswiu would follow up his victory in 655 by taking plunder from Penda's British allies in the following years.[62] Only if it has to be the same collection of events in the two sources does Hughes's analysis command assent; and yet the proposition that it was the same information drawn by the two texts from a lost source was precisely what she was attempting to prove. There was an element of circularity in her argument.

The alleged joint dependence of *Annales Cambriae* and the *Historia Brittonum* is still an open question. If the proposed source was a set of annals, it would make it easier to suppose that *Annales Cambriae* took material from it. Yet there is also every chance that any such material was subject to abbreviation in *Annales Cambriae*. As Table 11.2 indicates, the change in *Annales Cambriae* about 775 to a scope confined to Wales is clear, but before that the text is best described as Annals of the Britons rather than a Northern British chronicle—or indeed, as yet, *Annales Cambriae.* The run of consecutive obits of kings of Dumbarton is confined to the eighth century, after the Northern History in the *Historia Brittonum* had ended its narrative. Before then there were as many obits of kings from Wales as from North Britain.

As this table indicates, two kinds of evidence need to be distinguished: for the sixth and seventh centuries the main interest is, as has been said, in the wars of the Britons against the Northumbrians; for the eighth century, there is the cluster of obits of kings of Dumbarton, but also several entries to do with Wales and Cornwall.[63] In the seventh century, kings of Gwynedd and Powys were more prominent, in this text, in the struggle against Northumbria than were the kings of Dumbarton.

Against Hughes's case stand three main arguments: the debt of *Annales Cambriae* to the Chronicle of Ireland was more extensive than she supposed; although *Annales Cambriae* had a British source for the period 614–777, it was probably annalistic and, at least in the main, contemporary; because *Annales Cambriae* give a severely abbreviated text, and the part of that abbreviation affecting the Clonmacnois Chronicle demonstrably occurred in the tenth century, it is unwise to infer too readily characteristics of the British source from the text as we have it. Instead of Kathleen Hughes's single retrospective source, we have at least two and perhaps three.

62 Compare AU 642. 4, and the note to this entry in Charles-Edwards, *The Chronicle of Ireland*, i. 143.

63 *AC s.aa.* 722 (where the use of *dexterales Brittones* suggests a Welsh standpoint), 754, 768, 775.

Table 11.2. Kingdoms of British kings 600–850

613	Selim f. Cinan	Powys (slain at Chester)?
616	Ceretic	Elmet
627	Belin	Allt Glud / Alclud (Dumbarton)?
631	Catguollaun	Gwynedd (usual view)[64]
632	Iudris	Meirionydd?[65]
682	Catgualart f. Catguolaun	Gwynedd
722	Beli f. Elfin	Allt Glud / Alclud
750	Teudubr f. Beli	Allt Glud / Alclud
754	Rotri, rex Brittonum	Gwynedd
760	Dumnagual f. Teudubr	Allt Glud / Alclud
775	Fernmail f. Iudhail	Gwent
797	Morgetiud r. Demetorum	Dyfed
798	Caratauc r. Guenedotae	Gwynedd
807	Arthgen r. Cereticiaun	Ceredigion
808	Regin r. Demetorum	Dyfed
811	Eugein f. Margetiud	Dyfed
814	Trifun f. Reyn	Dyfed
	Griphiud f. Cincen	Powys
816	Cinan	Gwynedd
825	Higuel	Gwynedd
842	Iudguallaun	?
844	Mermin	Gwynedd
848	Iudhail r. Guent	Gwent
849	Mouric	(a common name in the Gwent dynasty)
850	Cinnen	Probably Cyngen of Powys

If we do accept, following Dumville, a common annalistic source for the *Annales Cambriae* and the *Historia Brittonum*, what can we say about the details in the latter that are not present in the former? If the source was as brief as the *Annales Cambriae*, then the further details may well have been provided by later elaboration of succinct earlier annal entries. In favour of this position, one might argue that the source may well have originated as brief marginal entries in an Easter table.[66] There are, however, important reasons for hesitation. As has just

[64] A. Woolf, 'Cædualla *Rex Brittonum* and the Passing of the Old North', *Northern History*, 41 (2004), 5–24, argues, in my opinion on weak grounds, that the Cadwallon of Bede, *HE* ii. 20, iii. 1–2, was a northern British king.

[65] Meirionydd according to Lloyd, *HW*[3] 251 and n. 123; and J. B. Smith and Ll. B. Smith (eds.), *History of Merioneth*, ii, *The Middle Ages* (Cardiff, 2001), 4.

[66] R. L. Poole, *Chronicles and Annals: A Brief Outline of their Origin and Growth* (Oxford, 1926), 27–9; D. Ó Cróinín, 'Early Irish Annals from Easter Tables: A Case Restated', *Peritia*, 2 (1983), 74–86.

been pointed out, the one thing we do know about *Annales Cambriae* is that the text was subject to radical abbreviation in the tenth century. The brevity exhibited by the surviving text does not reproduce the brevity of any original set of annals. Moreover, although it is true that Easter tables were a source of chronicling in Britain and Ireland, another was the pattern set by late Antique chronicles; and these, although succinct, allowed space for considerably longer entries than any in the *Annales Cambriae*. It is entirely possible to suppose British annals for 614–777 that were much fuller in style than the *Annales Cambriae* or the Chronicle of Ireland. Such annals could have been the source for the Northern History in the *Historia Brittonum*.

2. THE HARLEIAN GENEALOGIES

As stated above, the date and place of this collection are very probably determined by its starting point: Owain ap Hywel Dda, king of Dyfed, 950–*c.* 970. It can profitably be compared, however, with two later collections, one, also from South Wales, in Jesus College, Oxford, MS 20, a fourteenth-century copy of a collection made in the thirteenth century, and an early thirteenth-century collection from Gwynedd found in copies of a lost manuscript, Hengwrt 33.[67] The latter, especially, contains material that evidently descends independently of the Harleian Genealogies from a source of a similar date.

To understand the early material in these collections, we need to anticipate political developments in Wales in the ninth and tenth centuries, which will be discussed in detail later.[68] From the sixth to the ninth century Gwynedd was ruled by a dynasty descended, so it was claimed, from Cunedda ab Edern, who migrated to Gwynedd from Manaw Gododdin. For most of the period, a branch of Cunedda's descendants called by later poets the Maelgyning, descendants of the Maelgwn Gwynedd denounced by Gildas, held the kingship, but the last known king from the dynasty descended from Cunedda (*alias* 'the First Dynasty of Gwynedd') was probably of a collateral line associated with Rhos, on the east side of the Conwy.[69] He died in 825, and the kingdom was then taken by Merfyn Frych, who was, very probably, from the Isle of Man. His descendants, known to later poets as the Merfynion (*alias* 'the Second Dynasty of Gwynedd'), ruled, with some interruptions, until the deaths of Llywelyn ap Gruffudd and his brother Dafydd in 1282–1283. In the early tenth century, a branch of the Merfynion took the kingdom of Dyfed, and it was to this branch that Owain ap Hywel belonged. His grandfather, Cadell ap Rhodri, had acquired Dyfed, and his father, Hywel ap

[67] Also, like the Harleian Genealogies, ed. Bartrum, *Early Welsh Genealogical Tracts*, 42–50, 95–110.

[68] Chapters 15 and 16.

[69] The pedigree HG 3 in *EWGT* 10 is entitled *Gwehelyth Rros* in ABT 25, *EWGT* 108; the position of the pedigree as the third in the Harleian Genealogies indicates its importance for the Merfynion; this would be explained by an identification of Hywel ap Caradog with the Hywel of *AC* 812–825 and of his father with the Caradog, king of Gwynedd, whose obit is at *AC* 798. See, further, below, 476–7.

Cadell, better known as Hywel Dda, had ruled it for much of the first half of the century; in the last eight years of his life, 942–950, Hywel had also ruled Gwynedd.

When the Harleian collection was made in the third quarter of the tenth century, therefore, the Merfynion had only ruled Gwynedd for about 130 years, and their acquisition of Dyfed was even more recent, only about forty years before the beginning of Owain ap Hywel's reign. This posed a problem for the tenth-century genealogist. The commonest form of genealogy was a simple agnatic pedigree, going back from an existing king to the founder of a dynasty or even beyond into the mists of legend. It exhibited the legitimacy of that king's rule; and it was thus of critical significance only during his reign. The form of this pedigree is thus 'X son of Y son of Z . . . ', and it was of immediate relevance during the reign of X. If X was succeeded by his son W, the relevant pedigree would then be 'W son of X son of Y son of Z'. Pedigrees of this kind were likely to be regularly updated. The *Historia Brittonum* described one such pedigree as a genealogy that 'runs backwards to the beginning'.[70] It was described as running backwards because a British genealogy of this kind differed from the most familiar genealogy of all, that of Christ at the beginning of the Gospel according to Matthew, which came forwards in time, from the ancestor to his descendant: 'Abraham begat Isaac; and Isaac begat Jacob; and Jacob begat Judas . . . And Jacob begat Joseph the husband of Mary, of whom was born Jesus, who is called Christ.'

The founder of the dynasty was typically the man who established the rule of his descendants over a particular territory, so that a pedigree took him as its point of origin—or the focal ancestor might be someone who had so enhanced the power of the dynasty that his descendants came to monopolize the kingship, whether for a period or permanently, as with King Alfred in England. Although, on the face of it, the pedigree was just a statement of descent, in effect it was a justification for rule over the land to which the dynasty claimed an ancestral right. Yet the Merfynion had no ancestral right either to Gwynedd or to Dyfed. Quite what the genealogist could do about this situation will be discussed when we have considered the other two forms of genealogy common among the Britons.

One is what I shall call 'the branching genealogy'. This does not 'run backwards to the beginning' but comes forward from an ancestor. Yet it was not just, as was Christ's pedigree, a version of the pedigree X son of Y son of Z, namely the one normal among the Welsh and Irish, but in reverse order (X begot Y, Y begot Z); instead it included more than one son of the ancestor and thus more than one line of descent. It did not exhibit the claim of an individual but the shape of a dynasty. One branching genealogy of major significance for the Harleian collection was that of 'the sons of Cunedda'. Cunedda was three generations further back behind the Maelgwn Gwynedd whom the *Annales Cambriae* noted as dying in 547 (not a date to be trusted). The final section of the Harleian Genealogies was the story of Cunedda and his sons, already quoted and discussed in the previous chapter.[71]

[70] *HB*, c. 49. [71] Above, 328–9.

Its picture of the dynasty was as follows, and the land division followed suit, except that the share of Einion Yrth was not mentioned:

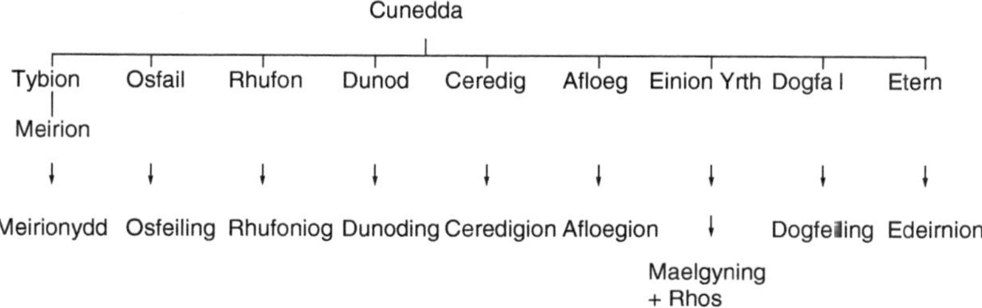

Figure 11.2. The sons of Cunedda and their lands

Crucial to understanding the point of this passage is to consider what divisions of Gwynedd were not stated as taking their names from this primitive land-sharing. The absences from the list are even more important than those present.

Map 21. The lands of the sons of Cunedda
From the sons of Cunedda the kings of Gwynedd up to AD 825 were supposedly descended, and so also were a range of lesser kingdoms. The latter were largely distributed around Cardigan Bay or in the interior of Gwynedd east of the Conwy. The only exception is Osfeilion in the east of Anglesey.

These territories (see Map 21) did not include any part of Arfon or Arllechwedd; in Anglesey there is only a small region in the east, Osfeilion, on the opposite side of the island from the later seat of kingship, Aberffraw.[72] In the Llŷn peninsula none of the northern coast was included. Instead there was a sequence of territories along the coastlands of Cardigan Bay, from Afloegion to Dunoding and Meirionydd, and then on to Ceredigion. In the lands to the east of the River Conwy, Rhufoniog and Dogfeiling lay away from the coast. The effect was that, apart from Osfeilion in Anglesey, no part of the northern coastlands from Bardsey to the border of Tegeingl was included. The contrast between the northern coastlands and those along Cardigan Bay gives the key to the underlying scheme, since the northern coastlands were the heart of Gwynedd, whereas the lands assigned to the sons, other than Einion Yrth, were peripheral. Einion Yrth, however, was the son from whom the Maelgyning derived and also the other dynasty which may have been based in Rhos, just to the east of the Conwy;[73] Hywel and his father Caradog, the last two descendants in the third pedigree in the Harleian Genealogies, have both been identified with kings of Gwynedd. Pedigrees associated with the other sons and their peripheral lands were confined to a later position in the Harleian collection (nos. 17, 18, 26, and possibly 20). The understanding, therefore, is that there was a radical difference in political status between the main lines of the dynasty, those not excluded from the kingship of Gwynedd, and the excluded branches. The latter might enjoy kingship in their peripheral territories, but they were not seen as possible contenders for the kingship of Gwynedd.[74]

Another branching genealogy appears in a section of a later Gwynedd collection, a section devoted to the sons of Rhodri Mawr, himself the son and successor of Merfyn Frych, the king of Gwynedd after whom the Merfynion, the Second

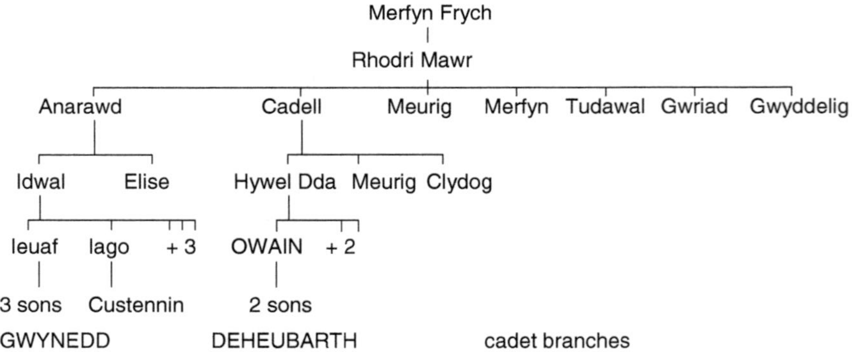

Figure 11.3. The Merfynion in the ninth and tenth centuries

[72] Richards, 'Early Welsh Territorial Suffixes', 209; *OP* ii. 296 n. 2.

[73] Kirby, 'British Dynastic History', 94.

[74] Lloyd, *HW*[3] i. 239, points out that the dynasty of Dunoding probably endured to the tenth century.

Dynasty of Gwynedd, were named.[75] It was with Rhodri Mawr that the Merfynion began to branch (see Figure 11.3).

Owain ap Hywel, the initial focus of the Harleian Genealogies, is in capitals; but in this genealogy, deriving from Gwynedd, he is given no special prominance, other than as one king among others. At least for the first part of the sequence of sons of Rhodri Mawr, they are likely to have been listed in order of seniority.[76] Anarawd was thus the eldest son and heir to Gwynedd; but Cadell, probably the second son, benefited from the territorial conquest by which the sons of Rhodri gained Ceredigion, Ystrad Tywi, and Dyfed. Cadell, too, ended his life as 'king of the Britons'.[77] This shows the principle on which the branching genealogy was constructed: the sons of kings were noted, but not the sons of those who were not kings. Their lines of descent fell out of the genealogical picture. This, therefore, is a form of genealogy that comes close to being a regnal list; but in this case it is complicated by conquest, so that two lines of descent are carried forward.

The genealogy of the descendants of Rhodri Mawr does, however, include brief notes on the other sons of Rhodri apart from Anarawd and Cadell, but these only reinforce the main message. From Merfyn ap Rhodri came the kindred of 'y Rhiw' in Llŷn; Meurig had no descendants; Tudawal, who was lamed in the Battle of the Conway in 881, was given 'the principal churches of Gwynedd' by his brothers; Gwriad, who was slain together with his father, Rhodri, in 878, was the ancestor of 'the men of the Nant Mawr in Twrcelyn in Môn'; and, finally, from Gwyddelig ap Rhodri derived the men of Penmon Lys, also in the east of Anglesey. The younger sons of Rhodri were, therefore, not the ancestors of kings but merely of local free kindreds, part of the *uchelwyr* of Gwynedd. None of them was associated with the peripheral lands along Cardigan Bay, nor with Rhufoniog or Dogfeiling. None of them was associated with Gwynedd east of the Conwy, in the lands which the dynasty of Rhos may have dominated before 825. There is no contrast between core and periphery here as in the account of the sons of Cunedda, only a unified kingdom of Gwynedd—a kingdom that remained unified by depressing the status of cadet lines.

The third kind of genealogy was designed to enhance the status and prestige of an individual and to display the alliances between kindreds through marriage of which he might be a beneficiary—what the Second Branch of the Mabinogi called *ymgyfathrachu* 'mutual-joint-inter-lineaging', linking lines of descent.[78] The assumption is that, although a man's right to succeed to high office or to inherit land is based on an agnatic pedigree, his descent goes back through his mother as well as his father. This form of genealogy, unlike the other two, admits, indeed thrives on, female links; and it is this form of genealogy, 'the status genealogy', that

[75] ABT 7 in *EWGT* 101–2.

[76] Cf. Asser, *Life of King Alfred*, ed. Stevenson, c. 80, 'Anaraut quoque filius Rotri, cum suis fratribus'.

[77] See below, 508–9, for all this.

[78] *PKM* 30. 19; and see above, 297–8.

is exemplified by the genealogies at the beginning of the Life of Gruffudd ap Cynan and the pair of lineages of Owain ap Hywel in the Harleian collection.[79] In that collection we never get Owain's agnatic lineage back to the ancestors of Merfyn Frych. Instead, the first pedigree traces his descent from the Maelgyning, the earlier dynasty of Gwynedd, via a daughter of Cynan Dindaethwy (the last king of Gwynedd from the Maelgyning). The second pedigree traces Owain's descent via his mother from the former kings of Dyfed. After that we go northwards, to a cadet line of the descendants of Cunedda, then to the Isle of Man, and to the dynasties of the northern Britons, first to the dynasty of Alclud, later Strathclyde, then to the Coeling, among whom pride of place was given to the pedigree of Urien ap Cynfarch, the Urien Rheged of the poetry. After the Coeling we return to Wales. Some of these dynasties were linked with the Merfynion by marriage: the fourth pedigree appears to be of a dynasty belonging to the Isle of Man, the island from which the Merfynion themselves very probably derived, a dynasty with which they were linked by marriage; but others, such as the dynasty of Alclud, were prominent simply because they were among the two or three leading royal kindreds of the Britons. The Harleian Genealogies thus have three aspects: they begin by upholding the status, in terms of descent, of one particular king, Owain ap Hywel, but they go on to give a broad survey of the royalty of the Britons, in a sequence roughly corresponding to the political status of the dynasties mentioned, and they conclude with the story of the migration of Cunedda.

3. EARLY WELSH POETRY: THE BOOK OF ANEIRIN

The earliest surviving British vernacular poetry may date from a period close to the lifetime of Gildas, but, if so, it does not survive in the form it had in the sixth century. According to the *Historia Brittonum*, four poets, Talhaearn Tad Awen, *Neirin* (Aneirin),Taliesin, and Cian 'who is called "Wheat of Poetry"', flourished during the reign of Ida, first Anglian king of Bernicia, that is, 547–559.[80] Surviving poetry is attributed to two of these poets, Aneirin and Taliesin. Among the poems attributed to Taliesin is a group in praise of Urien, king of Rheged—the Urien who is said in the *Historia Brittonum* to have fought against Hussa, king of Bernicia 585–592—and in praise, also, of Owain, his son. Urien was apparently slain by the treachery of a fellow-British king, Morgan, in the course of an expedition during Hussa's reign, perhaps that which led to the siege of *Medcaut* or Lindisfarne.[81] However, the poetry ascribed to Aneirin and Taliesin is preserved in manuscripts of the thirteenth and fourteenth centuries: 'The Book of Aneirin', a manuscript very

[79] For the Life of Gruffudd ap Cynan, see above, 333–4.

[80] *HB*, c. 62.

[81] *HB*, c. 63; the Irish attestations in *The Martyrology of Tallaght*, ed. H. J. Lawlor and R. I. Best, Henry Bradshaw Society 68 (London, 1931), and *The Martyrology of Oengus the Culdee*, ed. W. Stokes, Henry Bradshaw Society, 29 (1905) both under 31 August, and in AU 632. 4, show that the correct spelling of the name is *Medcaut*, as in § 65, not *Metcaud* as in § 63.

probably from Gwynedd and dated to the second half of the thirteenth century, and 'The Book of Taliesin', which dates from the first half of the fourteenth century and was written somewhere in South Wales.[82] Because of the many centuries separating the purported date of the poets and the manuscript copies of what is claimed to be their poetry, serious difficulties attend any attempt to use it as historical evidence. Moreover, as we have seen, there are further problems over the information given in the *Historia Brittonum*, information that is critical for the historical context of the poetry.

It is common ground that the texts, especially the *Gododdin*, include both early and late features; what is not agreed is the relative weight to be attached to these contrary indications. Recent scholarship is thus divided between two tendencies: one is cheerfully constructive, impressed by early features, happy to extend a line of argument from one ingenious suggestion to another; the other is sceptical, gives more weight to later features, and tends to see the texts as primarily late Old Welsh poems with only possible early antecedents.[83] The evidence of the poetry cannot be neglected by the historian of early medieval Wales, but the difficulties need to be brought out into the open.

The principal poem in the Book of Aneirin was at an early date entitled 'The Gododdin' after the name of one of the peoples between the Forth and the Tyne: in the manuscript the poem is introduced with the words 'This is the *Gododdin*; Aneirin sang it'.[84] I shall use Gododdin for the people and *Gododdin* for the poem. The latter has traditionally been understood to be a series of laments for warriors who died in a battle at Catterick in the North Riding of Yorkshire, and therefore within the territory that, in the seventh century, belonged to the kingdom of Deira. It exists in two different scribal versions in the one manuscript, both scribes belonging to the second half of the thirteenth century. One scribe, Hand A, began copying the text at the beginning of the manuscript, wrote the whole of quires 1 and 2, and continued writing in quire 3 as far as the sixth line of the second last page. Hand B completed quire 3. Hand A resumed at the beginning of quire 4

[82] *Llyfr Aneirin: A Facsimile/Llyfr Aneirin: Ffacsimile*, ed. D. Huws ([Cardiff and Aberystwyth], 1989); D. Huws, *Five Ancient Books of Wales*, H. M. Chadwick Memorial Lectures, 6 (Cambridge, 1995), 11–14, reprinted, with an important addition, in his *Medieval Welsh Manuscripts* (Cardiff, 2000), 72–5 (for the localization of the MS see p. 75); *Facsimile and Text of the Book of Taliesin*, ed. J. Gwenogvryn Evans (Llanbedrog, 1910); M. Haycock, 'Llyfr Taliesin', *National Library of Wales Journal*, 25 (1987–8), 357–86; *Legendary Poems from the Book of Taliesin*, ed. and trans. M. Haycock (Aberystwyth, 2007), 1–11.

[83] The principal contribution in the 'cheerfully constructive' camp is J. T. Koch's edition, translation and discussion of the *Gododdin*: *The Gododdin of Aneirin: Text and Context from Dark-Age Britain* (Cardiff, 1997); recent sceptics are O. J. Padel, 'A New Study of the *Gododdin*' [review of Koch], *CMCS* 35 (Summer 1998), 45–55, and G. Isaac, 'Readings in the History and Transmission of the *Gododdin*', *CMCS* 37 (Summer 1999), 55–78.

[84] *Llyfr Aneirin*, ed. Huws, p. 1, line 1 of the facsimile and of Gwenogvryn Evans's transcript; Gwenogvryn Evans's text, attached to the facsimile, is the only one to present the material in the order of the manuscript. For the likelihood that the manuscript was written in Gwynedd, see Huws, *Medieval Welsh Manuscripts*, 75. The standard edition remains *CA*; for Koch's edition see the previous note; the most accessible is Jarman, *Gododdin*; I shall use Jarman's translation unless otherwise indicated. A good translation, which has the great virtue of separating the A and B versions is by J. P. Clancy, *Medieval Welsh Poems* (Dublin, 2003), 45–76.

and continued as far as line 11 of page 30. His text in quire 4 was not, however, the *Gododdin* itself but the *Gorchanau* 'songs', beginning with *Gorchan Tudfwlch*; but when Hand B completed quire 4, he was continuing his copy of the *Gododdin* and was not copying further *gorchanau*. Quire 5 was written entirely by Hand B, but it now lacks the last five folios, namely folios 4–8 (what would have been folios 39–42 of the whole manuscript). There is nothing to show whether there was originally another quire. It is demonstrable, however, that the loss of folios in quire 5 has given us an incomplete text. The folios were not 'cancelled'; that is, the scribe did not decide that they were unnecessary to complete the task of copying and then remove the folios so that they could be used elsewhere; instead the text has been truncated by physical loss subsequent to the date of writing.[85] Yet, even though the manuscript is incomplete, there are enough stanzas written by Hand A that also appear in Hand B's text to show that we have two distinct versions of the one poem. By 'stanzas' I mean what Ifor Williams called *awdlau*, and in the manuscript itself were called *odleu*, the old plural of *awdl*; they have also been called 'verses'.[86] They vary in length but many are about ten lines in length. The metrical patterns are varied. Normally, however, one stanza has a single metrical form as well as being marked by a large initial.[87]

The manuscript, therefore, has given with one hand but taken away with the other: it is an immense benefit that we can compare two versions; but analysis is hampered by the incomplete state of the B text—indeed, it is even conceivable that Hand A may have contributed to the missing folios. Table 11.3 gives Daniel Huws's collation of the manuscript together with the sequence of *awdlau*:

Table 11.3. Collation of the Book of Aneirin

quires	pages	text	Awdlau	Hands
1^4	1–8	Gredyf gwr . . . a gwryen [catchword *a gwynn*]	A1–A30	A
2^4	9–16	a gwynn . . . vab llywri [catchword *ardyledawc*]	A30–A65	A
3^4	17–24	Ardyledawc . . . gwenabwy mab gwen*n* [no catchword]	A66–A88 + B1–B6	A→B (23.6)
4^4 (of which ff. 2 and 3 are singletons)				
	25–32	Aryf angkynnull . . . na deliis march [catchword lost?]	*Gorchanau* (A) + B7–B18	A→B (30.11)
5^8 wanting ff. 4–8.				
	33–38	neb march . . . budit did dr	B18–B42	B

[85] Compare Koch, *Gododdin*, 26 (the two texts at the foot of the page); Clancy, *Medieval Welsh Poems*, 76.

[86] Jarman, *Gododdin*, uses 'stanza', Jackson, *Gododdin*, 'verse', Ifor Williams, *CA*, *awdl* but also *pennill*. For the manuscript's *odleu*, used by Hand A, see *Llyfr Aneirin*, ed. Huws, 28. 16.

[87] An exception is LXXXV in *CA* (Jarman, *Gododdin*, no. 83; Koch, *Gododdin*, A 84).

The existence of two versions of the poem has given editors a problem. Ifor Williams kept relatively close to the order of the manuscript. He thus put the A text first, with the *awdlau* numbered in roman numerals, I–LXXXIX. Where an *awdl* existed in both versions, he again gave the A version first, but he attached to it the B version, for example LV. A and LV. B. This had the effect of taking the B *awdl* out of the sequence of that version into the sequence of the A version.[88] Finally, he gave the B *awdlau* that had no counterpart in the A version. An alternative plan is to give precedence to the B version, since, as we shall see, it appears to have preserved the original sequence of the *awdlau* better. This plan was first adopted in the translation by Kenneth Jackson.[89]

In a very few cases there appear to be more than two versions of the one stanza, which, in the principal edition by Sir Ifor Williams, are labelled A, B, C, etc. The distinctions between B, C etc. are, however, not on the same plane as the distinction between the A and B texts: the latter corresponds to the difference of scribes, the former does not. Invariably the stanzas labelled C etc. were written by Hand B (XLV, A–C, LI, A–C, LXIII, A–E).[90] Their existence, however, has prompted the theory that at least two sources were used by Hand B: by one scholar these are labelled B^1 and B^2.[91] A further consideration in favour of this idea is that the later stanzas in Hand B tend to be in more archaic spelling. If this theory were adopted, we should have an A version of 88 stanzas, a B^1 version of only 23 stanzas, and a B^2 version of 19 stanzas that is incomplete because of loss of folios; if it originally extended to the end of the quire, it would have had about 59 stanzas, still well short of the 88 in the A version but more than double the 23 of the B^1 version. However, the theory of the two sources used by Hand B is far from certain: rather than two extended sources, he may have used a single exemplar which had noted some variants in the margins. If one takes all the variants into account and still proposes to ascribe them to separate sources, it will then be far from clear that there were only two sources.[92] Another difficulty is that it is not easy to distinguish separate versions of the one stanza from what is called 'incremental repetition', the practice of following one stanza by another that repeats much of the wording of the first in order to build up a cumulative effect.[93]

Prefixed to the B version are two stanzas.[94] The first has nothing to do with the *Gododdin*: it is a celebration, from the point of view of the Britons of Alclud, of

88 There were a few other adjustments which meant that his numeration does not correspond entirely to that of the A version: his XXXIX. B is, in fact, a variant from the A version and his XL and XLI are from the B version but shifted by him into the sequence of the A version. What he has done is clear from marginal references to the pages of the manuscript.

89 He justified his procedure at Jackson, *Gododdin*, 95.

90 Jarman, *Gododdin*, 39–41, regards LXIII C–E as separate stanzas.

91 Koch, *Gododdin*, pp. lxvi–lxxv, following G. Isaac, '*Canu Aneirin* awdl LI', *Journal of Celtic Linguistics*, 2 (1993), 65–91.

92 The conclusion of Isaac, 'Readings in the History', 77–8.

93 Cf. K. H. Jackson, 'Incremental Repetition in the Early Welsh *Englyn*', *Speculum*, 16 (1941), 304–21.

94 *Llyfr Aneirin*, ed. Huws, 23. 6–14; *CA* stanzas LXXIX A and B, LV A and B; Jarman, *Gododdin*, stanzas 1 and 102; Koch, *Gododdin*, B^1.1 and B^1. 2; R. G. Gruffydd, 'The Strathcarron Interpolation (*Canu Aneirin*, Lines 966–77)', *Scottish Gaelic Studies*, 17 (1996), 172–8.

their victory over Domnall Brecc (Dyfnwal Frych) at the battle of Strathcarron, which is dated to 642.[95] The second is in the voice of a reciter who is about to sing the *Gododdin*. For that reason it is usually called 'The Reciter's Prologue'. One significant feature of this Prologue is that it addresses the poem in the second person and names it as *Gododdin*, referring also to Aneirin as someone who has died:[96]

> *Gododdin*, I make claim on thy behalf
> In the presence of the throng boldly in the court:
> And the song of the son of Dwywai, of high courage,
> May it be manifest in the one place that it vanquishes.
> . . .
> Since earth covered Aneirin,
> Poetry is now parted from the Gododdin.

The Prologue shows the feature known in Irish as *dúnad*, by which a word at the beginning is repeated at the end.[97] But this example has a special twist, since *Gododdin* at the beginning is the poem, while Gododdin at the end is the people.

In the A version, both of these stanzas—the Strathcarron verse and the Reciter's Prologue—recur, only now they are placed separately among the stanzas of the *Gododdin* itself. The stanza which follows the Reciter's Prologue in the B version also occurs in the A version, but in yet another position. So far, it seems that the B version preserves an early order, whereas the A version must have been disarranged. On the other hand, the A version begins, after a single initial stanza (*Greddf gŵr*), with stanzas which are, for the most part, in two evidently coherent sequences; the first sequence begins with *Caeog, cynhorog* 'wearing a brooch, in the forefront' (varied by *caeog cynifiad*) and the second initially by *Gwŷr a aeth Ododdin* 'men went to Gododdin' and then *Gwŷr a aeth Gatraeth* 'men went to Catraeth'. None of them occurs in the surviving portion of the B version. This has led to the suggestion that they are a later stratum in the textual tradition of the poem.[98] Since the earlier order—as it existed at the time when the Strathcarron stanza and the Reciter's Prologue were prefixed to the poem—is reflected in the B version, but disordered in the A version, a serious question can be raised about the status of these two sequences in the latter. The A version would appear to have been disarranged before the two coherent sequences, which have not suffered disarrangement, were added at the beginning of the A version. This may well be the case, although it leads

[95] AU 642. 1. Since it is combined with the obit of Domnall mac Áeda, which is likely to be correct, the date can probably be trusted. For the chronological problems of this section of the annals see Charles-Edwards, *The Chronicle of Ireland*, i. 38–9, 55–6, and for an argument that Domnall may have died in 643 see N. Evans, *The Present and the Past in Medieval Irish Chronicles* (Woodbridge, 2010), 178–9 (but this is unlikely in my view given the general run of external checks on the annalistic dates at this period).

[96] Trans. Jarman, *Gododdin*, 2; I do not accept Koch's view, *Gododdin*, p. liv, that a particular Votadinian is being addressed: the lines that follow refer to the poem and its triumph.

[97] J. Morris-Jones, *Cerdd Dafod* (Oxford, 1925), §§ 104, 508.

[98] Koch, *Gododdin*, p. xcv.

to the slightly uncomfortable conclusion that the most memorable poetry in the *Gododdin* is a later addition.

Another issue which arises from the two initial stanzas in the B version is the reason why the Strathcarron stanza was placed not just before the *Gododdin* but before the Reciter's Prologue. Since it occurs before the Reciter's Prologue, it is not presented by the B version as part of the poem introduced by the Prologue.[99] It is, however, easy to imagine it being added to an early manuscript as a separate text, perhaps in the top margin of the first page. Such a theory has, however, important consequences, if we add that both the Strathcarron stanza and the Reciter's Prologue also occur in the A version, but in separate and inappropriate positions. Both versions, on this explanation of the Strathcarron stanza, go back to a single manuscript text, namely the one which first received the marginal addition.[100] Moreover, it is likely that the Strathcarron stanza was added to a text which already had the Reciter's Prologue; in other words, there were now two separate additions at the beginning, the first (in time) being the Reciter's Prologue (conceived as introducing the poem) and the second being the Strathcarron stanza (unrelated to the *Gododdin*). Similarly, the short poem known as *Pais Dinogad*—a lullaby, and yet also a lament for a dead husband—occurs almost at the end of the A version and may again have been originally a marginal addition;[101] the references to a husband going out hunting are all to what he used to do in the past, so that the element of lament may have suggested to a scribe a kinship with the *Gododdin* itself.

The local associations of the added stanzas offer clues to the paths of transmission. The Strathcarron stanza was presumably composed for an audience in the victorious kingdom of Alclud (Dumbarton). *Pais Dinogad* includes a reference to the Falls of Derwennydd; and Derwennydd is a British river-name preserved in English as Derwent. There are several rivers of this name, but the most likely candidate to be identified as Rhaeadr Derwennydd, the Falls of Derwennydd, is the Lodore Cascade at the south-eastern end of Derwentwater in Cumbria, that is, very probably, in the early medieval kingdom of Rheged.[102] The B version thus probably came to Gwynedd via Alclud (later Ystrad Glud), while the A version may have gone from Alclud via Rheged to Gwynedd. It has been proposed that the transmission of the B version to Gwynedd from Strathclyde can be dated to the late

99 Koch, *Gododdin*, p. lx, suggests that the Strathcarron poem was part of a single performance on the occasion on which the Reciter declaimed his prologue followed by the *Gododdin*; the B version in the thirteenth-century Welsh manuscript would thus reflect a particular oral performance in the kingdom of Alclud in the seventh century, but this supposition is hazardous and unnecessary.

100 This was clearly seen by D. N. Dumville, 'Early Welsh Poetry: Problems of Historicity', in B. F. Roberts (ed.), *Early Welsh Poetry: Studies in the Book of Aneirin* (Aberystwyth, 1988), 6.

101 *Llyfr Aneirin*, ed. Huws, 22. 12–20; *CA* LXXXVIII; Jarman, *Gododdin*, stanza 103; Koch, *Gododdin*, A 87; for the explanation as a marginal addition, see *CA* l–li, Jackson, *Gododdin*, 46–7, Jarman, *Gododdin*, p. lxii. One cannot say confidently that this addition was originally made at the end of a manuscript text of the *Gododdin*, because the disarrangement that appears to have afflicted the A version prevents any conclusion about its sequence of stanzas before the disarrangement occurred.

102 R. G. Gruffydd, 'Where was *Rhaeadr Derwennydd* (*Canu Aneirin*, line 1114)?', in A. T. E. Matonis and D. F. Melia (eds.), *Celtic Language, Celtic Culture: A Festschrift for Eric P. Hamp* (Van Nuys, Cal., 1990), 261–66.

ninth century; but this rests on very late and untrustworthy evidence.[103] A further theory argues that the A version arrived in Wales more than two centuries earlier, after which the early sequence, *Caeog, cynhorog*, was added in the mid-seventh century.[104] This depends largely on the appearance of the same two adjectives in the same sequence in a poem in praise of a king of Gwynedd, Cadwallon (*ob.* 634), together with the participation of a slightly later king of Gwynedd, Cadafael, in Penda's campaign against Oswiu in 655, which reached the Forth.[105] The evidence is not sufficient to pin the date down even to a single century: repetition of a formula proves little; and the campaigns of Penda, with his Welsh allies, into northern Bernicia at best provide a context for something which might have happened—poets in Gwynedd might have given a welcome at that time to a poem celebrating the Gododdin. Yet it is unlikely that we shall ever be able to move from 'might' to 'did' or even to 'probably did'. What is crucial for present purposes is not, however, the particular paths of transmission—interesting though that is for cultural connections between the British kingdoms—but the fundamental point that the versions have diverged very considerably. This is what encourages us to allow considerable time for such divergence.

Sir Ifor Williams maintained that the spelling used in some of the B stanzas indicated derivation from a written text no later than the ninth century. This has been questioned on the grounds that Old Welsh orthography was not entirely abandoned until the middle of the thirteenth century, and if the issue is the date of Hand B's immediate exemplar, the criticism is correct.[106] Williams's argument, however, may be put in terms of how far back elements of the spelling used by Hand B will carry us along a sequence of copying, and then there are good but far from conclusive reasons for thinking that he was right. Essentially, late Old Welsh orthography—as represented by the Computus Fragment and the verse on St Padarn's staff, the latter from late eleventh-century Llanbadarn—was gradually extending the use of the letter *y* from one context to another.[107] Although even the more archaic part of the B text uses *y*, there is no context in which it is used regularly; this pattern, then, may be interpreted as having been created by sporadic modernization of an earlier orthography which did not use the letter *y* at all.[108] If that is correct, the evidence of spelling may carry the B version back to *c.* 900.

[103] Jackson, *Gododdin*, 65–7; M. Miller, 'Historicity and the Pedigrees of the Northcountrymen', *BBCS* 26 (1974–6), 273–80; Koch, *Gododdin*, pp. lxxxix, xc–xci; Charles-Edwards, 'The Authenticity of the *Gododdin*', 53–4.

[104] Koch, *Gododdin*, pp. xcii–ciii.

[105] For Iddew, see above, 7–8. The *Merin Iddew* of Jarman, *Gododdin*, line 944, = *CA* 1209, is therefore understood as the Firth of Forth.

[106] Dumville, 'Palaeographical Considerations', 249–50; Charles-Edwards, 'The Authenticity of the *Gododdin*', 50–1.

[107] P. Kitson, 'Old English Literacy and the Provenance of Welsh *y*', in P. Russell (ed.), *Yr Hen Iaith* (Aberystwyth, 2003), 49–65, esp. 49–53.

[108] Dumville, 'Palaeographical Considerations', 249, claims that 'The single stanza of Welsh verse in C.C.C.C. 199, in fact, shows no radical divergence in orthography from that of pre-950 sources.' There may be room for disagreement on what will count as radical, but the change is indubitably significant, especially because it marks a further stage in a process beginning with the Computus Fragment and ending with Middle Welsh.

The evidence of the two hands, A and B, with their different versions of the poem, leads to a difficult problem. The degree of divergence between the two versions, in the wording and also in the order of their stanzas, would be easier to explain if one assumed that oral transmission played some part in the transmission of the poem. Yet, the existence of the Reciter's Prologue and the Strathcarron stanza in both versions argues strongly in favour of a common ancestor which took the form of a manuscript copy. Moreover, a sequence of manuscript copies seems to lie behind the B version. Some mixture of oral and written transmission is, therefore, likely—perhaps more oral transmission for the A version, more written transmission for the B version. The B version is the one which has further variants within its text (those labelled C etc. in *Canu Aneirin*); these may be attributed to the same desire to recover as much of the text as possible that has been seen as lying behind the manuscript of the Book of Aneirin as a whole.[109] It may be compared with the noting of variant versions for parts of the text in the Lebor na hUidre copy of the Irish saga, *Táin Bó Cúailnge*; this, too, was a scholarly exercise within a written culture.[110] If the act of bringing together variants within the B version of the *Gododdin* is attributed to an earlier copyist rather than to Hand B himself, that will add to the orthographical argument for a sequence of manuscript copies lying behind the B text. Moreover, a manuscript transmission is also likely for the later stages of the A version.[111]

Yet, some kind of oral transmission may also have been behind our texts; and we need to consider what processes might have been involved.[112] At one extreme is the case in which the poem is recomposed in the act of performance, as in the Yugoslav epics made familiar by Parry and Lord; then there is one which is more likely for medieval Celtic literature, in which stories were not told in verse and therefore there were no epics: a memorized poem passes from one reciter to another without any intervention of a written text. At the other extreme, there may be a written text which is revised for oral performance, after which a new fair copy is made of the revised version. Since both versions appear to go back to a manuscript copy, the first and second scenarios are out of the question. The disarrangement of the order evident in A's positioning of the Strathcarron stanza and the Reciter's Prologue suggests that an orality confined to performance, while the actual transmission was effected by copying and revision of a written text, is insufficient to explain the final result in the Book of Aneirin. The extant evidence for transmission therefore makes the following stages a reasonable hypothesis, starting from the manuscript to which the Reciter's Prologue and the Strathcarron stanza were prefixed. Before that point transmission may have been purely oral:

[109] Huws, *Medieval Welsh Manuscripts*, 75.

[110] G. Toner, 'The Ulster Cycle: Historiography or Fiction?', *CMCS* 40 (2000), 1–20.

[111] As in *CA* line 620, *men* for *mein*; cf. *CA* lxvi.

[112] Cf. D. H. Green, 'Orality and Reading: The State of Research in Medieval Studies', *Speculum*, 65 (1990), 267–80.

I. The common manuscript origin of the A and B versions.

1. A manuscript copy, beginning with the Reciter's Prologue, received the further addition of the Strathcarron stanza no earlier than 642 (the date of the battle commemorated). Both it and the Reciter's Prologue are most likely to have been added in the kingdom of Alclud. Since this remained partially Brittonic-speaking up to the twelfth century, there is a long period during which these additions might have been made. We may suspect, from the degree of divergence between the two versions, that the common ancestor, with the Strathcarron stanza, was not written later than the ninth century, but so far this remains just a suspicion.

II. The A version.

2. A copy of this text may have been made in the kingdom of Rheged: if *Pais Dinogad* is a lament for a dead husband cast into the form of a lullaby, a husband who lived within an area likely to have belonged to Rheged, it is easiest to suppose that it was within Rheged that a manuscript received the addition of this extraneous poem. This copy was the source of the A version. Since the B version is incomplete at the end, we cannot be certain that it, too, did not derive from an exemplar containing *Pais Dinogad*, but there is no reason to think that it did. Since the kingdom of Rheged was conquered or absorbed into Northumbria in the mid-seventh century, stage 2 is more easily envisaged as occurring before that date. If that is true, stages 1 and 2 will have followed on each other quite quickly, and therefore the Strathcarron stanza will have been contemporary or near-contemporary with the battle it commemorates, and it will have been written into the common archetype lying behind both versions soon after composition. But this is very far from being a proof.
3. This early manuscript copy of the A version passed into oral currency, namely by passing from one reciter to another. This was the period at which the sequence of stanzas in the A version was seriously disarranged; since the main body of the *Gododdin* consists of a series of individual laments, such disarrangement could easily happen. If the series of stanzas beginning with *Caeog cynhorog* and *Gwŷr a aeth Ododdin/Gatraeth* were already part of the poem, they may have escaped disordering because they were evidently two sequences. Alternatively, they may have escaped because they were additions after the disordering had already occurred in the period of oral transmission.
4. A manuscript copy of this disarranged version was made, so that the final stage of transmission to the extant A version was a written one; this period of written transmission probably included the changeover in Wales from Insular script to late Caroline in the twelfth century.

III. The B version

5. The B Version shows more signs of written transmission than the A Version: it preserves the sequence at the beginning left by the manuscript additions. Its orthography retains evidence for a manuscript copy

> in Old Welsh no later than the beginning of the tenth century and probably a written transmission between then and the second half of the thirteenth century. It is possible that this version was solely preserved by writing.

Since there is some reason to think that the two versions parted company in the seventh century, comparison between them may well yield early material, which deserves to be taken into account by any historian of northern Britain in the period.[113] It should be stressed, however, that the suggested dating of the common ancestor rests on a conception of what is the easiest working hypothesis, not on any arguments that even approach being conclusive.

The interpretation of the *Gododdin* that prevailed from the date of Sir Ifor Williams's *Canu Aneirin* until recently understood the poem as being about a single event, an expedition sent by a ruler called Mynyddog from Edinburgh to attack the Deirans, an expedition that ended in a great battle at Catterick.[114] The core of Mynyddog's army was a force of three hundred mounted warriors, called 'The Retinue of Mynyddog', *Gosgordd Mynyddog*. Mynyddog had assembled this retinue, primarily from his own kingdom, but also from others, and had feasted them for a year. The warriors were 'reared on mead' and 'reared on wine'; but after the year almost all the three hundred were slain in the battle at Catterick. They were overwhelmed by superior numbers, but only after they themselves had inflicted casualties more numerous than themselves. The poem itself consisted of a series of laments for the deaths of Mynyddog's warriors, the members of his war band, who died at Catterick.

The date of the battle was assigned to about 600; this was before Æthelfrith of Bernicia annexed Deira and certainly before the later years of Edwin, his successor, since Bede records Paulinus baptizing many in the Swale, near Catterick.[115] By then, Catterick was securely and irrevocably in English hands. The assumption was that Catterick had been British up to the reign of Urien, who was described in a poem in his praise as lord of Catterick,[116] but that, after his death, it was taken by the Deirans. The impression given by the *Historia Brittonum* is that Urien was killed during the reign of Hussa in Bernicia and thus no earlier than 585 and no later than 592.[117] The date was therefore placed between the reign of Urien and the later years of Edwin, and hence the common date of *c.* 600.

This, it was also argued, was how the expedition and the poem that gave it lasting fame were remembered: a poem in praise of Cadwallon, who was killed in 634,

[113] Rollason, *Northumbria, 500–1100*, 101, takes an extreme position in regarding references to an expedition to Catterick as just as likely to be fictional as historical.

[114] *CA* xxiii–xlviii; Jackson, *Gododdin*, 3–25.

[115] Bede, *HE* ii. 14.

[116] *The Poems of Taliesin*, ed. I. Williams, English version by J. E. Caerwyn Williams (Dublin, 1968), viii. 9 (*llyw Katraeth*), ruling over 'the men of Catraeth' (*gwyr Katraeth*), ii. 1.

[117] Working from the regnal chronology of Bede and from the Bernician regnal list in the Moore Memoranda and in later manuscripts, Hussa's reign is given as 585–592.

recalled 'the disaster of Catterick, great and famous'.[118] In the twelfth century, a poem ascribed to the Powysian ruler, Owain Cyfeiliog, lamented those who had died in an expedition mounted by Owain to liberate a prisoner. His war band had fought no less gloriously than had the Gododdin:[119]

> I have heard of a payment for mead for an expedition to Catterick,
> True their boast, stained weapons.
> The retinue of Mynyddog, in return for their death-sleep,
> Won their fame, noble warriors hateful to the enemy.
> No worse did my warriors in the hard battle of Maelor,
> Releasing a prisoner in a manner deserving of praise.

In the early thirteenth century, Dafydd Benfras, poet to Llywelyn ab Iorwerth, asked God for inspiration to 'sing praise as once Aneirin did, on the day he sang *Gododdin*'.[120]

Nevertheless, almost everything in this interpretation has been questioned. Williams came to his date on the grounds that it fell between the reign of Urien, when he held Catterick, and the later years of Edwin, when it had become part of Deira. Yet excavations at Catterick indicated that the English occupation was no later than *c.* 500, a whole century before the proposed date for the expedition of the Gododdin.[121] Even if Urien did temporarily regain control of Catterick at some point in the second half of the sixth century, that would not offer a *terminus post quem*, since the Gododdin might have attacked Deirans at Catterick before Urien gained control of the area. Another difficulty is to explain why the Gododdin should have attacked the Deirans *c.* 600, during the reign of Æthelfrith in Bernicia, when the Bernicians were like a cancer within the body of the Gododdin. For this reason, it has been pointed out that it would be easier to explain the expedition against the Deirans if it occurred earlier in the sixth century before Bernicia was a threat.[122] These difficulties need to be acknowledged and a more systematic understanding must be developed.

The approach to the *Gododdin* appropriate for an historian is to proceed stage by stage. First, those *awdlau*, stanzas, for which there are both A and B versions, need to be analysed to reveal the social values and the references to contemporary conditions that both versions share. Secondly, the *awdlau* only found in the B version need to be analysed to determine whether they differ in any significant way from those shared by the A and B versions; and, thirdly, the same needs to be done for the A version.

The *awdlau* common to both versions show quite clearly that the poem is not a narrative. Neither Welsh nor Irish verse was normally used for narrative, so this is

[118] R. G. Gruffydd, 'Canu Cadwallon ap Cadfan', in R. Bromwich and R. Brinley Jones (eds.), *Astudiaethau ar yr Hengerdd / Studies in Old Welsh Poetry cyflwynedig i Syr Idris Foster* (Cardiff, 1978), 29–32.

[119] CBT II. 14. 123–8.

[120] CBT VI. 25. 1–6.

[121] P. R. Wilson et al., 'Early Anglian Catterick and *Catraeth*'.

[122] Dumville, 'Early Welsh Poetry', 1–4; N. J. Higham, *The Kingdom of Northumbria, AD 350–1100* (Stroud, 1993), 93.

only to be expected. If we wish to use the *Gododdin* as evidence for the history of events, we shall be relying on mere allusions. Most *awdlau* have a person who is the subject of praise, but this is not always true. In particular, it is not true of the *awdl* that appears to have been the original beginning of the poem. It exists in three versions, but, unfortunately, it is also very difficult and, for that reason, was omitted by Jarman from his text. Enough can be rescued, however, to show that the *Gododdin* began with a celebration of Lleuddinion, Lothian, and the principal fortress of Lothian. The short opening lines consist of a series of short phrases, mostly just nouns, that play upon the word *lleu*. The word *lleu* has been taken to mean 'open' as in *lleudir* 'open land'; but here we are dealing with a land by the Forth, part of the northern frontier of the Gododdin, so that it is scarcely credible that the poet is not referring to Lothian, Lleuddinion, 'the land of Lleu's fort'. On the other hand, we need not go to the extreme of supposing that the poet was an active worshipper of the pagan Celtic god Lleu (*Lugus), since Lleu survived in Welsh narrative long enough to become a major part of the Fourth Branch of the Mabinogi. The opening lines may be translated as follows:[123]

> The rock of Lleu's people,
> The people of Lleu's hill,
> The borderland of the Gododdin.
> The borderland was held;
> Counsel was taken,
> Counsel for a storm,
> A vessel from over the Forth,
> A host from over the Forth,
> . . .

After this, for several stanzas there is no reference to Catterick or to Mynyddog, the ruler supposed to have sent the expedition southwards. Instead, the Irish and Picts beyond the northern frontier are named; and there may also be a reference to fighting on the River Forth.[124] In B 7 we finally hear of battle against the English, and it seems as though Addonwy, the subject of this stanza, has been challenged to fight as courageously against the English as Bradwen and Morien fought against the Irish and the Picts.[125] That is not to say that the text in both versions did not mourn the deaths and celebrate the deeds of those who fought at Catterick: it did, but it was not until B 14 that it concerned itself with a battle against the Deirans, and it was not until B 20 that it named Catterick.[126] When we turn to the text

123 This translation is closer to Koch, *Gododdin*, 3, than to Clancy, *Medieval Welsh Poems*, 67.

124 B5, *CA* 474; *prif eg weryt* in the A version, *CA* 467, is more likely to mean 'a leader on the Forth' rather than 'a chief in the earth' as Jarman, *Gododdin*, 445, translates.

125 *CA* 634–5; Jarman, *Gododdin*, 527–8.

126 The identification of Catraeth with Catterick has been rejected: C. Cessford, 'Yorkshire and the *Gododdin* Poem', *Yorkshire Archaeological Journal*, 68 (1996), 241–3; but this was on the basis of an etymological speculation by E. P. Hamp, 'Catraeth', *BBCS* 40 (1993), 119. Hamp was setting out to explain the ancient forms of the name for Catterick; his translation of his reconstructed form of the name was then deemed by Cessford to be likely to be common (with no evidence supplied) and so might well not be Catterick.

preserved only in the B version, the situation is similar: Catterick is named, but it is far from clear that all the warriors praised in the poem died in that battle.[127] The A version is the reason why the whole poem has been understood as a lament for the battle at Catterick, especially because of the series of stanzas beginning *Gwŷr a aeth Gatraeth*, 'Men went to Catterick'.[128] The implication of examining the strata of text step by step is that the content was progressively simplified, so that it came to be about one battle rather than about a gallery of warriors from one people, warriors who died in different circumstances.

In one respect, however, the poem was not simplified but made more complicated: the enemy. In the B version as a whole, including those stanzas that also appear in the A version, the English against whom the host of the Gododdin fought were Deirans. In the stanzas that only appear in the A version they were both Deirans and Bernicians. This, however, gives some comfort, since from the reign of Æthelfrith the Bernicians were by far the most dangerous enemies of the Gododdin. Yet the B version of the poem was able to see past this situation to an earlier one, when the Deirans were much more powerful than the Bernicians. It is scarcely likely that any poet composing after the reign of Edwin, king of Northumbria, would have been in a position to reconstruct a political map of the previous century.

When we turn from events and places to values, the contrast between the different strata is less marked, but it is still significant and can be traced through the social vocabulary used in the text. However, it is useful here to refine the methodology a little further. The strongest evidence, as we have seen, comes from stanzas which occur in both the A and B versions; sometimes, however, only the B version of the stanza has the crucial word. The presence of the stanza in both versions is strong evidence that the stanza itself is old; and since the B version has already been revealed as the more conservative of the two, a word found in its version is quite likely to have been in the text of the poem from which both the A and the B version derived. This is a stronger case than if the word occurs in a stanza of the B version for which we have no pair in the A version, but a weaker case than when both versions have the stanza together with the particular word. If the word also occurs elsewhere in the A version, in addition to appearing in the B version of a stanza in both versions, the argument is stronger than when only the B version has the word. The different levels of evidence may be set out in a sequence running from stronger to weaker:

1. The word occurs in both the A and B versions of a stanza itself preserved in both.
2. The stanza appears in both versions; the word itself is lacking in the A version of the stanza but occurs elsewhere in the A version.
3. The stanza appears in both versions but the word only in the B version.

[127] *CA* 1175 (Jarman, *Gododdin*, 914), 1197 (Jarman, 932); Deira, 1216 (Jarman, 950).

[128] *CA* 68, 74, 84, 90, 97, 105, 121 (Jarman, *Gododdin*, 78, 84, 94, 100, 107, 115, 131; Koch, *Gododdin*, A 8–14).

4. The stanza and the word only appear in the B version.
5. The stanza and the word only appear in the A version.

With these aids to weighing up the evidence, we may go on to investigate the attestations of the central ideas.

A common stanza in the A version celebrates a warrior, whose name is often withheld to the end, for his heroism in battle and his gentleness and good living in the hall. The two are linked because the warrior who has been brave in battle has earned the mead that he drank in the hall:[129] to live with a king and to live like a king requires one to be willing to die for a king. By displaying the ferocity of a wild beast at bay, the warrior will keep his side of the contract, *amod*, with his king.[130] In the hall the warrior may make an *arfaeth*, a vow or declaration about the deeds he will perform.[131] If he fulfils his *amod* and his *arfaeth*, he will deserve *adrawdd*, fame in the sense that men will report his heroic deeds.[132] He will have honour, *wyneb*, literally 'face'.[133] The poet will look upon him with admiration; and the terms used, *ceinmygu*, *edmygu*, and *ermygu*, all favourable compounds of a verb signifying 'to look', contrast with the unfavourable *tremygu* 'to look through, to despise' and *dirmygu*.[134] Fame partakes of both senses, hearing and seeing. The warrior who has earned his mead (*talu medd*) and has survived will bask in the warm and approving eyes of his people as well as in what they say. The dead warrior, who has also earned his mead, will live on in memory and speech.

Some of these ideas are confined to the A version: only there are the *amod* 'contract' and the *arfaeth* mentioned. Confined to a single mention in the B version is the *cyfran clodfan*, literally 'the share of the peak of glory', taken to be equivalent to 'the champion's portion' of the early Irish saga, *Fled Bricrenn*.[135] The various compound verbs in *-mygu*, *ceinmygu*, *edmygu*, and *ermygu* are attested in both versions, but there are no stanzas where the same word appears in the same place, nor even stanzas occurring in both versions where the word occurs in the B version. The same is true of *wyneb* 'face' and thus 'honour'. The most secure attestation is for *adrawdd*, both as noun and as verb, for *gosgordd Mynyddog* 'the war band of Mynyddog', and for the concept of earning one's mead, *talu medd*. The fundamental conception of the warrior is not different in the two versions, but it is more sharply and fully articulated in the A version. That someone in the war band of Mynyddog should earn his mead suggests that he has kept his agreement, *amod*, with Mynyddog himself, but the term *amod* only occurs twice and only in the A version. The notion of honour as lying in the way other Gododdin looked at the person concerned is sufficiently widely attested in the compounds of *mygu* to make

129 On *talu medd*, 'being worth one's mead', see *CA* xlviii–xlix.

130 *CA* 32, 217 (Jarman, *Gododdin*, 42, 227).

131 *CA* 33, 111, 217, 295, 364 (Jarman, *Gododdin*, 43, 121, 227, 286, 348).

132 *CA* 1191 (Jarman, *Gododdin*, 926).

133 *CA* 213, 1149 (Jarman, *Gododdin*, 224, 888).

134 *CA* 145, 1149 (*ceinmygu*); 56, 178, 1129, 1246 (*edmygu*); 435 (*ermygu*): Jarman, *Gododdin*, 155, 853; 66, 188, 976; 413.

135 *CA* 1155 (Jarman, *Gododdin*, 894).

it likely that it occurred in the first written version of the poem, but it was not as prominent as the other concept of honour by which it lived in the way the Gododdin reported someone's bravery.

An aesthetic response to the poem should be consciously distinct from the historian's judgement. The finer expression of the poem is the A version: nearly all the most memorable lines are found there. The historian, however, must use the B version as his basis for a judgement about the original context of the poem. Finally, however, the two approaches may come together as both recognize the superior authenticity of the B version for the sixth century but recognize also the interest of the poem's subsequent development. We are extraordinarily lucky that the B version survived, even in an incomplete state, for it enables us to perceive the way a poem about a northern British people, which was destroyed as a political entity in the seventh century, was subsequently remoulded by other Britons. It was probably the A version that Cynddelw, the Welsh poet of the second half of the twelfth century, knew and valued.[136]

4. EARLY WELSH POETRY: TALIESIN

The Book of Taliesin—National Library of Wales, Peniarth MS 2—is an early fourteenth-century manuscript containing poetry of several kinds.[137] One is prophetic, often connected with the name of Taliesin, but also Myrddin (Geoffrey of Monmouth's Merlin).[138] The most important example is *Armes Prydein Vawr*, 'The Great Prophecy of Britain', a political poem of the tenth century which will be given detailed discussion in Chapter 16. Another group presupposes a narrative about Taliesin and how he gained his gifts of prophecy and shape-shifting. Building on this foundation, others treat Taliesin as the paradigm of poets, a figure through whom later poets could express their ideas about what a poet ought to be and how he should be respected, even feared, by ordinary Britons.[139] For Ifor Williams, a yet further group, mostly found as a single sequence (poems nos. 34–42 in the manuscript), stood apart from the rest. This was a group of praise-poems ascribed in many cases to Taliesin and praising Urien of Rheged and another king called Gwallog; with this group Williams associated others, another poem to Gwallog, one to Cynan Garwyn, and a lament for Urien's son, Owain (nos. 13, 26, and 48 in the manuscript). Instead of the mysterious powers of the poet himself, these poems praised their subjects as heroic warriors and generous kings. That is not to say that the poems of this group avoided all claims for the poet: one, *Dadolwch Urien*, 'The Re-Praise of Urien', a poem reclaiming a place as Urien's poet, a place that, for some reason, he had lost or abandoned, asserts the privileges of the poet as much as

[136] H. E. Means, 'Perceptions of the British Heroic Age in the Work of the Gogynfeirdd', unpublished D.Phil. Thesis, University of Oxford (2003), 83, 85 (on Cynddelw).

[137] *The Book of Taliesin*, ed. J. Gwenogvryn Evans (Llanbedrog, 1910); one version of this diplomatic edition was accompanied by a facsimile of Peniarth MS 2.

[138] M. Haycock, *Prophecies from the Book of Taliesin* (forthcoming).

[139] Haycock, *Legendary Poems*.

the grandeur of the king.[140] Moreover, the role such poems had for the person who made the collection preserved in the Book of Taliesin seems to have been as exemplary praise ascribed to a poet who stood for his profession. Yet, as has been noted, it is unlikely that Taliesin would have become, as a poet, the subject of saga if no poems by him had been preserved.[141]

For Ifor Williams, the praise-poems in the Book of Taliesin had a much better claim than any of the rest to be the work of an historical Taliesin, namely the Taliesin mentioned in the northern history in the *Historia Brittonum* as flourishing in the reign of Ida, the first king of Bernicia, 547–559. It has been observed that the form of the reference in the northern history to the four poets, including Aneirin and Taliesin—*Tunc XYZ in poemate claruerunt*—was characteristic of late Roman annalistic writing.[142] It has also been suggested that the author of the *Historia Brittonum* was directly indebted to such models, so that he, in the ninth century, need not have been drawing on an earlier source for the information the alternative would be that late Antique annals were most directly the model for early medieval annals, and that the references to the four poets were thus likely to be derived from those annals used to compile the Northern History. A final decision between these two interpretations is not possible, but the second has a good chance of being correct. If it is, that would not make the source a contemporary annal entry, since it is only with the seventh century that we have good reason to think that British annals became contemporary.

Yet, even if the reference to the four poets is credible on the grounds that it may have been written within a hundred years of their lifetimes, it does not follow that the texts in the fourteenth-century manuscript are usable evidence for an historian. Other poems in the manuscript show that Taliesin acquired a persona; that this persona was used to construct an image of early British poetry; and that poems praising a heroic king of the North could have been part of the later development of Taliesin's long-lived persona rather than compositions of the sixth-century poet. Urien of Rheged became a character in saga poetry, whereas the warriors praised in the *Gododdin*, so far as we can tell, did not.[143] There is no other textual witness to the poems purporting to be by an historical, sixth-century Taliesin, as the different versions of the *Gododdin* offer a check on each other. What can be done is, first, to compare the values implicit in the Taliesin poems to Urien, Owain, and Gwallog with those of the *Gododdin*. These poems, in other words, are more convincing evidence for the history of aristocratic values and their celebration by poets than they are for the history of events. It may also be reasonable to use the poems as evidence for the approximate whereabouts of Urien's kingdom. As with the *Gododdin*, there is a mixture of the old and the new. A good example of a convincing

140 *The Poems of Taliesin*, ed. I. Williams, no. IX; trans. Clancy, *Medieval Welsh Poems*, 43–4.
141 P. Sims-Williams, *Irish Influence on Medieval Welsh Literature* (Oxford, 2011), 91.
142 Dumville, 'The Historical Value of the *Historia Brittonum*', 17.
143 Rowland, *Early Welsh Saga Poetry*, ch. 2.

old feature is the use of *gwlad* to mean 'lord' rather than just 'country', since this variation of meaning is also present in its Old Irish cognate, *flaith*.[144]

The poems elsewhere in the manuscript that present Taliesin as the model poet have considerable importance for the historian of early British culture.[145] The parallels with some early Irish material on poets are very striking.[146] This material will take its place in the discussion of early Welsh poetry in Chapter 20 alongside two poems of lament, also from the Book of Taliesin, both of which may be datable.

The most sceptical view of the British evidence for the period 550–685 would dismiss the poetry ascribed to Aneirin and Taliesin as of dubious authenticity and date and would regard the *Annales Cambriae* and the northern material in the *Historia Brittonum* and in the Chronicle of Ireland as three later texts derived from one lost original of *c.* 800, more than a century after the end of the period. Such a view cannot be shown conclusively to be wrong, but a good case can be made that the *Gododdin* is an illuminating and very early text for the historian of culture, though less helpful for the history of events; and that the *Annales Cambriae* and the Northern History in the *Historia Brittonum* are not sister texts to the northern strand in the Chronicle of Ireland; the strongest element in the sceptical case is that there may be a textual relationship between the *Annales Cambriae* and the Northern History. A history of the relationship between the Britons and the English between the Justinianic plague and the battle of Nechtanesmere which balances British evidence against English evidence is a possibility.

[144] *Poems of Taliesin*, ed. Williams, vii. 53, reading (to get a rhyme): *gwacsa gwlat da wrth Uruöen*, 'useless is a good lord compared to Urien'; and see above, 321.

[145] Haycock, *Legendary Poems*.

[146] The shape-shifting poem put into the mouth of Amairgen, *Am gáeth i mmuir*, ed. R. Thurneysen, *Mittelirische Verslehren*, ii. 123, and ed. and trans. R. A. S. Macalister, *Lebor Gabála*, v (Irish Texts Society, 1956), 110–13, is comparable with the shape-shifting passages in *Kat Godeu*, ed. Haycock, *Legendary Poems*, no. 5.

12

The Britons, the Northumbrians, and the Rise of Mercia, 550–685

In 550, British kings still ruled an unbroken swathe of territory on the western side of Britain, from Stirling on the borders of Pictland to Cornwall; and, beyond Cornwall, British immigrants now controlled a new Britain across the sea. At the end of the 540s plague had devastated Ireland as well as Britain. The political and social repercussions of the disaster may have given the English an opportunity to make new inroads on British territory; but plague was not necessarily more damaging for the Britons than for their neighbours. It is, however, true that in the middle of the century, according to Bede, a new royal dynasty was established in the north, in what is now Northumbria and County Durham; that between then and *c.*600, the kingdom of Hwicce extended from its probable beginnings in the Cotswolds and the valley of the Warwickshire Avon to embrace part of the lower valley of the Severn; and the kingdom of the Gewisse in the Upper Thames area may have defeated the Britons in the area between Cirencester and Bath.[1] The entry in the Anglo-Saxon Chronicle for 577, which claims that kings of the Gewisse captured Gloucester, Cirencester, and Bath cannot be contemporary, but the forms of the British kings' names are early;[2] and yet the core of the kingdom of the Gewisse remained the Thames valley around Dorchester as late as the 630s.[3] At the same period and as part of the same process, the familiar early Anglo-Saxon kingdoms known from Bede were being consolidated, not just territorially but in their social and political organization.

A temptation is to translate back into the early seventh century the shape of Anglo-British relations as it existed in Bede's lifetime. By then it was clear that power had shifted from the south-eastern kingdoms towards the west and north—towards, that is, those kingdoms with a frontier across which Britons could be

[1] The Gewisse and the Hwicce had a common frontier by *c.* 600: *HE* ii. 2 (where *Occidentales Saxones* probably stands for the Gewisse), but this would have been as true before their expansion (Woodstock, close to the south-eastern edge of Wychwood, 'The Forest of the Hwicce', was also on the edge of the early territory of the Gewisse) as afterwards, when the boundary included the Avon at Bristol. Cf. Map 43 in E. O'Brien, *Post-Roman Britain to Anglo-Saxon England: Burial Practices Reviewed*, BAR British Series 289 (Oxford, 1999), 156, and B. Yorke, *Wessex in the Early Middle Ages* (London, 1995), 34–6, 57–60.

[2] A comparison of the Chronicle's Farinmail with Asser's contemporary Fernmail, *Asser's Life of King Alfred*, ed. W. H. Stevenson (Oxford, 1904), c. 80, suggests that the former is unlikely to be later than the seventh century.

[3] *HE* iii. 7.

raided or forced to pay tribute, and new territory conquered.[4] The pattern established by the eighth century was that three principal English kingdoms, Northumbria, Mercia, and Wessex, each had a British hinterland: the northern Britons for Northumbria, Wales for Mercia, and the Britons of Dumnonia for the West Saxons. The temptation to assume that this was true for the seventh century is all the more alluring because, to a considerable extent, that was the way political relations were developing. Yet, three qualifications must be made to this picture. First, the expansion in the north was much more rapid than elsewhere; secondly, Northumbria, as it existed in Bede's lifetime, did not exist in the sixth century and was only a fragile conjunction of two distinct kingdoms in the first half of the seventh; and, thirdly, the ambitions of the Northumbrian kings of the seventh century were far from being confined to the north but extended over the Welsh borderlands.

1. THE ORIGINS OF NORTHUMBRIA

Before 651, in terms of political power, and before Bede in terms of contemporary perception, we must think, not of Northumbria, but of two kingdoms, Bernicia and Deira. Both had pre-English names, but Deira was the first of the two to attain territorial cohesion. The earliest English presence in Deira was probably of two kinds and dated from the fifth century: on the one hand, early English cemeteries have been discovered close to the Roman city of York, and further evidence indicates an early presence further north and west at the Roman town at Catterick; on the other hand, there is a good spread of cemeteries in eastern Yorkshire from the North York Moors south to the Humber.[5] By contrast, a British kingdom, Elmet, covered much of West Yorkshire into the reign of Edwin (616–33).[6] The difference between the lands east and west of York is apparent even in Bede's *Historia Ecclesiastica*: Beverley, in the former East Riding, was called *In Dera Uudu* 'In the Wood of the Deirans'; in or near Leeds, then a district name, was 'The Wood of Elmet'.[7]

If eastern Yorkshire was the core of Deira, the origins of Bernicia may well lie between the eastern sector of Hadrian's Wall and the Tees. First, if eastern Yorkshire was the core of Deira, a core that did not, to judge by the distribution

4 J. R. Maddicott, 'Two Frontier States: Northumbria and Wessex, *c.* 650–750', in J. R. Maddicott and D. M. Palliser (eds.), *The Medieval State: Essays presented to James Campbell* (London, 2000), 25–45.

5 O'Brien, *Post Roman Britain to Anglo-Saxon England*, 71–7; S. Lucy, 'Changing Burial Rites in Northumbria AD 500–750', in J. Hawkes and S. Mills, *Northumbria's Golden Age* (Stroud, 1999), 12–43; the heartlands of Deira and Bernicia described by D. Rollason, *Northumbria, 500–1100* (Cambridge, 2003), 43–53, are those of the kingdom in Bede's time.

6 *HE* iv. 23/21, the 'king of the Britons, Cerdic' is likely to be the 'Certic', king of Elmet, of *HB* 63; O'Brien, *Post Roman Britain to Anglo-Saxon England*, map 17, p. 71.

7 *HE* ii. 14; v. 2. It is quite wrong to say that Bede 'refers to Elmet as the name of a forest', Rollason, *Northumbria*, 86; similarly, Deira was not the same as *Dera Wudu* and *Hwicca Wudu* was not the same as the Hwicce.

of furnished burials, extend north of the North Yorkshire Moors, the next area to the north that contains a good spread of such burials from the fifth or sixth century extends from the Tees northwards to the Tyne.[8] Secondly, it appears from Bede's narrative of the end of the Deiran dynasty in 651 that the Deiran army took up a position not far from Catterick to await a Bernician attack; even then, therefore, the Tees is likely to have been the boundary—a boundary that survived in the ecclesiastical domain, since it divided the dioceses of York and Hexham.[9] Within this core area Bede was born, in the lands belonging to the monastery of Wearmouth, in 671 or 672.

It has been argued that the early Anglo-Saxon furnished burials within Bernicia, although relatively few, were also relatively rich.[10] The implication may simply be that they were also relatively late, since the late sixth and seventh centuries seems to be the period, across much of England, in which such rich burials occurred; however, more recent excavations of cemeteries at Norton and Easington do not bear out Alcock's picture of a few rich burials.[11] Apart from a spread of early burials from the Tyne between Hexham and the North Sea, and also south to the Tees, another much smaller cluster was further north, on the slopes of the Cheviots, in an area also distinguished by the presence of the early royal vill at Yeavering and the later one at Milfield.[12] Although Yeavering is mentioned by Bede in his account of the later years of Edwin's reign, after his baptism in 627, Edwin himself belonged to Deira and is likely to have taken over Yeavering when, at his accession in 616, he drove out the sons of his Bernician enemy and predecessor, Æthelfrith.[13]

The 'Northern History' in the *Historia Brittonum* offers a curious detail about Ida, the founder of the Bernician dynasty (547–559): 'he joined Din Guayroi to Bernicia'.[14] Din Guayroi is very likely to be the British name for Bamburgh, later the principal centre of power in Bernicia, on the coast a little over ten miles east of Yeavering.[15] Bernicia, as its British name implies, had been in the Roman period a subdivision either of the land of the Gododdin or of the Brigantes. The former stretched from near Stirling to Hadrian's Wall; and it included at least two other named districts: Manaw around the upper Forth estuary and Lleuddinion, namely

[8] O'Brien, *Post Roman Britain to Anglo-Saxon England*, 62–70, and map 16, p. 68; Lucy, 'Changing Burial Rites', 17, fig. 2. 2.

[9] *HE* iii. 14.

[10] L. Alcock, *Economy, Society and Warfare among the Britons and Saxons* (Cardiff, 1987), 255–66.

[11] Lucy, 'Changing Burial Rites', 14; R. Cramp, 'Anglo-Saxon Settlement', in J. C. Chapman and H. C. Mytum (eds.), *Settlement in North Britain 1000 BC–AD 1000*, BAR British Ser. 118 (Oxford, 1983), 266–71, emphasized the small numbers of burials and thus the difficulty in making any classification.

[12] Lucy, 'Changing Burial Rites', 34–5, 40: Galewood, NT 912 324; 37, Milfield North, NT 934 348; and 54, Yeavering; NT 925 305, of which Milfield North is assigned to the seventh century; B. Hope-Taylor, *Yeavering: An Anglo-British Centre of Early Northumbria* (London, 1977); *HE* ii. 14; C. Scull, 'Post-Roman Phase 1 at Yeavering: A Reconsideration', *Medieval Archaeology*, 35 (1991), 51–63, argues that Phase 1 need not have been British.

[13] *HE* ii. 14; iii. 1.

[14] *HB*, c. 61.

[15] Jackson, 'The Northern History', 27–8; Bamburgh is *regia urbs*, *HE* iii 6, 16; *regia ciuitas*, iii. 12.

Lothian. The Brigantes had, in the first century AD, included all of northern Britain from the Tyne–Solway gap down to the Humber; but this exceptionally large *civitas* had been divided during the Romano-British period: the north-west, from the Wall to the valley of the Lune, became the *civitas Caruetiorum.*[16] *Berneich*, Bernicia, might have owed its origin to a similar detachment of territory from the Brigantes in the area behind the eastern part of the Wall; alternatively, if the Votadini/Gododdin took over the eastern part of the Wall in the post-Roman period, they may have extended their territory south to the Tees. Yet, whether Bernicia was, in origin, a territory within the lands of the Brigantes or of the Votadini, it did not originally include Bamburgh. A possibility, then, is that this early Bernicia stretched approximately from the Tyne to the Tees; that its name, 'Gap-land' or 'Pass-land', derived from its position at the east end of the Solway–Tyne gap;[17] and that it developed into a serious power only in the mid-sixth century, when it came to include the lands around Yeavering, Bamburgh, and Lindisfarne. According to the *Historia Brittonum*, Æthelfrith (592–616) gave Din Guayroi to his queen Bebba, and that was how it acquired its English name, *Bebbanburh*, Bamburgh.[18] None of this is a matter of contemporary record, but even a later British text, used by the *Historia Brittonum*, may have known what area was covered by the name Berneich (Bernicia), itself a British name, before it expanded under English rule. A tentative conclusion, therefore, is that Bernicia was, in origin, only one region within the lands of the Gododdin or Brigantes; that that region did not initially include Bamburgh; and that the *Historia Brittonum*'s statement about Ida may have had a basis in fact.

The Northern History also records a siege at some point between 572 and 592 in which Urien (in the poems in his praise known as the ruler of Rheged, Erechwydd, Llwyfennydd, and Catterick) besieged the Bernicians on the island of Lindisfarne, between Bamburgh and Berwick. Lindisfarne is here given a British name, in Modern Welsh spelling Meddgawd.[19]

> Against him[20] four kings fought: Urien and Rhydderch Hen and Gwallog and Morgan. Theodric: against him Urien, with his sons, fought bravely.[21] At that time sometimes the enemy, sometimes the citizens were defeated;[22] and he besieged them (sc. the enemy) for three days and three nights on the island of Meddgawd; and, while he was on campaign, he was killed at the instigation of Morgan on account of envy, for in him, beyond all kings, was the greatest power in pursuing a war.

[16] See above, 11–12.

[17] *LHEB* 701–5; N. J. Higham, *Northumbria*, 82, regards the lands between Hexhamshire and the Tees as the original core of Bernicia.

[18] *HB*, c. 63.

[19] *HB*, c. 63.

[20] The Harleian MS has *illum*, 'him', which should refer back to Hussa; MS *H* of Mommsen's edition has *illos*, which would refer to all the kings of Bernicia at least from Adda onwards.

[21] Morris's translation of this sentence is likely to be wrong: Deodric (Ðeodric for Theodric) is part of the regnal list, not the subject of *dimicabat*.

[22] A clear echo of Gildas, *De Excidio*, c. 26.

There are points at which both text and translation are uncertain; but what seems to be stated is that Urien besieged Theodric (572–579) on Meddgawd/Lindisfarne. A striking feature of this passage is the claim that Urien, who did not belong to the Gododdin, took the lead in attacking Bernicia.

A possible reconstruction is that the history of Bernicia falls into three periods: first, before Ida added the lands further north, around Bamburgh and Lindisfarne. At this stage it was only one district among several within a larger British kingdom; it may already have been settled by the English, but it was still no match for the Gododdin in territorial extent. The tentative attribution by Dumville of the Gododdin expedition to Catraeth to the end of this first phase is attractive.[23] The second phase follows this extension of Bernicia northwards to include Bamburgh, attributed by the *Historia Brittonum* to Ida; and Ida was the founder of the dynasty according to Bede. Effective Bernician kingship may thus have begun in the mid-sixth century, when Bernicia expanded north and so became a serious threat to the Gododdin. Even in this second stage, however, a British alliance led by Urien could imperil the new kingdom. The third phase followed the major extension of Bernician territory under Æthelfrith, grandson of Ida. This was twofold: first, so Bede wrote, he conquered more British territory than any English king before him, making some of it tributary and some of it available for English settlement; and, second, halfway through his reign, he took the kingdom of Deira, driving Edwin into exile.[24] His enemies were both British and English. By the end of his reign, Bernicia was the most powerful kingdom in northern Britain and embraced the lands of the Gododdin up to the Lammermuirs. The Tweed valley may be divided into two parts: up to and including Melrose probably had been part of the Gododdin kingdom and was now under Æthelfrith's authority; west of Melrose, around Selkirk, was a forest; and west of the forest is an area in which inscriptions attest British survival.[25] Although some of these inscriptions are likely to belong to a period before Æthelfrith, the contrast between the high rate of survival of British place-names in the upper Tweed basin and the lower rate in the lower part, east of Dere Street, indicates that anglicization was earlier and more thorough in the east.[26]

It is unlikely that the battle of Catterick, referred to in both versions of the *Gododdin*, belonged to the last of these three phases. One of the differences between the A and B versions of the *Gododdin* is that the B version only mentions Deira among the enemies of the Gododdin, whereas the A version mentions both Deira and Bernicia. The battle in which the forces of the Gododdin were heavily defeated

[23] D. N. Dumville, 'Early Welsh Poetry: Problems of Historicity', 2–3.

[24] *HE* i. 34; ii. 12; *HB*, c. 63.

[25] Nos. 9–12 in C. Thomas, 'The Early Christian Inscriptions of Southern Scotland', *Glasgow Archaeological Journal*, 17 (1991–2), 1–10, including two stones at Peebles, one at Yarrow, and one by Newholm Hope Burn. Ettrick Forest, then a hunting reserve but containing considerable woodland, was known in the twelfth and thirteenth centuries as Selkirk Forest: J. M. Gilbert, *Hunting and Hunting Reserves in Medieval Scotland* (Edinburgh, 1979), 129. C. E. Stancliffe, *Bede and the Britons*, Whithorn Lecture (Whithorn, 2007), 33–6.

[26] Stancliffe, *Bede and the Britons*, Map 2, pp. 26–7.

was at *Catraeth*, agreed to be the Roman town of Catterick;[27] and, since the boundary between Bernicia and Deira probably lay on the Tees, Catterick was in Deira and it seems only to be expected that the Deirans should have been the enemy. Moreover, an English settlement at Catterick is unlikely to be later than the end of the fifth century.[28] Before Æthelfrith's reign, however, Deira is likely to have been a much stronger kingdom than Bernicia; and there may even have been periods when the emerging English kingdom of Bernicia was subject to the Gododdin. At that stage, war between the Gododdin and Deira would be unsurprising.

A further complicating item of evidence is that, in the poems ascribed to Taliesin, Urien was described as lord of Catterick, namely of the former Roman town where the battle took place.[29] Moreover, Urien belonged to a dynasty called the Coeling; the father of the common ancestor, Coel, is named as Godebog in the Harleian genealogies; and his descendants may be named in the A version of the *Gododdin*:[30]

> Of the land of Catraeth it is related
> That hosts fell, long was the grief for them.
> In hardship, in ease, they fought for their land
> With the sons of Godebog, an evil people.

This seems to indicate that the Coeling were enemies of the Gododdin host at Catterick. On this basis it has been proposed that the enemies of the Gododdin in the battle of Catterick were an alliance of Britons and English, namely of Urien of Rheged together with the Deirans.[31] Similarly, any Bernician participation—if, indeed, there was any—could have been on the side of Gododdin. Finally, it has been proposed that a poem in the Taliesin corpus celebrates Urien's victory in the same battle.[32] A parallel is provided by the alliance between Mercia and the Britons that opposed Northumbria in the period 633–655. How much weight to grant this argument is uncertain: the crucial stanza in the poem is only in the later A version and different translations have been proposed.[33] The implication is that the battle of Catraeth occurred in the second phase of Bernician history distinguished above, between the accession of Ida and the reign of Æthelfrith, but another view would place it even earlier, towards the end of the first phase.[34] Indeed, the defeat of the Gododdin—so it could be surmised—might have been the occasion exploited by Ida to conquer more Gododdin territory, including Bamburgh; and that would

[27] On the Swale near Catterick Bridge, SE 22 99. In principle, *catraeth* might be *cad* 'battle, army' + *traeth* 'beach' and thus a kenning for any battle, but the compound appears not to be attested and Catraeth was clearly taken to be a place-name by the poet who composed the lament for Cadwallon (above, 373–4).

[28] See above, 11, 374.

[29] *Poems of Taliesin*, ed. Williams, viii. 9; cf. ii. 1.

[30] HG 8, 10; A 15 in Jackson, *Gododdin*, and Koch, *Gododdin*; Jarman, *Gododdin*, 141–4; *Canu Aneirin*, ed. Williams, 131–4.

[31] Koch, *Gododdin*, pp. xvii–xxxiv.

[32] *Poems of Taliesin*, ed. Williams, no. ii; also ed. and trans. Koch, *Gododdin*, pp. xxvi–xxviii.

[33] R. Bromwich, 'Cynon fab Clydno', in Bromwich and Jones (eds.), *Astudiaethau ar yr Hengerdd*, 157–8, discussed by Koch, *Gododdin*, p. xxv.

[34] Dumville, 'Early Welsh Poetry', 2–3.

account for the way in which Aneirin and his three fellow-poets were placed by the *Historia Brittonum* within the reign of Ida. Finally, although Catraeth was mentioned in both the A and B versions of the *Gododdin*, it was only in the A version that it became the dominant theme of the poem almost to the exclusion of any other. What may well be the opening stanza, itself attested in both versions, is likely to be praise of Lothian and makes no reference to Catraeth.[35]

2. MERCIANS, NORTHUMBRIANS, AND THE BORDERLANDS OF WALES

The core region from which the Mercian kingdom emerged by the early seventh century was probably in the valley of the Trent around Repton.[36] By the end of the seventh century, however, although the Mercians had expanded south-west to include the area around Lichfield, the Mercians were no longer strictly the 'Marcher People', *Mierce*.[37] They now had western satellites, some of them revealed by a document known as the Tribal Hidage, from the Cheshire Plain over into the Severn Valley and down as far as the mouth of the Wye: Wreocensæte, Magonsæte, and Hwicce.[38] A rough approximation, good enough for most purposes, is that the Wreocensæte occupied central and northern Shropshire, and just possibly also Cheshire, the Magonsæte Herefordshire, north of the Wye, and southern Shropshire, while the Hwicce, a more powerful people than the other western satellites, now held a broad territory represented by the medieval diocese of Worcester, not just Worcestershire, but also Gloucestershire—in modern terms, from Birmingham to Bristol. The Magonsæte were, on one view, the Westerne of the Tribal Hidage, a relatively large people of 7,000 hides; but another opinion would place the Westerne in the Cheshire plain.[39] The Magonsæte, whether or not they were the Westerne, maintained some independence in that their territory lay within a

[35] *Canu Aneirin*, ed. Williams, LI. A–C; Koch, *Gododdin*, 2–3.

[36] O'Brien, *From Roman Britain to Anglo-Saxon England*, map 21, p. 86.

[37] N. P. Brooks, 'The Formation of the Mercian Kingdom', in S. Bassett (ed.), *The Origins of Anglo-Saxon Kingdoms* (Leicester, 1989), 162.

[38] Texts: D. N. Dumville, 'The Tribal Hidage: An Introduction to Its Texts and Their History', in Bassett (ed.), *The Origins of Anglo-Saxon Kingdoms*, 225–30. Discussion: C. R. Hart, 'The Tribal Hidage', *TRHS*[5] 21 (1971), 133–57; W. Davies and H. Vierck, 'The Contexts of the Tribal Hidage: Social Aggregates and Settlement Patterns', *Frühmittelalterliche Studien*, 8 (1974), 223–93; Brooks, 'The Formation of the Mercian Kingdom', 159, 160–1, 167; A. R. Rumble, 'An Edition and Translation of the Burghal Hidage together with Recension C of the Tribal Hidage' and 'Appendix III. The Tribal Hidage: An Annotated Bibliography', in D. Hill and A. Rumble (eds.), *The Defence of Wessex: The Burghal Hidage and Anglo-Saxon Fortifications* (Manchester, 1996), 14–35, 182–8; P. Featherstone, 'The Tribal Hidage and the Ealdormen of Mercia', in Brown and Farr (eds.), *Mercia*, 23–34.

[39] For the Westerne being the Magonsæte, Pretty, 'Defining the Magonsæte', 181; for the Cheshire plain, Stenton, *Anglo-Saxon England*, *296*, P. Sims-Williams, *Religion and Literature in Western England 600–800* (Cambridge 1990), 18; M. Gelling, *The West Midlands in the Early Middle Ages* (Leicester, 1992), 83–4. The sequence of the list is the strongest argument against identifying the two, since it suggests that the Westerne lay between the Wreocensætan and the Pecsætan, 'the Peak-Dwellers' of Derbyshire.

bishopric for 'the people beyond the Severn', which came to be centred at Hereford, a diocese distinct from the bishopric of central Mercia, Lichfield, as well as of the bishopric of Hwicce, at Worcester.[40] The Wreocensæte, however, may perhaps have been split between Lichfield and Hereford, in that the medieval boundary of the diocese of Hereford runs straight across the Wrekin, but this may be a later extension northwards.[41] Most of the Wreocensæte, if not all, were attached to Lichfield, the episcopal see for Mercia proper, as were the Westerne if they are to be located in Cheshire.[42] Among these dependencies of Mercia, therefore, three levels of political subordination can be distinguished: the least subordinate were the Hwicce, with sub-kings and their own bishopric; the Magonsæte had a bishopric and, at least briefly, their own king, but it is not clear that they had a long-lasting dynasty, and it may, in any case, have been formed by a cadet line of the Iclingas, the Mercian royal kindred, in the generation of Penda or of his sons;[43] finally, the Wreocensæte, and probably the Westerne, were subordinate even in the ecclesiastical sphere.

Yet, although the neighbours of the Welsh were the Mercians and their satellites, the borderlands between the Welsh and the English were for more than a generation, *c.* 610–658, and perhaps as late as 679, the target of Northumbrian military intervention. To define the point more precisely, the target of Northumbrian intervention was the borderland that became the territories of the Westerne (if located in Cheshire) and the Wreocensæte, namely those western satellites that were later to be kept under the closest Mercian control. Northumbrian territorial ambitions were not, therefore, confined to northern Britain. Moreover, as references in the narratives of Bede and the *Life of Wilfrid* indicate, Northumbrian ambition to control the British borderlands as far south as Shropshire developed into an ambition to dominate the entire island: not just Britons but also Picts, the Irish of Britain, and, of course, the English. In 684 Northumbrian military aggression would even extend to Ireland.[44]

The first attested intervention led to the battle of Chester, the final victory of Æthelfrith, 'the most rapacious wolf', 'most desirous of glory, who ravaged the people of the Britons more than all the leaders of the English.'[45] For Bede, Æthelfrith's opponents in the battle were simply Britons;[46] the Chronicle of Ireland, here probably derived from Iona annals, dated the battle to 613 and stated

[40] 'Walhstod is bishop of those peoples who live beyond the Severn to the west,' *HE* v. 23; Sims-Williams, *Religion and Literature*, 39–40; Hereford may not have been the original see: ibid. 90–1.

[41] Sims-Williams, *Religion and Literature*, 44, who suggests that the early boundary ran along Wenlock Edge.

[42] *HE* v. 23. Cf. K. Pretty, 'Defining the Magonsæte', and M. Gelling, 'The Early History of Western Mercia', in Bassett (ed.), *The Origins of Anglo-Saxon Kingdoms*, 171–83, 184–201.

[43] H. P. R. Finberg, 'St Mildburg's Testament' and 'The Princes of the Magonsæte', in his *Early Charters of the West Midlands* (Leicester, 1961), 197–217 and 217–25; Sims-Williams, *Religion and Literature*, 47–51; Pretty, 'Defining the Magonsæte', 175–7; Gelling, *The West Midlands*, 81–2.

[44] On all this, see below, 409.

[45] *HE* i. 34. For the nature and background to this story see C. Stancliffe, 'The British Church and the Mission of Augustine', in R. Gameson (ed.), *Saint Augustine of Canterbury and the Conversion of England* (Stroud, 1999), 124–30.

[46] *HE* ii. 2.

that Selyf ap Cynan was killed.[47] Many of its annals at this period are placed two to three years too early, so that the true date may be 615, only one year before Æthelfrith's own death in the battle of the Idle against Rædwald, king of the East Anglians and overlord of the provinces up to the Humber.[48]

The Welsh genealogies attribute Selyf to a dynasty later associated with Powys, a kingdom not named in a contemporary source until the ninth century.[49] Yet, if the name Powys is correctly derived from the Latin word *pagenses*, 'country people', as seems very probable, it is likely to be older than the seventh century.[50] The presence of Selyf at the battle of Chester is consistent with the notion that the kingdom of Powys was the successor to the Romano-British *civitas* of the Cornovii, and that Chester, a former legionary fortress, had been annexed to the Cornovii no later than the fifth century.[51] It should not be inferred from Bede's narrative that the area around Chester now became part of the Northumbrian kingdom. What the victory is more likely to have achieved is, first, largely unimpeded plundering by the Northumbrians, and perhaps, for the short period until Æthelfrith's death, a tributary relationship between defeated and victor. Æthelfrith's victory thus threatened to establish Northumbrian rather than Mercian overlordship over a territory—that of the former Cornovii, by now probably already called Powys—covering the Welsh borderlands all the way from the Wirral to southern Shropshire.

Although Æthelfrith died in battle in 616, and his successor was of the Deiran rather than the Bernician dynasty, this made no apparent change to Northumbrian interest in the Britons. Indeed, Edwin, king of Northumbria 616–633, remained until the end of the Middle Ages the emblem of English hostility to the Welsh.[52] His power appears to have exceeded anything achieved by his predecessor: according to Bede he subjugated Anglesey, the heart of Gwynedd, as well as the Isle of Man, also British territory, and so established Northumbrian power in the Irish Sea.[53] A poem in praise of Cadwallon implies that he had had difficulty in

[47] AU 613. 3.

[48] Charles-Edwards, *The Chronicle of Ireland*, i. 128 n. 1; *HE* ii. 5.

[49] Selyf's pedigree is HG 22 in *Early Welsh Genealogical Tracts*, ed. Bartrum, 12, but the dynastic history of Powys is controversial (see below, 447–51); the first attestation of the name Powys is *HB*, c. 35; this name (unlike the dynastic name Cadelling) was not used in the early, but probably not contemporary, *Marwnad Cynddylan*.

[50] See above, 16, for Powys < *pagenses*, and for the possibility that the Cornovii were remembered in a poem ascribed to Taliesin.

[51] M. Gelling, *The West Midlands* 27–8, outlines the issues. Chester may have lost its legion in the late fourth century: P. Salway, *Roman Britain*, (Oxford, 1981), 404.

[52] Reginald of Durham's Life of St Oswald, c. 9, ed. Arnold, *Symeonis Monachi Opera Omnia*, i. 345, claimed that Edwin was fostered by Cadfan along with his son, Cadwallon. On this Life and its sources, see V. Tudor, 'Reginald's *Life of Oswald*', in C. Stancliffe and E. Cambridge (eds.), *Oswald: From Northumbrian King to European Saint* (Stamford, 1995), 178–94. Its account of Cadfan, Cadwallon, and Edwin is partly indebted to Geoffrey of Monmouth, *Historia Regum Britanniae*, c. 190, but Geoffrey made Edwin a son of Æthelfrith. A similar story appears to have been current among the Welsh at a similar period: *TYP*, 3rd edn., 339–41.

[53] *HE* ii. 5, 9. For the possible significance of this achievement, see Maddicott, 'Two Frontier States: Northumbria and Wessex, *c.* 650–750', 39–40.

withstanding Edwin's onslaught.[54] When Edwin was killed at the battle of Hatfield in 633, his defeat came about through an alliance of the king of Gwynedd, Cadwallon, and a young Mercian prince, Penda.[55] The leading role played by a king of Gwynedd, rather than a king of Powys, in the defeat and death of Edwin in 633 suggests that the alliance between Gwynedd and Penda was, for Cadwallon, a reaction against Edwin's subjugation of Anglesey, but, for Penda, a reaction against the Northumbrian threat to Mercian independence. If Edwin's campaign in north-west Wales involved an army coming by land from Northumbria as well, perhaps, as a fleet, it must have come via territory that the Mercians aspired to control, although they are not likely to have achieved a continuous domination in the first half of the seventh century. Edwin's defeat and death led to a year during which Northumbria was increasingly dominated by Cadwallon until, late in 634, he unexpectedly fell in battle against Oswald, Æthelfrith's son.[56]

Bede described the end of Edwin's reign as a rebellion against an imperial authority, reminiscent of Roman power, by former subjects of the overlord.[57] Although this may be interpreted as merely Bede's desire to associate English power with Rome, it is possible that Edwin himself sought to represent his authority in Roman terms. The archaeology of the conversion period shows that the English were then concerned to establish links with the Mediterranean world and that this both preceded and assisted conversion to Christianity.[58] Moreover, other evidence indicates that a rebellion within Mercia may have precipitated Edwin's defeat. The *Historia Brittonum* makes Penda's brother, Eowa, king of the Mercians until the battle of Cogwy (Bede's Maserfelth), in which Oswald was killed, namely until 642.[59] This may be linked with Bede's statement that, at the time of the battle of Hatfield in 633, Penda was not yet king but only 'an exceedingly energetic man of the royal kindred of the Mercians'; for Bede he became king in the aftermath of the battle.[60]

On the other hand, whereas Bede makes Penda's reign last for twenty-two years, from 633 to 655, the *Historia Brittonum* confines it to ten years.[61] In assessing this conflict of evidence we need to remember that among Eowa's descendants were the

[54] 'Canu Cadwallon ap Cadfan', ll. 24–8, ed. R. G. Gruffydd in R. Bromwich and R. Brinley Jones (eds.), *Astudiaethau ar yr Hengerdd* (Cardiff, 1978), 29–32.

[55] The proposal by A. Woolf, 'Caedwalla *Rex Brettonum* and the Passing of the Old North', *Northern History*, 41 (2004), 5–24, that Cadwallon was not king of Gwynedd but belonged to northern Britain, depends on an approach to the *Historia Brittonum* and the *Annales Cambriae* which I would not share (see the previous chapter) and on seeing in Bede's account implications which, to me, are invisible.

[56] *HE* iii. 1.

[57] *HE* ii. 20.

[58] H. Geake, *The Use of Grave-Goods in Conversion-Period England, c. 600–c.800*, BAR, Brit. Ser. 261 (Oxford, 1997), 120–2; N. P. Brooks, 'Canterbury, Rome and the Construction of English Identity', in J. M. H. Smith (ed.), *Early Medieval Rome and the Christian West: Essays in Honour of Donald A. Bullough* (Leiden, 2000), 221–46.

[59] *HB* c. 65.

[60] *HE* ii. 20.

[61] There is yet another chronology in the Anglo-Saxon Chronicle, but that has been explained away by Brooks, 'The Formation of the Mercian Kingdom', 165–6.

great Mercian kings of the eighth century, Æthelbald and Offa, whereas from Penda's day up until Æthelbald's accession in 716 it had been Penda's offspring that had ruled Mercia. Their power had led to the expulsion of Æthelbald from his native kingdom.[62] Although Bede was writing during Æthelbald's reign, his concern as an historian was with Penda and his sons. His understanding of Mercian dynastic history was formed by sources emanating from Lichfield, a church founded under Wulfhere son of Penda *c.* 670, whereas the church especially favoured by Æthelbald was Repton.[63] The *Historia Brittonum* was perhaps more concerned with Eowa's branch of the dynasty: it gave the pedigrees of both Ecgfrith son of Offa and Æthelbald as well as a highly unfavourable account of Penda.[64] It has also been proposed that Eowa was aligned with Northumbria, while Penda was linked with Cadwallon; and that the initial period of Penda's rule in Mercia only lasted until early in Oswald's reign, after which Northumbrian power ensured that Eowa was king until Oswald and Eowa were defeated and killed by Penda in 642.[65] The *Historia Brittonum*'s statement about Penda that 'he was the first to separate the kingdom of the Mercians from the kingdom of the Northerners' [namely, the Northumbrians] could then be explained as referring to Penda's reversal of his brother's subjection to Oswald. The reign of ten years assigned to Penda by the *Historia Brittonum* would still be too short to cover the years between 642 and Penda's defeat and death in 655, but the discrepancy would be much reduced.

Oswald was described by Bede as enjoying a power similar to that of Edwin.[66] That this entailed intervention in the Welsh borderlands emerges from the location of his last battle, fought in 642, in which he was killed, so Bede wrote, 'by the same pagan people and pagan king of the Mercians, by whom his predecessor Edwin had been killed', namely by Penda.[67] Clare Stancliffe has reconsidered the evidence for the location of Maserfelth and has confirmed the traditional site of Oswestry.[68] The situation of the battle, close to what became the western boundary of one of the Mercian satellites, either of the Westerne or of the Wreocensæte, has reasonably been explained in the context of an alliance between Penda and the Welsh, including, at least, the men of Powys.[69] It was very probably still Welsh territory in 642, since early Anglo-Saxon cemeteries are not attested in Shropshire, and even in Staffordshire are confined to the north-eastern and eastern edges of the county.[70] Not only does Bede tell a story of a Briton passing by the site of Oswald's death, but

62 Felix, *Life of Saint Guthlac*, ed. and trans. B. Colgrave (Cambridge, 1956), chs. 40, 45, 49.

63 *HE* iv. 3; ASC 755 = 757. 64 *HB*, cc. 60, 65.

65 Brooks, 'The Formation of the Mercian Kingdom', 166–8.

66 *HE* ii. 5; iii. 6. 67 *HE* iii. 9; *AC*, *s.a.* 644; *HB*, c. 65.

68 C. Stancliffe, 'Where was Oswald killed?', in Stancliffe and Cambridge (eds.), *Oswald: From Northumbrian King to European Saint*, 84–96. A different view, but after much less thorough discussion, is taken by M. Gelling, 'The Early History of Western Mercia', in Bassett (ed.), *The Origins of Anglo-Saxon Kingdoms*, 188–9. The argument by T. J. Clarkson, 'Locating Maserfelth', www.mun.ca/mst/heroicage/issues/9/clarkson.html (2006), accessed 21/04/2010, fails to note the range of Welsh evidence for the name *Cogwy*, found not only in the *Historia Brittonum* and the *Annales Cambriae*, but also in *Canu Heledd*, *CLlH* XI. 111, Rowland, *Early Welsh Saga Poetry*, 445.

69 Rowland, *Early Welsh Saga Poetry*, 124–5; Stancliffe, 'Oswald, "Most Holy and Most Victorious King"', in Stancliffe and Cambridge (eds.), *Oswald: From Northumbrian King to European Saint*, 56.

70 Gelling, *The West Midlands*, 29–30.

he envisages this Briton as coming to a nearby village, entering a house in which the local people were feasting, where he was welcomed; to these people he was later able to explain where he had been; and the likelihood is that they also were Britons.[71] Bede does not allude to any alliance between Welsh and Mercians in 642: its existence is inferred from the site of the battle, much later Welsh sources, which on their own would not merit any confidence, and the analogy of the alliance between Penda and Cadwallon in 633.[72] There are also internal reasons for doubting whether Bede's attribution of Oswald's defeat and death solely to the Mercians is correct. The strong rhetorical stress that he places on 'the same pagan people, and the same king of the Mercians' means that he fails to recall here the British leadership of the 'rebellion' against Edwin, a leadership that he had earlier acknowledged at the end of Book II and the beginning of Book III. The suggestion is, therefore, that the alliance of 633 against one Northumbrian king and his Mercian client, Eowa, was repeated, though perhaps with different Welsh participation, in 642 against Eowa and another Northumbrian king, Oswald. Both in 633 and in 642 the force behind the alliance was the desire to resist and, if possible, to destroy a military hegemony established by the Northumbrians.

The same king Oswald may well have been the conqueror of Lothian, the last independent remnant of the kingdom of the Gododdin or Votadini. His brother and successor, Oswiu, was to extend overlordship over the Picts, north of the Forth; and, as we shall see, he may have been driven by Penda's last great attack to take refuge in the fortress of Stirling. If this is correct, Lothian must have been conquered by 655. St Cuthbert is recorded as herding the sheep of his master near the Leader Water on the southern slopes of the Lammermuirs at the time of Aidan's death, 31 August 651; there is no hint in the story that he was near a frontier.[73] The Chronicle of Ireland, here probably drawing on an Iona chronicle that had an interest in Oswald and Northumbria, records, under the year before Oswald's defeat and death in battle, 'the siege of Etin'.[74] Entries recording sieges were a characteristic feature of the Iona chronicle.[75] It is more likely that Oswald was besieging Britons than that, say, Picts were besieging Northumbrians, since at this stage Oswald was, as far as we can tell, much more likely to be on the attack rather than the reverse.[76] That this entry represented the conquest of Lothian is likely but not certain. The dating of the Chronicle of Ireland was probably running

[71] Bede, *HE* iii. 10.

[72] The earliest Welsh source to imply actual Welsh participation in the battle is a verse attached to *Canu Heledd* (*Canu Llywarch Hen*, XI. 111 = Rowland, *Early Welsh Saga Poetry*, 445):

Gweleis ar lawr Maes Cogwy	I saw on the ground of Maes Cogwy
Byddinawr, a gawr gymwy.	Hosts, and strife of battle
Cynddylan oedd kynnorthwy.	Cynddylan gave assistance.

[73] Anonymous Prose Life, i. 5, ed. and trans. B. Colgrave, *Two Lives of Saint Cuthbert: A Life by an Anonymous Monk of Lindisfarne and Bede's Prose Life* (Cambridge, 1940), 69.

[74] AU 638. 1 (+ AT, CS); K. H. Jackson, 'Edinburgh and the Anglian Occupation of Lothian', in P. Clemoes (ed.), *The Anglo-Saxons: Studies presented to Bruce Dickins* (London, 1959), 35–47.

[75] J. Bannerman, *Studies in the History of Dalriada* (Edinburgh, 1974), 15–16.

[76] *HE* iii. 6 on the scope of his power; Oswald was not merely *sanctissimus* but also *uictoriosissimus*, iii. 7; when he was killed in battle, he was on the offensive.

three years too early at this stage, so the correct date is likely to be 641. If he did conquer Lothian, Oswald's aggressive stance towards the Britons extended from the Forth to northern Shropshire.

The contexts of the two battles, of Hatfield in 633 against Edwin and of Maserfelth in 642 against Oswald were, however, different. In 633, Cadwallon and Penda were challenging an overlord whose ancestral kingdom was Deira, and they were making this challenge close to the Deiran frontier.[77] In 642 Oswald, like Edwin king of the Northumbrians, but himself a Bernician rather than a Deiran, had led an army to a site situated in the borderlands between the Mercians and the Welsh. By 642, if we can trust Bede, the leadership of the alliance resisting Northumbrian power had passed to the Mercian ruler Penda: he only mentions Penda and the Mercians as Oswald's enemies. But it is much less clear if we can trust the *Historia Brittonum*'s statement that Eowa, king of the Mercians, was not killed until this battle.

According to the *Historia Brittonum*, in 655 the king of Gwynedd, Cadafael, was one of Penda's many allies in his last expedition, which issued in Penda's defeat and death at the hands of Oswald's younger brother Oswiu, at the battle of the Winwaed, close to Leeds.[78] By this time the Welsh appear to have been clients of the Mercian king. Both Mercia and the Welsh were, therefore, involved in the struggle for military overlordship in Britain in the period *c.* 625–679; the alliance between Penda and the Britons appears to have been a consistent feature; but the leadership was only British at the outset, or, at the very latest, up to 642.

The Mercians came to secure their overlordship over 'the Southern English' by opposing the Northumbrian ambition to dominate the English frontier zone with the Britons from Lothian to Shropshire. As the career of Cadwallon demonstrated, the rule of the English in Northumbria remained fragile. Until Edwin conquered Elmet and Oswald (so it seems) subjugated the last remaining territory of the Gododdin, English Northumbria was nearly surrounded by British kingdoms.[79] The rapidity of Northumbrian advance between the beginning of the reign of Æthelfrith in 592 and the death of Oswald fifty years later suggests that power must have been built around regular plunder and huge land grants available to the king's military followers. Its expansion was so fast that it cannot have been sustained by a war of English peasants seeking to drive British peasants off the land. To a somewhat lesser extent the same must be true of Wessex, where a British element in the population is well attested in Ine's laws (688 × 694).[80]

There was no reason why extensive conquests of British territory in northern Britain should not be followed by conquest of British territory in what became Wales: one has to remember that there was no such thing as Wales in the later

[77] 'Hatfield-land' was a district name and was assessed together with Lindsey in the Tribal Hidage: Dumville, 'The Tribal Hidage', 227; *The Earliest Life of Gregory the Great*, ed. B. Colgrave (Cambridge, 1985), c. 18, 'in regione illa que dicitur Hedfled' (for *Hedfeld*).

[78] *HB* 65; cf. *HE* iii. 24.

[79] For Elmet, see *HE* ii. 14; iv. 23/21; *HB*, c. 63.

[80] Ine's Laws, 23. 3; 24. 2; 32; 33; 54. 2; 74, ed. F. Liebermann, *Die Gesetze der Angelsachsen* (Halle, vol. i, 1903; ii, part i, 1906; ii, part ii, 1912; iii, 1916), i. 100–2, 114, 120; Yorke, *Wessex*, 72.

sense, and no reason to think that while, say, Elmet or the Gododdin were reasonable targets for Northumbrian attack, Powys and Gwynedd were not. Nor was it inevitable that Mercia would ally with the Welsh against northern kings from Æthelfrith to Oswald: Eowa, a Mercian king, may well have supported the Northumbrians.[81] The fact remains that Penda did ally with the Welsh and that his alliance set him on the road to overlordship over England south of the Humber.

Penda's concern for his British allies emerges from the *Historia Brittonum*'s account of the battle of the Winwæd in 655, if we take it in combination with Bede. In 655, Penda of Mercia, in alliance with British and other English kings, led a great campaign from the south against his rival Oswiu, king of Northumbria, a campaign that reached as far as 'the fortress which is called *Iudeu*'. On Bede's evidence, *Giudi*, his spelling for *Iudeu*, Modern Welsh Iddew, was on the northern frontier of Bernicia, on the Forth.[82] According to the *Historia Brittonum*, 'on that occasion Oswiu handed back all the treasures that were with him in the stronghold into Penda's hand, and Penda distributed them to the kings of the Britons, that is, "The Restitution of Iddew".' Yet Penda was defeated and killed by Oswiu on his way back south, when he had got as far as the River *Winwæd* (probably the Went), a battle also described by Bede as lying *in regione Loidis*, within the district of Leeds; this is very likely to have been in the former British kingdom of Elmet. Also killed in the battle were all his allied British kings, except for Cadafael, king of Gwynedd. 'Cadafael alone, king of the land of Gwynedd, together with his army, escaped, setting off by night; and for that reason he was called 'Battle-Seizer, Battle-Shirker'. The implication of this text, if we accept the identification of Bede's site for the battle, is that all Penda's British allies came from Wales or the south-west, not from the north, and that they had previously been subject to a Northumbrian attack. No northern British allies would have marched with Penda back southwards from the Forth until they came to disaster to the south-east of Leeds. Indeed, the topography may explain Cadafael's escape, provided we accept the identification of the *Win-* in *Winwæd* as the River Went.[83] The Roman road from York to Manchester, and then on to Chester and North Wales, branched off a few miles to the north of the battlefield. If Penda was following the Roman road southwards towards Mercia, the battle would have been where it crosses the River Went, just to the south of Pontefract. Cadafael, however, should have turned off in a south-westwards direction close to the modern Leeds.

Penda's campaign was one of a series of attacks on Northumbria, one of which reached as far as Bamburgh in the period before Aidan's death in August 651.[84] By the time of the campaign in which he met his death, Penda had secured one of

[81] Brooks, 'The Formation of the Mercian Kingdom', 166.

[82] See above, 7–8.

[83] The identification, made by J. Raine, *Dictionary of Christian Biography*, ed. W. Smith and H. Wace, 4 vols. (London, 1877–87), iv. 166, *s.v.* Oswy, is accepted by Rollason, *Northumbria*, 35–6, and by A. Breeze, 'The Battle of the *Uinued* and the River Went, Yorkshire', *Northern History*, 41 (2004), 377–83. Plummer was sceptical: *Baedae Opera Historica*, ii. 183.

[84] *HE* iii. 16. The later attack on the same region mentioned in *HE* iii. 17 may have been part of the 655 campaign.

Oswiu's sons as a hostage;[85] Œthelwald, son of Oswald, and now ruler in much, at least, of Deira, was his ally (he also, like Cadafael, is unlikely still to have been in Penda's army by the time the latter had got as far south as the Winwæd);[86] another ally was Æthelhere, king of the East Angles, whose predecessor, Anna, Penda had killed in battle not long before.[87] On the other hand, there are also likely to have been raids by Oswiu against Penda and his allies. Indeed, just by chance Bede revealed that Oswiu led an army to the site of his brother's defeat, Oswestry, in 643, only a year after the battle of Maserfelth.[88] The raid or raids against the British kings before 655 assumed by the phrase, 'the Restitution of Iddew', would have been part of this pattern of raid and counter-raid.

There is one straight contradiction between Bede and the *Historia Brittonum*: according to the *Historia Brittonum*, Penda compelled Oswiu to give his plunder back to the British kings; according to Bede, Oswiu was finally compelled by Penda's attacks to offer him vast treasures provided he would return home, but Penda refused the offer. 'He had decided to destroy and exterminate his [Oswiu's] entire people, both children and adults.'[89] Oswiu, however, put his trust in the mercy of God rather than of Penda and won a battle against huge odds. The main difficulty in accepting this story as it stands is topographical: Oswiu is said to have been forced to offer the treasure to Penda after he had been driven to a desperate extremity by savage attacks. Yet, the site of the battle was in the south-west of Deira, a kingdom in which one of his enemies, Œthelwald, was king. The people that Penda was supposed to be bent on destroying was hardly the Northumbrians as a whole, again since many of the Deirans were his own allies.[90] Moreover, the site of the battle was about sixty miles south of the Bernician frontier, not a plausible location for a desperate attempt to prevent the extermination of the Bernicians. As soon, therefore, as we accept Bede's location of the battle in the district of *Loidis*, his narrative becomes barely credible.[91] If we accept the *Historia Brittonum*, however, in thinking that Oswiu's offer of treasure was accepted, and that the offer was made at the northern extremity of his kingdom, Oswiu's success in defeating Penda becomes intelligible: Penda would have been on his way home; and some of his allies would have left his army, not out of treachery but for straightforward geographical reasons. In this instance, at least, the *Historia Brittonum* emerges as

85 Ecgfrith, the later king, *HE* iii. 24.

86 *HE* iii. 23 (*Oidiluald, filius Osualdi regis, qui in Derorum partibus regnum habebat*); iii. 24.

87 *HE* iii. 18, 24 and ASC 654.

88 *HE* iii. 12 (the issue, for Bede, was the fate of Oswald's body).

89 *HE* iii. 24: *qui totam eius gentem a paruo usque ad magnum delere atque exterminare decreuerat.*

90 Bede was normally very careful to describe Bernicia and Deira as *prouinciae*, not *gentes*, but he did describe Bernicia as a *gens* in *HE* iii. 2; cf. J. M. Wallace-Hadrill, *Bede's* Ecclesiastical History of the English People: *A Historical Commentary* (OMT, Oxford, 1988), 226–8; for *prouincia* see J. Campbell, 'Bede's Words for Places', in *Places, Names and Graves*, ed. P. H. Sawyer (Leeds, 1979), 48; reprinted in his *Essays in Anglo-Saxon History* (London, 1986), 113.

91 Jackson, 'On the Northern British Section in Nennius', 37–8. The difficulty posed by Bede's account explains the suggestion by W. Skene, *Celtic Scotland: A History of Ancient Alban*, 3 vols. (Edinburgh, 1876–80), i. 254–5, that *Loidis* might be Lothian, but that is not acceptable on linguistic grounds, and, as Skene noted, it requires one to believe that the *regio quae uocatur Loidis* of *HE* ii. 14 was quite different from the *regio Loidis* of *HE* iii. 24.

a credible and independent source, offering information most unlikely to be of early ninth-century origin. The implication is that Oswiu had, by astute tactics, achieved an unexpected victory immediately after a humiliation; Penda's campaign had, however, revealed the continuing fragility of Northumbrian power and the possibility of a British revival in the north.

Penda's son and ultimate successor, Wulfhere, pursued a similar policy to his father but perhaps with a significant difference. After Oswiu's death in 670 and before his own in 675, Wulfhere 'roused all the southern peoples' against Northumbria and attacked the new king, Ecgfrith, but was defeated.[92] 'All the southern peoples' might have included the Welsh, but there is no corroboration that it did. The years after this battle and especially after Wulfhere's death in 675, and before Ecgfrith's defeat at the hands of the Mercians at the Battle of the Trent in 679, were the last period in which the power of Northumbria extended as far as Wales.[93]

3. THE CHURCH AND RELATIONS BETWEEN THE BRITONS AND THE ENGLISH

By the 670s, conditions were much less favourable for an alliance between Mercians and Britons. In 664 the Easter dating followed by the Britons and by the northern Irish was condemned at the Synod of Whitby. In the aftermath of the synod, Oswiu wrote to the pope declaring his allegiance to the Roman Easter. To judge by the pope's reply, Oswiu also signified that he would use his military power over his neighbours in northern Britain to induce them to follow suit.[94] When Archbishop Theodore arrived in England from Rome in 669, he came with the firm belief that the Britons were both heretics and schismatics.[95] Wilfrid, who was established as bishop of York in 670, took the same view.[96] Because of Ecgfrith's power in northern Britain, Wilfrid was able to claim an authority extending over the northern Britons, as well as Picts and the Irish of Dál Riata.[97] In the 670s, the English Church was organized apart from the Britons and had already taken a stance that implied a much harsher policy towards them. As late as 664–665, after the Synod of Whitby, it was still considered acceptable in Wessex for Chad to be consecrated a bishop by one English and two British bishops.[98] Yet, for Theodore and for Wilfrid, Chad's consecration was illegitimate, and Theodore reconsecrated him, before he was sent to be bishop of the Mercians and to establish his see at Lichfield.[99] This could not have been done unless the Britons were considered to be

92 Stephen, *Vita Wilfridi*, c. 20.

93 Stephen, ibid., says that after Wulfhere's defeat Mercia became tributary to Northumbria, but that after Wulfhere's death Ecgfrith 'exercised a wider authority for some time in peace'. This must have extended to the boundaries of Wales, and perhaps further.

94 *HE* iii. 29.

95 *ECI* 410.

96 Stephen, *Vita Wilfridi*, cc. 10, 12.

97 Ibid. c. 21.

98 *HE* iii. 28.

99 *HE* iv. 2; Stephen, *Vita Wilfridi*, c. 15.

heretics. Although Theodore may have softened his stance later, he still regarded the Britons as schismatics, and such views, whether the more severe one that Wilfrid continued to champion or the more moderate later view of Theodore, were dominant in the English Church well into the eighth century.[100]

Even at Lindisfarne, where their first bishop, Aidan, continued to be revered even though he had followed the same Easter dating as the Britons, care had to be taken not to be identified as fellow-travellers of the schismatical Britons and Irish.[101] Bede, in his Prose Life of St Cuthbert, puts into the saint's mouth a deathbed speech, in which Cuthbert commands his brethren to 'have no communion with those who depart from the unity of the Catholic peace, either in not celebrating Easter at the proper time or in evil living'.[102] Bede himself was accused by a cleric in Wilfrid's household of paschal error.[103] To understand Bede's attitude to the Britons, it is essential to realize that, even late in his lifetime, when he was composing the *Ecclesiastical History*, he was writing after a period in which they had been regarded as schismatics and even as heretics.[104] What he wrote on Bishop Aidan explicitly contradicted the authoritative view of Theodore and Wilfrid.[105] His exculpation of the Britons and the Irish had, however, its limits. The Irish (and therefore also the Britons) were, for Bede, wrong on Easter but not heretical; moreover, the Irish could be excused because error was balanced by energy in spreading the gospel to the English. British error was accompanied by no such virtue. The Britons refused to assist Augustine of Canterbury in preaching to the English; 'and, indeed,' wrote Bede, 'even to this day it is the habit of the Britons to consider the faith and devotion of the English as of no value, and to have no more to do with them than with pagans'.[106]

This cannot always have been true, as is demonstrated by Bede's own story of the first consecration of Chad.[107] Moreover, it is probably indicative of British attitudes to the Irish mission to Northumbria that the Irish almost certainly knew Lindisfarne not as Lindisfarne but by its British name, Meddgawd.[108] Northumbria in Aidan's day must have included many British Christians; indeed, if Lothian was conquered by Oswald towards the end of his reign, further British territory will have been incorporated into Aidan's diocese during his episcopate. We have no

[100] A change in Theodore's position is argued by C. Stancliffe, *Bede, Wilfrid, and the Irish*, Jarrow Lecture 2003, 11–17.

[101] For fellow-travellers, see the speech put into Wilfrid's mouth by Stephen, *Vita Wilfridi*, c. 12.

[102] Bede, *Vita S. Cuthberti*, c. 39, ed. and trans. B. Colgrave, *Two Lives of Saint Cuthbert*, 284/285.

[103] Bede, *Epistola ad Pleguinum*, ed. C. W. Jones, *Bedae Venerabilis Opera, Pars VI, Opera Didascalica*, iii, CCSL 120C (Turnhout, 1980), 617–26.

[104] Similarly, Aldhelm, *Ep*. 4, ed. R. Ehwald, *Aldhelmi Opera Omnia*, MGH AA xv (Berlin, 1919), 480–7, trans. M. Lapidge and M. Herren, *Aldhelm: The Prose Works* (Ipswich, 1979), 155–60.

[105] *HE* iii. 17 (last paragraph) excludes heresy; and what he writes about Aidan's friendly relations with Honorius, bishop of Canterbury, and Felix, bishop of the East Angles, in *HE* iii. 25, excludes schism.

[106] *HE* ii. 20.

[107] *HE* iii. 28.

[108] Inis Medcóit: *Félire Óengusso Céli Dé: The Martyrology of Oengus the Culdee*, ed. W. Stokes, Henry Bradshaw Society 29 (London, 1905), 31 August (p. 179); *The Martyrology of Tallaght*, eds. R. I. Best and H. J. Lawlor, Henry Bradshaw Society 68 (London, 1931), 67 (31 August).

reason whatever to suppose that British clergy did not collaborate with the new mission. It has also been convincingly suggested that the Hwicce are likely to have been converted by Britons.[109]

However, that Canterbury, at an early date, faced a refusal on the part of the Britons to communicate with them is clear from the letter of Laurence, Mellitus, and Iustus to the Irish Church;[110] and it is also clear that information from Canterbury, including documents such as this very letter, had a major influence on Bede's *Ecclesiastical History*.[111] Yet Canterbury was in a specially disadvantageous position to gain the cooperation of the Britons. First, as the letter of Laurence and his companions makes clear, its views were influenced by tensions in Francia, notably by the opposition to the Irish abbot of Luxeuil, Columbanus, whose community included Britons.[112] There had long been tension, both political and ecclesiastical, between Franks and Gallo-Romans, on the one side, and Bretons on the other; and, here again, we must remember that contemporaries had no term for Bretons other than Britons and thought of them all as one people. Secondly, when in 601 it was clear to Gregory the Great that his mission was having major success, he planned the organization of the Church in Britain on the basis of a particular phase in the organization of Roman Britain. He took it for granted that bishoprics and ecclesiastical provinces should mirror the *civitates* and *provinciae* of the Empire. Hence, London and York were to be the metropolitan sees, each with its own province. As it happened, his plan seems to have been dictated by an account of the provincial structure of Britain as it stood before the changes of the early fourth century, so that there were only two provinces (equivalent to the old *Britannia Superior* with London as its capital and *Britannia Inferior* with York as its capital).[113] If he had been working from a fourth-century list of provinces, he would have had four, or even five, instead of only two; and one of them, *Britannia Prima*, would have been largely British. Moreover, Gregory was working through his Frankish contacts, and he was responding to feelers put out by some English ruler, very probably Æthelberht of Kent, whose wife was a Frankish princess and a Christian.[114] These circumstances, in combination, ensured that the Church in Britain would have two provinces, those of York and of Canterbury (the latter instead of London). Canterbury, the former Roman capital of Kent, was made by Gregory's disciples into an English reflection of Rome itself.[115]

[109] P. Sims-Williams, *Religion and Literature*, 75–9.

[110] *HE* ii. 4.

[111] As shown, for example, by the Preface to the *Ecclesiastical History*, where Bede describes Albinus, abbot of the monastery of St Peter and St Paul, Canterbury, as 'auctor ante omnes ac adiutor opusculi huius'.

[112] *ECI* 366, 371; Jonas, *Vita Columbanii*, i. 20 (ed. Krusch, MGH SRG, 196).

[113] Salway, *Roman Britain*, Map VII.

[114] *Reg.* vi. 49, 57 (as Plummer saw, *Baedae Opera Historica*, ii. 41, probably Frankish because, also in vi. 49, Gregory refers to his instruction to Augustine to take *presbyteros e uicino* as interpreters, and these are very likely to have been Franks, as Bede, *HE* i. 25, assumed). N. P. Brooks, 'Canterbury, Rome and the Construction of English Identity', 243–4 n. 57, still thinks that the *sacerdotes e uicino* of Gregory the Great, *Registrum*, vi. 51, 60, were British bishops, not Frankish; but see I. N. Wood, 'The Mission of Augustine of Canterbury', *Speculum*, 69 (1994), 8, who agreed with Plummer.

[115] Brooks, 'Canterbury, Rome and the Construction of English Identity', 244–6.

The implication of the revision of Gregory's plan, by which Canterbury, rather than London, was to be the metropolitan see, entailed a close tie between the new ecclesiastical structure and the power of Æthelberht, currently the leading English king south of the Humber.[116] Indeed, Gregory the Great himself, in a letter to Æthelberht, made it plain not only that he believed the king to have authority over other kings and peoples, but that he relied upon that authority to extend Christianity.[117] When Augustine, bishop of Canterbury, met British bishops and scholars, he did so 'with the aid of King Æthelberht';[118] and when Edwin of Northumbria was converted, his adoption of Christianity came about through a marriage alliance with Kent. The new bishop, Paulinus, took York as his see; and, if Bede is to be believed, the newly Christian kingship of Northumbria promptly embraced Roman symbols of authority.[119] Rome's connections with Britain were now overwhelmingly with the English, not the Britons; and, as we saw in Chapter 6, the Britons themselves had gradually come to be regarded more as another barbarian people than as citizens of an Empire that, by right, still extended far beyond the reach of its armies. In his *Moralia in Iob*, Gregory the Great rejoiced in the success of the English mission; but he did so in terms that implicitly cast into oblivion British Christianity before 597:[120]

> Britain's tongue, which had known nothing other than to rage with barbarian fury, now begins to echo the Hebrew Alleluia in the divine praises.

Here, Christian Britain was English Britain.

Augustine's meeting with the Britons occurred in two stages; and it appears that Bede had a source written not long after the events; a suggestion as to its nature is that it was a Canterbury document, written up in a hagiographical style, with miracles and prophecies, but based on a British informant or text.[121] First, he met 'the bishops and teachers of the nearest kingdom of the Britons'. Secondly, he met a larger synod, including 'seven British bishops and a larger group of very learned men, especially from their most prestigious monastery, which is called in English *Bancornaburg*'. Plummer suggested that Augustine organized the meeting after he had received from Gregory a set of replies to questions as to how he should proceed, now that he was established as bishop in his English see, in other words, not at the outset of the mission but when Gregory had replied to his question 'How should we act in relation to the bishops of the Gallic and British provinces?'[122] Gregory replied that Augustine should not claim any authority over the bishops of Gaul, but that he should assist the bishop of Arles, the papal vicar for Gaul, in promoting

[116] *HE* i. 25; ii. 3, 5.

[117] *HE* i. 32.

[118] *HE* ii. 2.

[119] *HE* ii. 14, 16.

[120] Gregory the Great, *Moralia in Iob*, XXVII. xii (21) (ed. M. Adraen, CCSL 143B, 1346).

[121] *HE* ii. 2; different views have been taken of the likely provenance of the document: C. Stancliffe, 'The British Church and the Mission of Augustine', 124–9; Wallace-Hadrill, *Commentary*, 52–3, 218–19.

[122] *HE* i. 27; Plummer, *Baedae Opera Historica*, ii. 73.

reform; as for Britain, 'However we entrust all the bishops of the British provinces to your fraternity, that the ignorant may be taught, that the weak may be strengthened by encouragement, and the perverse may be corrected.' The terms in which Gregory wrote suggest that his replies were sent with extra personnel, and also with the papal letter given by Bede in Book I, chapter 29—namely the letter by which Gregory set out the provincial structure of the Church in Britain and granted Augustine a pallium. Moreover, the letter included a sentence giving Augustine, for his lifetime only, authority over the bishop of York (yet to be consecrated) and all the bishops of Britain:

> However, you, my brother, are to have under your authority not just the bishops you have ordained, and not just those ordained by the bishop of York, but also all the bishops of Britain, by the authority of Our Lord and God, Jesus Christ.

This entirely accords with the response given by Gregory to Augustine's question, and it confirms that the pope consciously intended to make the British churches subject to Augustine in his lifetime and subject subsequently to the two metropolitan sees. The churches of the Bretons might maintain an effective independence of their canonical superior, the bishop of Tours;[123] and the pope may have contemplated the possibility that a similar independence might be sought by the Britons north of the Channel; but, if so, he categorically rejected it. In any case, Plummer was very probably right in seeing a link between the particular authority given to Augustine in 601 and the latter's approach to the Britons. Augustine did not merely seek British cooperation in his mission, but he did so in the course of claiming the authority over the Britons that the pope had given him. If Bede's story is accurate, he failed in the end to win over the Britons not so much because of their disagreements over Easter, but because he would not lay aside the high dignity of his office when approached by the British bishops and scholars. The Britons had determined in advance, on the advice of a hermit, that they would not cooperate if, when they came into his presence, he remained seated. Parallels from early Irish texts indicate that the Britons would have regarded remaining seated as a declaration by Augustine of his authority over themselves.[124]

If the provincial organization of the fourth-century British Church corresponded to the provinces as they were at the time, rather than to the third-century structure followed by Gregory the Great; and if the fourth-century provinces then survived in the ecclesiastical sphere, even though the imperial administration in Britain had receded into a remote past—if, that is, British Britain was, to this extent, like Gaul—then the authority claimed by Augustine will have come as a complete surprise to the Britons. If, on the other hand, all provincial organization had disappeared, or if it corresponded to the main political divisions, as in Ireland, it

[123] It is possible that Augustine visited Tours on his way to England: R. Gameson, 'Augustine of Canterbury: Context and Achievement', in Gameson (ed.), *St Augustine and the Conversion of England*, 10–12.

[124] *Críth Gablach*, ed. D. A. Binchy (Dublin, 1941), ll. 604–6; *Frithfholad*, § 9, ed. J. G. O'Keeffe, in J. Fraser, P. Grosjean and J. G. O'Keeffe (eds.), *Irish Texts*, i (London, 1931), 20. Cf. Suetonius, *De Vita Caesarum*, Tiberius, 31.

will also have been a surprise. In the long term, the Gregorian plan was not accepted by the Britons, as is evident from references to archbishops in Wales in the late eighth and late ninth centuries.[125] Relations only got worse when Theodore arrived in 669 with a new status, that of archbishop of the island of Britain.[126] The Gregorian scheme was, for the time being, abandoned in favour of a different application of the Roman past: Theodore's archbishopric corresponded to the late Roman diocese of the Britains.[127] For Theodore in the years immediately after his arrival, as we have seen, the Britons were not just rebelling against his authority but were heretics and schismatics.

The Canterbury condemnation of the Britons provoked a reaction. The letter of Lawrence, bishop of Canterbury, includes a passage explaining that an Irish bishop, Dagán, had come to them, and that through him and 'Abbot Columbanus in Gaul', they had discovered that the Irish Church did not differ from the British. Dagán, indeed, had refused to take food with them or to sleep in the same building. This is the mirror image of the command put by Bede into the mouth of the dying St Cuthbert: his monks were to 'have no communion with those who depart from the unity of the Catholic peace, either in not celebrating Easter at the proper time or in evil living'.[128] It is also reminiscent of the standpoint of the Breton king Iudicael, who refused to partake of Dagobert's hospitality by eating at his table, 'because Iudicael was a devout man and greatly feared God'; instead, he went to eat with Dado, Dagobert's referendary, 'whom he knew to be an adherent of holy religion'.[129] For Iudicael it was a matter of morals rather than of doctrine. Dagán's behaviour in refusing to eat or share sleeping quarters with Lawrence and his companions is best explained on the basis that he already knew that Augustine had condemned the British Church, with which the Irish had long and friendly links.

Bede's *Ecclesiastical History*, however, was designed to make a firm distinction between the Irish and British Churches. Bede believed, on the good authority of Gildas, that the Britons had lost most of Britain as a divine punishment for their sins. He also wrote:[130]

> among the other unrelatable offences that their historian, Gildas, describes in mournful prose, they were also adding this: that they never handed on by preaching the word of faith to the people of the Saxons or English, which inhabited Britain along with them. But nevertheless divine mercy did not abandon His people whom He foreknew, but rather sent much more worthy heralds of the truth to the aforementioned people, through whom it might believe.

125 See below, 593.

126 *HE* iv. 17/15 (Theodore's title at the Council of Hatfield).

127 A. Thacker, 'Gallic or Greek? Archbishops in England from Theodore to Ecgberht', in P. Fouracre and D. Ganz (eds.), *Frankland: The Franks and the World of the Early Middle Ages. Essays in Honour of Dame Jinty Nelson* (Manchester, 2008), 44–69.

128 Bede, *Vita S. Cuthberti Prosaica*, c. 39, ed. and trans. B. Colgrave, *Two Lives of Saint Cuthbert*, 284/285.

129 Fredegar, *Chronica*, iv. 78; discussed above, 240–1.

130 *HE* i. 22.

The much more worthy heralds were the Gregorian missionaries and also Aidan and the other Irish churchmen who came to England.

Bede had a particular reason for his concern with the sins of the Britons. He feared that the Northumbrians, too, might come to utter disaster, as they so nearly did at the hands of Cadwallon in 633–634, and as they did to a lesser extent in 685 at the hands of the Picts. His fear, as his letter to Bishop Ecgberht makes very evident, was that Northumbrian sins, like those of the Britons, cried to heaven for punishment.[131] There was an urgency behind his condemnation of the Britons and the contrast he made between Britons and Irish: a real danger troubled Bede that his own people, the Northumbrians, might be the Britons of the next generation, a people condemned by God to lose its land. This fear also explains why another Ecgberht, in voluntary exile in Ireland since the plague of 664, should have been a pivotal figure in the *Ecclesiastical History*: this Ecgberht not only pleaded with the king of Northumbria, Ecgfrith, not to attack the Irish in 684, but was himself, from Ireland, the inspiration behind the English mission to the Frisians, and would later, in 716, persuade the community of Iona to adopt the Roman Easter.[132] Because of Ecgberht and his like, there was always the chance that when God weighed whole peoples in the balance, as he weighed Sodom and Gomorrah, a new Abraham might be able to plead that the English, in spite of their many sins, resembled not Gildas's Britons but the Irish.

Bede may also have shared an antipathy felt by his own people to the Britons, together with a fear that the kingdom of Alclud could be a major threat to Northumbria.[133] The English of Northumbria were, even more than most of their southern neighbours, a people settled among Britons and claiming a political and social superiority over them, and yet, at the same time, perceiving them as dangerous enemies. For Bede, the sins of the Britons meant that the power of God was in alliance with the power of the English in reducing many of the Britons to a position of servitude to their English masters; and the Britons, for their part, had a *domesticum odium* for the English, a hatred as of unreconciled enemies forced to share the same house; thus the Britons and the English shared the one island in intimate hostility.[134]

This hostility makes it easier to explain why Bede made so fundamental a distinction between the Irish and the Britons. Although his defence of Aidan's Easter customs applied, in principle, just as much to the Britons, and though Bede never himself condemned the Britons as heretics, this mitigation of their condemnation, as they had been condemned by Theodore and Wilfrid, was outweighed by their refusal to preach to the English—and this in addition to all those grave sins recounted by 'their historian', Gildas. All this was in spite of Bede's acknowledgement in passing that, around the time of Theodore's death, some of the Britons, as

[131] J. Campbell, 'Bede I', in his *Essays in Anglo-Saxon History* (London, 1986), 15–19.
[132] *HE* iii. 27; iv. 27/24; v. 9, 22.
[133] Stancliffe, *Bede and the Britons*, 12–32.
[134] *HE* v. 23.

well as many of the Irish in Ireland, had accepted the Roman Easter.[135] In the chapter in which he mentions this, he goes on to explain how many of the Irish changed their stance, but in that chapter he never expands his brief notice of the British change. Plummer considered it probable that the Britons of the kingdom of Alclud were intended, but that it was possible that Bede was thinking of the Britons converted to the Roman Easter by Aldhelm, when he was abbot of Malmesbury.[136] Those Britons, however, were subject to the West Saxons, which evidently in reality, and perhaps also in Bede's mind, would put them in a rather different category. Bede's account would allow Aldhelm's 'excellent book against the error of the Britons' and his 'conversion of many of the Britons subject to the West Saxons' to be separate though broadly related achievements, one directed at subject Britons, the other at Britons in general. It is tempting to identify 'the book' with the letter Aldhelm wrote to Geraint, king of Dumnonia, and this may perhaps be correct.[137] Yet, there is no certainty that the conversion flowed from the book, and still less that those converted were the Britons of Dumnonia.

In general, British Christianity after the Gregorian mission was only mentioned by Bede in order to condemn it. Thus, when he refers to the consecration of the first English bishop of Whithorn, Pehthelm, who was a significant informant for the *Ecclesiastical History*, Bede explains it by writing that Whithorn 'has, with the multiplication of communities of the faithful, been made into an episcopal see and has him [Pehthelm] as its first bishop'.[138] Bede is here echoing the terms of the ninth chapter of the Synod of Hertford: 'That with the increasing number of the faithful more bishops should be added'.[139] And, yet, Bede had already told his readers that Whithorn had been a British church; indeed, he believed that a bishop of Whithorn, Ninian, had 'been correctly educated at Rome in the faith and the mysteries of the truth', and that, at Whithorn, a church dedicated to St Martin, Ninian 'rested with very many holy men'.[140] Bede believed, that is, that Whithorn had long been an episcopal centre of British Christianity and that only 'now does

[135] *HE* v. 15. The date is not closely specified, but the 'Quo tempore' at the beginning of the chapter probably continues the 'Eo tempore' of chapter 9 and the 'His temporibus' of chapter 12 rather than the reign of Coenred, 704–709, mentioned in chapter 13, since the Northumbrian king to whom Adomnán came (chapter 15) was Aldfrith, 685–705. If this is granted, the chronological anchor would be the death of Theodore, reported in chapter 8.

[136] In his commentary on the passage in *HE* v. 15, *Baedae Opera Historica*, ii. 301. Stancliffe, *Bede and the Britons*, 24–5, argues that Bede was referring to the Britons of Dumnonia

[137] Lapidge and Herren, *Aldhelm: The Prose Works*, 140–3, accept the identity of the letter with Bede's 'book'; Stancliffe, *Bede and the Britons*, 24 and n. 90.

[138] *HE* v. 23; cf. D. Brooke, 'The Northumbrian Settlements in Galloway and Carrick', *Proceedings of the Society of Antiquaries of Scotland*, 121 (1991), 295–27, who distinguishes between areas of strong and weak Northumbrian settlement.

[139] *HE* iv. 5. *Fideles* is used throughout the *Historia Ecclesiastica* in the sense of 'Christians' as opposed to *infideles*, 'non-Christians' (who refuse to accept faith (*fides*) in Christ). To contrast the orthodox with the unorthodox, further terms have to be used, as in *fideles catholici* in Book i. 17 where it contrasts with Pelagians (in text taken from Constantius's Life of St Germanus). It also needs to be remembered that, for Bede, the Britons and the Irish were not heretical on the date of Easter, merely wrong, and, in the case of the Britons, obstinately wrong. *Fideles* is used for Britons, who are wrong on Easter, in Book ii. 2.

[140] *HE* iii. 4.

the English people take control'.[141] In spite of these beliefs, however, he could treat 'the multiplication of communities of the faithful' as a recent event. Bede could write in one mode of the distant past, even claiming that Ninian had converted the southern Picts, and in quite a different mode of his own day, when the British Christians around Whithorn were as if they did not exist, Pehthelm was the first bishop of Whithorn, and the Britons in general had condemned themselves by not preaching the faith to their neighbours.[142]

The probability, then, is that relations between Britons and English in Northumbria were very different in 700 from what they had been in 650. In 650 the Britons in Northumbria are likely to have constituted a considerable portion of the population, and an even higher proportion of the Christian population, both of Deira and of Bernicia. In 700 the assimilation of Britons to the English was that much further advanced; and, on the ecclesiastical side, those Britons within the kingdom who still kept to the traditional Easter of their people were now subject to fierce condemnation as heretics.

What this might mean for the Britons can be surmised on the basis of Stephen's *Life of Wilfrid.* This was written after the death of Wilfrid in 709 and before the death of Ælffled, abbess of Whitby, in 715. It was written primarily for the community of Wilfrid's church at Ripon, in Deira, but also for other adherents of the saint, within and without Northumbria, notably Acca, formerly Wilfrid's priest, and now bishop of Hexham. It is a defence of the memory of a highly controversial figure, someone twice exiled by kings of Northumbria, someone who came into conflict with two archbishops of Canterbury, Theodore and Berhtwald, and someone whose brief rule over Lindisfarne in 687–688 left a deep scar on that community. There can be little doubt that Bede had major reservations about aspects of Wilfrid's career, and yet, as the leading champion of Rome and Roman ways in Northumbria during his episcopate at York, 670–678, his achievements were unquestionable. Bede's sympathies, therefore, were for Eata and the other bishops who replaced Wilfrid after his expulsion in 678—including, for two years, 685–687, an indubitable saint, Cuthbert—but he handled the career of Wilfrid always with a respectful circumspection and, when possible, with warm approbation. The *Life of Wilfrid* has an immense value, when set alongside the *Ecclesiastical History*, partly because of its early date, and also because it gives us some idea of the standpoint of those in Northumbria who, unlike Bede, condemned both the Britons and the Irish as heretics.

Ten chapters of the *Life*, 15–24, cover the eight years from Wilfrid's installation by Theodore as bishop of York in 670 to his expulsion by a combination of King Ecgfrith and the same Theodore in 678. Four of these chapters, 17–19 and 21, are of importance for his relations with the Britons. The first described a great feast held to celebrate the completion of his stone church at Ripon and its dedication to

141 Ibid. *iam nunc Anglorum gens obtinet.*

142 Similarly, he writes as if there were no churches in Deira before Edwin's conversion even though he goes on to mention Elmet, the British kingdom conquered by Edwin only a few years before, and although he knew of Cerdic, the previous British king: *HE* ii. 14; iv. 23/21.

St Peter. About ten years earlier, Alhfrith, then ruling Deira as sub-king, had expelled the earlier community, including Eata and Cuthbert, and had given Ripon to Wilfrid; and he had also given him forty hides of land.[143] In the meantime, however, Ahlfrith had rebelled against his father, Oswiu; and Wilfrid, although consecrated bishop, had spent three years in Gaul, 664–667, and then three years, 667–670, as abbot of Ripon.[144] Although Ripon had been the gift of the disgraced Alhfrith, this feast, some time after Wilfrid had been installed as bishop of York in 670, demonstrated to everyone that the gift had the full support of the current kings, Ecgfrith, king of Northumbria, and his younger brother, Ælfwine, who may have been king of Deira. They confirmed the earlier gifts, amounting to forty hides, and added more of their own. Before they all got down to three days of feasting, Wilfrid proclaimed before the people the generosity of kings:[145]

> And so the holy bishop Wilfrid, standing before the altar, turned to the people and listed in the presence of the kings the *regiones* which, for their souls, kings granted to him both previously and subsequently on that very day with the consent and over the subscription of bishops and all the *principes*. And he also clearly listed those holy places in various *regiones*, which the British clergy, fleeing from the sharp edge of the hostile sword wielded by the hand of our people, abandoned. It was indeed a gift pleasing to God that the pious kings had made over so many lands to God for the service of our bishop, and these are the names of the *regiones*: by the Ribble, and Yeadon (?), and in the *regio* of the *Dunutingas* (Dent?), and *In Caetlaeuum* (Catlow) and in other places.

These identifications are not certain;[146] but if *In Gaedyne* is in fact Yeadon, they included an estate probably within the Elmet conquered by King Edwin fifty or more years previously.[147] Yeadon would have been a neighbouring *regio* to the *Loidis regio* in which there was a royal vill.[148] These *regiones* appear to have been areas normally with more than one settlement but organized around a central *villa* or *tun*, to which food-renders and light services were delivered by the free and to which unfree tenants, owing much heavier services, were attached, the 'small shires'

[143] *Vita Wilfridi*, c. 8; *HE* iii. 25; Anonymous Monk of Lindisfarne, *Vita S. Cuthberti*, ii. 2; Bede, *Vita S. Cuthberti Prosaica*, c. 7; ed. and trans. Colgrave, *Two Lives of Saint Cuthbert*, 76–7, 174–7.

[144] *HE* iii. 14; *Vita Wilfridi*, c. 14.

[145] *Vita Wilfridi*, c. 17, modifying Colgrave's translation a little.

[146] They were suggested by H. M. Chadwick: see Colgrave's note to his edition, p. 164; A. H. Smith, *The Place-Names of the West Riding of Yorkshire*, iv (Cambridge, 1961), pp. xi, 155; vii (Cambridge, 1962), 76 n. 1, in the end agreed with Chadwick; I. N. Wood, 'Anglo-Saxon Otley: An Archiepiscopal Estate and its Crosses in a Northumbrian Context', *Northern History*, 23 (1987), 20–38, at 24, and P. Sims-Williams, 'St Wilfrid and Two Charters dated AD 675 and 680', *Journal of Ecclesiastical History*, 39 (1988), 180–3, doubt the Yeadon identification; Sims-Williams also doubts the Ribble identification; the Yeadon identification has been defended by G. R. J. Jones, 'Some Donations to Bishop Wilfrid in Northern England', *Northern History*, 31 (1995), 22–38, esp. 30–6. Cf. B. Cox, 'The Place-Names of the Earliest English Records', *Journal of the English Place-Name Society*, 8 (1975–6), 29.

[147] Yeadon is just to the north-west of Leeds, the *regio Loidis* of *HE* ii. 14 and iii. 24, Barwick-in-Elmet is just to the north-east of Leeds.

[148] *HE* ii. 14.

or 'multiple estates'.[149] These *regiones* were the building blocks of kingdoms, but they were also coming to perform the same role for the Church.[150]

This passage is not just important for the scale of royal generosity to Wilfrid or for the relationship between a written charter and a public proclamation.[151] What needs to be considered is the relationship between the list of *regiones* given to Wilfrid and the 'holy places' abandoned by the British clergy in the face of the Northumbrian army. Probably the churches were within the *regiones*. This is not explicitly stated, however, and one might conceive of churches being handed over, even though they were outside the lands given to Wilfrid. Yet, this seems rather less likely, since then they would probably have been handed over to him *qua* bishop of York rather than, as they seem to have been, *qua* abbot of Ripon. We still have two problems, however, first of the circumstances in which, and the date at which, British clergy were driven by force from their churches, and, secondly, of what happened to their churches and, in particular, how these churches fared in a Church organized around minsters and their *parochiae*.

For the first problem, two possibilities suggest themselves: first, this might simply have been an aspect of the conquest of those territories. In the case of Yeadon, therefore, it would have occurred in the reign of King Edwin, when Elmet was conquered. Then, however, we should have the problem of how these abandoned 'sacred places' were still recognizable as such some fifty years later. Second, the alternative is that the British clergy were driven out at a later period, close to the date of the grant. A possibility is that they were expelled because they were now, since the arrival of Theodore in 669, followed by Wilfrid gaining possession of the see of York, regarded as heretics. The event would probably have been very recent, and we should then have an easy explanation for the terms in which they are described. The sequence of events suggested by the second explanation is that, before 669, it was entirely possible for British clergy to collaborate, within Northumbria, with the bishops sent from Iona, Aidan, Fínán, and Colmán. After 664, it may have taken a few years before any drive against the heretical British clergy was fully under way: it does not seem likely that Chad, consecrated by two British bishops and one English bishop, and someone who, according to the *Life of Wilfrid*, was promoted to the bishopric of York by the machinations of the heretics, would have encouraged any such plan of action.[152] On the other hand, the basis for such a policy is present in Pope Vitalian's letter to Oswiu, *c.* 666, which was a reply to a

[149] Above, 289–92.

[150] J. Blair, 'Anglo-Saxon Minsters: A Topographical Review', in J. Blair and R. Sharpe, *Pastoral Care before the Parish* (Leicester, 1992), 226–66; id., *The Church in Anglo-Saxon Society* (Oxford, 2005), 153–60.

[151] Ibid. 87, on grants of estates between 50 and 100 hides to minsters in the late seventh century; the major royal grants were a feature of a short period, 670–700, and the gifts of Ecgfrith and Ælfwine were at the beginning of this period. For the charters of the period, see P. Wormald, *Bede and the Conversion of England: The Charter Evidence*, Jarrow Lecture (Jarrow, 1984), reprinted, with additions, in his *The Times of Bede: Studies in Early Christian Society and its Historian*, ed. S. Baxter (Malden MA, 2006), ch. 4.

[152] Stephen, *Vita Wilfridi*, c. 14.

lost letter from Oswiu.[153] It is plain from the pope's reply that Oswiu had offered to use his power in the island of Britain to secure the adoption of the Roman Easter. The Picts, the northern Britons, and the Irish of Dál Riata were tributary to Oswiu, and this relationship was very probably the power he offered to use; but a king who sought to influence tributary kingdoms was also likely to enforce orthodoxy within his own kingdom. However, as we shall see, the full development of the new policy came with Oswiu's son and successor, Ecgfrith (670–685). This, then, seems the most likely answer to the first problem: the British priests were driven from their church in the period from 670 because they were deemed to be heretics and schismatics: it was the local working out of a policy which saw not just Colmán compelled to leave Northumbria but also the English monks who still adhered to the Easter customs introduced from Iona.[154]

The second problem was how the abandoned churches fitted into the structure based on minsters. There is a suggestive chronological coincidence between the period of maximum pressure on these British and Irish heretics and schismatics and the period in which, as we have seen, most major royal land-grants occurred and so began to build the economic foundations of the minsters, 670–700. For Northumbria, at least, the answer may have been different in different areas. In the areas most immediately subject to Wilfrid's power as bishop of York, place-names in *eccles* came to denote minor churches; in Lothian and Tweeddale they were more likely to end up as mother-churches.[155] If we accept that, in the area around Ripon and York from 670 until at least 850, pastoral care was provided by minster churches, it follows that these minor *eccles* sites would not have continued as important churches after Wilfrid's time as bishop of York. As we shall see in the next chapter, the contrast between Deira east of the Pennines and Lothian can be extended when we examine the survival of British place-names.

After the chapter on the dedication of the new church at Ripon, the *Vita Wilfridi* goes on to recount a miracle story.[156] Wilfrid was riding round, baptizing and confirming, when he came to a vill called *On Tiddanufri*, where he met a woman lamenting the death of her first-born son; the bishop revived the child by his prayers, and gave him to the mother, extracting a promise from her that the boy would be given back to himself when he reached the age of seven.[157] The mother, however, 'being persuaded by the evil advice of her husband, when she saw how handsome the boy was, despised this promise and fled from her land'. 'The bishop's reeve, Hocca, went in search of the boy and found him hiding among others of the Britons, took him away by force, and brought him to the bishop.' The boy

153 *HE* iii. 29.
154 *HE* iii. 26, iv. 4.
155 Blair, *The Church in Anglo-Saxon Society*, 30–1; Stancliffe, 'Oswald "Most Holy and Most Victorious King"', 78.
156 *Vita Wilfridi*, c. 18.
157 Wilfrid may have regarded Eodwald as a first-born to be offered to the Lord: Exodus, 13: 1–2. For the identification of *On Tiddanufri* as Tidover in the parish of Kirkby Overton, on the north side of the River Wharfe and further east than Yeadon, see Jones, 'Some Donations to Bishop Wilfrid in Northern England', 23–6; and A. H. Smith, *The Place-Names of the West Riding of Yorkshire*, v (Cambridge, 1961), 43, vi (Cambridge, 1962), 32, 76 n. 1.

subsequently lived at Ripon, with the name Eodwald and the additional name 'Son of the Bishop', until he died 'of the great plague', probably that of 684–685. The critical phrase here is *latentem sub aliis Bryttonum*, 'lying hid among others of the Britons'. The implication appears to be that the boy and his parents were British, so that his English name, Eodwald, may not have been the one used by his own family.[158] The story is a striking example of the power of an early English lord over subject Britons, and of the way that power could be used to extract a British boy from his family and give him a new English identity.

The next three chapters were designed to demonstrate that Ecgfrith's power came to its apogee and endured while he was on good terms with Wilfrid.[159] First, 'the bestial peoples of the Picts' tried to use Ecgfrith's succession to his father to throw off their tributary subjection to Northumbria but were routed by a small cavalry force led by Ecgfrith and the sub-king, Beornhæth. Secondly, Wulfhere, king of the Mercians, brought 'all the southern peoples' to attack Northumbria, but was defeated and compelled to pay tribute. And so:

> Just as, under the most pious king Ecgfrith, the kingdom was extended by triumphant victories to the north and to the south, so also, under Bishop Wilfrid of blessed memory, a kingdom of churches was multiplied to the south over the English and to the north over Britons and Irish and Picts. . . . Almost all the abbots and abbesses of monasteries took a vow that either they should retain their property although under his name [as owner], or that they would choose to have him as their heir after their deaths. And secular leaders also, noble men, gave him their sons to be brought up, so that either, if they so wished, they might serve God, or, if they preferred, he might commend them, when grown up, to the king as armed men.

As the bishop's retinue contained both young nobles training to be warriors and others training to be clerics, so the reach of the bishop, both south over the English and north over the Celtic peoples, went hand-in-hand with the military power of the king.

In the episcopate of Wilfrid, therefore, an ecclesiastical authority that now saw itself as embattled against the heretics worked alongside a royal authority that aimed to maintain a military and tributary hegemony in northern Britain. The scale of the ambition is foreshadowed by the letter of Pope Vitalian, but it is most explicitly revealed by a confession of faith made by Wilfrid in Rome in 680. This was after his expulsion from Northumbria, in 678, but at a time when he had every hope of being restored through papal authority; he thus made his confession as the rightful bishop of York:[160]

[158] This depends upon *aliis* not having a sense that it could have in Hiberno-Latin, 'some'. We can be reasonably confident of this since it would otherwise be phrased *sub aliis Bryttonibus*. We are told that Wilfrid baptized the child, and so may have been responsible for giving the name at that point, but it is perhaps more likely that he acquired it at Ripon.

[159] *Vita Wilfridi*, cc. 19–21.

[160] Stephen, *Vita Wilfridi*, c. 53. For further discussion, see Charles-Edwards, *Early Christian Ireland*, 416–38.

> Wilfrid, beloved of God, bishop of York . . . confessed the true and catholic faith for the whole northern part of Britain and Ireland and for the islands which are inhabited by the peoples of the English and the Britons, and also the Irish and the Picts, and he corroborated it with his signature.

The inclusion of the northern part of Ireland can be explained on the basis that the southern part of Ireland, but not the northern, had adopted the Roman Easter many years before.[161] Wilfrid's claim to an authority over the northern parts of both islands is likely to have some connection with Ecgfrith's attack in 684 on Brega, then the leading kingdom of the northern half of Ireland; it was the kingdom that included Tara itself and it was also the kingdom to which belonged the current king of Tara, Fínsnechtae Fledach. If we may trust the claim of the *Life of Wilfrid* that, in the reign of Ecgfrith, ecclesiastical power went hand in hand with secular power, and if we may apply the linkage between orthodoxy and Northumbrian hegemony apparently promised by Oswiu to Pope Vitalian to the reign of Oswiu's successor, it is very likely that the attack on Brega was planned with this justification. If so, Ecgfrith intended his invasion to induce the king of Tara to give hostages and the northern Irish churches to adopt the Roman Easter.

The link between paschal orthodoxy and English power can be traced from the small scale to an ambition that straddled the Irish Sea—from the British clergy forced to flee their churches by a Northumbrian army all the way to other Northumbrian armies seeking to dominate the northern parts of the two islands, Britain and Ireland. Relations between the Britons and the English may have fallen, therefore, into two phases. In the earlier phase, some British communities existed within some English kingdoms with their own nobles and their own priests and churches; other British communities are likely to have been granted to English nobles, but they might still retain their own priests. In this phase, therefore, many Britons in English kingdoms will have been able to retain their own identity, language, and traditions. After 664, and still more after 670, they entered a new phase, when their religious traditions had been anathematized as heretical, their priests expelled, some of their churches abandoned and others handed over to an English ecclesiastical authority that considered their form of Christianity deplorable. If they still had British nobles, those nobles are unlikely to have been able to gain access to their English king without abandoning their British Christianity. In these circumstances, assimilation of British communities to a dominant English culture and language is likely to have become much more rapid.

The evidence for these changes comes mainly from Northumbria, and even then it is more indicative than conclusive. The severity of the change is likely to have been most acute in Northumbria, since it was expanding very rapidly: only in Æthelfrith's reign is it likely to have conquered all the Tweed valley up to the forest around Selkirk; only in Edwin's reign was Elmet conquered, and only in Oswald's reign was Lothian taken; and, yet, by the time Bede was writing a new English bishop was in place at Whithorn and English communities were multiplying in

[161] *HE* ii. 19; iii. 3.

what is now Galloway. Similar attitudes, however, are likely to have prevailed by the late seventh century in Mercia and in Wessex: we have direct evidence for Wessex;[162] and, in the eighth century, it will be possible to see the effects of these changes also in Mercia.

[162] Bede, *HE* v. 18; Aldhelm, *Ep.* 4, ed. R. Ehwald, *Aldhelmi Opera Omnia*, MGH AA xv (Berlin, 1919), 480–7, trans. M. Lapidge and M. Herren, *Aldhelm: The Prose Works* (Ipswich, 1979), 155–60.

13

The Britons and their Neighbours under the Mercian Hegemony, 685–825

The history of the Britons between the battle of Nechtanesmere and Mercia's defeat by Ecgberht of Wessex in 825 has a different shape from the previous period. After the battle of the Trent in 679, and still more after the death of Ecgfrith in battle against the Picts at Nechtanesmere in 685, Northumbria ceased to be a threat to the Southumbrian hegemony of the Mercian kings. No longer did the Welsh and the Mercians make common cause in order to withstand Northumbrian invasion. From 679 it seems to have been usual for Northumbrian ambitions to be confined to maintaining their power over the northern Britons, while the Mercians sought to control Wales, and the West Saxons extended their conquests in the south-west. This is the period of which it may be said that the three leading English kingdoms each had its British hinterland, which each sought to exploit by a mixture of conquest, raiding, and tribute-taking.[1] Although Mercian authority over Wales continued, with gaps, for nearly a century after 825, it did so in a different context: no longer was Mercia the leading kingdom in England; and a new dynasty in Gwynedd soon revealed an ambition to dominate Wales.

Mainly because of Bede, there are fragments of narrative material for the late seventh and early eighth centuries; for the late ninth century Asser's Life of King Alfred is brief but invaluable on Wales, the author's native country;[2] the Anglo-Saxon Chronicle, compiled in Alfred's reign, has entries dealing with the Britons of the south-west; similarly the late eighth-century Northumbrian annals known as the Continuation of Bede have some important entries mentioning the Britons of what is now Scotland, and so also do the northern annals that survive under the name of Simeon of Durham and those transmitted in the D and E versions of the Anglo-Saxon Chronicle; by then, also, the *Annales Cambriae* were becoming a slightly less exiguous record. Alongside such standard sources we have some sculpture and a few inscriptions, notably the Pillar of Eliseg, although the richest period in British epigraphy was over by 650; a tenth-century collection of royal genealogies;[3] the *Historia Brittonum* of 829–830 (and also later versions), which

[1] J. R. Maddicott, 'Two Frontier States: Northumbria and Wessex, *c.* 650–750', in J. R. Maddicott and D. M. Palliser (eds.), *The Medieval State: Essays Presented To James Campbell* (London, 25–45).

[2] Asser, *Life of King Alfred*, ed. W. H. Stevenson (Oxford, 1904), esp. cc. 79–80, tr. S. Keynes and M. Lapidge, *Alfred the Great: Asser's* Life of King Alfred *and Other Contemporary Sources*, Penguin Classics (Harmondsworth, 1983), 93–6.

[3] *EWGT* 9–13.

displayed more interest in Northumbria than in Mercia;[4] and some charters, of varying reputation.[5] In addition, there is the single best-known monument of the period, Offa's Dyke; yet this has usually been better appreciated for what it tells us of the governmental capacities deployed by a Mercian king than for any light it sheds on conditions in Wales.

1. THE WELSH AND THE RISE OF MERCIA

By the time of the Tribal Hidage, which may belong to the late seventh century, the Mercians were no longer strictly the 'Marcher People', *Mierce*.[6] They now had western satellites from the Cheshire Plain over into the Severn Valley and down as far as the mouth of the Wye: Westerne, Wreocensæte, Magonsæte, and Hwicce.[7] Nevertheless, the Welsh frontier in the late seventh century was a place where ambitious princes of the Iclingas, the Mercian royal lineage, might hope to make a reputation as war leaders. They might also take refuge across the frontier: St Guthlac's knowledge of Welsh was acquired during his period as a young Icling, leading his own war band and thus possibly making a bid for the kingship of Mercia; the consequence for him, as it was, slightly later, for Æthelbald, was exile; in Guthlac's case this was among the Britons. His experience of Wales is all the more striking because his parental residence was among the Middle Angles, to the east of the Mercian heartland.[8] The situation of the royal exile is also instructive, since it is easy to suppose that war between Britons and English would take the form of clashes between armies led by kings, as in the Battle of Chester. Yet, aspirants to kingship, with their own war bands, rivals of the current kings and thus often out of their control, may have been responsible for much of the violence and instability on the frontier. Cædwalla first attacked Sussex and killed its king when he himself was not yet king of the Gewisse, but merely a royal exile; when he became king, he continued the same onslaught.[9]

The Mercian hegemony had three zones. In the centre was Mercia proper, including such places as Repton, Lichfield, and Tamworth, the land that was Mercia before Penda and his sons made their kingdom the dominant force in southern England. Wrapped around this core were satellite peoples, probably

[4] *Historia Brittonum*, ed. E. Faral, *La Légende arthurienne*, 3 (Paris, 1929), 4–62 (Chartres, as far as it goes, in parallel with Harleian). Faral's Harleian text is reprinted with a translation in *Nennius, British History, and the Welsh Annals*, ed. and tr. J. Morris (London, 1980); a later recension is *The Historia Brittonum*, 3, *The 'Vatican Recension'*, ed. D. N. Dumville (Cambridge, 1985).

[5] See above, Ch. 7.

[6] N. P. Brooks, 'The Formation of the Mercian Kingdom', in S. Bassett (ed.), *The Origins of Anglo-Saxon Kingdoms* (Leicester, 1989), 162.

[7] See above, 387–8.

[8] Felix, *Life of St Guthlac*, ed. and trans. B. Colgrave (Cambridge, 1956), cc. 16–18, 34 (to be driven into exile was a common fate of members of a dynasty contending for the kingship; similarly Æthelbald, Felix, *Life*, c. 40; for the tensions arising from the presence of exiles in another country, see the letter of Waldhere, bishop of London, to Berhtwald of Canterbury, *EHD* i, no. 164, and Bede, *HE* ii. 12).

[9] *HE* iv. 15.

mostly with their own rulers, but often colonized by Mercian nobles. Beyond this zone lay another, more loosely dependent, indeed sometimes entirely independent, consisting of kingdoms with their own dynasties, quite separate from that of the Mercians. Around the core, therefore, there was an inner and an outer zone. The inner zone consisted of such peoples as those who inhabited the various Middle Anglian regions, Surrey and Essex, also the Hwicce and, along the Welsh border, the Wreocensæte and Magonsæte, and also the Westerne if they were distinct from the Magonsæte. In the outer zone lay the kingdoms of Kent, Sussex, the East Angles, and Wessex. The rulers in the inner zone, even if they started as kings, were reduced to sub-royal status; and some may never have had kings but only *principes* or *duces*; the rulers in the outer zone were kings, and when the Mercians imposed their own candidates, this was violently resented.

What is difficult to determine is whether the Welsh were part of this structure. If they were, they belonged to the outer zone; if they were not, they belonged to a different political sphere, as did the Northumbrians. Another complication is that the kingdoms in the outer zone were not in the same degree of subservience to the king of the Mercians. Kent was a special case because of the desire of Mercian kings to impose their own candidates as archbishops of Canterbury. The evidence is not sufficient to sustain definite conclusions, but a case can be made for seeing the Welsh kingdoms as part of the outer zone of the Mercian hegemony, just as the northern Britons were sometimes subject to the Northumbrians, sometimes to the Picts, and occasionally resisted both their powerful neighbours.

In the mid-seventh century, as we have seen, leadership in the alliance between the Welsh of Gwynedd and Powys and the Mercians shifted from Gwynedd to Mercia. The effect was that the north Welsh kings, those principally concerned with Northumbrian aggression, were normally, though perhaps not invariably, clients of the king of the Mercians. Their clientship may not have extended beyond the military sphere: when Penda summoned kings and 'royal leaders' for his great invasion of Northumbria in 655, Welsh kings received the summons along with English rulers, both of the outer and the inner zones.[10] At the end of the period, in the late ninth century, we can trace the outlines of a process by which Mercian authority in Wales was undermined. By this stage, it seems that Welsh subjection to Mercian kings had been more widespread geographically and more extensive in terms of the obligations imposed than it had been in the mid-seventh century. The clientship that Welsh kings sought to escape in the ninth century was not the same as the clientship of the age of Penda. Unfortunately, we have only the odd hint to guide us to an understanding of what had happened in between 679 and 850, between the end of Northumbrian overlordship in southern England and the years immediately preceding the arrival of the Great Army. To clarify the issues I shall present two rival accounts of relations between the Welsh and the Mercians; but, first, we need to consider two major items of evidence: the Pillar of Eliseg and Offa's Dyke.

[10] Bede, *HE* iii. 24; *Historia Brittonum*, cc. 64–5. There is nothing to prove that any Welsh were also included in 'all the southern peoples' summoned by Wulfhere to fight against Northumbria (Stephen, *Life of Wilfrid*, c. 20), but it is quite likely that some were.

2. THE PILLAR OF ELISEG[11]

The Pillar of Eliseg is the name given to an inscribed pillar, of local stone and oval in section, now situated in the parish of Llantysilio-yn-Iâl (Grid reference SJ 2026 4452) to the east of a road leading north to the Horseshoe Pass.[12] It stands on top of a barrow and would have dominated that part of the valley. Because it is oval in section, it is unlikely to be a reused Roman pillar. On the other hand, it may very well be an imitation of a Roman monument; and the type that would fit the function of the Pillar would be one celebrating a victory. It is a century or so earlier than the pillar crosses of north-west Mercia and cannot, therefore, be imitating them. By the fifteenth century, the monument was known as 'the old cross', *hen groes.*[13] It was also the cross that gave its name to the nearby abbey of Valle Crucis founded in 1201.

Fortunately, the inscription, although now illegible, was read, so far as was then possible, by Edward Lhuyd in the late seventeenth century; he made two copies, which agree in all essentials.[14] Also, fortunately, the inscription tells us who ordered it to be erected and who did the lettering (or, rather, so it seems, painted the letters then inscribed by another). The patron was Cyngen ap Cadell, king of Powys, and the inscription began with his genealogy, taken back to Elise ap Gwylog. Elise's name does not appear in the annals, but Cyngen's father, Cadell, is likely to be the Cadell 'of Powys', or 'king of Powys', who died in 808.

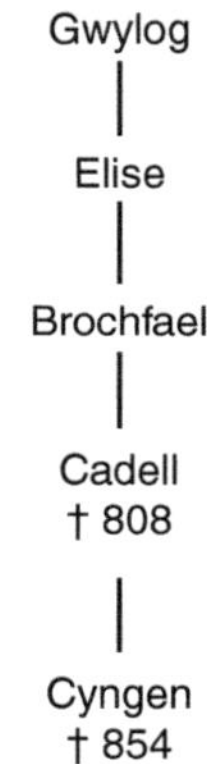

Figure 13.1. Kings of Powys on the Pillar of Eliseg

[11] N. Edwards, 'Rethinking the Pillar of Eliseg', *Antiquaries Journal*, 89 (2009), 1–35; ead., 'Early-Medieval Inscribed Stones', 36–8. See also O. W. Jones, 'The Pillar of Eliseg and the History of Early Powys', *Welsh History Review*, 24: 4 (2009), 41–80; D. Howlett, *Cambro-Latin Compositions* (Dublin, 1998), 27–32; D. Hill, 'Offa's Dyke: Pattern and Purpose', *Antiquaries' Journal*, 80 (2000), 202–5.

[12] *ECMW*, no. 182; Edwards, 'Early-Medieval Inscribed Stones', 36–8. For the following details, see N. Edwards, 'Rethinking the Pillar of Eliseg', and the *Corpus*, iii (forthcoming).

[13] Gutun Owain in the Black Book of Basingwerk version of *Brenhinedd y Saeson,* ed. T. Jones, p. 196, *s.a.* 1200, 'Dôl yr Hengroes yn Iâl'; *Gwaith Guto'r Glyn*, ed. I. Williams and J. Ll. Williams (Cardiff, 1939), cxv. 38.

[14] London, British Library, Harleian MS 3780, f. 95; Bangor, University Library, Penrhos MS v, 872.

The inscription, therefore, supplies enough detail to identify Cyngen with a man whose pedigree is given in the Harleian Genealogies.[15] The genealogies in Jesus College MS 20 that focus upon Rhodri Mawr claim that Rhodri's mother was Nest, the daughter of Cadell ap Brochfael ab Elise;[16] in other words, Nest would then be the sister of the Cyngen who had the inscription made. This makes it probable that the Cyngen of the inscription was the Cyngen, king of Powys, who died in Rome in 854.[17]

The base letterforms are those of half-uncial (Lhuyd's transcripts make it quite clear that the inscription had the **oc** type of **a**); but it used majuscule **R** and a curious **N** like an upside down reversed **h**;[18] his **u** is exactly an **h** turned 180 degrees, a mirror letter to his **N**. The total effect is of a formal half-uncial. The following transcription follows the line-divisions of Lhuyd's transcripts.

+CONCENN FILIUS CATTELL CATTELL
FILIUS BROHCMAIL BROHCMAL FILIUS
ELISEG ELISEG FILIUS GUOILLAUC
+ CONCENN ITAQUE PRONEPOS ELISEG
EDIFICAUIT HUNC LAPIDEM PROAUO
SUO ELISEG IPSE EST ELISEG QUI NEC(R?)
XIT HEREDITATEM POUOS . . . IPC . . . MORT
CA\V/TEM PER VIM E POTESTATE ANGLO
[RUM . . .] IN GLADIO SUO PARTA IN IGNE
[+ QUICU]MQUE RECIT[A]UERIT MANESCR[I]P/
[TUM . . .][19]EM DET BENEDICTIONEM SUPE
[R ANIMA]M ELISEG + IPSE EST CONCENN
[. . . . .] MANU
[. . . . .]E AD REGNUM SUUM POUOS
[. . . . .] ET QUOD
[. . . . .]
[. . . . .] MONTEM
[one or more lines missing]
[. . . . .] MONARCHIAM
[. . . . .]AIL MAXIMUS BRITTANNIAE

[15] *EWGT*, p. 12, HG 27.

[16] *EWGT*, pp. 46–7, JC 17–23.

[17] *AC* 854 (MS *A* is the only witness that spelt the name *Cinnen*; others have forms of Cyngen). For parallels, see C. Stancliffe, 'Kings who opted out', in P. Wormald et al. (eds.), *Ideal and Reality in Frankish and Anglo-Saxon Society: Studies presented to J. M. Wallace-Hadrill* (Oxford, 1983), 154–76.

[18] Also found in a ninth-century inscription from Ceredigion, Tregaron 2, 995/133/CD33, and in an earlier inscription from Dyfed, Llanychâr 1, 440/335/P48. It is ultimately from New Roman Cursive (see above, 167–8).

[19] LAPID]EM or CRUC]EM are possible restorations.

[CONCE]NN PASCEN[T] MAUN ANNAN
[+] BRITU A[U]T[E]M FILIUS GUARTHI
[GIRN] QUE*M* BENED[IXIT] GERMANUS QUE*M*
[QU]E PEPERIT EI SE[V]IRA FILIA MAXIMI
[RE]GIS QUI OCCIDIT REGEM ROMANO
RUM + CONMARCH PINXIT HOC
CHIROGRAFU*M* REGE SUO POSCENTE
CONCENN + BENEDICTIO D*OMI*NI IN CON
CENN ET *SIMILITE*R[20] (?) I*N* TOTA FAMILIA EIUS
ET IN TOTA RAGIONE*M*[21] POUOIS
USQUE IN [DIEM IUDICI AMEN (?)]

The epigraphy is consistent with a ninth-century date. The inscription belongs to the later group of inscriptions, namely those which used half-uncial, a book script. Even though we are dependent on Lhuyd's two transcriptions, the characteristic **oc** form of **a** is clearly shown. It is, however, a relatively formal type of half-uncial, which used majuscule **R** and, normally, majuscule **N** and **U**.[22] To judge by Lhuyd's transcription, the inscription was reasonably well preserved in his time at the beginning and at the end.[23] He shows it as having been divided into thirty-one horizontal lines; he transcribed the whole of the first eight lines; then his transcript becomes progressively more truncated at the beginning of each line until the eighteenth line, of which he could transcribe nothing; after that there is a recovery, so that of the last five lines only the last is incomplete.[24] The transcript also shows crosses being used at the beginning of some sentences, including the first: they may mark the start of distinct sections of the text. These are numbered in the translation given below, together with line numbers in square brackets. It should be noted, however, that section 5 almost certainly would be divided into more than one section if we had the complete text:[25]

1. [1] † Cyngen son of Cadell, Cadell [2] son of Brochfael, Brochfael son [3] of Elise, Elise son of Gwylog.
2. [4] † Cyngen, therefore, great-grandson of Elise, [5] erected this stone to his great-grandfather, [6] Elise.

[20] This extension of the abbreviation assumes that, because it is an abbreviation, minuscule **r** was used instead of the majuscule **R** used elsewhere in the inscription.

[21] *Sic* in spite of the transcription by Bartrum; the **R** has, instead of a diagonal stroke descending from the bottom of the bow, a low and horizontal right-hand stroke.

[22] The letter **e** is normally represented by a form resembling a Greek minuscule epsilon, but an **E** appears quite often.

[23] A photograph of Lhuyd's transcription is given before p. 1 of *EWGT*.

[24] The damage to the last line was different in that it was to the end, not, as previously, to the beginning.

[25] The line numbers are sometimes only in an approximately correct position, since the order of words in Latin cannot always be reproduced in English. They should, however, facilitate comparison of the translation with Lhuyd's transcript.

3. † It is the same Elise who seiz[7]ed the inheritance of Powys *ipc . . mort* [8] *ca\v/tem* by force . . . from the power of the English [9] . . . in the sword, [a power] born in fire.
4. [10] [† Who]ever has read out [this stone/cross] inscribed by hand, [11] let him give a blessing on [12] [the soul] of Elise.
5. † It is the same Cyngen [13] [who] . . . with his hand [14] . . . to his kingdom of Powys [15] . . . and which [16] . . . [17] . . . the mountain [18] . . . [19] . . . the monarchy . . . [20] . . . *ail* Maximus of Britain
6. [21] [Cynge]n, Pasgen . . . *maunannan*
7. [22] [†] Brydw, however, son of Gwrtheyrn, [23] was the one whom Germanus blessed [24] and whom Sevira bore to him, the daughter of Maximus, [25] [the ki]ng who killed the king of the Rom[26]ans.
8. † Cynfarch painted this [27] handwriting on the order of his king, [28] Cyngen.
9. † The blessing of the Lord on Cyn[29]gen and his people, on his entire household [30] and on the whole land of Powys [31] until the [day of judgement.]

Interpretation of the inscription as a whole is made difficult by its partially illegible state even in Lhuyd's time. However, one principal purpose was to celebrate the achievement of Cyngen's great-grandfather, Elise ap Gwylog, in restoring the kingdom of Powys by war against the English. Elise is not mentioned in the annals, but he should have belonged to the eighth century and his achievement is relevant to the issue of relations between the Welsh and the Mercians at that period. The dating of the restoration of Powys depends exclusively on the number of generations between Cyngen, who had the Pillar set up, and who may be identified with the king of Powys who died in 854, and his great-grandfather, Elise, who recovered Powys from the English; the year 757, in which Æthelbald, king of Mercia, was murdered and his successor, Beornred, driven from the kingship by Offa, may have been a favourable moment for the recovery of Powys.[26] This aspect of the inscription will, therefore, be considered in this chapter, leaving until later its significance for the time at which it was erected, namely in the ninth century.[27]

The crucial section now is the third (line numbers are again given in square brackets): [6] . . . '† It is the same Elise who seiz[7]ed (?) the inheritance of the men of Powys *ipc . . mort* [8] *ca\v/tem* by force[28] from the power of the English [9] in the sword, a power born in fire (*parta in igne*).' The word *parta*, of whose significance I am not sure, ought to be the past participle of *pario* 'beget, obtain'; it appears to agree with the word translated 'power', namely *potestate*. Unless, therefore, there is serious grammatical confusion, the phrase *parta in igne* refers to the nature of the

[26] Continuation of Bede, *s.a.* 757, ed. Colgrave and Mynors, 574.

[27] See below, 447–51.

[28] *VIM* has also been read as *VIIII* and understood, as in *ECMW*, no. 182, as 'throughout nine [years (?)]'.

previous English power over Powys, not to the manner in which Elise recovered his inheritance. Also, since the text did not contain a possessive pronoun *suam* after *hereditatem*, Powys is more likely to be a plural or collective noun (from Latin *pagenses*), rather than a singular noun standing for the kingdom (with *suam* it would have meant 'his inheritance, Powys', much as, in line 14, *regnum suum Pouos* is 'his kingdom of [the men of] Powys', namely Cyngen's kingdom).

In spite of the complications it may be possible to decide whether, within this section, there is a statement that 'Elise seized the inheritance of the men of Powys by force from the power of the English'. On the whole, this seems to be very probable, provided that we take *Pouos* to refer to the men of Powys: Elise is undoubtedly being praised, and if he merely 'seized the inheritance of the men of Powys' that would hardly be a laudable act unless it was 'from the English' or some other invader. Hence there is a strong argument for taking 'from the power of the English' with 'seized the inheritance of the men of Powys', even though 'from the power of the English' is at the end of the next line. It may be added that the word translated 'of the English' is *Anglorum*, not the usual Welsh term for their neighbours, namely 'Saxons'. This makes even more likely what was in any case extremely probable, namely that the Anglian Mercians were the people concerned.[29]

However, another problem is whether it is correct to translate what Elise did as 'seized'. The verb in question comes at the end of line 6 and runs over to the beginning of line 7. What Lhuyd has is (showing the line break by /): *necr/xit*. This is clearly a verb in the perfect tense and the third person, but what comes before it, *necr*, makes no clear sense. One solution, which has generally been adopted, is to omit the *r* and to take the resulting *necxit* as the verb *necto*, which has forms giving, for example, the *nex* of English 'annex'.[30] One should distinguish here between what is fairly secure, namely that it is a verb and that Elise is the subject, what is probable, given the context, namely that it meant something such as 'seized' or 'recovered', and what is uncertain, namely which Latin verb was intended.[31]

The implication, if this interpretation is correct, is that the English, namely the Mercians, had taken direct power over Powys before it was recovered by Elise, and that this recovery of Powys by Elise was remembered as a major, and presumably lasting, achievement approximately a hundred years later. However, another similar episode occurred early in the ninth century. In 822, according to the *Annales Cambriae*, 'The fortress of the Decanti is destroyed by the English, and they took the kingdom of Powys into their power.' It is conceivable that the largely lost middle portion of the inscription may commemorate a recovery from this later episode, a recovery which might have marked the beginning of Cyngen's reign. In

[29] Compare *AC* 894.

[30] As in the transcriptions by Bartrum, *EWGT*, p. 2, Macalister, *CIIC*, no. 1000, *ECMW* 182, and *CIB*, p. 379.

[31] If the letter read as *n* by Lhuyd were an Insular *r*, and if Lhuyd's *xi* were an error for *ea*, the *e* being reversed, as in line 29 (*eius*), the verb might be *recreat* from *recreare*, but, if Lhuyd is right, the inscription kept to majuscule *R*. Moreover, one would expect a past tense when referring to the deeds of Cyngen's great-grandfather, Elise.

that case, Cyngen's achievement would have paralleled that of his great-grandfather and the inscription, though primarily erected to commemorate Elise, might also have celebrated the patron, Cyngen. This is, however, speculative.

No source gives a date for the reign of Elise, so here, too, the best that can be achieved is to suggest a context in which his recovery of Powys from the Mercians might have occurred. The most likely one includes the final years of the reign of Æthelbald. As we shall see when discussing the history of the northern Britons in the eighth century, a rebellion occurred in 750 against the authority over southern Britain exercised by Æthelbald, itself allied with the authority of Óengus, king of the Picts, over northern Britain. In the same year, the West Saxons rebelled in the south and, in the north, the Britons of Alclud won a victory against the Picts. As far as we can tell, Æthelbald did not recover his power over southern Britain before he was killed in 757. The last seven years of Æthelbald's reign were succeeded by the brief reign of Beornred, which lasted less than a year, before Æthelbald's cousin, Offa, took the kingship. We can deduce from the evidence of the Pillar of Eliseg and the annal for 822 in the *Annales Cambriae* that there were at least two periods when the Mercians took direct control over Powys, one probably within the first half of the eighth century, the other in 822, only three years before the Mercians lost their power over south-eastern England.

3. OFFA'S DYKE[32]

> There was in Mercia in fairly recent times a certain vigorous king called Offa, who terrified all the neighbouring kings and provinces around him, and who had a great dyke built between Wales and Mercia from sea to sea.[33]

Asser, the earliest written source for the Dyke, was writing in Wessex for the king of the West Saxons; and he was himself, as he perceived it, from the people on the far side of Offa's Dyke. Elsewhere in his Life of Alfred Asser shows himself to be delighted at the decline of Mercian power over Wales, a power that had extended, as he says Offa's Dyke extended, 'from sea to sea'. Yet modern archaeological survey has shown that Offa's Dyke did not extend from sea to sea. In the north, there was another dyke, perhaps earlier, called Wat's Dyke, which Offa's Dyke partially overlaps; but while Wat's Dyke does reach the sea not far from Holywell, Offa's

[32] C. Fox, *Offa's Dyke* (London, 1955); D. Hill, 'Offa's and Wat's Dykes—Some Exploratory Work on the Frontier between Celt and Saxon', in *Anglo-Saxon Settlement and Landscape*, ed. T. Rowley, BAR 6 (Oxford, 1974), 102–7; id., 'The Interrelation of Offa's and Wat's Dyke', *Antiquity*, 48 (1974), 309–12; id. 'Offa's and Wat's Dykes: Some Aspects of Recent Work, 1972–1976', *Transactions of the Lancashire and Cheshire Antiquarian Society*, 79 (1977), 21–33; id. 'Offa's and Wat's Dyke', in J. Manley, S. Grenter, and F. Gale (eds.), *The Archaeology of Clwyd* (Mold, 1991), 142–56; id., 'Offa's Dyke: Pattern and Purpose', *Antiquaries' Journal*, 80 (2000), 195–206; D. Hill and M. Worthington, *Offa's Dyke: History and Guide* (Stroud, 2003); F. Noble, *Offa's Dyke Reviewed*, ed. M. Gelling, BAR, Brit. Ser. 114 (Oxford, 1983); M. Gelling, *The West Midlands in the Early Middle Ages* (Leicester, 1992), 101–19; W. Davies, *Patterns of Power in Early Wales* (Oxford, 1990), 62–7.

[33] Asser, *Life of King Alfred*, ed. W. H. Stevenson (Oxford, 1904), c. 14, trans. S. Keynes and M. Lapidge, *Alfred the Great*, 71.

Dyke comes to an end about twelve miles to the south-south-east, close to the road from Treuddyn to Llanfynydd.[34] Moreover, although Wat's Dyke is apparently a defensive work against people to the west and probably belongs to the Anglo-Saxon period, there is no reason to think that it formed part of the plan behind Offa's Dyke. If it had formed part of the plan, one would have expected Offa's Dyke to link up with Wat's Dyke.

In the south, also, Offa's Dyke did not reach the Bristol Channel. It appears to have come to an end on Rushock Hill, just to the north of Kington.[35] Between that point and where the boundary between Gwent and Gloucestershire reaches the sea, close to the mouth of the Wye, there were only 'short ditches', sometimes running across valley bottoms; but these were not themselves part of a unified scheme.[36]

What makes the contradiction between the actual extent of the Dyke and how it was described by Asser even more interesting is, first, that Asser did not himself derive from Powys, a kingdom that did indeed face the Dyke along the full stretch of its eastern border, but from the south-west; secondly, that we know that at least once, and probably several times, he crossed the frontier between England and Wales south of the termination of Offa's Dyke;[37] and, thirdly, that later evidence from Gwynedd also regarded *Clawdd Offa*, Offa's Dyke, as a frontier. A section of *Llyfr Iorwerth*, a lawbook from thirteenth-century Gwynedd, discusses the position of aliens, foreigners from outside Wales:[38]

> If the aliens want to depart from their lords before they are proprietors [after which they could not leave], it is right for them to leave half their goods to their lords. And if they come from this island, they are not entitled to stay in any place on this side of Offa's Dyke. And if they come from overseas, they are not entitled to stay here, save until the first wind by which they can go to their own country.

A further oddity of this passage is that, when it was written, Welsh settlement extended well to the east of the Dyke from the Severn Valley northwards as far as the end of the Dyke at Treuddyn. Offa's Dyke, therefore, acquired and retained a significance not fully justified by its original extent: from the days of Asser in the late ninth century to the last century of Welsh independence Offa was regarded as having established the eastern frontier of Wales. Moreover, the very fact that reality did not correspond with Asser's 'from sea to sea' makes it likely that it was an echo of Gildas's description of Hadrian's Wall as 'from sea to sea'.[39]

Frontiers, however, may be of very different kinds. The recent interpretation of Offa's Dyke by Hill and Worthington is that it was a defensive work undertaken to meet the threat from a resurgent Powys. Another kind of frontier might be marked

[34] The furthest north that it has been found by excavation is at SJ 267 577, in the parish of Treuddyn, but the precise termination is uncertain: Hill and Worthington, *Offa's Dyke*, 87.

[35] SO 289 595, Hill and Worthington, *Offa's Dyke*, 131–4.

[36] Hill and Worthington, *Offa's Dyke*, 131–54.

[37] Asser, *Life of King Alfred*, c. 79, assuming that *Wintonia* was Caerwent as argued by Stevenson, 313–14, and by Keynes and Lapidge, 261 n. 175.

[38] D. Jenkins, *The Law of Hywel Dda: Law Texts from Medieval Wales* (Llandysul, 1986), 116.

[39] Gildas, *De Excidio*, 18. 2, quoted by Bede, *HE* i. 12.

by the limit beyond which a Mercian king ceased to be able to take tribute as from his own people. Beyond that limit he might take tribute from other kings and their peoples, but that expression of overlordship would not change the boundary of his kingdom. Here, however, we meet a problem: the Mercian kingdom was composed of a Mercian core and a periphery of subordinate peoples, such as the Hwicce and the Magonsæte. From the point of view of a boundary between England and Wales, these other peoples would be on the English side; and yet they might also have been seen as owing tribute to the king of the Mercians as a subject people to its overlord. The temptation is, therefore, to focus on a distinction between two nations, the Welsh and the English: the Hwicce, the Magonsæte, and the Mercians shared the same language and religious customs. Moreover, other evidence shows that Offa had personal possessions within the territory of the Hwicce, which he is unlikely to have had in Welsh territory.[40]

Once, however, we bring into the discussion the boundary between Britons and English, other complications arise. Up to the eighth century it is likely that there was no straightforward boundary between Britons and English. Not only were there British enclaves in English territory, but there were British peasants subject to English lords. In the seventh century, the frontier between the two peoples was as much internal, within English kingdoms, as external, between English and British kingdoms. At that period, therefore, the link between the difference between peoples and the division between kingdoms was much less clear.

This complication is related to a contrast that may be of great importance for understanding Offa's Dyke: between, on the one hand, Shropshire and, on the other, Herefordshire. It is a remarkable fact that, away from the immediate area of the frontier, there are fewer British place-names surviving in Shropshire than in Staffordshire to the east.[41] This is not true to the south, where Herefordshire has a considerably higher rate of survival for British place-names than Shropshire.[42] Cheshire seems to be intermediate, in that it again has fewer British place-names than Staffordshire, but those that exist may be of greater significance than their Shropshire counterparts in that they are attached to places of administrative importance; however, some Brittonic place-names in Cheshire may be of more recent origin.[43] The intensity of anglicization appears to have been highest in Shropshire and to decline both northwards and, more especially, to the south. This may be expressed in a different way: the lands on the English side of the frontier between Wales and the Greater Mercia (including the Hwicce and the Magonsæte) that were defended by Offa's Dyke were also those in which anglicization was most complete. Just as the Dyke did not extend further south than

[40] S 116 = *Cart. Sax.* 236.

[41] Gelling, *The West Midlands*, 66–71.

[42] For Herefordshire, see the district names in B. Coplestone-Crow, *Herefordshire Place-Names* (2nd edn. Almeley, 2009), 11–26.

[43] Gelling, *The West Midlands*, 62–6; J. McN. Dodgson, *The Place-Names of Cheshire*, English Place-Name Society, 44–8, 54, 74 (5 vols. in 7, Nottingham and Cambridge, 1970–97), v, part 2 (1997), 288–98, 354–70, esp. 368.

Rushock Hill, north of Kington, so the strong anglicization of the lands subject to the Mercian kings was characteristic of Shropshire rather than Herefordshire.

The contrast between Shropshire and the boundary further south can also be discerned in a document probably of the late tenth century concerning relations between Welsh and English components of the *Dunsæte* or *Dunsætan*.[44] It is the Old English record of an agreement made by English and Welsh counsellors (*witan*, *rædboran*) within the territory of the Dunsætan. The text allows one to deduce its context and purpose. Welsh and English territories were separated by a river; also, the land of the Dunsætan bordered on Gwent, which 'at one time' belonged to the Dunsætan (§ 9). This makes it virtually certain that the Dunsætan included the lands on either side of the Wye upriver from Monmouth. The Monnow formed the northern boundary of Gwent, and to the north of the Monnow lay Archenfield (Welsh Ergyng), which is shown by Domesday Book to have had a Welsh population.[45] On the other hand, further upstream Domesday Archenfield did not extend right up to the Wye at Hereford; this makes it likely that the land of the Dunsætan lay on the Wye between Monmouth and Hereford, but not as far as the latter, and Noble may well have been correct in arguing that the English part of the territory corresponded to the deanery of Ross and the Welsh part to the deanery of Archenfield, both in the diocese of Hereford.[46] It may be significant that the Roman town, Ariconium, that gave its name to the territory of Ergyng, lay at Weston-under-Penyard, on the English side of the Wye to the north-east of Ross; the original Ergyng, that is, will have included land to the east of the Wye, and may have roughly corresponded to the territory of the Dunsætan.[47]

The Old English text records the agreement from the English side: it presents itself as belonging on the English side of the river and it uses English social categories. To judge by what is said of Gwent, the Welsh of the area within which the Dunsætan were to be found were tributary to the English. Yet it is relatively even-handed: there is no suggestion that the Welsh are to be treated as inferiors; and, therefore, there is no echo of Ine's laws, where the Britons have wergilds inferior to those of the corresponding English, even though Ine's laws formed part of Alfred's *domboc* and are echoed in the *Norðleoda laga*, associated with Archbishop Wulfstan II of York and likely to have been compiled in the early eleventh century.[48] Officially, therefore, they were still valid in the tenth century.

In the Dunsætan Agreement we have a boundary between English and Welsh communities that lay on the Wye and divided two parts of the one territorial unit. The boundary between English and Welsh had not rendered the territory of the

44 The text is edited and translated by Liebermann, *Gesetze*, i. 374–9; an English translation with facing facsimile of Corpus Christi College, Cambridge, MS 383, is given by F. Noble, *Offa's Dyke Reviewed*, 104–9; Charles-Edwards and Russell (eds.), *Tair Colofn Cyfraith*, 45–8, 52–9, includes my translation; see also Gelling, *The West Midlands*, 111–19; for the textual associations and probable late tenth-century date of the collection of texts of which it forms a part, see Wormald, *The Making of English Law*, 232–3, 381–2.

45 DB i. 179b, 181a.

46 Noble, *Offa's Dyke Reviewed*, 17.

47 Gelling, *West Midlands*, 114–16.

48 Liebermann, *Gesetze*, i. 460; *EHD* i, no. 51.

Dunsætan obsolete. It could be held together by an agreement designed to reduce tensions between the two communities on either side of the Wye. No dyke is mentioned. On the other hand, special measures had to be put into place to cope with the coexistence of two distinct nations within the one local district. For example, only half the wergild was due when a slayer belonged to the other side of the river:[49]

> If a Welshmen should slay an Englishman, he is not obliged to hand over to this side [of the river] except a half-wergild, nor an Englishman any more over there for a Welshman, whether he be born a thegn or a *ceorl*; half the wergild ceases to be due.

The clear assumption behind the text is that there was interaction across the river; and this will presumably have been peaceful and cooperative as well as the kind of wrong-doing that was the concern of the agreement.

A further element in the context of frontiers is dynastic conflict. As we saw in the previous section, a recurrent theme of early English politics was the royal exile leading his own war band on raiding expeditions, both against his own people and against others, in the hope of enforcing his claims to the kingship. This included exile across the Welsh frontier, as in the case of St Guthlac.[50] Offa was notorious for the violent action he took against dynastic rivals;[51] and, yet, even he was unable to enforce his son's succession to the kingship of the Mercians for more than one brief season. Other examples indicate that the borderlands of a kingdom were where rivals could best exploit the weaknesses in a regime.[52] Control of a frontier, not just against the Welsh but also against such rivals, would thus have enhanced the stability of royal power.

The earlier interpretation of the Dyke, by Sir Cyril Fox, differed from the recent one in two ways. First, it regarded the Dyke as following an agreed frontier. It was a defensive work carried out by the Mercians, but at certain points it did not take the most advantageous route from a military point of view. These divergencies included Pen-y-gardden fort, about six miles east of the Pillar of Eliseg, where the Dyke turns north-north-east to pass below the fort on the English side.[53] This argument has not been undermined. Secondly, although Fox took the view that most of the gaps in the Dyke were of more recent origin, he considered that a few were original.[54] Some movement across the Dyke, including perhaps trade, was permitted. It was, however, closely controlled. Hill and Worthington, on the other hand, claim that there are no gaps which can be shown to be original. The gap claimed by Fox at Orseddwyn, Selattyn (SJ 251 339) was excavated, but the results did not vindicate Fox's interpretation.[55]

The context of royal power in the western kingdoms of the English was, at first, of a landscape in which there was not yet a sharp divide between Britons and

49 Dunsætan Agreement, § 5.

50 *Felix's Life of St Guthlac*, ed. Colgrave, cap. 34, and see above 412 n. 8.

51 Alcuin, *Ep.* 122, ed. E. Dümmler, MGH Epp. iv.

52 Cædwalla: *HE* iv. 15.

53 Fox, *Offa's Dyke*, 81–2, 279–81. Pen-y-gardden fort is at SJ 297 448.

54 Ibid. 74–5.

55 Hill and Worthington, *Offa's Dyke*, 76.

English. There were still many pockets of British speakers, illustrated by place-names such as Walton, as well as many Britons mixed with, and often the tenants of, English neighbours.[56] This was especially so in Northumbria: in terms of population, Bernicia, the most successfully aggressive English kingdom of the seventh century, was the least English. Northumbrian kings intermarried with their British and Pictish neighbours; and that indicates that there was no social bar on marriage between English and British noble or peasant families.[57] In the mid-seventh century, also, English Christianity was assisted, though not usually initiated, by British neighbours and subjects.[58]

In the period 670–768 Christianity came to divide Britons from English, no longer as pagan versus Christian, as in the sixth century, but as two Churches that refused communion one with the other on the grounds of heresy.[59] Churches that in the middle of the seventh century are likely to have had close and cooperative relations with their British neighbours now cut off those relations.[60] In the same period, the landscape on the English side of the frontier was systematically anglicized, yielding a situation in which British place-names were rarer in Shropshire than they were in Staffordshire further east and much rarer than in Herefordshire to the south. Quite contrary to England as a whole, and quite contrary also to the Mercian dependencies of the Hwicce and Magonsæte to the south-west, British place-names in central and western Mercia get less common as one goes west towards Wales until one reaches the frontier zone itself.[61]

4. TWO VIEWS OF RELATIONS BETWEEN MERCIA AND WALES

Two stories may be told on the basis of the extant evidence. They are entirely incompatible, but neither is demonstrably wrong. They may be set out briefly so that a judgement can be made as to which is the more likely to be correct.

[56] Gelling, *The West Midlands*, 106–11.

[57] At the royal level this is exemplified by the union of Rhiainfellt with Oswiu: Ecgfrith is also said by the *Historia Brittonum*, c. 57, to have fought his *fratruelis* Bridei son of Bile at Nechtanesmere, and Bridei, who was king of Pictish Fortriu, may have belonged to the dynasty of Alclud by patrilineal descent. Although the link which made Bridei Ecgfrith's *fratruelis* cannot be identified, there is no reason to suspect the evidence of the *Historia Brittonum*: N. Evans, 'Royal Succession and Kingship among the Picts', *Innes Review*, 59 (2008), 29–33.

[58] P. Sims-Williams, *Religion and Literature in Western England, 600–800* (Cambridge, 1990), 54–86; Bede, *HE* iii. 28 (consecration of Chad). In Northumbria, the use of the British name of Lindisfarne in the Irish annals (here very probably derived from Iona annals) is probably symptomatic of contact between Aidan and the Britons *CI* 632. 4.

[59] The initial date, 670, is chosen because it was with the arrival of Theodore in 669, and the installation of Wilfrid in the see of York in 670, that a hard line began to be adopted; 768 derives from an entry in the *Annales Cambriae* recording the adoption of the Roman Easter in Gwynedd.

[60] Sims-Williams, *Religion and Literature*, 114: 'Only the influence of the neighbouring Welsh church is conspicuous by its absence.'

[61] Gelling, *The West Midlands*, 66–9.

The first story denies the existence of any settled Mercian overlordship over Wales in the period 679–796, from the battle of the Trent to the death of Offa, succeeded after a few months by Cenwulf.[62] In order to sustain its view of what happened, the first story draws a sharp contrast between the Welsh as military clients of Mercia in the mid-seventh century and the much more extensive subjection of the ninth. The military clientship of the seventh century was a voluntary arrangement dictated by Northumbrian aggression. Its voluntary character is underlined by changes in leadership: Penda had been a client of Cadwallon; he became the overlord of Cadafael.

In linguistic and cultural terms the frontier became much more sharply defined and much more impervious in the eighth century. At the very same period as the Northumbrian threat was removed, so also was any military necessity for an alliance. The warfare that is attested between Cenred (704–709), Æthelbald (716–757), Offa (757–796), and the Welsh was just conflict between independent kingdoms, not an attempt to restore an overlordship against the threat of rebellion.[63] One episode in that warfare was the recovery by its native dynasty from the English of control over Powys, a recovery recorded on the Pillar of Eliseg, an inscription of the ninth century, but celebrating a recovery by the Welsh of the land of Powys which should itself be dated to the end of the reign of Æthelbald or to the years immediately after his death, when first Beornred and then Offa became king.[64] Offa's Dyke was a defensive structure and did not merely delimit the boundary, as Fox believed; it was designed to keep an habitually hostile power at bay, above all from the central area of the frontier, the very area that was undergoing a thorough anglicization.[65]

This story switches direction, however, in the ninth century. It has to explain why, by *c.* 850, there was a traditional Mercian overlordship over most of Wales.[66] This overlordship it attributes not to the Mercian hegemony as a whole, stretching back to the seventh century, but to the victories of Cenwulf, the last great Mercian king. The last part of his reign saw successive campaigns in Gwynedd (816, 822), Dyfed (818), and in Powys (822).[67] These are not to be compared with his

[62] See F. M. Stenton *apud* C. Fox, *Offa's Dyke*, pp. xx–xxi; P. Wormald, 'The Age of Offa and Alcuin', in J. Campbell (ed.), *The Anglo-Saxons* (Oxford, 1982), 119; W. Davies, *Patterns of Power*, 62–71.

[63] Felix, *Life of Saint Guthlac*, ed. Colgrave, c. 34 (that Guthlac was an exile among the Britons is evidence that the Britons in question were independent of Cenred); *Annales Cambriae*, *s.aa.* 722, 760, 778, 784, 797 = 796.

[64] See above, 414–19.

[65] D. Hill (above n. 32).

[66] Cf. ASC 853 with 830.

[67] This information derives mainly from the B recension of the *Annales Cambriae*, mostly supported by the C recension; these were, however, independent versions and there is no textual reason to think that the extra information they contain was a later addition; the earliest version (A) has been thoroughly abbreviated. The further material in the other versions are to be found in the old and unsatisfactory edition by J. Williams ab Ithel, *Annales Cambriae*, Rolls Series (London, 1860) and in the much better edition by D. N. Dumville, *Annales Cambriae, A.D. 682–954: Texts A–C in Parallel* (Cambridge, 2002).

campaign of 798 to re-establish Mercian control over Kent.[68] That occurred two years after his accession in 796, when Mercian overlordship over the outer zone of its hegemony was in peril. His Welsh campaigns took place at the zenith of his power, and they should therefore be interpreted as new conquests rather than as attempts to hold on to old lordship. On this view, the Mercian hegemony reached its greatest territorial extent in the years immediately before it lost almost all authority south of the Thames.

The other story, however, sees the ninth-century Mercian hegemony in Wales as the lineal descendant of the authority acquired by Penda over southern England. In the first place, there is no mention in the sources, exiguous though they are, of any great rebellion, when the Welsh threw off the overlordship of the Mercians. The Welsh recovery of Powys, apparently after a period of direct English rule, recorded on the Pillar of Eliseg, may be compared with other periods when Mercian kings displaced local English dynasties;[69] and, in any case, it refers solely to Powys. Similar incidents were to occur in the ninth century, when the Mercian overlordship over much of Wales can hardly be denied.[70] On the other side, the famous list of so-called 'Bretwaldas', that notoriously ends with Oswiu of Northumbria, cannot be argued to indicate an end to English overlordship over the Britons after Oswiu's death: that list was probably taken by Bede from a Kentish document of *c.* 670, and Ecgfrith of Northumbria was to enjoy an overlordship over the southern English between 675 and 679 very similar to that held by his father 655–658.[71] Secondly, it appears that Æthelbald claimed an overlordship over southern Britain and not merely the southern English.[72] Bede's description of the territorial scope of his authority first details all the dioceses of the southern English (specified in terms of kingdoms, *prouinciae*), and then adds 'and the other southern provinces up to the boundary of the River Humber'; the latter ought to be British.[73] The Anglo-Saxon

[68] ASC, *s.a.* 798; S. Keynes, 'The Control of Kent in the Ninth Century', *Early Medieval Europe*, 2 (1992), 113.

[69] e.g. Kent from 785 to 796 (Stenton, *Anglo-Saxon England*, 206), East Anglia after 794, when the king was beheaded by command of Offa (ASC).

[70] *Annals of Ulster*, ed. S. Mac Airt and G. Mac Niocaill (Dublin, 1983), *s.a.* 865.4, if this refers to Wales rather than to the northern Britons.

[71] Stephen, *Life of Wilfrid*, c. 20, where Ecgfrith is said (a) to have made Mercia tributary after defeating Wulfhere's attack on Northumbria, and (b) after Wulfhere's death (675) to have 'ruled in peace for some time more widely'; Bede, *HE* ii. 5; as is well known, this list occurs in Bede's text associated with the death of a Kentish king (the only one to appear in the list); it shows a notable sensitivity to Kentish interests (Kent was the only part of Britain not subject to Edwin); and it ignores not just Æthelbald, mentioned later by Bede as having a similar authority (*HE* v. 23), but also Ecgfrith, the principal benefactor of Wearmouth-Jarrow. The nine years assigned to Ecgfrith in *HB* c. 65 may perhaps be explained not as a scribal error but as a statement from a north Welsh perspective, according to which the battle of the Trent put an end to Northumbrian overlordship.

[72] The Ismere charter, Sawyer, *Anglo-Saxon Charters*, no. 89, *EHD* i, no. 67; T. M. Charles-Edwards, 'The Continuation of Bede', in A. P. Smyth (ed.), *Seanchas: Studies . . . in Honour of Francis J. Byrne* (Dublin, 2000), 137–9; F. M. Stenton, 'The Supremacy of the Mercian Kings', *EHR* 33 (1918), 438–44 = Stenton, *Preparatory to Anglo-Saxon England* (Oxford, 1970), 53–8.

[73] Bede, *HE* v. 23: 'Et hae omnes prouinciae [the English dioceses/ kingdoms] ceteraeque australes ad confinium usque Hymbrae fluminis cum suis quaeque regibus Merciorum regi Aedilbaldo subiectae sunt.' The list even includes kingdoms currently without a bishop (Sussex, the Isle of Wight); the only frontier mentioned is to the north, the Humber.

Chronicle has an annal for 743 stating that 'Æthelbald and Cuthred fought against Britons': the Mercian king was assisting his West Saxon client against the Britons of the south-west. It is comparable with an entry to be discussed later recording the help Alfred's father, Æthelwulf, gave to the Mercians to enforce submission on the part of the Welsh.

Offa's warfare in Wales is likely to have had a similar background to his warfare in southern England: Kent threw off his overlordship for a time after defeating Offa in 776; under Cynewulf the West Saxons appear to have remained independent, in spite of defeat at Bensington in 779.[74] Even in the twelfth century, when English overlordship over Wales was very rarely questioned, campaigning was often necessary to support one ruler against another.[75] Offa's Dyke, even if it be admitted to be defensive, did not mark the limit of English settlement: numerous such settlements survived on the western side of the Dyke. On the other hand, the Dyke may be associated with Welsh rebellion and with the desire to protect those lands in Shropshire that had been systematically anglicized under royal authority.

After 768, when paschal differences no longer divided the Welsh and English,[76] but the Welsh still kept their independence of Canterbury, Offa is shown as having influence in Wales at the very least. The papal legates who came to Britain in 786 divided their efforts between the province of Canterbury, where Offa and Cynewulf collaborated to receive them in a special council, and Northumbria, the kingdom of Ælfwold. After attending the council with Offa and Cynewulf, 'when counsel had been taken with the aforesaid kings, bishops and elders of the land, we, considering that that corner of the world extends far and wide, allowed Theophylact, the venerable bishop, to visit the king of the Mercians and the parts of Britain.'[77] Having already conducted the formal business in council, Theophylact went first to Offa and then to 'the parts of Britain'. It may reasonably be inferred that these 'parts of Britain' were other than the English dominions already dealt with in the council and that they were in fact the non-English parts of Britain subject to Offa, namely Wales. They were treated independently from the areas covered by the council because they were not, in practice, part of the province of Canterbury, and perhaps also because they were solely the business of Offa and not of Cynewulf.

Cenwulf's aggression against the Welsh did not begin, as the first story would suggest, in 816, but immediately after his accession. Just as he attacked Kent, deposed the Kentish king Præn, and brought him back in chains into Mercia, so

74 Stenton, *Anglo-Saxon England*, 208.

75 An exception to the norm was the alliance sought by Owain Gwynedd with Louis VII: H. Pryce, 'Owain Gwynedd and Louis VII: The Franco-Welsh Diplomacy of the First Prince of Wales', *Welsh History Review*, 19/1 (1998), 1–28.

76 Assuming that the adhesion of Gwynedd to the Roman Easter, recorded in *Annales Cambriae*, *s.a.* 768, was the final episode: the northern Britons may have conformed much earlier under the influence of Adomnán of Iona, if they were the 'nonnulla [pars] etiam de Brettonibus in Brittania' of Bede, *HE* v. 15. See above, 402–3.

77 *Epistolae Karolini Aevi*, ed. E. Dümmler, MGH, Epp. 4 (1895), 20 (*Alcuini Epistolae*, no. 3), '... permisimus Theophylactum, venerabilem episcopum, regem Merchiorum et Britanniae partes adire'; trans. *EHD* i, no. 191.

also he or his subordinates slew the king of Gwynedd, Caradog.[78] Cenwulf's campaigning later in his reign may thus be seen as an attempt to maintain by violence an hegemony that was under severe threat.[79]

Both stories have their good points. In favour of the first is the strong possibility that the Mercians lost their authority over Wales in the reign of Cenred. Yet the arguments for the second account of events seem more convincing. In particular, the second story allows for periods when Mercian power collapsed in Wales as it did elsewhere in the outer zone; it does not assert that Mercian hegemony was uninterrupted, only that it was the settled ambition of Mercian rulers to dominate Wales and that, for most of the time, they had the power to attain that ambition.

5. THE WEST SAXONS AND THE *WESTWALAS*

In the late seventh century the West Saxons still faced a kingdom of Dumnonia across their western frontier. When he was still abbot of Malmesbury, namely before he was consecrated as bishop of Sherborne in 705, Aldhelm wrote a letter on the instructions of a council to Geraint, king of Dumnonia, and his bishops.[80] It was after an episcopal council, apparently one of those summoned by Theodore, archbishop of the island of Britain; the role of Aldhelm was to persuade the Britons of Dumnonia to abandon the Celtic Easter and tonsure in favour of Roman custom. Bede mentions a 'book', *liber*, written by Aldhelm, approximately for the same purpose, but he adds that Aldhelm succeeded in converting many Britons 'who are subject to the West Saxons'.[81] This *liber* was perhaps distinct from the extant letter, in that the letter did not purport to be directed to Britons subject to the English, but rather to an independent kingdom. Its independence is suggested by an entry in the Anglo-Saxon Chronicle for 710, according to which King Ine and his kinsman, Nun, fought against Geraint, 'king of the *Walas*'.[82]

There are other reasons for thinking that subject Britons existed within the West Saxon kingdom. First, there are the British inscriptions at Wareham in the east of Dorset: what may be the earliest of them already has Insular letterforms and is unlikely to be any earlier than the late seventh century.[83] By this date, eastern Dorset had long been under West Saxon rule. Secondly, Ine, king of the West

[78] *Annales Cambriae*, *s.a.* 798.

[79] For Cenwulf's dispute with Wulfred, archbishop of Canterbury, whose loyalty was crucial, see N. Brooks, *The Early History of the Church of Canterbury* (Leicester, 1984), 175–80; Keynes, 'The Control of Kent', 117–18.

[80] Aldhelm, Letter IV, ed. R. Ehwald, *Aldhelmi Opera Omnia*, MGH AA xv (Berlin, 1919), 481, 484, trans. M. Lapidge and M. Herren, *Aldhelm: The Prose Works* (Ipswich, 1979), 155, 158.

[81] Bede, *HE* v. 18.

[82] ASC DE 710: . . . ⁊ Ine ⁊ Nun his mæg gefuhton wið Gerente Weala cyninge . . .

[83] 1061/DSD–15; C. A. Ralegh Radford and K. H. Jackson, 'Early Christian Inscriptions', in The Royal Commission for Historical Monuments, *An Inventory of Historical Monuments in the County of Dorset*, ii, *South-East*, Part ii (London, 1970), 310–12; *CIB* 201. Against the theory that they were erected by Breton immigrants in the tenth century, E. McClure, 'The Wareham Inscriptions', *English Historical Review*, 22 (1907), 728–30, and D. N. Dumville, *Wessex and England from Alfred to Edgar* (Woodbridge, 1992), 157, see Yorke, *Wessex in the Early Middle Ages*, 69; D. Hinton, 'The Inscribed

Saxons, refers in his laws to different grades of Britons (*Walas, Wilisc*): there are British nobles as well as freemen and slaves within his kingdom.[84] In the years around 700, therefore, some areas, at least, of the kingdom were British; and, moreover, they had remained faithful to the traditional Easter dating followed by the Britons, the Irish, and the Picts even though the West Saxon Church had long followed Roman practice. By the end of the ninth century, however, the British kingdom of Dumnonia had long since been conquered, and King Alfred even had estates on the eastern side of Cornwall.[85] Before he was king, between about 863 and 868, Alfred went hunting in eastern Cornwall, where he prayed at the church of St *Gueriir* (later the church of St Neot).[86] The territorial expansion of Wessex in the eighth and ninth centuries was much more extensive than any expansion on the western borders of Mercia or Northumbria: the major gains of those two kingdoms had come earlier. As we shall see, however, the nature of the West Saxon expansion changed between the eighth and the ninth century.

The *Annales Cambriae* have an entry for 722 which records, first, the death of a king of Alclud, Beli son of Elffin, and then three battles: the battle of *Hehil* among the *Cornuenses*, the battle of Garth Maelog and the battle of *Pencon* among the 'southern Britons', 'and the Britons were victorious in those three battles'. The one annal thus ranges across much of the British world, from Alclud in the north to Cornwall in the south. As it stands, the annal betrays a Welsh standpoint: the term 'southern Britons' is here apparently being used for the southern Welsh. An obit for Beli is also in the Irish annals, here derived very probably from earlier Iona annals, so that we have independent confirmation of the date of his death. The notice of a battle among the Cornishmen is, however, striking at this early date, only twelve years after the Anglo-Saxon Chronicle noted Ine and Nun fighting against Geraint.[87] The form of the name used, *Cornuenses*, is purely Latin, *cornu* 'horn' with the common suffix for peoples, *-enses*. It is likely that Cornwall formed a subdivision within the kingdom of Dumnonia.[88] When the main portion of the kingdom fell to the West Saxons, Cornwall emerged as a new British kingdom. The battle of *Hehil* among the Cornishmen, won by the Britons, not long after Geraint was last attested as king of Dumnonia, may indicate two things: first, that Dumnonia had fallen by 722 and, secondly, that the British victory of 722 secured the survival of a kingdom of Cornwall for another hundred and fifty years. The likeliest date for the fall of the British kingdom of Dumnonia is, therefore, the early eighth century,

Stones in Lady St. Mary Church, Wareham', *Proceedings of the Dorset Natural History and Archaeological Society*, 114 (1992), 260.

[84] Ine's Laws, 23. 3; 24. 2; 32; 33; 54. 2; 74, ed. F. Liebermann, *Die Gesetze der Angelsachsen* (Halle, vol. i, 1903; ii, part i, 1906; ii, part ii, 1912; iii, 1916), i. 100–2, 114, 120.

[85] Stratton in Triggshire, no. 1, and no. 18, the lands in Cornwall attached to Lifton, in map 5, p. 176, of King Alfred's Will, S. D. Keynes and M. Lapidge, *Alfred the Great*, 174–8; *EHD* i, no. 96.

[86] Asser, *Vita Ælfredi*, c. 74.

[87] Cf. H. P. R. Finberg, *Early Charters of Devon and Cornwall*, p. 16, no. 73, in which Ine is said to have granted land near the Tamar, compared with no. 72, in which the grantor of land, also near the Tamar, was Geraint; these charters are discussed by Finberg, *Lucerna*, 100–4.

[88] See above, 22, on the evidence of Aldhelm.

although the first mention in the Anglo-Saxon Chronicle of the men of Devon as part of Wessex does not come until 825.

Records of fighting between the West Saxons and the *Walas*—in these instances referring to Cornishmen—continue intermittently during the rest of the eighth century. In general they are uninformative, because the exceptionally succinct style of the Anglo-Saxon Chronicle at this date did not permit the inclusion of any background. Until his rebellion against Æthelbald in 750, Cuthred was subject to the Mercian king. One symptom of this subjection was that Æthelbald and Cuthred are said to have fought against the Britons in 743. Since it appears in a West Saxon source, this is more likely to refer to Mercian assistance to the West Saxons against the Cornishmen rather than to Cuthred giving aid to Æthelbald against the Welsh. Admittedly, in the mid-ninth century, Æthelwulf of Wessex would aid Burgred against the Welsh, but then the enemy is explicitly named as the *Norþwalas*, the 'North Welsh' being a West Saxon term for the Welsh as opposed to the 'West Welsh', the Cornishmen. Cuthred is also said by the Chronicle to have fought against the 'Welsh' in 753, namely after his rebellion against Æthelbald. In this annal, the circumstances show that the Cornishmen were intended, and yet exactly the same formula is used ('fought against *Walas*'). This makes it more likely that the earlier entry also concerned the Cornishmen.

Cuthred died the next year, 754. His successor, Sigeberht, only lasted for a single year, but the next king, Cynewulf, had a long reign, 755–784. The beginning was marked in the Anglo-Saxon Chronicle by an exceptionally long and vivid narrative, already incorporated into the Chronicle in Alfred's reign, but shown by its style and length to have come from a non-annalistic source. It begins with the way in which Cynewulf removed his predecessor and then rapidly jumps to the end of the reign, 784. There was, however, a real connection between the beginning and the end, since Cynewulf was killed by a brother of Sigeberht, called Cyneheard, who himself made a bid for the kingship. Only a single sentence joins the story of the accession to power in 755 and his violent death in 784: 'and the said Cynewulf often fought against the Britons in major engagements'. This is interesting because none of these major engagements receives a separate notice in the Chronicle, even though the narrator saw Cynewulf's battles against the Britons as the memorable characteristic of the reign, apart from its beginning and end. The impression given is that relations between the Cornishmen and the West Saxons were uniformly hostile during his reign, an impression shared by a charter by which Cynewulf gave lands to Wells *c.* 766, 'for certain harassment of our enemies, the race of the Cornish'.[89]

A detail within the story of his death may, however, give a different impression. His kinsman and enemy, Cyneheard, managed to surprise the king when, with only a small bodyguard at hand, he was enjoying the company of a woman. Both the

[89] S 262, *EHD* i, no. 70. The translation proposed by H. P. R. Finberg, *The Early Charters of Wessex* (Leicester, 1964), no. 394, is 'in expiation of his sins and of his regrettable harassing of the Cornish enemy'. If the original grant were to Sherborne, as proposed by H. Edwards, *The Charters of the Early West Saxon Kingdom*, BAR, Brit. Ser., 198 (1988), 259–61, it would become more likely that the grant was partly to offset losses suffered by Sherborne; this would make Finberg's translation less attractive (it is certainly not necessitated by the Latin).

king and his bodyguard were slain to a man by Cyneheard, 'except for one British hostage—and he was severely wounded'. If the British hostage was given by the Cornishmen, it would suggest a less unremittingly hostile relationship between the two peoples than was indicated earlier. On the other hand, if it was given by a British group within the West Saxon kingdom, such as those 'subject to the West Saxons' *c.* 700 according to Bede, it would be surprising that a community of Britons sufficiently important to be giving a hostage should still survive within the West Saxon kingdom as late as 784.

A Cornish kingdom survived to the late ninth century. Ecgberht, Alfred's grandfather, is recorded as having ravaged Cornwall in 815 'from the east to the west'.[90] This may have been the annal entry that prompted William of Malmesbury to claim that Ecgberht subjugated Cornwall a century before Æthelstan.[91] However, the *Annales Cambriae* record the drowning of *Dungarth, rex Cerniu,* under 875; this entry, which is likely to be contemporary, is of much greater authority than William's claim, made from the distance of the early twelfth century. Admittedly Alfred had been able to visit eastern Cornwall for entirely peaceful purposes in the decade before Dungarth's death; presumably the latter was an under-king subject to the king of the West Saxons. Earlier in the century, the Anglo-Saxon Chronicle itself shows the Cornishmen fighting the men of Devon in 825 and subsequently in alliance with 'a great ship-army' of Vikings in 838, an alliance defeated by the West Saxons at Hingston Down.[92] A final subjection of Cornwall may thus be dated to the middle of the ninth century, a subjection followed a few years later by the loss of its status as a client-kingdom. That Cornwall was becoming more subject to the West Saxons by the late ninth century is supported by a profession of obedience to Canterbury made between 833 and 870 by Kenstec, bishop 'in the Cornish race in the monastery, which in the language of the British is called *Dinuurrin*.'[93] Between 885 and 893 Alfred gave his Welsh bishop, Asser, the church of Exeter 'with all the territory that belonged to it in England and in Cornwall'.[94] A more complete ecclesiastical subjection had to wait, however, until 905, when King Edward the Elder created the see of Crediton for Bishop Eadwulf, and gave him estates 'so that there, every year, he should visit the Cornish people, to stamp out their errors, for previously they resisted the truth as much as they could and did not obey papal decrees'.[95] If this phrase is authentic, this charter is remarkable as showing that the ecclesiastical antipathies created by the paschal

[90] ASC 813 = 815.

[91] William of Malmesbury, *Gesta Regum*, ed. Mynors et al. § 106. 3 (p. 152).

[92] Probably the Hingston Down to the north-east of Callington in the east of Cornwall, SX 37 71 and SX 38 71.

[93] *Canterbury Professions*, ed. M. Richter (London, 1973), p. 24, no. 27. For discussion, see L. Olson, *Early Monasteries in Cornwall* (Woodbridge, 1989), 51–6.

[94] Asser, *Vita Ælfredi*, c. 81.

[95] S 1451a, *CS* 614, is the Latin counterpart of an English text, S 1296, *EHD* i, no. 229. The English version regards the bad behaviour of the Cornishmen as secular rather than ecclesiastical: 'because its people had previously been disobedient, without awe of the West Saxons' (trans. Whitelock, who notes the difference and suggests that the Latin version 'gives a more convincing motive'). It would be possible to regard the English version here as more likely.

dispute in the seventh century still cast a long shadow even as far as the tenth century, long after the adoption of the Roman Easter by Gwynedd in 768.

There are, however, reasons for thinking that old antipathies were becoming less sharp. Dumnonia, which was incorporated in Wessex in the eighth century and became a West Saxon shire, Devon, *Defna scir*, was thoroughly anglicized. Cornwall, which was incorporated little more than a century later, retained its form of British in the western hundred of Penwith until *c.* 1800; and the place-names, apart from one or two areas, such as the far north-east, in the hundred of Stratton, frequently remained British.[96] The contrast between Devon and Cornwall after the English conquest can be seen as being between a subjection when the independent Britons of the south-west were still regarded as heretics, as they were by Aldhelm, and a later subjection when they were not, even though their former sins were remembered. Although William of Malmesbury regarded Æthelstan as taking a strong line against the Cornish, expelling them from Exeter and setting the Tamar as a boundary, this is an improbable story. As we have seen already, Alfred was able to visit eastern Cornwall with impunity before he was king.

6. THE NORTHERN BRITONS AND THEIR NEIGHBOURS

After the battle of Nechtanesmere or Dún Nechtain in May 685 a portion of the northern Britons gained independence from Northumbria. Bede's statement is as follows:[97]

> From this time (*sc.* May 685) the confidence and strength of the kingdom of the Angles began 'to melt away and, having fallen backwards, to go into reverse'. For the Picts recovered the land they had possessed which the Angles took, and the Irish, who are in Britain, and a portion of the Britons (*Brettonum pars nonnulla*) also recovered their freedom.

The Britons in question were presumably those of northern Britain, since, after the battle of the Trent in 679, Ecgfrith no longer exercised overlordship south of the Humber. There are, however, two ways of reading this passage, so far as the 'portion of the Britons' is concerned. It is evident that another portion of the Britons did not recover their freedom in 685. The contrast may be between the Irish in Britain, who all recovered their liberty, and the Britons, only some of whom did so, namely those previously subject to the Northumbrians as opposed to the Britons of Wales and Dumnonia. In that case, Bede would not be implying that some northern Britons remained subject to the Northumbrians after 685: they might have done, but, so far as his words go, all the northern Britons might have escaped Northumbrian overlordship in 685. The other way of reading the passage argues from the premiss that the Britons of whom Bede was speaking were those who were subject to the Northumbrians before the

[96] O. J. Padel, 'Cornwall as a Border Area', *Nomina*, 6 (1982), 18–22.
[97] Bede, *HE* iv. 24.

battle of Nechtanesmere; of these a portion recovered their liberty. In that case, Bede would be implying that some northern Britons now escaped the overlordship of the Northumbrians and some did not. On the whole, the second interpretation seems to be the better, since the Britons of Wales and Dumnonia were not directly involved in the consequences of Nechtanesmere. A possibility is that the kingdoms of Alclud and of the Isle of Man ceased to be tributary, but that any remnants of the kingdoms of Rheged and of the Gododdin did not.

Earlier a contrast was pointed out between the British place-names surviving in Shropshire and Staffordshire and between Shropshire and Herefordshire. Much the same contrast as that between Shropshire and Staffordshire was also noted in the south-west, between Devon and Somerset and Dorset. In the cases of Shropshire and Devon, the county closest to the frontier with Wales and Cornwall had the fewer British place-names. The same contrast did not exist in Herefordshire. Here Lothian, the frontier province of Northumbria against Picts to the north of the Forth and against the Britons to the west, undoubtedly resembles Herefordshire rather than Shropshire.[98] In the previous chapter we saw that there seems to have been more continuity between the British Church and the Northumbrian in Lothian than in Deira east of the Pennines. The border regions of Northumbria were unlike the lands sheltered by Offa's Dyke; and, in the ecclesiastical sphere, the most striking case is Whithorn, where the cult of a British saint was given a strong Roman colouring and was taken up with enthusiasm by the first English bishop, Pehthelm. In Chapter 3 we met the memorial inscription of the *sacerdos* Neitan, found at Peebles in the upper waters of the Tweed, Peebles probably being a British place-name containing a word borrowed from Latin, Modern Welsh *pebyll*.[99]

Although the battle of Nechtanesmere is likely to have been fought far to the north, as a consequence of Ecgfrith's decision to attack Bridei son of Bile, king of Fortriu, whose base was north of the Mounth, it is not surprising that the consequences should benefit Alclud.[100] Bridei's father is said in a verse quoted in a tenth-century Life of Adomnán, abbot of Iona, to have been king of Alclud, and this may well be correct, since the name Bile is very likely to be a version of the British name Beli.[101] Moreover, the *Historia Brittonum* says that Ecgfrith was attacking his *fratruelis*.[102] This was usually a term for a paternal cousin: the *fratrueles* were sons of *fratres*, brothers. However, Isidore of Seville defined it,

[98] Watson, *The History of the Celtic Place-Names of Scotland*, ch. 11, 'British Names', provides ample examples.

[99] Ibid. 383, regarded as uncertain by Jackson, *LHEB* 553, though he uses the etymology, with hesitation, at 613.

[100] A. Woolf, 'Dún Nechtain, Fortriu and the Geography of the Picts', *Scottish Historical Review*, 85 (2006), 182–201, esp. 182–8.

[101] *Betha Adamnáin: The Irish Life of Adamnán*, ed. M. Herbert and P. Ó Riain, Irish Texts Society, liv (London, 1988), line 199. Cf. the poem quoted in *Fragmentary Annals*, ed. J. Radner, 54, which clearly refers to Nechtanesmere, but is misplaced as referring to Aldfrith; Evans, 'Royal Succession and Kingship among the Picts', 26 (with references to earlier discussions).

[102] *HB*, c. 57.

very oddly, as sons of someone's maternal aunt.[103] Precisely how Bridei and Ecgfrith were related is uncertain, but the fact remains that the ruler of Alclud in 685 was probably the nephew of the king of Fortriu, the victor in the battle, a king who, on his father's side, belonged to the dynasty of Alclud. Alclud, therefore, undoubtedly gained its independence because of the weakening of Northumbrian military power, but perhaps also because the nephew gained from the victory of his uncle.

The battle of Nechtanesmere initiated a period in which the Picts were, on the whole, the dominant power in northern Britain. This lasted until 750, when, in the words of the Continuation of Bede, namely eighth-century Northumbrian annals added to some manuscripts of Bede:[104]

> In the year 750 Cuthred king of the West Saxons rose against King Æthelbald and Óengus. Tewdwr and Eanred died. Eadberht added the plain of Kyle together with other districts to his kingdom.

This has to be interpreted together with two entries for the same year, 750, in the Annals of Ulster (the first entry was also in the Annals of Tigernach and thus must go back to the Chronicle of Ireland, apart from the words in round brackets, which were only in the Annals of Ulster and those in italics, which were only in the Clonmacnois group of chronicles):[105]

> 4. The battle (of Catohic) between Picts and Britons, in which Talorgan son of Forgus, brother of Óengus, fell, *and, along with him, a slaughter of other Picts.*
> 11. The ebbing of the power of Óengus.

These entries indicate a complex but important shift of power throughout Britain all occurring in the one year. The persons involved were as follows: Óengus son of Forgus was king of the Picts (he was also known by the Pictish form of his name, Unust or Unuist or Onuist son of Uurgust); Talorgan, killed in battle with the Britons, was his brother; Æthelbald was the king of the Mercians, Cuthred the king of the West Saxons, Tewdwr king of Alclud, and Eadberht king of the Northumbrians. That Cuthred rebelled against both Æthelbald and Óengus can best be explained on the supposition that Óengus and Æthelbald were not simply in alliance but had agreed to divide the overlordship of Britain between them: Æthelbald was overlord of the provinces south of the Humber, Óengus overlord of those to the north of the river, including Northumbria and the northern Britons.[106] The allied kings, Óengus and Æthelbald, were attacked in the one year by the West Saxons in the south and the Britons in the north. The conquest of

[103] *Origines*, 9. 6. 15.

[104] *Bede's Ecclesiastical History*, ed. and tr. B. Colgrave and R. A. B. Mynors (Oxford, 1969), 574.

[105] The translation is from my *Chronicle of Ireland.*

[106] T. M. Charles-Edwards, 'The Continuation of Bede, *s.a.* 750: High-Kings, Kings of Tara and "Bretwaldas"', in A. P. Smyth (ed.), *Senchas: Studies in Early and Medieval Irish Archaeology, History and Literature in Honour of Francis J. Byrne* (Dublin, 1999), 137–45; for a different view, see D. N. Dumville, 'The English in Inter-Ethnic *Imperium* in the Early Middle Ages: A Mid-Eighth-Century Case Study', in his *Anglo-Saxon Essays, 2001–2007* (Aberdeen, 2007), 47–54.

Kyle by Eadberht needs to be set in this context rather than being seen as a further extension of Northumbrian power. If we assume that Kyle had previously belonged to the kingdom of Alclud, it is easy to suppose that, while that kingdom was involved in a major conflict with the Picts, the king of the Northumbrians exploited his opportunity to attack in the rear. The annal, by itself, will not show whether this conquest was lasting, since the context in which it occurred was temporary: the Britons of Alclud won the battle 'of Catohic' against the Picts in the same year.

The main theme of northern political history in the years between Nechtanesmere and 750 was conflict between the Northumbrians and the Picts, interrupted by periods of peace. One of these periods still lasted when Bede was finishing his *Historia Ecclesiastica*: 'at this time,' wrote Bede, 'the Pictish nation has a treaty of peace with the English people'.[107] However, Bede also records the death of a major Northumbrian leader, Berhtred, in battle against the Picts in 698.[108] In 711 the annals of Ulster record, 'A slaughter of the Picts in the Plain of Manu, where Finnguine son of Deile Roith met an untimely death.'[109] The same battle is recorded by Bede, who gives the name of the victor as Berhtfrith, probably a kinsman of Berhtred, and also by the northern annals in some versions of the Anglo-Saxon Chronicle.[110] The latter place the battle 'between the Avon and the Carron', namely in the area of Falkirk, on the south side of the Forth. The 'plain of Manu', *Mag Manann*, of the Annals of Ulster was the former Manaw Gododdin, namely a district which had belonged to the kingdom of the Gododdin, conquered by the Northumbrians about eighty years earlier. It appears to have included both Clackmannan, to the north of the Forth, and Slamannan to the south.[111] The land 'between the Avon and the Carron' belonged to the southern part of Mag Manann, *alias* Manaw Gododdin. There is every reason to suppose, therefore, that this was a secure Northumbrian possession before 685 but was now in dispute. The main conflict now was along the fault line of the Forth estuary, and this might have left Alclud, further south-west, out of danger.

The treaty of peace recorded by Bede in 731 did not last more than a few years. This was the period of the rise to power in Pictland of Unust son of Uurgust (Onuist or, in a Gaelic form, Óengus mac Forggusso), who mounted a major attack on Dál Riata in 736 and followed it up with a crushing victory in 741.[112] War between Unust and Northumbria broke out by 740: Æthelbald, king of the Mercians, invaded Northumbria when the Northumbrians were engaged in an expedition against the Picts.[113] This was presumably part of the alliance between the Picts and the Mercians that enabled them to divide between them the overlordship of Britain. No expedition by Unust against the Britons of Alclud is recorded

[107] *HE* v. 23.

[108] Bede, *HE* v. 24; also AU 698. 2.

[109] AU 711. 3.

[110] Bede, *HE* v. 24, *s.a.* 711; ASC DE 710.

[111] See above, 4–6; Jackson, *Gododdin*, 69–75; Watson, *History of the Celtic Place-Names*, 103–4.

[112] AU 736. 1, 741. 11; Fraser, *From Caledonia to Pictland*, 287–312.

[113] Cont. Bede, 740: Aedilbaldus rex Merciorum per impiam fraudem uastabat partem Nordanhymbrorum; eratque rex eorum Eadberctus occupatus cum suo exercitu contra Pictos.

explicitly, but one such may lie behind the curt report of a battle between Picts and Britons in 744;[114] and it is hardly likely that they escaped the power of their neighbour to the north-east. That they were subject to Unust is made all the more likely by the annal of 750, already noted, by which a Pictish defeat at the hands of the Britons was associated with an entry later in the same annal recording the 'ebbing of the power of Óengus' (Unust).

After 750 and before the death in 761 of Unust, 'tyrant and butcher', as the Continuation of Bede described him, northern annals in Simeon of Durham record another disaster for the Northumbrians, in 756. This, however, was apparently at the hands of the Britons of Alclud. Eadberht, king of the Northumbrians, and Unust, king of the Picts, led an army against Alclud and imposed terms on the Britons on 1 August. The Northumbrian army then returned to home but were largely destroyed in battle. The usual identification of the place-names *Ovania* and *Niwinbirig* in the annals implies that Eadberht's return march took him from Govan, on the Clyde, to Newbrough near Hexham.[115] If we are to understand that the army of Alclud followed the returning Northumbrians as far as Hexhamshire and there achieved a complete victory over their opponents, the tactics echo the famous victory of Oswiu over Penda at the Winwæd a century earlier. That the Britons had come so well out of this joint attack by their neighbours to the north-east and the south-east demonstrates their military effectiveness. It is also striking that in this period, after the ebbing of the power of Unust in 750, the pattern of alliances was quite different from that revealed by the campaign of 740.

After 761 there is less surviving information about northern affairs. The Iona annals come to an end *c.* 740; the *Annales Cambriae* ceased to record the kings of Alclud after 760, although we have a pedigree in the Harleian Genealogies; the Continuation of Bede ends in 766. It may well be the case that, with the decline of Pictish power, and internal struggles in Northumbria, the Britons of Alclud were now for a time relatively secure. The next crisis in their affairs of which we know—no doubt there were many of which we are entirely ignorant—would not come until 870.

The Isle of Man is mentioned in the northern annals in 792, when King Osred, deposed and exiled in 790, returned hoping to claim again the kingship but was defeated and killed.[116] This can be compared with entries recording Northumbrian exiles taking refuge among the Picts.[117] The natural inference is that Man was independent of Northumbrian power, otherwise it would not have offered a refuge for dynastic rivals. It is thus likely still to have been under British rule, as will be confirmed by the evidence for Merfyn Frych's origin in Man.[118]

114 Simeon of Durham, *s.a.* (*EHD* i, no. 3).

115 A. Breeze, 'Simeon of Durham's Annal for 756 and Govan, Scotland', *Nomina*, 22 (1999), 133–7; see also K. Forsyth, 'Evidence of a Lost Pictish Source in the *Historia Regum Anglorum*', in S. Taylor (ed.), *Kings, Clerics and Chronicles in Scotland, 500–1297* (Dublin, 2000), 29–31. A. Woolf, 'Onuist son of Uurguist: *Tyrannus Carnifex* or a David for the Picts?' in D. Hill and M. Worthington (eds.), *Æthelbald and Offa: Two Eighth-Century Kings of Mercia*, BAR, Brit. Ser. 383 (Oxford, 2005), 39, proposes Newborough, about 15 miles north of Lichfield, in the Mercian heartland, and therefore suggests that the Northumbrian army, perhaps augmented by Britons, immediately attacked Mercia.

116 Simeon of Durham, *s.a.* 792 and cf. 790.

117 Ibid. 774, 796.

118 See below, 467–71.

14

Two Ninth-Century Writers

In 829–830, the fourth year of the reign of Merfyn as king of Gwynedd, an anonymous Welsh scholar wrote 'The History of the Britons', *Historia Brittonum.*[1] In 893, a Welsh bishop, Asser, wrote a Life of Alfred, 'king of the Anglo-Saxons'.[2] Both wrote in periods of momentous change for Britain; both, in very different ways, reveal the culture of the Welsh Church in the ninth century; but both wrote a Latin that betrays that they were British-speakers and learnt their Latin from books.[3] The *Historia Brittonum* was written shortly after a new dynasty had taken power in Gwynedd, after the political shape of England had been changed for good, as it turned out, by Ecgberht of Wessex's defeat of Beornred of Mercia, and as the Viking threat in the Irish Sea was becoming more acute. Asser's Life of Alfred celebrated the achievement of the king, first in war against the Vikings and, secondly and more especially, in 'wisdom', namely the cultivation of the mind as a foundation for the better worship of God and for just judgement of men. It was written after a period of peace as a new Viking onslaught on Britain was getting under way.

1. THE *HISTORIA BRITTONUM*

The *Historia Brittonum* survives in numerous manuscripts and in successive versions.[4] The earliest is the Harleian version, named after its oldest manuscript copy, British Library, Harleian MS 3859, which also contains, attached to the *Historia Brittonum*, the earliest copy of *Annales Cambriae* and the Harleian Genealogies.[5]

[1] For the date, see D. N. Dumville, 'Some Aspects of the Chronology of the *Historia Brittonum*', *BBCS* 25 (1972–4), 439–45. *HB*, c. 4 gives a date of AD 831, disagreeing with other data; Dumville explains this as a miscopying of xxix as xxxi.

[2] Asser, *De Rebus Gestis Ælfredi*, ed. W. H. Stevenson, *Asser's Life of King Alfred* (Oxford, 1904; repr. with an article on recent work by D. Whitelock, 1959); trans. S. Keynes and M. Lapidge, *Alfred the Great: Asser's Life of King Alfred and Other Contemporary Sources*, Penguin Classics (Harmondsworth, 1983).

[3] Well shown by R. L. Thomson, 'British Latin and English History: Nennius and Asser', in R. L. Thomson (ed.), *A Medieval Miscellany in honour of John Le Patourel*, Leeds Philosophical and Literary Society, Proceedings 18: 1 (1982), 38–53.

[4] D. N. Dumville, 'The Historical Value of the *Historia Brittonum*', *Arthurian Literature*, 6, ed. R. Barber (Cambridge, 1986), 1–26; id., '*Historia Brittonum*: An Insular History from the Carolingian Age', in A. Scharer and G. Scheibelreiter (eds.), *Historiographie im frühen Mittelalter* (Munich, 1994), 406–34.

[5] *Historia Brittonum*, ed. E. Faral, *La Légende arthurienne*, 3 (Paris, 1929), 4–62 (Chartres, as far as it goes, in parallel with Harleian). Faral's Harleian text is reprinted with a translation in *Nennius, British History, and The Welsh Annals*, ed. and trans. J. Morris (London, 1980).

Since these latter texts date from the reign of Owain ap Hywel Dda, king of Dyfed, 950–988, the combination with the *Historia Brittonum* must be secondary: quite apart from the dates of the texts, the *Historia Brittonum* was written in Gwynedd, but the combination with *Annales Cambriae* and the Harleian Genealogies was created in Dyfed. A text which does not survive as such was produced in Gwynedd in the reign of Anarawd ap Rhodri, 'king of Anglesey, who now rules the kingdom of the land of Gwynedd', in his thirtieth year, which is given as 912.[6] A further version, the Vatican recension, can be attributed to England and the reign of Edmund, 939–946.[7] Another version, the 'Nennian recension', is only preserved in an Irish translation and in additions to a copy of yet another version, the Gildasian recension. A preface to the Nennian recension ascribes the authorship of the text to 'Ninnius, disciple of St Elfoddw', presumably the Elfoddw 'Archbishop of Gwynedd' who died in 809; the problem with accepting it as authentic is that it only appears in a later version.[8] On one theory the Nennian version originated in North Wales so that the Irish translation attests scholarly connections between Gwynedd and Ireland, but, on another, it was made in northern Britain through connections between the kingdom of Scots and Cumbria.[9] By the end of the eleventh century, therefore, the *Historia Brittonum* had attracted readers in England and among Gaelic-speakers as well as in Wales.

Although it was written in Gwynedd in 'the fourth year of King Merfyn', it was a history of the Britons as a whole and a history of an already remote past. It did not celebrate the achievements of the new king. Relations between the Britons and the English were a central theme, but not those between the Welsh and the Mercians; its concern was with the fifth to the seventh century. The latest event mentioned is the battle of *Lin(n) Garan*, namely Nechtanesmere, where, in 685, Ecgfrith of Northumbria perished at the hands of the Picts.[10] As this example shows, the geographical scope of the *Historia Brittonum* extended beyond the lands of the Britons; indeed, it even extended to Ireland, since one section gave a summary account of the earliest history of Ireland and another recounted the mission of St Patrick. It was more a history of the Britons than of Britain, but it was one in which their relationships with other peoples—with the Romans, the English, and the Irish—occupied the centre of the stage. The effect was that it ranged over the British Isles as a whole and gave the Britons a place in the scheme of world history.

[6] Dumville, '"Nennius" and the *Historia Brittonum*', 86; *HB*, ed. Mommsen, p. 146 (MSS D^2, G): . . . ab incarnatione autem eius anni sunt DCCCCXII usque ad XXX annum Anaaurauht regis Moniae, id est Mon, qui regit modo regnum Wenedotiae regionis, id est Gue(r)net: fiunt igitur anni ab exordio mundi usque in annum praesentem VI (milia) CVIII. See also H. Zimmer, *Nennius Vindicatus: Über Enstehung, Geschichte und Quellen der Historia Brittonum* (Berlin, 1893), 44.

[7] *The Historia Brittonum*, iii, *The 'Vatican Recension'*, ed. D. N. Dumville (Cambridge, 1985).

[8] D. N. Dumville, 'Nennius and the *Historia Brittonum*', *Studia Celtica*, 10/11 (1975–6), 78–95; on the other hand, P. J. C. Field, 'Nennius and his History', *Studia Celtica*, 30 (1996), 159–65, defends the authenticity of the preface.

[9] D. N. Dumville, 'The Textual History of "Lebor Bretnach": A Preliminary Study', *Éigse*, 16 (1975–6), 255–73, sees the link as being between North Wales and Ireland; T. O. Clancy, 'Scotland, the "Nennian" recension of the *Historia Brittonum*, and the *Lebor Bretnach*', in S. Taylor (ed.), *Kings, Clerics and Chronicles in Scotland, 500–1297* (Dublin, 2000), 87–107, as being in northern Britain.

[10] *HB*, c. 57.

Box 14.1. The shape and scope of the *Historia Brittonum*

I. Introduction
   1. Ages of the World (cc. 1–5)
   2. Description of Britain (cc. 6–9)

II. The origins of the peoples of Britain and Ireland and the settlement of the two islands
   3. Settlement of Britain and Ireland
      i. 'The Annals of the Romans', *Annales Romanorum*: Britto, ancestor of the Britons (c. 10)
      ii. Synchronism for Britto (c. 11)
      iii. Picts (c. 12)
      iv. Irish
         (a) in Ireland (c. 13)
         (b) in Britain (c. 14)
         (c) Ireland, 'as the most learned of the Irish have informed me', *sic mihi peritissimi Scottorum nuntiauerunt* (c. 15)
   4. Chronology (c. 16)
   5. Frankish Table of Nations (c. 17) (British descent: from Brutus in the first sentence; but Britto in the text). *aliud experimentum inueni de isto Bruto... Hanc peritiam inueni ex traditione ueterum.* Appendix of genealogy (c. 18) tracing descent from Brutus. §§ 4 and 5 represent a conscious digression (the beginning of c. 19, 'and let me now return to the point from which I have digressed' probably refers back to the end of c. 15).

III. Roman Britain. Seven emperors (cc. 19–27)
   6. (1) Julius Caesar (cc. 19–20)
   7. (2) Claudius (c. 21)
      Lucius, king of the Britons (c. 22)
   8. (3) Severus (c. 23)
   9. (4) Karitius/Carutius (c. 24)
   10. (5) Constantinus Constantini magni filius (c. 25)
   11. (6) Maximus (c. 26)
   12. (7) Maximianus (c. 27)
      Roman version: nine emperors: + a second Severus and Constantius
   13. Concluding notes (cc. 28–30)

IV. After Rome, an intertwined narrative: Vortigern and Hengest vs. Germanus and Ambrosius, cc. 31–49
   14. Vortigern and Hengest (c. 31)
   15. Germanus, Benlli, and Cadell Ddyrnllug (cc. 32–5)
   16. The Saxons obtain Kent in exchange for Hengest's daughter; more Saxons come and are settled by the Wall (cc. 36–8)
   17. Germanus and Vortigern's son conceived in incest with his daughter (c. 39)
   18. Vortigern, Ambrosius, and Caer Emrys (cc. 40–2)
   19. Vortimer expels the Saxons from Kent to Thanet (cc. 43–4)
   20. Vortigern's leaders slain by Hengest in a feast (cc. 45–6)

(continued)

Box 14.1. continued

21. Final end of Vortigern, who flees to Gwerthrynion, 'with his wives, . . . as I have discovered in the Book of the Blessed Germanus. Others, however, tell it differently.' Other versions. His sons and the kings of Gwerthrynion and Buellt. 'Enough has been said about Vortigern and his kindred. After that man's death, St Germanus returned to his own country.'

V. St Patrick (cc. 50–5)

22. Patrick and Palladius (c. 50)
23. Patrick sent by Pope Celestine to Ireland to replace Palladius, 'on the advice and through the persuasion of St Germanus', is consecrated bishop and takes the name of Patrick in Gaul (c. 51)
24. Goes to Ireland; chronology (cc. 52–3)
25. Summary of his life in Ireland (c. 54)
26. Ways in which Patrick resembled Moses (c. 55)

VI. Arthur

27. His twelve battles (c. 56)

VII. The genealogies of the English kings, cc. 57–61. 2

28. Bernicia 1, from Ida to the sons of Oswiu, with notes (i) on Ecgfrith and *Gueith Linn Garan* (AD 685) and (ii) on the two wives of Oswiu (c. 57)
29. Kent, East Angles, Mercians, Deirans, with a note on the battle of *Meicen* (cc. 58–61)
30. Bernicia 2, the descendants of Oswiu and the collateral lines (c. 61. 2)

VIII. The regnal list of Bernicia and Northumbria with notes on northern history

31. Ida, the four British poets, and Maelgwn (cc. 61. 3–62)
32. Adda, Æthelric, Theodric, Frithuwald and the Gregorian mission (c. 63. 1),
33. Hussa and the four British kings (Urien, Rhydderch Hen, Gwallog, and Morgan) (c. 63. 2)
34. Æthelfrith in Bernicia and Deira; Bamburgh (c. 63. 3)
35. Edwin and his baptism (c. 63. 4)
36. Oswald and the battle of *Cantscaul*; Oswiu, the plague, the Winwæd and the expedition to *Iudeu* (cc. 64–5); Ecgfrith, Cuthbert and Nechtanesmere (c. 65).
37. Penda and the battle of Cogwy (c. 65)

[IX. Chronology. This is the Harleian MS's chronological introduction to the *Annales Cambriae*, which are inserted here together with the Harleian Genealogies (c. 66).]

X. 38. The 28 cities (c. 66a)

XI. Marvels

39. The thirteen marvels of Britain (cc. 67–74)
40. The four marvels of Anglesey (c. 75)
41. The marvels of Ireland (c. 75)

Although the title was not in the Harleian manuscript, the text was indeed primarily a history of the Britons. Yet it began more as a history of Britain. After a brief account of the six ages of the world, bringing the chronology of the world down to the time of writing, it begins with a description of Britain.[11] We are then given a history of the settlement of the island, first by the Britons and then by the Picts. Since the Irish also settled in Britain, the *Historia Brittonum* adds an account of the settlement of Ireland. At the end of this section it gives a summary:[12]

> The Britons came to Britain in the third age of the world; the Irish, however, settled Ireland in the fourth age.[13] The Irish, who are in the west, and the Picts in the north were fighting in alliance and in an unceasing and combined onslaught against the Britons, because the Britons did not make use of weapons.[14] And after a considerable interval of time the Romans took the monarchy of the entire world.

In this way, the *Historia Brittonum* gets all its characters, apart from the English, on to the stage before Julius Caesar even set foot in Britain; it was to be more a history of the relationships of peoples than a history of individuals, although in the central section (IV in Box 14.1 above) Vortigern, St Germanus, Hengest, and Ambrosius would play a major role. Moreover, the rule of Rome was only an interval in a longer conflict: the attacks of the Irish and the Picts on the unwarlike Britons.

One would have expected the text to move smoothly onwards to the history of Roman Britain, but in fact it gives, as if as an appendix to the previous section, a different account of the origins of the Britons, one derived from the so-called 'Frankish Table of Nations'.[15] Although the closest textual link for the *Historia Brittonum*'s text is with the Italian branch of the tradition, that branch itself is derived from the Frankish version of the text.[16] In the Frankish Table, the *Brittones* are made to descend from *Istio* (*Hessitio*), ancestor also of the Franks, the Alamans, and the *Romani*. As has been noted, this looks very much as if it grouped together the peoples within the Frankish kingdom after Clovis's victories but before its major expansion in the 530s.[17] If so, the *Brittones* were originally those Britons in north-western Armorica, the Bretons; but, for the *Historia*, they were the Britons as a whole.

The history of Roman Britain is, at first sight, startlingly remote from anything that might appear in a modern textbook, but this is for interesting reasons. Even in

[11] The figures for the number of years in each age are a problem: the first is that of the Septuagint and thus Eusebius, but the rest correspond neither to Eusebius nor to Bede's *Hebraica ueritas*.

[12] *HB*, c. 15.

[13] The implication of *HB*, c. 12, is that the Picts arrived in the fifth age, but this is not stated here. Indeed, it is clear from the beginning of c. 13 that the Picts were at that point thought to arrive before the Irish settled Ireland.

[14] Based on Gildas, *De Excidio*, 6. 2; 18. 1; 19. 2.

[15] *HB*, c. 17, with a genealogy of Brutus attached as c. 18. That this was a digression is noted at the beginning of c. 19 (*Et redeam nunc ad id de quo digressus sum*); this looks back to the end of c. 15, before the chronological summary and the Table of Nations. On the other hand, this alternative explanation was already anticipated in the first sentence of c. 10.

[16] W. Goffart, 'The supposedly Frankish Table of Nations: An Edition and Study', in his *Rome's Fall and After* (London, 1989), 133–64, at 144, 149, 162.

[17] Ibid., 154.

Gildas's account of the Romans in Britain, written about three hundred years before the *Historia Brittonum*, the Romans were thought to have been inclined to conquer Britain, impose order, and then go away.[18] At first, the order was imposed on the Britons, subsequently on Irish and Pictish invaders, but the pattern remained the same. In the *Historia Brittonum* the pattern became more explicit and took a different form. First, because of the story of Lucius, king of the Britons, asking for Christian missionaries from the pope and the senate in the second century, it became accepted that British kings had continued to rule under Roman authority. The story arose from a simple confusion in the *Liber Pontificalis*, the series of short biographies of the popes, but it was as authoritative for Bede as it was for the *Historia Brittonum*.[19] Secondly, a new complication was introduced: there were Roman emperors, but there were also British emperors. Claudius may have conquered Britain, even to the point of making the Orkney Islands pay tribute, but in his time 'tribute ceased to be paid to the Romans from Britain, but it was paid to British emperors'.[20] A sequence of seven emperors in Britain (whether deriving from Britain or coming from outside) was attributed to 'the old tradition of our elders', but it is then immediately said that 'the Romans' say that there were nine, adding a second Severus and Constantius.[21] After Constantius we are told that 'the Romans ruled among the Britons for 409 years. The Britons, however, rejected Roman rule and did not give tribute to them nor did they accept their kings.'[22] This would have been an appropriate conclusion to the Roman section, but, as in the previous section there is an appendix, consisting of further details on Maximianus *alias* Maximus and then on the help given by the Romans to the Britons against the Irish and Picts. In this latter section there is a direct echo of Gildas.[23]

The next section is the most ambitious and the one most concerned with individuals, but it also sees the arrival of the last of the nations of Britain, the English. The British king Vortigern and the Saxon exile Hengest are pitched against St Germanus from Gaul and Ambrosius, the boy destined to be a great king, born of a virgin birth in Glamorgan.[24] The story has an intertwined structure: we begin

[18] Gildas, *De Excidio*, 6. 1; 7; 16; 19. 1.

[19] Bede, *HE* i. 4; *HB*, c. 22; Harnack, 'Der Brief des britischen Königs Lucius'.

[20] *HB*, c. 21.

[21] *HB*, c. 27.

[22] *HB*, c. 28. The 409 years is presumably a confusion with AD 409 and derives from Bede, whose 409 = 410, the sack of Rome and the end of Roman rule in Britain (see above, 39).

[23] *HB*, cc. 29–30; in 30, *cum sablonibus super capita sua* echoes *De Excidio*, 17. 1, *opertisque sablone capitibus*.

[24] It has often been supposed that the St Garmon attested in several place-names, such as Llanarmon (all six), was a different saint from St Germanus of Auxerre: Bartrum, *A Welsh Classical Dictionary*, 269–70. This is exceedingly improbable: if one considers the hagiographical persona of Germanus in the Patrician legend, in the *Historia Brittonum*, and on the Pillar of Eliseg, it is evident that they are concerned with the same man, and that he is the saint of Auxerre. To suppose otherwise would be to deprive the British Germanus/Garmon of almost all the significance he possessed in the eyes of the hagiographers. It is true that the failure of lenition to appear in Garmon is a problem: the name should have been Gerfon or Garfon, as noted by Ifor Williams, 'Hen Chwedlau', *THSC 1946–7*, 53. The *a* in place of *e* is easily paralleled in Bede, *HE* v. 9 (and see *LHEB*, p. 281, for Latin parallels). For the *-m-* see H. Lewis, *Yr Elfen Ladin yn yr Iaith Gymraeg* (Cardiff, 1943), 19, who cites *salm* as

with Vortigern (Gwrtheyrn) receiving the exiled Hengest kindly and giving him Thanet, but then we switch to St Germanus confronting a wicked king, Benlli, and also converting Benlli's slave, Cadell. Benlli is destroyed and Cadell is promised that he will be the ancestor of the kings of Powys 'right up to the present day'. Once Cadell has been raised to kingship we return to Vortigern and Hengest: the numbers of the Saxons had multiplied through further immigration and the Britons could no longer feed them; Hengest then planned with his leading men to break the peace treaty with Vortigern. The first step was to induce Vortigern to fall in love with Hengest's daughter so allowing Hengest to demand Kent as a bride-price; the next move was to persuade Vortigern to invite more Saxons and place them in the north, near the Wall, to repel the Irish and the Picts. We then return briefly to Germanus, now in direct conflict with Vortigern. The king had committed incest with his daughter and so fathered a son; this incurred condemnation by all the British clergy and a great synod was summoned. Vortigern persuaded his daughter to accuse Germanus of fathering the child, but, by a miracle, the saint got the infant to declare that Vortigern was his father.[25]

Vortigern then found a new opponent by taking seriously a druidic prophecy. Paying too much attention to druids was a standard characteristic of pagan kings in Irish hagiography;[26] it would be remarkable if Vortigern were being portrayed as a pagan, some three centuries after Lucius, the first Christian king of the Britons, but that other wicked king confronted by Germanus, Benlli, was clearly presented as a pagan. It may well be that the narrative scheme of the Christian saint confronting the pagan king, as in Patrick confronting Lóegaire, was dictating the story of Germanus and Vortigern. Interaction between the hagiographical traditions of Germanus and Patrick is very probable, since, by the late seventh century, Germanus was depicted as playing an important role in Patrick's career.[27] If a narrative scheme was responsible, there is an odd feature in this version, because the person who defeats the druids at their own game—normally a feat performed by the saint—is here Ambrosius. Moreover, Ambrosius is a very strange figure, in that he is Christlike to an extraordinary extent, being born of a virgin, and being led off to be sacrificed so that the king's fortress could be built; and yet he becomes a great king who, as the author of the *Historia Brittonum* knew from Gildas, fought the English. His encounter with Vortigern is also odd. He reveals something the druids do not know (as Daniel revealed to Nebuchadnezzar the meaning of a dream that his *magi* could not interpret): that the king's fortress cannot be built because it was built upon an underground lake, and in the lake there were two tubs and a folded cloth, and in the cloth were two serpents, one white and the other red. The two

another exception to the normal rule. The association of Garmon with Powys, extending south into Rhwng Gwy a Hafren, is the effect of the story of Germanus, Cadell Ddyrnllug, and Vortigern: it is not testimony to another saint.

[25] For the details of this story, see above, 300–1.

[26] As in Muirchú's Life of St Patrick, i. 10, 15–17, ed. L. Bieler, *The Patrician Texts in the Book of Armagh* (Dublin, 1979), 74–6, 84–90, an eighth-century version of which will have been known to the author of the *Historia Brittonum*, although he does not include it in his account of St Patrick.

[27] Muirchú, i. 6–8, ed. and trans. Bieler, 70–3.

serpents began to fight; the white serpent first drove the red one to the edge of the cloth, but then the red one revived and drove the white serpent off the cloth. The druids were then asked by Ambrosius to explain the significance of what they had seen and were quite unable to do so. Thereupon Ambrosius declared that the white serpent stood for the English, the red one for the Britons; that the English would at first prove stronger than the Britons, but that, in the end, the Britons would drive their enemies back across the sea.[28]

The story of Ambrosius and Vortigern is the climax of this section and so of the entire text. After Ambrosius, Vortigern continues on his disastrous way. Whereas his son Vortimer (Gwerthefyr) defeats the Saxons of Kent in four great battles, Vortigern remains their friend 'on account of his wife'; once his son is dead he allows them to resettle, is tricked into a feast at which his nobles are all slain and he is compelled to ransom himself by ceding territory which becomes Essex and Sussex. In this way, Hengest becomes the ruler of almost all of what was known by the West Saxons after they conquered it in 825 as 'the East Kingdom': Kent with Sussex, Essex and also Surrey.[29]

Germanus then intervenes again: he tries and fails to persuade Vortigern to 'turn to the Lord and abstain from illicit sex'; Vortigern flees to Gwerthrynion, the district in Wales named after him, where he is confronted by Germanus and all the clergy of Britain. He flees again to the 'Fortress of Vortigern' in Dyfed; Germanus and the other clergy pursue him there and fast against him for three days and nights *causaliter*, which may mean 'in legal mode', *causa* being the standard term for a legal case: fasting was a legal process in early Irish law and may well have been so also in Welsh law at this early period.[30] On the fourth night, Vortigern, his wives, and his fortress were all destroyed by lightning. 'This is the end of Vortigern, as I found it in the Book of the Blessed Germanus. Others, however, say otherwise.' The *Historia* then gives two more versions of Vortigern's death. And that might have been the end of the section, except that there is again an appendix, on Vortigern's descendants.

St Germanus returned home to Gaul in time to persuade the pope to send St Patrick as a missionary to Ireland in place of the failed first missionary bishop, Palladius. Hence we then get, in the next section, an outline of the story of Patrick, roughly as it is known in the *Vita Tripartita*: the author of the *Historia Brittonum* probably had access to the late eighth-century forerunner of that Life.[31] After Patrick came Arthur, who in twelve battles defeated the English in the generation after Vortigern and Hengest; but the only effect was that the English sought help from Germany and their numbers were constantly increased. 'They also brought

[28] I. Williams, 'Hen Chwedlau', 40. Serpents were as characteristic of British hagiography as demons were of Frankish, for example, *Vita Prima S. Samsonis*, i. 32, 50, 58–60.

[29] ASC 893 (cf. 825, 839).

[30] A notorious example is in the Tripartite Life of St Patrick: *Bethu Phátraic*, ed. K. Mulchrone (Dublin, 1939), 71–5. D. A. Binchy, 'A Pre-Christian Survival in Mediaeval Irish Hagiography' in D. Whitelock et al. (eds.), *Ireland in Early Mediaeval Europe* (Cambridge, 1982), 165–78; F. Kelly, *A Guide to Early Irish Law* (Dublin, 1988), 182–3. For *causa* cf. *cyngaws*, *cynghawsedd*, and *cyngheusaeth*.

[31] D. N. Dumville, 'St Patrick in the *Historia Brittonum*: Three Texts', in D. N. Dumville et al., *Saint Patrick, A.D. 493–1993* (Woodbridge, 1993), 221.

kings over from Germany to rule over them in Britain up to the time when Ida reigned, who was son of Eobba. He was the first king in Bernicia, that is, in *Berneich*.'[32] And so the way is prepared for the last major section of history before a concluding collection of marvels: the genealogies and history of the English kings and their wars, especially those between the kings of Bernicia and Deira, on the one hand, and the Britons on the other. It ends with Penda, king of the Mercians, who defeated Oswald 'by demonic arts. He had not been baptized and never believed in God.'[33] By ending with the last pagan king of a major English kingdom, the *Historia Brittonum* looks forward to a new era, a wholly Christian Britain. It also looks forward to an immediate future in which the boundary between the Britons and the English will remain much more static: but in the longer term, in terms of the prophecy of Ambrosius, the days of the triumph of the white serpent are now almost over and soon, perhaps, the red serpent will begin to revive his strength and push his enemy back towards the North Sea.

The *Historia Brittonum* is, deliberately, a highly compressed text. Of Patrick it states: 'The subject demanded that one should speak at greater length about St Patrick, but nevertheless I wished to keep it short for the sake of brevity.'[34] The succinct nature of the text makes literary debts less evident, yet several are clear, only some of which will be mentioned here. Verbal borrowings from Gildas are few, but well scattered and unmistakable.[35] The *Historia Brittonum* used, as we have seen, the Frankish Table of Nations alongside another version, which it calls the 'Annals of the Romans', a title which recurs in the early eighth-century *Collectio Canonum Hibernensis*.[36] To judge by the material attributed to it, it must have contained an origin-legend of the Britons; one is reminded of the seventh- and eighth-century development of the legend of the Trojan origin of the Franks.[37] A British counterpart would not be surprising. Then he had an early version of what would become the *Lebor Gabála Érenn*, 'The Book of the Settlement of Ireland'.[38] His whole approach to the earliest history of Britain was very much in accord with this Irish tradition of scholarship by which a grand scheme was created into which every royal genealogy, every tale about the gods, the heroes, and the kings of ancient Ireland could be fitted. He also had an early Life of St Patrick, as we have seen, to place alongside his 'Book of the Blessed Germanus'. The latter was combined with a Kentish, and also English, origin-legend, which has been argued to have been composed in Canterbury in the reign of the first English Christian

[32] *HB*, c. 56.

[33] *HB*, c. 65.

[34] *HB*, c. 55.

[35] For example, *HB*, c. 63, *In illo autem tempore aliquando hostes, nunc cives vincebantur*, and Gildas, *De Excidio*, 26. 1, *Ex eo tempore nunc cives, nunc hostes, vincebant.*

[36] *Collectio Canonum Hibernensis*, ed. H. Wasserschleben (2nd edn. Leipzig, 1885), lxiii. 2 *b*; ed. R. Flechner, 62. 2.

[37] R. A. Gerberding, *The Rise of the Carolingians and the* Liber Historiae Francorum (Oxford, 1987), 13–30.

[38] J. Carey, *The Irish National Origin-Legend: Synthetic Pseudohistory*, Quiggin Lecture (Cambridge, 1994), 5–9.

king, Æthelberht.[39] As a framework for the English kings and their wars with the Britons, he had an early version of 'The Anglian Collection of Genealogies and Regnal Lists' dating from 796.[40]

The most intriguing debt, apart perhaps from that to Gildas, was to Bede. Two works by the Northumbrian scholar were potentially important: the *Chronica Maiora* of 725 and the *Historia Ecclesiastica* of 731. Both came to be widely read in the British Isles: the *Chronica Maiora* was one of the texts used for the Chronicle of Ireland; and a fragment of an Irish translation of the *Historia Ecclesiastica* survives.[41] For that reason, it would be surprising if an historian of Britain and the Britons, writing a hundred years after Bede, did not make use of his work. The *Historia Brittonum* does not acknowledge Bede as a source, but then neither did it acknowledge Gildas. A detail of chapter 63, in a passage about the Northumbrian kings, indicates a debt. According to the *Historia Brittonum*, Edwin's daughter, Eanfled, was baptized 'on the twelfth day after Pentecost'. What Bede has in the *Historia Ecclesiastica*, is that Eanfled, daughter of King Edwin, was baptized with twelve others on Pentecost Sunday. There is no information on the baptism of Eanfled in the *Chronica Maiora*, where only Edwin's baptism is noted.[42] The phrase in the *Historia Brittonum* looks like a straightforward slip by someone who had access to Bede's *Historia Ecclesiastica*.

If the author of the *Historia Brittonum* knew Bede's historical works, it complicates judgement on his aims and achievement. Bede, after all, had, as a major theme, a condemnation of the Britons, because 'Among the innumerable sins they committed, which their historian, Gildas, describes in lacrimose language, they added this one as well: that they never preached the word of faith to the people of the Saxons or English, who along with them inhabited Britain.'[43] Bede, like the author of the *Historia Brittonum*, was concerned with the relationships between the peoples of Britain: the Irish had preached the gospel to the English, and so it was only a merited reward when their paschal errors were corrected by the preaching of an Englishman, Ecgberht; the Britons had refused to discharge this elementary duty of Christian charity and so deservedly remained in error, habitually hostile to the English. Even when the English became Christian, the Britons held their Christianity as of no account.[44] The *Historia Brittonum* tackles this accusation head-on. 'If anyone wishes to know who baptized them, Rhun son of Urien baptized them, and for forty days he did not cease from baptizing all the people of the Northumbrians, and by his preaching many believed in Christ.'[45]

[39] N. P. Brooks, 'The English Origin Myth', in his *Anglo-Saxon Myths: State and Church* (London, 2000), 79–89.

[40] His Mercian genealogy in c. 60 ends with Offa's son Ecgfrith, who ruled very briefly after his father's death in 796, and does not, as in English versions of the same collection, contain Cenwulf's genealogy (Mercia IV): see D. N. Dumville, 'The Anglian Collection of Royal Genealogies and Regnal Lists', *Anglo-Saxon England*, 5 (1976), 40–1.

[41] O. J. Bergin, 'A Middle-Irish Fragment of Bede's Ecclesiastical History', *Anecdota from Irish Manuscripts*, 3 (Halle, 1910), 63–76.

[42] Bede, *HE* ii. 9, v. 24; *Chronica Maiora*, ed. Mommsen, *Chron. Min.*, iii. 311 (§ 541).

[43] Bede, *HE* i. 22. [44] Bede, *HE* ii. 20. [45] *HB*, c. 63.

Bede's accusation gained force from his reliance on 'their historian'. The sin of not preaching to the English was only in addition to those already catalogued by Gildas. The *Historia Brittonum* also has an answer here. The central section on Vortigern, Hengest, St Germanus, and Ambrosius has plenty of British sin, but it is largely concentrated in one man, King Vortigern, who was, moreover, the friend of the English.[46] Whereas, for Gildas, the disasters of the Britons were just punishment meted out by God for their assiduous and wide-ranging sinfulness, for the *Historia Brittonum*, it was more the inscrutable workings of divine providence: the barbarians 'occupied Britain not because of their strength, but because it was the will of God. Who will have the power to resist the will of God, even if he has attempted such a thing? But God has done what he wished, and he rules and governs all peoples.'[47] It is not even merely the case that kings sin and churchmen rightly reprove them: to the minor wicked king, Benlli, is opposed the good king in the making, Cadell; to the wicked king Vortigern is opposed the 'great king' Ambrosius. The *Historia Brittonum* is much readier to accept Gildas's accusation that the Britons were unwarlike, but it places this characteristic in the pre-Roman past and it accepts it as a simple lack of any experience in the use of arms, not, as in Gildas, lack of courage.[48]

If one purpose of the *Historia Brittonum* was to offer an *apologia pro gente sua*, there was also much more. The central section is a highly effective compound of an origin-legend from England, a British Life of St Germanus, international folk tale motifs, and prophetic history. The whole text gained authority from its habit of citing variant opinions ('others say otherwise') and the statements of learned scholars ('as the most learned of the Irish have informed me'). The style and diction echoes that of the Latin Bible.[49] Although the language is plain, quite unlike the high style of Gildas, it does not thereby lack authority. Even though its subject might be a people on the western fringes of Europe, its range of allusion and literary manipulation of sources, its geographical scope, and the many centuries it covered, all compressed into a short text, made it highly effective.

It should not be supposed, however, that its version of events was the only one current in ninth-century Wales. As we have seen, the *Historia Brittonum* itself noted the existence of other opinions; and one difference of viewpoint is shown by the later section of the Pillar of Eliseg.[50] We have already met the earlier part of the inscription, which celebrated a recovery of territory, probably in the middle of the eighth century, on the part of Elise ap Gwylog, king of Powys. The inscription then became progressively illegible until the eighteenth line, after which Edward Lhuyd managed to read more and more until the end, which for several lines is

[46] Since Vortigern's iniquities replace those attributed by Bede to the Britons, the reference to Vortigern, c. 39, *super omnia mala adiiciens*, may be an echo of Bede, 'Inter alia inenarrabilium scelerum facta ... et hoc addebant ... ', *HE* i. 22.

[47] *HB*, c. 45.

[48] Compare *HB*, c. 15, *sine armis utebantur Brittones*, with Gildas, *De Excidio*, 5. 2, 18. 1, 19. 2.

[49] *Factus est autem ...*, cc. 31, 36, 45; cf. D. Howlett, *Cambro-Latin Compositions: Their Competence and Craftsmanship* (Dublin, 1998), 69–83.

[50] See above, 416–17.

largely complete. The inscription was put up, it will be remembered, by Elise's great-grandson, Cyngen ap Cadell, very probably the Cyngen, king of Powys, who died in Rome in 854. The inscription, therefore, was contemporary with the *Historia Brittonum.* It presents, in the latter part of its exceptionally long text, some references to the history of Britain in the fifth century which contradict the account in the *Historia Brittonum.* In the latter, the confrontation between St Germanus and Vortigern did not issue in the conversion of the king or, indeed, in anything positive. One of its climaxes was Vortigern's attempt, with his daughter and concubine, to accuse the saint of fathering the child born of incest. Neither the daughter nor her son was named in chapter 39, although we are later told that the son's name was Faustus (that is, the Faustus who was later abbot of Lérins and bishop of Riez).[51] The seventh section of the inscription, however, was read by Lhuyd as:

> ... britu a.t.m filius guarthi/ ... que*m* bened ... germanus que*m*/ . . peperit ei se.ira filia maximi/ . . gis qui occidit regem romano/rum

This, with some fairly secure completions of illegible letters, may be translated:

> [†] Brydw, however, son of Gwrtheyrn (Vortigern), was the one whom Germanus blessed and whom Sevira bore to him, the daughter of Maximus, the king who killed the king of the Romans.

The Brydw of the inscription appears to be the counterpart to the Faustus of the *Historia Brittonum.* Even though the latter's Faustus was the child of incest, St Germanus did not impute the sins of the parents to the son. Instead 'he baptized, reared, and taught him'.[52] Since Faustus, according to the *Historia Brittonum*, was the first head of a major church, he was not seen as the ancestor of a dynasty. If one may argue by Irish parallels, this would have made all the difference to the significance, for him as opposed to Vortigern, of his incestuous birth. For a saintly churchman, to be born of incest could be a hagiographical commonplace; for the ancestor of a royal line, it would condemn the descendants to political clientship.[53] In the inscription, however, the child blessed by the saint was not the offspring of incest. Instead, his mother was the daughter of Maximus, the king who killed 'the king of the Romans'. In other words, Sevira (a good Late Latin spelling of Severa) was the daughter of Magnus Maximus, who killed the emperor Gratian. In the *Historia Brittonum*, however, Magnus Maximus is split into two emperors, Maximus and Maximianus; the latter is the one who is said to have killed Gratian.

A further complication is that the Pillar includes the name Pasgen and possibly the name Cyngen in the previous line, and Maximus again in the line before that:

51 *HB*, c. 48, where *Renis*, the Rhine, is a result of confusion with Riez. For the historical Faustus of Riez, see above, 199–202.

52 *HB*, c. 48.

53 Compare *Vita Ailbei*, c. 1, ed. Heist, *Vitae Sanctorum Hiberniae*, p. 118; Ailbe was the child of fornication between two slaves; similarly, the conception of St David through the rape of his mother by Sant, Rhigyfarch's Life of St David, ed. and trans. Sharpe and Davies, § 4.

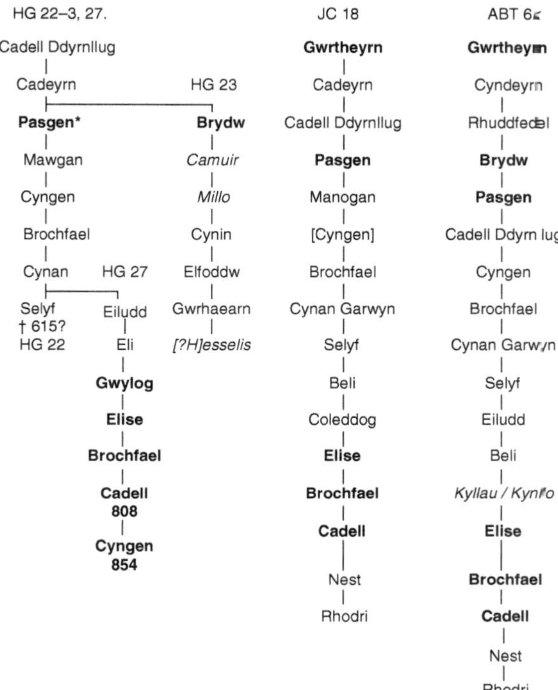

Figure 14.1. Genealogies of Powys compared*

* Names which recur on the Pillar of Eliseg are in bold.

Note *HB* 48: Tres filios habuit [Guorthigirnus], quorum nomina sunt Guorthemir, qui pugnabat contra barbaros, ut supra diximus, secundus Categirn, tertius Pascent, qui regnauit in duabus regionibus Buelt et Guorthegirniaun post mortem patris sui ... Quartus fuit Faustus, qui a filia sua genitus est illi....

[20] ... *ail* Maximus of Britain
6. [21] [Cynge]n, Pasgen ... *maunannan*

It looks as though there has been some linkage, or interference, between the genealogies of Powys, on the one hand, and Gwerthrynion on the other. This may be echoed in much later versions of the genealogy of the kings of Powys.

ABT is a collection of genealogies preserved in early modern copies of a lost late medieval manuscript.[54] It appears, however, to be derived ultimately from a collection put together in the first half of the thirteenth century, perhaps by Einion ap Gwalchmai ap Meilyr Brydydd of the well-known poetic family.[55] JC is a collection of roughly the same early thirteenth-century date, but from South

[54] *EWGT*, pp. 75–80.
[55] If ABT and Hen Lwythau in *EWGT* were compiled by the same man; cf. *EIWK* 207.

Wales, preserved in a late fourteenth-century manuscript. JC's version of the Powys pedigree is evidently related, but also usually superior, to the version in ABT. One source of error, which they share, is a tendency to make a brother into a member of the main line: Selyf ap Cynan is brought into the main line by both, but, in this instance, JC does this by omitting Eiludd, while ABT merely inserts Selyf. Here, then ABT is superior. On the other hand, ABT has inserted Brydw into the main line, which JC has not; and, moreover, JC gets the name of Gwrtheyrn's son, Cateyrn, right, whereas ABT does not.

What they both share is the view that Cadell, after whom the early dynasty of Powys was called the Cadelling, was descended from Gwrtheyrn (Vortigern). The much earlier Harleian Genealogies do not share this idea; moreover it is incompatible with the *Historia Brittonum*, in which Vortigern and Cadell were contemporaries and the former was the ancestor of the kings of Buellt and Gwerthrynion, not Powys. The issue, however, is whether the Pillar of Eliseg betrays a quite different view of the origins of the dynasty of Powys, according to which it was descended from Vortigern, not the incestuous Vortigern of the *Historia Brittonum*, but a Vortigern who was legitimately married to the daughter of Maximus.[56] We have seen already that the Pillar and the *Historia Brittonum* are in disagreement about Vortigern's sexual relationships. It may be argued that it would not be surprising if they also disagreed about the origins of the kings of Powys. If this were the view presented on the Pillar, put up by a king of Powys in the first half of the ninth century, it would appear to be the official view of the royal dynasty at that period. One would then be tempted to argue that the appearance of Gwrtheyrn (Vortigern) as an ancestor of the kings of Powys in JC and ABT was not mere late confusion, but an understandable attempt to marry together two incompatible views, both going back at least to the ninth century. Kirby, for example, has argued that the ascription of the ninth-century kings of Powys to the Cadelling was a fabrication created in Gwynedd (and thus found in the *Historia Brittonum*), whereas the Cadelling had been displaced in the mid-eighth century by Elise ap Gwylog, the hero of the Pillar, the first of the descendants of Vortigern to rule Powys.[57]

The role given to the Emperor Magnus Maximus in other Welsh genealogies offers some support to this idea. He seems to have been important as an emperor (or king) whose power took its origin from Britain: to be descended from him was to be linked with a Roman past but one with a British aspect.[58] For example, he appears in the Harleian Genealogies as an ancestor of the kings of Dyfed.[59] There he is the father of *Dimet*, namely Dyfed, the eponymous ancestor. He is also an ancestor for what appears to be the dynasty of the Isle of Man; there it is added, almost exactly as the Pillar of Eliseg puts it, that he 'killed Gratian, the king of the

56 D. N. Dumville, 'Sub-Roman Britain: History and Legend', *History*, 62 (1977), 185–7.

57 D. P. Kirby, 'British Dynastic History in the Pre-Viking Period', *BBCS* 27, 106–9.

58 Compare *EWGT* 44, JC 4: Maxen wledic brenhin y Brytanyeit, a gwedy hynny yn amherawdyr yn Rufein.

59 *EWGT* 10, HG 2 (reading *Maxim guletic* as in HG 4).

Romans'.[60] In this collection it may even be significant that Maximus is only given as an ancestor of dynasties connected with the Merfynion.

We cannot, however, push this argument for disagreement between the *Historia Brittonum* and the Pillar of Eliseg much further. First, the poor state of the text in the middle of the inscription makes interpretation uncertain. There is a pedigree at the beginning, but we cannot have any confidence that this pedigree was pursued backwards, as a straightforward patriline, to Vortigern, adding his father-in-law Maximus at the end.[61] There might, for example, be a female link indicating 'mutual-inter-lineaging', *ymgyfathrachu*, between the Cadelling and the descendants of Vortigern. Furthermore, it would be odd if the royal dynasty of Gwerthrynion had taken over the heartland of Powys, displacing the Cadelling, and had then handed over Powys to a remote collateral line descended from a different son of Vortigern.[62] If St Germanus's blessing of Brydw on the Pillar had the function which his blessing of Cadell had in the *Historia Brittonum*, Brydw must have been claimed as the ancestor of the kings of Powys. Yet, this too is very uncertain: only ABT had him in the main line, and the textual history indicates that the agreement of HG and JC on this point against ABT is decisive. Moreover, the tendency, as we have seen, was to incorporate collaterals into the main line; one would thus expect the Harleian Genealogies to have the better version when it allows Brydw to be a brother of Pasgen. He would not then be the ancestor of the later kings, and any blessing of Brydw would hardly validate their power. Instead the blessing might have the function which St Germanus's rearing of Faustus has in the *Historia Brittonum*.

Finally, there is a problem about the standpoint of the *Historia Brittonum*. Its story about Germanus blessing Cadell, ancestor of the kings of Powys, is likely to be part of the material derived from the *Liber Beati Germani*. The tendency is for Welsh saints' Lives to be written in, or on behalf of, their principal churches. One of the main churches associated with St Germanus, Llanarmon-yn-Iâl, was quite close to the site of the Pillar. One would expect such hagiography to respect the official pedigree of a dynasty with which it was on good terms and whose support it needed. The story in the *Historia Brittonum* can reasonably be interpreted in such a light: St Germanus was playing the role of the prophet Samuel, deposing a wicked king and raising up the humble servant to be king, as Samuel was the voice of God in deposing Saul and raising the shepherd boy David. To interpret the claim that Cadell was a slave as a Gwynedd attack on the dynasty of Powys, which, perhaps, it already proposed to supplant, is to ignore an Old Testament parallel that would have sprung immediately to the mind of many early medieval clerics. We can indeed use the Pillar of Eliseg to show that beliefs were current in ninth-century Wales about the post-Roman history of Britain other than those advanced in the

60 Ibid. HG 4.

61 As assumed by Kirby, 'British Dynastic History', 101.

62 Kirby, ibid. 107, shows the two lineages, one descended from Brydw (*Britu*) son of Vortigern and the other from his brother, Pasgen (*Pascent*).

Historia Brittonum; but we cannot use it to uncover some supposed political propaganda on behalf of Merfyn, the new king of Gwynedd.

2. ASSER'S LIFE OF ALFRED

Asser, who wrote the Life of King Alfred in 893, was probably a native of Dyfed.[63] He himself says that he was 'brought up, educated and tonsured, and eventually ordained' at St Davids;[64] and, in the same chapter, he describes a kinsman, Nobis, as archbishop and includes him among those bishops of St Davids who were expelled by Hyfaidd, king of Dyfed. Later, probably in the 890s, Asser was appointed bishop of Sherborne by King Alfred, but he may already have been a bishop before he first came to Alfred's court as a mature scholar in 885.[65] He outlived the king, dying in 908 or 909.[66] It is reasonable, therefore, to place his birth in the second quarter of the ninth century.

According to William of Malmesbury, Asser helped Alfred with his translation of Boethius's *Consolation of Philosophy*, and also, according to the king himself, he helped with the translation of Gregory the Great's *Pastoral Care*.[67] Yet he is known first and foremost for his Life of Alfred, the first biography of an English king. Only in ninth-century Francia had royal biography become a genre practised alongside, and initially in strong contrast to, the Lives of the Saints.[68] For students of early medieval Wales, the Life of Alfred has a double importance. Although what it says about Wales is exceedingly succinct, it provides crucial information permitting an understanding of important political changes in Wales during the first great Viking onslaught in the second half of the ninth century. But even more important is the evidence it offers for Welsh scholarship at St Davids and elsewhere. One readership intended by Asser for the Life was Welsh: this is suggested not merely by his tendency to give Welsh names to English places but by his evident sensitivity to possible charges that he neglected his duties in Wales and by his open support for Welsh independence from Mercian overlordship, even though Æthelred, ealdorman of the Mercians, was Alfred's son-in-law and ally.[69]

[63] *Asser's Life of King Alfred*, ed. W. H. Stevenson (Oxford, 1904 and reprints), trans. S. Keynes and M. Lapidge, *Alfred the Great: Asser's Life of King Alfred and Other Contemporary Sources*, Penguin Classics (Harmondsworth, 1983), c. 91. This translation will be the one used, in general, in what follows.

[64] *Life*, c. 79.

[65] Keynes and Lapidge, *Alfred the Great*, 213–14 n. 24.

[66] ASC 909; AC 908.

[67] William of Malmesbury, *Gesta Regum Anglorum*, ed. R. A. B. Mynors et al. (OMT; Oxford, 1995), i. 190, § ii. 122. 4, and the *Gesta Pontificum Anglorum*, ed. M. Winterbottom and R. M. Thomson (OMT; Oxford, 2007), Bk. ii. 801, p. 278/9; M. Godden, 'Alfred, Asser and Boethius', in K. O'Brien O'Keeffe and A. Orchard (eds.), *Latin Learning and English Lore: Studies in Anglo-Saxon Literature for Michael Lapidge* (Toronto, 2008), i. 326–48; for British interest in Boethius, see F. Kerlouégan, 'Une citation de la *Philosophiae Consolatio* (III, mètre 9) de Boèce dans la *Vita Pauli* d'Uurmonoc', *Études Celtiques*, 24 (1987), 309–14; P. Sims-Williams, 'A New Brittonic Gloss on Boethius: *ud rocashaas*', *CMCS* 50 (Winter 2005), 77–86.

[68] W. Berschin, *Biographie und Epochenstil im lateinischen Mittelalter*, 3 vols. (Stuttgart, 1986–91), iii. 416–21 (on Asser).

[69] Cf. Keynes and Lapidge, *Alfred the Great*, 41–2, 56.

Before we consider Asser as a biographer, two obstacles need to be cleared from the path. The first is the issue of authenticity. It has been claimed, notably by Galbraith in 1964 and in 1995 by Smyth, that the Life was not by Asser but was a later concoction.[70] These claims occasioned vigorous rebuttals and it seems clear that the case for authenticity is overwhelming.[71] I shall not rehearse the arguments. What will become evident when we consider the political history of Wales in Asser's lifetime is that the understanding of events implied by the Life could hardly derive from someone working a century or more later (the period to which Galbraith and Smyth would assign the work). The Welsh dimension of the work, whether we examine the forms of the names used or the fortunes of Welsh kingdoms, is perhaps the strongest argument for its authenticity.

The second problem is posed by the possibility that the distinctive features of the Life stem from Asser's Frankish colleagues in Alfred's household. As we shall see, the plan of the Life is an adaptation of the one employed by Einhard in his Life of Charlemagne, written between 817 and 833. Moreover, a very strong case has been made for Asser's indebtedness to Sedulius Scottus's *Liber de rectoribus Christianis*, the work of an Irish scholar settled in Francia.[72] This was a 'mirror for princes', written in 869–870, and it has been argued that the prince in question was Charles the Bald.[73] King Alfred's scholars included at least two from the Frankish kingdoms, Grimbald and John the Old Saxon.[74] Hence it is reasonable to suppose that Asser's Life reflects the intellectual cross-fertilization possible in Alfred's household rather than the culture of St Davids.

Up to a point, this argument is entirely sound. What is unacceptable, however, is an assumed premiss, lying half-hidden in the background, namely that only by coming to England could a Welsh scholar hope to come into contact with books and ideas from Francia. It is this hidden premiss alone that could suggest that the major Frankish elements in the Life must signify Asser's huge intellectual debt to his contacts in Alfred's household. What is wrong with this assumption is, first, that it neglects the traffic of scholars and books between Francia and Ireland which had been going on for centuries and was especially busy in the ninth century. In this interchange, St Davids was favourably placed. Gwynedd earlier in the ninth century had links with Francia through the Irish scholars who travelled between their

[70] V. H. Galbraith, *An Introduction to the Study of History* (London, 1964), 85–128; A. P. Smyth, *King Alfred the Great* (Oxford, 1995).

[71] C. Plummer, *The Life and Times of Alfred the Great*, 14–53; D. Whitelock, *The Genuine Asser* (Reading, 1968); S. Keynes, 'On the Authenticity of Asser's *Life of King Alfred*', *Journal of Ecclesiastical History*, 47 (1996), 529–51; D. N. Dumville, *CMCS* 31 (Summer 1996), 90–3; D. R. Howlett, *English Historical Review*, 112 (1997), 942–4; J. L. Nelson, 'Review Article: Waiting for Alfred', *Early Medieval Europe*, 7/1 (1998), 115–24.

[72] Sedulius Scottus, *Liber de Rectoribus Christianis*, ed. S. Hellmann, Quellen und Untersuchungen zur lateinischen Philologie des Mittelalters 1 (Munich, 1906), 19–91; A. Scharer, 'The Writing of History at King Alfred's Court', *Early Medieval Europe*, 5 (1996), 177–206, at 191–204.

[73] Sedulius Scottus, *Collectaneum Miscellaneum*, ed. D. Simpson, CC Cont. Med. 67 (Turnhout, 1988), xxiv n. 41; N. Staubach, *Rex Christianus: Hofkultur und Herrschaftspropaganda im Reich Karls des Kahlen. II: Die Grundlagen der 'religion royale'*, Pictura et poesis 2 (Cologne, 1993), 105–12.

[74] *Life*, c. 78.

homeland and the Continent.[75] This scholarly traffic continued into and beyond Asser's lifetime. Similarly, ties between Wales and Brittany had not been ruptured in the ninth century, when Brittany came under much stronger Carolingian influence. The presence of a Breton scholar in a Welsh church is attested, as Helen McKee has argued, in the Juvencus manuscript now in Cambridge.[76] The contacts available to Asser when he went to Alfred's court fitted into a long-term pattern of intellectual interchange between the British Isles and Francia. As we saw earlier, the *Historia Brittonum* of 829 or 830 appears to have derived its text of the so-called Frankish Table of Nations from Francia via Italy. In a later chapter a Welsh manuscript containing Book I of Ovid's *Ars Amatoria* will be considered for the light it throws on Welsh learning and book production. This was written in the second half of the ninth century or the beginning of the tenth in what has been described as 'Welsh reformed minuscule';[77] it may well, therefore, have been written during the lifetime of Asser. The text contained in this manuscript and other early copies is thought to derive from an exemplar written on the Continent, probably in Francia, about 800.[78] The Welsh manuscript has numerous glosses, mainly in Latin but also in Old Welsh. These glosses have been copied from an earlier manuscript. The Welsh transmission, therefore, goes back at least one stage before the existing copy. A text whose dissemination was part of the Carolingian Renaissance, found its way to Wales during the ninth century and was copied more than once. Of course, it might have travelled via England, but there is no good reason to prefer that route over any other.

Asser, therefore, when he met the other scholars who worked for Alfred, may have come, in his own words, from 'the furthest western parts of Wales',[79] but that does not mean that he emerged from intellectual backwoods to be transformed in his outlook by a far more cosmopolitan group of scholars. It is, in general, impossible to tell which books he read at St Davids and which he read in England;[80] but his culture was essentially formed by the time he met Alfred: the king was not anxious to import scholars from outside his kingdom for their intellectual benefit but for that of Wessex.[81]

[75] N. K. Chadwick, 'Early Culture and Learning in North Wales', in N. K. Chadwick (ed.), *Studies in the Early British Church* (Cambridge, 1958), 94–103.

[76] H. McKee, 'Scribes and Glosses from Dark Age Wales: The Cambridge Juvencus Manuscript', *CMCS* 39 (Summer 2000), 9–10; *The Cambridge Juvencus Manuscript Glossed in Latin, Old Welsh, and Old Irish: Text and Commentary*, ed. H. McKee (Aberystwyth, 2000), 20–3.

[77] D. N. Dumville, *A Palaeographer's Review: The Insular System of Scripts in the Early Middle Ages* (Osaka, 1999), 124–6.

[78] L. D. Reynolds (ed.), *Texts and Transmission: A Survey of the Latin Classics* (Oxford, 1983), 259.

[79] 'de occiduis et ultimis Britanniae finibus', *The Life*, c. 79.

[80] M. Lapidge, 'Asser's Reading', in T. Reuter (ed.), *Alfred the Great: Papers from the Eleventh-Centenary Conference*, Studies in Early Medieval Britain 3 (Aldershot, 2003), 27–47, esp. 28 and 42–3, suggests that his reading was more considerable than previously allowed and that Orosius and the *Proverbia Grecorum* were probably read at St Davids; but for the rest it is impossible to tell; see also Lapidge, *The Anglo-Saxon Library* (Oxford, 2006), 115–20, 237–9.

[81] As the Preface to his translation of Gregory the Great's Pastoral Care makes plain: *EHD* i, no. 226.

By whatever route he came to read Einhard's Life of Charlemagne, it undoubtedly gave him a crucial idea about how a royal biography might be written; it is likely, indeed, to have given him the idea that the Life of a king was a fit subject for a Christian scholar. The Life of Charlemagne is thus a key to understanding the Life of Alfred.[82]

Here again there are potential misunderstandings to be cleared out of the way. Historians who seek to trace the influences of one writer on another are understandably prone to argue in terms of degrees of indebtedness. Thus Scharer, in putting an entirely sound case for Asser's use of Sedulius Scottus's *Liber de Rectoribus Christianis*, writes:[83]

> Although Asser knew and used Einhard's Life of Charlemagne and although his conclusion bears resemblances to that of Einhard, he is more indebted to the model provided by the *speculum principis* [namely, Sedulius Scottus's book].

In terms of the way Asser wished to present Alfred as a very particular kind of king, as the Solomon of the English, this is entirely just. On the other hand, by arguing simply in degrees of indebtedness, it misses one important use of such a model as Einhard's Life of Charlemagne: once one knows that a writer in a particular genre has read and pondered another work in the same genre, the differences between them become much more significant. Intellectual history, after all, is not just a matter of borrowings; what is often very rewarding is to watch a writer setting out to do something different from his model. The combination of indebtedness and independence is especially revealing.[84]

Einhard's Life of Charlemagne is utterly remote from any modern notions of biography.[85] In essence it aims at being a static, and thus monumental character sketch. It does not set out to pursue the chronological sequence of Charlemagne's actions and experiences. Any narrative is limited and subordinate. A Life, for Einhard, was very different from history. While the latter was composed of events in chronological order, the former offered an account of someone's manner of life; and, even though Einhard was concerned with character, he had no intention of pursuing, or even alluding to, any development in Charlemagne's personality. Even Einhard, it is true, was unable or unwilling to dismiss all events from his work, but they were almost entirely relegated to the first half of the Life, a half which Einhard himself regarded as subordinate to the second.

The two principal divisions of the Life are, first, Charlemagne's *res gestae*, his public actions, and, secondly, his *vita*, the sketch of his manner of life, his *mores et studia*, 'habits and concerns'. I shall refer to these two halves as the Deeds and the

[82] Cf. J. Campbell, 'Asser's *Life of Alfred*', in C. Holdsworth and T. P. Wiseman (eds.), *The Inheritance of Historiography, 350–900* (Exeter, 1986), 115–35, who, on pp. 117–20, compares Asser's Life not only with Einhard but also with the Lives of Louis the Pious by Thegan and the Astronomer, and with Notker's Life of Charlemagne.

[83] Scharer, 'The Writing of History at Alfred's Court', 204.

[84] This has long been recognized: see the observation by Jaffé on an argument of Ranke about Einhard's debt to Suetonius, noted by Plummer, *The Life and Times of Alfred the Great*, 10.

[85] S. Hellmann, 'Einhards literarische Stellung', *Historische Vierteljahrschrift*, 27 (1932), 40–110, remains fundamental.

Life, using initial capital letters to indicate that these are sections of the work consciously distinguished by the author himself.[86] He was unusually open about the plan of the work, so that we can be sure both about his intentions for the arrangement of his text and about the way it was understood by his contemporaries. To avoid the difficulty that the Life, in the sense just explained, was itself part of 'The Life of Charlemagne', I shall use the Latin word *Vita*, 'Life', for the whole text, reserving the English 'Life' for the second principal section of the *Vita*. Similarly, I shall also use the Latin titles, *Vita Karoli* and *Vita Ælfredi*. The latter is chosen in preference to the attested title *De Rebus Gestis Ælfredi*, because *res gestae* refer only to one dimension of the *Vita*.

The Deeds consist of the wars waged by Charlemagne together with his diplomacy and his public building works. Yet these wars are described one by one in an order dictated by the dates when they broke out. The war against the Avars was covered quite separately from the war against the Saxons; yet the latter lasted far longer and so was not just under way before the Avar war began, but also was not completed until years after the Avars had been defeated. Although we are told that the Saxon war often flared up again when it was thought to be over, Einhard does not tell us how these successive emergencies interacted with Charlemagne's other commitments. That could be inferred from the annals; but though Einhard used the Frankish Royal Annals, he distanced his text from his source by the device of treating each war as a single separate entity, however many phases it might have had.

Although the wars occupy so large a part in the Deeds, the division between the first half of the work and the Life was not one between military and civil concerns. Nor, indeed, was it a division between public and private. Rather the distinction was between public and domestic, between those things that concerned Francia and her neighbours beyond the royal household and those things that pertained to a domestic sphere that was itself exceedingly un-private. Within the Life, it is true, Einhard makes a further distinction between *domestica vita*, 'the manner of life within the household', and *interior vita*, the personal manner of life of Charlemagne.[87] The first covered his family in a broad sense—concubines as well as wives—and thus included the education of the children; but it also covered his hospitality to foreigners, for they, having been made welcome, became part of the life of the household. The second, the *interior vita*, described Charlemagne himself, beginning with his bodily characteristics and then going outwards to clothing, food, and drink. From his accessibility (attached to the section on food and drink) Einhard went on to describe Charlemagne's mind via the books that were read to him while he ate.[88] His intellectual concerns are presented as a constant habit, not a developing enquiry.

According to one of his statements of literary intention, Einhard was to proceed from the Life to an account of Charlemagne's administration and, finally, to his death.[89] Yet, quite contrary to the interests of modern historians, he passed over the

[86] Einhard, *Vita Karoli*, ed. O. Holder-Egger, MGH SRG in usum scholarum (Hanover, 1911), c. 4; cf. c. 18.

[87] Ibid. c. 18. [88] Ibid. cc. 24–5. [89] Ibid. c. 4.

government of Francia and the Empire with quite remarkable rapidity, confining it to a single paragraph.[90] The account of Charlemagne's death acts more as a frame to the work than as a self-standing section. Hence the main plan proceeds, not chronologically from birth to death, but from public deeds to personal characteristics. This pattern—moving from public to individual—was only slightly relieved when, in the physical description of Charlemagne, Einhard adopted a descriptive sequence working from the body outwards.

Einhard's *Vita Karoli* is a succinct and tightly constructed text. It is also, for its time, astonishingly secular. As we shall see, Asser understood but radically changed the structure and entirely rejected the secularity of his model.

Asser's text is organized around Einhard's distinction between Deeds and Life, but also according to stages in a life cycle: birth; childhood up to marriage; adulthood after marriage but before Alfred began *lectio*; adulthood after *lectio*.[91] *Lectio* we shall discuss later, but briefly it did not mean 'reading' so much as 'study of Latin texts'. This life cycle did two things to Asser's text: it reintroduced a chronological scheme in place of Einhard's static portrayal; but it also implied that there had been a change in the central concerns of the king. Personal development as well as time shaped Asser's *Vita Ælfredi.* What kind of development Asser considered significant emerges from his choice of which stages of life he would consider. They correspond only in part to the scheme of the seven ages of man, already standard by the ninth century. Any scholar of Asser's day knew what they were from Isidore of Seville's *Etymologies*, if not from other sources as well.[92] Asser, however, lumped together the standard 'infancy' and 'childhood' and entirely omitted 'adolescence'. Marriage was not a normal rite of passage in a man's life cycle, although it was for a woman: rites associated with the taking of arms and thus warfare were the norm for a man, leaving those associated with sexuality and domesticity to women.[93] Asser also makes his dividing points shift from the purely chronological (birth, infancy, childhood) to the sexual and domestic (the political aspects of marriage remained in the background), and finally to the intellectual, *lectio*. The standard scheme of the seven ages of man, however, remained straightforwardly chronological throughout, old age succeeding maturity. We shall return later to consider why Asser employed this plan, but first we must consider the general shape of the *Vita*.

Einhard had eschewed chronology as far as possible even for the Deeds of Charlemagne. He had thus made his text more timeless and so more monumental

90 The first paragraph of c. 29.

91 M. Schütt, 'The Literary Form of Asser's "Life of Alfred"', *English Historical Review*, 72 (1957), 209–20, remains interesting but does not, to my mind, pursue the Frankish connections vigorously enough. D. R. Howlett analyses 'Biblical Style' as practised by Asser, *Cambro-Latin Compositions*, 84–94; cf. id. 'Alfredian Arithmetic—Asserian Architectonics', in T. Reuter (ed.), *Alfred the Great: Papers from the Eleventh-Centenary Conference*, Studies in Early Medieval Britain 3 (Aldershot, 2003), 49–61; A. Scharer, *Herrschaft und Repräsentation: Studien zur Hofkultur König Alfreds des Grossen = Mitteilungen des Instituts für Österreichische Geschichtsforschung*, Ergänzungsband 35 (Vienna, 2000), 62–66.

92 Isidore, *Origines*, XI. Ii, 'De aetatibus hominum'.

93 *EIWK* 175–7 (though marriage is important in the Fourth Branch of the Mabinogi, ibid. 178).

than his model, Suetonius's *Lives of the Caesars*. His Frankish emperor was to be an even more dominating figure than the emperors of Ancient Rome. Asser, however, was not concerned with emperors, ancient or contemporary, even though Bede and the Anglo-Saxon Chronicle offered him the opportunity. What mattered to him were the kings of Israel and Judah, pre-eminently Solomon, not Augustus or Trajan or Constantine. This was a deliberate choice: quite apart from earlier English aspirations to *imperium*, there is evidence for ninth-century Welsh interest in Roman emperors in the *Historia Brittonum*. Asser's outlook did not have to be so biblical, even though his education at St Davids probably impelled him in that direction. Biblical kings were not timeless monuments exhibited for the admiration of later generations. The more we are told about them the more they are seen to change: they are men who sin and repent; and God, if not ordinary politics, ensures that their lives are dominated by connections between past actions and actions, or sufferings, in the future. Asser's Alfred was driven by temptation and by suffering, even though he was not a sinner-king like David or Solomon: although there is sexual temptation, there is no Bathsheba in Asser's *Vita Ælfredi*.[94]

Because Asser was not concerned to present a timeless portrayal of Alfred, he could make open use of annals. The Deeds of Alfred are thus mostly a Latin version of the Alfredian Chronicle, written in English at, or by someone with very close connections with, Alfred's court.[95] This was the basis of what we know as the Anglo-Saxon Chronicle. It is revealing of the way in which the Chronicle had already made Alfred into the central figure of a narrative that Asser could make only fairly minor adjustments to when he turned his source into a Latin Deeds of Alfred. These Deeds were, however, divided by Asser into three separate blocks, placed alongside sections of the Life. The resulting scheme is best shown by two tables, the second of which also includes a simplified version of David Howlett's analysis of the text:

Box 14.2. The Structure of Einhard's *Vita Karoli*

A. Prologue: 'The Life and the way he lived and to a considerable degree the Deeds . . . ', *Vitam et conversationem et ex parte non modica res gestas . . .*

B. Frame: the Merovingians and the Carolingians: 1–3. The plan of the work: 4

C. The *res gestae*, 'Deeds'

- (a) external, *foris*:
  - (i) the wars, *bella*:
    - (a) 'the war in Aquitaine', *bellum Aquitanicum*: 5
    - (b) 'the war against the Lombards', *bellum contra Langobardos*: 6

(continued)

[94] Scharer, 'The Writing of History at King Alfred's Court', 186–91. On the significance of Alfred's physical suffering, see further P. Kershaw, 'Illness, Power and Prayer in Asser's *Life of King Alfred*', *Early Medieval Europe*, 10 (2001), 201–24.

[95] This is not to say, as James Campbell does, that the Life as a whole has 'a basically annalistic structure', 'Asser's *Life of Alfred*', 118.

Box 14.2. continued

(c) 'the Saxon war', *bellum Saxonicum*: 7–8
(d) 'the war in Spain and against the Basques', *bellum in Hispania et contra Wascones*: 9
(e) 'he also subdued the Bretons', *domuit et Brittones*: 10
(f) 'he threatened war against the Beneventans', *bellum Beneventanis comminatus est*: 10
(g) 'the Bavarian war', *Baioaricum bellum*: 11
(h) 'the war against the Welatabi (Wilzi)', *bellum contra Welatabos (Wilzos)*: 12
(i) 'the war against the Avars or Huns', *bellum contra Avares sive Hunos*: 13
(j) 'the war against the Northmen', *bellum contra Nordmannos*: 14
c. 15 is a summary of the *bella*.

(ii) 'Kings and peoples rendered friendly by alliance', *reges ac gentes per amicitiam conciliatae*: 16
Hadefonsus, king of Galicia and Asturia
The kings of the Irish
'Aaron, king of the Persians' (Harun al-Rashid, the caliph)
The emperors of Constantinople

(b) '[Deeds] at home: works conducive to the adornment and prosperity of the kingdom', *[res gestae] domi: opera ad regni decorem et commoditatem pertinentia*: 17:
(i) 'among these special works may be considered the basilica of the holy mother of God at Aachen . . . and the bridge on the Rhine at Mainz', *inter quorum praecipua videri possunt basilica sanctae Dei genetricis Aquisgrani . . . et pons apud Moguntiacum in Rheno.*
(ii) the others:
(a) *palatia* at Ingelheim and Nijmegen
(b) fleets and coastal watchpoints built for the *bellum Nordmannicum* and in the Mediterranean against the Moors

D. 'His personal and household manner of life'/'manner of life and way of living'/'habits and concerns', *Interior atque domestica vita/vita et conversatio/mores et studia*:
(i) manner of life in his household *domestica vita*: 18–21
(a) brother: 18
(b) wives, concubines and their children (listed)
(c) mother
(d) sister
(e) children's upbringing: 19
(f) Pope Hadrian (whose death Charlemagne mourned 'as if he had lost a brother or a most dear son', *ac si fratrem aut carissimum filium amisisset*, c. 19): an illustration of his *amicitiae*, 'alliances of friendship', and in particular, of his ability to make such a friend and ally into a virtual member of his immediate family
(g) criticism of his refusal to let his daughters marry
(h) Pippin the Hunchback, the cruelty of Queen Fastrada (to which Charlemagne gave his consent), and conspiracies: 20

(continued)

Box 14.2. continued

(i) hospitality to *peregrini* (this is placed where it is as a counterweight to the criticism of Charlemagne for having consented to the cruelty of Fastrada, and also because it is a household matter and thus belongs to *domestica vita*): 21

(ii) 'personal manner of life', *interior vita*:

(1) physical description (goes outwards from the body to clothing and then to the more social matter of eating and drinking, in which note the reference to music and to reading):

(a) body and bodily exercise: 22

(b) clothing: 23

(c) food and drink: 24

His accessibility (c. 24 last para.) provides a link to:

(2) 'qualities of mind', *animi dotes* (cf. c. 18): 25–7

(a) speech and knowledge of languages: 25

(b) 'the liberal arts', *artes liberales*

(c) 'Christian worship', *religio Christiana*: 26

(d) 'generosity bestowed gratis', *gratuita liberalitas* especially towards St Peter's, Rome: 27

The passage on his love of Rome leads to c. 28, the account of the imperial coronation, and so on to the topic of

E. 'The government of the kingdom', *regni administratio*: c. 29.

(1) Defective attempts to reform the laws

(2) vernacular grammar and names of months and winds

F. 'His end', *finis*: 30–3

Box 14.3. The Structure of the *Vita Ælfredi*: 'Deeds' versus 'Life'

What Asser made of Einhard	Howlett: 2-part structure
A. Birth (849 = 1st year) and lineage: chapters 1–2	i. A, B
B. The first stage of life:	
(1) Deeds = annals from 851 to 866 = 3rd–18th year: chapters 3–21	C–H
(2) Life as a boy (both 'infancy' and 'boyhood'): chapters 21–25	I
C. The second stage of life:	
(1) Deeds = annals 867–884 = 19th–36th year: chapters 26–72	H'–B'
(2) Life after marriage (in 20th year) and before *lectio*: chapters 74–81	B'–A' + ii. A–B5
D. The third stage of life:	
(1) Deeds = annals 886–7 = 38th–39th year: chapters 82–86	B4'
(2) Life after *lectio* in 39th year: chapters 87–106	B3'–A'

There is, however, an odd chronological dislocation between the three blocks of annals, on the one hand, and the three stages of Alfred's Life on the other:

Stages of life	Deeds	Life
Infancy and boyhood	851–866	
After marriage	867–884 (885 is missing)	marriage in 868 = Alfred's 20th year
After *lectio*	886–887	*Lectio* begins in 887 = Alfred's 39th year

Various considerations can be advanced to explain why the blocks of the Life begin one year after the corresponding blocks of Deeds. The last annal in the childhood Deeds records the accession of Alfred's brother, Æthelred, to the kingship of Wessex and the concomitant accession of Alfred himself to the position of heir-apparent; but it also records the coming of the Viking 'Great Army' to England. The second block of Deeds covers the struggles of the English kingdoms against the Great Army until the decisive battle of Edington in 878, but it also stretches beyond that year, going right up to, but not including, the missing annal for 885, in the middle of a peaceful period in Alfred's reign. The best guess is that 885 is likely to be the year in which Asser first met the king, although he did not take up residence with Alfred until 886. At all events, it is hard to avoid the conclusion that the second division of the Deeds has to do with Asser's arrival as a royal adviser. The pattern once established, it allows the third section of Deeds to begin with Asser firmly established at court and to end, one year later, with Alfred achieving *lectio*. Here, at least, the structure works well.

What we may call the Einhardian plan of Asser's *Vita Ælfredi* is not the same as the analysis proposed by David Howlett in his *Cambro-Latin Compositions*. For him, the *Vita* falls into two parts, chapters 1–75.16 and chapters 75.16–106 in Stevenson's edition. Each part has the chiastic structure characteristic of 'Biblical Style' (ABCB'A'). The division between the two parts comes within what I have called, on the Einhardian side of the Table, C (2), namely in the second section of the Life as opposed to the Deeds. Hence the last bit of Howlett's Part I and the first bit of his Part II are both within the section that corresponds to Einhard's *domestica uita*, the manner of life of the household.

The two analyses of the structure do, however, have important points of contact. Thus the crux, the chiastic midpoint, of Howlett's Part I contains the famous story of Alfred, his mother and the book of poetry; and this lies at the heart of the Einhardian B (2). The crux of Part II is the arrival of Asser at Alfred's court, including the brief account of Welsh politics in c. 81; and this is the culmination of the Einhardian C (2). I therefore see these two analyses as different but compatible. To take one further example, Howlett's Part II opens inside the Einhardian *domestica uita*, as we have seen, but it does so at the point when Asser describes the education of Alfred's children. The corresponding passage in Einhard's *Vita Karoli* was not one of any great consequence, but in Asser's *Vita Ælfredi* it was critical.

The crucial position played in the structure of the Life by Asser's own first appearance at Alfred's court is consistent with his open avowal that what concerned him most was the Life rather than the Deeds. In this he followed Einhard but for quite different reasons.[96] What mattered to Asser emerges as soon as we analyse the three blocks devoted to the Life. They cover, respectively, (1) the reasons why Alfred did not learn to read Latin in his youth, but only to love, memorize, recite, and read English poetry; (2) the education of Alfred's children and how Alfred came to assemble a group of scholars; (3) how Alfred himself came to read and to expound Latin texts. The central theme for Asser was Alfred's intellectual development. One might be tempted to dismiss this preoccupation as merely the view of a scholar who found it difficult to enter into concerns outside scholarship, if it were not for three things: first, that Alfred himself was deeply concerned with scholarship; secondly, that Asser's picture of a king's struggle to become a wise ruler can easily be paralleled in what Alfred wrote about kingship; and, finally, that, once we examine the content and uses of wisdom, *sapientia*, as Asser conceived that central idea of the *Vita Ælfredi*, it soon becomes apparent that it extended far beyond a narrow concern for an ability to read and understand Latin texts.

Alfred's prose preface to the translation of Gregory the Great's *Regula Pastoralis* is only the most famous of his expressions of concern for the state of what he called *wīsdōm*, Latin *sapientia*. This was a virtue which embraced a disciplined and well-trained concern for truth as such and also a capacity to relate particular practical issues to general principles. Although the ninth-century term *wīsdōm* looks deceptively close to modern 'wisdom', the associations of the term are far less esoteric. Moreover, the word ties together two things which we tend to separate: the first is being a good man of business, a discerning judge of practical isses and energetic in getting things done; the second is being someone who minds very much about the right answers to problems concerning the ultimate principles on which one should act. Alfred's wise man does not have a narrow wisdom or a narrow curiosity. For accidental reasons, also, there was a special association of wisdom with judgement, since the suffix *-dōm*, as in *wīsdōm*, was derived from the ordinary word for judgement, *dōm* (modern English 'doom' as in Doomsday, 'Day of Judgement'). That the search for wisdom undertaken by Asser's King Alfred should end in a concern that local judges had the intellectual equipment to judge wisely was entirely natural within the conceptual framework of ninth-century Wessex, just as it was natural as soon as King Solomon was taken as a primary model for kings.

In the translation of the Pastoral Care, Alfred's principal concern was for the Church, as befitted a circular letter sent to bishops together with copies of the translation. Gregory the Great's text was about the proper discharge of a bishop's

[96] Einhard's relative valuation of the two main sections of his work is suggested at the very beginning of the Preface: 'Vitam et conversationem et ex parte non modica res gestas domini et nutritoris mei Karoli....' It is made more explicit in c. 6: Italiam intranti quam difficilis Alpium transitus fuerit... hoc loco describerem, nisi vitae illius modum potius quam bellorum quae gessit eventus memoriae mandare praesenti opere animo esset propositum. Cf. Asser, *Life*. c. 73, quoting Einhard's Preface. But in c. 21 he also is more explicit: 'ad id, quod nos maxime ad hoc opus incitavit, nobis redeundum esse censeo, scilicet aliquantulum, quantum meae cognitioni innotuit, de infantilibus et puerilibus domini mei venerabilis Ælfredi, Angulsaxonum rex, moribus hoc in loco breviter inserendum esse existimo.'

duties, and Alfred is here urging English bishops to a greater concern for education. But in the translation of Boethius's *Consolation of Philosophy*, in which his principal helper was said by William of Malmesbury to be Asser, it is made clear that the concept of wisdom was one that applied to kings as much as to bishops.[97] Moreover, even in the Preface to the Pastoral Care, secular concerns were not forgotten. Alfred looked back on the golden age of seventh-century England and remembered 'how they succeeded both in warfare and in wisdom'.[98]

Asser's own concept of wisdom was as broad as it could very well be. At one end was the traditional Irish and British notion of the *sapiens*, the wise man, as the scholar educated in a syllabus of Latin studies culminating in biblical exegesis. In that sense the Northumbrian king Aldfrith was, as Bede described him, 'most wise'; he deserved this description, not because, as Bede also says, 'he nobly restored his kingdom' after the catastrophic defeat of Nechtanesmere in 685, but because he had been the recipient, to a high level, of the traditional Latin education. This concept of wisdom as the proper end of a Latin education underlies Asser's *Vita*, only it is modified to include the study of vernacular as well as Latin texts.[99] Its beginnings are even situated in Alfred's love of an orally performed vernacular poetry. Alfred thus crossed two crucial bridges on his journey to wisdom: from an appreciation of orally performed poetry to a desire to own and to master a book in which such poems were written; and, secondly, from the vernacular to Latin, to the language in which, for western Europeans, were to be found the intellectual riches of Antiquity, both pagan and Christian, and also the works of such earlier English scholars as Bede, for whom the king had a particular reverence. When, therefore, Alfred began, in 887, 'to read and to interpret', it went without saying that he was reading and interpreting Latin texts, such as Gregory the Great's *Pastoral Care* or Boethius's *Consolation of Philosophy*, as well as, most important of all, the Latin Bible.

Yet, because such works were translated into English under Alfred's aegis, though not always by him, the wisdom embodied in Latin could increasingly inform the minds of those who could only read the vernacular. For this reason, too, the last part of Asser's *Vita*, the third block, extends the demands made by the virtue of wisdom from Latin *lectio*, in which Alfred and Asser spent the king's rare leisure moments, all the way to the level of the ealdormen and reeves. The end of the *Vita* was not Alfred's furthest exploration of the resources of Christian Latin, but the demands of wisdom on local judges. We have seen that the Old English notion of *wīsdōm* was naturally associated with judgement, and that such an association led on to another, namely with King Solomon, of whom the Bible said that 'all Israel heard of the judgement

[97] The authorship of the translation, let alone whether Asser played any role in it, is a vexed question: M. Godden, 'Alfred, Asser and Boethius', i. 326–48; *The Old English Boethius: An Edition of the Old English Version of Boethius's* De Consolatione Philosophiae, ed. M. Godden and S. Irvine, 2 vols. (Oxford, 2009), i. 59–61, 140–51.

[98] Keynes and Lapidge, *Alfred the Great*, 124; *EHD* i, no. 226.

[99] D. A. Bullough, 'The Educational Tradition in England from Alfred to Ælfric: Teaching *Utriusque Linguae*', *Settimane di studio sull' alto medioevo*, 19 (1972), 460, notes the lack of precedent for *utraque lingua* (Asser, c. 75).

which the king had judged; and they feared the king; for they saw that the wisdom of God was in him, to do judgement.'[100]

It has been shown that, in their concern for kingly wisdom, Alfred and Asser were following recent Frankish fashion: Charles the Bald (the father-in-law of Æthelwulf, and thus the father of Alfred's stepmother) embraced the biblical ideal of Solomon rather than that of David, which, two generations earlier, had been applied to Charlemagne.[101] Asser's most important immediate source for the Solomonic ideal of kingship appears to have been Sedulius Scottus's *Liber de Rectoribus Christianis*; but Sedulius stood in a tradition of Irish writing on the wisdom of kings.[102] There are also more distant indications that the ideal of the wise king was present in Wales as well as in Ireland. One is the seventh-century inscription at Llangadwaladr in Anglesey, praising Cadfan as 'the wisest of kings'. The superlative, *sapientissimus*, makes it likely that the reference was to the Solomonic ideal of the king as just judge rather than merely to expertise in Latin *lectio*.[103] This interpretation is rendered more probable by the earlier occurrence in Wales of Solomon as a royal name.[104]

It is also worth remembering the role played by Solomon in Gildas's *De Excidio*, especially because Gildas was read by Bede and Alcuin in the eighth century, by the author of the *Historia Brittonum* in the ninth, and by Wulfstan II of York a hundred years after Alfred.[105] Asser's own fondness for the simile of a ship finding its way to its harbour as a marker of major textual divisions may derive from Gildas.[106] The section directed at kings contains a block of quotations from Solomon, *qua* author of the Book of Proverbs, and another block from Solomon *qua* author of the Book of Wisdom.[107] True, Gildas also referred to Solomon's personal decline from virtue, but his readers were left in no doubt of the applicability of his teaching to kings—and of his role as a positive example in his youth and a warning in his maturity.[108] One block of Solomonic quotations was directed at Maelgwn, a king who not only had received his education from 'the refined master of almost all Britain' but had also briefly converted to the monastic life. Immediately after recalling Maelgwn's education Gildas began to deploy his quotations from Solomon:[109]

> Yet surely you have had no lack of warnings: for you have had as your teacher the refined master of almost all Britain. Therefore beware lest what is noted by Solomon

[100] 1 Kings, 3: 28 (3 Kings in the Vulgate).

[101] Scharer, 'The Writing of History at King Alfred's Court', 191–9; id., *Herrschaft und Repräsentation*, 83–108.

[102] L. Davies, 'Sedulius Scottus: *Liber de Rectoribus Christianis*, Carolingian or Hibernian Mirror for Princes?', *Studia Celtica*, 26–7 (1991–2), 34–50.

[103] 1/3 Kings 3:12: God promised to make Solomon uniquely wise.

[104] AU 613. 3.

[105] *De Excidio*, 36. 1; 36. 4; 39. 4; *Sermo Lupi ad Anglos*, ed. D. Whitelock (3rd edn. London, 1963), p. 65, l. 184.

[106] Gildas, *De Excidio*, 65; Asser, *Life of Alfred*, cc. 21, 73.

[107] Gildas, *De Excidio*, 36, 62–3.

[108] Ibid. 39. 4.

[109] Ibid. 36. 1.

> befall you: 'Like one who wakes a sleeper from deep slumber is he who tells a fool wisdom. For at the end of the story he will say: What was it you said first?'

Gildas's appeal to kings, judges, and priests was not merely to justice but also to wisdom, that they should open 'the eyes of the soul'.[110] It is worth noting, also, that, as Asser finishes with Alfred's concern that judges should acquire wisdom, so Gildas finished his section on kings with an appeal to both kings and judges that they judge justly.[111]

The importance of the Old Testament background and its exploitation by scholars, most recently in the Carolingian Empire, is undoubted; but Asser himself (as well as his master, King Alfred) had specific ideas on how to turn biblical exegesis into political policy. The king's wisdom was God's personal gift, conferring authority but also entailing obligations. Asser presents in direct speech the king's invocation of divine authority in a challenge to judges. They had, through ignorance, passed unjust judgements:[112]

> I am astonished at this arrogance of yours, since through God's authority and my own you have enjoyed the office and status of wise men, yet you have neglected the study and application of wisdom.

This challenge was effective because of the use of *wita*, plural *witan* in Old English. The *witan* were the *sapientes*, 'wise men', of Bede and Asser; they participated in counselling the king before any major decision. When the king settled a great issue, he was expected to seek out and profit by the wisdom of his counsellors. Notions of wisdom both in government in general and in judgement in particular were ubiquitous, and for that very reason rhetorically useful. An ignorant *wita* could thus be presented as a contradiction in terms.

An over-mechanical view of Asser's Life of Alfred might claim that it was Einhard modified in accordance with Sedulius Scottus. A just view would give full recognition to Insular traditions of wise kingship, themselves linked with the Old Testament king and judge, Solomon.[113] It would also give full recognition to the role of *wīsdōm*, *sapientia*, in ordinary English political discourse of the time.

Alfred's cultivation of wisdom offered opportunities sufficient to draw Asser from St Davids. These were partly to do with the vulnerability of St Davids to the oppression of Hyfaidd, king of Dyfed, and, more generally, with the possibility of creating a peaceful settlement in Wales. Other inducements were the possibilities of collaboration with the other scholars at the court and, above all, with the king himself. From Alfred's point of view, however, Asser was worth bringing into his household for one reason only: because he already had, from his education at St Davids, the scholarship with the aid of which the king hoped to develop *wīsdōm*. In the following century other Britons, Welsh, Cornish, and Breton, would find their

110 Ibid. 74. 4.

111 Ibid. 63.

112 *Life*, c. 106, trans. Keynes and Lapidge, *Alfred the Great*, 110.

113 Scharer, *Herrschaft und Repräsentation*, 95–103, on the influence of the Hiberno-Latin text, *Prouerbia Grecorum*; he also suggests, 102–3, that Asser may have known the *Collectio Canonum Hibernensis*.

way to major English centres, showing that the old antipathies between the two peoples no longer formed so great a barrier as they did in the eighth century.[114]

Both the *Historia Brittonum* and Asser's Life of Alfred were addressed to a Welsh readership, though not exclusively so. Both were designed to persuade that readership of a case. The *Historia Brittonum* incorporated the Britons into world history and presented the relationship of the Britons with the Romans and with the English in a much more favourable light than did two important sources, Gildas's *De Excidio Britanniae* and Bede's *Historia Ecclesiastica*. Asser's Life of Alfred portrayed Alfred as someone who was a champion of Christians against pagan invaders and as a benevolent and wise protector of Welsh kings. Both texts, therefore, took a relatively hopeful view of the relationship between the Welsh and the English, especially when compared with Gildas and Bede in earlier centuries or, as we shall see in Chapter 16, *Armes Prydein* in the tenth century. Both engaged with texts both Insular and continental. Yet a vast difference remains. In spite of its focus on the personal relationships between Vortigern, Hengest, St Germanus, and Ambrosius, the *Historia Brittonum* was concerned above all with the relationships between peoples. Asser's Life of Alfred was not unconcerned with peoples—the wars of the English with the Vikings and the movement of the Welsh towards submission to, and support for, Alfred—but the intellectual and spiritual growth of the king was central.

[114] See below, Ch. 19.

15

The Transformations of the Ninth Century

1. MERFYN FRYCH AND THE MERFYNION

The first half of the ninth century in Wales saw the arrival of a new dynasty in Gwynedd. The descendants of Cunedda were replaced by Merfyn Frych and his descendants, later called after their ancestor the Merfynion.[1] About 825, Merfyn Frych, son of Gwriad, took the kingship of Gwynedd in obscure circumstances. It was later claimed, as in the poem *Cyfoesi Myrddin a Gwenddydd ei Chwaer*, that Merfyn came from the Isle of Man.[2] According to the most recent edition of the poem, the earliest stratum of the text is tenth century.[3] What makes the claim of a Manx origin for Merfyn distinctly plausible is a combination of four things:[4] first, an inscription on the Isle of Man called 'the Cross of Gwriad', which has been taken to be a memorial to Merfyn's father, the Gwriad ab Elidyr known from a later Welsh genealogy;[5] second, a verse written into the margin of the primary manuscript of the Annals of Ulster;[6] third, later Welsh evidence supporting the *Cyfoesi* and not known to be derived from it;[7] and, finally, the general shape of events. None of these offers a complete proof, either singly or cumulatively; yet, when taken together, they provide enough weight of evidence for present purposes.[8]

[1] CBT I. 7. 102 n. (the note gives further later examples).

[2] *The Poetry in the Red Book of Hergest*, ed. J. Gwenogvryn Evans (Llanbedrog, 1911), p. 2, col. 578. 40.

[3] Above, 337 n.134.

[4] P. Sims-Williams, 'Historical Need and Literary Narrative: A Caveat from Ninth-Century Wales', *WHR* 17/1 (1994–5), 11–20; B. L. Jones, 'Gwriad's Heritage: Links between Wales and the Isle of Man in the Early Middle Ages', *THSC* 1990, 29–44.

[5] *CIIC* 1066, Maughold 1 (from Port e Vullen, approx. SC 473 928): P. M. C. Kermode, 'A Welsh Inscription in the Isle of Man', *ZCP* 1 (1897), 48–51; *Manx Crosses*, no. 48 and Appendix A; *EWGT* 46, § 17.

[6] AU 878.

[7] CBT VII. 48. 21. The note *ad loc.* notes quite correctly that there might be a reference to Gruffudd ap Cynan's maternal descent from 'Avloed, vrenhin dinas Dulyn a phymhet ran Ywerdon ac enys Vanaw', *Historia Gruffud vab Kenan*, ed. D. S. Evans (Cardiff, 1977), § 2, but it should be noted that the text of the Latin version, *Vita Griffini Filii Conani*, ed. and trans. P. Russell (Cardiff, 2005), § 4, at once goes on to say 'qui e Scotia genus ducebat', '(Olaf) who derived his ancestry from Scotland', while the Welsh version, *Historia Gruffud vab Kenan*, has 'a hanoed gynt o deyrnas Prydein', 'who formerly derived from the kingdom of Britain'.

[8] The Manx origin of Merfyn is doubted by Thornton, *Kings, Chronologies, and Genealogies*, 94–5, but he takes no account of the Irish evidence; cf. D. Kirby, 'Vortigern', *BBCS* 23 (1968–70), 51; id. 'British Dynastic History in the Pre-Viking Period', *BBCS* 27 (1976–8), 97; however, the argument for a special connection between Merfyn and Powys has been undermined by P. Sims-Williams, 'Historical Need', 6–30).

Gwriad is a name attested in the period, and the inscription does not supply the name of his father, so the first item of evidence is not strong on its own. Merfyn's father was, however, named as Gwriad in later Welsh genealogies and the name was borne by other members of the dynasty; moreover, the only other Gwriad in the early collections of genealogies is likely to be an incorrect insertion.[9] The marginal verse in the Annals of Ulster could well have been composed close to the events it records, namely the deaths of four kings or princes in the years 877–878.[10] One of them was named in the annal entry *Ruaidhri mac Muirminn, rex Brittonum*, 'Rhodri son of Merfyn, king of the Britons'. In the verse, however, he was called *Ruaidri Manann*, 'Rhodri of Man'.[11] Since Rhodri was king of Gwynedd, it is hard to see any reason for calling him 'of Man' other than that his kindred came from the island and perhaps still had authority over it. Finally, considerably later Welsh evidence describes Merfyn as 'of Man'.[12]

The fourth support for accepting a Manx origin for Merfyn is the general shape of events. It is worth thinking of the western parts of Britain and the eastern coast of Ireland as they might have appeared to a Viking leader about 820, looking in his mind's eye southwards from the Isle of Skye. This Viking leader has already come across the North Sea to the Orkney Islands; and from there he has been part of the conquests which were, in the opening decades of the ninth century, turning the Hebrides into *Innsi Gall*, 'the Islands of the (Scandinavian) Foreigners' or, from a northern standpoint, the Suðreyar, 'The Southern Islands', by contrast with the Orkneys and the Shetland Islands.[13] To understand his view of the Irish-Sea world, one must turn the map upside down and look from the north southwards rather than from the south northwards (see Map 22).

In the foreground, with the island monastery of Iona on the horizon, were the Southern Islands. The Suðreyar were to give their name to one part, namely the northern part, of the medieval diocese of Sodor and Man, Sodor being derived from the Old Norse Suðreyar. Further south, beyond the Suðreyar, lay Kintyre, the northern and north-eastern coastlands of Ireland, what later became Galloway but

[9] *EWGT*, 36, § 2 (*Historia Gruffud vab Kenan = Vita Griffini Filii Conani*, ed. Russell, § 3); p. 46, JC §§ 17, 19; p. 101, ABT §§ 7*a*, *s*; *AC* 877 = 878. The Gwriad ap Brochfael of JC § 9 does not appear in HG § 29.

[10] It has the *aicill* rhyme *flatha : Macha* for eighth-century Irish *flatho : Machae*, but this would certainly be possible even in strict verse by the end of the tenth century and such rhymes appear in *Pangur Bán*, a less formal ninth-century poem contemporary with Rhodri. The name Barrfhinn Bili (so reading to get rhyme with *cridi*) may well be a nickname for a monk of Movilla, Mag mBili, the patron of which was St Findbarr: A. Woolf, *From Pictland to Alba* (Edinburgh, 2007), 116–17. The four persons commemorated were: (1) Rhodri; (2) Áed mac Cinadan, king of Picts (the united kingdom of Scotia, still called 'of Picts' until *c.* 900); (3) Donnchad mac Áedacáin maic Conchobair, 'material of a king', who belonged to Cland Cholmáin of Mide; (4) Garbsith mac Maíl Brigte, king of Conailli Muirthemni. It is hardly likely that a poet later than the ninth century would have had much interest in Donnchad mac Áedacáin.

[11] The other Manu, genitive Manann, namely Welsh Manaw Gododdin, cannot have had anything to do with Rhodri.

[12] P. Bartrum, *A Welsh Classical Dictionary* (Aberystwyth, 1993), 473–4.

[13] For the date of the Viking conquest of the Hebrides, see J. Graham-Campbell, 'The Irish-Sea Vikings: Raiders and Settlers', in T. Scott and P. Starkey (eds.), *The Middle Ages in the North West* (Oxford, 1995), 67; the historical evidence is of attacks on Iona (AU 802. 9; 806. 8).

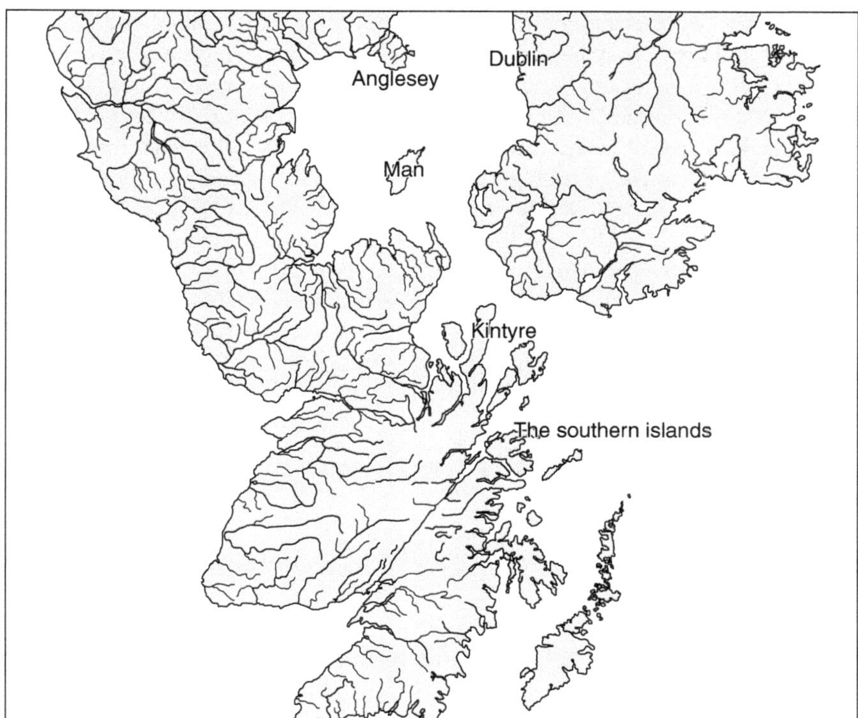

Map 22. The View from Orkney: the Suðreyar and the Irish Sea (upside down)
The Old Norse name for the Hebrides, 'The Southern Islands', Suðreyar, immediately implies a view of Britain and Ireland quite unfamiliar to us, from the north southwards. The map depicts the western maritime route from the Orkneys to Dublin and to Gwynedd.

was then part of a much wider region, the western coastlands of English Northumbria, the Isle of Man, the rich eastern midlands of Ireland, and Gwynedd. And the heart of Gwynedd was the island of Anglesey, almost midway between England and Ireland, looking north to the Isle of Man, east towards the Dee estuary and the Wirral, and west towards Dublin. In 825 Dublin was still a minor local church on the northern border of Leinster, but in 841 it would become the principal *longphort*, 'ship-port', of the Vikings in Ireland.[14]

In the northern part of this maritime zone, the southern Hebrides had long been settled by the Irish and drawn into the Irish kingdom of Dál Riata. In the ninth century, however, as the Hebrides became, for the Irish, 'The Islands of the Foreigners', the kings of Scottish Dál Riata decamped eastwards and became the rulers of Pictland.[15] Fifty years after Cináed mac Ailpín became king 'in the east',

[14] AU 841. 4.

[15] The origins of the later dynasty of Scotland, descended from Cináed mac Alpín, in the Dál Riata dynasty called Cenél nGabráin or, at least, in the latter's core kingdom of Kintyre are reflected in the

his kingdom became the core of a new Scotland, a new land of the Gaels, the *Scotti*.[16] Similarly, it may be suggested, the former British rulers of the Isle of Man decamped southwards and became the new dynasty of Gwynedd. The Gaels of Dál Riata may have conquered the Picts by force, and the triumph of Merfyn may have been just as violent.[17] This new dynasty of Gwynedd, the Merfynion, would become in the course of a single century the rulers of most of Wales. Viking power down the western seaboard of Britain made the Merfynion into a purely Welsh dynasty just as the very same period saw the descendants of Cináed mac Alpín become a dynasty based in eastern Scotland.

There is perhaps one objection to the notion of a Manx origin for Merfyn, namely that in the Harleian Genealogies there is another pedigree, quite distinct from the ancestors of Merfyn, that has been ascribed by modern scholars to Man.[18]

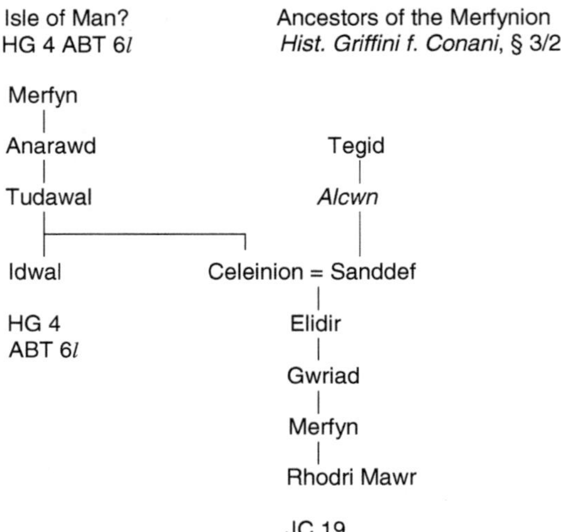

The identification of HG 4 as the royal pedigree of Man depends, first, on a further identification, namely of the Merfyn who was the great-grandfather of Idwal with the Merfyn (*Muirmin*) slain *inmano* (probably for *in Manu*) in 682 according to the

same marginal poem in AU 878, in which Áed mac Cináeda, entitled in the annal itself *rex Pictorum*, is called 'Áed from the lands of Kintyre', *Áed a críchaib Cinn Tíre*, Kintyre being the heartland of Cenél nGabráin.

16 A. Woolf, *From Pictland to Alba, 789–1070*, ch. 3.

17 P. Wormald, 'The Emergence of the *Regnum Scottorum*: A Carolingian Hegemony?', in B. E. Crawford (ed.), *Scotland in Dark-Age Britain* (St Andrews, 1996), 131–60. Other views of the change from Pictland to Scotland or Alba see the process as much more gradual, e.g. D. Broun, 'Alba as "Britain" after 900 and the Pictish Antecedents of the Kingdom of the Scots', in D. Broun, *Scottish Independence and the Idea of Britain* (Edinburgh, 2007), 71–97. For my view, see T. M. Charles-Edwards, 'Picts and Scots', *Innes Review* 59 (2008), 168–88.

18 HG 4 in *EWGT* 10; JC 19 in *EWGT* 46; *Vita Griffini filii Conani*, ed. P. Russell (Cardiff, 2005), p. 52, § 3; *OP* ii. 210; H. M. Chadwick, *Early Scotland* (Cambridge, 1949), 146.

Annals of Ulster.[19] The second reason, however, depends on positing a Manx origin for Merfyn Frych, whose great-grandfather married the earlier Merfyn's great-granddaughter. This connection would be easier to explain if both lines of descent belonged to Man. The Isle of Man has two areas of relatively good land, one at the north end of the island and the other in the south, split by a range of mountains running west to east from near Peel to Maughold, of which Snaefell is the highest. It would thus be easy to suppose two ruling kindreds with their core territories either side of these mountains; but, by the time of Gwriad, Merfyn's father, the distribution of power may have changed. If the father of Merfyn was the person commemorated in the inscription, the Maughold area, where the *Crux Guriat* was situated, may have been the centre of his power; and from Maughold, at the eastern end of the central mountain range, control could be maintained over both the north and the south.

Two contexts for Merfyn Frych's acquisition of the kingship of Gwynedd need to be considered: the Irish-Sea region in the years when Viking attacks were accelerating and the Mercian hegemony in the years when it was, for a time, shattered by the victories of Ecgberht, king of Wessex. The date at which Merfyn Frych became king of Gwynedd, 825, came six years after the death of Áed Oirdnide, and two years after a most unusual change of leadership within Áed Oirdnide's dynasty, Cenél nÉogain. Áed Oirdnide had dominated the northern half of Ireland since the end of the previous century; and, as part of this domination, he had exercised authority over the affairs of Ulster.[20] His power in the Irish coastlands facing the Hebrides may well have discouraged any serious attack. If Cenél nÉogain had retained the kingship of Tara, the opportunities for the Vikings might have been less promising; but instead Conchobor mac Donnchada, of the midland dynasty of Cland Cholmáin, succeeded to the kingship; and Cland Cholmáin kings were much less likely to intervene in Ulster. Murchad mac Maíle Dúin of Cenél nÉogain failed in his challenge to Conchobor in 820 and again in 822; in 823 'Niall son of Áed and the Cenél nÉogain removed Murchad son of Máel Dúin from the kingship'.[21] After this, Viking attacks on Ireland increased in frequency, in seriousness, and in their range. In 825 Vikings were campaigning in Ulster, just to the west of the Isle of Man, where they sacked Downpatrick and Movilla. In 827 the Vikings attacked eastern Brega and eastern Leinster.[22] They were thus able to challenge the authority of the Uí Néill both in the midlands and in the north-east. In 841, after a period of intense raiding, the Vikings established their *longphoirt* 'ship-ports' at Dublin and at Lind Duachaill (Annagassan, Co. Louth), on the northern and southern boundaries of Brega: Dublin looked east

[19] AU 682. 2; the main entry can be ascribed with confidence to the Chronicle of Ireland, but the detail about *Muirmin* is not in any of the Clonmacnois group: see *CI* 682. 2. It is, however, much more likely to have been omitted in the course of transmission rather than added in a forerunner of the Annals of Ulster: *CI* i. 19–20.

[20] As in AU 809. 7.

[21] AU 820. 2; 822. 3; 823. 7.

[22] AU 827. 3, 9.

towards Gwynedd, Lind Duachaill north-east towards Man. By this date, it can be argued, the Isle of Man must have become a Viking base.

Yet it has been claimed that the archaeological evidence for a Viking presence on Man only begins in the tenth century.[23] This raises the possibility that Rhodri Mawr was not said to be 'of Man' in the Irish verse merely because of the earlier home of his dynasty, by now more than fifty years in the past, but because he and his father, Merfyn Frych, had ruled both Gwynedd and Man. The implications are intriguing: any ruler who controlled both Anglesey and Man was in a powerful position within the Irish-Sea region as a whole. Indeed, such dual rule across the sea could hardly be sustained without an effective fleet. The prime targets of Viking raiding might be the rich coastal kingdoms of Ulster and Brega, but the island dominion of Merfyn and his son Rhodri would have to be challenged by the Vikings if they were to raid in relative security, still more if they were to conquer and settle.

Just as the means by which the land of the Picts became a new land of the Gaels are deeply controversial, so also there are profound obscurities covering the relationship of Man and Gwynedd in the ninth century. It is perhaps best to set out two possible reconstructions of the broad shape of events. The first will stem from a hypothesis that the Vikings did indeed drive Merfyn from Man even if they did not settle the island permanently until about 900. They might, for example, have established their own puppet-ruler over Man rather than take direct power themselves. The second reconstruction, however, will proceed on the basis outlined above, namely that Merfyn and Rhodri retained power in Man until much later in the ninth century. Both reconstructions will assume that in the early ninth century Man remained a British island as it had been in the seventh.[24] On the other hand, Irish influence had been strong, as it was in other British coastal regions; and the later emergence of Manx as a Gaelic language may stem, in part, from this early Irish settlement as well as from later Irish-speaking settlers in the Viking period.[25] In 825 the population may have remained partly British-speaking and partly Irish-speaking (as it did not in ninth-century Wales), and probably partly bilingual, although under British rule. This supposition will help to explain what appears to be an absence of British place-names on the Isle of Man: if we assume that many places had both Irish and British names, the destruction of the British elite *c.* 900 may have allowed the Irish names to survive, where they were not replaced by Norse names, while British names perished.

The first reconstruction assumed that Merfyn appeared in Gwynedd because he was driven from Man by Vikings. It gained strength from the close coincidence in time between the beginning of his reign in Gwynedd and the rising tempo of

[23] J. Graham-Campbell, 'The Irish-Sea Vikings: Raiders and Settlers', 75–8; id., 'The Early Viking Age in the Irish Sea Area', in H. Clarke et al. (eds.), *Ireland and Scandinavia in the Early Viking Age* (Dublin, 1998), 116–18.

[24] Bede, *HE* ii. 5; AU 682. 2.

[25] See above, 148–51; R. L. Thomson, 'The Continuity of Manx', in C. Fell et al. (eds.), *The Viking Age in the Isle of Man* (London, 1983), 169–74; and N. J. Williams, 'An Mhanainnis', in K. McCone et al. (eds.), *Stair na Gaeilge in ómos do Pádraig Ó Fiannachta* (Maynooth, 1994), 703–44, at 739–41.

Viking attacks in the Irish Sea. As we saw above, these included a sustained raid on Ulster in 825, including both Mag nInis around Downpatrick and the more northerly lands of the Ulaid, from Nendrum to the southern skirts of Belfast, ruled by the Uí Blathmeic branch of their dynasty. Ulster had old connections with the Isle of Man as well as geographical proximity; and one might well suppose that control of an island in the north of the Irish Sea would precede a major attack on the Irish kingdom most prone to seek naval power in the region.[26] If this were the case, Merfyn might have been dislodged from Man by 825.

The difficulty with this explanation is that Merfyn must first be supposed to have sought refuge in Gwynedd, presumably with the consent of its ruler or rulers, and then to have succeeded in taking over the kingdom itself. He must be supposed first to have lost the territorial base of his power on the Isle of Man and only later to have taken power in Gwynedd. Also, if we begin with the premiss, based on the Chronicle of Ireland, that Viking activity in the Irish Sea increased sharply after the death of Áed Oirdnide and the final failure of his successor as ruler of Cenél nÉogain in 823, there is very little time left before the beginning of Merfyn's rule after the death of Hywel in 825.

A traditional escape route from this difficulty is to suppose that Merfyn's succession was peaceful rather than a military conquest or coup d'étât. The first pedigree in the Harleian Genealogies gives the paternal side of Owain ap Hywel Dda's descent.[27] It is entirely patrilineal in accordance with what one would expect from a Welsh royal pedigree, except that Merfyn is said to be the son of *Etthil merch Cinnan map Rotri*; and Rhodri's line is taken back to Maelgwn and to the latter's great-grandfather Cunedda, who is said to have come from Manaw Gododdin. In the terms used by the Gogynfeirdd, the pedigree attaches the Merfynion to the Maelgyning via *Etthil*. The same linkage is made elsewhere in later genealogies only in a slightly different form: in these texts *Etthil* was the wife of Merfyn rather than of his father, Gwriad.[28] If they are correct, Merfyn himself, as opposed to his descendants, was not descended from the Maelgyning.

To assess the nature of the pedigree we need to bear in mind the fundamental distinction between the kinship of inheritance, including the inheritance of office, and the kinship of status and alliance. The former is reflected in patrilineal pedigrees—X son of Y son of Z—the latter in genealogies which begin from a particular person, the focus of the whole statement, and take his various lines of descent back through females as well as through males. When this takes the form of single female links connecting a group of patrilineal pedigrees, it is an expression of *ymgyfathrachu*, 'mutual-joint-inter-lineaging', marriage alliances between agnatic lineages.[29] When there is more than one female link, the function is less as evidence for alliance, more to display the genealogical status of the person taken as the focus.

[26] *Chronicle of Ireland*, 784. 8 n.

[27] *EWGT* 9 (HG § 1).

[28] *EWGT* 36 (and *Vita Griffini Filii Conani: The Medieval Latin Life of Gruffudd ap Cynan*, ed. and trans. P. Russell (Cardiff, 2005), § 3), 38 (Mostyn MS 117), 95 (ABT § 1); but *EWGT* 47 (JC § 22) agrees with HG § 1.

[29] See above, 298, 334.

A directly relevant example is given by the genealogies in Jesus College, Oxford, MS 20.[30] The focus here was Rhodri Mawr, son of Merfyn. A succession of pedigrees had the following functions:

(1) Rhodri's patrilineal descent via Merfyn ap Gwriad ab Elidyr back to Llywarch Hen and thus to Coel Hen, ancestor of the Coeling. The pedigree thus makes Rhodri a patrilineal descendant of one of the principal ancestors ascribed to northern British dynasties.

(2) Rhodri's maternal ancestry: his mother is given as Nest, daughter of Cadell of Powys; and her patrilineal pedigree goes back to Gwrtheyrn Gwrthenau, namely one of the ancestors claimed for the royal line of Powys.[31]

(3) This pedigree starts along the same 'patriline' as (1) but then diverges via Celeinion, the mother of Elidyr, Rhodri's great-grandfather; she is claimed to belong to a dynasty attested in the Harleian Genealogies, which has also been connected with the Isle of Man.[32]

(4) Rhodri's sons are divided according to their mothers, the main one being Angharad ferch Feurig; her patriline is given back to Ceredig ap Cunedda, the eponym of Ceredigion.[33]

(5) Finally, Rhodri's descent is given via *Ethellt merch Cynan Tintaethwy*, namely the link back into the Maelgyning, 'the first dynasty of Gwynedd'.

This group of pedigrees, focused on Rhodri Mawr, is designed to exalt his status. In its present form it was not produced for Rhodri himself but probably for one or other of his southern descendants from the Dyfed branch of the Merfynion, the branch whose ancestor was Rhodri's son Cadell. Cadell was put first in the list of sons in (4), whereas Anarawd, ancestor of the Gwynedd branch of the Merfynion, was placed third.

Similarly, the first two pedigrees in the Harleian collection give the Gwynedd and the Dyfed sides of the descent of Owain ab Hywel Dda. Owain succeeded his father in 950 and died in 988. The collection as a whole probably belongs to his reign. The first pedigree took his ancestry back, via *Etthil* to the Maelgyning, to Cunedda and then to Beli Mawr; the second took it back via his mother, Elen, into the royal lineage of Dyfed. The impression given is that Owain's ancestors made their way into the royal seats of Gwynedd, Dyfed, and Powys as valued allies, not as enemies and usurpers. Yet, none of these marriages and the consequent pedigrees through female links gave them the right to succeed, or even to compete to succeed, to the kingship either of Gwynedd or of Dyfed.[34] The genealogical language of alliance and high royal status is used to smooth over a political hiatus. In the twelfth century, again, the genealogies prefixed to the Life of Gruffudd ap Cynan displayed his royal status through royal ancestresses:

[30] *EWGT* 46–7, JC §§ 17–22.

[31] Similarly *EWGT* 100, ABT 6*k*.

[32] *EWGT* 10, § 4; similarly *EWGT* 100, ABT 6*l*.

[33] Similarly *EWGT* 100, ABT 6*j*.

[34] The grounds on which later writers have claimed that the successions of the Merfynion to kingdoms outside Gwynedd were lawful have been scrutinized and found wanting by Thornton, *Kings, Chronologies, and Genealogies*, ch. 4.

the presupposition was that if one's family was in the habit of marrying royalty, it was itself accepted as royal. The Life also contained sustained propaganda against those whom it portrayed as usurpers in Gwynedd, because they were not descended in the male line from Anarawd ap Rhodri Mawr. For this propaganda against usurpers, only Gruffudd's descent in the male line mattered.

As we shall see later, the acquisition of the kingship of Dyfed by the Merfynion came in the early tenth century after sustained military pressure.[35] It was certainly not a smooth succession by right of descent through a woman. One context in which the later Welsh laws allowed for the son of a woman of the kindred to share its lands was when they gave her in marriage to an alien. The assumption, however, in such cases was that the alien had settled in his wife's native kingdom as someone who was landless except through her. This has nothing to do with the situation when a king's daughter was given to a prince of another dynasty, as Owain's mother, Elen, was given, so we may presume, to Hywel Dda, son of Cadell ap Rhodri Mawr ap Merfyn Frych, and still less with the situation when a royal woman was part of the booty taken by the conqueror. That Rhodri Mawr's connection through *Etthil* with the Maelgyning gave him no right to rule in Gwynedd is apparent from the appearance of a parallel link with the lineage of Dyfed: there we know from a good contemporary source, Asser, that the Merfynion planned to conquer Dyfed well before they were eventually successful.[36] The proposed escape route, therefore, is a mere cul-de-sac.

The second reconstruction would see Merfyn taking power in Gwynedd while still the ruler of Man. There is no problem here about his base from which to gain power in Gwynedd, since he would have retained Man. It might still be a reaction to the Viking threat, in that a ruler of Man might seek to strengthen his power in the Irish Sea against that threat by taking power over Anglesey and so obtaining two bases, one northern and one southern. A difficulty remains, however, in that the reconstruction does not touch on the issue of how it might be possible for a ruler of Man to acquire power in Gwynedd. To make progress on this aspect of the problem, we need to turn to the relationship between Gwynedd, Mercia, and Wessex and also to the internal politics of Gwynedd.

Hywel, perhaps the last ruler of Gwynedd from the descendants of Cunedda, died in 825.[37] In the same year Mercian power collapsed after their king was defeated by Ecgberht, king of the West Saxons, in the battle of *Ellendun*, now Wroughton in Wiltshire.[38] Immediately afterwards a Mercian client-ruler, King Baldred, was driven from Kent, and the East Angles then renounced Mercian overlordship and slew the Mercian king, Beornwulf. After Beornwulf's death the last vestiges of Mercian authority in Kent came to an end.[39] In 830 Ecgberht even led an expedition into Wales, presumably to claim for himself the overlordship previously exercised by the Mercians.[40] These events may have had some effect on

[35] See below, 507–9. [36] Asser, *Life*, c. 80.
[37] *AC* 825. [38] ASC 825.
[39] S. Keynes, 'The Control of Kent in the Ninth Century', *Early Medieval Europe*, 2: 2 (1993), 220.
[40] ASC 828 = 830.

Gwynedd, where an earlier period of dynastic strife had overlapped with Mercian military pressure.

In 813 the annals record a battle between Hywel and Cynan, in which Hywel was the victor. In the next year 'Hywel from the island of Anglesey was victorious and expelled Cynan from there with major losses to his army.' In 816 Hywel was in turn expelled from Anglesey, but 'Cynan son of Rhodri, king of the Britons' died in the same year.[41] Also in 816, according to the *B* version of the *Annales Cambriae* and the *Brut*, the English 'invaded the mountains of Eryri and the kingdom of Rhufoniog'.[42] The English in question are likely to have been the Mercians, either led or sent by their king, Cenwulf, who also laid waste Dyfed in 818. The impression given by these terse annal entries is that Hywel and Cynan were principally fighting for control of Anglesey. When either of them was driven from Anglesey, as Cynan was in 814 and Hywel was in 816, they had some other territorial base to which they could retire. There is some evidence, mostly late, and always fragmentary and unsatisfactory, that Hywel's native territory may have been Rhos, which, at this date, is likely to have included the fortress of Degannwy.[43] Against this one must set the phrase 'Hywel from Anglesey', *Higuel de Monia insula*, in the *Annales Cambriae*, *s.a.* 814.[44] This, although probably contemporary, is not conclusive, provided that we accept that Hywel was the victor in the battle of 813 and that, in general, they were fighting over Anglesey. He might well have taken Anglesey as the prize of his victory in 813, before he was attacked there by Cynan in 814, when, again victorious, he was described as *de Monia*. It may be significant that, almost a century later, Anarawd ap Rhodri was described as 'king of *Monia*, that is, Môn, who now rules the kingdom of Gwynedd', a description all the more striking because it comes from 908, just after the invasion of Anglesey by Ingimund in 902.[45] The implication may be that already in the ninth century Anglesey contained what the Irish called 'the seat of kingship', as, by the twelfth century, Aberffraw undoubtedly had that role and was called 'the special seat', *eisteddfa arbennig*, of the kingdom of Gwynedd.[46]

When Cynan ap Rhodri died in 816, he was very probably supreme ruler of Gwynedd, since he was described by the Annals of Ulster as 'king of the Britons',

[41] AU 816. 1, supplies the patronymic, which is lacking from AC. This supports the pedigree, *EWGT* 9, HG § 1.

[42] *Annales Cambriae, A.D. 682–954*, ed. Dumville, 10–11, *s.a.* 816.

[43] Thornton, *Kings, Chronologies, and Genealogies*, 78–87; Kirby, 'British Dynastic History', 94; the suggestion is based on identifying our Hywel with the person whose pedigree is given at *EWGT* 10 (HG § 3) and 108 (ABT, § 25); it is only the latter which describes the pedigree as pertaining to Rhos. Degannwy was later in the small commote of Creuddyn, attached to the cantref of Arllechwedd although it was east of the Conwy; but it would more naturally go with Rhos, and Creuddyn may be a later creation designed to prevent Degannwy from being a centre rivalling Aberffraw but in Gwynedd east of the Conwy.

[44] The versions of the *Brut* indicate that the *B* version of *Annales Cambriae* was alone in changing *de Monia* to *in Monia*.

[45] See D. N. Dumville, 'The Corpus Christi "Nennius"', *BBCS* 25 (1972–4), plate I, 3 (opposite p. 376), provides a photograph of the addition in the Sawley MS.

[46] *Llyfr Iorwerth*, § 3/4–5; trans. *LTMW* 5–6; *The Latin Texts of the Welsh Laws*, ed. H. D. Emanuel (Cardiff, 1967), 207. 27–9; 317. 30–2.

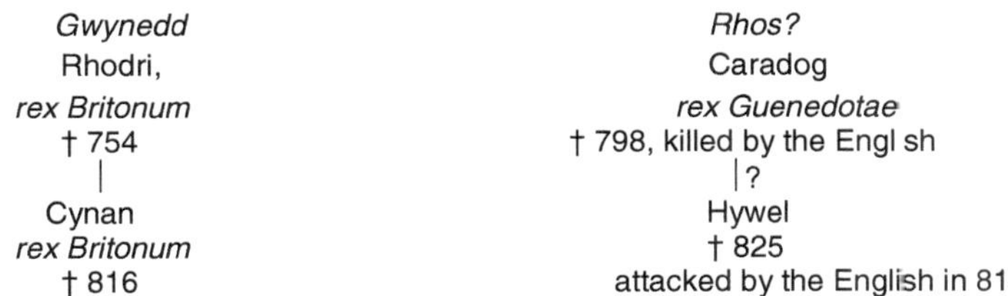

Figure 15.1. The Maelgyning and the dynasty of Rhos, 750–825

not a title accorded by the Irish chronicles to minor kings.[47] After his death Hywel may have emerged as sole ruler of Gwynedd. But, if so, this was not without some opposition, for the English invasion of Gwynedd occurred in the same year, 816, but apparently after Cynan's death. Moreover, if Hywel's ancestral land was Rhos, and if Degannwy belonged to Rhos, an entry in *Annales Cambriae* for 822 gains further significance: 'The fortress of the Decanti is destroyed by the English, and they brought the kingdom of Powys under their power.' There is a possible pattern to the interventions of the English, namely the Mercians, in Gwynedd. If Hywel has been correctly identified with the subject of the third pedigree in the Harleian Genealogies, his father was called Caradog ap Meirion. In 798, immediately after Cenwulf's accession to power in Mercia, 'Caradog, king of Gwynedd, is killed by the English'.[48] Unfortunately, the entry does not supply the name of Caradog's father, but, even so, there is a serious possibility that this Caradog was Caradog ap Meirion and was the father of Hywel, also king of Gwynedd.[49] No English attacks on Cynan are recorded during his reign; but, as soon as he was dead, they began again.

It looks as though Caradog's rule was entirely acceptable to Offa, but he was killed by the Mercians soon after Cenwulf had taken power in opposition to Offa's son Ecgberht. On the other hand, Cynan's rule was acceptable to Cenwulf. This pattern gives rise to the hesitant suggestion that factions within Gwynedd were aligned with factions in Mercia.

It is worth pursuing the implications of this suggestion a little further. The destruction of Degannwy by the Mercians occurred in 822, the year after Cenwulf's death and the succession of his presumed close kinsman, Ceolwulf. Ceolwulf, however, was deposed in 823, perhaps in favour of a collateral line.[50] Mercian royal rivalries provided the opportunity for Ecgberht of Wessex to make his challenge, to win the battle of Ellandun in 825, and to take supremacy over the

[47] For the Irish use of such titles, see *EIWK* 101–2; for examples, see *The Chronicle of Ireland*, trans. Charles-Edwards, ii. 121. No such argument holds for English usage, as in Bede's description of Cerdic (Ceredig), king of Elmet, as *rex Brettonum*, *HE* iv. 23/21.

[48] *AC* 798.

[49] Thornton, *Kings, Chronologies, and Genealogies*, 79–82.

[50] This depends on the uncertain business of deducing lines of descent within the royal lineage of Mercia from the forms of names, and so positing a 'C-branch' opposed by a 'B-branch': Cenwulf and Ceolwulf would belong to the former, Ceolwulf's successor, Beornwulf, to the latter. For discussion and references to earlier work, see S. Keynes, 'Mercia and Wessex in the Ninth Century', in Brown and Farr (eds.), *Mercia: An Anglo-Saxon Kingdom in Europe*, 315–20.

south-east of England away from the Mercians. The emergence of a different royal line in Mercia and the more general decline of Mercian power may have made it easier for Hywel to survive as king of Gwynedd.

Hywel's death in 825, however, was the occasion on which Merfyn appears to have seized the kingship. The marriage alliance between Merfyn and Cynan is most likely to have been created before Cynan's death in 816; it may well have been made in order to strengthen Cynan in his struggle with Hywel. On the one hand, Cynan was probably, as we have seen, a loyal client of Cenwulf, king of the Mercians; on the other, he now had an ally across the sea to the north. The acquisition of power in Gwynedd by Merfyn in 825 perhaps saw the triumph of what might be called Cynan's faction even after his death: Merfyn got his foot into the door of Gwynedd through his alliance with Cynan; and Cynan's other former allies and clients may have helped him to the kingship in 825. His triumph indicates that there was no close kinsman of Cynan, no member of the Maelgyning, who could make an equally effective, and moreover legitimate, bid for the kingship. This is unlikely to be because there were no such kinsmen: to judge by the sexual habits of later Welsh kings and contemporary Irish ones, as well as by the eligibility of the sons born of secondary unions, it is most unlikely that there were, simply in terms of descent, no plausible heirs. The situation is easiest to understand if we suppose that Merfyn could rely on the power he enjoyed as ruler of Man to make sure that he was the most powerful figure in the alliance built up by Cynan. Hence the second reconstruction is the most likely: Merfyn was still ruler of Man when he became king of Gwynedd.

It may be worth bearing in mind the possibility of an explanation that takes something from both these rival explanations. Merfyn, on this view, was the ruler of Man or part of Man, but he was also a client of the Vikings that were attacking the east coast of Ireland. If this were the case, it would help to explain why he still held his base in Man when the Vikings had already gained power in the Irish Sea. Viking power might then have helped Merfyn to gain power in Gwynedd. On this interpretation, everything suggested about the relationship between Merfyn and, first, the struggle for power between the Maelgyning and the dynasty of Rhos, and, secondly, the kings of Mercia may still be true: the role of the Vikings might simply be a further element in the situation.

The difficulty with the idea that the Vikings were part of the explanation for Merfyn's acquisition of power is the information in the Irish annals about the relationship between his son, Rhodri Mawr, and the Vikings. A Viking leader, Orm, was killed by Rhodri in 856.[51] In 877 Rhodri was driven by Vikings to take refuge in Ireland.[52] The only answer might be that the Viking enemies of Rhodri on both these occasions were the *Dubgennti* or *Dubgaill*, the 'Dark Heathen' or 'Dark Foreigners'. On the second occasion, there was fighting between the Fair Heathens and the Dark Heathens in Strangford Lough.[53] The latter could have

[51] AU 856. 6. [52] AU 877. 3. [53] AU 877. 5.

been Rhodri's enemies while the rival Vikings, the *Findgennti* or 'Fair Heathens' were his and his father's allies or overlords.

2. THE BRITONS AND ALFRED, *c.* 850–900

The century between 858, when Alfred's father Æthelwulf died, and 958, by which time Northumbria had been incorporated into the Anglo-Saxon kingdom, saw the creation of the English state.[54] In 858 England was still, as it had been for centuries, a collection of kingdoms. The English had long been a distinct people, but their identity had neither given rise to, nor had it been confirmed by, a single government. The English, that is, had been like the Britons. West of Offa's Dyke there was another distinct people; yet, again, national identity had neither led to, nor had it been created by, a single government or state. The English Channel had been, ever since the conquests of Clovis, a boundary in political culture. South of the Channel, Frankish, Lombard, Visigoth, Burgundian identities had all found expression in—indeed had sometimes been created by—a unity of government. By the mid-tenth century that boundary in political affairs had moved north-westwards: it now coincided with the boundary between the English and the Welsh.

The nature of Anglo-Welsh relations had, therefore, changed; and it had done so in a way that was to shape the political relationship until the end of an independent Gwynedd in 1282–1283. From the mid-tenth century onwards a single English government capable of shaping local as well as national politics, of redrawing political maps, of enforcing a single coinage and making it widely available throughout its territory, was confronted by a single people, the Welsh, but several kingdoms, for long essentially coinless and apparently faithful to ancient political boundaries. The relationship between the English and the Welsh had been transformed because one partner to that relationship had undergone a major change while the other partner had not. Because the crucial differences between the 850s and the 950s were seen among the English rather than among the Welsh, a full discussion belongs to a history of England rather than of Wales. Yet the Welsh were involved in the process by which the relationship was transformed. In the Viking Age the Irish Sea played a major military role; and Gwynedd especially was an important power within that zone.

In 850 there were still four English kingdoms ruled by their own separate dynasties: Northumbria from the Firth of Forth to the Humber; Mercia between the Welsh border, the Humber, the Fens, and the Thames valley; East Anglia beyond the Fens; and Wessex from the Thames valley southwards. Apart from the Welsh border, two areas were subject to a marked instability: the central lowland belt of what is now Scotland and the Thames valley. The central belt of Scotland—roughly Glasgow to Edinburgh—was where the early medieval nations of Britain met: Britons, Irish, Picts, and English all had a toehold in or on the edge

[54] J. Campbell, 'The Late Anglo-Saxon State: A Maximum View', *Proceedings of the Bristish Academy*, 87 (1995), 39–65.

of this zone. Just before the beginning of the period, the *Historia Brittonum* still paid more attention to Anglo-British relations in the north than to those between Wales and Mercia. The medieval kingdom of the Scots was, in these very years in the middle of the ninth century, forming on the northern edge of the central belt and would habitually seek to expand southwards across it.

In 870 two Viking kings based in or near Dublin, Olaf and Ivar, besieged Alclud and, 'at the end of four months they destroyed and plundered the fortress'.[55] For more than two centuries Alclud, alias Dún mBretan, 'the fortress of the Britons', Dumbarton, had been the centre of British power in the north. Their kings, if they were referred to by something more precise than merely 'kings of the Britons', were known as kings of Alclud or, in a longer form, Allt Glud (Irish *Ail Chlúathe*): they struck contemporaries as kings of a fortress, and only secondarily as kings of a people or of a territory.[56] The time taken by the Vikings to capture the fortress indicates both its formidable defences and its importance to Olaf and Ivar—an importance that one can well understand, since Alclud lay on the north bank of the Clyde as it is broadening out into the Firth. The two kings did not immediately depart with their plunder. Only in the the next year did they return 'to Dublin from Britain with two hundred ships; and a very great prey of the English and the Britons and the Picts was brought with them in captivity to Ireland'.[57] The capture of Alclud had facilitated the exploitation of northern Britain as a whole: those newly enslaved came from three of the four nations of Britain. Slaves were not, however, all that the Vikings desired from northern Britain. Four years earlier, in 866, Olaf and another Viking king, called by the Irish annalist *Auisle*, 'went into Fortriu with the Foreigners of Ireland and Britain and they plundered the whole Pictish people and took their hostages'.[58] The intention was both exploitation and political domination. When Ivar died in 873, the Chronicle of Ireland termed him 'king of the Northmen of all Ireland and Britain'—and this was after the campaigns of the Great Army in England had been under way for seven years.

In 872 the northern British king Arthal 'was killed at the instigation of Constantine son of Cináed', namely the king of the Picts.[59] (The dynasty of Cináed mac Ailpín, known later as Clann Chináeda, although Gaelic in cultural affiliation, retained at first the title of 'king of the Picts'; the first to be recorded in the Chronicle of Ireland as 'king of Alba' was Constantine's son, Domnall, who died in 900.)[60] The title given to Arthal in the Chronicle of Ireland was quite new: 'the king of the Britons of Srath Clúade', namely Strathclyde, Welsh Ystrad Glud. In 875, according to the Anglo-Saxon Chronicle, the portion of the Great Army under Healfdene, which had established its winter camp by the Tyne in the autumn of the previous year, 'frequently harried the Picts and the Strathclyde Welsh'.[61] Here, too, a change of name was registered in a quite independent and contemporary source. The implication seems to be that the Britons were not able to rebuild their fortress

[55] AU 870. 6; cf. *AC* 870. Olaf had a fort at Clondalkin, close to Dublin, AU 867. 8.

[56] AU 658. 2; 694. 6; 722. 3; AT 752.

[57] AU 871. 2.

[58] AU 866. 1.

[59] AU 872. 4.

[60] AU 900. 6.

[61] ASC 875.

at Allt Glud (Alclud); the kingdom could no longer be centred upon its great stronghold. Admittedly, the old name does not entirely vanish from the sources: *Armes Prydein*, a political poem of the tenth century, retains the old name, Alclud, alongside one for the people, Cludwys, the people of the Clyde.[62]

A major centre for the new kingdom of Strathclyde has been identified at Govan, on the south bank of the Clyde and much further up the river than Dumbarton, not far from what would, in the twelfth century, become the principal church of Strathclyde, Glasgow. An important collection of sculpture, associated with what may be a combined ecclesiastical and royal complex, suggests that this was the new centre for this renamed and restructured kingdom.[63] The immediate hinterlands of the old and new centres were different: Alclud, further down the Clyde and on the north bank, looked northwards towards Lennox and to Loch Lomond, in Welsh Llyn Llumonwy, for the *Historia Brittonum* the first of 'the marvels of Britain'.[64] All the good land around the lake was very probably within its territory.[65] For Govan, however, on the south bank, the valley of the Clyde and Renfrewshire formed the natural hinterland. This, it has been suggested, is the reason why the name changed from Alclud or Allt Glud to Ystrad Glud.[66]

The new kingdom of Strathclyde enjoyed a remarkable territorial expansion in the late ninth and early tenth century. The details are obscure, but it is probable that the southern boundary of the kingdom, also known to contemporaries as Cumbria, reached as far south as Penrith by 927.[67] The expansion was at the expense of the old Northumbria but in the quite new conditions created by the Viking capture of York; this led to a Viking Northumbria in which the Viking army and its kings were firmly in control of what had been Deira, while other northern rulers took control in the north, the Britons in Cumbria and the English in northern Northumbria.

It is possible to take different views about when and how the new wider Cumbria emerged. One view would see Cumbria as aligned with the principal Viking powers of the day from soon after the capture of Alclud in 870. The simplest argument for this position comes from a comparison between the outcome of the Viking victories at York and Alclud of 867–870. The victory at York led to the contraction and fragmentation of Northumbria; the capture of Alclud was followed by expansion to the south. One might argue that this could not have happened if the new Strathclyde had been in long-term conflict with the Vikings of Northumbria.

62 *Armes Prydein*, ed. Williams, lines 11 (Cludwys), 151 (Alclud). A still later example is CBT I. 9. 145 (Gwalchmai ap Meilyr, twelfth century).

63 A. Ritchie (ed.), *Govan and its Early Medieval Sculpture* (Stroud, 1994).

64 *HB*, c. 67.

65 W. J. Watson, *The History of the Celtic Place-Names of Scotland* (Edinburgh, 1926), 15, suggested that Clach na mBreatan in Glenn Falloch, the pass between Loch Lomond and Crianlarich, marked the boundary with Dál Riata. See above, 8.

66 Woolf, *From Pictland to Alba*, 109–11.

67 See below, 511–12. It has sometimes been claimed that Cumbria was distinct from Strathclyde, but this was refuted by P. A. Wilson, 'On the Use of the Terms "Strathclyde" and "Cumbria"', *Transactions of the Cumberland and Westmorland Antiquarian and Archaeological Society*, NS 66 (1966), 57–92.

Admittedly, the conflict between the Vikings and Strathclyde lasted after 870: as we saw above, in 875 the Vikings led by Healfdene 'frequently harried the Picts and the Strathclyde Welsh'.[68] The argument would then be that it was only after 875 that the hostilities between Strathclyde and the Vikings came to an end. To judge by the sculpture at Govan and by its political behaviour in the period 919–945, Strathclyde or Cumbria tended to align with the Vikings of Ireland and Northumbria, and this alignment was prepared by the capture of Alclud in 870 and the attacks of the Vikings in Northumbria on the northern peoples in 875.[69] Much of what had been British territory in 600 and was then subjugated by Northumbria was now taken again by the Cumbrians. This Cumbrian acquisition of so much of what was formerly north-western Northumbria was probably by agreement with the new rulers of Northumbria and on condition that Cumbria remained faithful to its Viking alliance. The Cumbrians did not participate in the Scottish campaign against the Vikings that led to the battle of the Tyne in 918.[70] One may compare also the alliance that, according to Asser, existed between Gwynedd and the Viking rulers of Northumbria, before Anarawd ap Rhodri submitted to Alfred *c.* 890.

Another view would be that the alignment of Strathclyde with the Vikings did not occur until the major Viking victories of 918–919, on the Tyne and at Dublin. The *Historia de Sancto Cuthberto* has a story about a Northumbrian nobleman called Ælfred son of Brihtwulf, who fled from 'pirates' and crossed 'the mountains in the west'. He received a group of vills between the Wear and the Tees and became St Cuthbert's 'faithful man'; subsequently, he led a force which fought against King Ragnall at the battle of the Tyne.[71] This might be taken to suggest a collapse of the power of an English elite in north-western Northumbria at the hands of Vikings in the early years of the tenth century after the dispersal from Dublin in 902 and before 918.[72] No positive evidence exists for any alignment between Strathclyde and the Vikings until the 920s and thus after the battle of the Tyne. After 918 the main concern of Ragnall and his successors was to maintain their hold over York against a challenge from the south: a readiness to allow the expansion of Strathclyde into what is now Dumfriesshire and Cumbria may have seemed politic when the main threat was from a resurgent Wessex and Mercia. The significance of 918–919 will be discussed further in the next chapter.

[68] ASC 875. It should be added that the supposed migration from Strathclyde to Gwynedd in the late ninth century and said to be recorded in *Brut y Tywysogion* (Jackson, *Gododdin*, 67; A. P. Smyth, *Warlords and Holy Men: Scotland AD 80–1000* (London, 1984), 217–18; A. Macquarrie, 'The Historical Context of the Govan Stones', in A. Ritchie (ed.), *Govan and its Early Medieval Sculpture*, 30) does not occur in any early version of the *Brut*. Jackson, Smyth, and Macquarrie all took it from A. O. Anderson, *Early Sources for Scottish History* (Edinburgh, 1922; repr. Stamford, 1990), i. 890, and Anderson took it from the 'Aberpergwm Brut' in the Myvyrian Archaeology: see Charles-Edwards, 'The Authenticity of the *Gododdin*', 53–4.

[69] The 'Scottish Chronicle', ed. Hudson, for Constantine's reign also indicates sustained pressure.

[70] AU 918. 4.

[71] *Historia de Sancto Cuthberto*, ed. and trans. T. Johnson South (Cambridge, 2002), § 22.

[72] For an early tenth-century Viking settlement in western Northumbria, see Graham-Campbell, 'The Irish-Sea Vikings: Raiders and Settlers', 72–5 (this would not exclude further settlement later: the issue is the start of a significant land-taking).

The Thames valley was the theatre for an earlier shift of power: in 820 it had still been dominated by the traditional leader in southern English politics, Mercia. Indeed, the great Mercian kings, Æthelbald, Offa, and Cenwulf, had all been overlords of Kent, Sussex, Surrey, and Essex. In the late 820s, however, power over south-eastern England had been seized by the West Saxons. In spite of the seriousness of the territorial loss suffered by the Mercians, the subsequent conflict had only resulted in serious violence for a short period; in the mid-ninth century both faced Viking attacks and were tending towards a firmer alliance.

In 850 southern England may have seemed to be on the road to stability, but this was soon to be reversed. In the 830s and 840s Vikings had been especially active in two areas: in Ireland and in Frisia. In 848, however, the Irish won some important, and also widely dispersed, battles.[73] With the transformation of Dublin in 841 from a minor church into a major Viking fortress and port, and then these defeats seven years later, the Norse–Irish relationship changed in character, from widespread campaigning and plundering to tribute-taking and more occasional raiding.[74] In Francia, after 866, the increased stability of Charles the Bald's kingdom made it a less promising target.[75] It was the misfortune of the peoples of Britain that Viking military power was displaced both from Ireland and from the Continent towards Britain at much the same time. While some Viking leaders had been prominent earlier in Ireland and in the central belt of Scotland, others may have been new arrivals either from Scandinavia or from Frisia.

From 865 to 878 the English suffered the campaigns of what the Anglo-Saxon Chronicle called 'the Great Army' or simply 'the army'. These fourteen years saw the conquest of Northumbria and East Anglia, the conquest of most of Mercia and the near conquest of Wessex. Both Northumbria and Mercia came to be partitioned, permanently weakening the two most powerful kingdoms of the previous centuries. In the north, this encouraged the Scots to seek conquests or else absorption of territory south of the Forth;[76] while the division of Mercia threw into question the relationship between the Welsh and their English neighbours. No longer was the kingdom that lay east across Offa's Dyke the most powerful in Britain. Whereas, in 850, Mercia was the equal partner of Wessex in an alliance, by 883 what remained outside Danish control was largely a satellite of its southern neighbour. West Saxon power over English Mercia, when added to the earlier acquisition of what the West Saxons called 'the Eastern Kingdom'—Kent, Sussex, Surrey, and Essex—was the launching pad for the late Anglo-Saxon kingdom of the English.[77] Because the English kingdom that had traditionally exercised overlordship over Wales, namely Mercia, was so gravely weakened by the Viking wars, and

[73] AU 848. 4–7; cf. *The Annals of St-Bertin*, trans. J. Nelson (Manchester, 1991), 66.

[74] AU 841. 4; C. Etchingham, *Viking Raids on Irish Church Settlements in the Ninth Century* (Maynooth, 1996), 9–11, 49–50.

[75] J. Nelson, *Charles the Bald* (London, 1992), 213.

[76] 'The Scottish Chronicle', ed. Hudson, 148, suggests that this had already begun in the reign of Cináed mac Alpín.

[77] Keynes, 'King Alfred and the Mercians', 31–6.

because the Vikings themselves were partly based in the coastlands of the Irish Sea, Wales was an essential part of the pattern of events.

In Wales, this period saw the triumph of a new dynasty, the Merfynion. In 825 Merfyn Frych son of Gwriad had, as we saw earlier, taken the kingship of Gwynedd in obscure circumstances.[78] Admittedly, neither Merfyn nor any of his descendants, right down to Llywelyn the Last Prince, would ever rule directly over the whole of Wales. Initially, Merfyn only ruled Gwynedd. In the course of the next century, 825–925, however, his descendants would come to rule over Powys, Ceredigion, Dyfed, and Ystrad Tywi. In 918 one version of the Anglo-Saxon Chronicle records the death of King Alfred's daughter, Æthelflæd, Lady of the Mercians, and the takeover of Mercia by her brother, Edward the Elder, and it adds that 'there sought Edward as lord the kings of the Welsh, Hywel, Clydog and Idwal'.[79] All three were grandsons of Rhodri Mawr, himself son of Merfyn Frych. In this century also Mercian hegemony over Wales was first replaced by the overlordship of the West Saxon, Alfred, and then by the overlordship of his descendants, kings of the English. It was also the same period in which Vikings conquered much of England and then later gradually lost ground to the West Saxons. Large-scale military activity was changing the political shape of the British Isles (see Map 23).

The first more particular question concerns the situation of Wales in the period from 866 to 878 in which the so-called 'Great Army' posed a major threat to all English kingdoms. In these years we enter one of those exceedingly rare periods for pre-Norman Welsh history when one can see in some detail what was going on. The story will set the scene for what happened after Alfred's victory over the Vikings in 878.

The Great Army was led by kings termed by the Irish and the Welsh annals 'Dark Heathens'. These Dark Heathens are first recorded as arriving in Dublin in 851, when they defeated their Viking opponents, the 'Fair Foreigners'.[80] This inaugurated a long period in which one of the principal powers of both Ireland and Britain was a Viking dynasty, known to the Irish as Uí Ímair, 'the descendants of Ímar', and it has been argued that 'the Dark Heathens' were those who gave their allegiance to Ímar and his heirs, the Uí Ímair.[81] The Ímar (Ívarr) in question was described by the Chronicle of Ireland, when recording his death in 873, as 'king of the *Nordmanni* of all Ireland and Britain'.[82]

In 856 the Irish annals tell us that 'Orm, leader of the Dark Heathens, was killed by Rhodri son of Merfyn, king of the Britons.'[83] These Dark Heathens were active

[78] See above, 471–9.

[79] ASC A 922 = 918.

[80] *The Chronicle of Ireland*, trans. Charles-Edwards, 851. 3.

[81] C. Downham, *Viking Kings of Britain and Ireland: The Dynasty of Ívarr to A.D. 1014* (Edinburgh, 2007), pp. xvi–xvii, on *Dubgennti*; D. N. Dumville, 'Old Dubliners and New Dubliners in Ireland and Britain: A Viking-Age Story', *Medieval Dublin*, 6 (2004), 97–116; reprinted in his *Celtic Essays, 2000–2007* (Aberdeen, 2007), 103–22.

[82] *The Chronicle of Ireland*, trans. Charles-Edwards, 873. 3.

[83] AU 856. 6.

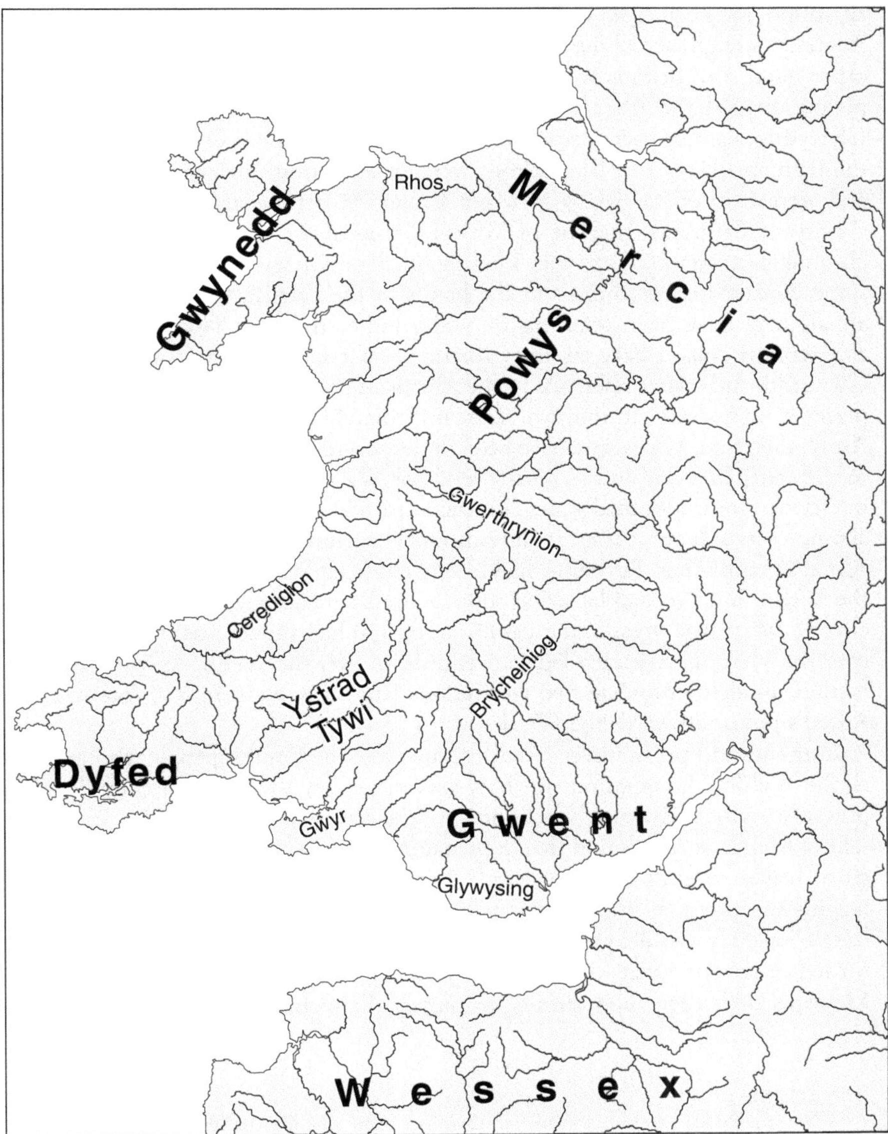

Map 23. The Welsh kingdoms, *c.* 840
In 840 Powys still confronted Mercia across Offa's Dyke, but Mercia was already extending its power in north-east Wales.

all round the Irish Sea, and it is hardly surprising that a king who ruled over Anglesey, straight across the water from Dublin, should be heavily involved. On the other hand, the Britons were also under pressure from the English in the same period. In 864 the *Annales Cambriae* record that someone called *Duta* ravaged Glywysing, namely part of south-east Wales.[84] The name is Old English.[85] In 865 the Irish annals say that 'the Britons were expelled from their land by the English and were reduced to slavery in Maen Conan.'[86] Britons at this period, just like Cymry or Cumbras, may be of Wales, Cornwall, or Strathclyde, but the close chronological conjunction of an English attack on Glywysing with this mention of some disaster for the Britons at the hands of the English suggests that the Irish annals may have been referring to Wales rather than the North; moreover the *Fragmentary Annals* have an entry for this year referring to an English attack on Gwynedd, and a later reference in the Annals of the Four Masters to Maen Conan places it in Wales.[87] In the two years immediately before the arrival of the Great Army, therefore, Wales may have been under severe pressure from the English both in the south-east and in the north-west. For Wales, at this period, the English in question were undoubtedly the Mercians. In 853 they had received West Saxon assistance in order to reassert their traditional hegemony in Wales.[88] Earlier, in 830, Alfred's grandfather, Ecgberht, had briefly enforced West Saxon overlordship over the Welsh, but this had lapsed as soon as the Mercians reasserted their independence.[89] What that West Saxon campaign in 830 had shown was that overlordship over the Mercians naturally led to overlordship over the Welsh. As it was recorded in the Alfredian chronicle two generations later, this event in 830 foreshadowed Alfred's policies towards the Welsh.

In the meantime, however, the Mercians were the English people who mattered to the Welsh. The question was how successful they would be in enforcing their power over the Welsh and how oppressive their overlordship would be. It has been said of Mercia at this period that 'a predatory power which had enjoyed its time of glory began to turn in on itself'.[90] For Mercian relations with their English neighbours this may indeed be so; but the Welsh of the ninth century would have been only too delighted if the predatory energies of the Mercians had been turned elsewhere. Even when pressure from the Great Army was at its height, the Mercians took every opportunity to pursue their objective of maintaining their

[84] AC 864.

[85] Namely Dudda (compare the ealdorman of that name who died in 835: ASC 836). The name occurs in the Book of Llandaff, as the father of a lay witness in 217 and as the father of two clerical witnesses in 218 (p. 221, ll. 8–9); but there are other English names among the witnesses to 217.

[86] AU 865. 4.

[87] *Fragmentary Annals of Ireland*, ed. J. Radner (Dublin, 1978), § 314; AFM *s.a.* 960 = 962. See also Moind Conáin (Main Conain), *The Book of Leinster, formally Lebar na Núachongbála*, eds. R. I. Best, O. J. Bergin, M. A. O'Brien, and A. O'Sullivan, 6 vols. (Dublin, 1954–83), i. 21, l. 656, and 24, l. 764, mentioned by R. Thurneysen, *Gúbretha Caratniad*, ed. and trans. R. Thurneysen, *Zeitschift für celtische Philologie*, 15 (1925), 302–70, at 338, where he takes it to be Anglesey.

[88] ASC 853.

[89] ASC 830.

[90] Keynes, 'King Alfred and the Mercians', 6.

power in Wales, including, probably, taking advantage of Viking attacks on Gwynedd. In 873 the Great Army marched into Mercia, drove King Burgred overseas and set up Ceolwulf as a client-king. This seems by now to have been Viking policy: after Halfdan settled his army in Northumbria in 876, an English client-king of Northumbria continued to rule, perhaps now based in the northern part of the kingdom.[91] For Asser, 'the Northumbrians' with whom Anarawd had an alliance up until *c.* 890 were the Viking rulers of the kingdom.[92] In the autumn of 877 the Vikings divided Mercia into two, leaving Ceolwulf in possession only of one part of the kingdom; however, this included the districts adjacent to Wales.[93] Both Northumbria and Mercia were now divided.

In 877 Rhodri Mawr was defeated in battle in Anglesey and driven to take refuge in Ireland.[94] His enemies were described in the Irish annals as 'Dark Foreigners', namely as belonging to the same group within the Vikings that had moved from Ireland to participate in the leadership of the Great Army; it was to this group, moreover, that Orm, killed by Rhodri Mawr in 856, had belonged. The most natural interpretation of these events is that the Viking leaders were behaving just as Ecgberht, king of the West Saxons, had behaved in 830. When he achieved an hegemony over the Mercians, he followed it up by enforcing on his own behalf the overlordship over the Welsh traditionally held by the Mercians. Similarly in 877 partition of the Mercian kingdom was associated with the attack on Anglesey in the same year, as a result of which Rhodri was compelled to flee to Ireland.[95] Hegemony in Wales by this time meant overlordship over Rhodri Mawr in particular, not because, as Lloyd maintained, he had already extended his power to the northern frontier of Dyfed on the Teifi, but because Gwynedd by this date threatened Powys, close neighbour to Mercia.[96] According to Asser, Powys was not among the Welsh kingdoms threatened either by Mercia or by Gwynedd in the 880s. The likely explanation is that it had already been incorporated into Gwynedd before 886.[97] As will be argued later, the absence also of Ceredigion from Asser's list of Welsh kingdoms subject to Alfred is much more likely to be explained by territorial expansion of Dyfed than by any conquest, as yet, by the Merfynion. Quite apart from the implications of overlordship over the Mercians, the leaders of the 'Dark Foreigners' may also have been led to attack Rhodri so that they could both take revenge for the killing of Orm and protect communications with Dublin by conquering Anglesey.

[91] Roger of Wendover, *Flores Historiarum*, ed. H. O. Coxe (London, 1841), *s.a.* 867, 872, 873, 874, *EHD* i, no. 4. A division between a Viking Deira and an English Bernicia very probably did not occur in 867, as stated by Simeon of Durham, *EHD* i, no. 3, *s.a.* 867: Woolf, *From Pictland to Alba*, 73–7.

[92] Asser, *Life*, c. 80.

[93] ASC 877.

[94] AU 877. 3. Since *AC* 877 is shown by AU 878. 1 to be for 878, I assume that *AC*'s annal for 876, 'The "Sunday Battle" on Anglesey', *Gueith Diu Sul in Mon*, was also one year too early. In that case, it very probably refers to the same event as AU 877. 3.

[95] AU 877. 3.

[96] Lloyd, *HW* i. 325.

[97] Asser, *Life*, c. 80.

In the winter of 877–878 the Great Army mounted the attack on Wessex that initially came close to conquest but which ended, in the early summer, in Alfred's decisive victory at Edington. In the autumn of 878, in accordance with the terms of the treaty made with Alfred after Edington, the Viking army moved from Chippenham to take up its winter camp at Cirencester. Also in 878, both the Irish and the Welsh annals record the killing of Rhodri Mawr by the English.[98] Alfred's involvement with the Great Army makes it inconceivable that he was responsible. But between January 878 when the final Viking attack on Wessex began and the autumn of the same year, Ceolwulf, king of the Mercians, may have had a relatively free hand. The same year, probably for a similar reason, namely that the Great Army was committed to its attempted conquest of Wessex, saw the return of Rhodri Mawr from exile in Ireland. The pattern of events shows the difficulty faced by the Great Army in enforcing its authority over the whole area in which it had been active, all the way from the Clyde to Wessex, from Anglesey to East Anglia. In other words, for Rhodri Mawr and Ceolwulf, once the Vikings had their hands full in Wessex, it was back to business as usual: Rhodri established himself in Gwynedd and Ceolwulf attacked him in order to reassert the old Mercian overlordship. In this attack Rhodri was killed, an outcome that apparently restored the Mercian hegemony in Wales. Yet Alfred's near-contemporaneous victory at Edington raised a question both over the Viking hold on Mercia and over their client-king's survival.

In 879 the Viking army moved from Cirencester to East Anglia, where they settled. They subsequently made the treaty with Alfred known after the kings on either side as Alfred-Guthrum—a treaty which used Watling Street as a boundary between Danish England and the part of Mercia now under the overlordship of Alfred. The extant treaty cannot be precisely dated and must be distinguished from the earlier agreement made by Alfred with Guthrum and his army in the summer of 878. We now approach the short but very interesting period of Anglo-Welsh relations illuminated by Asser's Life of King Alfred.[99]

Asser wrote his Life of Alfred in 893.[100] He had probably first met the king in 885, but had only been regularly present in his household from 886. As is well known, he divided his time between Alfred's court and St Davids, either six months in Wales and six in England or three months in turn in each.[101] That Asser had a Welsh readership in mind for his work is, I think, well established.[102] Whether he also intended it for those at court, including the king himself, who could read Latin is disputed; it is also an issue intimately related to what Asser has to say about Anglo-Welsh relations. What we have in Asser's Life, then, is an account of the

[98] AU 878. 1; *AC* 877 = 878.

[99] W. Davies, 'Alfred's Contemporaries: Irish, Welsh, Scots and Breton', in T. Reuter (ed.), *Alfred the Great: Papers from the Eleventh-Centenary Conference*, Studies in Early Medieval Britain 3 (Aldershot, 2003), 323–37; R. Abels, *Alfred the Great: War, Kingship and Culture in Anglo-Saxon England* (London, 1998), 182–3, 186–7.

[100] Keynes and Lapidge, *Alfred the Great*, 269–70 n. 218.

[101] This arrangement was not rigidly adhered to: Asser stayed at Alfred's court for eight months in 886–887: Asser, *Life*, c. 81. 10.

[102] Keynes and Lapidge, *Alfred the Great*, 56, and cf. above, 452.

reign at the point when a period of warfare up to 878 had been succeeded by a period of relative peace, from 878 to 892. The situation in 893 accorded well with the portrait of the king that Asser wished to convey. As we have seen, instead of one diptych of public deeds versus manner of life Asser had three successive diptychs, in each one of which Deeds were succeeded by Life. The reason for this was to display the king as a latter-day Solomon, a pursuer of wisdom. Asser naturally considered a preoccupation with warfare, the main topic of the Deeds, to be thoroughly inimical to scholarship; moreover, in a tradition long since established in Wales and Ireland, he considered *sapientia*, 'wisdom', to be primarily a scholarship whose summit was the understanding of the Bible, an understanding not normally gained by any direct personal inspiration but by the hard grind of learning and study.[103] Hence the period of incessant warfare up to 878 was explicitly regarded by Asser as incompatible with the pursuit of wisdom.[104] For Asser, the period of peace between 878 and 892 was, therefore, the culmination of Alfred's reign, a period in which a relaxation of external pressure allowed Alfred to learn to read Latin.

Unfortunately for Asser, the autumn of 892 was the start of the second great Viking assault on England in Alfred's lifetime. The next few years were not propitious for even those short intervals of unhurried intellectual enquiry possible for a busy king in the 880s. Asser's view of the situation is, therefore, particular to one period within Alfred's reign, and this is, as we shall see, as true of what he says about Wales as it is for his understanding of Alfred's life as a whole. The crucial section of the Life for Welsh history is at the end of the second of the three diptychs. Asser is explaining how Alfred gathered together a group of scholars at his court, first four Mercians—Werferth, later bishop of Worcester, Plegmund, later archbishop of Canterbury, Æthelstan, and Werwulf, priests and chaplains—then subsequently scholars from outside England, Grimbald and John from Francia and, finally, Asser himself from St Davids. The reason why the community of St Davids was willing to allow Asser leave of absence was that they were subject to the oppression of the king of Dyfed, Hyfaidd, and hoped to use Asser's influence with Alfred to secure themselves against any further unfriendly attentions. Asser then explains the context which made it reasonable for St Davids to look to a king of the West Saxons in order to compel Hyfaidd to treat the main church of his own kingdom with greater benevolence:[105]

> For at that time (namely 886), and for a considerable period beforehand, all the kingdoms of southern Wales belonged to Alfred and they still do. For Hyfaidd, with all the inhabitants of the kingdom of Dyfed, had submitted to the king's overlordship, driven by the military power of the sons of Rhodri. Hywel ap Rhys, also, the king of Glywysing, and Brochfael and Ffernfael, kings of Gwent, driven by the military power and tyranny of Ealdorman Æthelred and the Mercians, of their own will sought out the king, so that they might have his lordship and protection from their enemies. Likewise Elise ap Tewdwr, king of Brycheiniog, driven by the military power of those same sons of Rhodri, of his own will sought the lordship of the king. Finally Anarawd

103 *Sapientia* is also practical wisdom: Asser, *Life*, c. 91. 69.
104 Ibid. c. 76. 1–12.
105 Asser, *Life*, c. 80.

son of Rhodri, together with his brothers, abandoned his alliance with the Northumbrians, from which he had had nothing but harm, eagerly sought the king's alliance and came to his presence. When he had been honourably welcomed by the king and had been received by him at the hand of a bishop as his son in confirmation, and had been enriched with many exceedingly precious gifts, he submitted himself to the king's lordship with all his people, namely [promising] that he would in every way be obedient to the king's will on the very same conditions as Æthelred and the Mercians.

This passage reveals the existence, in the early 880s, of two earlier spheres of power in process of giving way to a third. First, there was the sphere of Anarawd and his brothers, sons of Rhodri Mawr. Hyfaidd, king of Dyfed and Elise ap Tewdwr, king of Brycheiniog, both feared the power of Gwynedd. On the other hand, the rulers of south-east Wales, Hywel ap Rhys, king of Glywysing, and Brochfael and Ffernfael, kings of Gwent, had been subject to pressure from Æthelred and the Mercians. The division is thus between south-west and central southern Wales, the target of Anarawd ap Rhodri and his brothers, and south-eastern Wales, the target of Æthelred and the Mercians.

The background to this state of affairs can be broadly reconstructed. In 878, as we saw earlier, Alfred defeated the Great Army at Edington, while Ceolwulf, king of the Mercians, defeated and killed Rhodri Mawr. At the time of his death Rhodri had barely recovered his position in Gwynedd after an earlier defeat and expulsion at the hands of the Dark Foreigners, namely a group among the Vikings also prominent in the leadership of the Great Army. Since Ceolwulf was a client-king of the Great Army, it is only reasonable to see the end of Rhodri's reign as coming about through the conjunction of Mercian and Viking power. Three years later, in 881, the sons of Rhodri defeated the Mercians in the battle of the Conwy, a battle described by the Welsh annals, in a wholly exceptional departure from their normal succinct and unemotional style, as 'revenge by God for Rhodri'. This interpretation of the battle as vengeance is remarkable, because the Mercian leader in 881 was not the King Ceolwulf who had led them to victory in 878. A Worcester king-list gives him a reign of five years, implying that it came to an end in 879.[106] A charter of 883, two years after the battle of the Conwy, shows that Ceolwulf had been replaced by Æthelred, and that Æthelred had by then already submitted to the overlordship of Alfred.[107]

Confirmation that Æthelred was the leader of the Mercians at the battle of the Conwy comes from a thirteenth-century collection of Welsh genealogies, in a section on the descendants of Rhodri Mawr:

Tudwal the Lame son of Rhodri was wounded in his knee in the battle of Cymrid Conwy, when the sons of Rhodri fought with Edryd Long-Hair, king of Lloegr, and

[106] Keynes, 'King Alfred and the Mercians', p. 12 n. 48. Keynes, ibid. 13–14, notes the coincidence of the end of Ceolwulf's reign with Guthrum's presence at Cirencester from the autumn of 878 to the autumn of 879 and wonders whether Guthrum might have been involved in removing him from power; an alternative is that Ceolwulf was ousted by the Mercians in the autumn of 879 when the Viking army removed itself to East Anglia.

[107] S 218, ed. and trans. F. E. Harmer, *Select English Historical Documents of the Ninth and Tenth Centuries* (Cambridge, 1914), no. 12; Keynes, 'King Alfred and the Mercians', 20.

from that wound he became lame. And for that reason his brothers gave him the chief churches of Gwynedd.[108]

Edryd Long-Hair is almost certainly Æthelred of Mercia, as shown by other spellings of the name in Asser in particular.[109] Lloyd, and more recently Simon Keynes, have quoted another, much later piece of Welsh evidence for Æthelred's participation in the battle;[110] this earlier genealogical item is far from contemporary, but the form of the section in which it occurs is similar to early Irish genealogies,[111] and the principal concern of the immediately preceding portion of the text with enhancing the status of Merfyn Frych, Rhodri Mawr and his sons suggests that it may derive ultimately from a tenth-century text.[112]

The Welsh annalist's interpretation of the Battle of Conwy as divine revenge cannot be explained on the grounds that Ceolwulf had been the client-king of pagan Vikings when he killed Rhodri and that God was thus angry with a Christian king who had submitted to pagan authority; the Mercian leader at the Battle of the Conway was Æthelred not Ceolwulf, and Æthelred was not a Viking client-king. Rather, it portrays the hostilities between the Mercians and Gwynedd as a blood-feud, and so foreshadows the attitudes expressed on a much grander scale in the tenth-century poem *Armes Prydein*; but it is also consistent with Asser's description of the power of Æthelred of Mercia in Wales as a military tyranny.[113] By some date before *c.* 886 that tyranny was exercised only over the south-eastern kingdoms of Gwent and Glywysing. The core of English Mercia was then the lower Severn valley, including the old kingdom of the Hwicce, around Gloucester and Worcester, but also neighbouring districts, such as the land of the Magonsæte, the diocese of Hereford. The centre of Æthelred's power lay adjacent to those south-eastern Welsh kingdoms on which he continued to exert pressure after his defeat at the Conwy in 881. Following that battle, the area of Mercian overlordship in Wales contracted in a way corresponding very closely with the territorial contraction of English Mercia itself. But even in this reduced condition Mercia did not cease to be a predatory power: overlordship over a portion of Wales briefly kept alive some shadow of its imperial past.

The Battle of the Conwy, therefore, had brought to an end any hope that Mercia could impose its authority on Gwynedd. Anarawd must have made his alliance with the Northumbrians shortly after the battle.[114] The alliance was presumably anti-

108 ABT 7 (q), ed. Bartrum, *EWGT* 101.

109 Eadred in Asser, Life, c. 80. 8 (also c. 75. 7), is an emendation for a probable Eudred in the Cottonian MS; Æthered in c. 80. 22 is also an emendation: the original probably had Œthelred. Æthered is a well-attested variant. This suggests a fluctuation between a more Welsh spelling such as Edred (misinterpreted by an English scribe as Eadred, miscopied as Eudred) and English spellings such as Æthelred, Æthered, and, mistakenly, Œthelred. The genealogist's Edryd is a further shift in a Welsh direction from something like Edred, where the medial *-d-* stands in this instance for /ð/.

110 Lloyd, *HW* i. 328 and n. 30; Keynes, 'King Alfred and the Mercians', 19 and n. 84.

111 In Irish terms it traces *cráeba coibnesa*, 'branches of kinship'.

112 Probably via an early twelfth-century intermediary to judge by its interest in Gruffudd ap Cynan and eleventh-century kings such as Llywelyn ap Seisyll and Gruffudd ap Llywelyn.

113 It was a matter of *vis et tyrannis*, Asser, Life, c. 80. 7–8.

114 It can hardly have been made by Rhodri, since Ceolwulf was the client of the Great Army, one section of which had taken over power in Northumbria; it is too early to consider Northumbrian

Mercian, at a time when the ruler of English Mercia was no longer a Viking client. Asser says that Anarawd got no benefit from the alliance, perhaps because Viking raids may have continued on Gwynedd.[115] What is evident from what Asser himself says is that for much of southern Wales, the threat of a predatory overlordship was now from Gwynedd rather than from Mercia. Moreover, it is noticeable that, for Wales outside the south, Asser need only mention Anarawd and his brothers, and they remained at this period an effective political unit. Asser's chapter is the clearest evidence that Gwynedd had already conquered or taken over Powys. While Lloyd maintained that this was Rhodri's achievement, there is much to be said for dating it later, to the period immediately after 881 when Mercian control of Wales outside the south-east had collapsed. Before then any Venedotian conquest of Powys would surely have been most firmly resisted by the English overlord.[116]

The Battle of the Conwy is, therefore, the key to Asser's Wales, namely the Wales of 881–893. The collapse of Mercian power was exploited by two neighbours: Alfred sought to displace Æthelred as overlord of the south-eastern Welsh kingdoms; Anarawd and his brothers likewise sought to replace Æthelred as overlord of Brycheiniog and Dyfed. Wessex and Gwynedd were now rivals for dominance in Wales. Æthelred of Mercia, for his part, submitted to Alfred no later than 883. Asser's evidence indicates that there was an interval after the Battle of the Conwy when Æthelred was still attempting to hold on to his overlordship at least over Gwent and Glywysing, although he now had no hope of maintaining Mercian power elsewhere in Wales. This limited hegemony, although critical for a kingdom whose centre of gravity was now in the lower Severn valley, was very rapidly undermined by Alfred. The contrast made by Asser between the 'force and tyranny' exercised by Æthelred and the Mercians and the benevolent lordship offered by Alfred suggests that Mercian power even in south-east Wales had been dangerously weakened after the Battle of the Conwy and was being enforced by unusual violence.

Presented with the possibility of a gentler overlord, the kings of Gwent and Glywysing could change allegiance without undermining the collaboration between Wessex and Mercia against the Vikings. All this suggests, without in any way proving it, that the submission of the kings of Gwent and Glywysing preceded the submission of Æthelred himself; on this view Alfred subverted the remnants of the traditional Mercian power in Wales when Æthelred was still attempting to act as an independent ruler. In that case, the submissions of the kings of Gwent and Glywysing may have been a significant element in the situation that caused the subsequent submission of Æthelred. Now Alfred had allies on the western frontier of Mercia to reinforce what was, after the defeat of the Vikings at Edington, a powerful West Saxon position on the

Vikings acting against those Vikings who were calling the tune in Mercia. Moreover, the Viking leaders in Northumbria were, for the *Annales Cambriae*, s.a. 867, 'Dark Heathens', of the same grouping that expelled Rhodri to Ireland in 877.

[115] None is recorded in the *Annales Cambriae*, but that source is too exiguous a record to support an argument *e silentio* on this point.

[116] Another possibility is that the British disaster of 865, recorded by the Irish annals, included a Mercian assumption of direct rule in Powys; in that event Anarawd would still have taken over from the Mercians after 881.

southern boundary of Mercia. As a result, the Mercians are likely to have perceived that independence was impossible for the time being.

It is possible, then, to suggest the following chronology of events:

881:	the Battle of the Conwy;
881–882:	Æthelred struggled to retain Mercian power over Gwent and Glywysing, but Alfred intervened to encourage Hywel ap Rhys, Brochfael ap Meurig and his brother Ffernfael to transfer their allegiance to himself;
882–883:	Æthelred accepted that West Saxon power rendered independence unsustainable and himself submitted.

The implication of all this is that the Mercian submission to Alfred—a crucial step in the creation of a single English kingdom—occurred not just because of one battle, Alfred's victory over the Great Army at Edington in 878, but also because of another, more distant battle, 'God's revenge' on the Mercians at the Conwy, when Anarawd of Gwynedd and his brothers defeated Æthelred and so brought about that collapse of the Mercian hegemony in Wales from which Alfred was only too pleased to profit.

Between the Battle of the Conwy in 881 and the end of 883, therefore, West Saxon overlordship had been extended northwards, first across the Bristol Channel to Gwent and Glywysing, and secondly over English Mercia. The treaty between Alfred and Guthrum, which fixed Watling Street as the limit of English Mercia, should be dated after these changes, almost certainly no earlier than 883, five years after the Battle of Edington and four years after Guthrum's army had moved from Cirencester to East Anglia.[117] In Wales, Alfred used against Gwynedd the same tactics that he had employed against Æthelred: Hyfaidd, king of Dyfed and Elise ap Tewdwr, king of Brycheiniog, submitted to Alfred in order to secure protection against Anarawd and his brothers. The geography of the situation suggests that these submissions occurred after the kings of Gwent and Glywysing had accepted Alfred's lordship. Asser puts them all together and dates them 'some considerable time' before the agreement with St Davids, *c.* 886, by which he was allowed to spend some months each year at Alfred's court. In this context, 'some considerable time' cannot mean more than a few years.

In Asser's account of Wales, however, the great prize was not any one of the southern Welsh kingdoms but Gwynedd. His words make it clear that a period intervened between Alfred's acquisition of overlordship over South Wales and the submission of Anarawd 'on the same conditions as Æthelred and the Mercians'. It has been suggested that Anarawd's abandonment of his alliance with the Northumbrian Vikings and his submission to Alfred may have been as late as 893, in other words only months at the most before Asser was writing.[118] Yet this is to

[117] D. N. Dumville, 'The Treaty of Alfred and Guthrum', in his *Wessex and England from Alfred to Edgar* (Woodbridge, 1992), ch. 1; Keynes, 'King Alfred and the Mercians', 31–4.

[118] Keynes and Lapidge, *Alfred the Great*, 287 n. 15. This is on the basis of what ASC A has to say about the Battle of Buttington, for which see below. A similar dating is advocated by D. P. Kirby, 'Asser and his Life of King Alfred', *Studia Celtica*, 6 (1971), 16–17, but his date for Æthelred's submission is three years too late.

imply that Anarawd's switch of allegiance came, not when Alfred's power was at its height, from 883 to 892, but precisely when a new Viking invasion was threatening West Saxon power. I think that a more likely reconstruction of events can be attempted, if we place Anarawd's submission *c.* 888–892. When trying to understand Gwynedd, it is always wise at this period to look at the Irish situation; 888 saw a serious defeat inflicted by the Vikings on the king of Tara, Flann Sinna.[119] The vernacular Welsh annals, but not *Annales Cambriae*, record an attack by the 'Dark Northmen' on Gwynedd in 892;[120] this attack may perhaps have been in Asser's mind when he noted that Anarawd gained no profit from his alliance with the Northumbrians.[121] It looks as though the situation in the Irish-Sea area was again becoming more dangerous, and this may well have propelled Anarawd to seek an alliance with Alfred.

Although Anarawd's submission was on the same terms as Æthelred's, he remained king of Gwynedd, whereas, in West Saxon eyes, Æthelred was not king of the Mercians. There was a difference of policy on the part of Alfred towards the Britons: the Cornish, whom he inherited as clients of the West Saxons, had no acknowledged king after the death of *Dungarth* in 875.[122] *Dungarth* was drowned, which may have been an accident, but at this period is attested in Ireland as a punishment for collaboration with the Vikings.[123] The Cornishmen seem, therefore, to have been treated as were the Mercians, in that they no longer had recognized kings. Welsh rulers, however, retained, even in West Saxon sources, their regal status: they might be 'under-kings' but they were still kings. On the other hand, when Mercia was considered from the west, looking eastwards, whether by the Welsh or by the Irish, Mercian rulers retained all their old regality until 918. As we shall see, from a western perspective this was entirely justifiable.

Two fleets, one from northern Francia and the other from the Loire, arrived in south-eastern England in the summer or early autumn of 892. The timber for the palisade at the crannog of the kings of Brycheiniog on Llangorse Lake was felled between 889 and 893, and this construction, unique for Wales, could have been a reaction to the new threat.[124] Viking forces were active in England, and also intermittently in Wales, for about four years, until 896. By the end of this phase of military activity, Alfred had little more than three years to live. The question is, therefore, how far, if at all, the Welsh settlement described by Asser was undermined, or at least threatened, in the period 892–896. There are two crucial pieces of evidence from within the period, while some later annals offer useful context.

119 AU 888. 5 (and cf. 888. 9).

120 *Brut, Pen. 20, s.a.* 890 (see Jones's note to the translation, where he notes that *Brenhinedd y Saeson* may offer some support to the Peniarth 20 version against the Red Book version, which in any case offers an impossible reading).

121 'ad postremum amicitiam Northanbymbrorum deserens, de qua nullum bonum nisi damnum habuerat', Asser, c. 80.

122 *AC* 875.

123 AU 851. 2.

124 M. Redknap, 'Viking-Age Settlement in Wales and the Evidence from Llanbedrgoch', in Hines et al. (eds.), *Land, Sea and Home*, 144–5.

The two primary items are, first, three successive entries in the *Annales Cambriae*, assigned by the editor, Egerton Phillimore, to the years 892, 894, and 895. The second is the annal in the A version of the Anglo-Saxon Chronicle for 893. The context is supplied by later annals and genealogies which show that, after some fighting, Cadell ap Rhodri replaced the sons of Hyfaidd as ruler of Dyfed. By 918/919, when Edward the Elder seized control of Mercia after the death of his sister Æthelflæd, the three Welsh rulers whose allegiance came with control of Mercia were Hywel ap Cadell, king of Dyfed, Clydog his brother, who may have been king of Powys, and Idwal ab Anarawd, king of Gwynedd.[125] Neither Gwent nor Glywysing are mentioned; by this time they seem to have become a single kingdom, ruled by Owain ap Hywel, son of the Hywel ap Rhys who was king of Glywysing in Asser.[126] South-eastern Wales, therefore, had remained under West Saxon overlordship, while the rest of Wales had moved back into a Mercian sphere.

There is a good case for concluding that this had happened during the period 892–896. Hyfaidd, king of Dyfed, died around 892;[127] the last attested king of Ceredigion, Gwgon, had died about 872. It is significant that Asser did not mention Ceredigion as one of the South-Welsh territories threatened by the Merfynion. The most likely reason for this silence is that by the time of his death Hyfaidd was ruler of Ystrad Tywi and at least overlord of Ceredigion. The deaths of two of Hyfaidd's sons are recorded in 903 and 904, suggesting that his line did not pass into obscurity at his death; moreover the death of Rhodri ap Hyfaidd in 904 occurred by violence in Arwystli: he is said to have been beheaded, which is more likely to have been the culmination of defeat in battle than an assassination or judicial execution.[128] If this is correct, the dynasty of Dyfed probably still controlled Ceredigion in 904; otherwise it would have been much more difficult to campaign in Arwystli. However, the succession to Hyfaidd offered an opportunity, which seems to have been seized by Anarawd. The entry in the *Annales Cambriae* for 894 says that 'Anarawd came with Englishmen to lay waste Ceredigion and Ystrad Tywi'. Although it has been suggested that Cadell ap Rhodri, of the Merfynion, already ruled Ceredigion, and that Anarawd's attack represented fraternal rivalry, the continued significance of Hyfaidd's sons in the early tenth century makes this very unlikely.[129] The English help given to Anarawd is also very unlikely

[125] See the next chapter, 498–9.

[126] The 'Uwen Wenta cyning' of ASC D 926 = 927. In Asser, Life, c. 80, the kings of Glywysing and Gwent belonged to two branches of the one dynasty: *EWGT*, pp. 12 and 45, HG 29, and JC 9.

[127] *AC* 892 (891 in Dumville's edition). If *AC* 895 is recording the Viking period in Wales mentioned in ASC A 893–894, that annal must be one year too late (hence 894 in Dumville's edition). This suggests that there is a chronological fault line in *AC* at 891–892: 889 in *AC* B (890 Dumville) = 891 (AU, ASC), and hence the record shifts from being one to two years too early to being one year too late (cf. Alfred's death under 900, when it occurred in the autumn of 899). The annalist clearly entered *an.* too many times between [895] and [896], but [896] may be approximately correct, so that one *an.* out of the four may be retained. Dumville removes two *anni* immediately after his 890.

[128] *AC* 904 (but the name of the father is not in MS *A*, although it is in the *Brut* under the form *Hennyth*). The term used is *decollatus* 'beheaded', which cannot be translated 'strangled' as it is by Thornton, *Kings, Chronologies, and Genealogies*, 110. For beheading as a consequence of defeat in battle, cf. AU 738. 4, Bede, *HE* iii. 12 (Oswald).

[129] Dumville, 'The "Six" Sons of Rhodri Mawr', 15.

to have been West Saxon, as has been suggested:[130] if Asser's account of Wales reflects Alfred's own understanding of the situation, the West Saxons would hardly have been found helping Anarawd to attack the dynasty of Dyfed, which Alfred had undertaken to defend from Anarawd and his brothers. On the other hand it is entirely possible that Anarawd had Mercian help (as, indeed, the use of *Angli* instead of the usual *Saxones* suggests). If this is correct, the two kingdoms that had lost ground to Alfred in the 880s were now seeking to undo his settlement of Welsh affairs.

The next crisis period for the West Saxon hegemony over southern Britain came in the early years of Edward the Elder's reign, when his cousin Æthelwald disputed the succession with Viking help.[131] In 902, probably as a result of the expulsion of Vikings from Dublin, a leader named in *Annales Cambriae* as Igmunt invaded Anglesey and defeated the Welsh near Llanfaes.[132] On the other hand, two of the sons of Hyfaidd of Dyfed died in 903–904, one of them violently. By 909 Cadell had acquired the kingdom of Dyfed,[133] so that it can be suggested that this final triumph of the Merfynion came at another period of West Saxon weakness, early in the reign of Edward the Elder.

By these successive stages Alfred's settlement of Wales had been largely undone. West Saxon, as opposed to Mercian, Wales had been confined to the south-east; the power of Gwynedd had triumphed, but within the terms of what seems to have been a Mercian alliance. At least by 918, after the deaths of both Cadell and Anarawd, the Merfynion were client-kings of Mercia. Edward the Elder displaced Æthelflæd's daughter, Ælfwyn, in 919 in a coup d'état, and so incorporated Mercia into a kingdom that was now looking more like the England of the future. By this act of what Mercians may have regarded as 'force and tyranny', he succeeded to a Mercian hegemony in Wales that had been rebuilt by Æthelred and Æthelflæd. The English tyranny of which *Armes Prydein* complained so fiercely some years later was more the heir of that Mercian tyranny of which Asser wrote than it was of Alfred's overlordship. His period of power in Wales was a short, if comparatively pleasant, period in Anglo-Welsh relations, a transition between two harsher regimes.

[130] D. P. Kirby, 'Political Developments', in J. L. Davies and D. P. Kirby (eds.), *Cardiganshire County History*, gen. ed. I. G. Jones, i, *From the Earliest Times to the Coming of the Normans* (Cardiff, 1994), 331 (English military aid was a 'reciprocal token on Alfred's part of his [Anarawd's] new relationship with the West Saxon king').

[131] Æthelwald was killed in 905.

[132] *AC* 902; for the location of Maes Osfeilion, see above, 328 n. 95; for the sculptural evidence for Viking influence in this area, see N. Edwards, 'Viking-Age Sculpture in North-West Wales: Wealth, Power, Patronage and the Christian Landscape', in F. L. Edmonds and P. Russell (eds.), *Tome: Studies in Medieval Celtic History and Law in Honour of Thomas Charles-Edwards* (Woodbridge, 2011), 73–87.

[133] This can be inferred from (1) his son Hywel's rule over Dyfed; (2) the terms in which his obit is given in *Chronicum Scotorum*; without a major kingdom of interest to the Irish he would not have been termed 'king of the Britons', especially since his brother Anarawd was still alive. He may earlier have been king of Powys, but that kingdom was too remote from Irish interests to justify such an obit.

16

The Britons and the Empire of Britain

1. FROM ALFRED TO EDWARD THE ELDER

Alfred's settlement of Wales after his victory at Edington was probably undermined, as we have seen, during a new phase of Viking aggression from 892 to 896. Both King Alfred and Æthelred, 'Lord of the Mercians', were active in opposing the Viking armies, but towards Wales their policies are likely to have diverged. Mercia now seems to have worked with Gwynedd and the Merfynion, whereas Mercia and Gwynedd had been in conflict before Alfred's brief hegemony over Wales.

In spite of the sparsity of evidence, it is possible to make a reasonable guess at the broad trend of events in the period 892 to 918, from the beginning of the second great Viking offensive to the death of Æthelflæd, Alfred's daughter and Æthelred's consort. This can only be done, however, if we begin at the end, in 918, and work backwards.

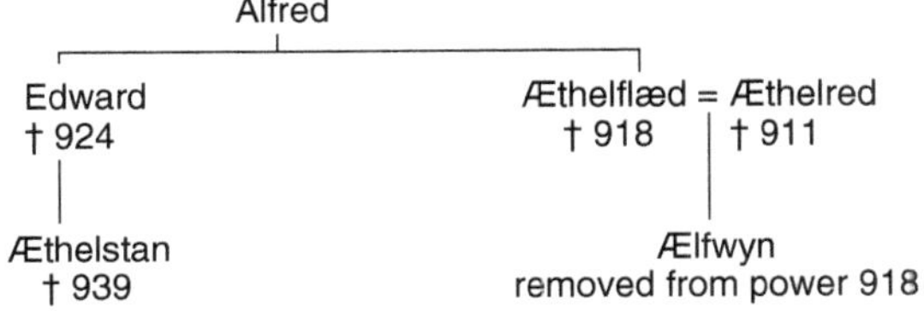

In recording Æthelflæd's death, Irish and Welsh annals are united in regarding her as a queen. English sources, however, do not give her this title. For the Parker Chronicle (the A version of the Anglo-Saxon Chronicle) this is unsurprising, since at this period it saw events from a strongly West Saxon point of view. Essentially, this part of the Chronicle, from 910 to 918, is a laudatory account of the campaigns of Edward the Elder, Alfred's eldest son and successor. One might well have supposed that it was betraying West Saxon bias in refusing the title of queen to Æthelflæd. Yet any such judgement is ruled out by another source, a set of Mercian annals incorporated into some of the other versions of the Anglo-Saxon Chronicle and known as 'the Mercian Register'.[1] The surviving portion of these annals concentrates on the last years of Æthelred, who died in 911, and the sole rule of Æthelflæd from 911 to 918. Yet, although they were written from a Mercian standpoint, they call her 'Lady of the Mercians' and not 'queen'.[2] The conflict is

[1] *EHD* 110–11 (2nd edn.145). [2] ASC in *EHD* i, no. 1, *s. aa.* 912, 913, 917.

thus between English and non-English sources and not between a West Saxon text and all others. We shall return to this problem at a later stage.[3]

Æthelflæd, Lady of the Mercians, died in June 918. She had just recovered control over Derby and Leicester; and the Mercian Register says that she had also made an agreement with the Vikings of York, by which they promised that they would act 'according to her counsel'.[4] Although her brother Edward had made major acquisitions of territory that had once been Mercian, these were in the south-east midlands and in the borderlands of East Anglia. The agreement with Viking York was an indication that the ruler of Mercia, not the king of the West Saxons, might perhaps prove to be the dominant influence north and west of a line from Cirencester to Northampton and on to Stamford.[5] As it happened, however, Æthelred and Æthelflæd had had no surviving son; according to the Mercian Register, Æthelflæd was succeeded by their daughter, Ælfwyn; but about six months after Æthelflæd's death, Edward mounted a coup by which he rode to Tamworth, deprived Ælfwyn of her authority in Mercia and led her away into Wessex.[6] The unity of Mercia with Wessex was achieved by violence, although it had been prepared by more peaceable means.[7]

The Parker Chronicle's account is different in that it makes no reference to Ælfwyn. We are told that, immediately after Æthelflæd's death, Edward rode to Tamworth, where his sister had died, took possession of the fort; 'and all the people in the land of the Mercians who had been subject to Æthelflæd turned to him; and the kings among the Welsh, Hywel and Clydog and Idwal, and all the Welsh people sought to have him as their lord.'[8] Quite apart from any omissions, this version sees affairs from a West Saxon standpoint: the point of the phrase 'the Mercians who had been subject to Æthelflæd' is that south-east Mercia was already subject to Edward, from Oxford and London northwards to Stamford. The Parker Chronicle joins together two political events: on the one hand, the Mercians previously subject to Æthelflæd 'turned to' Edward, and, on the other, the Welsh kings and all the Welsh people 'sought him as their lord'. In both cases the initiative is presented as coming from those submitting rather than from the new ruler of Mercia. The terms used are, however, interestingly different: *cirran* 'turn' is the most neutral and purely political of the verbs used by the annalists for submission; to 'seek a lord' is, however, a standard phrase for commending oneself to a lord, whether that lord is a king or not.[9] The Chronicle therefore portrays the Welsh kings and people as more emphatically subject to Edward than were the Mercians.

[3] Below, 505–7.

[4] The *Eforwicingas* promised to be 'on hyre rædenne', ASC C 918.

[5] ASC A 911 (Oxford), 915 (Bedford), 917 (Northampton), 918 (Stamford).

[6] ASC C *s.a.* 919 (probably referring to 918, since the annal begins 'Her eac . . .', 'In this year also . . .').

[7] Keynes, 'King Alfred and the Mercians'.

[8] ASC A *s.a.* 922 = 918.

[9] For *cirran* see ASC A *s.aa.* 823, *Cantware him to cirdon*, 886, *him all Angel cyn to cirde*; for 'seeking someone as a lord' see ASC A 918 = 914, *Þurcytel eorl hine gesohte him to hlaforde*; cf. 'choosing someone as king', ASC D 924 (*Æþelstan wæs gecoren to cynge of Myrcum*), and the oath of fidelity to a lord in *Swerian* (ed. Liebermann, *Gesetze*, i. 396).

There was no suggestion here of any such equality in the terms of submission as had existed, according to Asser, between Anarawd of Gwynedd and Æthelred of Mercia.

Whatever the terms of subjection, there was no pretence on the part of the Parker Chronicle that the three Welsh kings, Hywel, Clydog, and Idwal, had been subject to Edward before his sister's death in 918. Since the Parker Chronicle's standpoint was strongly sympathetic to Edward himself, we can accept this negative fact with confidence, however tendentious the annal may be in other ways. What is less certain is whether the submission of the three Welsh kings immediately followed Edward's acquisition of royal authority over all Mercia. That is the implication of the Parker Chronicle: for it, the three kings must have been subject to Æthelflæd and thus naturally submitted to her brother and successor; one overlordship was followed without dispute by another. Yet the Mercian Register shows that the succession did not take place without dispute: Ælfwyn was Æthelflæd's immediate successor and Edward only gained power by deposing her. Moreover, if we follow the Mercian Register's account, the Welsh submission to Edward can hardly have occurred in 918, as the Parker Chronicle implies, since Edward's coup occurred in December, and there would not have been time for any Welsh submission until 919. At the very least, therefore, the Parker Chronicle must be compressing into the one annal what, in reality, was a sequence of events running on from June 918 into 919.

The crucial question, however, is not one of chronology but of the interrelatedness of events. The Parker Chronicle may have foreshortened its narrative, and also have left out Ælfwyn entirely, yet it could still be true that Edward's acquisition of power in Mercia led directly and without delay to the submission of the Welsh kings. There are arguments in both directions. Edward was undoubtedly active on the border of North Wales in the six remaining years of his reign. In 919 a burh were built at Thelwall, on the Mersey by Warrington, and the Roman fort at Manchester was repaired, and in 921 the Mercian Register shows him building 'the *burh æt Cledemuþan*'.[10] *Cledemuþa* has been interpreted as 'the mouth of the Clwyd' and identified with a site at Rhuddlan.[11] The interpretation is very likely indeed and the identification is probable. In 924 Edward died at Farndon, on the east bank of the River Dee, opposite Holt and a few miles north of Bangor-is-Coed.[12] The *Annales Cambriae* are skimpy at this point, but they record a 'battle of the New Fortress' under 921, and this new fortress could be the new *burh* at Rhuddlan. If one were to accept such a linking of the Welsh and English evidence, one could go on to argue that the fort at Rhuddlan was not established on territory

[10] ASC A 919, ASC C 921.

[11] F. T. Wainwright, 'Cledemutha', *EHR* 65 (1950), 202–12; D. Griffiths, 'The North-West Mercian Burhs: A Reappraisal', *Anglo-Saxon Studies in Archaeology and History*, 8 (1995), 75–86; id., 'The North-West Frontier', in N. J. Higham and D. H. Hill (eds.), *Edward the Elder, 899–924* (London, 2001), 167–87; H. Quinnell and M. R. Blockley, *Excavations at Rhuddlan, Clwyd, 1969–73: Mesolithic to Medieval*, CBA Research Report 95 (York, 1994).

[12] ASC BCD 924; *The Chronicle of John of Worcester*, ii, ed. R. R. Darlington and P. McGurk, OMT (Oxford 1995), 384, AD 924. That this Farndon is meant is indicated by William of Malmesbury, *Gesta Regum*, ii. 133.

already subject to Mercia but was part of new English aggression. In turn, that might lead one to suppose that Idwal ab Anarawd, king of Gwynedd, had not submitted to Edward in 919 but did so only after the battle of 921 at the earliest. William of Malmesbury has an unsupported story that, just before Edward's death, he suppressed a revolt at Chester, in which the rebels had relied on Welsh help.[13] Yet, even William does not say whether the rebels' trust in their Welsh allies was well founded.

The arguments in favour of the Parker Chronicle's statement about the three Welsh kings are more convincing. Edward the Elder's activity in north-west Mercia may have been directed at enhancing royal power in north-western Mercia with Vikings in mind rather than the Welsh. In 902 the Vikings of the early *longphort* at Dublin had been expelled: 'The heathens were driven from Ireland, that is from the *longphort* of Áth Cliath, by Máel Finnia son of Flannacán with the men of Brega and by Cerball son of Muirecán with the Leinstermen.'[14] This expulsion of Vikings in 902 appears to have led to renewed attacks on Anglesey, since an entry in the *Annales Cambriae* for that year declares that 'Igmunt came into the island of Môn and settled Maes Osmeliaun'.[15] There may have been other incursions elsewhere along the North Welsh coast. The same dispersal of Vikings probably led, also, to their settlement on the Isle of Man, in parts of Cumbria, in the Wirral, and perhaps also to an attack on Chester.[16] Not all of those involved in such settlements are likely to have come from Dublin; but the Dublin expulsion seems to have precipitated a new phase of Viking settlement in the Irish-Sea region, drawing in Vikings from elsewhere, just as, later, the renewed Viking activity in Ireland from 914 drew in support from Britain and Brittany. The early Viking archaeology of Man divides into a Christian phase, beginning about 930 and a preceding pagan phase.[17] The material remains of the pagan phase accord with those from tenth-century Dublin, established on a new site in 917, rather than with the ninth-century Viking cemeteries at Islandbridge and Kilmainham.[18] This makes it likely that this phase on Man lasted for less than a generation, between no earlier than 902 and *c.* 930; and, if the Vikings only settled Man *c.* 902, one may suppose that before 902 the Merfynion retained control of their ancestral island. Some support for this supposition comes from the verse attached to the Annals of Ulster for 878

[13] William of Malmesbury, *Gesta Regum*, ii. 133.

[14] AU 902. 2 (also CS); Downham, *Viking Kings of Britain and Ireland: The Dynasty of Ívar to A.D. 1014* (Edinburgh, 2007), 26–31.

[15] AC 902.

[16] Modern understanding owes much to F. T. Wainwright, 'North-West Mercia, 871–924', *Trans. Hist. Soc. of Lancashire and Cheshire*, 94 (1942), 3–56; id., 'Ingimund's Invasion', *EHR* 63 (1948), 145–69; both reprinted in id., *Scandinavian England: Collected Papers by F. T. Wainwright*, ed. H. P. R. Finberg (Chichester, 1975), 63–129, 131–61. See also the recent summary by Downham, *Viking Kings of Britain and Ireland*, 83–5, and F. L. Edmonds, 'History and Names', in J. Graham-Campbell and R. Philpott, *The Huxley Viking Hoard: Scandinavian Settlement in the North-West* (Liverpool, 2009), 5–7.

[17] J. Graham-Campbell, 'The Early Viking Age in the Irish-Sea Area', 116–20.

[18] AU 917. 4.

describing Rhodri as 'of Man'.[19] If this reconstruction is correct, the Merfynion were principal victims of the 902 Viking diaspora.

Moreover, Viking settlement also occurred on their other island in the Irish Sea, Anglesey. A generation later, *Armes Prydein* was to speak of the 'Gwyddyl of Ireland, Môn and Prydyn' as part of the proposed grand coalition against the heirs of Alfred.[20] This is odd unless one supposes, first, that, by 'Gwyddyl', the poet is thinking of those who speak Gaelic (Irish), and, secondly, that the Viking settlers of the tenth century included, or brought with them, many Irish speakers.[21] The upshot of the Viking settlement on Man was clearly a bilingual society, Irish and Norse, in which the Irish-speaking element eventually came to predominate; ultimately the population of Man became monolingual speakers of a Gaelic dialect, the forerunner of Manx. Similarly, place-name evidence indicates that the 'Hiberno-Norse' settlement of north-western England included an Irish-speaking element.[22] The evidence for a Viking presence on Anglesey has recently been considerably augmented by excavations in the east of the island at Llanbedrgoch.[23]

A settlement on the farm of Glyn, Llanbedrgoch, was discovered as the result of discoveries of coins and lead weights in three fields on the farm. This lies less than a mile from Red Wharf Bay, where the gently shelving sandy beach would have provided easy access for ships of the Viking period. After a preliminary investigation in 1994, excavation of five areas took place between 1995 and 2001. The history of the settlement is divided into two distinct phases, but there is no reason to posit an interval between them. The early medieval settlement was established before 600. In the sixth or seventh century the site, roughly one hectare, was enclosed by a ditch and bank. Within the enclosure there were at least two buildings, a small round-house and a larger rectangular hall. The inhabitants maintained themselves by farming. This was the pre-Viking phase at Llanbedrgoch.

In the ninth century, the bank was replaced by a stone wall more than two metres wide that could have carried a wall walk. The construction of this impressive defensive feature marked the change to the Viking period. At least five buildings were found belonging to this phase, together with a paved road and a stone-lined

[19] See ch. 15, 468.

[20] *Armes Prydein*, ed. I. Williams, trans. R. Bromwich (Dublin, 1972), line 10 (but I have sometimes used my own translation); A. Breeze, '*Armes Prydein*, Hywel Dda and the Reign of Edmund of Wessex', *Études Celtiques*, 33 (1997), 210, translates line 10, 'The Irish of Ireland and Man and Scotland', implicitly emending *Mon* to *Manaw*; but this is unnecessary and may have the unfortunate effect of removing valuable evidence (valuable precisely because initially unexpected); a text and a new translation by G. Isaac, '"Armes Prydain Fawr" and St David', is in Evans and Wooding (eds.), *St David of Wales*, 170–81.

[21] See also below, 503.

[22] G. Fellows-Jensen, *Scandinavian Settlement Names in the North-West* (Copenhagen, 1985), 303–6.

[23] M. Redknap, 'Glyn, Llanbedrgoch, Anglesey', *Archaeology in Wales*, 34 (1994), 58–60; id., 'Glyn, Llanbedrgoch, Anglesey', *Archaeology in Wales*, 35 (1995), 58–9; id., *Vikings in Wales: An Archaeological Quest* (Cardiff, 2000), 68–80; id., 'Viking-Age Settlement in Wales and the Evidence from Llanbedrgoch', in J. Hines, A. Lane, and M. Redknap (eds.), *Land, Sea and Home: Settlement in the Viking Period* (Leeds, 2004), 139–75; id. 'Viking-Age Settlement in Wales: Some Recent Advances', *THSC 2005*, New Ser. 12 (2006), 5–35.

pool fed by a spring. This last feature was built before the Viking period, but a silver penny of Edmund in the upper silt indicates that it remained in use through the first half of the tenth century. Five skeletons—four adults and one child—were found buried in shallow graves in the ditch outside the wall on the western side of the settlement. They may belong to the late tenth century and they seem to have died through violence; they were buried in a non-Christian form. In the period between the construction of the wall and the five burials, the settlement was active in a corridor of exchange stretching west–east, from Dublin to the Chester area and on to York. A wide range of artefacts have been recovered, all typical of the Hiberno-Norse diaspora around the Irish Sea. The excavations did not show that the change between the pre-Viking and Viking phases, a change signified by the construction of the wall, accompanied a change of population, but it is clear that the economic relations of the inhabitants were transformed.

A section of the *Fragmentary Annals of Ireland* has a story of the expulsion of Vikings from Ireland towards the beginning of the tenth century (here attributed to a holy man, Céle Dabaill). It is a later source, perhaps from the kingdom of Loíchsi on the north-western frontier of Leinster and to be dated to the eleventh century; while it contains early material, such as entries from the Chronicle of Ireland, it has also made sagas out of historic events, a fashion which took root in Clonmacnois in the tenth century, although there are earlier examples.[24] The leader of the Vikings is called Ingimund, which looks very much like the Igmunt of the *Annales Cambriae*.[25] Ingimund was met in Wales by an army under, so the *Fragmentary Annals* claim, 'the son of Cadell son of Rhodri', namely either Hywel or Clydog, rather than, as would be expected, Anarawd ap Rhodri.[26] A hard battle against the Welsh persuaded Ingimund to go to Æthelflæd, 'Queen of the English', from whom he obtained lands near Chester. The Cuerdale hoard, found in 1840 on the bank of the Ribble near Preston, combined arm-rings and hack-silver, very probably from Dublin, with recent coins from York.[27] It suggests that relations between the Vikings of the Irish-Sea littoral and York were established very soon after 902; this, together with the coin evidence, led to the proposed dating *c.* 905–910. The purpose of the assemblage of bullion in the hoard is not entirely clear, but a plausible suggestion is that it was the treasure chest from which a Viking army was to be paid.[28]

The reaction of Æthelflæd was focused on building up Mercian power in the north-west. Chester 'was restored' in 907; Eddisbury and Runcorn were built in 914 and 915 respectively.[29] After the refoundation of Chester the Vikings decided to attack the city, an attack which, according to the *Fragmentary Annals*, failed

[24] *Fragmentary Annals of Ireland*, ed. J. N. Radner (Dublin, 1978), pp. xxii–xxv; F. L. Edmonds, 'History and Names', 6.

[25] In Old and Middle Welsh *g* may stand for *ng*, as in Chad 2 *tagc* for *tangc*.

[26] *Fragmentary Annals of Ireland*, ed. Radner, § 429.

[27] M. M. Archibald, 'Dating Cuerdale: The Evidence of the Coins', in J. Graham Campbell (ed.), *Viking Treasure from the North West: The Cuerdale Hoard in its Context* (Liverpool, 1992), 15–20.

[28] Graham-Campbell, 'The Cuerdale Hoard: Comparisons and Context', ibid. 114.

[29] ASC C (the Mercian Register), 907, 914, 915.

when Æthelflæd and her husband, Æthelred, persuaded the Irish contingent in the besieging army to change sides.[30] The combination of the entry in the *Annales Cambriae* naming Igmunt, place-name evidence for Viking settlement in the Wirral, and the evident concern of, first, Æthelflæd and then Edward the Elder for north-west Mercia indicates that there is some truth in this story in the *Fragmentary Annals*, even though it is likely that the more famous Hywel Dda has been substituted for his uncle, Anarawd.

The subsequent Viking resettlement of Dublin (on a new site) heralded a period of still closer links between Dublin and York. The resettlement of Dublin appears to have been part of the second great wave of Viking attacks on Ireland which began about 913. In that year 'the heathens routed the crews of a fleet of Ulstermen on the coast of England', showing that the most maritime province in the northern half of Ireland was unsuccessfully disputing control of the Irish Sea.[31] In 917 'Sitriuc ua hÍmair entered Áth Cliath', an entry which very probably marks the resettlement.[32] This phase was to lead to renewed Viking settlement at Waterford as well as at Dublin and, in 919, to perhaps the worst defeat of the Irish at the hands of the Vikings, when Niall Glúndub, king of Tara, was killed in battle at Dublin. A king of Tara was not able in 919 to repeat the earlier success of the kings of Brega and Leinster in 902. A year earlier, in 918, Sihtric's brother, Ragnall ua hÍmair, now described as of 'the foreigners of Loch dá Cháech', namely Waterford Harbour, had won a hard-fought battle on the River Tyne against the Scots; and from 918 or 919 to 921 he was established as king in York.[33] In 919 Edward the Elder, who had taken power in Mercia in the previous year, sent a Viking army to Manchester, within Northumbria, where they repaired existing defences and installed a garrison.[34] This all suggests an intention on the part of Edward to interpose his men between two Viking forces: those who occupied the coastlands of the Irish Sea and those of Northumbria. The boundary between Mercia and Northumbria in the west may have been moved north at this point from the Mersey (literally, the 'march' or 'boundary river') to the Ribble.[35] Since Gwynedd was also threatened by Viking aggression, one would have expected an alliance between Edward and Idwal, who had succeeded his father, Anarawd, in 916. The 'battle of the New Fortress' briefly mentioned in *Annales Cambriae* under 921 could as well have been fought between Welsh allied with Edward against Vikings as between the Welsh and the English.[36]

30 *Fragmentary Annals*, ed. Radner, § 429.

31 AU 913. 5.

32 AU 917. 4.

33 AU 918. 4; cf. Simeon of Durham, *Historia Regum*, *s.a.* 919 (*EHD* i, no. 3), ASC D 924 = 923, Her Regnold cyning gewan Eoforwic; Downham, *Viking Kings of Britain and Ireland*, 91–5.

34 ASC A 923 = 919.

35 See N. J. Higham, 'The Cheshire *Burhs* and the Mercian Frontier to 924', *Transactions of the Lancashire and Cheshire Antiquarian Society*, 85 (1988), 212–14, for the view that the land between the Mersey and the Ribble became part of Mercia and thus of the diocese of Lichfield under Edward the Elder.

36 'Gueith Dinas Neguid', *Annales Cambriae*, 921.

Finally, however, the most powerful argument that Idwal was one of the group which submitted in 918 is the one with which we began, that the Parker Chronicle's statement suggests that the submission of the Welsh was not a West Saxon achievement but flowed directly from Edward's assumption of authority in Mercia. Yet the whole burden of the Parker Chronicle's account of Edward the Elder's reign from 910 to 924, after the difficulties of his early years, was of repeated acquisition of territorial power by the West Saxon king's own forces. The Mercian expansion of the same years was not recorded in the Parker Chronicle. Hence, when it avoided making the extension of Edward's power over the three Welsh kings an achievement of West Saxon military power, there is a very strong presumption that it was telling the truth. We may therefore proceed with considerable confidence on the assumption that the three Welsh kings had previously been subject to Æthelflæd and that they transferred their allegiance to Edward her brother after the latter's coup against Ælfwyn early in December 918. What Edward gained was thus the inheritance of Mercian power over the Welsh. From this basis we may work back in time towards the Wales described by Asser, always taking into account the Viking pressure on Gwynedd and north-west Mercia.

The three Welsh kings were, in order, Hywel, Clydog, and Idwal. These all belonged to the Merfynion, descendants of Merfyn Frych, king of Gwynedd. Hywel and Clydog were sons of Cadell ap Rhodri, Idwal of Anarawd ap Rhodri. Cadell had died in 909; the *Chronicum Scotorum* described him as 'king of the Britons', a title the Irish annals generally reserved for the most powerful kings among the Britons of Wales and of Strathclyde.[37] Anarawd died a few years later, and the *Chronicum Scotorum* also proclaimed him as 'king of the Britons', agreeing here with the *Annales Cambriae*.[38] Hywel, Clydog, and Idwal thus belonged to the next generation after those 'sons of Rhodri' whose ambitions had driven the kings of Dyfed and Brycheiniog into the arms of Alfred. Hywel ap Cadell would reign until 950;[39] Idwal would be killed, together with his son Elise, probably in 942, by the English; Clydog, however, was killed in 919 or 920—according to a later genealogy, at the hands of his brother Meurig.[40] The *Annales Cambriae*, *s.a.* 934, have an entry recording the deaths of Hyfaidd ap Clydog and Meurig; these events may, perhaps, have been further episodes in an intra-familial feud. Yet, whatever the conflicts between the Merfynion in later years, the Parker Chonicle for 918 presents them as a unified group, just as Asser had portrayed their fathers' generation, the sons of Rhodri Mawr.

The Parker Chonicle implies that the three Welsh kings brought with them the submission of all the Welsh: 'and the kings among the *Norþwealas*, Hywel and Clydog and Idwal, and the entire *Norþweallcyn*, sought him as their lord.' It is as if the three kings from the Merfynion were the only kings in Wales, since *Norþwealas* was the Chronicle's standard term for the Welsh as opposed to the *Westwealas*, the

[37] *CS* 908 = 909.
[38] *CS* 915 = 916; AC 915 = 916.
[39] D. Thornton, 'The Death of Hywel Dda: A Note', *Welsh History Review*, 20: 4 (2001), 743–9.
[40] *EWGT* 101 (ABT § 7*l*).

men of Cornwall. A comparable entry occurs in the Parker Chronicle's annal for 920: 'the king of the Scots and all the people of the Scots chose him (Edward) as father and lord'; similarly, in the same annal, 'and also the king of the Strathclyde Welsh and all the Strathclyde Welsh'. It was common in these years for the Chronicle to couple together ruler and people in its record of such submissions. Yet, although the identity of rulers and the entire Welsh people is implied by the Chronicle, this can hardly be the literal truth. It can only be explained in terms of the respective spheres of influence in Wales enjoyed by Æthelflæd and Edward in the years before 918. The witness lists to some charters of Æthelstan and his successors show, as we shall see, that south-east Wales continued to have its own dynasty: the Morgan who would give his name to Morgannwg (alternatively, Gwlad Forgan, Glamorgan, 'the country of Morgan'), witnessed between 931 and 956.[41] A charter of 934 was attested by Tewdwr, who was probably king of Brycheiniog.[42] The evidence of the charters accords with that of the Anglo-Saxon Chronicle. The D version of the Chronicle, *s.a.* 926 (= 927), names an Uwen, very probably Owain, as king of Gwent.[43] The genealogies suggest that the Morgan who attested Æthelstan's charters was son of Owain, who in turn was son of the Hywel ap Rhys named by Asser.[44] In Asser's day, Hywel ap Rhys was king of Glywysing, while his first cousins, Brochfael and Ffernfael, sons of Meurig, were kings of Gwent. The annal for 927 indicates, therefore, that, since Hywel's son Owain now ruled Gwent and there is no mention of any other ruler of his rank in the south-east, Glywysing and Gwent had been reunited under a single king.

Similarly, the Mercian Register suggests that Brycheiniog had possessed its own king under Æthelflæd. In 916, perhaps in punishment for the killing of an abbot Ecgbryht and his companions, Æthelflæd sent an army which broke into the royal fort on Llangorse Lake, burnt it, and took captive the queen and thirty-three others.[45] It is conceivable that the king of Brycheiniog was already one of the Merfynion, but the later appearance of a Tewdwr as a witness to a charter of Æthelstan in 934 makes this very unlikely.[46] In 918, therefore, two kingdoms in south-east Wales, Gwent and Brycheiniog, were ruled by kings who did not belong to the Merfynion and were not among the group said to have submitted to Edward after he gained power in Mercia.

Two different explanations, one for Gwent and the other for Brycheiniog, can be offered to account for their kings' absence from the Parker Chronicle's annal for

41 The earliest is likely to be S 413 (20 June 931), the last S 633 (956). Several of these charters are discussed by H. R. Loyn, 'Wales and England in the Tenth Century: The Context of the Æthelstan Charters', *WHR* 10 (1980–1), 283–301.

42 S 425 (at Winchester, before the Scottish campaign).

43 The identification is complicated by William of Malmesbury's statement that Owain of Strathclyde was present at the meeting (see below, 521–2); but both Owains might well have been present.

44 *EWGT* 45–6 (JC 9–14).

45 ASC C 916 (Mercian Register).

46 Tewdwr was a favourite name in the royal dynasty of Brycheiniog, and this Tewdwr may be the Tewdwr ap Griffri whose pedigree is given in JC § 8, *EWGT* 45. His grandfather, Elise ap Tewdwr was king in the early 880s: Asser, *Life*, c. 80; above, 489–90.

918. An earlier entry in the same chronicle, for 914, records the arrival at the mouth of the Severn of a Viking fleet, led by two earls, Ohtor and Hroald. From there they harried the Welsh and captured Bishop Cyfeilliog, who was probably bishop of Ergyng or, at least, captured in Ergyng. Cyfeilliog was taken to the ships but was ransomed by Edward the Elder for the princely sum of 40 pounds of silver. We may reasonably infer from this episode that the far south-east of Wales was within Edward's sphere of power and not that of his sister Æthelflæd. Supporting evidence comes from the Dunsæte Agreement, a local regulation of border arrangements in an area, that of the Dunsæte, 'Hill People', which apparently bordered on Gwent.[47] The text may belong to the eleventh or the late tenth century; but it still maintained the idea that Gwent belonged to the West Saxons while its neighbours, the Dunsæte themselves, did not. This notion is readily explicable as a survival of the division of Wales between Mercian and West Saxon spheres before 918.

For Brycheiniog the explanation must be different, since the Mercian Register's account of the capture of Llangorse Lake in 916 is good evidence that Brycheiniog, unlike Gwent, was subject to Æthelflæd. The single appearance of Tewdwr among the witnesses of Æthelstan's charters suggests two things: that the dynasty of Brycheiniog was not ended by the capture of the royal crannog in 916, and that Brycheiniog was less significant in English eyes than such kingdoms as Gwent, Gwynedd, and Dyfed. The single appearance was in 934 at Winchester, at an assembly before the start of Æthelstan's campaign against the Scots. Yet, although the kings of Dyfed, Gwent, and Gwynedd also attested another charter later that same year, at Nottingham on the way north, Tewdwr either did not attest or his name was omitted as of lesser importance.[48] It may also be true that, in the years immediately after the capture of the royal crannog in 916, the hold on power of the king of Brycheiniog was especially weak. Whereas, therefore, Gwent was an important kingdom, but lay outside Æthelflæd's reach, Brycheiniog, subject to Mercia, was not on a level with the Merfynion in power or prestige, especially after 916.

The murkiest problem affecting this whole period from *c.* 890 to 918 is that of the rise of the Merfynion to the power they held at Æthelflæd's death. We have to explain the change from Asser's Wales, when Alfred's power secured the south Welsh kingdoms from the aggression of the Merfynion against Dyfed and Brycheiniog and the aggression of the Mercians against Gwent and Glywysing. The latter two kingdoms, now reunited as Gwent, apparently remained under direct West Saxon overlordship, as suggested by the ransoming of Cyfeilliog; Brycheiniog remained under its native dynasty but subject to Mercia; Dyfed, however, had almost certainly passed under the rule of the Merfynion. The oddest aspect of the change between 893 and 918 is, therefore, this: those south-eastern kingdoms previously threatened by Mercia remained under West Saxon overlordship, while those threatened by the Merfynion had mostly fallen to them, but were, nevertheless, under Mercian overlordship. The kings of the West Saxons, Alfred and Edward, had protected the south-east from Mercia, but they had allowed most of the rest of

[47] See above, 422. [48] S 407.

south Wales to pass under Mercian overlordship, which now extended precisely over those areas not threatened by Mercia after the Battle of the Conwy in 881.

The rough shape of what must have happened between 893 and 918 is revealed by the situations in those two years. Mercia (ruled by Æthelred and Æthelflæd) must have come to an arrangement with the Merfynion by which the latter were enabled to make further conquests in south-west Wales in exchange for a recognition of Mercian overlordship. The victims of this arrangement were, on the one hand, the previous Welsh rulers of Dyfed, the son or sons of Asser's bête noire Hyfaidd, and, on the other, the king of Wessex. In 893 Alfred's authority had extended over all Wales; before December 918 Edward's power only extended over Gwent (here including Glywysing).

What remains uncertain is quite how and when this radical change occurred. Under the year 892 the *Annales Cambriae* record the death of Hyfaidd, presumably the king of Dyfed to whose protection Alfred had committed his authority. The exact date is, however, uncertain. At the end of the 880s the *Annales Cambriae* were one to two years too early: the annal for 887 should have appeared under 888, and that for 889 should have been under 891.[49] Hyfaidd's death may have occurred in 893 or even as late as 894, so explaining why Asser, writing in 893, seems to be unaware of any such development. By the end of the 890s, however, any such chronological distortion seems to have been rectified, perhaps excessively: Alfred's death is recorded under 900 whereas it occurred in October 899. The next crucial annal after Hyfaidd's obit, that for 894, may be in its correct place. It records a campaign into south-west Wales: 'Anarawd came with *Angli* to lay waste Ceredigion and Ystrad Tywi'. Apparently he was not yet attacking the core of Dyfed, to the south of the Teifi and westwards from Carmarthen. Nevertheless, the threat to the dynasty of Hyfaidd was evident. The annalist's choice of *Angli* in preference to *Saxones* is striking: the latter was his standard word for the English as a whole, while he termed the West Saxons the *Giuoys* (for Old English Gewisse). The term *Angli* may have been chosen to indicate that Anarawd's allies were not the English in general, and certainly not the West Saxons, but rather the (Anglian) Mercians. If this is correct, the arrangement between the Mercians and the Merfynion can be traced back to 894, a year in which Alfred's energies were absorbed by the Viking offensives.

It may even go back to the previous year, 893, the very year when Asser was writing. In that year Ealdorman Æthelred, Ealdorman Æthelhelm, and Ealdorman Æthelnoth besieged a Danish army at Buttington, just to the east of Welshpool, where Offa's Dyke reaches the Severn. They did so in conjunction with 'some portion of the Welsh people'.[50] Given the situation of Buttington, on the border of Powys, by now ruled by the Merfynion, the 'portion of the Welsh people' must have been some or all of those under their authority; and, for the same reason, as well as the order of the names in the

49 The annal for 887 is an obit for Cerball mac Dúngaile, king of Osraige, AU 888.6; that for 889 is an obit for Suibne, a Clonmacnois scholar whose death is recorded both in AU 891. 8, and in ASC, 891. In his edition, *Annales Cambriae, A.D. 682–954*, 14, Dumville removes two annals marked by *an.* between the obit of Suibne and that of Hyfaidd, thus making the latter die in 891

50 ASC A (CD), 893 (*sum dæl þæs Norðwealcynnes*). Buttington is SJ 24 08.

Parker Chronicle, Æthelred, Ealdorman of the Mercians, is likely to have had the leading role among the English. In 893, therefore, we may see those ancient enemies, the Merfynion and the Mercians coming together in the face of the Viking threat. Anarawd's campaign in Ceredigion and Ystrad Tywi with the help of *Angli* may have stemmed from this new alliance.

There is no reference to Dyfed as such in contemporary sources between Asser's remarks in 893 and an annal for 952. By the latter date Hywel Dda was dead and his sons were fighting a war against the sons of his first cousin Idwal ab Anarawd (Idwal Foel). The Merfynion, hitherto the dominant force in Welsh politics, had broken apart. The seeds of this development probably lay in the domination of Welsh affairs by Hywel Dda, the firmest ally of the English 'emperors of Britain' among all the kings of his day. His first cousin, Idwal ab Anarawd, king of Gwynedd, had been killed by the English, probably in 942. Subsequently, Idwal's sons, Ieuaf and Iago, had been expelled from Gwynedd by Hywel.[51] After the latter's death in 950, however, Ieuaf and Iago recovered Gwynedd and proceeded to take revenge on Owain ap Hywel and his brothers. In 952 this led to them ravaging Dyfed. It is fair to conclude, therefore, that the political base of Owain ap Hywel and of his father lay in Dyfed.

We can perhaps push the acquisition of Dyfed by the Merfynion back one generation further. Hywel may himself have inherited Dyfed from his father, Cadell ap Rhodri. Cadell died in 909 and the *Chronicum Scotorum* termed him 'king of the Britons', indicating that he was a major ruler.[52] Yet it is hard to see how he could have been of such rank in Irish eyes unless he had been king of Dyfed, so matching his brother Anarawd, king of Gwynedd, also termed 'king of the Britons' by the *Chronicum Scotorum* in his obit in 916.[53] The acquisition of Dyfed by the Merfynion is thus likely to have occurred between 894, the year of Anarawd's expedition against Ceredigion and Ystrad Tywi, and 909, the year of Cadell's death. In 894 the attack was directed at what were probably dependent territories of Dyfed, since Asser does not mention them as separate South Welsh kingdoms, and the last-attested king of Ceredigion, Gwgon, was drowned in 871.[54] He is the latest in the pedigree of the kings of Ceredigion.[55] We can narrow the date down a little further, since Hyfaidd may not have been the last king of Dyfed before the Merfynion conquest: his son, Llywarch ap Hyfaidd, is given an obit under 903; it was Llywarch's daughter, Elen, whom Hywel ap Cadell was to marry.[56] Another son of Hyfaidd, Rhodri, was decapitated in Arwystli in 904.[57] Cadell's final taking

[51] The direct evidence for this is confined to one version of *Annales Cambriae* (B), which, *s.a.* 950, says of the two sons of Idwal, Iago and Ieuaf, that they were expelled by Hywel. This is confirmed by the absence of any separate ruler of Gwynedd among the Welsh kings attesting English royal charters after 942 (S 520, 544, 552a) until Iago appears in S 566 (AD 955).

[52] CS 908 = 909.

[53] CS 915 = 916.

[54] AC 871; drowning was a punishment used in Ireland in the ninth century (AU 845. 8; 851. 2); Gwgon's drowning cannot be taken to be a mere accident.

[55] *EWGT* 12 (HG § 28).

[56] *EWGT* 9 (HG § 2).

[57] AC 904; this may have been in battle (cf. AU 738. 4).

of Dyfed could thus have been as late as 906, when a battle is recorded by the *Annales Cambriae* in the same entry as an attack on St Davids.

These laconic notices suggest, therefore, that the Merfynion renewed their attack on Dyfed in 894, shortly after Hyfaidd's death. Their opportunity to challenge Alfred's settlement of Wales was offered by the Viking campaigns of 892–896. The final success of their designs on Dyfed only came, however, in the early years of Edward the Elder's reign. When Llywarch ap Hyfaidd died in 903, and when his brother Rhodri was decapitated in the next year, Edward the Elder had his hands full with the attacks mounted against him by his first cousin, Æthelwald. He was in no position to intervene in Wales. Any English influence was much more likely to be exerted by Æthelred of Mercia than by the West Saxons; and Æthelred is likely already to have been allied with the Merfynion, as suggested by the annals for 893 and 894. By the time Asser, by now bishop of Sherborne, died in 909, his native Dyfed was almost certainly ruled by Cadell ap Rhodri. The sketch of Wales Asser drew in 893 was now wholly out of date and never again bore any resemblance to the current shape of Welsh politics; that is indeed a major reason for believing in its authenticity. As for Anarawd, Cadell's brother and the leader of the expedition of 894, if he had entertained hopes of ruling Dyfed as well as Gwynedd, he would have found it exceedingly difficult to implement any such ambitions. As we have seen, in 902 the Vikings were expelled from Dublin; and in the same year the *Annales Cambriae* record a major Viking attack on Anglesey.

The rise of the Merfynion may thus be divided into three phases. Merfyn Frych belonged to the Isle of Man but gained power in Gwynedd in 825. From his point of view, the move from Manaw to Môn may have been partially defensive, as the Viking attacks in the Irish Sea gathered strength in the years after the death of Áed Oirdnide in 819. By then the Isle of Man is likely to have been a target, although nothing is known in detail, and the full Viking settlement of the island probably did not occur until *c.* 902. Although the move to Môn may have been defensive, it is not likely that Merfyn had been expelled from Man by Viking attacks. Instead, he may have desired to gain power in Gwynedd so that, holding two islands in the Irish Sea, he could better withstand the Viking storm. Secondly, and probably immediately after the Battle of the Conwy in 881, Anarawd and his brothers gained control over Powys. This was at the expense of the native dynasty, the Cadelling, and also of the Mercians, previously their overlords. Once they were in control of Powys, they immediately began to threaten Brycheiniog and Dyfed. At this point, however, Alfred's power arrested the expansion of the Merfynion for a few years. The third phase began with the second great Viking offensive (892–896). The two predatory powers which had previously been restrained by Alfred, the Merfynion and Mercia, combined to attack the outer defences of Dyfed, Ystrad Tywi, and Ceredigion. In the early years of Edward the Elder's reign, when he was preoccupied with threats to his kingship, the conquest of Dyfed was accomplished, very probably with the consent if not the active participation of the Mercians, as in 894. In the first phase, in 825, English policy may not have played a significant role, except in so far as Gwynedd had recently suffered from Cenwulf's attacks and factions within Mercia may have been aligned with factions within Gwynedd. In the second phase, the Merfynion triumphed at the expense of Mercia. In the third, they shared a common frontier and, so far as their ambitions in Wales went, common rivals, Alfred and his son Edward, and common enemies, the Vikings.

2. ÆTHELSTAN'S INHERITANCE IN WALES

When Edward the Elder died in 924 at Farndon on the Dee, not far from Welsh territory, the succession to the kingdom was confused. First, Ælfweard, who may well have been the heir-apparent, at least to Wessex, died at Oxford shortly after the death of his father.[58] His other son, Æthelstan, may have been fostered in the household of Æthelred and Æthelflæd.[59] At any rate he was 'chosen as king by the Mercians' in 924 and only consecrated as king of the English in September 925.[60] Whether Edward intended his two sons to succeed to two different kingdoms, Ælfweard to Wessex and Æthelstan to Mercia, we cannot say, but the possibility should not be forgotten. It is conceivable that his primary desire was to exalt his descendants rather than to unify Wessex and Mercia. In that case, Edward's coup against Ælfwyn in 918 may have been directed towards preparing the ground for Æthelstan's succession as king of Mercia. In any event, after the death of his brother, Æthelstan succeeded to a kingdom whose Mercian component, evidently still capable of decisive and independent political action, had willingly supported his kingship. So far as Wales was concerned, the conditions obtaining at Æthelstan's succession favoured a substantial continuity with the Mercian hegemony, as it existed under Æthelflæd, rather than any return to Alfred's policy towards Wales.

There are, moreover, definite indications that the English hegemony over Wales in the middle years of the tenth century, from the accession of Æthelstan to Mercia in 924 until the death of Edgar in 975, was essentially that bequeathed by Æthelflæd to her daughter Ælfwyn in 918, which passed, after his capture of Ælfwyn, to her brother Edward. These indications are the primacy of Hywel ap Cadell among the Welsh kings and the continuance of an administrative distinction between Gwent and the rest of Wales inherited from the early tenth century.

Of the kings of the Merfynion listed in the Parker Chronicle for 918 the first named was Hywel ap Cadell, later called Hywel Dda, 'Hywel the Good'. He took precedence of his brother Clydog and his first-cousin Idwal, even though the latter's kingdom, Gwynedd, was the basis of Merfynion power and had usually been the strongest among the Welsh kingdoms. The preeminence of Hywel lasted until his death in 950. In those charters of Æthelstan witnessed by both Hywel and Idwal,

[58] ASC D 924; Dumville, *Wessex and England*, 146; S. Keynes, 'King Athelstan's Books', in M. Lapidge and H. Gneuss (eds.), *Learning and Literature in Anglo-Saxon England* (Cambridge, 1985), 186–7.

[59] This depends on the testimony of William of Malmesbury, *Gesta Regum*, ii. 133; it is doubted by Dumville, *Wessex and England*, 146, who admits that 'much would be explained thereby', but suspects that William made a plausible guess. It is not obvious, however, what would have either enabled or encouraged him to make such a guess.

[60] S 394, a grant made on the day of the consecration, 4 September 925.

Hywel invariably attested before his cousin, and also before the king of Gwent, Morgan ab Owain.[61]

In the D version of the Anglo-Saxon Chronicle, *s.a.* 926 but to be corrected to 927, there is an entry recording the death of Sihtric, the Viking king of Northumbria, and Æthelstan's subsequent acquisition of his kingdom. We are then given a résumé of Æthelstan's successes in establishing his authority over the other rulers in Britain:[62]

> and he subjected all the kings that reigned in this island, first Hywel, king of the *Westwalas*, and Costantín, king of Scots and Owain, king of Gwent, and Ealdred Ealdulfing from Bamburgh; and with pledge and with oaths they established a peace in the place which is called Eamont on the 12th day of July.

The River Eamont flows eastwards out of Ullswater to join the Eden; it passes Penrith and also Brougham, the Roman fort of Brocauum at the junction of Roman roads coming from the south—from Manchester, refortified under Æthelstan's father—and from the south-east, namely from Catterick in the kingdom of York.

There are three distinct elements in this annal: first, the résumé of royal subjections, at least partially in chronological order, since Hywel's priority over Constantine (Costantín) was not one of power or status but merely that his submission was earlier in time. Secondly, the rest of the list, from Constantine to Ealdred, appears to be ordered according to power or status: the king of the Scots is the most powerful; Owain is a king; Ealdred was not regarded as king, at least not by the southern English. The third strand in this web is the peace established at the River Eamont by Æthelstan and the named kings. There is no solid reason why this particular meeting should have been the occasion on which all of the named rulers submitted to Æthelstan, certainly not Hywel, whose submission had presumably been inherited from Edward the Elder. On the other hand, this annalist, generally well informed on northern affairs, is likely to be telling the truth in that there was a royal meeting by the River Eamont to establish peace upon Æthelstan's accession as king of Northumbria the same year. That accession meant that all the rulers in Britain from the king of Scots southward (excluding Orkney and the Isles) were now Christian and that Æthelstan was evidently the leading king among them. There is no reason to deny that Hywel and Owain could have been involved in a meeting held so far to the north.[63] We know from charter evidence that Hywel, Idwal of Gwynedd, and Morgan of Gwent (Owain's son and successor), accompanied Æthelstan on his 934 campaign into Scotland, at least as far as Nottingham; and nothing suggests that they stopped there.[64] The pattern of events was partially similar in 927: first Sihtric, king of York, died; then Guthfrith, king of Dublin,

61 For example, S 400, 413.

62 *The Anglo-Saxon Chronicle: A Collaborative Edition*, 6, *MS D*, ed. G. P. Cubbin (Cambridge, 1996), *s.a.* 926 (= 927). A related list appears in *The Chronicle of John of Worcester*, ed. Darlington et al., 386–7 (both are texts associated with Worcester).

63 It is denied by A. P. Smyth, *Scandinavian York and Dublin* (New Jersey, 1979), ii. 12.

64 S 407.

attempted to succeed him; he was, however, driven out and was back in Dublin six months after leaving. Hence we may reasonably suppose that Hywel and Owain had marched in Æthelstan's army to take control of Northumbria and defeat Guthfrith in 927 as Hywel and Owain's son, Morgan, would march in the army which invaded Scotland in 934.[65]

On the other hand, William of Malmesbury, depending on a different source, since he talks of Dacre (an important church just by the River Eamont) as the place of the meeting, gives no list of kings but makes it clear that the persons whom Æthelstan wished to overawe were Constantine, king of Scots, and a different Owain, namely the king of the Cumbrians.[66] Given the site of the meeting, the presence of the Cumbrian ruler is exceedingly probable. The best explanation is that there were two Owains present at Dacre by the Eamont, one, Owain king of Gwent, in Æthelstan's army, and the other, Owain king of the Cumbrians, the person whose support for Guthfrith had principally angered Æthelstan. The D version of the Anglo-Saxon Chronicle or its source understandably combined the two. The site of the meeting is best understood on two assumptions: first, that Owain, king of the Cumbrians, was present; and, secondly, that the River Eamont was the frontier—and therefore that Dacre was close to the frontier—between the lands now ruled by Æthelstan and the newly expanded kingdom of Cumbria or Strathclyde.[67] That the second assumption is correct is confirmed by the contemporary poem, *Carta, dirige gressus*, according to which the Scottish king, Constantine, 'rushed to Britain' to submit to Æthelstan; the Britain in question can hardly have been the island but was rather, as in the Scottish Chronicle, Cumbria.[68] On these two assumptions, the meeting would fall into an old pattern of kings or their representatives meeting on frontiers, a pattern attested across Europe in the early and central Middle Ages, including Wales:[69]

> The King's worth is his sarhaed [insult-payment] three times. In three ways sarhaed [insult] is done to the King . . . A second is when two kings meet on their common boundary to negotiate, and in the presence of the two kings a subject of one kills a subject of the other.

As for Hywel's role in the annal for 927, three things are striking: first, as we have seen, he was perceived as Æthelstan's earliest sub-king; secondly, he was the only king among the Merfynion to be mentioned, even though Æthelstan is likely to have succeeded to his father's and aunt's overlordship over Idwal of Gwynedd; thirdly, Hywel was called 'king of the *Westwalas*'. In a West Saxon context, the

[65] That Æthelstan came north with an army, which one could in any case presume, is implied by the contemporary Latin poem, *Carta, dirige gressus*, stanza 4, ed. and trans. M. Lapidge, 'Some Latin Poems as Evidence for the Reign of Athelstan', *Anglo-Saxon England*, 9 (1981), 89.

[66] William of Malmesbury, *Gesta Regum*, ii. 134. 2 (ed. Mynors et al., 214–15).

[67] F. M. Stenton, *Preparatory to Anglo-Saxon England*, 217–18.

[68] Lapidge, 'Some Latin Poems', 90; and cf. above, 2.

[69] D. Jenkins, *The Law of Hywel Dda: Law Texts from Medieval Wales*, 5, translating Ior 3/2–3; J. Barrow, 'Chester's Earliest Regatta: Edgar's Dee-Rowing Revisited', *Early Medieval Europe*, 10: 1 (2001), 84–9; T. M. Charles-Edwards, 'Alliances, Godfathers, Treaties and Boundaries', in M. A. S. Blackburn and D. N. Dumville (eds.), *Kings, Currency and Alliances: History and Coinage of Southern England in the Ninth Century*, Studies in Anglo-Saxon History, 9 (Woodbridge, 1998), 47–62.

Westwalas were the Cornishmen; but here it is likely to refer to the people of Dyfed, south-west Wales, as opposed to Gwent in south-east Wales. The geographical viewpoint of the annalist is Mercian rather than West Saxon, more that of Worcester than that of Winchester or Sherborne.[70]

A possible interpretation of Hywel's primacy among the Merfynion, and also among all the Welsh kings of his time, is that such a primacy was one element in Æthelflæd's policy for Wales. There had, so I have argued, been an agreement with the Merfynion allowing them to conquer Dyfed, including Ystrad Tywi and Ceredigion. Hywel and his father, Cadell, had been the beneficiaries of this agreement. The conquest in turn allowed Æthelflæd to treat Hywel ap Cadell as the chief among the Merfynion. This would have had two benefits: Dyfed was, of all the Welsh kingdoms, the one most remote from Mercia; and Dyfed was not the traditional basis of Merfynion power. The primacy of Dyfed was more likely to endure with English support; and it would thus tend to strengthen the peace between Dyfed and, first, Mercia, and then the kingdom of the English as a whole. This primacy of Dyfed is first seen in the Parker Chronicle for 918, then in the D version of the Chronicle for 927, and in charters from 928 to 935. It was thus an enduring element in Anglo-Welsh relations from the time when Æthelflæd, Lady of the Mercians, was the dominant figure in western Britain north of the Brecon Beacons to the heyday of Æthelstan's power; in different forms it would endure until Hywel's death in 950.[71]

A further, more particular detail suggests that English hegemony over Wales was inherited from Æthelflæd. In the document known as 'The Dunsætan Agreement', variously dated to the tenth or the eleventh century, it is said that[72]

> At one time the inhabitants of Gwent belonged among the Dunsætan, but that district belongs more justly to the West Saxons. They should deliver tribute and hostages there.

The implication is that hegemony over the Welsh was still divided between a West Saxon overlordship and another, presumably Mercian in origin. Since it is unlikely that the text could be as old as 918, the division between Wext Saxons and others, presumably Mercians, cannot be that Mercia still had its separate ruler. Instead, an explanation must be sought in administrative arrangements for tribute collection. These must have been divided between one arrangement for tribute paid to the West Saxon section of a unified kingdom and another arrangement for the Mercian section. When the Mercians and Northumbrians insisted on having Edgar rather than Eadwig as their king, he was 'king of the Mercians and Northumbrians and Britons'.[73] Most of

[70] G. P. Cubbin, in his edition of ASC D, *The Anglo-Saxon Chronicle: A Collaborative Edition*, 6, *MS D*, lxxviii–lxxix, associates D with Aldred, bishop of Worcester, *c.* 1046 to 1062, and archbishop of York, 1061–1066. He sees this particular annal as either a final borrowing from the Mercian Register or from northern annals such as those which descended through Byrhtferth of Ramsey to the *Historia Regum* ascribed to Simeon of Durham, ibid. p. xxxi.

[71] S 552a (Barking, not yet printed), dated to the year of Hywel's death, 950, has him and Morgan attesting.

[72] Dunsætan Agreement, c. 9, ed. Liebermann, *Gesetze*, i. 378, for which see above, 422–3.

[73] S 677, trans. Whitelock, *EHD* i, no. 109.

Wales went with Mercia. Just as Mercia came to be subject to powerful ealdormen, Ælfhere and his brother-in-law Ælfric, in the second half of the tenth century, and to earls Leofwine and Ælfgar in the eleventh, so there were Welsh tributes paid to Mercian officials. The division between Gwent, which owed tribute to Wessex, and the neighbouring lands to the north, which owed tribute to Mercia, must descend from the days when Edward the Elder was overlord of Gwent and Æthelred and Æthelflæd were Lord and Lady of the Mercians. It makes no sense in the Wales of Asser, when West Saxon power extended over all Wales, nor at any earlier period, when Gwent would have been subject to Mercia rather than to Wessex.

This division between most of Wales subject to Mercia and the far south-east subject to Wessex may explain a particular aspect of Anglo-Welsh relations even as late as Domesday Book, 1086. At that date, Robert of Rhuddlan, currently dominant in Gwynedd, owed £40 for North Wales, while Rhys ap Tewdwr, king of Dyfed, also owed £40 apparently as tribute for South Wales. One would expect South Wales (Deheubarth, *Dextralis Pars*) always to include Gwent and Glamorgan, but it usually refers to a political grouping centred on Dyfed or the heirs of Dyfed. The reason may be the division referred to in the Dunsæte Agreement: Gwent (including Glamorgan) was out of the picture, since it owed tribute and hostages to Wessex. Among the other Welsh kingdoms, Dyfed was the dominant force in the south. Hence, for the purposes of the Mercian as opposed to the West Saxon tribute, Dyfed and its satellites were South Wales, Deheubarth.

In the reigns of Æthelstan and his brother Edmund this division between south-east Wales and the rest may perhaps have been partly submerged. *Armes Prydein*, a Welsh poem composed in opposition to Hywel's pro-English policy, has an extremely hostile sketch of the methods employed by the English overlord in order to gather tribute (as we shall see, this overlord was either Æthelstan or his brother and successor, Edmund). It appears that the tax-gatherers were based at Cirencester, Caer Geri, which was traditionally part of Mercia, although close to the boundary with Wessex.[74] On the other hand, the poem also imagines the tax-gatherers fleeing to Winchester after they have been put to flight by a Welsh uprising; and the poem refers to Dyfed and Glywysing as if they were both to be part of the uprising against 'the reeves of the great king'. At this stage, therefore, a single English government imposed its will on its Welsh client-kingdoms. Gwent and Glywysing remained, however, outside the reach of the Merfynion.

When Welsh kings witnessed Æthelstan's charters, the order in which they did so is significant. In charters of this reign, under-kings witness after archbishops, but before bishops. Like the king himself, they are separated from non-regal lay magnates by churchmen.[75] In Edmund's reign, however, the sequence changes: for example, in the will of Æthelgifu (S 1497), Hywel witnessed after the bishops and thus at the head of the laity, immediately before *Eadgarus æþeling*, namely the

[74] When the Viking army under Guthrum left Wessex for Mercia in 879, after the Battle of Edington and the baptism of Guthrum, it went to Cirencester: Asser, *Life*, cc. 56 (the promise to leave Wessex), 57 (departure from Chippenham for Cirencester), ASC 878, 879.

[75] S 426, preserved in two Glastonbury cartularies.

future king. The different sequences were not, therefore, random, but were ordered according to a deliberate scheme. One may reasonably argue that the same goes for the sequence in which under-kings attest, especially if the sequence is regular. On the other hand, one caveat is especially important: what is not in general significant is the absence of a name from a witness list. If the text comes from a cartulary rather than being contemporary, there is every possibility that names will have been omitted. For example, one charter, drawn up immediately after the Scottish campaign of 934, was witnessed by Constantine, *subregulus*, namely the king of Alba. There are no other names in the two surviving cartulary copies, but it is most likely that the original had a witness list of normal length.[76]

Table 16.1. Sub-kings attesting English charters

400	413	416	417	418a	420	
16.4.28	20.6.31	12.11.31	30.8.32	9.11.32	16.12.33?	
Exeter	Worth, Ha	Lifton, De	Milton	Exeter	Kingston	
Hywel	Hywel	Hywel	Hywel	Hywel	Hywel	
Idwal	Idwal	Idwal	Idwal	Idwal		
	Morgan		Morgan	Morgan		
Gwriad	*Eugenius*		Gwriad			
425	407	426	427	1792	434	
28.5.34	7.6.34	12.9.34	16.12.34	? 935	21.12.35?	
Winchester	Nottingham	Buckingham	Frome	Cirencester	Dorchester	
Hywel	Hywel	Constantine	Hywel	Constantine	Eugenius	
Idwal	Morgan			*Eugenius*	Hywel	
Morgan	Idwal			Hywel	Morgan	
Tewdwr				Idwal	Idwal	
				Morgan		
Edmund	Eadred				Eadwig	
1497	520	544	550	552a	566	633
c. 946	946	949	949	950	955	956
Kirtlington	Kingston, Su	?Somerton, Som.	?	Abingdon	?	Cirencester
Hywel	Hywel	Hywel	Hywel	Hywel	Morgan	Morgan
	Morgan	Morgan	Morgan	Morgan	Owain	
	Cadmo[n]	*Cadmon*			*Syferth*	
					Iago	

[76] The basis of this table is S. D. Keynes, *An Atlas of Attestations in Anglo-Saxon Charters, c. 670–1066*, rev. edn. (Cambridge, 2002), Table XXXVI; an earlier discussion is H. R. Loyn, 'Wales and England in the Tenth Century, 283–301.

Hywel was the king whose presence was most frequently noted and he was regularly placed first. There are two interesting exceptions: S 1792, in which Constantine and *Eugenius* come first and second; and S 434, a charter in favour of Malmesbury whose authenticity has been doubted, but whose witness list is not a straight copy from any extant charter, since here *Eugenius* precedes Hywel and the others. The name may be Gaelic, Éugan or Éogan, or else Old Welsh or Cumbric Eugen or Eugein (the modern Owain). He ought, therefore, to have been a relatively important king, even though he is placed last on his first appearance as a witness (S 413). There is no plausible Éogan, but there were three Owains of the requisite stature alive in the middle years of the tenth century (925–975): Owain ap Hywel ap Rhys, the king of Gwent of the meeting by the River Eamont; Owain ap Hywel ap Cadell, the son of Hywel Dda, who succeeded his father in 950; and Owain ap Dyfnwal, king of the Cumbrians, who was already king in 927 and was still king at the date of Brunanburh, 937.[77] The attestations of *Eugenius* run from 931 to 935, which makes it very probable that he was Owain king of the Cumbrians: when *Eugenius* attested in 931, Morgan ab Owain had already succeeded his father as king of Gwent; on the other hand, Owain ap Hywel Dda would not succeed his father until 950, fifteen years after the later attestations of *Eugenius*.

A mysterious under-king was the Syferth who attested S 566 (AD 955) after Morgan and Owain, but before Iago. He is very probably the King Sigeferth who committed suicide in 962 according to the Anglo-Saxon Chronicle. The name is Germanic and he is thus likely to have been a Viking ruler, Sigeferth being the Old English form of a Scandinavian name. At all events, he was neither Welsh nor Cumbrian.

The other names, Gwriad, Tewdwr, and *Cadmon* always come last among the under-kings. There is some chance that Gwriad, who only appears early (928 and 932) was a kinsman and ally of Hywel Dda; he may have been king of Powys or Ceredigion. Gwriad was a name used by the Merfynion and he may perhaps have been a son of Hywel's brother Clydog, who was one of the three Merfynion kings who submitted to Edward the Elder in 918.[78] Tewdwr attested once, at the assembly at Winchester which immediately preceded the Scottish campaign of 934, in which he therefore probably took part, even though he is not recorded as attesting at Nottingham on the way north; he is likely to be Tewdwr ab Elise, king of Brycheiniog, son of the Elise ap Tewdwr mentioned by Asser.[79] It has been

[77] *Historia Dunelmensis Ecclesiae*, ii. 18, ed. Arnold, *Symeonis Monachi Opera Omnia*, i. 76.

[78] The suggestion that it might have been Ceredigion is based on the *Brut*, *s.a.* 954, and the corresponding entries in *Annales Cambriae*, B and C: Anarawd ap Gwriad was killed, apparently in the battle of Nant Conwy, in which the sons of Idwal appear to have defeated the sons of Hywel, thereby driving them out of Gwynedd. Anarawd's death appears to have led to the ravaging of Ceredigion in the same year, and this leads to the supposition (1) that his father was the *subregulus* Gwriad of Æthelstan's charters, and (2) that he ruled Ceredigion (though this second suggestion can only be put very hesitantly, since Ceredigion could have been ravaged because it was under Owain ap Hywel Dda's control). It seems unlikely that Gwgon ap Gwriad, who was killed in 957, can have been the son of the Gwriad ap Rhodri Mawr killed in 878, as indicated in ABT 7*r*, *EWGT* 101. He is more likely to have been another son of our Gwriad.

[79] *LL* 237b, JC 8 (where he should be brother of Griffri ab Elise); there is no need to identify him with Tewdwr ap Griffri ab Elise, since the name Tewdwr was clearly a favourite in the dynasty, but Tewdwr ap Griffri is a possibility.

suggested that the name *Cadmon*, which appears twice for a sub-king in the reigns of Edmund and Eadred, may be a misspelling for *Caducaun*: a Cadwgan son of Owain was killed by the English in 951;[80] a brother of Morgan ab Owain bearing this name is attested with the title *rex* in one of the Llandaff charters, which shows him exercising authority near Merthyr Mawr, at the western end of the Vale of Glamorgan,[81] and a further brother, Gruffudd ab Owain died in 935 and was also entitled *rex* in a charter which suggests that he may have ruled in Gŵyr.[82] It looks as though Morgan ab Owain was the king of the entire kingdom but allowed his brothers to be sub-kings in parts of his dominion.[83] What would be surprising would be that someone who, from Edmund's or Eadred's point of view, was under-king of an under-king should attest charters ahead of his greatest magnates. The spelling of the name may, therefore, be correct—most English spellings of these tenth-century Welsh sub-kings are accurate—in which case it should represent Welsh Cadfan. No king of this name is known in the period, and no royal dynasty in power in the tenth century is known to have used the name, but neither of these are conclusive arguments. It is worth noting that, while *Eugenius* attests under Æthelstan, *Cadmon* does so under Eadred, in 946 and 949; perhaps there was a Cadfan, king of Cumbria, who succeeded Owain, conceivably after Edmund ravaged Cumbria in 945.[84]

Nearly all the attestations were for transactions explicitly said to have been agreed at great assemblies. These were characteristic of Æthelstan's reign, occasions of grand festivity as well as serious business.[85] Moreover the position in which the under-kings attest indicate the rank they were assigned in the festivities themselves. The main divisions of lay authority were marked by the clergy: Æthelstan came first, above the archbishops (we may contrast, for example, the norm for south-eastern Welsh charters of the period, in which a clerical list preceded a lay list, and the king was put at the head of the lay list). After the archbishops but before the bishops came the under-kings; other lay magnates were placed after the clerical section of the list. Æthelstan's position is not surprising: he was a crowned and anointed king.[86] Although his early charters style him 'king of the Anglo-Saxons', or 'of the Angles and Saxons', or even just 'of the Angles', in the 930s he was entitled 'emperor of Britain' or by some equivalent term. To that extent, the under-kings were not so much degraded—they attested ahead of the bishops—but rather remained at a merely royal level, inferior to the emperor of Britain. They were not,

[80] Lloyd, *HW* i. 338 n.; *AC* 951.

[81] *LL* 224, which indicates that he ruled in Glywysing rather than in Gwent.

[82] *AC* BC, *Brut*, 935; *LL* 239.

[83] For this pattern see *Vita S. Gundleii*, § 1, ed. and trans. Wade-Evans, *Vitae Sanctorum Britanniae*, 172–3.

[84] The next attested king of Cumbria was Dyfnwal or Dwnwallon ab Owain, who died in 975: AU 975.2; *Brut*, 975. Someone called Meurig ap Cadfan died in 963 (*AC* B and *Brut*).

[85] Stenton, *Anglo-Saxon England*, 345–8.

[86] J. Nelson, *Politics and Ritual in Early Medieval Europe* (London, 1986), 357; M. Hare, 'Kings, Crowns and Festivals: The Origins of Gloucester as a Royal Ceremonial Centre', *Trans. of the Bristol and Gloucestershire Archaeological Society*, 115 (1997), 41–78.

therefore, less kingly, but rather merely kingly: the *under* in *undercyning* referred to their political subordination rather than any diminution of their kingly status. There is, however, a difficulty in that the implications of a title may differ between Latin and the vernacular. Hywel Dda and the other Welsh kings were called *subreguli* in the witness lists of Æthelstan's charters, and *regulus* suggests someone with less authority and status than a full *rex*; but the Old English counterpart was probably *undercyning* and this could be used as soon as one king submitted in any form to an overlord.[87] The active connotation of the term for those actually present at these assemblies would have been that of the Old English word for which the Latin was a translation. Moreover, it was appropriate to Æthelstan's conception of imperial dignity that there should be under-kings—kings subject to the emperor of Britain. The significance of the Britons in the reign of Eadred was still recognized in a charter of Eadred drawn up at a great assembly, probably at Somerton, Somerset, in 949, which refers to Eadred as 'king of the Anglo-Saxons and emperor of the Northumbrians, governor of the pagans, and protector of the Britons'.[88] Both Hywel Dda and Morgan ab Owain were present on this occasion.

The danger was, however, that kings who were not crowned and anointed would come to be regarded not as normal kings but as inferior kings. In the twelfth and thirteenth centuries, the kings of Scots were crown-wearing even if they were not made kings by a coronation, but they were not anointed; and the English king protested vigorously to the pope when the Scots proposed that their kings should be anointed.[89] Middle Welsh literature would distinguish, for the pre-Roman period, between 'the crowned king of London' and other rulers.[90] The latter were entitled *arglwyddi* rather than *brenhinoedd*, lords rather than kings, perhaps because the accepted view of the remote past was, by then, of a single king of the Britons, such as the Lucius, king of the Britons, who, by a scribal error in the *Liber Pontificalis*, found a place in the authoritative pages of Bede and in the *Historia Brittonum*. Although the distinction was made of the remote pre-Roman past, it might fit the eleventh and twelfth centuries—and, with the exception of London, it might also fit the reign of Æthelstan—provided the under-kings became mere lords.

Finally, there were preconditions before Welsh and other kings could attend Æthelstan's court. For Hywel to reach England, he would probably have crossed either Brycheiniog or Gwent, territories ruled by his fellow under-kings Tewdwr and Morgan or, previously, the latter's father, Owain. An overlordship of the kind enjoyed by Æthelstan required a secure peace between his under-kings. The implication is that one can, at least to some extent, judge the effectiveness of English overlordship by the frequency of conflict among Welsh kings; and, indeed,

[87] As indicated by its use for Gruffudd ap Llywelyn, ASC C 1056: *Griffin swor aðas þæt he wolde beon Eadwarde kingc hold underkingc*. Hywel was described as an *undercyning* in S 706, namely the Old English version of S 705.

[88] S 549, *Charters of Burton Abbey*, ed. P. H. Sawyer (Oxford, 1979), no. 8: Ealdredus rex Ængulsæxna ond Norðhymbra imperator, paganorum gubernator, Brittonumque propugnator.

[89] *Anglo-Scottish Relations, 1174–1328: Some Selected Documents*, ed. and trans. E. L. G. Stones, 2nd edn. (Oxford, 1970), no. 9.

[90] *Pedeir Keinc y Mabinogi*, ed. Williams, 29, 49–51.

to judge by the sparse record of the annals, there was very little conflict between *c.* 910 and 950. Apart from those kings killed by the English, there were two poisonings and at least one family killing;[91] otherwise kings seem to have died peacefully in their beds. Even more significantly, perhaps, not a single kingdom is recorded in this period as being ravaged by another Welsh king. As we shall see later, the contrast with the second half of the tenth century is very striking.

3. *ARMES PRYDEIN VAWR*

Armes Prydein Vawr, 'The Great Prophecy of Britain', was the title given in the Book of Taliesin, an early fourteenth-century manuscript, to a prophetic poem of just under two hundred lines. It opens with the statement that 'they' will hasten:

> The *Awen* foretells that they will hasten.
> We shall have wealth and property and peace.

Who 'they' may be is only revealed later: they are two ancient kings, Cynan of Brittany and Cadwaladr of Gwynedd.[92] The same opening is found elsewhere, in a poem clearly composed by a supporter of the Merfynion of Gwynedd, and it seems likely that an audience could be expected to know who 'they' were.[93]

That the role of Cynan of Brittany was already traditional is likely to be the explanation of the apparent contradiction between the poem's reference to Brittany and the strong Breton–English alliance in the reign of Æthelstan.[94] Brittany had been conquered by the Franks, first by Charlemagne in 786, and again by his son, Louis the Pious, in 818.[95] Yet, during the long decline of the Carolingian empire the rulers of Brittany had gained a very large measure of independence and had considerably expanded their territory. As a result of that expansion there was a solidly Romance-speaking Brittany in the east alongside a Breton-speaking Brittany in the west. The Bretons failed to retain all of this acquired territory in the east after their recovery from the Viking domination of the peninsula between 919 and 936. Yet, they did keep the counties of Rennes and Nantes, and in the course of the

[91] Clydog ap Cadell was killed, probably in 920 (*AC* ed. Phillimore, 919 = 920, ed. Dumville), by his brother Meurig according to ABT 7; what may be the same Meurig and Hyfaidd ap Clydog died in 938 (939, ed. Phillimore = 938, ed. Dumville); they are not said to have been killed, but, given the killing of 920, it would not be surprising if this were a new round in a family feud; Cadell ab Arthfael was poisoned in 942 (*AC*, ed. Phillimore, 943 = 942, ed. Dumville); Cyngen ab Elise was poisoned in 945 (*AC*, ed. Phillimore, 946 = 945, ed. Dumville).

[92] The two kings are not named until later in the poem: *Armes Prydein*, ed. Williams, ll. 89, 91; for material on them see Bartrum, *Welsh Classical Dictionary*, 80–1, 165–6.

[93] *Facsimile and Text of the Book of Taliesin*, ed. J. Gwenogvryn Evans (Llanbedrog, 1910), 70. 16–19; *Armes Prydein*, ed. Williams, p. xlii.

[94] D. N. Dumville, 'Brittany and "Armes Prydein Vawr"', *Études Celtiques*, 20 (1983), 145–59.

[95] *Annales Regni Francorum*, ed. F. Kurze, MGH, SRG (Hanover, 1895), *s.aa.* 786, 818; Ermold the Black, *In Honorem Hludowici Christianissimi Caesaris Augusti . . . Elegiacum Carmen*, ed. E. Faral, *Ermold le Noir: Poème sur Louis le Pieux et épitres au roi Pépin* (Paris, 1932), 98–123; J. M. H. Smith, *Province and Empire: Brittany and the Carolingians* (Cambridge, 1992), 58–9, 65–6.

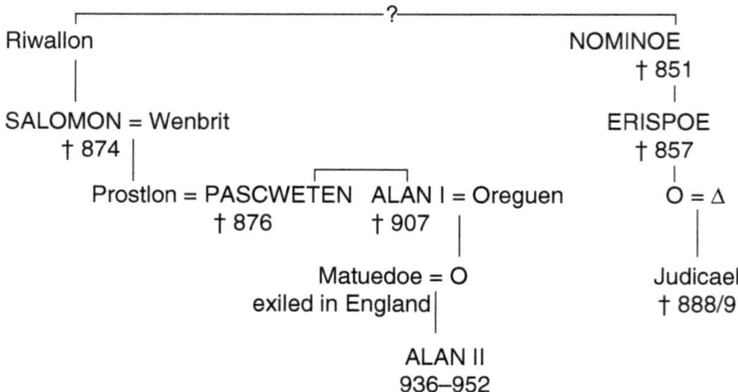

Figure 16.1. The rulers of Brittany

tenth century first Nantes and then Rennes emerged as the principal centre of power.

The period of Viking domination in Brittany was brought to an end in 936–937 by Alan II (Barbetorte), who had been in exile in England ever since his father, Matuedoe, count of Poher (around Carhaix), had fled to England with his son in 919. Alan's return to Brittany was with the support of Æthelstan. He took Nantes in 937, the very year in which the battle of Brunanburh was fought. His main base in Brittany came to be in the south-east, in the county of Nantes rather than in his father's lands in the north of Cornouaille.[96] From his time on, the rulers of Brittany took their place among the regional powers of north-western France, the counts of Anjou and Chartres and the dukes of Normandy. Whether these rulers were Frankish or Scandinavian or Breton in origin, through intermarriage and emulation they came to share in large measure one Francophone culture. Any expectation that the Bretons would join the other Britons in their attempt to throw off West Saxon domination cannot have been founded on contemporary reality but rather on the established conventions of the genre.

The belief in a restoration of British power over Britain by the return of two ancient kings was thus part of the background of the poem, as, perhaps, was the conception of Myrddin as the prophet. He was also the prophet in *Cyfoesi Myrddin a Gwenddydd ei Chwaer*, a poem, as we have seen, likely to belong, before it was extended, to the tenth century.[97]

Armes Prydein has generally been dated either to the reign of Æthelstan or to that of his successor, Edmund, although recently an eleventh-century date has also been proposed.[98] The date is based principally on the references in the poem to a

[96] Smith, *Province and Empire*, 139; N. S. Price, *The Viking in Brittany* (London, 1989), 42–4, 46–8.
[97] Above, 335–9.
[98] *Armes Prydein*, ed. Williams, pp. xii–xx; D. N. Dumville, 'Brittany and "Armes Prydein Vawr"', 145–59; A. Breeze, '*Armes Prydein*, Hywel Dda, and the Reign of Edmund of Wessex', *Études Celtiques*, 33 (1997), 209–22; C. Etchingham, 'Viking-Age Gwynedd and Ireland: Political Relations', in K. Jankulak and J. Wooding (eds.), *Ireland and Wales in the Middle Ages* (Dublin,

coalition of forces against an English overlord: the composition of the coalition resembles, up to a point, those put together by Olaf Guthfrithsson in 937 and 939–940, designed, respectively, to attack the power of Æthelstan and then Edmund. But, to judge the probable date and purpose of the poem, we need to understand the evolving struggle between the Viking dynasty of Dublin, the Uí Ímair, to which Olaf belonged, and the West Saxon kings, Æthelstan and Edmund.[99]

The struggle is best understood as a contest in seven rounds. The first was in 927 and was occasioned by the death of Sihtric, grandson of Ivar (ua hÍmair), the current king of York and also Æthelstan's brother-in-law; the issue was who would now take the kingdom of York. One claimant was Guthfrith, king of Dublin and likewise a grandson of Ivar. He left Dublin for York, probably accompanied, not just by a fleet from Dublin itself but also by the entire fleet of the Viking *longphort* at Linn Duachaill, by Annagassan in Co. Louth.[100] With these forces he attempted to gain the kingship in succession to Sihtric (who may, indeed, have been his brother). Æthelstan, however, also intended to gain power in York. The exact succession of events in this year is unclear: much depends on how far William of Malmesbury's account is to be believed. My own judgement is that, while William very probably had at least one tenth-century source in addition to a version of the Anglo-Saxon Chronicle, he fundamentally misunderstood the situation: he gave the impression that Guthfrith was in York when Sihtric died, which is contradicted by the Annals of Ulster, a contemporary source; and he may also have accentuated the likely West-Saxon bias of the text or texts he was using.[101] The most important item of evidence may be, not William's detailed story, but a single phrase in the northern annals which came down, via Byrhtferth of Ramsey, to Simeon of Durham: according to this Guthfrith was driven out by Æthelstan 'from the kingdom of the Britons', probably Cumbria; according to the Annals of Ulster he was back in Dublin six months after leaving.[102] The implication of saying that Guthfrith was driven out 'from the kingdom of the Britons' when put together with

2007),164–6, suggests that a period in the eleventh century is also a possibility (a very remote one in my view); H. Fulton, 'Tenth-Century Wales and *Armes Prydein*', *THSC 2000*, NS 7 (2001), 5–18, argues that it was composed on the occasion of Hywel Dda's death in 950 (also much less likely than the date proposed by Sir Ifor Williams).

99 Downham, *Viking Kings of Britain and Ireland*, 89–112.

100 AU 927. 2.

101 For discussion of the value of William's narrative, see R. M. Thomson's commentary, in William of Malmesbury, *Gesta Regum*, ed. Mynors, Thomson, and Winterbottom, ii. 116–18, and the works referred to there.

102 The phrase 'from the kingdom of the Britons' occurs only in Simeon of Durham, *Historia Regum*, *s.a.* 927, ed. Arnold, *Symeonis Monachi Opera Omnia*, ii. 93 (*EHD* i, no. 3). It is, rightly I think, interpreted as a reference, natural in a northern source, to Cumbria by Smyth, *Scandinavian York and Dublin*, ii. 11–12. It is inconsistent with William of Malmesbury's story. *Historia Regum*, ii. § 134, according to which Guthfrith fled to Scotland, apparently from York and shortly after Sihtric's death; Æthelstan demanded from Constantine and from Owain of Cumbria that Guthfrith be handed over. He was to be brought to the meeting at Dacre by the Eamont, but escaped back to York, where he was driven off and eventually came to Æthelstan's court, where he was feasted for four days and permitted to return to Dublin. The impression given by William that Guthfrith was in York when Sihtric died suggests a misunderstanding of the context and thus a mistaken interpretation of whatever source he may have had. See also ASC E 927; AU 927. 3.

the Anglo-Saxon Chronicle is, as Alfred Smyth saw, that Æthelstan took an army north, which included Hywel Dda and a Welsh contingent; that this army invaded or overawed Cumbria and thus drove out Guthfrith, who promptly took to his ships and returned to Dublin. Since six months would be more than enough time for Guthfrith to get his forces from Dublin to Cumbria and back again, he probably did indeed get as far as York, from where he was either repelled by the people of the kingdom of York or driven in flight by Æthelstan, and, in either case, made his way to Cumbria. The underlying suggestion is, therefore, that the Cumbrians had given Guthfrith some support. The meeting at the River Eamont, probably at the church of Dacre, as William of Malmesbury states, would then follow both Guthfrith's attempt on York and his being driven both from York and from Cumbria. Only at that point would Æthelstan have been in a position to induce the northern kings, Constantine of Alba and Owain of Cumbria, to come to the meeting at the River Eamont and to make an alliance. The principal target of that alliance must have been Guthfrith, who had so recently taken refuge in Cumbria. When the D version of the Anglo-Saxon Chronicle says that the kings assembled by the Eamont 'renounced all idolatry', it is hardly implying that any of them had previously been given to such practices. What it is rather doing—and doing deliberately—is coupling together two concerns that the northern kings preferred to keep separate: the cause of Æthelstan's power in Northumbria and the cause of Christianity in opposition to Scandinavian paganism. The thoroughly contentious implication was that any of the northern kings who gave aid to Guthfrith rather than to Æthelstan was favouring idolatry. The presupposition is that Guthfrith was not a Christian.

At this point it may be helpful to recall again the various forms taken by overlordship, such as Æthelstan sought in Britain.[103] The mildest was to claim the position of being the focus of an alliance. Such an alliance aimed to bind the participants to share the same friends and enemies as the king who was the focus: the alliances and hostilities of the others were to be dependent upon his.[104] An example of such overlordship as the focus of an alliance was the agreement made at Chester in 973, where 'six kings came to meet him (Edgar) and promised him that they would work with him on sea and on land'.[105] The second level of overlordship went a bit further: the overlord claimed the right to summon his clients, as I shall call them, to march in his armies, as Hywel Dda and other Welsh kings marched in Æthelstan's army in 934, when it invaded Scotland.[106] The third level included the first two but added another element, that hostages should be given by the client to the overlord, as Constantine, king of Alba, gave his son after Æthelstan's 934 Scottish campaign. The fourth required the client-kings to attend their overlord's court on special occasions. Charter witness lists indicate that for part, at least, of

[103] See above, 326–7.

[104] Note that the undertaking to have the same allies and enemies was similar to the oath of fealty in *Swerian*, ed. F. Lieberman, *Die Gesetze der Angelsachsen* (Halle, 1903–16), i. 396, where the person becoming a lord's man swears: ic wille beon N. hold ⁊ getriwe ⁊ eal lufian ðæt he lufað ⁊ eal ascunian ðæt he ascunað, 'I will be faithful and true to N and love all that he loves and reject all that he rejects'.

[105] ASC D (E), *s.a.* 972 = 973.

[106] S 407, *EHD* i, no. 104.

Æthelstan's reign, Hywel Dda, Idwal of Gwynedd, and Morgan of Gwent, regularly performed this duty.[107] According to Roger of Wendover (who was, no doubt, keeping one eye on his own day as he wrote), Edgar received Cináed mac Maíl Choluim, king of Alba, as his guest, gave him princely gifts, and granted him Lothian, formerly part of Northumbria, 'on this condition, that every year at the principal festivals, when the king and his successors wore their crowns, they (the kings of the Scots) should come to the court and joyfully celebrate the feast with the rest of the nobles of the kingdom'.[108] A fifth level of overlordship included the first four but added tribute; the first two levels were honourable forms of subjection, the third and fourth were less favourable, but the fifth was considered to bring a servile element into the relationship. It was this aspect of overlordship which attracted the special indignation of the poet of *Armes Prydein*.

Yet another element, namely that the client-ruler was denied the status or, less severely, the full status of king, might add a sixth level: he was a *dux* or perhaps a *subregulus*, an *undercyning* 'under-king', as Welsh kings were often described by English sources in the tenth century. This level, however, was capable of being seen differently by the overlord and his client: for the Welsh and the Irish, Hywel Dda was a full king. In such a case denying kingship to a subordinate ruler was more a style of overlordship than a level. But when, for example, the ruler of the Hwicce ceased to be regarded as a king, that did indeed add another level to his subjection to Mercian overlordship. In the seventh and final level, princes, officials and perhaps also nobles of the overlord's kingdom gained authority within the client-kingdom: this also happened to the kingdom of the Hwicce in the eighth century.[109] There were, therefore, both different levels of overlordship, some lighter, some heavier, and different ways of exercising power over a client-king, ways which were alternative devices rather than different levels of power.

If, then, we consider the meeting by the Eamont against this measuring rod, it seems likely that the kings of Alba and Cumbria were being induced to become client-allies at the first level, whereas Hywel, by marching in Æthelstan's army, showed that he was at least at the second level; and, through his attendances at Æthelstan's court, he showed himself to have reached the fourth.

The second of the seven rounds in the conflict between the Uí Ímair and the West Saxons occurred in 934, the year in which Guthfrith, 'the most cruel king of the Northmen', died, according to the Irish annalists, of an appropriately painful illness.[110] His son, Olaf, thereby became the leading figure among the Uí Ímair, but he was not in a position to challenge Æthelstan at the beginning of his reign. Instead, in 934 Constantine, king of Alba, was humbled when Æthelstan led an army as far as Dunottar, a major fortress on the east coast near Stonehaven, and sent his fleet to ravage Scotland 'as far as Caithness'.[111] The king of Scots was forced to

107 For example S 413, 416, 417.

108 Roger of Wendover, *Flores Historiarum*, *s.a.* 975, trans. *EHD* i, no. 4.

109 S 116 = *CS* 236.

110 AU 934. 1; CS 933 = 934; AClon 929 = 934.

111 Symeon of Durham, *Historia Regum*, *s.a.* 934, ed. Arnold, *Symeonis Monachi Opera Omnia*, ii. 124. What may be an earlier campaign was recorded in the *Annals of Clonmacnoise*, *s.a.* 928 = 933:

submit and give his son as a hostage, and to appear in person at a meeting of 'all the magnates' at Buckingham on 12 September, who were celebrating Æthelstan's triumph and Constantine's humiliation by enjoying a feast provided by 'royal munificence'; this indicated that his clientship had reached the third, and even, in the aftermath of defeat, the fourth level described above.[112] He attended Æthelstan's court again in 935, when he attested a charter in first place among the under-kings, followed by his neighbour and ally, Owain of Cumbria, both of whom took precedence of the Welsh kings, Hywel, Idwal, and Morgan.

The campaign of 934 was probably a consequence of Constantine's previous and otherwise unrecorded switch of alliance back from Æthelstan to the Uí Ímair, thus undoing the agreement made at the meeting at Eamont in 927.[113] At some point, possibly during his father's reign and thus before 934, Olaf Guthfrithsson married a daughter of Constantine.[114] His use of marriage alliances would again be illustrated when, as part of his second attempt in 939–940, according to Roger of Wendover, Olaf married Aldgyth, daughter of Earl Orm, 'with the support of whose aid and counsel he had obtained the aforesaid victory'—namely the campaign by which he gained England north of Watling Street.[115] So major a campaign as the one mounted by Æthelstan in 934 would hardly have been attempted if Constantine had remained faithful to the terms agreed by the River Eamont; and, on the other hand, Constantine would hardly have switched alliance after he had heard of Guthfrith's illness. The change perhaps occurred later than the first appearance of a king called *Eugenius* in a West Saxon witness list on 20 June 931.[116] Since this was almost certainly Owain, king of Strathclyde, it would offer a plausible *terminus post quem* for Constantine's abandonment of the alliance with Æthelstan, since Owain probably changed alliance at the same time as Constantine. A reasonable hypothesis is that in 932 or 933 Constantine allied himself with Guthfrith; but, when the latter fell mortally ill in 934, Constantine was left exposed to a West Saxon invasion (which came from eastern Northumbria and advanced up the east coast of Alba, far from any intervention via the Irish Sea). As *Britannia* might mean both Britain and Wales, so Alba was still ambiguous in the early tenth century, both

'Adalstan king of Saxons preyed & spoyled the kingdom of Scotland to Edenburrough, yett the Scottishmen compelled him to return without any great victory.' There is nothing to corroborate this entry in CS or AFM. Smyth, *Scandinavian York and Dublin*, ii. 64–5, takes it to be a reference to the Dunottar campaign of 934, which is possible, but it would have to have been placed a year too early.

[112] *Symeonis Monachi Opera Omnia*, ed. Arnold, ii. 93; *The Chronicle of John of Worcester*, ed. Darlington and McGurk, ii. 388–90; ASC *s.a.* 934. In S 426, 12 September 934, immediately after the campaign, *Constantinus subregulus* witnessed.

[113] *The Chronicle of John of Worcester*, *s.a.* 934, ed. Darlington and McGurk, ii. 388, 'quia rex Scottorum Constantinus foedus quod cum eo pepigerat dirupit', may be making the same inference rather than reporting a contemporary source, but he had apparently sound information for the reign going beyond what is found elsewhere (see next note).

[114] This information is only in *The Chronicle of John of Worcester*, ii. 392–3. It is discussed by Smyth, *Scandinavian York and Dublin*, ii. 43–4.

[115] Roger of Wendover, *Flores Historiarum*, ed. H. O. Coxe (London, 1841), *s.a.* 940; trans. *EHD* i, no. 4.

[116] S 413: Old Welsh spellings of the name Owain include Ougen (*AC* A 736) and Eugein (Harl. Gen. § 5).

Scotland and Britain. When after the campaigns of 927 and 934, Æthelstan used the title *rex totius Albionis*, 'king of all Britain', the Scots of Alba, 'Scotland', could now know who ultimately ruled Alba, 'Britain'.[117] When it was used in a charter for St German's in Cornwall, the Britons of the south-west might know who ruled the whole island of their forefathers.[118]

The third round, Olaf's campaign in 937, led to his defeat at Brunanburh, probably Bromborough in the Wirral.[119] In the fourth, in 939–940 after Æthelstan's death, he was largely successful: Watling Street was established as the boundary between Olaf's sphere and that of Edmund, but Olaf then died in 941.[120] In both campaigns, Olaf's first base was Dublin, but he aimed not just to establish himself as king of York but also to challenge the West Saxon supremacy in Britain.

The pattern of events before, during, and after these two campaigns, of 937 and 939–940, indicate that the politics of Britain and Ireland were interdependent. They also show that the actual timing of a campaign was uncertain until not long before it was mounted, since it was contingent on other events. Olaf succeeded his father in 934, and, in the very next year, took and plundered the 'seats of kingship' of his Irish neighbours to the north, Lagore and Knowth.[121] In 936 he plundered Clonmacnois and early in 937 gained the allegiance of the Vikings of Lough Ree.[122] Olaf's expedition to Britain in 937 only came, therefore, after vigorous campaigning in Ireland. Similarly, although the kings of Tara and 'the North' of Ireland, Donnchad mac Maíl Shechnaill and Muirchertach mac Néill, ravaged the territory of Dublin in 938, the year after Olaf's defeat at Brunanburh, the next year Muirchertach had the indignity of seeing his own royal seat, Ailech, taken by storm, being himself taken captive to the Viking ships, and having to pay a ransom to secure his freedom.[123] This reverse to the most effective Irish enemy of the Hiberno-Norse should have made it easier for Olaf to embark on the second and more successful campaign in England. Both in 937 and in 939–940 the conditions had to be favourable, and it cannot, therefore, have been clear for a long time previously that such elaborate expeditions were imminent: although long-term diplomacy, as with Constantine, king of Alba, could be conducted well in advance,

117 S 421 (AD 933), a grant of privileges to Crediton, in which, in the body of the charter, Æthelstan is described as *per omnipatrantis dexteram apice totius Albionis sublimatus*, a variant on a common formula which uses *totius Britanniae*. The source of the terminology was presumably the opening sentence of Bede, *HE* i. 1; Bede took it from Pliny the Elder; J. C. Crick, 'Edgar, Albion and Insular Dominion', in D. Scragg (ed.), *Edgar, King of the English 959–975: New Interpretations* (Woodbridge, 2008), 158–70.

118 O. J. Padel, 'Two New Pre-Conquest Charters for Cornwall', *Cornish Studies*, 6 (1978), 20–7. One, a charter of Æthelstan, 936, to St German's, gives his title as *Rex totius Albionis*.

119 J. McN. Dodgson, 'The Background of *Brunanburh*', *Saga-Book of the Viking Society*, 14 (1957), 303–16, repr. in P. Cavill, S. E. Harding, and J. Jesch (eds.), *Wirral and its Viking Heritage* (Nottingham, 2002), 60–9; P. Cavill, S. E. Harding, and J. Jesch, 'Revisiting *Dingesmere*', *Journal of the English Place-Name Society*, 36 (2003–4), 25–38.

120 CS *s.a.* 940 = 941.

121 AU 935. 4.

122 CS 935 = 936, 936 = 937.

123 AU 939.

the agreement with allies on strategy and timing is likely to have taken months rather than years.

On both occasions when Olaf led combined armies against the West Saxons, the leading king in Wales, Hywel ap Cadell, remained faithful to his English overlord. If, therefore, *Armes Prydein* belongs to this period, it gives urgent voice to a policy contrary to that which prevailed, except that Idwal Foel ab Anarawd, king of Gwynedd, may well have participated in the campaign of 939–940. At all events, in 942, and thus in the year after Olaf's death, 'Idwal and his son Elisedd were slain by the English', probably punishment meted out for earlier hostile actions by Idwal.[124] This was effectively the fifth round in the struggle, a round in which one of the allies of the Uí Ímair was destroyed. So far as Edmund's reign was concerned, the last rounds came in 944, when he conquered the kingdom of York, and in 945, when he ravaged Cumbria 'and granted it all to Malcolm, king of the Scots, on condition that he should be his ally both on sea and on land', so reviving the first level of overlordship, as at the Eamont, over Constantine's successor, but with the major sweetener that Malcolm (Máel Coluim mac Domnaill) gained a recognized overlordship over Cumbria.[125]

It is easy to see why Idwal, a ruler based in north-west Wales, might have been more likely to ally himself with Olaf Guthfrithson than was Hywel Dda, based in the south-west. A crucial difference between them was that Anglesey, the traditional seat of the kingship of Gwynedd, had been settled by 'the men of Dublin' in 902; it also lay on an important route between Dublin, from which Olaf came, and York, where he intended to base his kingship. Even before 902, Anarawd, Idwal's father, had been allied with the Viking ruler of York until *c.* 890. The Merfynion had old links with the Isle of Man, now undoubtedly under Viking rule. Gwynedd was thus in the core of the Irish-Sea region in the Viking era; Dyfed was marginal. This may have been one reason why the hegemony of a king of Dyfed within Wales was welcome to an English king.

This summary of the successive rounds in the struggle between the Uí Ímair and their allies, on the one hand, and the English kings and their consistent South-Welsh allies, Hywel Dda and Morgan ab Owain, makes two things clear. First, it is evident how much the northern kings disliked the emerging West Saxon hegemony in Britain. The contrary hegemony of a Viking ruler from Dublin, who aimed to base himself in York, seemed much less threatening. The degree of antipathy to West Saxon domination increased the closer one got to the main part of the Irish Sea: Cumbria was even more hostile than was Alba further north and east, Gwynedd was hostile, but Dyfed and Gwent remained allied with the English. Secondly, the context makes it plain what the purpose of *Armes Prydein* must have been if it belonged to this period: to rally the Welsh to the cause of Olaf Guthfrithsson.

[124] *AC* A 943 = 942: Et Iudgual et filius eius Elized a Saxonibus occiduntur. The addition in the *B* MS after Iudgual, *filius Rodri*, is an error; contrast the correct version in *The Annals of Clonmacnoise*, ed. Murphy, *s.a.* 935 = 942, 'Idvall m^{c} Anoroit, prince of Brittons, was killed by the Saxons'.

[125] ASC 945.

For various reasons, it is not easy to date the poem exactly. The match between the allies of Olaf, whether in 937 or in 939–940, and the allies envisaged in *Armes Prydein* is only partial. The principal participants in the anti-English alliance in 937 are mentioned in the Old English poem on the battle of Brunanburh included in the Anglo-Saxon Chronicle.[126] They were Olaf Guthfrithson himself and Constantine, king of Alba. Owain, king of the Cumbrians, is mentioned by the *Historia Dunelmensis Ecclesiae*, and also simply as 'the king of the Cumbrians' in the *Historia Regum*; a king of 'the Islands', presumably the Hebrides, called *Gebeachan* is among the participants listed by the Annals of Clonmacnois.[127] Essentially, this was an alliance of Vikings, Gaels (both of Ireland and Britain), and Cumbrians.

In *Armes Prydein*, however, the allies of the Cymry are divided into two groups: the first were those with whom the Cymry had made a *cymod*, 'alliance' (often after hostilities and, in that case, a 'reconciliation'), namely 'the men of Dublin, the Gaels of Ireland, of Anglesey and of (mainland) Britain'.[128] The phrase 'the Gaels of Anglesey' (*Gwydyl Mon*, modern *Gwyddyl Môn*) has caused difficulties. One reaction has been to propose an emendation: Manaw, 'Man', in place of Môn, 'Anglesey', but an emendation of this kind should only be adopted as a last resort.[129] Moreover, it is not clear that in the tenth century the situation of Man was so very different from that of Anglesey: both had been British islands and both were subject to Viking conquest and settlement. If a Welshman thought of seeking help from Man, it is unlikely that he would think first of the Gaelic settlers rather than of their Viking overlords.

Another has been to shift the date later, to a period when Irish kings controlled Dublin and its overseas dependencies.[130] In that case, the term *Gwyddyl* would have been adopted because of the leadership of Irish kings whose power over Dublin extended to Viking settlements east of the sea. Brian Bóraime (Brian Boru), king of Munster and subsequently 'emperor of the Irish', and Diarmait mac Maíl na mBó, king of Leinster, have been proposed as possible examples. Brian was described in his obit in the Annals of Ulster as 'high-king of the Gaels of Ireland and of the Foreigners and of the Britons'.[131] In 984 'the sons of Harald', Guthfrith and Maccus, had appeared with a fleet at Waterford and had there exchanged hostages with Brian as a guarantee of an alliance against the Dublin Vikings.[132]

126 *The Battle of Brunanburh*, ed. A. Campbell (London, 1938).

127 *Symeonis Monachi Opera Omnia*, ed. Arnold, i. 76; *The Annals of Clonmacnoise*, ed. Murphy, *s.a.* 931 = 937, gives a standard Irish annalist's casualty list, namely the most distinguished on the defeated side. *Gebeachan* may be for Giblechán (as in AU 890. 4) or Gébennach (as in AU 973. 2), but there is a word *gebech* for a type of craftsman, which might have yielded a derivative name in *-án*. At all events, the name is Irish, which means that he cannot have come from the Orkneys.The entry in *The Annals of Clonmacnoise* is helpfully discussed by Smyth, *Scandinavian York and Dublin*, ii. 39–40.

128 *Armes Prydein*, ed. Williams, lines 9–10 (where *Prydyn* may be for Scotland (Alba), but since it certainly means 'Britain' later in the poem, line 67, it seems better to take it the same way here; the Scots were by far the most important set of 'Gaels of Britain'. In both cases *Prydyn* is in rhyming position and cannot be emended to *Prydein*.)

129 See above, 501 n. 20.

130 Etchingham, 'Viking-Age Gwynedd and Ireland', 164–6.

131 AU 1014. 2.

132 AI 984. 2.

Guthfrith's son, Ragnald, died as 'king of the Isles' in 1004 or 1005, apparently in Munster, ruled by Brian. The leading Irish ruler was thus seeking to bind to himself the Vikings of the Isles and so discourage them from allying with the Vikings of Dublin over whom he had placed his son Murchad as ruler after entering the city in 999. Similarly, Diarmait mac Maíl na mBó, king of Leinster, established his son, also called Murchad, as ruler of Dublin in 1052; and in 1061 Murchad made an expedition to Man, where he exacted tribute and defeated Echmarcach mac Ragnaill.[133] The Life of Gruffudd ap Cynan claims that his maternal grandfather, Olaf, king of Dublin, had built a castle in Gwynedd, called after him 'Olaf's Castle'.[134] All this is wholly correct and will form an important theme in the next chapter; yet there is no reason to think that Irish political dominance exercised through control of Dublin by rulers based in Ireland provides any explanation of the crucial phrase 'the Gaels of Anglesey'. Moreover, it is noticeable that in lines 129–31 the Irish allies will follow the banner of David, but that is not said of the *gynhon Dulyn*. Although the term *gynt*, with its alternative plural *gynhon*, properly 'heathens', was still used out of habit after the Hiberno-Norse had embraced Christianity, the sequence of thought here suggests that the Dubliners still were pagan, otherwise they, too, would have followed David's banner; and that implies a tenth-century rather than an eleventh-century date.

A third argument relies on the premiss that *Goídil* 'Gaels' in ninth-century Irish sources encompassed the entire Gaelic-speaking community, east as well as west of the sea, whereas such terms as *Érennach*, 'inhabitant of Ireland' could cover non-Gaelic-speakers in Ireland as well as the Gaelic-speaking majority.[135] Ever since the seventh century there had been three coexisting conceptions of Irishness: one linguistic, a second in terms of descent, and a third territorial. The territorial conception was especially associated with Armagh: Patrick was seen as the apostle of Ireland because Armagh's authority was confined to the island. It was natural that the authority of Armagh should be expressed by the story of his circuit round the country, first just the northern half and then including Leinster and Munster. The territorial sense of Irishness, in competition with a non-territorial sense, is illustrated by a note added to Tírechán's *Collectanea* stating that the relics of Columba from Britain (*Albu*) would be brought back at the Day of Judgement to lie with those of Patrick 'and all the saints of Ireland' at Saulpatrick (in Co. Down).[136] The premier Irish-born saint of Britain would be an Irishman back in the soil of Ireland, when Christ came to judge mankind.

If, then, we take *Gwyddyl* to reflect the linguistic definition of Irish *Goídil*, the phrase *Gwyddyl Môn* indicates that there was a Gaelic-speaking settlement in Anglesey as well as in mainland Britain as part of, or in the wake of, Ingimund's

[133] AT 1052, 1061.

[134] *Vita Griffini filii Conani*, ed. Russell, § 4.

[135] M. Herbert, 'Sea-divided Gaels? Constructing Relationships between Irish and Scots *c.* 800–1169', in B. Smith (ed.), *Britain and Ireland 900–1300* (Cambridge, 1999), 87–97; ead. '*Rí Éirenn, Rí Alban*: Kingship and Identity in the Ninth and Tenth Centuries', in S. Taylor (ed.), *Kings, Clerics and Chronicles* (Dublin, 2000), 62–72.

[136] Notes supplementary to Tírechán, § 55. 2, ed. Bieler, *The Patrician Texts*, 164.

invasion in 902. The *Fragmentary Annals* envisaged a sizeable Irish element in Ingimund's army besieging Chester.[137] All this is far from being unlikely: such names as Ireby in Cumbria or Irby in the Wirral ('farm of the Irish') offer a parallel, since they are best explained on the supposition that the dispersal of the men of Dublin in 902 included Irish-speaking contingents.[138] The men of Dublin are unlikely to have been Irish-speaking at this date, but they had subjugated the neighbouring Irish; and it was probably for that reason also that the Viking conquest and settlement of Man may have reinforced the position of Gaelic in the island: British rather than Gaelic was the victim of Viking settlement in Man.[139]

This first group among the allies I shall call 'the associates'; it combined together, in addition to the men of Dublin, not just the Gaels of northern Britain, subjects of Constantine, king of Alba, but also those who had come across the Irish Sea only a generation ago as subjects of the Hiberno-Norse. The other group among the allies embraced the Cornishmen and the Cumbrians, the *Cludwys*: they were to be 'included among us'.[140] Later in the poem 'a brave company from Brittany' was also said to be going to come;[141] and, indeed, their participation could be assumed from the start, since one of the two ancient kings who would rise again to lead the Cymry was Cynan of Brittany. Those 'included among us' were, therefore, the other Britons as a whole, whereas 'the associates' were the non-British allies.

The way the distinction is made between the two groups of allies can probably be illuminated from later Welsh law: a kinsman so distant that he was almost ruled out from making a claim to a share of the kindred's land might give 'a shriek over the Otherworld'; 'and then the law hears that shriek and grants him inclusion (*cynnwys*), that is to say, as much as each of their number who are settled there before him'.[142] The one term, *cynnwys*, is used in the poem to express the relationship between the other Britons and the Welsh and in the later laws for the recognition of the distant kinsman as a fellow-heir to the ancestral land. The Cornishmen, the Cumbrians—and presumably also the Bretons—were to be accepted as having a hereditary right, along with the Welsh, to their ancient inheritance, the Island of Britain. The poem, in its use of the term Cymry, seems to allow the same ambiguity as *Britannia* had for Asser: as that was, at one and the same time, both Britain and Wales, so the Cymry of Wales would 'include', *cynnwys*, the other Britons as one people, Cymry, and one set of heirs with them.[143] This is hardly surprising, since in the tenth century those whom the poem calls *Cludwys*, 'people of the Clyde', were

137 *Fragmentary Annals*, § 429, ed. and trans. Radner 172, 173.

138 Armstrong et al., *The Place-Names of Cumberland*, 299–300; Edmonds, 'History and Names', 8–10.

139 See above, 472.

140 *Armes Prydein*, ed. Williams, line 11 (*eu kynnwys genhyn*).

141 Ibid. line 153.

142 *Llyfr Iorwerth*, ed. Wiliam, § 85/6; for this ritual 'shriek' or 'cry' over the Otherworld, see *EIWK* 403–4, and compare the threat made by Culhwch in *Culhwch and Olwen: An edition and Study of the Oldest Arthurian Tale*, ed. R. Bromwich and D. S. Evans (Cardiff, 1992), ll. 104–13.

143 The translation 'welcome' favoured by Bromwich and Isaac is entirely acceptable but perhaps does not convey the full flavour; similarly the early examples that concern acceptance into heaven may well be based on the same idea as found in the laws: *CA* 341 and n., 1005.

known to the English as *Cumbras*, a name derived from an early form of Cymry. In this instance, English terminology is likely to have reflected the Cumbrians' sense of who they were, Cymry.

The match between the poem and the allies of 937 was probably perfect in the first group, the associates. One need only assume that Irish settlers in Anglesey joined hands with the men of Dublin. The mismatch, interestingly, came in the second group, those who were to be included as joint-heirs along with the Welsh. Neither the Welsh nor the other Britons of Cornwall and Brittany came out against Æthelstan; only the Cumbrians of Strathclyde, often allies or clients of the Scots, marched into England. So far as the Bretons were concerned, as we have seen, any participation was quite out of the question. 937 was also the year in which Alan II, who had returned to Brittany from exile in England the previous year, took Nantes.[144] Alan was a former guest at Æthelstan's court and was an ally of the English.

In 939–940 it is more difficult to know who joined Olaf. There are, however, indications that his allies on this occasion did not include the Scottish king, Constantine, who would shortly abdicate and be succeeded by Máel Coluim, who came of a different branch of the dynasty.[145] The allies probably did include, however, the Cumbrians and the men of Gwynedd. In 945, as we have seen, Edmund 'ravaged all *Cumbra land* and granted it to Máel Coluim, king of the Scots, on condition that he should be his ally both on sea and on land'.[146] This could be explained on the basis that the Cumbrians were being punished for earlier hostility to Edmund, while Máel Coluim was being rewarded because the Scots had not, this time, marched south to support Olaf; in addition, Edmund was extending a hand of friendship to a new king in Scotland. An implication is that the Cumbrians were capable, on occasion, of following a policy different from that of the Scots.

The brief entry in the *Annales Cambriae* recording that Idwal, king of Gwynedd, and his son Elisedd were killed by the English in 942, suggests that Gwynedd sided with Olaf Guthfrithson in 939–940. A further possible comparison is with an entry in *Chronicum Scottorum*, the principal representative of 'the Clonmacnoise Chronicle' at this period. Having recorded the death of Olaf in 941, its next entry is about a fleet sent by the main enemy of the Vikings among the Irish kings, Muirchertach mac Néill, king of 'The North' and heir-apparent to the kingship of Tara. This fleet took plunder from 'the Isles of Alba', probably referring in particular to the southern Hebrides, those closest to the northern coast of Ireland. Here one may recall the presence among the allies of 937 of a 'king of the Islands', *Gebeachan*. It is possible that the enemies of the Uí Ímair, English and Irish, may have concerted their efforts at this favourable moment, after Olaf's death.

[144] N. S. Price, *The Vikings in Brittany* (London, 1989), 46–8.

[145] The chronology is uncertain but the abdication occurred 940 × 943. That it was an abdication is stated by the Scottish Chronicle, ed. Anderson, *Kings and Kingship in Early Scotland*, 251, ed. B. T. Hudson, 'The Scottish Chronicle', *SHR* 77 (1998), 150; this is confirmed by the *Prophecy of Berchán*, ed. and trans. B. T. Hudson (Westport, Connecticut, 1996), stanza 156, pp. 47, 87; but stanza 154 may also give a clue that Máel Coluim had temporarily taken control of Alba by force after Brunanburh (see Hudson's discussion, ibid. 210).

[146] ASC ABCD 945.

The match is thus better in 937 for the allies, since the Scots were then principal members of the coalition against Æthelstan, but it is somewhat better in 939–940 for the Britons, if one accepts that the men of Gwynedd as well as the Cumbrians were then allies of Olaf. It has been argued by Breeze that the poem's references to a place called *Lego* and to a river called *Ailego* are to *Legora ceaster*, Leicester, or the district around the river Leire (close to Leicester, a tributary of the Soar on which Leicester stands).[147] The English, according to the poem, 'will be put to flight as far as the river Ailego'; 'an eager *llynges* will come from Lego'.[148] In the 939–940 campaign Olaf's army took up its position in Leicester, where it was opposed by Edmund; a peace was then negotiated which made Watling Street the boundary. *Llynges*, 'fleet', could refer to the army which Olaf had brought by sea from Dublin, although that will have been much augmented from the kingdom of York and the Five Boroughs, leaving aside any help from the Cumbrians or from Gwynedd. However, in the form in which the case has been put, it asks us to accept an emendation of Ailego to Arlego, and to regard Arlego as the land near the river Lego (compare the relationship between Arfon and Môn); yet this theory cannot account for the particular wording of the poem: the name given in the poem to the river (*ffrwt*) is Ailego, but this according to Breeze was the name of a district near a river, not the river itself (which was called Lego). This attempt to resolve the problem of date is not persuasive, and the precise date of the poem has not, therefore, been determined. A more promising suggestion is that Lego is for Legio, and that it stands for Chester or Caerleon, both called Caer Llion in Middle Welsh, Caer Legion in Old Welsh.[149] Yet, one would expect *Leg(i)on* rather than *Leg(i)o*, as in the paragon of courage, Lleon, presumably based on the place-name.[150]

On the other hand, the reference to 'the men of Dublin' demonstrates that it must be later than 841, when the first Viking *longphort* was founded. The West Saxons and the Mercians are acting as one force to oppress the Welsh, but the West Saxons have the leading role: the tribute-gatherers 'will flee to Winchester'.[151] The context can hardly, therefore, be Burgred of Mercia's imposition of his authority in 853, backed up by West Saxon help. The nature of the English domination of Wales, portrayed as a harsh, tribute-gathering regime, does not fit the reign of Alfred. Likewise, the poem envisages a single English overlord, which indicates that it is no earlier than 918. There is a very good chance that it refers to the situation created by the alliance between the Uí Ímair and Constantine, king of Alba, and Owain, king of Cumbria. As we have seen, that was divided into several phases: in 927 when, so it seems, the northern kings favoured Guthfrith's succession to York; in 932 or 933 to 934, when they again went over to Guthfrith, only to be undermined by his death, and in 937 in the Brunanburh campaign, when they fought with Guthfrith's son, Olaf. In 939–940, so it seems, only

[147] Breeze, '*Armes Prydein*', 215–17.

[148] *Armes Prydein*, ed. Williams, lines 106, 149.

[149] *HB* § 66a; Isaac, 'Armes Prydain Fawr', 165 n. 8 (but his preference for Caerleon over Chester takes no account of the Viking interest in the former).

[150] CBT I. 1. 46 and n.; R. G. Gruffydd and B. F. Roberts, 'Rhiannon gyda Theyrnon yng Ngwent', *Llên Cymru*, 13 (1974–81), 289–91; Bartrum, *Welsh Classical Dictionary*, 407.

[151] *Armes Prydein*, ed. Williams, line 96.

the Cumbrians supported Olaf. The earlier phases of northern support for Guthfrith would have been enough to enable the poet of *Armes Prydein* to envisage the composition of those whom I have called 'the associates'; and, on the other hand, the combination of 'the men of Dublin', Alba, and the Cumbrians in opposition to the English was hardly a serious issue for the Welsh until Æthelstan made his successful bid for York in 927.

The switch of alliance by Constantine in 932 or 933, the participation of the Cumbrians in both of Olaf's campaigns, in 937 and in 939–940, the likelihood that Idwal of Gwynedd also participated in 939–940, and the support given by Wulfstan, archbishop of York, to Guthfrith, all go to show that Æthelstan's imperial policies, continued by his brother Edmund, provoked strong opposition in the northern half of Britain. That hostility, shared by the Cumbrians and by Gwynedd, finds it fullest expression in the poem, just as the most vivid expression of English imperial triumph is the Old English poem on the Battle of Brunanburh. The best hypothesis about the date of *Armes Prydein* is that it is no earlier than 927 and no later than 942, the date at which Idwal and his son were killed by the English.

The crucial point is that the poem appears to be serious practical propaganda, in spite of its more visionary component; and after Idwal's death there was no prospect of any Welsh uprising against the English in alliance with 'the associates'. Moreover, in the second half of the tenth century the Vikings who would have a major impact on Wales were not the men of Dublin but, as we shall see in the next chapter, the rulers of 'the Isles'. In the eleventh century the name Glywysing had given way to Morgannwg.[152]

It has been claimed that the poet came from South Wales.[153] The argument depends, however, upon a hidden premiss: that what determines the rhetoric used by a propagandist poet is his own geographical situation rather than his sense of what will best persuade his target audience. The premiss needs only to be brought out into the open for it to be apparent that it is an example of what we may call the authorial fallacy: that it is the author's personal preferences to the exclusion of those of his intended audience which determine the character of the text. It is quite true

[152] Phillimore *apud* Owen, *Pembrokeshire*, i. 208; W. Davies, *An Early Welsh Microcosm* (London, 1978), 92. Cf. *Brut*, 992, 1043. These are, on their own, insufficient examples, since the *Brut* represents a much later version of the original annals, but since the Morgan after whom Morgannwg was named is likely to have been the tenth-century Morgan ab Owain, who died in 974, the change is likely in any case to be no later than *c.* 1000. Etchingham's rejection of this dating evidence, 'Viking-Age Gwynedd', 165, relies on Dumville's correct explanation of the appeal to Breton support in the poem as invoking legendary convention; but the rejection is hardly persuasive: he has no evidence that Glywysing was used after AD 1000 as part of any convention. The only exception is where descent from Glywys is in question, as in Lifris's *Vita Cadoci*, Pref., §§ 13, 69, ed. and trans. Wade-Evans, *Vitae Sanctorum Britanniae*, 24/25, 54/55, 138/9 (Cadog was son of Gwynllyw son of Glywys).The earliest of the Gogynfeirdd attests the change, CBT I. 1. 9, 45, as does Lifris himself when he is referring to the eleventh century: § 7, ed. and trans. Wade-Evans, *Vitae*, 38/9 (*ad tempus Hiuguel regis, filii Ougueni, regis Morganensium*—Hywel died in 1043).

[153] *Armes Prydein*, ed. Williams, pp. xxiv–xxvi; D. N. Dumville, 'Brittany and "Armes Prydein Vawr"', *Études Celtiques*, 20 (1983), 148; Breeze, '*Armes Prydein*', 217–18, Isaac, '"Armes Prydain Fawr" and St David', 162.

that one trump card deployed in the poem, St David, might indicate South-Welsh allegiances:[154]

> Why have they trampled upon the status of our saints?
> Why have they broken the laws of David?

Similarly it says of the Cymry:[155]

> To God and to David they commend themselves.

St David was primarily the saint of what Asser called the archbishopric of St Dewi to be compared with, and distinguished from, the archbishopric of Gwynedd mentioned by the *Annales Cambriae*, although it is possible that some northerners would have accepted that St David was the premier saint of Wales.[156] There are also specific references to the kingdoms of the south:[157]

> The allies of the Cymry (will be) careless of their lives:
> the men of the South will withhold their taxes.

And similarly,[158]

> Let not Dyfed or Glywysing tremble.

These are enough, perhaps, especially the last one, to suggest that it was the allegiance of Dyfed and Glywysing that the poet wished to change—away from the English overlord and towards those whom I have called 'the associates'. But that concerns the target of the propaganda, not the domicile of the propagandist. It is entirely conceivable that *Armes Prydein* may have been the work of a poet from Gwynedd in 939, a year in which Gwynedd but neither Dyfed nor Glywysing supported Olaf; and it is worth remembering that the other poem to use the same opening lines was clearly from Gwynedd.[159]

The broad argument of the poem, however, was so angled as to appeal to all the Britons—to the Welsh in the first place, and more distantly to the Cumbrians and the Cornishmen. The Bretons were in a different category: they were not mentioned in the opening section of the poem; indeed they were closely allied with Æthelstan, because of their own Viking problem; and it is very likely that they only appeared later because the genre of *armes*, already traditional, made it imperative.[160] In any case, they

[154] *Armes Prydein*, ed. Williams, lines 139–40. I have preferred to translate *reitheu Dewi* by 'the laws of David' rather than 'the rights of Dewi' (Bromwich) or 'the rights of David' (Isaac), since, although *reith* is cognate with English 'right' it is not clear that it ever has that meaning ('right' in the sense meant is *dylyed* in Middle Welsh). On the other hand, Irish saints did have laws, for example *recht Adamnáin*, *Críth Gablach*, ed. Binchy, line 524; and, at an early period, *reith* will have had the meaning later taken over by its compound *cyfraith*.

[155] *Armes Prydein*, ed. Williams, lines 50–1.

[156] Asser, *Life*, c. 79; *AC* 809.

[157] Ibid. line 78.

[158] Ibid. line 99.

[159] *Armes Prydein*, ed. Williams, line 27, *Gwrtheyrn Gwyned*, does not pose a serious objection: see the note to the line in the edition; N. Tolstoy, 'When and where was *Armes Prydein* composed?', *Studia Celtica*, 42 (2008), 145–9.

[160] Dumville, 'Brittany and "Armes Prydein Vawr"', 151–58; above, 519–20.

were not victims of English overlordship and thus the first main argument of the poem had no purchase on them. This argument was against the tribute demanded by the English overlord. It thus presumed that the Welsh kingdoms were in a relatively servile form of political clientship. The second argument went much further and had much more ancient roots: the English were illegitimate intruders on the land of Britain, to which they had no right, either by inheritance or by contract.

The poem combines prophecy, ascribed to Myrddin, history, and legal argument. There is both the history of the remote past, of Vortigern, Hengest, and the first settlements of the English in Britain, and an imagined sequence of events, set within the prophecy, a narrative of how the rising of the Cymry against the English will progress. The metre divides the poem into nine sections each with a single rhyme.[161] It begins by invoking the alliance between 'the associates' and the Cymry and then turns to the narrower issue of tribute: a meeting at Aber Peryddon will bring about a confrontation between the Cymry and 'the reeves of the great king', who will attempt to collect the taxes, but none of the Cymry will pay.[162] The second section turns to ancient history: Hengest and Horsa made a deceitful contract when they acquired Thanet in exchange for fighting on behalf of the Britons. They did not fulfil the contract, but betrayed the Britons. Hence their claim to Thanet, to British soil, immediately became invalid. In the third and fourth sections, the poem turns back to prophesying the confrontation with the tribute-gathering reeves: to avoid 'infamy', *goeir*, the Cymry will not make peace. Instead they will fight against 'the reeves of Cirencester'. In the fifth section prophecy continues: the English reeves will flee to Winchester; they may have started out from Cirencester, in Mercia, but they will flee back to Wessex. In the sixth and seventh sections, it is prophesied that the men of Wessex and Mercia will unite to avenge the defeat of the tribute-gatherers, but they will be met by the Cymry with what are presented as legal charges—that they have taken land without any right, either by inheritance or by contract; moreover they have insulted the saints and have broken the laws of David. The prophesied quasi-legal confrontation thus turns to an argument from history. The final culmination of the poem in the last two sections brings allies from Ireland, Strathclyde, and Brittany (the Scots are not mentioned at this point); and the allied army, under the *revenant* leaders, Cynan and Cadwaladr, will achieve a final and enduring victory for the Cymry. The Cymry will possess their inheritance 'from Manaw to Llydaw', that is, from Manaw Gododdin around the upper Forth estuary to Brittany.[163]

As the summary reveals, the poem has no overt interest in the aims of 'the associates'. There is no mention of the kingdom of York. Even the Cumbrians, as well as the men of Dublin and the Bretons, will appear late on the scene to reinforce

[161] The edition divides lines 17–24 (line 24 being an insertion) from lines 1–16, but there is a single rhyme from 1–23, and lines 17–23 would be an improbably short section by comparison with the others.

[162] The phrase *meiryon mechteyrn* (lines 18 and 100) is better not translated 'the stewards of the Great King' (thus Bromwich and Breeze), since a steward was a household officer and the *maer* was not; compare Wulfric 'the Welsh-reeve', *Wealh-gerefa*, ASC BCD 896 (A has *gefera* for *gerefa*).

[163] *Armes Prydein*, ed. Williams, line 172: o Vynaw hyt Lydaw.

a Welsh uprising. More immediately and more realistically, what the poem is arguing for is an end to the tribute; the further claim to repossess the land 'from Manaw to Llydaw' seems much more impractical. Yet, there may be some contemporary basis even to this argument: the northern boundary of Cumbria may well have been on Mynydd Bannog, the hills from which Bannockburn flows down into Manaw. The southern boundary may already have come down as far as the River Eamont, that is to the Lake District mountains, and even to Stainmoor. Further south, in the old south-west of Northumbria, were the western appendages of the kingdom of York and the northern marches of Mercia, a land with many Hiberno-Norse settlers, who looked to the west, to Dublin and to Man, as well as to the east, to York, and who had natural affinities with Cumbria, since its southern territories also included many Hiberno-Norse and had links also with North Wales and its Scandinavian settlements. Much of the coastland of the Irish Sea, from the Clyde down to the Lake District, and from the Dee to Land's End, was within the domain of the Cymry in the wider sense of that term, both Cumbrians and Welsh; and part of the remaining coastland was potentially controlled by the 'associates'. An Irish-Sea world offered an appealing counterweight to the growing English empire. Moreover, there are slight indications that the poet was well aware of contemporary conditions: the Cymry will take the land 'from the Wall to the Forth', suggesting that, south of the Wall, in the kingdom of York, and north of the Forth, in Alba, they would allow others to rule.[164] Yet, the visionary element is very strong: the argument is ultimately about the right to all of Britain south of the Forth; the objection was not just to an English empire but to England as such. The Cymry were the Palestinians of early medieval Britain.

Armes Prydein is remarkable because we date it by allusions to the historical context, but its central arguments make very little reference to that context. A rebellion against the overlordship of the new England created by the combination of Wessex and Mercia was a practical proposition only because of the Men of Dublin and the Viking diaspora around the Irish Sea. Yet the arguments of the poem are all about the grievances of the Welsh and the immemorial claims of the Britons to Britain. It may well be that this disjuncture between what might move the Welsh to rebel and what might enable the opposition to Æthelstan and Edmund to be successful was replicated, with appropriate variations, among all the actual and potential allies of the Men of Dublin. That would explain why it was only at particular moments in the second quarter of the tenth century that the Men of Dublin could muster the opposition. The achievements of Olaf must have rested more on diplomacy than on mere force: *Armes Prydein* was one of the tools of persuasion which that diplomacy could employ.

[164] *Armes Prydein*, ed. Williams, line 174.

17

Wales from 950 to 1064

1. THE DECLINE OF WEST SAXON POWER OVER WALES

The death of Hywel Dda in 950 marked a major change in the politics of Wales and the relationship with England. Although the political unity of Mercia and Wessex, for which Alfred and Edward the Elder had worked, was to endure, its continuance could not be taken for granted. In 955, after Eadred's death, Eadwig became king of the English, but in 957 Edgar 'succeeded to the kingdom of the Mercians'—Edgar only succeeded to Wessex as a result of Eadwig's death in October 959.[1] During the period between 957 and 959 Edgar was entitled 'king of the Mercians and Northumbrians and Britons' in a charter preserved in a contemporary hand.[2] We may conclude that most of Wales was subject to Edgar, although the south-east was probably, as we have seen, under Eadwig's authority; 'Britons', however, would include the Cumbrians.

From his appointment by Eadwig early in 956 until his death in 983, Ealdorman Ælfhere of Mercia seems to have been the most active English figure in most of Wales.[3] Even though he was closely connected with Eadwig, his authority remained unharmed when Edgar became king of the Mercians. At this period, more than in the reigns of Æthelstan and Edmund, the kingdoms of the Merfynion were again subject, in practice, to Mercian authority. That authority was, however, less effective than it had been for more than half a century. It had been restored, apparently in the 890s, through an agreement between Æthelred and the sons of Rhodri Mawr at the expense, primarily, of Hyfaidd, king of Dyfed. From the death of his uncle Anarawd in 916 until his own death in 950, Hywel Dda had been the leading king among the Merfynion. Yet, reliance on the authority of one king within the dynasty had its drawback. When Idwal ab Anarawd became entangled with the enemies of King Edmund, but Hywel Dda remained faithful to the English king, the political unity of the Merfynion came to an end. One of the side effects of the struggle between Olaf Guthfrithsson and the 'emperors of Britain' was that the Merfynion, who had driven southern Welsh kings into the hands of

[1] ASC BC 955, 957.

[2] S 677, trans. *EHD* i, no. 109 (AD 958).

[3] *AC* C, *Brut*, 967; *AC*, *Brut*, 983; for his career, see A. Williams, '*Princeps Merciorum*: The Family, Career and Connections of Ælfhere, Ealdorman of Mercia, 956–983', *Anglo-Saxon England*, 10 (1982), 143–72. For Æthelmund, ealdorman of north-western Mercia 940 × 965, see C. R. Hart, *The Early Charters of Northern England and the North Midlands* (Leicester, 1975), 287–8, Keynes, *Atlas*, Tables XLII, XLV, XLVIIa and b, L, LII, LVI.

Alfred and had defeated the Mercians at the battle of the Conwy, ceased to act as a single political force. For a few years this did not matter: in 942 Hywel became king of all Wales outside the south-east.

When Hywel died in 950, his son, Owain ap Hywel, succeeded to Dyfed without any recorded opposition. He did not, however, retain Hywel's power over Gwynedd. Already in 951 'the sons of Hywel' fought a battle against 'the sons of Idwal' at Carno—probably the Carno in Arwystli, on one of the main routes between Gwynedd and the south; and since, in the next year, 952, Iago and Ieuaf, sons of Idwal, ravaged Dyfed, the battle of Carno is likely to have been a defeat for Hywel's sons, as one version of *Annales Cambriae* openly says that it was.[4] In 954 the sons of Hywel fought a battle by the River Conwy, after which Ceredigion was ravaged by the sons of Idwal. After this triumph for the northern branch of the Merfynion, any attempt by Owain ap Hywel and his brothers to retain power in Gwynedd seems to have been abandoned. In 955 Morgan, Owain, and Iago appeared at Eadred's court, where they attested a grant in that order (except that Iago came after Sigeferth, who followed Owain).[5] This shows that since the death of Hywel Dda a new political order existed in Wales, at least in the view of the English overlord. Morgan, much the senior ruler in terms of years in power, came first; Owain ranked ahead of Iago, just as Hywel had ranked ahead of Idwal in the 930s. Although the annals may tend to talk of 'the sons of Idwal', one of them, Iago, was recognized by the English as king of Gwynedd. The situation was probably similar to that existing in Gwent, where Morgan was king of Gwent but two of his brothers, Cadwgan and Gruffudd were, at least for a time, lesser kings with a more circumscribed authority.[6]

Between 956, when Ælfhere was appointed ealdorman of the Mercians by Eadwig, and 973, the date of Edgar's coronation at Bath and his meeting at Chester with six (or eight) kings, Welsh affairs were characterized by intermittent violence from two sources: external attacks on Gwynedd and conflict in the south in the fault line marked by the territory of Gŵyr (Gower) and, further east, Margan and then Gwrinydd (in modern terms, from Cowbridge to Neath, inclusive). To judge by a difficult entry in the *Brut* for 960, Gwrinydd was ravaged by Owain ap Hywel, king of Dyfed, in 960; but in 970 and 977 his son, Einion ab Owain was attacking Gŵyr, further west.[7] We noted earlier a charter in the Book of Llandaff, which

[4] *AC* C, *s.a.* 950, which runs together two separate annals.

[5] S 566.

[6] *LL* 239.

[7] In 960 *AC* C has *Goher*, but *Brut, Pen. 20, Gorwyð, BS Gorynyd* (v. l. y Gorvynydd). The entry is not in *AC* B or in *Brut, RBH*. Lloyd, *History of Wales*, i. 345 n. 85, suggested that *BS*'s *Gorynyd* was closest to the original Old Welsh *Guorinid* (*LL* 32. 21; 42. 16; 202) later reformed as Gorfynydd and Gronedd (the rural deanery of Groneath); cf. Llyswyrny < Llyswrinydd, 'The court of Gwrinydd'; the deanery of Groneath in *PW* is bounded on the west by the deanery of Gower in the diocese of St Davids, but in the early-medieval period the western portion of the deanery, from the Ogwr to the Nedd, constituted a separate territory of Margan (modern Margam): *LL* 224 and P. Jenkins, 'Regions and Cantrefs in Early Medieval Glamorgan', *CMCS* 15 (Summer 1988), 31–7, 47 (who prefers the Tawe as the western boundary of Margan). If *BS* is correct, Owain ap Hywel may still have controlled Gower and have been attacking a district that unquestionably belonged to Gwent / Glywysing. Cf. *AC*, *Brut* 970, 977.

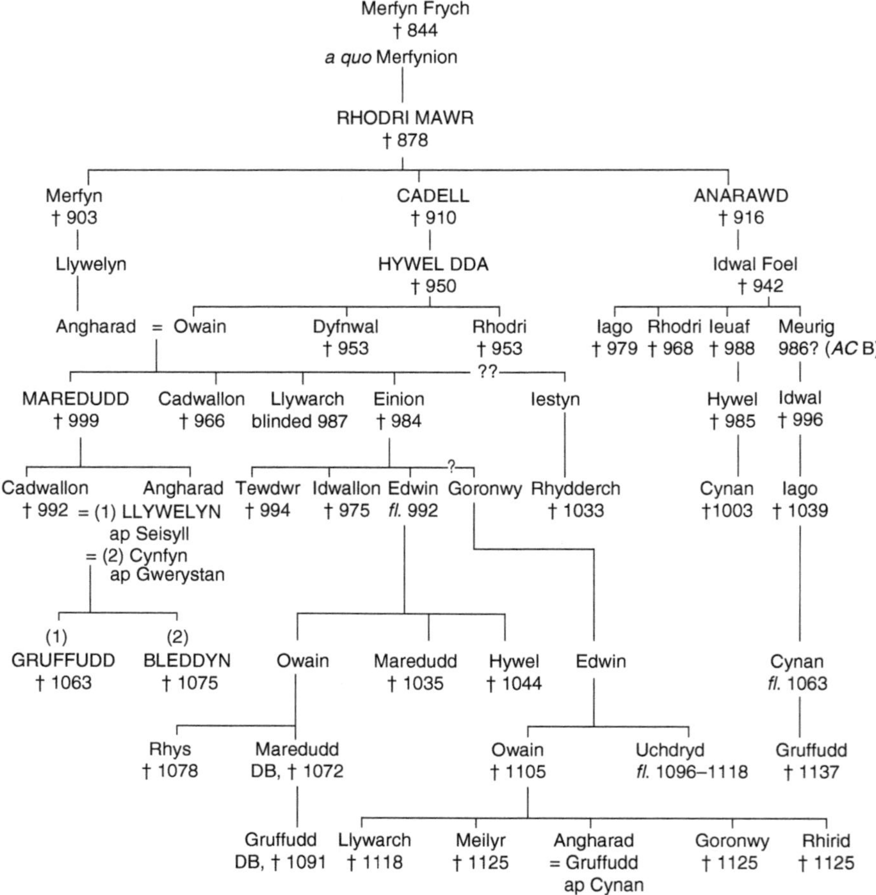

Figure 17.1. The Merfynion and their affines[8]

Note: a name in capitals designates a person described as *rex Britonum/Britanniae/rí Bretan*

indicated that Gŵyr was within the sphere allocated to one of Morgan ab Owain's brothers, Gruffudd ab Owain, earlier in the century.[9] Morgan himself did not die until 974; and it is a reasonable inference from the annalistic entries recording ravaging expeditions from Dyfed that in the 970s Gŵyr was attached to Gwent but was claimed by Dyfed. If the raid by Owain on Gwrinydd in 960 signified that Gŵyr, further to the west, was part of Owain ap Hywel's kingdom in 960, it would make it likely that, in the second half of the tenth century, Gŵyr shifted back and forth between Gwent and Dyfed.

[8] P. C. Bartrum, *Welsh Genealogies, A.D. 300–1400* (Cardiff, 1974). i. 41–2

[9] *LL* 239.

The other source of violence was external: attacks on Gwynedd by, first, 'the sons of Olaf', who sacked Caergybi and ravaged Llŷn in 961, of whom one raided Gwynedd again in 962, and then by an English army, led by Ælfhere, which ravaged 'the kingdom of the sons of Idwal' in 967.[10] Finally there were two Viking attacks on Anglesey in successive years, first in 971 by Maccus son of Harald, who sacked Penmon at the eastern end of Anglesey, and secondly, in 972, by his brother, Guthfrith son of Harald, who ravaged Anglesey and made it pay a large tribute.[11] It is possible that these entries, one for 961 in the Welsh chronicles and the other for 962, in the Annals of the Four Masters refer to the same attack, but this should not be assumed too readily: one may compare the successive attacks by the sons of Harald in 971 and 972. If we keep them separate, the sons of Olaf first ravaged Caergybi and Llŷn in 961, then went to the east coast of Ireland in 962, from where one of them raided *Moin Conáinn* in Gwynedd in 962.

It is not clear what was the context of Ælfhere's ravaging of the lands subject to the sons of Idwal in 967, except that it indicates that in the period since the appearance of Iago at Eadred's court in 955 the normal clientship of the Welsh kings had broken down so far as the northern branch of the Merfynion were concerned. We may suppose that their victories over their southern kinsmen in the previous decade had given them control over Powys as well as Gwynedd, and this might well have seemed menacing to an ealdorman of Mercia, but there is no direct evidence.

Rather more can be said about the Viking attacks on Gwynedd. These had different leaders in the 970s from those active in the 960s: in 961 the attackers were led by 'the sons of Olaf' and in 962 by 'the son of Olaf', but from 971 Wales was subject to attack from two sons of Harald, Guthfrith and Maccus. All the plausible candidates in Irish sources who can be identified with the leaders of these attacks recorded in the Welsh annals belonged to one or other of the many branches of a single dynasty, Uí Ímair, 'the descendants of Ívarr'.[12] The obvious candidate to be identified as the Olaf whose sons laid waste Caergybi (Holyhead) and Llŷn in 961, one of whom raided again in 962, is Olaf Cuarán. He was king of Dublin at intervals until his abdication in 980 to go in pilgrimage to Iona, where he died. An alternative is the Olaf Guthfrithsson who died in 941.[13] The advantage of the latter

[10] *Brut*, 961 (*ac y diffeithwyd Kaer Gybi a Lleyn y gan veibyon Abloyc*, where *Abloyc* is for an Old Welsh form such as *Abloib*, similar to Irish *Amlaib*); AFM 960 = 962 refers to a single son of Olaf; *AC* B, *Brut* 967; *AC* C's version is here unlikely to be correct, since it is contradicted both by *AC* B and the *Brut*. For the form Alfre, *Brut*, 967, cf. Keynes, *The Diplomas of King Æthelred*, 50 n. 98, on Ælfre in S 594, 608, probably referring to Ealdorman Ælfhere.

[11] *Brut*, Pen. 20, where Madoc has been substituted for Maccus, and *BS* (see Jones's note to p. 8. 21–2 of his translation of the Peniarth 20 *Brut*).

[12] C. Downham, *Viking Kings of Britain and Ireland: The Dynasty of Ívarr to A.D. 1014* (Edinburgh, 2003), 186–90, confirms the usual view of the descent of Maccus and Guthfrith, against B. T. Hudson, *Viking Pirates and Christian Princes* (Oxford/New York, 2005), 65–70; ch. 7 of Downham's book covers the dealings of Uí Ímair with Wales.

[13] C. Etchingham, 'North Wales, Ireland and the Isles: The Insular Viking Zone', *Peritia*, 15 (2001), 168–9; id., 'Viking-Age Gwynedd and Ireland: Political Relations', in Jankulak and Wooding (eds.), *Ireland and Wales in the Middle Ages*, 154–6; A. Woolf, 'Amlaíb Cuarán and the Gael, 941–81', in S. Duffy (ed.), *Medieval Dublin III* (Dublin, 2002), 34–43.

alternative is that, according to the Annals of the Four Masters, 'the son of Olaf' had come with 'the Lawmen', probably elected leaders of each island community in *Innsi Gall*, the Islands of the Foreigners, and had raided down the east coast of Ireland, including territory just to the north of the Liffey within the kingdom of Dublin.[14] If, then, Olaf Cuarán was king of Dublin in 962, it is somewhat improbable that his own sons should be laying waste his territory.

The difficulty is that it is not certain that Olaf Cuarán was king of Dublin in 962: he was expelled from York in 952, and his brother Guthfrith, ruler of Dublin probably from 948, died soon after a defeat in 951.[15] It is thus easy to suppose that Olaf Cuarán returned to Dublin from York in 952. Yet the first definite and trustworthy evidence that he again ruled Dublin does not come until 964.[16] In the Annals of the Four Masters, the Dublin king responsible for killing Conchobor mac Maíl Mithig in 956 is named as *Amhlaoibh mac Gofradha*, namely Olaf Guthfrithsson.[17] The well-known Olaf Guthfrithsson had died in 941, but Olaf Cuarán's brother Guthfrith may well have had a son Olaf, who could have succeeded his father. On the other hand, the same Annals of the Four Masters report a Dublin attack in 953 on south Leinster in alliance with a north Leinster king and name Olaf Cuarán as the Dublin king.[18]

It is a difficult issue whether one of these identifications in the Annals of the Four Masters is incorrect, and, if so, which one.[19] If the Olaf Guthfrithsson of the 956 annal entry is the result of confusion with the famous Olaf Guthfrithsson who died in 941, we should accept the identification of the Dublin king in 953 as Olaf Cuarán. Yet the same argument of confusion with a better-known Olaf could be advanced against that entry. When Olaf Guthfrithsson died in 941, his sons might have found a refuge in the Hebrides and so have been in a position to bring a fleet including the Lawmen of the Isles south into the Irish Sea in 962; but so also might Olaf Cuarán and his sons have found their way to the Hebrides when he was expelled from York in 952.

The sons of Harald probably belonged to a branch of Uí Ímair which, earlier in the century, had been based at Limerick, though again this is not certain. The Harald who is likely to have been their father was Olaf Cuarán's brother but was

[14] D. Ó Murchadha, 'Lagmainn, Lögmenn', *Ainm*, 2 (1987), 136–40; Downham, *Viking Kings of Britain and Ireland*, 184–5; A. Woolf, *From Pictland to Alba*, 212–13.

[15] ASC E 952; CS 950 = 951.

[16] CS 962 = 964.

[17] AFM 954 = 956: *Slóiccheadh la Conghalach mac Maoilmithigh, rí Ereann, co Laighnibh, 7 iar n-ionnradh Laighen 7 iar n-aighe aonaigh Life fri tríbh láibh do cós ó Laighnibh co Gallaibh Atha Cliath, 7 tuccsat Amhlaoibh mac Gofradha, tighearna Gall, cona Ghallaibh, 7 ro hindleadh caithedarnnaigh leó fór cind Congalaigh, conidh triasin ceilcc sin tairus é cona maithibh oc Tigh Gioghrann.* 'A hosting led by Congalach mac Maíl Míthig, king of Ireland, to Leinster, and having ravaged Leinster and having held the Fair of Liffey for three days they set out for [the land of] the Foreigners of Dublin, and Olaf son of Guthfrith, ruler of the Foreigners, went with his Foreigners and an ambush was laid by them for Congalach, so that he fell victim to that stratagem at Tech Giograinn' (Tech Gioghrann is unidentified but presumably within Fine Gall).

[18] AFM 951 = 953: *Orgain Insi Doimhle 7 Insi Uladh la hAmhlaibh Cuaráin 7 la Tuathal mac Ugaire.* Tuathal mac Úgaire belonged to the Uí Muiredaig branch of Uí Dúnlainge: *CGH* 12.

[19] See n. 14 above.

killed when still young; now, however, their main centre was the Hebrides, with a further ambition to control the Isle of Man, and this would explain their attacks on Gwynedd.[20]

The pattern behind all these events is, first, that Dublin enjoyed a pre-eminence among the Viking settlements in Ireland and along the western coastlands of Britain: the king of Dublin was *rí Gall* 'the king of the Foreigners', but the ruler of the Hebrides was *rí Innse nGall* 'the king of the Isles of the Foreigners'.[21] Secondly, Dublin's authority over the Viking diaspora varied: sometimes contingents came from the Isles to help Dublin, as they came to support Olaf Cuarán at the Battle of Tara in 980 and Sihtric Olafsson at the Battle of Clontarf in 1014;[22] at other times the Isles could be the base for an expedition hostile to Dublin, as in 962. In 980 Olaf Cuarán retired to Iona in pilgrimage and died there; Iona, after all, lay in Innsi Gall, 'the Isles of the Foreigners', so that he was going to the principal monastery in a kingdom from which he had drawn a contingent earlier that year; but in 986 a newly arrived fleet of Danes plundered Iona on Christmas Night, killing the abbot and fifteen senior monks.[23] Yet in 987 what appear to be the same Danes then worked with Guthfrith Haraldsson, king of the Isles, to win a battle on the Isle of Man, perhaps thereby detaching the island from Dublin control.[24] In 995 Swein Forkbeard, later king of Denmark and (briefly) England, and also father of Cnut, ravaged Man.[25] Æthelred II's fleet ravaged Man in 1000 as part of a campaign whose primary target was Strathclyde.[26] If we had more evidence, we should probably be able to see interactions between Dublin and the Viking settlements on Man, in Cumbria, and in north-east Wales in the second half of the tenth century. The Isle of Man is represented by a single entry in the Annals of Ulster; but its strategic significance is indicated by the fact that Swein and Æthelred both attacked it (the one attack noted in a Welsh source, the other in an English source).

Finally, the power of Dublin within Ireland received a major blow at the Battle of Tara in 980. The site and the participants indicate the context: Olaf Cuarán was almost at the end of his career: he would resign the next year and, as we have seen, go in pilgrimage to Iona, where he died; he was king of Dublin but his sons led the Dublin

[20] This is based, first, on supposing that the Harald of CS *s.a.* 939 = 940, AClon *s.a.* 933 = 940, was their father, and, secondly, that Guthfrith son of Harald was the *Gofraidh m. Arailt, ri Innsi Gall*, who was killed in Dál Riata: AU 989. 4; CS *s.a.* 987 = 988; AClon 982 = 989. The interest in the Isle of Man is revealed by AU 987. 1. See D. Thornton, 'Edgar and the Eight Kings, AD 973: *Textus et Dramatis Personae*', *Early Medieval Europe*, 10/1 (2001), 72–3; id., 'Hey, Mac! The Name *Maccus*, Tenth to Fifteenth Centuries', *Nomina*, 20 (1997), 67–98; Etchingham, 'North Wales, Ireland and the Isles', 168–80; Woolf, *From Pictland to Alba*, 206–7; Downham, *Viking Kings of Britain and Ireland*, 185–93.

[21] AU 989. 3 and 4 (AT 989, CS 987 = 989).

[22] AU 980. 1: 'the Foreigners of Áth Cliath and the Isles'; in 1014 the Viking allies came from even further afield, from the Orkneys and Scandinavia.

[23] AT 980, AU 986. 3.

[24] AU 987. 1.

[25] *AC* B, *Brut*, 995 (with Ywein for Swein in the Peniarth 20 version, Yswein in the RBH version, Suein in *BS*).

[26] ASC CDE 1000.

army;[27] Máel Sechnaill mac Domnaill was king of Mide (Meath) and, in 980, succeeded Domnall ua Néill (of the Northern Uí Néill dynasty of Cenél nEógain) as king of Tara. To fight a battle against a new king of Tara at Tara itself was to challenge his authority in the most direct form possible. Yet, it is also clear that Olaf Cuarán had exercised power over the area close to Tara.[28] Olaf's challenge was not something unprepared, an entirely novel intervention within the structure of Irish politics at the highest level. In the event, Olaf Cuarán was defeated. According to the Annals of Tigernach and Chronicum Scotorum, both sources favourable to Máel Sechnaill, the latter then besieged Dublin and extracted the liberation of 'the hostages of Ireland', including Domnall Cláen, king of Leinster, the release of 'the sureties of the Uí Néill', and also 'the freedom of the Uí Néill from the Shannon to the sea'. In triumphalist mode the annalist added, 'That harrying was the harrying of the Babylon of Ireland. It was like the Harrying of Hell.'[29]

This contemporary annalist was based at Clonmacnois, a monastery with close ties with the ruling dynasty of Mide. What is most remarkable, however, is the implication that, before the battle, Olaf Cuarán had held the king of Leinster as a hostage and had held the *aitiri*, hostage-sureties, of the Southern Uí Néill. If Máel Sechnaill had won the freedom of the Southern Uí Néill in 980, in some sense they must have been unfree before 980. No such acknowledgement of Irish subjection to the Vikings had been made by an Irish annalist since 853, when an earlier Olaf, 'son of the king of Lochlann', came to Ireland, and the Vikings gave him hostages while the Irish gave him tribute.[30] It cannot be the case that the Uí Néill had been continuously subject to the Vikings of Dublin from 853 to 980, if only because the Irish had succeeded in ejecting the Vikings from Dublin in 902. The power enjoyed by the Babylon of Ireland up to 980 was much more recent. In 970 Olaf Cuarán and his neighbour and ally in Brega had defeated the king of Tara, Domnall ua Néill, in a major battle, probably at Kilmoone in Co. Meath, close to Tara.[31] Earlier in the same year Olaf had sacked Kells and defeated the Uí Néill at Ardmulchan, on the Boyne between Navan and Slane.[32] In 976 Olaf had captured the king of Leinster, Úgaire son of Tuathal, and in 977 he had killed two 'royal materials' of the Uí Néill, one a son of Domnall ua Néill and the other of the royal

[27] AT 980, CS 978 = 980.

[28] As shown by Cináed ua hArtacáin's poem on Achall, where the Columban monastery of Scrín Cholaim Chille, was situated, a poem that incorporates praise of Olaf, *Metrical Dinnsheanchas*, ed. E. J. Gwynn, i. 46–53; it was attacked in 976, very probably because of its association with Olaf: CS 974 = 976; E. Bhreathnach, 'The Documentary Evidence for Pre-Norman Skreen, County Meath', *Ríocht na Midhe*, 9: 2 (1996), 37–41; ead. 'Columban Churches in Brega and Leinster: Relations with the Norse and the Anglo-Normans', *JRSAI* 129 (1999), 8–9.

[29] AT 980; CS omits the Harrying of Hell, but the close agreement otherwise suggests that something approximating to the wording of AT was in the contemporary tenth-century chronicle, composed at Clonmacnois, a monastery closely linked with the Clann Cholmáin of Mide. The translations in AT and CS are wrong: *brat* here has its older sense, and Máel Sechnaill was thus the Cyrus of Ireland.

[30] AU, CS 853.

[31] AU 970. 4, CS 968 = 970.

[32] CS 968 = 970; Ard Máelchon (Ardmulchan) is at N 90 70.

dynasty of North Brega.[33] In 978 the men of Dublin killed the king of Leinster in battle, and in 979 they seized the next king of Leinster, Domnall Cláen, the one who was released in 980 after the Battle of Tara and the siege of Dublin.[34] In one decade Olaf Cuarán had reduced the Leinstermen to abject submission and had humiliated and defeated the Uí Néill, including the king of Tara, Domnall ua Néill. It was hardly surprising that in 980, when Domnall ua Néill died 'after penitence', Olaf Cuarán and his sons should challenge Máel Sechnaill at Tara.[35]

In 973, during this period of exceptional Dublin military success, there occurred the famous meeting at Chester, at which six (or, in some sources, eight) kings promised to be *efenwyrhtan*, 'co-workers', with Edgar by sea and by land.[36] That is to say, an agreement was made at the first level of overlordship described in Chapter 10, for which use of the terms *efenwyrhta* and its synonym *midwyrhta* was characteristic.[37] Edgar was the focus of an alliance; but, because he was the focus, he was the leader. For the identity of the kings we are dependent on twelfth-century historians, in particular John of Worcester and William of Malmesbury, who are also our earliest sources for the story that Edgar acted as steersman when he was rowed on the River Dee by the kings.[38] John and William were in touch with each other and are thus not independent sources.[39] The kings, with suggested identifications, are as follows:[40]

	John	William	Identification
A.	*Subreguli*		
1.	Kynath, rex Scottorum	=	Kenneth II / Cináed mac Maíl Choluim (971–995)
2.	Malcolm, rex Cumbrorum	=	Máel Coluim mac Domnaill / ap Dyfnwal (d. 997)
3.	Maccus, plurimarum rex insularum	Mascusius archipirata	Maccus son of Harald, king of Innsi Gall
B.	*Alii*	*Walenses*	
4.	Dufnal	Dufnal	Dyfnwal, father of no. 2, Máel Coluim?

[33] AT 975 = 976, AU 977. 1.

[34] AU 978. 3; AT 978 = 979; CS 977 = 979.

[35] Woolf, 'Amlaíb Cuarán and the Gael, 941–81', 42–3.

[36] J. Barrow, 'Chester's Earliest Regatta: Edgar's Dee-Rowing Revisited', *Early Medieval Europe*, 10/1 (2001), 81–93; Thornton, 'Edgar and the Eight Kings', 49–79; A. Williams, 'An Outing on the Dee: King Edgar at Chester, AD 973', *Medieval Scandinavia*, 10 (2004), 229–44; S. Matthews, 'King Edgar, Wales and Chester: The Welsh Dimension in the Ceremony of 973', *Northern History*, 44: 2 (2007), 9–26.

[37] *Midwyrhta*, ASC A, 945.

[38] *The Chronicle of John of Worcester*, ed. and trans. Darlington et al., ii. 422–5; William of Malmesbury, *Gesta Regum Anglorum*, ii. 148, ed. and trans. Mynors et al., 238–9.

[39] M. Brett, 'John of Worcester and his Contemporaries', in R. H. C. Davis and J. M. Wallace-Hadrill (eds.), *The Writing of History in the Middle Ages: Essays presented to R.W. Southern* (Oxford, 1981), 101–26.

[40] This is based on Thornton, 'Edgar and the Eight Kings', 64–74.

5.	Siferth	Giferth	If we prefer John of Worcester's version here, an otherwise unknown Sigfrith/Sigferth,[41] probably a Viking, perhaps from Man or Galloway; if we prefer William of Malmesbury, perhaps an error of transmission for Guthfrith son of Harald (d. 989, king of Insi Gall)?
6.	Huuual	Huual	Hywel ab Ieuaf, nephew of Iago
7.	Iacob	Iacob	Iago ab Idwal, king of Gwynedd (*fl.* 942–979)
8.	Iuchil	Iudethil	perhaps an otherwise unknown Ithel (Old Welsh *Iudhail*)

If the identifications are correct, it may be possible to explain the difference between the D version of the Anglo-Saxon Chronicle and later accounts, in that the Chronicle has six kings attending the meeting, while the later versions have eight. Máel Coluim was son of Dyfnwal and Hywel was the nephew of Iago. Both may have been involved as heirs-apparent; both would very soon assume power and thus become the important personages for anyone recording what had happened.

The meeting at Chester represented a diplomatic effort to impose an English-led peace upon as many as possible of the kings of the Irish-Sea area and northern Britain. Earlier, in 970, Edgar seems to have attempted to exert his influence on the politics of northern Britain: Máel Coluim, king of Strathclyde, appeared at his court in that year, and so, probably, did Cináed mac Maíl Choluim, another of those who also appeared at Chester in 973, but who was not yet king in 970: the Malcolm *dux* who appears as a witness to a charter of 970 is likely to be Máel Coluim, king of Strathclyde; and 970 was also the year in which Lothian appears to have been granted to Cináed son of Máel Coluim, not yet king of Scots.[42]

Although the identity of *Iuchil/Iudethil* is quite unknown and that of *Dufnal* is not certain, it seems that the southern Welsh kings, Owain ap Hywel and Morgan ab Owain, were not present.[43] There is, however, no reason why they should have been at Chester, since they may well have been at the coronation at Bath, which was much closer.[44] The kingdoms certainly represented at Chester were also those that had been allied with Olaf Guthfrithsson of Dublin either in 937 or 939–940 or both. When the probable participation of Idwal ab Anarawd in the campaign of

[41] Downham, *Viking Kings of Britain and Ireland*, 182–3; it cannot be the King Sigeferth who 'killed himself, and his body is buried at Wimborne', ASC (A) 962.

[42] S 779; S. Keynes, 'Edgar, *Rex Admirabilis*', in Scragg (ed.), *Edgar, King of the English*, 50 n. 232, 51; Culén mac Illduilb was killed by Britons in battle in 971: AU 971. 1. Woolf, *From Pictland to Alba*, 211.

[43] I am not persuaded by the identifications of Hywel and Iuchil proposed by A. Breeze, 'Edgar at Chester in 973: A Breton Link', *Northern History*, 44 (2007), 153–7; if the southern Welsh kings did not attend, there is even less reason to suppose that Bretons would have been present.

[44] Thornton, 'Edgar and the Seven Kings', 70; cf. W. Davies, *Patterns of Power*, 75.

939–940 was discussed, it became apparent that Gwynedd was central within the Irish Sea, whereas Dyfed and even more Gwent were not. Yet, for the meeting at Chester, the principal source of concern lay further north: the three principal kings were the king of Scots, the king of Cumbria, and the king of the Isles. Gwynedd was subject to attack from the Isles; no doubt part of the motivation for those attacks was plunder, especially in the form of captives for the slave market, but the attacks may also have been designed to bring parts of Gwynedd under submission.[45]

Another reason for the meeting at Chester may well have been reports of the victories of Olaf Cuarán and the men of Dublin. From that point of view, the most important of those to attend at Chester was Maccus Haraldsson, 'king of very many isles'. On the other hand, the attacks by Maccus and Guthfrith on Anglesey in 971 and 972, especially that of Guthfrith, did not indicate that the powers of the Irish Sea and the Hebrides were all about to ally of their own accord against the king of the English: there was no sign of an alliance between Gwynedd and the Uí Ímair against England, still less the kingdoms of South Wales, and Maccus and Guthfrith were rivals of Olaf Cuarán and his sons.[46] What probably lay behind the meeting at Chester was, first, that a recently crowned and thus all the more imperial king of the English wished to demonstrate that his authority, not Olaf Cuarán's, extended over the powers of the Irish Sea and northern Britain, and, secondly, the challenge posed by the attacks of Maccus and Guthfrith on one of his subject kingdoms, Gwynedd, and the advantage of gaining their allegiance against any move from Dublin to gain power east of the Irish Sea, especially by an alliance with the Scots and Cumbrians.

Perhaps in part because of the renewed Viking onslaughts, Gwynedd was itself unstable.[47] Nearly twenty years previously, Iago ab Idwal had appeared as a witness to a charter of Eadred; he then acted as the king of Gwynedd, even though the Welsh annals talked of 'the sons of Idwal' as a collective group. Among the kings at Chester, however, Iago came after someone named Hywel, who is very likely to have been his nephew, Hywel ab Ieuaf ab Idwal. Hywel's father, Ieuaf ab Idwal, who acted in concert with Iago earlier in their careers, was imprisoned by him in 969. That event signalled the breakdown of the unity hitherto displayed by the sons of Idwal. In 974, the year after the meeting at Chester, Iago was expelled from his kingdom, which was taken over by Hywel: if, as I have suggested, Iago sought to heal the rift with Hywel by making him heir-apparent, he did not succeed. Furthermore, if Iago was the king of all Gwynedd and Hywel king only of one area, Iago is likely to have been the person most directly damaged by the onslaughts on Anglesey, the innermost core of Gwynedd.

[45] As suggested by Davies, *Patterns of Power*, 57–58, and Etchingham, 'North Wales, Ireland and the Isles', 173–6; K. L. Maund, 'Dynastic Segmentation and Gwynedd, *c.* 950 – *c.* 1000', *Studia Celtica*, 32 (1998), 164–6, is inclined to the view that no actual domination was achieved.

[46] This makes it unlikely that *Armes Prydein* belongs to this period.

[47] Maund, 'Dynastic Segmentation', 160–1.

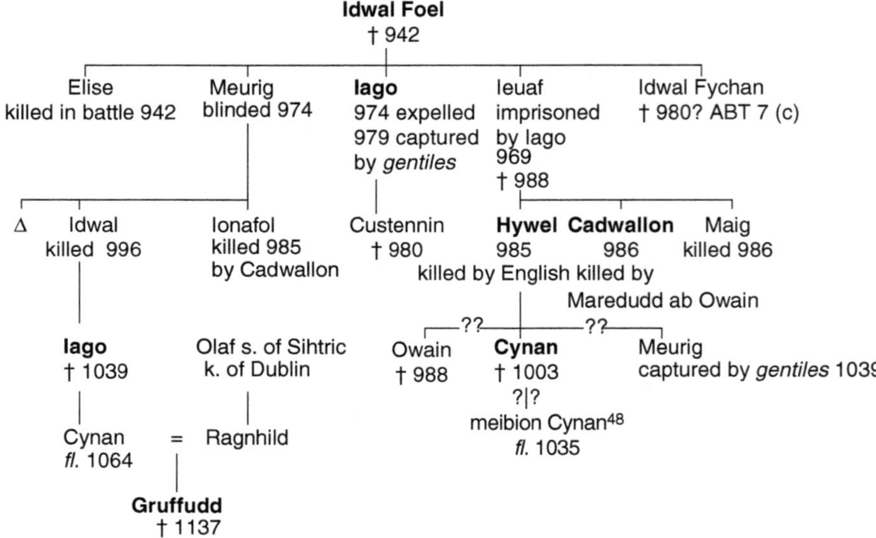

Figure 17.2. The Merfynion of Gwynedd 940–1063
Note: names in bold are of those who ruled or probably ruled Gwynedd

In 971 Maccus had sacked Penmon, an important church in the east of Anglesey. The elaborate cross at Penmon belongs approximately to this period and has been placed within a group of 'crosses of Anglo-Viking character distributed along the western seaboard of Northumbria and the adjacent coastal region of North Wales'.[49] Another cross, also at Penmon, has been compared with sculpture in the Isle of Man in the period *c.* 950–1050 and with Irish and Scottish sculpture of the Viking period.[50] These crosses indicate that Penmon was a major church with significant patronage; the Viking connections recall the earlier Viking presence not far to the north-west at Llanbedrgoch, but the probability of local Welsh political backing is illuminated by a note in a thirteenth-century collection of genealogies, stating that Gwyddelig, son of Rhodri Mawr, was the ancestor of 'the men of Penmon Lys', the court of Penmon.[51] In other words, there was a *llys*, a court (usually royal), at Penmon, to which a cadet branch of the Merfynion was attached. Similarly, when the annals tell us that in 978 'Guthfrith again ravages Llŷn', it is important to remember that Llŷn was also the home of another cadet branch of the Merfynion, one descended from Merfyn ap Rhodri Mawr.[52] If a king of Gwynedd could not defend the lands of his kinsmen, his authority was inevitably gravely weakened. External attacks, if successful, contributed to internal weakness.

[48] More likely to be sons of Cynan ap Seisyll: see below, 561.
[49] *ECMW*, no. 37; N. Edwards, 'Viking-Influenced Sculpture in North Wales, its Ornament and Context', *Church Archaeology*, 3 (1999), 5–16.
[50] *ECMW*, no. 38.
[51] ABT 7 (t) in *EWGT* 102.
[52] *Brut*, 978 (assuming that *Gwrmid* was Guthfrith); ABT 7 (o), in *EWGT* 101.

If Edgar's intervention at Chester in 973 was intended to arrest the political dissolution of Gwynedd, it was a failure. Admittedly Maccus Haraldsson was busy elsewhere in 974, sacking Scattery Island, a major monastery in the Shannon estuary attached to Limerick. He was accompanied by 'the Lawmen of the Isles'.[53] In 975 Edgar died, and in 978, as we have seen, Guthfrith Haraldsson 'again ravaged Llŷn'; and, in the same year, 'Hywel ab Ieuaf and the English sacked Clynnog Fawr', the monastery of St Beuno lying at the western end of Arfon, close to the boundary with Llŷn.[54] On 18 March in 978 or 979 Edward, son of Edgar, king of the English, was assassinated at Wareham; he was succeeded by his younger half-brother, Æthelred II 'the Unready'.

The annalistic evidence, sparse though it is, allows one to suggest a possible context for the double attack on western Gwynedd in 978. First, although Iago ab Idwal was present at Chester, he was, as we have seen, no longer the principal ruler of Gwynedd and in 974 was expelled from his kingdom. He must, however, have recovered his position, at least in part, by 978, since in the next year 'Iago was captured by the *Gentiles* [Vikings] having been defeated by Hywel ab Ieuaf, who took possession of his kingdom'.[55] The wording suggests cooperation between the Vikings and Hywel ab Ieuaf against Iago; and, if so, Iago was perhaps based in Llŷn and Arfon, attacked respectively by Guthfrith and Hywel ab Ieuaf in 978.

A similar pattern of internal disunity and external intervention in combination is seen in 980, the year of the Battle of Tara. First, one of the sons of Idwal Foel, Idwal Fychan, was slain; then Iago's son Custennin, together with Guthfrith Haraldsson, ravaged both Llŷn and Anglesey; and, finally, Custennin was slain in battle by Hywel ab Ieuaf.[56] Whereas, in 978, the Vikings were probably collaborating with Hywel ab Ieuaf, in 980 Guthfrith was clearly allied with Custennin ab Iago against the latter's first cousin, Hywel ab Ieuaf. Perhaps the *Gentiles* of 979 were a different set of Vikings from the fleet of Guthfrith Haraldsson. They are unlikely to have come from Dublin, which was fully engaged in Ireland; but they might well have come from Waterford, where the local ruler, Ímar ua hÍmair, was beginning to emerge as a major power: he would sack Kildare in 982 and his death in 1000 would, unusually for an Irish Viking, be recorded in the *Brut*.[57] Different contenders for power among the Merfynion of Gwynedd may have had different Viking backers. An alternative explanation, however, would see a single set of Vikings encouraging instability among the northern Merfynion by backing now one contender for power and then another. This might be with the ultimate aim of taking control of territory in Gwynedd.[58]

[53] AFM 972 = 974, AI 974.

[54] *Brut*, 978.

[55] *AC* B and *Brut*, 979, which agree quite closely against *AC* C, except that both *AC* C and *Brut* have Hywel ab Ieuaf, whereas *AC* B has Hywel ab Idwal.

[56] Apart from the death of Idwal, all of this is only in *Brut*.

[57] AU 982. 4; AT 981 = 982; CS 980 = 982; *Brut* 1002 = 1000.

[58] Cf. W. Davies, *Patterns of Power*, 58–60.

According to the annals, Gwynedd enjoyed relative peace from 980 until 985, when Hywel ab Ieuaf was killed by the English.[59] His death was followed by a struggle between his brother, Cadwallon ab Ieuaf, and his first cousin, Ionafol ap Meurig, in which Cadwallon was victorious and slew his rival. In the next year, 986, another of the northern Merfynion, a brother of Cadwallon, Maig ab Ieuaf, was killed; and after that Maredudd ab Owain ap Hywel Dda killed Cadwallon ab Ieuaf and took possession of his kingdom.[60] A grandson of Hywel Dda had reunited Gwynedd and Deheubarth, but in far less propitious circumstances.

An explanation of the background to the rise of Maredudd ab Owain should start in 982, when Guthfrith Haraldsson ravaged Dyfed including St Davids.[61] Viking attacks had hitherto been concentrated on North Wales; now the south-west would begin to be the object of serious raids. In 983 Hywel ab Ieuaf, together with the English, who were led by the Mercian ealdorman Ælfhere in his last expedition before his death in the same year, ravaged 'Brycheiniog and all the lands of Einion ab Owain', namely Maredudd's brother. Both versions of *Annales Cambriae* agree with the *Brut* that Einion ab Owain 'slew many of them'; the source of the annals was still being written at St Davids and therefore within the core territory of the southern Merfynion.[62] In two years, the Vikings, the English, and the northern Merfynion had all attacked lands held by the heirs of Hywel Dda.

The background of the campaign of 983 cannot be securely reconstructed, in spite of its evident importance. First, Einion's father, Owain ap Hywel Dda did not die until 988. He might have resigned his kingship earlier, but it is on the whole likely that he had not, and therefore that, in 983, he was still king. Einion's ravaged territory probably lay outside Dyfed, Ystrad Tywi, and Ceredigion. The old dynasty of Brycheiniog cannot be traced beyond 934 and may well have been ejected by Hywel Dda, even though it had survived the sacking in 916 of its 'seat of kingship' on Llangorse Lake.[63] It may also be significant that one of Einion's sons was given the name Tewdwr, characteristic of the old dynasty of Brycheiniog.[64] The phrase 'Brycheiniog and all the lands of Einion ab Owain' is, however, ambiguous.[65]

[59] *AC* B and *Brut* 985; *AC* C does not mention the English and runs together the annals for 985 and 986. The *Brut* says that the English slew Hywel 'by a trick'.

[60] The name Maig ab Ieuaf is only in the *Brut*; *AC* B has instead Meurig ab Idwal. Both occur in ABT 7 (c) and (d), but Meurig had been blinded in 974.

[61] *AC* B 982 has *Gothrit et Haraldus* and *Brut* just Harald, but *AC* C has *Godisric filio Haraldi*. On Maredudd, see D. E. Thornton, 'Maredudd ab Owain (d. 999): The Most Famous King of the Welsh', *WHR* 18 (1996–7), 567–91.

[62] *AC* B and C, *Brut*, 983.

[63] *LL* 237b, dated to the episcopate of *Libiau*, that is, according to the chronology of *LL*, 927 × 929 (*c.* 925 in Davies, *A Welsh Microcosm*, 60), concerns a king of Brycheiniog called Tewdwr ab Elisedd, very probably son of the Elisedd ap Tewdwr who was named by Asser, *Life of Alfred*, c. 80. Tewdwr ab Elisedd was probably the Tewdwr who witnessed a charter of Æthelstan in 934 (see above, 505). The genealogy given by Jesus College MS 20, JC 8 in *EWGT* 45, is of a Tewdwr ap Griffri ab Elise ap Tewdwr. Either Griffri is an error (perhaps for Tewdwr a Griffri ab Elise, 'Tewdwr *and* Griffri ab Elise) or the Tewdwr of *LL* was an uncle of the Tewdwr of the pedigree.

[64] D. E. Thornton, 'Predatory Nomenclature and Dynastic Expansion in Early Medieval Wales', *Medieval Prosopography: History and Collective Biography*, 20 (1999), 1–22; *AC*, *Brut*, 994, *EWGT* 101, ABT 7 *m*, *n*.

[65] Thornton, 'Maredudd ab Owain', 574.

Taken one way it would mean 'Brycheiniog and all the *other* lands of Einion ab Owain'; taken the other way it would imply that Brycheiniog was not one of his territories: it would be 'Brycheiniog (ruled by someone unnamed) and all the lands of Einion ab Owain'. The balance of probability is in favour of the first alternative; for one thing, we know from Asser that Brycheiniog was threatened by the Merfynion even in the 880s and early 890s. If we follow the first alternative, therefore, the other lands apart from Brycheiniog might well have included Buellt and Elfael, and perhaps further territories between the Wye and the Severn. The disposition of lands held by the southern Merfynion would thus have reflected that habit of Welsh kings by which sons were put in charge of peripheral territories: Owain ap Hywel Dda would have ruled the south-western core and his son Einion would have ruled the more recently acquired territory further east.

Such a conglomeration of territories in South Wales would have been a threat to Gwent and Morgannwg. In 970 and 977 Einion ab Owain had attacked Gŵyr, evidence that it was then attached to Morgannwg; by 992 Gŵyr was one of the territories of Maredudd ab Owain and had therefore been taken from Morgannwg, the Welsh kingdom that, in the tenth century was most enduringly aligned with the English.[66] It is conceivable that English involvement in the campaign of 983 had something to do with south-east Wales, while the participation of Hywel ab Ieuaf from Gwynedd arose from the rivalry between the northern and southern Merfynion. At all events, in the next year Einion was slain by the nobles of Gwent.[67] Earlier pressure by Einion on Gwent might easily have provoked an English response.

In 983, therefore, Hywel ab Ieuaf, king of Gwynedd, was working as the ally of Ælfhere, ealdorman of the Mercians; but in 985, after Ælfhere's death, Hywel was killed by the English.[68] That was the signal for a new bout of dynastic infighting among the northern Merfynion: Cadwallon ab Ieuaf, brother of Hywel, killed Ionafol ap Meuryg, and in 986 Maig ab Ieuaf was killed.[69] This gave Maredudd ab Owain the opportunity to intervene: in 986 he slew Cadwallon ab Ieuaf and took possession of Gwynedd. It looks as though Cadwallon's succession to his brother had aroused opposition within the dynasty, and Maredudd may have been able to use this discontent to facilitate his conquest. In 987, however, Maredudd's power in Gwynedd was challenged by Guthfrith Haraldsson, king of Innsi Gall. In the same year, probably before an attack on Gwynedd, Guthfrith had won 'the battle of Man' in alliance with the Danish force now operating in the Hebrides and the Irish Sea.[70] In 987, according to the Welsh chronicles, Guthfrith together with 'the Black

[66] *AC* B, *Brut*, 992.

[67] *Brut*, 984.

[68] *AC* B and the *Brut* agree that the English were responsible; *AC* C does not state who was responsible.

[69] These killings are both in the *Brut*; *AC* B names the victim of 986 as *Meuric filius Idwal*, following its habit of giving Idwal as the father of all the northern Merfynion. I have followed the *Brut*.

[70] AU 987. 1; *AC* C 987, refers to an attack by the 'Black Gentiles' on *Menauia*, while the other Welsh chronicles have *Mon*; in the light of the entry in the Annals of Ulster, the one fleet may have ravaged both *Manaw*, Man, and *Mon*, Anglesey.

Gentiles' ravaged Anglesey and took 2,000 captives.[71] In the decade after the Battle of Tara, 980, and the consequent political and military decline of Dublin, the rival Viking dynasty to Dublin, the Haraldssons, kings of Innsi Gall, were again extending their power from the Hebrides into and across the Irish Sea. We do not know what Guthfrith Haraldsson did with his captives: probably most were sold into slavery; but the noblest may have been given their freedom in return for ransom payments and perhaps political influence.

In 988 Vikings sacked a series of leading southern monasteries: Mynyw, Llanbadarn, Llanilltud, Llancarfan, and Llandudoch (St Dogmael's); and in the next year, Maredudd ab Owain paid tribute to 'the Black Gentiles', who may have been the Danes who were allied with Guthfrith Haraldsson.[72] In the same year, 989, however, the position of Dublin received a further setback: Glún Iairn, king of the Gaill, was slain when drunk by his own slave; and Máel Sechnaill, king of Tara, again attacked the town and compelled the Dubliners to promise 'an ounce of gold for every *garðr* every Christmas'.[73] Both the Chronicles that report this last detail were supportive of Máel Sechnaill. What they did not report but is noted in the Annals of Ulster is the further information that, in the same year, Guthfrith Haraldsson was killed in Dál Riata, in territory that would be renamed 'The Coastland of the Gaels', Airer Gáedel, Argyll, by contrast with Innsi Gall, 'The Islands of the (Viking) Foreigners'. Both the leading branches of the Uí Ímair, therefore, those of Dublin and of the Isles, suffered major reverses in 989. To judge by the order of entries in the *Brut*, the death of Glún Iairn occurred before Maredudd paid tribute to the Black Gentiles. In the Annals of Ulster, the death of Guthfrith Haraldsson is noted immediately after the entry on the killing of Glún Iairn. Maredudd might, therefore, have paid tribute to Guthfrith. But it might well have been paid to the Danes: their fleet was active in the west until 990, when they sacked Derry.[74] From the 990s more powerful Viking leaders were appearing. In 995 Swein, the future king, ravaged Man.[75] Moreover, in 991 Olaf Tryggvason attacked south-eastern England; after which Viking attacks occurred in most years up to the accession of Cnut in 1017. The Welsh chronicles do not report a significant Viking attack for the next decade until 999: in the year in which Maredudd ab Owain died, St Davids was sacked and its bishop killed by unspecified *gentiles*. This ten-year respite may be partly because of the weakness of the Irish and Hebridean Vikings, and partly because Vikings were attracted away to the English campaigns; but there is an account in the C, D and E versions of the Anglo-Saxon

[71] That the Battle of Man and the attack on Anglesey occurred in the same year is confirmed by the notice in the *Brut* of a cattle plague that is also noted in AU 987. 2.

[72] The fuller list of monasteries sacked in 988 is in *AC* B and the *Brut*. *AC* C omits the monasteries in Morgannwg: Llanilltud and Llancarfan. *AC* C and the *Brut* agree that Maredudd paid tribute, as against *AC* B which describes the payment as a ransom-payment. See Thornton, 'Maredudd ab Owain', 578–9.

[73] AT 988 = 989; CS 987 = 989. The killing of Glún Iairn but not Máel Sechnaill's triumph is in AU. The killing was also noted in the *Brut* but not in the surviving versions of *AC*.

[74] AU 990. 1.

[75] *AC* B 995; the *Brut, Pen. 20* has *Ywein* in place of Swein, but BS is correct while the RBH version has *Yswein*.

Chronicle for 997 of ravaging in the south-west, including the Welsh side of the Severn Estuary. This was not reported in the Welsh annals, which are even thinner in their information than before. The apparent respite from Viking attacks on Wales is thus partly to be attributed to the scarcity of good annalistic information.

Maredudd faced a major attack in 992 from a combination of the English, probably led by someone named Æthelsige, who may have been in charge of Mercia, and Edwin ab Einion ab Owain.[76] This may have been, for the English, retaliation for offensive action by Maredudd in 991, when he ravaged Maes Hyfaidd, a name which was subsequently changed by misinterpretation into Maesyfed.[77] At this date the name referred to the valley around New Radnor, which had been settled by the English. The B version of *Annales Cambriae* agrees with the *Brut* that the invading army of 992 ravaged 'all the lands of Maredudd', namely Dyfed, Ceredigion, Gŵyr, and Cedweli. What is interesting in the light of the warfare of 983 is that Brycheiniog is not listed among the lands of Maredudd in 992. It may, therefore, have been held by Edwin ab Einion in succession to his father. This campaign of 992, however, marks a breakdown in the dynastic coherence of the southern Merfynion, echoing the earlier and much more serious breakdown among their northern cousins. According to the *Brut* Edwin took hostages from the whole of Maredudd's kingdom; but he seems not to have gained any lasting power in the south-west. Maredudd replied by ravaging Morgannwg with the help of a Viking fleet which he had hired. Ultimately, Edwin ab Einion did not succeed in establishing himself in his father's kingdom. He is next attested in the reign of Cnut (1016–1035) in Herefordshire, involved in a suit against his own mother, an Englishwoman.[78] By this stage Edwin was presumably without any foothold in Wales.

In 993 the sons of Meurig ab Idwal Foel made an attack on Gwynedd—that is, they aimed to retake the kingdom of their grandfather and their kinsmen. The extent of their success is obscured by the disagreements among the versions of the *Brut* and the absence of a corresponding entry in the *Annales Cambriae*.[79] In 994, Maredudd was defeated in battle against the sons of Meurig at a place called Llangwm, probably Llangwm Dinmael in the valley of the Clwyd. Maredudd may have lost power in Gwynedd, but Idwal ap Meurig was killed in 996, and Maredudd may well have regained power in the north and held it until his own death in 999.[80]

The history of the Merfynion in the late ninth and tenth centuries repeats a pattern. First, the unity of a group of brothers facilitates military and political

[76] *AC* B, *Brut* 992; Thornton, 'Maredudd ab Owain', 581–5, discusses the variations between the annals, the sequence of events, and the possible identity of Æthelsige (*Edelisi, Edylfi* etc.)

[77] H. W. Owen and R. Morgan, *Dictionary of the Place-Names of Wales*, 348–9, *s.v.* New Radnor.

[78] *EHD* i, no. 135. Since Einion was killed in 984 and Edwin was sufficiently old to lead a campaign in 992, the document about the latter's suit against his mother is likely to have been relatively early in the reign of Cnut; an English noblewoman with estates in Herefordshire would have made a suitable alliance for a ruler of Brycheiniog. See below, 554, for the details

[79] Thornton, 'Maredudd ab Owain', 587–9.

[80] The killing of Idwal ap Meurig and the death of Maredudd were reported in both versions of *Annales Cambriae* and the *Brut*.

success, as with the sons of Rhodri Mawr from 881 to 939. Then that unity breaks down and a phase of family feuding and violent competition for the kingship takes its place. The unity of the sons of Idwal from 950 to 969 gives way to a struggle between uncle and nephew or between brother and brother or cousin and cousin for the kingship of Gwynedd. Hywel is said to have expelled his uncle, Iago, and taken over the kingdom of Gwynedd in 974, the very year after the meeting at Chester; moreover it was already clear at Chester that Iago had lost his preeminence in Gwynedd: both of them were listed, and Hywel was put first. Feuding within the northern Merfynion eventually led in 986 to the conquest of Gwynedd by Maredudd ab Owain, king of Dyfed. Yet, he would only hold it with difficulty against Viking attack and his northern cousins; and it is not certain that he ruled Gwynedd continuously until the date of his death in 999. The empire of Britain that reached its apogee under Æthelstan and his immediate successors, Edmund and Eadred, had as one of its props an alliance with Hywel Dda and, initially, also with his cousin Idwal Foel. In spite of Alfred's policy as portrayed by Asser, in the end the Merfynion rose to power in the South with the blessing of Æthelred and Æthelfled, rulers of Mercia. From *c.* 910 to 950 stability in Wales had gone together with a consistency in English policy towards Wales. From 950 until 999 there was no unity among the Merfynion and no consistency in English policy towards Wales. Hywel Dda in the south-west and Morgan ab Owain in the south-east were neither undermined by shifts in their relations with the English nor were they themselves untrustworthy allies; the English after 950 were changeable in their Welsh alliances and content with short-term advantage.

2. THE ELEVENTH CENTURY: NEW DYNASTIES

Wales in the eleventh century (see Map 24) was marked by dynastic change, as were Ireland and England at much the same date. In the course of the ninth and tenth centuries, the Merfynion, descendants of Merfyn Frych, had taken power in Gwynedd, then Powys, Ceredigion, Dyfed, and, finally, Brycheiniog. Powys is never mentioned in *Annales Cambriae* or in the *Brut* between 854, the death of Cyngen in Rome, and 1069, and then only as an appendage of Gwynedd; it was not named as an independent entity until 1102, shortly after Henry I came to the throne of England.[81] As far as one can tell, the kingdom of Gwynedd included Powys for much or all of this period. One dynasty ruled Wales outside the south-east; indeed, for a few years, 942–950, a single king, Hywel Dda, had ruled all the lands of the Merfynion. The lawyers of the twelfth and thirteenth centuries looked back to the last years of his reign as the time when he employed his authority to promulgate a law for all the Welsh. As we have seen, however, the second half of the tenth century had seen the progressive decay of the unity and of the power of the

[81] The 1069 reference is only in the RBH version of the *Brut*; the 1102 reference is in all versions of the *Brut*, in the context of the promises made by Henry I to Iorwerth ap Bleddyn as Henry sought to put down the Montgomery revolt (the earl of Shrewsbury and Arnulf of Pembroke).

Map 24. Wales, *c.* 1000
After victory against the Mercians in the battle of the Conwy in 881, Gwynedd seems to have absorbed Powys and so became a threat to the southern Welsh kings, driving them to submit to Alfred. Powys remained part of Gwynedd until the end of the eleventh century.

Merfynion, and the decay, also, of English power in Wales. In the eleventh century new dynasties emerged to challenge the Merfynion; and, in the middle years of the century, Gruffudd ap Llywelyn, from the most successful of these new dynasties, would enjoy a power in Wales even more extensive than that gained by Hywel Dda. His relationship with the English would, however, be very different from that of Hywel.

Interpretation of the history of Wales in the period 1000 to 1064 has been hampered by the sparsity of contemporary evidence and by the long shadow cast backwards in time by the Life of Gruffudd ap Cynan (1054/5–1137), who re-established the power of the Merfynion in Gwynedd, but not in Powys. The original Latin Life is most likely to have been composed by a cleric associated with St Davids, between 1137, when Gruffudd died, and 1148.[82] One of its purposes was to assert that Gruffudd's Welsh rivals in the struggle for power in Gwynedd were illegitimate intruders.[83] This standpoint affected Sir John Lloyd's account of eleventh-century Wales.[84] But it has rightly been argued that this is to accept too hastily a partisan version of events.[85]

In perhaps 999, Maredudd ab Owain, 'the most praiseworthy king of the Britons', died.[86] Cynan ap Hywel, of the northern Merfynion, took the kingship of Gwynedd in 1000, but he was killed in 1003 and there is no record of any successor. Neither do the chronicles reveal who succeeded Maredudd in Dyfed and its appendages. Maredudd's nephew, Edwin ab Einion, had ravaged all Maredudd's lands in 992; and he was still alive at the beginning of Cnut's reign, when he brought a case in the shire court of Herefordshire against his mother, a kinswoman of Leofflæd, wife of Thurkil the White.[87] His grandson and great-grandson are recorded in Domesday Book holding lands in Herefordshire; and it seems likely, therefore, that this branch of the southern Merfynion had a long-term connection with Herefordshire throughout much of the eleventh century.[88] The connection is consistent with the likelihood, as we have seen, that Edwin ab Einion had ruled Brycheiniog, bordering on Herefordshire, in the years running up to 992. One may compare the possessions held by the branch of the northern Merfynion near

82 *Vita Griffini Filii Conani: The Medieval Latin Life of Gruffudd ap Cynan*, ed. and trans. P. Russell (Cardiff, 2005), 46–7.

83 *Vita Griffini*, ed. Russell, § 10 ('iniuste ac indebite').

84 Lloyd, *HW*, ii. 358; id., 'Wales and the Coming of the Normans, 1038–1093', *THSC* (1899–1900), 154.

85 K. L. Maund, 'Trahaearn ap Caradog: Legitimate Usurper?', *Welsh History Review*, 13 (1986–7), 468–76; ead., '"Gruffudd, Grandson of Iago": *Historia Gruffudd vab Kenan* and the Construction of Legitimacy', in ead. (ed.), *Gruffudd ap Cynan: A Collective Biography* (Woodbridge, 1996), 109–16.

86 *Brut*, 999; but the chronology at this stage is uncertain: the burning of Armagh recorded in 996 may be the event in AU 996. 1, but it could be 998. 3; the laying waste of Dublin in 1000 ought to refer to the aftermath of the battle of Glenn Máma, at the very end of December, 999: AU 999. 8. The death of Ímar of Waterford, recorded in the *Brut* for 1002, is AU 1000. 3.

87 *EHD* i, no. 135; Robertson, *Anglo-Saxon Charters*, no. 78.

88 *DB* i. 180 c, 183 d, 184 d, 187 a, c (where Maredudd ab Edwin is described as a king, whereas his son, Gruffudd, is not); D. E. Thornton, 'Some Welshmen in Domesday Book and Beyond: Aspects of Anglo-Welsh Relations in the Eleventh Century', in Higham (ed.), *Britons in Anglo-Saxon England*, 153, 157–60.

Swords within the territory of Dublin in the middle of the century.[89] Both were available as refuges when the dynasties were excluded from the kingship and driven into exile.

No doubt Edwin ab Einion hoped to succeed Maredudd as ruler of Dyfed, but there is no positive evidence that he did.[90] Gwynedd is only marginally less obscure. As argued in a later chapter, the Aeddon mourned in a poem in the Book of Taliesin is likely to be the same person as the Aeddan ap Blegywryd killed in battle by Llywelyn ap Seisyll in 1017 or 1018.[91] He appears from the poem to have ruled Anglesey and to have led an army from Arfon to his last and fatal battle at Caer Seon, on the west side of the Conwy close to its mouth, nearly opposite Degannwy. His power had lain, therefore, in the heart of Gwynedd uwch Conwy, Gwynedd west of the Conwy. Provided that the Aeddon of the poem was indeed the Aeddan of the annal entry, we have one possible ruler of Gwynedd in the obscure period 999–1017 and, also, a hint that Llywelyn ap Seisyll may have had his base east of the Conwy. His son, Gruffudd ap Llywelyn, had an important centre of his power in 1063 at the former Mercian *burh* at Rhuddlan.[92] This was probably not part of the land he acquired, probably in 1056, along the Dee estuary east of Wat's Dyke but an earlier gain.[93] Some of the land acquired by the Welsh in the eleventh century probably changed hands in the troubled later years of Æthelred II.[94] These scraps of evidence allow at least a hypothesis, first, that the base of Llywelyn ap Seisyll and his son Gruffudd was in north-east Wales and, secondly, that extension of territory at the expense of the English helps to explain the rise of that dynasty.

Both father and son would gain a supremacy over the south as well as Gwynedd. Although their dynastic origins are wholly obscure, it is known that Llywelyn married a daughter of Maredudd ab Owain: though both father and son were initially kings of Gwynedd, they were linked through Angharad, daughter of Maredudd, to the southern rather than to the northern Merfynion, and specifically to a branch of the southern Merfynion primarily associated with Dyfed in opposition to another branch probably associated with Brycheiniog.[95] The conflict

89 *Vita Griffini Filii Conani*, ed. Russell, § 1; cf. M. T. Flanagan, '*Historia Gruffud vab Kenan* and the Origins of Balrothery', *CMCS* 28 (Winter 1994), 71–94, ABT 2 *p*, for the continuance of links between Gwynedd and the area north of Dublin even into the thirteenth century.

90 Maund, *Ireland*, 115, speculates that Edwin ab Einion or his brother Cadell or the latter's son Tewdwr might have held power in parts of the south in the period 999–1023.

91 Below, 665–6. For a very different view, see Maund, *Ireland*, 90.

92 H. Quinnell and M. R. Blockley, *Excavations at Rhuddlan, Clwyd, 1969–73: Mesolithic to Medieval*, CBA Research Report 95 (York, 1994), 8, claim that 'In 1015 Llywelyn ap Seisyll of Gwynedd built a stronghold (*palatium*) at Rhuddlan, perhaps sited on Twt Hill which commanded the Clwyd ford.' Similarly on p. 213. They give no reference. It seems to derive from Camden's *Britannia*, 2nd edn. rev. by E. Gibson (London, n.d.), ii. 823. The same story is in T. Pennant, *A Tour in Wales*, 2 vols. (London, 1784), ii. 10–11.

93 See below, 565–6.

94 As suggested by the reference to the three manors of Chirbury, Maesbury, and Whittington as having paid the *firma* of half a night in the time of Æthelred, as if that was the last time that the English could exact revenue, DB 253c, under Whittington; C. P. Lewis, 'English and Norman Government in the Welsh Borders, 1039–1087', unpublished D.Phil. Thesis, University of Oxford (1985), 147–9.

95 *Brut*, 1116 (and cf. 1109); *EWGT* 47 (JC 27), 96 (ABT 1 *e*, 2 *f*, 7 *k*).

within the southern Merfynion between Einion ab Owain and his son Edwin, on the one side, and Maredudd ab Owain, on the other, may be part of the explanation why Maredudd's son-in-law, married to his daughter Angharad, gained power in the south even though Edwin ab Einion had a strong claim. Less certain is the evidence that Llywelyn ap Seisyll's mother was Prawst, daughter of Elise ab Anarawd and thus from the northern Merfynion, although of a cadet branch; yet, if the information is sound, it suggests that Seisyll as well as his son, Llywelyn, may have aspired to royal status.[96]

Llywelyn ap Seisyll gained power in the south by defeating 'Rhain the Irishman', who 'said' or 'lied' that he was the son of Maredudd ab Owain.[97] It is an index of the achievement of Maredudd that, if Llywelyn's power in the south was through his connection with Maredudd, so too did Rhain's claim depend upon a king who had died twenty-three years earlier. The source most favourable to Rhain is the C version of *Annales Cambriae*, which neither labels him an Irishman (which implies that he was not the son of Maredudd) nor says that he lied about his being a son of Maredudd; it merely declares that he was proclaiming himself to be Maredudd's son. The B version and all the vernacular annals agree that he was Irish and did lie. Yet the vernacular annals certainly, and the B text of *Annales Cambriae* probably, were also agreed that the southern Welsh accepted Rhain as their king and, by implication, as the son of Maredudd. These same versions are so written as to encourage the reader to suppose that Rhain had only just imposed himself on the southern Welsh when Llywelyn challenged him at the mouth of the Gwili and defeated him; but it is conceivable that he had been reigning over the South for some time, though probably not ever since the death of his supposed father, Maredudd ab Owain. To add to the confusion, Rhain could be either a native Welsh name or an unrelated Irish name in Welsh form.[98] He certainly had Irish support and, unusually, this seems to have been from native Irish rulers rather than the Hiberno-Norse.[99] According to the B version of *Annales Cambriae* Rhain was killed in the battle, but the *Brut*, although elsewhere in agreement with this unfavourable account, explicitly says that Rhain was not found in the rout.

In the same year *Eilaf* 'came into Wales (*in Britanniam*) and laid waste Dyfed, and Mynyw was wrecked'.[100] *Eilaf* is likely to be the earl Eilífr Thorgilsson, who was associated with Gloucestershire and was a major figure in England from the beginning of Cnut's reign to 1024, after which he disappears from witness lists; his brother, Ulf, was married to Estrith, Cnut's sister, and his own sister, Gytha, was married to Earl Godwine; his link with Cnut is underlined, in spite of his disappearance from witness lists, by a later entry in the *Brut* recording that he left England for

[96] *EWGT* 101 (ABT 7 *f*).

[97] For this episode see D. E. Thornton, 'Who was Rhain the Irishman?', *Studia Celtica*, 34 (2000), 131–48, whose interpretation I follow here.

[98] Thornton, 'Who was Rhain the Irishman?', 136–42, against S. Duffy, 'Ostmen, Irish and Welsh in the Eleventh Century', *Peritia* 9 (1995), 383.

[99] S. Duffy, 'Ostmen, Irish and Welsh', 382–4.

[100] This is a reconstruction of the likely form of the entry lying behind the extant versions, following *AC* C, except that it probably wrongly makes Mynyw the victim of Eilaf's forces.

Germania in flight after Cnut's death in 1035.[101] There is no evident connection between his invasion and the battle of Aber Gwili, in which Llywelyn ap Seisyll defeated Rhain, but it has been suggested that there was some alliance between Cnut and the Irish.[102] At the very least, he may have been fishing in waters that he knew to be troubled. The previous such expedition was that of 992, directed against Maredudd ab Owain by a combination of his nephew, Edwin ab Einion, and an English nobleman, Æthelsige. It too failed to change the distribution of power in South Wales. It is worth remembering that, in 1022, the same Edwin ab Einion is likely to have been an exile in Herefordshire. The expedition shows that Wales remained of concern to the political leaders of England in Cnut's reign, and yet beyond their power to control.

In 1022 Llywelyn ap Seisyll had imposed his power over the former territories of the Merfynion from the north coast to the far south-west. Yet, he himself did not come from the Merfynion, and whereas Maredudd ab Owain and Hywel Dda in the previous century had gained a similar power, they had done so from a base in Deheubarth, whereas Llywelyn was primarily king of Gwynedd. Llywelyn died, apparently peacefully, in 1023, the year after his victory at Aber Gwili and his conquest of the South.[103] The power of Gwynedd outside the North did not survive his death; it would not be recreated until the reign of Llywelyn's son, Gruffudd.

After Llywelyn's death another new dynasty emerged in the South. The chronicles do not reveal directly from where the new king of the South, Rhydderch ab Iestin, came. His descendants in the twelfth century were mainly based in Gwent, and this seems already to have been true in the reign of William the Conqueror to judge by a reference in the Book of Llandaff. This is in a record of ordinations by Herewald, bishop of Llandaff, who died in 1104 after an episcopate of forty-eight years.[104] Here we are told that, in the reign of William the Conqueror, while Cadwgon ap Meurig ruled Glamorgan, 'King Caradog was ruling in Ystrad Yw, Gwent uwch Coed, and Gwynllŵg, but Rhydderch in Ewyas and Gwent is Coed'. Their relationships to each other, to their grandfather, Rhydderch ab Iestin, and to the latter's other descendants are shown in Figure 17.3, and the intertwining of their lands are shown in Map 25.

The greater power of Caradog ap Gruffudd is suggested by the way his three territories kept the two territories of his cousin Rhydderch apart and by the way they included Gwynllŵg, considered at the time to be the senior cantref in

[101] On Eilaf (Eglaf, Aglaf) = Eilífr see *Encomium Emmae*, ed. A. Campbell, Camden Society, 3rd Ser. lxxii (London, 1949), 82, 86–7; cf. *Vita S. Cadoci*, c. 40, ed. Wade-Evans, *VSBG*, 110–12; S. Keynes, 'Cnut's Earls', in A. Rumble (ed.), *The Reign of Cnut, King of England, Denmark and Norway* (London, 1994), 58–60. For the connection with Gloucestershire, see S 1424, printed in *Historia et Cartularium Monasterii Sancti Petri Gloucestriae*, ed. W. H. Hart, Rolls Ser., 3 vols. (1863–7), i. 9.

[102] C. Downham, 'England and the Irish Sea Zone in the Eleventh Century', *Anglo-Norman Studies*, 26 (2003), 64.

[103] AU 1023. 7; AT 1023 (both entitle him 'king of the Britons').

[104] *LL*, p. 279. 1–3.

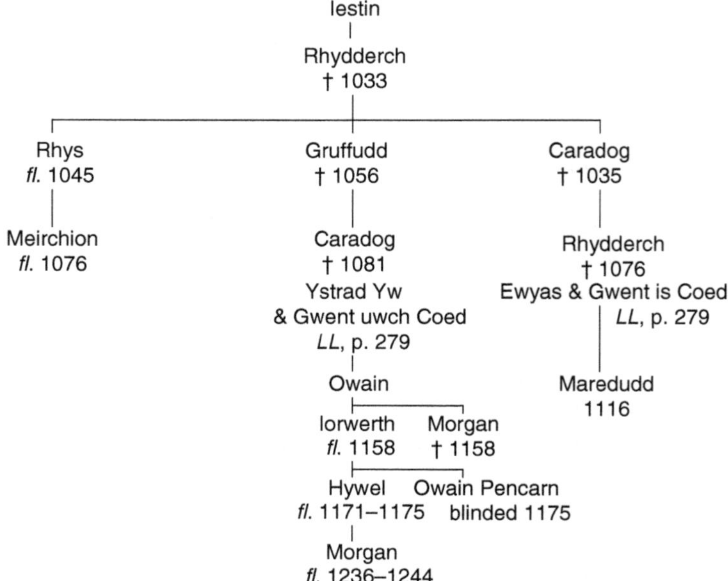

Figure 17.3. The descendants of Rhydderch ab Iestin (based on ABT 17 and the *Brut*)[105]
Cf. Brut, RBH 1158: tir Caer Llion a holl gyuoeth Ywein, 'the land of Caerlleon and the whole realm of Owain'.

Glamorgan (see Map 25).[106] On the other hand, Rhydderch 'held the South' together with Rhys ab Owain after the killing of Bleddyn ap Cynfyn in 1075, even though it was Caradog who, with 'the French', slew Maredudd ab Owain, king of Deheubarth, in 1072 on the banks of the Rhymni.[107] Earlier, in 1065, the same Caradog had destroyed the hunting lodge being built by Harold son of Godwin at Portskewett in Gwent is Coed, even though, according to the Book of Llandaff, it was within his cousin's territory of Gwent is Coed.[108] At all events, the combination of annalistic evidence from Wales and England with the Book of Llandaff is enough to confirm that the kindred descended from Rhydderch ab Iestin were based in the south-east, in Gwent and in neighbouring territories, at the end of the reign of Edward the Confessor.

In 1023, then, after the death of Llywelyn ap Seisyll, 'Rhydderch ab Iestin gained the kingdom of the Southern Britons'.[109] This is close to the time when a likely rival, Edwin ab Einion of the southern Merfynion, was disputing his mother's lands

[105] Principally *Brut*, 1072: Caradawc vab Gruffuð ap Ryderch; *Brut*, 1116: Maredud vab Ryderch vab Karadawc; *Brut*, 1171: Ior*werth* ap Ywein ap Karadawc ap Gruffud.

[106] 'Primogenitus quippe Gundleius primariam regni genitoris sui sedem, videlicet Gundliauc, sortitur', *Vita S. Cadoci*, Pref., ed. and trans.

[107] *Brut*, 1072, 1075.

[108] ASC CD 1065 (24 August).

[109] The likely wording behind *AC* BC and the *Brut*, 1023.

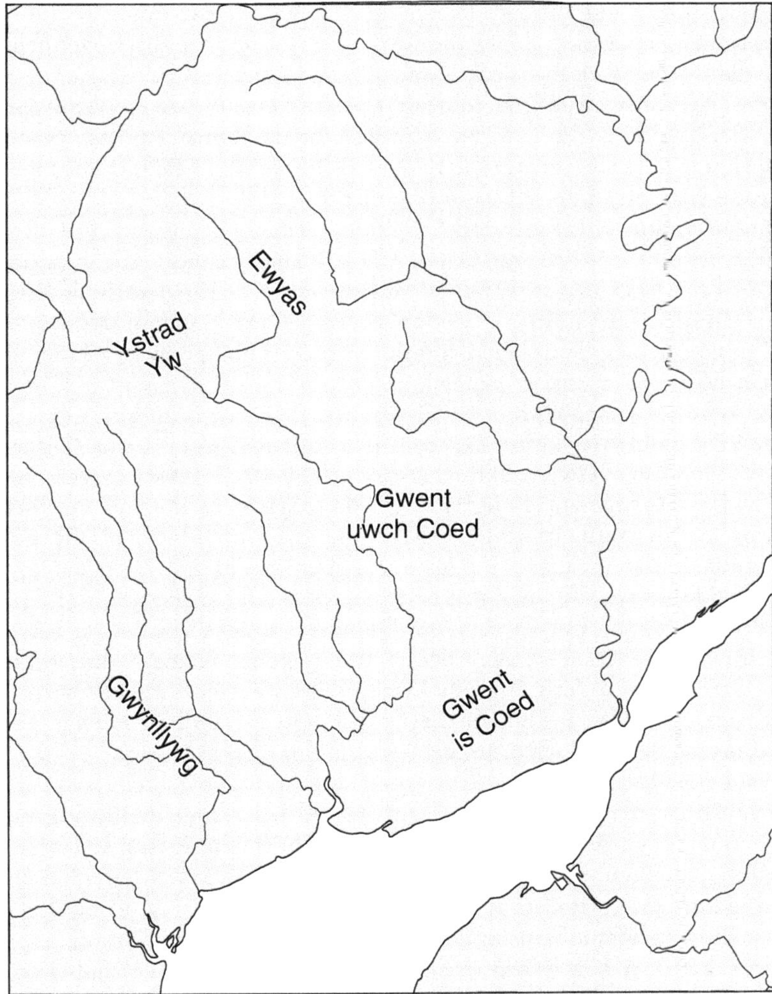

Map 25. The lands of Caradog and Rhydderch[110]

in the shire court of Herefordshire. Rhydderch, therefore, whose base was in the south-east, successfully excluded from power a great-grandson of Hywel Dda. Edwin's ambition, from his lands in Herefordshire, must have been to gain power in Dyfed, Ystrad Tywi, and Brycheiniog; yet Rhydderch's home territory in the south-east lay in his path. Rhydderch is likely to have gained Brycheiniog on

[110] Ystrad Yw in *WATU* = Cwm-du + Afon Crawnon = parishes of Llanfihangel Cwm-du and Llangynidr; but in *LL*, p. 279, it includes Llanbedr (SO 23 20), Llangedwyn = Llangenni (SO 24 18), Merthyr Issw = Partrishow (SO 27 22), and thus abuts Ewyas on the west.

his way to power and was thus in a position to bar the two doorways into South Wales from Herefordshire, along the Wye valley north of the Black Mountains and along the Usk between the Black Mountains and Bannau Brycheiniog, the Brecon Beacons. As for Rhydderch, the route to power in the south-west probably lay along the Usk and across to the Tywi, the way taken by the Roman road and the modern A 40, although he also seems to have reduced Hywel ab Owain, of the main royal lineage of Glamorgan, to the status of under-king.[111]

The succession to Llywelyn ap Seisyll in Gwynedd is unclear. The only hints are, first, an obit for Cynan ap Seisyll in 1027, and, secondly, the implication of the annal for 1033 that it was only after the death of Rhydderch ab Iestin that Iago ab Idwal, of the northern Merfynion, gained the kingdom of Gwynedd. In 1027 Cynan ap Seisyll was killed, but the chronicles do not say by whom. Since at this period they do not, in general, record the deaths of laymen of non-royal status, it is a fair inference that Cynan was Llywelyn's brother and that he succeeded Llywelyn as king of Gwynedd. If this is right, the two brothers had held the kingship of Gwynedd for a decade, 1017–1027. If we can trust the Book of Llandaff, Rhydderch ab Iestin succeeded Cynan as king of Gwynedd, in addition to his southern realm, except that Iago ab Idwal, of the northern Merfynion, held Anglesey.[112] This succession should not be taken to imply that Rhydderch was the unnamed person responsible for the death of Cynan ap Seisyll: in 1030 the English and the Dubliners attacked Wales;[113] Rhydderch himself would be killed 'by the Irish' in 1033; and an alliance between the Irish and Hiberno-Norse with Iago ab Idwal could well have killed Cynan.[114] In Cnut's reign it looks as though the English and the Dubliners were prone to combine together to attack prominent Welsh kings, perhaps because they seemed a threat to the English.

After Rhydderch's death at the hands of the Irish, Iago ab Idwal gained the kingdom of Gwynedd, and the sons of Edwin ab Einion, Hywel and Maredudd, gained the kingdom of the South.[115] In 1033, therefore, the Merfynion regained power in both Gwynedd and the South. In 1034, however, Hywel and Maredudd were obliged to fight a battle against the sons of Rhydderch ab Iestin; and in the next year Maredudd ab Edwin was killed 'by the sons of Cynan' and Caradog ap Rhydderch was killed by the English.[116] These two events are recorded before the notice of Cnut's death in the same year and the subsequent flight of Eilífr, who may still have held authority in Gloucestershire.[117] The whole sequence of entries under

[111] 'Hiuel subreguli regis Morcannuc', *LL* 252b; Hywel died 'in his old age' in 1043, *Brut*; *AC* B has a bare obit.

[112] *LL* 253.

[113] AT 1030.

[114] 1033 was the year when the king of Osraige, Donnchad mac Gilla Phátraic, gained the kingship of Leinster and demonstrated his authority by celebrating the Fair of Carman, AU 1033. 4.

[115] *Brut*, 1033, *AC* C 1033; *AC* B excludes all mention of Iago and so suggests that Rhydderch's death was of no consequence for Gwynedd, but the substantial agreement of *AC* C with the *Brut* makes this unlikely.

[116] *AC* BC, *Brut*, 1035.

[117] Eilífr's flight is only in the *Brut*.

this year, apart from the death of Cnut, thus seems to refer to South Wales, to the two main dynasties of the South and to the Anglo-Scandinavian Eilífr who was probably the person among the English elite most concerned with South Wales. The killing of Caradog ap Rhydderch could be construed as English help designed to keep the southern Merfynion in power. As for 'the sons of Cynan', they should, in the context, be the sons of the last-named Cynan, namely Cynan ap Seisyll. He, however, as we have seen, had probably been king of Gwynedd and his family seems to have been based in the north; yet in 1035 we see the sons of Cynan killing Maredudd, one of the sons of Edwin ab Einion, rulers of the South. It is tempting to suppose that these events were connected—that the sons of Cynan were in alliance with Caradog ap Rhydderch, that the killing of Maredudd endangered the power of the southern Merfynion, and that their position was safeguarded by an English expedition that succeeded in killing Caradog—but there is no way to confirm such a theory. At all events, Hywel ab Edwin survived the death of his brother and Iago ab Idwal continued to rule Gwynedd: the Merfynion, northern and southern, remained in power for another four years, until 1039.

In 1039, *gentiles*, namely Vikings, captured Meurig ap Hywel, probably the king of Morgannwg; and, in what is likely to have been an entirely unconnected event, Iago ab Idwal, king of Gwynedd, was killed; we are not told by the Welsh chronicles who slew him, but his successor was Gruffudd ap Llywelyn ap Seisyll.[118] The Annals of Ulster, *Chronicum Scotorum*, and the Annals of Tigernach report the killing and say that he was slain *a suis*, that is to say, by the men of Gwynedd; they all entitle him 'king of the Britons'.[119] Kings of Gwynedd in this period had a good chance of being given an obit in the Irish chronicles, whereas such major southern-based figures as Maredudd ab Owain and Rhydderch ab Iestin, even though they gained power in the north, went unrecorded. Gwynedd and its dynasties were of greater significance in the Irish-Sea region than were southern Welsh rulers.

Gruffudd ap Llywelyn was the most long-lasting Welsh king of the eleventh century and the one who made the greatest impression on his English neighbours. As a result, the evidence, though still sparse, is far better than for his immediate predecessors. His domination of Tegeingl is obliquely referred to in Domesday Book, which records that in the hundred of *Atiscros* King Gruffudd had one manor at Bistre and one plough in demesne, while 'his men' had six ploughs. 'When the king himself used to come there, each plough used to pay him two hundred *hesthas* and one vat full of ale and one vessel of butter.'[120] To judge by the Welsh laws, this was a *dawnbwyd* render, though perhaps incompletely specified, and the *hesthas* should have been some form of loaf of bread.[121] To judge by Domesday, Gruffudd ap Llywelyn had ruled north-east Wales, old Mercian territory, from the *burh* at Rhuddlan almost to the gates of Chester.[122]

118 Meurig and the killing of Iago: *AC* C, *Brut*. The succession of Gruffudd: *AC* BC, *Brut*.

119 AU 1039. 1; *CS* 1037 = 1039; AT 1039.

120 DB 269 b. 121 Cf. *EIWK* 386–90, 395–400.

122 DB 263a: Rex E*dwardus* ded*it* regi Grifino tota*m* t*er*ram quæ jacebat trans aqua*m* quæ De uocatur. Sed postq*uam* ipse Grifin forisfecit ei, abstulit ab eo hanc t*er*ram, et reddidit *episcopo* de Cestre et om*ni*b*us* suis ho*min*ib*us* qui antea ipsa*m* tenebant'; the gift probably concerned not just *Exestan*

The tenor of the new reign was indicated in the very first year, 1039, when Gruffudd fought and won a battle against the English at Rhyd y Groes, 'the Ford of the Cross', on the Severn, probably near Buttington.[123] This may be the same battle as that recorded in the C version of the Anglo-Saxon Chronicle: 'And the Welsh killed Edwin, Earl Leofric's brother, and Thurkil and Alfgeat and very many good men with them.'[124] The C Chronicle was compiled by someone sympathetic to Leofric, Earl of Mercia, so this notice is excellent evidence.[125] Gruffudd, therefore, began his reign with a victory against the Mercians, although from 1055 to at least 1058 he would be an ally of Earl Leofric's son and successor, Ælfgar.

In 1039 Gruffudd also launched an attack on Hywel ab Edwin, king of Deheubarth, and drove him to flight; however, he was again obliged to defeat Hywel in 1041 in the battle of Pencadair, showing that Hywel did not finally lose all his territory until later; in 1039, therefore, Gruffudd may only have succeeded in permanently taking Ceredigion, while Hywel recovered control of Dyfed and Ystrad Tywi.[126] In 1042 Hywel defeated Vikings who were ravaging Dyfed; and in the same year Gruffudd was captured by the men of Dublin, who presumably allowed him to ransom himself, even though they may already have been sheltering his main rival from Gwynedd, Cynan ab Iago.[127] In 1043 Gruffudd appears finally to have driven Hywel out of Dyfed, since in 1044 Hywel brought a Viking fleet from Ireland to the mouth of the Tywi and began to ravage the country. There he was met by Gruffudd, who therefore seems already to have held Ystrad Tywi, and was killed with considerable slaughter on both sides.[128]

Gruffudd ap Llywelyn still had a rival in the South, namely Gruffudd ap Rhydderch ab Iestin, brother of the Caradog ap Rhydderch killed by the English in 1035; another brother, Rhys, was still active: he would be killed in 1053 on the orders of Edward the Confessor.[129] Gruffudd ap Rhydderch witnesses one charter

hundred, to which this statement immediately pertains, but also the hidated portion of *Atiscros* along the Dee estuary as far as Wat's Dyke: Lewis, 'English and Norman Government', 122–3; B. E. Harris and A. T. Thacker (eds.), *A History of the County of Chester*, i, (VCH; London, 1987), 262–3; J. Tait, 'Flintshire in Domesday Book', *Flintshire Historical Society Publications*, 11 (1925), 1–37; Lewis, 'English and Norman Government', 122–3, 140–6, 153–62.

123 *AC* B and *Brut*, 1039 (Rhyd y Groes in *Brut RBH* and *BS*, Rhyd y Grog in *Brut, Pen. 20*; Lloyd, 'Wales and the Coming of the Normans', 129–31.

124 ASC C 1039. S. Baxter, *Earls of Mercia: Lordship and Power in Late Anglo-Saxon England* (Oxford, 2007), 31–2, suggests that Edwin was sheriff of Shropshire.

125 S. Baxter, 'MS C of the Anglo-Saxon Chronicle and the Politics of Mid-Eleventh-Century England', *EHR* 122 (2007), 1189–227.

126 *AC* BC, *Brut*, 1039, 1041. The statement in *AC* B and the *Brut* that Gruffudd 'conquered Deheubarth' and expelled Hywel suggests that the latter managed to recover territory before 1041, perhaps in the way other eleventh-century Welsh kings achieved such a result—with Irish or Hiberno-Norse help.

127 *AC* B, *Brut*, 1041; in *AC* C the annals for 1041 and 1042 have been conflated.

128 *AC* B, *Brut* 1044 (the Peniarth 20 version has *bonhedigyon*, the Red Book version *kenedyl*, both incorrect translations of *gentiles*, as shown by *AC*).

129 ASC C *s.a.* 1052 (before Easter 1053); John of Worcester, ii. 574–5.

in the Book of Llandaff, in which he is entitled king of Morgannwg.[130] Hostility between them broke out in 1045, when 'there was great deceit between Gruffudd and Rhys, sons of Rhydderch, and Gruffudd ap Llywelyn'.[131]

The C version of the Anglo-Saxon Chronicle has a notice referring to 1046, the year after hostility between Gruffudd ap Llywelyn and the sons of Rhydderch came out into the open, and a year before Gruffudd's men were killed in Ystrad Tywi: 'In this year, Earl Swein went into Wales and Gruffudd, the northern king, accompanied him and hostages were given to him/them.' The Old English *him*, used in this entry, may be singular or plural, so it is difficult to be sure whether Swein alone or Swein and Gruffudd were given hostages.[132] Swein was the eldest son of Earl Godwine and Gytha, sister of Eilífr. By 'the northern king' the Chronicle is making it clear that the Gruffudd in question was Gruffudd ap Llywelyn rather than Gruffudd ap Rhydderch. The Chronicle entry does not specify where in Wales Swein went, other than leaving it to be understood that it was not in North Wales. The entry could refer to a joint expedition into south-east Wales, by Swein from Gloucester, where he was earl, and by Gruffudd from Gwynedd. It is important to notice that Gloucester was the seat of an earldom separate from Mercia; this may well have already been the case in Cnut's reign, when Eilífr was probably earl. It is also important to remember that the earldom included Herefordshire, where the branch of the southern Merfynion descended from Einion ab Owain ap Hywel Dda had taken refuge. Since Swein was cooperating with Gruffudd ap Llywelyn, he was not concerned at that stage to support the Merfynion against Gruffudd.

In 1047 'about seven score men of Gruffudd ap Llywelyn's war band were slain through the treachery of the leading men of Ystrad Tywi'.[133] The sons of Rhydderch ab Iestin may have been implicated: their lineage would retain an interest in Ystrad Tywi into the twelfth century.[134] Yet, Gruffudd's reaction, as described in the Welsh chronicles, does not point in this direction, since he ravaged Dyfed as well as Ystrad Tywi in revenge, and not Morgannwg or Gwent; and it needs to be remembered that in Herefordshire there were members of the lineage of Edwin ab Einion, whose kinsman, Hywel ab Edwin, Gruffudd had slain.

In 1051, Earl Godwine and his sons were driven into exile. Of the sons, Swein, Tostig, and Gyrth accompanied their father to Bruges in Flanders, Harold and Leofwine went to Ireland.[135] When, in the next year, Godwine and his sons returned to England, Swein went on pilgrimage to Jerusalem and died on the way. In the same year, according to the D version of the Anglo-Saxon Chronicle, 'Gruffudd, the Welsh king, raided in Herefordshire and he came very close to

[130] *LL* 264a.

[131] *Brut* (for differences between the Welsh chronicles here, see Jones's note to his translation of the Peniarth MS 20 version, to 14. 9–11).

[132] The translation in *EHD* ii, no. 1, *s.a.* 1046, assumes that they were given only to Swein.

[133] Maund, *Ireland*, 128, proposed that the expedition with Swein, 1046 in the ASC C, and the events placed by the corrected dates in the *Brut* in 1047 should be placed in the same year; but the evidence on the chronology of the *Brut* set out at the end of this chapter shows that this is improbable.

[134] *Brut* 1116 on Maredudd ap Rhydderch ap Caradog.

[135] ASC CDE 1051.

Leominster'. He was opposed by the men of the shire and also 'the Frenchmen from the castle', which the new earl, Ralph, was building. This Gruffudd is usually taken to be Gruffudd ap Llywelyn, but this may well be untrue, since Gruffudd ap Rhydderch and his brother Rhys also had a record of attacking the earldom.[136] In 1049 Gruffudd 'the Welsh king' had joined forces with a fleet of thirty-six ships from Ireland who had entered the River Usk; the location of the fleet shows that this Gruffudd is very likely to be the son of Rhydderch ab Iestin. In January 1053, the year after the raid on Herefordshire, 'Rhys, the king's brother' was slain by the English on King Edward's orders and his head was brought to Gloucester.[137] The Rhys in question must be Rhys ap Rhydderch, brother of Gruffudd ap Rhydderch. Later the same year 'Welshmen slew many Englishmen from the patrols at Westbury'.[138] The pattern of events suggests that the Gruffudd who raided Herefordshire in 1052 was Gruffudd ap Rhydderch, not Gruffudd ap Llywelyn. The son of Rhydderch was finally slain by the son of Llywelyn in 1055;[139] after that the power of Gruffudd ap Llywelyn extended from the north of Anglesey to the Severn estuary.

Gruffudd was also remembered as a great enemy of the *gentiles*, the men of the Viking towns in Ireland, of Man, and of the Hebrides. Since the men of Dublin sheltered his rival, Cynan ab Iago, this would not be surprising. But in reality his relationships with the Norse were more complex. For one thing, there were rivalries among the Vikings: the principal Hiberno-Norse dynasty, the Uí Ímair, lost control of Dublin in 1036–1038 and again from 1046 to Echmarcach mac Ragnaill, who is likely to have been a grandson of the Guthfrith who, with his brother Maccus, raided Wales in the previous century.[140] He, in turn, was driven out of Dublin by Diarmait mac Maíl na mBó, king of Leinster, in 1052. He appears to have withdrawn to the Isle of Man: in 1061, Murchad, son of Diarmait, attacked Man and defeated Echmarcach, who was associated with the Rhinns of Galloway at his death in 1064.[141] When, in 1042, Gruffudd ap Llywelyn was captured by the Dubliners, their ruler was Ímar mac Arailt of Uí Ímair; when Harold and Leofwine, sons of Earl Godwine, sailed to Ireland from Bristol in 1051, the ruler of Dublin was Echmarcach mac Ragnaill; but Echmarcach, as we have seen, was expelled by Diarmait mac Maíl na mBó in 1052, probably before Harold and Leofwine returned from Ireland to England in that year. Diarmait is the person most likely

[136] D. G. Walker, 'A Note on Gruffudd ap Llywelyn (1035–63)', *Welsh History Review*, 1 (1960–3), 88–9; Lewis, 'English and Norman Government', 120–1.

[137] ASC D 1053; John of Worcester, ii. 572.

[138] ASC C 1053. This is Westbury-on-Severn, SO 716 139 (church).

[139] The *Brut* places this event in 1056 but before the battle between Ælfgar and his allies, on one side, and Earl Ralph on the other; this battle occurred on 24 October 1055. The *Brut* may have confused the battle with Ralph in 1055 with that against Leofgar, bishop of Hereford, which took place in 1056.

[140] B. T. Hudson, 'Cnut and the Scottish Kings', *English Historical Review*, 107 (1992), 355–6; Downham, *Viking Kings of Britain and Ireland*, 193; S. Duffy, 'Irishmen and Islesmen in the Kingdoms of Dublin and Man, 1052–1171', *Ériu*, 43 (1992), 95–6, associated Echmarcach mac Ragnaill with the Waterford branch of Uí Ímair.

[141] Duffy, 'Irishmen and Islesmen', 94–101, on the period when the Leinstermen controlled Dublin.

to have supplied the ships and men to enable them to return. Diarmait and his son Murchad controlled Dublin when, in 1054 or 1055, a son, Gruffudd, was born to Cynan ab Iago and his wife Ragnhild, probably daughter of Olaf son of Sitriuc son of Olaf Cuarán.[142]

The relationship which brought Gruffudd ap Llywelyn to the peak of his power was with Ælfgar.[143] The latter was earl of East Anglia in 1051–1052, during the exile of the family of Earl Godwine, then from 1053, when Harold succeeded Godwine as earl of Wessex; Ælfgar succeeded his own father, Leofric as earl of Mercia in 1057, whereupon Harold's brother Gyrth succeeded to East Anglia.[144] Ælfgar's relations with the sons of Godwine, and Harold in particular, were fragile at best. In 1055 Ælfgar, now earl of East Anglia, was outlawed, 'without any fault' according to the version of the Chronicle most favourable to his family.[145] He imitated Harold and Leofwine by going to Ireland, where he was given eighteen ships; he then made for Wales and successfully sought the aid of Gruffudd ap Llywelyn. Perhaps in 1055 Gruffudd married Ealdgyth, Ælfgar's daughter.[146] Ælfgar, with his Irish and Welsh allies, then attacked Hereford, where they defeated Earl Ralph on 24 October and sacked the town. Harold assembled an army at Gloucester 'from very nearly all England' but a peace was negotiated at Billingsley, between Ludlow and Bridgnorth.[147]

From this point Gruffudd's relationship with the family of Godwine was permanently damaged: as we have seen, he had joined Swein, eldest son of Godwine, on a campaign in 1046, but from 1055 his fortunes were tied to those of Ælfgar, and both of them were threatened by the rising power of Harold. In 1055 Siward, earl of Northumbria, died and was succeeded by Tostig, son of Godwine: opposition to this appointment may have precipitated Ælfgar's outlawry.[148] In June 1056 the new bishop of Hereford, Leofgar, previously Harold's chaplain, decided to invade Wales but was routed by Gruffudd and himself killed 'together with his priests and Ælfnoth the sheriff and many good men'.[149] Although peace was made by Earl Leofric, Earl Harold, and Bishop Ealdred, the humiliating defeat and death of Harold's former chaplain was another issue between him and Gruffudd; it may have been at this point that Gruffudd acquired the Domesday hundred of Exestan and the hidated part of Atiscros; Rhuddlan and Bistre are likely to have been earlier acquisitions, perhaps in the reign of Æthelred II, when the Welsh seem

[142] D. E. Thornton, 'The Genealogy of Gruffudd ap Cynan', in K. L. Maund (ed.), *Gruffudd ap Cynan: A Collaborative Biography* (Woodbridge, 1996), 87–90.

[143] K. L. Maund, 'The Welsh Alliances of Earl Ælfgar of Mercia and his Family in the Mid-Eleventh Century', *Anglo-Norman Studies*, 11 (1988), 181–90.

[144] Baxter, *The Earls of Mercia*, 43, 45.

[145] ASC C 1055; D modifies this verdict slightly, E is less favourable.

[146] *The Ecclesiastical History of Orderic Vitalis*, ed. M. Chibnall, 6 vols. OMT (Oxford, 1969–80), ii. 138, 216; William of Jumièges, *The Gesta Ducum Normannorum of William of Jumièges, Orderic Vitalis, and Robert of Torigni*, ed. E. M. C. van Houts, 2 vols., OMT (Oxford, 1992–5), ii. 160–2.

[147] ASC C.

[148] Baxter, *The Earls of Mercia*, 46.

[149] ASC C 1056.

to have acquired land further south, near Oswestry and to the east of Montgomery.[150] On this theory, Llywelyn ap Seisyll acquired formerly Mercian land around Rhuddlan and Bistre, as well as, in Shropshire, Whittington, Maesbury, and Chirbury earlier in the eleventh century, while his son, Gruffudd, acquired Exestan and the hidated part of Atiscros, perhaps in 1056. However, when Earl Leofric died on 30 September 1057 and Earl Ralph died soon afterwards, on 21 December, Ælfgar, now earl of Mercia, was succeeded in East Anglia by Gyrth, Harold's brother, while Harold himself took over Ralph's earldom in addition to his own. The power of the sons of Godwine was yet further increased.

In 1058 Ælfgar was again expelled, and 'soon came back in again with Gruffudd's help'.[151] Gruffudd's support should have been anticipated by Harold. What could not have been foreseen was the appearance in the Irish Sea of a fleet led by Magnus, son of Harald Hardrada, king of Norway, 'with the Foreigners of the Orkneys and of the Hebrides and of Dublin'; the Annals of Tigernach add that this was 'in order to seize the kingdom of England, but God did not permit that'.[152] The annalist was probably exaggerating: what the combined support of Gruffudd and Magnus assured was the return of Ælfgar to power in Mercia; there is no reason to think that Magnus attempted to conquer England.

The last that is heard of Ælfgar is that he, together with Harold, counselled the appointment of Wulfstan to the bishopric of Worcester in 1062.[153] He may have died the same year; Mercia passed to his son Edwin. This allowed Harold and Tostig to attempt a coup against Gruffudd at Christmas 1063.[154] Earl Harold, with a small band of horsemen, set out 'after Christmas from Gloucester to Rhuddlan, where Gruffudd was' with the intention of killing the king.[155] The point of this would appear to be that it was known to Harold that Gruffudd would, as was normal for a Welsh king, be celebrating Christmas and the New Year with a great feast, and that it was also known that the feast would be at Rhuddlan. This suggests that either Rhuddlan was the regular place for the Christmas feast in Gruffudd's reign or that Harold had special intelligence. Harold succeeded in burning Gruffudd's court and his ships, but, according to John of Worcester, 'Gruffudd, forwarned of their arrival, took flight with his men, boarded a ship, and just managed to make his escape'. This bold attempt on Gruffudd's life had failed. It had been mounted from Gloucester, within Harold's own territories, and probably required no prior arrangement with the earl of Mercia.

[150] See above, 555 nn. 94, 122.

[151] ASC D. [152] AT 1058.

[153] *The Vita Wulfstani of William of Malmesbury*, ed. R. R. Darlington (London, 1928), 18.

[154] Much the most detailed account is in ASC D 1063. John of Worcester, ii. 592–3, is shorter but also adds the odd detail. ASC E is very brief and entirely omits the midwinter raid. *Vita Ædwardi Regis/ The Life of King Edward*, ed. F. Barlow, Nelson's Medieval Texts (London, 1962), 57–8, is much vaguer but has some interesting details. For problems of chronology and detail see B. T. Hudson, 'The Destruction of Gruffudd ap Llywelyn', *WHR* 15 (1991), 331–50; K. L. Maund, 'Cynan ab Iago and the Killing of Gruffudd ap Llywelyn', *CMCS* 10 (Winter 1985), 57–65.

[155] The intention is stated by John of Worcester but is merely implicit in ASC D. John also specifies the use of a band of horsemen.

The second stage in the downfall of Gruffudd came in Rogationtide, in the week beginning with the 5th Sunday after Easter, 1064. Harold set out with a fleet from Bristol to sail round Wales so as to attack Gwynedd. Meanwhile, his brother, Tostig, led an army by land into North Wales. The latter presumably required the agreement of the Mercians; and it is to be noted that the land in north-east Wales won back by this expedition from the Welsh was in the possession of Edwin, Ælfgar's son and successor, in 1066. Edwin, it seems, had been bought off and had left his father's friend to his fate. The Welsh, according to the D version of the Chronicle, sued for peace and gave hostages, apparently in response to Harold's expedition by sea; but perhaps the placing by the chronicler of this submission after Harold's expedition and before Tostig's was merely to exalt the achievement of Harold.

The final stage came in the autumn, when Gruffudd was killed 'by the treachery of his own people'.[156] According to the Annals of Ulster, 'the son of Llywelyn, king of the Britons, was killed by the son of Iago', almost certainly Cynan ab Iago intervening from his base north of Dublin.[157] Yet Cynan did not achieve what must have been his aim, the kingship of Gwynedd. Edward the Confessor gave the succession to Bleddyn ap Cynfyn and his brother Rhiwallon, Gruffudd's uterine brothers. They received Gwynedd with Powys, while Maredudd ab Owain ab Edwin gained the kingship of Deheubarth. At the end of its entry the D version of the Chronicle notes that Bleddyn and Rhiwallon 'swore oaths and gave hostages to the king and to the earl that in all ways they would be faithful to them . . . and would pay from that land what used to be paid before to any other king'.[158] The emphasis on the earl, Harold, is notable as is the presupposition that, in normal times, tribute was paid. The time of Gruffudd ap Llywelyn had, it appears, not been normal.

The contest between Harold and Gruffudd had an epilogue. In 1065, before Lammas (1 August), Harold decided to build a grand hunting lodge at Portskewett in the far south-east of Wales. There he proposed to entertain King Edward at a great hunt. But Caradog ap Gruffudd ap Rhydderch attacked the place, killed most of the builders and took the great stock of wealth that Harold had placed there. 'And soon after that' the thegns in Yorkshire and all Northumbria came together and outlawed Tostig and summoned Morcar, Ælfgar's other son, and chose him as earl. They then marched southwards, gathering to their cause Nottinghamshire, Derbyshire, and Lincolnshire, until they arrived at Northampton. There they were joined by Earl Edwin and the Mercians, 'and also many Britons came with them', led, according to Ordericus Vitalis, by Gruffudd ap Llywelyn's half-brother and successor, Bleddyn ap Cynfyn.[159]

[156] *On herfeste*, ASC D; *dolo suorum*, *AC* B (similarly the *Brut*).

[157] AU 1064. 8.

[158] This may be compared with the £40 paid, according to Domesday Book, for South Wales by Rhys ap Tewdwr and for North Wales by Robert of Rhuddlan.

[159] ASC D 1065; John of Worcester, ii. 596–9; *The Ecclesiastical History of Orderic Vitalis*, ed. M. Chibnall, ii (OMT 1969), 214–17 (which says that Bleddyn ap Cynfyn led them).

No other Welsh king known to history ruled more of his country than did Gruffudd ap Llywelyn. Not even the two Llywelyns in the thirteenth century came near to rivalling the geographical extent of his power, for by then much of Wales lay in the March. The memory of his power may have encouraged William the Conqueror to establish three great earldoms at Chester, Shrewsbury, and Hereford—first, Hereford, and then, later, Shrewsbury and Chester.[160] He was remembered, too, by Walter Map in the reign of Henry II; but it may be asked whether he left any lasting impression on Wales to compare with the law attributed to Hywel Dda, who came nearest among earlier kings to matching the extent of his rule.

One possibility is that he was responsible for the system of cantref and commote, the local territorial divisions, which covered the entire country from the commote of Talybolion in the north-west of Anglesey to Portskewett (Porth Ysgewin) in the far south, east of Gwent. Throughout the country the same division applied, into, first, cantrefs, and, secondly, of the cantrefs into commotes. The system was not of immemorial age but was an effort at securing some measure of uniformity; although Sir John Lloyd described them as 'the tribal divisions of Wales', they were often of recent and artificial origin, as he clearly saw.[161] In some areas, the cantref is manifestly older than the commote: an example is the cantref of Arfon, divided by the River Gwyrfai into the commotes of Uwch Gwyrfai and Is Gwyrfai, 'Above Gwyrfai' and 'Below Gwyrfai'. In other areas, however, as in Anglesey, across the Menai Strait from Arfon, the commotes seem to be the older units: their names at least appear to be more ancient. In some areas, such as Llŷn, both cantref and commote names seem to be ancient: Llŷn itself, and one of the commotes, Dinllaen, both derive their names from the earlier period of Irish settlement.[162] In the *Historia Brittonum* and *Annales Cambriae* local districts were called 'regions', *regiones*, whether they were small, as was Gwerthrynion, or large, such as Gwynedd.[163] Gwerthrynion was later reckoned to be a commote. So also was Afloegion in Llŷn, one of the portions assigned to the sons of Cunedda, whereas Rhufoniog, another portion, was a cantref, with two of its three commotes divided by the River Aled into Rhufoniog Uwch Aled and Rhufoniog Is Aled. The name of the cantref, Rhufoniog, occurs in both versions of the *Gododdin*. I suggest, therefore, that it was Gruffudd ap Llywelyn who, with his power over all Wales, was responsible for the fully-developed and universal system of cantref and commote. In some cases, this system merely used existing names, as in Llŷn; but in others new divisions were introduced.

The words, *cwmwd* and *cantref*, are not likely to have been coined in the eleventh century. The literal sense of *cwmwd* was 'being together' or 'living together'; its

160 M. Lieberman, *The March of Wales, 1067–1300* (Cardiff, 2008), 20–2.

161 Lloyd, *HW* 229–82. is a splendid description of these divisions, once they are removed from the period 650–850, to which Lloyd ascribed them (p. 229), and placed in the mid-eleventh century.

162 See above, 176.

163 *HB* 40 'ad regionem quae vocatur Guined', 47 'in regione Demetorum', 'ad regionem quae a nomine suo accepit nomen Guorthigirniaun'. It is possible that, with the loss of the distinction between long and short vowels, *regio* came to be associated more closely with *regnum*, and thus conceived as a district, large or small, over which a king, *rex, regis*, might rule.

Breton cognate, *compot*, is attested in ninth-century charters and is there used for a small unit of land, although how the *compot* was related to other small territorial units is unclear.[164] The other term, *cantref*, has its cognate in Old Irish, *céttreb*, in a document about the kindreds and the military obligations of Dál Riata, *Senchas Fer nAlban*.[165] As far as one can tell, the correspondence between *cantref* and *céttreb* is an outcome of counting in fives, and the natural use of a hundred for a large unit. The words themselves may not have been new, but as parts of a system of territorial units in which the cantref was divided into commotes, they probably were new.

When Melville Richards analysed those commote names that consist of the cantref name together with 'above' and 'below' some river or, less commonly, a wood, he came to the conclusion that a commote that was 'above' a river was not in any sense higher than one that was 'below' the river.[166] He argued that, instead, 'below' meant 'nearer' and 'above' meant 'further' in the sense that, normally, the main royal centre of the cantref would be situated in the commote that was below the river. In relation to that centre, the 'below' commote was closer.[167] This generally works well; yet when we come to the name of an entire kingdom, Gwynedd was divided into Gwynedd uwch Conwy, 'Gwynedd above the Conwy' and Gwynedd is Conwy, 'Gwynedd below the Conwy': and the portion 'above the Conwy' lay to the west of that river and the portion 'below the Conwy' lay to the east, as if the more important royal *llys* was east of the Conwy. Normally, that was manifestly untrue: the main centres, such as Aberffraw, were to the west. But there was one period in which this seems not have been the case: Gruffudd ap Llywelyn's main *llys* appears to have been Rhuddlan, the former Mercian *burh*. That may be the clue to the age of the whole system.

3. THE FATE OF CUMBRIA

By 1064 the situation of each of 'the small Britains'—Cumbria, Wales, Cornwall, and Brittany—differed fundamentally from the others. Cornwall was an English county, even though it largely retained its Brittonic language, and its religious landscape remained quite different from that of its neighbour, Devon. Although the Cornish hundreds might seem at first sight as if they were English creations,

164 L. Fleuriot, *Dictionnaire des gloses en vieux breton*, 88, under (2) **bot**; W. Davies, *Small Worlds*, 66–7.

165 J. Bannerman, *Studies in the History of Dalriada* (Edinburgh, 1974), 142–3; D. N. Dumville, 'Ireland and North Britain in the Earlier Middle Ages: Contexts for *Míniugad Senchasa Fher n-Alban*', *Rannsachadh na Gàidhlig, 2000: Papers read at the Conference Scottish Gaelic Studies 2000 held at the University of Aberdeen 2–4 August*, ed. C. Ó Baoill agus Nancy R. McGuire (Aberdeen, 2002), 185–211, includes a new edition.

166 M. Richards, 'The Significance of *Is* and *Uwch* in Welsh Commote and Cantref Names', *Welsh History Review*, 2 (1964–5), 9–18.

167 Compare *gwarthaf* 'uppermost' in the sense of 'furthermost', as in Cantref Gwarthaf, the furthest east of 'the seven cantrefs of Dyfed', and *PKM* 71. 3, *hyt ygwarthaf Keredigyawn*, 'to the furthest part of Ceredigion'.

their origins almost certainly lay in the remote past.[168] The place-names, apart from the north-east of the county, remain largely Brittonic. Its native aristocracy was not swept away, as is illustrated by a grant of King Edgar to Ælfheah Gerent, his man, and Ælfheah's wife, Moruurei, of land at Lamorran and Trenowth in Probus, Cornwall.[169] Ælfheah was his English name, but in Cornish he was Gerent; and his wife's name suggests that his Cornish identity came first. The experience of Cornwall under English rule was thus very different from that of its neighbour, Devon. It was argued above that this was primarily a consequence of the date at which it was incorporated within Wessex—after the Britons conformed to the Roman Easter and tonsure.

Brittany had been conquered by the Franks, first by Charlemagne in 786, and again by his son, Louis the Pious, in 818.[170] Yet, during the long decline of the Carolingian empire the rulers of Brittany had gained a very large measure of independence and had considerably expanded their territory. As a result of that expansion there was a solidly Romance-speaking Brittany in the east alongside a Breton-speaking Brittany in the west. Even in the west some reorientation of cultural links away from Ireland and Celtic Britain had occurred and was permanent: the monks of Landévennec now lived by the Rule of St Benedict, mandatory in the Carolingian empire, although they remembered their previous 'Irish' monastic rule.[171]

In the late ninth and early tenth century Cumbria saw an even more dramatic expansion than did Brittany. Its history in this period offers the sharpest contrast with that of Wales, and it thus deserves more detailed consideration. From its core in the Clyde valley it took over former Northumbrian territory in what is now south-west Scotland and north-west England. In the latter, to judge by place-names, it had re-established Cumbric in some areas, in the later wards of Cumberland (south-east of Carlisle as far as the River Wampool), Leath (in the valley of the Eden), and Eskdale (north-east of Carlisle): the deanery of Cumberland and the ward of Cumberland (which did not cover the same territory, and both of which were only districts within the later shire of Cumberland), probably indicate two areas of relatively strong Cumbrian control and settlement within the region covered by the later county. Some British place-names are likely to be of this phase of Cumbrian expansion rather than survivals from the sixth and early seventh century.[172] There seems to have been an arrangement that left the coastal belt largely to the Hiberno-Norse, while the Cumbrians

[168] See above, 23.

[169] S 770 = Birch, *Cartularium Saxonicum*, 1231.

[170] *Annales Regni Francorum*, ed. F. Kurze, MGH, SRG (Hanover, 1895), *s.aa.* 786, 818; Ermold the Black, *In Honorem Hludowici Christianissimi Caesaris Augusti . . . Elegiacum Carmen*, ed. E. Faral, *Ermold le Noir: Poème sur Louis le Pieux et épitres au roi Pépin* (Paris, 1932), 98–133; J. M. H. Smith, *Province and Empire: Brittany and the Carolingians* (Cambridge, 1992), 58–9, 65–6.

[171] Wrdisten, *Vita S. Winwaloei*, ii. 12–13, ed. C. De Smedt, *Analecta Bollandiana*, 7 (1888), 226–7.

[172] Following K. H. Jackson, 'Angles and Britons in Northumbria and Cumbria' in J. R. R. Tolkein et al., *Angles and Britons: O'Donnell Lectures* (Carditt, 1963), 73–7, 80–2, and A. Breeze, 'Britons in the Barony of Gilsland, Cumbria', *Northern History* 43 (2006), 327–32, as against Phythian-Adams, *Land of the Cumbrians*, 77–87, and J. M. Todd, 'British (Cumbric) Place-Names in the Barony of Gilsland, Cumbria', *TCWAAS* 3rd Ser. 5 (2005), 89–102.

settled in the interior. There they lived side by side with English-speakers, if the name of the forest to the south of Carlisle, Inglewood, 'The Forest of the English', was so named to distinguish it from lands under direct Cumbrian or Hiberno-Norse control. Although the wards are not attested until the reign of Edward I, the division between Allerdale 'below Derwent' and 'above Derwent', the latter being the ward furthest away from Carlisle, is reminiscent of Welsh commote and cantref names; and Allerdale itself is attested in the eleventh century by Gospatric's Writ.[173]

The greater Cumbria of the tenth century was, therefore, a land of many peoples. Ethnically it was much less Cumbrian as a result of its huge expansion; indeed, the lands that were mainly English-speaking were probably more extensive than those that were strongly Cumbric-speaking. On the other hand, the appearance of new British place-names even in the southern region around Carlisle indicates that a dominant element within the aristocracy of the kingdom was Cumbric in language.[174]

Welsh, English, and Irish annals allow us to reconstruct the Cumbrian royal genealogy with some certainty for the tenth century and reasonable probability for the first half of the eleventh.[175] Rhun ab Arthal was the latest name in the pedigree of the northern British kings given in the Harleian Genealogies. That pedigree thus crossed the divide between the old Alclud, the Rock of the Clyde, and the new kingdom of Strathclyde, the Clyde valley, that emerged out of the disaster in 870, when Alclud was taken by the Vikings. As we saw in Chapter 16, the border of Cumbria, alias Strathclyde, was probably on the River Eamont, near Penrith, by 927. As far as we can tell, the expanded Cumbria endured into the eleventh century. The great victory of Carham in 1018, which assured control of Lothian to the king of Scots, was won with the aid of Owain Foel, king of the men of the Clyde.[176] The dynasty appears to have lasted until 1054 at least, when Siward defeated Macbeth and 'made Malcolm, son of the king of the Cumbrians, king [of Scots], as the king [Edward the Confessor] had commanded'.[177] (Macbeth, however, rapidly recovered his kingdom.)[178] Yet, by 1070 Cumbria, including what later became English Cumberland, was under the control of the Scots—from a Northumbrian standpoint 'not possessed by right but subjugated by violence'—and the *Historia Regum* records a raid in that year by Gospatric, earl of Northumbria, into a Cumberland under the authority of the

[173] M. Richards, 'The Significance of *Is* and *Uwch* in Welsh Commote and Cantref Names', 9–18; Gospatric's Writ, ed. and trans. F. E. Harmer, *Anglo-Saxon Writs* (Manchester, 1952), 419–24; ed. and trans. B. Dickins, *The Place-Names of Cumberland*, 3 vols. (Cambridge, 1950–2), iii, pp. xxvii–xxx.

[174] Jackson, 'Angles and Britons in Northumbria and Cumbria', 81–3; the map in the pocket at the end of vol. iii of A. H. Armstrong et al., *The Place-Names of Cumberland* (Cambridge, 1950–52), shows both old British names and those that are likely to belong to the Strathclyde period.

[175] D. Broun, 'The Welsh Identity of the Kingdom of Strathclyde *c.* 900 – *c.* 1200', *Innes Review*, 55 (2004), 135; A. A. M. Duncan, *The Kingship of the Scots, 842–1292: Succession and Independence* (Edinburgh, 2002), 29, 37–40; A. Macquarrie, 'The Kings of Strathclyde, *c.* 400–1018', in A. Grant and K. Stringer (eds.), *Medieval Scotland: Crown, Lordship and Community. Essays Presented to G. W. S. Barrow* (Edinburgh, 1993), 1–19.

[176] Simeon, *Historia Regum*, *s.a.* 1018, *Opera*, ii. 156 (*EHD* i, no. 3, *s.a.* 1018).

[177] John of Worcester, *Chronicle*, *s.a.* 1054, ed. Darlington and McGurk, ii. 574.

[178] Woolf, *From Pictland to Alba*, 261–2.

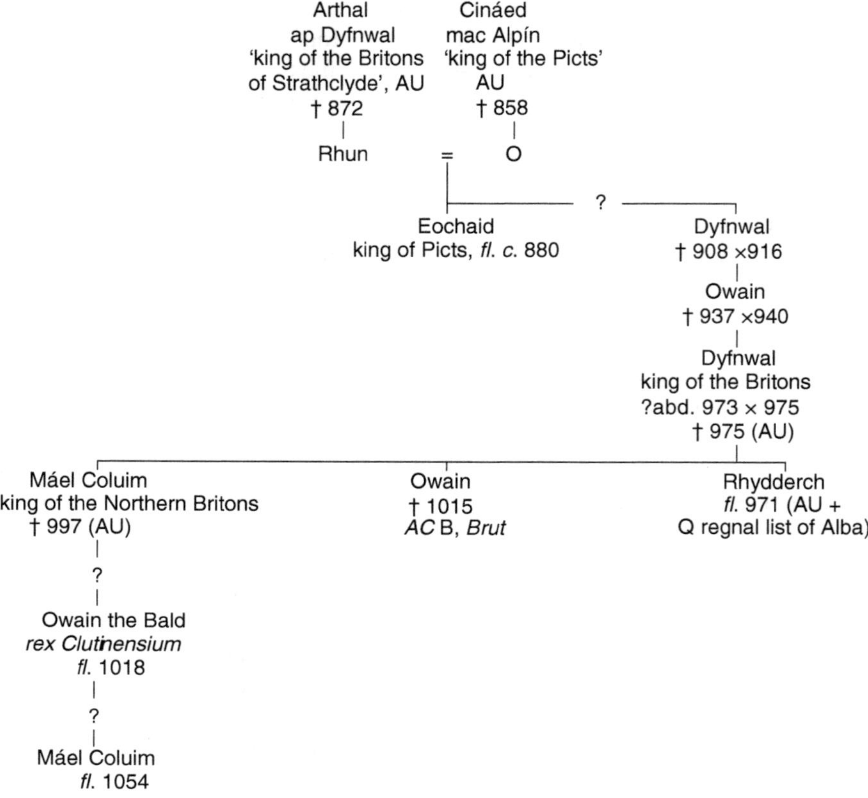

Figure 17.4. The Dynasty of Cumbria/Strathclyde

Scots.[179] It has been suggested that it was taken by Malcolm III, king of the Scots, in 1061, when Tostig, the new earl of Northumbria, was on pilgrimage to Rome, and that it would remain Scottish until, in 1092, William Rufus 'with a great army went north to Carlisle, and restored the city and erected the castle, and drove out Dolfin who had ruled the country'.[180] The date 1061 for Scottish acquisition is possible; yet Simeon of Durham, our authority for the Scottish campaign of 1061, did not mention Cumbria; his only detail is that the Scottish army caused damage to Lindisfarne, on the North Sea coast.

Two developments seem to have weakened Cumbria in the middle years of the eleventh century. The first was the emergence of 'the Rhinns' as a separate entity in

[179] Simeon, *Opera*, ii. 191.

[180] Simeon, *Historia Regum*, *s.a.* 1061, *Opera*, ii. 174–5; W. E. Kapelle, *The Norman Conquest of the North: The Region and its Transformation, 1000–1135* (Chapel Hill, 1979), 92–3; ASC E 1092. Duncan, *The Kingship of the Scots*, 45–6, denies that Malcolm controlled the lands around Carlisle for more than a few months, but this is to push the balance of Simeon's evidence too far.

the south-west. The context was the relationship between Leinster, Dublin, the Isle of Man, the Hebrides, and the Rhinns.[181] In 1064 two men 'reckoned not ignoble among their own people', died on pilgrimage to Rome: Donnchad son of Brian Bórama, formerly king of Munster, and Echmarcach son of Ragnall, 'king of the Rhinns'.[182] Echmarcach was very probably a grandson of the Guthfrith son of Harald, who, with his brother Maccus, had ravaged Gwynedd in the late tenth century. At this period, 'the Rhinns' seem to have included the area around Whithorn as well as what are now known as the Rhinns of Galloway. Echmarcach had earlier been king of Dublin, and then, when driven out by Diarmait mac Maíl na mBó and his son, Murchad, in 1052, he had retained the kingship of Man. But in 1061 he was driven out of Man by Murchad, and the Rhinns seem to have been the final remnant of his former dominions.[183] By 1061 at the latest, therefore, the far south-west of Cumbria had become part of the complex of territories ranging from Dublin itself to the Hebrides, territories often attached to Dublin; and in 1061 it acquired a separate identity as a kingdom as a result of the expulsion of Echmarcach from Man.

Earlier, in 1034, an obit in the Irish annals describes Suibne son of Cináed as 'king of the Gallgáedil, 'Foreign Irish'.[184] This is the Gaelic name that lies behind Galloway, and the latter is securely attested in the twelfth century as the name for a kingdom or territory in the south-west of the kingdom of the Scots.[185] It is tempting to suppose that these Gallgáedil over whom Suibne ruled were the dominant element in Galloway *c.* 1030. This, however, is far from certain.[186] The previous attestations of Gallgáedil were in Irish annal entries in the middle years of the ninth century; and those Gallgáedil were active in Ireland.[187] The Gallgáedil of twelfth-century Galloway appear to have been predominantly Gaelic-speakers: Gaelic survived there into the early modern period. The Scots, however, were unambiguously Gáedil, without the Scandinavian admixture suggested by the first element *Gall*; and in the twelfth century, the Gallgáedil remained a people separate from the Scots, even though they fell under the rule of the Scottish king. Their separateness seems to have been established not by language but by their links with Man, Dublin, and the *Innsi Gall*, the Hebrides: they were part of a Hiberno-Norse Irish-Sea world, and their laws may well have been quite distinct from those

[181] S. Duffy, 'Irishmen and Islesmen', 93–133.

[182] Echmarcach is 'king of the Foreigners' in his obit in AU 1064.9, but *rex inna Renn* in *Mariani Scotti Chronicon*, ed. G. Waitz, MGH SS 5 (Hanover, 1844), 559.

[183] AT 1052, 1061; F. J. Byrne, 'Onomastica 2: Na Renna', *Peritia*, 1 (1982), 267; S. Duffy, 'Irishmen and Islesmen', 98–101.

[184] AU, AT 1034.

[185] T. O. Clancy, 'The Gall-Ghàidheil and Galloway', *The Journal of Scottish Place-Name Studies*, 2 (2008), 19–50.

[186] Ibid.; Woolf, *From Pictland to Alba*, 253–4.

[187] AU 856, 857; CS 858.

of the Gáedil of Scotland.[188] It is not necessary to invoke the Gallgáedil of the mid-ninth century to account for the Gallgáedil of the eleventh and twelfth.

The interval between Echmarcach's kingdom of the Rhinns and the kingdom of Fergus of Galloway in the twelfth century is admittedly far briefer than the interval between Suibne and the ninth-century Gallgáedil. The place-names of south-western Scotland indicate a stronger Viking settlement in Dumfriesshire and along the coast of Cumberland than in the Rhinns and in the Machars around Whithorn; and this can be interpreted as evidence that any Scandinavian influence in the far south-west was later, eleventh rather than tenth century.[189] Suibne mac Cináeda and his Gallgáedil of 1034 may have been behind the creation of Galloway; and the Gallgáedil of 1034 should then be associated with the Rhinns of 1064 and the Galloway of the twelfth century rather than with the Gallgáedil of ninth-century Ireland.

Suibne's Gallgáedil, however, may not have been in the Rhinns. Echmarcach, who was to die as king of the Rhinns, is likely to have been the 'Iehmarc' who, according to the Anglo-Saxon Chronicle, was one of three kings who submitted to Cnut when he went north into Scotland in 1031.[190] At this date, Echmarcach would appear to have been a king in northern Britain: he was probably based in the Rhinns or in the Hebrides, where his grandfather had ruled. The only certain point is that Echmarcach could retire to what was later Galloway but was at the time called 'the Rhinns' after being expelled from Man in 1061. His possession of the Rhinns from 1061 to 1064 may have been due to his earlier position as king of Dublin rather than to his ancestral connection with the Hebrides.

A recent explanation of the origins of Galloway begins from two pieces of evidence at first sight very distant from each other.[191] In the twelfth century Galloway could include 'the whole of Scotland south and west of Clydesdale and Teviotdale.[192] In the *Martyrology of Tallaght*, a text of the early ninth century, one of the saints included under 10 August was 'Blaan, bishop of Kingarth among the Gallgáedil'.[193] If the phrase 'among the Gallgáedil' was part of the original text, the implications are far-reaching. In the ninth-century Irish annals, the Gallgáedil were a set of people with no apparent territorial connection. Yet, in the Martyrology, the situation of Kingarth, the principal ancient church on the isle of Bute, can be explained by saying that it was 'among the Gallgáedil'; here Gallgáedil plainly does have a topographical sense: the people have become attached to a region; and, moreover, the region in question was

[188] H. L. MacQueen, 'The Laws of Galloway: A Preliminary Study', in R. D. Oram and G. P. Stell (eds.), *Galloway: Land and Lordship* (Edinburgh, 1991), 131–43.

[189] G. Fellows-Jensen, 'Scandinavians in Dumfriesshire and Galloway: The Place-Name Evidence', ibid., 77–95.

[190] ASC E 1031, Hudson, 'Cnut and the Scottish Kings', 350–60.

[191] Clancy, 'The Gall-Ghàidheil and Galloway'.

[192] *Regesta Regum Scottorum*, i. *The Acts of Malcolm IV*, ed. G. W. S. Barrow (Edinburgh, 1960), 38–9 and no. 131; *The Charters of King David I*, ed. G. W. S. Barrow (Woodbridge, 1999), no. 57. The smaller Galloway was defined by the diocese of Whithorn.

[193] *The Martyrology of Tallaght*, ed. R. I. Best and H. J. Lawlor, Henry Bradshaw Society, 88 (London, 1931), 62.

not Galloway. The argument, therefore, is that the term Gallgáedil first acquired a topographical sense in Bute and probably Cowal, on the Firth of Clyde. Across the Firth lay the northern districts of the later 'Greater Galloway'. Instead of Galloway being initially the district that became the diocese of Whithorn, more or less the modern Galloway, it was further north. The implications for Cumbria are considerable, since the argument implies that the lands from Strathgriff down to Carrick were taken by the Gallgáedil of Bute and probably Cowal. Only later, perhaps in the early twelfth century, were the Rhinns added to form the Greater Galloway. Whithorn would then have been, in origin, the diocese of the Rhinns.

Much depends on the phrase in the Martyrology of Tallaght. It is preserved in the Book of Leinster and, partially, in an early modern manuscript that derives indirectly from the Book of Leinster.[194] We are thus dependent on a single primary copy of the text. It is entirely possible that the phrase *i nGallgáedelaib*, 'among the Gallgáedil', was added in the tenth or eleventh century, before the Greater Galloway was created. Yet, even if this were so, it would still be good evidence for the presence of the Gallgáedil in the Firth of Clyde at a date when the modern Galloway was known as 'the Rhinns'; it would still be possible to argue strongly for a Greater Galloway created from the north and thus for a sequence of events that would have greatly reduced the area covered by Cumbria.

The second change that weakened Cumbria also occurred sometime in the mid-eleventh century: Siward, the earl of the Northumbrians, gained power over the whole of Cumbria; he is likely to have taken direct possession of lands around Carlisle, the southern (and later the English) portion of Cumbria, and this is likely to have been accompanied by an overlordship over the rest of the kingdom.[195]

The mixture of influences in eleventh-century Cumbria is illustrated by Gospatric's writ, a unique document for the area and date.[196] Unfortunately, the identity of the Gospatric in question has been controversial, although current opinion favours Gospatric son of Maldred rather than Gospatric son of Uhtred;[197] and the text of the writ, which only survives in a later copy of an Old English original, may be corrupt in places. The Gospatric of the writ held authority in Cumbria at a date when the part that was later the English county was no longer ruled by the Cumbrians. This is shown by the salutation at the beginning:

> Gospatric sends friendly greetings to all my *wassenas* and to every man, free man and dreng, dwelling in the lands that were Cumbrian, and to all my kindred.

The name Gospatric is Cumbric, 'Servant of Patrick'; and yet the known Gospatrics who might have held power in Cumberland in the eleventh century were all attached to the Northumbrian family descended from Uhtred, earl of

194 *The Martyrology of Tallaght*, ed. Best and Lawlor, p. xviii.

195 Kapelle, *The Norman Conquest of the North*, 27–49.

196 Gospatric's Writ, ed. and trans. F. E. Harmer, *Anglo-Saxon Writs* (Manchester, 1952), 419–24; ed. and trans. B. Dickins, *The Place-Names of Cumberland*, 3 vols. (Cambridge, 1950–2), iii, pp.xxvii–xxx.

197 H. W. C. Davis, 'Cumberland before the Norman Conquest', *English Historical Review*, 20 (1905), 61–5, for Gospatric son of Uhtred; C. Phythian-Adams, *Land of the Cumbrians: A Study in British Provincial Origins A.D. 400–1120* (Aldershot, 1996), 174–81, for Gospatric son of Maldred.

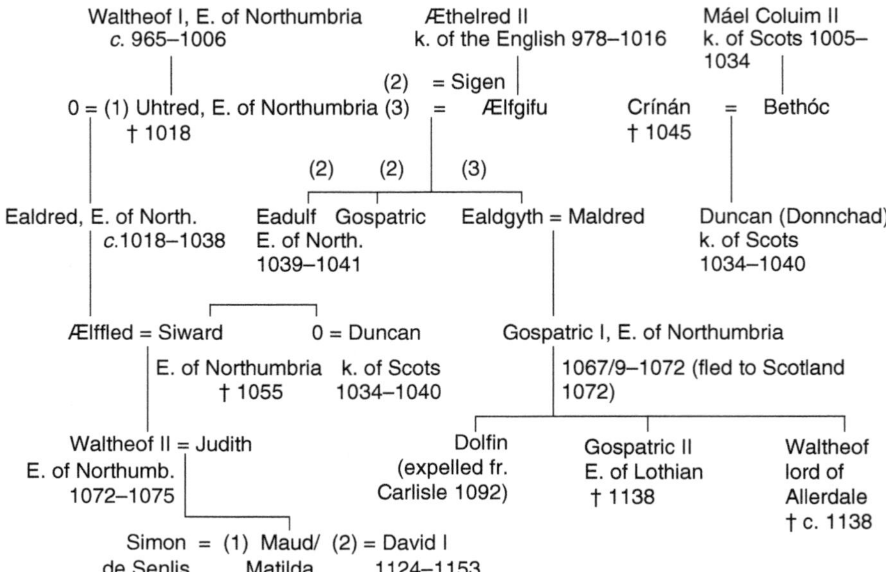

Figure 17.5. The earls of Northumbria

Northumbria.[198] The first known Gospatric was a son of Uhtred, earl of Northumbria, and himself a powerful Northumbrian thegn murdered in Edward the Confessor's court on 28 December 1064 because he had crossed Tostig, earl of Northumbria and brother of the future King Harold; the murder precipitated the rebellion against Tostig the next year in which the Welsh participated.[199] The second was a grandson of Uhtred through a daughter and himself earl of Northumbria, appointed by William the Conqueror (as earl of Northumbria and ancestor of the earls of Dunbar he is usually known as Gospatric I). Although he was a grandson of Uhtred, his father, Maldred, may have borne a Cumbrian name.[200]

The first addressees of the writ were Gospatric's *wassenas*: this is an Old English plural form of a Cumbric word referring to his retainers: in Welsh *gwas* has a suffix with a vowel + *n* in both the *gwasan-* in *gwasanaeth* 'service' and in the Welsh plural *gweision* 'servants'. *Dreng* is an English word derived from Old Norse *drengr*, which itself meant 'young man'—originally, therefore, more or less synonymous with Welsh *gwas*, but here clearly a distinct group. To judge by later evidence drengs were subject to relatively light agricultural services to their lords and some military

198 F. L. Edmonds, 'Personal Names and the Cult of Patrick in Eleventh-Century Strathclyde and Northumbria', in S. Boardman, J. R. Davies, and E. Williamson (eds.), *Saints' Cults in the Celtic World* (Woodbridge, 2009), 43.

199 ASC D 1065; John of Worcester, ii. 596–9, *s.a.* 1065; see above, 567; R. Fletcher, *Bloodfeud: Murder and Revenge in Anglo-Saxon England* (Oxford, 2003), 157–62.

200 Edmonds, 'Personal Names and the Cult of Patrick', 56–7.

obligations.[201] The *wassenas* appear to have been closer to their lord than were the drengs. Cumbrian society and political structures still had a partially Cumbrian character even though these were lands which 'were Cumbrian' (in the past). The principal beneficiary of the writ was a man called Thorfynn mac Thore, two good Scandinavian names joined together by a Gaelic word for 'son'. Those who called him by this name should have been Gaelic speakers. Thorfynn was to be 'as free in all things that are mine in Allerdale as any man may be'. Allerdale was south-west of the Wampool and beyond, therefore, the later ward of Cumberland; it was part of the coastal belt heavily settled by the Norse, probably in the tenth century after the dispersal from Dublin in 902—a dispersal that also brought Scandinavians to Anglesey and to Man. Thorfynn and his men, however, lived just to the north-east of the Wampool at Cardew and Cumdivock, two good Cumbric place-names; Cardew, at least, was introduced in the period of Strathclyde rule and was not a survival from the seventh century.[202] Thorfynn mac Thore had also been granted a peace by Siward, earl of Northumbria, who died in 1055. The crucial point here—and it is independent of the identity of Gospatric—is, therefore, that Siward had exercised direct authority within what became Cumberland before his death. Indeed Siward had been heavily involved in Cumbrian and Scottish affairs: in 1054 he had attempted, as we have seen, to put Malcolm 'son of the king of the Cumbrians' on the throne of Scotland in opposition to Macbeth; and he had previously attempted to replace Macbeth by another man in 1046.[203] He was married to a sister of Donnchad I (Duncan I). During the time when Cynesige was archbishop of York (1051–1060), he is said to have consecrated two bishops, Magsuen and John, to Glasgow.[204] If the Gospatric in question was the son of Uhtred, he may have been collaborating with Siward in giving his peace to Thorfynn mac Thore; if he was the son of Maldred, he may also have been active in Cumbria in the period of Scottish rule, which probably stretched from no later than 1070 until 1092, when this Gospatric's son, Dolfin, was driven from Carlisle by William Rufus.[205]

What the writ reveals is not just a society of different languages but also, first, a society understood in terms derived from Cumbric, English, and Norse, and, secondly, an elite which, whatever its genealogical origins, could reach out to other linguistic and cultural communities. The first Gospatric, the son of Uhtred, was presumably given that name because Uhtred wished his dynasty to be acceptable to the Cumbrians as a whole; the cult of Patrick flourished among the Hiberno-Norse of the Cumbrian coast but was also popular among the British Cumbrians;

201 Cf. F. M. Stenton, *The First Century of English Feudalism*, 2nd edn. (Oxford, 1961), 146–89; C. W. Hollister, *Anglo-Saxon Military Institutions* (Oxford, 1962), 34–7; G. W. S. Barrow, 'Northern Society', in his *Scotland and its Neighbours in the Middle Ages* (London, 1992), 136–7.

202 Jackson, 'Angles and Britons in Northumbria and Cumbria', 82.

203 A. O. Anderson, *Scottish Annals from English Chroniclers* (London, 1908), 84.

204 Hugh the Chantor, *The History of the Church of York, 1066–1127*, ed. C. Johnson (London, 1961), 32.

205 That Dolfin was the son of Gospatric son of Maldred is supported by R. Sharpe, *Norman Rule in Cumbria, 1092–1136*, Cumberland and Westmorland Antiquarian and Archaeological Society, Tract Series, 21 (Carlisle, 2006), 34–5 n. 80.

and the name 'Gospatric', (Cumbric) 'Servant of Patrick', thus included both communities. Cumbria was part of Uhtred's plans for the future: the naming of his son is not evidence that he already exercised power in the Carlisle region.[206] The second Gospatric (Gospatric I) was the son of Maldred and a daughter of Uhtred, and Maldred's name may be Cumbrian.[207] Someone whom the Cumbrians may even have regarded as one of themselves could become earl of Northumbria. The various nationalities of the lands from southern Alba to the River Eamont were linked by marriage and bonds of lordship. Up to 1092, whether Cumbria as a whole, from around Carlisle to Glasgow and beyond, was ultimately subject to the English or the Scottish king, it was in practice controlled by this intermarried local aristocracy.

Cumbria and Brittany were, in territorial terms, the British successes of the period from the ninth to the eleventh century. By their very success they became open to external influence and a dilution of their British identity. Wales, under Llywelyn ap Seisyll and his son, Gruffudd ap Llywelyn, also enjoyed a territorial expansion, but it was far more modest. When Mercia was weakened by Viking attacks in the ninth century, the Merfynion profited by gaining control of most of Wales, including some lands previously subject to the Mercian kings. They did not gain extensive territories east of Offa's Dyke as the dynasty of Strathclyde took over much of north-western Northumbria. Instead, it was the West Saxons who brought Mercia under their power: first, under Alfred, the western and south-western lands, and then, in the tenth century, the rest. West Saxon power meant that there could be no Welsh counterpart to Cumbrian expansion. As we have seen, the Welsh may well have expanded their territory into Shropshire in the reign of Æthelred II, profiting from that king's inability to repel Scandinavian attacks, yet this expansion was insignificant in comparison with that achieved by their fellow-Britons of the North. Llywelyn ap Seisyll and Gruffudd ap Llywelyn made gains in Tegeingl at the expense of the Mercians, but that was, again, a modest expansion and was partially reversed after Gruffudd's death.[208] The relative power of the West-Saxon kingdom of England when compared with Northumbria is thus one explanation for the territorial and linguistic continuity of Wales. Another, however, is the different fortunes of the Scandinavian and, in particular, Hiberno-Norse settlements in Wales and Cumbria. The Hiberno-Norse settlement in the coastlands of Dumfries and (the modern) Cumberland were more widespread in the tenth century than were the corresponding settlements in Anglesey and Tegeingl and they were more enduring. Wales saw no equivalent to the expansion of the Gallgáedil into Galloway. The shape of Wales in 1064 was caused as much by the history of Britain and Ireland in the Viking era as it was by Welsh resistance to English conquests in the sixth and seventh centuries.

Wales in 1064 was much more British than was Cumbria for two principal reasons: first, because much less Welsh territory had been conquered by Vikings and for a much briefer period, after which Welsh control was reasserted; and, secondly, because there was no expansion of Welsh rule into English Mercia as extensive as that of Cumbria into English Northumbria. Northern Britain between

206 Edmonds, 'Personal Names and the Cult of Patrick', 54.
207 Ibid. 56–7.
208 See above, 365–6.

the ninth and the twelfth century was the graveyard of two languages, Pictish and Cumbric. Even Cornwall, under West Saxon rule since the ninth century, and Brittany, conquered by Charlemagne and his son, kept their Brittonic languages far longer than did Cumbria. At this period, extensive bilingualism, even multilingualism, was more dangerous for the survival of languages than was alien rule. Earlier, after the end of Roman rule, the direction of linguistic change throughout north-western Europe had been towards the consolidation of monolingual populations—at the expense of Celtic languages in Gaul and in England, at the expense of Romance in Wales, Cornwall, and most of Brittany. In twelfth-century Cumbria, whether in the portion under the rule of Scottish kings or the portion within England, the long-term victor among the languages was English, except for Galloway, which retained its Gaelic until the early-modern period.

Appendix: The Chronology of Annales Cambriae and the *Brut*

Chronology in the A version is fixed by (1) years counted from 444 given every decade and (2) *an.* prefixed to each annal (not *Kal.* as in most Irish chronicles); this can be checked (3) by corresponding AU dates, since *AC* is in part derived from the Chronicle of Ireland. These criteria do not always yield the same result. For early entries in the *Brut* but not in any version of *AC*, see the *Brut, Pen. 20 Trans.* p. xlii, where they are listed and briefly discussed. Most, since they have to do with Irish affairs, were fairly clearly in the original grand-daughter of the Chronicle of Ireland (Chronicle of Ireland → Clonmacnois Chronicle of the tenth century → a Welsh copy). *B* and *C* do not use *A*'s decades from 444; chronology after the end of *A* is based purely on a succession of *ann'* for *annus*, namely *A*'s method (2). At this period, the chronicles are not derived from the Chronicle of Ireland and thus (3) does not apply. What is crucial at this period is the use of external controls to fix the AD dates of particular annals. These are usually from English or Irish chronicles, but the English ones especially, the different derivatives from the Anglo-Saxon Chronicle, have their own chronological problems—in particular, they do not all start a new annal from the same day of the year.

The *Brut* has rather more aids. It has its own method of dating by decades only these are not counted from 444 but rather the AD dates are given every ten years, for example, 980, 990, 1000. These are, however, consistently one to two years late when compared with external sources. It also sometimes notes which year it is in a nineteen-year paschal cycle, and these are correct once the two-year correction has been made: thus the corrected date 1007 is indeed the first year in the cycle.

The chronology of the *Brut*

Brut corrected	*Brut* decades	*Brut* 19-year cycle	External controls
956			AU 956.3 (ob. Congalach)
962	960		
972	970		
973			ASC D (Edgar at Chester)

975			ASC (ob. Edgar) AU 975.2 (pilgrimage)
982	980		
983			ASC 983 (ob. Ælfhere)[209]
987			AU 987.1 ?= *AC* C AU 987.2 (cf. ASC 986)
989			AU 989.3 (ob. Glún Iairn)
991	990		
996			AU 996. 1 (but cf. 998. 3)
1000			AU 999. 8 ref. to 1000
1001	1000		
1002			AU 1000.3 (ob. Ímar)
1007		correct 1st of cycle	(cf. AU 1014.1)
1012	1111		
1013			ASC 1013 (flight of Æthelred) ASC 1014 (ob. Swein)
1014			AU 1014. 2 (Clontarf)
1016			ASC 1016 (accession of Cnut)
1022	1020		
1023			AU 1023.7 (ob. Llywelyn)
1026		correct 1st of cycle	
1033	1031		
1035			ASC 1035, AU 1035.1 (ob. Cnut)
1039			AU 1039. 1 (ob. Iago)
1042	1040		
1047			AU 1047. 1 (snow)
1052	1050		
1056			ASC 1055 (battle vs. Ralph)
1058			AT 1058 (Magnus's fleet)
1063	1061		

The external controls confirm Jones's corrected chronology, with just two exceptions, the obit of Ímar of Waterford (1002 in the *Brut*; 1000 in AU and AT), and the battle against Ralph near Hereford in 1055 (1056 in the *Brut*). The latter is easily explained: the *Brut* is likely to have conflated the battle in 1056, in which Gruffudd killed the new bishop of Hereford, with the battle the previous year in which he defeated Ralph. The *Brut* does not refer to the battle against the bishop, but the date 1056 indicates that a source probably noted the events of both 1055 and 1056.

209 The obit provides a terminus for the entry in the Welsh chronicles, not an absolute date.

PART IV

THE WELSH CHURCH AND CULTURE

18

The Organization of the Church

1. BISHOPS

In the early fourth century the Council of Nicaea partly assumed and partly prescribed a congruence between the episcopal organization of the Church and the local organization of the Empire. Each semi-self-governing city and territory was to have its bishop; his see was to be in the city itself, while his authority was to extend as far as the bounds of the city's territory. As the Empire was divided into provinces, so were the bishops to be gathered together in provincial synods at regular intervals under a presiding metropolitan bishop. The three British bishops who attended the Council of Arles in 314 were the bishops of London, York, and, probably, Lincoln, all capitals of fourth-century provinces; they may already have had metropolitan status and would, in any case, have been likely to acquire such a status by the end of the fourth century.[1] There were no archbishops in Gaul or Britain at this period. The bishop who is likely to have come from Lincoln was accompanied by a *presbyter* and a deacon, showing that those three orders were already part of the personnel of an episcopal church. By the time of the Council of Tours in 461, at which Mansuetus, bishop of the Britons, was present, only bishops or their representatives were named among the subscriptions to councils.[2] By the sixth century this pattern of one bishop to a *civitas*, presiding over the other orders, priests, deacons, and the rest, was already traditional in Gaul and can be followed in the works of Gregory of Tours and in the Gallic councils. The *ecclesia* was the bishop's church in the city, what we would call the cathedral;[3] other churches within the walls and in the suburbs were not *ecclesiae* but *basilicae*; those in the suburbs were often associated with cemeteries, in which many of the holy slept in death, and were thus *basilicae sanctorum*. The distribution of English place-names in *eccles*, however, makes it unlikely that *ecclesia* in British Latin always retained the old meaning it has in the work of Gregory of Tours.[4] In the countryside in Gaul well-established churches were called *parochiae*, the source of our term 'parishes' but not meaning the same thing. For Gregory, it was inconceivable that there

[1] *Concilia Galliae, A. 314–A. 506*, ed. C. Munier, 15, 18, 20; H. Williams, *Christianity in Early Britain* (Oxford, 1912), 141–3; J. C. Mann, 'The Administration of Roman Britain', *Antiquity*, 35 (1961), 316–20.

[2] *Concilia*, ed. Munier, 147–8.

[3] *ECI* 249, 378.

[4] K. Cameron, 'Eccles in English Place-Names', in Barley and Hanson (eds.), *Christianity in Britain, 300–700*, 87–92; and see below, 611.

should be a *parochia* in the city; the *parochia* was essentially, and indeed etymologically, in the country away from the city; and the typical *parochia* had more than one priest and might well be headed by an archpriest. It was distinguished from the oratory, a church probably with a single resident priest and without a clerical community, a church likely to have been established by a landowner for himself and his household, and thus sometimes called an 'estate-church' by modern scholars.

The best guide to the situation in late Roman Britain is to compare our scraps of British evidence with the fuller record for Gaul and also for Ireland. In the latter case this is because the early Irish Church was largely created by British missionaries and was for some time under strong British influence. In addition, connections between Ireland and western Britain remained strong right up to the twelfth century. We shall come across some particular examples later. Ireland was never part of the Roman Empire; it was not subject, therefore, to that imperial policy which prescribed that each local people should have an urban centre as its political capital. Even so, the terminology of city versus *parochia* (also spelt *paruchia* and *parrochia*) is attested in Irish sources.[5] This is a strong argument for believing that this terminology was so firmly established in late Roman Britain that it was easier for missionaries in Ireland to find some equivalent for the city than to abandon the conception of church organization of which it was so crucial a part.

From the earliest Irish sources, which include one that belongs to the missionary period, we can detect an assumption that the *parochia* is not, as in Gaul, a particular country church, but rather the entire territory attached to a major church and over which the bishop of that church had jurisdiction and the duty of pastoral care.[6] It is still not quite what we mean by a diocese because it did not include the episcopal centre itself, the equivalent of the late Roman city. On one interpretation, this conception of the bishop and his *parochia* is also attested in Wales, when Asser, in his Life of King Alfred, composed in 893, wrote of St Davids as 'the monastery and *parochia* of Dewi'[7]; this might mean 'the monastery and diocese of St David'; yet, as we shall see, there is another interpretation of Asser's *parochia*. *Parochia* as 'diocese' is also attested, however, in the Synod of Hertford in seventh-century England.[8] The broad contrast between city and *parochia* therefore appears to have worked rather differently north and south of the English Channel: in Frankish Gaul in the sixth century the *parochia* was a particular country church, properly organized and with a group of clerics often headed by an archpriest; in the British Isles, irrespective of whether the population was British or Irish or English, it is usually the entire territory attached to an episcopal church and subject to a bishop. In Ireland and in

[5] *Collectio Canonum Hibernensis*, ed. H. Wasserschleben, *Die irische Kanonensammlung*, 2nd edn. (Leipzig, 1885), i. 22; xx. 2; xxxvii. 14.

[6] 'Synodus I S. Patricii', c. 30, ed. and trans. L. Bieler, *The Irish Penitentials* (Dublin, 1963), 58/59; cf. C. Etchingham, 'The Implications of *Paruchia*', *Ériu*, 44 (1993), 139–62, and his *Church Organization in Ireland, AD 650 to 1000* (Maynooth, 1999), 105–30.

[7] *Asser's Life of King Alfred*, ed. W. H. Stevenson (Oxford, 1904), c. 79.

[8] As in the second decree of the Synod of Hertford, Bede, *Historia Ecclesiastica* [hereafter *HE*], iv. 5.

western Britain, the episcopal *civitas* was likely to consist, in practice, of a major monastery, as at St Davids or at Kildare.[9]

Yet, there are also indications of yet another meaning for *parochia* in Britain, including Anglo-Saxon England, and also in Ireland. Wilfrid, bishop of York, was expelled from his diocese in 678, whereupon Archbishop Theodore divided the huge diocese of York, consecrating Bosa to York (for Deira), Eata to Lindisfarne (for Bernicia), and Eadhæd to Lindsey.[10] Wilfrid immediately appealed to Rome. There were several grounds for the appeal, but one of them was that Archbishop Theodore had consecrated to 'his own *loca* belonging to his *episcopatus*' 'three bishops found from elsewhere and not from the subjects of that *parrochia*'; and the effect of their actions was that King Ecgfrith and Archbishop Theodore had, 'like robbers, deprived him of the possessions with which, for God's sake, kings had endowed him'.[11] This is clarified, and at the same time complicated, by the rather different terms of the appeal Wilfrid is said to have made when he had finally arrived in Rome: if his former diocese, *parrochia*, had to be divided, 'the usurpers' should be driven out, and new bishops should be chosen 'from our own clergy'.[12] Now, it is abundantly evident that Stephen was using *parrochia* in two different senses. One was a normal sense of the word, as found in the acts of the Synod of Hertford: there *parrochia* means diocese, or perhaps rather the territory attached to the see.[13] The other, however, was equivalent to Wilfrid's own property and his supporters, both clergy and monks. This has to be so, since everyone would have known that the bishops consecrated in 678 by Theodore to replace Wilfrid, Eata for the Bernicians, Bosa for the Deirans, and Eadhæd for Lindsey, all belonged to Wilfrid's *parrochia* in the first sense. Taking *parrochia* as diocese, these bishops were not 'found from elsewhere' (*aliunde inuentos*) and were not 'intruders' (*inuasores*). Stephen's account only makes sense if we recognize the systematic ambiguity of the word *parrochia*. In the sense of a community of people and property defined by allegiance to Wilfrid, it stretched beyond the bounds of the diocese, *parrochia*, of York, for Wilfrid had several monasteries in Mercia.

A similar ambiguity was also present in Ireland and, probably, in Wales. When, in 787, the abbot of Clonard 'visited the *paruchia* of the land of Munster', he was very probably visiting the churches, lands, and *manaig* (church-tenants) within the province of Munster that were attached to Clonard, a great monastery of Meath.[14] This *paruchia* was outside the province to which Clonard itself belonged and cannot have been part of a territorially unified diocese centred on the monastery. Yet, earlier in the same century, *parochia* retained the meaning of a territory subject

[9] *Vita S. Dauid*, § 41, ed. and trans. Sharpe and Davies, 136–7; cf. *Vita S. Cadoci*, § 13, ed. A. W. Wade-Evans, *Vitae Sanctorum Britanniae et Genealogiae*, History and Law Series 9 (Cardiff, 1944), 54: 'Dauid . . . magnam sinodum in Ciuitate Breeui congregauit.'

[10] *HE* iv. 12.

[11] *VW*, c. 24.

[12] *VW*, c. 30; C. Cubitt, 'Wilfrid's "Usurping Bishops": Episcopal Elections in Anglo-Saxon England *c.*600–*c.*800', *Northern History*, 25 (1989), 18–38.

[13] Bede, *HE* iv. 5 (canons 2 and 6). The cautionary note is because of the older sense, still preserved in Hiberno-Latin of the period, in which the *urbs* or *civitas* is distinct from the *parochia* attached to it.

[14] AU 787. 5.

to a bishop, the equivalent of our 'diocese'.[15] In the seventh century it was also used for the jurisdiction over the whole island claimed by Kildare and Armagh.[16] There was, therefore, a considerable flexibility in the use of the term.

With this in mind, we may return to Asser. The context of his reference to 'the monastery and *parochia* of St David' was the injuries perpetrated by Hyfaidd, king of Dyfed, on St Davids. Hyfaidd plundered the monastery and the *parochia*, and he also expelled its bishops, for example 'Archbishop Nobis my kinsman', and members of the community, including Asser himself. The immediate context of Asser's *parochia* of St David is thus the economic and personal injuries committed by Hyfaidd. *Parochia* may refer, as we have seen, to the lands, local rights, and persons belonging to a great ecclesiastical lordship and this may be its meaning here. If we take Asser's *parochia* as 'diocese', the sequence of thought runs less easily, since it is very likely that the diocese of St Davids included the whole of Hyfaidd's kingdom. The plunder taken by Hyfaidd was the particular property of St Davids rather than the property of others within the diocese. There is no reason to think that there is any difference between this use of *parochia* and Asser's later reference to Alfred's gift to him of 'Exeter with all the *parochia* belonging to it in England and in Cornwall'.[17]

This compels us to ask a crucial question, namely, was the post-Roman Church in Celtic Britain organized in essentially the same way as in sixth-century Gaul, even if one has to allow for differences of terminology, as in the case of *parochia*? From the modern historian's point of view, it would be helpful if the answer were an unambiguous 'yes'. The same governmental assumptions had, after all, been inherited by both. Just as the Arverni of the Auvergne, a Gaulish people, came to have their urban centre at Clermont, and therefore by the fourth century their bishop was there also, so too Venta Silurum, Caerwent, was the capital of the Silures. Its status as the *civitas*-capital is exemplified by the inscription put up by the *ordo*, the local aristocratic council;[18] likewise, its importance in the late Roman period is shown by the way it gave its name to the kingdom of Gwent.[19] In the period up to the ninth century, Gwent seems to have embraced both what later remained as Gwent and also Glamorgan or Glywysing, and it sometimes had that wider meaning even later.[20] Similarly there should have been a bishop of the Demetae at Moridunum, the later Carmarthen.[21] It is less easy to say what will have been the situation further north, since it is unclear where the capitals of the

[15] *Hib.* i. 8, 22.

[16] Cogitosus, *Vita Brigidae*, Prologue (ed. Bollandists, *Acta Sanctorum*, Feb. i. 135); *Liber Angeli*, § 28, ed. Bieler, *The Patrician Texts from the Book of Armagh*, 188.

[17] Asser, *Life of King Alfred*, c. 81; O. J. Padel, 'Asser's *Parochia* of Exeter', in F. L. Edmonds and P. Russell (eds.), *Tome: Studies in Medieval Celtic History and Law in Honour of Thomas Charles-Edwards* (Woodbridge, 2011), 65–72.

[18] *RIB*, No. 311 = A. R. Burn, *The Romans in Britain: An Anthology of Inscriptions*, 2nd edn. (Oxford, 1969), no. 67.

[19] *Vita I S. Samsonis*, i. 1 (ed. P. Flobert, *La Vie ancienne de Saint Samson de Dol* (Paris, 1997), 146).

[20] For the complexities, see W. Davies, *An Early Welsh Microcosm* (London, 1978), 65–98. Glywysing is likely to have been, in origin, a dynastic name and thus not on the same level as Gwent.

[21] *RIB* no. 412.

Ordovices and the Deceangli were; and they may well never have had them at all, remaining under military rule; but Wroxeter is likely to have had a bishop, and so also, perhaps, did the old legionary fortress at Chester.[22] Gwynedd is especially problematic, since it was a creation of the post-Roman period.

If the British Church were like the Church of Gaul, it should also have had ecclesiastical provinces headed by a metropolitan bishop (not to be confused at this stage with an archbishop). It is probable, as we have seen, that the bishops of London, York, and (probably) Lincoln, who attended the Council of Arles in 314, did so because those cities were the capitals of their respective imperial provinces; and these imperial provinces were therefore in process of begetting their ecclesiastical counterparts. The concept of a metropolitan bishop with his province is well attested in eighth-century Ireland;[23] and this makes it more likely than not that there were ecclesiastical provinces in Britain by *c.* 500.

If we then compare the presumed situation in South Wales *c.* 400 with the actual situation after our period, *c.* 1150, there is a resemblance in the scale of the bishoprics, one for the south-east and another for the south-west, but no resemblance in where those bishops had their sees: instead of Caerwent we have Llandaff; instead of Carmarthen St Davids. What is perhaps more serious, it can be shown that the resemblance in the area covered by the bishoprics does not indicate a direct continuity. What the Norman rearrangement of dioceses effected in South Wales was essentially the reversal of changes which had occurred between 400 and the seventh century. Very broadly, the situation obtaining in 1150 by which the Welsh Church was divided between four dioceses resembled the situation that can probably be posited for the late fourth century, but it was markedly different from the pattern obtaining in the early medieval period.

Crucial evidence for this contrast comes from a letter of Aldhelm, written when he was still abbot of Malmesbury—that is, before 705, when he became bishop of Sherborne but possibly to be dated as early as the 670s.[24] It was addressed to Geraint, king of Dumnonia, and to his *sacerdotes*. Dumnonia, it should be noticed, was a kingdom which was a continuation of a Romano-British *civitas*, a city-cum-territory (I shall call it a city-territory for short). It should have had its capital and therefore its episcopal see at Exeter.[25] We can fairly safely assume that a single bishop is what Dumnonia had by the end of the fourth century. *Sacerdos* can refer to priests as well as bishops: for example, the early eighth-century *Collectio Canonum Hibernensis*, in its Book I, 'On the bishop', remarks, 'It should be noted that *episcopi* are called *sacerdotes*, and also *prespiteri* are assigned the name of *sacerdotes*.'[26] Viventius and Mavorius at Kirkmadrine were *sacerdotes* and may have been

[22] On the assumption that it was ecclesiastically independent of Wroxeter; for the latter see *RIB* no. 288.

[23] *ECI* 126.

[24] Aldhelm, Letter IV, ed. R. Ehwald, *Aldhelmi Opera Omnia*, MGH AA xv (Berlin, 1919), 481, 484, trans. M. Lapidge and M. Herren, *Aldhelm: The Prose Works* (Ipswich, 1979), 155, 158.

[25] Cf. P. Salway, *Roman Britain* (Oxford, 1981), 495 n. 3.

[26] *Collectio Canonum Hibernensis*, ed. H. Wasserschleben, *Die irische Kanonensammlung* (Leipzig, 1885), i. 1.

bishops.[27] In this letter, Aldhelm seems to use *sacerdotes* for bishops: at the beginning of the letter he writes that he had been present at a council of *episcopi*, but then notes in the same sentence that, at this council, a great company of *sacerdotes* had assembled. The *sacerdotes* appear to be the same as the *episcopi*; and this suggests that Lapidge and Herren, in their translation, were right to render both by 'bishops'. If this is correct, by the late seventh century, Dumnonia had a plurality of bishops. Aldhelm addressed himself, as directed by a council of bishops in England, to 'all the bishops (*sacerdotes*) of God abiding throughout Dumnonia'; it would be natural to assume that bishops address bishops rather than priests. Similarly he remarks that 'the bishops (*sacerdotes*) of Dyfed . . . detest our communion'. Two old Romano-British city-territories, both now kingdoms, had a plurality of bishops.

Supporting evidence comes from Bede's account of the negotiations between Augustine of Canterbury and the Britons; and this is especially important because of the ambiguity of the term *sacerdos* in Aldhelm's letter.[28] The situation faced by Augustine and his British opposite numbers was, as we saw in Chapter 12, a virtually inescapable but most unfortunate side effect of Gregory the Great's plans for the mission to the English. The mission was possible because the Pope could work via the Franks of Burgundy and Austrasia so as to send a mission to the king of Kent, Æthelberht, the son-in-law of a former Frankish king.[29] The Franks did not want to mount their own mission but were happy to support one coming from Rome.[30] Gregory the Great had high hopes for his mission precisely because Æthelberht had a powerful position in southern England. Moreover, his proposed organization of his new Church, once it was fully off the ground, envisaged a revival of a Roman pattern: the metropolitan bishops were to be at London and York, probably reflecting the division between the third-century provinces of Britannia Inferior, with its capital at York, and Britannia Superior, with its capital at London.[31] It looks as though Gregory cannot have had access to a document which would have given him the fourth-century division, since he could then have made separate provision for a metropolitan province roughly reproducing the western province of Britannia Prima and that would have gone some way to solving the problem of the Britons.[32] Whatever the precise reason, the effect of a mission that came through Francia to Kent, in the south-east corner of the island, was to precipitate a conflict between Augustine, claiming authority over the British bishops through Gregory's express instructions,[33] and the Britons themselves, who are unlikely to have been willing to subject themselves to a metropolitan

[27] See above, 141.

[28] Bede, *HE* ii. 2, on which see the excellent commentary by C. Stancliffe, 'The British Church and the Mission of Augustine', in R. Gameson (ed.), *Saint Augustine and the Conversion of England* (Stroud, 1999), 124–34.

[29] The initial scheme is likely to have been hatched when Childebert II was ruling both Burgundy and Austrasia (593–596); see I. N. Wood, 'The Mission of Augustine of Canterbury', *Speculum*, 69 (1994), 1–17.

[30] Gregory, *Reg.* vi. 51, 60.

[31] See above, 398.

[32] See map VII in P. Salway, *Roman Britain*.

[33] Bede, *HE* i. 27 (Interrogatio VII).

bishop closely associated with an ambitious English overking.[34] Bede evidently had a good source for his account of the negotiations; whatever its ultimate origin, it probably came to him from Canterbury, but it shows a close interest in, and even some very mild and limited understanding of, the British reaction to Augustine. The first two stages of the affair are what concern us. In the first, Augustine used the good offices of King Æthelberht to arrange a meeting with, in Bede's words, 'the bishops and teachers of the neighbouring British kingdom'.[35] At this point only one British kingdom was involved; but that one kingdom had a plurality both of bishops and of teachers, *doctores*, present at the meeting. These bishops and teachers were unwilling to take a decision on their own, so a subsequent synod was arranged at which more British kingdoms would be represented. Bede, citing an unnamed source, says that 'there came, as it is related, seven British bishops and many very learned men, especially from their most distinguished monastery, which is called in English *Bancornaburg*, over which Dinoot is said to have ruled as abbot at that time'. The impression given is that the rise in numbers on this second occasion was not so much achieved by the participation of many more bishops as a great increase in the number of learned men present; but it would be hard to suppose that seven British bishoprics at the level of an entire major kingdom, reflecting the ancient *civitas*, were represented at this synod. Moreover, there is no need to search for seven major kingdoms, such as Dyfed or Gwent, since we already know from Bede's account of the earlier synod that one kingdom could send more than one bishop. Bede's account thus confirms the interpretation given above of Aldhelm's letter, by which his *sacerdotes* were bishops, and also adds something extra to what Aldhelm's letter revealed, namely the right of ecclesiastical scholars to participate as full members of synods.[36] The kingdom, often continuing an old Roman-British city-territory as we have seen, remained an important unit in ecclesiastical as well as secular affairs, but its supreme ecclesiastical authority appears to have been a synod rather than a single bishop; to such a synod both bishops and learned men belonged; and where an issue proved too difficult for one such synod, it might be remitted to be decided by a larger synod embracing more than one kingdom. The authority of ecclesiastical scholars may have had its beginnings in Antiquity: in some areas the title *doctor* was simply another term for the bishop, but in others it was distinct.[37] It would be easier to understand the post-Roman situation in Britain if, in the fourth century, its *doctores* had been distinct from its bishops.

What is striking is that the conclusion to which I have just come might be taken as a paraphrase of the relevant section of the *Collectio Canonum Hibernensis*, compiled between 716 and 725. In Ireland, too, the counterparts of such kingdoms

[34] Cf. Bede, *HE* ii.5.

[35] 'Kingdom' translates Bede's *prouincia* in *HE* ii. 2, which is not to be confused with the metropolitan province.

[36] In England or in Francia others might attend synods but they did not subscribe to any decrees unless they deputized for bishops; Aldhelm himself wrote the letter to Geraint because he had just attended such a synod and had been asked to make the approach.

[37] J. Gaudemet, *L'Église dans l'empire romain, IVe–Ve siècles*, Historie du droit et des institutions de l'Église en Occident, gen. ed. G. Le Bras (Paris, 1958), 102.

as Dumnonia or Dyfed might contain more than one bishop; and a synod might be attended by ecclesiastical scholars as well as bishops.[38] As Huw Pryce has shown, there is some evidence indicating a relatively early reception of this collection in Wales, just as it is well attested in Brittany by the ninth century.[39] All this, together with Bede's evidence, suggests that the change away from the late Roman pattern of one bishop to one city-territory had occurred in the fifth and sixth centuries, during the period in which Ireland was converted. It would not have been surprising if there had been some division of old city-territories. In Frankish Gaul, Gregory of Tours thought that Dijon should have been made into an episcopal city; and, at the same period, Châteaudun briefly made itself independent of Chartres.[40] What is surprising is that the change seems to have been general, attested both in Dumnonia and in Dyfed, and also in Ireland. It was not caused by a collapse of the city-territory itself, since such territories frequently became kingdoms, as they did both in Dumnonia and in Dyfed.

Up to now I have tried the strategy of moving from Roman Britain forwards in time, but now I shall turn to examine the contemporary evidence from after the post-Roman period and also, with caution, move from the twelfth century backwards. This will consider four aspects of the major churches: first the bond between church and patron-saint; secondly, the link between a bishop and his church; thirdly, the role of the cemetery attached to a church; and finally the membership of the church community.

As is well known, the English and Welsh names of St Davids express different aspects of the church: St Davids, and also the Welsh Tyddewi, express a connection with a saint, whereas Mynyw is topographical.[41] Although the attestation of the name Tyddewi is late, the association of church and saint was made by Asser in the late ninth century: his church was the *monasterium* of St Dewi.[42] Similarly, with a church that attained episcopal status in the twelfth century, St Asaph's expresses a relationship with the saint, but Llanelwy is topographical, the *llan* by the River Elwy.

The best example of the role of the saint as patron of church and community comes from one of the documents added in the margins of the Lichfield Gospels when that manuscript was at Llandeilo Fawr in Carmarthenshire in the ninth and early tenth centuries. The fifth of these documents was discussed above—the manumission of one Bleiddudd ap Sulien in exchange for a payment of 4 pounds and 8 ounces of silver.[43] The clerical witness list was headed by Nobis, *episcopus*

[38] T. M. Charles-Edwards, *Early Christian Ireland* (Cambridge, 2000), 265–81.

[39] H. Pryce, 'Early Irish Canons and Medieval Welsh Law', *Peritia*, 5 (1986), 107–27; see also below, 641–2.

[40] Gregory of Tours, *Hist.*, iii. 19; vii. 17; Council of Paris, AD 573, ed. C. de Clercq, *Concilia Galliae, A. 511–A. 695*, CCSL 148A (Turnhout, 1963), 212–17.

[41] On Tyddewi, see T. Roberts, 'Welsh Ecclesiastical Place-Names and Archaeology', in Edwards and Lane, *The Early Church in Wales and the West*, 43, who notes that it is only recorded from the fifteenth century but is paralleled by such Irish names for churches as Tech Munnu 'Munnu's house', Taghmon.

[42] Cf. 'episcopus Dauid Lunberth nomine', *The Text of the Book of Llan Dâv*, 237b (p. 238).

[43] *LL* xlvi, and see above, 247.

Teiliau and *Saturnguid sacerdos Teiliav*. Anyone who flouted the terms of the contract was threatened with the curse of God and of Teilo 'in whose gospel book it has been written'. Another of the documents in the Lichfield Gospels refers to the original gift of the gospel book 'on the altar of Saint Teilo'; and here one needs to remember that one church might have altars dedicated to different saints, as shown for the twelfth century by Llywelyn Fardd's *awdl* in praise of Cadfan of Tywyn.[44] Yet another document in the Lichfield Gospels refers to the community as the *familia*, the household, of Teilo.[45] Land and food-renders given to Llandeilo were given to God and to St Teilo.[46] At Llandeilo Fawr in the ninth century the identification of church, land, and community with the patron-saint was complete: the bishop and the *sacerdos* (here apparently a rough equivalent to the modern dean of a cathedral) were the bishop and the *sacerdos* of Teilo; the community was the saint's community; the gospel book, having been placed on Teilo's altar by the original donor, became the property of the saint, and documents written into it had his sanction behind them.[47]

To judge by the witness lists in the documents written into the Lichfield Gospels, Llandeilo Fawr did not always have a bishop at its head. The *sacerdos* heads the clerical witness list in nos. 3 and 4; only in no. 5 does Teilo's bishop appear. It is entirely possible that this evidence is somewhat deceptive: Teilo had other churches apart from Llandeilo Fawr and his bishop could not always be present there, even if it was his principal church: his role as an itinerant supreme pastor is likely to have been complemented by that of the *sacerdos*, permanently resident and thus responsible for the liturgy. On the other hand, the evidence accords very well with the Irish situation, where an episcopal church enjoyed its high rank even if it did not currently have a living bishop.[48] It was enough that it had had bishops, that those bishops lay buried in the cemetery of the church, and that it might again have a bishop.[49] Some churches were episcopal in that they had been the sees of bishops even though there was little expectation that they would again be ruled by bishops. Coleraine seems to have been an early example, a bishop's see in the second half of the sixth century but living on past glory by the late seventh.[50] The very greatest churches might have an uninterrupted succession of bishops—St Davids is a likely example—but other churches might only have resident bishops at intervals.[51]

Similarly, while Asser's evidence indicates that the bishop of Mynyw was the principal bishop of St David, it does not prove that there was no other bishop of St David. Asser describes his kinsman, Nobis, as archbishop, a term to which we

44 Chad 1; CBT ii. 1. 25–6.

45 Chad 2.

46 Chad 3.

47 He heads the witness list in Chad 2; his curse forms part of the sanction in Chad 5.

48 *ECI* 132–3; and cf. poetic families without a current poet, *Uraicecht na Ríar*, ed. and trans. L. Breatnach (Dublin, 1987), §§ 7–9.

49 *Collectio Canonum Hibernensis*, ed. Wasserschleben, xliv.8 (and the expanded version from Redaction B).

50 *ECI* 55–60.

51 Gerald of Wales claimed to have a continuous list of the bishops of St Davids: *Itinerarium Kambrie*, ii. 1 (ed. J. Dymock, *Giraldi Cambrensis Opera*, vi. 102–4).

shall return shortly. A charter discussed above, recording a grant made by Æthelred the Unready in 1005 to 'the episcopal church' of Dewistow suggests that other churches than Mynyw might be both episcopal and also be St David's churches.[52] The grant was of land at Over, on the English side of the Severn estuary, very close to where the M4 approaches the bridge. Just on the Welsh side of the estuary is a place called Dewstow, earlier Dewistow. It used to be thought that the church which was the beneficiary of Æthelred's grant must be St Davids;[53] it was, after all, episcopal, and everyone knew that St David's bishop was to be found at St Davids; but the topography prompted Dorothy Whitelock to propose that Dewistow was indeed the Dewistow lying only a few miles from Over.[54] Dewistow simply means 'St David's place'; and if it was episcopal, as it is described in the charter, it is possible that a bishop of St David might be found there, in Gwent Is Coed, as well as at Mynyw. This does not mean that one would always find a bishop there, only that it was a church capable of having a bishop.

There may be a connection here with the development attested by Aldhelm and Bede, whereby a single former city-territory, now a kingdom, might have more than one bishop. That would allow, for example, Gwent to have both a bishop of St David and also a bishop of, say, St Teilo.[55] If the *familiae* of David and Teilo had both acquired churches within Gwent which were of episcopal status, they might well both have their bishops within the one kingdom. An Irish parallel may help to give concrete shape to these uncertain inferences. In 875 the Annals of Ulster recorded the death of two bishops of Kildare, the leading church of Leinster: Robartach was bishop of Kildare and also head of the church of Cell Achaid in the far north-west of Leinster; Lachtnán was bishop of Kildare and head of the church of Ferns in south-east Leinster. Lachtnán (the one mentioned second) may have been bishop for less than a year and so died in the same calendar year as his predecessor, but the way they combined their positions at Kildare with responsibilities elsewhere allows for another interpretation. According to this second view, both Robartach and Lachtnán were members of the community of Kildare, they were both bishops at the same time, and their episcopal status thus added to the prestige of their church. It was important to Kildare that they were bishops of Kildare. On the other hand, their headships of the churches of Cell Achaid and Ferns sustained the position of Kildare in another way, showing how its men held power right across the province. This example is not unique: an earlier annal entry for 787 also records the obits of two bishops of Kildare.

An example, covering the period up to the mid-eleventh century, of the bishop of a saint, and of the churches and people owing allegiance to that saint, is preserved

[52] For the two versions of the charter, ed. N. R. Ker, 'Hemming's Cartulary', in R. W. Hunt, W. A. Pantin, and R. W. Southern (eds.), *Studies in Medieval History presented to F. M. Powicke* (Oxford, 1948), 73–4, see above, 254–6.

[53] So Ker, 'Hemming's Cartulary', 73; H. P. R. Finberg, *The Early Charters of the West Midlands* (Leicester, 1961), no. 147; S 913.

[54] D. Whitelock, *English Historical Documents, c.500–1042*, 1st edn. (London, 1955), 352.

[55] Since *esgob Dewi* should normally mean 'the bishop of Dewi' rather than 'a bishop of Dewi', it might be proposed that there would only be one bishop of a given saint within one kingdom.

in a short text from a Douai manuscript.[56] 'These are the names of the bishops of the community (*clas*) of Cynidr: *Brecchert, Keneder*... [10 names] ... *Tremerin*, and from there he departed to Hereford'. The last part of this list is confirmed by an entry in the C and D versions of the Anglo-Saxon Chronicle under 1055: 'In the same year died Tremerig, the Welsh bishop, soon after the devastation [24 October]—he was Bishop Athelstan's deputy after he became infirm.'[57] The principal church of St Cynidr was Glasbury, Y Glas ar Wy, 'The community on the Wye'.[58] But he also had churches in Archenfield, at Kenderchurch, and Llangynidr in Brycheiniog.[59] Cynidr is said to have been from Maelienydd, one of the lands 'between the Wye and the Severn'. Glasbury was in Elfael, on the north side of the Wye and thus in *Rhwng Gwy a Hafren*. On the other hand, according to the *Generatio S. Eguini*, Cynidr was a brother of Egwine, the saint of Llaneigion (Llanigon), on the other side of the Wye, and of St Cadog of Llancarfan, who also had churches at Llangatwg and Llanspyddig in Brycheiniog;[60] and in Lifris's Life of Cadog Cynidr appears as a witness for Cadog to guarantee the sanctuary obtained from Arthur, Maelgwn, Rhun, and Rhain.[61] The supposed kinship of Cynidr, Cadog, and Egwine is a formula expressing an alliance between their churches, an alliance whose significance is clear from the topographical closeness of their churches and from the way that Cynidr's churches crossed the boundary between Elfael and Brycheiniog and extended east into Ergyng. Glasbury may have been the principal church of Elfael, while the saint was attributed to Maelienydd, Elfael's northern neighbour, but the significance of Cynidr's bishop was not limited to one *cantref* or *gwlad*.

Two Welsh archbishops are attested from the ninth century: Asser's kinsman Nobis, whose see was St Davids; and, in *Annales Cambriae*, *s.a.* 809, the obit of Elfoddw, 'archbishop of the land of Gwynedd'. It is striking that our two Welsh archbishops belonged respectively to the south-west and the north-west of the country. The scale of Elfoddw's authority corresponds to the *civitas* and its territory in late Antiquity, all the more so if we remember the inscription in which Gwynedd appeared as a *civitas* with its complement of 'citizens'.[62] From this starting point, the natural deduction would be that an archbishop stood to lesser bishops within a major kingdom, such as Gwynedd, as a major king, a king of Gwynedd, stood to lesser kings, a *brenin* to a mere *rhi*. The position of an archbishop would be the corollary of the plurality of bishops within a former *civitas* discussed above. Yet, there may be more to this title than that. From 735 England, too, was divided between two archbishops, of Canterbury and York. In Ireland, in the seventh century, Armagh in the north and Kildare in the south-east had both claimed to

[56] L. Fleuriot, 'Varia: I. Les Éveques de la "Clas Kenedyr", évêché disparu de la région de Hereford', *Études Celtiques*, 15 (1976–8), 225–6.

[57] *EHD* ii, no. 1, *s.a.* 1055.

[58] SO 177 391.

[59] Kenderchurch, *Lann Cinitr*, *LL* 277: SO 403 284; Llangynidr: SO 155 194.

[60] *EWGT* 21; *Vita S. Cadoci*, § 11, for the saint and Brycheiniog.

[61] Llangatwg, SO 200 179, a parish in the deanery of Brecon Third Part, *PW* 37, and Llanspyddid SO 012 282, a parish in the deanery of Brecon First Part, *PW* 37; *Vita S. Cadoci*, §§ 22, 25.

[62] See above, 177–8.

be archbishoprics, superior to mere metropolitan bishoprics. Between 669 and 735 the issue of archbishoprics had been very much alive in England and Ireland; and it is possible that the two Welsh archbishops may be an echo of those grand causes in the neighbouring countries. The title 'archbishop' strongly indicates such a link, since it was only used in the British Isles from the late seventh century.[63] Even before the title 'archbishop' was introduced, there could have been superior bishops of, say, Dyfed or Gwent, alongside more local bishops, and these superior bishops may have been called 'high bishops' or 'metropolitan bishops' as in Ireland. Only subsequently did they acquire the new title of 'archbishop'.

Some pattern of this kind, with two grades of bishop, may indeed be true of the south-east. The Book of Llandaff claimed that there was a single succession of bishops whose authority covered all the lands between the Wye and the Tywi; yet this claim is unlikely to be true.[64] One of the bishops in its list was Cyfeilliog, assigned to the early tenth century.[65] He is very likely indeed to have been the Cyfeilliog recorded in the A version of the Anglo-Saxon Chronicle as having been captured in 914 by a Viking fleet brought from Brittany by two leaders, Ohter and Hroald, taken to the ships, and then ransomed by Edward the Elder for £40. He is described as bishop of Archenfield.[66] The grants made to him suggest that he was also active in Gwent. Indeed, he may have played a similar role to Tremerin of Clas Cynidr—that is, he may have been primarily bishop of Gwent or part of Gwent but have ministered with the consent of the bishop of Hereford to the inhabitants of Ergyng, who long remained Welsh in language and custom, even though under English rule. An English source might then think of him as bishop of Archenfield, the Welsh Ergyng.

Some progress can be made with the south-eastern bishops of the tenth century by tracing links between episcopal households. In many of the charters of this period, titles are given to the principal members of the episcopal household: *sacerdos* (sometimes *presbyter*), *lector* (occasionally *scriptor*), responsible for teaching, and *equonimus*, responsible for the economic needs of the community. If two bishops had, in their *familiae*, the same persons as principal office-holders, there is a good chance that their bishoprics were the same. In this way *Libiau* (Llifio), Wulfrith, and Pater can be linked through *Dimin* (*Diuin*), their *sacerdos*, and *Dissaith*, their *lector*.[67] There was a change of *equonimus*: Cerennyr under Llifio was succeeded by

[63] A. Thacker, 'Gallic or Greek? Archbishops in England from Theodore to Ecgberht', in P. Fouracre and D. Ganz (eds.), *Frankland: The Franks and the World of the Early Middle Ages. Essays in Honour of Dame Jinty Nelson* (Manchester, 2008), 44–69; *ECI*, ch. 10.

[64] Davies, *An Early Welsh Microcosm*, 150–9.

[65] *LL* contains an obit, 927, after 237a. He may be the priest Cyfeilliog who annotated the Cambridge Juvencus manuscript: H. McKee, *The Cambridge Juvencus Manuscript Glossed in Latin, Old Welsh, and Old Irish: Text and Commentary* (Aberystwyth, 2000), 27–9.

[66] ASC A, originally 914, changed to 918, 'Cameleac biscop on Ircinga felda'. For the use of *on*, cf. 909 (> 910), 'Her feng Friðestan to biscopdome on Winteceastre'. The A version, the Parker Chronicle, is the one aligned with Edward the Elder, the ransomer.

[67] *LL* 237b, 239 (Llifio), 222, 223, 224 (Wulfrith), 217, 218, 221 (Pater). It should be noted that the twelfth-century Llandaff sequence appears to be the reverse of the historical one; and Bishops Nudd and Cyfeilliog were inserted between Wulfrith and Llifio.

Cynwal (*Congual, Cingual*) under Wulfrith and Pater.[68] The bishop who succeeded Pater, Gwgon, still had *Dissaith* as his *lector* at the beginning of his episcopate, but he seems then to have been succeeded by *Eidef lector urbis Guenti*, namely *Eidef*, *lector* of Caerwent.[69] This was the church in which Asser was tended in the previous century, when for a little over a year he was gravely ill.[70] It may be that *Eidef* was described as being 'of Caerwent' because that was not the normal base of this episcopal community. Wendy Davies suggested that either Llandogo (on the west bank of the Wye in Gwent Is Coed) or St Maughan's (in Gwent Uwch Coed) was the see of these tenth-century bishops.[71] The reference in one charter to King Nowy ap Gwriad despoiling *Arcoit* the son of *Dissaith* in Treleck argues in favour of Llandogo; *Dissaith* the *lector* was one of the witnesses of this charter, issued during the episcopate of Pater.[72]

The witness lists, therefore, suggest a succession to a single bishopric, Llifio—Wulfrith—Pater—Gwgon. The extent of this bishopric is not entirely clear. First, Morgan ab Owain was, as we saw in Chapter 16, king of Glywysing with Gwent for much of the century, from no later than 931 until his death in 974.[73] Considering the length of his reign, it is remarkable that no charters recording grants made by him were recorded in the Book of Llandaff.[74] The relationship of our succession of tenth-century bishops to the principal king of the period thus remains obscure. Their grants came from different kings. Llifio was associated with a brother of Morgan, Gruffudd ab Owain, who died in 935 and seems to have ruled Gŵyr;[75] Wulfrith was associated with another of Morgan's brothers, Cadwgon, and the grant concerned Merthyr Mawr at the south-eastern end of the district of Margam (*in Marcan*);[76] Wulfrith was thus active in western Glywysing. In two other charters, however, Wulfrith was associated with another sub-king, perhaps also in Glywysing, Cadell ab Arthfael;[77] and Pater dealt with a sub-king, Nowy ap Gwriad, who appears to have been based in Gwent.[78] A possible interpretation is that this bishopric covered all the south-east.

The situation before Llifio is unclear. He may well have overlapped with Cyfeilliog, who had predecessors in Nudd and Cerennyr. Cyfeilliog's household was quite different from those of Llifio and his successors. It seems to split his episcopate into early and late periods. In the later period, *Catgen* was his *lector*, but he did not appear in the witness lists after Cyfeilliog. In the earlier period, *Bleinguid*

68 Cerennyr was given his title in *LL* 239 but is also among the clerical witnesses in 237b. Cynwal is given his title in 217 (Pater), but is present in two charters during Wulfrith's episcopate, 223 and 224.

69 *LL* 245 (*Dissaith*), 244 and 243 (*Eidef*).

70 Asser, *Life of King Alfred*, c. 79.

71 Davies, *A Welsh Microcosm*, 154.

72 *LL* 217.

73 See above, 515, 538.

74 As Wendy Davies notes, *Llandaff Charters*, 125, *LL* 240 is not a proper charter: it is a narrative introducing a series of boundary clauses of estates that are said to have been restored to Llandaff by Morgan; there is no witness list.

75 *LL* 239.

76 *LL* 224.

77 *LL* 222, 223.

78 *LL* 217, 218, 221.

(who may have been *Catgen*'s father) and *Tuted* were prominent and were both inherited from the household of Bishop Cerennyr, while *Tuted* also appeared in the household of Bishop Nudd.[79] Nudd himself is likely to have been the *lector* in the household of Bishop Grecielis, and a cleric of the same name was also important under Cerennyr.[80] In the whole period from the mid-ninth century to *c.* 920, the attested overlap between episcopal households, the number of clerical witnesses shared between bishops, *c.* 850–*c.* 920, was as follows:[81]

Cerennyr—Nudd	12
Cerennyr—Grecielis	7
Nudd—Grecielis	5
Cerennyr—Cyfeilliog	3
Nudd—Cyfeilliog	3

One might suppose from the high number of shared witnesses that Nudd must have succeeded Cerennyr, who in turn succeeded Grecielis. This was not, however, the conclusion that Wendy Davies drew. For her Grecielis was active in Gwent and Ergyng, as was Nudd, his former *lector*, and also Cyfeilliog. Cerennyr, however, was active over the south-east as a whole; and she suggested that in some of the charters in which Nudd's name followed that of Cerennyr, he might have witnessed as a local bishop, while Cerennyr witnessed as the superior bishop.[82] This may well be the case, but the degree of overlap in the households would then indicate that these two bishops operated out of the same church, just as we saw earlier Kildare providing the base for two bishops, one for north-west Leinster, the other for the south-east.

The possibility of the existence of two grades of bishop, one local, the other more wide-ranging, and, secondly, of an episcopal church as one which can have a bishop but does not necessarily always have one, may help us to understand another puzzling text, 'The Seven Bishop-Houses of Dyfed'.[83] This is undated, but it appears to stem from a period at which Dyfed remained a Welsh kingdom, and may thus be put before the Norman conquest of 1093. It was preserved in some lawbooks, apparently as an interesting antiquarian item—an item which was, however, of possible contemporary use in that it upheld the primacy of St Davids among Welsh churches.[84] It lists seven churches all of which deserved the title of

[79] Davies, *Llandaff Charters*, 61–3.

[80] Ibid. 59–62, *LL* 169b, 170. Grecielis was placed much earlier in *LL* because his charters came from a different archive from those from which the documents of his successors derived.

[81] Ibid. 70–1. I have subtracted the laymen from her figures.

[82] Davies, *Llandaff Charters*, 71, referring to *LL* 199b ii, 214, 216a, and 216b. In 216b Nudd also follows *Nouis*, but he may also have been a local bishop, the Nobis whom the compilers made into the nineteenth bishop of Llandaff, *LL* 217. In 214 Nudd follows the three abbots, of Illtud, Cadog, and *Docunni*, but their insertion is suspect since their names are in the ablative, not in the nominative as in the rest of the list: Davies, *Llandaff Charters*, 119.

[83] T. M. Charles-Edwards, 'The Seven Bishop-Houses of Dyfed', *BBCS* 24 (1970–2), 247–62; H. Pryce, *Native Law and the Church* (Oxford, 1993), 146–7, 179, 188 n.

[84] Cf. R. R. Davies, *Conquest, Coexistence, and Change*, 188–91.

esgopty, 'bishop-house'. On the other hand, the heads of all of them, apart from Mynyw, are called abbots rather than bishops. One way to interpret this apparent contradiction is to suppose that, in the eyes of the lawyer who composed the text, the six churches apart from Mynyw were known to be of episcopal status because they had bishops buried in their cemeteries. There may have been little or no expectation that they would again have living bishops as their heads, but their episcopal character nonetheless remained. The explanation can hardly be that these were churches with communities, each headed by an abbot, but all subject to the one bishop of St Davids because they lay in Dyfed, since there were plenty of other churches within Dyfed that would then have qualified for the same title. Moreover, there is no reason to think that these seven churches included all the major churches of Dyfed: that is evidently not the case, since they do not, for example, include Nevern, centre of the cult of St Brynach, very strong in the cantref of Cemais, or the important Teilo church of Penally, both of them associated with pre-Norman sculpture. The point of the text is that these seven were churches of specially high status and that this high status was linked with their being in some way episcopal.

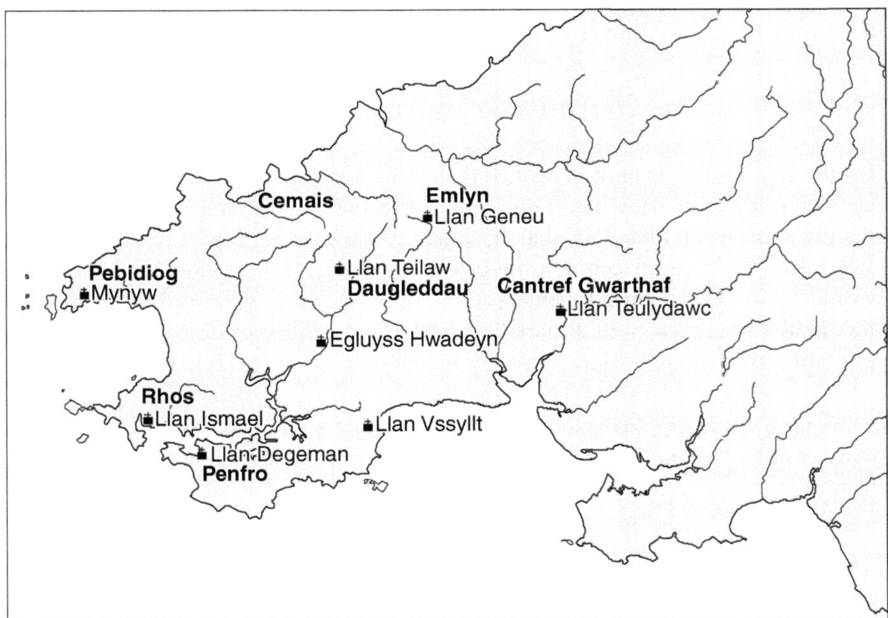

Map 26. The seven bishop-houses of Dyfed
The map shows the situation of 'the bishop-houses of Dyfed' listed in a short legal text dating from before the Norman conquest of Dyfed in 1093. In general there is one bishop-house to each cantref.

In general, the sequence of bishop-houses follows a pattern by which there is one 'bishop-house' for each of the seven cantrefs of Dyfed (see Map 26).[85] The Dyfed in question was the core of the kingdom: it included Llandeulyddog in Carmarthen, perhaps the former episcopal see, but nothing further east. An alternative explanation of this pattern is, however, worth pursuing. It relies on an analogy with the *cylch* or 'circuit' of kings. In the twelfth- and thirteenth-century laws, it is understood that in each commote the king will have a court, *llys*. The spread of such courts around his kingdom offers the basis on which he and his men can go on circuit. Similarly, one might suppose, the seven bishop-houses, one to a cantref, might be so named because the bishop had the right to visit each on his circuit. A bishop had the obligation to travel round his diocese, and these bishop-houses might have made this easier, as well as less burdensome for the people under his care.[86] Yet, there does not seem to be any connection between these bishop-houses and the post-Norman estates of the Bishop of St Davids. In the twelfth century and later, the cantref of Pebidiog was St David's special land, 'Dewisland'; and that was wholly in line with the pattern we have met already of great churches claiming authority over a whole cantref, and it is therefore likely to be a claim that goes back before the Norman conquest of Dyfed. Moreover, the text on the Seven Bishop-Houses was concerned above all with the exalted status of the heads of these churches. It does not mention any episcopal *cylch*. The first explanation thus seems the more likely.

2. CHURCHES AND CEMETERIES

By the tenth and eleventh centuries there had been another major change in the character of Welsh churches. This is related to the issues that arise over the Seven Bishop-Houses of Dyfed in that it concerns burial practices.[87] In England and Ireland in the seventh century there was no general expectation that Christians would be buried in church cemeteries.[88] In Wales, it is striking that some early medieval cemeteries were situated around prehistoric monuments, which were probably still visible.[89] Most laymen continued to be buried where their kinsmen

[85] The distribution of the bishop-houses should be compared with the fuller picture of early churches in N. Ludlow, 'Identifying Early Medieval Ecclesiastical Sites in South-West Wales, in N. Edwards (ed.), *The Archaeology of the Early Medieval Celtic Churches: Proceedings of a Conference on the Archaeology of the Early Medieval Celtic Churches, September 2004*, Society for Medieval Archaeology Monographs, 29 (Leeds, 2009), 62 (Figure 4. 1).

[86] For this circuit, cf. *Synodus I S. Patricii*, c. 25, ed. and trans. Bieler, *The Irish Penitentials*, 58/59.

[87] For the archaeological evidence, see H. James, 'Early Medieval Cemeteries in Wales', in Edwards and Lane, *The Early Church in Wales and the West*, 90–103, and D. Longley, 'Early Medieval Burial in Wales', in Edwards (ed.), *The Archaeology of the Early Medieval Celtic Churches*, 105–32.

[88] J. Blair, *The Church in Anglo-Saxon Society* (Oxford, 2005), 228–45; E. O'Brien, 'Pagan and Christian Burial in Ireland during the First Millennium AD: Continuity and Change', in Edwards and Lane (eds.), *The Early Church in Wales and the West*, 130–62; ead., 'Pagan or Christian? Burial in Ireland during the 5th to 8th Centuries AD ', in Edwards (ed.), *The Archaeology of the Early Medieval Celtic Churches*, 135–54.

[89] Examples include: Tandderwen, NGR SJ 0815 6613, K. S. Brassil, W. G. Owen, and W. J. Britnell, 'Prehistoric and Early Medieval Cemeteries at Tandderwen, near Denbigh, Clwyd', *Archaeological Journal*

had been buried, whereas members of church communities, perhaps including tenants, would be buried in the cemeteries of their churches. The post-Roman memorial inscriptions, unlike their later successors, were not in general associated with church sites.[90] By the twelfth century this had all changed to the situation which we take for granted, or have taken for granted until recently. It is impossible to say exactly how this happened, but it is likely that two influences were at work: first, churches were built in some cemeteries previously unattached to a church;[91] and, secondly, some old non-ecclesiastical cemeteries were abandoned in favour of neighbouring churchyards. In other words, sometimes new churches went to old cemeteries; sometimes old churches attracted all local burials to their churchyards. These two influences varied from region to region in their effectiveness.[92]

So far we are looking at a broad trend common to much of north-western Europe. We can, however, put further Welsh flesh on the bare bones of general supposition by considering the term *llan*. To judge by the Book of Llandaff this had become the normal term for a local church complex by the eleventh century.[93] It is, however, most unlikely that this situation goes back to the fifth and sixth centuries, since seventh-century and later evidence for Irish churches shows that the Irish counterpart, *land* (*lann*), was only one of several words in use. Where it does occur, as at Lann Elo, Lynally, in Co. Offaly, or Lann Léire in what is now Co. Louth, it is not in composition with a saint's name:[94] the Irish pattern agrees with Llanelwy rather than with, say, Llandeilo or Llanarmon. In compounds, such as *perllan* 'orchard', Welsh retains the older meaning of 'enclosed land'.[95] There were also older terms, notably *domnach* borrowed from the Latin *dominicum*, 'the Lord's place', corresponding exactly in its literal meaning to the Greek *kuriakon* which gave English 'church'. This passed out of use after the conversion phase in which relations between the churches in Ireland and Celtic Britain were especially close; but, as a normal term for a church and its appurtenant buildings, Irish replaced it by *cell* from Latin *cella* rather than by *land*. The counterparts of *llan* are common in Cornwall and in Brittany;[96] but in the former it has been questioned whether the

148 (1991), 46–97 (inhumation cemetery, 62–7 and discussion, 87–91); Plas Gogerddan near Aberystwyth, NGR SN 6264 8351, K. Murphy, Plas Gogerddan, Dyfed: A Multi-Period Burial and Ritual Site', *Archaeological Journal*, 149 (1992), 1–38 (inhumation cemetery: 15–22).

90 See above, 125.

91 C. Thomas, *The Early Christian Archaeology of North Britain* (London, 1971), 48–90, remains an excellent guide. An example of an early cemetery which acquired a church later, probably not before the twelfth century, is Capel Maelog: W. J. Britnell, 'Capel Maelog, Llandrindod Wells, Powys: Excavations 1984–7', *Medieval Archaeology*, 34 (1990), 27–96. An early cemetery which had a wooden structure, perhaps a memorial chapel, over a special grave, which was itself the focus of other burials, is Capel Eithin: S. I. White and G. Smith, 'A Funerary and Ceremonial Centre at Capel Eithin, Gaerwen, Anglesey: Excavations of Neolithic, Bronze Age, Roman and Early Medieval Features in 1980 and 1981', *Transactions of the Anglesey Antiquarian Society and Field Club* (1999), 156–8.

92 See above, 123–5.

93 As in *LL* 275 (the list of churches in Ergyng).

94 L. Mac Mathúna, 'Observations on Irish *Lann* "(Piece of) Land; (Church) Building" and Compounds', *Ériu*, 48 (1997), 153–60.

95 Roberts, 'Welsh Ecclesiastical Place-Names and Archaeology', 43.

96 O. J. Padel, 'Cornish Language Notes: 5. Cornish Names of Parish Churches', *Cornish Studies*, 4/5 (1976–7), 15–27; id., *Cornish Place-Name Elements*, English Place-Name Society, 56/57

word had yet acquired a strictly ecclesiastical sense; and in the latter many local names are compounded with *plou* (from Latin *pleb-em, pleb-is*, the oblique stem of *plebs* 'people') in origin a term for the local community.[97] Very early Irish evidence shows *plebs* as the counterpart of *túath* (Welsh *tud*), a word that was used for the people of a minor kingdom but also for the lay people as the recipient of the pastoral care, and subject to the authority, of a bishop.[98] It was a secular community, but, by virtue of the reciprocal contract between clergy and laity, it was also very much part of how contemporaries understood the role of the Church.[99] The type of name exemplified by Llandeilo, namely *llan* compounded with the name of the saint, is not, therefore, to be assumed to have descended from some early Age of the Saints. On the other hand it accords very well with the evidence of the ninth-century documents in the Lichfield Gospels; there we had Teilo's bishop, Teilo's *sacerdos*, Teilo's altar, Teilo's gospel book, and Teilo's community.[100] As it happens we did not have Teilo's *llan*, but it was probably already the name for the church, Llandeilo.

In the Life of St Cadog, the saint began the construction of his monastery at Llancarfan by making the cemetery:[101]

> Hence the venerable man began to raise up a huge heap of earth, and to make in the same a very beautiful cemetery dedicated to the honour of God, wherein the bodies of the faithful might be buried around the church.

This priority is explained by the extensive claims made in the Life to burial rights (the saint's father, Gwynllyw, is on his deathbed and is blessing his son in the style of an Old Testament patriarch):[102]

> From the spring, which in British is called Ffynnon Hen, that is, from the old well, till one reaches the mouth of the River Naddawan, all kings and their companions, also

(Nottingham, 1985), 142–5; id., 'Local Saints and Place-Names in Cornwall', in Thacker and Sharpe (eds.), *Local Saints and Local Churches*, 306–7; B. L. Olson and O. J. Padel, 'A Tenth-Century List of Cornish Parochial Saints', *CMCS* 12 (Winter 1986), 33–71; B. Tanguy, *Dictionnaire des noms de communes, trèves et paroisses des Côtes d'Armor* (Douarnenez, 1992); id., *Dictionnaire des noms de communes, trèves et paroisses du Finistère: origine et signification* (Douarnenez, 1990); J.-Y. Le Moing, *Les noms de lieux breton de Haut-Bretagne* (Spezed, 1990), 166–7, 180–1.

[97] A. Preston-Jones, 'Decoding Cornish Churchyards', in Edwards and Lane, *The Early Church in Wales and the West*, 108; W. Davies, *Small Worlds: The Village Community in Early Medieval Brittany* (London, 1988), 63–7, 81–5, and her 'Priests and Rural Communities in East Brittany in the Ninth Century', *Études Celtiques*, 20 (1983), 177–97.

[98] *Synodus I S. Patricii*, cc. 24, 27, ed. and trans. Bieler, *The Irish Penitentials*, 58/59; cf. the *parruchia* of c. 30.

[99] T. M. Charles-Edwards, 'The Pastoral Role of the Church in the Early Irish Laws', in J. Blair and R. Sharpe (eds.), *Pastoral Care before the Parish* (Leicester, 1992), 63–80.

[100] See above, 247–8.

[101] *Vita S. Cadoci*, § 9; Brassil et al., 'Prehistoric and Early Medieval Cemeteries at Tandderwen', 86–7, note the association, at that site, of a mound, within a 'rectilinear causewayed enclosure', with the inhumation cemetery; they cite this passage of the Life of St Cadog and speculate that the mound might have been used as a place of assembly and termed a *gorsedd*; for the term *gorsedd*, see T. M. Charles-Edwards, '*Gorsedd, Dadl*, and *Llys*: Assemblies and Courts in Medieval Wales', in A. Pantos and S. Semple (eds.), *Assembly Places and Practices in Medieval Europe* (Dublin, 2004), 95–105.

[102] *Vita S. Cadoci*, § 28.

nobles and leading men, and also all the members of their households, shall be buried in the cemetery of your monastery of Llancarfan.

The Naddawan was the old name for the river Thaw, which divided the cantref of Penychen from its neighbour to the west, Gwrinydd, in which the cemetery of Llanilltud Fawr was the most prestigious burial place. What should be noted is that these two passages reveal two different stages in the rise of churchyard burial. In the second passage, the claim is that the elite of the cantref of Penychen should be buried in the cemetery of their greatest monastery. Burial in the monastic cemetery was a right and a duty attached to high status. In the first passage, however, the purpose with which Cadog made his cemetery was to accommodate the bodies of the faithful at large, not just the elite; it seems to assume the ubiquity of churchyard burial, which is a later stage than churchyard burial as a privilege for the elite.

The link with the cantref is found elsewhere: for Llancarfan, the cantref was Penychen by virtue of the situation of the monastery, but also Gwynllŵg by virtue of Cadog's father, the eponymous Gwynllyw. A short distance north of Llanilltud Fawr was Llyswrinydd (Llysworney), the royal *llys* of Gwrinydd. In the twelfth century, Llanbadarn Fawr still claimed the northernmost cantref of Ceredigion, Penweddig, as its own *parochia*, but with a special claim, by virtue of a gift by Maelgwn Gwynedd, to the land between the Rheidol and the Clarach; the Life of St Padarn also boldly claimed that Seisyllwg (Ceredigion with Ystrad Tywi) was Padarn's diocese.[103] In Anglesey, the churches of St Cybi's named disciples—Caffo, Maelog, Llibio, Peulan, and Cyngar—were strung out across the west and south of the island from the River Alaw to the Braint, and inland as far as Llangefni.[104]

The conception of the layout of a church indicated by the Life of Cadog reappears in a more elaborate form in the Welsh laws, in a section on the compensation to be paid for an offence within a church.[105] The plan was concentric: the outermost zone was the *noddfa*, the 'safe-conduct place' (*nawdd* + *ma*), in Latin the *refugium*. It was there that the *nawddwyr* of the church, those who had resorted to sanctuary within the *noddfa*, were to be found. An especially important church would claim a correspondingly extensive *noddfa*; and here it is significant that St Cadog's successive conflicts with earthly kings, Arthur, Maelgwn, Rhun, and Rhain, all ended by the extension or confirmation of his *noddfa*. To judge by eighteenth-century evidence, the *noddfa* attached to Llanelwy, later the see of St Asaph, was also very large, embracing the townships of Brynpolyn, Gwerglefryd, Gwerneigron, and the two Talars.[106] It was not confined to the tongue of land between the Elwy and the Clwyd. Within the *noddfa* lay the *mynwent*, by this date referring to the cemetery immediately around the church, as at Llancarfan. *Mynwent* is a loanword from Latin *monumentum* in the sense of a tomb, perhaps from

103 *Vita S. Paterni*, §§ 19, 30, *VSBG* 258, 266; R. R. Davies, *Conquest, Coexistence and Change*, 174.

104 *Vita S. Kebii*, §§ 5, 16, *VSBG* 236, 244.

105 The best text is in the Bodorgan MS of *Llyfr Cyfnerth* (*Mk*), 95. 8–19; it is printed by Pryce, *Native Law and the Church*, 180 n. 86, and see more generally ibid. 179–85.

106 J. Wyn Evans, 'The Early Church in Denbighshire', *Denbighshire Historical Society Transactions*, 35 (1986), 80. Brynpolyn, SY 04 73; Gwerneigron, SJ 02 75.

the plural *monumenta*.[107] The shift of meaning to ecclesiastical cemetery reflects parallel changes in burial practice.

Cadog's church at Llancarfan was said to have three altars, one for Cadog himself, one dedicated to his disciple Elli, and another to Macmoil.[108] On the other hand, it was also possible for a single cemetery to contain more than one church. The list of churches in Ergyng at the end of the Book of Llandaff includes one notable case (and here *llan* is clearly the church itself, not the whole complex):[109]

> In the time of Edward, king of England, and of Gruffudd king of Wales, Bishop Herwald consecrated Henllan Dyfrig and Llandeilo within one cemetery, and he ordained Einion ap Cyngen to be priest; the heirs to the lands of those churches remained under the authority of Bishop Herwald, Moriddig ap Cyni, Morfran ab *Audi* and his brother Cyni, and Marchwain ab Elgu and *Podin*, all of whom rendered the food-rent of the bishop together with the bishop's entitlement.

The implication of this and similar cases is that it was exceptional for more than one church (*llan*) to lie within one cemetery; the norm was one church within one cemetery, the whole complex being termed a *llan*.[110] Yet, as in this passage, it was possible, though exceptional, for *llan* to refer just to a church, not to the whole complex. The normal language used for church settlements in the twelfth century had undergone major changes to fit the new situation, in which church, cemetery, and saint were bound together in one whole; and it looks as though these changes may have been in full swing in the eighth and ninth centuries. The insights afforded by the Lichfield Gospels and by Asser may thus be into a new ecclesiastical order.

3. *CLAS* CHURCHES

Relatively grand churches, with cemetery and sanctuary, are, in modern scholarship, sometimes called *clas* churches, *clasau*. These so-called *clas* churches have also sometimes been presented as if they were survivals from a primitive age of monasticism. As has been pointed out, *clas* was a term for a community, especially but not solely an ecclesiastical community.[111] In one version of the legal text on the compensation to be paid for an offence committed within a church, the term *clas* is used:[112]

[107] H. Lewis, *Yr Elfen Ladin yn yr Iaith Gymraeg* (Cardiff, 1943), § 8 and p. 43.

[108] On Macmoil, see *Vita S. Cadoci*, § 11. The name is presumably derived from an Irish name of the type Mac Máel(e) X.

[109] *LL* 275.

[110] *Lan* (cognate with Welsh *llan*) is stated to be equivalent to *cimiterium* in the Gotha Life of St Petroc: P. Grosjean, 'Vies et miracles de S. Petroc', *Analecta Bollandiana*, 74 (1956), 153: 'Incolarum enim lingua Lan Wethinocke Cimiterium Wethinoci exprimit'. In ninth-century Brittany it was equated with *monasterium*: 'Iste est locus qui nunc monasterium sive vulgato nomine Lanna Pauli in plebe Telmedoviæ dicitur': *Vita S. Pauli*, ed. C. Cuissard, *Revue Celtique*, 5 (1881–3), 440.

[111] J. Wyn Evans, 'The Survival of the *Clas* as an Institution in Medieval Wales', in Edwards and Lane (eds.), *The Early Church in Wales and the West*, 33–40; id., 'The Early Church in Denbighshire', 61–81, esp. 70–4; Pryce, *Native Law and the Church*, 186–8.

[112] *Llyfr Iorwerth*, ed. Wiliam, 43/10–12 (but I have translated the version in MSS *A* and *E*).

> Whoever does wrong to a mother-church, let him pay fourteen pounds, one half to the abbot, if he be a devout and literate man, and the other between the priest and the *clas*. If wrong be done in the cemetery, seven pounds in two halves, like the other [fine]. Whoever does wrong in another church, let him pay seven pounds, one half to the priest and the other to the parson.

Here the term *clas* seems to refer to the community of the mother-church; it is not used of a lesser church. Like many such communities, the Welsh *clas* appears to have had its own complicated history. I shall avoid most of the complications and look at the main lines of development.

Not all churches supported a community, but from the documents in the Lichfield Gospels, the Lives of St Cadog and St David, from the earliest versions of the Welsh laws, and from the Book of Llandaff, we can form some idea of what was the standard personnel of a well-provided and important church in the period between the ninth and eleventh centuries. It might be headed by a bishop; if not the superior was usually called an abbot or a *princeps*.[113] Examples occur in early Ergyng charters of important local churches headed by abbots and *principes*.[114] These look like the Welsh counterparts to the Gaulish *parochiae* or the minsters of eighth-century England. The *sacerdos*, probably the priest in charge of liturgical and sacramental provision in the church, might come second in rank; he might also be the head of the church.[115] Two other officials are quite often named: one provided for the educational and scholarly aspect of the church, and is variously named as the *lector* or the *magister*, the *scriba* or the *scholasticus*;[116] in Welsh this person seems to have been known as the *athro*, which etymologically means 'foster-father'—he was the foster-father of his pupils.[117] The other official looked after the material needs of the community; he was known as the *oeconomus* (usually in the form *equonimus*). A much more rarely attested official, but one who was probably more common than the evidence would suggest, was the *sepeliarius*, the sexton.[118] The documents appended to the Life of St Cadog mention *legati*, 'messengers', who were sent with relics wherever they might be needed.[119]

When we go from officials to the ordinary members of the community, what is striking is that they are often, especially in Welsh, known by terms which originally meant pupils in a school. The oldest such term may be *meibion lleyn*, literally 'sons

113 *Princeps*: *AC s.a.* 856 = 858; *Vita S. Cadoci*, § 67; *LL* 149, 151b, 164.

114 *LL* 163b, 164.

115 Chad 4, 5.

116 *Lector* is the most common term in *LL*; also *Vita S. Cadoci*, §§ 57, 61. *Magister* occurs in Gildas, *De Excidio Britanniae*, § 36, and in Asser, *Vita Ælfredi*, § 23 (for an English teacher), §§ 25, 75; it is occasionally used in *LL*, as for Lifris, the author of the *Vita S. Cadoci*, *LL* 269; also in the Life itself, § 65; note also the portion at Llanrhaeadr-ym-Mochnant, known as that of 'Emeystr' (A. N. Palmer, 'The Portionary Churches of Mediæval North Wales', *AC* (1886), reprinted as an appendix to his *The History of the Parish Church of Wrexham* (Wrexham n.d.), 21); *scholasticus* is used in Chad 5 and in *Vita S. Cadoci*, § 27; *scriba* is used in Rhigyfarch's *Vita S. Dauidis*, § 10.

117 In *Brut Dingestow*, ed. H. Lewis (Cardiff, 1942), 62. 11, *athro* translates *doctor*; *WML* 88. 5–6 (important ex.). Note the way Asser, speaking of his own education at St Davids, couples together *nutritus et doctus*, *Life*, § 79. For fosterage, including its ecclesiastical form, see above, 299–300.

118 *Vita S. Cadoci*, § 12.

119 Ibid. § 50.

of literature'.[120] A common term in Middle Welsh was *ysgolheigion*; by then, however, this very often just meant 'clerics', as it does in the Third Branch of the Mabinogi. To make it quite clear that it still had its etymological meaning the texts are sometimes forced to use the phrase *ysgolheigion ysgol*, 'scholars of a school'.[121]

The best guide to the character of such a church in the eleventh century is provided by a text appended to the Life of St Cadog.[122] This begins by declaring that Cadog instituted thirty-six canons and established for them

> thirty-six *atria*, in which the canons should have their buildings, and the same number of parcels of land, in which were eighty acres, which from ancient times were called the properties of the *atria*, and which gardeners cultivated, who had the job of laying out orchards and gardens, and looking after the guest-chambers; and in addition the same number of vills, from which they (the canons) had what they needed in the way of clothing and food.

From the Life itself we can gather what Welsh term was rendered by the Latin *atrium*, 'an enclosed area with an open space within it'. This contains a miracle story telling how a swineherd of the saint's uncle, *Poul Pennychen*, Paul of Penychen, threatened Cadog with a spear, was blinded and paralysed, and was sent back to his master to be healed.[123] He came to the gate of the *atrium* where Paul lived, was admitted by the gatekeepers, and then proceeded to the hall. This indicates that *atrium* stood for *llys*, 'court', in the sense of an enclosed settlement, within which was the *neuadd*, the hall, and the other buildings.

Table 18.1. The prebends of Llancarfan

	person	*atrium/llys*	*parcel of land*	*vill*
1.	The abbot	The *Llys* of the *Diserth*	—	*Treimgueithen*
2.	The Teacher	The *Llys* of *Benignus*	a parcel in the *castellum*[124]	—
3.	The *sacerdos*	The *Llys* by the hazel	—	—
4.	(A canon)	Aidan Bloch's *llys*	*Niaysgurthin*[125]	Further *Pennon*
5.	(A canon)	*Atrium Album* (*Llys Wen*)	*Cruc y Greif*	Nearer *Pennon*
6.	The cook?	The *Llys* of the Kitchen	Parcel to the south towards *Talcatlan*	*Pencrychgel*

[120] *WML* 113.19–114.7; for the text of a better MS see Pryce, *Native Law and the Church*, 180 n. 86; see also his discussion, ibid. 180–2.

[121] *WML* 88. 5–6.

[122] *Vita S. Cadoci*, §§ 48–52; J. K. Knight, 'Sources for the Early History of Morgannwg', in *Glamorgan County History*, gen. ed. Glanmor Williams, ii, *Early Glamorgan*, ed. H. N. Savory (Cardiff, 1984), 395–8.

[123] Ibid. § 8.

[124] For the *castellum*, 'castle', see ibid. § 9. It appears to have been an area surrounded by a rampart, similar in construction to the cemetery, which was also surrounded by a rampart. Could it be Castle Ditches, just to the east of Llancarfan?

[125] Perhaps for *Maysgurthin*.

7.	The cook?	A second *llys* of the kitchen	*Cayr i Coc*	*Pellussen*
8.	*Consul* (*maer*)[126]	*Atrium consulatus*	Parcel by *Talcathlan*	*Talpontymit*
9.	(A canon)	The *Llys* of *Tref y Crugau*	—	*Tref y Crugau*
10.	(A canon)	The *Llys* of *Treflech*	Parcel beyond the cross	*Treflech*
11.	(A canon)	*Llys Samson*	*Cymmyoucti*	—
12.	(A canon)	*Llys Elphin*	—	*Cestyll Dingad*
13.	(A canon)	*Atrium Chincencoh*	—	—
14.	(The baker?)	The Llys of the Bakery	—	*Tref Nantbucelis*
15.	The abbot	Llys Talcadlan	—	Talcadlan
16.	Gwrgi, *sacerdos*	Llys Gwrgi	Caer Arthan	*Pencrycgel* + Pistyll Cadwg
17.	(A canon)	Llys Arwystl	*Ygrestyl*	*Hendref Dumbrych*
18.	(A canon)	Llys Nestreg	parcel beyond the ditch of *Pulltauus*	Brynsychan
19.	(A canon)	Llys Elda	—	*Trefhinun*
20.	(A canon)	Llys *Cair Guicou*	—	*Ecclus Silid*
21.	(A canon)	Llys Alfryd ap Cynwyd	—	Allt Cynwyd
22.	(A canon)	Llys Cyndraeth	Nant Cyngar	*Pencrycgel* + *Cilbleingurth*
23.	(A canon)	Llys Ellybr	—	Tref Ellybr
24.	(A canon)	Llys Cruginan	—	Tref Crugbilia
25.	(A canon)	Llys *Medgarth*	—	Tref *Medgarth*
26.	(A canon)	Llys *Cairdicycit*	—	Tref *Cairdicit*[127]
27.	(A canon)	Llys Cynflwst	—	Tref Celli Dremiog i.e. Nant Carthau

The appendix to the Life then goes on to list twenty-seven *atria*, beginning with the one belonging to the abbot, which it calls the *atrium deserti*, 'the *llys* of the *diserth*'. For some *atria* it specifies also a parcel of land and the vill, and some of these it names. In Table 18.1 *atrium* is translated as *llys* unless it occurs within a Latin phrase.

What this text shows is that a complete prebend contained three elements: first was the *llys*, in Latin *atrium*; the second was the parcel of land used as a garden; and the third was the *tref*, in Latin *villa*. As nos. 7 and 16 show, the second, the parcel of

[126] For *consul* = *maer*, see *Braint Teilo*, *LL* 118, *sine consule sine proconsule* = 120 *heb mair . heb cyghellaur*. The use in *atrium consulatus* of the term for the office, *consulatus*, rather than the officer, *consul*, emphasizes that the *atrium* was attached to the office.

[127] These are presumably the same name, but which is correct I cannot tell.

land, was called in Welsh a *caer*.[128] Normally in Old Welsh this renders *civitas*, in a sense covering both city and fortress: this is clear from c. 66a of *Historia Brittonum*, where the names of twenty-eight *civitates* of Britain all begin with *cair*. The use of *caer* in this text, however, is much closer to its Breton cognate, *kêr*, commonly used in place-names for an enclosed farmstead.[129] Yet the equivalent of the farmstead itself is here the *atrium* or *llys*, while the farm is the *tref* or *villa*. The distinction between the *caer* and the *tref* is probably not just a matter of what was produced—garden vegetables and fruits as opposed to grain and meat—but of the method of cultivation. The *caer* is likely to have been dug, while the arable in the *tref* would have been ploughed. To judge by the introductory passage the average *caer* was a little more than two acres, while the *tref* is likely to have been considerably larger. One *tref* was sometimes split between two or more prebends: this is obvious in the case of nos. 4 and 5, Further *Pennon* and Nearer *Pennon*, but *Pencrychgel* was also split between nos. 6, 16, and 22.

The names for the different elements of a prebend are sometimes entirely separate, as with no. 16, where the *llys* is called after a person, Gwrgi, but the *caer* after a different person, Arthan. Sometimes, however, one element seems to take precedence: the *llys* in no. 20 is 'of *Cair Guicou*'; and, although no *caer* is specified, one may suppose that it was called *Cair Guicou*. In no. 26, again no *caer* is specified and yet both the *llys* and the *tref* are 'of *Cairdicit*' (or *Cairdicycit*). In no. 9, the *llys* is named after the *tref*.

The personal names used do not, in general, offer any help to explaining the arrangement of the prebends. They do not appear in the clerical sections of the Cadog charters, nor do they include the names of Cadog's principal disciples, Finnian, Macmoil, and Gnauan.[130] A clue, however, is offered by no. 21, where the *llys* is the *llys* of Alfryd ap Cynwyd, but the *tref* is called Allt Cynwyd, presumably after the father. This suggests a family element. Perhaps the personal names after which the different elements are called were the names of ancestors of kindreds with a stake in the church of Llancarfan.

Much of the text suggests that the canons lived separate lives. Yet the details about the kitchen indicate that this cannot be entirely true. Two prebends are devoted to the upkeep of the kitchen and a third to the support of the bakery. The canons may, therefore, have had a common table. The practice of eating together at a common table spread in the post-Roman period.[131] However, no *equonimus* (*oeconomus*) is mentioned in the text, and this may have meant that the cook had some responsibility for the lands of Llancarfan, unless that was the duty of the *maer*, which it may well have been.

One notable feature of the arrangement of the prebends is the name of the first *llys* attached to the office of abbot, *Atrium Deserti*, the *llys* of the *diserth*. When referring to churches or elements within a church, *diserth* may be an invention of

[128] For the senses of *caer* see Padel, *Cornish Place-Name Elements*, 50–4 (but I do not accept that *caer* glosses *atrium* in the *Vita S. Cadoci* as there claimed).

[129] Cf. above, 286, on *Cairnonui* in *LL* 221.

[130] Cf. *Vita S. Cadoci*, § 11.

[131] Cf. Gregory of Tours, *Hist.*, x. 31, where Baudinus, the sixteenth bishop, instituted the *mensa* for the canons of Tours cathedral.

the ninth century. In Ireland, churches called 'The Desert of X' are well attested in the annals, but not before the ninth century.[132]

What is striking about the personnel of a well-provided Welsh church is how closely it resembled its Irish counterpart. Almost always the same names are used; sometimes the resemblance extends to details of spelling. One might be uncertain quite what were the *meibion lleyn* were it not that they correspond to the Irish *maic légind*. The form *lleyn* rather than the normal *llên* was probably directly influenced by the Irish form.[133] There may be a further resemblance. Sometimes the word *clas* seems to be used for the community of a church, but in one or two cases something more specific seems to be intended. In the Life of Gruffudd ap Cynan there is an account, highly tendentious in some ways, of events leading up to the battle of Mynydd Carn in 1081. In the Welsh version we are told that Gruffudd ap Cynan was welcomed by a deputation consisting of Rhys ap Tewdwr, king of Deheubarth, and of the bishop and his *athrawon* and the whole *clas* of the Lord Dewi and that of the Church of Mynyw; in the Latin original, however, *holl clas er argluyd Dewi* was *chorus universus Sancti Davidis*, while *ac vn eglvys Vynyv* was *clericique omnes Menevenses*.[134] In the Welsh there appear to be two *clasau*, that of the saint and that of the church, but the word *clas* itself seems to be non-technical, just 'community'. Many Irish churches had distinct attached groups with carefully graded claims to supply an abbot: one was the kindred of the saint, another the tenants of the church.[135] There may have been some such division at St Davids. The claim, presumably fictitious, by which St David was attached to the old royal kindred of Ceredigion may have been designed to give that dynasty a claim to supply the bishop.

This situation is not surprising: there were British churches, let alone individual churchmen, in Ireland, such as the Cell Mór Mochop in Meath, attached to Caergybi, where Mochop is an early pet name of the saint, Cybi, or 'The House of the Britons' at Kells.[136] There were churches in Wales with Irish connections, such as Diserth Cwyfien, Cwyfien being very probably the Cóemgen or Kevin who was the patron-saint of Glendalough.[137] Llancarfan claimed to have a special

[132] AU 819. 6, 842. 11, 857. 2, 870. 5. Cf. *Tír an Dísirt*, 'The Land of the Dísert', *Betha Colmáin maic Lúatháin*, ed. K. Meyer (Dublin, 1911), §§ 53, 54.

[133] For the normal development, see *LHEB* § 76.

[134] *Historia Gruffud ap Kenan*, ed. D. S. Evans (Cardiff, 1977), 13: 'Ac ena y kerdus Rys m. Teudur, brenhin Deheubarth Kemry, a'r escop a'e athraon a holl clas er argluyd Dewi ac vn eglvys Vynyv, hyt e borth', translating *Vita Griffini filii Conani*, ed. Russell, § 17/2, 'Ad cuius adventum Rysus ap Theodvr, rex australium Cambrorum, Menevensis episcopus, doctores, chorus universus Sancti Davidis, clericique omnes Menevenses, in portum sunt profecti.'

[135] Cf. T. M. Charles-Edwards, '*Érlam*: The Patron-Saint of an Irish Church', in A. Thacker and R. Sharpe (eds.), *Local Saints and Local Churches in the Early Medieval West* (Oxford, 2002), 267-90.

[136] *Vita S. Kebii*, c. 13, *VSBG* 240; for the identification, see *Corpus Genealogiarum Sanctorum Hiberniae*, ed. P. Ó Riain (Dublin, 1985), 317; *Félire Óengusso Céli Dé: The Martyrology of Oengus the Culdee*, ed. W. Stokes, Henry Bradshaw Society (London, 1905). Notes, 26 Oct.

[137] J. Lloyd-Jones, *Geirfa Barddoniaeth Gynnar Gymraeg*, 192; CBT I. 27. 92, where the note simply follows E. G. Bowen, *The Settlements of the Celtic Saints in Wales* (Cardiff, 1954), 84, quite wrongly in my opinion; cf. *LBS* ii. 201–2. For the phonology, cf. *maccwyf* < Ir. *macccem*; for this and for the confusion with Cwyfan < Cóemán, see *CIB* 167 and n. 998; D. Longley, 'Llangwyfan—the Church in the Sea', *Transactions of the Anglesey Antiquarian Society and Field Club* (2008), 77–88. For

relationship with the great monastery of Clonard in Meath: 'The learned men of the Irish who live at Clonard in the monastery of his (Cadog's) disciple, the blessed Finnian, testify that, if any of the clergy of St Cadog should go to them, they receive him with honour and make him an heir, just like one of themselves.'[138] The link is confirmed by the Life of St Finnian.[139] The suggestion here is that the community of Llancarfan was also made up of 'heirs'. The Life of St Cadog also claims that Llancarfan possessed land by the Liffey.[140]

All this, however, pertains to the great churches, those which were staffed by whole communities. When one comes to smaller, more local churches, the forerunners of the parish churches of the twelfth century, there is much less evidence. However, the Book of Llandaff contains a list of churches in Ergyng, a formerly royal territory that is called a *parochia*.[141] To this it adds a further list of churches in Ystrad Yw, Gwent, and Gwynllŵg.[142] Ergyng appears from this document to have been well populated with churches. A typical entry is the one concerning Kilpeck: 'In the time of King William, he (Bishop Herwald) consecrated *Cilpedec*, and ordained *Morcenoui* as priest; and when he died, he ordained his son, Einion'. Such succession of son to father was the norm. There were, however, differences among the local churches, as emerges from the following passage:[143]

> In the time of King Harold, he likewise consecrated Llansanffraid, and ordained in it *Guollguinn* as priest, and after him his son Ieuan. In the time of King Harold, he consecrated Llanbedr 'under the heir', *Cidrich* son of *Gunncu*, and Cadien and his sons, *Gunna*, and *Eutut*, and his sons Meirchion and Custennin; and he handed over the care of the church to the aforesaid priest *Guollguinn*.

The relationship of *Guollguinn* to the two churches seems to have been different: in Llansanffraid he appears to be simply the priest, ordained by the bishop, and succeeded by his son; in Llanbedr he officiated as priest, but the lordship over the church was held by a set of kinsmen, pre-eminent among them, perhaps, 'the heir', *Cidrych* son of *Gunncu*. There is no mention here of *Guollguinn*'s son, Ieuan, succeeding his father.

A tenth-century list of saints drawn up by a Cornishman or Breton may refer to a group of churches.[144] When plotted on a map, they seem to cluster especially in central southern Cornwall, where they indicate a good coverage of that area. In the development of parishes, three things need to be distinguished: first, the distribution of churches offering a regular liturgy; secondly, the development of the canon

Glendalough's connections with Wales and Cornwall, cf. A. Mac Shamhráin, *Church and Polity in Pre-Norman Ireland: The Case of Glendalough* (Maynooth, 1996), 124–5.

138 *Vita S. Cadoci*, § 43.

139 Heist, *Vitae*, pp. 82 (= *De Tribus Ordinibus*), 97–9 (Life of St Finnian of Clonard, §§ 4–6, 9, 11 (Cathmaelus)), p. 182 (Life of St Cainnech, § 4 [Docc]).

140 *Vita S. Cadoci*, § 43.

141 *LL* 275–8; for *parochia Ercycg*, see 278, l. 15, 279, l. 6.

142 Ibid. 278. 26–280, 3.

143 Ibid. 276. 1–8.

144 B. L. Olson and O. J. Padel, 'A Tenth-Century List of Cornish Parochial Saints', 33–71; Olson, *Early Monasteries in Cornwall*, 56–60.

law classification of churches according to their rights and duties; and thirdly, the shifting impact of that classification on the churches in an area. A mere list of this kind cannot show us much, if anything, about the second and the third, but it is precious evidence about the first. In the tenth century, Cornwall appears to have had a good supply of churches, so that, if the list is typical of Cornwall as a whole, most Cornish people would not have had to travel far to hear mass.

This Cornish example raises the question whether those areas of Britain that remained British resembled more in their ecclesiastical structure Anglo-Saxon England or Ireland. A contrast has been argued by Tomás Ó Carragáin between pre-Viking Ireland and the England of the same period portrayed in John Blair's book, *The Church in Anglo-Saxon England*.[145] Blair argued that the early English Church was dominated by minsters—churches with a community, the equivalent of the *parochiae* of Gaul, but with a monastic ethos, stronger in some cases, more attenuated in others. The minsters served *regiones*, 'small shires'. They were established by royal authority, either as royal minsters or as foundations by bishops or nobles. Within a typical *regio*, the minster was the church: there was, as yet, no multiplication of lesser churches within the territory; and, in particular, the estate-church founded by a noble family on the site of an old cemetery, common in Gaul, is not attested in England. From the minster, priests went round the *regio*, which, in an ecclesiastical context, was termed a *parochia*, to preach, to say mass, and to administer the sacraments. Some 'cult-sites', such as holy wells, were acknowledged to have been present in the *parochia* as well as the minster. Sometimes, to judge by Theodore's Penitential, chapels were attached to old cemeteries, but these rarely gave rise to parish churches.[146] The only ecclesiastical settlements with a future in front of them were the minsters. From the ninth century onwards, however, the minster tended to lose its monopoly within the *regio*, quickly in some areas, more slowly in others. It survived better in more upland areas in the north; but even where other churches were founded within the *regio*, the minster's rights as the mother-church often preserved a memory of the older state of affairs.

Ireland, however, seemed from Ó Carragáin's work to be characterized by a plethora of small local churches combined with cemeteries and houses within 'cemetery-settlements'. These cemetery-settlements were zoned, so that the cemetery and the oratory were in one part, houses in another, but in their approach to the relationship between the living and the dead they were very different both from traditional practice in the Roman Empire and from Iron-Age practice within Ireland itself, which kept the dead apart from the living. These cemetery-settlements were not old pre-Christian cemeteries that had been rendered Christian by the building of a church in association with the cemetery, but new Christian

145 Blair, *The Church in Anglo-Saxon Society*, 118–21, 149–60; T. Ó Carragáin, 'Cemetery Settlements and Local Churches in Pre-Viking Ireland in Light of Comparisons with England and Wales', in J. Graham-Campbell and M. Ryan (eds.), *Anglo-Saxon/Irish Relations before the Vikings*, 329–66; id. 'A Landscape Converted: Archaeology and Early Church Organization on Iveragh and Dingle, Ireland', in M. Carver (ed.), *The Cross goes North*, 127–52.

146 J. Blair, 'Minster Churches in the Landscape', in D. Hooke (ed.), *Anglo-Saxon Settlements* (Oxford, 1988), 52–3.

foundations. The area he studied, the Dingle and Iveragh peninsulas in Co. Kerry, parts of the early medieval kingdom of Corcu Duibne, were admittedly remote. But, if we remember that, in England, the old minsters survived longest in upland areas, the remote situation of the area he studied only strengthens the argument for a contrast. Moreover, he was able to cite an earlier study on the south-east of Co. Dublin (part of the early medieval district of Cualu in the north-east of Leinster).[147] This lay in a relatively fertile part of the country open to influence from Roman Britain and probably among the earliest districts to be influenced by Christianity. The evidence, also mainly in the east of the country, thrown up by rescue excavations in advance of road building, suggested that there, also, cemetery-settlements were common.

The contrast made between Ireland and England is, therefore, on several levels. In Ireland, there might be, according to a legal reference, 'a chief church of the *tuath*', a minor kingdom similar in extent to the English *regio*, but there was no single minster excluding the foundation of other churches in Ireland; again, there was no sign of royal control on the multiplication of churches.[148] In the small kingdom of Eilne, between the lower Bann and the Bush in the north of Co. Antrim, Coleraine was an early episcopal church, but others were recorded as early foundations by Tírechán at the end of the seventh century.[149] The density of pre-Viking churches was thus much higher in Ireland than in England. The relationship of the living to the dead was also quite different. What is lacking in England, but present in Gaul, is chapels built by aristocrats at existing cemeteries descending from the pagan period. The move to Christian burial in England went at varying speeds and took different forms, but, by the time Bede was writing his *Ecclesiastical History*, the norm was unfurnished burial, probably in a shroud, in small cemeteries away from settlement-sites.

The contrasts between Ireland and England and between England and Gaul raise the question what pattern was followed in the lands of the Britons: did it resemble Irish or English or Gaulish practice? This may be considered under four headings: first, royal control over the alienation of land in order to found churches; secondly, the position of a church served by a community, *clas* or minster, within a local district (since *regio* is, as we have seen, used in Wales for all territories from Gwynedd to Gwerthrynion, I shall refer to the more local territory as the *pagus*, Welsh *pau*); thirdly, the density of churches within a *pagus*; whether, as in Gaul, there were estate-churches, often on the site of old cemeteries, or churches founded by kindreds, as probably in Ireland; and, finally, the issue of what Ó Carragán has called 'cemetery-settlements'.

[147] E. O'Brien, 'Churches of South-East County Dublin, Seventh to Twelfth Century', in G. Mac Niocaill and P. F. Wallace (eds.), *Keimelia: Studies in Medieval Archaeology and History in Memory of Tom Delaney* (Galway, 1988), 506–22.

[148] CLH 577. 34; but note *Additamenta*, § 8, in *Patrician Texts*, ed. Bieler, 172, where the king freed the grant made by Caíchán (probably the client, *aithech*, of § 8. 3) and Mac Caírthinn (probably the lord, *flaith*).

[149] Tírechán, *Collectanea*, § 48. 2–3, ed. Bieler, *Patrician Texts*, 160; Adomnán, *Life of St. Columba*, i. 50.

Wendy Davies argued from the evidence of the Llandaff charters that kings of Gwent and Glywysing were successful in maintaining a control over the alienation of land until the eighth century.[150] This would suggest that the Welsh pattern might well resemble the English. We have no evidence to show whether this was also true of the rest of Wales, except that the Llandeilo documents in the Lichfield Gospels do not indicate that royal participation or consent was required. The greater Gwent (including Glywysing), with its stronger Roman inheritance, may well have been different.

Clasau sometimes seem to resemble early English minsters in that they dominated a local district or *pagus*. The positions of Llanbadarn in northern Ceredigion or of Basaleg in Gwynllŵg exemplify the pattern. Another influence on the situation, however, that of the fragmentation of dioceses, needs to be taken into account. The Roman *civitas* seems to have survived better as the post-Roman major kingdom—Dyfed, the greater Gwent, Gwynedd, Powys—than it did as the episcopal territory. If the interpretation of the evidence proposed above is correct, a *pagus* could have its own bishop, so that there could be more than one bishop in what had been a *civitas*; the unity of the *civitas* survived in the synod of a single kingdom, such as the first one to meet with Augustine of Canterbury. In England, however, large bishoprics were the rule, sometimes continuing Roman *civitates*, as in Kent or Lindsey. An echo of this situation may be the use of *ecclesia* in names of churches. As we noted earlier, in sixth-century Gaul this was traditionally used for the bishop's see in the capital of the *civitas*. Other words, such as *basilica*, *parochia*, and *oratorium* were used for other churches. If we bear in mind the change in Britain from *civitas*-bishopric to *pagus*-bishopric, observations made about *eglwys* in Welsh place-names and *eccles* in Lancashire place-names take on a new interest. Tomos Roberts noted that 'I have noticed that there is never more than one *Eglwys*-name in a commote'.[151] In Lancashire it has been noted that there was just one *eccles* in a hundred.[152] Eglwys Nynnid in Glamorgan may well be an ancient church: the name is likely to precede its medieval use as a grange of Margam Abbey; the associated stones include an early bilingual (Irish and Latin) inscription and a later half-uncial inscription.[153] On the other hand, by the eleventh century, *eglwys* was not used specifically for a church of high status, let alone episcopal: *Ecclus Silid*, in the list of prebends attached to the Life of St Cadog, was the name of a *villa* or *tref*, and may have been a minor estate-church.[154] *Ecclesia* was probably losing its special sense in the sixth and seventh centuries, but retained it longer in some areas than others.

The possibility that episcopal authority was often circumscribed by the *pagus* rather than the major kingdom, implies that the *clas* might be distinguished as a potential bishop's see rather than by any exclusion of other churches within its

150 Davies, *An Early Welsh Microcosm*, 50, 104–5.
151 Roberts, 'Welsh Ecclesiastical Place-Names and Archaeology', 42.
152 Blair, *The Church in Anglo-Saxon Society*, 31 n. 86.
153 Margam (Eglwys Nynnid) 1, 409/198/Gse-12/G86, and 2, 1020/200/G87.
154 *VSBG* 120.

territory. In Dyfed, bishop-houses seem to have coexisted with other churches, some of them of considerable importance, in the same cantref.[155] In Ergyng, a prime example of a *pagus*, witness lists to charters from the early seventh century supply evidence for several major churches, with communities headed by abbots or *principes* (see Maps 27 and 28). Two lay close to each other in the northern zone, on the south side of the Wye, Moccas and Bellamore or Byecross, two others also close to each other in the far south, close to Monmouth, Welsh Bicknor (perhaps earlier Hentland in Goodrich) and Little Doward, with a sprinkling of others in between, Llandinabo (or Bredwardine), Garway (or Eaton Bishop), Ballingham (or Carey within the parish of Ballingham), and Much Dewchurch.[156] This looks like a much denser distribution of community churches, equivalent to English minsters, than one would expect in England even in the eighth century. Moccas and Bellamore in the north were less than three miles apart (and Byecross even closer), Welsh Bicknor and Doward in the south about three miles as the crow flies, though the twists of the Wye would have made it a longer journey (Hentland to Little Doward is a mile and a half with the same proviso). If this were generally the case, we would expect a denser distribution of old churches in pre-Viking Wales than in England. Both Wales and Cornwall may have approximated more closely to the Gaulish and Irish patterns, though these differed from one another. Yet, there remains so much uncertainty over the age of most church sites that this can only be a provisional conclusion.

As for cemetery-settlements, these seem to be a distinctively Irish type. St Davids was surrounded by satellite chapels, and these do seem to have been linked with long-cist cemeteries, but they look more like Charles-Thomas's 'developed cemeteries', old cemeteries with a new chapel, than they do Ó Carragáin's cemetery-settlements, which were newly founded as such by Christians.[157] It has been suggested by excavators, as at Llandegai in Gwynedd, that remains of wooden structures in a cemetery may indicate the presence of a church, but this remains quite uncertain.[158] At Plas Gogerddan in Ceredigion, it was not clear whether the three early-medieval structures included a church or were simply special graves.[159] The church excavated at Capel Maelog may be as late as the twelfth century, after the period of this book.[160] The provisional conclusion must be that Wales still adhered to the normal separation of the living and the dead, a separation which

[155] H. James, 'The Geography of the Cult of St David: A Study of Dedication Patterns in the Medieval Diocese', in Evans and Wooding, *St David of Wales*, 47.

[156] *LL* 163b (*Comereg [abbas] Mochros, Iudnou abbas Bolcros, Helhearn abbas Lannguorboe, Guordoce abbas Lanndeui, Bithen princeps Landougarth, Guenuor abbas Lanngarthbenni*), similarly 164. Of these, *Lanngarthbenni* (Welsh Bicknor) in the south of Ergyng and *Mochros* (Moccas) in the north have hints of episcopal status (72a, and the *Comereg*, abbot of Moccas in 63b and 64 is likely to be the bishop of 165). The initial identifications are those of Davies, *An Early Welsh Microcosm* and *Llandaff Charters*, those in brackets are revisions suggested by B. Coplestone-Crow, *Herefordshire Place-Names*, 2nd edn. (Almeley, 2009). The map follows Coplestone-Crow, but the broad distribution is not affected.

[157] James, 'The Geography of the Cult of St David', 49–51; James, 'The Cult of St David', 105–11.

[158] C. Houlder, 'The Henge Monuments at Llandegai', *Antiquity*, 42 (1968), 221.

[159] K. Murphy, 'Plas Gogerddan, Dyfed, 22.

[160] W. J. Britnell, 'Capel Maelog, Llandrindod Wells, Powys: Excavations 1984–7', 27–96.

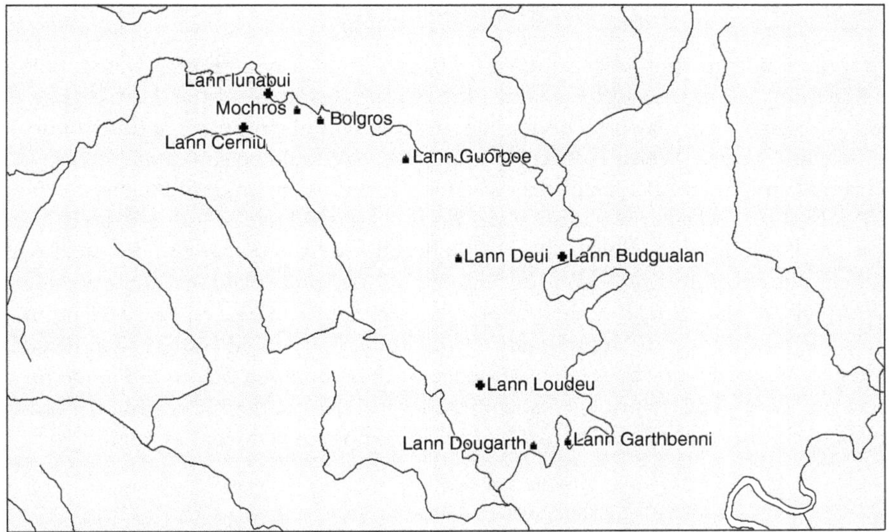

- Seventh-century churches with abbots or *principes*
- Other major seventh-century churches

Map 27. Major early churches in Ergyng
Seventh-century charters reveal the existence in Ergyng of churches served by communities and headed by abbots or *principes*. They are distributed across the old Ergyng and show a concentration along the Wye west of Hereford, an area taken by the English in the eighth century.

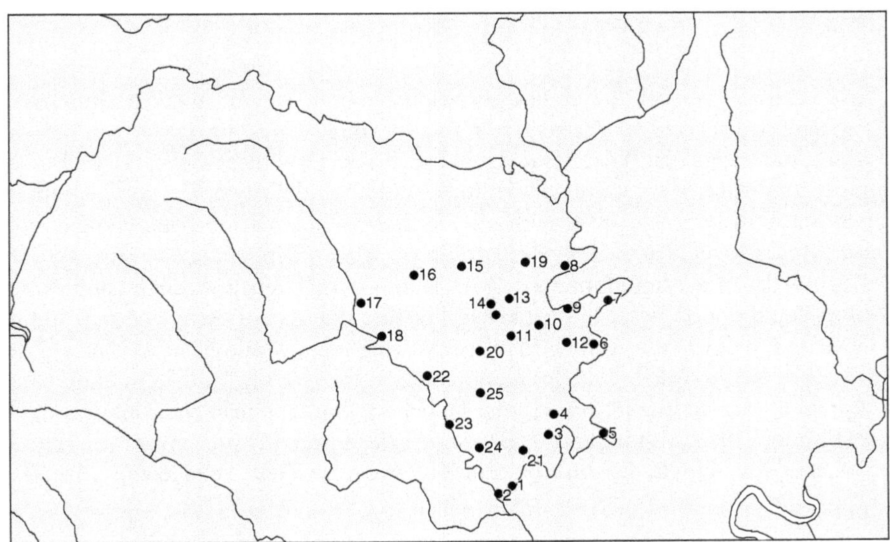

Map 28. Ergyng churches, *c.* 1100
The distribution of churches in Ergyng claimed by the bishop of Llandaff in the twelfth century is much denser than those attested at an early date, but it does not include the lands in the north of the old Ergyng lost to the English.

meant that the monastic cemetery, adjacent to the community, stood out as something new, quite different from the normal treatment of the dead.

Although there may have been much continuity in the practices and personnel of the pre-Norman Welsh Church, two periods saw major change: one was in the immediate post-Roman centuries, when the ecclesiastical unity of the city-territory was broken; the other was around the ninth century. That period saw the culmination of a long-term process by which churches were increasingly identified with their patron-saints. Not just the church, its personnel and its lands were the property of the saint, but the cemetery was particularly his, especially if he, too, lay there expecting the resurrection of the body;[161] to lie in his, or in some cases her, cemetery was to claim the patronage of the saint even before the judgement-seat of God. This standpoint is expressed with clarity about Ynys Enlli, Bardsey Island, in the twelfth century in the Death-Bed poem of Meilyr Brydydd:[162]

> May I be in that dwelling awaiting the call,
> The abbey where the tide beats against it:
> Secluded it is, its fame undimmed,
> Its graveyard in the breast of the brine.
> Fair Mary's isle, saintly isle of the saints,
> Expecting resurrection, it is splendid there.

It was the same attitude which encouraged the renaming of many churches as *llannau* of saints. The early medieval barrier in death between the clergy and monks on the one hand and the ordinary laity on the other was now removed.

4. SAINTS AND THEIR CULTS

In Chapter 7 we met the close association between a saint and his church, an association displayed in charters, not just in saints' Lives, liturgical commemoration, and calendars. That association had a background of belief as well as of customary ritual, such as annual commemoration on the day of the saint's death or pilgrimage to sites associated with his life. It is an assumption behind the cult of saints that the souls of the holy dead can know what is happening on earth. To pray to saints that they should intercede with God on one's behalf would be pointless if saints could not be aware of the prayer. The idea that a saint owns a church and its lands, that a dead saint is the lord of many living men, would be a silly fancy if the saint had no knowledge of, let alone concern for, earthly lands and those who supposedly served him in those lands. To believe that Llandeilo was Teilo's church, its bishop Teilo's bishop, and its peasants Teilo's peasants presumes that Teilo is aware of his church, his bishop, and his peasants. That Teilo could witness a

[161] In the tract *Bonedd y Saint*, *EWGT* 51–67, this is often indicated, as in similar Irish texts, by saying that the saint is 'in such-and-such a place', for example, § 9, 'King Einion in Llŷn, and Seiriol in Penmon, and Meirion in the Cantref'.

[162] CBT i. 4. 29–34, trans. J. Clancy, *Medieval Welsh Poems*, 123.

transaction on earth and his name could thus be entered among the witnesses in his gospel book would be an absurdity unless it was generally believed that heaven and earth were intimately connected through the concern of the holy dead for the living. A difference between an ecclesiastical lordship and its secular counterpart lies in this belief: the secular lord may be the heir of some earlier lord, but that earlier lord plays no significant role in the present except as ancestor; the ecclesiastical heir, however, is but the deputy of a lord in heaven, who, through his holiness on earth, has the ear of God himself.

This belief did not go unchallenged, as any British reader of the *Collectio Canonum Hibernensis* would have realized. The compilers of the *Hibernensis* admittedly had a fondness for issues that could be argued one way or the other. One such issue was whether the dead have any knowledge of what happens on earth.[163] If the holy dead are in the bliss of heaven, how can they know what is going on on earth and still remain in bliss? If all their attention and delight was absorbed in the contemplation of God, how could the affairs of the earth concern them at all? And, assuming such objections could be overcome, how could incorporeal spirits know what was happening on earth? Perhaps the saints in heaven depended upon reports brought by the newly dead. Or perhaps they were allowed to share even in God's foreknowledge, so that they were aware not only of what had already happened and of what was currently happening but even of what was going to happen in the future. Since it was in any case a mystery how a God existing in infinite happiness could know and be concerned about all the unhappinesses of this world, it was not much more of a problem to understand how the saints, whose own bliss was a sharing in the happiness of God, could also have some knowledge of the affairs of the earth.

It is important that theological belief was not static and unquestioned. Yet, the usual view was increasingly that the holy dead both knew and cared about what was happening on earth. Although they might be incorporeal spirits, they retained many of the allegiances they had had in the body. They could be expected to care particularly for their kindreds and their servants. Of course, the overriding solidarity was between those who delighted in the presence of God and those who hoped to do so when they had died, but that great solidarity—the solidarity of the Church as a whole, living and dead—did not preclude others. The saints cared about their peoples as the patriarch Abraham cared for all his descendants, though they were as numerous as the stars in heaven.[164] An awareness that a people's saints were a distinct group within the great host of heaven was an important manifestation of the consciousness of being a people. The Britons on earth should venerate the Britons in heaven, although they might also venerate some saints belonging to neighbouring peoples as well as the great saints of the universal Church. The Irish *Martyrology of Tallaght*, of the first half of the ninth century, lists the saints under

[163] *Collectio Canonum Hibernensis*, ed. Wasserschleben, xlix. 12–14, using quotations attributed to Jerome (not traced) and Augustine, *De Cura Mortuis Gerenda*, first sentence of x, § 12, CSEL xli. 641, combined with the first sentence of xv, § 18, CSEL xli. 650.

[164] Luke, 16: 19–31.

the day of the month on which they died to this world and were reborn in paradise. It divides the list into two: the universal saints and the saints of the Irish; but, among the latter, it admitted a few British saints—Gildas, David, Beuno, and Daniel—and a few English ones, such as the great saint of the Northumbrians, Cuthbert of Lindisfarne, and Wilfrid of York.[165]

No Welsh equivalent of the *Martyrology of Tallaght* has survived, but place-names allied with later calendars suggest that, if it had, it also would have contained some non-British saints: by the eleventh century Brigit of Kildare was venerated from Anglesey to Gwent, while Cóemgen (Kevin) of Glendalough had his followers in the north, from Anglesey to Tegeingl. Some great saints, indeed, moved between the two peoples, Patrick above all, but also perhaps Carannog of Llangrannog in Ceredigion.[166] St Cybi, as we have seen, had his church in Meath. It has been argued that many of the saints of Ceredigion were Irish in origin, but this is controversial.[167] Some sense of the range of British saints can be obtained from their genealogies recorded in *Bonedd y Saint* 'The Lineage of the Saints', a text probably of the thirteenth century.[168] Its counterparts in Ireland are rather earlier, from the Viking period up to the twelfth century. By comparing *Bonedd y Saint* with the assumptions behind the eleventh-century Welsh saints' Lives and the assumptions held by neighbouring peoples, Irish and English, it is possible to come to a reasonable estimate of how this British contingent in the host of heaven was viewed in the Wales of the eleventh century.

Unsurprisingly, since the saints were understood to care for their earthly kin and countrymen, this British heavenly contingent was marshalled according to categories familiar on earth. It began with St David leading the saints descended from Ceredig ap Cunedda.[169] Long after the death of the last king of Ceredigion descended from Ceredig, the lineage lived on in its saints. The great dynasties of Wales had their members in heaven. Thus the saints descended from Ceredig were followed by saints descended from Einion Yrth ap Cunedda, ancestor of the two royal dynasties of Gwynedd, the Maelgyning and the dynasty of Rhos, two for the Maelgyning and three for the dynasty of Rhos.[170] Here, too, the dynasties in their merely terrestrial form had come to an end in the ninth century; yet they remained influential in heaven. Then the text turns to the saints descended from the northern Britons,[171] after which it moves from one end of the British lands to the other, to

[165] *The Martyrology of Tallaght*, eds. R. I. Best and H. J. Lawlor, Henry Bradshaw Society, 68 (London, 1931), 29 January (Gildas), 1 March (David), 20 March (Cuthbert), 21 April (Beuno), 24 April (Wilfrid), 11 September (Daniel).

[166] K. Jankulak, 'Carantoc *alias* Cairnech? British Saints, and the Irish in Wales', in Jankulak and Wooding (eds.), *Ireland and Wales*, 116–48, provides a critical assessment of the evidence for the identity of Carannog and Cairnech (hence my 'perhaps').

[167] P. Ó Riain, 'The Church in Ceredigion: b. The Saints of Cardiganshire', in J. L. Davies and D. P. Kirby (eds.), *Cardiganshire County History*, gen. ed. I. G. Jones (Cardiff, 1994), 378–96.

[168] *EWGT* 51–67; the earliest manuscript, Aberystwyth, National Library of Wales, Peniarth MS 16, Part iv, is dated to the second half of the thirteenth century, Huws, *Medieval Welsh Manuscripts*, 58.

[169] *Bonedd y Saint*, §§ 1–8.

[170] Ibid. §§ 9–11.

[171] Ibid. §§ 12–18.

Brittany, and lists the saints descended mainly from Emyr Llydaw but also Gwyndaf Hen o Lydaw and Ithael Hael o Lydaw; and they are followed by saints descended from Custennin of Cornwall.[172] *Bonedd y Saint*, therefore, is a list of British, not just Welsh, saints.

The interest of *Bonedd y Saint* is not confined to lineage: often it also adds where a saint is—and by 'is' it means where the saint is buried. Thus later copies of the text added two of the saints who, by lineage, were Bretons, 'Cristiolus in Lledwigan in Anglesey and Rhystud in Ceredigion in Deheubarth'.[173] For someone who knew his Welsh geography, that would be enough to recall Llangristiolus, to the south-west of Llangefni, and Llanrhystud on the coast to the south of Aberystwyth. If he also knew a text such as *Englynion y Beddau*, he could populate the Wales of his imagination with the graves of warriors as well as the graves of the saints;[174] yet it is important that these two populations of the dead were kept apart, just as, in the hagiography of the eleventh century, kings, even Arthur himself, were more likely to be the opponents of saints than their allies. Only some of the warriors were described as being buried in a churchyard: they remained close to the burial customs of Wales as they existed before the ninth century. There is, however, a major difference between the resting places of the saints and their lineages: the latter, as we have seen, encompassed all the British lands from Scotland to Brittany; the former were in Wales. The saints of *Bonedd y Saint* were British by birth but Welsh in death.

The notion of an 'Age of Saints' has been prominent in both scholarly and popular writing about Wales and the other Celtic countries in the early Middle Ages. To a considerable extent this idea reflects something that, for British saints, can be followed back well into the early medieval period itself—to the late ninth century in the earlier Breton saints' Lives, to the early ninth century or even into the eighth century in the references to British saints in Irish saints' Lives as well as in the hagiographical component in the *Historia Brittonum*, and, finally, into the seventh century in the earlier Life of St Samson. The reasons why a saint mattered varied from one group to another: the saint might be the founder of a monastic way of life, as David was remembered in Rhigyfarch's Life of the saint, and that mattered primarily for his own community, though it also mattered for those who asked for the prayers of those ascetic monks who lived by his rule. The saint might be remembered as the founder of a monastery and as its present lord, and that also mattered primarily to his community, though from a different point of view, and for the lay element in that community as much as for monks or clerics; and it also mattered to those who might bury their kin in the monastic cemetery. The saint might be remembered through stories in which the saint was linked to different places in the landscape, and that mattered to those who lived in or visited that landscape.

It is evident from the Lives of British saints, whether they were written in Brittany in the ninth century or Wales in the eleventh, that one concern of a saint's community

172 Ibid. §§ 19–25; 26–7.

173 Ibid. § 24a.

174 T. Jones, 'The Black Book of Carmarthen "Stanzas of the Graves"', *Proceedings of the Britioh Academy*, 53 (1967), 97–137.

was his relationship with other saints. This took different forms: prophecy of one saint by another, godparenthood, spiritual direction, teaching, and even mere meetings were all put to good use. Claims to a relationship with another saint might be reciprocated, suggesting that some alliance between their communities was historical fact: the claims in the Life of St Cadog to a close alliance with Clonard, the most important monastery in East Meath, are echoed in the Life of Finnian, the patron saint and founder of Clonard: both Lives portray Finnian as the disciple of Cadog.[175] The purpose of these saintly connections varied. An important example is the role of St Germanus of Auxerre as the guardian of orthodoxy against the Pelagians. Germanus was the subject of a textual source used in the *Historia Brittonum* of 829–830. The *Liber Beati Germani* there cited must, therefore, be no later than the early ninth century. To judge by the material taken from the *Liber*, it was a British Life of the saint, not a copy of Constantius's *Vita S. Germani*. The First Life of St Samson claims that Samson's teacher, St Illtud, was a disciple of Germanus and that Germanus himself had ordained him to the priesthood.[176] The importance of Germanus is further confirmed by his role as the teacher of St Patrick according to the late seventh-century Life of Patrick by Muirchú.[177] The significance of portraying St Germanus as a teacher rather than in another role was his defeat of the British Pelagians. This may have mattered all the more because Pelagius continued to be read in Wales and Ireland up to the eighth century.[178]

The British saints, therefore, were not just holy individuals; they were also members of a society, the section of the Church that was already in heaven. Their interrelatedness on earth was only the beginning of the interrelatedness of the blessed in heaven. Yet someone's particular patron among the saints might perform the most crucial of all roles—to be the defender of the soul at the point of death. This is most clearly revealed in some early Irish rather than British saints' Lives, but associated ideas are also well attested in Wales. In the Lives of Beuno, David, Gwynllyw, and Cybi, the dying saint is met by a company of angels who conduct him from this world to heaven. This theme is especially prominent in the third book of Adomnán's Life of St Columba and its significance is there fully revealed. In one of the chapters in that book, Adomnán told a story about a vision that the saint had, when he was still alive and living on Iona.[179]

> Once, when St Columba was living in Iona, he was suddenly aroused and had the brethren gathered together by ringing the bell.
>
> 'Now,' he said to them, 'we must bring the help of our prayers to some of St Comgall's monks who are drowned in Belfast Lough at this time. See, even now,

[175] *Vita S. Cadoci*, ed. Wade-Evans, *VSBG*, §§ 11, 12, 17, 43; *Vita S. Finniani*, ed. W. W. Heist, *Vitae Sanctorum Hiberniae ex Codice olim Salmanticensi nunc Bruxellensi* (Brussels, 1965), 96–107, §§ 4, 5, 6, 9, 11.

[176] *Vita Prior S. Samsonis*, ed. Flobert, i. 6.

[177] Muirchú, *Vita S. Patricii*, i. 6 (ed. Bieler, *The Patrician Texts in the Book of Armagh*, 70/71). In *HB*, c. 50, Patrick receives a theological education at Rome, but is sent to Ireland by Pope Celestine on the advice of Germanus.

[178] D. N. Dumville, 'Late-Seventh- or Eighth-Century Evidence for the British transmission of Pelagius', *CMCS* 10 (Winter 1985), 39–52.

[179] Adomnán, *Vita S. Columbae*, iii. 13, trans. R. Sharpe, *Adomnán of Iona: Life of St Columba*, Penguin Classics (London, 1995), 215.

they are battling in the air against the powers of the Adversary who are seeking to snatch away the soul of a visitor who was drowned along with them.'

He prayed earnestly, not without tears, then rose quickly in front of the altar while the rest of the brethren were still lying on the ground in prayer. His face was lit up with joy, and he said:

'Give thanks to Christ. For holy angels have met the souls of these saints and have been victorious in the battle. Even the visitor who was seized by the battling demons has been saved.'

This was an example of what was elsewhere called 'the battle over a soul'.[180] The drowned monks of St Comgall of Bangor were relatively safe, but the visitor's hope of salvation would evidently have been slim had he not been in holy company, had he not been the beneficiary of the prayers of Columba and his monks, and had not Christ sent his angels to defeat the demons. The prospect of 'the battle over a soul' was terrifying even for the moderately virtuous layman. We shall come shortly to a passage in Rhigyfarch's Life of St David which could offer some comfort; but, first, it is vital to see that, in the mental world of Adomnán and many others in Wales as in Ireland and Scotland, death was not just something for the individual and God. If it had been, the visitor would have been damned. Although each human being brought his own sins, his own repentance, and his own virtuous acts before the judgement-seat of God, the prayers of others moved the mercy of Christ. That Christ sent his angels marked a decision to grant mercy, and the decision came after the drowned monks had fought to save their companion and after the monks of Iona, with their abbot, had prayed for the dead. The visitor on his own, unprayed for and unaccompanied, would have met in Christ a just judge; what saved him was the spiritual solidarity in prayer of all Christians, for that solidarity included the resurrected Christ, the lord of the angels, now at the right hand of God, and yet still bearing the wounds of his passion.

As this example illustrates, a saint's Life could include narratives that had a significance far beyond the story itself. We shall consider shortly the meanings conveyed by the Life of St David; but the Life must be prefaced with a brief account of the sources for St David before Rhigyfarch. In the *Annales Cambriae* the saint's death was placed under a year corresponding to AD 601, in the same year as it placed the death of Gregory the Great (who actually died in 604); but in the Irish Annals of Tigernach and other annals of the Clonmacnois group it was placed under a year corresponding to 589.[181] Presumably an entry recording the death of St David would have been part of *Annales Cambriae* at least from the time it became a St Davids text in the late eighth century. The dating of the *Annales Cambriae*, however, is very defective at this stage, and we do not know the source used by the Clonmacnois chronicler in the tenth century. It is worth noting, however, that Rhigyfarch has St David die on a Tuesday, 1 March, and that 1 March was a

[180] *Contentio animae*, equivalent to Irish *cath anmae*, *Vita S. Cainnechi*, c. 48 (ed. W. Heist, *Vitae Sanctorum Hiberniae*, 195).

[181] Dumville, *St David of Wales*, 3 (repr. 37) n. 9.

Tuesday in 604, the year of Gregory the Great's death;[182] but the first secure attestation of St David comes in Irish saints' Lives which are likely to belong to the eighth century or the early ninth and in Irish martyrologies.[183] The Life of St Ailbe of Emly, the premier saint of Munster, contains a version of the story that Rhigyfarch told in his Life of St David about Gildas being unable to preach when Nonnita (Non), pregnant with David, entered the church; in the Life of St Ailbe the priest unable to speak is nameless and he is celebrating mass rather than preaching, but otherwise it is the same story.[184] In the earlier Life of St. Lugaid (Mo Lua moccu Óche of Clonfertmulloe and Drumsnat), Áed of Ferns in southern Leinster wished to go to David so that the latter might be his 'soul-friend', namely spiritual director, but an angel redirected him to St Lugaid.[185] In Rhigyfarch's Life Áed (Máedóc) of Ferns is one of David's principal disciples, as he is in the Life of Máedóc himself.[186] In the Martyrology of Tallaght, a ninth-century reworking of material derived from Iona (and ultimately from Northumbria), as well as in the vernacular verse derivative, the Martyrology of Óengus, St David of Cell Muine ('the church of Mynyw') is entered under 1 March. Of the standard coordinates of a saint, the feast day and the place of burial, we have supporting evidence from Irish sources in the first half of the ninth century: to call the saint 'David of Cell Muine' does not prove that he was buried at Mynyw, but it makes it likely. Much of Rhigyfarch's Life is, therefore, likely to consist of older material that he has reworked, as he himself declared.[187]

As we saw in Chapter 3, St David was also named in an inscription from Llanddewi Brefi, which cannot be dated earlier than the ninth century.[188] It refers to plunder taken from St David, presumably because the church at Llanddewi Brefi was already his. If we accept that the church the Irish called Cell Muine was at or very close to St Davids, in the far west of Dyfed, this inscription attests his lordship of another major church, but this time in the east of Ceredigion, which, however, before the middle to late eighth century, may well have belonged to Dyfed.[189]

The Llandaff charters, however, suggest that the cult of St David had, long before the ninth century, transcended the limits of Dyfed at its widest. A charter assigned to the early eighth century recorded a grant by King Meurig in the presence of the *seniores* of Glywysing.[190] It is an unusual text, since in specifying the saintly beneficiaries, the twelfth-century editors seem to have been less than

[182] C. R. Cheney, *A Handbook of Dates*, rev. M. Jones (Cambridge, 2000), 156.

[183] R. Sharpe, *Medieval Irish Saints' Lives: An Introduction to Vitae Sanctorum Hiberniae* (Oxford, 1991), ch. 10; M. Herbert, 'Literary Sea Voyages and Early Munster Hagiography', in R. Black et al. (eds.), *Celtic Connections: Proceedings of the 10th International Congress of Celtic Studies: Language, Literature, History, Culture* (East Linton, 1999), 182–9.

[184] *Vita S. Albei*, § 21, ed. Heist, *Vitae Sanctorum Hiberniae*, 123.

[185] *Vita I S. Lugidi*, ed. Heist, ibid. 140.

[186] Rhigyfarch, *Vita S. David*, § 15, *Vita S. Aedui siue Maedoc*, §§ 11–20 (ed. Plummer, *Vitae Sanctorum Hiberniae*, ii. 297–300).

[187] Rhigyfarch, *Vita S. David*, § 66.

[188] See above, 164–6, Llanddewi Brefi 9.

[189] See above, 20.

[190] *LL* 190a.

careful in getting rid of any name other than Dyfrig, Teilo, and Euddogwy. The grant was to *sanctis Dubricio, Teliauo, et Oudoceo Deuioque*, 'Saints Dyfrig, Teilo, Euddogwy, and Dewi'. The first clerical witness after Bishop Berthwyn was *Morheb abbas podii Deui*, 'M. abbot of Llanddewi'.[191] Llanddewi is likely to be Much Dewchurch in Ergyng, for it appears in witness lists to early seventh-century charters, where the principal clerical witnesses were the abbots of *Mochros*, *Bolgros*, *Lannguorboe*, *Langarthbenni*, and *Lanndeui*, together with the *princeps* 'superior' of *Lanndougarth*.[192] If these places are all correctly identified as Moccas, Bellamore (Bellimoor), Garway, Welsh Bicknor, Much Dewchurch, and Doward, they were distributed across much of Ergyng, including the land just to the south of the Wye west of Hereford, which was lost to Ergyng before Domesday Book. One of the principal early churches of Ergyng, therefore, belonged to St David in the seventh century, not long after the saint's death.

From the ninth century, St David and his principal church are relatively well attested: his bishops have their obits in the *Annales Cambriae*, and Asser throws some light on the culture and status of the community at the end of the century. David is a figure of importance in Wrmonoc's Life of Paul Aurelian written in 884.[193] In the tenth century, as we saw in Chapter 16, his name is invoked in *Armes Prydein* as the chief of the saints of Britain, a saint under whose banner the Irish, not just the Britons, would be willing to march. The significance of the central role of St David in the poem is sometimes minimized by claiming that, because he saw St David in this role, the poet must have been a member of the community of St Davids: he, as a member of that community, naturally believed David to be the saintly leader of the Welsh, but those outside the community would be unlikely to take the same view.[194] As pointed out in Chapter 16, this is to forget that the poem was a serious attempt to rally the Welsh to the support of the Uí Ímair: to be effective the poet had to consider the assumptions and the loyalties of his target audience. His own sympathies, apart from hostility to the English, were of comparatively little significance. In spite of the view taken in recent scholarship, there is every reason to regard *Armes Prydein* as good evidence for the pre-eminence of St David among the saints of the Welsh.

The Life of St David was constructed by Rhigyfarch within a hagiographical tradition that anyone familiar with Irish saints' Lives would have understood. It was, however, particularly rich in reference and rewards close reading. I shall take a few passages as examples. The Life begins with the claim that David was predestined to be a great saint; this matches the final climax of the Life, when David triumphed at the Synod of Llanddewi Brefi against the Pelagians. Quite how great a saint David was going to be is demonstrated by a story about St Patrick: he is said to

[191] Davies, *The Llandaff Charters*, 112, notes that the names between Berthwyn and *Morheb* should be moved to the lay section. She dates the charter *c.* 728. The place, *Villa Bertus*, is unidentified.

[192] *LL* 163b, 164; Davies, *Llandaff Charters*, 104–5.

[193] *Vita S. Pauli Aureliani*, ed. C. Cuissard, 'Vie de S. Paul de Léon en Bretagne', *Revue Celtique*, 5 (1881–83), 421.

[194] A. O. H. Jarman, review of *Armes Prydein*, ed. I. Williams, *Llên Cymru*, 4 (1956), 57, and *The Welsh Life of St David*, ed. D. S. Evans (Cardiff, 1988), p. xix.

have wished to settle in the valley where Mynyw would later be founded but to have been told by an angel that it was reserved for one yet to be born; instead Patrick was shown by the angel a vision of Ireland, predestined to be his sphere of work.

These preliminaries are followed by the story of David's conception: he was the child of rape; his father raped his mother and then disappeared from the Life. The significance of the story, however, lies in its claims about the holiness of the mother, Nonnita (Non). When she was raped, it was the only sexual contact of her life. In terms of voluntary action she remained a virgin. The story becomes intelligible once the patristic background in the ideas of Jerome and Augustine about sexuality is appreciated.[195] These ideas resemble to some extent modern debates about the relative parts played by genetic inheritance and environment in forming the moral character of a person, but they also addressed the relative significance of voluntary action as compared with a physical event. Augustine argued that sinfulness was transmitted at conception through the unregulated passion of the parents. The disordered nature of human sexuality explained how evil could be passed by sexual intercourse from one generation to the next. This was the theory against which Pelagius reacted, as we have seen.[196] Since sexual passion was critical, Jerome could argue that a virgin forced into intercourse lost physical virginity but not its moral essence; and the argument mattered, since if the physical change were taken as being crucial, the raped woman would lose her honour—and in most Mediterranean societies the loss of sexual honour destroyed a woman's social standing. Whereas the behaviour of David's father entirely exemplified unregulated sexual desire, that of Nonnita was its opposite. Even David's father was said by Rhigyfarch to have later abdicated his throne and turned to the religious life. In that way he belatedly grew into his (artificial) name, Sanctus 'holy'; but Nonnita (Non is simply *nonna* 'nun' made into a name, while Nonnita is derived from *nonna*) was holy throughout her life; no unregulated passion of hers transmitted original sin to her son.

Pregnancy, birth, and baptism offered other opportunities to display David's relationships with other holy men. Gildas could not preach when the pregnant Non entered the church, 'for God has given him [David] the privilege, sovereignty and princely dignity of all the saints of Wales for ever'.[197] This theme was picked up again at the Synod of Llanddewi Brefi, where David alone was able to preach effectively (preaching being the special duty of the bishop, this was appropriately rewarded by the archiepiscopal title). David was baptized by Ailbe 'bishop of Munster' while being held by Mo Bí, the saint of Glasnevin, just to the north of the Liffey and thus in the early medieval province of Brega; both thus became godparents, spiritual fathers of the child. The spiritual kinship of the leading Welsh saint was wholly Irish. Among his other saintly connexions were a friendship with

[195] Jerome, *Commentarium in Matheum Libri IV*, ii, on Matthew 11: 30 (ed. D. Hurst and M. Adraen, CCSL 77, Turnhout, 1969, 87), contrasting the New Testament with the Old, cited by *Collectio Canonum Hibernensis*, ed. Wasserschleben, xlvi. 21. Cf. P. R. L. Brown, *The Body and Society: Men, Women and Sexual Renunciation in Early Christianity* (London, 1989), 407, on the difference between Augustine and Ambrose.

[196] See above, 196–9.

[197] Rhigyfarch, *Vita S. David*, § 5, trans. Sharpe and Davies.

Brendan the Navigator, saint of Clonfert in Connaught but himself the leading saint of West Munster, and with Bairre of Cork; his teaching of Áedán (Máedóc) of Ferns in South Leinster and Mo Domnóc of Osraige, the kingdom in the east of Munster that later became part of Leinster, gave him a particular affinity with south-eastern Ireland. David's spiritual ties covered Munster and South Leinster and just extended into the northern half of Ireland at Glasnevin. Unlike some other Welsh saints, however, David was not taught in Ireland but by Paulinus, disciple of St Germanus.

Like the Patrick portrayed by Tírechán, St David went on a circuit founding churches.[198] Whereas the beginning of his life looked westwards towards Ireland, this circuit went east, across South Wales and into England. Apart from Glastonbury, all the churches he was said to have founded, Bath, Crowland, Repton, and Leominster, belonged to the former kingdom of Mercia. After the circuit, Rhigyfarch turned to the foundation of Mynyw. First he found his nephew, Bishop Gwystli, living in the place, 'The Old Grove', from which David had set out. But that site was rejected:

> The angel of the Lord has told me, 'From the place where you intend to serve God, scarcely one out of hundred will be able to ascend to the kingdom of God.' Instead, he showed me a place from where few will go to perdition; for everyone who is buried in good faith in the graveyard of that place will obtain forgiveness.

This is a classic motif of Irish hagiography from the eighth century onwards and it proclaims the power of a cemetery where a saint lay buried to draw to itself the burials of lay people as well as monks.[199]

Rhigyfarch's Life of St David was written in a high Latin style and therefore for scholars rather than for the ordinary clergy, let alone for the laity. It ensured that the saint was remembered in fine Latin prose, as was only appropriate for the intellectual grandchild of St Germanus and the one who, in his preaching surpassed all his contemporaries. The Welsh translation of the Life was not made until later, although some episodes were celebrated in the *awdl* by Gwynfardd Brycheiniog in the second half of the twelfth century.[200] If we ask what sustained the popular cult of St David, one answer is the topography of the cult.[201] The difficulty here is that, apart from places mentioned in Rhigyfarch's Life, it is hard to give any chronological precision to the material. From the Life, however, one can surmise that the topography of St David was well developed but not necessarily completely developed by the late eleventh century. Stories attached to places, which the saint's follower could visit, places that prompted remembered stories for one person to tell

[198] Ibid. § 13.

[199] *Additamenta*, § 14, in *Patrician Texts*, ed. Bieler, 176/177; *Vita S. Fintani Cluana Ednig*, ed. Heist, *Vitae Sanctorum Hiberniae*, 146–7.

[200] *The Welsh Life of St David*, ed. Evans; CBT ii. 26; N. A. Jones and M. E. Owen, 'Twelfth-Century Welsh Hagiography: The Gogynfeirdd Poems to the Saints', in Cartwright (ed.), *Celtic Hagiography*, 45–76, esp. 61–7.

[201] James, 'The Cult of St David'; similarly, for Brittany, J. M. H. Smith, 'Oral and Written: Saints, Miracles and Relics in Brittany, *c.* 850–1250', *Speculum*, 65 (1990), 309–43.

another—these sustained the cult as a whole. There may have been a linguistic and stylistic gulf between such stories and the mannered Latin prose of Rhigyfarch, but the latter's Life offered plenty of topographically anchored narrative, such as St Patrick's seat near St Davids or the hill at Llanddewi Brefi. True, it did not explain the origins of St Justinian's Chapel, but it did explain the relationship to David of his disciples, Ishmael, Máedóc, and Teilo. The Life did not embrace the whole cult, but it was part of it for a special readership.

This chapter has attempted to gain some sense of the general trends in the development of the Welsh Church between the fourth century and the eleventh. Precision in dating the changes and in detecting local variations has been hampered by the lack of evidence. That has encouraged a reliance on comparing Wales with neighbouring countries; and the danger of the comparative approach is that aspects of the Welsh Church that could be illuminated by that route may have been given undue prominence. If we knew more about the British Christianity that was submerged or even repressed in England, especially after 664, it would help to gain a sense of what changes had occurred by the seventh century. There is some hope that close study of the landscape of early English Christianity, allied with survey and excavation, may help the Welsh historian. Some things are, however, quite clear from this chapter and those dealing with the post-Roman period. There is no good reason to think that British Christianity was seriously reversed as a result of the disaster of 367. Instead, the geographical reach of Christianity was steadily extended westwards until, through St Patrick, it reached the Atlantic coast of Ireland. The close links with Irish Christianity created in the fifth century remained throughout the period up to 1064, whereas the links with English Christianity were abruptly cut in the aftermath of the condemnation of the Britons and the Irish as heretics, a condemnation that remained in force for a generation after 669. Relations between the English and the British Churches were imperilled from the start by political tensions in both Britain and Gaul; but the fatal step was taken by men such as Wilfrid of Ripon and Archbishop Theodore. As we shall see in the next chapter, better relations were established from the late ninth century, but by then the damage had been done.

19

Latin Learning in Wales, *c.* 400–1100[1]

1. THE DEATH OF BRITISH LATIN AND ITS CONSEQUENCES

A change which transformed the conditions underlying the culture of the Britons was the slow decline and eventual death of British Latin as a language of the home. In Chapter 2 it was argued that British Latin survived into the seventh century as a regional form of Romance, a spoken form of Latin learnt in childhood within the family, and a language that had undergone major changes since Classical Latin. The evidence came from inscriptions showing developments in British Latin parallel with those in other regional forms of Romance and often parallel with those undergone by British Celtic at the same period. The number of inscriptions, however, was sharply reduced in the seventh and eighth centuries, and this makes it more difficult to date the death of British Latin. A clue is the First Life of St Samson, which I would date to the seventh century.[2] Although the Latin of this text is relatively correct, it includes a number of words and phrases that indicate that British was the writer's first language; for example, *ipse solus* is used to mean 'himself', a usage which mimics the British forerunner of Middle Welsh *e hunan*, *ehun*, Middle Breton *(h)e hunan*.[3] Admittedly some such Brittonic influences on his Latin may go back earlier to a time when there were numerous speakers bilingual in Latin and British. What is persuasive is the combination of a general correctness in his Latin with evidence of an underlying British influence. His Latin is certainly not derived from a spoken British Romance, in which British Celtic influences might be expected. When such influences appear, therefore, they are more easily explained as evidence of a native speaker of British Celtic who has learnt Latin. The same can be said of the *Historia Brittonum* of 829 or 830, whereas Gildas's Latin was indeed grammatically correct, but did not exhibit such British influences.[4]

[1] I am grateful for advice generously given by Helen McKee. There is a helpful survey of the subject by H. Pryce, 'The Origins and the Medieval Period', in P. H. Jones and E. Rees (eds.), *A Nation and its Books* (Aberystwyth, 1998), 1–7, and of more palaeographical and codicological aspects by D. Huws, 'The medieval manuscript', ibid., 25–8, reprinted in his *Medieval Welsh Manuscripts* (Cardiff, 2000), 1–23.

[2] See above, 238–9.

[3] *Vita Prima S. Samsonis*, ed. P. Flobert, *La Vie ancienne de Saint Samson de Dol* (Paris, 1997), 66–8.

[4] *HB* cap. 37, *ipse solus* = *e hun(an)*, cap. 73, *ego solus* = *fy hun(an)*. F. Kerlouégan, 'Le Latin du De Excidio Britanniæ de Gildas', in M. W. Barley and R. P. C. Hanson (eds.), *Christianity in Britain, 300–700* (Leicester, 1968), 172, concludes 'c'est en gros le latin d'un bon auteur du Vème finissant, avec cette différence importante que Gildas n'est pas à l'écoute d'une langue parlée', 'taken as a whole,

When this proposed seventh-century date for the death of British Latin is tested against the evidence of South-Welsh inscriptions from the eighth to the eleventh century, the results are mixed. I shall take three relatively long and well-preserved inscriptions in what may be their chronological order. The first is an inscription at Llanilltud Fawr, the earlier of two which show that monastery as the burial place of kings.[5]

IN NOM/INE D(*e*)I SU/MMI INCI/PIT · CRU/X · SAL/UATO/RIS · QUA/E PREPA/RAUIT / SAMSO/NI:· APA/TI PRO / ANIMA / SUA : [ET P]/RO ANI/MA IU/THAHE/LO REX:. / ET ART/MALI :. ET / TEC[A]/N[I]/ +

In the name of the supreme God (the text) begins. The cross of the Saviour which Abbot Samson had put up for his own soul and for the soul of King Ithael and Arthfael and Tegan.

This inscription may be dated to the middle of the eighth century, the earliest datable Welsh inscription in half-uncial.[6] Its dependence on scribal traditions is shown by the use of an *incipit* formula ('begins'). The Latin, however, is of poor quality: QUAE is a mistake for QUAM, SAMSONI for SAMSON, APATI for ABBAS (of which APAS would be an acceptable variant), IUTHAHELO for IUTHHAELI, REX for REGIS. Adams's charge against the post-Roman inscriptions, that they exhibited an ignorance of Latin morphology and therefore of Latin, might have missed the mark there, since Latin was by then a variety of Romance, but it would be entirely fair if applied to this inscription. It is, however, noticeable that 'epigraphic -I' still seems to be present in SAMSONI; yet IUTHAHELO, which should have had an ending -I, has an -O, which, in earlier British Latin inscriptions, appears in place of the nominative -US as well as continuing the ablative -O. Poor Latin rather than any continuance of British Romance seems to be the explanation here. The poor quality of the Latin is remarkable given the elevated status of the people concerned and the reputation of Llanilltud Fawr as a place of high Latin culture: in the First Life of St Samson, the saint is taken to study under Illtud in 'the school of the distinguished teacher of the Britons'.[7] Although the twelfth-century Life of Illtud has relatively little to say about his excellence as a teacher, it does make the king declare that 'your *gimnasium* will be revered'.[8] The intellectual decline at this church between the sixth century and the seventh appears to have been calamitous.

An inscription on Caldey Island, Ynys Bŷr, off the coast of Dyfed (see Illustration 19.1), is noted for the unusual excellence of its lettering, showing strong geometrical influence and reminiscent of Insular display letters in grand gospel books.[9] It may be important, however, that it has lost the upper part of the stone. In the *Corpus* it is dated to the eighth or early ninth century.[10]

it is the Latin of a good writer of the late-fifth century, with the important difference that Gildas was not accustomed to hear the spoken language'. This issue needs to be considered further.

5 Llantwit Major 3, 1012/223/G65.

6 See above, 138.

7 *Vita Prima S. Samsonis*, ed. Flobert, i § 7, 156.

8 *Vita S. Iltuti*, § 10, ed. and trans. Wade-Evans, *VSBG* 208.

9 427/301/P6.

10 Cf. *LHEB*, p. 293, *CIB*, p. 197.

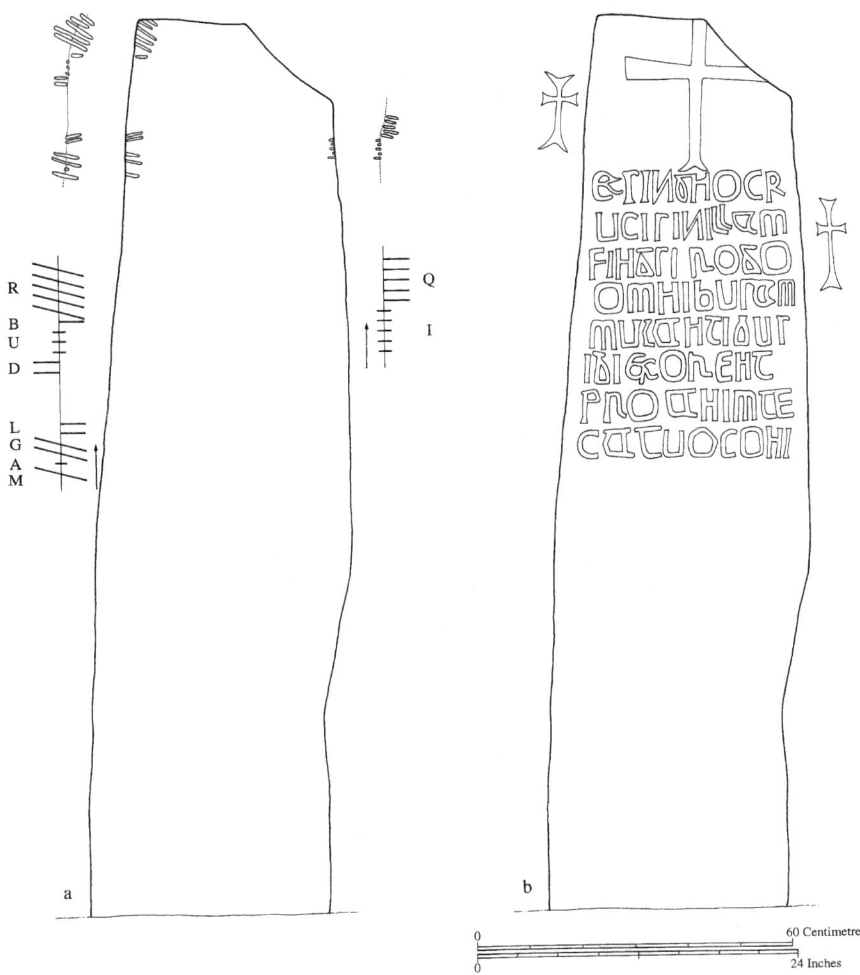

Illustration 19.1. This stone comes from Caldey Island off the south coast of Pembrokeshire, which, from the sixth century, was home to a monastic community recorded in the First Life of St Samson. The stone contains two inscriptions, an early ogham inscription, probably fifth century, and one with a base of half-uncial but strongly influenced by geometrical letterforms; the inscription has been dated to the eighth or early ninth century. It is reminiscent of the decorative drawn letters used in Insular gospel books. © Crown copyright: Royal Commission on the Ancient and Historical Monuments of Wales.

ET SINGNO CR/UCIS IN ILLAM / FINGSI ROGO / OMNIBUS AM/MULANTIBUS / IBI EXORENT / PRO ANIMÆ / CATUOCONI

The translation preferred in the *Corpus* takes this as: 'With the sign of the cross I fashioned on that [?] I ask all walking there that they pray for the soul of

Catuoconus'. The first part of the translation is influenced by proposals made by David Howlett, who understands the Latin *et* as 'with', which would reflect the instrumental use of Welsh *a*(*c*).[11] The translation preferred by Nash-Williams was 'And by the sign of the cross (which) I have fashioned upon that (stone) I ask all who walk there that they pray for the soul of Catuoconus'. He compared the similar request for prayer associated with a cross on the Llanwnnws stone in Ceredigion.[12] That inscription asked the person who explained the abbreviated name IHS XRS (Iesus Christus) at the top of the cross to give a blessing for the soul of HIROIDIL FILIUS CAROTINN. It is not impossible that the ET 'and' at the beginning of the Caldey inscription is to be explained by words which were on the lost top of the stone and that the feminine gender of ILLAM is also to be explained by the lost text. This would go some way to justify Nash-Williams's translation, but it remains true that both translations imply that a relative pronoun has been omitted (as shown by Nash-Williams's (which)); this may be explained by the influence of the vernacular, in which, with a compound verb in the relative clause, there could be no relative pronoun or particle.[13] It remains possible that SINGNO is a Late Latin form of SINGNUM. That would suggest that the old spoken British Latin survived.

The final phrase of the inscription, PRO ANIMÆ CATUOCONI has caused some difficulty. The translations by Nash-Williams and in the *Corpus* presuppose that ANIMÆ is for ANIMA, since the preposition *pro* takes the ablative. Howlett, however, sees ANIMÆ as composed of two words, ANIMA and E, even though E is ligatured with the preceding A, with E postponed after the word it governs (ANIMA). The reason for this, at first sight unlikely, proposal is that he believes that the inscription is metrical, made up of syllabic adonics.[14] The classical adonic line had five syllables, but with the further provision that it was composed of a long syllable followed by two short ones and then two long ones: ¯ ˘ ˘ | ¯ ¯. The old distinction between long and short vowels had been lost, as we have seen, long before the date of this inscription, and a simpler, syllable-counting metre was a natural result. Howlett's metrical line division is thus as follows:

ET SINGNO CRUCIS
IN ILLAM FINGSI
ROGO OMNIBUS
AMMULANTIBUS
IBI EXORENT
PRO ANIMA E
CATUOCONI

This proposal is, however, very difficult to accept because of the last two lines. Although it restores a correct ANIMA, it does so at the price of breaking up the

11 D. Howlett, *Cambro-Latin Compositions* (Dublin, 1998), 23–5. Cf. D. S. Evans, *Grammar of Middle Welsh* (Dublin, 1964), § 201.

12 994/125/CD27.

13 Evans, *Grammar of Middle Welsh*, § 65, n. 1.

14 Cf. J. Rhys, *The Origin of the Welsh Englyn and Kindred Metres* (*Y Cymmrodor*, 18 [1905]), 56–7, who also proposed a metrical analysis, but a quite different one.

standard formula *pro anima X* 'for the soul of X'; and if E is understood as the preposition, *e, ex* 'out of', either ANIMA must be governed by two prepositions at once, PRO and E, or CATUOCONI now has the wrong case. Moreover, it requires CATUOCONI to be five syllables, so that U would have to be understood as /uw/. This is theoretically possible for an early inscription, but at this date it can safely be discounted, and with that the metrical interpretation of this inscription falls.[15]

The inscription, however, remains very interesting for Welsh Latin. SINGNO is for standard SIGNO and FINGSI for standard FINXI, but in both cases NG would be a good phonetic spelling for Classical Latin.[16] The -MM- of AMMULANTIBUS shows a British sound-change, *-mb- > -mm-*, but its use as an ordinary verb of going can be paralleled in Late Latin.[17] If we except ANIMÆ for ANIMA, a spelling for which Nash-Williams was able to cite non-British parallels, the inscription reveals a relatively correct Late Latin.[18] This was probably a Latin learnt in a school but nevertheless used in speech—presumably, given the site, in a monastery—but SINGNO may perhaps reveal the survival of the old spoken Latin. If we compare it with the Llanilltud inscription already discussed, it shows a distinctly higher level of Latin.

A rather later Llanilltud inscription can be dated because it was made at the command of Hywel ap Rhys, named as king of Glywysing by Asser, in memory of his father and thus probably close to the beginning of his reign.[19] He may be the Hywel who died in Rome in 886.[20] The date of his father's death is not recorded, but it may be assigned to the second or third quarter of the ninth century.

[I]N INOMINE D PATRIS ET
[S]PERETUS SANTDI ANC
[C]RUCEM HOUELT PROPE[R]
ABIT PRO ANIMA RES P[A]
[TR]ES EUS

In the name of the Father and of the Holy Spirit. Hywel had this cross made for the soul of his father, Rhys.

An important key to this inscription is the spelling of the name of Hywel's father, Rhys, as RES rather than, as with Asser, *Ris*. This shows that a centralized /ï/, namely the 'clear *y*' of the medieval Welsh grammarians, a sound still preserved in North Welsh, could be spelt as E, something well attested in vernacular Welsh manuscripts of the thirteenth century.[21] The same spelling explains [S]PERETUS for standard SPIRITUS and PATRES for PATRIS.[22] The initial I- of INOMINE is not necessarily an error, since the addition of a 'prosthetic' vowel, as in Middle

[15] *CIB*, p. 128 n. 726; linguistic commentary in Edwards, *Corpus*, ii, P6.
[16] W. S. Allen, *Vox Latina: The Pronunciation of Classical Latin* (Cambridge, 1965), 23–5.
[17] *CIB*, p. 74; Väänänen, *Introduction au latin vulgaire*, § 141.
[18] The grammatical index to H. Dessau, *Inscriptiones Latinae Selectae*, 4th edn. (Dublin/Zürich, 1974), iii. 807, has two examples of <ae> for /a/.
[19] 1011/220/G63, Llantwit Major 1.
[20] *AC*, ed. Dumville, 12–13.
[21] *LHEB*, 283 n. 2.
[22] In Welsh the first *i* of *spiritus* was syncopated, but when pronouncing the Latin word a Welshman would probably have said /spïrïdus/ or /espïrïdus/.

Welsh *ynifer* for *nifer* (from Latin *numerus*), is already attested at this period.[23] The prosthetic vowel is first attested in Late Latin, and one might, therefore, regard this example as evidence for the survival of British Romance. Yet, although the prosthetic vowel in Welsh before /s/ + stop is very probably due to Latin influence, its appearance before /n/ was specifically Welsh; by this date the Welsh vowel may be affecting the pronunciation of Welsh Latin. This inscription does not attest, therefore, the survival of British Latin. These examples merely suggest that the person who composed this inscription used a pronunciation of Latin strongly influenced by Welsh. He also, however, used Old Welsh spelling conventions, as in EUS for standard EIUS, which can most easily be explained by the practice of writing *e* for /ei/.[24] Similarly, Old Welsh spelling sometimes disregarded an /h/ at the beginning of a word, as in the Juvencus gloss *anter* on Latin *semi-*, Middle Welsh *hanher*.[25] SANTDI for standard SANCTI is also readily explicable: Welsh *sant* shows that the complex consonantal cluster /nkt/ was simplified in British Latin, as elsewhere (for example Italian *santo*). The use of TD for /t/ is merely a quirk of spelling: SPERITUS SANTI occurs at Merthyr Mawr, a few miles west-north-west of Llanilltud Fawr.[26]

A rather more complex problem is offered by PROPARABIT in place of a standard PRAEPARAUIT (allowing for the normal Late Latin *pre-* for *prae-*, the standard Latin form was attested in Llantwit Major 3, discussed above). Two divergencies from PREPARAUIT stand out: PRO- instead of PRE- and -ABIT instead of -AUIT. PRO- instead of PRE- may perhaps be nothing more than a confusion between their abbreviations; and that could suggest that an *ordinator* misunderstood the abbreviated *pre-* on the wax tablet, and, therefore, that he was a different person from the author of the text. An alternative is to suppose a reduction of the unstressed vowels of both PRE- and PRO- to a 'murmer vowel', /ə/ (as in the second syllable of English 'father', /fa:ðə/), so that both were pronounced /prə/ and were thus interchangeable.[27] The use of -ABIT in place of -AUIT is more difficult, although it is also attested in an inscription further west at Margam.[28] Normally in Late Latin a /w/, spelt *u*, developed to a /v/, but this change is not normally reflected in loanwords from British Latin, not only in loans into British, which might well have been early enough to escape this change, but in loans into Irish or into English (as in *wic* < *uicus*), which were generally late. A retention of /w/ in British Latin would simply reflect its retention in British Celtic—another example of how the two languages influenced each other. The easiest explanation of -ABIT,

[23] In the Juvencus glosses, *LHEB*, pp. 527–8; but the redating of the accent-shift to the ninth century means that the prosthetic vowel must have been well established before then, and, as Jackson notes, it is paralleled in Late Latin. The Juvencus example follows the usual Late Latin pattern whereby such a vowel developed before consonantal clusters of *s* + stop: Väänänen, *Introduction au latin vulgaire*, §§ 82–5; Evans, *Grammar of Middle Welsh*, § 15.

[24] *LHEB*, pp. 587–8.

[25] *Juvencus: Text and Commentary*, ed. H. McKee (Aberystwyth, 2000), fo. 42r23 and p. 471.

[26] 1022/240/G100.

[27] *LHEB* § 202 (but the reduction must have been complete before the shift of the accent, now thought to be ninth century in date: see above, 92).

[28] 1015/233/G81, Margam 4, the 'Grutne stone'.

however, is to suppose a speaker of Old Welsh for whom /v/ was the lenited counterpart of /b/. He could then write -ABIT and pronounce it /avit/ or perhaps rather /avid/. But such an explanation requires that -AUIT was pronounced in a way characteristic of Late Latin outside Britain, as /avit/ or /avid/ (compare French *avoir* from Latin *habere*). If all this can be granted, then we have a speaker who would make no distinction in pronunciation between -AUIT and -ABIT. Continental influence on early Welsh pronunciation of Latin after it had died out as a native spoken language in Britain is not difficult to accept: it might have come *via* Brittany.

Most of this inscription can be explained on the basis of Old Welsh. What is striking is the change from the post-Roman period: then Latin was the language of higher status, a language that appeared on the memorial stones of an Irish settler elite, often, but not always, alongside Irish. The tools of literacy, spelling included, were primarily those of Latin, only secondarily those of British, as seen in proper names. In this ninth-century inscription, however, Latin was impregnated with Welsh phonology and, even more surprising, Welsh spelling habits. Once this has been recognized, however, the Latin appears to be better than on the earlier cross put up by Abbot Samson for his king, Ithel. Yet the final element in the explanation has compelled us to turn to the Continent; and this indicates that Llanilltud Fawr was not purely Insular in its culture. What remains very odd, and presumably a testament to the carelessness of those responsible for the text of the inscription rather than a revelation of a heterodox theology, is the complete omission of the Second Person of the Trinity.

Two general conclusions can be drawn from these three inscriptions. First, the old native British Latin was dead in South Wales by the eighth century. Latin was spoken as well as read, but it was learnt in a school and its pronunciation was now largely dictated by Welsh. Perhaps the last British inscription to suggest that the old British Latin was alive is, strangely, from Peebles in the north, where an inscription, probably of the second half of the seventh century, commemorating NEITANO SACERDOS has the characteristic -O for -US.[29] The best explanation for this inscription is that clergy in late Antiquity were drawn from clerical families, and that, even beyond Hadrian's Wall, such families may sometimes have preserved for a time a bilingualism after the rest of British society had become monolingual. The end of the old native British Latin will have varied in date between different groups in society and different areas, but by *c.* 700 it is likely to have been complete. Secondly, the level of Latin culture even in the principal monasteries of South Wales varied considerably: the Latin of the Caldey inscription was superior to the earlier Llanilltud inscription; but the later Llanilltud inscription suggested a recovery.

Irish was attested in Wales in inscriptions, but these, apart from the odd exception, are all dated before *c.* 600. Some forms of the Cunedda legend, whose original version has been tentatively dated to the eighth century, state that Cunedda and his sons drove out the Irish. By the eighth century, probably, Irish was no longer a normal language of the home in Wales. The shift in Wales from three

[29] 2025/Scot12, K. H. Steer, 'Two Unrecorded Early Christian Stones', *Proceedings of the Society of Antiquaries of Scotland*, 101 (1968–9), 127–8.

languages to one language may all be part of one process—a process that may be assigned to the seventh century.[30] The end of British Latin tended to separate the Britons from Romance-speaking Gaul, and the death of Irish in Wales must similarly have weakened ties across the Irish Sea.

2. SCRIPTS AND BOOKS

The end of the old British Latin and the abandonment of roman capitals for inscriptions both came in the seventh century and were part of a loosening of the ties with the Roman past. In the fifth and sixth centuries, as we saw in Chapter 3, cursive letters sometimes intruded into inscriptions whose base letterforms were capitals.[31] The appearance of such intrusive cursive was geographically unevenly spread and it was mainly a matter of the use of two cursive letters, **f** and **s**, **f** being commonly found in the word *filius*, genitive *fili*, where the **f** was ligatured with the following **i**. The significance of such intrusions was that they revealed the continued use in Britain of New Roman cursive, a form of script introduced *c.* 300 and employed by the imperial administration, but also found in such private texts as the Bath curse tablets.

Cursive played an important role in the shaping of the Insular version of half-uncial, what was by the seventh century the script used for grand books. It is also from *c.* 600 that we get our earliest Insular manuscripts, not in Celtic Britain but in Ireland. Yet the date is sufficiently close to the time of the conversion of Ireland to make it likely that Irish scribal practice remained close to its British parent; and, in any case, Irish and Welsh scribal habits advanced in parallel until *c.* 1000.[32] Analogy with the inscriptions also makes it easier to visualize the development of Insular book scripts in the fifth and sixth centuries, and thus to perceive the continuity between fourth-century Britain and seventh-century Ireland and Britain. The intrusion of cursive into capitals was explained as an outcome of the process by which an inscription was made: the author of the text wrote it on a wax tablet in cursive; the *ordinator* then took this text and laid it out on the stone. In general, he changed the letterforms to fit the context, replacing cursive by capital letters; sometimes, however, and especially in such regularly repeated words as *filius*, he allowed the cursive of the tablet to remain at the stage of *ordinatio*. The lapidary then inscribed the stone.

A similar process is likely to have formed Insular half-uncial. A text was first drafted in cursive on wax tablets and only subsequently written in a formal book script on parchment. This sequence made it easy for cursive letterforms to intrude into half-uncial or minuscule. By the seventh century this process was complete for such letters as **g**, **r**, and **s**. In half-uncial the cursive forms of **r** and **s** continued to

[30] See above, 114–15.

[31] Above, 119–27.

[32] D. N. Dumville, *A Palaeographer's Review: The Insular System of Scripts in the Early Middle Ages*, i (Osaka, 1999), 125–6.

coexist with majuscule forms, **R** and **S**, but in minuscule the cursive forms carried all before them except in some very grand varieties. This pattern, with the process of infiltration from below being most complete in Insular minuscule and incomplete in half-uncial, suggests that a hierarchy of scripts already existed in the fifth and sixth centuries, that the infiltration of cursive proceeded upwards, first into relatively rapidly written minuscule, then into more stately forms of minuscule, and finally into half-uncial. It was a gradual development, so that a British half-uncial manuscript of the fifth century, at the top of the hierarchy, may still have been indistinguishable from one in Gaul. Such a gradual process presupposes that a hierarchy of scripts and therefore, more generally, of book production already existed in the fifth and sixth centuries. Only the last stages, such as the development of the Insular serif, can be traced in the manuscripts of the seventh century.

The best, and only direct, evidence for the role of the wax tablet in Insular writing is from northern Ireland, the Springmount Bog tablets.[33] These, however, may well date from the sixth century and thus from a period when relations between Ireland and Celtic Britain were especially close.[34] The first hand (there is more than one) was very competent with the stylus but had not yet learnt how to write a book hand. This is shown by his attempt to imitate a book-hand serif on an ascender (such serifs were foreign to the type of ascender used on wax tablets, which instead employed approach-strokes). He produced his imitation-serif but put it on the wrong side of the ascender.[35] The implications of this example are, first, as has been noted, that the inscribing technique with the sharp-pointed stylus upon wax produced a partially different set of letterforms; secondly, that many may have been competent with a stylus but entirely, or almost entirely, without experience in writing on parchment; and, thirdly, that we can, therefore, grade the literate into three broad categories: those who only read; those who read and inscribed with stylus and wax tablet; those who read, inscribed with stylus, and wrote with quill on parchment. Wax tablets were used in education (the Springmount Bog tablets probably belong to this category), in literary composition,[36] and, probably, for correspondence. A gloss in the early tenth-century Welsh copy of Ovid, *Ars Amatoria*, Book I, explained *tabellas* by *aepistolas* 'letters' (fo. 42r22, to l. 383 of the text) but also (fo. 38r2 to l. 71) by Old Welsh *cloriou* 'surfaces', where *tabellae*, in the context, refers to pictures on the *Porticus Liviae* (in other words, the glossing was not mechanical but sensitive to the particular references of the text). The explanation of *tabellas* by *aepistolas* thus makes it likely that wax tablets were commonly used to write letters. The wax tablet was intended to be reused; for this reason it was unlikely to end up in an administrative archive or a library book cupboard. Its original ubiquity is intimately related to the reason why hardly any examples survive.

33 *CLA* Suppl. 1684; D. G. Charles-Edwards, 'The Springmount Bog-Tablets: Their Implications for Insular Epigraphy and Palaeography', *Studia Celtica*, 36 (2002), 27–45.

34 Dumville, *A Palaeographer's Review*, 31–5.

35 D. G. Charles-Edwards, 'The Springmount Bog Tablets', 31.

36 Adomnán, *De locis sanctis*, Praef. and II. 2 (ed. and trans. D. Meehan, *Adamnan's* De locis sanctis [Dublin, 1958], 36 and 42).

Once the convention that roman capitals were used for epigraphy had broken down it begins to be possible to trace other characteristics in Insular scribal practice from their reflexes in stone. The angular letterforms sometimes found as an intrusion in earlier inscriptions, and probably derived, as argued above, from lettering in wood, took on a life of their own as an especially grand form, drawn in manuscript display letters and also inscribed on stone. The Caldey Island inscription discussed earlier was heavily influenced by such angular forms; and the Ramsey Island inscription was entirely inscribed in 'geometrical' letterforms.[37] The exceptional form of the **A** in the Llangadwaladr inscription in memory of Cadfan, king of Gwynedd, who died *c.* 625, is directly paralleled by a majuscule **A** used in a 'diminuendo' effect in the Cathach of St Columba—a practice whereby a large initial letter was followed by letters still relatively large but gradually decreasing towards the normal text size.[38] This **A** ultimately derived from uncial; yet uncial itself, so far as we know, was never used by Insular scribes in the seventh century; but this distant echo of the grandest script for ecclesiastical texts in the late Empire survived to reappear in manuscript in Ireland or Gaelic northern Britain and in stone in Anglesey.[39] Whereas the link with Roman epigraphy was broken in the seventh century, the scribal tradition was continuous from the fourth century until the eleventh. The earliest charters preserved in the archives, mainly in Gwent and Ergyng, that were taken by the clerics of Llandaff in the eleventh and early twelfth centuries, and were then used to construct the Book of Llandaff, might well originally have been written in cursive; even in the twelfth century, the Caroline script used by the Llandaff scribes sometimes reveals that they themselves had been first trained to write Insular scripts.[40]

The student of Latin learning in early medieval Wales, and also in those other areas that remained British-speaking, has to cope with an inconvenient gap in the evidence: there are no surviving books known to have been written in Wales or Cornwall before the ninth century.[41] From the British-speaking kingdoms of northern Britain there survive no books at all. The earliest history of the British book must, therefore, be reconstructed by circuitous processes of reasoning: by inference from the links between letterforms in inscriptions on stone and those used in books or on tablets and by comparison with Ireland. The comparison with Ireland is justified because it was part of the one Insular cultural province; not only did it have the same scripts, largely the same orthography for Latin texts, the same methods of constructing a codex, but scribal practice evolved in the same direction and at much the same time.[42] Moreover, in the early part of our period, there were

[37] See above, 127. Cf., for Ireland, D. G. Charles-Edwards, 'The East Cross Inscription from Toureen Peacaun: Some Concrete Evidence', *Journal of the Royal Society of Antiquaries of Ireland*, 132 (2002), 114–26.

[38] An example is on fo. 48, the beginning of psalm 90, in the first **a** of *Qui habitat.*

[39] See above, 132–4.

[40] Huws, *Medieval Welsh Manuscripts*, 135, 142–3.

[41] As we shall see, Wales and Cornwall were too closely linked up to the tenth century for it to be helpful to consider them apart.

[42] A good example from the ninth century is pointed out by Dumville, *A Palaeographer's Review*, 125–6.

Irish colonies in Britain, including Wales, and British missionaries in Ireland; even in a later period, there is ample evidence of continued scholarly and ecclesiastical links across the Irish Sea.[43] Although the main epigraphic evidence for the Irish in Britain belongs to the post-Roman period, Irishmen in South Wales are also attested later by inscriptions at Llanllŷr in Ceredigion, dated to the late seventh or early eighth century, and Penally in Dyfed, dated to the late ninth or first half of the tenth century; these are likely to have been churchmen.[44] Irish personal names were among those borne by men of importance in the Llandaff charters.[45]

Pre-Norman manuscripts from Wales survived only if they were taken to England in the tenth century and were there preserved in ecclesiastical libraries that had a continuous history until the Reformation.[46] It was not only books but teachers that took the road to England: as well as Asser at Alfred's court, a teacher called Iorwerth is attested at Winchester in the tenth century.[47] In tenth-century England, Welsh manuscripts might find a home alongside Breton manuscripts and Welsh scholars meet Bretons.[48] Sometimes it is difficult to know whether a British scholar was from Wales or Brittany, as with one of the leading scholars of the tenth century in northern Europe, Israel the Grammarian, who left England for the Continent at Æthelstan's death and became the tutor of Bruno, the future archbishop of Cologne and younger brother of Otto I.[49] Similarly, it is broadly true that early Irish books survived only if they were taken to Francia or to Italy in the eighth or ninth centuries. English books survived somewhat better because they travelled along both routes to preservation, to Francia in the eighth and ninth centuries and into the libraries of reformed English monasteries and cathedrals in the tenth century. There is a well-known chronological horizon for the survival of books, namely the establishment of churches, monasteries, or cathedrals, which had a tolerably uninterrupted physical and institutional existence until the early-modern or, at best, the French Revolutionary period. In other words, what made books survive was not anything to do with either book production or book

43 Sims-Williams, *Irish Influence*, 17–18; T. M. Charles-Edwards, 'Britons in Ireland, *c.* 550–800', in J. Carey, J. T. Koch, and P.-Y. Lambert (eds.), *Ildánach Ildírech: A Festschrift for Proinsias Mac Cana* (Andover and Aberystwyth, 1999), 15–26; K. Grabowski and D. N. Dumville, *Chronicles and Annals of Mediaeval Ireland and Wales: The Clonmacnoise-Group Texts* (Woodbridge, 1984), 209–26, on the Irish connections of *Annales Cambriae*; N. K. Chadwick, 'Early Culture and Learning in North Wales', in N. K. Chadwick (ed.), *Studies in the Early British Church* (Cambridge, 1958), 93–110, on Irish scholars at the court of Merfyn Frych, king of Gwynedd, and their links with other Irish scholars in the Carolingian empire. Llangrannog in Ceredigion remembered that it had the same founder as Dulane, just to the north of Kells (in the kingdom of Brega), *Vitae Sanctorum Britanniae*, ed. Wade-Evans, 146, § 6. For the Irish connections of Caergybi (Holyhead) and Llancarfan, and the presence of a 'house of Britons' at Kells, see above, 607–8.

44 993/124/CD20; 1038/365/P83.

45 Mailbrigit, *sacerdos*, LL 239, probably for Irish Máel Brigte.

46 Good examples are the Lichfield Gospels (Lichfield Cathedral Library, MS. 1), since, irrespective of its place of writing, it was at Llandeilo Fawr in the ninth century, and two of the sections that made up 'St Dunstan's Classbook' (Oxford, Bodleian Library, Auct. F. 4. 32).

47 M. Lapidge, 'Three Latin Poems from Æthelwold's School at Winchester', *Anglo-Saxon England*, 1 (1972), 115, n. on l. 52.

48 As shown by 'St Dunstan's Classbook': the first section of the manuscript is Breton.

49 M. Lapidge, 'Israel the Grammarian in Anglo-Saxon England', in H. J. Westra (ed.), *From Athens to Chartres: Neoplatonism and Medieval Thought* (Leiden, 1992), 97–114; reprinted in his *Anglo-Latin Literature, 900–1066* (London, 1993), 87–104.

use, but rather what happened to the places in which out-of-date texts happened to be preserved through laudable inertia.

These considerations matter because they explain not just the overall scarcity of books but also the imbalance, both geographical and chronological, in direct manuscript evidence. The libraries that gave hospitality to surviving pre-Norman Welsh manuscripts were generally those of churches reformed in the tenth century; these, however, were concentrated in Wessex, the lower Severn valley, and in the Fenlands. Hence it was, predominantly if not exclusively, southern British books that survived, those from South Wales and Cornwall.[50] Similarly, the influence of Welsh reformed minuscule in the creation of English square minuscule in the late ninth century is likely to have come from South Wales to southern England.[51] Political and ecclesiastical links were also usually stronger with southern than with central and northern Wales, while Cornwall was fully incorporated into the English kingdom in the tenth century.[52] It is not surprising, therefore, that no early book survives from Cumbria (Strathclyde); and, yet, the textual history of the *Gododdin* makes it likely that such a book existed in the mid-seventh century; and, moreover, that it was that very rare thing at this early period, a manuscript containing, perhaps with other material, a vernacular text in verse.

The Irish mission-field of the fifth and sixth centuries, however, must have generated a demand for books, a demand likely to have encouraged the further development of a minuscule script as the supply of parchment had to keep pace with the spread of Christianity westwards. These were not only liturgical, biblical, and patristic texts. The Irish were not Latin-speakers but they were now being drawn into the Latin Church: they therefore needed grammars and word lists. This reinforced a trend under way at home in Britain. As Ireland and Pictland came into the Latin Church, the Britons, former citizens of the Empire, moved away from their past, a past in which bilingualism in Latin and British had been widespread. One foundation underlying the Insular cultural province was that the Irish learnt a Latin that their first teachers pronounced in a British manner: for that reason alone an Irish student of Latin in the seventh century would have understood a British fellow-student more easily than a Gallo-Roman. To the issue of pronunciation should be added the fact that, increasingly as the old British Latin died, both Britons and Irishmen learnt Latin using the same grammars. If they learnt Latin well, they acquired a relatively correct form of the language by classical standards. When that is contrasted with the developments in Gallo-Romance exemplified by a seventh-century author such as Fredegar, it becomes quite unsurprising that the

[50] Examples are: the Lichfield Gospels from Llandeilo Fawr; the copy of Ovid, *Ars Amatoria*, Book I, in 'St Dunstan's Classbook' to be discussed below, shown to be from South Wales by the dialect form *ceintiru*; Oxford, Bodleian Library MS 572, Cornish but with Welsh glosses in one section; for the Juvencus MS see H. McKee, 'Scribes and Glosses from Dark Age Wales: The Cambridge Juvencus Manuscript', *CMCS* 39 (Summer 2000), 1–22.

[51] D. N. Dumville, 'English Square Minuscule Script', *Anglo-Saxon England*, 16 (1987), 148–50, 159–61.

[52] As illustrated by the career of Asser; by Edward the Elder's ransoming of Cyfeilliog, above, 506, 594; by S 913, the grant of land to Dewstow, above, 254–6; H. P. R. Finberg, *The Early Charters of the West Midlands*, no. 147; *EHD* i, p. 352 and nos. 115, 131; and by Bishop Tremerin, above, 593.

Britons (including the Bretons) and the Irish formed one cultural province. For the same reasons, the newly converted English would come to be part of the same province in the seventh century.

3. THE CURRICULUM

Within the early phase up to the seventh century, developments occurred that were to be crucial in shaping Welsh culture until the Norman Conquest and the full impact of the Gregorian Reform. In Italy, Gaul, and Spain, the old municipal education of Antiquity—with its strong bias towards the arts of verbal persuasion and the word-for-word study of a narrow canon of literary texts—barely survived into the sixth century.[53] In Latin-speaking Europe the Church was not committed to a syllabus often seen as too pagan; and it was not dependent on the old syllabus and its teachers, the grammarian and the rhetor, to provide literate priests equipped to celebrate the Latin liturgy. Gregory of Tours excused his Latin style by referring to the nature of his education: 'I have not been polished by the cultivated reading of secular writers; instead the blessed father Avitus, bishop of Clermont, exhorted me to study ecclesiastical works.'[54] West and south of the Rhineland and north-eastern Gaul, almost everyone who mattered now spoke Latin.[55] In Britain the Church had no such comfort: although some spoke Latin as well as British, they were a declining minority; and by about 700 they had ceased to exist. The old municipal system of education was not, therefore, left to wither with the imperial government, the *civitates* and their aristocratic *ordines* or *curiae*, for whom it had existed. If the British Church were to retain a Christianity that was part of Latin Christendom, it had to have its own schools in which Latin was taught. In the British Isles the Church had to take the place of the *civitates* of late Antiquity—one reason among others why the principal churches were called *civitates*.

The British Church thus retained the schools but it partially reconstructed the syllabus: biblical exegesis was now the culmination of study. This can be inferred from odd scraps of evidence offered by Gildas, Bede, and the Life of St Samson, and from the pattern of education established in Ireland during the period when the British Church played the major role in conversion.[56] There were three main stages

[53] For these schools see H.-I. Marrou, *A History of Education in Antiquity* (London, 1956), 305; for their demise, P. Riché, *Éducation et culture dans l'occident barbare, vi^e–viiie siècles*, 3rd edn. (Paris, 1962), 62–78; English trans. by J. J. Contreni, *Education and Culture in the Barbarian West: From the Sixth through the Eighth Century* (Columbia, S. Carol., 1976), 24–38.

[54] Gregory of Tours, *Vita Patrum*, ii. pref., MGH SRM i. 2, pp. 218–19; trans. E. James, *Gregory of Tours, Life of the Fathers* (Liverpool, 1985), 35–6.

[55] Gogo, the *nutritor* of the child-king Childebert II, *Epistolae Austrasicae*, ed. W. Gundlach, MGH Epp. i, no. 16, refers to himself, in consciously elaborate Latin, as 'a barbarian writer who has rather learnt from Dodorenus the languages of barbarian tribes than from Parthenius of good memory to master rhetorical composition'. His Latin epistolary style was designed to demonstrate that he had, in fact, learnt both.

[56] In the *Vita Prima S. Samsonis*, ed. P. Flobert i. 7, 156, *philosophia* includes the seven liberal arts and is placed alongside study of the Bible; T. M. Charles-Edwards, 'The Context and Uses of Literacy in Early Christian Ireland', in H. Pryce (ed.), *Literacy in Medieval Celtic Societies*, 66–8.

in the education offered: the first or elementary stage, the *rudimenta*, gave the pupil a capacity to read and write Latin, and to do some arithmetic; this was also when one learnt the Latin psalms by heart.[57] The Life of St Samson has the saint entering the school of St Illtud as a young boy. He first learnt his letters and then went on to learn how to put them together into syllables and words; after that he went on to learn the psalms.[58] This was the stage which bequeathed the word *egwyddor* to Welsh, a borrowing from Latin *(ab)ecedarium*, 'the ABC'.[59] The young St David learnt 'the rudiments, the psalms, the readings of the whole year, the masses, and the divine office'.[60] The effect was to enable David to participate in the Latin liturgy.

The second stage was grammar, which involved not just grammar in our sense, but the close study of central school texts. In late Antiquity the principal, and often the only, such text was Virgil's *Aeneid*. Virgil was the only pagan Latin poet whose work Gildas and Columbanus can be shown to have studied; he was still the only pagan poet widely attested in texts from ninth-century Brittany.[61] There were also Christian Latin poets, whose work could be studied. As we shall see, there is good evidence for the study of a late Roman Christian poet, Juvencus, in ninth-century Wales, and both he and other Christian writers were also studied in Brittany.[62] St Cadog's education, as described by Lifris in the eleventh century, distinguished the different stages by making Cadog move from place to place and teacher to teacher. The 'rudiments' were, as often, passed over in silence, but with Meuthi he studied 'Donatus, Priscian, and the other arts' close to home, namely grammar and then the other subjects (*artes*) of the standard curriculum bequeathed to the Latin world by the Hellenistic schools. Donatus, a fourth-century Latin grammarian, provided the standard elementary works; Priscian's grammar, his *Institutiones Grammaticae*, was more advanced and was favoured by the ninth-century Irish schools.[63] From Ireland the study of Priscian extended to the Britons: a surviving manuscript exhibits layers of glossing, in which Irish glosses belong to an early layer, Breton ones to a later layer, and Welsh glosses to the latest layer.[64] Similarly, the Breton glosses on a copy of Philargyrius's commentary on Virgil show Breton glosses at a

[57] Bede, *HE* iii. 5: 'ut omnes qui cum eo [Aidan] incedebant, siue adtonsi, seu laici, meditari deberent, id est, aut legendis scripturis aut psalmis discendis operam dare.

[58] *Vita S. Samsonis*, ed. Flobert, i. 10.

[59] In Old Irish, *aipgitir*, used from a very early period for any elementary work; G. Márkus, 'What were Patrick's Alphabets', *CMCS* 31 (Summr 1996), 1–15.

[60] *Vita S. Dauid*, § 7, ed. and trans. R. Sharpe and J. R. Davies, 'Rhygyfarch's "Life" of St David', 117.

[61] N. Wright, 'Gildas's Prose Style and its Origins', in Lapidge and Dumville (eds.), *Gildas: New Approaches*, 112–14; M. Lapidge (ed.), *Columbanus: Studies on the Latin Writings*, 66–87, 278–81; F. Kerlouégan, 'Les citations d'auteurs latins profanes dans les Vies de saints breton carolingiennes', *Études Celtiques*, 18 (1981), 181–95.

[62] F. Kerlouégan, 'Les citations d'auteurs chrétiens dans les Vies de saints breton carolingiennes', *Études Celtiques*, 19 (1982), 215–57 (Juvencus 246–7).

[63] V. Law, *The Insular Latin Grammarians* (Woodbridge, 1982), 21.

[64] P.-Y. Lambert, 'Les gloses du manuscrit BN Lat. 10290', *Études Celtiques*, 19 (1982), 173–213, esp. 180–1.

late stage of the transmission, Irish glosses at an earlier stage.[65] A Breton manuscript of Orosius contains a gloss on *Eburacum*, York, namely *Cairebrauc*, which is Old Welsh rather than Old Breton.[66]

The third stage in the ancient curriculum was rhetoric. St Cadog left Wales for Ireland, where he studied all the seven liberal arts with various Irish teachers, in particular at Lismore.[67] But, once he was back in Wales, he studied in Brycheiniog with a *rethoricus* called Bachan, who came from Italy, and was thus able to teach Latinity *Romano more*, 'in the Roman manner'.[68] Lifris's account of Cadog's education includes a manifest anachronism in that Cadog, supposed to belong to the sixth century, studied under Mo Chutu of Lismore, who belonged to the seventh; but in the way he makes Cadog move from teacher to teacher and place to place he echoes Jonas's seventh-century account of Columbanus's education. What is striking is the stability of the curriculum over the centuries from the fifth to the eleventh century. Lifris cannot make the difference between grammar and rhetoric clear: both taught Latinity, and rhetoric was only different in that the Latinity came from a more exotic and prestigious source. His rhetoric was not the rhetoric Gildas learnt; and, yet, Lifris felt the need to make Cadog learn rhetoric, since his saint could not be found wanting in learning, and rhetoric was, as everyone knew, the 'liberal art' that with grammar and logic made up the *trivium*. This curriculum was typical for Latin Christendom;[69] the only special characteristic was the need to learn Latin as a foreign language.

A biblical element appeared in the curriculum almost from the start, when the child began to learn the psalms. Some grammars even set out to replace examples from classical authors by biblical texts.[70] The culmination of study was, however, biblical exegesis. In the Life of St David, the saint was said to have been taught by a *scriba*, Paulentus, who instructed him 'in the three parts of *lectio* until he (David) was a *scriba*; it is not entirely clear what were 'the three parts of *lectio*'—perhaps 'the Law and the Prophets' from the Old Testament and the New Testament as the third. David remained there many years studying the Bible.'[71] The term *scriba* for a scriptural scholar was derived from the scribes of the New Testament, masters of Mosaic law, and was standard in Ireland, where major churches in the eighth century would all hope to have a *scriba*.[72] The *Collectio Canonum Hibernensis* reveals the *scriba* as a judge employing a law largely based on the Bible.

Outside the sequence of the seven liberal arts lay medicine. Here British interest is attested by the Leiden Leechbook, a single bifolium written in Insular minuscule no earlier than the mid-ninth century.[73] It contains two collections of medical remedies and a list of Egyptian days (unfortunate days according to astrologers) and

[65] P.-Y. Lambert, 'Les gloses celtiques aux commentaires de Virgile', *Études Celtiques*, 23 (1986), 91.

[66] Paris, BN 4877: P.-Y. Lambert, 'Gloses à Orose: Résultats d'enquête', *Études Celtiques*, 25 (1988), 213–20, at 216.

[67] *Vita S. Cadoci*, § 10.

[68] Ibid. § 11.

[69] Riché, *Éducation et culture dans l'occident barbare, VIe–VIIe siècles*, 510–30.

[70] Law, *Insular Latin Grammarians*, ch. 3.

[71] *Vita S. Dauidis*, § 10.

[72] The first obit for a *scriba* in the Annals of Ulster is 697; obits are frequent from 724.

[73] *The Leiden Leechbook*, ed. A. Falileyev and M. E. Owen (Innsbruck, 2005).

dietary rules.[74] One of the lists of remedies is in a mixture of Latin and British, the latter being probably Cornish, since, as far as we know, Insular scripts had been abandoned in Brittany in favour of Caroline in the first half of the ninth century. The scripts are easiest to parallel in early tenth-century Welsh manuscripts, but the linguistic evidence is against Welsh being the primary language.[75] An Old Irish gloss, however, indicates that the history of the text is not confined to one Celtic country; and it may be that the manuscript itself is Welsh, but a copy of a Cornish or Breton exemplar, and thus is yet another manuscript that attests intellectual interchange between the Celtic countries. The *Vita Tertia* of St Patrick contains two Brittonic phrases, *pop iou* 'every Thursday', and *pop Saturn* 'every Saturday'.[76] This Life also changed an earlier *Aralanensis insula* to *Tamerensis insula*, 'island in the Tamar', which suggests that the text had a Cornish connection.

4. THE TEACHERS

Major churches in Wales appear to have had a figure equivalent to the Irish *scriba*. Most of the Llandaff witness lists before the eleventh century derived, as we have seen, from archives not at Llandaff but at churches in Ergyng (now south-west Herefordshire) and Gwent.[77] Of these, many included a *lector* within the clerical section of the list, generally placed immediately after a bishop or abbot and before the ordinary clergy.[78] Other terms for what is likely to be the same office were *magister* in early charters (and also in a very limited revival in the eleventh century), and in a small interconnected group of ninth-century charters, *scriptor*.[79] Of these the earlier term, *magister*, recalls the *magister elegans*, 'refined teacher', mentioned by Gildas as having instructed 'almost all Britain' and, in particular, Maglocunus, the future king of Gwynedd, and the *magister*, identified as Illtud, said to have been the teacher of St Samson of Dol.[80] Another term, probably for the same office, was

[74] Ibid. 5–9.

[75] Ibid. 85–7 (language), 88–94 (scripts).

[76] *Four Latin Lives of St. Patrick*, ed. L. Bieler (Dublin, 1971), 179, 184, §§ 83, 88 (preserved in both branches of the textual tradition); on which see P.-Y. Lambert, 'Rencontres culturelles entre Irlandais et Bretons aux IXe et Xe siècles: le témoignage des gloses', in C. Laurent and H. Davis (eds.), *Irlande et Bretagne: vingt siècles d'histoire* (Rennes, 1994), 98–100.

[77] Probably including Welsh Bicknor / Llangystennin Garth Benni in Ergyng and Llandogo in Gwent: W. Davies, *An Early Welsh Microcosm: Studies in the Llandaff Charters* (London, 1978), 151–9.

[78] *Liber Landavensis*, ed. J. Gwenogvryn Evans and J. Rhys, *The text of the Book of Llan Dâv* (Oxford, 1893), [161a = the first charter to begin on p. 161], 161, 162a, 169b, 170 etc. *Lector* is also used in one charter in the Llancarfan collection, *Vitae sanctorum Britanniae et genealogiae*, ed. Wade-Evans, p. 130, § 62, but there Pill *lector* is the last of the clerical witnesses. In the *De Raris Fabulis*, no. I in *Early Scholastic Colloquies*, ed. W. H. Stevenson (Oxford, 1929), 1–11, ed. and trans. S. Gwara, De Raris Fabulis, *'On Uncommon Tales': A Glossed Latin Colloquy Text from a Tenth-Century Cornish Manuscript* (Cambridge, 2005), the teacher is *lector* or *doctor*, the pupils *scholastici*.

[79] *Magister*: *Liber Landavensis*, ed. Evans and Rhys: 127b (highly suspect text); 140, 164, 174b (all seventh or very early eighth century); 269, 271, 274 (all late eleventh century and associated with Lifris of Llancarfan and Bishop Herewald of Llandaff); *scriptor*, 224, 239, 245 (all referring to the same person, and associated with Gower and western Glamorgan).

[80] *Vita Prima S. Samsonis*, ed. Flobert, i. 7, 156.

scholasticus, found in one of the documents added to the Lichfield Gospels when they were at Llandeilo Fawr in Carmarthenshire.[81]

Intimately associated with the importance of a *lector* within major churches was the right of a leading ecclesiastical scholar to be a full member of a synod. This was crucial because, in addition to episcopal authority, both the British and Irish Churches were governed by synods.[82] On the evidence of Bede, the British Church allowed learning as well as episcopal orders to qualify someone for participation in the supreme decision-making bodies of the Church.[83] Yet this would hardly have been conceivable if the syllabus had remained what it had been before the triumph of Christianity, vulnerable to the damning criticisms levelled by St Augustine in his *De Doctrina Christiana* and his *De Civitate Dei*. On a grand scale, beyond that of the local synod, Gildas's *De Excidio Britanniae* reveals the new Christian scholar in action, able to interrogate scriptural authority as a basis on which to pass judgement on those who had strayed, whether they were Gildas's adulterous and murderous kings or Cummian's holy but heretical monks.

In Chapter 5 we saw how Gildas employed an argumentative strategy by which he assembled scriptural and other ecclesiastical texts and also *exempla*—instances in scripture or ecclesiastical history that could be taken to exemplify some rule—to pass judgement upon the shortcomings of different orders within a Christian society. The *De Excidio* excoriates these orders in turn: kings, judges, bishops, priests, and deacons. The same argumentative strategy underlay Cummian's Letter to Ségéne and Béccán, written in 632 or 633, and reached its fullest expression in the early eighth-century *Collectio Canonum Hibernensis*.[84] One of the latter's sources was a collection ascribed to Gildas.[85] It has been proposed that the *Hibernensis* was intended for the British as well as for the Irish Church.[86] This seems unlikely, in that the timing of the text's composition seems to be directly related to the adoption by Iona of the Roman Easter; and the Britons are condemned within the text for their failure to follow Roman practice; yet the manuscript tradition demonstrates that it was rapidly received in Brittany, while later evidence suggests a fairly early reception in Wales as well.[87] This, together with the

81 No. 5, printed in Evans and Rhys, *The Text of the Book of Llan Dâv*, p. xlvi.

82 For a general survey, see D. N. Dumville, *Councils and Synods of the Gaelic Early and Central Middle Ages*, Quiggin Pamphlets, 3 (Cambridge, 1997).

83 See above, 589.

84 The two types of evidence on which the *Hibernensis* depended were texts, *testimonia*, from authoritative sources, and *exempla* from the Bible or the history of the Church: T. M. Charles-Edwards, 'The Construction of the *Hibernensis*', *Peritia*, 12 (1998), 209–37; for similar use of *exempla* in Gildas, see *De Excidio*, c. 73.

85 R. Sharpe, 'Gildas as a Father of the Church', in M. Lapidge and D. Dumville (eds.), *Gildas: new approaches* (Woodbridge, 1984), 194–6.

86 M. P. Sheehy, 'The *Collectio Canonum Hibernensis*: A Celtic Phenomenon', in H. Löwe (ed.), *Die Iren und Europa*, 2 vols., Veröffentlichungen des Europa Zentrums Tübingen (Stuttgart, 1982), ii. 527–8.

87 H. Bradshaw, *apud* H. Wasserschleben, *Die irische Kanonensammlung*, 2nd edn. (Leipzig, 1885), pp. lxiii–lxxv; D. N. Dumville, 'Ireland, Brittany and England: Some Questions of Transmission', in C. Laurent and H. Davis (eds.), *Irlande et Bretagne: vingt siècles d'histoire* (Rennes, 1994), 85–95; W. Stokes, *The Breton Glosses at Orléans*, repr. separately from *Transactions of the Philological Society*

importance of Gildas in the formation of this kind of law, makes it fair to ask whether the same fundamental conditions that produced the *Hibernensis* in Ireland might have encouraged its reception in Wales. While Irish canon law was a law of the Church, it was quite as prepared to lay down rules for kings as it was for bishops and other clergy. Moreover, the *Hibernensis* was compiled for a Church which did not use Roman law in the way that was taken for granted in Gaul or Italy. In the later Roman Empire and in its successor states, bishops had secular as well as ecclesiastical judicial authority, and therefore employed the law of the Empire alongside the canons of the Church.[88] Yet Gildas says that the Britons 'gave only superficial obedience to the edicts of the Romans', while later Welsh law is much more Celtic than Roman.[89] In Britain, as in Ireland, it was not possible for the canons to be an ecclesiastical adjunct to the law of an emperor who was the head of the Christian world, who summoned councils and took a strong line with popes. The British Church was more dependent on biblical scholarship than were its continental counterparts, while it was increasingly, and soon wholly, dependent on its teachers to provide clergy who were *litterati*. This state of affairs, common to Wales and Ireland, explains why Middle Welsh *yscolheic*, while etymologically meaning 'man trained in a school', actually meant 'cleric', and why a Welsh vernacular term for the pupils in an ecclesiastical school was *meibion lleyn*, 'sons of learning', a direct counterpart to Irish *maicc legind*;[90] it also explains why the scholar might be admitted to participate alongside bishops and leading abbots in the synods of the Church. This authority of the scholar in synod, an authority which seems to have been common to Ireland and Wales, is probably intimately related to the form of law found in the *Hibernensis* and, so far as surviving texts go, founded by Gildas.[91] If we then add the good evidence for the Breton transmission of the text, it becomes more likely than not that the *Hibernensis* was received early into Wales.

The trend of these developments was to drive clerical and secular society further apart. The Church had a law of books backed up by the penitentials; the latter's textual tradition went back to sixth-century Wales. Lay society lived by a law that was probably still oral; and although, in Ireland, a written ecclesiastical law, a 'lettered law',[92] soon engendered a written secular law, there is no evidence for Welsh lawbooks until the tenth century; and even then the later tradition ascribing

1885–7; L. Fleuriot, *Dictionnaire des gloses en vieux breton* (Paris, 1964), 4–6; H. Pryce, 'Early Irish Canons and Medieval Welsh Law', *Peritia*, 5 (1986), 107–27.

[88] Gregory of Tours, *Vita Patrum*, VIII, on Nicetius, bishop of Lyons, as a judge; Council of Orléans I (AD 511), c. 1; *Lex Ribvaria*, § 61. 1 (ed. F. Beyerle and R. Buchner, MGH, Leges in Quarto, I. 3, 2, pp. 108–9).

[89] Gildas, *De Excidio*, c. 5. See also above, 40–1, 318.

[90] *Pedeir Keinc y Mabinogi*, ed. I. Williams (Cardiff, 1930), 244, n. on 61. 17; compare also Irish *scolóc*; *Welsh Medieval Law*, ed. A. W. Wade-Evans (Oxford, 1909), 114. 3, *meibon lleyn yr egl6ys*.

[91] The words of Patrick in his *Epistola ad Milites Corotici*, 9, 'Longum est per singula discutere uel insinuare, per totam legem carpere testimonia de tali cupiditate', suggests that Gildas's approach would not have been entirely foreign even in the previous century.

[92] 'Introduction to the *Senchas Már*', ed. and trans. R. Thurneysen, *Zeitschrift für celtische Philologie*, 16 (1927), 175, § 1.

a foundational Welsh lawbook to the authority of Hywel Dda (*ob.* 950) is, in the eyes of some scholars, complete fiction, although others would give it some credence.[93]

Yet there was never a complete divide between a clerical order, for whom books were a central element in daily experience, and a secular order in which they were not. In the sixth century, Gildas's 'refined teacher' had a future king as his pupil; another of Gildas's wicked kings spent some time under monastic vows.[94] Later, although there was sometimes conscious opposition between ecclesiastical scholar and professional vernacular poet, the latter was also ready to depreciate other poets and was anxious to display a learning largely derived from Latin sources;[95] and the Latin scholar, for his part, seems sometimes to have taken on something of the magical persona of the druid.[96] The existence of a single standard orthography for Old Welsh, Old Cornish, and Old Breton (with some variations) implies a tradition of writing in the vernacular.[97] It is also likely that this tradition included more than merely the proper names, interlinear glosses and marginal verses in which Old Welsh largely survives. It has to be remembered, yet again, that the route to preservation via tenth-century England was open to Latin, not vernacular, manuscripts.

5. SOME EARLY WELSH MANUSCRIPTS

Surviving manuscripts from the ninth and tenth centuries show that the various dividing lines between clerical and lay, Latin and vernacular, literate and non-literate, did not coincide. Apart from the 'Computus Fragment', they contain Latin texts;[98] the presence of Welsh is marginal or interlinear. Yet we have to ask what this implies. Does it signify that the role of the vernacular within the ecclesiastical community from which the books came was indeed marginal? Or does it suggest, at the other extreme, that Latin texts existed within communities that, outside the liturgy, spoke only Welsh, and thus that Latin books were studied in clerical communities that never spoke Latin except to God?

As we have seen already, spoken British Latin, as a language of the home, was dead, probably by *c.*700. Whatever the failings in the Latinity of the inscriptions discussed earlier, they indicated that ecclesiastical teachers taught their pupils to speak as well as to read Latin. We may now ask whether, if Latin was spoken, it was

[93] See above, 268–70.

[94] Gildas, *De Excidio*, cc. 28, 36.

[95] M. Haycock, '"Preiddeu Annwn" and the Figure of Taliesin', *Studia Celtica*, 18/19 (1983–4), 52–78, and ead. *Legendary Poems*, no. 18; also hostile to Latin scholars, nos. 1, l. 38, 5, ll. 7ff.; hostile to other poets, nos. 2, 7, 26.

[96] T. Jones, '*Llyfrawr* < *Librarius*', *BBCS* 11 (1941–4), 137–8, on the evidence of *Armes Prydein Fawr*, ed. I. Williams (Cardiff, 1955), l. 193, and *Vita Prima S. Samsonis*, ed. Flobert, §§ 2 and 3 (*librarius* as 'sorcerer').

[97] P. Sims-Williams, 'The Emergence of Old Welsh, Cornish and Breton Orthography, 600–800: The Evidence of Archaic Old Welsh', *BBCS* 38 (1991), 20–86.

[98] The Computus Fragment, Cambridge University Library, Additional MS 4543, a single leaf: I. Williams, 'The Computus fragment', *BBCS* 3 (1926–7), 245–72.

a language customarily used within the school, if not in the ecclesiastical community as a whole. Two categories of evidence offer the possibility of an answer to this and other questions—glossed manuscripts and colloquies designed as aids to the teaching of Latin.[99] Yet although glossing may often bear some relationship to teaching, the evidence needs to be scrutinized.[100] Two rather different examples are the Cambridge Juvencus and the Oxford Ovid.[101] The latter consists of a copy of Ovid, *Ars Amatoria*, Book I, on a single quire forming the last section of 'St Dunstan's Classbook', so called because the different sections of the manuscript were brought together by St Dunstan before he ceased to be abbot of Glastonbury in 957, and presumably before he was temporarily exiled in 956. The Juvencus is a complete manuscript of fifty-five folios, of which two are missing;[102] the glosses were written by several hands, but the main text was written by a single scribe, who wrote a colophon in which he named himself as Nuadu and asked for prayers. The name is Irish, but the request was made in Old Welsh. Similarly, the glosses are mainly in Latin; most of those in the vernacular are in Welsh but a few are in Old Irish.[103] The evidence offered by this manuscript that an ecclesiastical community within Wales might contain Irishmen as well as Welshmen, and probably one Breton, has been challenged, but on insufficient grounds.[104]

In two ways, the manuscripts are quite different. It has been thought that a single scribe wrote the entire quire in St Dunstan's Classbook containing Ovid's *Ars Amatoria*, Book. I, apart from the last leaf;[105] the latter is in an Anglo-Caroline hand which has been identified as that of St Dunstan. Yet it seems more likely that three Insular hands contributed: Hand A, an exceptionally accomplished scribe,

[99] P.-Y. Lambert, 'Les gloses grammaticales brittoniques', *Études Celtiques*, 24 (1987), 285–308, provides a very useful survey of one important category.

[100] Cf. M. Lapidge, 'The Study of Latin texts in Late Anglo-Saxon England: 1. The Evidence of Latin glosses', in N. Brooks (ed.), *Latin and the Vernacular Languages in Early-Medieval Britain* (Leicester, 1982), 99–140 (the Welsh Juvencus MS in Cambridge, is discussed on pp. 111–13); P.-Y. Lambert, 'La typologie des gloses en Vieux-Breton', *Britannia Monastica*, 1 (1990), 13–21.

[101] Cambridge University Library MS Ff. 4. 42 (saec. IX^2 and X^1); for a facsimile and edition, see *Juvencus: Codex Cantabrigiensis Ff.4.42*, ed. H. McKee (Aberystwyth, 2000); *Juvencus: Text and Commentary*, ed. H. McKee (Aberystwyth, 2000); the last section of Oxford, Bodleian Library MS Auct. F. 4. 32 (S.C. 2176), saec. X^1; a facsimile is *Saint Dunstan's Classbook from Glastonbury*, ed. R. W. Hunt, Umbrae Codicum Occidentalium IV (Amsterdam, 1961).

[102] For a discussion of the MS see Helen McKee's introduction to her facsimile edition (above, n. 101), and her 'Scribes and Glosses from Dark Age Wales'.

[103] The Welsh glosses were edited by W. Stokes, 'Cambrica, I. The Welsh Glosses and Verses in the Cambridge Codex of Juvencus', *Transactions of the Philological Society*, 1860–1, 204–32; the Irish glosses by W. Stokes and J. Strachan, *Thesaurus Palaeohibernicus* (Cambridge, 1901–3), ii. 44.

[104] A. Harvey, 'The Cambridge Juvencus glosses—Evidence of Hiberno-Welsh Literary Interaction?' in P. S. Ureland and G. Broderick (eds.), *Language Contact in the British Isles* (Tübingen, 1991), 181–98. For the interpretation of the glossators' backgrounds and activities followed here, see McKee, 'Scribes and Glosses from Dark Age Wales', and the introduction to *Juvencus: Text and Commentary*, ed. H. McKee (Aberystwyth, 2000).

[105] This is asserted without discussion by M. Budny, '"St Dunstan's Classbook" and its Frontispiece: Dunstan's Portrait and Autograph', in N. Ramsay et al. (eds.), *St Dunstan: His Life, Times and Cult* (Woodbridge, 1992), 103–42, at 115; the only dissentient voice of which I am aware is G. Conway, 'Towards a Cultural Context for the Eleventh-Century Llanbadarn Manuscripts', *Ceredigion*, 13/1 (1997), 15, who distinguishes two scribes, of whom the first is clearly Hand A in my classification.

wrote the text up to fo. 42r18; Hand B from fo. 42r19 to the end of fo. 46r; Hand C wrote fo. 46v, while Hand D (St Dunstan) wrote the final page, fo. 47r.[106] Most of the glosses are in the section copied by Hand A (ll. 1–379 of Ovid's text). Once Hand B took over, he added glosses on seven further lines, ll. 383–9; then there was a long gap without any glosses until the last lines of fo. 45r. At that point there are glosses on ll. 623–52 (fo. 45r36–45v26). A possible partial explanation of this last burst of glossing is that, in the exemplar used by Hand B, there was one page of approximately thirty lines towards the end of Book I that contained glosses. In Hand B's copy, the thirty lines with glosses were not on a single page even though he wrote thirty-nine lines to a page. The exemplar may have been a smaller manuscript. Hands C and D wrote no glosses at all. In examining the glosses, therefore, we may be looking beyond the existing manuscript to one or more earlier books; the immediate exemplars were still Welsh, since both Hand A and Hand B copied Welsh as well as Latin glosses in their own sections of the text, and there is no positive evidence that either added glosses beyond what they found before them. The Juvencus is a more live text, even though it is a much less elegant production. The number of glossing hands working on a text that they themselves had not written contrasts with the Ovid manuscript, in which Hands A and B copied glosses on a text that they themselves had written. Whereas the Ovid manuscript is prodigal of space (the text is written by metrical lines), the Juvencus is not. The Ovid, then, is more likely to have been a patron's book, whereas the Juvencus was a school text.[107] Yet, behind the Ovid, there must have been an exemplar which, in some fundamental ways, was more like the Juvencus, a text in which the interpretation conveyed by the glosses was still being elaborated; and, on the other hand, some of the Juvencus glosses, too, have been shown to have been copied.[108] As we saw when considering Asser's scholarship, the extant textual tradition of Ovid, *Ars Amatoria*, is thought to derive from a Carolingian manuscript of *c.* 800.[109] Some of the Latin glosses in the Oxford manuscript may go back to the continental stage of transmission. Yet, the fact that the Welsh glosses, not just the Latin ones, were copied by our scribes from an exemplar reveals the former existence of at least one further Welsh Ovid manuscript.

These two manuscripts thus suggest a hierarchy within Welsh book production: the Ovid manuscript suggests a patron capable of paying for a manuscript expensively produced and elegantly written, and containing a text that was not likely to be studied in an ecclesiastical community; behind this book, however, there may well have been a scholar's working copy, to which the Oxford Ovid owed its glosses. Then, finally, there would be the school text, as in the case of the Juvencus, with its numerous contributing hands among the glosses and its inexpensive production.

106 Among other points of difference, Hand A and Hand B formed the letter **a** differently, while Hands B and C were much less accomplished scribes than Hand A.

107 Cf. Lapidge, 'The Study of Latin Texts', 126, who would deny the title 'classbook' to the St Dunstan manuscript as a whole; G. R. Wieland, 'The Glossed Manuscript: Classbook or Library Book', *Anglo-Saxon England*, 14 (1985), 153–73.

108 Lapidge, 'The Study of Latin Texts', 111–13.

109 See above, 454.

Then there is the further distinction between a text accompanied, as in the Juvencus, by an accumulating interpretation, and a text, such as the Ovid, whose interpretation has been arrested. But the character of the glossing, even when arrested, enables us to look behind the surviving manuscript to earlier books. Many of the glosses in the Ovid manuscript are elementary parsing, identifying cases of nouns and adjectives or identifying parts of speech.[110] On the first page, but hardly, if at all, later, there are also what have been called 'syntax marks' or 'construe marks', namely marks to indicate syntactical relationships, such as agreement between a noun and adjective or a noun and a verb.[111] Of the lexical glosses most offer straightforward equivalents. When, therefore, these glosses or marks were first written, as opposed to when they were copied into our manuscript, they were usually of an elementary character, designed to aid a more correct and rapid reading.

Some glosses, however, suggest a more scholarly level of understanding. A good example is the distinction made between 38ᵃ20, where *guaroimaou* (literally 'play-places') glosses *theatris* and 38ᵃ34 where *estid* 'sitting' glosses *theat(h)ro*.[112] In the first case, the glossator understands the Latin word to refer to theatres, places where plays are put on; in the second, which talks of *uela* which hang over the *marmoreo . . . theatro*, he correctly understands that the 'sails' are awnings over the seating area, not the theatre as a whole.

The idea that the glosses on the Ovid text derive from an earlier manuscript, or several, is supported by one more surprising example. In line 76, standard editions read:

> cultaque Iudaeo septimo sacra Syro

The last word, *Syro*, appears only in our manuscript, and even then only as a gloss: *deo* is what Hand A wrote in his text. What the exemplar may have had was not so much a gloss as an emendation, something such as *uel Syro*, 'or (rather) *Syro*'. This was then taken to be a gloss on *deo*, 'to the (Syrian) god'.

Indirectly, therefore, one surviving manuscript can tell us something about other manuscripts now lost—about a tradition of copying, of textual explanation, and of annotation. The contrast between the Juvencus and the Ovid manuscript, in terms of the quality of the penmanship and the relationship of the glossing hands to text hands, suggests a corresponding difference in their use. The Juvencus manuscript was a working copy actually studied within a community, while the Ovid manuscript is more likely to have derived its glosses from a scholar's copy and was itself a grander product, betraying no evidence of current use, and perhaps belonging to an individual of high rank. In both manuscripts Latin glosses outnumbered Welsh ones, from which it may be inferred that both languages were used in schools, but that Latin had precedence.

110 Cf. P.-Y. Lambert, 'Les gloses grammaticales brittoniques', 285–308; R. J. Hexter, *Ovid and Medieval Schooling: Studies in Medieval School Commentaries on Ovid's* Ars Amatoria, Epistulae ex Ponto, *and* Epistulae Heroidum, Münchener Beiträge zur Mediävistik und Renaissance-Forschung, 38 (Munich, 1986), 26–41 (33–5 on the Old Welsh glosses).

111 M. Draak, 'Construe-Marks in Hiberno-Latin Manuscripts', *Medelingen der Koninklijke Nederlandse Akademie van Watenschappen afdeling Letterkunde*, Niewe Reeks, 20 (1957), 261–82.

112 Lambert, 'La typologie des gloses', 15.

Another indication that Latin had priority within pre-Norman Welsh education is the 'scholastic colloquy' entitled *De Raris Fabulis*, 'On rare expressions', known from Oxford, Bodleian Library MS 572.[113] This is a Cornish manuscript but is itself a collection of distinct sections, containing quite different texts.[114] *De Raris Fabulis* is one of these texts, contained in its own section of the manuscript; it has numerous Welsh as well as a few Cornish and English glosses. These glosses are especially frequent on those lists of recondite words that gave the whole work its title. Although the glosses are mainly Welsh, the manuscript is written in a number of hands, partly Insular, but in the case of the *De Raris Fabulis*, Anglo-Caroline; moreover, the scribe that wrote the Welsh glosses also wrote the text. The likelihood, therefore, is that our portion of the manuscript was written in the second half of the tenth century in Cornwall.[115] Since the glosses were almost all written by the text hand, there is no difficulty in supposing that they were copied from the exemplar; and since the glosses are mainly Welsh, that exemplar is likely to have come from Wales.

The tradition of the colloquy as an aid in teaching a foreign language goes back to Antiquity.[116] The *De Raris Fabulis*, however, is very much a text of its place of composition, Celtic Britain,[117] and of the centuries between the end of spoken British Latin and the Norman Conquest. It delights in a (probably fictional) defeat of the English at the hands of the Britons, and it assumes that the teaching of Latin takes place within an ecclesiastical community of a distinctly unascetic tone. The terminology used for a church and its personnel is recognizably British.[118] Yet, though the immediate context is British, the individual scholar is assumed to be mobile. For the purposes of the dialogue, the pupil is to imagine himself as a

[113] *S. C.* 2026; ed. W. H. Stevenson, *Early Scholastic Colloquies*, 1–11; ed. and trans. S. Gwara, De Raris Fabulis, *'On Uncommon Tales': A Glossed Latin Colloquy-Text from a Tenth-Century Cornish Manuscript* (Cambridge, 2005); cf. S. Gwara, *Education in Wales and Cornwall in the Ninth and Tenth Centuries: Understanding* De raris fabulis, Kathleen Hughes Memorial Lectures 4 (Cambridge, 2004); M. Lapidge, 'Colloquial Latin in the Insular Latin Scholastic *Colloquia*' in E. Dickey and A Chahoud (eds.), *Colloquial and Literary Latin* (Cambridge, 2010), 406–18; L. Olson, *Early Monasteries in Cornwall* (Woodbridge, 1989), 60–2; H. Lewis, 'Glosau Rhydychen', *BBCS* 3 (1926–7), 1–4; I. Williams, 'Glosau Rhydychen', *BBCS* 5 (1929–31), 1–8. M. Winterbottom, 'On the *Hisperica Famina*', *Celtica*, 8 (1968), 126–39, offers an important discussion of another Insular colloquy (the 'Hisperic Colloquy'), no. II in Stevenson's collection, with connections with the *Hisperica Famina*.

[114] W. Lindsay, *Early Welsh Script*, 26–32, and plates XIV and XV.

[115] Lindsay, *Early Welsh Script*, 28, argued against this position, but on grounds that, to my mind, cannot prevail against the combined evidence of the text's association with unquestionably Cornish sections of the MS and the Anglo-Caroline script. The latter had some impact in Wales, probably in the south-east, before the Norman Conquest, as shown by Cambridge, Corpus Christi College MS 153, Martianus Capella: T. A. M. Bishop, 'The Corpus Martianus Capella', *Trans. Cambridge Bibliographical Soc.*, 4 (1964–8), 257–75, whose Hand C, illustrated in Lindsay, *Early Welsh Script*, plate IX/1, wrote in hybrid Insular-Caroline.

[116] Marrou, *A History of Education in Antiquity*, 263–4, 268–7.

[117] Mention of the *comes* as being in charge of a *civitas* and the *dux* in charge of twelve *civitates* suggests a Frankish link, and that might favour Brittany as the ultimate place of origin, if it were not for mention of the Britons defeating the English, *De Raris Fabulis*, ed. Stevenson, *Early Scholastic Colloquies*, § 24, ed. Gwara, § 22 (these *Saxones* are unlikely to be the Saxons of the Bessin, in spite of Gregory of Tours, *Hist.* x. 9). Perhaps the text has been shaped both by Bretons and by Welshmen, before finding its home in Cornwall.

[118] e.g. 'abbas huius podi uel princeps huius loci', *Early Scholastic Colloquies*, ed. Stevenson, *De Raris Fabulis*, § 5, ed. Gwara, § 6 (fo. 42r).

foreigner, a *peregrinus*, who begs for the help of the *princeps*, the head of the church to which he has come. The *princeps* replies, 'Where were you?' To this the pupil answers, 'Till now I was reared or fostered [he is made to use two words to extend the range of vocabulary covered] in Ireland or in Britannia or in Francia.'[119]

The relationship between teacher and taught is usually presented as one between two individuals, as analogous to fosterage rather than to simple inclusion within a group over which the teacher presides. Indeed, the connection between teaching and the ubiquitous institution of fosterage is likely to be one of the social foundations of early medieval Welsh (and Irish) culture.[120] Welsh *athro*, used in Middle Welsh for a teacher and a spiritual director, is in origin a 'fosterer'; since the meaning of the Breton cognate, *aotrou*, is very different, the semantic development of the word in Welsh is likely to have occurred during the Old Welsh period. Yet, while the primary relationship was a personal one, between teacher and pupil, there were physical accoutrements: someone might be instructed to look after, not merely the teacher's goods, but 'especially the *scola* and the *bibliothicae librorum*',[121] the room in which instruction was given. In that room the book cupboards, *bibliothecae*, were kept, including *libri canonici* (books of the canonical scriptures) and the *liber grammaticus, id est, Donaticus*, 'grammar book, i.e. book of Donatus'.[122] In this *scola* the pupil would be taught 'the law of Latinity' as well as, later, the exegesis of the Bible. The colloquy was itself part of this instruction in 'the law of Latin', and must have been intended by its author to find a place in the *scola*'s book cupboard, alongside the *Ars Minor* and *Ars Maior* of Donatus and other works. It shows that the intention remained to instruct the pupil to speak as well as to read and write Latin.

Yet the Latin culture of pre-Norman Wales remained very closely attached to the book. In the *De Raris Fabulis* the pupil asks to read, *legere*, with his teacher, *lector* 'reader'; what they are engaged in is *lectio*.[123] In a more general sense, *lector* could, occasionally, be used of the pupil himself. What they studied was, in Welsh, *llên*, from Latin *legenda*, 'those things that should be read'. When a teacher, such as the outstanding *magister* mentioned by Gildas, had more than one or two pupils, we must not imagine them all with copies of the text being studied, but rather that the teacher dictated a passage from a book, which he alone possessed, to be copied by each pupil on his wax tablet. Then he could proceed to expound the current portion of text: 'we shall leave nothing doubtful or obscure in it'.[124] The glosses suggest that the main language of exposition was Latin, but with occasional explanations of words by their Welsh equivalents.

This education was still intact at Llanbadarn Fawr in Ceredigion, and at Llancarfan in Morgannwg in the mid- to late eleventh century. Llanbadarn was

[119] *De Raris Fabulis*, ed. Stevenson, § 14, ed. Gwara, § 16.

[120] F. Kerlouégan, 'Essai sur la mise en nourriture et l'éducation dans les pays celtiques d'après le témoignage des textes hagiographiques latins', *Études Celtiques*, 12 (1968–9), 101–46.

[121] *De Raris Fabulis*, ed. Stevenson, § 4, ed. Gwara, § 5.

[122] *De Raris Fabulis*, ed. Stevenson, § 6, ed. Gwara, § 7; Middle Welsh *dwned* is a loan from ME, but there may well have been an earlier borrowing directly from Latin, **Dunodig*.

[123] *De Raris Fabulis*, ed. Stevenson, § 6, ed. Gwara, § 7.

[124] *De Raris Fabulis*, ed. Stevenson, § 6, ed. Gwara, § 7.

the home of the best-known scholarly family of Wales before the Gregorian Reform, which in alliance with Anglo-Norman control of the Church, introduced fundamental change. This family is known to us principally through a Latin poem by Ieuan ap Sulien, *Carmen Iohannis de uita et familia Sulgeni*.[125] In this poem Ieuan celebrates his native kingdom, Ceredigion, and declares that his father, Sulien, was born at Llanbadarn Fawr 'of a distinguished stock of parents', who were 'always wise'.[126] Here *sapiens* is likely, on Irish evidence, to mean 'scholar' in the sense of someone who had the attainments required to give him high rank through his learning. This was the public recognition that had enabled his predecessors to appear alongside bishops, anchorites, and the greater abbots in synods. Sulien, therefore, came from a family of scholars, but his own learning was not merely home-grown. When, as an *infans* (up to seven years), he learnt his Latin psalter, he was also taught to write it out.[127] He then went to other Welsh schools; and subsequently, although intending to go to study in Ireland, he was blown off course to Scotland, where he studied the traditional seven liberal arts for five years. He subsequently went to Ireland, where he studied the Bible. There is nothing fundamental to distinguish either the curriculum or the mobile pattern of study from the experience of the young Leinsterman, Columbanus, in the third quarter of the sixth century or that imagined by Lifris in the eleventh century for his saint, Cadog. Stages in education might be punctuated by journeys from one teacher to the next. The education of Sulien also illustrates the enduring connections between those Celtic countries that had been brought closer together by the great missionary campaigns of the fifth and sixth centuries. There were to be signs in the twelfth century that Armagh might have developed a university, but by then Wales, at least for Latin studies, was no longer part of the same cultural province.[128]

The Norman invasion of Dyfed in 1093 was a disaster for the old learned tradition, based as it was on family tradition allied with hereditary church possessions. At least one member of the family would hold an important ecclesiastical office in the new Wales,[129] but the hold of the family on the church of Llanbadarn was threatened. Another poem, by a brother of Ieuan, Rhigyfarch (who also wrote the Life of St David), is a lament for a Wales subjected to the Norman yoke:[130]

125 It is edited and translated by M. Lapidge, 'The Welsh-Latin Poetry of Sulien's Family', *Studia Celtica*, 8–9 (1973–4), 68–106, at 80–9.

126 *Carmen*, ll. 86–7.

127 I thus interpret *edidit*, l. 88.

128 This is suggested by the ruling of the Synod of Clane, recorded in the Annals of Ulster, *s.a.* 1162, that 'no one should be a lector in any church in Ireland unless he were an alumnus of Armagh', and the grant made by Ruaidrí Ua Conchobair, king of Ireland (Annals of Ulster, *s.a.* 1169), 'to the lector of Armagh, in honour of St Patrick, to provide teaching to students from Ireland and Scotland'.

129 Daniel ap Sulien died in 1127 as archdeacon in Powys (*Brut y Tywysogion: Peniarth MS. 20 version*, trans. T. Jones [Cardiff, 1952], *s.a.*); his son, Cedifor ap Daniel, died in 1163 as archdeacon of Ceredigion (ibid. *s.a.* 1162 = 1163).

130 *Planctus Ricemarch*, ed. and trans. Lapidge, 'The Welsh-Latin Poetry of Sulien's Family', 88–91, ll. 8–17.

Nothing is of any use to me now but the power of giving: neither the law, nor learning, nor great fame, nor the deep-resounding glory of nobility, not honour formerly held, not riches, not wise teaching, not deeds nor arts, not reverence of God, not old age; none of these things retains its station, nor any power. Now the labours of earlier days are despised; the people and the priest are despised by the word, heart and work of the Normans.

20

Poets and Storytellers

1. PROBLEMS OF TIME AND SPACE

Very little Welsh vernacular literature is contained in manuscripts dated before 1250, almost two centuries after the terminal date of this book. What survives from manuscripts before 1100 is marginal—literally, in the sense that it survived by being written into the margins of pages devoted to Latin texts. It is also confined to a single family of metres, the englyn. Two sets of englynion were written into the margins of the Juvencus manuscript *c.* 900 and a single englyn on St Padarn's staff is in the top margin of a manuscript written by Ieuan ap Sulien in the late eleventh century.[1] The absence of Welsh vernacular manuscripts before 1250 is not surprising, but it certainly hampers any effort to write a history of pre-Norman Welsh literature. Those Welsh manuscripts that survive from before 1063 did so because they were taken to England in the tenth century and there found a home in monastic libraries that endured until the Reformation. English scholars of the tenth century were interested in acquiring Latin manuscripts; they would have had no use whatsoever for Welsh vernacular manuscripts.[2]

The textual history of the *Gododdin* provides good reason, however, to think such manuscripts existed.[3] That example raises two central issues: location and dating. The first is the easier: much of the poetry that survives in Welsh manuscripts after 1250 and yet was composed before 1063 is better described as British rather than Welsh. The Welsh manuscript tradition of the late thirteenth and fourteenth centuries preserved poems from the northern Britons, from what I have chosen to call Cumbria. Indeed, only if early British literature from outside Wales found its way into Welsh manuscripts did it survive. All this, however, only mirrors the history of the Britons in general, with the one exception that it is remarkable how little vernacular material survived in Brittany, particularly since the history of

[1] For the Juvencus MS see above, 644–6, and for the englynion, I. Williams, *The Beginnings of Welsh Poetry*, ed. R. Bromwich (Cardiff, 1972), 89–121, and *Blodeugerdd Barddas o Ganu Crefyddol Cynnar*, ed. M. Haycock ([Y Bala], 1994), no. 1; for the englyn on Padarn's staff, Williams, *The Beginnings of Welsh Poetry*, 181–9, and Haycock, *Blodeugerdd*, no. 23.

[2] P. Sims-Williams, 'The Uses of Writing in Early Medieval Wales', in H. Pryce (ed.), *Literacy in Medieval Celtic Societies*, Cambridge Studies in Medieval Literature 33 (Cambridge, 1998), 20–1.

[3] See above, Ch. 11, § iii.

the Arthurian legend and its transmission from British sources into medieval French texts suggests that it must have existed.[4]

The really difficult problem is dating. It is clear enough that some texts preserved in manuscripts after 1250 were composed before 1064, but which ones? And if we can identify them, where in the many centuries before 1064 should they be placed? Unless some rough chronology can be established, no history is possible; and, yet, as has recently been observed, 'It has long been something of an embarrassment that we lack a set of agreed and dependable linguistic dating criteria for pre- *c.* 1100 Welsh verse.'[5] To take just one crucial example of the difficulties: it is very likely that between the ninth century and the twelfth a major change in word order occurred by which the unmarked order of the ordinary positive sentence changed from Verb + Subject (+ Object) to one in which the verb came second but could have one of a range of constituents before it, subject, object, adverb, or adverbial phrase.[6] Even though very little Old Welsh prose survives, its word order appears to be sufficiently attested;[7] and the difference between it and early Middle Welsh prose is clear. In the poetry of the Gogynfeirdd, however, both the Old Welsh and the Middle Welsh word order were possible. Conversely, it has been argued that in Old Welsh verse a similarly free word order obtained, so that what would have been a marked word order in prose could be used without restriction in verse.[8] The effect is that what might have been a precious clue to the dates of texts is largely nullified.

In the middle of the twentieth century there was a broadly accepted chronology for Old Welsh verse, thought to have been established by the work of Morris-Jones and, above all, by his pupil Ifor Williams.[9] It formed the basis for the first chapter of Thomas Parry's standard *Hanes Llenyddiaeth Gymraeg*.[10] There was the early poetry of Aneirin and 'the historical Taliesin' as well as the elegies for Cadwallon (d. 633) and Cynddylan, together with some other poems preserved in the Book of Aneirin alongside or mixed in with the *Gododdin*, such as the Strathcarron poem; all this comprised the poetry of the earliest *Cynfeirdd*, the earliest, that is, of the surviving British poets from before *c.* 1100. From *c.* 1100 began the far better dated *Gogynfeirdd*, the poets who praised Welsh rulers in the twelfth and thirteenth centuries.[11]

[4] Particularly if P. Sims-Williams, 'Did Itinerant Breton *Conteurs* transmit the *Matière de Bretagne*?', *Romania*, 116 (1998), 72–111, is right in thinking that written texts were more important in this transmission than has been widely supposed.

[5] *Legendary Poems from the* Book of Taliesin, ed. and trans. M. Haycock (Aberystwyth, 2007), 21.

[6] D. W. E. Willis, *Syntactic Change in Welsh: A Study of the Loss of Verb-Second* (Oxford, 1998), 10–11 and 50–101.

[7] T. A. Watkins, 'Constituent Order in the Old Welsh Verbal Sentence', *BBCS* 34 (1987), 51–60.

[8] J. T. Koch, 'The Cynfeirdd Poetry and the Language of the Sixth Century', in B. F. Roberts, (ed.), *Early Welsh Poetry*, 28–35.

[9] J. Morris-Jones, 'Taliesin', *Y Cymmrodor*, 28 (1918); Ifor Williams edited *Canu Llywarch Hen* (Cardiff, 1935), *Canu Aneirin* (Cardiff, 1938) and *Canu Taliesin* (Cardiff, 1960); English version by J. Caerwyn Williams, *The Poetry of Taliesin* (Dublin, 1968).

[10] First published Cardiff, 1944; translated by H. I. Bell, *A History of Welsh Literature* (Oxford, 1955). Also in A. O. H. Jarman and G. R. Hughes (eds.), *A Guide to Welsh Literature*, i (Swansea, 1976), chs. 2–5, esp. pp. 51–2; A. O. H. Jarman, *The Cynfeirdd* (Cardiff, 1981).

[11] The first dated *Gogynfardd* poem probably comes from 1101 and is praise for Hywel ap Goronwy, one of the leaders of the Welsh counter-attack of 1096 against the Normans, on the occasion of his succession to Brycheiniog in 1101: CBT i. 1; D. Stephenson, '*Mawl Hywel ap Goronwy*:

Between the early *Cynfeirdd* and the *Gogynfeirdd* lay two main bodies of verse: first, the englyn cycles associated with the names of Llywarch Hen, Urien Rheged, and Heledd as well as other, less extensive material in the same family of metres;[12] and, secondly, the poetry of the 'Taliesin persona', namely a body of verse, not in englyn metres, that presented a Taliesin who was a prophet and a shape-shifter—the bearer of supernatural knowledge and power.[13] Both these bodies of verse were assigned to the ninth century or, at least, to a period centring on the ninth century; and both were seen as different from the earliest *Cynfeirdd* in that they presupposed a body of narrative: in the case of the englynion this narrative was heroic saga;[14] but with the Taliesin persona it was held to be a story about how Taliesin acquired and used his mysterious powers.[15] In the tenth and eleventh century came 'the Gap', a period from which only a few poems survived, such as *Armes Prydein*.

Some portions of this scholarly structure have survived better than others. A detailed analysis of the saga englynion by Jenny Rowland has defended and refined Ifor Williams's view that they were verse utterances in a narrative setting; and she has proposed a more detailed chronology in five phases, of which the first three fall within our period: late eighth century to mid-ninth century; mid-ninth century to late ninth century; and tenth century.[16] The englynion have the great advantage that they can be closely compared with the slight remains of Old Welsh poetry contained in Old Welsh manuscripts, since the latter are also englynion. The date of the *Gododdin*, however, is the subject, as we have seen, of active debate, as are the dates of the poems ascribed by Williams to 'the historical Taliesin'.[17] Perhaps the greatest change affects the Taliesin persona: Marged Haycock argues in her edition of the legendary poems that some of this material may well have been composed by the *Gogynfardd* Prydydd y Moch (*c.* 1175–*c.* 1220).[18] This is part of a more general shift: differences that were once thought to be chronological are now more likely to be ascribed to genre, and in particular to the difference between the grand eulogistic style of the *Gogynfeirdd* and more popular poetry of the same period. The effect is that much of the scholarship that previously made possible a history of Welsh poetry before 1064 has now been reapplied to refining the history of Welsh poetry in the twelfth and thirteenth centuries.

Similar problems have affected prose. The view of Ifor Williams was that the Four Branches of the Mabinogi were probably the creation of 'a man from Dyfed who brought together old tales of Gwent, Dyfed, and Gwynedd about 1060, when

Dating and Context', *CMCS* 57 (Summer 2009), 41–9; N. A. Jones, 'Golwg Arall ar "Fawl Hywel ap Goronwy"', *Llên Cymru*, 21 (1998), 1–7.

[12] *Canu Llywarch Hen*, ed. Williams; J. Rowland, *Early Welsh Saga Poetry*.

[13] M. Haycock, 'Llyfr Taliesin', *National Library of Wales Journal*, 25 (1988), 357–86; id., *Legendary Poems*; id. *Prophecies from the Book of Taliesin*, ed. and trans. M. Haycock (forthcoming).

[14] I. Williams, 'The Poems of Llywarch Hen', *Proceedings of the British Academy*, 18 (1933), 7–12, id., *Lectures on Early Welsh Poetry* (Dublin, 1944), 22–4.

[15] Ifor Williams, *Chwedl Taliesin* (Cardiff, 1957), argued that this was an earlier version of what survives as a much later narrative about Taliesin: *Ystoria Talesin*, ed. P. K. Ford (Cardiff, 1992).

[16] Rowland, *Early Welsh Saga Poetry: A Study and Edition of the Englynion* (Cambridge, 1990), 388–9.

[17] See above, 364–80.

[18] Haycock, *Legendary Poems*, 27–36.

the three countries were united'—the Four Branches, on his view, belonged to the reign of Gruffudd ap Llywelyn and thus, conveniently, to the final period of this book.[19] This view reigned supreme for a generation, and *Culhwch ac Olwen* was dated by Idris Foster to the late eleventh century or the very beginning of the twelfth, about a generation later than Williams's date for the Four Branches.[20] The standard view of the date of the earliest prose tales prevailing in the mid-twentieth century has been assailed, notably by Saunders Lewis for the Four Branches and more recently by Simon Rodway for *Culhwch*.[21] In 1972 I suggested a slightly later date for the Four Branches, but my arguments were in turn questioned by Sims-Williams.[22] He has also put forward a strong argument for associating the Fourth Branch, *Math*, with the most important church of western Arfon, Clynnog Fawr, the principal church of St Beuno; and Brynley Roberts has, partly for the same reasons, preferred Gwynedd to Dyfed as the home of the author of the Four Branches as a whole.[23] It has also been seriously questioned whether the Four Branches were composed by the same person.[24] While few, perhaps, would deny that much of the material in the Four Branches and in *Culhwch* is older than the existing texts, most scholars have thought it better not to follow W. J. Gruffydd in reconstructing earlier forms of the narrative but rather to elucidate the texts as we have them.[25] One aspect of Gruffydd's views in particular has come under sustained attack: he relied very heavily on Irish comparisons and this was carried further by Proinsias Mac Cana, who argued for actual borrowing as well as 'affinities'.[26] This was countered by Sims-Williams in a series of articles: he did

[19] *PKM* xli.

[20] I. Ll. Foster, 'Culhwch and Olwen and Rhonabwy's Dream', in R. S. Loomis (ed.), *Arthurian Literature in the Middle Ages* (Oxford, 1959), 38–9; id., 'Culhwch ac Olwen', in G. Bowen (ed.), *Traddodiad Rhyddiaith yn yr Oesau Canol* (Llandysul, 1974), 65–81, at 65; similarly R. Bromwich and D. S. Evans, *Culhwch and Olwen: An Edition and Study of the Oldest Arthurian Tale* (Cardiff, 1992), pp. lxxvii–lxxxiii.

[21] Saunders Lewis, *Meistri'r Canrifoedd: Ysgrifau ar Hanes Llenyddiaeth Gymraeg*, ed. R. G. Gruffydd (Cardiff, 1973), chs. 1–4; S. Rodway, 'The Date and Authorship of *Culhwch ac Olwen*: A Reconsideration', *CMCS* 49 (Summer 2005), 21–44. On the other side, cf. P. Mac Cana, 'On the Early Development of Written Narrative Prose in Irish and Welsh', *Études Celtiques*, 29 (1992), 64 n. 38; T. M. Charles-Edwards, 'The Date of *Culhwch ac Olwen*', in W. McLeod, A. Burnyeat, D. U. Stiùbhairt, T. O. Clancy and R. Ó Maolalaigh (eds.), *Bile ós Chrannaibh: A Festschrift for William Gillies* (Ceann Drochaid, 2010), 45–56.

[22] T. M. Charles-Edwards, 'The Date of the Four Branches of the Mabinogi', *THSC, 1970*, 263–98; P. Sims-Williams, 'The Submission of Irish Kings in Fact and Fiction: Henry II, Bendigeidfran, and the Dating of *The Four Branches of the Mabinogi*', *CMCS* 22 (1991), 31–61; revised version in his *Irish Influence*, 209–29.

[23] P. Sims-Williams, 'Clas Beuno and the Four Branches of the Mabinogi', in B. Maier and S. Zimmer *150 Jahre 'Mabinogion'—Deutsch-Walische Kulturbeziehungen* (Tübingen, 2001), 111–27; B. F. Roberts, 'Where were the Four Branches of the Mabinogi written?', in J. F. Nagy (ed.), *The Individual in Celtic Literatures* (Dublin, 2001), 61–75.

[24] S. Davies, '*Pedeir Keinc y Mabinogi*—A Case for Multiple Authorship', in G. W. MacLennan (ed.), *Proceedings of the North American Congress of Celtic Studies* (Ottawa, 1988), 443–59.

[25] W. J. Gruffydd, *Math vab Mathonwy* (Cardiff, 1928); id. *Rhiannon: An Inquiry into the First and Third Branches of the Mabinogi* (Cardiff, 1953); the current approach is best followed via S. Davies, *The Four Branches of the Mabinogi*: Pedeir Keinc y Mabinogi (Llandysul, 1993), and P. Mac Cana, *The Mabinogi*, rev. edn. (Cardiff, 1992).

[26] P. Mac Cana, *Branwen Daughter of Llŷr* (Cardiff, 1958).

not deny that there was some borrowing but, in his view, its importance had been much exaggerated.[27] On the other hand, a case has recently been made for accepting such borrowing in one particular narrative sequence, the stories about Brân and the Cauldron of Rebirth.[28]

The argument for the role of Clynnog in the formation of the Fourth Branch has, however, important further implications. Considerable progress has been made by placing medieval Welsh narrative against a background of oral performance.[29] The performance under investigation has been that of the *cyfarwydd*, the storyteller, or the poet acting, in one of his roles, as a *cyfarwydd*.[30] Yet, if a church had the major role in the formation of the Fourth Branch, perhaps the tendency to keep separate Latin ecclesiastical learning from vernacular narrative and non-religious poetry needs to be questioned; and, once the barrier has been crossed between vernacular narrative and poetry, on the one hand, and, on the other, the *ysgol* where *llên* was taught to *meibion llên*, 'sons of literature', we shall be in an institution with close links to Irish learning, as we saw in the previous chapter. It is entirely possible, therefore, for good scholars to take very different views of the history of British literature before the Norman conquest. What follows is, even more than usual, one person's ideas. It aims to be illustrative rather than a survey of the whole field.

2. METRICS[31]

Welsh scholars have with good reason reacted against the notion that a similarity between their early literature and that of the Irish is, other things being equal, to be explained by borrowing—by Welsh poets or storytellers taking themes or stories or metrical ornaments from the Irish. Similarities are, however, when taken as a whole, incontrovertible in metrics and they may provide a help in judging other similarities elsewhere. Moreover, these metrical resemblances exist against a broader background: there is no equivalent to *Beowulf* or to the Old Norse heroic edda poetry in either Welsh or Irish. Except in special circumstances neither the Welsh nor the Irish used verse to tell a story; narrative was in prose, although heightened utterance by characters within narrative could be in verse; and, although verse could allude to

[27] For example, P. Sims-Williams, 'A Riddling Treatment of the "Watchman Device" in *Branwen* and *Togail Bruidne Da Derga*', *Studia Celtica*, 12/13 (1977/8), 83–117; id., 'The Significance of the Irish Personal Names in *Culhwch ac Olwen*', *BBCS* 29 (1982), 600–20; id. 'The Evidence for Vernacular Irish Influence on Early Medieval Welsh Literature', in D. Whitelock et al., *Ireland in Mediaeval Europe* (Cambridge, 1982), 235–57. These have been updated and brought together in his *Irish Influence on Medieval Welsh Literature* (Oxford, 2011).

[28] J. Carey, 'Bran son of Febal and Brân son of Llŷr', in Jankulak and Wooding (eds.), *Ireland and Wales in the Middle Ages*, 168–79; id., *Ireland and the Grail* (Aberystwyth, 2007), 43–66.

[29] S. Davies, *Crefft y Cyfarwydd* (Cardiff, 1995).

[30] As Gwydion does at the court of Pryderi: *PKM* 69. This evidence was queried by Bromwich, *Trioedd Ynys Prydein*, 1st edn. pp. lxxxiii–lxxxv, but I am not convinced.

[31] The standard account is J. Morris-Jones, *Cerdd Dafod* (Oxford, 1925); for Ireland, G. Murphy, *Early Irish Metrics* (Dublin, 1961).

events within the narrative, it did not carry the story forward from event to event.[32] The exceptions are religious poems retelling a biblical or hagiographical story.[33]

The metrical similarities between early Irish and Welsh verse may be divided into three classes: general characteristics, rhyme, and alliteration.

In the first category we may place such general points as the combination of stanzaic and non-stanzaic verse: in Irish the four-line stanza is ubiquitous, the three-line stanza less frequent; in Early Welsh the three-line englyn is more common, although four-line englynion also occur and become more usual by the twelfth century.[34] The Welsh *awdl*, on the other hand, consists of longer sequences of lines, although these may be broken up into sections, each of which has its own end-rhyme; into this category fall, for example, the Lament for Cynddylan, *Armes Prydein*, and the poems I shall discuss shortly, one in praise of Tenby, its lord, Bleiddudd, and its warriors, the other a lament for the death of a Gwynedd ruler called Aeddon. An Irish example of non-stanzaic verse is the poem in praise of Indrechtach mac Muiredaig, king of the Connachta, who died in 723.[35]

Overlapping with this distinction is that between verse with a regular number of syllables per line and verse in which the number of stresses rather than of syllables is crucial. An example of the latter, common in early Irish verse but also found in Welsh, is the line of two stresses in which the beginning of the second stressed word alliterates with the first stressed word of the following line; this is found as early as the sixth century in Ireland.[36] In early Welsh verse one may also have, instead of a fixed number of syllables, verse in which a regular syllable-count is the norm, but some variation is allowed, as in *Armes Prydein*, where nine-syllable lines prevail but ten syllables are also quite common. In addition, Irish verse includes a mixed type in which syllable counting coexists with a stress pattern, as in the seven-syllable line with a caesura after the fourth syllable and then three syllables of which only the first carries the stress. Finally, a particular device by which the beginning of a poem is echoed at the end is very common in Irish but is also found in Welsh verse: the poem ends with the word with which it began.[37]

[32] P. Mac Cana, 'Notes on the Combination of Prose and Verse in Early Irish Narrative', in S. N. Tranter and H. L. C. Tristram, (eds.), *Early Irish Literature—Media and Communication/ Mündlichkeit und Schriftlichkeit in der frühen irischen Literatur*, ScriptOralia 10 (Tübingen, 1989), 125–47; id., 'Prosimetrum in Insular Celtic Literature', in J. Harris and K. Reicht (eds.), *Prosimetrum: Crosscultural Perspectives on Narrative in Prose and Verse* (Cambridge, 1997), 99–129.

[33] In Irish, *Saltair na Rann*, ed. W. Stokes, Anecdota Oxoniensia (Oxford, 1883); in Welsh, Haycock, *Blodeugerdd*, no. 9, no. 14, lines 29–36, 53–78.

[34] An Irish example of the three-line stanza is G. Murphy, *Early Irish Lyrics* (Oxford, 1956), no. 35.

[35] ed. K. Meyer, *Die älteste Irische Dichtung*, ii. 25; also ed. Murphy, *Early Irish Lyrics*, p. xiii. The subject must be Indrechtach mac Muiredaig who died in 723 rather than the Indrechtach mac Dúnchada, who died in 707, since this Indrechtach evidently belonged to the Uí Briúin.

[36] In the poem *Luin oc elaib*, 'Blackbirds compared with swans', attributed to Colmán mac Lénéni, *ob*. 604 (the poem was composed 565–566 if this Domnall was, as seems likely, the king of Tara of those dates). For Welsh stress metres, see M. Haycock, 'Metrical Models for the Poems in the Book of Taliesin', in B. F. Roberts (ed.), *Early Welsh Poetry*, 155–77, esp. 162–8.

[37] A Welsh example is provided by the *Cyngogion* from the Black Book of Carmarthen, ed. M. Haycock, *Blodeugerdd*, no. 27; Morris-Jones, *Cerdd Dafod*, 294–6; this is the *dúnad* 'closing' of early Irish verse: Murphy, *Early Irish Metrics*, 43–5.

Two aspects of rhyme are shared by Irish and some Welsh verse. The first is called 'generic rhyme': rhyming consonants need not be identical but must belong to the same class, so that, for example, unvoiced stops may rhyme (*p* with *t* and *k*). The second is the device by which the end of one line rhymes with an internal syllable in the next. This is especially characteristic of certain metres, such as *rannaigecht mór* in Irish and the *awdl-gywydd* in Welsh. Alongside these aspects of rhyme, there are similarities in the use of alliteration. The most striking is alliteration across lenition ('soft mutation'). As we saw in Chapter 2, both Welsh and Irish had systematic changes of consonants at the beginning of words in particular syntactical contexts. A consonant could, however, alliterate with its lenited or nasalized counterpart. In combination with generic rhyme this produced a metrical system in which rhyme and alliteration revealed the consonantal systems of the two languages. So, for example, in Welsh a *p* could alliterate with a lenited *p*, namely *b*, or a nasalized *p*, namely *mh*; it could not rhyme with a *b* but could rhyme with *t*:

(p ~ t = p rhymes with t; p ↔ b = p alliterates with b)

p ~ t ~ k ~ rhyme
↕ ↕ ↕
↕ alliteration b ~ d ~ g

p ~ t ~ k
↕ ↕ ↕
mh ~ nh ~ ngh

Figure 20.1. Alliteration across mutations

Three examples of alliteration across mutations from the elegy of Meilyr Brydydd for Gruffudd ap Cynan are:

Ac ail dra **d**rymaf **t**rengi meddwawd, CBT I. 3. 9
A nw neud **gw**eryd yn **w**arweiddiawg, 83 (the soft mutation of *gw-* is *u-*)
Ny thorraf â'm **c**ar fy **ngh**erennydd, 156

One of generic rhyme from the same poem is:

Cnöynt frain friwg**ig** o l**id** llawrydd, 116

In this last example, *friwgig* and *lid* have generic rhyme, while *frain* and *friwgig* show normal alliteration, and *lid* and *llawrydd* show alliteration across a mutation. Another way in which alliteration worked with the similarity rather than the identity of sounds was that, in both Irish and Welsh, any initial vowel could alliterate with any other.[38]

Other ways in which rhyme and alliteration were complementary affected both lines and stanzas. In the line, alliteration at the beginning was widely used to

[38] *Pace* Morris-Jones, *Cerdd Dafod*, § 342, who took no account of the Irish parallel.

connect one line with another as rhyme linked lines at the end; on the other hand, both rhyme and alliteration were used as ornament within lines. Just as we had alliteration of the final stressed word in one line with the initial stressed word in the next, so this device was also used to link one stanza to the next.[39]

All this evidence, taken in combination and set against a comparison with Germanic and Classical Latin verse, makes it hard to deny that in the technique of verse, as elsewhere, Wales and Ireland formed one cultural province. Some of these similarities, at least, were fading by *c.* 1100—for example, generic rhyme in Welsh. But others appeared later. It is characteristic of one form of englyn and of what became the most popular type of *cywydd* metre in Welsh, and likewise of the very common *deibide scaílte* in Irish that rhymes were arhythmic, in the sense that in a rhyming couplet a stressed syllable rhymed with an unstressed syllable. This cannot be as old in Welsh as it may have been in Irish, for the simple reason that before the accent shift from the final to the penultimate syllable, probably in the ninth century, no such rhyme was possible in Welsh; in Irish, however, there are good ninth-century examples.[40]

An historical judgement on the links between Welsh and Irish metrics should not be made, however, before a third player is introduced: Insular Latin. A hymn in praise of St Martin of Tours was composed by Óengus mac Tipraite, abbot of Clonfad in Westmeath, who died in 746.[41] It is in quatrains with seven-syllable lines; the second line of a stanza rhymes with the fourth.[42] I shall take the second stanza as an illustration of the metrical ornaments already available to the poet in Latin as well as the vernacular.

End of Stanza 1: . . . **_m_atrem.**
*M*artinus *m*irus *m*ORE
ORE laudauit D**eum**;
puro *c*orde *c*antAUIT
*a*tque *a*mAUIT **_e_um**.

*E*lectus . . .

Note: Bold = end-rhyme; caps. = internal rhyme + *aicill*-rhyme (end with interior); italics = alliteration.

I have added the last word of the first stanza and the first of the third to show how alliteration is used to link one quatrain with another. The example chosen does not exhibit generic rhyme, but the poem on the community of Bangor (Co. Down) in the late seventh-century Antiphonary of Bangor, shows a neat combination of regular with generic rhyme.[43] Here too we have quatrains with seven-syllable lines.

[39] As in *Cyngogion Elaeth: Llyfr Du Caerfyrddin*, ed. A. O. H. Jarman (Cardiff, 1982), no. 19.

[40] *Early Irish Lyrics*, ed. and trans. G. Murphy (Oxford, 1956), nos. 1, 36.

[41] *Liber Hymnorum*, ed. J. H. Bernard and R. Atkinson, Henry Bradshaw Society 13 (London, 1898), i. 47.

[42] Cf. *rannaigecht mór*, Murphy, *Early Irish Metrics*, § 15 (+ Thurneysen's quoted remark about early exx.), and *dían airseng*, ibid. § 2.

[43] *The Oxford Book of Medieval Latin Verse*, ed. F. J. E. Raby (Oxford, 1959), no. 50, p. 69.

Domus deliciis plena,
super petram constructa,
necnon uinea uera
ex Aegypto transducta.

The full rhyme is between the second and fourth lines (constr**ucta** / transd**ucta**), while the first and third have generic rhyme (pl**ena** / u**era**). These examples, from different provinces, are enough to show that, in Ireland, Latin and vernacular metrics evolved together. Since Latin was a language common to Ireland and Wales, it could have been the means by which metrical innovation spread across the Irish Sea, in either direction.

There is no need for a single explanation of the similarities between Welsh and Irish poetry. A common inheritance from the pre-Roman period very probably made its contribution; to this one may add the Irish settlements in Britain and the close relationship between Ireland and Celtic Britain created by the spread of Christianity to Ireland in the fifth century; and, as we have seen, links between Ireland and Wales remained strong in subsequent centuries. If we leave aside the pre-Roman era, at some subsequent periods British influence on Ireland was stronger, at others Irish influence on Britain. In material culture in the post-Roman world the importance of an Insular dimension alongside work more characteristic of one people, such as Pictish sculpture, has long been recognized. There is no reason to think that poetry was different.

3. TWO BARDIC PRAISE-POEMS: *EDMYG DINBYCH* AND *ECHRYS YNYS*

Two poems in the Book of Taliesin concern particular people and places in the pre-Norman period other than Urien and the others celebrated by 'the historical Taliesin'. *Edmyg Dinbych* celebrates a fortress largely surrounded by the sea and called 'The Small Fortress', *Dinbych*.[44] There is one and only one Dinbych that could be so described, Tenby in south Pembrokeshire. A lord of this Dinbych is named, Bleiddudd (lines 36, 54); yet, as we shall see, he is not the current lord but has died, probably very recently, and the poem is thus partly a lament for his death, a *marwnad*. Bleiddudd's successor is likely to be the great-grandson of Owain mentioned at the end (line 57). He is never named directly.

The date of the poem depends on the status of Bleiddudd and his fort: was it royal? If it was, and if, as one may presume, the rich agricultural land of south Pembrokeshire formed an indispensable part of the core of Dyfed, Bleiddudd

[44] R. Geraint Gruffydd, *'Edmyg Dinbych': Cerdd Lys Gynnar o Ddyfed*, Darlith Goffa J. E. Caerwyn a Gwen Williams 2001 (Aberystwyth, 2002); English version, '"The Praise of Tenby": A Late-Ninth-Century Welsh Court Poem' in J. F. Nagy and L. E. Jones (eds.), *Heroic Poets and Poetic Heroes in Celtic Tradition: A Festschrift for Patrick K. Ford*, CSANA Yearbook, 3–4 (Dublin, 2005), 91–202; I. Williams, 'Two Poems from the Book of Taliesin', in his *The Beginnings of Welsh Poetry*, 155–72.

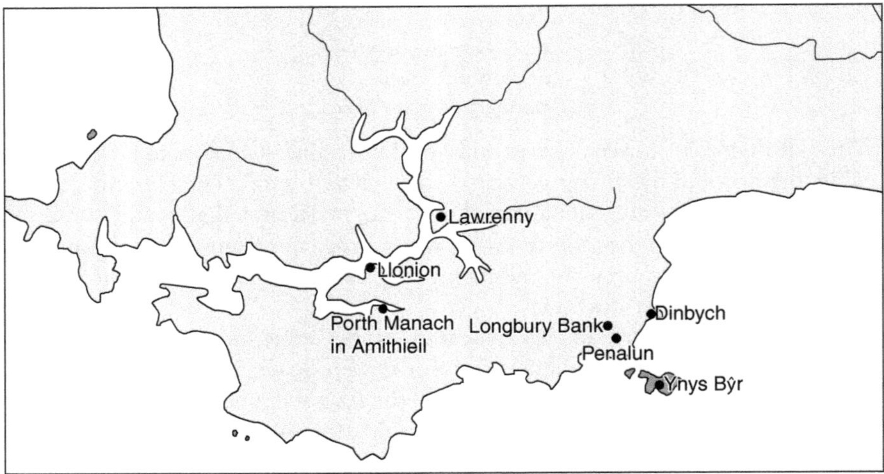

Map 29. The context of *Edmyg Dinbych*

should have been a king of Dyfed.[45] Some help in answering this question comes from the post-Roman period, some from sculpture dated to the late ninth century or the first half of the tenth, some from a text no later than the eleventh century and preserved as a fragment in Latin Redaction B of the Law of Hywel Dda.[46]

Longbury Bank was an undefended site close to Dinbych, where the finds showed that it participated in both the Mediterranean imports into south-western Britain between the late fifth and the mid-sixth century and the later wider imports to royal sites in Ireland and western Britain (without the earlier concentration on south-west Britain).[47] These later imports are associated with E-ware and glass and are dated between the late sixth and some date in the eighth century. Medieval ploughing meant that hardly any structures would have survived, if they existed originally, but it is clear that it was not fortified. A combination of undefended site, royal seat, and important church is likely in south Pembrokeshire (the medieval Penfro). Four sites are in close proximity: the Dinbych of the poem (Tenby), Longbury Bank, Penally (Penalun), and Caldey Island (Ynys Bŷr). Penally is one and a half miles west-south-west of Dinbych; Longbury Bank is less than a mile north-north-west of Penally, while Caldey Island lies just over two miles due south of Dinbych and about a mile and a half south-east of Penally (see Map 29).

Penally, apart from the sculpture of the late ninth or tenth century, is best attested in the witness list to a charter which has been dated to the late seventh century: one of the witnesses was *guonocatui princeps aluni capitis*, namely

[45] See above, 157.

[46] E. Campbell and A. Lane, 'Excavations at Longbury Bank, Dyfed, and Early Medieval Settlement in South Wales', *Medieval Archaeology*, 37 (1993), 15–77; Edwards, *Corpus*, ii. 410–21, P82–4; *The Latin Texts of the Welsh Laws*, ed. H. Emanuel (Cardiff, 1967), 248–9.

[47] E. Campbell, *Continental and Mediterranean Imports to Atlantic Britain and Ireland,* AD *400–800,* CBA Research Report 157 (York,

'*Guonocatui* head (of the church) of Penalun'.[48] However, it was still a church that the bishops of Morgannwg wished to claim in the eleventh century on account of its connection with the early life of St Teilo.[49] The church is likely to have had a continuous history from the seventh to the eleventh century (and beyond). Ynys Bŷr (Caldey Island) is mentioned in the seventh-century Life of St Samson; and the author of the Life claims to have been there himself.[50] A long and exceptionally well-designed inscription has been dated to the eighth or early ninth century.[51] The letterforms are based on half-uncial with a strong geometrical character: that is, its associations are with grand Insular manuscripts. It suggests that such manuscripts were accessible, if not produced, in Dyfed.

The legal evidence consists of a text about the *galanas* 'wergild' payable for *prepositi* (probably Welsh *meiri*) in charge of royal sites in Dyfed. These include Dinbych, *Llonion* (probably Llanion now swallowed up in Pembroke Dock), *Leurenni* (probably Lawrenny), and *Amiteil*, probably the district on the south side of Pennar Pill (the estuary of the Pembroke River) including Monkton.[52] The identified sites run across the neck of the medieval *cantref* of Penfro, but the lawbook adds, 'and the same amount for the *galanas* of the *prepositi* of all Dyfed'. Penfro fell to the Norman invasion of 1093 and was never recovered by the Welsh. The material can hardly, therefore, derive from a source written after 1093.

The evidence suggests that for most of the period from the fifth to the eleventh century Dinbych was an important royal site, very much as the Four Branches refer to Arberth as a *priflys* 'a chief court', not the chief court, of the ruler of Dyfed.[53] If we then ask when someone called Bleiddudd might have been the ruler of Dyfed, the most likely period is between 814 and *c.* 870.[54] By this stage the importance of Longbury Bank was at an end, but both Penally and Caldey Island are likely to have been active.

The last obit of someone from the old dynasty of Dyfed is that of Triffun in 814 or 815.[55] Hyfaidd, who died *c.* 892, is known to have been ruling before 874, since Asser tells us that he expelled Nobis, bishop (or archbishop) of St Davids, who held that position from 840 until his death in 873 or 874.[56] Triffun's first cousin, Tangwystl, married Bleddri, the father of Hyfaidd, and it has been proposed that

[48] *LL* 151b; Davies, *An Early Welsh Microscosm*, 169, who notes errors in the lay part of the witness list, including the placing of *Guonocatui* in the lay section.

[49] *LL* 253 (p. 255), 269 (p. 270).

[50] *Vita Prima S. Samsonis*, i. 20.

[51] Edwards, *Corpus*, ii. 294–9, P6; above, 626–9 and Illustration 19.1.

[52] *OP* ii. 421, citing the *Amithieil* of *LL* 123 (p. 124), 253 (p. 255). The text of Latin B should, therefore, have the word division emended to read *Amiteil Lonion*. Cf. *6y g6nant aer ar vrys am lys lonyon*, 'they will wreak slaughter in haste about the court of Llonion', *The Book of Taliesin*, ed. J. Gwenogvryn Evans (Llanbedrog, 1910), 73. 5–6, a poem dated by Ifor Williams, *The Poems of Taliesin*, pp. xxvi–xxvii, to 942–950 (but one should include the next decade, 950–960). Cf. *OP* ii. 545 on 'Pennar Mowth'. Llonion is also mentioned in the triad of 'The Three Powerful Swineherds of the Island of Britain', *TYP*, no. 26.

[53] *Priflys idaw* not *y briflys*.

[54] N. Tolstoy, *The Oldest British Prose Literature: The Compilation of the Four Branches of the* Mabinogi (Lampeter, 2009), 495–540, prefers a later date, at the beginning of the eleventh century.

[55] *AC*, ed. Phillimore, 814 = 815, *AC*, ed. Dumville; HG 2; cf. Kirby, 'British Dynastic History', 86–7.

[56] Asser, *Life*, c. 79; *AC* 840; *AC*, ed. Phillimore, 873 = 874 *AC*, ed. Dumville.

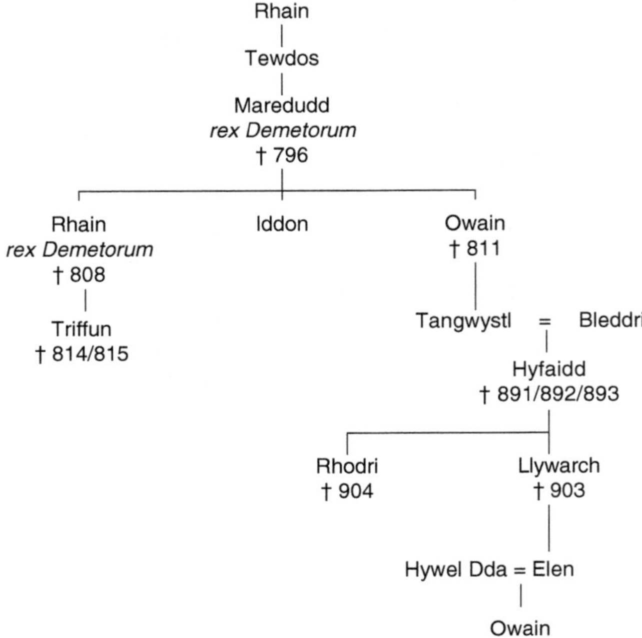

Figure 20.2. Rulers of Dyfed from the eighth to the tenth century

the name *Bledri* or *Bledric* given by *Brut y Tywysogion* to the father of Hyfaidd was an error for Bleiddudd.[57] Yet, this is unnecessary: Bleiddudd may well have belonged to the same family as Bleddri: their names share the same first element, *blaidd* 'wolf', but have different words for a ruler as the second element, *udd* and *rhi*. After the death of Hyfaidd's sons, Llywarch and Rhodri, in 903 and 904, the father of Hywel Dda, Cadell ap Rhodri ap Merfyn Frych, gained control of Dyfed.[58] Two changes of dynasty occurred in Dyfed between 814 or 815 and *c.* 904, the first in favour of the family of Bleddri and Hyfaidd, and the second in favour of a branch of the Merfynion. From *c.* 870 until the end of our period there is no room for a Bleiddudd as ruler of Dyfed. A date for the poem between 815 and *c.* 870 is thus probable, although it is just possible that Bleiddudd, as a kinsman of Bleddri, Hyfaidd, and his son Llywarch, held Penfro as a subordinate ruler at some date during their reigns.

The poem is divided into seven sections each defined by the end-rhyme and by an invocation of the fortress itself. The first section begins and ends by addressing God. At the beginning the poet declares that he has a petition to present to God; and, at the end, he states it: he wishes for reconciliation once he has fulfilled his side

[57] *Bledri*, *Brut RBH*, *Bledric*, *Brut, Pen. 20* and *BS s.a.* 893; Gruffydd, *Edmyg Dinbych*, 15; id., 'In Praise of Tenby', 93.
[58] See above, 507–9.

of the *amod*, the bargain or contract. What the *amod* entailed is not stated: perhaps the bargain was with Bleiddudd to sing his praises and finally his *marwnad*. The context is the great feast at the New Year, *Calan*, which is likely to have extended from Christmas to the New Year. Later, in the twelfth and thirteenth centuries, this seems to have been the greatest of 'the three principal feasts': Christmas, Easter, and Whitsun.[59] In the Arthurian tale *Culhwch ac Olwen*, New Year's Day was the only day in the entire year on which Glewlwyd Gafaelfawr, the Porter, performed his duties in his own person, the rest of the year being left to deputies, and New Year's Day was chosen by Culhwch to make his arrival at Arthur's court. He had a special gift to ask of Arthur; and New Year's Day was sufficiently important in the calendar of royal generosity to produce a special word, *celennig*, for a gift made on *Calan*, 1 January—a word used in the poem (line 44).[60] On this New Year the sea was angry; and the poets were happy to make a festive clamour above their mead cups and to leave the sea to 'a fleet of Picts'. There still was a Pictish kingdom in the ninth century, but this phrase suggests more the conditions of the fourth and fifth centuries than those of the ninth.[61] Perhaps, just as early medieval historical sources called the Avars Huns, so the poet may have used the name of the old marauders from the north for their contemporary equivalents, the Vikings, especially since Gildas had described the Picts as coming to northern Britain by sea, settling there, and subsequently attacking the Britons by sea.[62] 'Picts' are mentioned elsewhere in poetry that is early, but nevertheless later than the end of the Pictish kingdom.[63]

As would be appropriate for any poem at *Calan*, this one combines praise of a generous ruler with praise of his war band and retinue. The feast has brought together the elite of Bleiddudd's kingdom with the ruler and with the poets. Our poet, however, claims a special position among them: he is 'a tongue for the poets of Britain', and it is his privilege to lie beside the king (the feasters recline in pairs), just like an Irish *ollam*, chief poet.[64] Yet, there is more than a hint that something has been wrong with the relationship of poet and king. Much of the poem reads initially as though Bleiddudd were the current king, presiding at the feast in his fortress. But some of the verbs are in the imperfect or past tense. The privilege of lying beside the king on the night of *Calan* wearing a purple mantle *was* the poet's; but it was precisely this past privilege that entitled him to 'become a tongue for the poets' in the present. Even more strikingly, 'before he went into *derwin llan* he *gave*

59 *Welsh Medieval Law*, ed. A. W. Wade-Evans, 2. 15; 87. 18–25 (where the feast of Christmas is defined as lasting from the night of Christmas Eve after Vespers to New Year's Day after Mass); *Llyfr Iorwerth*, ed. Wiliam, §§ 2, 66, trans. Jenkins, *LTMW* 5, 76; Haycock, *Legendary Poems*, no. 14. 49; M. E. Owen, 'Literary Convention and Historic Reality: The Court in the Welsh Poetry of the Twelfth and Thirteenth Century', *Études Celtiques*, 29 (1992), 83.

60 *GPC* under *calennig*; Haycock, *Legendary Poems*, no. 14, l. 49, and n. p. 385.

61 Compare the Pict, *illius nefarie gentis princeps*, who is made in the Life of Teilo, when Teilo and David are both studying with *Poulinus* (*LL* 99–100), to play the part attributed in the Life of David to the Irishman Boia.

62 Gruffydd, *Edmyg Dinbych*, 24, id., 'The Praise of Tenby', 99; Gildas, *De Excidio*, §§ 14; 19. 1; 21. 1.

63 Haycock, *Legendary Poems*, no. 1, l. 68 and n. on p. 70.

64 Gruffydd, *Edmyg Dinbych*, 29, id., 'The Praise of Tenby', 95; cf. P. A. Breatnach, 'The Chief's Poet', *PRIA* 83 C (1983), 45–8.

me mead and wine from a glass goblet'.[65] *Derwin llan* 'oaken church-enclosure' must be a church (and in this context a cemetery), just as Old Irish *dairthech*, literally 'oak-house', was a church or oratory, and hence Bleiddudd must be dead. The poet, therefore, is parading his past privileges before a new ruler, who may be the one said to descend, probably not in the male line, from 'the son of Erbin', presumably the famous Geraint ab Erbin, king of Dumnonia (line 14); and he also is likely to be the great-grandson of Owain mentioned at the end. Kirby argued, however, that the Erbin who appears in the genealogy of Dyfed in two later versions, but is omitted in the two earlier ones, was probably the brother of Aergol Lawhir, not his son, and thus the progenitor of a collateral line, to which the new ruler would have belonged.[66] This is possible, but it would imply that the kingship reverted to a branch of the old dynasty after the death of Bleiddudd. This is perhaps not the most likely explanation, though one must admit that the genealogical background of Hyfaidd ap Bleddri is not known.[67]

The difficulty the poet faces in negotiating his way into a favour with the new ruler that would match the position he held under Bleiddudd forms a central strand of the poem. The poet therefore emphasizes his solidarity with the war band and the others present at the feast:

> They take no pleasure in causing shame,
> It is not their custom to be niggardly.
> I shall not utter a falsehood against my sustenance:
> A slave in Dyfed is better than yeomen in Deudraeth (lines 21–4).

Deudraeth was a district in the northern part of Ardudwy, part of Gwynedd, the kingdom that, by the 880s was showing such evident ambition to conquer Dyfed that Hyfaidd ap Bleddri was driven to submit to King Alfred and seek his protection.[68] The happy past under Bleiddudd is the basis for the poet's claims under the new ruler:

> Mine were the privileges that I used to desire—
> I shall not speak of legal entitlement—I used to maintain law.
> He who does not know this is not entitled to a *celennig* (lines 42–4).

Those present at the feast are called to witness to his past privileges and his past respect for law. Although he will not speak of *taith*, what is legally right, he clearly implies that he has rights. These lines are immediately followed by three others of particular historical interest which complete section VI of the poem:

> The written text (*ysgrifen*) of Britain (is) the chief object of concern,
> Where the waves make their tumult;
> The cell I used to visit will long endure (or: may it long endure!).

65 For the glass drinking vessel, cf. Campbell, *Continental and Mediterranean Imports*, ch. 4.

66 D. P. Kirby, 'British Dynastic History in the Pre-Viking Period', *BBCS* 27 (1976–8) 84.

67 Triad no. 68 in *Trioedd Ynys Prydein*, ed. Bromwich, gives as one of three kings sprung from *meibion eillion* Hyueid ap Bleidic yn Deheubarth, but this evidence is too late for confidence.

68 Asser, *Life*, c. 80.

Ysgrifen is from Latin *scribendum* 'what should be written', just as *llên* is from Latin *legendum* 'what should be read'. It may refer to a letter or a charter. The second is the more likely here; and the sequence of thought would be clear if one could assume that the *ysgrifen* of Britain was kept in the place mentioned as 'the cell I used to visit'. If it were a church—and Penally has been proposed—its endurance would guarantee the survival of the charter.[69] The Britain mentioned is very likely to be Wales, but, even so, the claim made here is a large one: if the charter enshrined the privileges of poets (among other things perhaps) and was seen as a model for the poets and their patrons throughout Wales, the terms used would be justified. It has even been suggested that the poem itself might have been written into a gospel book and so have survived;[70] but perhaps it is too oblique in expression to have fulfilled such a role.

Echrys Ynys, also preserved in the Book of Taliesin, is a poem in two sections marked by end-rhyme and shared opening words, *echrys ynys* 'desolate the island'. It is similar to *Edmyg Dinbych* in one major respect: the context is the death of a ruler, the obligation of the poet to praise him in death, and the difficulty of the transition to a new regime. It concerns, however, the north-west not the south-west of Wales. It has been dated to the period from the ninth to the mid-eleventh century by its most recent editor; Ifor Williams tentatively favoured the eleventh century.[71] The ruler is called Aeddon. He had ruled Anglesey before his death in battle, but when he met his death in battle at 'Seon's stronghold' he had come from 'Gwydion's land' (Arfon, especially Arfon uwch Gwyrfai).

Echrys Ynys may be datable, if the Aeddon of the poem is the Aeddan ap Blegywryd who, together with his four sons, was killed by Llywelyn ap Seisyll in 1017.[72] This possibility was entertained by Sir Ifor Williams, and then rejected.[73] He did so partly because of the final syllable, *-on* in the poem (confirmed by rhyme) rather than *-an* as in the annal, partly because he followed Lloyd-Jones in taking *aeddon* to be a common noun, and partly because of the form *archaedon* in lines 5 and 17. Geraint Gruffydd, however, distinguishes between the name Aeddon and the common noun *archaddon* 'lord'; there is no need for the latter to interfere with our judgement of the former: both are present in the poem but they are quite distinct. The first of Williams's difficulties remains; but a possible solution may be found by considering the textual history of *Brut y Tywysogion*, in its two versions, and *Brenhinedd y Saeson*. These give us three independent translations of a Latin original related to, but not identical with, the B and C versions of *Annales Cambriae*. The surviving texts all stem from a Latin chronicle; and it may be

[69] Gruffydd, *Edmyg Dinbych*, 26; cf. Sims-Williams, 'The Uses of Writing', 29–30. *Cell*, from Latin *cella*, is used for a storehouse in Middle Welsh, as in *Llyfr Iorwerth*, ed. Wiliam, §§ 44, 51, 139, 143. Perhaps it was used in a Welsh monastery for the room where the book cupboards and their contents were kept, but it may be used here, as in Irish, for an entire complex of church buildings.

[70] Gruffydd, ibid.

[71] R. G. Gruffydd, 'A Welsh "Dark Age" Court Poem', 42–3; Williams, *The Beginnings of Welsh Poetry*, 177.

[72] *Brut*, *s.a.* 1017; *AC* [1017].

[73] Williams, *The Beginnings of Welsh Poetry*, 179–80.

suggested that the form *Aidan* or *Aedan* was far better known in Latin sources than *Aedon*. Both are likely to be borrowings from Irish at a period when Welsh had no long *ā*, so that either *-an* with a short *a* or the well-known native suffix *-on* (as in the divine names, Mabon son of Modron, Teyrnon, Gofannon) was substituted for *-ān*.[74] The advantage of this proposal is that Aeddan ap Blegywryd was killed by Llywelyn ap Seisyll and Llywelyn was subsequently entitled king of Gwynedd.[75] The poem, as we have seen, shows that Aeddon had ruled Anglesey and probably Arfon, both in the core of Gwynedd; yet there is no period between 800 and 1064 other than the beginning of the eleventh century when it is easy to think of a ruler of Anglesey and probably also of Arfon who did not belong to a well-recognized dynasty, such as the Maelgyning and their kinsmen from Rhos up to the beginning of the ninth century, the Merfynion from 825 until the end of the tenth century and from 1033 to 1039, and Llywelyn ap Seisyll and his son Gruffudd ap Llywelyn from 1017 to 1023 and 1039 to 1064. The rulers of Gwynedd after Gruffudd ap Llywelyn are well known: there is no later period into which Aeddon could be fitted. One answer that has been given to this difficulty is that 'Aeddon, though clearly of high status, was of less than royal rank'.[76] Yet he is termed *gwledig* and evidently ruled Anglesey, and probably Arfon as well. There is one much later period when rulers of Anglesey did not always rule Gwynedd as a whole, namely the strife among the sons of Owain Gwynedd after the death of their father and the killing of Hywel ab Owain,[77] but any ruler then was a son or grandson of Owain Gwynedd; there is no Aeddon who, like them, might have ruled Anglesey as an *arglwydd* under a brother. It is much easier to suppose that the two forms of the name refer to the same person than that there was an Aeddan and an Aeddon both involved in the struggle for domination in Gwynedd at the beginning of the eleventh century. Once we accept this dating, however, the poem becomes precious evidence for the history of Welsh literature, both verse and prose, before 1064.

The poem seems to be an odd mixture of lament for the dead Aeddon and negotiation of the poet's way into a new reign (19, 26–7). If so, the task was a delicate one, and was perhaps fittingly performed through reference to ancient tradition. As we have seen, Aeddon 'came from Gwydion's land to Seon's stronghold', namely from Arfon, and especially Arfon uwch Gwyrfai, intimately connected with Gwydion ap Dôn, the central figure of the Fourth Branch of the Mabinogi, to 'Seon's stronghold'.[78] It seems as though Caer Seon, facing

[74] The other suffix *-awn*, later *-on*, may have been avoided because it was used in the names of lineages, for example, Merfyniawn, Merfynion.

[75] *Brut*, *AC s.a.* 1022.

[76] Gruffydd, 'A Welsh "Dark Age" Court Poem', 41.

[77] *Brut*, *s.aa.* 1174, 1175, 1193.

[78] Gruffydd, 'A Welsh "Dark Age" Court Poem', line 7; Gruffydd follows B. F. Roberts, 'Rhai o Gerddi Ymddiddan Llyfr Du Caerfyrddin', in R. Bromwich and R. Brinley Jones (eds.), *Astudiaethau ar yr Hengerdd* (Cardiff, 1978), 319–22; Haycock, *Legendary Poems*, 345–6 (n. on poem 11. 91) gives good reason to revert to Ifor Williams's identification of 'Seon tewdor' with the Caer Seon named in the Dialogue of Taliesin and Ugnach in the Black Book of Carmarthen, *Llyfr Du Caerfyrddin*, ed. A. O. H. Jarman (Cardiff, 1982), no. 36. 13–15, and both with the hill fort on Conwy Mountain, named as Caer Seion on Ordnance Survey maps (SH 760 779).

Degannwy across the estuary of the River Conwy, is where Aeddon met his death in battle.[79] The poem thus suggests a ruler who controlled Gwynedd west of the Conwy meeting his death in battle close to the mouth of the Conwy. If Aeddon was Aeddan ap Blegywryd, his opponent, Llywelyn ap Seisyll, may then have been based in Gwynedd east of the Conwy.

The poet goes on to compare the justice of Aeddon's rule to the time of Gwydion and Amaethon, when 'counsel used to prevail'.[80] He also seems to compare his own role as poet to that of Taliesin, 'a generous utterer', whom 'Math and Eufydd fashioned by magic'.[81] The legendary Taliesin triumphed at Degannwy, just across the estuary from Caer Seon, and in *Canu y Gwynt* he calls himself 'the sage of Seon'.[82] The fortresses either side of the Conwy were as closely associated with Taliesin as Arfon uwch Gwyrfai was with Gwydion and Math. If, therefore, the real battle in which Aeddon died was at or near Caer Seon, it might be natural for Aeddon's poet to evoke the memory of Taliesin.

Quite what would be the lot of the poet after the death of Aeddon is far from clear in the poem, and perhaps was unclear to the poet himself when he composed this *marwnad* for Aeddon. The first section of the poem (lines 1–17) is unambiguously a lament for his dead lord and king. The poet himself appears to have had a special link with Anglesey for the island 'is desolate' after the death of its just ruler: this may be the theme of the justice of the ruler assuring the fertility of the land known from thirteenth-century Welsh poetry as well as from early Irish texts.[83] In its last two lines the poet prays for his own salvation, 'an apostle's lot', just as he expresses confidence that 'the generous and most just one shall be received by angels'—the standard welcome into heaven given to the saved. The poet's own eternal future is placed side by side with that of Aeddon. The second section of the poem (lines 18–29), however, refers to a victor, *buddwas*, which might be the new victor or the old king, previously victorious.[84] At the end of this section the poet again prays for his own salvation. He is not without concern, however, for the temporal prosperity of the kingdom in the aftermath of Aeddon's death: he puts before his audience two questions, 'who will restore order?' and 'who will defend Anglesey of abundant wealth?' Effectively he challenges the new king to rule as justly as Aeddon did in his lifetime assuring for Anglesey a similar prosperity. This challenge gives an extra point to his use of ancient tradition: that, as we have seen,

[79] In the context the 'four bare-headed women in the midnight hour' of line 8 are more likely to be supernatural creatures resembling Valkyries than arrogant former slave girls, or else his daughters, who had an undue influence on Aeddon (possibilities canvassed by Ifor Williams, *The Beginnings of Welsh Poetry*, 179); I take their feasting mentioned in line 22 to be the battle itself. Given the Viking settlements on Anglesey, it is far from impossible that these figures are derived from the Valkyries.

[80] Gruffydd, 'A Welsh "Dark Age" Court Poem', line 11.

[81] Gruffydd, 'A Welsh "Dark Age" Court Poem', line 10; cf. *Kat Godeu*, ed. Haycock, *Legendary Poems*, no. 5, lines 151–77.

[82] Haycock, *Legendary Poems*, 11. 91.

[83] See above, 324–6.

[84] Although Gruffydd translates *aros ara* at the end of the same line (19) as 'it was pleasant to remain', thus restricting its application to Aeddon, it is literally just 'a pleasant remaining' with no tense specified.

had a precise topographical reference, and the poem thus voices the hopes of a kingdom that the death in battle of a just king will not mean the end of just rule.

What is most remarkable for the history of Welsh literature is that the poet was prepared to bring together two very different periods in the history of the Britons—a history divided into three principal epochs: before Rome, Roman Britain, and after Rome. Gwydion, Eufydd, and Math were assigned in the Four Branches to the period immediately before Rome, but Taliesin belonged to the time of Maelgwn Gwynedd in the sixth century. So to say that Taliesin was created by the magic of Math and Eufydd seems to muddle two eras. The Taliesin of *Echrys Ynys*, however, is very much the legendary Taliesin, who lived through many ages; and this legendary Taliesin is thus shown to have been a well-developed figure by the early eleventh century. *Echrys Ynys* is also crucial for the background of the Four Branches, for it shows that the association of Gwydion with Arfon was already well established in the early eleventh century. The topography of the Fourth Branch, *Math*, was an inherited element in the story and cannot be used to place the author of the Four Branches in Gwynedd.

Echrys Ynys, like the poem in praise of Dinbych, is a subtle and delicate response to the death of a ruler. The ambiguities of the poem reflect the uncertainties of the situation, and the references to persons and places of tradition place the concerns of an ancient kingdom before a new regime.

4. LLYWARCH AND GWÊN: OLD AGE AND YOUTH

The dialogue between Llywarch and his son Gwên and the subsequent lament by Llywarch for his son, both dated by Rowland to the late eighth or early ninth century,[85] could hardly be a greater contrast with *Echrys Ynys* and the poem in praise of Dinbych. In the place of allusions to tradition we have here a ruthless concentration on one issue, the relationship between father and son.

In the manuscripts, the cycle of englynion in the voices of Llywarch Hen and two of his sons opens with two poems, Llywarch's lament for his old age and a dialogue between Llywarch and Gwên.[86] These were the poems entitled, in the White Book of Rhydderch, 'The *englynion* of Llywarch'.[87] Yet, since Llywarch's son was dead at the time of 'The Song of the Old Man' but was alive and speaking in the dialogue, the manuscript order needs to be reversed.[88] In the copies of the dialogue, the second poem in the White Book and in the Red Book of Hergest, Gwên speaks first, but in a copy of a lost medieval manuscript made by Dr John

[85] Rowland, *Early Welsh Saga Poetry*, 388–9.

[86] In the Red Book of Hergest 'The Song of the Old Man', *Cân yr Henwr*, comes before 'Llywarch and Gwên', and the same sequence was followed in the lost section of the White Book, to judge by copies, but in *Canu Llywarch Hen*, ed. I. Williams (Cardiff, 1935), and in J. Rowland, *Early Welsh Saga Poetry*, text 404–5, trans. 468–9, 'Llywarch and Gwên' is placed first.

[87] *CLlH*, p. li.

[88] *CLlH*, p. li; Rowland, *Early Welsh Saga Poetry*, 11 and n. 16.

Davies of Mallwyd in the early seventeenth century, the sequence opens with an englyn by the father, Llywarch.[89]

Although it was only inserted in the margin of one early-modern version of the poem, it provides a dramatically effective beginning to the verbal cut-and-thrust between father and son:[90]

> Over the left side of my body the shield is thin.
> Though I be old, I can do it:
> I shall stand guard on Gorlas Ford.[91]

The issue is who will watch the ford over which the enemy is expected to come. Behind that question lie others: whether the old man is still physically capable of fighting or the young man is now willing to risk his life on the border. Llywarch's initial stance is that, just perhaps, he may still have the strength to uphold the role he had discharged triumphantly years before, when he too was a young man. Yet this is only an opening move: the truth is (and the first line effectively admits as much) that he is too decrepit to ward off any enemy seeking to cross Gorlas Ford. The Llywarch of this dialogue is hardly younger than the Llywarch of the 'Song of the Old Man'; the only thing he will wield is a stick, much needed to sustain his uncertain walk. His place is by the fire not the ford.

Even though the old man may need a stick, his tongue needs no support; and though he may not be able—in spite of his somewhat hesitant initial boast—to defend the ford, the power of his words may ensure that someone else is there to await the enemy that night. His power is not that of a king over his people, but of a father over his sons. He cannot give orders but he can needle: he can cast doubt on their manliness and he can invoke the memory of his own heroism in a distant youth; and he can go even further than his own personal achievement, or his son's lack of anything to match it. He can invoke the authority, universal and impersonal, of proverbial wisdom.[92]

The wisdom of Llywarch comes in two forms, truths about the natural world and truths about human beings. For example the sixth and seventh englynion exhibit the way in which, even when he has secured from his son Gwên an express resolve to defend the ford, Llywarch cannot resist puncturing the moral value of that resolve by adopting the role of the sceptical sage.

> Gwên
> I shall not shame you battle-ready-man;
> When the brave man arms for the border,
> I shall endure hardship before I shift my ground.

[89] NLW MS 4973B, written 1617 × 1634: D. Huws, 'John Davies and his Manuscripts', in C. Davies (ed.), *Dr John Davies of Mallwyd: Welsh Renaissance Scholar* (Cardiff, 2004), 107.

[90] For this reason it is placed first by Rowland, *Early Welsh Saga Poetry*, 11–12 and 404. In *CLlH* this englyn occurs at V. 10.

[91] On the name of the ford see P. Sims-Williams, 'The Provenance of the Llywarch Hen Poems: A Case for Llan-gors, Brycheiniog', *CMCS* 26 (Winter, 1993), 27–64, at 44.

[92] S. L. Higley, *Between Languages: The Uncooperative Text in Early Welsh and Old English Nature Poetry* (University Park, PA, 1993), 174.

Llywarch
The wave has a free run along the beach.
Soon a boasted plan is broken,
Battle-fragile: it's usual for one full of talk to flee.

This interchange shows how the young man, too, has his verbal weapons to hand: Gwên is a true son of Llywarch in more than mere stalwart courage. The language of these englynion may be difficult (at least for us), but it is not usually ornate. The grand nominal compounds or collocations of professional praise poetry are not its style. Yet Gwên's first line quoted above has a model example of such grand diction: 'battle-ready-man', *trin wosep wr*. Instead of a normal word-order—man ready for battle—the order is reversed and the head-word, 'man', kept to the end. The phrase cannot be understood *seriatim* but must be comprehended as a single complex whole. These were words appropriate for a professional poet to address to his patron setting out for battle. Yet Llywarch will not set out for battle brandishing his spear; he was not in the slightest battle-ready; he will sit by the fire twisting his stick in his hands till he hears what has happened to his son.

There are many things conspicuously absent from this dialogue. 'Battle-ready-men' usually went out to fight in the ranks of an army. Llywarch vainly imagined that he might go out; Gwên, his son, did indeed go out, but he went out alone. There was no army, no king, no one beyond the one family, even the single pair of father and son. There is nothing to suggest that Gwên will defend the ford because, on this particular night, the job has been allotted by some higher authority to him. It may be that the guarding of this particular ford has fallen, by lot or by higher command, to Llywarch's kindred, but, if so, that was in the prose or perhaps entirely undisclosed.[93] The line, 'When the brave man arms for the border', is a way of saying that he will not be behindhand, that he will behave as any brave man would. It does not imply a battalion of other brave men in the background. Llywarch never appeals to any political bond to persuade Gwên to fight. On his side, Gwên does not make his promise to fight to some commander but only to Llywarch, his father. The line, 'I shall not shame you, battle-ready-man', is half-satirical, praise so ludicrously inappropriate to its subject that it becomes satire, half a sad acknowledgement of what Llywarch once was, a great warrior, and therefore a man whose face should not be shamed by his son.

Llywarch, however, would not accept any such double-edged compliment. He seizes upon the last phrase in Gwên's englyn, 'before I shift my ground'. He does not respond, however, on the same moral level but himself shifts into a proverbial mode. The wave, the incoming tide, will run smoothly over the beach; no small obstacle set up by a pygmy human resolve will delay it for a moment. The proverb about nature provides an authoritative grounding for one human proverb and then another. Everything Llywarch says in this englyn purports to be calm, immemorial wisdom. He never says, 'Perhaps you, Gwên, will not stand firm when the attackers

[93] Some organization is suggested by the term *gwylfa*, 'watch place', in *Braint Teilo*, *LL* 120: the church of Llandaf claimed exemption from such watch duty (*heb guylma* in the Welsh version corresponds to *sine uigilanda regione* in the Latin, ibid. 118).

try to rush the ford.' He not only keeps his distance from his son but even increases it: when he uses a poetic compound, 'battle-fragile' *cadangdo*, he is uttering a universal truth. Yet it is abundantly obvious that all this impersonal wisdom has only one target, his son.

Llywarch may be the master of proverbial wisdom, but the first to appeal to its authority was Gwên:

> Do not arm after dinner; let not your mind be sad.
> Keen is the breeze; bitter is poison.[94]
> My mother declares that I am your son.

It is possible, since we do not have the narrative context, to imagine that Gwên has long been absent and that he is not immediately recognized by his father, Llywarch.[95] It is not necessary, however, to suppose that Gwên was doing anything more than adopting the pose of the unrecognized and unacknowledged son. Welsh medieval children might be affiliated by the formal oath of the mother, and Gwên may be alluding to some such statement.[96] In any case, Llywarch does acknowledge kinship in his reply:

> Indeed, I recognize by my heart
> That we come from one line.
> You hang around a good long time, O Gwên!

Once acknowledged, Gwên declares his *arfaeth*: what, on pain of shame, he vows to perform:

> Keen my spear, flashing in battle.
> I vow to watch the ford.
> Though I may not survive, God be with you!

Llywarch, as is the habit of both speakers, picks on the last line of the other's englyn:

> If you survive, I shall see you.
> If you have been killed, I shall mourn you.
> Do not lose the honour of a man in the face of hardship.

Llywarch, apparently, can handle whatever Fate has in store. What matters more than whether his son lives or dies is whether he keeps the honour of a man. It is to this last line that Gwên in turn retorts, in the englyn already quoted, 'I shall not shame you, battle-ready-man.'

Llywarch may have the greater proverbial authority by virtue of age, past achievements, and ample memories. Yet Gwên too has his strong ground. Llywarch

[94] I am not sure of the exact significance of *gwenwyn* 'poison' unless it is making the dinner that Llywarch has just eaten the equivalent of the fatal mead drunk by the warriors of the Gododdin, before they rode off to their deaths: *Glasfedd eu hancwyn a gwenwyn fu*, Jarman, *Gododdin*, line 79 = *CA*, line 69.

[95] *CLlH* pp. lii–liii; Williams, *Lectures on Early Welsh Poetry* (Dublin, 1944), 37–8.

[96] Ior § 100, *LTMW* 132–3.

has invoked the honour of a man, a warrior—something which combines masculinity and physical courage. The one who cannot endure hardship, *gnif*, even to the point of death is no man. Yet the ancient Llywarch is not the man he once was: no girl loves him; his spear does not flash in the battle. He must appeal to his memories:

> When I was at the age of yonder youth,
> Who puts on his spurs of gold,
> Swiftly would I rush to my spear.

To which Gwên replies, so ending their exchange:

> Your assertion is utterly certain,
> You being alive and your witness dead!
> No old man was feeble when young.

Once Llywarch shifts his ground from universal wisdom to personal assertion, from what is always true for all things and all humanity to what was once true of himself, he loses authority. When Llywarch questions Gwên's authority in the present, and then goes on to boast of his own resolve in the past, he renders himself vulnerable to this conclusive rejoinder.

Only when the dialogue had almost reached its end was it revealed who the enemy was:

> In spite of horror at conflict against the warriors of England,
> I shall not ruin my high rank.
> I shall not wake girls.

There is no pretence here that a brave warrior does not experience fear: it is not a poem of unreal heroism. In the poem, the identity of the enemy is not of huge consequence: what matters more is that Gwên, as Llywarch's son, is a great man, someone of high lineage, who will not bring shame upon his rank by shrieking in fear and so waking girls—or old men. Llywarch's lament for his son, spoken the next morning, when he knows that his son did watch the ford, did fight the English, and was slain, refers regularly to the dialogue, and yet it makes no reference at all to the identity of the enemy, other than by saying that he who killed Gwên was no kinsman.

Much of the power of this lament derives from its inversion of the stance taken by Llywarch in the dialogue. Gwên is now no mere lad showing off his golden spurs:

> Four and twenty sons used to be mine,
> Golden-torqued princely chieftains.
> Compared to Gwên they were little lads (*gweisionein*).

Yet it also, in part, continues themes contained within the dialogue. There, Llywarch recognized his son as his at the outset and his lament is as much concerned with his son's relationship to himself as with Gwên's death as such.

The lament opens with three englynion which use the device known as incremental repetition.[97] In the first Llywarch brings out an inner tension of his lament—at once praise of a warrior and misery for a lost son—with one ambiguous phrase:

Gwên stood watch by the Llawen last night.
  In spite of the onslaught he did not flee—
Sad the report/cold the fame—on Gorlas dyke.

Adrawdd is translated both 'report' and also 'fame' because the former is its normal and literal meaning, whereas the second is a meaning it has in early Welsh verse, notably in the *Gododdin*. *Oer* is translated both as 'cold' and as 'sad', similarly combining literal and metaphorical senses, but since English 'cold' can also be used metaphorically, the translation which best conveys the sharpness of Llywarch's words is probably 'cold the fame'.

The second and third englynion develop the tension:

Gwên stood watch by the Llawen last night,
  With his shield on his shoulder.
Since he was a son of mine, he was ready.

Gwên stood watch by the Llawen last night
  With his shield up to his chin.
Since he was a son of mine, he did not escape.

A son of Llywarch would be ready for any combat and Gwên was true to his birth: he finally confirmed his lineage in death. Yet the word used for 'escape' is picked up in a later englyn:

Gwên, I know your nature,
You were as the rush of an eagle in estuaries.
I would have been happy had you escaped.

As so often, the englyn deliberately contradicts itself: 'the rush of an eagle in estuaries', *rhuthr eryr yn ebyr*, evokes the grandeur and dominance of the sea eagle, larger even than the golden eagle. It is found as a term of heroic praise in the *Gododdin*, and here it is used to place Gwên in that world.[98] The warriors of the *Gododdin* did not escape either, but no claim was made in that poem that anyone would have been happy if they had survived; for them heroic death was all that could be desired. Llywarch undermines his own claims to heroic stature, made only the night before, by the admission made in the last line. In the dialogue Llywarch asserted that he was a great warrior and that Gwên still had everything to do to match his paternity; here, in acknowledging Gwên's claim to be every bit as great a warrior as he, Llywarch, had ever been in his prime, he also acknowledges that now, in his old age, thoughts of the heroism of his son cannot assuage his grief.

[97] K. H. Jackson, 'Incremental Repetition in the Early Welsh *Englyn*', *Speculum*, 16 (1941), 304–21.
[98] Jarman, *Gododdin*, line 41 = *CA*, line 31.

In the dialogue the image of the wave running over the shore evoked the fate against which no man can stand. Here a similar image is developed for a quite different purpose:

> The wave is in tumult; the breaking sea covers [the shore].
> When warriors go into battle,
> Gwên, woe for an old man who grieves for you.
>
> The wave is in tumult; the sea-flood covers [the shore].
> When warriors go on a mission,
> Woe for one too old who has lost you.

In the end, Llywarch was a father first and a proud old warrior second.

Canu Heledd, the cycle of englynion spoken by Heledd, sister of Cynddylan ap Cyndrwyn, is in many ways a contrast with *Canu Llywarch Hen*. In the Llywarch cycle we had the dialogue with Gwên before the catastrophe of his killing. In the Heledd cycle disaster has already struck. Cynddylan is dead and his land is aflame in the very first englyn. The Llywarch cycle began by concentrating on a relationship between persons, between father and son; the Heledd cycle mourns place almost as much as person. For that reason, although there is just about enough evidence to argue that the earliest Llywarch material has Brycheiniog as its background, it is wholly evident that the Heledd cycle belongs to a greater Powys that embraced Shropshire as far as the Wrekin. The lost lands of Powys were, however, remembered across a great divide created by the thorough anglicization of this central part of the march between Mercia and Powys. *Eglwysau Bassa*, 'the churches of Bassa', now Baschurch, belong to the ninth and tenth centuries not, as *Canu Heledd* would have it, to the seventh, for Bassa is an English personal name. The Heledd cycle aspires to recall the land of Cynddylan, but it can only achieve a partial recovery. The Llywarch cycle is not concerned to recall in painful memory a lost British landscape, only sons lost through deaths brought about by their own father. Shared, however, between the two cycles is the agony of the survivor still living after all that has been loved has been destroyed.

5. POET, STORYTELLER, AND LATIN LEARNING

Behind the dialogue of Llywarch and Gwên and Llywarch's lament for his dead son lay narrative, as argued by Ifor Williams and Jenny Rowland. We have to rely on educated guesswork to reconstruct the story but it is believed that the original audience did not. As we have seen, praise poems such as *Edmyg Dinbych* and *Echrys Ynys* were also directly responding to events, but these were in the real world; what distinguishes the saga poetry is that the verse is in the voice of a character in a narrative and that the events to which it responds are within that same narrative. Saga poetry thus raises the issue of the relationship between poet and storyteller, between *bardd* and *cyfarwydd*.

The same issue is raised in another form by *Echrys Ynys*. A real kingdom, Gwynedd, is evoked through allusion to narrative—a narrative about the characters of the Fourth Branch. The status of the poet, his relationship to Gwynedd, and perhaps his right to speak for Gwynedd is also conveyed obliquely through the figure of Taliesin and an allusion to a story about his creation. Narrative is presupposed, since the audience will not appreciate the significance of the poem unless they have some knowledge of the persons and events which the poet mentions. The authority of the poet is bound up with a narrative tradition of which he is a master but in which his audience share.

In the Fourth Branch, Gwydion travels south to ask a great gift of Pryderi, king, by now, of all South Wales and inheritor of his father's friendship with Arawn, king of the Otherworld. Gwydion and his companions go in disguise, as a company of poets. They find Pryderi in the south of Ceredigion, at Rhuddlan Teifi, a court of his. Gwydion evidently acted as the leader of the company, for he was placed to sit beside Pryderi himself.

> 'Well,' said Pryderi, 'we should like to have story-telling from some of those young men over there.' 'We have a custom, Lord,' said Gwydion, 'that on the first night when one comes to a great man the chief poet should speak. I shall gladly tell a tale.' He, Gwydion, was the best story-teller in the world. And that night he entertained the court with delightful dialogues and story-telling until he was praised by all the members of the court and Pryderi was pleased to converse with him.

What Pryderi and his court want from these poets is not some grand praise-poem but stories, and what Gwydion, in the character of a chief poet, gives them is a mixture of dialogues and storytelling. They all take it for granted that storytelling is a job performed by a poet. What is also striking, however, is that Gwydion gives them, besides stories, dialogues, *ymddiddanau*. This is reminiscent of such poems as *Ymddiddan Myrddin a Thaliesin*, 'The Conversation of Myrddin and Taliesin', but also of the dialogue between Llywarch and Gwên. The *ymddiddan*, like *cyfarwyddyd* 'storytelling', was part of the repertoire of the *pencerdd*, the highest-ranking poet. If Pryderi thought that storytelling was provided by lesser *cerddorion* within the company led by the *pencerdd*, that was not the custom invoked by Gwydion.[99]

Gwydion used the disguise of a poet on another occasion, when he was trying to break the fate imposed on Lleu by his mother, Aranrhod. Gwydion and Lleu presented themselves at the gate to Caer Aranrhod as 'poets from Morgannwg', and they were given a great welcome. After the main part of the meal, Aranrhod and Gwydion talked about *chwedlau a chyfarwyddyd* 'tales and storytelling'; and the story reminds us that 'He, Gwydion, was a fine storyteller.'[100] The evidence of the Fourth Branch accords perfectly with that of *Echrys Ynys*: there might be a *cyfarwydd* who was not a poet, but a *bardd* was expected to tell tales as well as

[99] Compare the Irish tale lists, which set out the tales that a poet should be able to tell: P. Mac Cana, *The Learned Tales of Medieval Ireland* (Dublin, 1980); G. Toner, 'Reconstructing the Earliest Irish Tale Lists', *Éigse*, 32 (2000), 88–120.

[100] *PKM* 82.

sing poems of praise. Similarly, the most probable view of 'The Triads of the Island of Britain' is that they were an index to narrative tradition for the use of poets—a narrative tradition that they mastered and on which they drew both for their own storytelling as well as for allusions in their poetry.[101]

The poet who praised the dead Bleiddudd and his fortress at Dinbych also claimed that he used to lie with his lord at the feast and that he was 'the tongue of the poets'.[102] In *Echrys Ynys* the poet, by aligning himself with Taliesin and speaking for Anglesey and Gwynedd, claimed the high status of a chief poet. In the laws such a poet was called a *pencerdd*, the teacher and the lord of other *cerddorion*, and, as teacher and head of his craft, entitled to a chair recalling the chair of the bishop as teacher of his flock and the chair of the rhetor and the grammarian in the schools of Classical Antiquity: he was a *bardd cadeiriog* 'chaired poet'.[103] Gruffudd ap Cynan's *pencerdd* Gellan fell in battle in Anglesey, fighting for his patron, and in the Life of Gruffudd ap Cynan he received an eloquent and highly classicizing obituary that makes it clear that he was both a harpist and a poet.[104] Gwydion, too, claimed to be a *pencerdd* accompanied by eleven other poets, just as the *pencerdd* was accompanied by his *cyweithydd*, a group of lesser poets who shared his journeys; and, as his fellow-*cerddorion* could not request gifts without his permission, so Gwydion as *pencerdd* decided that he should show his power of words first and thus be entitled to make his request before anyone else.

Many of the characteristics of the Welsh *pencerdd* have their counterparts in the Irish *ollam ríg*, 'king's poet', as bed-fellow, as counsellor of the king, and as one entitled to hold his land free of render. The curious *cyfarws neithior* that he could claim from the virgin bride after the first night on which she slept with her husband has its direct parallel in Ireland.[105] But in one way the Welsh *pencerdd* seems to be rather different from the Irish *ollam ríg*, 'king's chief poet'. In Ireland, the *ollam* as holding the highest rank in his profession was distinct from the *ollam ríg*, for the latter was bound to his king by contract to praise him in life and lament him in death, whereas the former had an independent authority because he was at the head of his craft and the teacher of lesser poets.[106] Admittedly the poet of *Edmyg Dinbych* may have understood himself as having a contract, *amod*, with Bleiddudd, but the legal evidence argues strongly that the Welsh *pencerdd* was more independent, more like the Irish chief poet than the king's chief poet, the *ollam* rather than the *ollam ríg*.[107] The *pencerdd* was not a regular member of the king's itinerant court, unlike

[101] *TYP*, 3rd edn., pp. liii–lxix.

[102] But in the Welsh Laws, the *pencerdd* merely sits with the heir-apparent, the *edling*, *Welsh Medieval Law*, ed. Wade-Evans, 33.14, or even with the court judge, *Llyfr Iorwerth*, ed. Wiliam, 40/2. This may represent a progressive degradation of his festive status.

[103] *Llyfr Iorwerth*, ed. Wiliam, 13/15; *LTWL* 330: *Bart* erit *penkert* cum in certamine cathedre uictor fuerit.

[104] *Vita Griffini filii Conani*, ed. Russell, § 23.

[105] P. Mac Cana, 'An Archaism in Irish Poetic Tradition', *Celtica*, 8 (1968), 174–81; id. 'Elfennau Cyn-Cristnogol yn y Cyfreithiau', *BBCS* 23 (1968–70), 316–20.

[106] Breatnach, 'The Chief's Poet', 37–9.

[107] D. Jenkins, '*Bardd Teulu* and *Pencerdd*', in T. M. Charles-Edwards, M. E. Owen, and P. Russell (eds.), *The Welsh King and his Court* (Cardiff, 2000), 142–66.

'a poet of the war band', *bardd teulu*. Instead, he had an area that was his *penceirddiaeth*, a *patria* or *gwlad*.[108] What made him a *pencerdd* was victory in a poetic contest, not a contract with his king.[109] When the king's court came to his *penceirddiaeth*, he had his place in the king's hall, but that was by the heir-apparent, the *edling*, or even the *ynad llys*, the court judge, rather than by the king.[110]

The position of the *pencerdd* may be illustrated by a poet recorded in the Gloucestershire section of Domesday Book. 'Berddig, the king's minstrel, has three vills, and, there, there are five plough-teams. He pays nothing'.[111] What is probably the same person appears in some witness lists in the Book of Llandaff, where he is known as *Berdicguent*, 'Berddig of Gwent'.[112] His name means 'Poetic' (*berddig* from *bardd*)' and this suggests that he may well have belonged to a kindred of poets, like most of his Irish counterparts.[113] That he is described as 'of Gwent' indicates that he may well have been the *pencerdd* of that *gwlad* or *patria*. Yet, Domesday Book described him as 'the king's minstrel'; and, even in the laws, his independence was not complete: according to one text, the king invested the *pencerdd* with his office.[114]

The links of Welsh poets to Latin learning are sometimes at their most clear in poems where there is evidence of rivalry. *Preideu Annwfyn* 'The Spoils of the Otherworld' is a title given by a later hand in the Book of Taliesin to a poem about Arthur's voyage to the Other World, named as *Caer Sidi*.[115] *Sidi* is a borrowing from the genitive of Irish *síd, síde*, a term for the Otherworld. *Preideu Annwfyn*, like *Echrys Ynys*, is important for the background to the Four Branches: it mentions Pwyll and Pryderi (l. 4), two principal figures of the First Branch, and also 'the Cauldron of the Head of Annwfn', *peir pen Annwfyn* (l. 15) and we are thus reminded of Pwyll's title *Penn Annwuyn*.[116] There is probably some relationship between this poem and the inclusion of Taliesin among the seven men who escaped from Ireland in *Branwen ferch Lyr*.[117] In his note on this latter passage, Ifor Williams cites another poem from the Book of Taliesin, *Golychaf i gul6yd argl6yd pop echen*, where Taliesin is made to declare, 'I was with Lleu and Gwydion in the battle of Goddau ... I was with Brân in Ireland', *Bum yg kat Godeu gan Lleu a G6ydyon ... Bum y gan Vran yn Iwerdon*.[118] It would be hard to deny, therefore,

[108] He is the *pencerdd* of a *patria*, *Latin Texts of the Welsh Laws*, ed. Emanuel, 330. 27, *pennkerd y wlat*, *Llyfr Blegywryd*, ed. Williams and Powell, 25. 13.

[109] *Welsh Medieval Law*, ed. Wade-Evans, 33. 20–1.

[110] Ibid. 33.14; *Latin Texts of the Welsh Laws*, ed. Emanuel, 110. 36–7; *Llyfr Iorwerth*, ed. Wiliam, 40/2.

[111] *DB* 162a, 'Berdic joculator regis h*abe*t .iii. uillas. 7 ibi .v. car*ucae*. nil reddit.'

[112] *LL* 270, 273, 274.

[113] *Uraicecht na Ríar*, ed. and trans. L. Breatnach (Dublin,1987), 102–8, §§ 3, 4, 7, 8, 12. The rank of a poet was based on three qualifications: *frithgnam, airchetal, cland*, 'study, poetic gift, family'.

[114] *AL* IV. ii. 26, 28.

[115] *BT* 54. 16 = BT fo. 25v16 (the later title is omitted from Gwenogvryn Evans's transcript but can be seen in his facsimile); Haycock, *Legendary Poems*, no. 18; also discussed and translated by Carey, *Ireland and the Grail*, 80–7; Sims-Williams, *Irish Influence on Medieval Welsh Literature*, 66–78.

[116] *PKM* 8. 25.

[117] *PKM* 44. 26.

[118] *BT* 33. 23–5; *Legendary Poems*, ed. Haycock, no. 8, ll. 29–31.

that the 'cauldron of the head of Annwfn', *peir pen Annwfyn*, of *Preideu Annwfyn* is likely to have something to do with the 'cauldron of rebirth', *peir dadeni*, of *Branwen* and perhaps also something to do with Pwyll who was *Pwyll Penn Annwuyn*.[119] Again, because Taliesin was one of the seven who came back from Ireland, and because the poem appears in the Book of Taliesin, there is a strong likelihood that the omnipresent 'I' of the poem was Taliesin himself.

The poem begins and ends with brief praise of God, but that seems to be essentially formulaic, a pious frame for a poem that is not in the slightest degree pious. Eight sections are defined by rhyme and by repeated opening phrases. The first lines will give a taste of the whole:[120]

I. *Golychaf wledic pendeuic gwlat ri* 'I praise the Lord, the Ruler of the kingly realm'

II. *Neut wyf glot geinmyn: cerd ochlywit*, 'I am splendid of fame—song was heard'

III. *Neut wyf glot geinmyn: kyrd glywanor*, 'I am splendid of fame: songs are heard'

IV. *Ny obrynaf-i lawyr llen Llywyadur*, 'I do not rate the pathetic men involved with religious writings'

V. *Ny obrynaf y lawyr llaes eu kylchwy*, 'I do not deserve to be stuck with pathetic men with their trailing shields/garments'[121]

VI. *Ny obrynafi lawyr llaes eu gohen*, 'I do not deserve to be stuck with pathetic men, with no go in them'

VII. *Myneich dychnut val cunin cor*, 'Monks congregate like a pack of dogs'

VIII. *Myneych dychnut val bleidawr*, 'Monks congregate like wolves'

A prevailing characteristic of the poem is its obliqueness of reference: narrative is invoked but no narrative is given; it is as if fragments of a story are paraded before the hearer. This is coupled with praise of the poet: 'I am splendid of fame: the song was heard in the four quarters of the fort' (11–12). By the time we get to sections V and VI, the tone has shifted: from display of knowledge of a narrative beyond our reach to denunciation of those who do not know the answers to various questions. Finally, in VII and VIII, we are introduced to those who most emphatically do not know the answers: monks.

The poet has been presented as a *bardd*, but also as one who knows far more natural philosophy and biblical chronology than any monk. That is, he knows his own craft but he is also a master of written texts; he is happy to use a phrase that is a mixture of Latin and Welsh, *traeth Mundi* 'the extent of the world'; he knows the answer to questions about Creation or the time of Christ's birth that the pathetic

119 *PKM* 8. 24–6: *y diffygwys y enw ef ar Pwyll, Pendeuic Dyuet, ac y gelwit Pwyll Penn Annwuyn o hynny allan.*

120 The translations are from Haycock, *Legendary Poems*, no. 18.

121 For the meanings of *kylchwy* see the note to line 35 in Haycock, *Legendary Poems*, 446. 'Garment' fits the context better.

monks do not know. The notion that a proper *bardd* should have a purely oral culture would horrify him.

Preideu Annwfyn implies close links between monastery and the professional poet even while insisting on the gulf between monkish incompetence and the superiority of the poet. The 'pathetic men', however, are not to be assumed to be solely monks: the grand professional poet was as likely, or even more likely, to cast scorn on less well-trained and less well-educated poets, just as, even in the fourteenth century, the Grammar of Einion Offeiriad draws a sharp distinction between the *prydydd* and the *clerwr*. A similar situation existed in Ireland: the *fili* insisted on the length of his education and it is likely that some part of that education might be spent in ecclesiastical schools.[122] The Irish *fili* was as prone as the trained Welsh *bardd* to assert his status by using difficult language and by strewing a composition with references to an esoteric learning beyond the grasp of his hearer. The same highly competitive learning, and the same propensity to demonstrate it by asking questions that, so it is hoped, the person interrogated will not be able to answer, is attested in the late tenth century in a verse altercation from Winchester. The dialogue is between a master and a pupil, and the master's name is Iorwerth:[123] according to the pupil, Iorwerth can count himself lucky to have come to England, but the master's learning lacks substance and can readily be exposed for the hollow thing that it is. The pupil uses rapid-fire questions as his main method of attack—and 'barrages of questions' have been noted as a characteristic of the legendary Taliesin.[124]

The legendary Taliesin was the creation of a poetic organization that was highly competitive, both within itself and with other men of learning. This Taliesin claimed to be the possessor of a wisdom and a learning that literally took more than one lifetime to acquire. He asserted his status, however, by oblique references to a knowledge that never had to be expounded. In the extremity of his claims he bears a distant but unmistakable resemblance to Llywarch, the old man boasting of the heroism of his youth and so rendering himself vulnerable to the crushing retort made by his son, Gwên.

The habit of Welsh and Irish poets to claim an expertise in the learning of the Latin scholar and yet to insist on the distinction between themselves and monks or churchmen has implications for the history of the culture that both Irish and Welsh poets shared. Though they might display the breadth of their learning by using the odd Latin word or phrase, the expertise of the professional poets was tied to the vernacular. The more we stress the role of the vernacular and of oral performance, the more likely we are to give a greater weight to a shared Celtic inheritance in creating two similar literary cultures on either side of the Irish Sea. The more we stress the links with ecclesiastical learning, on the other hand, the more natural it becomes to ascribe similarities to a cultural interchange across the sea throughout the period between the fifth and the eleventh century.

122 *Uraicecht na Ríar*, ed. L. Breatnach, 87.

123 Lapidge, 'Three Latin Poems from Æthelwold's School', 98–9 (for the literary type), and 108–25 for the text.

124 Haycock, *Legendary Poems*, 11.

Select Bibliography

I. General and Introduction
This includes works on the geography of the British territories and those relevant to more than one section of the book.
II. The late-Roman and post-Roman periods, 350–550
III. Early Welsh society
IV. The Britons and their neighbours, 550–1064
V. The Church and its culture, poets, and storytellers

I. GENERAL AND INTRODUCTION

A. General Guides to Bibliography, Prosopography and Genealogy, Chronology, Place-names and Topography, and Archaeology

1. Bibliography

Bibliography of the History of Wales, 2nd edn. (Cardiff, 1962). Supplements in *BBCS* 20, 22–3, 25; also regular lists of 'Articles relating to the History of Wales', in the *Welsh History Review*.

Emanuel, H. D., 'Studies in the Welsh Laws', *Celtic Studies in Wales*, ed. E. Davies (Cardiff, 1963), 73–100.

Hughes, M. B., and Williams, J. E. C., *Llyfryddiaeth yr Iaith Gymraeg* (Cardiff, 1988).

Lapidge, M., and Sharpe, R., *A Bibliography of Celtic-Latin Literature 400–1200* (Dublin, 1985).

Parry, T., and Morgan, M., *Llyfryddiaeth Llenyddiaeth Gymraeg* (Cardiff, 1976), with G. O. Watt, 'Atodiad I', *BBCS* 30 (1983), 55–121.

Sawyer, P. H., *Anglo-Saxon Charters: An Annotated List and Bibliography* (London, 1968); an updated version is online at: http://www.trin.cam.ac.uk/kemble/

Sharpe, R., *A Handlist of the Latin Writers of Great Britain and Ireland before 1540*, Publications of the Journal of Medieval Latin, 1 (Turnhout, 1997).

2. Prosopography and Genealogy

Bartrum, P. C., *Welsh Genealogies, A.D. 300–1400* (8 vols., Cardiff, 1974).

——*A Welsh Classical Dictionary: People in History and Legend up to about A.D. 1000* (Aberystwyth, 1993).

3. Chronology

Fryde, E. B. et al. (eds.), *Handbook of British Chronology*, 3rd edn. (London, 1986), 49–54.

4. Place-Names and Topography

Armstrong, A. M., Mawer, A., Stenton, F. M., and Dickins, B., *The Place-Names of Cumberland*, 3 vols, English Place-Name Society, 20–2 (Cambridge, 1950–2).

Charles, B. G., *Non-Celtic Place-Names in Wales* (London, 1938).

—— *The Place-Names of Pembrokeshire* (Aberystwyth, 1992).

Coates, R., and Breeze, A., *Celtic Voices, English Places* (Stamford, 2000).

Coplestone-Crow, B., *Herefordshire Place-Names*, BAR, Brit. Ser., 214 (Oxford, 1989; 2nd edn. Almeley, 2009).

Cox, B., 'The Place-Names of the Earliest English Records', *Journal of the English Place-Name Society*, 8 (1975–6), 12–66.

Davies, Ellis, *Flintshire Place-Names* (Cardiff, 1959).
Davies, Elwyn, (ed.), *Rhestr o Enwau Lleoedd/A Gazetteer of Welsh Place-Names* (Cardiff, 1957).
Ekwall, E., *Scandinavians and Celts in the North-West of England* (Lund, 1918).
Gelling, M., *Signposts to the Past: Place-Names and the History of England*, 2nd edn. (Chichester, 1988).
——and Cole, A., *The Landscape of Place-Names* (Stamford, 2000).
Jones, G. T., and Roberts, T., *Enwau Lleoedd Môn / The Place-Names of Anglesey* (Bangor, 1996).
Jones, N. A., 'An Index to the Discussion on Place-Names by Henry Owen and Egerton Phillimore in *The Description of Pembrokeshire by George Owen of Henllys*', *Nomina*, 15 (1991–2), 107–24; a Welsh version is in *Studia Celtica*, 26/27 (1991–2), 214–25.
Le Moing, J.-Y., *Les noms de lieux breton de Haut-Bretagne* (Spezed, 1990).
Lewis, H., 'Buellt', *BBCS* 8 (1935–7), 229.
Lhuyd, E., *Parochialia*, ed. R. H. Morris (London, 1909–11).
Lloyd, J. E., 'Welsh Place-Names: A Study of Common Name-Elements, with Additional Notes by Egerton Phillimore', *Y Cymmrodor*, 11 (1892), 15–60.
Lloyd-Jones, J., *Enwau Lleoedd Sir Gaernarfon* (Cardiff, 1928).
McDodgson, J. McN., *The Place-Names of Cheshire*, English Place-Name Society, 44–8, 54, 75 (5 vols. in 7, Nottingham and Cambridge, 1970–97).
Morgan, R., *Welsh Place-Names in Shropshire* (Cardiff, 1997).
——*A Study of Radnorshire Place-Names* (Llanrwst, 1998).
——*A Study of Montgomeryshire Place-Names* (Llanrwst, 2001).
——and Powell, R. F. P., *A Study of Breconshire Place-Names* (Llanrwst, 1999).
Nicolaisen, W. F. H., 'Scottish Place-Names: 24. *Slew-* and *Sliabh*', *Scottish Studies*, 9 (1965), 91–106.
——'Gaelic Place-Names in Southern Scotland', *Studia Celtica*, 5 (1970), 15–35.
——*Scottish Place-Names* (London, 1976).
——and MacQueen, J., '*Kirk-* and *Kil-* in Galloway Place-Names', *Archivium Linguisticum*, 8 (1956), 139–49.
[Ordnance Survey], *Map of Britain in the Dark Ages*, 2nd edn. (London, 1966); includes a useful gazetteer.
Ordnance Survey, *Roman Britain*, 5th edn. (Southampton, 2001).
Owen, H. W., *The Place-Names of East Flintshire* (Cardiff, 1994).
——and Morgan, R., *Dictionary of the Place-Names of Wales* (Llandysul, 2007).
Padel, O. J., 'Cornwall as a Border Area', *Nomina*, 6 (1982), 18–22.
——*Cornish Place-Name Elements*, English Place-Name Society, 56/57 (Nottingham, 1985).
——*A Popular Dictionary of Cornish Place-Names* (Penzance, 1988).
Picken, W. M. M., 'The Names of the Hundreds of Cornwall', *Devon and Cornwall Notes and Queries*, 30 (1965–7), 36–40, reprinted in his *A Medieval Cornish Miscellany*, ed. O. J. Padel (Chichester, 2000), 76–80.
Pierce, G. O., *The Place-Names of Dinas Powys Hundred* (Cardiff, 1968).
Rees, W., *An Historical Atlas of Wales* (Cardiff, 1951).
Richards, M., '*Hafod* and *Hafoty* in Welsh Place-Names: A Semantic Study', *Montgomeryshire Collections*, 56:1 (1959), 13–20.
——'Gwrinydd, Gorfynydd and Llyswyrny', *BBCS* 18 (1960), 383–6.
——'*Meifod, Lluest, Cynaeafdy* and *Hendre* in Welsh Place-Names', *Montgomeryshire Collections*, 56: 2 (1960), 177–87.
——'Sgeibion, Llanynys', *Denbighshire Historical Society Transactions*, 9 (1960), 187–8.

Richards, M., 'Norse Place-Names in Wales', in *Proceedings of the First International Congress of Celtic Studies* (Dublin, 1962), 51–60.

——'The Significance of *Is* and *Uwch* in Welsh Commote and Cantref Names', *Welsh History Review*, 2 (1964–5), 9–18.

——'Early Welsh Territorial Suffixes', *Journal of the Royal Society of Antiquaries of Ireland*, 95 (1965), 205–12.

——'Gwŷr, Gwragedd a Gwehelyth', *THSC*, 1965, 27–45.

——'The Population of the Welsh Border', *THSC*, 1970, 77–100.

——*Welsh Administrative and Territorial Units: Medieval and Modern* (Cardiff, 1969).

——*Enwau Tir a Gwlad*, ed. B. L. Jones (Caernarfon, 1998).

Rivet, A. L. F., and Smith, C., *The Place-Names of Roman Britain* (London, 1979).

Smith, A. H., *The Place-Names of the West Riding of Yorkshire*, 8 vols., English Place-Name Society, 30–7 (Cambridge, 1961–3).

——*The Place-Names of Westmorland*, English Place-Name Society, 42–3 (Cambridge, 1967).

Tanguy, B., *Dictionnaire des noms de communes, trèves et paroisses du Finistère: origine et signification* (Douarnenez, 1990).

——*Dictionnaire des noms de communes, trèves et paroisses des Côtes d'Armor* (Douarnenez, 1992).

Thomas, C., 'Settlement-History in Early Cornwall, I. The Antiquity of the Hundreds', *Cornish Archaeology*, 3 (1964), 70–9.

Thomas, R. J., *Enwau Afonydd a Nentydd Cymru* (Cardiff, 1938).

Wade-Evans, A. W., 'Parochiale Wallicanum', *Y Cymmrodor*, 22 (1910), 22–124.

Watson, W. J., *The History of the Celtic Place-Names of Scotland* (Edinburgh, 1926).

Williams, I., *Enwau Lleoedd* (Liverpool, [1945]).

Williams, S. J., 'Some Breconshire Place-Names', *Brycheiniog*, 11 (1965), 155–67.

Wmffre, I., *The Place-Names of Cardiganshire*, 3 vols., BAR 379 (Oxford, 2004).

5. Archaeology: collections of inscriptions, general surveys, and excavation reports

(i) *Stone monuments*

(a) *Celtic inscriptions:*

Celtic Inscribed Stones Project: www.ucl.ac.uk/archaeology/cisp

Corpus Inscriptionum Insularum Celticarum, ed. R. A. Macalister, 2 vols., Irish Manu scripts Commission (Dublin, 1945–9). Reviews by Ifor Williams, *THSC, 1943–4*, 152–6, and by K. H. Jackson, *Speculum*, 21 (1946), 521–3 (vol. 1), *Speculum*, 24 (1949), 598–601 (vol. 2).

(b) *British inscriptions:*

Tedeschi, C., *Congeries Lapidum: Iscrizioni Britanniche dei Secoli V–VII*, 2 vols. (Pisa, 2005).

(c) *Wales (the main collections of inscriptions and other monuments)*

Edwards, N., *A Corpus of Early Medieval Inscribed Stones and Stone Sculpture*, ii, *South-West Wales* (Cardiff, 2007).

——*A Corpus of Early Medieval Inscribed Stones and Stone Sculpture*, iii, *North Wales* (Cardiff, forthcoming).

Nash-Williams, V. E., *The Early Christian Monuments of Wales* (Cardiff, 1950).

Redknap, M., and Lewis, J. M., *A Corpus of Early Medieval Inscribed Stones and Stone Sculpture*, i, *South-East Wales and the English Border* (Cardiff, 2007).

The Royal Commission on Ancient and Historical Monuments in Wales, *Anglesey* (Cardiff, 1937).

——*An Inventory of the Ancient Monuments in Glamorgan*, i. 3, *The Early Christian Period* (Cardiff, 1976).

Thomas, W. Gwyn, 'The Early Christian Monuments', in J. L. Davies and D. P. Kirby (eds.), *Cardiganshire County History*, gen. ed. I. G. Jones, i, *From the Earliest Times to the Coming of the Normans* (Cardiff, 1994), 407–20.

(d) *Brittany and South-West Britain (inscriptions)*

Davies, W., et al., *The Inscriptions of Early Medieval Brittany* (Oakville, CT, and Aberystwyth, 2000)

Okasha, E., *Corpus of Early Christian Inscribed Stones of South-West Britain* (London, 1993).

(e) *Isle of Man (inscriptions and other monuments)*

Kermode, P. M. C., *Manx Crosses* (London, 1907; repr. Belgavies, 1994).

(f) *Northern Britain (inscriptions and other monuments)*

Allen, J. Romilly, and Anderson, J., *The Early Christian Monuments of Scotland* (Edinburgh, 1903; repr. in 2 vols., Belgavies, Angus, 1993).

Thomas, C., 'The Early Christian Inscriptions of Southern Scotland', *Glasgow Archaeological Journal*, 17 (1991–2), 1–10.

(g) *Inscriptions of Gaul*

Le Blant, E., *Inscriptions chrétiennes de la Gaule antérieures aux VIIIe siècles*, 2 vols. (Paris, 1856–65).

(ii) *General works on early-medieval Welsh archaeology*

Arnold, C. J., and Davies, J. L., *Roman and Early Medieval Wales* (Stroud, 2000).

Edwards, N. (ed.), *Landscape and Settlement in Medieval Wales* (Oxford, 1997).

——and Lane, A. (eds.), *Early Medieval Settlements in Wales, AD 400–1100* (Bangor and Cardiff, 1988) [gazetteer of sites].

—— ——(eds.), *The Early Church in Wales and the West* (Oxford, 1992).

Musson, C. R., *Wales from the Air: Patterns of Past and Present* (Aberystwyth, 1994).

(iii) *Excavation reports*

Alcock, L., *Dinas Powys: An Iron Age, Dark Age and Early Medieval Settlement in Glamorgan* (Cardiff, 1963).

——*'By South Cadbury is that Camelot': Excavations of Cadbury Castle, 1966–70* (London, 1972).

——and Alcock, E. A., 'Reconnaissance Excavations on Early Historic Fortifications and Other Royal Sites: 4, Excavations at Alt Clut, Clyde Rock, Strathclyde, 1974–75', *Proceedings of the Society of Antiquaries of Scotland*, 120 (1990), 95–149.

Brassil, K. S., Owen, W. G., and Britnell, W. J., 'Prehistoric and Early Medieval Cemeteries at Tandderwen, near Denbigh, Clwyd', *Archaeological Journal*, 148 (1991), 46–97.

Britnell, W. J., 'Capel Maelog, Llandrindod Wells, Powys: Excavations 1984–7', *Medieval Archaeology*, 34 (1990), 27–96.

Campbell, E., and Lane, A., 'Excavations at Longbury Bank, Dyfed, and Early Medieval Settlement in South Wales', *Medieval Archaeology*, 37 (1993), 15–77

——and Macdonald, P., 'Excavations at Caerwent Vicarage Orchard Garden, 1973: An Extramural Post-Roman Cemetery', *Archaeologia Cambrensis*, 142 (1993), 74–98.

Cane, J., 'Excavations on Wat's Dyke at Pentre Wern, Shropshire in 1984/5', *Trans. of the Shropshire Archaeological and Historical Society*, 71 (1996), 10–21.

Casey, P. J., and Davies, J. L., with Evans, J., *Excavations at Segontium (Caernarfon) Roman Fort, 1975–1979*, CBA Research Report, 90 (London, 1993).

Frere, S. S., *Verulamium Excavations*, 3 vols. (London, 1972, 1983, 1984).

Hill, P., *Whithorn and St Ninian: The Excavation of a Monastic Town, 1984–91* (Stroud, 1997).

Hogg, A. H. A., 'The Llantwit Major Villa: A Reconsideration of the Evidence', *Britannia*, 5 (1974), 225–50.

Holbrook, N., and Thomas, A., ''An Early Medieval Monastic Cemetery at Llandough, Glamorgan: Excavations in 1994', *Medieval Archaeology*, 49 (2005), 1–92.

Hope-Taylor, B., *Yeavering: An Anglo-British Centre of Early Northumbria* (London, 1977).

Houlder, C., 'The Henge Monuments at Llandegai', *Antiquity*, 42 (1968), 216–21.

James, H., 'Excavations at Caer, Bayvil, 1987', *Archaeologia Cambrensis*, 136 (1987), 51–76.

Longley, D., The Excavation of Castell, Porth Trefadog, a Coastal Promontory Fort in North Wales', *Medieval Archaeology*, 35 (1991), 64–85.

Murphy, K., 'Excavations at Llanychlwydog Church, Dyfed', *Archaeologia Cambrensis*, 136 (1987), 77–93.

——'Plas Gogerddan, Dyfed: A Multi-Period Burial and Ritual Site', *Archaeological Journal*, 149 (1992), 1–38.

National Monuments Record of Wales: Royal Commission on the Ancient and Historical Monuments of Wales, Plas Crug, Aberystwyth, Ceredigion, SY23 1NJ
websites: http://www.rcahmw.org.uk
http://www.coflein.gov.uk (for the National Monuments Record itself)

Quinnel, H., Blockley, M. R., and Berridge, P., *Excavations at Rhuddlan, Clwyd, 1969–73, Mesolithic to Medieval*, CBA Research Report 95 (London, 1994).

Rahtz, P., 'Cannington Hillfort, 1963', *Somerset Archaeology and Natural History*, 113 (1969), 56–68.

——et al., *Cannington Cemetery: Excavations 1962–3 of Prehistoric, Roman, Post-Roman, and Later Features at Cannington Park Quarry, near Bridgwater, Somerset*, Britannia Monographs 17 (London, 2000).

Robinson, D. M. (ed.), *Biglis, Caldicot and Llandough: Three Late Iron Age and Romano-British Sites in South-East Wales. Excavations 1977–79*, BAR British Series, 188 (Oxford, 1988).

Savory, H. N., 'Excavations at Dinas Emrys, Beddgelert (Caerns.), 1954–56', *Archaeologia Cambrensis*, 109 (1960), 13–77.

——*Excavations at Dinorben* (Cardiff, 1971).

Schlesinger, A., and Walls, C., 'An Early Church and Medieval Farmstead Site: Excavations at Llanelen, Gower', *Archaeological Journal*, 153 (1996), 104–47.

Wainwright, G. J., *Coygan Camp* (Cardiff, 1967).

White, R. B., 'Excavations at Arfryn, Bodedern', *Transactions of the Anglesey Antiquarian Society and Field Club* (1969–70), 257–8.

——'Excavations at Arfryn, Bodedern, Long-Cist Cemeteries and the Origins of Christianity in Britain', *Transactions of the Anglesey Antiquarian Society and Field Club* (1971–72), 19–51.

White, S. I., and Smith, G., 'A Funerary and Ceremonial Centre at Capel Eithin, Gaerwen, Anglesey: Excavations of Neolithic, Bronze Age, Roman and Early Medieval Features in 1980 and 1981', *Transactions of the Anglesey Antiquarian Society and Field Club* (1999).

Wilkinson, P. F., 'Excavations at Hen Gastell, Briton Ferry, West Glamorgan', *Medieval Archaeology*, 39 (1995), 1–50.

B. Primary written sources (those beginning before 550 and encompassing later periods)

Anderson, A. O., *Early Sources of Scottish History, A.D. 500 to 1286*, 2 vols. (Edinburgh, 1922; repr. Stamford, 1990).

The Annals of Ulster (to A.D. 1131), ed. S. Mac Airt and G. Mac Niocaill, Part I, Text and Translation (Dublin, 1983).

Bede, *Historia Ecclesiastica*, ed. C. Plummer in *Venerabilis Baedae Opera Historica*, 2 vols. (Oxford, 1896); also ed. and trans. B. Colgrave and R. Mynors, *Bede's Ecclesiastical History of the English People* (Oxford Medieval Texts, 1969).

C. Secondary Sources (including collected papers referring to more than one period)

Bowen, E. G., *Britain and the Western Seaways* (London, 1972).
Chédeville, A., and Guillotel, H., *La Bretagne des saints et des rois, Ve–Xe siècle* (Paris, 1973).
Cunliffe, B., *Facing the Ocean: The Atlantic and its Peoples. 8000 BC–AD 1500* (Oxford, 2001).
Davies, J. L., and Kirby, D. P. (eds.), *Cardiganshire County History*, gen. ed. I. G. Jones, i, *From the Earliest Times to the Coming of the Normans* (Cardiff, 1994).
Davies, W., *Wales in the Early Middle Ages* (Leicester, 1982).
——*Patterns of Power in Early Wales* (Oxford, 1990).
——*Welsh History in the Early Middle Ages: Texts and Societies*, Variorum Collected Studies (Farnham, 2009).
——*Brittany in the Early Middle Ages: Texts and Societies*, Variorum Collected Studies (Farnham, 2009).
Dumville, D. N., *Histories and Pseudo-Histories of the Insular Middle Ages*, Variorum Collected Studies (Aldershot, 1990).
——*Britons and Anglo-Saxons in the Early Middle Ages*, Variorum Collected Studies (Aldershot, 1993).
——*Celtic Essays, 2001–2007*, 2 vols. (Aberdeen, 2007).
Durtelle de Saint Sauveur, E., *Histoire de Bretagne* 2 vols (Rennes, 1935).
Edwards, N., 'Anglesey in the Early Middle Ages: The Archaeological Evidence', Trans. *Anglesey Antiquarian Society and Field Club* (1986), 19–41.
Fahy, D., 'When did Britons become Bretons?', *WHR* 2 (1964–5), 111–24.
Fraser, J. E., *From Caledonia to Pictland: Scotland to 795* (Edinburgh, 2009).
——'Bede, the Firth of Forth, and the Location of *Urbs Iudeu*', *Scottish Historical Review*, 87 (2008), 1–25.
Frere, S. S., 'Civitas—A Myth?', *Antiquity*, 35 (1961), 29–36.
Griffiths, R. A. (gen. ed.), *The Gwent County History*, i, *Gwent in Prehistory and Early History* (Cardiff, 2004).
Gruffydd, R. G., 'In Search of Elmet', *Studia Celtica*, 28 (1994), 63–79.
Higham, N. J., 'Continuity Studies in the First Millennium A.D. in North Cumbria', *Northern History*, 14 (1978), 1–18.
——*The Northern Counties to A.D. 1000* (London, 1986).
——*The Kingdom of Northumbria, A.D. 350–1100* (Stroud, 1993).
——'Britons in Northern England in the Early Middle Ages: Through a Glass Darkly', *Northern History*, 38 (2001), 5–25.
——(ed.), *The Britons in Anglo-Saxon England* (Woodbridge, 2007).
——and Jones, B., *The Carvetii* (Gloucester, 1985).
Hind, J. G. F., '*Elmet* and *Deira*—Forest Names in Yorkshire?', *BBCS* 28 (1979–80), 541–52.
Hogg, A. H. A., 'Llwyfenydd', *Antiquity*, 20 (1946), 210–11.
Jackson, K. H., *Language and History in Early Britain* (Edinburgh, 1953).
——'The Britons of Southern Scotland', *Antiquity*, 29 (1955), 77–88.
Jankulak, K., and Wooding, J. (eds.), *Ireland and Wales in the Middle Ages* (Dublin, 2007).
Jarrett, M. G., and Mann, J. C., 'The Tribes of Wales', *WHR* 4 (1968–9), 161–71.

Jenkins, P., 'Regions and Cantrefs in Early Medieval Glamorgan', *CMCS* 15 (Summer 1988), 31–50.

Kirby, D. P., 'Strathclyde and Cumbria: A Survey of Historical Development to A.D. 1092', *Transactions of the Cumberland and Westmorland Antiquarian and Archaeological Society*, NS 62 (1962), 77–94.

Lloyd, J. E., *A History of Wales*, 3rd edn. (London, 1939).

Lloyd-Jones, J., 'Nefenhyr', *BBCS* 14 (1950–2), 35–7.

McCarthy, M., *Roman Carlisle and the Lands of the Solway* (Stroud, 2002).

——'Rheged: An Early Kingdom near the Solway', *PSAS* 132 (2002), 357–81.

Phythian-Adams, C., *Land of the Cumbrians: A Study in British Provincial Origins, AD 400–1200* (Aldershot, 1996).

Pryce, H., 'British or Welsh? National Identity in Twelfth-Century Wales', *EHR* 116 (2001), 775–801.

Quaghebeur, J., and Merdrignac, B. (eds.), *Bretons et Normands au Moyen Âge* (Rennes, 2008).

Rhys, J., *Celtic Britain* (London, 1882).

Richmond, I. A., 'Queen Cartimandua', *Journal of Roman Studies*, 44 (1954), 43–52.

Rollason, D. W., *Northumbria 500–1100: Creation and Destruction of a Kingdom* (Cambridge, 2003).

Sargent, A., 'The North-South Divide Revisited: Thoughts on the Character of Roman Britain', *Britannia*, 33 (2002), 219–26.

Savory, H. N. (ed.), *Glamorgan County History*, gen. ed. G. Williams, ii, *Early Glamorgan* (Cardiff, 1984).

Smith, J. B., and Smith, Ll. B. (eds.), *History of Merioneth*, ii, *The Middle Ages* (Cardiff, 2001).

Wilson, P. A., 'On the Use of the Terms "Strathclyde" and "Cumbria"', *Transactions of the Cumberland and Westmorland Antiquarian and Archaeological Society*, NS 66 (1966), 57–92.

Woolf, A., *Where was Govan in the Early Middle Ages?* (Govan, 2007).

II. THE POST-ROMAN PERIOD

A. Primary Sources

Ammianus Marcellinus, *Res Gestae*, ed. W. Seyfarth, 2 vols. (Leipzig, 1978); ed. and trans. J. C. Rolfe, 3 vols. Loeb, rev. edn. (Cambridge, Mass., 1935–39).

Concilia Galliae A. 314–A. 506, ed. C. Munier, CCSL 148 (Turnhout, 1963).

——*511–A. 695*, ed. C. de Clercq, CCSL 148A (Turnhout, 1963); also ed. and trans. J. Gaudemet and B. Basdevant, *Les Canons des conciles mérovingiens (VIe–VIIe siècles)*, 2 vols. (Paris, 1989).

Constantius, *Vita S. Germani*, ed. W. Levison, MGH SRM 7, pp. 285–83; ed. R. Borius, *Constance de Lyon: Vie de S. Germain*, Sources chrétiennes, no. 112 (Paris, 1965).

Eusebius Gallicanus, *Collectio Homiliarum*, ed. F. Glorié, CCSL 101, 101A, and 101B (Turnhout, 1970–71).

Faustus of Riez: *Fausti Reiensis praeter Sermones Pseudo-Eusebianos Opera*, ed. A. Engelbrecht, CSEL 21 (Vienna, 1891).

Gallic Chronicle of 452, ed. Th. Mommsen, *Chronica Minora*, i, MGH, AA 9 (Berlin, 1892), 617–62; 'The Gallic Chronicle of 452', ed. R. W. Burgess, in R. W. Mathisen and

D. Shanzer (eds.), *Society and Culture in Late Antiquity: Revisiting the Sources* (Aldershot, 2001), 39–84.

Gildas, *De Excidio Britanniae*, ed. Th. Mommsen, *Chronica Minora Saec. IV. V. VI. VII*, iii, MGH AA 13 (Berlin, 1898), 1–85; ed. and trans. H. Williams, *Gildae De Excidio Britanniae, Fragmenta, Liber De Paenitentia, Lorica Gildae*, Cymmrodorion Record Series, 3 (London, 1899); ed. and trans. M. Winterbottom, *Gildas: The Ruin of Britain and Other Works* (London and Chichester, 1978).

Gregory of Tours, *Libri Historiarum Decem*, ed. B. Krusch and W. Levison, MGH SRM i. 1 (Hanover, 1951); ed. and trans. R. Buchner, *Gregor von Tours: Fränkische Geschichte*, 2 vols. (Darmstadt, 1955–56); trans. L. Thorpe, *Gregory of Tours: History of the Franks* (London, 1974).

——*Miracula*, ed. B. Krusch, MGH SRM i. 2.

Marius of Avenches, *Chronica*, ed. Th. Mommsen, *Chronica Minora*, ii, MGH AA xi (1894), 225–39.

Notitia Galliarum, ed. Mommsen, *Chronica Minora*, i, MGH AA ix. 584–612.

Patrick, *Libri Epistolarum* (incl. the *Confessio* and the *Epistola ad Milites Corotici*), ed. L. Bieler, *Libri Epistolarum Sancti Patricii Episcopi*, 2 vols., Irish Manuscripts Commission (Dublin, 1952; repr. Dublin, 1993).

Ed. and trans. R. P. C. Hanson with C. Blanc, *Saint Patrick: Confession et lettre à Coroticus*, Sources chrétiennes, 249 (Paris, 1978).

Ed. and trans. D. R. Howlett, *The Book of Letters of Saint Patrick the Bishop* (Blackrock, Co. Dublin, 1994).

English translations by L. Bieler, *The Works of St Patrick*, Ancient Christian Writers, 17 (London, 1963) and by R. P. C. Hanson, *The Life and Writings of the Historical Saint Patrick* (New York, 1983).

Procopius, *The Wars*, ed. and trans. H. B. Dewing, Loeb, 5 vols. (Cambridge, Mass., 1914–28).

Prosper, *Chronicon*, ed. Th. Mommsen, *Chronica Minora*, i, MGH, AA 9 (Berlin, 1892), 341–485.

——*De Gratia Dei et Libero Arbitrio contra Collatorem, PL* li, 213–76.

——*De Vocatione Omnium Gentium, PL* li. 647–722; trans. P. de Letter, *St Prosper of Aquitaine: The Call of All Nations* (London, 1952).

Venantius Fortunatus, *Opera Poetica*, ed. F. Leo, MGH AA iv.1 (Berlin, 1881); ed. and trans. C. Nisard, *Venance Fortunat: poésies mêlées* (Paris, 1887); partially translated by J. W. George, *Venantius Fortunatus: Personal and Political Poems*, Liverpool Translated Texts (Liverpool, 1995).

Vita Eligii, ed. B. Krusch, SRM iv. 634–761.

Vita Prima S. Samsonis, ed. and trans. P. Flobert, *La Vie ancienne de Saint Samson de Dol* (Paris, 1997); trans. T. Taylor, *The Life of St Samson of Dol* (London, 1925; reprinted Felinfach, 1991).

Zosimus, *Historia Nova*, ed. and trans. F. Paschoud, *Zosime: Histoire nouvelle* (Paris, 1971–89; new edn. Paris, 2000–), English trans. R. T. Ridley, *Zosimus: New History* (Sydney, 1982).

B. Discussions of Primary Sources

Burgess, R. W., 'The Dark Ages return to Fifth-Century Britain: The "Restored" Gallic Chronicle exploded', *Britannia*, 21 (1990), 185–95.

Deanesly, M., and Grosjean, P., 'The Canterbury Edition of the Answers of Pope Gregory', *JEH* 10 (1959), 1–49.

Duine, F., *Origines bretonnes. Études des sources: II. La Vie de saint Samson. Sources, époque et langue de la Vita* (Paris, 1914; repr. from *Annales de Bretagne*, 30 (1914–15), 123–64).

Goffart, W., *The Narrators of Barbarian History (A.D. 550–800): Jordanes, Gregory of Tours, Bede, and Paul the Deacon* (Princeton, 1988).

Jones, M. E., and Casey, P. J., 'The Gallic Chronicle Restored: A Chronology for the Anglo-Saxon Invasions and the End of Roman Britain', *Britannia*, 19 (1988), 367–98.

——'The Gallic Chronicle Exploded?', *Britannia*, 22 (1991), 212–15.

Kerlouégan, F., 'Les Vies de saints bretons les plus anciennes dans leurs rapports avec les Îles Britanniques', in M. Herren (ed.), *Insular Latin Studies, 550–1066* (Toronto, 1981), 195–213.

Knight, J. K., 'Sources for the Early History of Glamorgan', in H. N. Savory (ed.), *Glamorgan County History*, gen. ed. G. Williams, ii, *Early Glamorgan* (Cardiff, 1984), 365–409.

Loth, J., 'La Vie la plus ancienne de Saint Samson', *Revue Celtique*, 40 (1923), 1–50.

Muhlberger, S., 'The Gallic Chronicle of 452 and its Authority for British Events', *Britannia*, 14 (1983), 22–33.

Poulin, J.-C., 'Hagiographie et politique: La première Vie de saint Samson de Dol', *Francia*, 5 (1977), 1–26.

——'Recherches et identifications des sources de la littérature hagiographique du Haut Moyen Âge: L'exemple breton', *Revue d'histoire de l'Église de France*, 71 (1985), 119–29.

——'Le Dossier de saint Samson de Dol', *Francia*, 15 (1987), 715–73.

——*L'Hagiographie bretonne du haut moyen âge. Repertoire raisonné*, Beihefte *Francia*, 69 (Osttildern, 2009).

Sowerby, R., 'The Lives of St Samson', *Francia*, 38 (2011), 1–31.

Wood, I. N., 'Continuity or Calamity? The Constraints of Literary Models', in J. F. Drinkwater and H. Elton (eds.), *Fifth-Century Gaul: A Crisis of Identity* (Cambridge, 1992), 9–18.

C. Secondary Sources

1 (a). *Britain, 350–550*

Alcock, E. A., 'Enclosed Places: AD 500–800', in S. T. Driscoll and M. R. Nieke (eds.), *Power and Politics in Early Medieval Britain and Ireland* (Edinburgh, 1988), 40–6.

Alcock, L., *Arthur's Britain* (London, 1971).

——'A Multi-Disciplinary Chronology for Alt Clut, Castle Rock, Dumbarton', *Proceedings of the Society of Antiquaries of Scotland*, 107 (1976), 103–13.

——'Cadbury-Camelot: A Fifteen-Year Perspective', *PBA* 68 (1982), 355–88.

——'Gwŷr y Gogledd: An Archaeological Appraisal', *Archaeologia Cambrensis* 132 (1983), 1–18.

——*Economy, Society and Warfare among the Britons and Saxons* (Cardiff, 1987).

——'The Activities of Potentates in Celtic Britain, AD 400–800: A Positivist Approach', in Driscoll and Nieke (eds.), *Power and Politics*, 22–39.

——*Bede, Eddius, and the Forts of the North Britons*, Jarrow Lecture 1988.

——*Kings and Warriors, Craftsmen and Priests in Northern Britain AD 550–850* (Edinburgh, 2003).

Allen, J. Romilly, 'Early Christian Art in Wales', *Archaeologia Cambrensis*, 5th Series 16 (1899), 1–69.

Atsma, H., 'Klöster und Mönchtum im Bistum Auxerre bis zum Ende des 6. Jahrhunderts', *Francia*, 11 (1983), 1–96.

Bachrach, B. S., 'Gildas, Vortigern and Constitutionality in Sub-Roman Britain', *Nottingham Medieval Studies*, 32 (1988), 126–40.
Bammersberger, A., and Wollmann, A. (eds.), *Britain 400–600: Language and History* (Heidelberg, 1990).
Barley, M. W., and Hanson, R. P. C. (eds.), *Christianity in Britain, 300–700* (Leicester, 1968).
Barrett, A., 'Saint Germanus and the British Missions', *Britannia*, 40 (2009), 197–217.
Bartholomew, P., 'Fifth-Century Facts', *Britannia*, 13 (1982), 261–70.
Birley, A., *The Roman Government of Britain* (Oxford, 2005).
Böhme, H., 'Das Ende der Römerherrschaft in Britannien und die angelsächsische Besiedlung Englands im 5 Jahrhundert', *Jahrbuch des Römisch-Germanischen Zentralmuseums Mainz*, 33 (1986), 469–574.
Boon, G. C., 'A Christian Monogram at Caerwent', *BBCS* 19 (1962), 338–44.
——'The Early Church in Gwent, I. The Romano-British Church', *The Monmouthshire Antiquary*, 8 (1992), 11–24.
Brewer, R., *Caerwent Roman Town* (Cardiff, 1992).
Brown, P. R. L., *The Rise of Western Christendom*, 2nd edn. (Oxford, 2003).
Campbell, E., 'The Archaeological Evidence for External Contacts: Imports, Trade and Economy in Celtic Britain A.D. 400–800', in Dark (ed.), *External Contacts*, 83–96.
——*Continental and Mediterranean Imports to Atlantic Britain and Ireland, AD 400–800*, CBA Research Report 157 (York, 2007).
Carey, J., Koch, J. T., and Lambert, P.Y. (eds.), *Ildánach, Ildírech: A Festschrift for Proinsias Mac Cana* (Andover, MA, and Aberystwyth, 1999).
Casey, P. J. (ed.), *The End of Roman Britain*, BAR 71 (Oxford, 1979).
——and Jones, M. E., 'The Date of the Letter of the Britons to Aetius', *BBCS* 37 (1990), 281–90.
Chadwick, N. K., 'The Name Pict', *Scottish Gaelic Studies*, 8 (1955–8), 146–76.
——*The Age of the Saints in the Early Celtic Church* (London, 1961).
——(ed.), *Studies in Early British History* (Cambridge, 1954; rev. imp. 1959).
——(ed.), *Celt and Saxon: Studies in the Early British Border* (Cambridge, 1963).
Charles-Edwards, T. M., 'Palladius, Prosper, and Leo the Great: Mission and Primatial Authority', in D. N. Dumville et al., *Saint Patrick, A.D. 493–1993* (Woodbridge, 1993), 1–12.
——'Language and Society among the Insular Celts, 400–1000', in M. Green (ed.), *The Celtic World* (London, 1995), 703–36.
——'Britons in Ireland, *c.*550–800', in J. Carey, J. T. Koch, and P.-Y. Lambert (eds.), *Ildánach Ildírech: A Festschrift for Proinsias Mac Cana* (Andover, Mass., 1999), 15–26.
——*Early Christian Ireland* (Cambridge, 2000).
——'Law in the Western Kingdoms between the Fifth and the Seventh Century', in A. Cameron, B. Ward-Perkins, and M. Whitby (eds.), *The Cambridge Ancient History*, xiv, *Late Antiquity: Empire and Successors, A.D. 425–600* (Cambridge, 2000), 260–87.
Cleary, A. S. Esmonde, *The Ending of Roman Britain* (London, 1989).
Coates, R., 'The Significance of Celtic Place-Names in England', in Filppula et al. (eds.), *The Celtic Roots of English*, 47–85.
——'Invisible Britons: The View from Linguistics', in Higham (ed.), *The Britons in Anglo-Saxon England*, 72–91.
——'Invisible Britons: The View from Toponomastics', in P. Cavill and G. Broderick, *Language Contact in the Place-Names of Britain and Ireland*, English Place-Name Society, Extra Ser. 3 (Nottingham, 2007), 43–55.

Cramp, R., 'Anglo-Saxon Settlement', in J. C. Chapman and H. C. Mytum (eds.), *Settlement in North Britain 1000 BC–AD 1000*, BAR British Series, 118 (Oxford, 1983), 263–97.

Dark, K. R., *Civitas to Kingdom: British Political Continuity, 300–800*, *Studies in the Early History of Britain* (Leicester, 1994).

——(ed.), *External Contacts and the Economy of Late Roman and Post-Roman Britain* (Woodbridge, 1997).

——*Britain and the End of the Roman Empire* (Stroud, 2000).

Davis, K. R., *Britons and Saxons: The Chiltern Region AD 400–700* (Chichester, 1982).

Drinkwater, J., and Elton, H. (eds.), *Fifth-Century Gaul: A Crisis of Identity?* (Cambridge, 1992).

Driscoll, S. T., and Nieke, M. R. (eds.), *Power and Politics in Early Medieval Britain and Ireland* (Edinburgh, 1988).

Dumville, D. N., 'Sub-Roman Britain: History and Legend', *History*, 62 (1977), 173–92; reprinted as no. I in his *Histories and Pseudo-Histories*.

——'On the Dating of the Early Breton Law Codes', *Études Celtiques* 21 (1984), 207–21.

——'Late-Seventh- or Eighth-Century Evidence for the British Transmission of Pelagius', *CMCS* 10 (Winter 1985), 39–52.

——et al., *Saint Patrick, A.D. 493–1993* (Woodbridge, 1993).

——*A Palaeographer's Review: The Insular System of Scripts in the Early Middle Ages*, i (Osaka, 1999).

——*Saint David of Wales*, Kathleen Hughes Memorial Lectures, 1 (Cambridge, 2001); reprinted in his *Celtic Essays, 2001–2007*, i. 35–71.

Ewig, E., 'Studien zur merowingischen Dynastie', *Frühmittelalterliche Studien*, 8 (1974), 15–59.

——*Spätantikes und fränkisches Gallien*, 2 vols. (Munich, 1976).

——*Die Merowinger und das Imperium* (Rhein.-westfäl. Akad. d. Wiss., Geisteswiss., Vortr., G 261; Opladen, 1983).

——*Die Merowinger und das Frankenreich*, Urban-Taschenbücher, 392 (Stuttgart, 1988)

——'Die Namengebung bei den ältesten Frankenkönigen und im merowingischen Königshaus', *Francia*, 18/1 (1991), 21–69.

Fahy, D., 'When did Britons become Bretons?', *WHR* 2 (1964–5), 111–24.

Filppula, M., Klemola, J., and Pitkänen, H. (eds.), *The Celtic Roots of English*, Studies in Languages 37 (Joensuu, 2002).

Foster, I. Ll., and Daniel, G. (eds.), *Prehistoric and Early Wales* (London, 1965).

Fox, A., 'The Siting of Some Inscribed Stones of the Dark Ages in Glamorgan and Breconshire', *Archaeologia Cambrensis* 94 (1939), 30–41.

Frere, S. S., 'Civitas—A Myth?', *Antiquity*, 35 (1961), 29–36.

——*Britannia: A History of Roman Britain*, 3rd edn. (London, 1987); 3rd edn. with further revisions (London, 1999) [not the same pagination].

Fuentes, N., 'Fresh Thoughts on the Saxon Shore', in V. A. Maxfield and M. J. Dobson (eds.), *Roman Frontier Studies 1989: Proceedings of the XVth International Congress of Roman Frontier Studies* (Exeter, 1991), 58–64.

Fulford, M. G., 'Byzantium and Britain: A Mediterranean Perspective on Post-Roman Imports in Britain and Ireland', *Medieval Archaeology*, 33 (1989), 1–6.

——and Clarke, A., 'Silchester and the End of Roman Towns', *Current Archaeology*, 14 (1999), 176–80.

—— ——and Eckhardt, H., *Life and Labour in late Roman Silchester: Excavations in Insula IX Since 1997*, Britannia Monograph Series 22 (London, 2001).

Fulford, M. G., and Sellwood, B., 'The Silchester Ogham Stone: A Reconsideration', *Antiquity*, 54 (1980), 95–9.
Geake, H., *The Use of Grave-Goods in Conversion-Period England, c.600–c.850*, BAR British Series, 261 (Oxford, 1997).
Gelling, M., *The West Midlands in the Early Middle Ages* (Leicester, 1992).
——'Why aren't we speaking Welsh?', in W. Filmer-Sankey (ed.), *Anglo-Studies in Archaeology and History*, 6 (1993), 51–6.
——*Signposts to the Past: Place-Names and the History of England*, 2nd edn. (Chichester, 1988).
Goffart, W., *Barbarians and Roman, A.D. 418–584. The Techniques of Accommodation* (Princeton, NJ, 1980).
——'The Supposedly "Frankish" Table of Nations: An Edition and Study', *Frühmittelalterliche Studien*, 17 (1983), 98–130, reprinted in his *Rome's Fall and After* (London, 1989), 133–65.
Goodburn, R., and Bartholomew, P. (eds.), *Aspects of the Notitia Dignitatum*, BAR Supplementary Series, 15 (Oxford, 1976).
Graham-Campbell, J., and Ryan, M. (eds.), *Anglo-Saxon/Irish Relations before the Vikings*, Proceedings of the British Academy, 157 (Oxford, 2009).
Halsall, G., *Early Medieval Cemeteries: An Introduction to Burial Archaeology* (Glasgow, 1995).
Hamp, E, 'Voteporigis Protictoris', *Studia Celtica*, 30 (1996), 293.
Härke, H., 'The Anglo-Saxon Weapon Burial Rite', *Past & Present*, 126 (1990), 22–43.
Harries, J., *The World of Sidonius Apollinaris* (Oxford, 1994).
Higham, N. J., 'Gildas, Roman Walls, and British Dykes', *CMCS* 22 (Winter 1991), 1–14.
——*Rome, Britain and the Anglo-Saxons* (London, 1992).
——*The English Conquest: Gildas and Britain in the Fifth Century* (Manchester, 1994).
Hills, C., *Origins of the English* (London, 2003).
Hines, J., 'Philology, Archaeology and the *Adventus Saxonum vel Anglorum*', in A. Bammersberger and A. Wollmann (eds.), *Britain 400–600*, 17–36.
Hodgson, N., 'The Notitia Dignitatum and the Later Roman Garrison of Britain', in V. A. Maxfield and M. J. Dobson (eds.), *Roman Frontier Studies 1989: Proceedings of the XVth International Congress of Roman Frontier Studies* (Exeter, 1991), 84–92.
Hodges, R., and Bowden, W. (eds.), *The Sixth Century: Production, Distribution and Demand* (Leiden, 1998).
Hogg, A. H. A., 'Llwyfenydd', *Antiquity*, 20 (1946), 210–11.
Jackson, K. H., 'The Site of Mount Badon', *Journal of Celtic Studies*, 2 (1953–58), 152–5.
——'Varia : 2. Gildas and the Names of the British Princes', *CMCS* 3 (Summer 1982), 30–40.
Jarrett, M. G., and Mann, J. C., 'The Tribes of Wales', *WHR* 4 (1968–69), 161–71.
Jones, M. E., 'The Historicity of the Alleluja Victory', *Albion*, 18 (1986), 363–73.
——'The Appeal to Aetius in Gildas', *Nottingham Medieval Studies*, 32 (1988), 141–55.
——*The End of Roman Britain* (Newy York, 1996).
Knight, J. K., 'Early Christian Origins and Society in South Wales', *Merthyr Historian*, 2 (1978), 101–10.
——'Glamorgan A.D. 400–1100: Archaeology and History', in Savory (ed.), *Glamorgan County History*, ii, 315–64.
——*The End of Antiquity: Archaeology, Society and Religion in Early Medieval Western Europe 235–700* (Stroud, 1999).

Knight, J. K., 'Britain's Other Martyrs: Julius, Aaron and Alban at Caerleon', in M. Henig and P. Lindley (eds.), *Alban and St Albans: Roman and Medieval Art and Archaeology*, trans. Brit. Arch. Assoc. 24 (2001), 38–44.
——'Basilicas and Barrows: Christian Origins in Wales and Western Britain', in M. Carver (ed.), *The Cross goes North: Processes of Conversion in Northern Europe AD 300–1300* (York, 2003), 119–26.
——'From Villa to Monastery: Llandough in Context', *Medieval Archaeology*, 49 (2005), 93–107.
Koch, J. T., '**Cothairche*, Esposito's Theory, and Neo-Celtic Lenition', in Bammersberger and Wollmann (eds.), *Britain 400–600*, 179–202.
——'The Early Chronology for St Patrick (*c.* 351–*c.* 428): Some New Ideas and Possibilities', in J. Cartwright (ed.), *Celtic Hagiography and Saints' Cults* (Cardiff, 2003), 102–22.
Leech, R., 'The Excavation of a Romano-Celtic Temple and a Later Cemetery on Lamyatt Beacon, Somerset', *Britannia*, 17 (1980), 259–328.
Le Menn, Gw., and Le Moing, J. Y., *Bretagne et les pays celtiques—langues, histoire, civilisation. Mélanges offerts à la mémoire de Léon Fleuriot* (Saint-Brieuc et Rennes, 1992).
Levison, W., 'Bischof Germanus von Auxerre und die Quellen zu seiner Geschichte', *Neues Archiv*, 29 (1903–04), 95–175.
Levy, E., *West Roman Vulgar Law: The Law of Property* (Philadelphia, 1951).
Little, Lester K. (ed.), *Plague and the End of Antiquity: The Pandemic of 541–750* (Cambridge, 2008).
Longley, D., *Hanging-Bowls, Penannular Brooches and the Anglo-Saxon Connection*, BAR British Series, 22 (Oxford, 1975).
——'The Mote of Mark: The Archaeological Context of the Decorated Metalwork', in M. Redknap et al. (eds.), *Pattern and Purpose in Insular Art*, 75–89.
Lovecy, I., 'The End of Celtic Britain: A Sixth-Century Battle near Lindisfarne', *Archaeologia Aeliana*[5], 4 (1976), 31–45.
Lucy, S., 'Changing Burial Rites in Northumbria AD 500–750', in J. Hawkes and S. Mills (eds.), *Northumbria's Golden Age* (Stroud, 1999), 12–43.
Mac Cana, P., 'Y Trefedigaethau Gwyddelig ym Mhrydain', in G. Bowen (ed.), *Y Gwareiddiad Celtaidd* (Llandysul, 1987), 153–81.
McCarthy, M., *Roman Carlisle and the Lands of the Solway* (Stroud, 2002).
Macmullen, R., 'Late Roman Slavery', *Historia*, 36 (1987), 359–82 (see also Samson).
Mann, J. C., 'The Administration of Roman Britain', *Antiquity*, 35 (1961), 316–20.
——'The *Notitia Dignitatum*—Dating and Survival', *Britannia*, 22 (1991), 215–19.
Mathisen, R. W., 'The Last Year of St Germanus of Auxerre', *Analecta Bollandiana*, 99 (1981), 151–9.
——*Studies in the History, Literature, and Society of Late Antiquity* (Amsterdam, 1991).
Matthews, J. F., 'Macsen, Maximianus and Constantine', *Welsh History Review*, 11 (1982–3), 431–48.
Maxfield, V. A., and Dobson, M. J. (eds.), *Roman Frontier Studies 1989: Proceedings of the XVth International Congress of Roman Frontier Studies* (Exeter, 1991).
Miller, M., 'The Last British Entry in the Gallic Chronicles', *Britannia*, 9 (1978), 315–18.
Moisl, H., 'A Sixth-Century Reference to the British *Bardd*', *BBCS* 29 (1980–82), 269–73.
Morice, H., *Mémoires pour servir de preuves à l'histoire ecclésiastique et civile de Bretagne*, 3 vols. (Paris, 1742–46).
Morris, J., 'Pelagian Literature', *Journal of Theological Studies*, NS., 16 (1965), 26–60.
——'The Dates of the Celtic Saints', *Journal of Theological Studies*, NS, 17 (1966), 342–91.

Morris, R., *The Church in British Archaeology* (London, 1983).
Murray, J. (ed.), *St Ninian and the Earliest Christianity in Scotland*, BAR British Series 483 (Oxford, 2009).
Nash-Williams, V. E., 'Some Dated Monuments of the "Dark Ages" in Wales', *AC* 93 (1938), 31–56.
O'Brien, E., 'Pagan and Christian Burial in Ireland during the First Millennium AD: Continuity and Change', in N. Edwards and A. Lane (eds.), *The Early Church in Wales and the West*, Oxbow Monograph, 16 (Oxford, 1992), 130–62.
——*Post-Roman Britain to Anglo-Saxon England: Burial Practices Reviewed*, BAR British Series, 289 (Oxford, 1999).
O'Sullivan, T. D., *The De Excidio of Gildas, Its Authenticity and Date* (Leiden, 1978).
Painter, K. S., 'Villa and Christianity in Roman Britain', *British Museum Quarterly*, 35 (1971), 157–75.
Pearce, S. M., *The Kingdom of Dumnonia: Studies in the History and Tradition in South-Western Britain AD 350–1150* (Padstow, 1978).
——(ed.), *The Early Church in Western Britain and Ireland*, BAR British Series, 102 (Oxford, 1982).
Penny, S., and Shotter, D. C., An Inscribed Roman Salt-Pan from Shavington, Cheshire', *Britannia*, 27 (1996), 360–5.
Philpott, R., *Burial Practices in Roman Britain: A Survey of Grave Treatment and Furnishing, A.D. 43–410*, BAR 219 (Oxford, 1991).
Plummer, C., 'On the Meaning of Ogam Stones', *Revue Celtique*, 40 (1923), 387–90.
Pohl, W., *Kingdoms of the Empire: The Integration of Barbarians in Late Antiquity* (Leiden, 1997).
——and Reimitz, H. (eds.), *Strategies of Distinction: The Construction of Ethnic Communities, 300–800* (Leiden, 1998).
Poulin, J.-C., 'Recherches et identifications des sources de la littérature hagiographique du Haut Moyen Âge: L'exemple breton', *Revue d'histoire de l'Église de France*, 71 (1985), 119–29.
Pryce, H. (ed.), *Literacy in Medieval Celtic Societies* (Cambridge, 1998).
Radford, C. A. R., 'Christian Origins in Britain', *Medieval Archaeology*, 15 (1971), 1–12.
Rahtz, P., 'Irish Settlements in Somerset', *Proc. Roy. Ir. Acad.*, 76, C (1976), 223–30.
——'Celtic Society in Somerset A.D. 400–700', *BBCS* 30 (1982–83), 176–200.
——'Pagan and Christian by the Severn Sea', in L. Abrams and J. Carley (eds.), *The Archaeology and History of Glastonbury Abbey: Essays in Honour of the Ninetieth Birthday of C. A. Ralegh Radford* (Woodbridge, 1991), 3–37.
Redknap, M., *The Christian Celts*, National Museum of Wales (Cardiff, 1991).
——'Glitter in the Dragon's Lair: Irish and Anglo-Saxon Metalwork from Pre-Viking Wales, *c.* 400–850', in Graham-Campbell and Ryan (eds.), *Anglo-Saxon/Irish Relations before the Vikings*, 281–309.
Reynolds, S., 'What do we mean by "Anglo-Saxon" and "Anglo-Saxons"?', *Journal of British Studies*, 24 (1985), 395–414.
Riché, P., *Education et culture dans l'occident barbare, vi^e^–viiie siècles*, 3rd edn. (Paris, 1962); English trans. by J. J. Contreni, *Education and Culture in the Barbarian West: From the Sixth through the Eighth Century* (Columbia, S. Carol., 1976).
The Royal Commission for Ancient and Historical Monuments of Wales, *An Inventory of the Ancient Monuments in Anglesey* (London, 1937).

The Royal Commission for Ancient and Historical Monuments of Wales, *An Inventory of the Ancient Monuments of Glamorgan*, i:3, *The Early Christian Period* (London, 1976).

——*An Inventory of the Ancient Monuments in Brecknock (Brycheiniog): The Prehistoric and Roman Monuments, Part II: Hillforts and Roman Remains* (London, 1986).

——*An Inventory of the Ancient Monuments in Brecknock (Brycheiniog): The Prehistoric and Roman Monuments, Part I: Later Prehistoric Monuments and Unenclosed Settlements to 1000 AD* (Stroud, 1997).

The Royal Commission on the Ancient and Historical Monuments of Scotland, *An Inventory of the Ancient and Historical Monuments of Selkirkshire* (Edinburgh, 1957).

——*The Archaeological Sites and Monuments of Upper Eskdale* (Edinburgh, 1980).

——*The Archaeological Sites and Monuments of Ewesdale and Lower Eskdale, Annandale and Eskdale* (Edinburgh, 1997).

Savory, H. N. (ed.), *Glamorgan County History*, ii, *Early Glamorgan: Pre-History and Early History* (Cardiff, 1984).

Smith, J. M. H. (ed.), *Early Medieval Rome and the Christian West: Essays in Honour of Donald A. Bullough* (Leiden, 2000).

Stanley, W. O., 'Towyn-y-Capel', *Archaeological Journal*, 3 (1846), 223–8.

Snyder, C. A., *Sub-Roman Britain (AD 400–600): A Gazetteer of Sites*, BAR British Series, 247 (Oxford, 1996).

——*An Age of Tyrants: Britain and the Britons AD 400–600* (University Park PA, 1998).

Thomas, C., 'The Context of Tintagel: A New Model for the Recognition of Post-Roman Mediterranean Imports', *Cornish Archaeology*, 27 (1988), 7–25.

Thompson, E. A., 'Britonia', in Barley and Hanson (eds.), *Christianity in Britain, 300–700*, 201–5.

——'Britain AD 406–410', *Britannia*, 8 (1977), 208–18.

——'Gildas and the History of Britain', *Britannia*, 10 (1979), 203–26, and 11 (1980), 344.

——'Procopius on Brittia and Britannia', *Classical Quarterly*, 30 (1980), 498–507.

——'Zosimus 6. 10. 2 and the Letters of Honorius', *Classical Quarterly*, 32 (1982), 445–62.

——'Fifth-Century Facts?', *Britannia*, 14 (1983), 272–4.

——*Saint Germanus of Auxerre and the End of Roman Britain*, Studies in Celtic History, 6 (Woodbridge, 1984). Note the review article by R. A. Markus, *Nottingham Medieval Studies*, 29 (1985), 115–22.

——'Ammianus Marcellinus and Britain', *Nottingham Medieval Studies*, 34 (1990), 1–15.

Ward-Perkins, B., 'Why did the Anglo-Saxons not become More British?', *English Historical Review*, 115 (2000), 513–33.

——*The Fall of Rome and the End of Civilization* (Oxford, 2005).

Watts, D. J., *Christians and Pagans in Roman Britain* (London, 1991).

——*Religion in Late Roman Britain: Forces of Change* (London, 1998).

Werner, J., 'Zur Enstehung der Reihengräberzivilisation', *Archeologia Geographica*, 1 (1950), 23–32.

White, R. H., *Roman and Celtic Objects from Anglo-Saxon Graves*, BAR British Series, 191 (Oxford, 1988).

Williams, H., *Christianity in Early Britain* (Oxford, 1912).

Wilson, P. A., 'On the Use of the Terms "Strathclyde" and "Cumbria"', *Transactions of the Cumberland and Westmorland Antiquarian and Archaeological Society*, NS 66 (1966), 57–92.

Wilson, P. R., Cardwell, P., Cramp, R. J., Evans, J., Taylor-Wilson, R. H., Thompson, A., and Wacher, J., 'Early Anglian Catterick and *Catraeth*', *Medieval Archaeology*, 40 (1996), 1–61.

Wood, I. N., 'The End of Roman Britain: Continental Evidence and Parallels', in M. Lapidge and D. Dumville (eds.), *Gildas: New Approaches*, 1–25.

——'The Fall of the Western Empire and the End of Roman Britain', *Britannia*, 18 (1987), 251–62.

——'The Channel from the Fourth to the Seventh Centuries AD', in S. McGrail (ed.), *Maritime Celts, Frisians and Saxons* (London, 1990), 93–7.

——'Britain and the Continent in the Fifth and Sixth Centuries: The Evidence of Ninian', in Murray (ed.), *St Ninian and the Earliest Christianity in Scotland*, 71–82.

Wooding, J. M., *Communication and Commerce along the Western Seaways, AD 400–899*, BAR, International Series, 654 (Oxford, 1996).

——'Cargoes in Trade along the Western Seaboard', in Dark (ed.), *External Contacts*, 67–82.

Woolf, A., 'The Britons: From Romans to Barbarians', in H.-W. Goetz, J. Jarnut, and W. Pohl (eds.), *Regna and Gentes: The Relationship between Late Antique and Early Medieval Peoples and Kingdoms in the Transformation of the Roman World* (Leiden, 2003), 345–80.

——'Apartheid and Economics in Anglo-Saxon England', in Higham (ed.), *The Britons in Anglo-Saxon England*, 115–29.

Yorke, B., 'Fact or Fiction? The Written Evidence for the Fifth and Sixth Centuries AD', *Anglo-Saxon Studies in Archaeology and History*, 6 (1993), 45–50.

Youngs, S. (ed.), *The Work of Angels: Masterpieces of Celtic Metalwork, 6th–9th Centuries AD* (London, 1989).

——'Britain, Wales and Ireland: Holding Things Together', in Jankulak and Wooding (eds.), *Ireland and Wales in the Middle Ages*, 80–101.

——'Anglo-Saxon, Irish and British Relations: Hanging-Bowls Reconsidered', in Graham-Campbell and Ryan (eds.), *Anglo-Saxon/Irish Relations before the Vikings*, 205–30.

1(b). *Early Brittany*

Brett, C., 'Soldiers, Saints, and States? The Breton Migrations Revisited', *CMCS* 61 (Summer 2011), 1–56.

Chédeville, A., and Guillotel, H., *La Bretagne des saints et des rois, Ve–Xe siècle* (Paris, 1973).

Duchesne, L., *Fastes épiscopaux de l'ancienne Gaule* 3 vols. (Paris, 1894–1915).

Duine, F., *Mémento des sources hagiographiques de l'histoire de Bretagne. I. Les fondateurs et les primitifs* (Rennes, 1918).

Fleuriot, L., 'Recherches sur les enclaves romanes anciennes en territoire bretonnant', *Études Celtiques*, 8 (1958), 164–78.

——'Old Breton Genealogies and Early British Tradition', *BBCS* 26 (1976), 1–6.

——*Les Origines de la Bretagne. L'émigration* (Paris, 1980).

Giot, P.-R., Guigou, P., and Merdrignac, B., *The British Settlement of Brittany: The First Bretons in Armorica* (Stroud, 2003).

Guigon, P., *Les Églises du haut moyen âge en Bretagne*, 2 vols., Les Dossiers du Centre Régional d'Archéologie d'Alet, Suppléments T and U (Saint-Malo, 1997–98).

Langouët, L., *Les Fouilles archéologiques de la zone des cathedrales d'Alet*, Les Dossiers du Centre Régional d'Archéologie d'Alet, Suppl. J (Saint-Malo, 1987)

——*Les Coriosolites: un peuple Armoricain de la période gauloise à l'époque gallo-romaine*, Les Dossiers du Centre Régional d'Archéologie d'Alet, Suppl. K (Saint-Malo, 1988).

——*La Cité d'Alet: de l'agglomeration gauloise à l'île de Saint-Malo*, Les Dossiers du Centre Régional d'Archéologie d'Alet, S (Saint-Malo, 1996).

——and Daire, M. Y., *La Civitas gallo-romaine des Coriosolites: le milieu rural* (Rennes, 1989).

Le Duc, G., 'L'évêché mythique de Brest', *Britannia Monastica*, 3 (1994), 169–99.

——'The Colonization of Brittany from Britain: New Approaches and Questions', in R. Black, W. Gillies, and R. Ó Maolalaigh (eds.), *Celtic Connections: Proceedings of the Tenth International Celtic Congress of Celtic Studies*, i, *Language, Literature, History, Culture* (East Linton, 1999), 133–51.

Lot, F., *Mélanges d'histoire bretonne (VIe–XIe siècles)* (Paris, 1907).

Loth, J., *L'Émigration bretonne en Armorique* (Rennes, 1883).

——'La Vie la plus ancienne de Saint Samson', *Revue Celtique*, 40 (1923), 1–50.

Pape, L., *La Civitas des Osismes à l'époque gallo-romaine* (Paris, 1978).

——*La Bretagne romaine* (Rennes, 1995).

2. *The Britons and their languages*

Adams, J. N., *The Regional Diversification of Latin* (Cambridge, 2007).

Blom, A., '*Lingua Gallica, Lingua Celtica*: Gaulish, Gallo-Latin, or Gallo-Romance?', *Keltische Forschungen*, 4 (2009), 7–54.

Bonnet, M., *Le latin de Grégoire de Tours* (Paris, 1890).

Evans, D. Ellis, 'A Comparison of the Formation of Some Continental and Early Insular Celtic Personal Names', *BBCS* 24 (1970–72), 415–34.

——'Insular Celtic and the Emergence of the Welsh Language', in A. Bammersberger and A. Wollmann (eds.), *Britain 400–600*, 149–77.

——'Language Contact in Pre-Roman and Roman Britain, in H. Temporini and W. Haase (eds.), *Aufstieg und Niedergang des römischen Welt. II. Prinzipat*, 29.2, *Sprache und Literatur*, ed. W. Haase (Berlin, 1983), 949–87.

Evans, D. S., *A Grammar of Middle Welsh* (Dublin, 1964).

Falileyev, A., *Etymological Glossary of Old Welsh* (Tübingen, 2000)

——*Le Vieux-Gallois* (Potsdam, 2008).

Fleuriot, L., *Dictionnaire des gloses en vieux breton* (Paris, 1964).

——*Le vieux breton* (Paris, 1964).

Forsyth, K., *Language in Pictland*, Studia Hameliana, 2 (Utrecht, 1997).

Greene, D., 'The Spirant Mutation in Brythonic', *Celtica*, 7 (1966), 116–19.

——'Some Linguistic Evidence Relating to the British Church', in Barley and Hanson (eds.), *Christianity in Britain, 300–700*, 75–86.

Hamp, E., 'Social Gradience in British Spoken Latin', *Britannia*, 6 (1975), 150–61.

Harvey, A., 'Aspects of Lenition and Spirantization', *CMCS* 8 (Winter 1984), 87–100.

Herman, J., *Vulgar Latin* (University Park, Pennsylvania, 2000).

Hines, J., 'The Becoming of the English: Identity, Material Culture and Language in Early Anglo-Saxon England', in W. Filmer-Sankey and D. Griffiths (eds.), *Anglo-Saxon Studies in Archaeology and History*, 7 (1994), 49–59.

——'Focus and Boundary in Linguistic Varieties in the North-West Germanic Continuum', in V. F. Faltings, A. G. H. Walker, and O. Wilts (eds.), *Friesische Studien*, ii (Odense, 1995), 35–62.

——'Welsh and English: Mutual Origins in Post-Roman Britain?', *Studia Celtica*, 34 (2000), 81–104.

Jackson, K. H., *Language and History in Early Britain* (Edinburgh, 1953).

——'The Pictish Language', in F. T. Wainwright, *The Problem of the Picts* (Edinburgh, 1955; repr. Perth, 1980), 129–66.

——'Some Questions in Dispute about Early Welsh Literature and Language', *Studia Celtica*, 8/9 (1973–74), 1–32.

——'The Date of the Old Welsh Accent Shift', *Studia Celtica*, 10/11 (1975–76), 40–53.

Koch, J. T., 'The Loss of Final Syllables and the Loss of Declension in Brittonic', *BBCS* 30 (1982–83), 201–33.

Laker, S., and Russell, P. (eds.), 'Special Issue: Languages of Early Britain', *Transactions of the Philological Society*, 109: 2 (2011).

Lambert, P.-Y., 'Vieux-Gallois *nou, nom, inno*', *BBCS* 30 (1983), 20–9.

——*La langue gauloise* (Paris, 1995).

——'The Old Welsh Glosses on Weights and Measures', in Russell (ed.), *Yr Hen Iaith*, 103–34.

Lewis, H., *Datblygiad yr Iaith Gymraeg* (Cardiff, 1931; rev. edn. 1946).

——*Yr Elfen Ladin yn yr Iaith Gymraeg* (Cardiff, 1943).

Mac Cana, P., 'Latin Influence on British: The Pluperfect', in J. J O'Meara and B. Naumann (eds.), *Latin Script and Letters AD 400–900: A Festschrift presented to Ludwig Bieler* (Leiden, 1976), 194–203.

——and Watkins, T. A., 'Cystrawennau'r Cyplad mewn Hen Gymraeg', *BBCS* 18 (1958–60), 1–25.

McCone, K., *Towards a Relative Chronology of Ancient and Medieval Celtic Sound Change* (Maynooth, 1996)

McManus, D., 'The Chronology of Latin Loan-Words', *Ériu*, 34 (1983), 21–71.

——'The so-called *Cothrige* and *Pátraic* Strata of Latin Loan-Words in Early Irish', P. Ní Chatháin and M. Richter (eds.), *Irland und Europa: Die Kirche im Frühmittelalter / Ireland and Europe: The Early Church*, Veröffentlichungen des Europa Zentrums Tübingen, Kulturwissenschaftliche Reihe (Stuttgart, 1984), 179–96.

——'*Linguarum Diversitas*: Latin and the Vernaculars in Early Medieval Britain', *Peritia*, 3 (1984), 151–88.

——*A Guide to Ogam*, Maynooth Monographs, 4 (Maynooth, 1991).

Martinet, A., 'Celtic Lenition and Western Romance Consonants', *Language*, 28 (1952), 192–217.

——*Économie des changements phonétiques: traité de phonologie diachronique*, 2nd edn. (Berne, 1964).

Morris-Jones, J., *A Welsh Grammar, Historical and Comparative* (Oxford, 1913).

Nielsen, H. F., *Old English and the Continental Germanic Languages*, Innsbrucker Beiträge zur Sprachwissenschaft, 33 (Innsbruck, 1981; 2nd edn. 1985).

——*The Continental Backgrounds of English and its Insular Development until 1154* (Odense, 1998).

Parsons, D. N., 'Sabrina in the Thorns: Place-Names as Evidence for British and Latin in Roman Britain', in Laker and Russell (eds.), 'Languages of Early Britain', 113–37.

Russell, P., 'Recent Work on British Latin', *CMCS* 9 (Summer 1985), 19–29.

——'A Footnote to Spirantization', *CMCS* 10 (Winter 1985), 53–6.

Russell, P., *An Introduction to the Celtic Languages* (London, 1995).
——(ed.), *Yr Hen Iaith: Studies in Early Welsh* (Aberystwyth, 2003).
——'Latin and British in Roman and Post-Roman Britain: Methodology and Morphology', in Laker and Russell (eds.), 'Special Issue: Languages of Early Britain', *Transactions of the Philological Society*, 109: 2 (2011), 138–57.
Schrijver, P., *Studies in British Celtic Historical Phonology* (Amsterdam, 1995).
——'Spirantization and Nasalization in British', *Studia Celtica*, 33 (1999), 1–19.
——'Geminate Spellings in the Old Welsh Glosses to Martianus Capella', *Études Celtiques*, 34 (1998–2000), 147–60.
——'The Rise and Fall of British Latin: Evidence from English and Brittonic', in Filppula, M. et al. (eds.), *The Celtic Roots of English*, 87–110.
——'What Britons spoke around 400', in Higham (ed.), *Britons in Anglo-Saxon England*, 165–71.
——'Celtic Influence on Old English: Phonological and Phonetic Evidence', *English Language and Linguistics*, 13: 2 (2009), 193–211.
Sims-Williams, P., 'Dating the Transition to Neo-Brittonic: Phonology and History, 400–600', in A. Bammersberger and A. Wollmann (eds.), *Britain 400–600: Language and History* (Heidelberg, 1990), 217–61.
——'The Emergence of Old Welsh, Cornish and Breton Orthography, 600–800: The Evidence of Archaic Old Welsh', *BBCS* 38 (1991), 20–86.
——'The Five Languages of Wales in the Pre-Norman Inscriptions', *CMCS*, 44 (Winter 2002), 1–36.
——*The Celtic Inscriptions of Britain: Phonology and Chronology, c. 400–1200*, Publications of the Philological Society 37 (Oxford: Blackwell, 2003).
——*Studies on Celtic Languages before the Year 1000* (Aberystwyth, 2007).
Smith, C., 'Vulgar Latin in Roman Britain: Epigraphic and Other Evidence', in H. Temporini and W. Haase (eds.), *Aufstieg und Niedergang des römischen Welt. II. Prinzipat*, 29.2, *Sprache und Literatur* (Berlin, 1983), 843–948.
Thomas, P. W., 'The Brythonic Consonant Shift and the Development of Consonant Mutation', *BBCS* 37 (1990), 1–42.
Thomson, R. L., 'The Continuity of Manx', in C. Fell et al. (eds.), *The Viking Age in the Isle of Man* (London, 1983), 169–74.
Tomlin, R. S. O., 'Was Ancient British ever a Written Language? Two Texts from Roman Bath', *BBCS* 34 (1987), 18–25.
Väänänen, V., *Introduction au latin vulgaire*, 2nd edn. (Paris, 1967).
Watkins, C., Review of *LHEB*, *Language*, 30 (1954), 513–18.
Watkins, T. Arwyn, 'Points of Similarity between Old Welsh and Old Irish Orthography', *BBCS* 21 (1964–65), 135–41.
——'The Accent in Old Welsh—its Quality and its Development', *BBCS* 25 (1972–74), 1–11.
——'The Accent-Shift in Old Welsh', in H. Pilch and J. Thurow (eds.), *Indo-Celtica: Gedächtnisschrift für Alf Sommerfelt* (Munich, 1972), 201–5.
——'Cyfnewidiadau Seinegol sy'n Gysylltiedig â'r "Acen" Gymraeg', *BBCS* 26 (1974–76), 399–405.
——'Constituent Order in the Old Welsh Verbal Sentence', *BBCS* 34 (1987), 51–60.
Williams, I., 'When did British become Welsh', in his *The Beginnings of Welsh Poetry*, ed. R. Bromwich (Cardiff, 1972)
Willis, D. W. E., *Syntactic Change in Welsh: A Study of the Loss of Verb-Second* (Oxford, 1998).
Ziegler, S., *Die Sprache der altirischen Ogam-Inschriften* (Göttingen, 1994).

3. *Inscriptions: Palaeography and Epigraphy*

Bischoff, B., *Mittelalterliche Studien: Ausgewählte Aufsätze zur Schriftkunde und zur Literaturgeschichte*, 3 vols. (Stuttgart, 1966–67, 1981).

——*Latin Palaeography: Antiquity and the Middle Ages*, trans. D. Ó Cróinín and D. Ganz (Cambridge, 1990).

Brown, T. J., 'The Irish Element in the Insular System of Scripts to *c.* AD 850', in H. Löwe (ed.), *Die Iren und Europa*, 101–19; reprinted in his *A Palaeographer's View*, 201–20.

——'The Oldest Irish Manuscripts and their Late Antique Background', in P. Ní Chatháin and M. Richter (eds.), *Irland und Europa*, 311–27, reprinted in *A Palaeographer's View*, 221–41.

——*A Palaeographer's View: The Selected Writings of Julian Brown*, ed. J. Bateley, M. Brown, and Jane Roberts (London, 1993).

Bu'lock, J. D., 'Early Christian Memorial Formulae', *Archaeologia Cambrensis*, 105 (1956), 133–41.

Charles-Edwards, D. G., 'The East Cross Inscription from Toureen Peacaun: Some Concrete Evidence', *JRSAI* 132 (2002), 114–26.

——'The Springmount Bog-Tablets: Their Implications for Insular Epigraphy and Palaeography', *Studia Celtica*, 36 (2002), 27–45.

Craig, D. J., 'The Provenance of the Early Christian Inscriptions of Galloway', in P. Hill, *Whithorn and St Ninian: The Excavation of a Monastic Town 1984–91* (Stroud, 1997), 614–19.

Davidson, A., 'Two Early Medieval Stones from Llandanwg', *Archaeology in Wales*, 48 (2008), 73–5.

Dumville, D. N., *A Palaeographer's Review: The Insular System of Scripts in the Early Middle Ages*, vol. i (Osaka, 1999).

——*Abbreviations used in Insular Script before A.D. 850: Tabulation based on the Work of W. M. Lindsay* (Cambridge, 2004).

Edwards, N., 'Early Medieval Inscribed Stones and Stone Sculpture in Wales: Context and Function', *Medieval Archaeology*, 45 (2001), 15–39.

Forsyth, K., '*Hic Memoria Perpetua*: The Early Inscribed Stones of Southern Scotland in Context', in S. M. Foster and M. Cross (eds.), *Able Minds and Practised Hands: Scotland's Early Medieval Sculpture in the 21st Century*, The Society of Medieval Archaeology Monograph, 23 (Leeds, 2005), 113–34.

——'The Latinus Stone: Whithorn's Earliest Christian Monument', in Murray (ed.), *St Ninian and the Earliest Christianity in Scotland*, 19–41.

Gameson, R. G., 'The Insular Gospel Book at Hereford Cathedral', *Scriptorium*, 56 (2002), 48–79 (59–60 and 67 on Lichfield Gospels).

Handley, M. A., 'The Early Medieval Inscriptions of Western Britain: Function and Sociology', in J. Hill and M. Swan (eds.), *The Community, the Family and the Saint: Patterns of Power in Early Medieval Europe* (Turnhout, 1998), 339–61.

——'The Origins of Christian Commemoration in Late Antique Britain', *Early Medieval Europe*, 10 (2001), 177–99.

——*Death, Society and Culture: Inscriptions and Epitaphs in Gaul and Spain, AD 300–750*, BAR International Series, 1135 (Oxford, 2003).

Higgitt, J., 'The Dedication Inscription at Jarrow and its Context', *The Antiquaries' Journal* 59 (1979), 343–74.

——'The Pictish Latin Inscription at Tarbat in Rossshire', *PSAS* 112 (1982), 300–21.

Higgitt, J., 'The Thornton le Moors inscription', in M. M. Brown and D. B. Gallagher, 'An Anglo-Viking Cross Shaft from Thornton le Moors, Cheshire', *Journal of the Chester Archaeological Society* 66 (1983), 26–9.

——'Words and Crosses: The Inscribed Stone Cross in Early Medieval Britain and Ireland', in J. Higgitt (ed.), *Early Medieval Sculpture in Britain and Ireland*, BAR, British Series 152 (Oxford, 1986), 125–52.

——'The Stone-Cutter and the Scriptorium: Early Medieval Inscriptions in Britain and Ireland', *Epigraphik*, 213 (1988), 149–63.

——'The Display Script of the Book of Kells and the Tradition of Insular Decorated Capitals', in F. O'Mahony (ed.), *The Book of Kells* (Aldershot, 1994), 209–33.

——'Monasteries and Inscriptions in Early Northumbria, the Evidence of Whitby', in C. Bourke, ed., *From the Isles of the North* (Belfast, 1995).

——(ed.), *Early Medieval Sculpture in Britain and Ireland*, BAR British Series, 152 (Oxford, 1986).

——Forsyth, K., and Parsons, D. N. (eds.), *Roman, Runes and Ogham: Medieval Inscriptions in the Insular World and on the Continent* (Donington, 2001).

Huws, D., *Medieval Welsh Manuscripts* (Cardiff, 2000).

Jackson, K. H., 'The Idnert Inscription: Date, and Significance of Id-', *BBCS* 19 (1960–62), 232–4.

Knight, J. K., 'The Early Christian Latin Inscriptions of Britain and Gaul: Chronology and Context', in Edwards and Lane (eds.), *The Early Church in Wales and the West*, 45–50.

——'Penmachno Revisited: The Consular Inscription and its Context', *CMCS* 29 (Summer 1995), 1–10.

——'Seasoned with Salt: Insular-Gallic Contacts in the Early Memorial Stones and Cross Slabs', in Dark (ed.), *External Contacts*, 109–20.

Lewis, J. M., 'An Early Christian Stone from Pen-y-Fai, Glamorgan', *Archaeologia Cambrensis*, 119 (1970), 71–4.

——'A Survey of Early Christian Monuments of Dyfed, West of the Taf', in G. C. Boon and J. M. Lewis (eds.), *Welsh Antiquity* (Cardiff, 1976), 177–92.

Lindsay, W. M., *Early Irish Minuscule Script* (Oxford, 1910).

——*Early Welsh Minuscule Script* (Oxford, 1912).

——'Irish Cursive Script', *ZCP* 9 (1913), 301–8.

Mallon, J., *La Paléographie romaine*, Monumenta et Studia, 3 (Madrid, 1952).

Okasha, E., 'A New Inscription from Ramsey Island', *Archaeologia Cambrensis*, 119 (1970), 68–70.

Rhŷs, J., *The Origin of the Welsh Englyn and Kindred Metres* (*Y Cymmrodor*, 18 [1905]).

Tedeschi, C., 'Osservazioni sulla palaeografia delle iscrizioni britanniche palaeocristiane (V–VII sec.). Contributo allo studio dell'origine delle scritture insulari', *Scrittura e civiltà*, 19 (1995), 67–121.

——'Some Observations on the Palaeography of Early Christian Inscriptions in Britain', in J. Higgitt et al. (eds.), *Roman, Runes and Ogham: Medieval Inscriptions in the Insular World and on the Continent* (Donington, 2001), 16–25.

——*Congeries Lapidum: Iscrizioni Britanniche dei secoli V–VII*, 2 vols. (Pisa, 2005).

Thomas, C., 'The Early Christian Inscriptions of Southern Scotland', *Glasgow Archaeological Journal*, 17 (1991–92), 1–10.

——*Whithorn's Christian Beginnings*, Whithorn Lecture (Whithorn, 1992).

——*And shall These Mute Stones speak? Post-Roman Inscriptions in Western Britain* (Cardiff, 1994).

——*Christian Celts: Messages and Images* (Stroud, 1998).

——*Silent in the Shroud: A Seventh-Century Inscription from Wales* (Balgavies, Angus, 1999).

——*Whispering Reeds, or The Anglesey Catamanus Inscription Stript Bare* (Oxford, 2002).

Tomlin, R. S. O., *Tabellae Sulis: Roman Inscribed Tablets of Tin and Lead from the Sacred Spring at Bath* (Oxford, 1988) (also published as Part 4 of B. Cunliffe (ed.), *The Temple of Sulis Minerva at Bath, II: Finds from the Sacred Spring* (Oxford, 1988)).

Williams, I., 'The Ogmore Castle Inscription', *Archaeologia Cambrensis*, 87 (1932), 232–8.

——'II. The Epigraphy of the Inscription', in C. Fox et al., 'The Domnic Inscribed Slab, Llangwyryfon, Cardiganshire', *Archaeologia Cambrensis*, 97 (1943), 205–12.

Wright, R. P., and Jackson, K. H., 'A Late Inscription from Wroxeter', *Antiquaries Journal*, 48 (1968), 269–300.

Wynne, W. W. E., 'Letters of E. Lhwyd', *Archaeologia Cambrensis*, 3 (1848), 309–13, 243–7.

4. *The Britons and the Irish*

Bateson, J. D., 'Roman Material from Ireland: A Reconsideration', *PRIA* 73, C (1973), 21–97.

——'Further Finds of Roman Material from Ireland', *PRIA* 76, C (1976), 171–80.

Carey, J., 'Nodons in Britain and Ireland', *ZCP* 40 (1984), 1–22.

Charles-Edwards, T. M., 'Britons in Ireland, *c*.550–800', in J. Carey, J. T. Koch, and P.-Y. Lambert (eds.), *Ildánach Ildírech: A Festschrift for Proinsias Mac Cana* (Andover, Mass., 1999), 15–26.

Coplestone-Crow, B., 'The Dual Nature of Irish Colonization of Dyfed in the Dark Ages', *Studia Celtica*, 16/17 (1981–82), 1–24.

Gruffydd, R. G., 'From Gododdin to Gwynedd: Reflections on the Story of Cunedda', *Studia Celtica*, 24/25 (1989–90), 1–14.

——'Why Cors Fochno?', *THSC* NS 2 (1996), 5–19.

McManus, D., *A Guide to Ogam*, Maynooth Monographs, 4 (Maynooth, 1991).

Ó Cathasaigh, T., 'The Déissi and Dyfed', *Éigse*, 20 (1984), 1–33.

Richards, M., 'The Irish Settlements in South-West Wales: A Topographical Approach', *Journal of the Royal Society of Antiquaries of Ireland*, 90 (1960), 133–62.

Sims-Williams, P., 'The Five Languages of Wales in the Pre-Norman Inscriptions', *CMCS*, 44 (Winter 2002), 1–36.

Thomas, C., 'The Irish Settlements in Post-Roman Western Britain: A Survey of the Evidence', *Journal of the Royal Institute of Cornwall*, 6 (1972), 251–74.

Wmffre, I., 'Post-Roman Irish Settlement in Wales: New Insights from a Recent Study of Cardiganshire Place-Names', in Jankulak and Wooding (eds.), *Ireland and Wales in the Middle Ages*, 46–61.

5. *From Pelagius to Gildas*

(a) General

Frend, W. H. C., '*Ecclesia Britannica*: Prelude or Dead End?', *Journal of Ecclesiastical History*, 30 (1979), 129–44.

——'Romano-British Christianity and the West: Comparison and Contrast', in S. M. Pearce (ed.), *The Early Church in Western Britain and Ireland*, BAR 102 (Oxford, 1982), 5–16.

——'Pagans, Christians and the "Barbarian Conspiracy" of AD 367', *Britannia*, 23 (1992), 121–31.

Frend, W. H. C., '*Altare subnixus*: A Cult of Relics in the Romano-British Church', *Journal of Theological Studies*, New Series, 48 (1997), 125–8.

——Roman Britain, a Failed Promise', in Carver (ed.), *The Cross goes North*, 79–91.

Lorenz, R., 'Die Anfänge des abendländischen Mönchtums im 4. Jahrhundert', *Zeitschrift für Kirchengeschichte*, 77 (1966), 1–61.

Markus, R. A., *The End of Ancient Christianity* (Cambridge, 1990).

Sharpe, R., 'Martyrs and Local Saints in Late Antique Britain', in Thacker and Sharpe (eds.), *Local Saints and Local Churches*, 75–154.

Stancliffe, C., 'The British Church and the Mission of Augustine', in R. Gameson (ed.), *Saint Augustine and the Conversion of England* (Stroud, 1999), 107–51.

——'Religion and Society in Ireland', in P. Fouracre (ed.), *The New Cambridge Medieval History*, vol. i (Cambridge, 2005), 397–425.

——'Christianity amongst the Britons, Dalriadan Irish and Picts', ibid. 426–61.

Thacker, A., and Sharpe, R. (eds.), *Local Saints and Local Churches in the Early Medieval West* (Oxford, 2002).

Thomas, [A.] C., 'An Early Christian Cemetery and Chapel on Ardwall Isle, Kirkudbright', *Medieval Architecture*, 11 (1967), 127–88.

——*The Early Christian Archaeology of North Britain* (Oxford, 1971).

——*Christianity in Roman Britain to A.D. 500* (London, 1981).

(b) Pelagius

i. Texts and Translations

An excellent collection in translation is:

Rees, B. R., *The Letters of Pelagius and his Followers* (Woodbridge, 1991).

Epistula ad Sacram Christi Virginem Demetriadem, *PL* xxx. 15–45; xxxiii. 1099–1120.

Expositiones XIII Epistularum Pauli, ed. A. Souter, *Pelagius's Expositions of the Thirteen Epistles of St. Paul*, 3 vols. Texts and Studies 9 (Cambridge, 1922–31), repr. *PLS* i. 1110–1374. The commentary of the Epistle to the Romans is translated and discussed by T. De Bruyn, *Pelagius's Commentary on St Paul's Epistle to the Romans* (Oxford, 1993).

Liber de Vita Christiana, *PL* xxiii. 1407–70.

ii. Secondary

Bonner, G., 'The Pelagian Controversy in Britain and Ireland', *Peritia*, 16 (2002), 144–55.

Brown, P. R. L., *Augustine of Hippo: A Biography* (London, 1967).

——'Pelagius and His Supporters: Aims and Environment', *Journal of Theological Studies*, New Series, 19 (1968), 93–114, reprinted *Religion and Society*, 183–207.

——'Aspects of the Christianization of the Roman Aristocracy', *Journal of Roman Studies*, 51 (1961), 1–11; reprinted in his *Religion and Society in the Age of St Augustine* (London, 1972), 161–82.

Duval, Y.-M., 'Pélage est-il le censeur inconnu de l'*Adversus Iovinianum* à Rome en 393? ou Du "Portrait-Robot" de l'hérétique chez S. Jérome', *Revue d'histoire ecclesiastique*, 75 (1980), 530–40.

Evans, R. F., *Pelagius: Enquiries and Reappraisals* (London, 1968).

Herren, M. W., and Brown, S. A., *Christ in Celtic Christianity: Britain and Ireland from the Fifth Century to the Tenth* (Woodbridge, 2002).

Liebeschuetz, [J. H.] W., 'Pelagian Evidence on the Last Period of Roman Britain', *Latomus*, 26 (1967), 436–47.

Löhr, W., *Pelagius—Portrait of a Christian Teacher in Late Antiquity*, The Alexander Souter Memorial Lectures on Late Antiquity 1 (Aberdeen, 2007).
Márkus, G., 'Review Article: Pelagianism and the "Common Celtic Church"', *Innes Review*, 56 (2005), 165–213.
Markus, R. A., 'Pelagianism: Britain and the Continent', *Journal of Ecclesiastical History*, 37 (1986), 191–204.
——'The Legacy of Pelagius: Orthodoxy, Heresy and Conciliation', in R. D. Williams (ed.), *The Making of Orthodoxy* (Cambridge, 1989), 214–34.
Plinval, G. de, *Pélage, ses écrits, sa vie et son reforme* (Lausanne, 1943).
Rees, B., *Pelagius: A Reluctant Heretic* (Woodbridge, 1988).

(c) **Faustus**

i. Texts

Fausti Reiensis praeter Sermones Pseudo-Eusebianos Opera, ed. A. Engelbrecht, CSEL 21 (Vienna, 1891).
Eusebius 'Gallicanus', *Collectio Homiliarum*, ed. F. Glorié, 3 vols., CCSL 101, 101A, 101B (Turnhout, 1970–1).

ii. Secondary

Courcelle, P., 'Nouveaux aspects de la culture lérinienne', *Revue des études latines*, 46 (1968), 379–409.
Engelbrecht, A., *Studien über die Schriften des Bischofes von Reii Faustus* (Vienna, 1889).
Mathisen, R. W., *Ecclesiastical Factionalism and Religious Controversy in Fifth-Century Gaul* (Washington, 1989).
Pricoco, S., *L'isola dei santi: il cenobio di Lerino e le origini del monachesimo gallico* (Rome, 1978).
Prinz, F., *Frühes Mönchtum im Frankenreich*, 2nd edn. (Darmstadt, 1988).
Smith, T. A., *De Gratia: Faustus of Riez's Treatise of Grace and its Place in the History of Theology*, Christianity and Judaism in Antiquity, 4 (Notre Dame, Indiana, 1990).
Stancliffe, C., 'The Thirteen Sermons Attributed to Columbanus and the Question of their Authorship', in M. Lapidge (ed.), *Columbanus: Studies on the Latin Writings*, Studies in Celtic History, 17 (Woodbridge, 1997), 93–202. (Includes important discussions of Faustus's authorship of some Pseudo-Eusebian homilies and of the date of Gildas, *De Excidio*.)
——'Faustus (400 × *c.* 490)', H. C. G. Matthew and B. Harrison (eds.), *Oxford Dictionary of National Biography*, vol. 19 (Oxford, 2004), 161–3.
Wood, I. N., 'Continuity or Calamity: The Constraints of Literary Models', in Drinkwater and Elton (eds.), *Fifth-Century Gaul*, 9–18.

(d) **Gildas**

i. Text

De Excidio Britanniae, ed. and trans. M. Winterbottom, *Gildas: The Ruin of Britain and Other Works* (London and Chichester, 1978). For other editions see above 1(a), Britain, 350–550.

ii. Secondary

Breeze, A., 'Where was Gildas born?', *Northern History*, 45 (2008), 347–50.
Brooks, D. A., 'Gildas's *De Excidio Britanniae*: Its Revolutionary Meaning and Purpose', *Studia Celtica*, 18/19 (1983–84), 1–10.
Burkitt, F. C., 'The Bible of Gildas', *Revue Bénédictine*, 46 (1934), 206–15.

Chadwick, O., 'Gildas and the Monastic Order', *Journal of Theological Studies*, NS 5 (1954), 78–80.

Daniell, C., 'The Geographical Perspective of Gildas', *Britannia*, 25 (1994), 213–16.

Gardner, R., 'Gildas's New Testament Models', *CMCS* 30 (Winter 1995), 1–12.

——'The New Testament Motivation of Gildas and His Friends', *THSC* NS 1 (1995), 1–26.

George, K., *Gildas's* De Excidio Britonum *and the Early British Church* (Woodbridge, 2009).

Herren, M., 'Gildas and Early British Monasticism', in A. Bammersberger and A. Wollmann (eds.), *Britain 400–600*, 65–78.

Higham, N. J., 'Gildas, Roman Walls, and British Dykes', *CMCS* 22 (Winter 1991), 1–14.

Kerlouégan, F., 'Le Latin du *De Excidio Britanniae* de Gildas', in Barley and Hanson (eds.), *Christianity in Britain, 300–700*, 151–76.

——*Le* De Excidio Britanniae *de Gildas. Les destinées de la culture latine dans l'île de Bretagne au VIe siècle* (Paris, 1987).

Lapidge, M., and Dumville, D. (eds.), *Gildas: New Approaches* (Woodbridge, 1984).

McKee, I., 'Gildas: Lessons from History', *CMCS* 51 (Summer, 2006), 1–36.

Miller, M., 'Starting to Write History: Gildas, Bede and Nennius', *Welsh History Review*, 8 (1976–7), 456–65.

Sims-Williams, P., 'Gildas and Vernacular Poetry' in Lapidge and Dumville, *Gildas: New Approaches*, 169–92.

Sharpe, R., 'Gildas as Father of the Church', in Lapidge and Dumville, *Gildas: New Approaches*, 191–205.

Williams, J. E. Caerwyn, 'Gildas, Maelgwn and the Bards', in R. R. Davies et al. (eds.), *Welsh Society and Nationhood* (Cardiff, 1984), 19–34.

Winterbottom, M., 'The Preface of Gildas' *De Excidio*', *THSC*, 1974–75, 277–87.

——'Columbanus and Gildas', *Vigiliae Christianae*, 30 (1976), 310–17.

——'Notes on the Text of Gildas', *Journal of Theological Studies*, 27 (1976), 132–40.

Woolf, A., 'An Interpolation in the Text of Gildas' *De Excidio*', *Peritia*, 16 (2002), 161–67.

Wright, N., 'Gildas's Geographical Perspective: Some Problems', in Lapidge and Dumville (eds.), *Gildas: New Approaches*, 85–105.

——'Gildas's Reading: A Survey', *Sacris Erudiri*, 32 (1991), 121–62.

——*History and Literature in Late Antiquity and the Early Medieval West*, Variorum (Aldershot, 1995) includes the foregoing two papers and others on Gildas.

6. *Rome and the Britons*

(i) ***Texts***

Epistolae Austrasicae, ed. W. Gundlach, in *Epistolae Merowingici et Karolini Aevi*, ed. E. Dümmler, MGH (Berlin, 1892).

The Irish Penitentials, ed. L. Bieler (Dublin, 1963).

Pactus Legis Salicae, ed. K. A. Eckhardt, MGH, Legum Sectio I, iv. 1 (Hanover, 1962); trans. T. J. Rivers, *Laws of the Salian and Ripuarian Franks* (New York, 1986).

Vita Secunda S. Samsonis, ed. F. B. Plaine, 'Vita Antiqua S. Samsonis Dolensis Episcopi', *Analecta Bollandiana*, 6 (1887), 77–150; also printed separately as *La très ancienne vie de S. Samson* (Paris, 1887).

(ii) Secondary

Cameron, K., 'The Meaning and Significance of Old English *walh* in English Place-Names', *Journal of the English Place-Name Society*, 12 (1980), 1–53.

Campbell, E., *Continental and Mediterranean Imports to Atlantic Britain and Ireland, AD 400–800*, CBA Research Report, 157 (York, 2007).

Charles-Edwards, T. M., 'Rome and the Britons, 400–664', in T. M. Charles-Edwards and R. J. W. Evans (eds.), *Wales and the Wider World: Welsh History in an International Context* (Donington, 2010), 9–27.

Dumville, D. N., 'On the Dating of the Early Breton Lawcodes', *Études Celtiques*, 21 (1984), 207–21.

Ewig, E., 'Volkstum und Volksbewusstsein im Frankenreich', *Settimane*, 5 (1958), 614–22, repr. E. Ewig, *Spätantikes und fränkisches Gallien*, 2 vols. (Zürich and Munich, 1976), i. 249–55.

Fasham, P. J., Kelly, R. S., Mason, M. A., and White, R. B., *The Graeanog Ridge: The Evolution of a Farming Landscape and its Settlements in North-West Wales*, Cambrian Archaeological Monographs, 6 (Aberystwyth, 1998).

Faull, M. L., 'The Semantic Development of Old English *wealh*', *Leeds Studies in English*, 8 (1975), 20–44.

Fleuriot, L., 'Un fragment en Latin de très anciennes lois bretonnes armoricaines du VIe siècle', *Annales de Bretagne*, 78 (1971), 601–60.

George, J. W., *Venantius Fortunatus: A Poet in Merovingian Gaul* (Oxford 1992).

Hutchinson, G., 'The Bar-Lug Pottery of Cornwall', *Cornish Archaeology*, 18 (1979), 81–103.

Ó Floinn, R., 'Patrons and Politics: Art, Artefact and Methodology', in M. Redknap, N. Edwards, S. Youngs, A. Lane, and J. K. Knight (eds.), *Pattern and Purpose in Insular Art: Proceedings of the Fourth International Conference on Insular Art* (Oxford, 2001), 1–14.

Padel, O. J., 'Appendix II: Tintagel — An Alternative View', in C. Thomas, *A Provisional List of Imported Pottery in Post-Roman Western Britain and Ireland* (Redruth, 1981).

Tugène, G., *L'Idée de nation chez Bède le Vénérable*, Études Augustiniennes (Paris, 2001).

Ward-Perkins, B., *The Fall of Rome and the End of Civilization* (Oxford, 2005).

White, R., and Barker, P., *Wroxter: Life and Death of a Roman City* (Stroud, 1998).

Wooding, J. M., *Communication and Commerce along the Western Seaways, AD 400–899*, British. Architecture. Rep. International. Series., 654 (Oxford, 1996)

Youngs, S. (ed.), *'The Work of Angels': Masterpieces of Celtic Metalwork, 6th–9th Centuries AD* (London, 1989).

——'Britain, Wales and Ireland: Holding Things Together', in Jankulak and Wooding (eds.), *Ireland and Wales in the Middle Ages*, 80–101.

III. EARLY WELSH SOCIETY

A. Primary Sources

Ancient Laws and Institutes of Wales, ed. A. Owen (London: Record Commission, 1841); this edn. was published in two forms, a single volume folio and a two-volume quarto. The first volume of the quarto contains the three codes distinguished by Owen (Venedotian Code = *Llyfr Iorwerth*, Dimetian Code = *Llyfr Blegywryd*, Gwentian Code = *Llyfr Cyfnerth*); the second volume contains 'Anomalous Laws', namely those which did not fit into any of the codes, and also three of the Latin lawbooks. It should be noted that Book XIII is an eighteenth-century forgery by Iolo Morgannwg. The pagination of the folio and the quarto versions is quite different. References are therefore given by means of the numbering of books, chapters and paragraphs used by Owen: e.g. *VC* III. i. 24 = Venedotian Code, Book III, chap. i, paragraph 24; *ALW* VII. i. 3 = *Ancient Laws and Institutes of Wales*, Book VII, chap. i, paragraph 3 (the 'Anomalous Laws' are Bks. IV–XIV).

The Book of Llandaff: *The Text of the Book of Llan Dâv*, ed. J. Gwenogvryn Evans and J. Rhys (Oxford, 1893; repr. Aberystwyth, 1979).

Collectio Canonum Hibernensis, ed. F. W. H. Wasserschleben, *Die irische Kanonensammlung*, 2nd edn. (Leipzig, 1885).

Corpus Iuris Hiberniae, ed. D. A. Binchy, 6 vols. (Dublin, 1979).

Councils and Ecclesiastical Documents relating to Great Britain and Ireland, ed. A. W. Haddan and W. Stubbs, 3 vols. (Oxford, 1869–78).

Domesday Book, ed. A. Farley and H. Ellis, 4 vols. (London, 1783–1816).

Early Welsh Genealogical Tracts, ed. P. C. Bartrum (Cardiff, 1966).

Die Gesetze der Angelsachsen, ed. F. Liebermann (Halle, vol. i, 1903; ii, part i, 1906; ii, part ii, 1912; iii, 1916).

Gwaith Cynddelw Brydydd Mawr, ed. N. A. Jones and A. Parry Owen, 2 vols., CBT iii–iv (Cardiff, 1995).

The Latin Texts of the Welsh Laws, ed. H. D. Emanuel, History and Law Series, 22 (Cardiff, 1967). Latin Redaction A has been translated by I. F. Fletcher, *Latin Redaction A* (Pamphlets on Welsh Law; Aberystwyth, 1986).

Lichfield Gospels: the marginal memoranda are in *The Text of the Book of Llan Dâv*, ed. J. Gwenogvryn Evans and J. Rhys (Oxford, 1893; repr. Aberystwyth, 1979), pp. xliii–xlviii.

Llyfr Iorwerth, ed. A. Rh. Wiliam (Cardiff, 1960).

Vitae Sanctorum Britanniae et Genealogiae, ed. A. W. Wade-Evans, History and Law Series, ix (Cardiff, 1944).

Welsh Medieval Law, ed. A.W. Wade-Evans (Oxford, 1909) [text of *Llyfr Cyfnerth* mainly from MS *V* supplemented from MS *W*].

B. Secondary Sources

Anderson, M. O., *Kings and Kingship in Early Scotland* (Edinburgh, 1973; rev. edn. 1980).

Andrews, Rh., 'Rhai Agweddau ar Sofraniaeth yng Ngherddi'r Gogynfeirdd', *BBCS* 27 (1976–78), 23–30.

——and Stephenson, D., '*Draig Argoed*: Iorwerth Goch ap Maredudd, *c.* 1110–1171', *CMCS* 52 (Winter 2006), 65–91.

Barker, P. A., and Lawson, J., 'A Pre-Norman Field System at Hen Domen, Montgomery', *Medieval Archaeology*, 15 (1972 for 1971), 58–72.

Barrow, G. W. S. 'Northern English Society in the Twelfth and Thirteenth Centuries', *Northern History*, 4 (1969), 1–28, repr. in his *Scotland and her Neighbours*, 127–53.

——*The Kingdom of the Scots* (London, 1973).

——*Scotland and her Neighbours in the Middle Ages* (London, 1992).

Bezant, J., *Medieval Welsh Settlement and Territory: Archaeological Evidence from a Teifi Valley Landscape*, BAR British Series, 487 (Oxford, 2009).

Binchy, D. A., 'The Linguistic and Historical Value of the Irish Law Tracts', *Proceedings of the British Academy*, 29 (1943), 195–227; repr. in *Celtic Law Papers*, ed. D. Jenkins, 73–107.

——'Some Celtic Legal Terms', *Celtica*, 3 (1956), 221–31.

——'Linguistic and Legal Archaisms in the Celtic Law-Books', *Transactions of the Philological Society*, 1959 (1960), 14–24.

——*Celtic and Anglo-Saxon Kingship* (Oxford, 1970).

Bollard, J. K., 'Sovereignty and the Loathly Lady in English, Welsh and Irish', *Leeds Studies in English*, 17 (1986), 41–59.

Broun, D., *The Charters of Gaelic Scotland and Ireland in the Early and Central Middle Ages*, Quiggin Pamphlets on the Sources of Mediaeval Gaelic History 2 (Cambridge, 1995).

Charles-Edwards, T. M., 'Some Celtic Kinship Terms', *BBCS*, 24 (1970–72), 105–22.

——'The Heir-Apparent in Irish and Welsh Law', *Celtica*, 9 (1971), 180–90.

——'Kinship, Status and the Origins of the Hide', *Past and Present*, 56 (1972), 3–33.

——'Native Political Organization in Roman Britain and the Origins of Middle Welsh *Brenhin*', in M. Mayrhofer et al. (eds.), *Antiquitates Indogermanicae* (Innsbruck, 1974), 35–45.

——'*Nei, Keifn* and *Kefynderw*', *BBCS* 25/iv (1974), 386–88.

——'Boundaries in Irish Law', in *Medieval Settlement: Continuity and Change*, ed. P. H. Sawyer (London, 1976), 83–87.

——'Nau Kynywedi Teithiauc', in *The Welsh Law of Women: Studies presented to Professor Daniel A. Binchy on his Eightieth Birthday, 3 June 1980*, ed. D. Jenkins and M. E. Owen (Cardiff, 1980), 23–39.

——*The Welsh Laws*, Writers of Wales (Cardiff, 1989).

——'Early Medieval Kingships in the British Isles', in S. Bassett (ed.), *The Origins of Anglo-Saxon Kingdoms* (London, 1989), 28–39.

——*Early Irish and Welsh Kinship* (Oxford, 1993).

——'Language and Society among the Insular Celts, 400–1000', in M. Green (ed.), *The Celtic World* (London, 1995), 703–36.

——'Law in the Western Kingdoms between the Fifth and the Seventh Century', in A. Cameron, B. Ward-Perkins, and M. Whitby (eds.), *The Cambridge Ancient History*, xiv, *Late Antiquity: Empire and Successors, A.D. 425–600* (Cambridge, 2000), 260–87.

——'*Gorsedd, Dadl*, and *Llys*: Assemblies and Courts in Medieval Wales', in A. Pantos and S. Semple (eds.), *Assembly Places and Practices in Medieval Europe* (Dublin, 2004), 95–105.

——'Dynastic Succession in Early Medieval Wales', in R. A. Griffiths and P. Schofield (eds.), *Wales and the Welsh in the Early Middle Ages* (Cardiff, 2011), 70–88.

——Owen, M. E., and Walters, D. B. (eds.), *Lawyers and Laymen: Studies in the History of Law presented to Professor Dafydd Jenkins* (Cardiff, 1986).

——Owen, M. E., and Russell, P. (eds.), *The Welsh King and his Court* (Cardiff, 2000).

Coe, J., 'Dating the Boundary Clauses in the Book of Llandaf', *CMCS* 48 (Winter 2004), 1–43.

Davies, J. R., 'The Book of Llandaf: A Twelfth-Century Perspective', *Anglo-Norman Studies*, 21 (1998), 31–46.

——'*Liber Landavensis*: Its Date and the Identity of its Editor', *CMCS* 35 (Summer 1998), 1–11.

——*The Book of Llandaf and the Norman Church in Wales* (Woodbridge, 2003).

Davies, S., *Welsh Military Institutions, 633–1283* (Cardiff, 2004).

Davies, W., '*Unciae*: Land Measurement in the *Liber Landavensis*', *Agricultural History Review*, 21/2 (1973), 111–21.

——'Braint Teilo', *BBCS* 26 (1974–76), 123–37.

——*An Early Welsh Microcosm* (London, 1978).

——'Land and Power in Early Medieval Wales', *Past & Present*, 81 (1978), 3–23.

——*The Llandaff Charters* (Aberystwyth, 1979).

——*Small Worlds: The Village Community in Early Medieval Brittany* (London, 1988)

Davies, W., 'Adding Insult to Injury: Power, Property and Immunities in Early Medieval Wales', in W. Davies and P. Fouracre (eds.), *Property and Power in the Early Middle Ages* (Cambridge, 1995).

Dumville, D. N., 'Kingship, Genealogies and Regnal Lists', in *Early Medieval Kingship*, ed. P. H. Sawyer and I. N. Wood (Leeds, 1977), 72–104; reprinted as no. XV in his *Histories and Pseudo-Histories*.

——'The Ætheling: A Study in Anglo-Saxon Constitutional History', *Anglo-Saxon England*, 8 (1979), 1–33.

Edwards, J. G., *Hywel Dda and the Welsh Lawbooks* (Bangor, 1929); reprinted in *Celtic Law Papers*, ed. D. Jenkins (ed.), *Celtic Law Papers*.

——'The Historical Study of the Welsh Lawbooks', *Transactions of the Royal Historical Society*, 5th Series, 12 (1962), 141–55.

——'Studies in the Welsh Laws since 1928', *Welsh History Review*, Special no. on the Welsh Laws (1963), 1–17.

Edwards, N. (ed.), *Landscape and Settlement in Medieval Wales* (Oxford, 1997)

Faith, R. J., *The English Peasantry and the Growth of Lordship* (London, 1997).

Gregson, N., 'The Multiple-Estate Model: Some Critical Questions', *Journal of Historical Geography*, 11 (1985), 339–51.

Hadley, D. M., 'Multiple Estates and the Origin of the Manorial Structure of the Northern Danelaw', *Journal of Historical Geography*, 22: 1 (1996), 3–15.

Harnack, A., 'Der Brief des britischen Königs Lucius an dem Papst Eleutherus', *Sitzungsberichte der königlich-preussischen Akademie der Wissenschaften* (19 May 1904), fasc. xxvii. 909–16.

Hoz, J. de, 'Did a **brigantīnos* exist in Continental Celtic?', in P. Anreiter and E. Jerem (eds.), *Studia Celtica et Indogermanica* (Budapest, 1999), 145–9.

Huws, D., 'The Making of *Liber Landavensis*', *The National Library of Wales Journal*, 25 (1987–88), 133–60; reprinted in his *Medieval Welsh Manuscripts*, 123–57.

Jenkins, D., 'Legal and Comparative Aspects of the Welsh Laws', *Welsh History Review*, Special no. on the Welsh Laws (1963), 51–9.

——'A Lawyer looks at Welsh Land Law', *Transactions of the Honourable Society of Cymmrodorion*, 1967, (1968), 220–47.

——*Cyfraith Hywel* (Llandysul, 1970).

——(ed.), *Celtic Law Papers introductory to Welsh Medieval Law and Government*, Studies presented to the International Commission for the History of Representative and Parliamentary Institutions, xlii (Brussels, 1973).

——*Hywel Dda a'r Gwŷr Cyfraith*, Inaugural Lecture (Aberystwyth, 1977).

——'The Significance of the Law of Hywel', *Transactions of the Honourable Society of Cymmrodorion* (1977), 54–76.

——'The Medieval Welsh Idea of Law', *Tijdschrift voor Rechtsgeschiedenis*, 49 (1981), 323–48.

——*Agricultural Co-operation in Welsh Medieval Law* (St. Ffagan's, Amgueddfa Genedlaethol Cymru, 1982).

——(trans.), *The Law of Hywel Dda: Law Texts from Medieval Wales* (Llandysul, 1986).

——'From Wales to Weltenburg? Some Considerations on the Origins of the Use of Sacred Books for the Preservation of Secular Records', in N. Brieskorn et al. (eds.), *Vom mittelaterlichen Recht zur neuzeitlichen Rechtswissenschaft: Bedingungen, Wege und Probleme der europäischen Rechtsgeschichte* (Paderborn, 1994), 75–88.

——'*Bardd Teulu* and *Pencerdd*', in Charles-Edwards et al. (eds.), *The Welsh King and his Court*, 142–66.

——'A Second Look at Welsh Land Law', *THSC, 2001* New Series, 8 (2002), 13–93.

——and Owen, M. E. (eds.), *The Welsh Law of Women: Studies presented to Professor Daniel A. Binchy on his Eightieth Birthday* (Cardiff, 1980).

————'The Welsh Marginalia in the Lichfield Gospels, Part I', *CMCS* 5 (Summer 1983), 37–66; 'Part II', 7 (Summer 1984), 91–120.

Jolliffe, J. E. A., 'Northumbrian Institutions', *English Hist. Rev.*, 41 (1926), 1–42.

Jones, E. D., 'The Book of Llandaff', *National Library of Wales Journal*, 4 (1945–6), 123–57.

Jones, G. R. J., 'Medieval Settlement in Anglesey', *Transactions of the Anglesey Antiquarian Society* (1955), 27–96.

——'The Tribal System in Wales: A Re-assessment in the Light of Settlement Studies', *Welsh History Review*, 1 (1960–63), 111–32.

——'The Distribution of Bond Settlements in North-West Wales', *Welsh History Review*, 2 (1964), 19–36.

——'The Llanynys Quillets: A Measure of Landscape Transformation in North Wales', *Denbighshire Historical Society Transactions*, 13 (1964), 133–58.

——'Post-Roman Wales', in *The Agrarian History of England and Wales*, i, part ii, A.D. 43–1042, ed. H. P. R. Finberg (Cambridge, 1972), 281–382.

——'Early Territorial Organization in Gwynedd and Elmet', *Northern History*, 10 (1975), 3–27.

——'Multiple Estates and Early Settlement', in Sawyer (ed.), *Medieval Settlement*, 15–40.

——'Celts, Saxons and Scandinavians', in *An Historical Geography of England and Wales*, ed. R. A. Dodgshon and R. A. Butlin (London, 1978), 57–79.

——'Early Customary Tenures in Wales and Open-Field Agriculture', in *The Origins of Open-Field Agriculture*, ed. T. Rowley (London, 1981), 221–5.

——'Continuity despite Calamity: The Heritage of Celtic Territorial Organization in England', *Journal of Celtic Studies*, 3 (1981/2), 1–30.

——'Nucleal Settlement and its Tenurial Relationships', in B. K. Roberts and R. E. Glasscock (eds.), *Villages, Fields and Frontiers*, BAR International Series, 185 (Oxford, 1983), 153–70.

——'The Ornaments of a Kindred in Medieval Gwynedd', *Studia Celtica*, 18/19 (1983–84), 135–47.

——'Multiple Estates Perceived', *Journal of Historical Geography*, 11 (1985), 352–63 [reply to N. Gregson, q.v.].

——'The Portrayal of Land Settlement', in J. C. Holt (ed.), *Domesday Studies: Papers read at the Novocentenary Conference of the Royal Historical Society and the British Institute of Geographers, Winchester 1986* (Woodbridge, 1987), 183–200.

——'The Models for Organization in *Llyfr Iorwerth* and *Llyfr Cyfnerth*', *EBCS* 39 (1992), 95–118.

——'"Tir Telych", the Gwestfâu of Cynwyl Gaeo and Cwmwd Caeo', *Studia Celtica*, 28 (1994), 81–95.

——'The *Gwely* as a Tenurial Institution', *Studia Celtica*, 30 (1996), 167–88.

Jones, M. L., *Society and Settlement in Wales and the Marches, 500 BC–AD 1100*, BAR British Series, 121 (Oxford, 1984).

Jones, Rh. A., 'Problems with Medieval Welsh Local Administration—the Case of the Maenor and the Maenol', *Journal of Historical Geography*, 24: 2 (1998), 135–46.

Kelly, F., *A Guide to Early Irish Law*, Early Irish Law Series, 3 (Dublin, 1988).

——*Early Irish Farming* (Dublin, 1998).

Kerlouégan, F., 'Essai sur la mise en nourriture et l'éducation dans les pays celtiques', *Études Celtiques*, 12 (1968–69), 101–46.

Macmullen, R., 'Late Roman Slavery', *Historia*, 36 (1987), 359–82 (see also Samson).

Mac Neill, E., 'Mocu, Maccu', *Ériu*, 3 (1907), 42–9.

——'Early Irish Population-Groups: Their Nomenclature, Classification and Chronology', *Proceedings of the Royal Irish Academy*, section C, 29 (1911), 59–114.

Maitland, F. W., 'The Laws of Wales, the Kindred and the Blood Feud', *Collected Papers*, ed. H. A. L. Fisher (Cambridge, 1911), i. 202–29.

——'The Tribal System in Wales', *Collected Papers*, iii. 1–10.

Maund, K. L., 'Fact and Narrative Fiction in the Llandaff Charters', *Studia Celtica*, 31 (1997), 173–93.

Musson, C. R., *Wales from the Air: Patterns of Past and Present* (Aberystwyth, 1994).

Mytum, H., 'Castell Henllys', *Archaeology in Wales*, 38 (1999), 124.

O'Brien, E., 'Pagan and Christian Burial in Ireland during the First Millennium AD: Continuity and Change', in N. Edwards and A. Lane (eds.), *The Early Church in Wales and the West*, Oxbow Monograph, 16 (Oxford, 1992), 130–62.

Owen, M. E., 'Y Cyfreithiau: Natur y Testunau' and 'Y Cyfreithiau: Ansawdd y Rhyddiaith', in *Y Traddodiad Rhyddiaith yn yr Oesau Canol*, ed. G. Bowen (Llandysul, 1974), 196–244.

Padel, O. J., *Slavery in Saxon Cornwall: The Bodmin Manumissions*, Kathleen Hughes Memorial Lectures, 7 (Cambridge, 2009).

Parkes, P., 'Fostering Fealty: A Comparative Study of Tributary Allegiances of Adoptive Kinship', *Comparative Studies in Society and History*, 45/4 (2003), 741–82.

——'Celtic Fosterage', *Comparative Studies in Society and History*, 48/2 (2006), 359–94.

Pierce, T. Jones, *Medieval Welsh Society*, ed. J. Beverley Smith (Cardiff, 1972).

Pryce, H., 'Early Irish Canons and Medieval Welsh Law', *Peritia*, 5 (1986), 107–27.

——'The Prologues to the Welsh Lawbooks', *BBCS* 33 (1986), 151–87.

——'The Context and Purpose of the Earliest Welsh Lawbooks', *Cambrian Medieval Celtic Studies*, 39 (Summer 2000), 39–63.

——'Lawbooks and Literacy in Medieval Wales', *Speculum*, 75 (2000), 29–68.

Rees, W., 'Survivals of Ancient Celtic Custom in Medieval England', in J. R. R. Tolkien et al., *Angles and Britons: O'Donnell Lectures* (Cardiff, 1963), 148–68.

Samson, R., 'Slavery: The Roman Legacy', in J. Drinkwater and H. Elton (eds.), *Fifth-Century Gaul*, 218–27.

Sawyer, P. H. (ed.), *Medieval Settlement: Continuity and Change* (London, 1976).

Seebohm, F., *The Tribal System in Wales*, 2nd edn. (London, 1904).

Sharpe, R., 'The Naming of Bishop Ithamar', *English Historical Review*, 117 (2002), 889–94.

Sims-Williams, P. P., Review of W. Davies, *The Llandaff Charters*, *Journal of Ecclesiastical History*, 23 (1982), 124–9.

——'Edward IV's Confirmation Charter for Clynnog Fawr' in C. Richmond and I. Harvey (eds.), *Recognitions: Essays presented to Edmund Fryde* (Aberystwyth, 1996), 229–41.

Smith, J. B., 'Dynastic Succession in Medieval Wales', *BBCS* 33 (1986), 199–232.

Stacey, R. Chapman, *The Road to Judgment: From Custom to Court in Medieval Ireland and Wales* (Philadelphia, 1994).

——'King, Queen and *Edling* in the Laws of Court', in Charles-Edwards et al. (eds.), *The Welsh King and his Court*, 29–62.

Stevens, C. E., 'A Possible Conflict of Laws in Roman Britain', *Journal of Roman Studies*, 37 (1947), 132–4.

——'The Social and Economic Aspects of Rural Settlement', in C. Thomas (ed.), *Rural Settlement in Roman Britain* (London, 1966), 108–28.
Walters, D. W., *The Comparative Legal Method: Marriage, Divorce and the Spouses' Property Rights in Early Medieval European Law and Cyfraith Hywel* (Pamphlets in Welsh Law; Aberystwyth, 1982).

IV. THE BRITONS AND THEIR NEIGHBOURS, 550–1064

A. Primary Sources

Achau Brenhinoedd a Thywysogion Cymru, ed. P. C. Bartrum, *BBCS* 19 (1960–62), 201–24 and in *EWGT*.

The Anglo-Saxon Chronicle:
References under the form ASC A etc. are to annals in the translation by D. Whitelock in *EHD* i and S. I. Tucker in *EHD* ii with the chronology there indicated. Editions of the separate versions include:
The Anglo-Saxon Chronicle: A Collaborative Edition, iv, *MS B*, ed. S. Taylor (Cambridge, 1983).
The Anglo-Saxon Chronicle: A Collaborative Edition, iii, *MS A*, ed. J. Bately (Cambridge, 1986).
The Anglo-Saxon Chronicle: A Collaborative Edition, vi, *MS D*, ed. G. P. Cubbin (Cambridge, 1996).
The Anglo-Saxon Chronicle: A Collaborative Edition, v, *MS C*, ed. Katherine O'Brien O'Keeffe (Cambridge, 2001).

Anderson, A. O., *Scottish History from English Chronicles* (London, 1908)
——*Early Sources of Scottish History, A.D. 500 to 1286*, 2 vols. (Edinburgh, 1922; repr. Stamford, 1990).
Annales Cambriae [A Version], ed. E. Phillimore, 'The *Annales Cambriae* and the Old Welsh Genealogies from Harleian MS. 3859', *Y Cymmrodor*, 9 (1888), 141–83.
Annales Cambriae, ed. J. Williams ab Ithel, Rolls Series. (London, 1860).
Annales Cambriae, A.D. 682–954: Texts A–C in Parallel, ed. and trans. D. N. Dumville (Cambridge, 2002).
The Annals of Ulster (to A.D. 1131), ed. S. Mac Airt and G. Mac Niocaill. Part I, Text and Translation (Dublin, 1983).
Armes Prydein, ed. I. Williams (Cardiff, 1955); English version with translation by R. Bromwich (Dublin, 1972); new text and translation by G. Isaac, '"Armes Prydain Fawr" and St David', in Evans and Wooding (eds.), *St David of Wales*, 170–81.
Asser, *De Rebus Gestis Ælfredi*, ed. W. H. Stevenson, *Asser's Life of King Alfred* (Oxford, 1904; repr. with an article on recent work by D. Whitelock, 1959); trans. S. Keynes and M. Lapidge, *Alfred the Great: Asser's Life of King Alfred and Other Contemporary Sources*, Penguin Classics (Harmondsworth, 1983).
The Battle of Brunanburh, ed. A. Campbell (London, 1938).
Bede, *Vita S. Cuthberti Prosaica*, ed. and trans. B. Colgrave, *Two Lives of Saint Cuthbert: A Life by an Anonymous Monk of Lindisfarne and Bede's Prose Life* (Cambridge, 1940).

Bodmin Gospels: the manumissions are ed. M. Förster, 'Die Freilassingsurkunden des Bodmin-Evangeliars', in N. Bøgholm et al. (eds.), *A Grammatical Miscellany offered to Otto Jespersen* (Copenhagen and London, 1930), 77–99.

Brut y Tywysogyon or The Chronicle of the Princes, Peniarth MS. 20 Version, trans. T. Jones (Cardiff, 1952). References simply to *Brut* are to this vol. under the year.

Editions of the Welsh texts are:

Brut y Tywysogyon, Peniarth MS. 20, ed. T. Jones (Cardiff, 1941).

Brut y Tywysogyon or The Chronicle of the Princes, Red Book of Hergest Version, ed. and trans. T. Jones (Cardiff, 1955).

Brenhinedd y Saeson or The Kings of the Saxons, ed. and trans. T. Jones (Cardiff, 1971).

Canu Aneirin, see *Gododdin*.

'Canu Cadwallon ap Cadfan', ed. R. G. Gruffydd in R. Bromwich and R. Brinley Jones (eds.), *Astudiaethau ar yr Hengerdd* (Cardiff, 1978), 25–43.

Canu Llywarch Hen, ed. I. Williams, 2nd edn. (Cardiff, 1953).

Canu Taliesin, ed. I. Williams (Cardiff, 1960); English version by J. Caerwyn Williams, *The Poetry of Taliesin* (Dublin, 1968). Translated M. Pennar, *Taliesin Poems* (Felinfach, 1988).

The Chronicle of John of Worcester, ii, *The Annals from 450 to 1066*, ed. R. R. Darlington and P. McGurk, trans. J. Bray and P. McGurk, Oxford Medieval Texts (Oxford, 1995).

Cyfoesi Myrddin a Gwenddydd ei Chwaer, ed. M. B. Jenkins, 'Aspects of the Welsh Prophetic Tradition in the Middle Ages', unpublished Ph.D. thesis, University of Cambridge (1990), 33–90.

Domesday Book, ed. A. Farley and H. Ellis, 4 vols. (London, 1783–1816).

Echrys Ynys, ed. R. G. Gruffydd, 'A Welsh "Dark Age" Court Poem', in J. Carey et al. (eds.), *Ildánach, Ildírech*, 39–48.

Edmyg Dinbych, ed. I. Williams, *BWP* 155–72; a text in modernized orthography is given by R. G. Gruffydd, *'Edmyg Dinbych': Cerdd Lys Gynnar o Ddyfed* (Aberystwyth, 2002).

Die Gesetze der Angelsachsen, ed. F. Liebermann (Halle, vol. i, 1903; ii, part i, 1906; ii, part ii, 1912; iii, 1916).

Y Gododdin: Llyfr Aneirin: A Facsimile/Llyfr Aneirin: Ffacsimile, ed. D. Huws ([Cardiff and Aberystwyth], 1989), includes both a facsimile and a transcript; ed. I. Williams, *Canu Aneirin* (Cardiff, 1938), the foundation of subsequent scholarship; an English translation of the poem, together with valuable further material, is provided by K. H. Jackson, *The Gododdin* (Edinburgh, 1969). A modernized text and a translation is given by A. O. H. Jarman, *Aneirin: The Gododdin* (Llandysul, 1988). An edition which seeks to restore the text to something like its original form is by J. T. Koch, *The Gododdin of Aneirin: Text and Context from Dark-Age North Britain* (Cardiff, 1997).

Historia Brittonum:

(a) ed. Th. Mommsen, *Chronica Minora Saec. IV. V. VI. VII.*, iii, MGH AA 13 (Berlin, 1898);

(b) ed. E. Faral, *La Légende arthurienne*, 3 (Paris, 1929), 4–62 (Chartres, as far as it goes, in parallel with Harleian). Faral's Harleian text is reprinted with a translation in *Nennius, British History, and the Welsh Annals*, ed. and trans. J. Morris (London, 1980).

(c) *The Historia Brittonum*, iii, *The 'Vatican Recension'*, ed. D. N. Dumville (Cambridge, 1985). [A tenth-century English version.]

Historia de Sancto Cuthberto, ed. T. Johnson-Smith, Anglo-Saxon Texts 3 (Cambridge, 2002).

Historia Gruffud vab Kenan, ed. D. S. Evans (Cardiff, 1977) [see also *Vita Griffini filii Conani* below].

Jocelin of Furness, *Vita S. Kentegerni*, ed. and trans. A. P. Forbes, *Lives of S. Ninian and S. Kentigern*, The Historians of Scotland, v (Edinburgh, 1874), 159–242.

Llyfr Aneirin: A Facsimile/Llyfr Aneirin: Ffacsimile, ed. D. Huws (Cardiff and Aberystwyth, 1989).

Marwnad Cynddylan, ed. R. G. Gruffydd, in R. G. Gruffydd (ed.), *Bardos*, 10–28.

Miracula Nynie Episcopi, ed. K. Strecker, MGH Poetae Latini Medii Aevi, iv. 943–61; trans. W. MacQueen in J. MacQueen, *St Nynia*, new edn. (Edinburgh, 2005), 88–101.

Nennius, see *Historia Brittonum.*

The Old English Boethius: An Edition of the Old English Version of Boethius's De Consolatione Philosophiae, ed. M. Godden and S. Irvine, 2 vols. (Oxford, 2009).

Roger of Wendover, *Flores Historiarum*, ed. H. O. Coxe (London, 1841).

The Scottish Chronicle/The Chronicle of the Kings of Alba, ed. M. O. Anderson, *Kings and Kingship in Early Scotland* (Edinburgh, 1973), 249–53; ed. and trans. B. T. Hudson, 'The Scottish Chronicle', *Scottish Historical Review*, 77 (1998), 129–61.

Simeon of Durham, *Historia Regum* ed. T. Arnold, *Symeonis Monachi Opera Omnia*, 2 vols., Rolls Series (London, 1885), ii. 2–283; the early annals are extracted and translated by D. Whitelock, *EHD* i, no. 3.

Vita Griffini Filii Conani: The Medieval Latin Life of Gruffudd ap Cynan, ed. and trans. P. Russell (Cardiff, 2005).

Vita S. Cuthberti Auctore Anonymo, ed. and trans. B. Colgrave, *Two Lives of Saint Cuthbert*, 60–139.

Vita S. Kentegerni (Anonymous), ed. and trans. A. P. Forbes, *Lives of S. Ninian and S. Kentigern*, The Historians of Scotland, v (Edinburgh, 1874), 243–52.

B. Discussions of Primary Sources

Baxter, S., 'MS C of the Anglo-Saxon Chronicle and the Politics of Mid-Eleventh-Century England', *EHR* 122 (2007), 1189–227.

Besly, E. 'Recent Coin Hoards from Wales, 1985–1992', *British Numismatic Journal*, 63 (1993), 84–90.

Blackburn, M., 'Currency under the Vikings. Part 3. Ireland, Wales, Isle of Man and Scotland in the Ninth and Tenth Centuries', *British Numismatic Journal*, 77 (2007), 119–49.

Blunt, C. E., 'The Coinage of Athelstan, 924–39: A Survey', *British Numismatic Journal*, 42 (1973), 35–160.

——'The Cabinet of the Marquess of Ailesbury and the Penny of Hywel Dda', *British Numismatic Journal*, 52 (1982), 117–22.

Charles-Edwards, T. M., 'The Authenticity of the Gododdin: An Historian's View', in *Astudiaethau ar yr Hengerdd/Studies in Old Welsh Poetry*, ed. R. Bromwich and R. Brinley Jones (Cardiff, 1978), 44–71.

Dumville, D. N., 'The Corpus Christi "Nennius"', *BBCS* 25 (1972–74) 369–80; reprinted as no. IX in his *Histories and Pseudo-Histories of the Insular Middle Ages* (Aldershot, 1990).

——'Some Aspects of the Chronology of the *Historia Brittonum*', *BBCS* 25 (1972–74), 439–45; reprinted as no. IV in his *Histories and Pseudo-Histories.*

——'Nennius and the *Historia Brittonum*', *Studia Celtica*, 10/11 (1975–76), 78–95; reprinted as no. X in his *Histories and Pseudo-Histories.*

Dumville, D. N., 'The Textual History of "Lebor Bretnach": A Preliminary Study', *Éigse*, 16 (1975–76), 255–73.

——'The Anglian Collection of Royal Genealogies and Regnal Lists', *Anglo-Saxon England*, 5 (1976), 23–50; reprinted as no. V in his *Histories and Pseudo-Histories*.

——'On the North British Section of the *Historia Brittonum*', *Welsh History Review*, 8 (1976–77), 345–54; reprinted as no. II in his *Histories and Pseudo-Histories*.

——'Palaeographical Considerations in the Dating of Early Welsh Verse', *BBCS* 27 (1976–78), 246–51.

——'Celtic-Latin Texts in Northern England, *c*.1150–*c*.1250', *Celtica*, 12 (1977), 19–49; reprinted as no. XI in his *Histories and Pseudo-Histories*.

——'Kingship, Genealogies and Regnal Lists', in *Early Medieval Kingship*, ed. P. H. Sawyer and I. N. Wood (Leeds, 1977), 72–104; reprinted as no. XV in his *Histories and Pseudo-Histories*.

——'The "Six" Sons of Rhodri Mawr: A Problem in Asser's *Life of King Alfred*', *CMCS* 4 (Winter 1982), 5–18.

——'Brittany and "Armes Prydein Vawr"', *Études Celtiques*, 20 (1983), 145–59.

——'The Historical Value of the *Historia Brittonum*', *Arthurian Literature*, 6, ed. R. Barber (Cambridge, 1986), 1–26.

——'Early Welsh Poetry: Problems of Historicity', in B. F. Roberts (ed.), *Early Welsh Poetry: Studies in the Book of Aneirin* (Aberystwyth, 1988), 1–16.

——'*Historia Brittonum*: An Insular History from the Carolingian Age', in A. Scharer and G. Scheibelreiter (eds.), *Historiographie im frühen Mittelalter* (Munich, 1994), 406–34.

Foley, W. T., and Higham, N., 'Bede on the Britons', *Early Medieval Europe*, 17: 2 (2009), 154–85.

Foster, I. Ll., 'Rhai Sylwadau ar yr Hengerdd', *Ysgrifau Beirniadol*, 5 (1970), 15–29.

Godden, M., 'Alfred, Asser and Boethius', in K. O'Brien O'Keeffe and A. Orchard (eds.), *Latin Learning and English Lore: Studies in Anglo-Saxon Literature for Michael Lapidge* (Toronto, 2008), i. 326–48.

Hughes, K., 'The Welsh Latin Chronicles: *Annales Cambriae* and Related Texts', *Proceedings of the British Academy*, 59 (1973), 233–58. Reprinted in her *Celtic Britain in the Early Middle Ages*, 67–85.

——*Celtic Britain in the Early Middle Ages: Studies in Scottish and Welsh Sources*, ed. D. N. Dumville, Studies in Celtic History, 2 (Woodbridge, 1980).

Jackson, K. H., 'The Sources for the Life of St Kentigern', in N. K. Chadwick (ed.), *Studies in the Early British Church* (Cambridge, 1958), 273–357.

——'On the Northern British Section in Nennius', in N. K. Chadwick (ed.), *Celt and Saxon: Studies in the Early British Border* (Cambridge, 1963), 20–62.

Kerlouégan, F., 'Grégoire le Grand et les pays celtiques', in J. Fontaine (ed.), *Grégoire le Grand* (Paris, 1986), 589–96.

Kershaw, P., 'Illness, Power and Prayer in Asser's *Life of King Alfred*', *Early Medieval Europe*, 10 (2001), 201–24.

Keynes, S. D., 'On the Authenticity of Asser's *Life of King Alfred*', *Journal of Ecclesiastical History*, 47 (1996), 529–51.

Kirby, D. P., 'Asser and his Life of King Alfred', *Studia Celtica*, 6 (1971), 12–35.

Koch, J. T., 'The Cynfeirdd Poetry and the Language of the Sixth Century', in B. F. Roberts, (ed.), *Early Welsh Poetry*, 17–41.

Lapidge, M., 'Some Latin Poems as Evidence for the Reign of Athelstan', *Anglo-Saxon England*, 9 (1981), 61–98.

——'Byrhtferth of Ramsey and the Early Sections of the *Historia Regum* attributed to Symeon of Durham', *Anglo-Saxon England*, 10 (1982), 97–122.

——'Asser's Reading', in Reuter (ed.), *Alfred the Great*, 27–47.

Liebermann, F., 'Nennius: The Author of the *Historia Brittonum*', in A. G. Little and F. M. Powicke (eds.), *Essays in Medieval History presented to Thomas F. Tout* (Manchester, 1925), 25–44.

Miller, M., 'Historicity and the Pedigrees of the Northcountrymen', *BBCS* 26 (1974–75), 255–80.

——'Date-Guessing and Pedigrees', *SC* 10/11 (1975/6), 96–109.

——'Starting to Write History: Gildas, Bede and Nennius', *WHR* 8 (1976–77), 456–65.

——'The Foundation Legend of Gwynedd in the Latin Texts', *BBCS* 27 (1976–78), 515–32.

——'Date-Guessing and Dyfed', *Studia Celtica*, 12/13 (1977–78), 33–61.

——'Consular Years in the *Historia Brittonum*', *BBCS* 29 (1980–82), 17–34.

——'Final Stages in the Construction of the Harleian *Annales Cambriae*: The Evidence of the Framework', *Journal of Celtic Studies*, 4 (2004), 205–11.

Morris-Jones, J., 'Taliesin', *Y Cymmrodor*, 28 (1918).

Roberts, B. F. (ed.), *Early Welsh Poetry: Studies in the Book of Aneirin* (Aberystwyth, 1988).

Rowland, J., *Early Welsh Saga Poetry: A Study and Edition of the Englynion* (Cambridge, 1990).

——'Warfare and Horses in the *Gododdin* and the Problem of Catraeth', *CMCS* 30 (Winter 1995), 13–40.

Scharer, A., und Scheibelreiter, G. (eds.), *Historiographie im frühen Mittelalter* (Vienna, 1994).

Thomson, R. L., 'British Latin and English History: Nennius and Asser', in R. L. Thomson (ed.), *A Medieval Miscellany in honour of John Le Patourel*, Leeds Philosophical and Literary Society, Proceedings 18: 1 (1982), 38–53.

Thurneysen, R., Review of H. Zimmer, *Nennius Vindicatus*, *Zeitschrift für deutsche Philologie*, 28 (1896), 80–113.

——'Zu Nemnius (Nennius)', *ZCP* 20 (1936), 185–91.

Tolstoy, N., 'When and where was *Armes Prydein* composed?', *Studia Celtica*, 42 (2008), 142–49.

Zimmer, H., *Nennius Vindicatus: Über Enstehung, Geschichte und Quellen der Historia Brittonum* (Berlin, 1893)

C. Secondary Sources

1. Pre-Viking

Alcock, L., 'Gwŷr y Gogledd: An Archaeological Appraisal', *Archaeologia Cambrensis* 132 (1983), 1–18.

——*Economy, Society and Warfare among the Britons and Saxons* (Cardiff, 1987).

Alexander, L. M., 'The Legal Status of Native Britons in Late Seventh-Century Wessex as reflected by the Laws of Ine', *Haskins Society Journal*, 7 (1995), 31–8.

Anderson, M. O., *Kings and Kingship in Early Scotland* (Edinburgh, 1973; rev. edn. 1980).

Bassett, S. (ed.), *The Origins of Anglo-Saxon Kingdoms* (London, 1989).

Baxter, S., Karkov, C. E., Nelson, J. E, and Pelteret, D. E. (eds.), *Early Medieval Studies in Memory of Patrick Wormald* (Farnham, 2009).

Blair, P. Hunter, *Anglo-Saxon Northumbria*, ed. M. Lapidge and P. Hunter Blair (London, 1984).

Breeze, A., 'Seventh-Century Northumbria and a Poem to Cadwallon', *Northern History*, 38 (2001), 145–52.

Brooke, D., 'The Northumbrian Settlements in Galloway and Carrick: An Historical Assessment', *Proceedings of the Society of Antiquaries of Scotland*, 121 (1991), 295–327.

——*Wild Men and Holy Places: St. Ninian, Whithorn and the Medieval Realm of Galloway* (Edinburgh, 1994).

Brooks, N. P., *Bede and the English*, Jarrow Lecture 1999 (Jarrow, 2000).

——'Canterbury, Rome and the Construction of English Identity', in J. M. H. Smith (ed.), *Early Medieval Rome and the Christian West: Essays in Honour of Donald A. Bullough* (Leiden, 2000), 221–46.

——'The English Origin Myth', in his *Anglo-Saxon Myths: State and Church* (London, 2000), 79–89.

Cessford, C., 'Torcs in Early Historic Scotland', *Oxford Journal of Archaeology*, 14 (1995), 229–42.

——'Pictish Silver and the Gododdin Poem', *Pictish Arts Society Journal*, 9 (Spring 1996), 30–1.

——'Yorkshire and *The Gododdin* Poem', *Yorkshire Archaeological Journal*, 68 (1996), 241–3.

Chadwick, N. K. (ed.), *Studies in Early British History* (Cambridge, 1954; rev. imp. 1959).

——(ed.), *Studies in the Early British Church* (Cambridge, 1958).

——(ed.), *Celt and Saxon: Studies in the Early British Border* (Cambridge, 1963).

Charles-Edwards, T. M., 'Bede, the Irish and the Britons', *Celtica*, 15 (1983), 42–52.

——'Early Medieval Kingships in the British Isles', in S. Bassett (ed.), *The Origins of Anglo-Saxon Kingdoms* (London, 1989), 28–39.

——'The Continuation of Bede, *s.a.* 750: High-Kings, Kings of Tara and "Bretwaldas"', in A. P. Smyth (ed.), *Senchas: Studies in Early and Medieval Irish Archaeology, History and Literature in Honour of Francis J. Byrne* (Dublin: Four Courts Press: 1999), 137–45.

Clemoes, P. (ed.), *The Anglo-Saxons: Studies in Some Aspects of their History and Culture presented to Bruce Dickins* (London, 1959).

Crawford, B. E. (ed.), *Scotland in Dark Age Europe*, (St Andrews, 1994).

——(ed.), *Scotland in Dark Age Britain* (St Andrews, 1996).

——(ed.), *Conversion and Christianity in the North Sea World* (St Andrews, 1998).

Dornier, A. (ed.), *Mercian Studies* (Leicester, 1977).

Dumville, D. N., 'The Ætheling: A Study in Anglo-Saxon Constitutional History', *Anglo-Saxon England*, 8 (1979), 1–33.

——'The Origins of Northumbria: Some Aspects of the British Background', in S. Bassett (ed.), *The Origins of Anglo-Saxon Kingdoms* (Leicester, 1989), 213–22.

——et al., *Saint Patrick, A.D. 493–1993* (Woodbridge, 1993).

Edwards, N., 'Rethinking the Pillar of Eliseg', *Antiquaries Journal*, 89 (2009), 1–35.

Fanning, S., 'Bede, *Imperium* and the Bretwaldas', *Speculum*, 66 (1991), 1–26.

Faull, M. L., 'The Semantic Development of Old English *wealh*', *Leeds Studies in English*, 8 (1975), 20–44.

——'British Survival in Anglo-Saxon Northumbria', in L. Laing (ed.), *Studies in Celtic Survival*, BAR 37 (Oxford, 1977), 1–55.

——'Place-Names and the Kingdom of Elmet', *Nomina*, 4 (1980), 21–3.

Field, P. J. C., 'Nennius and his History', *Studia Celtica*, 30 (1996), 159–65.

Finberg, H. P. R., *The Early Charters of Devon and Cornwall*, Dept. of English Local History, Occasional Papers, no. 8 (Leicester, 1953). Supplement in Hoskins, *The Westwards Expansion of Wessex*, 23–35.

——*The Early Charters of the West Midlands* (Leicester, 1961).
——*Lucerna: Studies in Some Problems in the Early History of England* (London, 1964).
Foster, I. Ll., 'Wales and North Britain', *Archaeologia Cambrensis*, 118 (1959), 1–16.
Fox, C., *Offa's Dyke* (London, 1955).
——and Phillips, D. W., 'Offa's Dyke: A Field Survey (Fifth Report)', *Arch. Camb.*, 85 (1930), 1–73.
Gameson, R. G. (ed.), *St Augustine and the Conversion of England* (Stroud, 1999).
Gelling, M., *The West Midlands in the Early Middle Ages* (Leicester, 1992).
Griffiths, D., 'Sand-dunes and Stray Finds: Evidence for Pre-Viking Trade?', in Graham-Campbell and Ryan (eds.), *Anglo-Saxon/Irish Relations before the Vikings* 265–80.
Grimmer, M., 'Britons in Early Wessex: The Evidence of the Law Code of Ine', in Higham, (ed.), *The Britons in Anglo-Saxon England*, 102–14.
Gruffydd, R. G., 'Canu Cadwallon ap Cadfan', in Bromwich and Jones (eds.), *Astudiaethau ar yr Hengerdd*, 25–43.
——'Marwnad Cynddylan', in R. G. Gruffydd (ed.), *Bardos*, 10–28.
——'Where was *Rhaeadr Derwennydd* (*Canu Aneirin*, line 1114)?', in A. T. E. Matonis and D. F. Melia (eds.), *Celtic Language, Celtic Culture: A Festschrift for Eric P. Hamp* (Van Nuys, Cal., 1990), 261–6.
——'In Search of Elmet', *Studia Celtica*, 28 (1994), 63–79.
——'The Strathcarron Interpolation (*Canu Aneirin*, Lines 966–77)', *Scottish Gaelic Studies*, 17 (1996), 172–8.
Hawkes, J., and Mills, S. (eds.), *Northumbria's Golden Age* (Stroud, 1999).
Higham, N. J., 'Medieval Overkingship in Wales: The Earliest Evidence', *WHR*, 16 (1992), 145–59.
——*Rome, Britain and the Anglo-Saxons* (London, 1992).
——*The Kingdom of Northumbria AD 350–1100* (Stroud, 1993).
——*An English Empire: Bede and the Early Anglo-Saxon Kings* (Manchester, 1995).
——*The Convert Kings: Power and Religious Affiliation in Early Anglo-Saxon England* (Manchester, 1997).
——'Britons in Northern England in the Early Middle Ages: Through a Glass Darkly', *Northern History*, 38 (2001), 5–25.
——(ed.), *The Britons in Anglo-Saxon England* (Woodbridge, 2007).
Hill, D., 'The Interrelation of Offa's and Wat's Dykes', *Antiquity*, 48 (1974), 309–12.
——'Offa's and Wat's Dykes—Some Exploratory Work on the Frontier between Celt and Saxon', in *Anglo-Saxon Settlement and Landscape*, ed. T. Rowley, BAR 6 (Oxford, 1974), 102–7.
——'Offa's and Wat's Dykes: Some Aspects of Recent Work', *Transactions of the Lancashire and Cheshire Antiquarian Society*, 79 (1977), 21–33.
——'Offa's and Wat's Dyke', in J. Manley, S. Grenter, and F. Gale (eds.), *The Archaeology of Clwyd* (Mold, 1991), 142–56.
——'Offa's Dyke: Pattern and Purpose', *Antiquaries' Journal*, 80 (2000), 195–206.
——'Mercians: The Dwellers on the Boundary', in M. P. Brown and C. A. Farr (eds.), *Mercia: An Anglo-Saxon Kingdom in Europe*, 173–82.
——and Worthington, M., *Offa's Dyke: History and Guide* (Stroud, 2003).
————(eds.), *Æthelbald and Offa*, BAR British Series, 383 (Oxford, 2005).
Hooke, D., *Anglo-Saxon Territorial Organization: The Western Marches of Mercia*, University of Birmingham Department of Geography, Occasional Publication, 22 (Birmingham, 1986).

Hoskins, W. G., *The Westwards Expansion of Wessex*, Dept. of English Local History, Occasional Papers, no. 13 (Leicester, 1960).

Jackson, K. H., 'Nennius and the Twenty-Eight Cities of Britain', *Antiquity*, 12 (1938), 44–55.

——'The Britons of Southern Scotland', *Antiquity*, 29 (1955), 77–88.

——'Edinburgh and the Anglian Occupation of Lothian', in P. Clemoes (ed.), *The Anglo-Saxons: Studies in Some Aspects of their History and Culture presented to Bruce Dickins* (London, 1959), 35–47.

——'Angles and Britons in Northumbria and Cumbria', in J. R. R. Tolkien et al., *Angles and Britons* (Cardiff, 1963), 60–84.

——'Lloegr', *BBCS* 23 (1968–69), 26–7.

——'Some Questions in Dispute about Early Welsh Literature and Language', *Studia Celtica*, 8/9 (1973–74), 1–32.

Jarman, A. O. H., 'The Heroic Ideal in Early Welsh Poetry', in W. Meid (ed.) *Beiträge zur Indogermanistik und Keltologie* (Innsbruck, 1967), 193–211; Welsh version: 'Y Delfryd Arwrol yn yr Hen Ganu', *Llên Cymru*, 8 (1965), 125–49.

John, E., *Orbis Britanniae and Other Essays* (Leicester, 1966).

Jones, G. R. J., 'Some Donations to Bishop Wilfrid in Northern England', *Northern History*, 31 (1995), 22–38.

Jones, O. W., '*Hereditas Pouoisi*: The Pillar of Eliseg and the History of Early Powys', *Welsh History Review*, 24: 4 (2009), 41–80.

Keynes, S. D., 'The Control of Kent in the Ninth Century', *Early Medieval Europe*, 2 (1993), 111–31.

——'Mercia and Wessex in the Ninth Century', in Brown and Farr (eds.), *Mercia*, 311–28.

——'The Kingdom of the Mercians in the Eighth Century', in Hill and Worthington (eds.), *Æthelbald and Offa*, 1–26.

Kirby, D. P., 'Strathclyde and Cumbria: A Survey of Historical Development to A.D. 1092', *Transactions of the Cumberland and Westmorland Antiquarian and Archaeological Society*, NS 62 (1962), 77–94.

——'British Dynastic History in the Pre-Viking Period', *BBCS* 27 (1976–8), 81–114.

——'British Bards and the Border', in A. Dornier (ed.), *Mercian Studies* (Leicester, 1977), 31–42.

——*The Earliest English Kings* (London, 1991).

Little, L. K. (ed.), *Plague and the End of Antiquity: The Pandemic of 541–750* (Cambridge, 2007).

Longley, D., *Hanging-Bowls, Penannular Brooches and the Anglo-Saxon Connection*, BAR British Series, 22 (Oxford, 1975).

——'The Mote of Mark: The Archaeological Context of the Decorated Metalwork', in M. Redknap et al. (eds.), *Pattern and Purpose in Insular Art*, 75–89.

Lovecy, I., 'The End of Celtic Britain: A Sixth-Century Battle near Lindisfarne', *Archaeologia Aeliana*^{5}, 4 (1976), 31–45.

Macquarrie, A., The Kings of Strathclyde, *c*.400–1018', in A. Grant and K. Stringer (eds.), *Crown, Lordship and Community in Medieval Scotland: Studies in Honour of G. W. S. Barrow* (Edinburgh, 1993), 1–19.

Maddicott, J. R., 'Plague in Seventh-Century England', *Past & Present*, 156 (1997), 7–54; repr. in Little (ed.), *Plague and the End of Antiquity*, 171–214.

——'Two Frontier States: Northumbria and Wessex, *c*.650–750', in J. R. Maddicott and D. M. Palliser (eds.), *The Medieval State: Essays Presented to James Campbell* (London, 2000), 25–45.

——'Prosperity and Power in the Age of Bede and Beowulf', *Proceedings of the British Academy*, 117 (2001 Lectures, 2002), 49–71.

Maund, K. L., *The Welsh Kings* (Stroud, 2000).

Means, H. E., 'Perceptions of the British Heroic Age in the Work of the Gogynfeirdd', unpublished D.Phil. thesis, University of Oxford (2003).

Miller, M., 'The Commanders at Arthuret', *Transactions of the Cumberland and Westmorland Antiquarian and Archaeological Society*, NS 75 (1975), 96–117.

Noble, F., *Offa's Dyke Reviewed*, BAR British Series, 114 (Oxford, 1983).

Padel, O. J., 'Place-Names and the Saxon Conquest of Devon and Cornwall', in Higham (ed.), *Britons in Anglo-Saxon England*, 215–30.

——'Two Devonshire Place-Names', *Journal of the English Place-Name Society*, 41 (2009), 119–26.

Pearce, S. M., *The Kingdom of Dumnonia: Studies in the History and Tradition in South-Western Britain AD 350–1150* (Padstow, 1978).

——*The Archaeology of South-West Britain* (London, 1981).

——*South-Western Britain in the Early Middle Ages* (London, 2004).

——(ed.), *The Early Church in Western Britain and Ireland: Studies presented to C. A. Ralegh Radford*, BAR British Series, 102 (Oxford, 1982).

Rollason, D. W., *Northumbria 500–1100: Creation and Destruction of a Kingdom* (Cambridge, 2003).

Sawyer, P. H. (ed.). *Early Medieval Kingship* (Leeds, 1977).

Scull, C., 'Post-Roman Phase I at Yeavering: A Reconsideration', *Medieval Archaeology*, 35 (1991), 51–63.

Sims-Williams, P. P., 'Historical Need and Literary Narrative: A Caveat from Ninth-Century Wales', *WHR* 17 (1994–95), 1–40.

——'The Death of Urien', *CMCS* 32 (Winter 1996), 25–56.

Stancliffe, C., 'Oswald, "Most Holy and Most Victorious King of the Northumbrians"', in Stancliffe and Cambridge (eds.), *Oswald: Northumbrian King to European Saint* (Stanford, Lincs., 1995), 33–83.

——'Where was Oswald killed?', in Stancliffe and Cambridge (eds.), *Oswald: Northumbrian King to European Saint* (Stanford, Lincs., 1995), 84–96.

——'The British Church and the Mission of Augustine', in R. Gameson (ed.), *Saint Augustine and the Conversion of England* (Stroud, 1999), 107–51.

——*Bede, Wilfrid, and the Irish*, Jarrow Lecture 2003 (Jarrow, 2004).

——*Bede and the Britons*, Whithorn Lecture 2005 (Whithorn, 2007).

——and Cambridge, E. (eds.), *Oswald: Northumbrian King to European Saint* (Stamford, Lincs., 1995)

Thacker, A. T., 'Bede, the Britons and the Book of Samuel', in S. Baxter et al. (eds.), *Early Medieval Studies in Memory of Patrick Wormald*, 129–47.

Thomson, R. L., 'British Latin and English History: Nennius and Asser', *Transactions of the Leeds Philosophical and Literary Society*, 18 (1982), 38–53.

Wallace-Hadrill, J. M., *Bede's Ecclesiastical History of the English People: A Historical Commentary* (Oxford, 1988).

Wood, I. N., 'Anglo-Saxon Otley: An Archiepiscopal Estate and its Crosses in a Northumbrian Context', *Northern History*, 23 (1987), 20–38.

Woolf, A., 'Cædualla *Rex Brittonum* and the Passing of the Old North', *Northern History*, 41 (2004), 5–24.

——'Apartheid and Economics in Anglo-Saxon England', in Higham (ed.), *The Britons in Anglo-Saxon England*, 115–29.

Wormald, P., *The Times of Bede: Studies in Early English Christian Society and its Historian*, ed. S. Baxter (Malden, MA, 2006).

Worthington, M., 'Wat's Dyke: An Archaeological and Historical Enigma', *Bulletin of the John Rylands University Library of Manchester*, 79:3 (1997), 177–96.

Wrenn, C. L., 'Saxons and Celts in South-West Britain', *THSC* (1959), 38–75.

Yorke, B., *Kings and Kingdoms of Early Anglo-Saxon England* (London, 1990).

—— *Wessex in the Early Middle Ages* (London, 1995).

2. Post-Viking

Abels, R., *Alfred the Great: War, Kingship and Culture in Anglo-Saxon England* (London, 1998).

Abrams, L., *Anglo-Saxon Glastonbury: Church and Endowment*, Studies in Anglo-Saxon History, 8 (Woodbridge, 1996).

——'The Conversion of the Scandinavians of Dublin', *Anglo-Norman Studies*, 20 (1997), 1–29.

Aird, W. M., 'Northern England or Southern Scotland? The Anglo-Scottish Border in the Eleventh and Twelfth Centuries and the Problem of Perspective', in J. C. Appleby and P. Dalton (eds.), *Government, Religion and Society in Northern England, 1000–1700* (Phoenix Mill, 1997), 27–39.

Bailey, R. N., *Viking Age Sculpture* (London, 1980).

Baldwin, J. R., and Whyte, I. D. (eds.), *The Scandinavians in Cumbria* (Edinburgh, 1985).

Barrow, J., 'Chester's Earliest Regatta: Edgar's Dee-Rowing Revisited', *Early Medieval Europe*, 10: 1 (2001), 81–93.

Baxter, S., *Earls of Mercia: Lordship and Power in Late Anglo-Saxon England* (Oxford, 2007).

Blackburn, M. A. S., and Dumville, D. N. (eds.), *Kings, Currency and Alliances: History and Coinage of Southern England in the Ninth Century*, Studies in Anglo-Saxon History, 9 (Woodbridge, 1998).

Breeze, A., '*Armes Prydein*, Hywel Dda, and the Reign of Edmund of Wessex', *Études Celtiques*, 33 (1997), 209–22.

Broderick, G., 'Irish and Welsh Strands in the Genealogy of Godfred Crovan', *Journal of the Manx Museum*, 8 (1980), 32–8.

Broun, D., 'The Welsh Identity of the Kingdom of Strathclyde, *c.*900–*c.*1200', *Innes Review*, 55 (2004), 111–80.

Brown, M. P., and Farr, C. A. (eds.), *Mercia: An Anglo-Saxon Kingdom in Europe* (London, 2001).

Bullough, D. A., 'The Educational Tradition in England from Alfred to Ælfric: Teaching *Utriusque Linguae*', *Settimane di studio sull' alto medioevo*, 19 (1972), 453–94.

Byrne, F. J., *Irish Kings and High-Kings* (London, 1973).

Campbell, E., and Lane, A., 'Llangorse: A Tenth-Century Royal Crannog in Wales', *Antiquity*, 63 (1989), 675–81.

Campbell, J., *Essays in Anglo-Saxon History* (London, 1986).

——'Asser's *Life of Alfred*' in C. Holdsworth and T. P. Wiseman (eds.), *The Inheritance of Historiography 350–900* (Exeter, 1986), 115–35.

——'The Late Anglo-Saxon State: A Maximum View', *Proceedings of the British Academy*, 87 (1995), 39–65; repr. in his *The Anglo-Saxon State*, 1–30.

—— *The Anglo-Saxon State* (London, 2000).

Cavill, P., Harding, S. E., and Jesch, J., 'Revisiting *Dingesmere*', *Journal of the English Place-Name Society*, 36 (2003–4), 25–38.

Charles, B. G., *Old Norse Relations with Wales* (Cardiff, 1934).

Charles-Edwards, T. M., 'Alliances, Godfathers, Treaties and Boundaries', in M. A. S. Blackburn and D. N. Dumville (eds.), *Kings, Currency and Alliances: History and Coinage of Southern England in the Ninth Century*, Studies in Anglo-Saxon History, 9 (Woodbridge, 1998), 47–62.

Clancy, T. O., 'The Gall-Ghàidheil and Galloway', *The Journal of Scottish Place-Name Studies*, 2 (2008), 19–50.

Clarke, H. B., Ní Mhaonaigh, M., and Ó Floinn, R. (eds.), *Ireland and Scandinavia in the Early Viking Age* (Dublin, 1998).

Crawford, B. E. (ed.), *Scandinavian Settlement in Northern Britain* (London, 1996).

Crick, J. C., 'Edgar, Albion and Insular Dominion', in D. Scragg (ed.), *Edgar, King of the English 959–975: New Interpretations* (Woodbridge, 2008), 158–70.

Davies, W., 'Land and Power in Early Medieval Wales', *Past & Present*, 81 (1978), 3–23.

——*Patterns of Power in Early Wales* (Oxford, 1990).

——'Franks and Bretons: The Impact of Political Climate and Historiographical Tradition on Writing the Ninth-Century History', in P. Fouracre and D. Ganz (eds.), *Frankland: The Franks and the World of the Early Middle Ages. Essays in Honour of Dame Jinty Nelson* (Manchester, 2008), 304–21.

——'Alfred's Contemporaries: Irish, Welsh, Scots and Breton', in Reuter (ed.), *Alfred the Great*, 323–37.

Dolley, M., and Knight, J. K., 'Some Single Finds of Tenth- and Eleventh-Century English Coins from Wales', *Arch. Camb.*, 119 (1970), 75–82.

Downham, C., 'The Chronology of the Last Scandinavian Kings of York', *Northern History*, 40 (2003), 25–51.

——'England and the Irish Sea Zone in the Eleventh Century', *Anglo-Norman Studies*, 26 (2003), 55–73.

——*Viking Kings of Britain and Ireland: The Dynasty of Ívarr to A.D. 1014* (Edinburgh, 2007).

Driscoll, S. T., 'Church Archaeology in Glasgow and the Kingdom of Strathclyde', *Innes Review*, 49 (1998), 95–114.

——*Govan from Cradle to Grave*, Annual Lecture to Friends of Govan Old (Govan, 2004).

Duffy, S., 'Irishmen and Islesmen in the Kingdoms of Dublin and Man, 1052–1171', *Ériu*, 43 (1992), 93–133.

——'Ostmen, Irish and Welsh in the Eleventh Century', *Peritia*, 9 (1995), 378–96.

Dumville, D. N., *Wessex and England from Alfred to Edgar: Six Essays on Political, Cultural, and Ecclesiastical Revival* (Woodbridge, 1992).

——'Vikings in the British Isles: A Question of Sources', in J. Jesch (ed.), *Scandinavians from the Vendel Period to the Tenth Century* (Woodbridge, 2002), 209–50.

——'Old Dubliners and New Dubliners in Ireland and Britain: A Viking-Age Story', *Medieval Dublin*, 6 (2004), 79–94, reprinted in his *Celtic Essays, 2001–2007*, i. 103–22.

Edmonds, F. L., 'Personal Names and the Cult of Patrick in Eleventh-Century Strathclyde and Northumbria', in Boardman et al., *Saints' Cults in the Insular World*, 42–65.

——'History and Names', in Graham-Campbell and Philpott (eds.), *The Huxley Viking Hoard*, 3–12.

Edwards, N., 'Viking-Influenced Sculpture in North Wales, its Ornament and Context', *Church Archaeology*, 3 (1999), 5–16.

——'Viking-Age Sculpture in North-West Wales: Wealth, Power, Patronage and the Christian Landscape', in F. L. Edmonds and P. Russell (eds.), *Tome: Studies in Medieval Celtic History and Law in Honour of Thomas Charles-Edwards* (Woodbridge, 2011), 73–87.

Etchingham, C., 'North Wales, Ireland and the Isles: The Insular Viking Zone', *Peritia*, 15 (2001), 145–87.

——'Viking-Age Gwynedd and Ireland: Political Relations', in K. Jankulak and J. Wooding (eds.), *Ireland and Wales in the Middle Ages* (Dublin, 2007), 149–67.

Fell, C. E., 'Old English *wicing*: A Question of Semantics', *Proceedings of the British Academy*, 72 (1986), 295–316.

——'Scandinavian Settlement in the Isle of Man and North-West England: The Place-Name Evidence', in Fell et al. (eds.), *The Viking Age in the Isle of Man*, 37–52.

——Foote, P., Graham-Campbell, J., and Thomson, R. L. (eds.), *The Viking Age in the Isle of Man* (London, 1983).

Fellows-Jensen, G., 'Scandinavian Settlement in Cumbria and Dumfriesshire: The Place-Name Evidence', in Baldwin and Whyte, *The Scandinavians in Cumbria*, 65–82.

Fletcher, R. A., *Bloodfeud: Murder and Revenge in Anglo-Saxon England* (London, 2003).

Graham-Campbell, J. (ed.), *Viking Treasure from the North-West: The Cuerdale Hoard and its Context* (Liverpool, 1992).

——'The Irish-Sea Vikings: Raiders and Settlers', in T. Scott and P. Starkey (eds.), *The Middle Ages in the North West* (Oxford, 1995), 59–83.

——'The Early Viking Age in the Irish Sea Area', in H. B. Clarke et al. (eds.), *Ireland and Scandinavia*, 104–30.

——and Philpott, R. (eds.), *The Huxley Viking Hoard: Scandinavian Settlement in the North-West* (Liverpool, 2009).

Griffin, T. D. 'Aber Peryddon: River of Death', *Proceedings of the Harvard Celtic Colloquium*, 15 (1995), 32–41.

Griffiths, D., 'Coastal Trading Ports of the Irish Sea Region', in Graham-Campbell (ed.), *Viking Treasure from the North-West*, 63–72.

——'The North-West Mercian Burhs: A Reappraisal', *Anglo-Saxon Studies in Archaeology and History*, 8 (1995), 75–86.

——'The North-West Frontier', in Higham and Hill (eds.), *Edward the Elder*, 167–87.

——'Settlement and Acculturation in the Irish Sea Region', in Hines et al. (eds.), *Land, Sea and Home*, 125–38.

——Philpott, R. A., and Egan, G., *Meols: The Archaeology of the North Wirrall Coast: Discoveries and Observations in the 19th and 20th Centuries, with a Catalogue of Collections* (Oxford, 2007).

Harris, B. E., Thacker, A. T., and C. P. Lewis (eds.), *A History of the County of Chester*, i–v, part 2 (VCH; London, 1987–2005).

Higham, N. J., 'Continuity Studies in the First Millennium A.D. in North Cumbria', *Northern History*, 14 (1978), 1–18.

——'The Scandinavians in North Cumbria: Raids and Settlement in the Later Ninth to Tenth Century', in Baldwin and Whyte (eds.), *Scandinavians in Cumbria*, 37–51.

——'The Cheshire Burhs and the Mercian Frontier to 924', *Transactions of the Lancashire and Cheshire Antiquarian Society*, 85 (1988), 193–222.

——'Northumbria, Mercia and the Irish Sea Norse 893–926', in Graham-Campbell (ed.), *Viking Treasure from the North-West*, 21–30.

——'Viking-Age Settlement in the North-Western Countryside: Lifting the Veil?', in Hines et al. (eds.), *Land, Sea and Home*, 297–311.

——'The Context of *Brunanburh*', in A. R. Rumble and A. D. Mills (eds.), *Names, Places and People: An Onomastic Miscellany in Memory of John McNeal Dodgson* (Stamford, 1997), 144–56.

——and Hill, D. H. (eds.), *Edward the Elder, 899–924* (London, 2001).

Hines, J., Lane, A., and Redknap, M. (eds.), *Land, Sea and Home: Settlement in the Viking Period* (Leeds, 2004).

Hudson, B. T., '*Elech* and the Scots in Strathclyde', *Scottish Gaelic Studies*, 15 (1988), 145–9.

——'The Destruction of Gruffudd ap Llywelyn', *WHR* 15 (1991), 331–50.

——'Cnut and the Scottish Kings', *English Historical Review*, 107 (1992), 350–60.

——*Viking Pirates and Christian Princes: Dynasty, Religion, and Empire in the North Atlantic* (Oxford, 2005).

——*Irish Sea Studies, 900–1200* (Dublin, 2006).

Jesch, J. (ed.), *The Scandinavians from the Vendel Period to the Tenth Century: An Ethnographic Perspective* (Woodbridge/San Marino, 2002).

Jones, A., 'The Significance of the Regal Consecration of Edgar in 973', *Journal of Ecclesiastical History*, 33 (1982), 375–90.

Jones, B. L., 'Gwriad's Heritage: Links between Wales and the Isle of Man in the Early Middle Ages', *THSC*, 1990, 29–44.

——and Roberts, T., 'Osmund's Air: A Scandinavian Place-Name in Anglesey', *BBCS* 28 (1978–80), 602–3.

Kapelle, W. E., *The Norman Conquest of the North: The Region and Its Transformation 1000–1135* (London, 1979).

Kenyon, D., *The Origins of Lancashire* (Manchester, 1991).

Keynes, S. D., *The Diplomas of King Æthelred 'the Unready' (978–1016): A Study in their Use as Historical Evidence* (Cambridge, 1980).

——'King Athelstan's Books', in M. Lapidge and H. Gneuss (eds.), *Learning and Literature in Anglo-Saxon England* (Cambridge, 1985), 186–7.

——'King Alfred and the Mercians', in Blackburn and Dumville (eds.), *Kings, Currency and Alliances*, 1–45.

——*An Atlas of Attestations in Anglo-Saxon Charters, c. 670–1066*, rev. edn. (Cambridge, 2002).

——'Edgar, *Rex Admirabilis*', in Scragg (ed.), *Edgar, King of the English*, 3–59.

Kirby, D. P., 'Hywel Dda: Anglophil?', *WHR* 8 (1976–7), 1–13.

Lewis, C. P., 'English and Norman Government and Lordship in the Welsh Borders, 1039–1087', unpublished D.Phil. thesis, University of Oxford (1985).

——'Welsh Territories and Welsh Identities in Late Anglo-Saxon England', in Higham (ed.), *Britons in Anglo-Saxon England*, 130–43.

Lloyd, J. E., 'Hywel Dda: The Historical Setting', *Aberystwyth Studies*, 10 (1928), 1–4.

Loyn, H. R., *The Vikings in Wales*, Dorothea Coke Memorial Lecture (London, 1976).

——'Wales and England in the Tenth Century: The Context of the Æthelstan Charters', *WHR* 10 (1980–81), 283–301.

Maund, K. L., 'Cynan ap Iago and the Killing of Gruffudd ap Llywelyn', *CMCS* 10 (Winter 1985), 57–65.

——'Trahaearn ap Caradog: Legitimate Usurper?', *Welsh History Review*, 13 (1986–87), 468–76.

——'The Welsh Alliances of Earl Ælfgar of Mercia and his Family in the Mid-Eleventh Century', *Anglo-Norman Studies*, 11 (1988), 181–90.

——*Ireland, Wales, and England in the Eleventh Century*, Studies in Celtic History 12 (Woodbridge, 1991).

——(ed.), *Gruffudd ap Cynan: A Collaborative Biography* (Woodbridge, 1997).

Maund, K. L., 'Fact and Narrative Fiction in the Llandaff Charters', *Studia Celtica*, 31 (1997), 173–94.

——'Dynastic Segmentation and Gwynedd, *c.* 950–*c.* 1100', *Studia Celtica*, 32 (1998), 155–67.

Moon, R., 'Viking Runic Inscriptions in Wales', *AC* 127 (1978), 124–6.

Nelson, J., *Politics and Ritual in Early Medieval Europe* (London, 1986).

Padel, O. J., 'Asser's *Parochia* of Exeter', in F. L. Edmonds and P. Russell (eds.), *Tome: Studies in Medieval Celtic History and Law in Honour of Thomas Charles-Edwards* (Woodbridge, 2011), 65–72.

Price, N. S., *The Vikings in Brittany* (London, 1989).

Quaghebeur, J., and Merdrignac, B. (eds.), *Bretons et Normands au Moyen Âge. Rivalités, Malentendus, Convergences* (Rennes, 2008).

Redknap, M., 'Glyn, Llanbedrgoch, Anglesey', *Archaeology in Wales*, 34 (1994), 58–60.

——'Glyn, Llanbedrgoch, Anglesey', *Archaeology in Wales*, 35 (1995), 58–9.

——*Vikings in Wales: An Archaeological Quest* (Cardiff, 2000).

——'Viking-Age Settlement in Wales and the Evidence from Llanbedrgoch', in Hines et al. (eds.), *Land, Sea and Home*, 139–75.

——'Viking-Age Settlement in Wales: Some Recent Advances', *THSC 2005*, NS 12 (2006), 5–35.

——'Silver and Commerce in Viking-Age North Wales', in Graham-Campbell and Philpott (eds.), *The Huxley Hoard*, 29–41.

——Campbell, E., and Lane, A., 'Llangorse Crannog', *Archaeology in Wales*, 29 (1989), 57–8.

Reuter, T. (ed.), *Alfred the Great: Papers from the Eleventh-Centenary Conference*, Studies in Early Medieval Britain 3 (Aldershot, 2003).

Ritchie, A. (ed.), *Govan and its Early Medieval Sculpture* (Stroud, 1994).

Scharer, A. 'The Writing of History at King Alfred's Court', *Early Medieval Europe*, 5/2 (1996), 177–206.

——*Herrschaft und Repräsentation: Studien zur Hofkultur König Alfreds des Grossen = Mitteilungen des Instituts für Österreichische Geschichtsforschung*, Ergänzungsband 35 (Vienna, 2000).

Scott, T., and Starkey, P. (eds.), *The Middle Ages in the North-West* (Oxford, 1995).

Scragg, D. G. (ed.), *Edgar, King of the English, 959–975: New Interpretations* (Woodbridge, 2008).

Smyth, A. P., *Scandinavian Kings in the British Isles, 850–880* (Oxford, 1977).

——*Scandinavian York and Dublin: The History and Archaeology of Two Related Viking Kingdoms*, 2 vols. (Dublin, 1975–79).

——*Celtic Leinster* (Dublin, 1982).

——*Warlords and Holy Men: Scotland AD 80–1000* (London, 1984).

Stafford, P., *Unification and Conquest: A Political and Social History of England in the Tenth and Eleventh Centuries* (London, 1989).

Stenton, F. M., *Anglo-Saxon England*, 3rd edn. (Oxford, 1971).

Stevenson, W. H., and Duignan, W. H., 'Anglo-Saxon Charters relating to Shropshire', *Transactions of the Shropshire Archaeological and Historical Society*, 4th Ser., 1 (1911), 1–22.

Suppe, F. C., 'Who was Rhys Sais? Some Comments on Anglo-Welsh Relations before 1066', *Haskins Society Journal*, 7 (1995), 63–73.

Tait, J., 'Flintshire in Domesday Book', *Flintshire Historical Society Publications*, 11 (1925), 1–37.

Thomas, G., 'Rhai Sylwadau ar Armes Prydein', *BBCS* 24 (1970–72), 263–7.
——'O Maximus i Maxen', *THSC* (1983), 7–21.
Thornton, D. E., 'The Genealogy of Gruffudd ap Cynan', in K. L. Maund (ed.), *Gruffudd ap Cynan*, 79–108.
——'Maredudd ab Owain (d. 999): The Most Famous King of the Welsh', *WHR* 18 (1996–97), 567–91.
——'Kings, Chronicles, and Genealogies: Reconstructing Mediaeval Celtic Dynasties', in K. S. B. Keats-Rohan (ed.), *Family Trees and the Roots of Politics* (Woodbridge, 1997), 23–40.
——'Orality, Literacy and Genealogy in Early Medieval Ireland and Wales', in H. Pryce (ed.), *Literacy in Medieval Celtic Countries*, Cambridge Studies in Medieval Literature, 33 (Cambridge, 1998), 83–98.
——'Predatory Nomenclature and Dynastic Expansion in Early Medieval Wales', *Medieval Prosopography: History and Collective Biography*, 20 (1999), 1–22.
——'Who was Rhain the Irishman?', *Studia Celtica*, 34 (2000), 131–48.
——'Edgar and the Eight Kings, AD 973: *Textus et Dramatis Personae*', *Early Medieval Europe*, 10/1 (2001), 49–79.
——*Kings, Chronologies, and Genealogies: Studies in the Political History of Early Medieval Ireland and Wales* (Oxford, 2003).
Tolstoy, N., 'When and where was *Armes Prydein* composed?', *Studia Celtica*, 42 (2008), 145–9.
Wainwright, F. T., 'North-West Mercia, 871–924', *Trans. Hist. Soc. of Lancashire and Cheshire*, 94 (1942), 3–56.
——'Ingimund's Invasion', *EHR* 63 (1948), 145–69.
——'Cledemutha', *EHR* 65 (1950), 202–12.
——'Æthelflæd Lady of the Mercians', in Clemoes (ed.), *The Anglo-Saxons*, 53–69.
——*Scandinavian England: Collected Papers of F. T. Wainwright*, ed. H. P. R. Finberg (Chichester, 1975).
Walker, S., 'A Context for "Brunanburh"?', in T. Reuter (ed.), *Warriors and Churchmen in the High Middle Ages* (London, 1992), 21–39.
Whitelock, D., 'The Dealings of the Kings of England with Northumbria in the Tenth and Eleventh Centuries', in Clemoes (ed.), *The Anglo-Saxons*, 70–88.
——'The Prose of Alfred's Reign', in E. G. Stanley (ed.), *Continuations and Beginnings: Studies in Old English Literature* (London, 1966), 57–90.
Williams, A., '*Princeps Merciorum*: The Family, Career and Connections of Ælfhere, Ealdorman of Mercia, 956–983', *Anglo-Saxon England*, 10 (1982), 143–72.
Wilson, D. M., *The Viking Age in the Isle of Man: The Archaeological Evidence* (Odense, 1974).
Wood, M., 'Brunanburh Revisited', *Sagabook of the Viking Society for Northern Research*, 20 (1980), 200–17.
——'The Making of King Aethelstan's Empire: An English Charlemagne?', in P. Wormald et al. (eds.), *Ideal and Reality in Frankish and Anglo-Saxon Society* (Oxford, 1983), 250–72.
Woolf, A., *From Pictland to Alba, 789–1070* (Edinburgh, 2007).

Websites

Prosopography of Anglo-Saxon England: www.pase.ac.uk

V. THE CHURCH AND ITS CULTURE, POETS, AND STORYTELLERS

A Primary Sources

1. Manuscripts

Cambridge University Library Ff. 4. 42 (the Cambridge Juvencus): *Juvencus: Codex Cantabrigiensis Ff.4.42*, ed. H. McKee (Aberystwyth, 2000); *Juvencus: Text and Commentary*, ed. H. McKee (Aberystwyth, 2000).

Oxford, Bodleian Library, MS Auct. F. 4. 32: R. W. Hunt, *Saint Dunstan's Classbook from Canterbury*, Umbrae Codicum Occidentalium, 4 (Amsterdam, 1961), and online at http://image.ox.ac.uk

Oxford, Bodleian Library, Bodley MS 572: online at http://image.ox.ac.uk

2. Printed Sources

(a) *The Church*

Councils and Ecclesiastical Documents relating to Great Britain and Ireland, ed. A. W. Haddan and W. Stubbs, 3 vols. (Oxford, 1869–78).

Rhigyfarch, *Vita Sancti Dauid*, ed. A. W. Wade-Evans, *VSBG* 150–70 (Vespasian Recension), trans. A. W. Wade-Evans, *Life of St. David* (London, 1923); ed. and trans. J. W. James, *Rhigyfarch's Life of St. David: The Basic Mid Twelfth-Century Text* (Cardiff, 1967) (the Nero-Digby Recension); ed. and trans. R. Sharpe and J. R. Davies, 'Rhygyfarch's *Life* of St David', in Evans and Wooding (eds.), *St David of Wales*, 107–55 (Vespasian Recension).

Victricius of Rouen, *De Laude Sanctorum*, ed. J. Mulders and R. Demeulenaere, CCSL 64 (1983), 53–93.

Vita S. Kentegerni (Anonymous), ed. and trans. A. P. Forbes, *Lives of S. Ninian and S. Kentigern*, The Historians of Scotland, v (Edinburgh, 1874), 243–52.

Vitae Sanctorum Britanniae et Genealogiae, ed. A. W. Wade-Evans, History and Law Series, ix (Cardiff, 1944).

(b) *Learning*

De Raris Fabulis, ed. Stevenson, *Early Scholastic Colloquies*, 1–11; ed. and trans. S. Gwara, *De Raris Fabulis, 'On Uncommon Tales': A Glossed Latin Colloquy Text from a Tenth-Century Cornish Manuscript* (Cambridge, 2005).

Early Scholastic Colloquies, ed. W. H. Stevenson (Oxford, 1929).

Juvencus: Codex Cantabrigiensis Ff.4.42, ed. H. McKee (Aberystwyth, 2000); *Juvencus: Text and Commentary*, ed. H. McKee (Aberystwyth, 2000).

The Leiden Leechbook, ed. A. Falileyev and M. E. Owen (Innsbruck, 2005).

The Psalter and Martyrology of Ricemarch, ed. H. J. Lawlor, Henry Bradshaw Society, 47–8 (London, 1914).

(c) *Literature*

i. Poetry

Blodeugerdd Barddas o Ganu Crefyddol Cynnar, ed. M. Haycock ([Y Bala], 1994).

The Book of Taliesin, ed. J. Gwenogvryn Evans (Llanbedrog, 1910).

Early Welsh Gnomic and Nature Poetry, ed. N. Jacobs (London, 2012).

Echrys Ynys, ed. R. G. Gruffydd, 'A Welsh "Dark Age" Court Poem', in J. Carey et al. (eds.), *Ildánach, Ildírech*, 39–48.

Edmyg Dinbych, ed. I. Williams, *BWP* 155–72; a text in modernized orthography is given by R. G. Gruffydd, '*Edmyg Dinbych*': *Cerdd Lys Gynnar o Ddyfed* (Aberystwyth, 2002). English version, '"The Praise of Tenby": A Late-Ninth-Century Welsh Court Poem', in

J. F. Nagy and L. E. Jones (eds.), *Heroic Poets and Poetic Heroes in Celtic Tradition: A Festschrift for Patrick K. Ford*, CSANA Yearbook, 3–4 (Dublin, 2005), 91–202; I. Williams, 'Two Poems from the Book of Taliesin', *BWP* 155–72.

Legendary Poems from the Book of Taliesin, ed. and trans. M. Haycock (Aberystwyth, 2007).

'Tri Englyn y Juvencus', ed. I. Williams, *BBCS* 6 (1933), 101–10; English version in *BWP*, chap. VII.

'Naw Englyn y Juvencus', ed. I. Williams, *BBCS* 6 (1933), 205–24; English version in *BWP*, ch. VII.

Williams, I., *The Beginnings of Welsh Poetry: Studies by Sir Ifor Williams*, ed. R. Bromwich (Cardiff, 1972) [*BWP*].

ii. Prose

Texts and a Translation of the Mabinogion as a whole:

The Text of the Mabinogion . . . from the Red Book of Hergest, ed. J. Rhŷs and J. Gwenogvryn Evans (Oxford, 1887).

The White Book Mabinogion, ed. J. Gwenogvryn Evans (Llanbedrog, 1907); reissued as *Llyfr Gwyn Rhydderch: Y Chwedlau a'r Rhamantau*, ed. J. Gwenogvryn Evans with an introduction by R. M. Jones (Cardiff, 1973).

Davies, S., *The Mabinogion*, The World Classics (Oxford, 2007).

Particular Texts:

Culhwch and Olwen: An Edition and Study of the Oldest Arthurian Tale, ed. R. Bromwich and D. S. Evans (Cardiff, 1992).

Pedeir Keinc y Mabinogi, ed. I. Williams (Cardiff, 1930).

Pwyll Pendeuic Dyuet, ed. R. L. Thomson (Dublin, 1957).

Branwen verch Lyr, ed. D.S. Thomson (Dublin, 1961).

Manawydan uab Llyr: Text from the Diplomatic Edition of the White Book of Rhydderch, by J. Gwenogvryn Evans, ed. P. K. Ford (Belmont, MA, 1999).

Manawydan uab Llyr: Trydedd Gainc y Mabinogi, ed. I. Hughes (Cardiff, 2007).

Math uab Mathonwy: Text from the Diplomatic Edition of the White Book of Rhydderch, by J. Gwenogvryn Evans, ed. P. K. Ford (Belmont, MA, 1999).

Math uab Mathonwy: Pedwaredd Gainc y Mabinogi, ed. I. Hughes (Aberystwyth, 2000).

Breudwyt Maxen Wledic, ed. B. F. Roberts (Dublin, 2005).

Cyfranc Lludd a Llefelys, ed. B. F. Roberts (Dublin, 1975).

Trioedd Ynys Prydein, ed. R. Bromwich (3rd edn., Cardiff, 2006).

Ystorya Taliesin, ed. P. K. Ford (Cardiff, 1992).

B. Secondary Sources

1. The Church

Baring-Gould, S., and Fisher, J., *Lives of the British Saints*, 4 vols. (London, 1907–13).

Blair, J., 'Minster Churches in the Landscape', in D. Hooke (ed.), *Anglo-Saxon Settlements* (Oxford, 1988), 35–58.

—— *The Church in Anglo-Saxon Society* (Oxford, 2005).

——(ed.), *Minsters and Parish Churches: The Local Church in Transition 950–1200*, OUCA Monograph 17 (Oxford, 1988).

——and Pyrah, C. (eds.), *Church Archaeology: Research Directions for the Future*, CBA Research Report 104 (York, 1996).

——and Sharpe, R. (eds.), *Pastoral Care before the Parish* (Leicester, 1992).

Boardman, S., Davies, J. R., and Williamson, E. (eds.), *Saints' Cults in the Celtic World* (Woodbridge, 2009).

Boon, G. C., 'The Early Church in Gwent, I. The Romano-British Church', *The Monmouthshire Antiquary*, 8 (1992), 11–24.

Bowen, E. G., *The Settlements of the Celtic Saints in Wales* (Cardiff, 1954).

——*Saints, Seaways and Settlements in the Celtic Lands* (Cardiff, 1977).

Cartwright, J. (ed.), *Celtic Hagiography and Saints' Cults* (Cardiff, 2003).

Carver, M. (ed.), *The Cross goes North: Processes of Conversion in Northern Europe AD 300–1300* (York, 2003).

Chadwick, N. K. (ed.), *Studies in the Early British Church* (Cambridge, 1958).

Chadwick, O., 'The Evidence of Dedications in the Early History of the Welsh Church', in N. K. Chadwick (ed.), *Studies in Early British History*, 173–88.

——'Gildas and the Monastic Order', *Journal of Theological Studies*, NS 5 (1954), 78–80.

Charles-Edwards, T. M., 'The Seven Bishop-Houses of Dyfed', *BBCS*, 24 (1970–2), 247–62.

Clancy, J. P. (trans.), *The Earliest Welsh Poetry* (London, 1970).

——*Medieval Welsh Poems* (Dublin, 2003).

Davies, J. R., 'Church, Property, and Conflict in Wales, AD 600–1100', *WHR* 18 (1996–97), 387–406.

——'The Saints of South Wales and the Welsh Church', in Thacker and Sharpe (eds.), *Local Saints and Local Churches*, 361–95.

——'Some Observations on the 'Nero', 'Digby', and 'Vespasian' Recensions of *Vita S. David'*, in Evans and Wooding (eds.), *St David of Wales*, 156–60.

——'Bishop Kentigern among the Britons', in Boardman *et al.*, *Saints' Cults in the Celtic World*, 66–90.

Davies, W., 'Property Rights and Property Claims in Welsh "Vitae" of the Eleventh Century', in *Hagiographie, cultures et sociétés, IVe–XIIe siècles*, Études Augustiniennes (Paris, 1981), 515–33.

——'Priests and Rural Communities in East Brittany in the Ninth Century', *Études Celtiques*, 20 (1983), 177–97.

——'Adding Insult to Injury: Power, Property and Immunities in Early Medieval Wales', in W. Davies and P. Fouracre (eds.), *Property and Power in the Early Middle Ages* (Cambridge, 1995).

Doble, G. H. *The Saints of Cornwall*, ed. D. Attwater, 5 vols. (Truro, 1960–70).

——*Lives of the Welsh Saints*, ed. D. S. Evans (Cardiff, 1971).

Driscoll, S. T., 'Church Archaeology in Glasgow and the Kingdom of Strathclyde', *Innes Review*, 49 (1998), 95–114.

Dumville, D. N., *Saint David of Wales*, Kathleen Hughes Memorial Lectures, 1 (Cambridge, 2001).

Edwards, N., 'Identifying the Archaeology of the Early Church in Wales and Cornwall', in J. Blair and C. Pyrah (eds.), *Church Archaeology: Research Directions for the Future*, 49–62.

——'11th Century Welsh Illuminated Manuscripts: The Nature of the Irish Connection', in C. Bourke (ed.), *From the Isles of the North: Early Medieval Art in Ireland and Britain* (Belfast, 1995), 147–55.

——'Monuments in a Landscape: The Early Medieval Sculpture of St David's', in H. Hamerow and A. MacGregor (eds.), *Image and Power in the Archaeology of Early Medieval Britain: Essays in Honour of Rosemary Cramp* (Oxford, 2001), 53–77.

——'Celtic Saints and Early Medieval Archaeology', in Thacker and Sharpe (eds.), *Local Saints and Local Churches*, 225–65.

Edwards, N. (ed.), *The Archaeology of the Early Medieval Celtic Churches: Proceedings of a Conference on the Archaeology of the Early Medieval Celtic Churches* (Leeds, 2009).

Edwards, N., and Lane, A. (eds.), *The Early Church in Wales and the West* (Oxford, 1991).

Emanuel, H. D., 'An Analysis of the Composition of the "Vita Cadoci"', *National Library of Wales Journal*, 7 (1951–52), 217–27.

——'Beneventana Civitas', *Journal of the Historical Society of the Church in Wales*, 3 (1953), 54–63.

Evans, J. W., 'The Early Church in Denbighshire', *Trafodion Cymdeithas Hanes Sir Ddinbych/Denbighshire Historical Society Transactions*, 35 (1986), 61–81.

——'The Early Church in Carmarthenshire', in H. James (ed.), *Sir Gâr: Studies in Carmarthenshire History*, Carmarthenshire Antiquarian Society, Monograph Series, 4 (Carmarthen, 1991), 239–54.

——'St David and St Davids: Some Observations on the Cult, Site and Buildings', in Cartwright (ed.), *Celtic Hagiography and Saints' Cults*, 10–25.

——and Wooding, J. (eds.), *St David of Wales: Cult, Church and Nation*, Studies in Celtic History 24 (Woodbridge, 2007).

Fleuriot, L., 'Les Éveques de la "Clas Kenedyr", évêché disparu de la région de Hereford', *Études Celtiques*, 15 (1976–78), 225–6.

Gruffydd, R. G., and Owen, H. P., 'The Earliest Mention of St. David?', *BBCS* 17 (1958), 185–93.

——'The Earliest Mention of St. David: An Addendum', *BBCS* 19 (1962), 231–2.

Guigon, P., *Les Églises du haut moyen âge en Bretagne*, 2 vols. (Saint-Malo, 1997, 1998).

Harris, S. M., 'The Kalendar of the *Vitae Sanctorum Wallensium*', *Journal of the Historical Society of the Church in Wales*, 3 (1953), 3–53 (the text of the calendar is ed. 46–53).

Henken, E. R., *Traditions of the Welsh Saints* (Woodbridge, 1987).

——*The Welsh Saints: A Study in Patterned Lives* (Cambridge, 1991).

Hughes, K. W., *The Church in Early Irish Society* (London, 1966).

——'The Celtic Church: Is this a Valid Concept?', *CMCS* 1 (Summer, 1981), 1–20.

Jackson, K. H., 'The Sources for the Life of St Kentigern', in N. K. Chadwick (ed.), *Studies in the Early British Church* (Cambridge, 1958), 273–357.

James, H., 'The Cult of St David in the Middle Ages', in M. Carver (ed.), *In Search of Cult* (Woodbridge, 1993), 105–12.

——'The Church in Ceredigion in the Early Middle Ages: c. The Archaeology of Early Christianity in Cardiganshire', in Davies and Kirby (eds.), *Cardiganshire County History*, i. 397–407.

——'The Geography of the Cult of St David: A Study of Dedication Patterns in the Medieval Diocese', in Evans and Wooding (eds.), *St David of Wales*, 41–83.

Jankulak, K., *The Medieval Cult of St Petroc* (Woodbridge, 2000).

Johns, C. N., 'The Celtic Monasteries of North Wales', *Transactions of the Caernarvonshire Historical Society*, 21 (1960), 14–53.

——'The Celtic Monasteries of North Wales: A Postscript', *Transactions of the Caernarvonshire Historical Society*, 23 (1962), 129–31.

Jones, N. A., and Owen, M. E., 'Twelfth-Century Welsh Hagiography: The Gogynfeirdd Poems to the Saints', in Cartwright (ed.), *Celtic Hagiography*, 45–76.

Kerlouégan, F., 'Les Vies de saints bretons les plus anciennes dans leurs rapports avec les Îles Britanniques', in M. Herren (ed.), *Insular Latin Studies. Papers on Latin Texts and Manuscripts: 550–1066* (Toronto, 1981), 195–213.

——'Grégoire le Grand et les pays celtiques', in J. Fontaine (ed.), *Grégoire le Grand* (Paris, 1986), 589–96.

Knight, J. K., 'St Tatheus of Caerwent: An Analysis of the Vespasian Life', *Monmouthshire Antiquary*, 3 (1970–71), 29–36.

——'Early Christian Origins and Society in South Wales', *Merthyr Historian*, 2 (1978), 101–10.

Knight, J. K., 'The Early Church in Gwent, II: The Early Medieval Church', *Monmouthshire Antiquary*, 9 (1993), 1–17.

——'Britain's Other Martyrs: Julius, Aaron and Alban at Caerleon', in M. Henig and P. Lindley (eds.), *Alban and St Albans: Roman and Medieval Art and Archaeology*, Trans. British Archaeology Association 24 (2001), 38–44.

——'Basilicas and Barrows: Christian Origins in Wales and Western Britain', in M. Carver (ed.), *The Cross goes North: Processes of Conversion in Northern Europe AD 300–1300* (York, 2003), 119–26.

——'From Villa to Monastery: Llandough in Context', *Medieval Archaeology*, 49 (2005), 93–107.

Largillière, R., *Les saints et l'organisation chrétienne primitive dans l'Armorique bretonne* (Crozon, 1995).

Longley, D., 'Llangwyfan—the Church in the Sea', *Transactions of the Anglesey Antiquarian Society and Field Club* (2008), 77–88.

Mac Cana, P., 'An Archaism in Irish Poetic Tradition', *Celtica*, 8 (1968), 174–81.

——'Elfennau Cyn-Cristnogol yn y Cyfreithiau', *BBCS* 23 (1968–70), 316–20 (on a Welsh counterpart to the Irish custom discussed in the previous article).

——'On the Early Development of Written Narrative Prose in Irish and Welsh', *Études Celtiques*, 29 (1992), 51–66.

McKee, H., 'Scribes and Glosses from Dark Age Wales: The Cambridge Juvencus Manuscript', *CMCS* 39 (Summer 2000), 1–22.

Merdrignac, B., *Recherches sur l'hagiographie armoricaine du VII*[e] *au XV*[e] *siècle. I. Les saints bretons, témoins de Dieu ou témoins des hommes?* (Saint-Malo, 1985).

——*Recherches . . . II. Les hagiographes et leurs publics en Bretagne au Moyen Âge* (Saint-Malo, 1986).

——'Saint Guénolé et les monachismes insulaires au haut Moyen Âge', *Annales de Bretagne et les pays de l'Ouest*, 95 (1988), 15–40.

——*La Vie des saints bretons durant le Haut Moyen Âge* (Rennes, 1993).

Morris, R., *The Church in British Archaeology* (London, 1983).

Ó Carragáin, T., 'A Landscape Converted: Archaeology and Early Church Organization on Iveragh and Dingle, Ireland', in Carver (ed.), *The Cross goes North*, 127–52.

——'The Architectural Setting of the Cult of Relics in Early Medieval Ireland', *JRSAI* 133 (2005), 130–76.

——'Church Buildings and Pastoral Care in Early Medieval Ireland', in E. FitzPatrick and R. Gillespie (eds.), *The Parish in Medieval and Early Modern Ireland* (Dublin, 2006), 91–123.

——'Cemetery Settlements and Local Churches in Pre-Viking Ireland in Light of Comparisons with England and Wales', in Graham-Campbell and Ryan (eds.), *Anglo-Saxon/Irish Relations before the Vikings*, 329–66.

Olson, L., *Early Monasteries in Cornwall* (Woodbridge, 1989)

——and Padel, O. J., 'A Tenth-Century List of Cornish Parochial Saints', *CMCS* 12 (Winter 1986), 33–71.

Ó Riain, P., 'The Church in Ceredigion: b. The Saints of Cardiganshire', in J. L. Davies and D. P. Kirby (eds.), *Cardiganshire County History*, gen. ed. I. G. Jones (Cardiff, 1994), 378–96.

——'Hagiography without Frontiers: Borrowing of Saints across the Irish Sea', in D. Walz (ed.), *Scripturus Vitam: Lateinische Biographie von der Antike bis in die Gegenwart. Festschift für Walter Berschin zum 65. Geburtstag* (Heidelberg, 2002), 41–8.

Padel, O. J., 'Cornish Language Notes: 5. Cornish Names of Parish Churches', *Cornish Studies*, 4/5 (1976–77), 15–27.
——'Local Saints and Place-Names in Cornwall', in Thacker and Sharpe (eds.), *Local Saints and Local Churches*, 303–60.
Palmer, A. N., 'The Portionary Churches of Mediaeval North Wales', *Arch. Camb.*, 5th series, 3 (1886), 175–209.
Petts, D., *The Early Medieval Church in Wales* (Stroud, 2009),
Pryce, H., 'Ecclesiastical Wealth in Early Medieval Wales', in Edwards and Lane (eds.), *The Early Church in Wales and the West*, 22–32.
——*Native Law and the Church in Medieval Wales* (Oxford, 1993).
——'The Church of Trefeglwys and the End of the "Celtic" Charter Tradition in Twelfth-Century Wales', *CMCS* 25 (Summer 1993), 15–54.
——(ed.), *Literacy in Medieval Celtic Societies* (Cambridge, 1998).
Radford, C. A. R., 'The Celtic Monastery in Britain', *Arch. Camb.*, 111 (1962), 1–24.
Redknap, M., *The Christian Celts*, National Museum of Wales (Cardiff, 1991).
Rees, R., *An Essay on the Welsh Saints* (London, 1836).
Richards, M., 'Ecclesiastical and Secular in Medieval Welsh Settlement', *Studia Celtica*, 3 (1968), 9–18.
——'Places and Persons of the Early Welsh Church', *WHR* 5 (1970–71), 333–49.
Ritchie, A. (ed.), *Govan and its Early Medieval Sculpture* (Stroud, 1994).
Sharpe, R., 'Martyrs and Local Saints in Late Antique Britain', in Thacker and Sharpe (eds.), *Local Saints and Local Churches*, 75–154.
Simon, M. (ed.), *Landévennec et le monachisme Breton dans le haut Moyen Age: actes du colloque du 15ème centenaire de l'abbaye de Landévennec, 25–26–27 avril 1985* (Landévennec, 1986).
Sims-Williams, P., 'The Uses of Writing in Early Medieval Wales', in Pryce (ed.), *Literacy in Medieval Celtic Societies*, 15–38.
——'A New Brittonic Gloss on Boethius: *ud rocashaas*', *CMCS* 50 (Winter 2005), 77–86.
Smith, J. M. H., 'Celtic Asceticism and Carolingian Authority in Early Medieval Brittany', in W. Shiels (ed.), *Monks, Hermits and the Ascetic Tradition*, Studies in Church History, 22 (Oxford, 1985), 53–63.
——'Oral and Written: Saints, Miracles, and Relics in Brittany, *c.* 850–1250', *Speculum*, 65 (1990), 309–43.
Thacker, A., 'Gallic or Greek? Archbishops in England from Theodore to Ecgberht', in P. Fouracre and D. Ganz (eds.), *Frankland: The Franks and the World of the Early Middle Ages. Essays in Honour of Dame Jinty Nelson* (Manchester, 2008), 44–69.
——and Sharpe, R. (eds.), *Local Saints and Local Churches in the Early Medieval West* (Oxford, 2002).
Thomas, [A.] C., 'An Early Christian Cemetery and Chapel on Ardwall Isle, Kirkudbright', *Med. Arch.*, 11 (1967), 127–88.
——*The Early Christian Archaeology of North Britain* (Oxford, 1971).
——*Christianity in Roman Britain to A.D. 500* (London, 1981).
——*Whithorn's Christian Beginnings*, Whithorn Lecture (Whithorn, 1992).
——*Christian Celts: Messages and Images* (Stroud, 1998).
Thomas, D. R., *The History of the Diocese of St Asaph*, 3 vols. (Oswestry, 1908–13).
Timbal Duclaux de Martin, P., *Le Droit d'asile* (Paris, 1939).
Turner, S., *Making a Christian Landscape: The Countryside in Early Medieval Cornwall, Devon, and Wessex* (Exeter, 2006).

Vendryes, J., 'A propos du verbe "croire" et de la "croyance"', *Revue celtique*, 44 (1927), 90–6.

Williams, H., *Christianity in Early Britain* (Oxford, 1912)

Williams, I., 'The Computus Fragment', *BBCS* 3 (1926–7), 246–72.

2. Learning

De Raris Fabulis, ed. Stevenson, *Early Scholastic Colloquies*, 1–11; ed. and trans. S. Gwara, De Raris Fabulis, *'On Uncommon Tales': A Glossed Latin Colloquy-Text from a Tenth-Century Cornish Manuscript* (Cambridge, 2005).

Early Scholastic Colloquies, ed. W. H. Stevenson (Oxford, 1929).

Juvencus: Codex Cantabrigiensis Ff.4.42, ed. H. McKee (Aberystwyth, 2000); *Juvencus: text and commentary*, ed. H. McKee (Aberystwyth, 2000).

The Leiden Leechbook, ed. A. Falileyev and M. E. Owen (Innsbruck, 2005).

Saint Dunstan's Classbook from Glastonbury, ed. R. W. Hunt, Umbrae Codicum Occidentalium iv (Amsterdam, 1961).

Berschin, W., *Greek Letters and the Latin Middle Ages* (Washington, 1988).

Bischoff, B., *Mittelalterliche Studien*, 3 vols. (Stuttgart, 1966–81).

Bishop, T. A. M., 'The Corpus Martianus Capella', *Transactions of the Cambridge Bibliographical Society*, 4 (1964–68), 257–75.

——'An Early Example of Insular-Caroline', *Transactions of the Cambridge Bibliographical Society*, 4 (1964–68), 396–400.

Blom, A. H., 'The Welsh Glosses in the *Vocabularium Cornicum*', *CMCS* 57 (Summer 2009), 23–40.

Bradshaw, H., *Collected Papers* (Cambridge, 1889).

Breen, A., 'The Liturgical Materials in MS Oxford, Bodleian Library, Auct. F. 4. 32', *Archiv für Liturgiewissenschaft*, 34 (1992), 121–53.

Budny, M., '"St Dunstan's Classbook" and its Frontispiece: Dunstan's Portrait and Autograph', in N. Ramsay, M. Sparks, and T. Tatton-Brown (eds.), *St Dunstan: His Life, Times and Cult* (Woodbridge, 1992), 103–42.

Charles-Edwards, T. M., 'The use of the Book in Wales, *c.* 400–1100.', in Gameson (ed.), *The Cambridge History of the Book in Britain*, i. 389–405.

Conway, G., 'Towards a Cultural Context for the Eleventh-Century Llanbadarn Manuscripts', *Ceredigion*, 13: 1 (1997), 9–28.

Dumville, D. N., 'English Square Minuscule Script: The Background and Earliest Phases', *Anglo-Saxon England*, 16 (1987), 147–79.

——'Ireland, Brittany and England: Transmission and Use of *Collectio Canonum Hibernensis*', in C. Laurent and H. Davis, *Irlande et Bretagne: Vingt siècles d'histoire* (Rennes, 1994), 85–95.

——*A Palaeographer's Review: The Insular System of Scripts in the Early Middle Ages*, i (Osaka, 1999).

——'Writers, Scribes, and readers in Brittany, AD 800–1100', in H. Fulton (ed.), *Medieval Celtic Literature and Society* (Dublin, 2005), 49–64.

Edwards, N., 'The Decoration of the Earlier Welsh Manuscripts', in Gameson (ed.), *The Cambridge History of the Book in Britain*, i. 224–8.

Falileyev, A., and Owen, M. E., *The Leiden Leechbook: A Study of the Earliest Neo-Brittonic Medical Compilation* (Innsbruck, 2005).

Fischer, B., 'Die Lesungen der römischen Ostervigil unter Gregor der Grosse', in B. Fischer and V. Fiala (eds.), *Colligere Fragmenta: Festschrift Alban Dold* (Beuron, 1952), 144–59.

Fleuriot, L., *Dictionnaire des gloses en vieux breton* (Paris, 1964).

Gameson, R. (ed.), *The Cambridge History of the Book in Britain*, i *c.* 400–1100 (Cambridge, 2012).

Gneuss, H., 'A Preliminary List of Manuscripts written or owned in England up to 1100', *Anglo-Saxon England*, 9 (1981), 1–60.

Gwara, S., *Education in Wales and Cornwall in the Ninth and Tenth Centuries: Understanding* De Raris Fabulis, Kathleen Hughes Memorial Lectures on Mediaeval Welsh History, 4 (Cambridge, 2004).

Harvey, A., 'The Cambridge Juvencus glosses — evidence of Hiberno-Welsh literary interaction?' in P. S. Ureland and G. Broderick (eds.), *Language Contact in the British Isles* (Tübingen, 1991), 181–98.

——'Latin literacy and the Celtic vernaculars around the year AD 500', in C. J. Byrne et al. (eds.), *Celtic Languages and Celtic Peoples: Proceedings of the Second North-American Congress of Celtic Studies, Halifax, 1989* (Halifax, Nova Scotia, 1992), 11–26.

Holtz, L., 'A l'école de Donat, de saint Augustin à Bède', *Latomus*, 36 (1977), 522–38.

——*Donat et la tradition de l'enseignement grammatical: Etude sur l'Ars Donati et sa diffusion (IV*[e]*–IX*[e] *siècles et édition critique* (Paris, 1981).

——'Les grammairiens hiberno-latins étaient-ils des Anglo-Saxons?', *Peritia*, 2 (1983), 169–84.

Howlett, D., '*Orationes Moucani*: Early Cambro-Latin Prayers', *CMCS* 24 (Winter 1992), 55–74.

——*The Celtic Latin Tradition of Biblical Style* (Blackrock, Co. Dublin, 1995).

——*Cambro-Latin Compositions: Their Competence and Craftsmanship* (Dublin, 1998)

——'Rhygyfarch ap Sulien and Ieuan ap Sulien', in Gameson (ed.), *The Cambridge History of the Book in Britain*, i. 701–5.

Huws, D., 'The Medieval Manuscript', in P. H. Jones and E. Rees (eds.), *A Nation and its Books* (Aberystwyth, 1998), 25–39, reprinted in his *Medieval Welsh Manuscripts*, 1–23.

——*Medieval Welsh Manuscripts* (Cardiff, 2000).

Jackson, K. H., *Language and History in Early Britain* (Edinburgh, 1953).

Jenkins, D., and Owen, M. E., 'The Welsh Marginalia in the Lichfield Gospels, Part I', *CMCS* 5 (Summer 1983), 37–66.

——'The Welsh Marginalia in the Lichfield Gospels, Part II: The "Surexit" Memorandum', *CMCS* 7 (Summer 1984), 91–120.

Jones, P. H., and Rees, E. (eds.), *A nation and its books* (Aberystwyth, 1998).

Jones, T., '*Llyfrawr "librarius"*', *Bulletin of the Board of Celtic Studies*, 11 (1941–44), 136–8.

Kerlouégan, F., 'Essai sur la mise en nourriture et l'éducation dans les pays celtiques d'après le témoignage des textes hagiographiques latins', *Études celtiques*, 12 (1968–69), 101–46.

——'Les citations d'auteurs latins profanes dans les Vies de saints breton carolingiennes', *Études Celtiques*, 18 (1981), 181–95.

——*Le* De Excidio Britanniae *de Gildas. Les destinées de la culture latine dans l'île de Bretagne au VI*[e] *siècle* (Paris, 1987).

Lambert, P.-Y., 'Les gloses du manuscrit BN Lat. 10290', *Études Celtiques*, 19 (1982), 173–213.

Lambert, P.-Y., 'Les commentaires celtiques à Bède le vénérable', *Études Celtiques*, 20 (1983), 119–43, and 21 (1984), 185–206.

——' "Thirty" and "sixty" in Brittonic', *CMCS* 8 (Winter 1984), 29–43.

——'Les gloses celtiques aux commentaires de Virgile', *Études Celtiques*, 23 (1986), 81–128.

——'Les gloses grammaticales brittoniques', *Études Celtiques*, 24 (1987), 285–308.

——'Gloses à Orose: résultats d'enquête', *Études Celtiques*, 25 (1988), 213–20.

——'Gloses en vieux breton (§ 6–9)', *Études Celtiques*, 27 (1990), 337–61.

——'La typologie des gloses en Vieux-Breton', *Britannia Monastica*, 1 (1990), 13–21.

——'Gloses en vieux breton', *Études Celtiques*, 30 (1994), 221–8.

——'Rencontres culturelles entre Irlandais et Bretons aux IXe et Xe siècles', in C. Laurent and H. Davis, *Irlande et Bretagne: vingt siècles d'histoire* (Rennes, 1994), 96–106.

——'The Old Welsh Glosses on Weights and Measures', in P. Russell (ed.), *Yr Hen Iaith: Studies in Early Welsh* (Aberystwyth, 2003), 103–34.

Lapidge, M., 'Three Latin Poems from Æthelwold's School at Winchester', *Anglo-Saxon England*, 1 (1972), 85–137; reprinted in his *Anglo-Latin Literature, 900–1066*, 225–77.

——'The Welsh-Latin Poetry of Sulien's Family', *Studia Celtica*, 8–9 (1973–74), 68–106.

——'Latin Learning in Dark-Age Wales: Some Prolegomena', in D. E. Evans et al. (eds.), *Proceedings of the Seventh International Congress of Celtic Studies, Oxford, 1983* (Oxford, 1986), 91–107.

——'Israel the Grammarian in Anglo-Saxon England', in H. J. Westra (ed.), *From Athens to Chartres: Neoplatonism and Medieval Thought* (Leiden, 1992), 97–114; reprinted in his *Anglo-Latin Literature, 900–1066*, 87–104.

——*Anglo-Latin Literature, 900–1066* (London, 1993).

——*Anglo-Latin Literature, 600–899* (London, 1996).

——*The Anglo-Saxon Library* (Oxford, 2006).

——'Colloquial Latin in the Insular Latin Scholastic *Colloquia*', in E. Dickey and A. Chahoud (eds.), *Colloquial and Literary Latin* (Cambridge, 2010), 406–18.

Law, V., *The Insular Latin Grammarians*, Studies in Celtic History 3 (Woodbridge, 1982).

——'Notes on the Dating and Attribution of Anonymous Latin Grammarians of the Early Middle Ages', *Peritia*, 1 (1982), 250–67.

——'Linguistics in the Earlier Middle Ages: The Insular and Carolingian Grammarians', *Transactions of the Philological Society* (1985), 171–93.

——'When is Donatus not Donatus? Versions, Variants and New Texts', *Peritia*, 5 (1986), 235–61.

——*Grammar and Grammarians in the Early Middle Ages* (London, 1997).

——*The History of Linguistics in Europe from Plato to 1600* (Cambridge, 2003).

Lowe, E. A., *Codices Latini Antiquiores: A Palaeographical Guide to Latin Manuscripts Prior to the Ninth Century*, 11 vols. plus supplement (Oxford, 1935–71).

McKee, H., 'Breton Manuscripts of Biblical and Hiberno-Latin Texts', in T. O'Loughlin (ed.), *The Scriptures and Early Medieval Ireland* (Turnhout, 1999), 275–90.

——'Scribes and Glosses from Dark Age Wales: The Cambridge Juvencus Manuscript', *CMCS* 39 (Summer 2000), 1–22.

——'Script in Wales, Scotland and Cornwall', in Gameson (ed.), *The Cambridge History of the Book in Britain*, i. 167–73.

——'The Circulation of Books between England and the Celtic Realms', in Gameson (ed.), *The Cambridge History of the Book in Britain*, i. 338–43.

McKee, H., and McKee, J., 'Counter Arguments and Numerical Patterns in Early Celtic Inscriptions: A Re-examination of *Christian Celts: Messages and Images*', *Medieval Archaeology*, 46 (2002), 29–40.
Márkus, G., 'What were Patrick's Alphabets?', *CMCS* 31 (Summer 1996), 1–15.
Marrou, H.-I., *A History of Education in Antiquity* (London, 1956).
Oates, J. C. T., 'Notes on the Later History of the Oldest Manuscript of Welsh Poetry: The Cambridge Juvencus', *CMCS* 3 (Summer 1982), 81–7.
Peden, A., 'Science and Philosophy in Wales at the Time of the Norman conquest: A Macrobius Manuscript from Llanbadarn', *CMCS* 2 (Winter 1981), 21–45.
Pryce, H., 'The Origins and the Medieval Period', in P. H. Jones and E. Rees (eds.), *A Nation and its Books* (Aberystwyth, 1998), 1–7.
Pryce, H. (ed.), *Literacy in Medieval Celtic Societies*, Cambridge studies in medieval literature 33 (Cambridge, 1998).
Richards, M., 'The "Lichfield" Gospels (Book of "Saint Chad")', *National Library of Wales Journal*, 18 (1973–74), 135–46.
Williams, I., 'Glosau Rhydychen: Mesurau a Phwysau', *Bulletin of the Board of Celtic Studies*, 5 (1929–31), 226–48.
—— *The Beginnings of Welsh Poetry*, ed. R. Bromwich (Cardiff, 1972).
Winterbottom, M., 'On the *Hisperica Famina*', *Celtica*, 8 (1968), 126–39.
——'Columbanus and Gildas', *Vigiliae Christianae*, 30 (1976), 310–17.
Wood, I. N., 'Administration, Law and Culture in Merovingian Gaul', in R. McKitterick (ed.), *The Uses of Literacy in Early Medieval Europe* (Cambridge, 1990), 63–81.

3. Literature

(a) *Poetry*

i. General

(For the *Gododdin* and the poems of Taliesin deemed 'historical' by Sir Ifor Williams see above, 712–15.)

Gruffydd, R. G. (ed.), *Bardos: Penodau ar y Traddodiad Barddol Cymreig a Cheltaidd cyflwynedig i J. E. Caerwyn Williams* (Cardiff, 1982).
Haycock, M., 'Llyfr Taliesin', *National Library of Wales Journal*, 25 (1987–88), 357–86.
Jarman, A. O. H., *The Cynfeirdd* (Cardiff, 1981).
Jones, T., 'The Black Book of Carmarthen "Stanzas of the Graves"', *Proceedings of the British Academy*, 53 (1967), 97–137.
Koch, J. T., 'When was Welsh Literature first written down?', *Studia Celtica*, 20/21 (1985–86), 43–66.
Morris-Jones, J., *Cerdd Dafod* (Oxford, 1925).
Owen, M. E., 'Literary Convention and Historic Reality: The Court in the Welsh Poetry of the Twelfth and Thirteenth Century', *Études Celtiques*, 29 (1992), 69–85.
Rowland, J., 'Genres', in Roberts (ed.), *Studies in Early Welsh Poetry*, 179–208.
——'Y Beirdd Enwog: Anhysbys a'i cant', in I. Daniel, M. Haycock, D. Johnston, and J. Rowland (eds.), *Cyfoeth y Testun: Ysgrifau ar Lenyddiaeth Gymraeg yr Oesoedd Canol* (Cardiff, 2003), 31–49.
Williams, I., *Chwedl Taliesin* (Cardiff, 1957).

ii. Saga Poetry

Ford, P. K., 'The Poet as *Cyfarwydd* in Early Welsh Tradition', *Studia Celtica*, 10/11 (1975–76), 152–62.
Jacobs, N., 'Celtic Saga and the Contexts of Old English Elegiac Poetry', *Études Celtiques*, 26 (1989), 95–142.

Jacobs, N., 'Clefyd Abercuog', *BBCS* 39 (1992), 57–70.

Rowland, J., 'The Prose Setting of the Early Welsh *Englynion Chwedlonol*', *Ériu*, 36 (1985), 29–43.

——*Early Welsh Saga Poetry: A Study and Edition of the Englynion* (Cambridge, 1990).

Sims-Williams, P., 'The Provenance of the Llywarch Hen Poems: A Case for Llan-gors, Brycheiniog', *CMCS* 26 (Winter, 1993), 27–64.

——'Historical Need and Literary Narrative: A Caveat from Ninth-Century Wales', *Welsh History Review*, 17 (1994–95), 1–40.

Williams, I., 'The Poems of Llywarch Hen', *Proceedings of the British Academy*., 28 (1932), 269–302; reprinted in his *The Beginnings of Welsh Poetry*, ed. R. Bromwich, ch. viii.

——*Lectures on Early Welsh Poetry* (Dublin, 1944).

iii. Other poetry

Breeze, A., 'Two Notes on Early Welsh Poetry: The Date of the Gododdin and the Poet and Patron in The Praise of Tenby' , *Studia Celtica*, 31 (1997), 269–82.

Gruffydd, R. G., 'A Welsh "Dark Age" Court Poem', in J. Carey et al., *Ildánach, Ildírech*, 39–48.

Jarman, A. O. H., *The Legend of Merlin* (Cardiff, 1960).

(b) *Prose*

i. General

Texts and Translations of the Mabinogion:

The Text of the Mabinogion . . . from the Red Book of Hergest, ed. J. Rhŷs and J. Gwenogvryn Evans (Oxford, 1887).

The White Book Mabinogion, ed. J. Gwenogvryn Evans (Lanbedrog, 1907); reissued as *Llyfr Gwyn Rhydderch: Y Chwedlau a'r Rhamantau*, ed. J. Gwenogvryn Evans with an introduction by R. M. Jones (Cardiff, 1973).

Davies, S., *The Mabinogion*, The World Classics (Oxford, 2007).

Bowen, G. (ed.), *Y Traddodiad Rhyddiaith yn yr Oesau Canol* (Llandysul, 1974).

Bromwich, R., Jarman, A. O. H., and Roberts, B. F. (eds.), *The Arthur of the Welsh* (Cardiff, 1991).

Davies, S., *Crefft y Cyfarwydd* (Cardiff, 1996).

Mac Cana, P., *The Mabinogi*, Writers of Wales, 2nd edn. (Cardiff, 1992).

Roberts, B. F., 'Tales and Romances' in A. O. H. Jarman and G. R. Hughes (eds.), *A Guide to Welsh Literature*, i (Swansea, 1976), 203–43.

——'Ystoria', *BBCS* 26 (1974–76), 13–20.

——'Culhwch ac Olwen, the Triads, Saints' Lives', in R. Bromwich et al. (eds.), *The Arthur of the Welsh*, ch. 3.

——*Studies on Middle Welsh Literature* (Lewiston, 1992).

Rodway, S., 'The Where, Who, When and Why of Medieval Welsh Prose Tales: Some Methodological Considerations', *SC* 41 (2007), 47–89.

Sims-Williams, P., 'Did Itinerant Breton *Conteurs* transmit the *Matière de Bretagne*', *Romania*, 116 (1998), 72–111.

ii. Culhwch ac Olwen

Culhwch and Olwen: An Edition and Study of the Oldest Arthurian Tale, ed. R. Bromwich and D. S. Evans (Cardiff, 1992).

Studies

Charles-Edwards, T. M., 'The Date of *Culhwch ac Olwen*', in W. McLeod, A. Burnyeat, D. U. Stiùbhairt, T. O. Clancy, and R. Ó Maolalaigh (eds.), *Bile ós Chrannaibh: A Festschrift for William Gillies* (Ceann Drochaid, 2010), 45–56.

Ford, P. K., 'On the Significance of Some Arthurian Names in Welsh', *BBCS* 30 (1983), 268–73.
——'A Highly Important Pig', in Matonis and Melia (eds.), *Celtic Language, Celtic Culture*, 292–304.
——and Hamp, E., 'Welsh *asswynaw* and Celtic Legal Idiom', *BBCS* 26 (1975), 147–53.
Foster, I. Ll., 'Culhwch ac Olwen' and 'Rhonabwy's Dream', in R. S. Loomis (ed.), *Arthurian Literature in the Middle Ages* (Oxford, 1959), 31–43.
Henry, P. L., 'Culhwch and Olwen: Some Aspects of Style and Structure', *Studia Celtica*, 3 (1968), 30–8.
Hunter, J., 'Dead Pigs, Place Names, and Sir John Rhys: Reconsidering the Onomastic Elements of *Kulhwch ac Olwen*', *Proceedings of the Harvard Celtic Colloquium*, 11 (1991), 27–36.
Ifans, D., 'Yr Anifeiliaid Hynaf', *BBCS* 24 (1972), 461–4.
Jackson, K. H., 'Rhai Sylwadau ar Culhwch ac Olwen', *Ysgrifau Beirniadol*, 12 (1982), 12–23.
Padel, O. J., 'The Nature of Arthur', *CMCS* 27 (Summer 1994), 1–32.
——*Arthur in Medieval Welsh Literature*, Writers of Wales (Cardiff, 2000).
Radner, J., 'Interpreting Irony in Medieval Celtic Narrative: The Case of *Culhwch ac Olwen*', *CMCS* 16 (Winter 1988), 41–59.
Rodway, S., 'The Date and Authorship of *Culhwch ac Olwen*: A Reconsideration', *CMCS* 49 (Summer 2005), 21–44.
Sims-Williams, P., 'The Significance of the Irish Personal Names in *Culhwch ac Olwen*', *BBCS* 29 (1982), 600–20.
——'The Irish Geography of Culhwch and Olwen', in D. Ó Corráin et al., *Sages Saints and Storytellers: Celtic Studies in Honour of Professor James Carney* (Maynooth, 1989), 412–26.

iii. Pedeir Keinc y Mabinogi, The Four Branches of the Mabinogi

(a) Texts

Pedeir Keinc y Mabinogi, ed. I. Williams (Cardiff, 1930).
Pwyll Pendeuic Dyuet, ed. R. L. Thomson (Dublin, 1957).
Branwen verch Lyr, ed. D. S. Thomson (Dublin, 1961).
Manawydan uab Llyr: Trydedd Gainc y Mabinogi, ed. I. Hughes (Cardiff, 2007).
Manawydan uab Llyr: Text from the Diplomatic Edition of the White Book of Rhydderch, by J. Gwenogvryn Evans, ed. P. K. Ford (Belmont, MA, 1999).
Math uab Mathonwy: Text from the Diplomatic Edition of the White Book of Rhydderch, by J. Gwenogvryn Evans, ed. P. K. Ford (Belmont, MA, 1999).
Math uab Mathonwy: Pedwaredd Gainc y Mabinogi, ed. I. Hughes (Aberystwyth, 2000).

(b) *Studies*

Bollard, J. K., 'The Structure of the Four Branches of the Mabinogi', *THSC, 1975*, 250–76.
——'The Role of Myth and Tradition in *The Four Branches of the Mabinogi*', *CMCS* 6 (Winter 1983), 67–86.
Carey, J., 'A British Myth of Origins?', *Journal of the History of Religions*, 31 (1991), 24–37.
Charles-Edwards, T. M., 'Honour and Status in Some Irish and Welsh Prose Tales', *Ériu*, 29 (1978), 123–41.
Davies, S., *The Four Branches of the Mabinogi/Pedeir Keinc y Mabinogi* (Llandysul, 1993).
——'Blodeuwedd a *Mabinogi Math*', *Barn*, 292 (1987), 185–90.
——'*Pedeir Keinc y Mabinogi* — A Case for Multiple Authorship', *Proceedings of the North American Congress of Celtic Studies*, ed. G. W. MacLennan (Ottawa, 1988), 443–59.
——'Ail Gainc y Mabinogi: Llais y Ferch', *Ysgrifau Beirniadol*, 17 (1990), 15–27.

Dumézil, G., 'La Quatrième Branche du Mabinogi et la Theologie des Trois Fonctions', *Rencontres de Religions*, ed. P. Mac Cana and M. Meslin (Paris, 1986), 25–38.

Fulton, H., 'The *Mabinogi* and the Education of Princes in Medieval Wales', in H. Fulton (ed.), *Medieval Welsh Literature and Society* (Dublin, 2005), 230–47.

Gruffydd, W. J., *Math vab Mathonwy* (Cardiff, 1928).

——*Rhiannon: An Inquiry into the First and Third Branches of the Mabinogi* (Cardiff, 1953).

Haycock, M., 'Dylan Ail Ton', *Ysgrifau Beirniadol*, 13 (1985), 26–38 (on a poem in the Book of Taliesin; secondarily on *Math*).

Keefer, S. L., 'The Lost Tale of Dylan in the Four Branches of *The Mabinogi*', *Studia Celtica*, 24/25 (1989/90), 26–37.

Koch, J. T., 'A Welsh Window on the Iron Age: Manawydan, Mandubracios', *CMCS* 14 (Winter 1987), 17–52.

——'Some Suggestions and Etymologies reflecting upon the Mythology of the Four Branches', *Proceedings of the Harvard Celtic Colloquium* 9 (1989), 1–11.

Lambert, P.-Y., 'Magie et pouvoir dans la Quatrième Branche du *Mabinogi*', *Studia Celtica*, 28 (1994), 97–107.

Mac Cana, P., *Branwen Daughter of Llŷr* (Cardiff, 1958).

McKenna, C., 'The Theme of Sovereignty in Pwyll', *BBCS* 29 (1980), 35–52.

——'Revising Math: Kingship in the Fourth Branch of the Mabinogi', *CMCS* 46 (Winter 2003), 95–117.

Maier, B., and Zimmer, S. (eds.), *150 "Mabinogion"—Deutsche-walische Kulturbeziehungen* (Tübingen, 2001).

Roberts, B. F., 'Where were the Four Branches of the Mabinogi written?', in J. F. Nagy (ed.),, *The Individual in Celtic Literatures* (Dublin, 2001), 61–75.

Sims-Williams, P., 'A Riddling Treatment of the "Watchman Device" in *Branwen* and *Togail Bruidne Da Derga*', *Studia Celtica*, 12/13 (1977/8), 83–117.

——'The Evidence for Vernacular Irish Influence on Early Medieval Welsh Literature', in D. Whitelock (*et al.*), *Ireland in Mediaeval Europe* (Cambridge, 1982), 235–57.

——'Some Functions of Origin Stories in Early Medieval Wales', in T. Nyberg et al., *History and Heroic Tale: A Symposium* (Odense, 1985), 97–131.

——'Fionn and Deirdre in Late-Medieval Wales', *Éigse*, 23 (1989), 1–15.

——'Cú Chulainn in Wales: Welsh Sources for Irish Onomastics', *Celtica*, 21 (1990), 620–33.

——'The Submission of Irish Kings in Fact and Fiction: Henry II, Bendigeidfran, and the Dating of *The Four Branches of the Mabinogi*', *CMCS* 22 (Winter 1991), 31–61.

——*The Iron House in Ireland*, H. M. Chadwick Memorial Lectures 16 (Cambridge, 2006).

——*Irish Influence on Medieval Welsh Literature* (Oxford, 2010).

Sullivan III, C. W., (ed.), *The Mabinogi: A Book of Essays* (New York, 1996).

Tolstoy, N., *The Oldest British Prose Literature: The Compilation of the Four Branches of the* Mabinogi (Lampeter, 2009).

Valente, R., 'Gwydion and Aranrhod: Crossing the Borders of Gender', *BBCS*, 35 (1988), 1–9.

Welsh, A., 'The Traditional Narrative Motifs of *The Four Branches of the Mabinogi*', *CMCS* 15 (Summer 1988), 51–62.

——'Traditional Tales and the Harmonizing of Story in *Pwyll Pendeuic Dyuet*', *CMCS* 17 (Winter 1989), 15–41.

——'Doubling and Incest in the *Mabinogi*', *Speculum*, 65 (1990), 344–62.

Winward, F., 'Some Aspects of the Women in *The Four Branches*', *CMCS* 34 (Winter 1997), 77–107.

iv. Breuddwyd Macsen Wledig and *Cyfranc Lludd a Llefelys:*

Breudwyt Maxen Wledic, ed. B. F. Roberts (Dublin, 2005).

Cyfranc Lludd a Llefelys, ed. B. F. Roberts (Dublin, 1975).

Jones, T., 'Historical Writing in Medieval Welsh', *Scottish Studies*, 12 (1968), 15–27.

Matthews, J. F., 'Macsen, Maximianus and Constantine', *Welsh History Review*, 11 (1982–83), 431–48.

Roberts, B. F., *Studies on Middle Welsh Literature*, ch. 2.

——'Historical Writing', in A. O. H. Jarman and G. R. Hughes (eds.), *A Guide to Welsh Literature*, i (Swansea, 1976).

——'*Breuddwyd Macsen Wledig*: Cymhellion yr Awdur', *Llên Cymru*, 26 (2003), 18–26.

——'*Breuddwyd Macsen Wledig*: Why? When?', in J. F. Nagy and L. E. Jones (eds.), *Heroic Poets and Heroic Heroes in Celtic Tradition: A Festschrift for Patrick K. Ford* (Dublin, 2005), 303–14.

Index

Note: in the alphabetical sequence, Old English *æ* is treated as *ae*, Old English œ as *oe*, Welsh *ll* as a pair of *l*s, and Welsh *rh* as *r* followed by *h*. Inscriptions separately discussed as opposed to merely being cited are listed by name of the place under 'inscriptions discussed'. Some, however, have more than one name; in such cases, for the first two volumes of the *Corpus of Early Medieval Inscribed Stones and Stone Sculpture*, and where possible the third, the names in the *Corpus* are given first and those of Nash-Williams second, separated by a slash. In the text, Nash-Williams's names are sometimes used, since it was largely written before the publication of the *Corpus*. Similarly, charters discussed as opposed to merely being cited are listed under 'charters discussed' referring to the archive and the number, and likewise manuscripts discussed under 'manuscripts discussed'. The documents from Llandeilo Fawr in the Lichfield Gospels are traditionally known as Chad (from the patron saint of Lichfeld) together with the number, for example, Chad 2.

Lightning Source UK Ltd.
Milton Keynes UK
UKHW020153161221
395483UK00011B/299

9 780198 704911